# THE BEST 351 COLLEGES

## THE PRINCETON REVIEW

# THE BEST 351 COLLEGES

### 2004 Edition

By Robert Franek,
Tom Meltzer, Roy Opochinski,
Tara Bray, Christopher Maier, Carson Brown,
Julie Doherty, K. Nadine Kavanaugh, Catherine Monaco,
and Dinaw Mengestu

Random House, Inc.
New York
www.PrincetonReview.com

Princeton Review Publishing, L.L.C.
2315 Broadway
New York, NY  10024
E-mail: bookeditor@review.com

© 2003 by Princeton Review Publishing, L.L.C.

All rights reserved under International and Pan-American Copyright Conventions. Published in the United States by Random House, Inc., New York, and simultaneously in Canada by Random House of Canada Limited, Toronto. This is a revised edition of a book first published in 1989.

ISBN 0-375-76337-6
ISSN 1093-9679

Editorial Director: Robert Franek
Editors: Robert Franek and Erik Olson
Production Editor: Julieanna Lambert
Production Coordinator: Scott Harris

Manufactured in the United States of America on partially recycled paper.

9 8 7 6 5 4 3 2 1

2004 Edition

# Foreword

Every year, about three million high school graduates go to college. To make sure they end up at the *right* school, they spend several billion dollars on the admissions process. This money pays for countless admissions officers and counselors, a bunch of standardized tests (and preparation for them), and many books similar to—but not as good as—this one.

It's so expensive because most admissions professionals have a thing about being in control. As a group, colleges resist almost every attempt to standardize or otherwise simplify the process. Admissions officers want you to believe that every admissions decision that they render occurs within systems of weights, measures, and deliberations that are far too complex for you to comprehend. They shudder at the notion of having to respond to students and their parents in down-to-earth language that might reveal the arbitrary nature of a huge percentage of the admissions and denials that they issue during each cycle. That would be admitting that good luck and circumstance play a major part in many successful applications. So, in flight from public accountability, they make the process a lot more mysterious than it needs to be.

Even the most straightforward colleges hide the information you would want to know about the way they'll evaluate your application: What grades and SATs are they looking for? Do their reported SAT averages include minority students, athletes, and legacies (kids whose parents went to their school)? Exactly how much do extracurricular activities count? What percentage of the aid that they give out is in loans and what percentage is in grants?

We couldn't get answers to these questions from many colleges. In fact, we couldn't get answers to *any* questions from some schools. Others who supplied this information to us for earlier editions of this guide have since decided that they never should have in the first place. After all, knowledge is power.

Colleges seem to have the time and money to create beautiful brochures that generally show that all college classes are held under a tree on a beautiful day. Why not just tell you what sort of students they're looking for, and what factors they'll use to consider your application?

Until the schools demystify the admissions process, this book is your best bet. It's not a phone book containing every fact about every college in the country. And it's not a memoir written by a few graduates describing their favorite dining halls or professors. We've given you the facts you'll need to apply to the few hundred best schools in the country. And enough information about them—which we gathered from hundreds of counselors and admissions officers and more than 100,000 college students—to help you make a smart decision about which school to attend.

One note: We don't talk a lot about majors. This is because most high school students really don't know what they want to major in—and the ones who do almost always change their minds by the beginning of junior year. Choosing a school because of the reputation of a single department is often a terrible idea.

If you're interested in learning about majors and the colleges that offer them, pick up our *Guide to College Majors* or visit our website, www.princetonreview.com, where we explain majors and list the colleges that offer them.

As complicated and difficult as the admissions process is, we think you'll love college itself—especially at the schools listed in this book.

Good luck in your search.

*John Katzman*
*June 2003*

# ACKNOWLEDGMENTS

I am blessed year after year with a talented group of colleagues working together to produce our guidebooks. Each involved in this effort—authors, editors, data collectors, production specialists, and designers—give so much more than is required to make *The Best 351 Colleges* the best student guidebook *ever*. This new edition yields, like it predecessors, what prospective college students really want: the most honest, accessible, and pertinent information on the colleges they are considering attending for the next four years of their lives. My sincere thanks go to the many who contributed to this tremendous project. I am proud to note here that we have again successfully provided an uncompromising look into the true nature of each profiled college or university based on the opinions of each institution's current students. I know our readers will benefit from our cumulative efforts.

A special thank you goes to our authors, Tom Meltzer, Tara Bray, Roy Opochinski, Christopher Maier, Carson Brown, Julie Doherty, Nadine Kavanaugh, Catherine Monaco, and Dinaw Mengestu for their dedication in sifting through thousands of surveys to produce the essence of each school in three paragraphs. Very special thanks go to two stellar producers from our editorial staff: Erik Olson and Erica Magrey. Erik, our Senior Editor, is an essential resource to our department and a clear driver of this book. I can always trust Erik to provide clear direction in both the voice and sensibilities of The Princeton Review; he has proven himself again here. Erica, in her freshman performance, took this trial by fire with grace and moxie. On a daily basis, Erica brought quiet competence to the student survey process, adhering meticulously to our standards and goals for each school's narrative profile.

Sincere thanks goes to Jillian Taylor, our Student Survey Manager. Jillian provided clear messaging on our survey methodology and editorial procedure, remaining even-handed and approachable throughout the process. A special note goes to Amy Kinney, a veteran student surveyor, for her unwavering dedication to relaying our mission to the schools included in these pages. She provided sincere representation of the mission of The Princeton Review. Michael Palumbo also deserves praise for his indispensable contributions in the last days of production.

My continued thanks go to our data collection staff—David Soto, Ben Zelavansky, and Yojaira Cordero—for their successful efforts in collecting and accurately representing the statistical data that appear with each college profile. In turn, my gratitude goes to Chris Wujciak for his competence in all of our book pours.

The enormity of this project and its deadline constraints could not have been realized without the calm presence of our production team, Julieanna Lambert and Scott Harris. Their ability to remain focused throughout the production of this project inspires and impresses me. They deserve great thanks for their flexible schedules and uncompromising efficiency.

Special thanks go to Jeanne Krier, our Random House publicist, for the work she has done on this book and the overall series since its inception. Jeanne continues to be my trusted colleague, media advisor, and friend. I would also like to make special mention of Tom Russell, our publisher, for his continuous investment and faith in our ideas.

Lastly, I thank John Katzman and Mark Chernis for their steadfast confidence in this book and our publishing department, and for always being the champions of student opinion. It is pleasure to work with you both.

Again, to all who contributed so much to this publication, thank you for your efforts; they do not go unnoticed.

Robert Franek<br>
Editorial Director<br>
Lead Author—*The Best 351 Colleges*

# Contents

**PART 1: INTRODUCTION**  1

A Parent's Guide to the College Search  3
Ap_lic_t_o_.  7
How We Produce This Book  9
How This Book is Organized  13
Glossary  23
About Those College Rankings  25

**PART 2: SCHOOLS RANKED BY CATEGORY**  29

**PART 3: THE BEST 351 COLLEGES**  45

**PART 4: "MY ROOMMATE'S FEET REALLY STINK."**  749

**PART 5: INDEXES**  765

Index of Schools  766
Index of Schools by Location  769

About the Authors  773

DOONESBURY © 1999 G.B. Trudeau. Reprinted with permission of UNIVERSAL PRESS SYNDICATE. All rights reserved.

# PART 1

# INTRODUCTION

# A Parent's Guide to the College Search: Why It Ought To Be An Enjoyable Year

*By Dan Lundquist, Dean of Admissions, Financial Aid, and Communications; and Peter Blankman, Director of Communications and Public Relations; Union College, Schenectady, NY. Reprinted with their permission from the Union College brochure of the same name.*

There are some 3,500 colleges and universities in the United States, and by the time you leave your son or daughter at new student orientation, you may feel that you've seen every one of them—or at least received mail from most of them!

We hope that by sharing a college's perspective, we can shed some light on the search process and help you understand it better. We hope these "educated insights" will help you approach the process in the most positive and productive way.

The college search process ought to be a positive, educational experience in itself, not just something to be "survived." At this point—the bridge between high school and college, adolescence and young adulthood—students have a remarkable range of options in front of them, and it's a shame when the excitement of this situation becomes anxiety.

While there's no sure-fire way to eliminate anxiety, we believe proper planning, combined with a realistic and appropriate attitude, can go a long way toward minimizing anxiety.

And that's a laudable goal in itself.

## Getting started

The college search needn't be that overwhelming—not if you start early, plan ahead, and take things one step at a time.

No question, you're facing a big change in your family's life. So how do you find a compass? How do you begin to sort through all the information and begin to make some choices that will make sense for you and your child?

There are a couple of first steps. One is to take a self-inventory. You and your child should ask yourselves realistic, sometimes tough, person-centered questions about interests, skills, values, and aspirations. Soon it will be appropriate to begin thinking about externally oriented issues like college size, location, and cost. And it's okay to admit that trepidation and uncertainty exist, even among "veteran" families.

Alongside the self-inventory is the gathering of objective information about colleges themselves—the kind of details that will help you narrow that list from 3,500 to perhaps a handful. This can be daunting. One of the overwhelming aspects of the college search is that there's so much information available. Sometimes it's hard to distinguish between what is and what isn't valuable.

One of the resources that too often is not used properly is your school counseling office. Nearly everything you need to start doing some preliminary sorting is here—an experienced college counseling staff, publications from colleges, guidebooks of all kinds, and electronic databases.

Along with the experiences of friends—students and adults—your own child's "instincts" are also resources to draw on. These anecdotal resources should not drive the search process, but you should feel free to start the preliminary list of colleges with some sentimental favorites.

As a goal begins to come into focus, sometimes working backward from that goal makes great sense. If your goal is to get to a small, liberal arts college in the Northeast, for example, start with a group of schools and work backward, applying increasingly personal, student-oriented questions to make distinctions and winnow the list.

## Let the student lead

It's important that the student take the lead in thinking critically to get down to the shortlist. Ultimately a student who's been spoon-fed is the one who's going to be disappointed in college when he or she discovers that other people's interests and values drove the college search.

One of your best strategies is to ask questions, keep your eyes open, and evaluate information and impressions. In the end, it's a question and answer process between family and college, parent and child.

Determining the fit between student and college depends on how you want to define the outcome of your child's college education. If you want to define it vocationally, you might look purely at statistics. To the extent that cost will be a factor, you will need to research tuition prices and/or financial aid policies. And if you want to define it as an academic, intellectual, personal, and cultural experience—and you are attuned to those values and clues that give you insights into a college's "character"—then your child's college years will be all the richer for that.

## No such thing as a perfect fit

Happily, for most students there is no one perfect fit. In fact, against the backdrop of so many fine options, your child certainly has the talent and flexibility to succeed at a number of colleges. Strange as it may sound now, some of the students who turn out the happiest, in fact, are the ones who thought they had lost the "admissions sweepstakes" at the end of their senior year. Hence the old college counseling truism: The vast majority of students are at their first-choice college by Halloween of their first year.

Even though your child could be happy at a number of colleges, you still have to focus the search. Rankings, objective data, and reputation are necessary, but not sufficient, to judge the correctness of the fit between the individual and institution.

In short, it's time to hit the road.

## Make those visits

Visiting a college is really the only way you're going to get a sense of the reality or the personality of the place—its strengths, its surprises, its life in and outside the classroom. From the time you first walk on campus, you will start picking up messages, from the quality of the facilities to the friendliness of the students to the physical care of the campus grounds.

A prospective student ought to ask, "Can I see myself here?" Look at the students; look at the announcements on the bulletin boards; feel comfortable asking questions about any issue, from housing and campus safety to graduate school placement. Try to get a handle on the tone of the campus, what the students care about and pay attention to, and help your child compare that with her needs and "comfort zone."

The same goes for an interview. Treat it as a conversation, not an inquisition. Who does well in an interview? A relaxed student armed with good questions and ready to speak articulately about his interests and aspirations.

Will you get straight answers to your questions? In the overwhelming number of cases, yes. Sure, we're recruiters—salespeople—but we're also counselors. We want to enroll students who are going to be happy at our college. Maybe that's one reason we're an admissions office, not a rejection office. An overarching goal of ours is that the college search process be a positive educational experience in itself.

## The "heart" quotient

A lot of people do a great job with the analytical part of the search, but they leave out the heart component, if you will. They are transfer students in the making!

When students are asked how they came to choose Union, they almost always cite the "smart," cognitive factors, such as academic program, size, and post-graduate placement.

That's fine. But we always discover that, as they narrowed it down, the answers come much more from the heart and describe how they felt when they first visited campus, or how much they liked the students and professors they met. If someone doesn't have a reasonable measure of that "heart" quotient, then college's general educational value, as a total experience, is going to be lessened.

## How we choose

At a certain point this whole process becomes more of an art than a science for you.

It's the same for us.

We have a parallel, shared process and goal. You are choosing a college, we are selecting students, and our goal—the best "match"—is the same.

Just like you, we begin by looking at the objective criteria (grades, quality of courses, and test scores) to see if there is an initial fit between your son or daughter and our college.

And like your college search, assembling a class is not a purely objective process. We want to bring together young men and women who have enough in common so that they're going to be good roommates, study partners, and friends, and support each other as they take the "prudent risks" that are an important part of the educational experience. We also want enough differences so they're going to educate each other in some subtle ways. That's the richness of a residential, undergraduate college.

Being a selective college means having a large enough applicant pool to select the students we think will be appropriate for our institution. It's important for parents to understand that at selective colleges the process is going to be just that—selective. And it is important to acknowledge that selective judgements based upon subjective evaluations are, to some extent, going to be "unfair." Coming to terms with that reality early on will help put any disappointments, if they come, into perspective later on.

### A good rule of thumb

From the start of the process, you should keep this thought in mind:

What is a realistic pool for my child?

Most counselors are going to recommend that you have four schools that look likely, have a reach or two (based on the objective data), and have a sure bet or two. That rule of thumb has been around all these decades because it's based on experience and realism.

### A positive experience

We hope that some of these comments help you approach the college search process from a positive, productive perspective. College counselors—admissions officers, recruiters, and guidance personnel—believe that it ought to be an enjoyable, educational experience, one guided by concerns for what's best for the student at this pivotal point between late adolescence and young adulthood.

Assaying one's options at this time of life ought to be exciting and fun—at least most of the time. It's true that choosing a college is a serious business, but that does not mean one must be deadly serious about it.

Best wishes, good luck, and don't forget, Halloween is just around the corner!

*For the past twenty years Dan Lundquist has worked at small, liberal arts colleges and Ivy League universities. He is now vice president of admissions, financial aid, and communications at Union College in Schenectady, NY.*

*A former reporter, Peter Blankman has been director of communications at Union College since 1981.*

# A P _ LIC _ T _ O _.

What's *that*?!?!

It's APPLICATION with P-A-I-N removed from the process.

We removed the paper, too.

With PrincetonReview.com's Online College Applications there are no endless piles to shuffle. No leaky pens, no hand cramps, no trying to figure out how many stamps to stick on that envelope.

The process is so painless, online applications practically submit themselves for you. Watch . . .

Type in your main contact information just once in our application profile and every subsequent application you file from our database—picking from hundreds of top schools—is automatically filled in with your information.

Not only are online applications:

- Faster to fill out
- Completely safe and secure
- Instantly trackable (check your application status online!)
- And . . . impossible to lose in the mail (they reach schools instantly)

But also: On PrincetonReview.com, there's no extra fee to submit your application online—our technology is totally FREE for you to use. In fact, some colleges even *waive* the application fee if you apply online.

---

Still have questions?

- Can I start an application now and finish it later?
- Are there easy-to-use instructions or someone I can call if I have a question? If I get stuck are there application instructions?
- Do schools *really* want to receive applications online?

Yes, yes, and yes!

---

It's easy to see the advantages of online applications. Almost as easy as actually applying.

Just log on and apply. It's that easy.

PrincetonReview.com—Applications without the pain.

# How We Produce This Book

When we first began work on this project in 1991, there was a void in the world of college guides (hard to believe, but true!). No one publication provided prospective college students with in-depth statistical data from the colleges on admission, financial aid, student body demographics, and academics, as well as narrative descriptions of college academic and social life on each campus based on the opinions of the very students who attend them. Thus *Best Colleges* was born. There wasn't then—and there still isn't now—any other college guide like this one.

The differences start right on the cover with the name—*The Best 351Colleges*. Why not *The Best 300 Colleges*? Or just *The Best Colleges*? And how did we arrive at 351? Well, to be honest, the original plan back at the beginning was to produce a guide entitled *The Best 300 Colleges*. An initial list of colleges to be included was compiled, and the authors got to work arranging for on-campus student surveys to be conducted. Since student feedback is such an integral part of the individual college entries and several other aspects of the guide, it was absolutely imperative that every campus intended for inclusion be surveyed by academic year's end. Alas, Mother Nature and other forces kept our surveyors off of many campuses that year, and a number of colleges could not be included in the first edition. Thus it was simply called *The Best Colleges*, sans number.

The guide enjoyed some early success, but it really needed a number in its title in order to help position it in relation to other guides on the shelves of your friendly neighborhood book superstore. The second edition was referred to as *The Best 286 Colleges*, and it's all history from there.

To determine which colleges and universities are included in *The Best Colleges*, we have avoided using any sort of mathematical calculations or formulas. The initial list was built through consultation with a variety of expert sources, including fifty independent educational consultants from throughout the nation. From that point, new institutions have been added annually; a few have been dropped. A careful review of the guide will reveal a wide representation of colleges in terms of geography and enrollment size. Inside, you will read about public and private schools, historically black colleges and universities, science and technology–focused institutions, nontraditional colleges, highly selective schools and those with virtually open-door admissions policies, great buys and the wildly expensive. We've added six schools to the guide this year: Flagler College, Manhattanville College, Marist College, Mercer University, Seattle University, and the United States Merchant Marine Academy. Like the other schools in this guide, all are institutions well worth considering. Though not every college included will appeal to every student, this guide represents our version of the cream of the crop—comprising the top 10 percent of all colleges in the nation—and our best 351.

In addition to closely monitoring the statistical data we collect on nearly 2,000 colleges, we meet with dozens of admissions officers and college presidents annually, and keep abreast of college news 24/7 throughout each year. As a result, we are able to maintain a working list of colleges to consider adding to or deleting from the guide for each subsequent edition. Any college we consider adding to the guide must agree to allow anonymous student surveys to be completed on campus; it is difficulty with this issue alone that explains why the United States Air Force Academy was conspicuously absent from *Best Colleges* for many years, while West Point and Annapolis were (and still are) included in the guide. We tried to survey there for three editions before we finally succeeded; it always deserved to be included in the guide—but only if and when it would allow student anonymity in response to our survey. We're very psyched that they're finally a part of our guide.

Hundreds of thousands of students in total have been surveyed on the various campuses that comprise the best 351. Each annual edition includes information based on the opinions of more than 100,000 students; we've surveyed anywhere from twenty-odd men at Deep Springs College in the California desert to thousands of collegians at places like Clemson University and the University of Michigan. It's a mammoth undertaking, but the launch a few years ago of our online student survey (http://survey.review.com), available 24/7, has made it possible for students to complete a survey anytime and anywhere an Internet-enabled computer can be found.

So how do we do it? Early on we surveyed at all of the included colleges and universities on our own, marshalling resources through our network of dozens of Princeton Review offices nationwide. Once we'd gone through a few editions, we switched to a two-to-three-year cycle for revisiting each campus. (The reality is that, unless there's been some grand upheaval at a campus, we've found that there's little change in student opinion from one year to the next.) Thus, each year we now survey on approximately 100 to 125 campuses. Colleges that wish to be resurveyed prior to their regular survey cycle are accommodated with an earlier visit if at all possible.

All colleges and universities we plan to visit are notified through established campus contacts that we wish to arrange a survey; we depend upon these contacts for assistance in identifying common, high-traffic areas on-campus in which to survey, and to help us make any necessary arrangements as required by campus policies. At colleges in the New York metropolitan area (we call it home), we most often send our own team to conduct the typically day long surveys; at colleges that are further afield, we hire current students to conduct the surveys if at all possible. In recent years, many schools have chosen to send an email to the entire student body notifying it of the availability of the survey, which in some cases yielded astonishing results.

The survey itself is extensive, divided into four fundamental sections—"About Yourself," "Your School's Academics/Administration," "Students," and "Life at Your School"—that collectively include more than seventy questions. We ask about everything imaginable, from "How many out-of-class hours do you spend studying each day?" to "How widely used is beer?" Most questions are multiple-response in nature, but seven offer students the opportunity to expand on their answers with narrative responses. These narrative responses are the sources of the student quotes that appear throughout each entry in *Best 351 Colleges*.

Once the surveys have been completed and the responses stored in our database, each college is given a grade point average (GPA) for its students' answers to each individual multiple-response question. It is these GPAs that enable us to compare student opinions from college to college, and to gauge which aspects of the complete experience at each college rate highest and lowest according to the institution's own students. Once we have this information in hand, we write the individual college entries. Student quotes expressed within the entries are not chosen for their extreme nature, humor, or singular perspective—in all cases the intention is that they represent closely the sentiments expressed by the majority of survey respondents from the college or that they illustrate one side or another of a mixed bag of student opinion, in which case one should also find a counterpoint within the text. And, of course, if they accomplish this *and* are noteworthy for their wittiness, they'll definitely make it into the guide.

The entries in general seek to accomplish that which a college admissions viewbook by its very nature can never really hope to achieve—to provide a (relatively) uncensored view of life at a particular college, and acknowledge that even the best of the best of America's 3,500 or so colleges have their drawbacks. Though some college administrators find this book hard to accept, most have come to recognize that college officials no longer enjoy the luxury of controlling every word that students hear or read about their institutions and that the age of consumerism in the college search process is here to stay.

Our survey is qualitative and anecdotal rather than quantitative. While this approach sometimes means we blow a result—such as when we surveyed at Stephens College during the week the administration was debating the abolition of women's studies as a major at that small women's college and (*suprise!*) the survey results indicated an unhappy student body—most of our results are confirmed by feedback we get from alums, current students, counselors, and prospective students who visit the campuses. In order to help guard against the likelihood that we produce an entry that's way off the mark for any particular college, we send administrators at each school a copy of the entry we intend to publish prior to its actual publication date, with ample opportunity to respond with corrections, comments, and/or outright objections. In every case in which we receive a reply, we take careful steps to insure that we review their suggestions and make appropriate changes when warranted.

Far more important than what college administrators think is what YOU think. Take our information on colleges as you should take information from all sources—as input that reflects the values and opinions of others, which may be helpful to you as you *form your own opinions* about the colleges you're considering. This guide is not an end point from which you should cull your list of colleges to apply to without referencing any other source or visiting any of the colleges covered here. Rather, it's a starting point, a tool that can help you to probe the surface and get a sense of the college experience. You simply must do your own investigation and develop your own list of best colleges. Only then will this book be the useful tool that it is intended to be.

# How This Book Is Organized

Each of the colleges and universities listed in this book has its own two-page spread. To make it easier to find information about the schools of your choice, we've used the same format for every school. Look at the sample pages below:

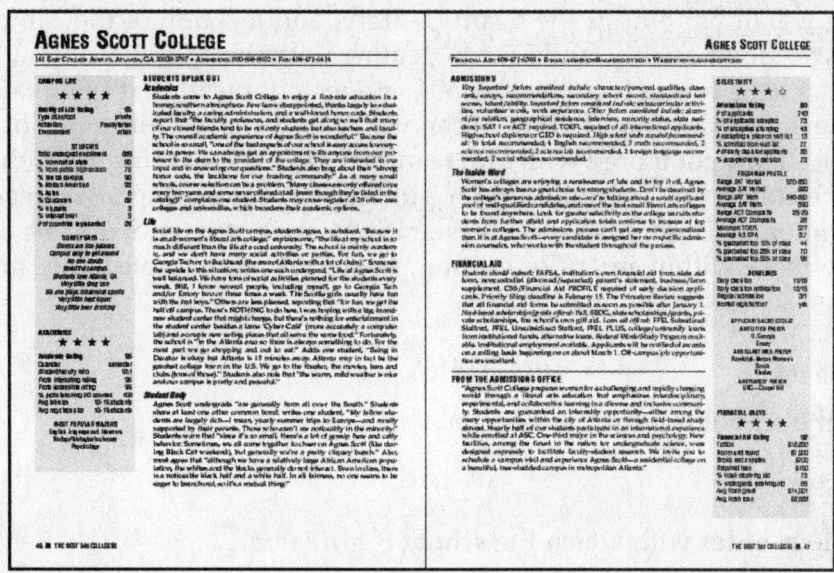

Each spread has nine major components. First, at the very top of the spread you will see the school's address, telephone, and fax numbers for the admissions office, the telephone number for the financial aid office, and the school's website and/or email address. Second, there are two sidebars (the narrow columns on the outside of each page, which consist mainly of statistics) divided into the categories of Campus Life, Academics, Selectivity, and Financial Facts. Third, there are four headings in the main body text or "write-up" called "Students Speak Out," "Admissions," "Financial Aid," and "From the Admissions Office." Here's what each part contains:

## The Sidebars

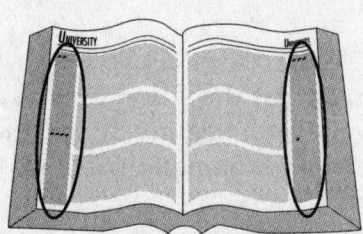

The sidebars contain various statistics culled from our own online student surveys and from questionnaires school administrators fill out. Keep in mind that not every category will appear for every school, since in some cases the information is not reported or not applicable.

Here is what each heading tells you:

## Quality of Life Rating

How happy students are with their lives outside the classroom. This rating is given on a scale of one to four stars. One star is the equivalent of a grade of 60 to 69; two are equivalent to a grade of 70 to 79; three are equivalent to a grade of 80 to 89; and four are equivalent to a grade of 90 or above. The ratings were determined using the results from our surveys. We weighed several factors, including students' overall happiness, the beauty, safety, and location of the campus, comfort of dorms, food quality, and ease in dealing with the administration. Note that even if a school's rating is in the low 60s, it does not mean that the quality of life is horrible—there are no "failing" schools. A low ranking just means that the school placed low compared with others in *Best 351 Colleges*. This individual rating places each college on a continuum for purposes of comparing all colleges within this edition only. Though similar, these ratings are not intended to be compared directly to those within any prior edition, as our ratings computations are refined and change somewhat annually.

## Type of school

Whether the school is public or private.

## Affiliation

Any religious order with which the school is affiliated.

## Environment

Whether the campus is located in an urban, suburban, or rural setting.

## Total undergrad enrollment

The total number of undergraduates who attend the school.

## "% male/female" through "# countries represented"

The demographic breakdown of the full-time undergraduate student body and what percentages of the student body live on campus, belong to Greek organizations, and, finally, the number of countries represented by the student body.

## Survey Says

Summarizes the results of our survey. This list shows what the students we surveyed felt unusually strongly about, both positively and negatively, at their schools (see the end of the introduction for a more detailed explanation of items on the list).

## Academic Rating

On a scale of one to four stars, how hard students work at the school and how much they get back for their efforts. The ratings are determined based on results from our surveys of students and administrators. Factors weighed included how many hours students studied and the quality of students the school attracts; we also considered students' assessments of their professors' abilities and helpfulness. This individual rating places each college on a continuum for purposes of comparing all colleges within this edition only. Though similar, these ratings are not intended to be compared directly to those within any prior edition, as our ratings computations are refined and change somewhat annually.

## Calendar

The school's schedule of academic terms. A "semester" schedule has two long terms, usually starting in September and January. A "trimester" schedule has three terms, one usually beginning before Christmas and two after. A "quarterly" schedule has four terms, which go by very quickly: the entire term, including exams, usually lasts only nine or ten weeks. A "4-1-4" schedule is like a semester schedule, but with a month-long term in between the fall and spring semesters. (Similarly, a 4-4-1 has a short term following two longer semesters.) When a school's academic calendar doesn't match any of these traditional schedules we note that by saying "other." For schools that have "other" as their calendar, it is best to call the admissions office for details.

## Student/faculty ratio

The ratio of full-time undergraduate instructional faculty members to all undergraduates.

## Profs interesting rating

Based on the answers given by students to the survey question, "In general, how good are your instructors as teachers?"

## Profs accessible rating

Based on the answers given by students to the survey question, "In general, how accessible are your instructors outside the classroom?"

## % profs teaching UG courses

Largely self-explanatory; this category shows the percentage of professors who teach undergraduates and eliminates any faculty whose focus is solely on research.

## % classes taught by TAs

Many universities that offer graduate programs use graduate students as teaching assistants (TAs). They teach undergraduate courses, primarily at the introductory level. This category reports on the percentage of classes that are taught by TAs instead of regular faculty.

## Average lab size; Average regular class size

College-reported figures on class size averages for regular courses and for labs/discussion sections.

## Most Popular Majors

The three most popular majors at the school.

## Admissions Rating

How competitive admission is at the school, on a scale of one to four stars. This rating is determined by several factors, including the class rank of entering freshmen, test scores, and percentage of applicants accepted. By incorporating all these factors, our competitiveness rating adjusts for "self-selecting" applicant pools. University of Chicago, for example, has a very high competitiveness rating, even though it admits a surprisingly large proportion of its applicants. Chicago's applicant pool is self-selecting; that is, nearly all the school's applicants are exceptional students. This individual rating places each college on a continuum for purposes of comparing all colleges within this edition only. Though similar, these ratings are not intended to be compared directly to those within any prior edition, as our ratings computations are refined and change somewhat annually.

## % of applicants accepted

The percentage of applicants to which the school offered admission.

## % of acceptees attending

The percentage of those who were accepted who eventually enrolled.

## # accepting a place on wait list

The number of students who decided to take a place on the wait list when offered this option.

## % admitted from wait list

The percent of applicants who opted to take a place on the wait list and were subsequently offered admission. These figures will vary tremendously from college to college, and should be a consideration when deciding whether to accept a place on a college's wait list.

### # of early decision applicants

The number of students who applied under the college's early decision or early action plan.

### % accepted early decision

The percentage of early decision or early action applicants who were admitted under this plan. By the nature of these plans, the vast majority who are admitted wind up enrolling. (See the early decision/action description that follows in this section for more detail.)

### Range/Average SAT Verbal, Range/Average SAT Math, Range/Average ACT Composite

The average and the middle 50 percent range of test scores for entering freshmen. Don't be discouraged from applying to the school of your choice even if your combined SAT scores are 80 or even 120 points below the average, because you may still have a chance of getting in. Remember that many schools emphasize other aspects of your application (e.g., your grades, how good a match you make with the school) more heavily than test scores.

### Minimum TOEFL

The minimum test score necessary for entering freshmen who are required to take the TOEFL (Test of English as a Foreign Language). Most schools will require all international students or non-native English speakers to take the TOEFL in order to be considered for admission.

### Average HS GPA

We report this on a scale of 1–4 (occasionally colleges report averages on a 100 scale, in which case we report those figures). This is one of the key factors in college admissions. Be sure to keep your GPA as high as possible straight through until graduation from high school.

### % graduated top 10%, top 25%, top 50% of class

Of those students for whom class rank was reported, the percentage of entering freshmen who ranked in the top tenth, quarter, and half of their high school classes.

### Early decision/action deadlines

The deadline for submission of application materials under the early decision or early action plan. Early decision is generally for students for whom the school is a first choice. The applicant commits to attending the school if admitted; in return, the school renders an early decision, usually in December or January. If accepted, the applicant doesn't have to spend the time and money applying to other schools. In most cases, students may apply for early decision to only one school. Early action is similar to early decision, but less binding; applicants need not commit to attending the school and in some cases may apply early action to more than one school. The school, in turn, may not render a decision, choosing to defer the applicant to the regular admissions pool. Each school's guidelines are a little different, and the policies of a few of the most selective colleges in the country have changed quite dramatically recently. Some colleges offer more than one early decision cycle, so it's a good idea to call and get full details if you plan to pursue one of these options.

### Early decision, early action, priority, and regular admission deadlines

The dates by which all materials must be postmarked (we'd suggest "received in the office") in order to be considered for admission under each particular admissions option/cycle for admission for the fall term.

### Early decision, early action, priority, and regular admission notification

The dates by which you can expect a decision on your application under each admissions option/cycle.

### Nonfall registration

Some schools will allow applicants or transfers to matriculate at times other than the fall term—the traditional beginning of the academic calendar year. Other schools will only allow you to register for classes if you can begin in the fall term. A simple "yes" or "no" in this category indicates the school's policy on nonfall registration.

### Applicants also look at

These lists were formulated with data from our student surveys and information solicited directly from the colleges. We asked students to list all the schools to which they applied and those at which they were accepted. Schools they named most often appear in these three lists. When students consistently rejected a school in favor of the featured school, that school appears under "and rarely prefer"; schools that split applicants on a relatively even basis with the featured school appear under "and sometimes prefer"; schools that students usually chose over the featured school appear under "and often prefer." For example, students who responded to our survey and who are accepted at both Princeton and Columbia more often chose Princeton. Therefore on Princeton's feature page, Columbia appears in the "and rarely prefer" category (because students rarely preferred Columbia to Princeton), and on Columbia's feature page, Princeton appears in the "and often prefer" category (because students often prefer Princeton to Columbia). Admissions officers are given the opportunity to annually review and suggest alterations to these lists for their schools.

### Financial Aid Rating

Based on school-reported data on financial aid and awards to students and students' satisfaction as collected through our survey with the financial aid they receive. Again, this is on a scale of one to four stars. This individual rating places each college on a continuum for purposes of comparing all colleges within this edition only. Though similar, these ratings are not intended to be compared directly to those within any prior edition, as our ratings computations are refined and change somewhat annually.

## Tuition, In-state tuition

The tuition at the school, or for public colleges, for a resident of the school's state. Usually much lower than out-of-state tuition for state-supported public schools.

## Out-of-state tuition

For public colleges, the tuition for a nonresident of the school's state. This entry appears only for public colleges, since tuition at private colleges is generally the same regardless of state of residence.

## Room & board

Estimated room and board costs.

## Books and supplies

Estimated annual cost of necessary textbooks and/or supplies.

## % frosh receiving aid

According to the school's financial aid department, the percentage of all freshmen who received need-based aid.

## % UG receiving aid

According to the school's financial aid department, the percentage of all undergrads who receive need-based financial aid.

## Avg frosh grant

The average grant or scholarship value.

## Avg frosh loan

The average amount of loans disbursed to freshmen.

## Students Speak Out

This section summarizes the results of the surveys we distributed to students at the school. When appropriate, it also incorporates statistics provided by the schools themselves. It is divided into three subheadings: Academics, Life, and Student Body. The Academics section reports how hard students work and how satisfied they are with the education they are getting. It also often tells you which 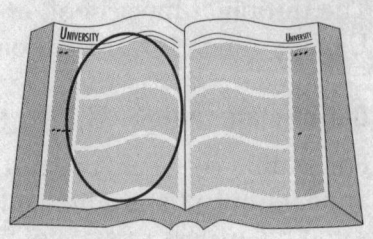 academic departments our respondents rated favorably. Student opinion regarding administrative departments often works its way into this section. The Life section describes life outside the classroom and addresses questions ranging from "How nice is the campus?" and "How comfortable are the dorms?" to "How popular are fraternities and sororities?" The Student Body section tells you about what type of student the school attracts and how the students view the level of interaction between various groups, including those of different ethnic origins.

All quotes in these sections are from students' essay responses to our surveys. **We choose quotes based on the accuracy with which they reflect our survey results.** Those students who wrote entertaining but nonrepresentative essays will find excerpts of their work in Part 4 of the book, a section titled "My Roommate's Feet Really Stink."

## Admissions

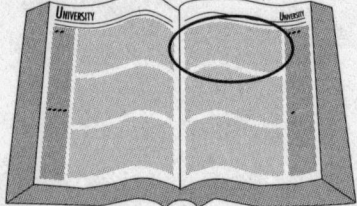 This section tells you what aspects of your application are most important to the school's admissions officers. It also lists the high school curricular prerequisites for applicants, which standardized tests (if any) are required, and special information about the school's admissions process (e.g., Do minority students and legacies, for example, receive special consideration? Are there any unusual application requirements for applicants to special programs?).

## The Inside Word

This section contains our own insights into each school's admissions process.

## Financial Aid

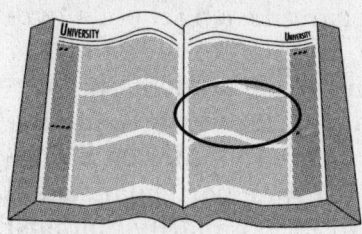

This section summarizes the financial aid process at the school: What forms you need and what types of merit-based aid and loans are available. Information about need-based aid is contained in the financial aid sidebar. While this section includes specific deadline dates for submission of materials as reported by the colleges, we strongly encourage students seeking financial aid to file all forms—federal, state, and institutional—as soon as they become available. In the world of financial aid, the early birds almost always get the best worms (provided, of course, that they're eligible for a meal!).

## From the Admissions Office

This section contains text supplied by the colleges in response to our invitation that they use this space to "speak directly to the readers of our guide." For schools that did not respond, we excerpted an appropriate passage from the school's catalog, website, or other admissions literature.

# Survey Says

Our Survey Says list, located in the Campus Life sidebar on each school's two-page spread, is based entirely on the results of our on-campus surveys. In other words, the items on this list are based on the opinions of the students we surveyed at those schools (*not* on any numerical analysis of library size, endowment, etc.). Items are defined as those that are popular or unpopular on a campus. The appearance of a Survey Says item in the sidebar for a particular school does not reflect the popularity of that item relative to its popularity amongst other schools' student bodies. For relative popularity of certain items, see the appropriate ranking (e.g., for the Survey Says item "Library needs improving," see the "This is a Library?" ranking). Some of the terms that appear on the list are not entirely self-explanatory; these terms are defined below.

**Diverse students interact:** We asked students whether students from different class and ethnic backgrounds interacted frequently and easily. When students' collective response is "yes," the heading "Diverse students interact" appears on the list. When student response indicates there are not many interactions between different students from different class and ethnic backgrounds, the heading "Students are cliquish" appears on the list.

**Cheating:** We asked students how prevalent cheating is at their school. If students reported cheating to be rare, "No one cheats" shows up on the list.

**Students are happy:** This category reflects student responses to the question "Overall, how happy are you with your school?"

**TAs teach upper-level classes:** At some large universities, you'll continue to be taught by teaching assistants even in your upper-level courses. It is safe to assume that when "Lots of TAs teach upper-level courses" appears on the list, TAs also teach a disproportionate number of intro courses as well.

**Students are very religious** or **Students aren't religious:** We asked students how religious they are. Their responses are reflected in this category.

**Diverse student body:** We asked students whether their student body is made up of a variety of ethnic groups. This category reflects their answers to this question. This heading shows up as "diversity lacking on campus" or "ethnic diversity on campus."

**Town-gown relations:** We asked students whether they got along with local residents; their answers are reflected by this category.

If you have any questions, comments, or suggestions, please contact us at Editorial Department, Admissions Services, 2315 Broadway, New York, NY 10024, or email us at bookeditor@review.com. We appreciate your input and want to make our books as useful to you as they can be.

# GLOSSARY

**ACT:** Like the SAT I but less tricky. Many schools accept either SAT or ACT scores; if you consistently get blown away by the SAT, you might want to consider taking the ACT instead.

**College-prep curriculum:** 16 to 18 academic credits (each credit equals a full year of a high school course), usually including: 4 years of English, 3 to 4 years of social studies, and at least 2 years each of science, mathematics, and foreign language.

**Core curriculum:** Students at schools with core curricula must take a number of required courses, usually in such subjects as world history, western civilization, writing skills, and fundamental math and science.

**CSS/Financial Aid PROFILE:** The College Scholarship Service PROFILE, an optional financial aid form required by some colleges in addition to the FAFSA.

**Distribution requirements:** Students at schools with distribution requirements must take a number of courses in various subject areas, such as foreign language, humanities, natural science, and social science. Distribution requirements do not specify which courses you must take, only which types of courses.

**FAFSA:** The Free Application for Federal Student Aid. Schools are required by law to accept the FAFSA; some require that applicants complete at least one other form (usually a CSS/Financial Aid PROFILE or the college's own form) to be considered for financial aid.

**4-1-4:** A type of academic schedule. It's like a semester schedule, but with a short semester (usually one month long) between the two semesters. Most schools offer internship programs or nontraditional studies during the short semester. A 4-4-1 schedule is similar to this one, except the short semester comes after the second long semester, usually in the late spring or early summer.

**GDI:** "Goddamned independents," a term frequently used by students in fraternities and sororities to describe those not in fraternities and sororities.

**Greek system, Greeks:** Fraternities and sororities.

**Humanities:** These include such disciplines as art history, drama, English, foreign languages, music, philosophy, and religion.

**Merit-based grant:** A scholarship (not necessarily full) given to students because of some special talent or attribute. Artists, athletes, community leaders, and geniuses are typical recipients.

**Natural sciences:** These include such disciplines as astronomy, biology, chemistry, genetics, geology, mathematics, physics, and zoology.

**Need-based grant:** A scholarship (not necessarily full) given to students because they would otherwise be unable to afford college. Student need is determined on the basis of the FAFSA. Some schools also require the CSS PROFILE and/or institutional applications.

**Priority deadline:** Some schools will list a deadline for admission and/or financial aid as a "priority deadline," meaning that while they will accept applications after that date, all applications received prior to the deadline are assured of getting the most thorough, in some instances potentially more generous, appraisal possible.

**RA:** Residence assistant (or residential advisor). Someone, usually an upperclassman or graduate student, who supervises a floor or section of a dorm, usually in return for free room and board. RAs are responsible for enforcing the drinking and noise rules.

**SAT I:** A college entrance exam required by many schools; most schools will accept either the ACT or the SAT I.

**SAT II: Subject Tests:** Subject-specific exams administered by the Educational Testing Service (the SAT people). These tests are required by some, but not all, admissions offices. English Writing and Math Level I or IIc are the tests most frequently required.

**Social sciences:** These include such disciplines as anthropology, economics, geography, history, international studies, political science, psychology, and sociology.

**Tuition GPA:** The competitiveness of the total cost of attending a college for one year as a resident undergrad with a meal plan, on a scale of 0.00 to 4.00. We calculate the average tuition actually paid by a student attending the college. Colleges offset their sticker prices by awarding both need-based and non-need-based gift aid (grants and scholarships) to undergraduates. We don't incorporate self-help aid (loans and work-study) in the GPA formula because these costs are ultimately the student's responsibility to meet. We only use the Tuition GPA in the formula that determines the schools on The Best Academic Bang for Your Buck list; you won't see it reported in this edition of the book. The lower the average tuition, the higher the Tuition GPA, which works to a school's favor in the ranking.

**TA:** Teaching assistant. Most often a graduate student, a TA will often teach discussion sections of large lectures. At some schools, TAs and graduate students teach a large number of introductory-level and even some upper-level courses. At smaller schools, professors generally do all the teaching.

**Work-study:** A government-funded financial aid program that provides assistance to financial aid recipients in return for work in the school's library, labs, etc.

# About Those College Rankings

We've shed some light on how we conduct our student survey and produce the entries and ratings that make up *Best Colleges*, as well as a sense of why we publish the guide; now we'd like to discuss how to use the information that we've compiled—specifically the rankings.

Perhaps no single element of our guide to *The Best 351 Colleges* gets more attention than the front section entitled "Schools Ranked By Category." Since it's become an annual subject addressed by the media, and subsequently college presidents, admission directors, public relations officers, students, and their parents, we want to share our own thoughts about it with the students and parents who have chosen this guide.

The "Schools Ranked By Category" section of *Best Colleges* includes sixty-three different rankings. (An additional "ranking" focuses on a single institution, Deep Springs College, the only two-year college ever included in the guide. Deep Springs is assigned its own "Honor Roll" list that includes all categories in which it placed highly, thus eliminating perpetual "apples and oranges" comparisons between it and the four-year colleges in the rankings.) All of the rankings are broad-based in their intent, designed to generally illustrate environmental considerations at the colleges across a wide variety of categories.

Fifty-eight of these lists are based entirely on either individual questions from our student surveys or are compiled from responses to several student survey questions. The other three lists include computations based on both student survey responses and statistical data provided by the colleges. Each list, even those entitled in a somewhat tongue-in-cheek manner, covers one of many aspects of a college's character that can be helpful in deciding if it's the right or wrong place for an individual student.

As the cost of attending college continues to rise at a pace exceeding that of inflation, and as students and their families must continue to approach college selection as consumers, it is important to recognize the schools that offer the greatest academic value for their students' dollars. Last year we introduced a new ranking highlighting those schools that offer the Best Academic Bang for Your Buck. We used three of our existing calculations to produce this new calculation: the Academic Rating, the Financial Aid Rating, and the Tuition GPA. (You can read about the Academic and Financial Aid Ratings in the "How This Book Is Organized" section and about the Tuition GPA on the previous page.) Together, these three calculations encompass a wide range of financial and academic data, both school-reported and student-opinion-based, for all 351 colleges in this book. We believe this ranking reveals the most accurate assessment of how pleased students are with the academic environment they get for what they actually pay. As with our other rankings, the Best Academic Bang for Your Buck ranking only shows how colleges stacked up against the other schools included in this edition.

The rankings are often misconstrued; many in the media and general public think that The Princeton Review annually deems colleges "party schools" or places where the "students never stop studying." Actually, the rankings are based directly upon what students on each campus tell us about their college. Besides inquiring about where else they applied for admission, we ask them only about the college they're attending. No students are asked to rate other colleges comparatively in terms of any of the items the lists rank. And compound rankings are just that—compound calculations based on responses to multiple questions. There's no individual "party school" question on the survey.

In case you haven't heard by now, the party school ranking draws lots of attention every year. It's even been the subject of a *Doonesbury* cartoon. Calls, email, and letters begin to arrive in our offices as soon as the first word of our rankings hits the media. Some contacts are from students who complain that their college didn't make the list, while others are from those who are irate because their college did. A *Washington Post* writer challenged WVU's number-one ranking in the 1998 edition as undeserved, contending that it's nothing like the good old days when he attended the university. Local media have touted the fact that nearby colleges didn't make the list when they aren't even in the guide in the first place, and thus were not surveyed at all. Many incorrectly assume that an institution that shows up on the party school ranking is a lousy college to attend—when the basic premise of the guide is to highlight colleges that The Princeton Review feels are among the top 10 percent of colleges and universities in the U.S.

*Best Colleges* begins with the best as its basis. Rankings that are among the less flattering of the sixty-three categories are not lists of bad schools—colleges on all of these lists are still among the best in the nation. This holds equally true for those on the party school list in particular. Remember our earlier comments about these rankings reflecting environmental considerations; broad categorizations of the college experience on each campus. Even schools placed at the top of the party school list are excellent places to pursue one's college career, and offer not only an exuberant social atmosphere but also a wide range of high-quality academic programs, as does every college or university that has ever appeared on this list in *Best Colleges*.

With few notable exceptions, no one should make the mistake of assuming that the colleges and universities that don't show up on the party school rankings are in any way insulated from the influences of alcohol and drugs on their student bodies and campuses. While a student who has little self-discipline or is easily led might be best off on a campus with a more distinctly academic emphasis, a glance at the news of the past academic year reveals that such considerations aren't often useful benchmarks.

The gaps aren't large in this regard, and tragedy is not exclusive. A Harvard University study has revealed that 44 percent of undergraduates in general binge drink (consume five or more alcoholic beverages in one sitting for men, four drinks or more for women). These facts are sobering, as they should be. Fingers can be pointed in many directions as concerns campus drinking and partying. "Dry campus" policies drive drinking off-campus, make it even more dangerous, and only exacerbate the problem by removing any opportunity to influence student behavior in this regard. If you're going off campus to drink, don't drive back drunk—get a designated driver. Wherever you're going to drink, do it safely, smartly, responsibly, and within the law. Don't let a peer situation (fraternity rush, etc.) put you in jeopardy—it's simply not worth it. Don't use alcohol or drugs as a badge of your coolness—there's not much of a fine line between someone who's socially engaging and someone who's totally disengaging because he or she has performed a chemically enabled auto-lobotomy. Lastly, don't simply take responsibility for yourself; remember to keep an eye on your friends, and never leave them passed out and alone.

Some critics contend that The Princeton Review glorifies drinking and partying with these rankings; we submit that we glorify important information for students preparing to make one of the biggest choices they'll ever make in their lives. What could be more useful to students choosing a college than the opinions of current college students about their campuses? College is an incredible growth experience, one that covers a significant portion of the full spectrum of life's lessons. It's much more than classrooms, books, and professors—it's a complete experience that you're bound never to forget. College—there's nothing like it.

# PART 2

# Schools Ranked by Category

One of the great things about a multiple-choice survey is that the results give you lots of numbers. We wanted to present those numbers to you in a fun and informative way; hence, the following rankings of schools in sixty-three categories. In the following lists, the top twenty schools in each category appear in descending order. Remember, of course, that our survey included only students at *The Best 351 Colleges*, and that all schools appearing on negative lists have many assets that counterbalance their various deficiencies.

Although these lists are presented mostly for fun, they can be used to help you clarify some of the choices you have to make in picking the right college. As you read through them, focus on those categories that are important to you: Do you want to go to a school where discussion takes up most of class time? Would you prefer only to be lectured to? Do you care? Do you want to go to a school where students party nonstop? Or would you rather go somewhere with a subdued social scene? By looking through these lists, you should be able to get a good idea of what are and are not important considerations to you.

We've broken the rankings down into nine categories: Academics; Administration; Quality of Life; Politics; Demographics; Social Life; Extracurriculars; Parties; and Schools by Type. Under each list heading, we tell you the survey question or assessment that we used to tabulate the list. For the Schools by Type rankings, we combined student responses to several questions to determine whether a school was a "jock" school, a "party" school, and so on. These lists have changed considerably since the first edition of this book, as we have had time to rethink what truly defines a school's character. For instance, we now factor students' answers to the question "How many hours a day do you study?" into our party-school calibrations. After all, as some of our readers have pointed out, at some schools students drink and do drugs to relieve the stress of their demanding curricula. And, in some cases, statistical data reported by the colleges is also factored in.

Be aware that all of these lists are based on our survey results. Therefore, they do not reflect our opinions, nor do they perfectly reflect reality; that is to say, we can't tell you at which schools registration is actually the biggest hassle. What we can tell you is the schools at which students are most pissed off about registration hassles. Our feeling is that students' self-perceptions are quite valuable. After all, what better way is there to judge a school than by how its students feel about it?

## ACADEMICS

### Best Overall Academic Experience For Undergraduates
*Based on The Princeton Review ACADEMIC RATING*

1. Yale University
2. Princeton University
3. Duke University
4. Amherst College
5. Massachusetts Institute of Technology
6. United States Air Force Academy
7. United States Coast Guard Academy
8. United States Naval Academy
9. United States Military Academy
10. Reed College
11. Wellesley College
12. Bates College
13. Williams College
14. Carleton College
15. Swarthmore College
16. Harvey Mudd College
17. Northwestern University
18. Columbia University
19. Haverford College
20. Dartmouth College

### The Toughest to Get Into
*Based on The Princeton Review ADMISSIONS RATING*

1. United States Military Academy
2. Princeton University
3. Harvard College
4. Yale University
5. United States Naval Academy
6. Massachusetts Institute of Technology
7. Davidson College
8. Stanford University
9. Dartmouth College
10. Cooper Union
11. Brown University
12. University of Pennsylvania
13. Duke University
14. United States Air Force Academy
15. Columbia University
16. Amherst College
17. Northwestern University
18. California Institute of Technology
19. Georgetown University
20. Williams College

## Their Students Never Stop Studying
*How many out-of-class hours do you spend studying each day?*

1. California Institute of Technology
2. Haverford College
3. Carnegie Mellon University
4. Swarthmore College
5. Wesleyan College
6. Scripps College
7. Worcester Polytechnic Institute
8. Colorado College
9. Knox College
10. St. Lawrence University
11. Rensselaer Polytechnic Institute
12. Colorado School of Mines
13. Earlham College
14. Bard College
15. Virginia Tech
16. Davidson College
17. Ohio Wesleyan University
18. Beloit College
19. Marquette University
20. Austin College

## Their Students (Almost) Never Study
*How many out-of-class hours do you spend studying each day?*

1. University of Colorado—Boulder
2. Indiana University—Bloomington
3. University of Florida
4. University of Illinois—Urbana-Champaign
5. Ohio State University—Columbus
6. University of North Dakota
7. University of Kentucky
8. Loyola University New Orleans
9. University of Connecticut
10. Temple University
11. Sonoma State University
12. TCU
13. Iowa State University
14. University of Dayton
15. American University
16. Clemson University
17. University of North Carolina—Asheville
18. The Evergreen State College
19. The College of New Jersey
20. Bellarmine College

## Professors Bring Material to Life
*Are your instructors good teachers?*

1. Middlebury College
2. Carleton College
3. Davidson College
4. Harvey Mudd College
5. Seattle University
6. The University of the South
7. Washington and Lee University
8. Whitman College
9. Wellesley College
10. United States Merchant Marine Academy
11. Kenyon College
12. Amherst College
13. Reed College
14. Smith College
15. New College of Florida
16. Wells College
17. Mount Holyoke College
18. Manhattanville College
19. Hampden-Sydney College
20. Wabash College

## Professors Get Low Marks
*Are your instructors good teachers?*

1. Stevens Institute of Technology
2. California Institute of Technology
3. Georgia Institute of Technology
4. New Jersey Institute of Technology
5. Montana Tech of the University of Montana
6. Florida A&M University
7. Stony Brook University (SUNY)
8. Webb Institute
9. Albertson College
10. Illinois Institute of Technology
11. Rider University
12. State University of New York at Albany
13. University of California—Riverside
14. University of Toronto
15. Stephens College
16. Michigan Technological University
17. Rensselaer Polytechnic Institute
18. Cooper Union
19. University of Nevada—Las Vegas
20. University of North Dakota

## Professors Make Themselves Accessible
*Are your instructors accessible outside the classroom?*

1. Franklin & Marshall College
2. Tulane University
3. Elon University
4. United States Air Force Academy
5. Washington and Lee University
6. Centre College
7. Harvey Mudd College
8. Wabash College
9. Davidson College
10. Kenyon College
11. Wellesley College
12. United States Naval Academy
13. Whitman College

14. Carleton College
15. College of the Holy Cross
16. The University of the South
17. Grinnell College
18. University of Richmond
19. Kalamazoo College
20. St. Olaf College

## Professors Make Themselves Scarce
*Are your instructors accessible outside the classroom?*

1. University of Iowa
2. University of Missouri—Rolla
3. Washington State University
4. Montana Tech of the University of Montana
5. Arizona State University
6. Florida State University
7. Kansas State University
8. Ohio State University—Columbus
9. Florida A&M University
10. University of Nevada—Las Vegas
11. Illinois Institute of Technology
12. Georgia Institute of Technology
13. University of Toronto
14. University of North Dakota
15. University of New Orleans
16. Eugene Lang College
17. Stevens Institute of Technology
18. University of Hawaii—Manoa
19. New Jersey Institute of Technology
20. State University of New York at Albany

## Class Discussions Encouraged
*How much of your overall class time is devoted to discussion as opposed to lectures?*

1. St. John's College (MD)
2. Sarah Lawrence College
3. Bard College
4. Hampshire College
5. Simon's Rock College of Bard
6. Goddard College
7. Bennington College
8. Marlboro College
9. St. John's College (NM)
10. Reed College
11. Guilford College
12. Rollins College
13. Eugene Lang College
14. Hollins University
15. Sweet Briar College
16. Wells College
17. Millsaps College
18. Colorado College
19. Wesleyan College
20. Earlham College

## Class Discussions Rare
*How much of your overall class time is devoted to discussion as opposed to lectures?*

1. University of Toronto
2. Georgia Institute of Technology
3. University of Missouri—Rolla
4. Stony Brook University (SUNY)
5. University of California—San Diego
6. Stevens Institute of Technology
7. McGill University
8. University of California—Davis
9. University of Hawaii—Manoa
10. Illinois Institute of Technology
11. California Institute of Technology
12. Virginia Tech
13. New Jersey Institute of Technology
14. University of Texas—Austin
15. Washington State University
16. University of California—Santa Barbara
17. Cal Poly
18. University of Washington
19. Case Western Reserve University
20. Texas A&M University—College Station

## Teaching Assistants Teach Too Many Upper-Level Courses
*What percentage of upper-level courses is taught by teaching assistants?*

1. University of Illinois—Urbana-Champaign
2. Ohio State University—Columbus
3. University of Kansas
4. University of Iowa
5. Purdue University—West Lafayette
6. University of New Mexico
7. University of Tennessee—Knoxville
8. University of Minnesota—Twin Cities
9. Florida State University
10. University of Connecticut
11. University of Arkansas
12. University of Kentucky
13. University of Michigan—Ann Arbor
14. University of Washington
15. University of Florida
16. University of Georgia
17. University of Montana—Missoula
18. Kansas State University
19. University of Nevada—Las Vegas
20. University of North Dakota

## ADMINISTRATION

### Great College Library
*Based on students' assessment of library facilities*

1. Dickinson College
2. Harvard College
3. Brigham Young University (UT)
4. Dartmouth College
5. Fordham University
6. Yale University
7. Cornell University
8. Stanford University
9. Princeton University
10. Smith College
11. University of Chicago
12. Mount Holyoke College
13. Wake Forest University
14. Wesleyan University
15. University of Virginia
16. Oberlin College
17. Bucknell University
18. University of New Hampshire
19. University of California—Berkeley
20. Auburn University

### This is a Library?
*Based on students' assessment of library facilities*

1. University of Dallas
2. Spelman College
3. Goddard College
4. Clarkson University
5. Bradley University
6. Florida A&M University
7. Stephens College
8. Whittier College
9. Duquesne University
10. Albertson College
11. Eckerd College
12. Fisk University
13. Stevens Institute of Technology
14. Wagner College
15. Valparaiso University
16. Hanover College
17. Lake Forest College
18. Pepperdine University
19. Illinois Institute of Technology
20. University of Redlands

### Students Happy with Financial Aid
*Based on The Princeton Review FINANCIAL AID RATING*

1. Knox College
2. Hollins University
3. Beloit College
4. Catawba College
5. Sweet Briar College
6. California Institute of Technology
7. Grinnell College
8. Susquehanna University
9. Mount Holyoke College
10. Lake Forest College
11. Whittier College
12. Agnes Scott College
13. Randolph-Macon Woman's College
14. The College of Wooster
15. Tulane University
16. Wofford College
17. University of New Orleans
18. DePauw University
19. Saint Louis University
20. Marlboro College

### Students Dissatisfied with Financial Aid
*Based on The Princeton Review FINANCIAL AID RATING*

1. Stony Brook University (SUNY)
2. Hampton University
3. Middlebury College
4. State University of New York at Albany
5. Temple University
6. State University of New York at Binghamton
7. Howard University
8. George Mason University
9. The Evergreen State College
10. Baylor University
11. Drexel University
12. Smith College
13. Colby College
14. Brown University
15. Villanova University
16. Reed College
17. Washington University
18. University of Rhode Island
19. The University of Scranton
20. University of Massachusetts—Amherst

### Best Academic Bang For Your Buck
*Based on students' assessment of financial aid, The Princeton Review FINANCIAL AID RATING and ACADEMIC RATING*

1. Marlboro College
2. Lake Forest College
3. University of North Carolina—Chapel Hill
4. Grinnell College
5. Brigham Young University (UT)
6. New College of Florida
7. Knox College
8. Grove City College
9. Rice University
10. Truman State University
11. Amherst College

12. City University of New York—Brooklyn College
13. University of California—Berkeley
14. University of Michigan—Ann Arbor
15. University of Virginia
16. The Evergreen State College
17. University of North Carolina—Asheville
18. Pennsylvania State University—University Park
19. University of Texas—Austin
20. Georgia Institute of Technology

### School Runs Like Butter
*Overall, how smoothly is your school run?*

1. University of Chicago
2. Pomona College
3. Washington University
4. Wabash College
5. Bowdoin College
6. Davidson College
7. Amherst College
8. Middlebury College
9. Williams College
10. Princeton University
11. Elon University
12. Claremont McKenna College
13. United States Naval Academy
14. Carleton College
15. Stanford University
16. Rose-Hulman Institute of Technology
17. University of Richmond
18. Washington and Lee University
19. Haverford College
20. Harvey Mudd College

### Long Lines and Red Tape
*Overall, how smoothly is your school run?*

1. Illinois Institute of Technology
2. Stony Brook University (SUNY)
3. Drexel University
4. Hampton University
5. Florida A&M University
6. University of Montana—Missoula
7. Northeastern University
8. McGill University
9. Stevens Institute of Technology
10. College of the Atlantic
11. Seton Hall University
12. Wagner College
13. City University of New York—Brooklyn College
14. City University of New York—Hunter College
15. Fisk University
16. Temple University
17. Rutgers University—New Brunswick

18. State University of New York at Albany
19. Loyola University of Chicago
20. University of Hawaii—Manoa

## QUALITY OF LIFE

### Happy Students
*Overall, how happy are you?*

1. DePaul University
2. Pomona College
3. Dartmouth College
4. William Jewell College
5. Whitman College
6. Stanford University
7. New College of Florida
8. Washington and Lee University
9. Wesleyan University
10. Brown University
11. Elon University
12. Carleton College
13. University of Tulsa
14. Davidson College
15. Centre College
16. Kenyon College
17. University of North Carolina—Chapel Hill
18. Ohio University—Athens
19. Wabash College
20. Barnard College

### Least Happy Students
*Overall, how happy are you?*

1. Montana Tech of the University of Montana
2. University of Missouri—Rolla
3. Albertson College
4. Illinois Institute of Technology
5. Fisk University
6. University of California—Riverside
7. Rochester Institute of Technology
8. Rider University
9. Goddard College
10. United States Military Academy
11. State University of New York at Albany
12. New Jersey Institute of Technology
13. University of Toronto
14. Webb Institute
15. Wittenberg University
16. Florida A&M University
17. Stevens Institute of Technology
18. Babson College
19. Eugene Lang College
20. University of North Carolina—Asheville

## Beautiful Campus
*Based on students' rating of campus beauty*

1. University of California—Santa Cruz
2. Elon University
3. Wagner College
4. Wellesley College
5. University of Miami
6. City University of New York—Brooklyn College
7. Mount Holyoke College
8. Washington and Lee University
9. Dartmouth College
10. Kenyon College
11. The University of the South
12. Wells College
13. Smith College
14. Colgate University
15. Williams College
16. Bryn Mawr College
17. Miami University
18. Bucknell University
19. Duke University
20. Stanford University

## Campus is Tiny, Unsightly, or Both
*Based on students' rating of campus beauty*

1. Illinois Institute of Technology
2. Drexel University
3. Rochester Institute of Technology
4. State University of New York at Albany
5. Cooper Union
6. Massachusetts Institute of Technology
7. New Jersey Institute of Technology
8. University of Dallas
9. State University of New York at Binghamton
10. Montana Tech of the University of Montana
11. Fisk University
12. University of Tennessee—Knoxville
13. University of Missouri—Rolla
14. Eugene Lang College
15. Rider University
16. Georgia Institute of Technology
17. North Carolina State University
18. Albertson College
19. Golden Gate University
20. Stephens College

## Great Campus Food
*Based on students' rating of campus food*

1. Bowdoin College
2. Colby College
3. Saint Anselm College
4. Wheaton College (IL)
5. Cornell University
6. Dartmouth College
7. Bryn Mawr College
8. Washington University
9. Dickinson College
10. Bates College
11. Bennington College
12. Gettysburg College
13. Tufts University
14. Loyola College in Maryland
15. St. Olaf College
16. Miami University
17. University of Notre Dame
18. James Madison University
19. Smith College
20. Macalester College

## Is It Food?
*Based on students' rating of campus food*

1. Saint Bonaventure University
2. State University of New York at Albany
3. Stevens Institute of Technology
4. Fordham University
5. Illinois Institute of Technology
6. New College of Florida
7. New Mexico Institute of Mining & Technology
8. Hampton University
9. Colorado School of Mines
10. New Jersey Institute of Technology
11. Catholic University of America
12. Johns Hopkins University
13. Hiram College
14. University of Missouri—Rolla
15. Centenary College of Louisiana
16. Oglethorpe University
17. California Institute of Technology
18. University of California—Berkeley
19. Carnegie Mellon University
20. University of Massachusetts—Amherst

## Dorms Like Palaces
*Based on students' rating of dorm comfort*

1. Loyola College in Maryland
2. Smith College
3. Bryn Mawr College
4. Scripps College
5. Agnes Scott College
6. Skidmore College
7. Claremont McKenna College
8. Bowdoin College
9. Mount Holyoke College
10. George Washington University
11. Randolph-Macon Woman's College
12. Williams College
13. Harvard College
14. Pomona College
15. Wellesley College

16. Pepperdine University
17. Dartmouth College
18. Boston University
19. Wells College
20. Sarah Lawrence College

**Dorms Like Dungeons**
*Based on students' rating of dorm comfort*

1. University of Missouri—Rolla
2. University of Oregon
3. State University of New York at Albany
4. Illinois Institute of Technology
5. Hampton University
6. University of Washington
7. Florida A&M University
8. University of Kentucky
9. University of Florida
10. City University of New York—Hunter College
11. Georgia Institute of Technology
12. Ohio State University—Columbus
13. Fisk University
14. United States Military Academy
15. University of Idaho
16. University of Oklahoma
17. University of South Dakota
18. University of Georgia
19. Florida State University
20. Indiana University of Pennsylvania

**Best Quality of Life**
*Based on The Princeton Review's QUALITY OF LIFE RATING*

1. Hollins University
2. Brigham Young University (UT)
3. University of Richmond
4. Dartmouth College
5. College of the Atlantic
6. Tuskegee University
7. Harvard College
8. Marlboro College
9. Skidmore College
10. Susquehanna University
11. Sweet Briar College
12. Williams College
13. Agnes Scott College
14. Calvin College
15. Claremont McKenna College
16. Macalester College
17. University of California—Santa Cruz
18. Amherst College
19. Rhodes College
20. Smith College

## POLITICS

**Students Most Nostalgic for Ronald Reagan**
*Based on students' assessment of their personal political views*

1. Washington and Lee University
2. Hampden-Sydney College
3. Brigham Young University (UT)
4. United States Naval Academy
5. Samford University
6. United States Air Force Academy
7. University of Mississippi
8. Texas A&M University—College Station
9. University of Dallas
10. Wheaton College (IL)
11. Furman University
12. Auburn University
13. Grove City College
14. Wabash College
15. Southern Methodist University
16. Allegheny College
17. University of Alabama—Tuscaloosa
18. Clemson University
19. Millsaps College
20. TCU

**Students Most Nostalgic for Bill Clinton**
*Based on students' assessment of their personal political views*

1. Bard College
2. Hampshire College
3. Sarah Lawrence College
4. New College of Florida
5. Wesleyan University
6. Grinnell College
7. Reed College
8. Macalester College
9. Oberlin College
10. Vassar College
11. Lewis & Clark College
12. Earlham College
13. Guilford College
14. Smith College
15. Bennington College
16. Goddard College
17. Carleton College
18. Scripps College
19. Connecticut College
20. Pomona College

**Most Politically Active**
*How popular are political/activist groups?*

1. Wesleyan University
2. Oberlin College
3. George Washington University

4. Bard College
5. Hampshire College
6. Grinnell College
7. New College of Florida
8. Smith College
9. Lewis & Clark College
10. Macalester College
11. Swarthmore College
12. American University
13. Guilford College
14. Sarah Lawrence College
15. University of California—Berkeley
16. University of Oregon
17. Vassar College
18. Georgetown University
19. University of California—Santa Cruz
20. Brown University

### Election? What Election?
*How popular are political/activist groups?*

1. Cooper Union
2. Stevens Institute of Technology
3. United States Naval Academy
4. Rose-Hulman Institute of Technology
5. New Jersey Institute of Technology
6. Colorado School of Mines
7. University of Missouri—Rolla
8. Clarkson University
9. California Institute of Technology
10. Webb Institute
11. United States Air Force Academy
12. Harvey Mudd College
13. Lehigh University
14. Illinois Institute of Technology
15. Hanover College
16. Babson College
17. Catawba College
18. Rensselaer Polytechnic Institute
19. New Mexico Institute of Mining & Technology
20. Susquehanna University

## DEMOGRAPHICS

### Diverse Student Population
*Is your student body made up of diverse social and ethnic types?*

1. Rutgers University—New Brunswick
2. George Mason University
3. University of Maryland, Baltimore County
4. City University of New York—Queens College
5. Occidental College
6. Temple University
7. New Jersey Institute of Technology
8. Clark University
9. University of Miami
10. State University of New York at Buffalo
11. University of Hawaii—Manoa
12. McGill University
13. Mount Holyoke College
14. New York University
15. University of San Francisco
16. Wesleyan University
17. Stony Brook University (SUNY)
18. DePaul University
19. University of Maryland—College Park
20. Columbia University

### Homogeneous Student Population
*Is your student body made up of diverse social and ethnic types?*

1. Grove City College
2. Providence College
3. Loyola College in Maryland
4. Wake Forest University
5. Washington and Lee University
6. Gettysburg College
7. College of the Holy Cross
8. Saint Anselm College
9. Villanova University
10. Fairfield University
11. Miami University
12. Westminster College
13. Muhlenberg College
14. University of Richmond
15. Bucknell University
16. University of Notre Dame
17. Saint Bonaventure University
18. Hanover College
19. University of San Diego
20. Rollins College

### Students from Different Backgrounds Interact
*Do different types of students (black/white, rich/poor) interact frequently and easily?*

1. McGill University
2. Clark University
3. United States Air Force Academy
4. Bennington College
5. Occidental College
6. Carleton College
7. United States Naval Academy
8. University of Hawaii—Manoa
9. Wabash College
10. Eckerd College
11. Hendrix College
12. Mount Holyoke College
13. Stanford University
14. Grinnell College
15. Whitman College

16. Bryn Mawr College
17. Wells College
18. University of California—Santa Cruz
19. Wesleyan University
20. Rice University

## Little Race/Class Interaction
*Do different types of students (black/white, rich/poor) interact frequently and easily?*

1. Trinity College (CT)
2. Wake Forest University
3. Vanderbilt University
4. Miami University
5. Hofstra University
6. Washington and Lee University
7. Hamilton College
8. College of the Holy Cross
9. Rollins College
10. Loyola College in Maryland
11. Fairfield University
12. Hanover College
13. Syracuse University
14. Baylor University
15. Denison University
16. Gettysburg College
17. University of Kentucky
18. Lehigh University
19. Duke University
20. Villanova University

## Gay Community Accepted
*Is there very little discrimination against homosexuals?*

1. New York University
2. Sarah Lawrence College
3. Mount Holyoke College
4. Smith College
5. University of California—Santa Cruz
6. New College of Florida
7. Grinnell College
8. Bryn Mawr College
9. Wells College
10. Wellesley College
11. Harvey Mudd College
12. Bard College
13. Boston University
14. Reed College
15. Barnard College
16. Vassar College
17. Macalester College
18. Carleton College
19. Emerson College
20. Haverford College

## Alternative Lifestyles Not an Alternative
*Is there very little discrimination against homosexuals?*

1. University of Notre Dame
2. Washington and Lee University
3. Grove City College
4. United States Naval Academy
5. Miami University
6. Montana Tech of the University of Montana
7. Hanover College
8. Wheaton College (IL)
9. Fisk University
10. College of the Ozarks
11. Baylor University
12. Texas A&M University—College Station
13. Providence College
14. Boston College
15. Brigham Young University (UT)
16. Birmingham-Southern College
17. University of Redlands
18. United States Military Academy
19. University of Utah
20. Hamilton College

## Students Pray on a Regular Basis
*Are students very religious?*

1. Brigham Young University (UT)
2. Wheaton College (IL)
3. Grove City College
4. University of Dallas
5. University of Notre Dame
6. Baylor University
7. Samford University
8. Calvin College
9. Pepperdine University
10. Furman University
11. United States Air Force Academy
12. Texas A&M University—College Station
13. Catholic University of America
14. Valparaiso University
15. Creighton University
16. Brandeis University
17. College of the Holy Cross
18. Providence College
19. William Jewell College
20. University of Utah

## Students Ignore God on a Regular Basis
*Are students very religious?*

1. Reed College
2. Lewis & Clark College
3. Simon's Rock College of Bard
4. New College of Florida
5. Vassar College
6. Bard College
7. Emerson College

8. Sarah Lawrence College
9. Hampshire College
10. Carleton College
11. Connecticut College
12. Grinnell College
13. Macalester College
14. Wesleyan University
15. Oberlin College
16. Pomona College
17. Swarthmore College
18. Colorado College
19. California Institute of Technology
20. Beloit College

## SOCIAL LIFE

### Great College Towns
*Based on students' assessment of the surrounding city or town*

1. New York University
2. Tulane University
3. Georgetown University
4. DePaul University
5. University of Miami
6. American University
7. Boston University
8. Columbia University
9. McGill University
10. The George Washington University
11. University of San Francisco
12. Cooper Union
13. Boston College
14. University of Texas—Austin
15. Southern Methodist University
16. Barnard College
17. University of Wisconsin—Madison
18. Harvard College
19. Indiana University—Bloomington
20. Simmons College

### More to Do on Campus
*Based on students' assessment of the surrounding city or town*

1. Rensselaer Polytechnic Institute
2. Earlham College
3. Union College (NY)
4. New Mexico Institute of Mining & Technology
5. Wheaton College (MA)
6. New Jersey Institute of Technology
7. Connecticut College
8. Truman State University
9. Hanover College
10. University of Missouri—Rolla
11. University of Connecticut
12. Trinity College (CT)
13. Vassar College
14. University of California—Riverside
15. Wittenberg University
16. Lehigh University
17. Beloit College
18. Albion College
19. DePauw University
20. University of Notre Dame

### Town-Gown Relations are Good
*Do students get along well with members of the local community?*

1. William Jewell College
2. Brigham Young University (UT)
3. Davidson College
4. US Merchant Marine Academy
5. Texas A&M University—College Station
6. St. Olaf College
7. United States Naval Academy
8. Samford University
9. Furman University
10. University of Tulsa
11. United States Air Force Academy
12. Calvin College
13. Hampden-Sydney College
14. Auburn University
15. Grove City College
16. Wells College
17. University of South Carolina—Columbia
18. Agnes Scott College
19. Creighton University
20. University of Mississippi

### Town-Gown Relations are Strained
*Do students get along well with members of the local community?*

1. Trinity College (CT)
2. Sarah Lawrence College
3. Fairfield University
4. Lehigh University
5. Vassar College
6. Union College (NY)
7. Duke University
8. Northwestern University
9. Gettysburg College
10. DePauw University
11. Connecticut College
12. Bard College
13. Simon's Rock College of Bard
14. Colorado College
15. Earlham College
16. State University of New York at Binghamton
17. Beloit College
18. Bates College
19. University of Pennsylvania
20. Hofstra University

# EXTRACURRICULARS

## Students Pack the Stadiums
*How popular are intercollegiate sports?*

1. University of Notre Dame
2. Pennsylvania State University—University Park
3. University of North Carolina—Chapel Hill
4. Duke University
5. Florida State University
6. Texas A&M University—College Station
7. University of Alabama—Tuscaloosa
8. Clemson University
9. University of Tennessee—Knoxville
10. University of Georgia
11. Boston College
12. University of Connecticut
13. University of Florida
14. University of Oklahoma
15. Syracuse University
16. University of Texas—Austin
17. Auburn University
18. Gonzaga University
19. University of Kansas
20. University of Wisconsin—Madison

## Intercollegiate Sports Unpopular or Nonexistent
*How popular are intercollegiate sports?*

1. New College of Florida
2. Reed College
3. Sarah Lawrence College
4. Simon's Rock College of Bard
5. Emerson College
6. Hampshire College
7. St. John's College (MD)
8. Bennington College
9. New York University
10. Eugene Lang College
11. Bard College
12. Oberlin College
13. Goddard College
14. California Institute of Technology
15. New Mexico Institute of Mining & Technology
16. University of Chicago
17. Cooper Union
18. St. John's College (NM)
19. University of California—Santa Cruz
20. Emory University

## Everyone Plays Intramural Sports
*How popular are intramural sports?*

1. Pennsylvania State University—University Park
2. University of Notre Dame
3. Wabash College
4. Whitman College
5. Carleton College
6. United States Naval Academy
7. Williams College
8. United States Air Force Academy
9. Colorado College
10. Grove City College
11. Iowa State University
12. Baylor University
13. Brigham Young University (UT)
14. Texas A&M University—College Station
15. University of Connecticut
16. Wake Forest University
17. Washington State University
18. Florida State University
19. Providence College
20. Centenary College of Louisiana

## Nobody Plays Intramural Sports
*How popular are intramural sports?*

1. Emerson College
2. Sarah Lawrence College
3. Simon's Rock College of Bard
4. Eugene Lang College
5. Goddard College
6. Bennington College
7. Bryn Mawr College
8. The Evergreen State College
9. New York University
10. Babson College
11. Reed College
12. Spelman College
13. Cooper Union
14. City University of New York—Queens College
15. Stephens College
16. Marlboro College
17. City University of New York—Brooklyn College
18. Whittier College
19. Guilford College
20. Scripps College

## Great College Radio Station
*How popular is the radio station?*

1. Emerson College
2. Saint Bonaventure University
3. DePauw University
4. Guilford College
5. Whitman College

6. Ithaca College
7. Seton Hall University
8. Skidmore College
9. Union College (NY)
10. Brown University
11. Grinnell College
12. Knox College
13. Florida A&M University
14. William Jewell College
15. Carleton College
16. Siena College
17. University of Mississippi
18. Denison University
19. Oberlin College
20. Alfred University

## Great College Newspaper
*How popular is the newspaper?*

1. University of North Carolina—Chapel Hill
2. Northwestern University
3. University of Pennsylvania
4. Arizona State University
5. Yale University
6. University of Kansas
7. University of California—Los Angeles
8. University of Georgia
9. Pennsylvania State University—University Park
10. Syracuse University
11. University of Kentucky
12. Howard University
13. University of Maryland—College Park
14. Tufts University
15. Auburn University
16. University of Arizona
17. University of Minnesota—Twin Cities
18. Indiana University—Bloomington
19. University of California—Santa Barbara
20. University of Florida

## Great College Theater
*How popular are theater groups?*

1. Emerson College
2. Vassar College
3. Yale University
4. Whitman College
5. Wesleyan University
6. Northwestern University
7. Oberlin College
8. Sarah Lawrence College
9. Skidmore College
10. Ithaca College
11. Catawba College
12. Brown University
13. Drew University
14. Muhlenberg College

15. Bennington College
16. Wagner College
17. New York University
18. Guilford College
19. Kalamazoo College
20. Harvard College

# PARTIES

## Lots of Beer
*How widely used is beer?*

1. University of Wisconsin—Madison
2. University of Texas—Austin
3. Washington and Lee University
4. Indiana University—Bloomington
5. Dartmouth College
6. Loyola College in Maryland
7. The University of the South
8. University of Georgia
9. Saint Bonaventure University
10. West Virginia University
11. University of Colorado, Boulder
12. University of Florida
13. University of Illinois—Urbana-Champaign
14. Louisiana State University—Baton Rouge
15. Pennsylvania State University—University Park
16. Clemson University
17. University of California—Santa Barbara
18. Colgate University
19. University of Dayton
20. McGill University

## Got Milk?
*How widely used is beer?*

1. Brigham Young University (UT)
2. Wheaton College (IL)
3. Spelman College
4. Grove City College
5. Hampton University
6. City University of New York—Brooklyn College
7. Samford University
8. Calvin College
9. Simmons College
10. Simon's Rock College of Bard
11. College of the Atlantic
12. Bryn Mawr College
13. City University of New York—Hunter College
14. Fisk University
15. United States Military Academy
16. College of the Ozarks
17. Wellesley College
18. Mount Holyoke College

19. Eugene Lang College
20. United States Naval Academy

## Lots of Hard Liquor
*How widely used is hard liquor?*

1. University of Wisconsin—Madison
2. University of Texas—Austin
3. The University of the South
4. University of Colorado, Boulder
5. Saint Bonaventure University
6. Washington and Lee University
7. Loyola College in Maryland
8. University of Alabama—Tuscaloosa
9. University of Mississippi
10. University of Michigan—Ann Arbor
11. DePauw University
12. University of Illinois— Urbana-Champaign
13. New York University
14. State University of New York at Albany
15. University of Georgia
16. Lehigh University
17. Louisiana State University—Baton Rouge
18. Clemson University
19. Colgate University
20. Bucknell University

## Scotch and Soda, Hold the Scotch
*How widely used is hard liquor?*

1. Brigham Young University (UT)
2. Wheaton College (IL)
3. Grove City College
4. Samford University
5. Spelman College
6. Calvin College
7. United States Naval Academy
8. Simmons College
9. College of the Atlantic
10. Simon's Rock College of Bard
11. Webb Institute
12. University of Utah
13. City University of New York— Brooklyn College
14. City University of New York— Queens College
15. Wesleyan College
16. Fisk University
17. United States Military Academy
18. College of the Ozarks
19. United States Air Force Academy
20. Wellesley College

## Reefer Madness
*How widely used is marijuana?*

1. Skidmore College
2. Lewis & Clark College
3. University of Colorado, Boulder
4. University of Wisconsin—Madison
5. University of Vermont
6. New College of Florida
7. Vassar College
8. State University of New York at Albany
9. Hampshire College
10. Reed College
11. Colorado College
12. University of Texas—Austin
13. University of Oregon
14. Ithaca College
15. Oberlin College
16. Wesleyan University
17. University of California—Santa Barbara
18. New York University
19. Indiana University—Bloomington
20. Guilford College

## Don't Inhale
*How widely used is marijuana?*

1. United States Air Force Academy
2. Brigham Young University (UT)
3. United States Naval Academy
4. Wheaton College (IL)
5. Grove City College
6. Samford University
7. Rose-Hulman Institute of Technology
8. University of Notre Dame
9. William Jewell College
10. Calvin College
11. Wellesley College
12. University of Dallas
13. New Jersey Institute of Technology
14. Agnes Scott College
15. Furman University
16. Valparaiso University
17. Sweet Briar College
18. Wesleyan College
19. Centre College
20. Texas A&M University—College Station

## Major Frat and Sorority Scene
*How popular are fraternities/sororities?*

1. DePauw University
2. Washington and Lee University
3. Indiana University—Bloomington
4. University of Colorado—Boulder
5. Southern Methodist University
6. University of Michigan—Ann Arbor
7. University of Alabama—Tuscaloosa
8. University of Illinois— Urbana-Champaign
9. Wake Forest University
10. Dartmouth College
11. Elon University

42 ■ THE BEST 351 COLLEGES

12. University of Mississippi
13. Bucknell University
14. University of Southern California
15. TCU
16. Miami University
17. University of Oklahoma
18. Pennsylvania State University—University Park
19. The University of the South
20. University of Wisconsin—Madison

## SCHOOL BY TYPE

### Party Schools
Based on a combination of survey questions concerning the use of alcohol and drugs, hours of study each day, and the popularity of the Greek system

1. University of Colorado, Boulder
2. University of Wisconsin—Madison
3. Indiana University—Bloomington
4. University of Illinois—Urbana-Champaign
5. Washington and Lee University
6. University of Texas—Austin
7. The University of the South
8. DePauw University
9. Saint Bonaventure University
10. University of Florida
11. University of Alabama—Tuscaloosa
12. University of Michigan—Ann Arbor
13. University of Mississippi
14. State University of New York at Albany
15. University of Georgia
16. Clemson University
17. Louisiana State University—Baton Rouge
18. New York University
19. Pennsylvania State University—University Park
20. University of California—Santa Barbara

### Stone-Cold Sober Schools
Based on a combination of survey questions concerning the use of alcohol and drugs, hours of study each day, and the popularity of the Greek system

1. Brigham Young University (UT)
2. Wheaton College (IL)
3. United States Naval Academy
4. United States Air Force Academy
5. Grove City College
6. Calvin College
7. Bryn Mawr College
8. Simmons College
9. Mount Holyoke College
10. Wellesley College
11. Agnes Scott College
12. Sweet Briar College
13. Wells College
14. St. Olaf College
15. Randolph-Macon Woman's College
16. United States Military Academy
17. Hollins University
18. College of the Atlantic
19. Webb Institute
20. Samford University

### Jock Schools
Based on a combination of survey questions concerning intercollegiate and intramural sports and the popularity of the Greek system

1. Pennsylvania State University—University Park
2. University of Notre Dame
3. Texas A&M University—College Station
4. Florida State University
5. University of Connecticut
6. University of Alabama—Tuscaloosa
7. University of North Carolina—Chapel Hill
8. Duke University
9. United States Naval Academy
10. United States Air Force Academy
11. Clemson University
12. University of Tennessee—Knoxville
13. University of Georgia
14. Ohio State University—Columbus
15. University of Florida
16. Iowa State University
17. Kansas State University
18. Auburn University
19. Boston College
20. Purdue University—West Lafayette

### Dodge-Ball Targets
Based on a combination of survey questions concerning intercollegiate and intramural sports and the popularity of the Greek system

1. Emerson College
2. Sarah Lawrence College
3. Simon's Rock College of Bard
4. New College of Florida
5. Bennington College
6. Reed College
7. Earlham College
8. Eugene Lang College
9. Goddard College
10. Hampshire College
11. Bard College
12. Marlboro College
13. Cooper Union
14. Oberlin College
15. Bryn Mawr College

16. Stephens College
17. The Evergreen State College
18. Babson College
19. Spelman College
20. City University of New York—Brooklyn College

## Future Rotarians and Daughters of the American Revolution

*Based on a combination of survey questions concerning political persuasion, the use of marijuana and hallucinogens, the prevalence of religion, the popularity of student government, and the students' level of acceptance of the gay community on campus*

1. United States Air Force Academy
2. United States Naval Academy
3. Brigham Young University (UT)
4. Wheaton College (IL)
5. University of Notre Dame
6. Samford University
7. Grove City College
8. Baylor University
9. Rose-Hulman Institute of Technology
10. Providence College
11. Creighton University
12. William Jewell College
13. University of Dallas
14. Valparaiso University
15. Hanover College
16. New Jersey Institute of Technology
17. Westminster College (PA)
18. Texas A&M University—College Station
19. Pepperdine University
20. Duquesne University

## Birkenstock-Wearing, Tree-Hugging, Clove-Smoking Vegetarians

*Based on a combination of survey questions concerning political persuasion, the use of marijuana and hallucinogens, the prevalence of religion, the popularity of student government, and the students' level of acceptance of the gay community on campus*

1. Lewis & Clark College
2. Hampshire College
3. New College of Florida
4. Oberlin College
5. Bard College
6. Reed College
7. Wesleyan University
8. Sarah Lawrence College
9. Vassar College
10. Earlham College
11. Macalester College
12. Grinnell College
13. University of California—Santa Cruz
14. The Evergreen State College
15. Simon's Rock College of Bard
16. University of Oregon
17. New York University
18. Guilford College
19. Skidmore College
20. Swarthmore College

## Deep Springs Honor Roll

*Since Deep Springs is a two-year college—the only one of its kind in The Best 351 Colleges—we've decided to remove it from the body of our individual rankings in order to avoid comparing "apples and oranges." Instead we've created this "honor roll," which includes all categories in which Deep Springs ranks high (or low, as it were) among the best colleges*

Best Overall Academic Experience for Undergraduates
The Toughest to Get Into
Election? What Election?
Best Academic Bang for Your Buck
Professors Make Themselves Accessible
Professors Bring Material to Life
School Runs Like Butter
Scotch and Soda, Hold the Scotch
Beautiful Campus
Students from Different Backgrounds Interact
Students Most Nostalgic for Bill Clinton
Great Food on Campus
Their Students Never Stop Studying
This is a Library?
Happy Students
Dodge-Ball Targets
Don't Inhale
Stone Cold Sober Schools
Gay Community Accepted
Got Milk?

## A Final Note

*The following schools have been excluded from our ranking lists dealing with financial aid:*

Cooper Union
United States Air Force Academy
United States Coast Guard Academy
United States Merchant Marine Academy
United States Military Academy
United States Naval Academy
Webb Institute

The reason—they're free!
We would like to commend each of these schools on their ability to do the seemingly impossible—not charge tuition. However, we thought it less than fair to include each of these schools in our financial lists, since each would have an unfair advantage over schools that charged even a moderate tuition.

# PART 3

# THE BEST 351 COLLEGES

# AGNES SCOTT COLLEGE

141 East College Avenue, Atlanta, GA 30030-3797 • Admissions: 800-868-8602 • Fax: 404-471-6414

## CAMPUS LIFE

| | |
|---|---|
| Quality of Life Rating | 93 |
| Type of school | private |
| Affiliation | Presbyterian |
| Environment | urban |

### STUDENTS

| | |
|---|---|
| Total undergrad enrollment | 869 |
| % from out of state | 50 |
| % from public high school | 76 |
| % live on campus | 90 |
| % African American | 22 |
| % Asian | 6 |
| % Caucasian | 62 |
| % Hispanic | 3 |
| % international | 5 |
| # of countries represented | 29 |

### SURVEY SAYS . . .
*Dorms are like palaces*
*Campus easy to get around*
*No one cheats*
*Beautiful campus*
*Students love Atlanta, GA*
*Very little drug use*
*No one plays intramural sports*
*Very little hard liquor*
*Very little beer drinking*

## ACADEMICS

| | |
|---|---|
| Academic Rating | 95 |
| Calendar | semester |
| Student/faculty ratio | 10:1 |
| Profs interesting rating | 96 |
| Profs accessible rating | 99 |
| % profs teaching UG courses | 100 |
| Avg lab size | 10-19 students |
| Avg reg class size | 10-19 students |

### MOST POPULAR MAJORS
English language and literature
Biology/biological sciences
Psychology

## STUDENTS SPEAK OUT

### Academics

Students come to Agnes Scott College to enjoy a first-rate education in a homey, southern atmosphere. Few leave disappointed, thanks largely to a dedicated faculty, a caring administration, and a well-loved honor code. Students report that "the faculty, professors, and students get along so well that many of our closest friends tend to be not only students but also teachers and faculty. The overall academic experience of Agnes Scott is wonderful." Because the school is so small, "one of the best aspects of our school is easy access to everyone in power. We can always get an appointment with anyone from our professor to the dean to the president of the college. They are interested in our input and in answering our questions." Students also brag about their "strong honor code, the backbone for our trusting community." As at many small schools, course selection can be a problem. "Many classes are only offered once every two years and some never offered at all (even though they're listed in the catalog)!" complains one student. Students may cross-register at 20 other area colleges and universities, which broadens their academic options.

### Life

Social life on the Agnes Scott campus, students agree, is subdued. "Because it is an all-women's liberal arts college," explains one, "the life at my school is so much different than the life at a coed university. The school is mainly academic, and we don't have many social activities or parties. For fun, we go to Georgia Tech or to Buckhead (the area of Atlanta with a lot of clubs)." Some see the upside to this situation; writes one such undergrad, "Life at Agnes Scott is well balanced. We have tons of social activities planned for the students every week. Still, I know several people, including myself, go to Georgia Tech and/or Emory two or three times a week. The Scottie girls usually have fun with the frat boys." Others are less pleased, reporting that "for fun, we get the hell off campus. There's NOTHING to do here. I was hoping with a big, brand-new student center that might change, but there's nothing for entertainment in the student center besides a lame 'Cyber Café' (more accurately a computer lab) and a couple new eating places that all serve the same food." Fortunately, the school is "in the Atlanta area so there is always something to do. For the most part we go shopping and out to eat." Adds one student, "Being in Decatur is okay, but Atlanta is 15 minutes away. Atlanta may in fact be the greatest college town in the U.S. We go to the theater, the movies, bars and clubs (tons of those)." Students also note that "the warm, mild weather is nice and our campus is pretty and peaceful."

### Student Body

Agnes Scott undergrads "are generally from all over the South." Students share at least one other common bond: writes one student, "My fellow students are largely rich—I mean, yearly summer trips to Europe—and mostly supported by their parents. Those who aren't are noticeably in the minority." Students warn that "since it's so small, there's a lot of gossip here and catty behavior. Sometimes, we all come together to cheer on Agnes Scott (like during Black Cat weekend), but generally we're a pretty cliquey bunch." Also, most agree that "although we have a relatively large African American population, the whites and the blacks generally do not interact. Even in class, there is a noticeable black half and a white half. In all fairness, no one seems to be eager to branch out, so it's a mutual thing."

46 ■ THE BEST 351 COLLEGES

# AGNES SCOTT COLLEGE

FINANCIAL AID: 404-471-6395 • E-MAIL: ADMISSION@AGNESSCOTT.EDU • WEBSITE: WWW.AGNESSCOTT.EDU

## ADMISSIONS

*Very Important factors considered include:* character/personal qualities, class rank, essays, recommendations, secondary school record, standardized test scores, talent/ability. *Important factors considered include:* extracurricular activities, volunteer work, work experience. *Other factors considered include:* alumni/ae relation, geographical residence, interview, minority status, state residency. SAT I or ACT required. TOEFL required of all international applicants. High school diploma or GED is required. *High school units required/recommended:* 16 total recommended; 4 English recommended, 3 math recommended, 2 science recommended, 2 science lab recommended, 2 foreign language recommended, 2 social studies recommended.

## *The Inside Word*

Women's colleges are enjoying a renaissance of late and to top it off, Agnes Scott has always been a great choice for strong students. Don't be deceived by the college's generous admission rate—we're talking about a small applicant pool of well-qualified candidates, and one of the best small liberal arts colleges to be found anywhere. Look for greater selectivity as the college recruits students from further afield and application totals continue to increase at top women's colleges. The admissions process can't get any more personalized than it is at Agnes Scott—every candidate is assigned her own specific admission counselor, who works with the student throughout the process.

## FINANCIAL AID

*Students should submit:* FAFSA, institution's own financial aid form, state aid form, noncustodial (divorced/separated) parent's statement, business/farm supplement. CSS/Financial Aid PROFILE required of early decision applicants. Priority filing deadline is February 15. The Princeton Review suggests that all financial aid forms be submitted as soon as possible after January 1. *Need-based scholarships/grants offered:* Pell, SEOG, state scholarships/grants, private scholarships, the school's own gift aid. *Loan aid offered:* FFEL Subsidized Stafford, FFEL Unsubsidized Stafford, FFEL PLUS, college/university loans from institutional funds, alternative loans. Federal Work-Study Program available. Institutional employment available. Applicants will be notified of awards on a rolling basis beginning on or about March 1. Off-campus job opportunities are excellent.

## FROM THE ADMISSIONS OFFICE

"Agnes Scott College prepares women for a challenging and rapidly changing world through a liberal arts education that emphasizes interdisciplinary, experimental, and collaborative learning in a diverse and inclusive community. Students are guaranteed an internship opportunity—either among the many opportunities within the city of Atlanta or through field-based study abroad. Nearly half of our students participate in an international experience while enrolled at ASC. One-third major in the sciences and psychology. New facilities, among the finest in the nation for undergraduate science, were designed expressly to facilitate faculty-student research. We invite you to schedule a campus visit and experience Agnes Scott—a residential college on a beautiful, tree-studded campus in metropolitan Atlanta."

### SELECTIVITY

| | |
|---|---|
| Admissions Rating | 80 |
| # of applicants | 743 |
| % of applicants accepted | 73 |
| % of acceptees attending | 43 |
| # accepting a place on wait list | 13 |
| % admitted from wait list | 77 |
| # of early decision applicants | 33 |
| % accepted early decision | 73 |

### FRESHMAN PROFILE

| | |
|---|---|
| Range SAT Verbal | 570-680 |
| Average SAT Verbal | 620 |
| Range SAT Math | 540-650 |
| Average SAT Math | 590 |
| Range ACT Composite | 23-29 |
| Average ACT Composite | 26 |
| Minimum TOEFL | 577 |
| Average HS GPA | 3.7 |
| % graduated top 10% of class | 44 |
| % graduated top 25% of class | 70 |
| % graduated top 50% of class | 95 |

### DEADLINES

| | |
|---|---|
| Early decision | 11/15 |
| Early decision notification | 12/15 |
| Regular admission | 3/1 |
| Nonfall registration? | yes |

### APPLICANTS ALSO LOOK AT AND OFTEN PREFER
U. Georgia
Emory

### AND SOMETIMES PREFER
Randolph-Macon Woman's
Smith
Rhodes

### AND RARELY PREFER
UNC—Chapel Hill

### FINANCIAL FACTS

| | |
|---|---|
| Financial Aid Rating | 92 |
| Tuition | $18,850 |
| Room and board | $7,500 |
| Books and supplies | $700 |
| Required fees | $150 |
| % frosh receiving aid | 73 |
| % undergrads receiving aid | 65 |
| Avg frosh grant | $14,001 |
| Avg frosh loan | $2,083 |

# ALBERTSON COLLEGE

2112 CLEVELAND BOULEVARD, CALDWELL, ID 83605 • ADMISSIONS: 208-459-5305 • FAX: 208-459-5757

## CAMPUS LIFE

| Quality of Life Rating | 78 |
|---|---|
| Type of school | private |
| Environment | suburban |

### STUDENTS
| | |
|---|---|
| Total undergrad enrollment | 841 |
| % male/female | 45/55 |
| % from out of state | 25 |
| % live on campus | 56 |
| % in (# of) fraternities | 20 (3) |
| % in (# of) sororities | 15 (4) |
| % Asian | 4 |
| % Caucasian | 80 |
| % Hispanic | 5 |
| % international | 2 |

### SURVEY SAYS . . .
Very little drug use
(Almost) no one smokes
Students don't like Caldwell, ID
Campus easy to get around
No one cheats

## ACADEMICS

| Academic Rating | 84 |
|---|---|
| Calendar | other |
| Student/faculty ratio | 12:1 |
| % profs teaching UG courses | 100 |
| Avg reg class size | under 10 students |

### MOST POPULAR MAJORS
Business administration/management
Biology/biological sciences
Psychology

## STUDENTS SPEAK OUT

### Academics
Albertson College's chief distinguishing characteristic is its location; the school has many peer institutions on the ivy-covered coasts, but precious few among the proverbial potato fields of Idaho. Like its peer schools, "the single greatest strength of Albertson is the undying commitment of our faculty to the cause of their students' education." As one student put it, "The professors are phenomenal. Many go by their first names, which breaks down the hierarchical barrier between student and professor. They treat each student as a soon-to-be colleague rather than an uneducated child." Students here undergo a rigorous program that "teaches writing across the curriculum; you write papers for every class and each one comes back with extensive comments, suggestions, and criticisms." Freshmen commence their work with the First Year Experience, a two-day mountain retreat followed by a sequence of special seminars and core courses. The goal is to rev recent high school grads up to college speed. "The First Year Experience can be a pain, but it gets you in touch with a lot of people and provides a good way to make friends," notes one undergrad. Asked to cite a weakness of ACI, many here finger the administration; a surprising number concurred that "this school is currently in budget crisis, and it's due to poor management." When all is said and done, however, students tell us that "when I look back on my days at Albertson College, I'm not going to remember the problems I had with deans, registrars, or the administration. Instead, I'm going to remember the professors."

### Life
Students make clear from the get-go that Albertson is no party school. Simply put, "There is a lot of homework, and the teachers expect a lot from you." When students do take some time to cut loose, they enjoy "lots of theme parties at the fraternities. They are immensely popular; just about everyone parties it up together." Students are also deeply involved in athletics, playing "flag football and volleyball intramurals, ultimate Frisbee, and basketball" regularly, as well as engaging in outdoor activities; many here report favorably on the "awesome trips to Idaho's unique areas (deserts, mountains, sand dunes, hot springs, stargazing, backpacking, rafting, mountain biking) run by the outdoor program." The student-run Program Council works hard to "put on events like Spring Fling, midnight movies, bowling nights, and they're all free." All this helps make up for the fact that hometown Caldwell "is really boring." Fortunately, "Boise is only 30 minutes away and there is generally plenty to do there. There are great restaurants, theaters, clubs, bars, sports venues, and anything else you could ever want. It's a great mix of rural and urban life." Faith-related activity plays a large role in many students' lives. Late Night, a weekly worship service, and Bible study groups help fill many students' extracurricular calendars. Albertson undergrads' biggest gripe: "Over half the campus goes home on weekends."

### Student Body
"The student body of Albertson College is very homogeneous: almost exclusively white, Republican, upper-middle-class Idahoans," concede most Albertson undergraduates. "We can be like a herd of sheep in that respect. But, hey, we all get along!" Students typically "fall into four overlapping categories to which they gravitate socially: bookish, artsy, jocks (almost everyone here plays sports or is involved in music), or party-oriented." While the student body consists of "definite groups, it's not like high school cliques. Just groups of people who have common interests." Undergrads report that "the school has worked hard to lure foreign and minority students with attractive aid packages. However, overall lack of diversity is obvious and very much a detraction." Financial aid has certainly helped to diversify the economic backgrounds of students: "A number of us come from rich families, but there are a number that are on scholarship as well," reports one student.

# ALBERTSON COLLEGE

FINANCIAL AID: 208-459-5308 • E-MAIL: ADMISSION@ALBERTSON.EDU • WEBSITE: WWW.ALBERTSON.EDU

## ADMISSIONS

*Very important factors considered include:* extracurricular activities, secondary school record. *Important factors considered include:* character/personal qualities, essays, geographical residence, interview, recommendations, standardized test scores, volunteer work, work experience. *Other factors considered include:* alumni/ae relation, class rank, talent/ability. SAT I or ACT required. TOEFL required of all international applicants. High school diploma or GED is required. *High school units required/recommended:* 12 total recommended; 4 English required, 3 math required, 2 science required, 3 science recommended, 2 science lab recommended, 2 foreign language recommended, 3 social studies required, 3 history required.

## The Inside Word

Albertson's open doors are a quirk of location. The college offers a challenging, high-quality academic program best suited to those who are intellectually curious and serious about their studies. The application process is relatively stress-free (Note: For now, enrollment is on the rise. If Albertson were closer to the nation's population centers, admission would be even more selective). As it is, the admissions committee is no less thorough than those at the highly selective level; its makeup consists of several deans and directors as well as faculty members. Students seeking to attend a small college in a rural setting near a small metropolitan area owe it to themselves to take a look. The admissions office points out that "although this college has a rolling admissions policy, it is to the applicant's advantage to apply by February 15 in order to be eligible for many scholarships."

## FINANCIAL AID

*Students should submit:* FAFSA, institution's own financial aid form. The Princeton Review suggests that all financial aid forms be submitted as soon as possible after January 1. *Need-based scholarships/grants offered:* Pell, SEOG, state scholarships/grants, private scholarships, the school's own gift aid. *Loan aid offered:* FFEL Subsidized Stafford, FFEL Unsubsidized Stafford, FFEL PLUS, Federal Perkins, alternative loans. Federal Work-Study Program available. Institutional employment available. Applicants will be notified of awards on a rolling basis beginning on or about April 1. Off-campus job opportunities are good.

## FROM THE ADMISSIONS OFFICE

"While the mission of Albertson College is traditional in that it remains committed to the teaching of the liberal arts, many of the approaches to accomplishing this goal are unique. Within the campus community is the creativity to create classroom opportunities for students that span the globe—both technologically and geographically. Here, students are just as apt to attend a biology class on campus as they are to hike in the nearby Owyhee or Sawtooth Mountains to carry out field research. And during the college's six-week winter term, more than 30 percent of the students are emailing friends and family from such locales as Australia, Israel, France, Ireland, England, Peru, or Mexico while taking part in faculty-led, multidisciplinary trips. Students are invited to visit the campus and the admissions counselors, either in person or by the website at www.albertson.edu."

### SELECTIVITY

| | |
|---|---:|
| Admissions Rating | 81 |
| # of applicants | 950 |
| % of applicants accepted | 77 |
| % of acceptees attending | 40 |

### FRESHMAN PROFILE

| | |
|---|---:|
| Range SAT Verbal | 510-630 |
| Average SAT Verbal | 571 |
| Range SAT Math | 510-616 |
| Average SAT Math | 563 |
| Range ACT Composite | 21-33 |
| Average ACT Composite | 24 |
| Minimum TOEFL | 550 |
| Average HS GPA | 3.6 |
| % graduated top 10% of class | 33 |
| % graduated top 25% of class | 66 |
| % graduated top 50% of class | 90 |

### DEADLINES

| | |
|---|---:|
| Priority admission | 2/15 |
| Regular admission | 6/1 |
| Nonfall registration? | yes |

### APPLICANTS ALSO LOOK AT AND OFTEN PREFER
Linfield
Willamette
Gonzaga
Whitman
U of Puget Sound

### AND SOMETIMES PREFER
Whitworth
Carroll
U of Idaho

### AND RARELY PREFER
Boise State
Northwest Nazarene

### FINANCIAL FACTS

| | |
|---|---:|
| Financial Aid Rating | 81 |
| Tuition | $13,900 |
| Room and board | $5,015 |
| Books and supplies | $650 |
| Required fees | $600 |
| % frosh receiving aid | 72 |
| % undergrads receiving aid | 69 |
| Avg frosh grant | $4,300 |
| Avg frosh loan | $3,420 |

THE BEST 351 COLLEGES ■ 49

# ALBION COLLEGE

611 EAST PORTER, ALBION, MI 49224 • ADMISSIONS: 800-858-6770 • FAX: 517-629-0569

## CAMPUS LIFE

| | |
|---|---|
| Quality of Life Rating | 77 |
| Type of school | private |
| Affiliation | Methodist |
| Environment | rural |

### STUDENTS

| | |
|---|---|
| Total undergrad enrollment | 1,548 |
| % male/female | 44/56 |
| % from out of state | 9 |
| % from public high school | 72 |
| % live on campus | 92 |
| % in (# of) fraternities | 40 (5) |
| % in (# of) sororities | 40 (6) |
| % African American | 2 |
| % Asian | 2 |
| % Caucasian | 86 |
| % international | 1 |
| # of countries represented | 19 |

### SURVEY SAYS . . .
Students don't get along with local community
(Almost) everyone smokes
Hard liquor is popular
Classes are small
Students don't like Albion, MI
Lousy off-campus food
Student government is unpopular

## ACADEMICS

| | |
|---|---|
| Academic Rating | 78 |
| Calendar | semester |
| Student/faculty ratio | 12:1 |
| Profs interesting rating | 69 |
| Profs accessible rating | 68 |
| % profs teaching UG courses | 100 |
| Avg lab size | 10-19 students |
| Avg reg class size | 10-19 students |

### MOST POPULAR MAJORS
Business administration/management
English language and literature
Biology/biological sciences

## STUDENTS SPEAK OUT

### Academics

Albion College's recently instituted core curriculum stresses the "liberal" in liberal arts, requiring courses not only in literature, the arts, and sciences, but also in gender studies, ethnic studies, global studies, and the environment. The curriculum kicks off with required freshman seminars and concludes with a "capstone experience" that emphasizes "integration, synthesis, and innovation" of thought. Students are generally positive about the curriculum: the seminars, writes one undergrad, "are excellent classes, small, creative, and fun." Some students complain that the requirements "take away from upper-class courses. There are not as many options once a student gets into the upper-level courses." Most students, however, simply appreciate the rigorous requirements, especially as presented by Albion's "caring," "passionate" faculty. Notes one student, "Albion has many strengths, the greatest being the faculty. We have a wealth of highly educated and friendly faculty . . . Albion is great for people who love people; as a student you get to know a lot of great folks in administration and faculty." Classes "are very tough, but the professors are very willing to help you out if you need it. They really want to make sure that we succeed here at Albion." There is a general sense among students that "our school strives to meet every student's individual goals. The faculty and administration will work with you to accomplish anything, within reason, and will generally fund your research or projects as well. Our school is very well endowed, financially. Therefore, we have more opportunities for success than many other schools." Students also appreciate the fact that, once they have graduated, the school's "many connections can help students get jobs."

### Life

Students agree that "Greek life is an important part of life at Albion. Basically, if you're not Greek, life at Albion can be pretty boring." Because "the surrounding town is completely dead," the social scene here "lacks resources aside from the weekend frat party. There really are no good bars in town, and you have to travel to Jackson, Ann Arbor, or Kalamazoo for something to do or somewhere to eat!" Beyond the frat system, collegiate sporting events are the campus' great unifiers: students are especially bullish about the football team, a Division III powerhouse. Undergrads also encouragingly note that "the school is getting better about bringing in outside entertainment for us. Last year, the band Vertical Horizon preformed. Also, the school shows recent movies every weekend and brings in comedians." Even so, many offer this advice to those seeking fun: "Leave the campus!" Nearby Ann Arbor provides big school fun, and the campus is roughly an hour from Detroit. Many students appreciate and enjoy the annual City Service Day, when "students beautify the land around the college community and around campus" by cleaning area parks and repairing homes of the needy and elderly.

### Student Body

As at many small private colleges, the student body at Albion "basically consists of upper- and middle-class white students; those students who do not fit that description tend to mingle with those who have a similar background." Most agree that "everyone is generally nice" and that "our students are like a big group of friends. There are only 1,500 students at this school and so it's hard not to know most of them. I have never felt lonely here, like some of my friends have said they felt at their larger schools." Those who don't fit in, however, have a tougher go of things. Complains one outsider, "There's a lot of social pretentiousness here, and a lot of students make it hard for us to kick the 'rich white kids' school' image. The Greek system is very restrictive and anti-unity; it breaks up an already small campus." Adds a fellow traveler, "A LOT of students are materialistic, sheltered, have unexpanded minds, thirst for social prestige . . . . There is a minority group of people on campus who are politically active, who are aware of current issues and who speak out against injustice. Those are the people that make this college great. The others are just background noise; they give us something to speak against."

# ALBION COLLEGE

Financial Aid: 517-629-0440 • E-mail: admissions@albion.edu • Website: www.albion.edu

## ADMISSIONS

*Very important factors considered include:* character/personal qualities, extracurricular activities, interview, secondary school record, standardized test scores, talent/ability, volunteer work. *Important factors considered include:* alumni/ae relation, class rank, essays, geographical residence, minority status, recommendations. *Other factors considered include:* work experience. SAT I or ACT required. TOEFL required of all international applicants. High school diploma or GED is required. *High school units required/recommended:* 15 total required; 17 total recommended; 4 English required, 2 math required, 3 math recommended, 2 science required, 3 science recommended, 1 science lab required, 2 foreign language recommended, 3 social studies required, 1 history required, 3 elective required.

### The Inside Word

Albion's approach to admissions is typical of many small colleges. Despite a very high admit rate, candidates can expect to undergo a thorough review, as matchmaking plays a strong part in the evaluation process here. Your personal side and extracurricular involvements count a great deal when an admissions committee is engaged in community building. Though the college is on a rolling admission schedule, we encourage you to apply early in order to have the best shot at both admission and financial aid. Albion will waive the application fee for candidates who apply online.

## FINANCIAL AID

*Students should submit:* FAFSA. The Princeton Review suggests that all financial aid forms be submitted as soon as possible after January 1. *Need-based scholarships/grants offered:* Pell, SEOG, state scholarships/grants, private scholarships, the school's own gift aid. *Loan aid offered:* Direct Subsidized Stafford, Direct Unsubsidized Stafford, FFEL Subsidized Stafford, FFEL Unsubsidized Stafford, FFEL PLUS, Federal Perkins, state loans. Federal Work-Study Program available. Institutional employment available. Applicants will be notified of awards on a rolling basis beginning on or about March 15. Off-campus job opportunities are good.

## FROM THE ADMISSIONS OFFICE

"Albion was the first private college in Michigan to have a chapter of Phi Beta Kappa, the oldest national honor society, founded in 1776. Albion's heavily endowed professional institutes in environmental science, public policy and service, professional management, pre-medical and healthcare studies, honors and education offer world-class internships and study abroad opportunities. Albion is among the top 85 private, liberal arts colleges for the number of alumni who are corporate executives, including top executives and CEOs of Newsweek, the Lahey Clinic (MA), PricewaterhouseCoopers, Dow Corning, the NCAA, NYNEX, and the Federal Accounting Standards Board (FASB). Albion's graduate school placement rates at 98 percent for law, 96 percent for dental and 89 percent for medical schools, including Harvard, Michigan, Columbia, Northwestern, Notre Dame, Vanderbilt, and Wisconsin. Albion was the top award winner at the 2001 Michigan Campus Compact, which includes public and private schools in Michigan committed to service and volunteerism. The long list of campus organizations includes Model United Nations, Fellowship of Christian Athletes, Canoe Club, Black Student Alliance, Equestrian Club, Medievalist Society, Ecological Awareness Club, and fraternity and sorority service organizations. Of particular note is Albion's athletics program, where in addition to dominating Division III football, women's soccer, and men's and women's golf and swimming, five varsity teams have earned the highest grade-point average in the MIAA conference, NCAA Division III, or any division nationwide."

### SELECTIVITY

| | |
|---|---|
| Admissions Rating | 80 |
| # of applicants | 1,297 |
| % of applicants accepted | 87 |
| % of acceptees attending | 40 |
| # of early decision applicants | 37 |
| % accepted early decision | 95 |

### FRESHMAN PROFILE

| | |
|---|---|
| Range SAT Verbal | 510-640 |
| Average SAT Verbal | 562 |
| Range SAT Math | 520-630 |
| Average SAT Math | 582 |
| Range ACT Composite | 22-27 |
| Average ACT Composite | 25 |
| Minimum TOEFL | 550 |
| Average HS GPA | 3.5 |
| % graduated top 10% of class | 31 |
| % graduated top 25% of class | 63 |
| % graduated top 50% of class | 88 |

### DEADLINES

| | |
|---|---|
| Early decision | 11/15 |
| Early decision notification | 12/15 |
| Priority admission | 4/1 |
| Regular admission | 5/1 |
| Nonfall registration? | yes |

### APPLICANTS ALSO LOOK AT AND OFTEN PREFER
U of Michigan
Indiana U at Bloomington
Grinnell
Purdue

### AND SOMETIMES PREFER
Oberlin
Kenyon
Miami of Ohio
Hope
Kalamazoo
Michigan State

### AND RARELY PREFER
Alma, Adrian, Olivet, Calvin

### FINANCIAL FACTS

| | |
|---|---|
| Financial Aid Rating | 87 |
| Tuition | $19,390 |
| Room and board | $5,604 |
| Books and supplies | $650 |
| Required fees | $230 |
| % frosh receiving aid | 65 |
| % undergrads receiving aid | 60 |
| Avg frosh grant | $16,823 |
| Avg frosh loan | $2,610 |

# ALFRED UNIVERSITY

ALUMNI HALL, ONE SAXON DRIVE, ALFRED, NY 14802-1205 • ADMISSIONS: 607-871-2115 • FAX: 607-871-2198

## CAMPUS LIFE

| Quality of Life Rating | 79 |
|---|---|
| Type of school | private |
| Environment | rural |

### STUDENTS
| | |
|---|---|
| Total undergrad enrollment | 2,080 |
| % male/female | 48/52 |
| % from out of state | 35 |
| % live on campus | 65 |
| % African American | 5 |
| % Asian | 2 |
| % Caucasian | 78 |
| % Hispanic | 4 |
| % international | 2 |

### SURVEY SAYS . . .
Lots of beer drinking
Students aren't religious
Campus easy to get around
High cost of living
Theater is unpopular
Class discussions encouraged
Lousy off-campus food
Political activism is (almost) nonexistent

## ACADEMICS

| Academic Rating | 76 |
|---|---|
| Calendar | semester |
| Student/faculty ratio | 12:1 |
| Profs interesting rating | 93 |
| Profs accessible rating | 92 |
| % profs teaching UG courses | 100 |
| Avg lab size | 10-19 students |
| Avg reg class size | 10-19 students |

### MOST POPULAR MAJORS
Business administration/management
Ceramic sciences and engineering
Fine/studio arts

## STUDENTS SPEAK OUT

### Academics
Alfred University, a school renowned for its ceramics and glassworks programs, provides a "stimulating and rewarding" academic experience. What makes Alfred unique is that it isn't only an art school. Students speak highly of the English and business departments and point out that science courses are quite challenging. The "brilliant" professors "know you on a first-name basis" and "are often available for help in a class. One-on-one sessions with professors are often available." Class sizes are small and TAs are uncommon. One first-year student writes, "I am a freshman and have already been to two of my professors' homes for dinner." The administration is "friendly" and "quite approachable." They are "willing to discuss any situation that might arise." Some students note that they would like to see more professors in order "to increase the diversity of classes." Several transfer students are extremely fond of AU: "Compared to my previous school, this is heaven." Students note that the computer and library facilities need improvement, as does the food. On-campus parking also needs to be expanded. A junior English major summarizes Alfred University thusly: "Alfred University is a wonderful institution. The buildings are nice-looking, the professors are knowledgeable, and the students are brilliant."

### Life
AU's location in a "small, rural town in upstate New York"—two hours away from both Buffalo and Rochester—doesn't inspire its students. "If you expect to have a thrill a minute, then this may not be the best place for you." Still, students say, "there is fun. You just have to find it." The university is aware that students don't have many entertainment options in the surrounding area, and so "they try to plan events for us." Students rent movies or go to AU's on-campus movie theater. Students also go to "the one or two bars in town." Those who partake in winter sports appreciate the campus' proximity to the nearby mountains.

### Student Body
Students looking for a diverse population won't find one at AU. "The students are mostly white kids from the East Coast who grew up in upper-middle-class families." Another student adds, "A large number of students have never encountered someone of a different ethnic background." The university's lack of diversity bothers many students. "The white kids mainly hang out with white kids, while black [kids] hang out with black [kids]." AU's small size—about 2,200 undergrads—means that students get to know their peers. "They are a great bunch of people," though "they are sometimes clique-ish." The art students are regarded as the most outgoing. "People mingle freely with ideas, are very friendly, and varied in their dress, interests, and opinions." At the same time, she points out that while "the art school is liberal . . . the school [itself] is rural and in a conservative area."

# ALFRED UNIVERSITY

FINANCIAL AID: 607-871-2159 • E-MAIL: ADMWWW@ALFRED.EDU • WEBSITE: WWW.ALFRED.EDU

## ADMISSIONS

*Very important factors considered include:* character/personal qualities, class rank, extracurricular activities, recommendations, secondary school record. *Important factors considered include:* essays, standardized test scores, volunteer work. *Other factors considered include:* interview, talent/ability, work experience. SAT I or ACT required. TOEFL required of all international applicants. High school diploma or GED is required. *High school units required/recommended:* 16 total required; 4 English required, 2 math required, 4 math recommended, 2 science required, 3 science recommended, 2 science lab required, 3 science lab recommended, 2 social studies required, 3 social studies recommended.

### The Inside Word

There's no questioning the high quality of academics at Alfred, especially in their internationally known ceramics program. Still, the university's general lack of name recognition and relatively isolated campus directly affect both the applicant pool and the number of admitted students who enroll, and thus keeps selectivity relatively low for a school of its caliber. (The exception is clearly in ceramic arts, where candidates will face a very rigorous review.) If you're a back-to-nature type looking for a challenging academic environment, AU could be just what the doctor ordered. And if you're a standout academically, you may find that they're generous with financial aid, too—they are serious about competing for good students.

## FINANCIAL AID

*Students should submit:* FAFSA, institution's own financial aid form, state aid form, noncustodial (divorced/separated) parent's statement, business/farm supplement. No deadline for regular filing. The Princeton Review suggests that all financial aid forms be submitted as soon as possible after January 1. *Need-based scholarships/grants offered:* Pell, SEOG, state scholarships/grants, private scholarships, the school's own gift aid. *Loan aid offered:* FFEL Subsidized Stafford, FFEL Unsubsidized Stafford, FFEL PLUS, Federal Perkins, college/university loans from institutional funds, private alternative loans. Federal Work-Study Program available. Institutional employment available. Applicants will be notified of awards on a rolling basis beginning on or about February 1. Off-campus job opportunities are fair.

## FROM THE ADMISSIONS OFFICE

"The admissions process at Alfred University is the foundation for the personal attention that a student can expect from this institution. Each applicant is evaluated individually and can expect genuine, personal attention at Alfred University."

---

### SELECTIVITY

★ ★ ☆ ☆

| | |
|---|---|
| Admissions Rating | 77 |
| # of applicants | 2,050 |
| % of applicants accepted | 65 |
| % of acceptees attending | 33 |
| # of early decision applicants | 45 |
| % accepted early decision | 93 |

### FRESHMAN PROFILE

| | |
|---|---|
| Range SAT Verbal | 490-640 |
| Range SAT Math | 490-640 |
| Range ACT Composite | 26-30 |
| Minimum TOEFL | 550 |
| % graduated top 10% of class | 23 |
| % graduated top 25% of class | 51 |
| % graduated top 50% of class | 83 |

### DEADLINES

| | |
|---|---|
| Early decision | 12/1 |
| Early decision notification | 12/15 |
| Priority admission | 2/1 |
| Nonfall registration? | yes |

### APPLICANTS ALSO LOOK AT
**AND OFTEN PREFER**
SUNY Geneseo
**AND SOMETIMES PREFER**
SUNY Buffalo
U of Rochester
Syracuse
St. Lawrence
**AND RARELY PREFER**
Rochester Institute of Technology
Clarkson
Rensselear Polytechnic Institute

### FINANCIAL FACTS

★ ★ ★ ☆

| | |
|---|---|
| Financial Aid Rating | 88 |
| Tuition | $18,498 |
| Room and board | $8,500 |
| Books and supplies | $700 |
| Required fees | $698 |
| % frosh receiving aid | 90 |
| % undergrads receiving aid | 90 |

THE BEST 351 COLLEGES ■ 53

# ALLEGHENY COLLEGE

OFFICE OF ADMISSIONS, MEADVILLE, PA 16335 • ADMISSIONS: 800-521-5293 • FAX: 814-337-0431

## CAMPUS LIFE

| | |
|---|---|
| Quality of Life Rating | 75 |
| Type of school | private |
| Affiliation | other |
| Environment | rural |

### STUDENTS

| | |
|---|---|
| Total undergrad enrollment | 1,924 |
| % male/female | 48/52 |
| % from out of state | 32 |
| % from public high school | 85 |
| % live on campus | 73 |
| % in (# of) fraternities | 26 (5) |
| % in (# of) sororities | 29 (4) |
| % African American | 2 |
| % Asian | 2 |
| % Caucasian | 94 |
| % Hispanic | 1 |
| % international | 1 |
| # of countries represented | 16 |

### SURVEY SAYS . . .
Athletic facilities are great
Frats and sororities dominate social scene
Classes are small
Student publications are ignored
Library needs improving
Lousy food on campus
Political activism is (almost) nonexistent
Lousy off-campus food
Diversity lacking on campus

## ACADEMICS

| | |
|---|---|
| Academic Rating | 83 |
| Calendar | semester |
| Student/faculty ratio | 14:1 |
| Profs interesting rating | 77 |
| Profs accessible rating | 87 |
| % profs teaching UG courses | 100 |
| Avg lab size | 10-19 students |
| Avg reg class size | 10-19 students |

### MOST POPULAR MAJORS
Biology/biological sciences
Psychology
Economics

## STUDENTS SPEAK OUT

### Academics
A warm communal feeling pervades the Allegheny academic setting, according to the school's satisfied undergraduates. One writes, "I consider many administrators and faculty good friends outside the academic realm. Allegheny is about people, not numbers. It is a gold mine waiting to be tapped." Students also appreciate that Allegheny is "really strong in the sciences, which gives us great placement for graduate schools," and are even happier for the support they receive in pursuit of their degree: "The professors are always willing to give their time to help and do their best to accommodate their schedules for you." All the assistance comes in handy at this "very academically challenging" school; students warn that "this place is very competitive. Many people double major, and classes can get rough." Adds another, "The workload here is intense, but the classes prepare you well for life beyond Allegheny." Students greatly value their "experiential learning opportunities [offered] through ACCEL (the Allegheny College Center for Experiential Learning)," which provides leadership training and internships in places including New York; Washington, D.C.; and Boston as well as spring term study tours both in and outside the United States. Almost everyone agrees that ACCEL "distinguishes Allegheny from other, larger schools." Several students note that the school's curriculum requirements help students develop a valuable generalist's perspective; "Instead of knowing a lot about something, I now know something about everything. That is Allegheny summed up to me," concludes one student.

### Life
Undergraduates overwhelmingly agree with the student who opines that "Academics are very important to Allegheny students, but I think there is a healthy balance between study and social activities." Elaborates a peer, "Life at Allegheny is stressful, but very rewarding. Everybody works hard during the week and plays hard on the weekends. There are plenty of parties, but there are also a lot of fun, school-sponsored events like movies, karaoke, and comedians." Because there is "not a whole lot to do in Meadville," students tend to find fun on and around campus. Some tell us that "people seem to have fun whatever they do. There is bowling, restaurants, ice skating, movies, and stuff on campus such as musicians, comedians, games, etc." An athletic type adds, "Depending on what the weather is like, we play football, go sledding, toss the Frisbee, that sort of thing. Most people here like sports." When the urge for big-city diversion takes them, Allegheny students drive to Pittsburgh or Cleveland, the two closest large cities, both about an hour and a half away.

### Student Body
Allegheny undergrads generally concede that theirs "is a 'cliquey' school." Explains one student, "I would say the mainstream social scene of fraternities and athletic groups can be very segregated at times." The glass-half-empty types among them observe with scorn that "students here tend to be rich and snobby" and that "the campus is very homogeneous as to types of students, and sometimes it seems everyone just thinks and acts the same way." To the majority of students, however, Allegheny is home to a "friendly, comfortable campus. When you walk down the street, most everyone says 'hi' and smiles." Notes one student, "I really was attracted to Allegheny's small campus. It's always nice to see a familiar face when you walk down the street."

54 ■ THE BEST 351 COLLEGES

# ALLEGHENY COLLEGE

FINANCIAL AID: 800-835-7780 • E-MAIL: ADMISS@ALLEGHENY.EDU • WEBSITE: WWW.ALLEGHENY.EDU

## ADMISSIONS

*Very important factors considered include:* class rank, secondary school record. *Important factors considered include:* character/personal qualities, extracurricular activities, interview, recommendations, standardized test scores. *Other factors considered include:* alumni/ae relation, essays, geographical residence, minority status, talent/ability, volunteer work, work experience. SAT I or ACT required; SAT II recommended. TOEFL required of all international applicants. High school diploma or GED is required. *High school units required/recommended:* 16 total required; 4 English required, 3 math required, 3 science required, 2 foreign language required, 3 social studies required, 1 elective required.

### The Inside Word

Don't be deceived by the fairly high admit rate here—Allegheny draws a strong pool of academically well-qualified applicants, and candidate evaluation here is rigorous and personalized. The admissions staff strongly recommends campus visits and interviews; students who visit the campus prior to Allegheny's application deadline receive application fee waivers. Given the highly personalized nature of candidate evaluation here, we'd suggest both the visit and taking the most challenging courses in high school in order to be as competitive in the applicant pool as possible.

## FINANCIAL AID

*Students should submit:* FAFSA. No deadline for regular filing. The Princeton Review suggests that all financial aid forms be submitted as soon as possible after January 1. *Need-based scholarships/grants offered:* Pell, SEOG, state scholarships/grants, private scholarships, the school's own gift aid. *Loan aid offered:* FFEL Subsidized Stafford, FFEL Unsubsidized Stafford, FFEL PLUS, Federal Perkins, state loans, private loans from commercial lenders. Federal Work-Study Program available. Institutional employment available. Applicants will be notified of awards on a rolling basis beginning on or about March 1. Off-campus job opportunities are excellent.

## FROM THE ADMISSIONS OFFICE

"Allegheny, the nation's 32nd oldest college, is a nationally recognized college of the liberal arts and sciences. Allegheny's nearly 2,000 students are active in social, economic, and environmental issues and work collaboratively with faculty as part of the learning process. The College's nationally recognized programs, such as the Center for Political Participation, the Center for Experiential Learning, and the Center for Economic and Environmental Development offer powerful and engaging out-of-classroom experiences. With about 40 programs of study and a capstone comprehensive senior project, the College's rigorous education results in benefits that include acceptance rates to medical and law school that are twice the national average. And Allegheny's geographic setting is ideal for our active student population, who enjoy biking, rock climbing, canoeing, and kayaking."

## SELECTIVITY

| | |
|---|---|
| Admissions Rating | 87 |
| # of applicants | 2,612 |
| % of applicants accepted | 80 |
| % of acceptees attending | 26 |
| # accepting a place on wait list | 62 |
| % admitted from wait list | 18 |
| # of early decision applicants | 102 |
| % accepted early decision | 97 |

### FRESHMAN PROFILE

| | |
|---|---|
| Range SAT Verbal | 550-650 |
| Average SAT Verbal | 598 |
| Range SAT Math | 550-650 |
| Average SAT Math | 600 |
| Range ACT Composite | 23-27 |
| Average ACT Composite | 25 |
| Minimum TOEFL | 550 |
| Average HS GPA | 3.7 |
| % graduated top 10% of class | 40 |
| % graduated top 25% of class | 74 |
| % graduated top 50% of class | 94 |

### DEADLINES

| | |
|---|---|
| Early decision | 1/15 |
| Early decision notification | 10/15 |
| Regular admission | 2/15 |
| Regular notification | 4/1 |
| Nonfall registration? | yes |

### APPLICANTS ALSO LOOK AT
**AND OFTEN PREFER**
Bucknell University, Dickinson College
Carnegie Mellon University
**AND SOMETIMES PREFER**
Pennsylvania State University—
University Park
Washington & Jefferson College
Gettysburg College, Denison University
Duquesne University, College of Wooster
**AND RARELY PREFER**
University of Pittsburgh—Pittsburgh
Westminster College, Miami University

### FINANCIAL FACTS

| | |
|---|---|
| Financial Aid Rating | 85 |
| Tuition | $23,100 |
| Room and board | $5,600 |
| Books and supplies | $700 |
| Required fees | $280 |
| % frosh receiving aid | 74 |
| % undergrads receiving aid | 71 |
| Avg frosh grant | $14,266 |
| Avg frosh loan | $3,062 |

# AMERICAN UNIVERSITY

4400 MASSACHUSETTS AVENUE, NW, WASHINGTON, DC 20016-8001 • ADMISSIONS: 202-885-6000 • FAX: 202-885-1025

## CAMPUS LIFE

| | |
|---|---|
| Quality of Life Rating | 80 |
| Type of school | private |
| Affiliation | Methodist |
| Environment | urban |

### STUDENTS
| | |
|---|---|
| Total undergrad enrollment | 5,872 |
| % male/female | 39/61 |
| % from out of state | 93 |
| % live on campus | 68 |
| % in (# of) fraternities | 17 (10) |
| % in (# of) sororities | 18 (12) |
| % African American | 6 |
| % Asian | 4 |
| % Caucasian | 58 |
| % Hispanic | 5 |
| % international | 9 |

### SURVEY SAYS . . .
Political activism is hot
Students are happy
Students are religious
Lots of classroom discussion
Great food on campus
Dorms are like palaces
Ethnic diversity on campus
Unattractive campus
Lots of long lines and red tape
Very little beer drinking

## ACADEMICS

| | |
|---|---|
| Academic Rating | 79 |
| Calendar | semester |
| Student/faculty ratio | 15:1 |
| Profs interesting rating | 78 |
| Profs accessible rating | 77 |
| % profs teaching UG courses | 95 |
| % classes taught by TAs | 5 |

### MOST POPULAR MAJORS
Business administration/management
International relations and affairs
Political science and government

## STUDENTS SPEAK OUT

### Academics
"So many academic and social opportunities" await one at American University, thanks in large part to its location in northwest Washington, D.C. Students have to be self-starters to take advantage of those opportunities, however; no one will hold your hand and accompany you to the threshold of learning here. "If you know what you want out of AU, you will get it," explains one student. Professors here ("about half are brilliant, and half are just okay," reports one undergrad) often have multiple commitments beyond campus. "We have lots of adjuncts who have super professional experiences, but who are inaccessible outside class," warns one student. Adds another, "Professors are not always approachable. Some have an attitude with students if they ask for help [or] if students do not agree with their views." Students don't feel completely ignored on the matter of their instructors, though, as "the school really takes the students' feedback on the professors very seriously," which means bad teachers often quietly and mysteriously disappear. And the faculty has plenty of bright lights, dedicated teachers who "are really amicable and cordial and are willing to help students. And many are leaders in their fields." Students generally dislike the administration, perceiving it as "much more concerned with the outward appearance of the school" than with current students' concerns. Some are willing to concede, however, "Although our president rules the school like a banana republic, he has brought about much-needed improvements in the community." The business department draws kudos, though science facilities reportedly need some TLC. The study abroad program and internship opportunities earn students' universal praise.

### Life
"D.C. is a great city to go to school in," AU students agree. "The city is the school's most valuable asset; it's got a life of its own, in contrast to many college towns. It really makes going to school here exciting." Students love Dupont Circle and the nearby neighborhood of Adams Morgan ("a big attention drawer because there are so many restaurants, clubs, bars, and poetry places") but find plenty to do all over town. As one student told us, "There are so many other things to do in D.C.! There are dozens of clubs, and hundreds of unique restaurants, many of which specialize in cultural goods." Another enthusiastic undergraduate adds, "It is not possible to go a single day without experiencing at least one aspect of a different culture." The city picks up the slack for the AU campus, which is often dormant: "Campus life itself isn't as exciting as a Big Ten school or something," concedes one student, "but that's because we're in a big city that actually has places to go [to] and hang out [in]." The campus is officially dry, a fact that further encourages this outwardly oriented student body to look for gathering places beyond the campus gates. With D.C. at the university's doorstep, partying away from school is a no-brainer. Students note that this is the type of campus where "we're more likely to attend Election Night parties than Super Bowl parties."

### Student Body
The "idealistic, smart, concerned" students at American University are "extremely politically involved. People here are passionate about various issues, due in no small part to our location." Most are to the left end of the political spectrum; one disaffected undergrad writes, "The typical student is a liberal tree-hugger who thinks he/she has an open mind but actually doesn't." A large international population ("lots of diplomats' kids"), along with smaller minority populations, engenders a diversity that is "wonderful; it makes political science classes quite invigorating!" When we asked what the typical American student was like, we typically got one of two responses. Some balked at the request: "This school is way too diverse to pinpoint the typical student," while others described a white kid from the "middle to upper middle class, interested in international relations, likes trying new things, [and] interested in community service."

56 ■ THE BEST 351 COLLEGES

# AMERICAN UNIVERSITY

FINANCIAL AID: 202-885-6100 • E-MAIL: AFA@AMERICAN.EDU • WEBSITE: WWW.AMERICAN.EDU

## ADMISSIONS

*Very important factors considered include:* secondary school record, standardized test scores. *Important factors considered include:* class rank, essays, extracurricular activities, recommendations, volunteer work. *Other factors considered include:* alumni/ae relation, character/personal qualities, interview, minority status, talent/ability, work experience. SAT I or ACT required; SAT II recommended. TOEFL required of all international applicants. High school diploma or GED is required. *High school units required/recommended:* 16 total required; 20 total recommended; 4 English required, 3 math required, 4 math recommended, 2 science required, 4 science recommended, 2 science lab required, 2 foreign language required, 3 foreign language recommended, 2 social studies required, 4 social studies recommended, 4 elective recommended.

### The Inside Word

Washington, D.C., is indeed a tremendous attraction for students who aspire to careers in government, politics, and other areas of public service. Georgetown skims most of the cream of the crop off the top of this considerable pool of prospective students, but American does quite nicely. Because the university is nationally known it also has formidable competition outside its own backyard, and as a result its yield of admits who enroll is on the low side. This necessitates a higher admit rate than one might expect at a school with considerable academic strength and an impressively credentialed faculty. If you're an active leadership type with a strong academic record the admissions process should be fairly painless—American offers a great opportunity for a quality educational experience without having to plead for admission.

## FINANCIAL AID

*Students should submit:* FAFSA, institution's own financial aid form. Regular filing deadline is March 1. The Princeton Review suggests that all financial aid forms be submitted as soon as possible after January 1. *Need-based scholarships/grants offered:* Pell, SEOG, state scholarships/grants, private scholarships, the school's own gift aid. *Loan aid offered:* Direct Subsidized Stafford, Direct Unsubsidized Stafford, Direct PLUS, Federal Perkins, college/university loans from institutional funds. Federal Work-Study Program available. Institutional employment available. Applicants will be notified of awards on or about April 1. Off-campus job opportunities are excellent.

## FROM THE ADMISSIONS OFFICE

"Our students learn how to turn ideas into action and action into service by interacting regularly with decision makers and leaders in every profession and from every corner of the world. If you are looking to be academically challenged in a rich multicultural environment, then American University is the place you want to be. Our expert teaching faculty provide a well-rounded liberal arts education, characterized by small classes, the use of cutting-edge technology, and an interdisciplinary curriculum in the arts, education, humanities, social sciences, and sciences. Not just a political town, Washington, D.C., offers a variety of internship opportunities in every field. And AU's World Capitals Program, with locations in 16 nations, lets you expand your studies into international settings. Because of these resources, AU enables you to put your education to work as nowhere else in the country."

### SELECTIVITY

| | |
|---|---|
| Admissions Rating | 83 |
| # of applicants | 9,879 |
| % of applicants accepted | 63 |
| % of acceptees attending | 21 |
| # of early decision applicants | 397 |
| % accepted early decision | 66 |

### FRESHMAN PROFILE

| | |
|---|---|
| Range SAT Verbal | 560-670 |
| Average SAT Verbal | 613 |
| Range SAT Math | 550-650 |
| Average SAT Math | 600 |
| Average ACT Composite | 27 |
| Minimum TOEFL | 550 |
| Average HS GPA | 3.3 |
| % graduated top 10% of class | 31 |
| % graduated top 25% of class | 66 |
| % graduated top 50% of class | 97 |

### DEADLINES

| | |
|---|---|
| Early decision | 11/15 |
| Early decision notification | 12/31 |
| Regular admission | 2/1 |
| Regular notification | 4/1 |
| Nonfall registration? | yes |

### APPLICANTS ALSO LOOK AT AND OFTEN PREFER

Boston U
George Washington
Georgetown U
NYU

**AND SOMETIMES PREFER**
Emory
Syracuse
Tufts
U of Maryland at College Park

**AND RARELY PREFER**
Fordham U
Ithaca College
Northeastern U, Penn State

### FINANCIAL FACTS

| | |
|---|---|
| Financial Aid Rating | 84 |
| Tuition | $23,068 |
| Room and board | $9,488 |
| Books and supplies | $600 |
| Required fees | $387 |
| % frosh receiving aid | 66 |
| % undergrads receiving aid | 62 |
| Avg frosh grant | $13,775 |
| Avg frosh loan | $5,791 |

# AMHERST COLLEGE

Campus Box 2231, PO Box 5000, Amherst, MA 01002 • Admissions: 413-542-2328 • Fax: 413-542-2040

## CAMPUS LIFE

| | |
|---|---|
| Quality of Life Rating | 92 |
| Type of school | private |
| Environment | rural |

### STUDENTS
| | |
|---|---|
| Total undergrad enrollment | 1,618 |
| % from out of state | 85 |
| % from public high school | 60 |
| % live on campus | 98 |
| % African American | 9 |
| % Asian | 13 |
| % Caucasian | 52 |
| % Hispanic | 8 |
| % international | 5 |
| # of countries represented | 34 |

### SURVEY SAYS . . .
Campus easy to get around
Registration is a breeze
Students are happy
Dorms are like palaces
No one cheats
Very little hard liquor
Very little drug use
Students aren't religious
Lousy food on campus
Student publications are ignored

## ACADEMICS

| | |
|---|---|
| Academic Rating | 99 |
| Calendar | semester |
| Student/faculty ratio | 9:1 |
| Profs interesting rating | 97 |
| Profs accessible rating | 96 |
| % profs teaching UG courses | 100 |
| Avg lab size | under 10 students |
| Avg reg class size | 10-19 students |

### MOST POPULAR MAJORS
English language and literature
Economics
Political science and government

## STUDENTS SPEAK OUT

### Academics
Small classes, great professors, as much academic freedom as students are willing to grab, and a beautiful campus; no wonder students say, "I could not, in my wildest dreams, imagine an environment better suited for a young adult to grow intellectually than Amherst College." Excellent professors dedicated to undergraduate teaching lie at the heart of the Amherst experience. "Professors make it their business to get to know students and show an interest in them," writes one undergrad. "They are very supportive." Recounts another, "When I wrote my math professor a panic-filled e-mail the night before a test, he called me to help at one in the morning." The administration aggressively encourages close student-teacher relationships, sponsoring "a program [that allows] students to take professors out to dinner and thus extend the educational realm beyond the classroom." Amherst's open curriculum means students "take every course by choice, not because it is required" and can easily "create [their] own interdisciplinary major." Classes are small and selection is limited, so classes close quickly. However, "while on paper it may seem [difficult] to get into classes, Amherst students take the words 'course closed' as a challenge. Here, the administration and many professors encourage us to whine and grovel to get what we want out of our academics. The rules are written so that anyone can be an exception." When students tire of their own college community, it is easy to take a class or audition for a play at one of the other four schools in the Five College Consortium (UMass—Amherst, Smith, Hampshire, and Mount Holyoke). The Five College system, according to students, "gives you all the opportunities of a large university, without any of the drawbacks."

### Life
According to most students, "Social life at Amherst isn't varied. Mostly it's either parties with lots of alcohol or else just hanging out with your group of friends and talking. But most people seem satisfied with this, and there are a few alternative social events for those who aren't." For fun, students "watch a lot of movies sponsored by campus groups, dance, and go out to dinner with friends." They also attend TAP, a.k.a. The Amherst Party, a regular campuswide blowout held in upper-class dorms. TAP "is huge here, as is drinking. But it's not as if drinking is mandatory for having a good time or fitting in." As an alternative, "some of the substance-free dorms run 'anti-parties' every Saturday in response to TAP." Otherwise, students engage in "lots of preppy activities, e.g. sailing, fencing, and crew"; take advantage of "the Five College system, which brings an endless stream of stuff to do to the Valley"; or just hang out in their amazing dorms. They do not, as a rule, date, since "dating is difficult at a school this small. Most people either randomly hook up on Saturdays or are in long-term relationships." When the campus social scene grows stifling, they head to the close-by fraternities of UMass.

### Student Body
Despite a minority population that is uncommonly large among New England private schools, Amherst students still complain that "this is not a very diverse school, and a lot of people don't make efforts to be friends with different kinds of people." Even the more generous undergrads qualify their praise, pointing out that "this school is more diverse than your average bear, but since it's in New England it's still pretty whitewashed." Students "get along very well" and appreciate the fact that their classmates are "very smart, somewhat intimidating, but great company." There are, notes one student, "lots of extremely talented students," and "many fun late-night discussions." Some warn that "too much political correctness is our biggest problem. Lots of complaining about nonexistent problems."

# AMHERST COLLEGE

FINANCIAL AID: 413-542-2296 • E-MAIL: ADMISSIONS@AMHERST.EDU • WEBSITE: WWW.AMHERST.EDU

## ADMISSIONS

*Very important factors considered include:* character/personal qualities, essays, extracurricular activities, recommendations, secondary school record, standardized test scores, talent/ability. *Important factors considered include:* alumni/ae relation, class rank, volunteer work. *Other factors considered include:* geographical residence, state residency, work experience. TOEFL required of all international applicants. *High school units required/recommended:* 4 English recommended, 4 math recommended, 3 science recommended, 1 science lab recommended, 4 foreign language recommended, 2 social studies recommended, 2 history recommended.

## The Inside Word

Despite an up-and-down fluctuation in application totals at most highly selective colleges over the past couple of years, Amherst remains a popular choice and very competitive. You've got to be a strong match all-around, and given their formidable applicant pool, it's very important that you make your case as direct as possible. If you're a special-interest candidate such as a legacy or recruited athlete, you may get a bit of a break from the admissions committee, but you'll still need to show sound academic capabilities and potential. Those without such links have a tougher task. On top of taking the toughest courses available to them and performing at the highest of their abilities, they must be strong writers who demonstrate that they are intellectually curious self-starters who will contribute to the community and profit from the experience. In other words, you've got to have a strong profile and a very convincing application in order to get admitted.

## FINANCIAL AID

*Students should submit:* FAFSA, CSS/Financial Aid PROFILE, noncustodial (divorced/separated) parent's statement, business/farm supplement, income tax returns, W-2 forms (or other wage statements). Regular filing deadline is February 15. The Princeton Review suggests that all financial aid forms be submitted as soon as possible after January 1. *Need-based scholarships/grants offered:* Pell, SEOG, state scholarships/grants, private scholarships, the school's own gift aid. *Loan aid offered:* Direct Subsidized Stafford, Direct Unsubsidized Stafford, Direct PLUS, Federal Perkins, college/university loans from institutional funds. Federal Work-Study Program available. Institutional employment available. Applicants will be notified of awards on or about April 8. Off-campus job opportunities are good.

## FROM THE ADMISSIONS OFFICE

"Amherst College looks, above all, for men and women of intellectual promise who have demonstrated qualities of mind and character that will enable them to take full advantage of the college's curriculum.... Admission decisions aim to select from among the many qualified applicants those possessing the intellectual talent, mental discipline, and imagination that will allow them most fully to benefit from the curriculum and contribute to the life of the college and of society. Whatever the form of academic experience—lecture course, seminar, conference, studio, laboratory, independent study at various levels—intellectual competence and awareness of problems and methods are the goals of the Amherst program, rather than the direct preparation for a profession."

### SELECTIVITY

| | |
|---|---|
| Admissions Rating | 99 |
| # of applicants | 5,238 |
| % of applicants accepted | 18 |
| # accepting a place on wait list | 321 |
| % admitted from wait list | 6 |
| # of early decision applicants | 368 |
| % accepted early decision | 36 |

### FRESHMAN PROFILE

| | |
|---|---|
| Range SAT Verbal | 660-770 |
| Average SAT Verbal | 710 |
| Range SAT Math | 650-770 |
| Average SAT Math | 707 |
| Range ACT Composite | 28-33 |
| Average ACT Composite | 30 |
| Minimum TOEFL | 600 |
| % graduated top 10% of class | 82 |
| % graduated top 25% of class | 98 |
| % graduated top 50% of class | 100 |

### DEADLINES

| | |
|---|---|
| Early decision | 11/15 |
| Regular admission | 12/31 |
| Regular notification | 4/3 |

### APPLICANTS ALSO LOOK AT AND OFTEN PREFER
Harvard
Princeton
Yale

### AND SOMETIMES PREFER
Brown
Williams
Stanford
Dartmouth

### AND RARELY PREFER
U. Virginia
Vassar
Tufts

### FINANCIAL FACTS

| | |
|---|---|
| Financial Aid Rating | 88 |
| Tuition | $27,800 |
| Room and board | $7,380 |
| Books and supplies | $850 |
| Required fees | $510 |
| % frosh receiving aid | 47 |
| % undergrads receiving aid | 49 |
| Avg frosh grant | $25,534 |
| Avg frosh loan | $2,150 |

# Arizona State University

PO Box 870112, Tempe, AZ 85287-0112 • Admissions: 480-965-7788 • Fax: 480-965-3610

## CAMPUS LIFE

| | |
|---|---|
| Quality of Life Rating | 78 |
| Type of school | public |
| Environment | suburban |

### STUDENTS

| | |
|---|---|
| Total undergrad enrollment | 36,802 |
| % male/female | 48/52 |
| % from out of state | 23 |
| % live on campus | 17 |
| % in (# of) fraternities | 6 (24) |
| % in (# of) sororities | 7 (18) |
| % African American | 3 |
| % Asian | 5 |
| % Caucasian | 74 |
| % Hispanic | 12 |
| % international | 3 |
| # of countries represented | 125 |

### SURVEY SAYS . . .
Students love Tempe, AZ
Athletic facilities are great
Everyone loves the Sun Devils
Popular college radio
Great library
Ethnic diversity on campus
Student publications are popular
Large classes
Lots of TAs teach upper-level courses
Dorms are like dungeons

## ACADEMICS

| | |
|---|---|
| Academic Rating | 68 |
| Calendar | semester |
| Student/faculty ratio | 22:1 |
| Profs interesting rating | 91 |
| Profs accessible rating | 88 |
| % profs teaching UG courses | 75 |
| Avg lab size | 20-29 students |
| Avg reg class size | 20-29 students |

### MOST POPULAR MAJORS
Communications studies/speech communication and rhetoric
Multi/interdisciplinary studies
Psychology

## STUDENTS SPEAK OUT

### Academics
"Walking to class in sunshine is great!" writes a first year. Indeed, among those surveyed, "temperature" and "weather" were some of the top reasons listed for choosing this huge (47,000 grad and undergrad combined) Pac-10 school located in Tempe, Arizona (quickly followed by "tuition, beer, parties, girls"—and in that order). This isn't to say ASU is only known for its sun-drenched, beer-soaked, bare-naked partying. A serious-minded senior argues: "There's a lot of people who complain that this is a party school. College is what you make of it. If you want to study, you can. If you want to party, you can. Thankfully, I've managed to balance the two." It's a sentiment that's echoed again and again. With its academic tutoring resources, relatively low cost, proximity to Phoenix industry, and strong programs (architecture, psychology, business administration, and the Walter Cronkite School of Journalism), Arizona State is a school with plenty of opportunities for an education—if, perhaps, a few more opportunities to have a good time. As with any school of its size, hassles with preregistration, overcrowded classes, inadequate facilities (especially the school's computer networking), and "too many teaching assistants" can lead to frustration. Still, say most, "at ASU professors care very much and they want students to succeed." As at any school, "There's a marked difference between mere professors and educators," concludes a junior. "All the people I learned from were the latter."

### Life
A first-year waxes profound: "Life is awesome here. Can't beat life in the sun." Tongue-tied from a bit too much of ASU's legendary partying? Perhaps. After all, Tempe's reputation as "extremely social" and "an excellent college town" is hard to live down. "The downtown area is spectacular," writes a freshman. "Lots of fun stuff to do. Lots of cool festivals, and, being close to Phoenix, many big musicians have concerts nearby." Of course, everyone's got a different pace, and ASU's size and diversity seems to be able to accommodate most. A junior describes her typical day: "People think about going to class, grades, studying, friends, relationships, parties, etc. We watch movies and TV, we exercise, [and] go out. We write, read, etc." So many people around all the time can put a strain on the facilities, and ASU's dorms bear witness to decades of wear. "Dorms here are essentially low-rent apartments in every sense of the word," gripes a sophomore. Still, when a first-year's only complaint is "more shade (it's really hot)," things can't be all bad.

### Student Body
"Lots of working out, tanning, dieting, highlighting, and plastic surgery. And everyone always seems to be on a cell phone." Is it all just a bunch of "Barbies & Kens," as one sick-of-it senior claims? We like this upperclassman's take on things: "Like any other place where there's a huge group of people, you learn patience. Sometimes people are really cool, sometimes they aren't." While some members of ASU's student body have been accused of "apathy" and of having a "safety-don't-talk-to-me bubble" around them, "many are ambitious and generally nice." A freshman concludes, "College is a slice of life. You run into everyone and every style of personality." Indeed, cultural, ethnic, and economic diversity is one of ASU's biggest strengths. An upbeat sophomore notes, "Students interact with a variety of others on a daily basis. There is more diversity here than anywhere else I have been."

# ARIZONA STATE UNIVERSITY

FINANCIAL AID: 480-965-3355 • WEBSITE: WWW.ASU.EDU

## ADMISSIONS

*Very important factors considered include:* class rank, secondary school record, standardized test scores. *Important factors considered include:* state residency. *Other factors considered include:* essays, extracurricular activities, interview, recommendations, talent/ability. SAT I or ACT required. TOEFL required of all international applicants. High school diploma or GED is required. *High school units required:* 16 total required; 4 English required, 4 math required, 3 science required, 3 science lab required, 2 foreign language required, 1 social studies required, 1 history required.

### The Inside Word

A college preparatory curriculum and solid grades should lead to hassle-free admission. ASU uses a formula and cutoff admission process. Candidates who don't fill the bill through the formula can appeal their denial and submit additional information for consideration.

## FINANCIAL AID

*Students should submit:* FAFSA. The Princeton Review suggests that all financial aid forms be submitted as soon as possible after January 1. *Need-based scholarships/grants offered:* Pell, SEOG, state scholarships/grants, private scholarships, the school's own gift aid, Federal Nursing. *Loan aid offered:* Direct Subsidized Stafford, Direct Unsubsidized Stafford, Direct PLUS, FFEL PLUS, Federal Perkins. Federal Work-Study Program available. Institutional employment available. Applicants will be notified of awards on a rolling basis beginning on or about March 15. Off-campus job opportunities are good.

## FROM THE ADMISSIONS OFFICE

"ASU is a place where students from all 50 states and abroad come together to live and study in one of the nation's premier collegiate environments. Situated in Tempe, ASU boasts a physical setting and climate second to none. ASU offers more than 150 academic programs of study leading to the BS and BA in eight undergraduate colleges and schools. Many of these programs have received national recognition for their quality of teaching, innovative curricula, and outstanding facilities. ASU's Barrett Honors College, the only Honors College in the Southwest that spans all academic disciplines, provides unique and challenging experiences for its students and was recently named one of eight 'best buys' in honors education by *Money* magazine."

---

### SELECTIVITY

| | |
|---|---|
| Admissions Rating | 79 |
| # of applicants | 18,155 |
| % of applicants accepted | 85 |
| % of acceptees attending | 41 |

### FRESHMAN PROFILE

| | |
|---|---|
| Range SAT Verbal | 480–590 |
| Average SAT Verbal | 538 |
| Range SAT Math | 490–610 |
| Average SAT Math | 551 |
| Range ACT Composite | 20–26 |
| Average ACT Composite | 23 |
| Minimum TOEFL | 500 |
| Average HS GPA | 3.4 |
| % graduated top 10% of class | 26 |
| % graduated top 25% of class | 52 |
| % graduated top 50% of class | 83 |

### DEADLINES

| | |
|---|---|
| Priority admission | 4/15 |
| Nonfall registration? | yes |

### APPLICANTS ALSO LOOK AT AND OFTEN PREFER
UCLA
U. Colorado—Boulder

### AND SOMETIMES PREFER
U. Southern Cal
BYU
UC—Irvine
U. Arizona

### AND RARELY PREFER
San Diego State
Northern Arizona

### FINANCIAL FACTS

| | |
|---|---|
| Financial Aid Rating | 81 |
| In-state tuition | $2,508 |
| Out-of-state tuition | $11,028 |
| Room and board | $5,866 |
| Books and supplies | $748 |
| Required fees | $77 |
| % frosh receiving aid | 32 |
| % undergrads receiving aid | 37 |
| Avg frosh grant | $4,638 |
| Avg frosh loan | $2,636 |

# AUBURN UNIVERSITY
202 MARY MARTIN HALL, AUBURN, AL 36849-5149 • ADMISSIONS: 334-844-4080 • FAX: 334-844-6179

## CAMPUS LIFE

| Quality of Life Rating | 77 |
|---|---|
| Type of school | public |
| Environment | suburban |

### STUDENTS
| | |
|---|---|
| Total undergrad enrollment | 18,922 |
| % male/female | 52/48 |
| % from out of state | 30 |
| % from public high school | 86 |
| % live on campus | 17 |
| % in (# of) fraternities | 21 (28) |
| % in (# of) sororities | 35 (19) |
| % African American | 7 |
| % Asian | 1 |
| % Caucasian | 90 |
| % Hispanic | 1 |
| % international | 1 |
| # of countries represented | 95 |

### SURVEY SAYS . . .
Everyone loves the Tigers
Frats and sororities dominate social scene
(Almost) everyone plays intramural sports
Great library
Students love Auburn, AL
Students get along with local community
Student publications are popular
Students are very religious
Large classes
Theater is unpopular

## ACADEMICS

| Academic Rating | 71 |
|---|---|
| Calendar | semester |
| Student/faculty ratio | 16:1 |
| Profs interesting rating | 92 |
| Profs accessible rating | 95 |
| % profs teaching UG courses | 98 |
| % classes taught by TAs | 10 |
| Avg lab size | 10-19 students |
| Avg reg class size | 20-29 students |

## STUDENTS SPEAK OUT

### Academics
When asked why she chose Auburn University, a land-grant institution located in the heart of Alabama, a sophomore explains, "The Blue and the Orange flows in my veins!" Strong on "people, atmosphere, education, and spirit," traditional, pragmatic Auburn inspires devotion among its undergrads, who are proud of the school's "great reputation" and "opportunity for advancement." Students must complete a core program of math, science, social science, fine arts, literature, and writing before they head off into one of 11 specialized schools (especially good are agricultural studies and agricultural engineering, veterinary medicine, engineering, architecture, nursing, and pharmacology). Classes are usually deemed "challenging, worthwhile, and fun," and profs are given high marks for teaching style and accessibility. "They are seriously interested in our education and personal lives," notes a junior. The administration, however, while considered "ambitious" in its quest to improve Auburn's program, has received flak in recent years for raising tuition. A senior sums up: "Auburn was great until proration hit. Now everything is expensive! Auburn has the potential to be one of the top schools. But as long as one trustee is running things . . . it won't happen."

### Life
A positive, symbiotic relationship between "town and gown" is one of the best aspects of life at Auburn; notes a junior, "The town of Auburn supports the university—which makes for a good college town setting and a friendly and safe atmosphere." "There's a great campus and community spirit," adds a senior. "You feel safe here." School spirit, too, runs high at Auburn, especially during football season. Regularly producing professional players, the Tigers provide a good rallying point for the students. Student government is also popular—a senior writes that "it's pretty political here." Despite their dissatisfaction with the current board of trustees, Auburn students find time to enjoy themselves on their "beautiful" campus. Greek life is popular, claiming about a quarter of the student body. Students more into "clubbing and bands" can also drive to Montgomery (about an hour away) or Atlanta (90 minutes).

### Student Body
"It's all about learning about yourself," writes a first-year, and the Auburn community seems to be uniquely suited to helping its undergrads achieve that goal. Maybe too suited. "Most people do not want to leave after graduation," writes a senior. While the school attracts a student body drawn mostly by the university's reputation of Southern traditionalism, and despite its mostly southern, white constituency, people are "warm" and "diverse," and "friendly smiles and faces are easily found." In recent years, Auburn's reputation and relatively low public tuition have enticed more out-of-state students, fueling a sense of its own growing potential as a high-caliber public institution.

# AUBURN UNIVERSITY

FINANCIAL AID: 334-844-4367 • E-MAIL: ADMISSIONS@AUBURN.EDU • WEBSITE: WWW.AUBURN.EDU

## ADMISSIONS

*Very important factors considered include:* secondary school record, standardized test scores. *Important factors considered include:* state residency. *Other factors considered include:* alumni/ae relation, geographical residence, minority status, talent/ability, volunteer work. SAT I or ACT required. TOEFL required of all international applicants. High school diploma or GED is required. *High school units required/recommended:* 12 total required; 15 total recommended; 4 English required, 3 math required, 2 science required, 3 science recommended, 1 foreign language recommended, 3 social studies required, 4 social studies recommended.

### The Inside Word

Auburn is another "follow the numbers" admission institution—if you have what they require, you're in with little sweat.

## FINANCIAL AID

*Students should submit:* FAFSA, institution's own financial aid form. No deadline for regular filing. The Princeton Review suggests that all financial aid forms be submitted as soon as possible after January 1. *Need-based scholarships/grants offered:* Pell, SEOG, state scholarships/grants, private scholarships, the school's own gift aid. *Loan aid offered:* FFEL Subsidized Stafford, FFEL Unsubsidized Stafford, FFEL PLUS, Federal Perkins, college/university loans from institutional funds. Federal Work-Study Program available. Institutional employment available. Off-campus job opportunities are excellent.

## FROM THE ADMISSIONS OFFICE

"Auburn University is a comprehensive land-grant university serving Alabama and the nation. The university is especially charged with the responsibility of enhancing the economic, social, and cultural development of the state through its instruction, research, and extension programs. In all of these programs the university is committed to the pursuit of excellence. The university assumes an obligation to provide an environment of learning in which the individual and society are enriched by the discovery, preservation, transmission, and application of knowledge; in which students grow intellectually as they study and do research under the guidance of competent faculty; and in which the faculty develop professionally and contribute fully to the intellectual life of the institution, community, and state. This obligation unites Auburn University's continuing commitment to its land-grant traditions and the institution's role as a dynamic and complex comprehensive university."

## SELECTIVITY

| | |
|---|---|
| Admissions Rating | 79 |
| # of applicants | 13,645 |
| % of applicants accepted | 76 |
| % of acceptees attending | 36 |
| # accepting a place on wait list | 459 |
| % admitted from wait list | 5 |

### FRESHMAN PROFILE

| | |
|---|---|
| Range SAT Verbal | 490-600 |
| Average SAT Verbal | 547 |
| Range SAT Math | 510-610 |
| Average SAT Math | 563 |
| Range ACT Composite | 21-26 |
| Average ACT Composite | 24 |
| Minimum TOEFL | 550 |
| Average HS GPA | 3.3 |
| % graduated top 10% of class | 26 |
| % graduated top 25% of class | 51 |
| % graduated top 50% of class | 80 |

### DEADLINES

| | |
|---|---|
| Early decision | 11/1 |
| Regular admission | 8/1 |
| Nonfall registration? | yes |

### APPLICANTS ALSO LOOK AT
### AND OFTEN PREFER
Florida State
University of Georgia
Mississippi State
U. Tenn—Knoxville
University of Florida
### AND SOMETIMES PREFER
U. Mississippi
Georgia Tech
### AND RARELY PREFER
U. Alabama

## FINANCIAL FACTS

| | |
|---|---|
| Financial Aid Rating | 84 |
| In-state tuition | $3,260 |
| Out-of-state tuition | $9,780 |
| Books and supplies | $900 |
| Required fees | $120 |
| % frosh receiving aid | 24 |
| % undergrads receiving aid | 29 |
| Avg frosh grant | $6,135 |
| Avg frosh loan | $2,931 |

THE BEST 351 COLLEGES ■ 63

# Austin College

900 North Grand Avenue, Suite 6N, Sherman, TX 75090-4440 • Admissions: 903-813-3000 • Fax: 903-813-3198

## CAMPUS LIFE

| | |
|---|---|
| Quality of Life Rating | 88 |
| Type of school | private |
| Affiliation | Presbyterian |
| Environment | suburban |

### STUDENTS

| | |
|---|---|
| Total undergrad enrollment | 1,241 |
| % male/female | 44/56 |
| % from out of state | 10 |
| % from public high school | 89 |
| % live on campus | 69 |
| % in (# of) fraternities | 27 (10) |
| % in (# of) sororities | 30 (7) |
| % African American | 4 |
| % Asian | 9 |
| % Caucasian | 78 |
| % Hispanic | 7 |
| % international | 2 |
| # of countries represented | 28 |

### SURVEY SAYS...
Campus easy to get around
Lots of beer drinking
Students are happy
(Almost) everyone smokes
Campus feels safe
Great library
Hard liquor is popular
Great computer facilities
School is well run
Diverse students interact

## ACADEMICS

| | |
|---|---|
| Academic Rating | 92 |
| Calendar | 4-1-4 |
| Student/faculty ratio | 13:1 |
| % profs teaching UG courses | 100 |
| Avg lab size | 10-19 students |
| Avg reg class size | 20-29 students |

### MOST POPULAR MAJORS
Business administration/management
Psychology
Biology/biological sciences

## STUDENTS SPEAK OUT

### Academics

Austin College, a small liberal arts school an hour north of Dallas, has long been known for its excellent pre-med program. "Most students are pre-med" here, and one in eight proceeds to medical school upon graduation. Biology and chemistry aren't the only star attractions here, however; offering a "high standard of academic integrity in a liberal, laid-back, personal environment," AC excels in all pre-professional areas, leading some boosters to dub it "The 'hidden' Ivy League school of the South." Unlike many Ivies, though, AC offers its students lots of individual attention. Professors "are very helpful and encouraging, and they promote a very casual atmosphere," particularly in the mentoring program, which "helps students get used to the school in their first year, and after that the mentor (an on-campus professor) becomes like a friend that you can talk to about anything, from personal matters to what classes to register for. I have enjoyed every minute of it." Students also praise AC's "holistic" approach to education. "Instead of forcing you to choose a path the first day of school, they make us take many compulsory subjects, which allow us to experience different parts of the spectrum," writes one undergrad. The popular study abroad program can send "AC students to study virtually anywhere in the world. Personally, I went to New Zealand for a semester. It was one of the best things that I have done in my life." Sums up one satisfied student: "This college has all of the perks of a large university within a small, intimate environment."

### Life

AC students agree on two things: While hometown Sherman "does not have much to offer," the school "does a pretty good job of finding things for us to do" on campus. "We have movie nights, bowling nights, and lots of performances, some by Austin College students and some brought in," explains one student. An active Greek scene keeps the parties hopping; notes one undergrad, "There are theme parties usually every weekend, so people focus more on costumes than drinking." Students admit, "If our football team wasn't so lame, maybe the student population would be more enthusiastic about being [Kanga]Roos," but add that "the soccer teams are growing in popularity. Intramural sports are always fun to watch, too." Immediately beyond campus, however, the pickings quickly grow slim. As one student put it, "For fun? Ha. Ha. We go to the local Wal-Mart or the deserted mall." Agrees another, "The only problem with AC is the location. The city of Sherman is small and does not have much to offer, but Dallas is only an hour away." Fortunately, "Dallas kicks ass. It has plenty of things to do: museums, clubs, restaurants, etc."

### Student Body

Austin undergrads pride themselves on their independence; writes one, "Individuality itself prospers in this environment, fostering an atmosphere that is considerably accepting and open." Students here are "a very diverse crop . . . from many different cultures and backgrounds," including economic: "While it is quite an expensive school, there is so much scholarship [money] that many different economic classes can come here," explains one undergrad. These predominantly pre-professional students are serious about work without getting all pointy-headed about it; as one undergrad put it, "Students here don't exactly ponder the meaning of life, but we have engaging discussions because everyone is pretty much on the same academic level. There's no 'super jock' group or 'super intellectual' group." While "the typical student is a conservative Southerner," particularly from Texas, there are also "many gays and lesbians and they all fit into the social atmosphere fine."

# AUSTIN COLLEGE

FINANCIAL AID: 903-813-2900 • E-MAIL: ADMISSION@AUSTINCOLLEGE.EDU • WEBSITE: WWW.AUSTINCOLLEGE.EDU

## ADMISSIONS

*Very important factors considered include:* secondary school record. *Important factors considered include:* character/personal qualities, class rank, essays, extracurricular activities, recommendations, standardized test scores, talent/ability. *Other factors considered include:* alumni/ae relation, geographical residence, interview, minority status, religious affiliation/commitment, state residency, volunteer work, work experience. SAT I or ACT required. TOEFL required of all international applicants. High school diploma or GED is required. *High school units required/recommended:* 4 English required, 3 math required, 4 math recommended, 3 science required, 4 science recommended, 2 science lab required, 3 science lab recommended, 2 foreign language required, 3 foreign language recommended, 2 social studies required, 3 social studies recommended, 1 elective required.

## The Inside Word

Austin continues to be a prize find among lesser-known colleges, but it isn't as much of a secret anymore. Freshman enrollment saw a major surge last year, which could translate into a somewhat tougher admissions committee. The college's emphasis on academic quality and its very sincere approach to recruitment of students has paid off handsomely. Efforts to increase minority representation on campus have been a big success—few small colleges have as impressive a level of diversity. Out-of-state students will continue to be appealing to the admissions committee, as their number is still rather low.

## FINANCIAL AID

*Students should submit:* FAFSA, institution's own financial aid form. The Princeton Review suggests that all financial aid forms be submitted as soon as possible after January 1. *Need-based scholarships/grants offered:* Pell, SEOG, state scholarships/grants, private scholarships, the school's own gift aid. *Loan aid offered:* FFEL Subsidized Stafford, FFEL Unsubsidized Stafford, FFEL PLUS, Federal Perkins, state loans, college/university loans from institutional funds, alternative loans, Premier Signature loans. Federal Work-Study Program available. Institutional employment available. Applicants will be notified of awards on a rolling basis beginning on or about March 1. Off-campus job opportunities are good.

## FROM THE ADMISSIONS OFFICE

"Students visiting Austin College immediately sense something different about the campus community. People look you in the eye. They call you by name. They want to see you succeed.

"That success comes from a strong academic foundation in the liberal arts and sciences, plus added opportunities like international study, January term, and close involvement with committed faculty who become your partners in learning.

"The comments on these pages from students make it clear that there is no 'typical' student at Austin College. Students can retain their individuality and still fit in. Our students value and respect differences of background, style, and belief. Campus organizations offer activities for all interests.

"Austin College prepares you to do more than make a living. It prepares you to make a difference in the place you work, in the community you call home, in the friends you make, and in the way you live. Service to others is an important part of campus life.

"Visit and discover Austin College for yourself!"

### SELECTIVITY

★ ★ ★ ☆

| | |
|---|---|
| Admissions Rating | 84 |
| # of applicants | 1,140 |
| % of applicants accepted | 78 |
| % of acceptees attending | 39 |
| # accepting a place on wait list | 16 |
| % admitted from wait list | 69 |
| # of early decision applicants | 25 |
| % accepted early decision | 92 |

### FRESHMAN PROFILE

| | |
|---|---|
| Range SAT Verbal | 560-660 |
| Average SAT Verbal | 614 |
| Range SAT Math | 570-660 |
| Average SAT Math | 613 |
| Range ACT Composite | 22-28 |
| Average ACT Composite | 25 |
| Minimum TOEFL | 550 |
| Average HS GPA | 3.4 |
| % graduated top 10% of class | 42 |
| % graduated top 25% of class | 75 |
| % graduated top 50% of class | 96 |

### DEADLINES

| | |
|---|---|
| Early decision | 12/1 |
| Early decision notification | 1/10 |
| Priority admission | 1/15 |
| Regular admission | 3/1 |
| Nonfall registration? | yes |

### APPLICANTS ALSO LOOK AT AND OFTEN PREFER
Trinity
Southwestern
**AND SOMETIMES PREFER**
UT Austin
Rice, Baylor
Texas A&M
Southern Methodist, TCU
**AND RARELY PREFER**
U of Dallas
Hendrix College

### FINANCIAL FACTS

| | |
|---|---|
| Financial Aid Rating | 90 |
| Tuition | $17,740 |
| Room and board | $6,822 |
| Books and supplies | $800 |
| Required fees | $160 |
| % frosh receiving aid | 60 |
| % undergrads receiving aid | 61 |
| Avg frosh grant | $11,877 |
| Avg frosh loan | $3,717 |

# BABSON COLLEGE

MUSTARD HALL, BABSON PARK, MA 02457-0310 • ADMISSIONS: 800-488-3696 • FAX: 781-239-4006

## CAMPUS LIFE

| | |
|---|---|
| Quality of Life Rating | 89 |
| Type of school | private |
| Environment | suburban |

### STUDENTS

| | |
|---|---|
| Total undergrad enrollment | 1,735 |
| % from out of state | 44 |
| % from public high school | 52 |
| % live on campus | 81 |
| % African American | 3 |
| % Asian | 11 |
| % Caucasian | 57 |
| % Hispanic | 4 |
| % international | 19 |
| # of countries represented | 64 |

### SURVEY SAYS . . .
Diverse students interact
Beautiful campus
Great computer facilities
Students are religious
Campus easy to get around
Campus feels safe
Lousy off-campus food
Theater is hot
Great library

## ACADEMICS

| | |
|---|---|
| Academic Rating | 87 |
| Calendar | semester |
| Student/faculty ratio | 13:1 |
| Profs interesting rating | 73 |
| Profs accessible rating | 73 |
| % profs teaching UG courses | 100 |
| Avg lab size | 10-19 students |
| Avg reg class size | 30-39 students |

### MOST POPULAR MAJOR
Business administration/management

## STUDENTS SPEAK OUT

### Academics

Entrepreneurship is the name of the game at Babson College. The college has strengths in other areas, surely, but most students arrive here hoping to learn the secret of establishing America's next Jiffy Lube or Continental Polymers (both of whose founders teach here). Babson stresses "hands-on experience" with a curriculum that "really plunges you into the real world, rather than teaching you theories. During first year you actually start a business and then learn how to manage it." (A few naysayers dismiss the freshman project as "small time. . . . The businesses tends to be more of peddle-shops than anything.") Starting a business is only part of a rigorous freshman year that students uniformly refer to as "business boot camp." Warns one undergrad, "Free time is very hard to come by at Babson. You'll always have a business plan to write, a group meeting to go to, or reading to do for a class." Professors are admired for their experience and expertise ("They are typically seasoned businessmen and businesswomen who have a genuine desire to teach students how to be successful in the real world"). While some here complain that "at times Babson can focus too much on 'street smarts' at the expense of 'book smarts'" and others assert that "Babson needs to improve the quality and quantity of the liberal arts curriculum," most here believe the school's assets far outweigh its drawbacks. As one student put it, "From great speakers, like the head of the NYSE, to programs like the Rocket Pitch Event, Business Plan Competition, and entrepreneurship conferences . . . Babson students get what they pay for."

### Life

Even though the Babson campus offers "tons of sports events, plays, concerts," and numerous active organizations (including Babson Dance Ensemble, the Babson Players, Student Government, and the Campus Activities Board), most students here agree that "There's lots of stuff offered on campus, but with such a diverse [international] population, it's hard to please everyone. Babson students are so spoiled in so many ways; we get very whiny and complain about things a lot, even though we have it so amazingly good." Some blame the situation on the school's small size; others finger the "super anal" campus police; still others say it's the grueling academic schedule ("Being both happy and successful at Babson requires 36 hours a day"). Fortunately, the school is "not quite in Boston, but close enough to all the action," at least for the majority of students who have cars ("the campus is isolated, so if you don't have a car, you are stuck here," warns one student). "Boston is the choice destination for partying," students tell us, warning that "clubs can set you back $100 in one night with cover charges, drinks, and shared cab fare." Students praise Babson's "small, beautiful campus" and the "extremely safe, lovely neighborhood" surrounding it.

### Student Body

The typical Babson undergrad is either "a white suburbanite from an East Coast private school" or "an international who smokes, is always on his/her cell phone, and wears designer threads." Students are "very conservative" and "extremely competitive," leading some to complain that "there are too many unfriendly people here. No one says hello when you walk by them and if you initiate a greeting, it is seldom returned." Reports one undergrad, "Many students are individualistic in nature. They could happily survive on a desert island with a computer, a cell phone, and caffeine." Given the school's focus on entrepreneurship, it is unsurprising that many here are also very materialistic. "If you want to be criticized for not ordering every new gadget in *Maxim* magazine, or for not having more than one car on campus, this is the place for you," is how one sardonic student here puts it.

# BABSON COLLEGE

FINANCIAL AID: 781-239-4219 • E-MAIL: UGRADADMISSION@BABSON.EDU • WEBSITE: WWW.BABSON.EDU

## ADMISSIONS

*Very important factors considered include:* essays, secondary school record, standardized test scores. *Important factors considered include:* class rank, recommendations. *Other factors considered include:* alumni/ae relation, character/personal qualities, extracurricular activities, geographical residence, interview, minority status, state residency, talent/ability, volunteer work, work experience. SAT I or ACT required; SAT II recommended. TOEFL required of all international applicants. High school diploma or GED is required. *High school units required/recommended:* 4 English required, 3 math required, 4 math recommended, 2 science required, 3 science recommended, 4 foreign language recommended, 2 social studies required, 3 social studies recommended.

## The Inside Word

Minority representation, including that of women, remains low, which makes for a very advantageous situation for such candidates. In this age of corporate "downsizing" it has become much more commonplace for students to pursue college programs that lead directly to career paths, and Babson has benefited handsomely from this trend. When this trend and the college's fine reputation are combined, the result is a relatively challenging admissions process despite a relatively modest freshman academic profile. On top of this, the college is also recruiting further afield than in the past. Be wary of overconfidence when applying.

## FINANCIAL AID

*Students should submit:* FAFSA, CSS/Financial Aid PROFILE, noncustodial (divorced/separated) parent's statement, business/farm supplement, federal tax returns, W-2s, verification worksheet. Regular filing deadline is February 15. The Princeton Review suggests that all financial aid forms be submitted as soon as possible after January 1. *Need-based scholarships/grants offered:* Pell, SEOG, state scholarships/grants, the school's own gift aid. *Loan aid offered:* FFEL Subsidized Stafford, FFEL Unsubsidized Stafford, FFEL PLUS, Federal Perkins, state loans. Federal Work-Study Program available. Institutional employment available. Applicants will be notified of awards on or about April 1. Off-campus job opportunities are good.

## FROM THE ADMISSIONS OFFICE

"In addition to theoretical knowledge, Babson College is dedicated to providing its students with hands-on business experience. The Foundation Management Experience (FME) and Management Consulting Field Experience (MCFE) are two prime examples of this commitment. During the FME, all freshmen are placed into groups of 30 and actually create their own businesses that they operate until the end of the academic year. The profits of each FME business are then donated to the charity of each group's choice.

"MCFE offers upperclassmen the unique and exciting opportunity to work as actual consultants for private companies and/or nonprofit organizations in small groups of three to five. Students receive academic credit for their work as well as invaluable experience in the field of consulting. FME and MCFE are just two of the ways Babson strives to produce business leaders with both theoretical knowledge and practical experience."

### SELECTIVITY

| | |
|---|---|
| Admissions Rating | 90 |
| # of applicants | 2,402 |
| % of applicants accepted | 48 |
| % of acceptees attending | 35 |
| # accepting a place on wait list | 268 |
| % admitted from wait list | 7 |
| # of early decision applicants | 122 |
| % accepted early decision | 58 |

### FRESHMAN PROFILE

| | |
|---|---|
| Range SAT Verbal | 550-630 |
| Average SAT Verbal | 600 |
| Range SAT Math | 600-690 |
| Average SAT Math | 640 |
| Minimum TOEFL | 550 |
| % graduated top 10% of class | 44 |
| % graduated top 25% of class | 81 |
| % graduated top 50% of class | 100 |

### DEADLINES

| | |
|---|---|
| Early decision | 12/1 |
| Early decision notification | 1/1 |
| Priority admission | 12/1 |
| Regular admission | 2/1 |
| Regular notification | 4/1 |

### FINANCIAL FACTS

| | |
|---|---|
| Financial Aid Rating | 80 |
| Tuition | $24,544 |
| Room and board | $9,226 |
| Books and supplies | $658 |
| % frosh receiving aid | 44 |
| % undergrads receiving aid | 42 |
| Avg frosh grant | $14,247 |
| Avg frosh loan | $2,887 |

THE BEST 351 COLLEGES ■ 67

# BARD COLLEGE

OFFICE OF ADMISSIONS, ANNANDALE-ON-HUDSON, NY 12504 • ADMISSIONS: 845-758-7472 • FAX: 845-758-5208

## CAMPUS LIFE

★ ★ ★ ☆

| | |
|---|---|
| Quality of Life Rating | 84 |
| Type of school | private |
| Environment | rural |

### STUDENTS

| | |
|---|---|
| Total undergrad enrollment | 1,454 |
| % male/female | 45/55 |
| % from out of state | 76 |
| % from public high school | 67 |
| % live on campus | 85 |
| % African American | 3 |
| % Asian | 4 |
| % Caucasian | 77 |
| % Hispanic | 5 |
| % international | 6 |
| # of countries represented | 48 |

### SURVEY SAYS . . .
(Almost) everyone smokes
Political activism is hot
Campus is beautiful
Campus feels safe
Lots of beer drinking
Students are happy
No one cheats
Hard liquor is popular

## ACADEMICS

| | |
|---|---|
| Academic Rating | 95 |
| Calendar | 4-1-4 |
| Student/faculty ratio | 9:1 |
| % profs teaching UG courses | 100 |
| Avg reg class size | under 10 students |

### MOST POPULAR MAJORS
Visual and performing arts
English language and literature
Social sciences

## STUDENTS SPEAK OUT

### Academics

Bard College, a Hudson Valley school that puts the "liberal" in "liberal arts," is a bastion of nonconformity and intellectualism. Explains one undergrad, "Bard is like [a] little village in the woods with an eclectic handful of buildings and equally strange and interesting people who are as motivated to delve into some existentialist discussion as they are to get trashed." Professors and academics, students tell us, "are both pretty amazing. All the professors seem willing to bend over backward for the students while being respectable members of academia in general." Undergrads may also love the faculty because "the professors are a reflection of the student body: a combination of above-it-all artists, leftist intellectuals, and downright nerds." Students here love the school's "general looseness, which makes it easy to do things—start a club, get a tutorial, make your own major, whatever." Recounts one student, "I wanted to transfer credits so I walked into the registrar's office and was out in five minutes. I wanted a Hebrew tutorial, I found the professor in his office, and he arranged it. . . . Every time I've needed anything, people have graciously given me their time and their advice, minus formality and bureaucracy." According to students, the only exception to the rule is course registration, "which is a nightmare. Professors sit in their offices, and it's first come, first served. Registration opens at noon. People camp out outside the offices up to six hours ahead of time. It's like a *Star Wars* premiere."

### Life

Because Bard is located "an hour from the nearest town that has more than 100 residents," the school "tries to be its own entertainment." The campus scene is enjoyable, if subdued, according to most; explains one undergrad, "For fun we have intellectual conversations, go to the movies, go to campus events, go to see bands, hang out in the library, drive around, go to thrift stores or to Wal-Mart, hang out in the campus center . . . and surf the Internet." There are "always movies at the theatre on weekends, and there are often theatrical productions, art openings, concerts, and lectures" as well. Even so, "It's the party/music scene that runs the place." There "are a lot of herbal activities" here, as "the policies on drugs and alcohol are lenient. For the most part, it should be noted, people respect themselves and one another and do not overuse." Several times a year the school unites for one big party; most popular of these is Drag Race, "where you cannot tell who really is female and who really is male, that is, as long as they have decided to wear clothes for the evening." Many traditional college diversions are absent here; as one student puts it, "These are things people are not into: football, television, dating, and fast food. Things people are into: dance parties, leftist politics, New York City, organic vegetables, and doing their own thang."

### Student Body

When conservatives complain about PC campuses and ultraliberal students, they might well be specifically describing Bard. It's the kind of place where students tell you that "we are more concerned with the terrorism for which our government is responsible than the terrorism that targets the United States," and mean it. Most Bard undergrads "didn't really fit in during high school" but feel right at home here among the "leftist white woman who goes to Green Party rallies weekly" and the "friendly white guys with dreadlocks . . . whose joys include learning, music, and getting stoned with close friends." Bard students describe themselves as cerebral, telling us that "a certain level of intellectualism prevails here, and you really feel that the people you are talking to know what they are talking about, and have done research on these topics. Debates get heated, but that's essential to really get to the depth of an issue anyway." Undergrads appreciate the fact that "There is a really high percentage of international students, which gives the Americans a different perspective of the world."

68 ■ THE BEST 351 COLLEGES

# BARD COLLEGE

FINANCIAL AID: 845-758-7526 • E-MAIL: ADMISSION@BARD.EDU • WEBSITE: WWW.BARD.EDU

## ADMISSIONS

*Very important factors considered include:* character/personal qualities, essays, extracurricular activities, recommendations, secondary school record, talent/ability, volunteer work. *Important factors considered include:* work experience. *Other factors considered include:* alumni/ae relation, class rank, geographical residence, interview, minority status, religious affiliation/commitment, standardized test scores, state residency. TOEFL required of all international applicants. High school diploma or GED is required. *High school units required/recommended:* 4 English recommended, 4 math recommended, 4 science recommended, 4 foreign language recommended, 4 social studies recommended, 4 history recommended.

### The Inside Word

Applicants tend to be cerebral sorts. Bard is highly selective, but it's the match that counts more than having the right numerical profile.

## FINANCIAL AID

*Students should submit:* FAFSA, CSS/Financial Aid PROFILE, state aid form, noncustodial (divorced/separated) parent's statement, business/farm supplement. Regular filing deadline is February 15. The Princeton Review suggests that all financial aid forms be submitted as soon as possible after January 1. *Need-based scholarships/grants offered:* Pell, SEOG, state scholarships/grants, private scholarships, the school's own gift aid. *Loan aid offered:* FFEL Subsidized Stafford, FFEL Unsubsidized Stafford, FFEL PLUS, Federal Perkins, college/university loans from institutional funds (for international students only). Federal Work-Study Program available. Institutional employment available. Applicants will be notified of awards on or about April 1. Off-campus job opportunities are fair.

## FROM THE ADMISSIONS OFFICE

"An alliance with Rockefeller University, the renowned graduate scientific research institution, gives Bardians access to Rockefeller's professors and laboratories, and to places in Rockefeller's Summer Research Fellows Program. Almost all our math and science graduates pursue graduate or professional studies; 90 percent of our applicants to medical and health professional schools are accepted.

"The Globalization and International Affairs (BGIA) Program is a residential program in the heart of New York City that offers undergraduates a unique opportunity to undertake specialized study with leading practitioners and scholars in international affairs and to gain internship experience with international-affairs organizations. Topics in the curriculum include human rights, international economics, global environmental issues, international justice, managing international risk, and writing on international affairs, among others. Internships/tutorials are tailored to students' particular fields of study.

"Student dormitory and classroom facilities are in Bard Hall, 410 West 58th Street, a newly renovated 11-story building near the Lincoln Center District in New York City."

## SELECTIVITY

| | |
|---|---:|
| Admissions Rating | 95 |
| # of applicants | 3,118 |
| % of applicants accepted | 36 |
| % of acceptees attending | 31 |
| # accepting a place on wait list | 216 |
| % admitted from wait list | 17 |

### FRESHMAN PROFILE

| | |
|---|---:|
| Range SAT Verbal | 650-750 |
| Average SAT Verbal | 670 |
| Range SAT Math | 590-690 |
| Average SAT Math | 630 |
| Minimum TOEFL | 600 |
| Average HS GPA | 3.5 |
| % graduated top 10% of class | 64 |
| % graduated top 25% of class | 90 |
| % graduated top 50% of class | 99 |

### DEADLINES

| | |
|---|---:|
| Regular admission | 1/15 |
| Regular notification | 4/1 |
| Nonfall registration? | yes |

### APPLICANTS ALSO LOOK AT AND OFTEN PREFER

Amherst
Yale
Harvard
Brown

### AND SOMETIMES PREFER

Reed
Boston U.
Vassar
Oberlin, NYU

### AND RARELY PREFER

Hampshire
Skidmore
Macalester
Ithaca
Sarah Lawrence

## FINANCIAL FACTS

| | |
|---|---:|
| Financial Aid Rating | 87 |
| Tuition | $26,900 |
| Room and board | $8,134 |
| Books and supplies | $700 |
| Required fees | $550 |
| % frosh receiving aid | 60 |
| % undergrads receiving aid | 61 |
| Avg frosh grant | $18,282 |
| Avg frosh loan | $3,351 |

# BARNARD COLLEGE

3009 BROADWAY, NEW YORK, NY 10027 • ADMISSIONS: 212-854-2014 • FAX: 212-854-6220

## CAMPUS LIFE

| | |
|---|---|
| Quality of Life Rating | 91 |
| Type of school | private |
| Environment | urban |

### STUDENTS

| | |
|---|---|
| Total undergrad enrollment | 2,297 |
| % from out of state | 65 |
| % from public high school | 58 |
| % live on campus | 88 |
| % African American | 5 |
| % Asian | 20 |
| % Caucasian | 65 |
| % Hispanic | 6 |
| % international | 3 |
| # of countries represented | 35 |

### SURVEY SAYS . . .
Students love New York, NY
Political activism is hot
Great off-campus food
(Almost) everyone smokes
Campus feels safe
Ethnic diversity on campus
Intercollegiate sports unpopular or nonexistent
Very little beer drinking
No one plays intramural sports

## ACADEMICS

| | |
|---|---|
| Academic Rating | 91 |
| Calendar | semester |
| Student/faculty ratio | 10:1 |
| Profs interesting rating | 94 |
| Profs accessible rating | 93 |
| % profs teaching UG courses | 100 |
| Avg lab size | under 10 students |
| Avg reg class size | 10-19 students |

### MOST POPULAR MAJORS
English language and literature
Psychology
Economics

## STUDENTS SPEAK OUT

### Academics

For those looking to be surrounded by "strong-willed, responsible, smart, and independent women" in a school boasting "all the advantages of an Ivy League school, as well as those of a small liberal arts school," look no further. Barnard women agree that their "classes are amazing" and that "the professors are young and excited to be teaching." Also, one student reflects the overwhelming feeling of the masses in saying that "administrators live to help their students." One of Barnard's big draws is its affiliation with across-the-street Columbia University. "Because of cross-registration with Columbia, the course offerings are endless." And the love flows both ways. One student confides, "Tons of Columbia students come over to Barnard for courses because our professors tend to be better teachers." The college "is very accommodating and open in terms of letting you study what you want." Students get their own "personal major advisor" whom " you don't have to utilize," but who "will ensure you don't get lost." Complaints? "The study abroad program is lacking . . . and [the sciences are] run more like a high school field program than a college science program." Most students agree, however, that "Barnard is one school that loves each student, viewing her as a powerhouse of potential and yearning to help her understand and realize that potential."

### Life

"If you can't find something to do in New York City, I really can't help you." That pretty much sums up life at Barnard. Located in the Morningside Heights neighborhood—little more upper than the Upper West Side—Barnard is "separated from the main distractions, but it's close enough to downtown that you can always find things to do." One student raves, "We live on the most exciting island in the world! You can do anything you can possibly imagine here." And while most will agree that "Barnard is all about life in New York City," many are disappointed with their actual campus life. Actually, according to some, "There is no real campus life . . . people come to Barnard because of New York City. As a result, sports . . . clubs in general, suffer from a lack of participation." Parties abound here, but to those intent on Barnard, "Don't come to NYC expecting kegs. Expect vodka." Despite the never-ending off-campus distractions, in-the-know students point out that "there are plenty of student organizations to choose from" (more than 125, actually), which "collectively provide plenty of things to do on campus almost every day and night of the week." Barnard dorms receive low marks. Warns one student, "A lot of the dorms haven't been maintained—rooms are small, there aren't common rooms, stoves/fridges don't work, there's mold everywhere, etc." Getting away from the mold doesn't seem to be too hard, though. Think "New York City: clubs, bars, theatre, opera, music, dance, parks, museums, shops, cruises, tours . . . . You get the idea, right?"

### Student Body

Comprising 2,297 individuals, Barnard's students describe themselves as "very diverse—except that we're all women!" These women refer to each other as "dynamic" and "the greatest I have ever known . . . well rounded, cultured, spunky, sophisticated, and fun loving." Here you'll find "liberal feminists, jocks, party girls, gay students, book worms, Orthodox Jews . . . the list goes on and on." One student notes, however, that "although we are friendly toward each other, most groups tend to stay close-knit and don't really diversify." Barnard students are driven; they are "sharks that carry a smile. They are confident, savvy, sophisticated. They embody the city in which they live, constantly evolving and transforming." Prospective students should expect "a very visible gay population," an "active Jewish religious presence," and "a strong feminist sector."

# BARNARD COLLEGE

FINANCIAL AID: 212-854-2154 • E-MAIL: ADMISSIONS@BARNARD.EDU • WEBSITE: WWW.BARNARD.EDU

## ADMISSIONS

*Very important factors considered include:* essays, recommendations, secondary school record, standardized test scores. *Important factors considered include:* character/personal qualities, class rank, extracurricular activities, talent/ability, volunteer work. *Other factors considered include:* alumni/ae relation, geographical residence, interview, minority status, state residency, work experience. TOEFL required of all international applicants. *High school units required/recommended:* 17 total recommended; 4 English recommended, 3 math recommended, 3 science recommended, 2 science lab recommended, 3 foreign language recommended, 2 social studies recommended, 2 history recommended.

### The Inside Word

As at many top colleges, early decision applications have increased at Barnard—despite the fact that admissions standards are virtually the same as for their regular admissions cycle. The college's admissions staff is open and accessible, which is not always the case at highly selective colleges with as long and impressive a tradition of excellence. The admissions committee's expectations are high, but their attitude reflects a true interest in who you are and what's on your mind. Students have a much better experience throughout the admissions process when treated with sincerity and respect—perhaps this is why Barnard continues to attract and enroll some of the best students in the country.

## FINANCIAL AID

*Students should submit:* FAFSA, institution's own financial aid form, CSS/Financial Aid PROFILE, state aid form, noncustodial (divorced/separated) parent's statement, business/farm supplement, parent's individual and corporate and/or partnership federal income tax returns. Regular filing deadline is February 1. The Princeton Review suggests that all financial aid forms be submitted as soon as possible after January 1. *Need-based scholarships/grants offered:* Pell, SEOG, state scholarships/grants, private scholarships, the school's own gift aid, New York Higher Educational Opportunity Program. *Loan aid offered:* FFEL Subsidized Stafford, FFEL Unsubsidized Stafford, FFEL PLUS, Federal Perkins, state loans, college/university loans from institutional funds. Federal Work-Study Program available. Institutional employment available. Applicants will be notified of awards on or about April 1. Off-campus job opportunities are excellent.

## FROM THE ADMISSIONS OFFICE

"Barnard College, a small, distinguished liberal arts college for women that is affiliated with Columbia University, and located in the heart of New York City. The College enrolls women from all over the United States, Puerto Rico, and the Caribbean. More than thirty countries, including France, England, Hong Kong, and Greece, are also represented in the student body. Students pursue their academic studies in over 40 majors, and are able to cross-register at Columbia University."

### SELECTIVITY

| | |
|---|---|
| Admissions Rating | 97 |
| # of applicants | 3,686 |
| % of applicants accepted | 34 |
| % of acceptees attending | 43 |
| # accepting a place on wait list | 484 |
| % admitted from wait list | 1 |
| # of early decision applicants | 317 |
| % accepted early decision | 45 |

### FRESHMAN PROFILE

| | |
|---|---|
| Range SAT Verbal | 630-710 |
| Average SAT Verbal | 660 |
| Range SAT Math | 620-700 |
| Average SAT Math | 670 |
| Range ACT Composite | 27-30 |
| Average ACT Composite | 29 |
| Minimum TOEFL | 600 |
| Average HS GPA | 3.9 |
| % graduated top 10% of class | 84 |
| % graduated top 25% of class | 98 |
| % graduated top 50% of class | 100 |

### DEADLINES

| | |
|---|---|
| Early decision | 11/15 |
| Early decision notification | 12/15 |
| Regular admission | 1/1 |
| Regular notification | 4/2 |
| Nonfall registration? | yes |

### APPLICANTS ALSO LOOK AT AND OFTEN PREFER
Brown, Columbia, Yale
Georgetown, Harvard
**AND SOMETIMES PREFER**
Cornell, NYU
Princeton, U of Chicago
Wesleyan
**AND RARELY PREFER**
Vassar, Northwestern, Tufts
George Washington U

### FINANCIAL FACTS

| | |
|---|---|
| Financial Aid Rating | 84 |
| Tuition | $24,090 |
| Room and board | $10,140 |
| Books and supplies | $900 |
| Required fees | $1,180 |
| % frosh receiving aid | 41 |
| % undergrads receiving aid | 41 |
| Avg frosh grant | $21,914 |
| Avg frosh loan | $2,625 |

# BATES COLLEGE

23 Campus Avenue, Lewiston, ME 04240-9917 • Admissions: 207-786-6000 • Fax: 207-786-6025

## CAMPUS LIFE

★ ★ ★ ☆

| | |
|---|---|
| Quality of Life Rating | 83 |
| Type of school | private |
| Environment | suburban |

### STUDENTS

| | |
|---|---|
| Total undergrad enrollment | 1,738 |
| % from out of state | 89 |
| % from public high school | 56 |
| % live on campus | 90 |
| % African American | 2 |
| % Asian | 4 |
| % Caucasian | 89 |
| % Hispanic | 2 |
| % international | 6 |

### SURVEY SAYS . . .
Dorms are like palaces
Everyone loves the Bobcats
Great food on campus
No one cheats
Campus feels safe
Low cost of living
Students don't get along with local community
Students don't like Lewiston, ME
Student publications are ignored

## ACADEMICS

| | |
|---|---|
| Academic Rating | 98 |
| Calendar | other |
| Student/faculty ratio | 10:1 |
| Profs interesting rating | 95 |
| Profs accessible rating | 98 |
| % profs teaching UG courses | 100 |
| Avg lab size | 10-19 students |
| Avg reg class size | 10-19 students |

### MOST POPULAR MAJORS
English language and literature
Psychology
Political science and government

## STUDENTS SPEAK OUT

### Academics

The happy students of Bates College agree that "Bates is the small academic atmosphere every liberal arts school brags about." Students' primary source of pride is the faculty, which is "exceptional. I'm taking introductory classes and my profs are all Ph.D.s from Harvard, Yale, and Tufts. I have thought to myself, 'Why are these brilliant people concerning themselves with dorky 18-year-olds?' [In addition], they relate to students very well. I genuinely feel taught, not just a target for information to be thrown at." Students also approve of the 4-4-1 calendar: two conventional semesters in the fall and spring, as well as a "short term" in May that provides students with opportunities to study less traditional topics, or to study or intern off campus. Writes one undergrad, "Short term in May is really fun. Your short term might be in India, or Ecuador, or sea kayaking in Maine. Short terms are great because you only have one class, and there is [a lot of] free time." The administration goes out of its way to involve students: writes one, "Students are involved in almost every single committee in the school, even search committees for professors and staff. I've been on search committees for tenure-track positions in the English and Chinese departments, which meant going for lectures and taking the candidates out to lunch with a couple of other students. My professors made the final decisions, but my opinion had a great deal of weight [with them]."

### Life

Bates' campus is a veritable beehive of extracurricular activity; explains one student, "There is always a diverse array of lectures, seminars, and performances (musical, theatrical, and otherwise) which I attend for fun. On any given day, there are a dozen activities in which students can participate, from club-sponsored movies and dinners to a capella group performances sponsored by the chaplain's office, to seminars targeting young feminists who want to end domestic violence." It's a good thing, too, because hometown Lewiston offers "nothing to do" other than shop at outlets (Patagonia, J.Crew, and especially L.L. Bean in nearby Freeport are campus faves); notes one student, "You can't really escape campus, so you have to be satisfied with on-campus things, like parties, etc., until it gets nice enough to be able to go hiking and so on." Many Bates undergrads are outdoor enthusiasts, and "a lot of people participate in sports, either intercollegiate or intramural as a way of unwinding at the end of the day." On weekends, "There is no doubt that Bates is a drinking school. Beer cans can be seen scattered around dorms on Sunday mornings, and empty beer boxes can be found in almost every trash can." Students appreciate the fact that major cities are not too far off: "People venture out to Freeport or Portland on the weekends, both of which are within an hour's drive, and the school runs shuttles in case you don't have a car." Boston is approximately 140 miles south.

### Student Body

Bates undergrads "range from being excessively rich, private boarding-school educated preppies to mountain crunchies who rush off to climb things between classes. Honest to God, there is a student here who looks like Paul Bunyan with his flannel and scruffy beard, and he will not put on shoes." Diversity also finds itself in a variety of "weird liberal types," as well as an unusual cross-section of "Trustifarian, want-to-be hippies." Students note that "lots of different people can interact together, although there is a sad lack of minority presence other than a very small number of foreign students." According to some, the absence of a Greek system here contributes to the "incredibly friendly" atmosphere; says one student, "There is no hierarchy. You can be friends with people in various groups." Adds another, "I have yet to meet a cruel person at Bates; I think they hide in the basement or something . . . ." Bates draws half of its students from New England. Only about 10 percent of the students are natives of Maine.

# BATES COLLEGE

FINANCIAL AID: 207-786-6096 • E-MAIL: ADMISSIONS@BATES.EDU • WEBSITE: WWW.BATES.EDU

## ADMISSIONS

*Very important factors considered include:* character/personal qualities, class rank, essays, extracurricular activities, interview, recommendations, secondary school record, talent/ability. *Other factors considered include:* alumni/ae relation, geographical residence, minority status, religious affiliation/commitment, standardized test scores, volunteer work. TOEFL required of all international applicants. High school diploma is required and GED is not accepted. *High school units required/recommended:* 15 total required; 19 total recommended; 4 English required, 3 math required, 4 math recommended, 2 science required, 3 science recommended, 1 science lab required, 2 foreign language required, 4 foreign language recommended.

## The Inside Word

With or without test scores, the admissions office here will weed out weak students showing little or no intellectual curiosity. Students with high SAT scores should always submit them. If you are curious about Bates, it is important to have solid grades in challenging courses; without them, you are not a viable candidate for admission. Tough competition for students between the College and its New England peers has intensified greatly over the past couple of years; Bates is holding its own. It remains a top choice among its applicants, and as a result selectivity is on the rise.

## FINANCIAL AID

*Students should submit:* FAFSA, CSS/Financial Aid PROFILE, noncustodial (divorced/separated) parent's statement, business/farm supplement. The Princeton Review suggests that all financial aid forms be submitted as soon as possible after January 1. *Need-based scholarships/grants offered:* Pell, SEOG, state scholarships/grants, private scholarships, the school's own gift aid. *Loan aid offered:* FFEL Subsidized Stafford, FFEL Unsubsidized Stafford, FFEL PLUS, Federal Perkins, state loans, college/university loans from institutional funds, private alternative loans. Federal Work-Study Program available. Institutional employment available. Applicants will be notified of awards on or about April 2. Off-campus job opportunities are good.

## FROM THE ADMISSIONS OFFICE

"The people on the Bates admissions staff read your applications carefully, several times. We get to know you from that reading. Your high school record and the quality of your writing are particularly important. We strongly encourage a personal interview, either on campus or with an alumni representative."

## SELECTIVITY

| | |
|---|---|
| Admissions Rating | 98 |
| # of applicants | 4,012 |
| % of applicants accepted | 28 |
| % of acceptees attending | 37 |
| # accepting a place on wait list | 300 |
| # of early decision applicants | 430 |
| % accepted early decision | 38 |

### FRESHMAN PROFILE

| | |
|---|---|
| Range SAT Verbal | 630-710 |
| Average SAT Verbal | 671 |
| Range SAT Math | 630-720 |
| Average SAT Math | 677 |
| Minimum TOEFL | 200 (CBT) |
| % graduated top 10% of class | 62 |
| % graduated top 25% of class | 93 |
| % graduated top 50% of class | 100 |

### DEADLINES

| | |
|---|---|
| Early decision | 11/15 |
| Regular admission | 1/15 |
| Regular notification | 4/1 |
| Nonfall registration? | yes |

### APPLICANTS ALSO LOOK AT AND OFTEN PREFER
Bowdoin

### AND SOMETIMES PREFER
Middlebury
Colby
Colgate

## FINANCIAL FACTS

| | |
|---|---|
| Financial Aid Rating | 82 |
| Comprehensive tuition | $37,500 |
| Books and supplies | $1,750 |
| Required fees | $0 |
| % frosh receiving aid | 46 |
| % undergrads receiving aid | 39 |
| Avg frosh grant | $21,160 |
| Avg frosh loan | $2,500 |

# BAYLOR UNIVERSITY

PO Box 97056, Waco, TX 76798-7056 • Admissions: 254-710-3435 • Fax: 254-710-3436

## CAMPUS LIFE

| | |
|---|---|
| Quality of Life Rating | 74 |
| Type of school | private |
| Affiliation | Baptist |
| Environment | suburban |

### STUDENTS

| | |
|---|---|
| Total undergrad enrollment | 11,987 |
| % male/female | 42/58 |
| % from out of state | 16 |
| % live on campus | 30 |
| % in (# of) fraternities | 15 (18) |
| % in (# of) sororities | 17 (15) |
| % African American | 6 |
| % Asian | 5 |
| % Caucasian | 78 |
| % Hispanic | 8 |
| % international | 2 |
| # of countries represented | 90 |

### SURVEY SAYS . . .
Frats and sororities dominate social scene
Very little drug use
(Almost) everyone plays intramural sports
Lots of conservatives on campus
Diversity lacking on campus
Students are very religious
Students don't like Waco, TX
Very little hard liquor
Very little beer drinking
(Almost) no one smokes

## ACADEMICS

| | |
|---|---|
| Academic Rating | 73 |
| Calendar | semester |
| Student/faculty ratio | 17:1 |
| Profs interesting rating | 93 |
| Profs accessible rating | 93 |
| % profs teaching UG courses | 90 |
| % classes taught by TAs | 6 |
| Avg lab size | 10-19 students |
| Avg reg class size | 20-29 students |

### MOST POPULAR MAJORS
Business administration/management
Biology/biological sciences
Psychology

## STUDENTS SPEAK OUT

### Academics
The biggest Baptist university in the world, Baylor strives to blend religion and scholarship. While some students praise the school for its "strong Christian education that does not impose close-mindedness on its students," others complain that the "Christian and conservative manner does not allow for certain points of view to be remotely discussed." A biology student is pleased that his professors "talk about evolution openly," even though disapproval is directed toward an Old Testament professor who subscribes to the Big Bang theory. Overall, faculty members "are not only concerned about my learning the material but [also] about my opinions and well-being." The Baylor Interdisciplinary Core gets rave reviews: "I love this curriculum as it has a more worldly emphasis and teaches you how to cope with other cultures." The administration has reportedly mastered "covering up scandal," though it is "friendly and open to questions and comments" and monitors student concerns with "discussion forums and surveys." The deep coffers keep financial aid flowing and allows, according to one skeptical student, "millions of dollars to be spent on things I really don't think we need."

### Life
As expected in a devout environment, "There are actually some parties without alcohol, and there will be hundreds of people there dancing and hanging out." "Christian sing-a-longs" and plenty of "Kool-Aid" are other key ingredients to the Baylor nightlife. At the same time, Greek affiliation means almost everything: "There are tables in the cafeteria where only certain people can sit depending on what Greek letters they are wearing." It is also reported that the "t-shirts that signify you were invited" to a Greek event are seen as "status symbols." Chivalry persists at Baylor—"Guys open doors for girls, and people still go out on real dates"—reminding some students of the "Leave It to Beaver days." Other throwbacks include restricted dorm visiting hours and the possible expulsion of women who get pregnant and their boy-toy partners. Bible study groups are popular, even if many students "go to church hungover on Sunday." Many undergraduates observe "growing dissension between the city of Waco and Baylor students," mainly rooted in the stark economic contrast between the two communities.

### Student Body
The stereotype of Baylor students is clear: "pretentious little children who carry the Bible in one hand and Daddy's credit card in the other." But the cliché doesn't necessarily play out in reality. "The typical Baylor student is an upper-class white Christian from Texas. I am none of these things, but I have still been able to find a niche at Baylor." Women reputedly arrive at Baylor husband hunting, which can be a challenge considering the 3 to 2 female to male ratio. A telling statistic lies in the fact that "there are [currently] no black students in any of the nine major sororities." One black student writes, however, "For once I can just be black in the presence of other blacks, whites, Hispanics, Asians, or a mixture thereof." Another student qualifies the racial situation very even-handedly: "Baylor could be considered segregated, but the segregation is not due to hatred or dislike of other groups but rather a preference of involvement in different activities." The W.W.J.D.-bracelet-wearing population can be "openly hostile about other religions, homosexuality, and even about left-wing politics," but they also undeniably "have manners."

# BAYLOR UNIVERSITY

FINANCIAL AID: 254-710-2611 • E-MAIL: ADMISSIONS_SERV_OFFICE@BAYLOR.EDU • WEBSITE: WWW.BAYLOR.EDU

## ADMISSIONS
*Very important factors considered include:* class rank, secondary school record, standardized test scores. *Other factors considered include:* alumni/ae relation, character/personal qualities, essays, extracurricular activities, geographical residence, interview, recommendations, religious affiliation/commitment, state residency, talent/ability, volunteer work. SAT I or ACT required. TOEFL required of all international applicants. High school diploma or GED is required. *High school units required/recommended:* 4 English required, 3 math required, 2 science required, 2 foreign language required, 1 social studies required, 1 history required.

## The Inside Word
A largely self-selected applicant pool and the need for a fairly large freshman class each year makes for a high admit rate. If your values reflect those of the community at Baylor, the chances are you will be offered admission.

## FINANCIAL AID
*Students should submit:* FAFSA. No deadline for regular filing. The Princeton Review suggests that all financial aid forms be submitted as soon as possible after January 1. *Need-based scholarships/grants offered:* Pell, SEOG, state scholarships/grants, the school's own gift aid, Federal Nursing. *Loan aid offered:* FFEL Subsidized Stafford, FFEL Unsubsidized Stafford, FFEL PLUS, Federal Perkins, Federal Nursing, state loans, college/university loans from institutional funds. Federal Work-Study Program available. Institutional employment available. Applicants will be notified of awards on a rolling basis beginning on or about March 1. Off-campus job opportunities are excellent.

## FROM THE ADMISSIONS OFFICE
"Baylor University, chartered by the Republic of Texas in 1845, is one of the world's major academic church-related institutions providing liberal arts and professional education in a Christian environment. Baylor's student body comes from all 50 states and 79 foreign countries. The university's number of National Merit Scholars places it in the top 1 percent of all colleges nationwide. . . . In addition, the Templeton Foundation has repeatedly named Baylor as one of America's top character-building colleges. Professors teach 93 percent of all courses; the student/faculty ratio is 18 to 1, and the typical class numbers 35. There are 162 bachelor's programs and 72 master's programs as well as numerous doctoral, professional, and specialist programs. More than 225 student organizations provide opportunities for social, intellectual, physical, spiritual, and professional development. One of the most inexpensive major private universities in the country, Baylor is consistently ranked by national organizations as one of the best buys in higher education. Take a closer look. . . . There is a place for you at Baylor."

### SELECTIVITY

| | |
|---|---|
| Admissions Rating | 81 |
| # of applicants | 7,431 |
| % of applicants accepted | 81 |
| % of acceptees attending | 43 |

#### FRESHMAN PROFILE
| | |
|---|---|
| Range SAT Verbal | 530-630 |
| Range SAT Math | 550-650 |
| Range ACT Composite | 22-27 |
| Minimum TOEFL | 540 |
| % graduated top 10% of class | 40 |
| % graduated top 25% of class | 68 |
| % graduated top 50% of class | 92 |

#### DEADLINES
| | |
|---|---|
| Priority admission | 3/1 |
| Nonfall registration? | yes |

#### APPLICANTS ALSO LOOK AT AND OFTEN PREFER
Texas A&M
U. Texas—Austin

#### AND SOMETIMES PREFER
U. Oklahoma
SMU
TCU

#### AND RARELY PREFER
Austin
Southwestern
Trinity U.

### FINANCIAL FACTS

| | |
|---|---|
| Financial Aid Rating | 78 |
| Tuition | $16,750 |
| Room and board | $5,434 |
| Books and supplies | $1,460 |
| Required fees | $1,680 |
| % frosh receiving aid | 49 |
| % undergrads receiving aid | 44 |

# BELLARMINE UNIVERSITY

2001 NEWBURG ROAD, LOUISVILLE, KY 40205 • ADMISSIONS: 502-452-8131 • FAX: 502-452-8002

## CAMPUS LIFE

| | |
|---|---|
| Quality of Life Rating | 80 |
| Type of school | private |
| Affiliation | Roman Catholic |
| Environment | suburban |

### STUDENTS

| | |
|---|---|
| Total undergrad enrollment | 2,905 |
| % male/female | 36/64 |
| % from out of state | 31 |
| % from public high school | 50 |
| % live on campus | 35 |
| % in (# of) fraternities | 3 (2) |
| % in (# of) sororities | 3 (1) |
| % African American | 4 |
| % Asian | 1 |
| % Caucasian | 86 |
| % Hispanic | 1 |
| % international | 1 |
| # of countries represented | 21 |

### SURVEY SAYS . . .
(Almost) everyone smokes
Great off-campus food
Lots of beer drinking
Students are cliquish
No one watches intercollegiate sports
Theater is unpopular
Very small frat/sorority scene
Lousy food on campus
(Almost) no one listens to college radio

## ACADEMICS

| | |
|---|---|
| Academic Rating | 77 |
| Calendar | semester |
| Student/faculty ratio | 12:1 |
| % profs teaching UG courses | 100 |
| Avg reg class size | 10-19 students |

## STUDENTS SPEAK OUT

### Academics
Bellarmine University, "a small, liberal arts college, designed to cater to the needs of its students," serves its predominantly Catholic, pre-professional student body with "small classes, a friendly staff, and students who all contribute to the university's unique atmosphere." Students brag about "excellent programs in accounting, education, and nursing," delivered through classes "small enough that you get to personally know your professors and fellow classmates." Although "academically, Bellarmine is challenging," most here are confident that "with the tutoring services and the willingness to help that our professors have, there is no reason one shouldn't succeed." Professors earn high grades here because they are "enthusiastic about their field, which truly sets a positive learning atmosphere in the classroom," and are also "most willing to help at any time." Students also appreciate the fact that all "classes are taught by professors; TAs are basically just gophers here." They are less complimentary of the administration, griping that it "is completely inaccessible. It is like pulling teeth to get anything done. . . . It seems as if we have to break down a brick wall to even get to the red tape."

### Life
"There is just a laid-back atmosphere" at Bellarmine, where a dry-campus policy, a tame Greek scene, and a large percentage of students who go home each weekend all contribute to the quietude. Most feel that "the school could work harder at trying to keep students here for the weekends" by "adding more social activities at school." Fortunately hometown Louisville makes up for the campus's shortcomings. According to those who live here, "Louisville is a great town. We go to bars to play pool and to clubs to dance and let loose. There are a lot of parks to go to when the weather is nice, and the art scene downtown is alive with new galleries. The city has lots of good restaurants, too. Bardstown Road is the place to go; there are tons of cool shops, bars, and clubs, all within walking distance." And, of course, "There's always [the Kentucky] Derby, the greatest day in Louisville, and the month before Derby there is always a festival going on. And by the way, we always get out of school before Derby (first Saturday in May), so that is definitely a plus!" For those rare college students who relish quiet, "Dorm life is almost the best part of school. We like to watch movies, or just sit around in the lobby or lounge and talk to the people passing by." A few undergrads complain about the school's strict social regulations: "They should allow alcohol on campus, allow 24-hour visitation in the dorms, and basically allow adult students to make grown-up decisions."

### Student Body
Bellarmine draws a predominantly local crowd. "I think that the student body is three-quarters white, upper-middle-class students from [within] an hour-and-a-half radius of Louisville," explains one student. Adds another, "Our typical student went to Assumption, Sacred Heart, St. X, or Trinity. They are people who have gone to Catholic schools all of their lives and have lived in Louisville all of their lives. They come to Bellarmine and attend school with all of their old high school classmates. Most drive either a Volvo or a BMW. They are very rich and they know it." Recent changes in the curriculum have helped the student body shed some of its "cookie-cutter" image; as one told us, "There are many 'atypical' students due to Louisville's growing creative/art movement. They fit into Bellarmine's environment easily but are sometimes looked down upon for not participating in University functions." There are also "tons more girls than guys–about [2:1] ratio the last I heard."

# BELLARMINE UNIVERSITY

FINANCIAL AID: 502-452-8124 • E-MAIL: ADMISSIONS@BELLARMINE.EDU • WEBSITE: WWW.BELLARMINE.EDU

## ADMISSIONS

*Very important factors considered include:* secondary school record, standardized test scores. *Important factors considered include:* class rank, essays, extracurricular activities, recommendations, volunteer work. *Other factors considered include:* alumni/ae relation, character/personal qualities, interview, minority status, talent/ability, work experience. SAT I or ACT required. TOEFL required of all international applicants. High school diploma or GED is required. *High school units required/recommended:* 4 English required, 3 math required, 4 math recommended, 2 science required, 3 science recommended, 2 foreign language recommended, 2 social studies required.

### The Inside Word

Bellarmine's admissions process follows the typical small liberal arts college approach fairly closely—solid grades, test scores, and course selection from high school combined with a broad complement of extracurriculars generally will add up to an admit. The applicant pool is very regional here; students who hail from outside the university's normal markets may benefit from the appeal that their relative scarcity brings to their candidacies.

## FINANCIAL AID

*Students should submit:* FAFSA. No deadline for regular filing. The Princeton Review suggests that all financial aid forms be submitted as soon as possible after January 1. *Need-based scholarships/grants offered:* Pell, SEOG, state scholarships/grants, the school's own gift aid. *Loan aid offered:* FFEL Subsidized Stafford, FFEL Unsubsidized Stafford, FFEL PLUS, Federal Perkins, college/university loans from institutional funds. Federal Work-Study Program available. Institutional employment available. Applicants will be notified of awards on a rolling basis beginning on or about April 1. Off-campus job opportunities are excellent.

## FROM THE ADMISSIONS OFFICE

"Bellarmine University is widely known for providing students outstanding personal attention in the classroom. However, for many out-of-town students, Bellarmine's outstanding location makes the difference. Just five miles from downtown Louisville, Kentucky, Bellarmine is near practically all the cultural and recreational offerings of the nation's 16th largest city, but the campus itself is set in the safe and beautiful Highlands neighborhood.

"The 135-acre campus features picturesque views of Beargrass Creek and the scenic rolling hills of Bellarmine's executive golf course. In all, the campus boasts 25 buildings, with the Norton Health Science Center opening for the fall 2003 fall semester. Bellarmine's campus also offers outstanding recreational facilities such as indoor and outdoor tennis courts, a fitness center, sand volleyball court, and athletic fields. Bellarmine also offers a full array of student activities. More than 50 clubs and organizations are active on campus and many students participate in intercollegiate athletics. Bellarmine fields 18 different teams at the NCAA Division II level, with most teams competing in the Great Lakes Valley Conference, easily one of the top Division II athletic conferences in the country.

"Students living on campus also will find a Bellarmine difference—namely resident students have several options with regard to living arrangements. Petrik Hall offers apartment-style living arrangements while Newman and Kennedy offer the traditional college-residence-hall layout. The new Anniversary Hall, meanwhile, offers residents the option of living in 'suites.' All residence halls offer amenities such as laundry facilities, computer labs, study rooms, and air conditioning."

### SELECTIVITY

| | |
|---|---:|
| Admissions Rating | 75 |
| # of applicants | 1,285 |
| % of applicants accepted | 80 |
| % of acceptees attending | 32 |

### FRESHMAN PROFILE

| | |
|---|---:|
| Range SAT Verbal | 500-600 |
| Average SAT Verbal | 576 |
| Range SAT Math | 490-620 |
| Average SAT Math | 576 |
| Range ACT Composite | 22-26 |
| Average ACT Composite | 24 |
| Minimum TOEFL | 550 |
| Average HS GPA | 3.5 |
| % graduated top 10% of class | 28 |
| % graduated top 25% of class | 55 |
| % graduated top 50% of class | 79 |

### DEADLINES

| | |
|---|---:|
| Priority admission | 2/1 |
| Early action | 11/1 |
| Regular admission | 8/15 |
| Nonfall registration? | yes |

### APPLICANTS ALSO LOOK AT AND OFTEN PREFER
U Dayton
Xavier U (OH)
U Kentucky
**AND RARELY PREFER**
Spalding U

### FINANCIAL FACTS

| | |
|---|---:|
| Financial Aid Rating | 84 |
| Tuition | $16,340 |
| Room and board | $5,300 |
| Books and supplies | $750 |
| Required fees | $670 |
| % frosh receiving aid | 97 |
| Avg frosh grant | $6,200 |
| Avg frosh loan | $2,600 |

# BELOIT COLLEGE

700 COLLEGE STREET, BELOIT, WI 53511 • ADMISSIONS: 608-363-2500 • FAX: 608-363-2075

## CAMPUS LIFE

★ ★ ★ ☆

| | |
|---|---|
| Quality of Life Rating | 84 |
| Type of school | private |
| Environment | urban |

### STUDENTS

| | |
|---|---|
| Total undergrad enrollment | 1,281 |
| % male/female | 38/62 |
| % from out of state | 80 |
| % from public high school | 80 |
| % live on campus | 93 |
| % in (# of) fraternities | 15 (3) |
| % in (# of) sororities | 5 (2) |
| % African American | 4 |
| % Asian | 4 |
| % Caucasian | 86 |
| % Hispanic | 3 |
| % international | 8 |
| # of countries represented | 54 |

### SURVEY SAYS . . .
Campus easy to get around
Lots of beer drinking
Campus feels safe
Campus is beautiful
Dorms are like palaces
Hard liquor is popular
(Almost) everyone smokes
Students are happy

## ACADEMICS

| | |
|---|---|
| Academic Rating | 87 |
| Calendar | semester |
| Student/faculty ratio | 11:1 |
| % profs teaching UG courses | 100 |
| Avg reg class size | 10-19 students |

### MOST POPULAR MAJORS
Creative writing
Psychology
Anthropology

## STUDENTS SPEAK OUT

### Academics

"Beloit seriously is about inventing yourself," writes one student, echoing the unofficial motto of this small southern Wisconsin liberal arts school. "Come to this school if you have initiative and motivation to do creative things of your own design. If you build it . . . they will pay for it to be done. I love it here." Agrees another undergrad, "Beloit College is a bombardment of opportunities, and if you are lucky and smart, you will take the opportunities that are best for you as a person and academically." Students here especially love the school's "multidisciplinary approach, which allows you to view events from the perspectives of different disciplines." They also appreciate the little things, from the academic advising to the uncommon sense of community that students, faculty, and administrators share ("Last weekend, all sophomores and a number of professors and administrators were treated to a weekend away from campus at a resort," reports a typical student.) Students also approvingly declare, "Beloit College runs based on the desires of the student body. Money is allotted to groups by student funding boards so that there isn't any discrepancy between the interests of the students and college bureaucracy about distribution of funds." Profs here, by all accounts, "are amazing. They will all take the time to talk to anybody about anything. They all really care about making the students interested in the material. Seriously."

### Life

Explains one student, "If you're okay with staying on campus all the time, Beloit's your school. If seeing the same places and the same people day after day after day bothers you, you might want to think over your decision to apply here." Given the situation, it's fortunate that "Beloit students are resourceful. Since there's not much to do in a dying town, we learn to entertain ourselves and each other. We love theme parties ('Come As Another Beloit Student,' 'Dress Like Your Celebrity Look-Alike'), and ultimate Frisbee has a cult-like participation and following." "Clubs and student organizations thrive on this campus," and "besides the many student clubs, there are establishments such as the Coughy-Haus (which serves alcohol, allows smoking, and features loud bands) and the Java Joint (quiet music, no smoking, no alcohol, good for studying or playing board games) that one can go to for fun." There's also "sporting events, theater choir and band performances, intramurals, talks, lectures, discussions, Greek-sponsored events, all-campus activities, and movies at cinema for additional entertainment. There's definitely always something going on at Beloit College." Students here appreciate the school alcohol policy, which is "to treat us like adults unless we give them a reason to do differently." Those with cars occasionally escape to "Rockford and Janesville, which are 20 minutes away. Also, Milwaukee, Madison, and Chicago are all within 90 minutes, so there's always chances for breaking out of the bubble."

### Student Body

Undergraduates insist, "There really is no 'typical student' at Beloit. People here are free to be whomever they want to be and definitely exercise that freedom." Most would concede, however, that the majority is a little on the nerdy side: "Beloit College is like high school, only now the misfits are the popular cliques, and they exclude people that seem too normal," notes one student. Many here are "always overly involved. I don't know anyone on campus that isn't involved in more than one club, sport, philanthropy, or Greek organization." The few conservative students warn, "A Beloit student will open his arms and celebrate just about any kind of person so long as that person is a liberal passionate activist who says he is open-minded. Oh yeah, and dreadlocks help." Beloit is also home to "a large, vocal international population [that] provides a worldview not available at most schools."

78 ■ THE BEST 351 COLLEGES

# BELOIT COLLEGE

FINANCIAL AID: 608-363-2500 • E-MAIL: ADMISS@BELOIT.EDU • WEBSITE: WWW.BELOIT.EDU

## ADMISSIONS
*Very important factors considered include:* essays, recommendations, secondary school record. *Important factors considered include:* class rank, interview, standardized test scores. *Other factors considered include:* alumni/ae relation, character/personal qualities, extracurricular activities, talent/ability, volunteer work, work experience. SAT I or ACT required. TOEFL required of all international applicants. High school diploma or GED is required. *High school units required/recommended:* 4 English recommended, 4 math recommended, 3 science recommended, 2 foreign language recommended, 4 social studies recommended, 4 history recommended.

### The Inside Word
Beloit expects to find evidence of sensitivity and thoughtfulness in successful candidates. There is tough competition for students among colleges in the Midwest, which gives those Beloit applicants who don't show consistent strength a bit of a break.

## FINANCIAL AID
*Students should submit:* FAFSA, institution's own financial aid form, state aid form. CSS/Financial Aid PROFILE is accepted. No deadline for regular filing. The Princeton Review suggests that all financial aid forms be submitted as soon as possible after January 1. *Need-based scholarships/grants offered:* Pell, SEOG, state scholarships/grants, private scholarships, the school's own gift aid. *Loan aid offered:* FFEL Subsidized Stafford, FFEL Unsubsidized Stafford, FFEL PLUS, Federal Perkins, college/university loans from institutional funds. Federal Work-Study Program available. Institutional employment available. Applicants will be notified of awards on a rolling basis beginning on or about April 1. Off-campus job opportunities are fair.

## FROM THE ADMISSIONS OFFICE
"While Beloit students clearly understand the connection between college and career, they are more apt to value learning for its own sake than for the competitive advantage that it will afford them in the workplace. As a result, Beloit students adhere strongly to the concept than an educational institution, in order to be true to its own nature, must imply and provide a context in which a free exchange of ideas can take place. This precept is embodied in the mentoring relationship that takes place between professor and student and the dynamic, participatory nature of the classroom experience."

### SELECTIVITY

| | |
|---|---|
| Admissions Rating | 80 |
| # of applicants | 1,677 |
| % of applicants accepted | 70 |
| % of acceptees attending | 26 |
| # accepting a place on wait list | 74 |
| % admitted from wait list | 61 |

### FRESHMAN PROFILE
| | |
|---|---|
| Range SAT Verbal | 590-690 |
| Average SAT Verbal | 640 |
| Range SAT Math | 560-650 |
| Average SAT Math | 610 |
| Range ACT Composite | 25-29 |
| Average ACT Composite | 27 |
| Minimum TOEFL | 525 |
| Average HS GPA | 3.5 |
| % graduated top 10% of class | 30 |
| % graduated top 25% of class | 68 |
| % graduated top 50% of class | 95 |

### DEADLINES
| | |
|---|---|
| Priority admission | 2/1 |
| Regular notification | 3/15 |

### APPLICANTS ALSO LOOK AT
**AND OFTEN PREFER**
Carleton
Colorado College
Kenyon
Northwestern
Oberlin
**AND SOMETIMES PREFER**
Macalester
Lawrence
Grinnell
**AND RARELY PREFER**
Ripon
Gustavus Adolphus
Lewis & Clark
U of Wisconsin
U of Illinois

### FINANCIAL FACTS

| | |
|---|---|
| Financial Aid Rating | 95 |
| Tuition | $23,016 |
| Room and board | $5,268 |
| Books and supplies | $400 |
| Required fees | $220 |
| % frosh receiving aid | 71 |
| % undergrads receiving aid | 70 |
| Avg frosh grant | $12,956 |
| Avg frosh loan | $2,920 |

THE BEST 351 COLLEGES ■ 79

# BENNINGTON COLLEGE

OFFICE OF ADMISSIONS AND FINANCIAL AID, BENNINGTON, VT 05201 • ADMISSIONS: 800-833-6845 • FAX: 802-440-4320

## CAMPUS LIFE

★ ★ ★ ☆

| | |
|---|---|
| Quality of Life Rating | 83 |
| Type of school | private |
| Environment | rural |

### STUDENTS

| | |
|---|---|
| Total undergrad enrollment | 580 |
| % male/female | 33/67 |
| % from out of state | 95 |
| % live on campus | 95 |
| % African American | 1 |
| % Asian | 1 |
| % Caucasian | 82 |
| % Hispanic | 2 |
| % international | 9 |
| # of countries represented | 19 |

### SURVEY SAYS . . .
Lots of classroom discussion
Student publications are popular
Political activism is hot
Students get along with local community
Students love Bennington, VT
Lousy food on campus
Campus difficult to get around
(Almost) no one smokes
Library needs improving

## ACADEMICS

| | |
|---|---|
| Academic Rating | 93 |
| Calendar | other |
| Student/faculty ratio | 9:1 |
| % profs teaching UG courses | 100 |
| % classes taught by TAs | 2 |
| Avg lab size | 10-19 students |
| Avg reg class size | 10-19 students |

### MOST POPULAR MAJORS
Multi/interdisciplinary studies
Visual and performing arts
Social sciences

## STUDENTS SPEAK OUT

### Academics
Bennington College has long been committed to "honoring individuality and the power to create your own education." Students at this unconventional school "don't ever officially declare majors," nor do they take final exams. "We do final projects instead," explained one undergrad. "I got to do a project imitating the style of my favorite poet and a psychological study about student drinking on campus. I feel so involved with my classes!" Instead of grades, students receive written evaluations of their work. Bennington's curriculum "is really dependent on the makeup of the faculty" because "there are not a lot of professors" and also because "the teachers 'teach what keeps them up at night.'" Profs here are "brilliant, amazing people who deeply care about their students"; undergrads also praise the Field Work Term ("a great program of going out for eight weeks to intern or work in your field or a field that you're interested in learning more about"). The visual arts program is one of the school's undisputed strengths. The VAPA (visual and performing arts) building is "open 24/7, and every studio, work space, or lab is open to everyone." Music and language arts instruction also receive praise; the sciences, on the other hand, are considered relatively weak. Many here worry that the student body is growing too rapidly ("We have 200 more students here this year than we had last year") without a proportionate increase in the faculty. "We need more professors," writes a typical student. "If the school is going to continue to accept more students, the college is going to change. Normalization is beginning, and that's sad."

### Life
Bennington's "small and secluded" campus is "absolutely beautiful. Imagine the most beautiful haven you have ever been to; that is Bennington in early May. Imagine Norman Rockwell paintings; that is our winter and fall." Students enjoy the luxury of living in actual houses rather than dormitories. "We have both barn houses built in the 1930s and modern houses that were built last year and were featured in architecture magazines," writes one student. All the same, because of the school's remote location, "most people have a really hard time adjusting to life, myself included. If you stick it out, it gets better. . . . There's a positive side to it: if I were in a larger city I would not be devoting as much time to my academics, which is the reason I came here." Bennington is "very isolated from the town, so there are a lot of on-campus events to keep one interested." Students mention "people screening independent films, stand-up comedy shows, and bands playing" as entertainment options. And "students are very supportive about attending others' performances." Undergrads also "tend to have small parties in their rooms, and every weekend, a house always throws a party." Because "constantly being on campus can get claustrophobic," "people with cars try to leave for the weekend." Many head to the campus of Williams College, about a half-hour drive to the south.

### Student Body
Bennington students range from "vegan, environmentally conscious punks that pretend to be hippies . . . to a significant group of students extremely passionate about their work." The tiny student body "gets oppressive at times, but is very comforting at others. You can say 'I was with Patrick,' and everyone will know who you are talking about." Students tend to subdivide into cliques: "I have a small but very lovable group of friends; that's the tendency here, to form cliques of friends . . . it's just the nature of a small school like this," explains one student. The atmosphere here is politically and socially liberal; "sexuality, religion, social class—none of that matters. I swear, it's like a hippie commune utopia . . . or at least another dimension from *The Matrix*," is how one student describes it.

# BENNINGTON COLLEGE

FINANCIAL AID: 802-440-4325 • E-MAIL: ADMISSIONS@BENNINGTON.EDU • WEBSITE: WWW.BENNINGTON.EDU

## ADMISSIONS

*Very important factors considered include:* character/personal qualities, essays, interview, secondary school record, talent/ability, volunteer work. *Important factors considered include:* alumni/ae relation, extracurricular activities, recommendations. *Other factors considered include:* class rank, standardized test scores, work experience. SAT I or ACT required. TOEFL required of all international applicants. High school diploma or GED is required. *High school units required/recommended:* 16 total recommended; 4 English recommended, 3 math recommended, 3 science recommended, 3 foreign language recommended, 3 social studies recommended.

## The Inside Word

For intellectually curious students Bennington can be a godsend, but for those who lack self-motivation it can represent a sidetracking of progress toward a degree. Admissions standards remain rigorous and enrollment is on an upswing. Candidates will encounter a thorough review process that places great emphasis on matchmaking, which means that strong essays and solid interviews are a must. Intellectual types whose high school grades are inconsistent with their potential will find an opportunity for forgiveness here if they can write well and demonstrate self-awareness and a capacity to thrive in the college's self-driven environment. Minority students are rarities in the applicant pool, and thus enjoy "most-favored candidate" status—provided they fit Bennington's profile.

## FINANCIAL AID

*Students should submit:* FAFSA, institution's own financial aid form, CSS/Financial Aid PROFILE, noncustodial (divorced/separated) parent's statement, parent and student federal tax returns and W-2s. CSS/Financial Aid PROFILE for Early Decision applicants only. The Princeton Review suggests that all financial aid forms be submitted as soon as possible after January 1. *Need-based scholarships/grants offered:* Pell, SEOG, state scholarships/grants, private scholarships, the school's own gift aid. *Loan aid offered:* FFEL Subsidized Stafford, FFEL Unsubsidized Stafford, FFEL PLUS, college/university loans from institutional funds. Federal Work-Study Program available. Institutional employment available. Applicants will be notified of awards on or about April 1. Off-campus job opportunities are fair.

## FROM THE ADMISSIONS OFFICE

"Bennington is designed for students with the motivation and maturity to give shape to their own academic lives. It invites you not merely to study the subject you are learning but to put into practice, to act, to compose, to write, to do science: to make the choices through which you become an educated person. Faculty guide the process, but students make it their own at every stage, leaving Bennington prepared to think and create for themselves."

### SELECTIVITY

| | |
|---|---:|
| Admissions Rating | 84 |
| # of applicants | 701 |
| % of applicants accepted | 70 |
| % of acceptees attending | 35 |
| # of early decision applicants | 49 |
| % accepted early decision | 86 |

### FRESHMAN PROFILE
| | |
|---|---:|
| Range SAT Verbal | 580-690 |
| Average SAT Verbal | 630 |
| Range SAT Math | 500-630 |
| Average SAT Math | 568 |
| Minimum TOEFL | 550 |
| Average HS GPA | 3.4 |
| % graduated top 10% of class | 40 |
| % graduated top 25% of class | 68 |
| % graduated top 50% of class | 89 |

### DEADLINES
| | |
|---|---:|
| Early decision | 11/15 |
| Early decision notification | 12/1 |
| Regular admission | 1/1 |
| Regular notification | 4/1 |
| Nonfall registration? | yes |

### APPLICANTS ALSO LOOK AT
**AND OFTEN PREFER**
Vassar
Smith
Bard
Swarthmore
**AND SOMETIMES PREFER**
Sarah Lawrence
Hampshire
NYU
Reed
Oberlin
**AND RARELY PREFER**
U New Hampshire
UConn
U Vermont

### FINANCIAL FACTS

| | |
|---|---:|
| Financial Aid Rating | 85 |
| Tuition | $28,030 |
| Room and board | $7,140 |
| Books and supplies | $800 |
| Required fees | $740 |
| % frosh receiving aid | 64 |
| % undergrads receiving aid | 59 |
| Avg frosh grant | $14,500 |
| Avg frosh loan | $2,977 |

THE BEST 351 COLLEGES ■ 81

# BENTLEY COLLEGE

175 FOREST STREET, WALTHAM, MA 02452-4705 • ADMISSIONS: 781-891-2244 • FAX: 781-891-3414

## CAMPUS LIFE

| | |
|---|---|
| Quality of Life Rating | 79 |
| Type of school | private |
| Environment | suburban |

### STUDENTS
| | |
|---|---|
| Total undergrad enrollment | 4,325 |
| % male/female | 57/43 |
| % from out of state | 40 |
| % from public high school | 70 |
| % live on campus | 71 |
| % African American | 4 |
| % Asian | 8 |
| % Caucasian | 78 |
| % Hispanic | 4 |
| % international | 8 |
| # of countries represented | 61 |

### SURVEY SAYS . . .
Musical organizations aren't popular
Classes are small
Great computer facilities
Students aren't religious
Ethnic diversity on campus
Theater is unpopular

## ACADEMICS

| | |
|---|---|
| Academic Rating | 77 |
| Calendar | semester |
| Student/faculty ratio | 14:1 |
| Profs interesting rating | 92 |
| Profs accessible rating | 91 |
| % profs teaching UG courses | 100 |
| Avg reg class size | 20-29 students |

### MOST POPULAR MAJORS
Accounting
International Studies
Marketing

## STUDENTS SPEAK OUT

### Academics
A primary focus of the educational process at Bentley College is preparing students for life in the business world. As one student writes, "people, technology, and business—that's what Bentley is about." Many undergraduates affirm that the on-campus trading floor drew them to Bentley. The college's 57-station trading floor is one of only a handful of such real-time trading floor facilities in the U.S. A NASDAQ stock market Premier Partner, Bentley's facility has live data feed from Bloomberg, Reuters, and Dow Jones, among others. Students frequently describe the school's technological and business resources as one of its major strengths. Of course, good technology is not enough to prepare prospective businesspeople. The students save their highest compliments for their professors. "They are all pretty much down to earth," one student writes, and another comments that "the professors are like our best friends. They are there when you need them." When describing professors, a favorite adjective of undergrads is "accessible." Writes one typical student, "All of the professors are extremely helpful and accessible." Classes and seminars are relatively small, which helps to increase student-faculty intimacy. "Because of the small size of our school, it is easy to develop a relationship outside of class between the students and teachers that is comfortable and very helpful." Most students are not as fond of Bentley's administrators, asserting that "it is virtually impossible to get things changed." In general, students believe that the school prepares them well for life after graduation. One muses that Bentley "builds a strong business foundation that will last for a lifetime."

### Life
Bentley is located in the small Massachusetts town of Waltham, but because of the school's proximity to Boston (about 20 minutes via a free shuttle), students "can always go there and have a good time." Many especially enjoy Boston's active club scene. Students describe the campus as beautiful and quiet, though many add that there is an obvious lack of school spirit, and according to one morose student, "fun at Bentley consists of sitting in a room and drinking." Still, other students believe that the active Greek life "keeps the campus busy with activities, charities, and parties" that allow them "to meet a lot of people and [enjoy] good times." However you slice it, drinking is a popular activity, and people "party every weekend through Monday." Students agree that the food at Bentley is less than satisfying, but the new residence halls and additional parking lots were the answer to their prayers. However, undergrads praise the feeling of safety that they have while on campus and the new Student Center (opening January 2002) will provide a better space for students. Overall, student sentiment about life on campus was perhaps best summarized by the student who told us "Bentley is definitely a fun school with a big party scene," but one which also provides "a very good academic foundation."

### Student Body
Though its technologically advanced business curriculum has gained national attention, Bentley remains a college that primarily attracts students from the Northeast. Students lean towards political conservatism, which isn't surprising considering that approximately three-quarters of the students come from New England. Many students list the student body's lack of diversity as one of Bentley's major weaknesses, saying undergrads tend to be very "cliquey, depending on what ethnicity you are." Others write that "everyone is pretty much white, preppy, and rich" and "if you can't afford all A&E and AF, then you won't interact with anyone." Still, most students agree that the campus is very friendly and that students should have "no problem making friends." One student told us, "the people are very nice." International students are not only accepted, but well respected. "The students [at Bentley] are very similar in nature. They all have a really competitive nature," one student wrote, but manage to remain "friendly."

82 ■ THE BEST 351 COLLEGES

# BENTLEY COLLEGE

FINANCIAL AID: 781-891-3441 • E-MAIL: UGADMISSION@BENTLEY.EDU • WEBSITE: WWW.BENTLEY.EDU

## ADMISSIONS
*Very important factors considered include:* class rank, essays, recommendations, secondary school record, standardized test scores. *Important factors considered include:* character/personal qualities, extracurricular activities, interview, talent/ability, volunteer work, work experience. *Other factors considered include:* alumni/ae relation, geographical residence, minority status, state residency. SAT I or ACT required. TOEFL required of all international applicants. High school diploma or GED is required. *High school units required/recommended:* 17 total required; 18 total recommended; 4 English required, 4 math required, 3 science required, 2 foreign language required, 3 foreign language recommended, 2 social studies required.

## The Inside Word
If you're a solid "B" student there's little challenge to encounter in the admissions process here. The College's appealing greater Boston location and career-oriented academic strengths account for a sizable applicant pool and the moderate selectivity that it enjoys.

## FINANCIAL AID
*Students should submit:* FAFSA, CSS/Financial Aid PROFILE, noncustodial (divorced/separated) parent's statement, business/farm supplement. Regular filing deadline is February 1. The Princeton Review suggests that all financial aid forms be submitted as soon as possible after January 1. *Need-based scholarships/grants offered:* Pell, SEOG, state scholarships/grants, private scholarships, the school's own gift aid. *Loan aid offered:* Federal Perkins, state loans. Federal Work-Study Program available. Institutional employment available. Applicants will be notified of awards on a rolling basis beginning on or about March 25. Off-campus job opportunities are excellent.

## FROM THE ADMISSIONS OFFICE
"Bentley College is a business university focusing on educating students interested in business and related professions, blending the broad curriculum and technological strength of a university with the values and student orientation of a small college. For students interested in business and related professions, Bentley does what the nation's leading technological universities do for students interested in science and engineering. A Bentley education is built on a strong foundation in the liberal arts with an unparalleled array of business courses and hands-on experience with technology. Concepts and theories that students learn in the classroom come alive in several hands-on, high-tech learning laboratories—each among the first of its kind in higher education. The financial Trading Room, a virtual laboratory of world financial markets, offers first-hand exposure to financial concepts such as risk management and asset valuation. In the Center for Marketing Technology, undergraduates learn the latest research tools and strategies in marketing and advertising. The Accounting Center for Electronic Learning and Business Measurement introduces students to the cutting-edge tools and technologies that have reshaped the profession of accounting. The Center for Language and International Collaboration is a key resource for language students, international studies majors, and anyone with an interest in international issues. And the Design and Usability Testing Center puts into students' hands the same applications employed by technical communicators. The Mobile Computing Program provides all Bentley freshmen with a network-ready laptop computer fully loaded with software. New athletic and recreation facilities complement the 22 varsity teams in Division I and II and the extensive intramural and recreational sports programs. Boston, just 10 miles from campus, and Cambridge, a regular trip on the free shuttle, are great resources for internships and jobs. More than 90 percent of Bentley students find employment within six months of graduation."

## SELECTIVITY

| | |
|---|---|
| Admissions Rating | 81 |
| # of applicants | 5,082 |
| % of applicants accepted | 46 |
| % of acceptees attending | 39 |
| # accepting a place on wait list | 936 |
| % admitted from wait list | 1 |
| # of early decision applicants | 162 |
| % accepted early decision | 65 |

### FRESHMAN PROFILE
| | |
|---|---|
| Range SAT Verbal | 520-600 |
| Average SAT Verbal | 559 |
| Range SAT Math | 560-650 |
| Average SAT Math | 603 |
| Range ACT Composite | 22-26 |
| Minimum TOEFL | 550 |
| % graduated top 10% of class | 31 |
| % graduated top 25% of class | 65 |
| % graduated top 50% of class | 95 |

### DEADLINES
| | |
|---|---|
| Early decision | 12/1 |
| Early decision notification | 11/15 |
| Priority admission | 2/1 |
| Regular admission | 2/1 |
| Regular notification | 4/1 |
| Nonfall registration? | yes |

### APPLICANTS ALSO LOOK AT AND OFTEN PREFER
Babson
Boston U
Boston College
**AND SOMETIMES PREFER**
Providence College
Villanova
NYU
**AND RARELY PREFER**
Northeastern
UMass at Amherst

## FINANCIAL FACTS

| | |
|---|---|
| Financial Aid Rating | 80 |
| Tuition | $20,880 |
| Room and board | $9,350 |
| Books and supplies | $900 |
| Required fees | $195 |
| % frosh receiving aid | 57 |
| % undergrads receiving aid | 50 |
| Avg frosh grant | $15,170 |
| Avg frosh loan | $2,810 |

# BIRMINGHAM-SOUTHERN COLLEGE

900 ARKADELPHIA ROAD, BIRMINGHAM, AL 35254 • ADMISSIONS: 205-226-4686 • FAX: 205-226-3074

## CAMPUS LIFE

| | |
|---|---|
| **Quality of Life Rating** | **87** |
| Type of school | private |
| Affiliation | Methodist |
| Environment | urban |

### STUDENTS

| | |
|---|---|
| Total undergrad enrollment | 1,395 |
| % male/female | 41/59 |
| % from out of state | 26 |
| % from public high school | 65 |
| % live on campus | 88 |
| % in (# of) fraternities | 53 (6) |
| % in (# of) sororities | 74 (7) |
| % African American | 6 |
| % Asian | 2 |
| % Caucasian | 90 |
| % Hispanic | 1 |

### SURVEY SAYS . . .
*Students are very religious*
*Students get along with local community*
*Students love Birmingham, AL*
*Campus feels safe*
*Athletic facilities are great*
*Theater is hot*
*Beautiful campus*
*Political activism is (almost) nonexistent*

## ACADEMICS

| | |
|---|---|
| **Academic Rating** | **86** |
| Calendar | 4-1-4 |
| Student/faculty ratio | 12:1 |
| Profs interesting rating | 96 |
| Profs accessible rating | 96 |
| % profs teaching UG courses | 100 |
| Avg lab size | 10-19 students |
| Avg reg class size | 10-19 students |

### MOST POPULAR MAJORS
Pre-law studies
Health/medical preparatory programs
Business administration/management

## STUDENTS SPEAK OUT

### Academics

Business and management studies earn star billing at Birmingham-Southern College, a small liberal arts school that emphasizes the importance of general knowledge and experiential learning. BSC's wide-ranging set of distribution requirements ("You are forced to endure the trial of a strict and laborious core requirement," writes one undergrad half-jokingly) in the humanities and social sciences keep future MBAs and their fellow students on their toes; these requirements may well play a key role in the high acceptance rate BSC students enjoy at MBA and other graduate programs. The cornerstone of the BSC program is Interim Term, a four-week January mini-mester during which students immerse themselves in a single subject or project. Students appreciate the school's philosophy but say the real reason to choose BSC is the faculty: explains one, "I will say the professors and faculty at Birmingham Southern College are wonderful. They are receptive and welcoming. I believe the majority strive to make the students' years beneficial, educational, and enjoyable." Agrees another, "The teachers are really part of what goes on here. They don't just show up for the lecture time and then disappear." Students also feel that "the administration is incredible. The president knows more about my college career than I do."

### Life

When a campus is so clearly dominated by the Greek system—65 of upperclassmen join a fraternity or sorority—students are bound to feel strongly about the benefits and drawbacks of Greek social life. Not surprisingly, most students love it: in fact, for many it is a primary reason they chose BSC. Writes one student, "Greek life is huge. Three nights a week, there is always something to do on fraternity row." Many agree that "the Greek system is pretty strong on our campus, but it's a good system and provides a lot of benefits for its members. We all get along well, and for the most part, everyone is friendly to each other." An adamant minority disagrees, complaining that "the male students who are in fraternities often associate solely with their fraternity brothers . . . . The independent population is generally very accepting of anyone who is independent, but less accepting of members of Greek organizations." When Greek life "gets old (which it does, more quickly for some than others), the SGA-sponsored 'drunk bus' is there to drive us to and from downtown Birmingham. There are concerts and bars and cool places to just hang out downtown. There are excellent places to eat around town, too, and many movie theaters and real theaters." High points of the school year include biannual "weekends of band parties on the dorm quad," for which "students get in free to see medium to big-name bands play right on our campus."

### Student Body

The "primarily affluent white students" who constitute the undergraduate population of BSC make for a "conservative liberal arts school." Notes one student, "We are a pretty homogeneous bunch. There is a strange mix of intellectual life with old-style Greek life on this small campus. It's possible to immerse yourself in one or the other or both." Students describe a pleasantly friendly atmosphere on campus, reporting that "people walk down the sidewalk, and even those whom you don't know (it's hard to believe that there are people you don't know, but there are a few) say hello." International students enhance student body diversity; explains one undergrad: "Birmingham Southern has a very diverse student population with students from all over the world."

# BIRMINGHAM-SOUTHERN COLLEGE

FINANCIAL AID: 205-226-4688 • E-MAIL: ADMISSIONS@BSC.EDU • WEBSITE: WWW.BSC.EDU

## ADMISSIONS
*Very important factors considered include:* essays, recommendations, secondary school record, standardized test scores. *Important factors considered include:* character/personal qualities. *Other factors considered include:* extracurricular activities, interview, state residency, talent/ability, volunteer work, work experience. SAT I or ACT required. TOEFL required of all international applicants. High school diploma or GED is required. *High school units required/recommended:* 16 total required; 4 English required, 4 math recommended, 4 science recommended, 2 foreign language recommended, 2 social studies recommended, 2 history recommended.

### *The Inside Word*
Birmingham-Southern's lack of widespread national recognition by students and parents results in a small applicant pool, the majority of whom are admitted. Most of the admits are looking for a quality southern college, recognize a good situation here, and decide to enroll. Our impression is that few regret their decision. In a reflection of the entire administration, the admissions staff is truly personal and very helpful to prospective students.

## FINANCIAL AID
*Students should submit:* state aid form. Regular filing deadline is May 1. The Princeton Review suggests that all financial aid forms be submitted as soon as possible after January 1. *Need-based scholarships/grants offered:* Pell, SEOG, state scholarships/grants, private scholarships, the school's own gift aid, United Negro College Fund. *Loan aid offered:* FFEL Subsidized Stafford, FFEL Unsubsidized Stafford, FFEL PLUS, Federal Perkins, college/university loans from institutional funds. Federal Work-Study Program available. Institutional employment available. Applicants will be notified of awards on a rolling basis beginning on or about February 1. Off-campus job opportunities are excellent.

## FROM THE ADMISSIONS OFFICE
"Respected publishers continue to recognize Birmingham-Southern College as one of the top-ranked liberal arts colleges in the nation. One guide highlights our small classes and the fact that we still assign each student a 'faculty-cum-mentor,' to assure individualized attention to our students. One notable aspect of our academic calendar is our January interim term, a four-week period in which students can participate in special projects in close collaboration with faculty members, either on or off campus. One dimension of Birmingham-Southern's civic focus is the commitment to volunteerism. In fact, former President George Bush visited the campus to present our Conservancy group with one of his 'Points of Light' volunteer service awards. The Center for Leadership Studies assists students in realizing their leadership potential by combining the academic study of leadership with significant community service."

### SELECTIVITY

| | |
|---|---:|
| Admissions Rating | 82 |
| # of applicants | 1,040 |
| % of applicants accepted | 90 |
| % of acceptees attending | 37 |

#### FRESHMAN PROFILE
| | |
|---|---:|
| Range SAT Verbal | 540-650 |
| Average SAT Verbal | 598 |
| Range SAT Math | 540-640 |
| Average SAT Math | 588 |
| Range ACT Composite | 23-29 |
| Average ACT Composite | 26 |
| Minimum TOEFL | 500 |
| Average HS GPA | 3.2 |
| % graduated top 10% of class | 38 |
| % graduated top 25% of class | 69 |
| % graduated top 50% of class | 89 |

#### DEADLINES
| | |
|---|---:|
| Priority admission | 1/15 |
| Nonfall registration? | yes |

#### APPLICANTS ALSO LOOK AT
**AND OFTEN PREFER**
Vanderbilt
Rhodes
**AND SOMETIMES PREFER**
Samford
U of Alabama
U of Auburn
U of the South
Furman
**AND RARELY PREFER**
LSU at Baton Rouge
Tulane

### FINANCIAL FACTS

| | |
|---|---:|
| Financial Aid Rating | 90 |
| Tuition | $17,650 |
| Room and board | $5,652 |
| Books and supplies | $600 |
| Required fees | $339 |
| % frosh receiving aid | 98 |
| % undergrads receiving aid | 38 |
| Avg frosh grant | $5,129 |
| Avg frosh loan | $2,517 |

# Boston College

140 Commonwealth Avenue, Devlin Hall 208, Chestnut Hill, MA 02467-3809 • Admissions: 617-552-3100 • Fax: 617-552-0798

## CAMPUS LIFE

| | |
|---|---|
| Quality of Life Rating | 80 |
| Type of school | private |
| Affiliation | Roman Catholic |
| Environment | suburban |

### STUDENTS

| | |
|---|---|
| Total undergrad enrollment | 8,916 |
| % from out of state | 73 |
| % from public high school | 60 |
| % live on campus | 73 |
| % African American | 5 |
| % Asian | 9 |
| % Caucasian | 75 |
| % Hispanic | 6 |
| % international | 2 |
| # of countries represented | 86 |

### SURVEY SAYS . . .
Lots of classroom discussion
Students love Chestnut Hill, MA
Great on-campus food
Everyone loves the Eagles
Political activism is hot
Students are cliquish
Student publications are ignored
(Almost) no one listens to college radio

## ACADEMICS

| | |
|---|---|
| Academic Rating | 92 |
| Calendar | semester |
| Student/faculty ratio | 13:1 |
| Profs interesting rating | 91 |
| Profs accessible rating | 89 |
| % profs teaching UG courses | 100 |
| Avg reg class size | 10-19 students |

## STUDENTS SPEAK OUT

### Academics

Boston College has long been known as one of the nation's more elite private undergraduate colleges. Don't let the name fool you, though; this is a research university. But don't let that fool you, either, because BC is as committed to teaching as it is to research. Steeped in strong Jesuit tradition, BC is known for its commitment to providing its students with a rigorous liberal arts curriculum aimed at teaching them not merely what to think, but how to think. Students at BC find some top notch professors, though one student cautions prospects to do their homework: "Research the good professors and take them." The majority of the faculty members at BC are known for taking their "jobs seriously" and being genuinely "interested in helping students learn." While not all the professors are easily accessible, there are definitely more than a handful [who] make the extra effort to reach out to their students. As one student notes, "My professors have been excellent and extremely accessible. I have attended pizza parties and barbecues at professors' homes on a number of occasions." Don't, however, expect to find the same level of openness and warmth with the administration. The students here are often more than just a little disenchanted at the relationship between students and administrators. "I don't know who the administration is really," writes one bewildered student. "They aren't involved much in student life." Many others describe the administration as "aloof" and "overly bureaucratic."

### Life

Despite its rigorous academics, BC is also known for its social scene. For many students here the weekend begins a bit prematurely ("weekends begin on Wednesday") and continue right on up to the last minute. Drinking, whether it's at house parties or Boston bars ("you need a fake ID"), tends to be the social lubricant of choice, especially in Cleveland Circle, where BC parties reign, or on campus in one of the senior student apartments known as "Mods." Now, the fact that BC students may have a readily available supply of alcohol doesn't mean the administration takes it lightly. Underage drinking policies, especially in dorm rooms, are strictly enforced. While much of student life may "revolve around the bottle," that by no means is the end of the story. This is, after all, Boston, "the best college city in the world." As one student notes, "The best thing about BC is that it's just right outside of Boston. Whenever campus gets dull you just hop on the T [Boston's public train system] and you're right in the center of one of the most incredible cultural cities in the country." Whether you're looking for a museum, café, club, or bar, you can bet that you'll be able to find it in Boston. In addition, true to its Jesuit heritage, BC maintains an active social presence through volunteering, with more than "500 students" participating in spring break in Appalachia.

### Student Body

The students at BC describe themselves as looking like they have all just stepped out of an "Abercrombie or J.Crew catalogue." As one student notes, "All of the students here look exactly alike. . . . There's pretty much no diversity." Undergrads call their classmates "very nice," while at the same time "rich and cliquish." And while BC certainly is objectively more ethnically and racially diverse than many of its peer institutions, its undergrads by and large don't see it. "This is a pretty cliquey school and groups are formed from freshman year," laments one typical survey respondent. "There's little interaction between different cliques. This is definitely not an ethnically diverse school, and there is often tension between races." For those wishing to break from this standard, student groups often provide a welcoming opportunity to reach across boundaries, regardless of race and background. "The most important thing to do is to get involved with lots of groups, clubs, or sports so that you always have another outlet."

86 ■ THE BEST 351 COLLEGES

# BOSTON COLLEGE

FINANCIAL AID: 800-294-0294 • E-MAIL: UGADMIS@BC.EDU • WEBSITE: WWW.BC.EDU

## ADMISSIONS
*Very important factors considered include:* character/personal qualities, secondary school record, standardized test scores. *Important factors considered include:* alumni/ae relation, class rank, essays, extracurricular activities, minority status, recommendations, religious affiliation/commitment, talent/ability, volunteer work, work experience. SAT I or ACT required. TOEFL required of all international applicants. High school diploma or GED is required. *High school units required/recommended:* 20 total recommended; 4 English recommended, 4 math recommended, 4 science recommended, 4 science lab recommended, 4 foreign language recommended.

### The Inside Word
While applications to BC in general have increased over the past couple of years, early action applications have risen more dramatically. Standards remain high, and we more than recommend a strong college-preparatory curriculum in high school—it's a must in order to have a shot. With a large percentage of its students coming from Catholic high schools such applicants are treated well, but there is little room for relaxation in the process. Applicants need to show strong SAT and SAT II scores, but keep the tests in perspective—BC is interested in the whole package.

## FINANCIAL AID
*Students should submit:* FAFSA, CSS/Financial Aid PROFILE, noncustodial (divorced/separated) parent's statement, business/farm supplement, parent and student tax returns and W-2 statements. The Princeton Review suggests that all financial aid forms be submitted as soon as possible after January 1. *Need-based scholarships/grants offered:* Pell, SEOG, state scholarships/grants, private scholarships, the school's own gift aid. *Loan aid offered:* FFEL Subsidized Stafford, FFEL Unsubsidized Stafford, FFEL PLUS, Federal Perkins, Federal Nursing, state loans. Federal Work-Study Program available. Institutional employment available. Applicants will be notified of awards on or about April 15. Off-campus job opportunities are good.

## FROM THE ADMISSIONS OFFICE
"Boston College students enjoy the quiet, suburban atmosphere of Chestnut Hill, with easy access to the cultural and historical richness of Boston. Junior Year Abroad and Scholar of the College Program offer students flexibility within the curriculum. Facilities opened in the past 10 years include: the Merkert Chemistry Center, a new dorm and dining hall facility, and a new library. Fifteen Presidential Scholars enroll in each freshman class with a half-tuition scholarship irrespective of need, and funding is available to meet full demonstrated need. These students, selected from the top 1 percent of the Early Action applicant pool, participate in the most rewarding intellectual experience offered at the university."

### SELECTIVITY

| | |
|---|---|
| Admissions Rating | 96 |
| # of applicants | 21,133 |
| % of applicants accepted | 32 |
| % of acceptees attending | 34 |

### FRESHMAN PROFILE
| | |
|---|---|
| Range SAT Verbal | 600-690 |
| Range SAT Math | 620-710 |
| Minimum TOEFL | 600 |
| % graduated top 10% of class | 72 |
| % graduated top 25% of class | 94 |
| % graduated top 50% of class | 99 |

### DEADLINES
| | |
|---|---|
| Regular admission | 1/2 |
| Regular notification | 4/15 |
| Nonfall registration? | yes |

### APPLICANTS ALSO LOOK AT AND OFTEN PREFER
University of Pennsylvania
Brown University
Georgetown University
Harvard College
University of Notre Dame
**AND SOMETIMES PREFER**
Tufts University
Cornell University
**AND RARELY PREFER**
Boston University
College of the Holy Cross
New York University

### FINANCIAL FACTS

| | |
|---|---|
| Financial Aid Rating | 84 |
| Tuition | $27,080 |
| Room and board | $9,300 |
| Books and supplies | $600 |
| Required fees | $442 |
| % frosh receiving aid | 60 |
| % undergrads receiving aid | 42 |
| Avg frosh grant | $15,880 |
| Avg frosh loan | $3,459 |

THE BEST 351 COLLEGES ■ 87

# BOSTON UNIVERSITY

121 BAY STATE ROAD, BOSTON, MA 02215 • ADMISSIONS: 617-353-2300 • FAX: 617-353-9695

## CAMPUS LIFE

★★★☆

| | |
|---|---|
| Quality of Life Rating | 84 |
| Type of school | private |
| Environment | urban |

### STUDENTS

| | |
|---|---|
| Total undergrad enrollment | 17,860 |
| % male/female | 40/60 |
| % from out of state | 76 |
| % from public high school | 70 |
| % live on campus | 74 |
| % in (# of) fraternities | 3 (9) |
| % in (# of) sororities | 5 (10) |
| % African American | 2 |
| % Asian | 12 |
| % Caucasian | 62 |
| % Hispanic | 5 |
| % international | 7 |
| # of countries represented | 101 |

### SURVEY SAYS . . .
Students love Boston, MA
Very little drug use
Lousy food on campus
Great off-campus food
Class discussions are rare
Ethnic diversity on campus
Unattractive campus
Large classes
Very small frat/sorority scene
Athletic facilities need improving

## ACADEMICS

| | |
|---|---|
| Academic Rating | 92 |
| Calendar | semester |
| Student/faculty ratio | 14:1 |
| Profs interesting rating | 91 |
| Profs accessible rating | 95 |
| % profs teaching UG courses | 74 |
| % classes taught by TAs | 7 |
| Avg lab size | 20-29 students |
| Avg reg class size | 10-19 students |

## STUDENTS SPEAK OUT

### Academics
Whether they love the school or simply love to hate it, students at BU know how to communicate their beliefs. On the quality of teaching: "Come here and have any life path available to you," writes a first year, "and brilliant, energetic, enthusiastic professors ready to give you the equivalent knowledge of a Ferrari to drive down it." Sound too good to be true? A sophomore puts it into perspective: "I guess the professors here are like those at any university. Some have been wicked funny, awe inspiring, and life changing. Of course there are also a fair share of pompous, misogynistic jerks—but that's why BU has such a great system for dropping classes." Also, "the school's administration resembles a small dictatorship of some Central American country," quips a sophomore. "It is rash, volatile, and hopefully it won't last long." Yet some appreciate the "generally well-run" nature of the school itself. As for the school's large size, one junior remarks, "BU is a large university that may appear overwhelming to a freshman just beginning; however, BU is actually a collection of tiny schools that make up one large institution. Each individual school looks after their individual students, making sure they are not just another number." Not so, counters a sage senior: "If you want individual attention, you need to seek it. Professors (and everyone, really) are receptive if you approach them, but since this is a big school with big classes, they won't seek you out." Most students seem to like the school's deep coffers—financial aid awards are often generous and widespread. Unfortunately, the money doesn't seem to trickle down to the physical plant: a fairly spread-out, urban school, Boston University seems to suffer in the eyes of its students from a lack of a central, well-maintained campus. Writes a senior, "It would be nice to have a campus . . . or at least a patch of shrubs."

### Life
While some students view the strictly enforced rules on alcohol, drugs, and guest visitation as providing a safe haven, others, like this sophomore, find the school's strict dorm regulations infantilizing and unnecessarily harsh: "The guest policy creates a type of environment not conducive to socializing or feeling laid-back. We live in a dictatorship!" Still, students at BU seem to get through; as a sophomore describes it, "During the week, students are very focused on class work and courses, but on the weekends, their mindset is completely different. All thoughts lean toward parties, sex, clubs, and alcohol. In short, good old-fashioned college fun." And for those not in the mood for body shots and early morning walks of shame, there's always Boston, "one of the best college towns in the country." Why go to BU? An answer from a particularly expressive senior: "The BU experience goes way beyond the classroom. Just in the last month, I've gone to see the Phantom of the Opera, gone skiing in Vermont, and gone to the Fogg Museum at Harvard. Its location is BU's greatest strength."

### Student Body
It might seem incredible that such a large and opinionated student body gets along as well as they do. Writes one junior, "Generally students are unique and independent and encourage healthy competition and collaboration on projects. They are easy to get along with." So it's just like the cast of *Friends* but on a really big scale? Well . . . not quite, according to a sophomore. "There are, of course, a few cliques on campus composed of students who obviously skipped the day in preschool when they taught 'How to Get Along With Others and Not Be a Eurotrashy Snot.'" Ouch. Fortunately, in a large school there's bound to be someone to click with. How does a typical BUer feel about his or her fellow students? We like this answer: "How should I know?" asks a first year. "Out of 15,000 undergraduates [sic] I have seen about 2,000, spoken to about 500, and hung around with 50." Really good odds, we'd say.

# BOSTON UNIVERSITY

FINANCIAL AID: 617-353-2965 • E-MAIL: ADMISSIONS@BU.EDU • WEBSITE: WWW.BU.EDU

## ADMISSIONS
*Very important factors considered include:* secondary school record. *Important factors considered include:* class rank, essays, recommendations, standardized test scores. *Other factors considered include:* alumni/ae relation, character/personal qualities, extracurricular activities, volunteer work, work experience. SAT I or ACT required. TOEFL required of all international applicants. High school diploma or GED is required. *High school units required/recommended:* 15 total required; 20 total recommended; 4 English required, 3 math required, 4 math recommended, 3 science required, 4 science recommended, 2 foreign language required, 4 foreign language recommended.

### The Inside Word
Boston is one of the nation's most popular college towns, and BU benefits tremendously. The university's last few entering classes have been chock-full of high-caliber students; despite a general decline in applications at colleges in the Northeast it will continue to be competitive to gain admission to BU, as applications keep a steady upward trend and entering class size is kept in check. Those who aren't up to traditional standards are sometimes referred to the less selective College of General Studies, which allows students to continue on to other divisions of the university once they prove themselves academically—but standards here are rising.

## FINANCIAL AID
*Students should submit:* FAFSA, CSS/Financial Aid PROFILE, state aid form, noncustodial (divorced/separated) parent's statement, business/farm supplement. The Princeton Review suggests that all financial aid forms be submitted as soon as possible after January 1. *Need-based scholarships/grants offered:* Pell, SEOG, state scholarships/grants, private scholarships, the school's own gift aid. *Loan aid offered:* Direct Subsidized Stafford, Direct Unsubsidized Stafford, Direct PLUS, Federal Perkins, state loans. Federal Work-Study Program available. Institutional employment available. Applicants will be notified of awards on a rolling basis beginning on or about March 22. Off-campus job opportunities are excellent.

## FROM THE ADMISSIONS OFFICE
"Boston University (BU) is a private teaching and research institution with a strong emphasis on undergraduate education. We are committed to providing the highest level of teaching excellence, and fulfillment of this pledge is our highest priority. Boston University has 11 undergraduate schools and colleges offering 250 major and minor areas of concentration. Students may choose from programs of study in areas as diverse as biochemistry, theater arts, physical therapy, elementary education, broadcast journalism, international relations, business, and computer engineering. BU has an international student body, with students from every state and more than 100 countries. In addition, opportunities to study abroad exist through 29 different programs, spanning 16 countries on 6 continents."

### SELECTIVITY

| | |
|---|---|
| Admissions Rating | 91 |
| # of applicants | 27,038 |
| % of applicants accepted | 58 |
| % of acceptees attending | 29 |
| # accepting a place on wait list | 558 |
| % admitted from wait list | 12 |
| # of early decision applicants | 399 |
| % accepted early decision | 47 |

### FRESHMAN PROFILE
| | |
|---|---|
| Range SAT Verbal | 590-680 |
| Average SAT Verbal | 634 |
| Range SAT Math | 610-690 |
| Average SAT Math | 647 |
| Range ACT Composite | 25-29 |
| Average ACT Composite | 28 |
| Minimum TOEFL | 550 |
| Average HS GPA | 3.5 |
| % graduated top 10% of class | 56 |
| % graduated top 25% of class | 90 |

### DEADLINES
| | |
|---|---|
| Early decision | 11/1 |
| Early decision notification | 12/15 |
| Regular admission | 1/1 |
| Nonfall registration? | yes |

### APPLICANTS ALSO LOOK AT AND OFTEN PREFER
Boston College
George Washington University
New York University

**AND SOMETIMES PREFER**
University of Pennsylvania
Syracuse University
Northeastern University

**AND RARELY PREFER**
Tufts University
University of Massachusetts
SUNY

### FINANCIAL FACTS

| | |
|---|---|
| Financial Aid Rating | 87 |
| Tuition | $28,512 |
| Room and board | $9,288 |
| Books and supplies | $753 |
| Required fees | $394 |
| % frosh receiving aid | 52 |
| % undergrads receiving aid | 46 |
| Avg frosh grant | $16,825 |
| Avg frosh loan | $4,614 |

# BOWDOIN COLLEGE

5000 COLLEGE STATION, BRUNSWICK, ME 04011-8441 • ADMISSIONS: 207-725-3100 • FAX: 207-725-3101

## CAMPUS LIFE

| | |
|---|---|
| Quality of Life Rating | 91 |
| Type of school | private |
| Environment | suburban |

### STUDENTS

| | |
|---|---|
| Total undergrad enrollment | 1,657 |
| % male/female | 49/51 |
| % from out of state | 86 |
| % from public high school | 54 |
| % live on campus | 90 |
| % African American | 4 |
| % Asian | 8 |
| % Caucasian | 77 |
| % Hispanic | 4 |
| % international | 3 |
| # of countries represented | 27 |

### SURVEY SAYS . . .
Great food on campus
Everyone loves the Polar Bears
Very little drug use
Athletic facilities are great
(Almost) no one smokes
Low cost of living

## ACADEMICS

| | |
|---|---|
| Academic Rating | 94 |
| Calendar | semester |
| Student/faculty ratio | 10:1 |
| Profs interesting rating | 94 |
| Profs accessible rating | 95 |
| % profs teaching UG courses | 100 |
| Avg lab size | 10-19 students |
| Avg reg class size | 10-19 students |

### MOST POPULAR MAJORS
Government and legal studies
English
Economics

## STUDENTS SPEAK OUT

### Academics

"Independence," "freedom," and "self-motivation" are words Bowdoin College students frequently associate with their undergraduate experience. Perhaps it has something to do with the size and location of the campus itself—a few miles from the coast of southern Maine (and its islands, lakes, and wilderness), tiny but highly selective Bowdoin prides itself on its "Walden Pond" atmosphere and challenges its students to, like Thoreau, find their own way. Notes one senior, "You are encouraged to explore all sorts of academic areas, and once you find something you love, you can run with it." Bowdoin's campus is, according to its students, "unbeatable." Remodeled buildings, "pretty good housing—especially for first years," and some of the best college food around all make Joe and Jane College's quest for knowledge a little more, well, comfortable. Professors are, for the most part, accessible (Brunswick is a small town—they can't go far) and full of encouragement. Writes another senior, "Professors are excellent. We've had them over to our house for dinner." Unfortunately, students also note that the "whale of a bureaucracy" at Bowdoin can make retaining such teaching excellence difficult. A savvy junior describes the situation as such: "Great professors, but the school's rush to determine whether to tenure or not leaves their status uncertain and hurries, regrettably, some good ones away."

### Life

As one would expect, a major aspect of Bowdoin's social life revolves around—you guessed it—the great outdoors. "There are great opportunities for getting outside," writes a senior. "With the Bowdoin Outing Club you can spend the weekend skiiing, camping, hiking, snowshoeing, rock climbing, hanging out at the Outing Club's cabin drinking hot chocolate all weekend." Athletics, too, seem to draw the campus together, whether it's "hockey on the town commons," playing on the rugby team and in other club sports, or watching Bowdoin continue an eons-old rivalry with nearby Colby College during one of their "especially insane" hockey matches. Of course, not everyone is thrilled about all this huffing and puffing in the name of good, clean fun; one junior makes it plain that "athletics and personal fitness activities are a little too popular." In terms of nightlife, there seems to be only a few options at Bowdoin, and most of those involve drinking. Though the administration and the recently transformed "social house" system (sororities and fraternities were banned a few years ago) try to promote non-alcoholic programming such as concerts, dances, and performances, many students stick close to the keg. "I drink for fun," writes a senior, and while one student's soused state might not speak for everyone, at least one first-year agrees: "There's a lot of drinking here."

### Student Body

"Everyone here is interesting," says a first year. "We can talk about girls on TV and China's foreign policy as it relates to European trade in the same moment." Another freshman provides a living example of Bowdoin's reputation for turning out aware and independent yet community-minded thinkers and doers: "I am an athlete, don't smoke, and voted Republican. I live next to a kid who smokes, listens to Phish, voted for Nader, and we are now best friends." Too bad much of Bowdoin's diversity is limited to political parties and smoking habits. Another freshman weighs in about what is increasingly seen as a major drawback to an otherwise excellent college experience: "Good thing this campus is traditionally liberal and open minded," she writes. "Otherwise, we would be confused with a white pride meeting." It's a negative the school's administration has not overlooked, and according to students, is working hard to change. "Only recently is Bowdoin attempting to push away from the stale, prep-school boy's attitude that it previously held. Yet the effort is commendable and noticeable." Besides, jokes a sophomore, "It turns out that white, New England prep-school kids are pretty nice. Who knew?"

90 ■ THE BEST 351 COLLEGES

# BOWDOIN COLLEGE

FINANCIAL AID: 207-725-3273 • E-MAIL: ADMISSIONS@BOWDOIN.EDU • WEBSITE: WWW.BOWDOIN.EDU

## ADMISSIONS

*Very important factors considered include:* character/personal qualities, class rank, essays, diversity of background, recommendations, secondary school record. *Important factors considered include:* alumni/ae relation, extracurricular activities, geographical residence, talent/ability, volunteer work. *Other factors considered include:* interview, standardized test scores, work experience. TOEFL required of all international applicants. *High school units required/recommended:* 20 total recommended; 4 English recommended, 4 math recommended, 4 science recommended, 3 science lab recommended, 4 foreign language recommended, 4 social studies recommended.

### The Inside Word

This is one of the 20 or so most selective colleges in the country. Virtually everyone who applies is well qualified academically, which means criteria besides grades and test scores become critically important in candidate review. Who you are, what you think, where you are from, and why you are interested in Bowdoin are the sorts of things that will determine whether you get in, provided you meet their high academic standards.

## FINANCIAL AID

*Students should submit:* FAFSA, institution's own financial aid form, CSS/Financial Aid PROFILE, noncustodial (divorced/separated) parent's statement, business/farm supplement. Regular filing deadline is February 15. The Princeton Review suggests that all financial aid forms be submitted as soon as possible after January 1. *Need-based scholarships/grants offered:* Pell, SEOG, state scholarships/grants, private scholarships, the school's own gift aid. *Loan aid offered:* FFEL Subsidized Stafford, FFEL Unsubsidized Stafford, FFEL PLUS, Federal Perkins, state loans, college/university loans from institutional funds. Federal Work-Study Program available. Institutional employment available. Applicants will be notified of awards on or about April 5. Off-campus job opportunities are fair.

## FROM THE ADMISSIONS OFFICE

"Each year Bowdoin sponsors myriad events, including performances by bands, comedians, artists, and dancers as well as lectures and film series, community service events, and the occasional scavenger hunt. Performers who have appeared at the College recently include Savion Glover, Jurassic 5, The Capitol Steps, and Mos Def. Speakers have included Doris Kearns Goodwin, Robert Reich, Spike Lee, Nobel Laureate Thomas Cech, and playwright Tony Kushner. The College has more than 100 active student organizations. About 70 percent of students participate in community service during their time at Bowdoin, and the College's many volunteer programs allow students to interact with the Brunswick community. Club and intramural sports and the Outing Club enable students to get involved in physical fitness without having to be star athletes. Bowdoin is determined to be a place that brings together people from widely diverse ethnic and economic backgrounds, from different parts of the country and the world, and with divergent political beliefs, a full range of religious identities, and broad academic interests."

## SELECTIVITY

| | |
|---|---:|
| Admissions Rating | 97 |
| # of applicants | 4,505 |
| % of applicants accepted | 25 |
| % of acceptees attending | 41 |
| # of early decision applicants | 627 |
| % accepted early decision | 28 |

### FRESHMAN PROFILE

| | |
|---|---:|
| Range SAT Verbal | 640-730 |
| Average SAT Verbal | 680 |
| Range SAT Math | 640-720 |
| Average SAT Math | 680 |
| Minimum TOEFL | 600 |
| % graduated top 10% of class | 72 |
| % graduated top 25% of class | 94 |
| % graduated top 50% of class | 100 |

### DEADLINES

| | |
|---|---:|
| Early decision | 11/15 & 1/1 |
| Early decision notification | 12/15 & 2/7 |
| Regular admission | 1/1 |
| Regular notification | 4/1 |

### APPLICANTS ALSO LOOK AT AND OFTEN PREFER
Brown
Dartmouth
Harvard
Williams

### AND SOMETIMES PREFER
Amherst
Middlebury
Princeton
Cornell U
Pomona

## FINANCIAL FACTS

| | |
|---|---:|
| Financial Aid Rating | 80 |
| Tuition | $28,070 |
| Room and board | $7,305 |
| Books and supplies | $850 |
| Required fees | $615 |
| % frosh receiving aid | 45 |
| % undergrads receiving aid | 40 |
| Avg frosh grant | $22,096 |
| Avg frosh loan | $2,891 |

# BRADLEY UNIVERSITY

1501 WEST BRADLEY AVENUE, PEORIA, IL 61625 • ADMISSIONS: 309-677-1000 • FAX: 309-677-2797

## CAMPUS LIFE

| Quality of Life Rating | 77 |
| --- | --- |
| Type of school | private |
| Environment | urban |

### STUDENTS

| Total undergrad enrollment | 5,190 |
| --- | --- |
| % male/female | 45/55 |
| % from out of state | 14 |
| % from public high school | 76 |
| % live on campus | 70 |
| % in (# of) fraternities | 34 (18) |
| % in (# of) sororities | 33 (12) |
| % African American | 5 |
| % Asian | 2 |
| % Caucasian | 85 |
| % Hispanic | 2 |
| % international | 2 |
| # of countries represented | 26 |

### SURVEY SAYS . . .
Frats and sororities dominate social scene
(Almost) everyone smokes
Popular college radio
Hard liquor is popular
Lots of beer drinking
Athletic facilities need improving
Library needs improving
Students don't like Peoria, IL
Lousy food on campus

## ACADEMICS

| Academic Rating | 69 |
| --- | --- |
| Calendar | semester |
| Student/faculty ratio | 14:1 |
| Profs interesting rating | 92 |
| Profs accessible rating | 93 |
| % profs teaching UG courses | 100 |
| Avg reg class size | 10-19 students |

### MOST POPULAR MAJORS
Elementary education and teaching
Psychology
Actuarial science

## STUDENTS SPEAK OUT

### Academics
Career-oriented undergraduates seeking the intimacy of a small college and the resources of a research institution might want to consider Bradley University. With just under 5,000 undergrads and nearly 1,000 grad students, Bradley is small enough to allow personal interaction between students and professors and big enough to offer more than 90 academic and pre-professional majors in five undergraduate colleges. Many who attend agree that "Bradley is the perfect size. The smaller school atmosphere has allowed me to get more involved in campus." Indicative of the level of intimacy here is the fact that "many professors include their home number on the syllabus so we can contact them. One even said we could call until 1 A.M. because they're on a college schedule, but after that to wait until the next day." The business, chemistry, and engineering departments all receive high marks here, and liberal arts faculty members have their advocates as well. Professors generally "are good. With small schools, the classes are small and close-knit, but class variety is limited. The trade-off is good, though." The administration gets mixed reviews; explains one student, "Academically, Bradley is run very well. But in the area of nonacademics, the administration needs to be more open." Writes another, "Administrators seem willing to hear students' questions but not necessarily as willing to do anything about them." Other student complaints center on the library ("out of date") and technology services. All in all, though, the students tell us that they're happy with the "memorable" and "excellent" academic experience that Bradley offers. "I love Bradley University," beams one sophomore. "I have never regretted my decision [to attend] at all."

### Life
Students describe a "laid-back," midwestern vibe permeating the "self-contained" and "pretty campus" at Bradley University. For some, especially those outside the Greek system, it's a little too laid back. Explains one student, "Bradley is a good school if you don't care about a social life." Those within Greek society, however, find plenty to fill their extracurricular hours. "Social life is somewhat Greek-oriented," concedes one frat member. Adds another student, "If you don't like Greek parties you are kind of screwed." For the alternatively inclined, "art parties are pretty hip, or you could go to local rock shows. Local bars are also popular." For all others, the school provides a few activities "specifically designed to get everyone on campus involved," but for the most part, students find few distractions enticing them from their studies. The gym facilities, a potential source of diversion, "need serious improvement." To make matters worse, most students agree that Peoria "is boring." On the positive side, it is "easy, quick, and convenient to get to and from class" at Bradley, especially considering the size of the undergraduate population. Also, brand new dorms are soon to be available for upperclassmen; in just a few years you'll be living in really swank digs.

### Student Body
"Most people are either athletes or Greeks" at Bradley, where the "atmosphere is on the conservative side, not so open to activism." However, "people are friendly for the most part," writes one student, and others further characterize their classmates as "outgoing," "courteous," "wealthy, educated," and "slightly motivated." Because the student body is small, "everyone knows everyone else [by the beginning of senior year], which can be a good thing or a bad thing." Some students say self-imposed racial and ethnic segregation is "obvious," but others feel that tolerance and unity are hallmarks here. "Bradley is like a family," coos a junior. "People from all different backgrounds are constantly interacting."

92 ■ THE BEST 351 COLLEGES

# BRADLEY UNIVERSITY

FINANCIAL AID: 309-677-3089 • E-MAIL: ADMISSIONS@BRADLEY.EDU • WEBSITE: WWW.BRADLEY.EDU

## ADMISSIONS

*Very important factors considered include:* secondary school record. *Important factors considered include:* class rank, standardized test scores. *Other factors considered include:* alumni/ae relation, character/personal qualities, essays, extracurricular activities, interview, personal experience and cultural background, recommendations, talent/ability, volunteer work, work experience. SAT I or ACT required. TOEFL required of all international applicants. High school diploma or GED is required. *High school units required/recommended:* 16 total required; 4 English required, 5 English recommended, 3 math required, 4 math recommended, 2 science required, 3 science recommended, 2 science lab required, 3 science lab recommended, 2 foreign language recommended, 2 social studies required, 3 social studies recommended, 2 history recommended.

### *The Inside Word*

Though students come here from far and wide, Bradley is best known within the Midwest and its reach is primarily regional. As a result, the admission process at Bradley is not super competitive; combined with solid academic quality and a broad range of offerings, this makes Bradley a worthwhile choice for those seeking to attend a strong school without running a grueling admissions gauntlet.

## FINANCIAL AID

*Students should submit:* FAFSA. The Princeton Review suggests that all financial aid forms be submitted as soon as possible after January 1. *Need-based scholarships/grants offered:* Pell, SEOG, state scholarships/grants, private scholarships, the school's own gift aid. *Loan aid offered:* Direct Subsidized Stafford, Direct Unsubsidized Stafford, Direct PLUS, Federal Perkins, Federal Nursing, college/university loans from institutional funds. Federal Work-Study Program available. Institutional employment available. Applicants will be notified of awards on a rolling basis. Off-campus job opportunities are good.

## FROM THE ADMISSIONS OFFICE

"Does the size of a college make a difference? Bradley's 5,000 undergraduates and 1,000 graduates think so. They like the opportunities, choices, and technologies of a larger university and the quality, personal attention, and challenge of a small, private college. Bradley's size makes so many things possible—recognition instead of anonymity, accessibility instead of bureaucracy, and academic choices instead of limits. Bradley students choose from more than 90 programs of study in the Foster College of Business Administration, Slane College of Communications and Fine Arts, College of Education and Health Sciences, College of Engineering and Technology, and Liberal Arts and Sciences. Clearly, size does make a difference."

## SELECTIVITY

| | |
|---|---|
| Admissions Rating | 77 |
| # of applicants | 5,506 |
| % of applicants accepted | 67 |
| % of acceptees attending | 30 |
| # accepting a place on wait list | 132 |
| % admitted from wait list | 33 |

### FRESHMAN PROFILE

| | |
|---|---|
| Range SAT Verbal | 540-650 |
| Average SAT Verbal | 597 |
| Range SAT Math | 550-670 |
| Average SAT Math | 610 |
| Range ACT Composite | 23-29 |
| Average ACT Composite | 25 |
| Minimum TOEFL | 500 |
| % graduated top 10% of class | 33 |
| % graduated top 25% of class | 68 |
| % graduated top 50% of class | 93 |

### DEADLINES

| | |
|---|---|
| Priority admission | 3/1 |
| Regular admission | rolling |
| Nonfall registration? | yes |

### APPLICANTS ALSO LOOK AT
**AND OFTEN PREFER**
University of Illinois—Urbana-Champaign
University of Iowa
Marquette University
**AND SOMETIMES PREFER**
Illinois State University
Illinois Wesleyan University
Depaul University
Purdue University—West Lafayette
**AND RARELY PREFER**
Northern Illinois University
Eastern Illinois University
Western Culinary Institute

## FINANCIAL FACTS

| | |
|---|---|
| Financial Aid Rating | 84 |
| Tuition | $16,800 |
| Books and supplies | $500 |
| % frosh receiving aid | 63 |
| % undergrads receiving aid | 71 |
| Avg frosh grant | $9,279 |
| Avg frosh loan | $3,671 |

# BRANDEIS UNIVERSITY

415 SOUTH STREET, MS003, WALTHAM, MA 02454 • ADMISSIONS: 781-736-3500 • FAX: 781-736-3536

## CAMPUS LIFE

| | |
|---|---|
| Quality of Life Rating | 80 |
| Type of school | private |
| Environment | suburban |

### STUDENTS

| | |
|---|---|
| Total undergrad enrollment | 3,057 |
| % male/female | 44/56 |
| % from out of state | 75 |
| % from public high school | 70 |
| % live on campus | 84 |
| % African American | 3 |
| % Asian | 10 |
| % Caucasian | 75 |
| % Hispanic | 3 |
| % international | 6 |
| # of countries represented | 54 |

### SURVEY SAYS . . .
Student publications are popular
Political activism is hot
Campus feels safe
Students are happy
Lots of classroom discussion
Students don't like Waltham, MA
No one watches intercollegiate sports
Students are cliquish
Very small frat/sorority scene
Very little drug use

## ACADEMICS

| | |
|---|---|
| Academic Rating | 83 |
| Calendar | semester |
| Student/faculty ratio | 8:1 |
| Profs interesting rating | 94 |
| Profs accessible rating | 97 |
| % profs teaching UG courses | 100 |
| Avg reg class size | 10-19 students |

### MOST POPULAR MAJORS
Biology/biological sciences
Economics
Political science and government

## STUDENTS SPEAK OUT

### Academics
Students who choose Brandeis expect both university-caliber facilities and a small-college experience. For the most part, they feel they get what they came for. "I love the fact that my school feels like a college, yet has so many resources," writes one undergrad. Muses another, "The school is large enough that it isn't stifling, but small enough that it is homey." Only a few complain that "Brandeis tries to be both a small liberal arts school and a research university. I think in trying to be both it succeeds at neither." Typical of a progressive university, "Brandeis has a continued commitment to improving the school. It is constantly reinventing itself." Students warn that "academics are tough and there's not much getting around it. Especially for pre-meds (computer science and biology students also complain of ultra-heavy workloads), things can get really stressful at times. However, the professors are very accessible and the advising, both peer and academic, is great." Economics, English, life sciences, theater arts, and Near Eastern and Jewish studies ("One of the best departments in the country!" raves one student) are among the many excellent majors here. Brandeis's core curriculum (math, science, humanities, and foreign language), which takes at least two semesters to complete, "makes sure we get a broad-based education." Students say the "wonderful professors" are "some of the biggest characters I've ever met" and are "genuinely concerned with the academic interests of their students." The administration "keeps the school running quite well, but they seem out of touch with the students."

### Life
Brandeis has long been known as a low-key campus, but things are gradually changing. "Social life at Brandeis has slowly been improving since my freshman year," reports one senior. Popular happenings include "the fall weekend, called 'Louie, Louie,' and the spring weekend, 'Bronstein,' " as well as the "The Less You Wear, the Less You Pay" dance, which students deem "very entertaining." Also, "volunteer groups are very popular here and so are student-run theater and a cappella groups," and "the opportunities to join clubs and associations are terrific." Fraternity members say that, though frats are underground, they "try to remain active [even though] the administration does a pretty good job of suppressing our existence and badmouthing us to each year's incoming freshmen." Despite all these options, though, many students still choose to seek entertainment off campus. "Brandeis students tend to fall into two groups: on- and off-campus socializers," points out one undergrad. "Some spend all their time on campus doing various activities and seem to forget about the outside world. Others spend all their time in town (Waltham) or in Boston, stepping foot on campus only for class." An on-campus commuter rail takes students into downtown Boston in a scant half hour. Boston has "so much to offer," but "most things tend to close early."

### Student Body
Because Jewish students make up about half the population here, "Brandeis has a reputation for being a solely Jewish school, but in the two months I've been here I've found an amazing[ly diverse] group of friends, and everyone is more than willing to talk about their differences and explain their beliefs. That's one of the main things I love about this place: the lack of intolerance." Efforts to create a more diverse student body appear to be working. Explains one undergrad, "This place may have a 'Jew U' feel, but it's weakening as the student body diversifies . . . it's not the shtetl it used to be." Politically, "Brandeis is for people who are leaning to the left." Students "are politically active and working for social justice and awareness. It's an amazing place to be when we rally for recycling, GLBT issues, abortion rights, whatever." They also "tend to be highly opinionated . . . and passionate about causes." Don't expect the sports teams to win any major championships, though, since "everyone here is someone in your high school PE class that was completely ostracized."

# BRANDEIS UNIVERSITY

Financial Aid: 781-736-3700 • E-mail: sendinfo@brandeis.edu • Website: www.brandeis.edu

## ADMISSIONS
*Very important factors considered include:* class rank, secondary school record. *Important factors considered include:* character/personal qualities, essays, extracurricular activities, recommendations, standardized test scores, talent/ability, volunteer work, work experience. *Other factors considered include:* alumni/ae relation, interview, minority status. TOEFL required of all international applicants. High school diploma or GED is required. *High school units required/recommended:* 16 total recommended; 4 English recommended, 3 math recommended, 1 science recommended, 1 science lab recommended, 3 foreign language recommended, 1 history recommended, 4 elective recommended.

## The Inside Word
While the university has a reputation for quality, the low yield of admits who actually choose to attend Brandeis results in a higher acceptance rate than one might expect. Weak students will still find it difficult to gain admission. The option of submitting ACT scores instead of SAT and SAT II: Subject Test scores should be the hands-down choice of any candidate who doesn't have to take SAT IIs for any other reason.

## FINANCIAL AID
*Students should submit:* FAFSA, CSS/Financial Aid PROFILE, noncustodial (divorced/separated) parent's statement, business/farm supplement. No deadline for regular filing. The Princeton Review suggests that all financial aid forms be submitted as soon as possible after January 1. *Need-based scholarships/grants offered:* Pell, SEOG, state scholarships/grants, the school's own gift aid. *Loan aid offered:* Direct Subsidized Stafford, Direct Unsubsidized Stafford, Direct PLUS, Federal Perkins, state loans, college/university loans from institutional funds. Federal Work-Study Program available. Institutional employment available. Applicants will be notified of awards on or about April 1. Off-campus job opportunities are excellent.

## FROM THE ADMISSIONS OFFICE
"Brandeis's top-ranked faculty focuses on teaching undergraduates and is accessible to students during classes, during office hours, and even at home. Students become involved in cutting-edge faculty research at the Volen Center for Complex Systems—studying the brain's cognitive process—and throughout the university. Brandeis has an ideal location on the commuter rail nine miles west of Boston; state-of-the-art sports facilities; and internships that complement interests in law, medicine, government, finance, the media, public service, and the arts. Brandeis offers broad renewable need-based financial aid and scholarships for domestic and international students."

### SELECTIVITY

| | |
|---|---|
| Admissions Rating | 91 |
| # of applicants | 6,080 |
| % of applicants accepted | 42 |
| % of acceptees attending | 33 |
| # accepting a place on wait list | 165 |
| % admitted from wait list | 33 |
| # of early decision applicants | 297 |
| % accepted early decision | 72 |

### FRESHMAN PROFILE
| | |
|---|---|
| Range SAT Verbal | 627-710 |
| Average SAT Verbal | 660 |
| Range SAT Math | 630-710 |
| Average SAT Math | 670 |
| Minimum TOEFL | 600 |
| Average HS GPA | 3.8 |
| % graduated top 10% of class | 62 |
| % graduated top 25% of class | 93 |
| % graduated top 50% of class | 100 |

### DEADLINES
| | |
|---|---|
| Early decision | 1/1 |
| Early decision notification | 2/1 |
| Regular admission | 1/15 |
| Regular notification | 4/1 |
| Nonfall registration? | yes |

### APPLICANTS ALSO LOOK AT
**AND OFTEN PREFER**
Cornell U, Columbia
U of Pennsylvania
Brown
Dartmouth
**AND SOMETIMES PREFER**
NYU
Tufts
Washington U in St. Louis
**AND RARELY PREFER**
Binghamton U
Boston U
Boston College

### FINANCIAL FACTS

| | |
|---|---|
| Financial Aid Rating | 85 |
| Tuition | $27,345 |
| Room and board | $7,849 |
| Books and supplies | $700 |
| Required fees | $820 |
| % frosh receiving aid | 50 |
| % undergrads receiving aid | 50 |
| Avg frosh grant | $15,012 |
| Avg frosh loan | $4,647 |

# BRIGHAM YOUNG UNIVERSITY

A-183 ASB, PROVO, UT 84602-1110 • ADMISSIONS: 801-378-2507 • FAX: 801-378-4264

## CAMPUS LIFE

| Quality of Life Rating | 96 |
|---|---|
| Type of school | private |
| Affiliation | Church of Jesus Christ of Latter-day Saints |
| Environment | urban |

### STUDENTS

| Total undergrad enrollment | 29,379 |
|---|---|
| % male/female | 50/50 |
| % from out of state | 70 |
| % live on campus | 20 |
| % Asian | 3 |
| % Caucasian | 91 |
| % Hispanic | 3 |
| % international | 3 |
| # of countries represented | 127 |

### SURVEY SAYS . . .
Students are very religious
Students get along with local community
Lots of conservatives
Everyone loves the Cougars
Great library
Very little beer drinking
Very little drug use
Very little hard liquor
Diversity lacking on campus

## ACADEMICS

| Academic Rating | 86 |
|---|---|
| Calendar | other |
| Student/faculty ratio | 18:1 |
| Profs interesting rating | 94 |
| Profs accessible rating | 87 |
| % profs teaching UG courses | 95 |
| % classes taught by TAs | 12 |
| Avg lab size | 20-29 students |
| Avg reg class size | 10-19 students |

### MOST POPULAR MAJORS
Business administration/management
Accounting
Teacher education and professional development, specific subject areas

## STUDENTS SPEAK OUT

### Academics
One can't separate Brigham Young University and the Church of Jesus Christ of Latter-day Saints, the school's sponsoring faith. From the student body to the "stringent" honor code (which regulates not only academic behavior but also dress, hair length, diet, and sexual activity) to the heavy religious studies requirement, BYU serves the needs of America's Mormon community first and foremost. For those within the religious community, BYU provides a comfortable environment in which to receive a reputable education at a discount price. Those few non-Mormons we heard from in our survey, on the other hand, suggest that outsiders considering the school strongly consider their ability to live within Mormonism's strict requirements. Notes one student, "People choose to come here; in a way, we are pledging to accept elite standards. I like that—it sets you apart and even testifies of your integrity." Students happily report that "professors are excellent. The classes may be bigger than a normal campus, but with 30,000 students, what do you expect?" Similarly, the "efficient and fair" administration is, according to one undergrad, "very available to the students and involved in school events. The degree of their accessibility has really amazed me at a school of almost 30,000." Some complain, however, that the university's "resources are spread incredibly thin among the 35,000 [sic] students (which is about 25,000 more than can fit)."

### Life
"Life at BYU is a lot different than a typical university life," explains a typical undergrad. "Students here do not participate in activities that are in contrast with our religious beliefs. For fun we will go to dances and parties that have a healthy environment (no drugs, alcohol, or sexual activities). We spend a lot of time in nature, hiking and such. We play games and go to the movies. It's a little different than most colleges, but that's why I decided to go to BYU." Students do find ways to have fun; notes one, "We do all the crazy things that other people do when they're drunk. The only difference is that we are sober." For various, mostly religious reasons, "marriage is on everyone's mind here." Writes one student, "People are into dating, but more than one date often constitutes a serious relationship. This gets particularly annoying when one is pursuing a friendship and doesn't want a serious relationship." Hometown Provo "is large enough to have many opportunities for entertainment but small enough that a friendly atmosphere persists." When free time presents itself, students are content to "get together with friends, watch movies, go dancing, or attend sports. I guess the atmosphere here at BYU is very wholesome."

### Student Body
Students report that BYU is "a very undiverse place: most people are white, middle-class Mormons . . . . With people from all over the United States, though, it's interesting to find what differences we have even without the more obvious ones, like race or sexual orientation." Students describe each other as "upstanding" and "extremely friendly"; writes one, "One of the main reasons that I chose to come to BYU was for the students. Nowhere else in the world is there such an amazing group of people that hold such high moral standards. People smile, say hello, hold the door open for each other, and are generally very respectful of one another." Some, however, warn that "the nonconformist will find a dull social life with difficulty finding someone that will be their friend, regardless of who they are or what they believe."

# BRIGHAM YOUNG UNIVERSITY

FINANCIAL AID: 801-378-4104 • E-MAIL: ADMISSIONS@BYU.EDU • WEBSITE: WWW.BYU.EDU

## ADMISSIONS

*Very important factors considered include:* character/personal qualities, interview, religious affiliation/commitment, secondary school record, standardized test scores. *Important factors considered include:* essays, extracurricular activities, minority status, recommendations, volunteer work. *Other factors considered include:* talent/ability, work experience. ACT required. TOEFL required of all international applicants. High school diploma or GED is required. *High school units required/recommended:* 4 English required, 3 math required, 4 math recommended, 2 science required, 3 science recommended, 2 science lab required, 3 science lab recommended, 2 foreign language required, 4 foreign language recommended, 2 history required.

### The Inside Word

Despite the high acceptance rate, this is a rigorous application process that will quickly and efficiently eliminate candidates who make a poor match. Most eliminate themselves by not applying to begin with, as the matchmaking places the greatest weight on the ideological fit.

## FINANCIAL AID

*Students should submit:* FAFSA, institution's own financial aid form. No deadline for regular filing. The Princeton Review suggests that all financial aid forms be submitted as soon as possible after January 1. *Need-based scholarships/grants offered:* Pell, state scholarships/grants, private scholarships, the school's own gift aid. *Loan aid offered:* FFEL Subsidized Stafford, FFEL Unsubsidized Stafford, FFEL PLUS, college/university loans from institutional funds. Federal Work-Study Program available. Institutional employment available. Applicants will be notified of awards on a rolling basis beginning on or about April 1. Off-campus job opportunities are good.

## FROM THE ADMISSIONS OFFICE

"The mission of Brigham Young University—founded, supported, and guided by the Church of Jesus Christ of Latter-day Saints—is to assist individuals in their quest for perfection and eternal life. That assistance should provide a period of intensive learning in a stimulating setting where a commitment to excellence is expected and the full realization of human potential is pursued. All instruction, programs, and services at BYU, including a wide variety of extracurricular experiences, should make their own contribution toward the balanced development of the total person. Such a broadly prepared individual will not only be capable of meeting personal challenge and change but will also bring strength to others in the tasks of home and family life, social relationships, civic duty, and service to mankind."

## SELECTIVITY

| | |
|---|---|
| Admissions Rating | 88 |
| # of applicants | 7,329 |
| % of applicants accepted | 73 |
| % of acceptees attending | 79 |

### FRESHMAN PROFILE

| | |
|---|---|
| Range SAT Verbal | 540-650 |
| Range SAT Math | 560-670 |
| Range ACT Composite | 25-30 |
| Average ACT Composite | 27 |
| Minimum TOEFL | 500 |
| Average HS GPA | 3.8 |
| % graduated top 10% of class | 54 |
| % graduated top 25% of class | 86 |
| % graduated top 50% of class | 99 |

### DEADLINES

| | |
|---|---|
| Regular admission | 2/15 |
| Nonfall registration? | yes |

### APPLICANTS ALSO LOOK AT AND OFTEN PREFER
U of Utah
Utah State
Utah Valley State College

### AND RARELY PREFER
Boston U
UT Austin
UC Berkeley
U of Michigan at Ann Arbor
U of Washington

## FINANCIAL FACTS

| | |
|---|---|
| Financial Aid Rating | 90 |
| Tuition | $3,150 |
| Room and board | $4,874 |
| Books and supplies | $1,110 |
| % frosh receiving aid | 5 |
| % undergrads receiving aid | 31 |
| Avg frosh grant | $2,803 |
| Avg frosh loan | $1,082 |

# BROWN UNIVERSITY

Box 1876, 45 Prospect Street, Providence, RI 02912 • Admissions: 401-863-2378 • Fax: 401-863-9300

## CAMPUS LIFE

| | |
|---|---|
| Quality of Life Rating | 87 |
| Type of school | private |
| Environment | urban |

### STUDENTS
| | |
|---|---|
| Total undergrad enrollment | 6,030 |
| % male/female | 45/55 |
| % from out of state | 96 |
| % from public high school | 60 |
| % live on campus | 85 |
| % in (# of) fraternities | 15 (10) |
| % in (# of) sororities | 5 (3) |
| % African American | 6 |
| % Asian | 15 |
| % Caucasian | 53 |
| % Hispanic | 7 |
| % international | 6 |
| # of countries represented | 72 |

### SURVEY SAYS . . .
Political activism is hot
Students aren't religious
Great off-campus food
Ethnic diversity on campus
Intercollegiate sports unpopular or nonexistent

## ACADEMICS

| | |
|---|---|
| Academic Rating | 96 |
| Calendar | semester |
| Student/faculty ratio | 8:1 |
| Profs interesting rating | 94 |
| Profs accessible rating | 90 |
| % profs teaching UG courses | 100 |
| % classes taught by TAs | 13 |

### MOST POPULAR MAJORS
Biology/biological sciences
International relations and affairs
History

## STUDENTS SPEAK OUT

### Academics
Brown's famous "open curriculum," which has no requirements outside of one's major, is "more rewarding for those students who know exactly what they wish to pursue academically." Those lacking the "incredible maturity" it takes "to balance all your courses and choose the right ones" can languish if they're used to rigid structure. Some students warn that good advisement is not always a given. The university, however, prides itself on "helping undergrads achieve their utmost potential." The emphasis is on quality of instruction rather than quantity, with small seminars available from day one of freshman year. Writes one academic junkie, "I go to class because I couldn't deprive myself of listening to what my professors have to say." Students also gush about their "godsend" of a new president, Ruth Simmons, who "simply rocks." Other administrators "understand students and are extremely tolerant of us." They "trust us to do what we want." Complaints primarily involve problems related to Brown's relatively small endowment, citing in particular poor financial aid packages. Students urge those in power to "go need-blind ASAP" in admissions (which the university approved in February 2002). Nonetheless, this "do-it-yourself" experience makes Brown "an Ivy League education without the pretense."

### Life
"If you understand how this school is both an old, stuffy Ivy League college for boring academics and a laid-back place for chill folk, then you understand Brown," explains one undergraduate. Brown maintains its reputation as a "touchy-feely kind of place" with an "emphasis on individuality and individual choice." Suggests one student, "Think theater, poetry slams, literature." Students beg for some improved facilities for these activities, though, including a concert hall, more meeting space, and easier access to music and sports equipment. In typical departure from the norm, three coed fraternities (two of which are literary in focus) are standard-bearers of the social life at Brown. With "everyone and their dog in an a cappella group," students still find time for politics, being "generally eager to protest anything and everything." Amid this PC climate, students sometimes feel that "debates and conversation are many times stilted by a pathological fear of offending anyone." The campus is "extremely connected to the community" of Providence, where the "weather sucks eight of the nine months you are here." For those with overcoats but without cars, however, inexpensive trolley service runs through the town.

### Student Body
Generally, students at Brown refuse to generalize when it comes to their peers, maintaining that "there is no typical Brown student—each individual here is truly unique." Considered a "Birkenstock-wearing, crunchy, granola-eating, nonflushing, tree-hugging crowd" by the outside world, many students contend that in reality "it's much more diverse than that." The population comprises "bright freaks" who are often "book worms with not a lot of social skills" and "rich snobs with little cell phones and fancy clothes." Ideologically, "there is no emphasis to conform to a certain stereotype, and we're quite accepting of all viewpoints." Some students would amend that evaluation by stating that the student body is indeed quite accepting—of liberal viewpoints: "Do not confuse the openness of the curriculum with immediate acceptance of all ideas," writes one undergrad. Though there is "more interracial and interclass mixing than in the 'real world,' " the "liberal and agnostic" majority sometimes shows disdain for "the following categories: varsity athletes, Christians, conservatives, frat boys, rich students, midwesterners, or southerners." But in an "activist" place where "everyone wants to change the world," broader acceptance may be the next step toward "unparalleled social consciousness."

# BROWN UNIVERSITY

FINANCIAL AID: 401-863-2721 • E-MAIL: ADMISSION_UNDERGRADUATE@BROWN.EDU • WEBSITE: WWW.BROWN.EDU

## ADMISSIONS

*Very important factors considered include:* character/personal qualities, secondary school record, talent/ability. *Important factors considered include:* class rank, essays, extracurricular activities, recommendations. *Other factors considered include:* alumni/ae relation, geographical residence, interview, minority status, standardized test scores, state residency, volunteer work, work experience. TOEFL required of all international applicants. High school diploma is required and GED is not accepted. *High school units required/recommended:* 16 total required; 19 total recommended; 4 English required, 3 math required, 4 math recommended, 3 science required, 4 science recommended, 2 science lab required, 3 science lab recommended, 3 foreign language required, 4 foreign language recommended, 2 history required, 1 elective required.

### The Inside Word

The cream of just about every crop applies to Brown. Gaining admission requires more than just a superior academic profile from high school. Some candidates, such as the sons and daughters of Brown graduates (who are admitted at virtually double the usual acceptance rate), have a better chance for admission than most others. Minority students benefit from some courtship, particularly once admitted. Ivies like to share the wealth and distribute offers of admission across a wide range of constituencies. Candidates from states that are overrepresented in the applicant pool, such as New York, have to be particularly distinguished in order to have the best chance at admission. So do those who attend high schools with many seniors applying to Brown, as it is rare for more than two or three students from any one school to be offered admission.

## FINANCIAL AID

*Students should submit:* FAFSA, CSS/Financial Aid PROFILE, noncustodial (divorced/separated) parent's statement, business/farm supplement. Regular filing deadline is February 1. The Princeton Review suggests that all financial aid forms be submitted as soon as possible after January 1. *Need-based scholarships/grants offered:* Pell, SEOG, state scholarships/grants, private scholarships, the school's own gift aid. *Loan aid offered:* Direct Subsidized Stafford, Direct Unsubsidized Stafford, Direct PLUS, Federal Perkins, state loans, college/university loans from institutional funds. Federal Work-Study Program available. Institutional employment available. Applicants will be notified of awards on or about April 1. Off-campus job opportunities are excellent.

## FROM THE ADMISSIONS OFFICE

"It is our pleasure to introduce you to a unique and wonderful learning place: Brown University. Brown was founded in 1764 and is a private, coeducational, Ivy League university in which the intellectual development of undergraduate students is fostered by a dedicated faculty on a traditional New England campus."

### SELECTIVITY

| | |
|---|---|
| Admissions Rating | 99 |
| # of applicants | 14,612 |
| % of applicants accepted | 17 |
| % of acceptees attending | 59 |
| # accepting a place on wait list | 400 |
| # of early decision applicants | 1,918 |
| % accepted early decision | 27 |

### FRESHMAN PROFILE

| | |
|---|---|
| Range SAT Verbal | 640-750 |
| Average SAT Verbal | 690 |
| Range SAT Math | 650-750 |
| Average SAT Math | 700 |
| Range ACT Composite | 26-32 |
| Average ACT Composite | 29 |
| Minimum TOEFL | 600 |
| % graduated top 10% of class | 87 |
| % graduated top 25% of class | 97 |
| % graduated top 50% of class | 100 |

### DEADLINES

| | |
|---|---|
| Early decision | 11/1 |
| Early decision notification | 12/15 |
| Regular admission | 1/1 |
| Regular notification | 4/1 |

### APPLICANTS ALSO LOOK AT AND OFTEN PREFER
Harvard
Princeton
Yale
Stanford

### AND SOMETIMES PREFER
Swarthmore
Amherst
Williams, Smith

### AND RARELY PREFER
Tufts
Georgetown U.
Bowdoin, Oberlin

### FINANCIAL FACTS

| | |
|---|---|
| Financial Aid Rating | 79 |
| Tuition | $27,856 |
| Room and board | $7,876 |
| Books and supplies | $960 |
| Required fees | $851 |
| % frosh receiving aid | 41 |
| % undergrads receiving aid | 40 |
| Avg frosh grant | $20,800 |
| Avg frosh loan | $2,700 |

# BRYANT COLLEGE

1150 DOUGLAS PIKE, SMITHFIELD, RI 02917 • ADMISSIONS: 401-232-6100 • FAX: 401-232-6741

## CAMPUS LIFE

| | |
|---|---|
| Quality of Life Rating | 86 |
| Type of school | private |
| Environment | suburban |

### STUDENTS

| | |
|---|---|
| Total undergrad enrollment | 2,912 |
| % male/female | 60/40 |
| % from out of state | 74 |
| % from public high school | 78 |
| % live on campus | 75 |
| % in (# of) fraternities | 8 (6) |
| % in (# of) sororities | 8 (3) |
| % African American | 3 |
| % Asian | 2 |
| % Caucasian | 86 |
| % Hispanic | 3 |
| % international | 4 |
| # of countries represented | 37 |

### SURVEY SAYS . . .
Lots of classroom discussion
Great computer facilities
Great library
Lots of beer drinking
Hard liquor is popular
(Almost) no one listens to college radio
Theater is unpopular
Student government is unpopular

## ACADEMICS

| | |
|---|---|
| Academic Rating | 79 |
| Calendar | semester |
| Student/faculty ratio | 16:1 |
| Profs interesting rating | 82 |
| Profs accessible rating | 86 |
| % profs teaching UG courses | 100 |
| Avg lab size | 20-29 students |
| Avg reg class size | 30-39 students |

### MOST POPULAR MAJORS
Business administration/management
Finance and financial management services
Marketing

## STUDENTS SPEAK OUT

### Academics
Bryant College's curriculum allows its undergraduates to have their "whole world . . . incorporated into business." Practical application is emphasized, with classes "always relating back to something you're going to need to know in real life." Professors are also stores of pragmatic knowledge: "Apart from teaching, they bring an overwhelming amount of experience on the subject matter we are learning since many of them have other jobs" in the real world. Some students feel the business focus is too tight, though. Writes one, "I realize this is a business school, but they should include some more liberal-arts-oriented courses. As a marketing major, I would like to take an art class or something that promotes creativity." Bryant prides itself on hooking its students up with plum jobs after they graduate. First off, "the career services office is phenomenal" in that they forge "really good connections to local companies that provide internships and possible future jobs." Students also enjoy "excellent networking" and an "extensive alumni network that supports the school and hires its graduates." As far as administrators go, "meeting with them with or without an appointment is never a problem," and "they are always asking students how they can better the school." Overall, Bryant students think "it's too bad that the school does not get the recognition it deserves" because it's "more rigorous academically than the numbers seem to show."

### Life
Tucked away on 392 acres outside of Providence, students agree that "you couldn't get a better location." The sense of safety is high, with one student commenting, "I have always liked how we have a one-entrance, guarded campus." In terms of social life, another undergrad explains, "We're out in the woods, so if you aren't clubbing in Providence, you are drinking or hooking up on campus." Reportedly, "the campus is a lot of fun whether you drink or not." The majority of students, however, count themselves among the nonteetotalers. School-sponsored activities are available but considered "childish" and are thus "not readily attended." Student clubs and organizations do exist, and students readily participate in sports, taking advantage of some of the "best athletic facilities in New England." One student writes, "Intramural sports always have a large number of teams, no matter what sport, and the gyms are in constant use, whether for varsity sports or just pick-up games." One of the only complaints is that the school "needs to work on our unity and school pride."

### Student Body
If you look at the approximately 3,000 undergrads here long enough, according to a lot of its constituents, you'll see that "there is definitely a 'Bryant type,'" since "everyone looks the same and does the same thing." One student writes, "I like the people I go to school with because they are a lot like me," meaning that the "majority are from New England" and most share a "sense of professionalism." Students that deviate from this description tend to stick together. "White, minority, and international students predominantly associate with themselves." One can break down social circles even further: "Greeks, sports teams, and multicultural students don't always hang out together." Despite this separation, one student reports, "As an openly gay male on a relatively straight campus, I have had no real incidents of discrimination." Another points out, "I suppose it is just a reflection of the student body being predominantly business students who are focused on money, but I feel as though many seem apathetic to greater social causes in the world." The upside of the homogeneity is a sense of "cohesiveness" and "students and alumni that are very loyal."

100 ■ THE BEST 351 COLLEGES

# BRYANT COLLEGE

FINANCIAL AID: 401-232-6020 • E-MAIL: ADMISSIONS@BRYANT.EDU • WEBSITE: WWW.BRYANT.EDU

## ADMISSIONS

*Very important factors considered include:* class rank, essays, recommendations, secondary school record, standardized test scores. *Important factors considered include:* alumni/ae relation, character/personal qualities, extracurricular activities, interview, talent/ability. *Other factors considered include:* geographical residence, minority status, volunteer work, work experience. SAT I or ACT required. TOEFL required of all international applicants. High school diploma or GED is required. *High school units required/recommended:* 16 total required; 4 English required, 4 years of math required, 3 science recommended, 2 lab sciences required, 2 foreign language required.

### The Inside Word

If you're a solid student you should meet little trouble getting into Bryant. The college's admissions effort has brought in qualified applicants from across the country, but the heaviest draw remains from New England. Students attending Bryant will receive a solid business education as well as precious connections in the corporate worlds of Providence and Boston.

## FINANCIAL AID

*Students should submit:* FAFSA, institution's own financial aid form. Regular filing deadline is February 15. The Princeton Review suggests that all financial aid forms be submitted as soon as possible after January 1. *Need-based scholarships/grants offered:* Pell, SEOG, state scholarships/grants, private scholarships, the school's own gift aid. *Loan aid offered:* Direct Subsidized Stafford, Direct Unsubsidized Stafford, FFEL PLUS, Federal Perkins. Federal Work-Study Program available. Institutional employment available. Applicants will be notified of awards on or about March 15. Off-campus job opportunities are good.

## FROM THE ADMISSIONS OFFICE

"Bryant College is a student-centered learning community that gives students the tools and resources they need to acquire knowledge, develop character, and achieve success—as they define it. In addition to a first-class faculty, state-of-the-art facilities, and advanced technology, Bryant offers stimulating classroom dynamics; internships at more than 200 companies; 60 student clubs and organizations; varsity, intramural, and club sports for men and women; and opportunities for community service.

"Bryant is the College of choice for individuals seeking the best combination of a business and liberal arts education. Bryant's rigorous academic standards have been recognized and accredited by AACSB International—The Association to Advance Collegiate Schools of Business. Our academic programs blend the practical with the theoretical; with degrees in business administration, applied psychology, communication, information technology, and liberal studies, Bryant offers academic studies for diverse interests and people.

"Technology is a fundamental component of the learning process at Bryant. Every entering freshman receives an IBM laptop to use through his or her first two years at Bryant, and is then issued a new laptop in the junior year, which can be purchased upon graduation.

"Our new Wellness Center employs a full-time wellness coordinator/health educator to help students keep a sense of balance throughout their educational experience.

"Bryant is situated on 392 acres of beautiful New England countryside and is only 15 minutes from Providence, one hour from Boston, and three hours from New York City and all of the cultural and social amenities of these major metropolitan areas."

## SELECTIVITY

★ ★ ☆ ☆

| | |
|---|---|
| Admissions Rating | 75 |
| # of applicants | 2,811 |
| % of applicants accepted | 74 |
| % of acceptees attending | 36 |
| # accepting a place on wait list | 283 |
| % admitted from wait list | 23 |
| # of early decision applicants | 14 |
| % accepted early decision | 93 |

### FRESHMAN PROFILE

| | |
|---|---|
| Range SAT Verbal | 480-560 |
| Average SAT Verbal | 522 |
| Range SAT Math | 510-610 |
| Average SAT Math | 557 |
| Range ACT Composite | 19-24 |
| Average ACT Composite | 22 |
| Minimum TOEFL | 550 |
| Average HS GPA | 3.0 |
| % graduated top 10% of class | 9 |
| % graduated top 25% of class | 36 |
| % graduated top 50% of class | 80 |

### DEADLINES

| | |
|---|---|
| Early decision & early action | 11/15 |
| Early decision notification | 12/15 |
| Regular admission | 2/15 |
| Regular notification | 3/15 |
| Nonfall registration? | yes |

### APPLICANTS ALSO LOOK AT AND OFTEN PREFER
Bentley College
Quinnipiac
Stonehill

### AND SOMETIMES PREFER
UMass at Amherst
Babson
St. Anselm

### AND RARELY PREFER
U of Rhode Island
U of Connecticut
Northeastern
Assumption, Roger Williams

## FINANCIAL FACTS

★ ★ ★ ☆

| | |
|---|---|
| Financial Aid Rating | 86 |
| Tuition | $21,160 |
| Room and board | $8,546 |
| Books and supplies | $900 |
| % frosh receiving aid | 65 |
| % undergrads receiving aid | 70 |
| Avg frosh grant | $7,774 |
| Avg frosh loan | $3,914 |

# BRYN MAWR COLLEGE

101 NORTH MERION AVENUE, BRYN MAWR, PA 19010-2899 • ADMISSIONS: 610-526-5152 • FAX: 610-526-7471

## CAMPUS LIFE

| Quality of Life Rating | 87 |
|---|---|
| Type of school | private |
| Environment | suburban |

### STUDENTS
| | |
|---|---|
| Total undergrad enrollment | 1,322 |
| % male/female | 2/98 |
| % from out of state | 80 |
| % from public high school | 56 |
| % live on campus | 98 |
| % African American | 4 |
| % Asian | 14 |
| % Caucasian | 66 |
| % Hispanic | 3 |
| % international | 8 |
| # of countries represented | 45 |

### SURVEY SAYS . . .
Theater is hot
No one cheats
Great food on campus
Dorms are like palaces
Campus feels safe
Very little beer drinking
No one plays intramural sports
Very little hard liquor
Intercollegiate sports unpopular or nonexistent

## ACADEMICS

| Academic Rating | 96 |
|---|---|
| Calendar | semester |
| Student/faculty ratio | 8:1 |
| Profs interesting rating | 96 |
| Profs accessible rating | 98 |
| % profs teaching UG courses | 100 |
| Avg lab size | 20-29 students |
| Avg reg class size | 10-19 students |

### MOST POPULAR MAJORS
English language and literature
Mathematics
Biology/biological sciences

## STUDENTS SPEAK OUT

### Academics
You'll find few colleges where more than a handful of overly exuberant students would refer to their professors as "gods and goddesses," but such overwhelming praise is precisely the case at Bryn Mawr. A small and very elite woman's college located just outside of Philadelphia, Bryn Mawr is known not only for challenging and difficult academics, but also for its commitment to its approximately 1,300 undergraduates. "The courses that are offered are extremely challenging and interesting," declares one student. And "the professors are dedicated individuals who always make themselves available." It's not just easy access, though, that makes the faculty and the academics here so inspiring for so many students. Perhaps more than anything else it's the level of instruction gauged to each student's abilities. As one student notes, "The profs at Bryn Mawr take everything to the next level. If you think you can get a B, they don't give you one until you have an A." And professors trust their students. The revered honor code allows undergraduates the freedom to schedule their own exams and ensure the integrity of their work. The college's close proximity to three other excellent schools (Haverford, Swarthmore, and the University of Pennsylvania) also provides students with the opportunity to enroll in classes not offered at Bryn Mawr. New freshmen should come prepared because "there is A LOT of work," and the competition and debates in class are intense, leaving little room for students who aren't interested in taking class seriously.

### Life
Bryn Mawr is known as a "quiet campus," where everyone is too busy studying or thinking about studying to go out and party. Students are not, however, hermits cloistered in their ivory towers. They do have a host of odd traditions like "lantern night" where students carry lanterns, don robes, and have a sing-along in the campus cloister. Sound strange? As any student here will tell you, you have to experience it to understand it. When the students at Bryn Mawr aren't walking around in the dark and singing, however, they are pretty much having a good time. Campus groups play a large and active role here, and freshman customs groups are a vital way of forming lifelong bonds between students. The city of Philadelphia is only a train ride away and offers a great and active getaway from the campus, as do the neighboring campuses of Haverford and U Penn. Most students wouldn't mind seeing campus life given a B-12 injection, but fortunately, as one student notes, "I think the campus activities have improved a lot in my time here."

### Student Body
Bryn Mawr may enroll only women, but it's definitely not lacking in diversity. The students at Bryn Mawr come from varied backgrounds, and if they share any common traits, it's probably a genuine "warmth," "openness," and liberalism. Many of the students here are just as in love with their peers as they are with their college and often describe the tenor of their campus as that of "one big sorority." They consider one another "brilliant," and for good reason, since almost all of them aren't afraid to roll up their sleeves and work out the challenges their professors lay before them (there's a reason why they call themselves "Mawrtyrs"). The women of Bryn Mawr may be open-minded and liberal and could care less about your sexuality or race, but conservative politics are a different story, and as one student notes, some of her classmates "are extremely close-minded to any views (particularly conservative or religious ones) and deride anything not related to the typical 'liberal' collegiate view."

102 ■ THE BEST 351 COLLEGES

# BRYN MAWR COLLEGE

FINANCIAL AID: 610-526-5245 • E-MAIL: ADMISSIONS@BRYNMAWR.EDU • WEBSITE: WWW.BRYNMAWR.EDU

## ADMISSIONS

*Very important factors considered include:* essays, recommendations, secondary school record. *Important factors considered include:* character/personal qualities, extracurricular activities. *Other factors considered include:* class rank, interview, standardized test scores, talent/ability, volunteer work, work experience. TOEFL required of all international applicants. High school diploma or GED is required. *High school units required/recommended:* 16 total recommended; 4 English recommended, 3 math recommended, 2 science recommended, 1 science lab recommended, 3 foreign language recommended, 2 social studies recommended, 2 history recommended, 2 elective required.

## The Inside Word

Do not be deceived by Bryn Mawr's admit rate; its student body is among the best in the nation academically. Outstanding preparation for graduate study draws an applicant pool that is well prepared and intellectually curious. The admissions committee includes eight faculty members and four seniors. Each applicant is reviewed by four readers, including at least one faculty member and one student.

## FINANCIAL AID

*Students should submit:* FAFSA, CSS/Financial Aid PROFILE, noncustodial (divorced/separated) parent's statement, business/farm supplement. Regular filing deadline is January 15. The Princeton Review suggests that all financial aid forms be submitted as soon as possible after January 1. *Need-based scholarships/grants offered:* Pell, SEOG, state scholarships/grants, the school's own gift aid. *Loan aid offered:* FFEL Subsidized Stafford, FFEL Unsubsidized Stafford, FFEL PLUS, Federal Perkins, college/university loans from institutional funds. Federal Work-Study Program available. Institutional employment available. Applicants will be notified of awards on or about April 1. Off-campus job opportunities are good.

## FROM THE ADMISSIONS OFFICE

"One wouldn't ordinarily assume that a small institution could offer as diverse a range of opportunities as many large universities, or that a campus that looks like the English countryside could exist within 20 minutes of downtown Philadelphia, but Bryn Mawr is far from ordinary. Prepare to be surprised. Innovative, creative, and purposeful, the students at Bryn Mawr inspire their peers as much and as often as any faculty member. Spirited intellectual inquiry, a commitment to academic excellence, and a desire to impact the world in a meaningful way are the hallmarks of this community of equals. Students at Bryn Mawr learn by doing and lead by example. They take full advantage of all that Bryn Mawr has to offer, including internship opportunities, an active Alumnae Association, a lively Community Service office and a consortium of schools that includes Haverford, Swarthmore, and the University of Pennsylvania. Bryn Mawr's Student Government Association is the oldest in the country and students participate in every aspect of the College's decision-making process, serving as representatives to Admissions, The Honor Board, The Curriculum Committee, and even The Board of Trustees. Bryn Mawr is a demanding and caring place where both ideas and individuals matter."

### SELECTIVITY

| | |
|---|---:|
| Admissions Rating | 93 |
| # of applicants | 1,743 |
| % of applicants accepted | 50 |
| % of acceptees attending | 35 |
| # accepting a place on wait list | 163 |
| % admitted from wait list | 26 |
| # of early decision applicants | 157 |
| % accepted early decision | 62 |

### FRESHMAN PROFILE

| | |
|---|---:|
| Range SAT Verbal | 630-730 |
| Average SAT Verbal | 672 |
| Range SAT Math | 600-690 |
| Average SAT Math | 638 |
| Range ACT Composite | 26-30 |
| Average ACT Composite | 28 |
| Minimum TOEFL | 600 |
| % graduated top 10% of class | 57 |
| % graduated top 25% of class | 93 |
| % graduated top 50% of class | 100 |

### DEADLINES

| | |
|---|---:|
| Early decision | 11/15 |
| Early decision notification | 12/15 |
| Regular admission | 1/15 |
| Regular notification | 4/1 |

### APPLICANTS ALSO LOOK AT
**AND OFTEN PREFER**
Brown
U of Pennsylvania
Harvard
**AND SOMETIMES PREFER**
Wellesley
Swarthmore
Smith
Mount Holyoke
Haverford
Scripps
**AND RARELY PREFER**
Oberlin, Vassar

### FINANCIAL FACTS

| | |
|---|---:|
| Financial Aid Rating | 80 |
| Tuition | $25,550 |
| Room and board | $8,970 |
| Books and supplies | $1,450 |
| Required fees | $670 |
| % frosh receiving aid | 64 |
| % undergrads receiving aid | 59 |
| Avg frosh grant | $19,738 |
| Avg frosh loan | $2,815 |

# BUCKNELL UNIVERSITY

FREAS HALL, LEWISBURG, PA 17837 • ADMISSIONS: 570-577-1101 • FAX: 570-577-3538

## CAMPUS LIFE

★ ★ ★ ★

| | |
|---|---|
| Quality of Life Rating | 91 |
| Type of school | private |
| Environment | rural |

### STUDENTS

| | |
|---|---|
| Total undergrad enrollment | 3,440 |
| % male/female | 51/49 |
| % from out of state | 68 |
| % from public high school | 76 |
| % live on campus | 89 |
| % in (# of) fraternities | 41 (13) |
| % in (# of) sororities | 45 (7) |
| % African American | 3 |
| % Asian | 6 |
| % Caucasian | 87 |
| % Hispanic | 2 |
| % international | 2 |
| # of countries represented | 34 |

### SURVEY SAYS . . .
Frats and sororities dominate social scene
Great food on campus
Great library
Low cost of living
Diversity lacking on campus

## ACADEMICS

| | |
|---|---|
| Academic Rating | 91 |
| Calendar | semester |
| Student/faculty ratio | 12:1 |
| Profs interesting rating | 95 |
| Profs accessible rating | 99 |
| % profs teaching UG courses | 100 |
| Avg lab size | 10-19 students |
| Avg reg class size | 10-19 students |

### MOST POPULAR MAJORS
Business administration/management
English language and literature
Economics

## STUDENTS SPEAK OUT

### Academics
Engineering, science, and business are among the top drawing cards at Bucknell University, where tomorrow's leaders (and the sons and daughters of today's leaders) enjoy a great faculty, up-to-date facilities, and—perhaps most important to students—"a great reputation. Everyone that goes here has worked hard in their life to actually make it here, so you know that they are smart." Professors here "are unbelievably enthusiastic and genuinely care about their students." Administrators receive similarly high praise. Reports one student, "I have eaten meals with school administrators. They are very accessible. If I ever need to speak with a dean, I never have to wait more than a couple of minutes even if I show up without an appointment." All of these institutional assets help students handle the "challenging" academic environment at Bucknell, which is definitely not for the faint at heart. "The workload is tough," warns one student, and competition for good grades is stiff.

### Life
On Bucknell's "gorgeous" campus, most agree that "the Greek system is everything." This helps make up for the fact that "there is not much to do in this area." Some warn that "the Greek stuff makes our school cliquey. It also makes dating a rare thing. Sororities are usually fun, except during rush, which is miserable. You are basically judged based on a short first impression." For those adverse to Greek life, "Bucknell is really good at having events on the weekends that people who do not want to participate in Greek life can attend. There are always movies being shown or comedians or musical entertainment." Adds one student, "Bucknell really tries to bring in programs that would be attractive for students to participate in," including the construction of "Uptown," a student nightclub. As far as hometown Lewisburg is concerned, "it's a quaint Victorian-style town, but it's rather lacking as far as activities go. There aren't really any stores of interest in town other than the CVS and grocery store. This makes it hard on freshman, since no cars are permitted first year. There is a mall, a Wal-Mart, and a K-mart in the area, but none are within walking distance." Reports one student, "The school needs to improve the relations between students and the town; there have been problems with off-campus houses and parties disrupting" members of the community.

### Student Body
A homogeneous, upper-crust student body has always been part of Bucknell's reputation. According to students, that reputation is justified. Writes one student, "Everyone here is pretty much the same. You wear J.Crew and Abercrombie, you join a frat or sorority, you have a stylish and conservative haircut. It sounds scary, but it really isn't." Jokes one undergrad, "It's kind of irritating that everyone here is so incredibly attractive, although you get used to it. Actually, I'm not complaining. It's weird to go home, though, and realize that in the real world not every girl is a size two and has long, blonde hair." Students are comfortable with their classmates, reporting that "most of the kids at Bucknell are nice. It's not the most intellectual school on the face of the planet, but the kids are friendly, 'good kids.' "

104 ■ THE BEST 351 COLLEGES

# BUCKNELL UNIVERSITY

FINANCIAL AID: 570-577-1331 • E-MAIL: ADMISSIONS@BUCKNELL.EDU • WEBSITE: WWW.BUCKNELL.EDU

## ADMISSIONS

*Very important factors considered include:* character/personal qualities, recommendations, secondary school record, standardized test scores, talent/ability. *Important factors considered include:* class rank, extracurricular activities, minority status, volunteer work. *Other factors considered include:* alumni/ae relation, essays, geographical residence, interview, work experience. SAT I or ACT required, SAT I preferred. TOEFL required of all international applicants. High school diploma or GED is required. *High school units required/recommended:* 16 total required; 20 total recommended; 4 English required, 3 math required, 4 math recommended, 2 science required, 3 science recommended, 2 foreign language required, 4 foreign language recommended, 2 social studies required, 2 history required, 1 elective required.

### The Inside Word

Each application is read by two admissions officers. If you are serious about attending Bucknell as well as strong grades and test scores, you'll need to take the most competetive courses available at your high school. Still, overconfidence or a so-so match can throw a wrench in the plans of some; recent trends show larger numbers on the university's wait list and a track record of increased competitiveness for admission.

## FINANCIAL AID

*Students should submit:* FAFSA, CSS/Financial Aid PROFILE, noncustodial (divorced/separated) parent's statement, business/farm supplement. Regular filing deadline is January 1. The Princeton Review suggests that all financial aid forms be submitted as soon as possible after January 1. *Need-based scholarships/grants offered:* Pell, SEOG, state scholarships/grants, private scholarships, the school's own gift aid. *Loan aid offered:* FFEL Subsidized Stafford, FFEL Unsubsidized Stafford, FFEL PLUS, Federal Perkins. Federal Work-Study Program available. Institutional employment available. Applicants will be notified of awards on or about April 10. Off-campus job opportunities are poor.

## FROM THE ADMISSIONS OFFICE

"Bucknell offers a unique learning environment and is one of a few primarily undergraduate colleges that offers the opportunity to investigate both the human and technical aspects of life in the 21st century. A major curricular revision was implemented by the faculty in 1993. All students enrolling in the College of Arts and Sciences will complete a first-year foundation seminar; distributional requirements which include four humanities courses, two social science courses, and three courses in natural science and mathematics; broadened perspectives for the 21st century consisting of one course each in natural and fabricated worlds and on human diversity; departmental, college, or interdepartmental majors; and a capstone seminar or experience during the senior year. Bucknell also requires all students to complete three writing emphasis courses."

### SELECTIVITY

| | |
|---|---|
| Admissions Rating | 91 |
| # of applicants | 7,760 |
| % of applicants accepted | 39 |
| % of acceptees attending | 30 |
| # accepting a place on wait list | 740 |
| # of early decision applicants | 693 |
| % accepted early decision | 52 |

### FRESHMAN PROFILE
| | |
|---|---|
| Range SAT Verbal | 590-670 |
| Average SAT Verbal | 631 |
| Range SAT Math | 620-700 |
| Average SAT Math | 659 |
| Minimum TOEFL | 550 |
| % graduated top 10% of class | 64 |
| % graduated top 25% of class | 94 |
| % graduated top 50% of class | 99 |

### DEADLINES
| | |
|---|---|
| Early decision | 11/15 |
| Early decision notification | 12/15 |
| Regular admission | 1/1 |
| Regular notification | 4/1 |

### APPLICANTS ALSO LOOK AT
**AND OFTEN PREFER**
Cornell U.
Middlebury
Duke
Dartmouth

**AND SOMETIMES PREFER**
Boston Coll.
Colgate
Villanova
Penn State—Univ. Park
Lehigh

**AND RARELY PREFER**
Lafayette

### FINANCIAL FACTS

| | |
|---|---|
| Financial Aid Rating | 82 |
| Tuition | $28,764 |
| Room and board | $6,302 |
| Books and supplies | $750 |
| Required fees | $196 |
| % frosh receiving aid | 55 |
| % undergrads receiving aid | 48 |
| Avg frosh grant | $19,629 |
| Avg frosh loan | $3,937 |

# CAL POLY

1 GRAND AVENUE, SAN LUIS OBISPO, CA 93407 • ADMISSIONS: 805-756-2311 • FAX: 805-756-5400

## CAMPUS LIFE

| | |
|---|---|
| Quality of Life Rating | 85 |
| Type of school | public |
| Environment | suburban |

### STUDENTS

| | |
|---|---|
| Total undergrad enrollment | 17,401 |
| % male/female | 56/44 |
| % from out of state | 6 |
| % from public high school | 91 |
| % live on campus | 16 |
| % in (# of) fraternities | 10 (25) |
| % in (# of) sororities | 9 (10) |
| % African American | 1 |
| % Asian | 11 |
| % Caucasian | 62 |
| % Hispanic | 10 |
| % international | 1 |

### SURVEY SAYS . . .
Very little drug use
Students love San Luis Obispo, CA
Athletic facilities are great
Class discussions are rare
Campus difficult to get around
Dorms are like dungeons
Registration is a pain
Lousy food on campus
Unattractive campus
Diversity lacking on campus

## ACADEMICS

| | |
|---|---|
| Academic Rating | 77 |
| Calendar | quarter |
| Student/faculty ratio | 19:1 |
| Profs interesting rating | 91 |
| Profs accessible rating | 94 |
| Avg lab size | 20-29 students |
| Avg reg class size | 20-29 students |

### MOST POPULAR MAJORS
Business administration/management
Architecture
Psychology

## STUDENTS SPEAK OUT

### Academics
"Cal Poly says it's really hands on, and it is." Students learn processes by doing, which gives them "a very good idea about the major they're studying." This real-world experience helps students a great deal when they graduate. The University encourages students to pursue co-op and internship opportunities. "Cal Poly grads get the job first because they know how to do it." Some students believe that the general education classes are "too broad and mostly boring." Also, some students have a difficult time getting into required, entry-level math and English courses that fill up quickly. The school operates on a quarterly calendar, and students quickly learn that they cannot fall behind in their studies. "There is so much information that the teachers want to go over, one lecture missed could be one entire chapter missed." The faculty is highly respected. "Most of the professors are here because they want to teach you," one student says. They are very accessible and not only go over theory but also explain how it relates to real-world experiences. Students' opinions about the administration are mixed. While some say that the "administration does a good job at involving students in decisions," others say that certain members of the administration are rarely seen.

### Life
"It's the classic college life," writes one student. "Go to school through the day and when the sun goes down, the drinking starts up." Fraternities and private houses often host large parties. For students over the age of 21, "the night life in San Luis Obispo is pretty good." On Thursday night, the Farmers' Market downtown is the place to be. Life at Cal Poly is laid back. The beautiful California weather combined with the university's location 15 minutes from the beach means that students take part in many outdoor activities. The nearby ocean "attracts a lot of surfers to San Luis Obispo." In addition, students enjoy having bonfires and partying on the beach. Hiking and rock climbing are other popular activities, and the ski club takes an annual week-long trip. Though students are not politically active, they do get down socially. Many volunteer with Habitat for Humanity, and the frats are especially active participants. ("Must be something about hammers and jocks," one student quips.) "On campus and in the surrounding area, you can go to the movies, go kayaking, go to the beach, build a computer, go clubbing, go camping, or shear some sheep." Off-campus housing is "very hard to find," and "what is available is expensive." However, the word is that new apartment-style, on-campus student housing will be available soon.

### Student Body
More than 80 percent of Cal Poly students live off campus, which means that students don't get to know each other. " You must join a club or an organization" if you want to make friends, according to one student. And students tend to befriend other students in their respective majors. Cal Poly students are very laid back and some are apathetic as regards the classroom. "There is a general trend for students here not to think for themselves, which means they're always smiling and easy to get along with." People are "very respectful of differences," though some of the on-campus religious groups "like to tell everyone else how awful they are." One student comments that most of the people in the "huge" Christian club on campus "are in it to hook up with people who believe in God."

# CAL POLY

FINANCIAL AID: 805-756-2927 • E-MAIL: ADMISSIONS@CALPOLY.EDU • WEBSITE: WWW.CALPOLY.EDU

## ADMISSIONS

*Very important factors considered include:* secondary school record, standardized test scores. *Other factors considered include:* extracurricular activities, talent/ability, volunteer work, work experience. SAT I or ACT required. TOEFL required of all international applicants. High school diploma or GED is required. *High school units required/recommended:* 15 total required; 4 English required, 3 math required, 3 science required, 1 science lab required, 2 foreign language required.

### The Inside Word

While it's tough to get admitted, Cal Poly doesn't spend much time on frills in the admissions process. Satisfy the formulas or else! As with all California public institutions, the banning of affirmative action will continue to roil the application process for the near future.

## FINANCIAL AID

*Students should submit:* FAFSA, institution's own financial aid form, by March 3. The Princeton Review suggests that all financial aid forms be submitted as soon as possible after January 1. *Need-based scholarships/grants offered:* Pell, SEOG, state scholarships/grants, private scholarships, the school's own gift aid. *Loan aid offered:* FFEL Subsidized Stafford, FFEL Unsubsidized Stafford, FFEL PLUS, Federal Perkins, college/university loans from institutional funds, alternative loans. Federal Work-Study Program available. Institutional employment available. Applicants will be notified of awards on a rolling basis beginning on or about May 1. Off-campus job opportunities are good.

## FROM THE ADMISSIONS OFFICE

"From row crops to computers, Cal Poly believes the best way for someone to learn something is to do it. That's been the school's philosophy since it began in 1901: Learn by Doing. Cal Poly students gain invaluable firsthand experience both on campus and off. On-campus opportunities such as the daily student-run newspaper and real-world agricultural projects such as the organic farm, thoroughbred breeding project, ranch horse training project, test bull project, and market beef, sheep, and swine projects as well as engineering opportunities like the Cal Poly CubeSat satellite-building project, make hands-on learning a daily reality, not just a catch phrase. Off-campus work with government agencies and major national corporations for both academic credit and a salary is available through various programs, including the largest cooperative education program in the western United States. With its successful, no-nonsense approach to education, Cal Poly has built a solid statewide and national reputation."

### SELECTIVITY

| | |
|---|---|
| Admissions Rating | 86 |
| # of applicants | 20,797 |
| % of applicants accepted | 37 |
| % of acceptees attending | 42 |
| # of early decision applicants | 2,726 |
| % accepted early decision | 19 |

### FRESHMAN PROFILE

| | |
|---|---|
| Range SAT Verbal | 580-640 |
| Average SAT Verbal | 594 |
| Range SAT Math | 580-700 |
| Average SAT Math | 639 |
| Range ACT Composite | 25-31 |
| Average ACT Composite | 28 |
| Minimum TOEFL | 550 |
| Average HS GPA | 3.8 |
| % graduated top 10% of class | 42 |
| % graduated top 25% of class | 85 |
| % graduated top 50% of class | 97 |

### DEADLINES

| | |
|---|---|
| Early decision | 10/31 |
| Early decision notification | 12/15 |
| Regular admission | 11/30 |
| Nonfall registration? | yes |

### APPLICANTS ALSO LOOK AT AND SOMETIMES PREFER

UCLA
UC Berkeley
UC Irvine
UC Davis
UC San Diego
UC Santa Barbara
Santa Clara U
USC

### FINANCIAL FACTS

| | |
|---|---|
| Financial Aid Rating | 81 |
| In-state tuition | $3,046 |
| Out-of-state tuition | $15,519 |
| Room and board | $7,119 |
| Books and supplies | $1,080 |
| Required fees | $2,877 |
| % frosh receiving aid | 29 |
| % undergrads receiving aid | 34 |

# CALIFORNIA INSTITUTE OF TECHNOLOGY

1200 EAST CALIFONIA BOULEVARD, PASADENA, CA 91125 • ADMISSIONS: 626-395-6341 • FAX: 626-683-3026

## CAMPUS LIFE

| | |
|---|---|
| Quality of Life Rating | 82 |
| Type of school | private |
| Environment | suburban |

### STUDENTS
| | |
|---|---|
| Total undergrad enrollment | 939 |
| % from out of state | 64 |
| % from public high school | 81 |
| % live on campus | 93 |
| % African American | 1 |
| % Asian | 27 |
| % Caucasian | 56 |
| % Hispanic | 7 |
| % international | 8 |

### SURVEY SAYS . . .
Campus is beautiful
Campus easy to get around
Great computer facilities
Lab facilities are great
Great library
Campus feels safe
Students love Pasadena, CA
Class discussions encouraged
Great off-campus food

## ACADEMICS

| | |
|---|---|
| Academic Rating | 97 |
| Calendar | quarter |
| Student/faculty ratio | 3:1 |
| % profs teaching UG courses | 100 |
| Avg lab size | 10-19 students |
| Avg reg class size | 10-19 students |

### MOST POPULAR MAJORS
Electrical, electronics, and communications engineering
Biology/biological sciences
Physics

## STUDENTS SPEAK OUT

### Academics
Students arrive at Caltech knowing what to expect—namely, academic boot camp—and few graduate disappointed. The school's "grueling" demands "prepare students to face far more challenges than they ever thought possible." The school operates on the quarter system, which means "classes go by quickly." Warns one student, "Stay on top of things because before you know it, it's midterms. Then finals. Rinse and repeat two times. Then you have a complete school year. Good luck, you'll be fine. Don't worry. Too much." The first two freshman quarters "are pass/fail, which is extremely helpful in learning to adjust to the workload at Tech and to college life in general." First year is also when students immerse themselves in core courses "which consist of roughly three lectures a week (taught by a professor to the entire freshman class, some 215 people) and then one or two recitation sections, in which Teaching Assistants (graduate students, or occasionally undergraduates or other professors) go over the material covered in lecture and answer questions. The system works, I guess, but there is a lot (and I do mean a lot) of homework involved." Students note, "The core professors aren't always the best around, but once you get into the more specialized major-specific or elective courses, the classes become much smaller and the professors are generally excellent teachers who genuinely care about the educational experiences of the students." Caltech's rigors are softened by the fact that "the environment is a very supportive one. Students here work together in many subjects and general activities."

### Life
"There is not a lot of time for extra activities" at Caltech. "A lot of people get beat down by the extreme workload." Writes one student, "Life is work. On an average day, the average Techer probably spends 8 to 10 hours on academic matters." As one undergrad joked, "We're not like MIT, where students take homework with them on dates. We generally bring our dates to work on our homework in group sessions." Social life "revolves around the housing system. All students join one of the seven Houses—they're kind of hybrids between dorms and frats—at the beginning of freshman year . . . . The system is a real blessing." Once they've found their cohort, "Techers enjoy a random life filled with random events that just happen. One day they may build a giant jungle gym on the lawn of the faculty club building. Another day they may pull a prank by sneaking a girl into a group of high school students and parents visiting Caltech, then 'kidnapping' the girl and yelling, 'We got one! We got one!'" Beyond campus, "Old Pas, Pasadena's shopping district, is a short walk away, is one of L.A.'s 'destinations' with good restaurants [and] movie theaters, and is just fun to walk around. If they get out, most students go there."

### Student Body
Techers may debate whether they are technically geeks or nerds, but nearly all agree that theirs is a truly odd lot. Reports one from the "geek" camp: "The typical student here is a geek. I'm a geek. You're probably a geek too, if you're considering Tech . . . . Of course, the list of things we do in our 'spare time' is diverse. You get geeks who play musical instruments, geeks who play sports, . . . geeks who drink beer and smoke pot, and geeks who run around in winged monkey suits saying 'Whee!' (I kid you not), but we're all geeks." Within these parameters, "There are a lot people here . . . who are interested in art, music, or literature, philosophy, history, and all manner of supposed humanities." As at most tech schools, "The guy-to-girl ratio is ridiculous. It creates an environment where guys can turn into infatuated/stalker types for a girl that would never get a second glance at her high school."

108 ■ THE BEST 351 COLLEGES

# CALIFORNIA INSTITUTE OF TECHNOLOGY

FINANCIAL AID: 626-395-6280 • E-MAIL: UGADMISSIONS@CALTECH.EDU • WEBSITE: WWW.ADMISSIONS.CALTECH.EDU

## ADMISSIONS

*Very important factors considered include:* character/personal qualities, essays, recommendations, secondary school record. *Other factors considered include:* class rank, extracurricular activities, minority status, standardized test scores, talent/ability, volunteer work, work experience. SAT I required. *High school units required/recommended:* 15 total required; 3 English required, 4 English recommended, 4 math required, 2 science required, 1 science lab required, 1 social studies required, 1 history required.

### The Inside Word

A mere glance at Caltech's freshman profile can discourage all but the most self-confident of high school seniors. It should. The impact of grades and test scores on the admissions process is minimized significantly when virtually every freshman was in the top fifth of his or her high school class and has a 1400 SAT. The admissions office isn't kidding when they emphasize the personal side of their criteria. Six students are on the admissions committee; every file is read at least twice. The process is all about matchmaking, and the Tech staff is very interested in getting to know you. Don't apply unless you have more than high numbers to offer.

## FINANCIAL AID

*Students should submit:* FAFSA, CSS/Financial Aid PROFILE, noncustodial (divorced/separated) parent's statement, business/farm supplement. Noncustodial parent's statement and business/farm supplement forms are required only when applicable. Regular filing deadline is March 2. The Princeton Review suggests that all financial aid forms be submitted as soon as possible after January 1. *Need-based scholarships/grants offered:* Pell, SEOG, state scholarships/grants, private scholarships, the school's own gift aid, United Negro College Fund. *Loan aid offered:* Direct Subsidized Stafford, Direct Unsubsidized Stafford, Direct PLUS, Federal Perkins, college/university loans from institutional funds. Federal Work-Study Program available. Institutional employment available. Applicants will be notified of awards on or about April 15. Off-campus job opportunities are excellent.

## FROM THE ADMISSIONS OFFICE

"Admission to the freshman class is based on many factors—some quantifiable, some not. What you say in your application is important! And, because we don't interview students for admission, your letters of recommendation are weighed heavily. High school academic performance is very important, as is a demonstrated interest in math, science, and/or engineering. We are also interested in your character, maturity, and motivation. We are very proud of the process we use to select each freshman class. It's very individual, it has great integrity, and we believe it serves all the students who apply. If you have any questions about the process or about Caltech in general, write us a letter or give us a call. We'd like to hear from you!"

### SELECTIVITY

| | |
|---|---|
| Admissions Rating | 99 |
| # of applicants | 2,615 |
| % of applicants accepted | 21 |
| % of acceptees attending | 45 |
| # accepting a place on wait list | 150 |

### FRESHMAN PROFILE

| | |
|---|---|
| Range SAT Verbal | 710-780 |
| Average SAT Verbal | 736 |
| Range SAT Math | 760-800 |
| Average SAT Math | 774 |
| % graduated top 10% of class | 99 |
| % graduated top 25% of class | 100 |

### DEADLINES

| | |
|---|---|
| Regular admission | 1/1 |
| Regular notification | 4/1 |

### APPLICANTS ALSO LOOK AT AND OFTEN PREFER
Stanford
Harvard
Princeton

### AND SOMETIMES PREFER
MIT
UC Berkeley
Harvey Mudd

### AND RARELY PREFER
Virginia Tech
RPI

### FINANCIAL FACTS

| | |
|---|---|
| Financial Aid Rating | 94 |
| Tuition | $23,901 |
| Room and board | $7,560 |
| Books and supplies | $1,005 |
| Required fees | $216 |
| % frosh receiving aid | 54 |
| % undergrads receiving aid | 57 |
| Avg frosh grant | $20,485 |
| Avg frosh loan | $1,404 |

# CALVIN COLLEGE

3201 Burton Street, SE, Grand Rapids, MI 49546 • Admissions: 616-526-6106 • Fax: 616-526-6777

## CAMPUS LIFE

| | |
|---|---|
| **Quality of Life Rating** | **93** |
| Type of school | private |
| Affiliation | other |
| Environment | suburban |

### STUDENTS

| | |
|---|---|
| Total undergrad enrollment | 4,286 |
| % male/female | 44/56 |
| % from out of state | 39 |
| % from public high school | 42 |
| % live on campus | 58 |
| % African American | 1 |
| % Asian | 2 |
| % Caucasian | 92 |
| % Hispanic | 1 |
| % international | 8 |

### SURVEY SAYS . . .
Students are very religious
Very little hard liquor
Very little beer drinking
(Almost) no one smokes
Lots of conservatives on campus
Classes are small
Diversity lacking on campus
Musical organizations are hot
Very little drug use

## ACADEMICS

| | |
|---|---|
| **Academic Rating** | **82** |
| Calendar | 4-1-4 |
| Student/faculty ratio | 13:1 |
| Profs interesting rating | 95 |
| Profs accessible rating | 97 |
| % profs teaching UG courses | 100 |
| Avg lab size | 20-29 students |
| Avg reg class size | 20-29 students |

### MOST POPULAR MAJORS
Business administration/management
Elementary education and teaching
English language and literature

## STUDENTS SPEAK OUT

### Academics
Christian values are certainly front-and-center at Calvin College, a midsize midwestern school affiliated with the Christian Reformed Church. Rigid dogma, however, is not on the agenda; writes one student, "Calvin gives students the opportunities to explore their faith at an academic and spiritual level. Students can take advantage of religion classes, Bible studies, and fun worship groups, or they can choose to ignore all of that." Agrees another, "Calvin gets people to think for themselves and not just regurgitate the political and religious ideals of their parents." Students praise requirements that "encourage you to delve into subjects you wouldn't have necessarily considered if you didn't have to take them for the fulfillment of the core curriculum." Of course, an excellent program can go only so far without an excellent faculty; fortunately, "Calvin College's professors are dedicated to serving the student body in any way possible." Notes one student, "Professors often have students to their house for dinner, eat in the cafeteria with students, keep their doors open, follow office hours, and accept home phone calls." Similarly, administrators are "always eager to help solve problems and give suggestions as to how to improve" the school, "know students by name," and "often attend student functions, like chapel and sports events. They aren't holed up in their offices; they are a part of the community."

### Life
Calvin undergrads appreciate the efforts their school makes to provide "plenty of things to do outside of the classroom. There is always a show of some sort, whether it is improv or a band." Adds one student, "Calvin offers great entertainment. The Student Activities Board brings in great concerts like Bela Fleck, Ben Harper, and Emmylou Harris. The Film Arts committee shows artsy movies every weekend, and the dorms all plan activities on the weekend, from floor dates for sundaes to massive broom ball tournaments." Students are especially grateful for on-campus diversions during the tundra-like winters, during which there is "way too much snow and the sun doesn't shine." (But hey, "that provides a great study environment.") Students enjoy a surprising amount of freedom on campus: explains one undergrad, "Our values are good, but we are a lot less strict than many Christian schools. Chapels are not mandatory, smoking is permitted, alcohol and most other policies are under 'responsible freedom' guidelines. The school trusts students to make their own decisions and expects that students want to learn." Despite its nickname of "Bland Rapids," hometown Grand Rapids earns the praise of many undergrads. Offers one, "Grand Rapids has one area of town, Eastown, which has lots of fun coffee shops and artsy shops, and is much more diverse than the rest of GR. A lot of Calvin students live there." The campus "is very beautiful, especially in the fall—great time to visit!"

### Student Body
A number of Calvin respondents this year noted a broadening of the school's traditionally narrow demographic. Wrote one, "Historically, Calvin has been a conservative, Christian, suburban, white school with few people from other religious denominations . . . [but] in the past few years, Calvin has taken great strides to promote a more diverse campus, and it shows. I think the students here are genuinely benefiting from the progress Calvin has made." Things haven't changed that much, though; you can still "learn Dutch without taking a class" here. As one would expect, students are religious, "but not freaky about religion. Calvin students are very intelligent, so they enjoy talking theology and philosophy, and such. Because of this, they are generally accepting of a lot of viewpoints."

# CALVIN COLLEGE

FINANCIAL AID: 616-526-6134 • E-MAIL: ADMISSIONS@CALVIN.EDU • WEBSITE: WWW.CALVIN.EDU

## ADMISSIONS

*Very important factors considered include:* religious affiliation/commitment, secondary school record, standardized test scores. *Important factors considered include:* character/personal qualities, essays, extracurricular activities, recommendations. *Other factors considered include:* class rank, volunteer work, work experience. SAT I or ACT required; ACT preferred. TOEFL required of all international applicants. High school diploma or GED is required. *High school units required/recommended:* 12 total required; 17 total recommended; 3 English required, 4 English recommended, 3 math required, 2 science required, 1 science lab recommended, 2 foreign language recommended, 2 social studies required, 3 social studies recommended, 3 elective required.

### The Inside Word

Calvin's applicant pool is highly self-selected and small. Nearly all candidates get in, and over half choose to enroll. The freshman academic profile is fairly solid, but making a good match with the college philosophically is much more important for gaining admission than anything else.

## FINANCIAL AID

*Students should submit:* FAFSA, institution's own financial aid form. No deadline for regular filing. The Princeton Review suggests that all financial aid forms be submitted as soon as possible after January 1. *Need-based scholarships/grants offered:* Pell, SEOG, state scholarships/grants, private scholarships, the school's own gift aid. *Loan aid offered:* Direct Subsidized Stafford, Direct Unsubsidized Stafford, Direct PLUS, Federal Perkins, state loans, college/university loans from institutional funds, private alternative loans. Federal Work-Study Program available. Institutional employment available. Applicants will be notified of awards on a rolling basis beginning on or about March 15. Off-campus job opportunities are excellent.

## FROM THE ADMISSIONS OFFICE

"Calvin's well-respected faculty, innovative core curriculum, and inquiring student body come together in an environment that links intellectual freedom with a heart for service. Calvin's 400-acre campus is home to more than 4,300 students and 300 professors who chose Calvin because of its national reputation for academic excellence and faith-shaped thinking. Calvin encourages students to explore all things and offers nearly 100 academic options to choose from, including accredited professional programs.

"Quality teaching and accessibility to students are considered top priorities by faculty members. More than 80 percent of Calvin professors hold the highest degree in their field, the student/faculty ratio is 13:1, and the average class size is 23. The College's 4-1-4 calendar offers opportunities for off-campus and international study, while service-learning projects draw Calvin students into the local community. Internships allow students to try their individual gifts in the workplace while gaining professional experience. In a recent survey, 96 percent of Calvin graduates reported that they had either secured a job or begun graduate school within six months of graduation. Calvin is among the top 3 percent of four-year private colleges in the number of graduates who go on to earn a PhD."

## SELECTIVITY

| | |
|---|---|
| Admissions Rating | 78 |
| # of applicants | 1,862 |
| % of applicants accepted | 98 |
| % of acceptees attending | 57 |

### FRESHMAN PROFILE

| | |
|---|---|
| Range SAT Verbal | 520-640 |
| Average SAT Verbal | 584 |
| Range SAT Math | 530-660 |
| Average SAT Math | 595 |
| Range ACT Composite | 22-28 |
| Average ACT Composite | 26 |
| Minimum TOEFL | 550 |
| Average HS GPA | 3.5 |
| % graduated top 10% of class | 27 |
| % graduated top 25% of class | 52 |
| % graduated top 50% of class | 81 |

### DEADLINES

| | |
|---|---|
| Regular admission | 8/15 |
| Nonfall registration? | yes |

### APPLICANTS ALSO LOOK AT AND OFTEN PREFER
Hope
### AND SOMETIMES PREFER
U of Michigan at Ann Arbor
Wheaton College (IL)
Grand Valley State
### AND RARELY PREFER
Michigan Tech
Michigan State

## FINANCIAL FACTS

| | |
|---|---|
| Financial Aid Rating | 90 |
| Tuition | $15,750 |
| Room and board | $5,485 |
| Books and supplies | $655 |
| % frosh receiving aid | 63 |
| % undergrads receiving aid | 64 |
| Avg frosh grant | $7,600 |
| Avg frosh loan | $4,700 |

THE BEST 351 COLLEGES ■ 111

# CARLETON COLLEGE

100 SOUTH COLLEGE STREET, NORTHFIELD, MN 55057 • ADMISSIONS: 507-646-4190 • FAX: 507-646-4526

## CAMPUS LIFE

★ ★ ★ ☆

| | |
|---|---|
| Quality of Life Rating | 89 |
| Type of school | private |
| Environment | rural |

### STUDENTS

| | |
|---|---|
| Total undergrad enrollment | 1,932 |
| % male/female | 48/52 |
| % from out of state | 77 |
| % from public high school | 74 |
| % live on campus | 90 |
| % African American | 4 |
| % Asian | 9 |
| % Caucasian | 82 |
| % Hispanic | 4 |
| % international | 3 |

### SURVEY SAYS . . .
(Almost) everyone plays intramural sports
No one cheats
Students aren't religious
Lab facilities need improving
Great computer facilities
Theater is hot
(Almost) no one smokes
Musical organizations are hot

## ACADEMICS

| | |
|---|---|
| Academic Rating | 98 |
| Calendar | other |
| Student/faculty ratio | 9:1 |
| Profs interesting rating | 94 |
| Profs accessible rating | 99 |
| % profs teaching UG courses | 100 |
| Avg lab size | 10-19 students |
| Avg reg class size | 10-19 students |

### MOST POPULAR MAJORS
Political science and government
Biology/biological sciences
English

## STUDENTS SPEAK OUT

### Academics

At this "blazingly liberal" college the classes are small, and the class discussions "well-modulated" and "enlightening." "WOW," says a student about the professors, who provide a "wonderful support system here for dealing with academic issues." Students have every right to be proud; Carleton is a nationally preeminent liberal arts college. It divides the academic year into trimesters, and students take only three classes per term, which "allows students to concentrate more fully on each subject." The workload's not light, though; students are "committed," and by the end of the term "the entire campus suffers from sleep deprivation." Students compete academically, "not with other students—but with themselves." And if one needs it, Carleton provides free tutoring in various academic subjects. Carleton has "first-rate everything," but in spirit the school "doesn't take itself too seriously." It is common for students to call professors by their first names, and professors often give out their home phone numbers. The administration is highly accessible, too, and even the president holds office hours every Tuesday. He also "read Winnie the Pooh stories to my floor last term, one Sunday evening—he does a great Eeyore." Students don't find much to complain about, though the library's resources are "limited," and the on-campus food "sucks."

### Life

"Ultimate Frisbee and Carleton are practically synonymous," so much so that entering students are each given a Frisbee. But Frisbee's not all that Carleton students ("Carls" for short) find to do in Northfield, Minnesota. On weekdays there is little drinking and few parties, as "people study all the time, but it's just considered normal." Students "always complain about having work to do, but the truth is, we love it and become totally engaged in it." During moments of free time and on the weekends, Carls find all sorts of "weird" ways to have fun. Hints one students, "A word to the wise—if streaking embarrasses you, stay away. Carls aren't afraid to bare all." When there's snow (and there's plenty of it) students go "traying," which is "sledding using a tray from the dining hall." Hungry in the middle of the night? There's Dace Moses House, where students can go whenever the urge strikes to "make cookies—chocolate chip, to be exact. The rule is that you have to leave what you don't eat at the house." And in the spring (when all that snow melts) there's "Rottblatt. A 'softball' game with an inning for each year the college has been in existence (135 in 2001). Traditionally, a keg is at each base, and it is an excuse to get up early on Saturday and drink." While "there is a lot of boozing around," Carls don't feel pressured to drink. Complaints? You guessed it: the "ridiculous cold." Minnesota winters are brutal. And, while the school does provide shuttle service for trips to the nearby Twin Cities and the Mall of America, it's "not very frequent or very cheap."

### Student Body

"People who go to Carleton know that they are smart and are willing to demonstrate it." The "quirky," "creative" students are "independent thinkers" and "share a respect for one another that seems unique to Carleton." Some students, however, can be arrogant about their high intelligence. Students dress "a little weird," with "bat ears" or "without shoes," but "no one can be placed by the way they look." The "traditional stereotypes don't apply at all to anyone. Everyone is much more deep and interesting than they first appear." And students are "so friendly, I feel like I'm in Mr. Roger's neighborhood." But while Carleton is "diverse in terms of personalities," the school is primarily Caucasian, and both students and administrators would like to see more racial and ethnic diversity. A gay student also warns that "it's really really really hard to hook up with another guy."

# CARLETON COLLEGE

FINANCIAL AID: 507-646-4190 • E-MAIL: ADMISSIONS@ACS.CARLETON.EDU • WEBSITE: WWW.CARLETON.EDU

## ADMISSIONS

*Very important factors considered include:* secondary school record. *Important factors considered include:* character/personal qualities, class rank, essays, extracurricular activities, minority status, recommendations, standardized test scores, talent/ability, volunteer work, work experience. *Other factors considered include:* alumni/ae relation, geographical residence, interview, state residency. SAT I or ACT required; SAT II recommended. TOEFL required of all international applicants. High school diploma or GED is required. *High school units required/recommended:* 4 English recommended, 3 math recommended, 3 science recommended, 1 science lab recommended, 3 foreign language recommended.

### The Inside Word

Admission to Carleton would be even more difficult if the college had more name recognition. Current applicants should be grateful for this, because standards are already rigorous. Only severe competition with the best liberal arts colleges in the country prevents an even lower admit rate.

## FINANCIAL AID

*Students should submit:* FAFSA, CSS/Financial Aid PROFILE, noncustodial (divorced/separated) parent's statement, business/farm supplement. Regular filing deadline is February 15. The Princeton Review suggests that all financial aid forms be submitted as soon as possible after January 1. *Need-based scholarships/grants offered:* Pell, SEOG, state scholarships/grants, private scholarships, the school's own gift aid. *Loan aid offered:* FFEL Subsidized Stafford, FFEL Unsubsidized Stafford, FFEL PLUS, Federal Perkins, state loans, college/university loans from institutional funds, Minnesota SELF Loan program. Federal Work-Study Program available. Institutional employment available. Applicants will be notified of awards on or about April 15. Off-campus job opportunities are good.

## FROM THE ADMISSIONS OFFICE

"In an annual college freshmen survey, Carleton students self-identify along the full conservative-to-liberal spectrum, with a majority identifying as moderate to liberal. Individualistic and energetic, Carls take academics seriously but not themselves. Participation in athletics, theater, or music and in activities from religious events to dining hall discussion over hearty fare marks the Carleton experience. More than two-thirds of students spend time studying abroad. Cool fact: More snow fell in the northeast than here in the past three years."

## SELECTIVITY

★ ★ ★ ★

| | |
|---|---|
| Admissions Rating | 97 |
| # of applicants | 4,170 |
| % of applicants accepted | 35 |
| % of acceptees attending | 35 |
| # accepting a place on wait list | 394 |
| % admitted from wait list | 3 |
| # of early decision applicants | 367 |
| % accepted early decision | 55 |

### FRESHMAN PROFILE

| | |
|---|---|
| Range SAT Verbal | 640-740 |
| Range SAT Math | 640-720 |
| Range ACT Composite | 27-31 |
| Minimum TOEFL | 600 |
| % graduated top 10% of class | 70 |
| % graduated top 25% of class | 93 |
| % graduated top 50% of class | 99 |

### DEADLINES

| | |
|---|---|
| Early decision | 11/15 |
| Early decision notification | 12/15 |
| Regular admission | 1/15 |
| Regular notification | 4/15 |

### APPLICANTS ALSO LOOK AT AND OFTEN PREFER
Williams
Brown
### AND SOMETIMES PREFER
Pomona
Bowdoin
### AND RARELY PREFER
Macalester
Bates

## FINANCIAL FACTS

| | |
|---|---|
| Financial Aid Rating | 83 |
| Tuition | $26,745 |
| Room and board | $5,535 |
| Books and supplies | $1,200 |
| Required fees | $165 |
| % frosh receiving aid | 55 |
| % undergrads receiving aid | 54 |
| Avg frosh grant | $17,184 |
| Avg frosh loan | $2,781 |

THE BEST 351 COLLEGES ■ 113

# CARNEGIE MELLON UNIVERSITY

5000 FORBES AVENUE, PITTSBURGH, PA 15213 • ADMISSIONS: 412-268-2082 • FAX: 412-268-7838

## CAMPUS LIFE

★ ★ ★ ☆

| | |
|---|---|
| Quality of Life Rating | 81 |
| Type of school | private |
| Environment | urban |

### STUDENTS

| | |
|---|---|
| Total undergrad enrollment | 5,475 |
| % male/female | 61/39 |
| % from out of state | 76 |
| % live on campus | 72 |
| % in (# of) fraternities | 14 (13) |
| % in (# of) sororities | 10 (5) |
| % African American | 5 |
| % Asian | 26 |
| % Caucasian | 48 |
| % Hispanic | 5 |
| % international | 11 |
| # of countries represented | 100 |

### SURVEY SAYS . . .
Great computer facilities
Ethnic diversity on campus
Campus easy to get around
Registration is a breeze
Lots of beer drinking
Campus feels safe
(Almost) everyone smokes
Great off-campus food
Hard liquor is popular
Students are happy

## ACADEMICS

★ ★ ★ ★

| | |
|---|---|
| Academic Rating | 94 |
| Calendar | semester |
| Student/faculty ratio | 11:1 |
| Avg lab size | 20-29 students |
| Avg reg class size | 10-19 students |

### MOST POPULAR MAJORS
Computer science
Computer engineering
Business administration/management

## STUDENTS SPEAK OUT

### Academics

The students of Carnegie Mellon University proudly report that their school fulfills the fundamental mission of the university: to offer excellent instruction in a wide variety of fields while also promoting cutting-edge research. "Of all the schools I've seen, no other is as well-known in so many different fields: architecture, engineering, drama, science, design, music, and business, just to name a few," is how one undergrad put it, adding, "If you couldn't decide what path to take in life, you could still come to Carnegie Mellon and have a world-class education in almost any interest." Students warn, "Academically, this school will push you to your limit." As one put it, "CMU is a very research-oriented university. . . . It has truly opened doors for me that I did not know were available. The professors are actively involved in the topics in which they teach. . . . There is no such thing as a 'basic' course at CMU." The school does a good job of recognizing the demands it makes, however, and "in many departments, professors actually coordinate their tests and papers so that there is very little overlap in workloads between classes." It's just such little touches that so endear CMU to its students. Another example: "The Business School's administration loves to send us notes about various types of opportunities for internships, jobs, and lectures through email." Students are also unanimous in their praise for online services: "You can register online, check your grades online, often get assignments online, and even check what movie is playing at school online," reports an undergrad.

### Life

Because of CMU's intense academic demands, "people here think about school 90 percent of the time. The other 10 percent is divided among when they're going to sleep next [and] how they're going to blow off some stress." Fortunately, there are lots of options for that scant 10 percent. Hometown Pittsburgh "is a great city if you let it be. There are many theaters, museums, and sporting events. Shops and great restaurants are all really close, and we get bus passes as students, so you can get anywhere." There are also many nearby bars, "most of which don't card." On campus, "people go to the fraternities on weekends." Also popular are one-dollar movies ("shown from Thursday to Sunday, which are a real great getaway from work, and they get good, recent movies") and student-produced plays. Student clubs and organizations also have their boosters; writes one student, "CMU has a lot of really fun, quirky organizations. . . . My two favorites are the Kiltie Band and KGB. The Kiltie Band is our band for nonmajors. As The Band Without Pants, we wear our kilts proudly, cheer giddily, click our heels, and beep when we back up. Talent for music and/or marching is not a requirement. . . . KGB stands for Keeping Geeks Busy. . . . Each semester, they host Capture the Flag with Stuff, a game that always attracts a large crowd." Although "there are sports games going on, no one ever knows when or cares to go."

### Student Body

"There are a few types that are typical," at CMU; identifiable factions include: "a large number of tech, math, and computer geeks . . . strange art students, loud drama students, and many Asian student groups." Most are "hardworking, bright, ambitious," and shy. Reports one undergrad, "Students here would be considered very friendly if they weren't so reserved. You'll find that the person who sits next to you in lecture is always really nice if either of you ever overcomes your shyness enough to say hello." Politically "there is a large minority of very left-wing, extremely active students who are responsible for most of what occurs on campus. Most students, however, are apathetic and very absorbed in their studies."

# CARNEGIE MELLON UNIVERSITY

FINANCIAL AID: 412-268-2068 • E-MAIL: UNDERGRADUATE-ADMISSIONS@ANDREW.CMU.EDU • WEBSITE: WWW.CMU.EDU

## ADMISSIONS
*Very important factors considered include:* secondary school record, standardized test scores. *Important factors considered include:* alumni/ae relation, character/personal qualities, class rank, extracurricular activities, recommendations, talent/ability, volunteer work, work experience. *Other factors considered include:* essays, interview, minority status. SAT I or ACT required, SAT II also required. TOEFL required of all international applicants. High school diploma or GED is required. *High school units required/recommended:* 4 English required, 4 math required, 3 science required, 3 science lab required, 2 foreign language required, 1 social studies required, 2 history required, 3 elective required, 4 elective recommended.

### The Inside Word
The Office of Admission reports that it uses "no cutoffs, no formulas" in assessing its applicant pool. Don't get too excited—that doesn't necessarily mean that applicants are looked at in a more personal fashion. Applications have seesawed here over the past couple of years, and to temper the effects of a decline in application totals on selectivity CMU maintains a huge wait list. A very low yield of admits who enroll keeps selectivity moderate, but you've got to have strong numbers to gain admission.

## FINANCIAL AID
*Students should submit:* FAFSA, institution's own financial aid form, parent and student federal tax returns, parent W-2 forms. Regular filing deadline is May 1. The Princeton Review suggests that all financial aid forms be submitted as soon as possible after January 1. *Need-based scholarships/grants offered:* Pell, SEOG, state scholarships/grants, private scholarships, the school's own gift aid. *Loan aid offered:* FFEL Subsidized Stafford, FFEL Unsubsidized Stafford, FFEL PLUS, Federal Perkins, GATE Loans. Federal Work-Study Program available. Institutional employment available. Applicants will be notified of awards on a rolling basis. Off-campus job opportunities are good.

## FROM THE ADMISSIONS OFFICE
"Carnegie Mellon is a private, coeducational university with approximately 5,100 undergraduates, 3,300 graduate students, and 778 full-time faculty members. The University's 103-acre campus is located in the Oakland area of Pittsburgh, five miles from downtown. The University is composed of seven colleges: the Carnegie Institute of Technology (engineering); the College of Fine Arts; the College of Humanities and Social Sciences (combining liberal arts education with professional specializations); the Graduate School of Industrial Administration (undergraduate business and industrial management); the Mellon College of Science; the School of Computer Science; and the H. Hohn Heina III School of Public Policy and Management."

## ADMISSIONS

| | |
|---|---|
| Admissions Rating | 92 |
| # of applicants | 14,271 |
| % of applicants accepted | 38 |
| % of acceptees attending | 25 |
| # accepting a place on wait list | 915 |
| % admitted from wait list | 16 |
| # of early decision applicants | 273 |
| % accepted early decision | 49 |

### FRESHMAN PROFILE
| | |
|---|---|
| Range SAT Verbal | 590-700 |
| Average SAT Verbal | 646 |
| Range SAT Math | 680-770 |
| Average SAT Math | 716 |
| Range ACT Composite | 27-32 |
| Average ACT Composite | 29 |
| Minimum TOEFL | 600 |
| Average HS GPA | 3.6 |
| % graduated top 10% of class | 72 |
| % graduated top 25% of class | 95 |
| % graduated top 50% of class | 100 |

### DEADLINES
| | |
|---|---|
| Early decision | 11/15 |
| Early decision notification | 12/15 |
| Regular admission | 1/1 |
| Regular notification | 4/15 |

### APPLICANTS ALSO LOOK AT AND OFTEN PREFER
Cornell U
MIT
U Penn
**AND SOMETIMES PREFER**
Northwestern
Washington U
**AND RARELY PREFER**
U Pittsburgh
Boston U
Syracuse
Penn State at University Park

## FINANCIAL FACTS

| | |
|---|---|
| Financial Aid Rating | 84 |
| Tuition | $26,910 |
| Room and board | $7,844 |
| Books and supplies | $880 |
| Required fees | $385 |
| % frosh receiving aid | 54 |
| % undergrads receiving aid | 49 |
| Avg frosh grant | $19,902 |
| Avg frosh loan | $4,021 |

THE BEST 351 COLLEGES ■ 115

# CASE WESTERN RESERVE UNIVERSITY

103 TOMLINSON HALL, 10900 EUCLID AVENUE, CLEVELAND, OH 44106-7055 • ADMISSIONS: 216-368-4450 • FAX: 216-368-5111

## CAMPUS LIFE

★ ★ ☆ ☆

| | |
|---|---|
| Quality of Life Rating | 70 |
| Type of school | private |
| Environment | urban |

### STUDENTS

| | |
|---|---|
| Total undergrad enrollment | 3,457 |
| % male/female | 61/39 |
| % from out of state | 40 |
| % from public high school | 70 |
| % live on campus | 78 |
| % in (# of) fraternities | 36 (18) |
| % in (# of) sororities | 15 (5) |
| % African American | 5 |
| % Asian | 15 |
| % Caucasian | 76 |
| % Hispanic | 2 |
| % international | 4 |
| # of countries represented | 89 |

### SURVEY SAYS . . .
Ethnic diversity on campus
Students love Cleveland, OH
Great library
Great computer facilities
Class discussions are rare
Intercollegiate sports unpopular or nonexistent
Registration is a pain
Campus difficult to get around
Unattractive campus

## ACADEMICS

★ ★ ★ ☆

| | |
|---|---|
| Academic Rating | 80 |
| Calendar | semester |
| Student/faculty ratio | 8:1 |
| Profs interesting rating | 88 |
| Profs accessible rating | 91 |
| % profs teaching UG courses | 72 |
| % classes taught by TAs | 5 |
| Avg lab size | 10-19 students |
| Avg reg class size | 10-19 students |

### MOST POPULAR MAJORS
Business administration/management
Biology/biological sciences
Psychology

## STUDENTS SPEAK OUT

### Academics
Though CWRU was officially born out of the union of the engineering-intense Case Institute of Technology and the liberal arts-focused Western Reserve University, there's no mistaking that the academic scales are tipped in favor of the former; the extensive engineering offerings leave some "humanities people feeling left in the dust." Many students choose CWRU for its strong academic reputation, but prospectives are advised by current students to do their homework before signing up for classes in any given department, as shown in their remarkably even-handed appraisal of instructional quality. While one complains that "some professors . . . don't speak English, don't teach, waste class time rambling about their native countries, or take pride in failing all their students," another beams, "Many of the professors are not only staggeringly intelligent and excited about their area of study, but are [also] eager to share their enthusiasm for their research with students." Students are equally split on the administration; descriptions of deans range from "always accessible" to "not terribly bright."

### Life
According to a female sophomore, "Case is fun if you make it fun, but it's not a top-ten party school. If you're looking for that, go somewhere else." Why? Academic demands dilute the bacchanalia that might otherwise go on in Cleveland. One student complains that life is "kinda boring" because there is "a lot to do but no time to do it." Those who make time for something besides studying, however, get involved in theater and music, hang out with friends, or go Greek. Writes one senior, "Greek life is fun. I am very involved with it and hang out with my sisters a lot." Beyond these activities, many feel "there is very little to do on campus" and turn to surrounding Cleveland for entertainment. "I don't understand how people are bored living in Cleveland. This city has so many possibilities . . . being bored on this campus is a choice," declares a senior. Another elucidates, "For fun, we spend time with friends, go to movies and plays, and go to Severance Hall to hear the world-class Cleveland Orchestra." Furthermore, the city provides a great opportunity for students who want to lend a hand in the greater community. Claims a sophomore, "I get involved in all the social and environmental justice activities I can. There's a small but growing group of very liberal activists on campus."

### Student Body
CWRU's diverse student population shares one thing in common: they are serious about school. While this seriousness means excellent classmates to some, it means a campus full of losers to others. Some undergrads say their fellow students are "centered and want to learn," "studious," and "respectful and friendly," while others describe them as "antisocial, unfriendly, and very self-centered." Given the conflicting attitudes, the campus has something of a split personality. A female junior sums it up: "It seems there is a dichotomy in the social life. Either you're very social and go out a lot or you never leave your room." A sardonic sophomore agrees, "There seem to be two distinct social groups here: people who accept that they are total dorks and the rest who try to party their dorkiness away."

# CASE WESTERN RESERVE UNIVERSITY

FINANCIAL AID: 216-368-4530 • E-MAIL: ADMISSION@PO.CWRU.EDU • WEBSITE: WWW.CWRU.EDU

## ADMISSIONS
*Very important factors considered include:* extracurricular activities, secondary school record, talent/ability, volunteer work, work experience. *Important factors considered include:* alumni/ae relation, character/personal qualities, class rank, essays, interview, minority status, recommendations, standardized test scores. SAT I or ACT required; SAT II recommended. TOEFL required of all international applicants. High school diploma or GED is required. *High school units required/recommended:* 16 total required; 4 English required, 3 math required, 4 math recommended, 3 science required, 1 science lab required, 2 science lab recommended, 2 foreign language required, 3 foreign language recommended, 3 social studies required, 4 social studies recommended.

### The Inside Word
Case Western faces tough competition, and they handle it very well. The university received a record number of applications last year, and as a result it's quite a bit tougher to get admitted. Even if you solidly meet the academic profile, don't be complacent—Case's freshman profile reflects well on the academic preparedness of its candidates, and due to their good fortune they've got an opportunity to be significantly more choosy about who gets an offer.

## FINANCIAL AID
*Students should submit:* FAFSA, CSS/Financial Aid PROFILE, noncustodial (divorced/separated) parent's statement, business/farm supplement, parent and student income tax returns and W-2 forms. Regular filing deadline is April 15. The Princeton Review suggests that all financial aid forms be submitted as soon as possible after January 1. *Need-based scholarships/grants offered:* Pell, SEOG, state scholarships/grants, private scholarships, the school's own gift aid. *Loan aid offered:* Direct Subsidized Stafford, Direct Unsubsidized Stafford, FFEL PLUS, Federal Perkins, Federal Nursing, state loans, college/university loans from institutional funds. Federal Work-Study Program available. Institutional employment available. Applicants will be notified of awards on a rolling basis beginning on or about March 15. Off-campus job opportunities are good.

## FROM THE ADMISSIONS OFFICE
"An important part of CWRU's philosophy is that education is best accomplished through experience. We've begun a new undergraduate program called SAGES that strives to blur the distinctions between learning and life. SAGES students engage with faculty, peers, and the larger Cleveland community through small seminars, research projects, internships, and community service. Their seminar professors serve as mentors, helping them design their educational plan. The opportunities CWRU students have to work with some of the top curators, scientists, musicians, educators, and professionals (to name a few) are truly exciting."

### SELECTIVITY

| Admissions Rating | 86 |
| --- | --- |
| # of applicants | 4,428 |
| % of applicants accepted | 78 |
| % of acceptees attending | 24 |
| # accepting a place on wait list | 177 |
| % admitted from wait list | 3 |
| # of early decision applicants | 108 |
| % accepted early decision | 86 |

### FRESHMAN PROFILE
| Range SAT Verbal | 590-710 |
| --- | --- |
| Range SAT Math | 630-730 |
| Range ACT Composite | 26-31 |
| Minimum TOEFL | 550 |
| % graduated top 10% of class | 66 |
| % graduated top 25% of class | 92 |
| % graduated top 50% of class | 99 |

### DEADLINES
| Early decision | 1/1 |
| --- | --- |
| Regular admission | 2/1 |
| Regular notification | 4/1 |
| Nonfall registration? | yes |

### APPLICANTS ALSO LOOK AT AND OFTEN PREFER
Cornell
Duke
**AND SOMETIMES PREFER**
Johns Hopkins
Northwestern
**AND RARELY PREFER**
Bucknell
Purdue
Ohio State

### FINANCIAL FACTS

| Financial Aid Rating | 82 |
| --- | --- |
| Tuition | $24,100 |
| Room and board | $7,660 |
| Books and supplies | $800 |
| Required fees | $242 |
| % frosh receiving aid | 63 |
| % undergrads receiving aid | 54 |
| Avg frosh grant | $15,865 |
| Avg frosh loan | $5,580 |

# CATAWBA COLLEGE

2300 WEST INNES STREET, SALISBURY, NC 28144 • ADMISSIONS: 704-637-4402 • FAX: 704-637-4222

## CAMPUS LIFE

| Quality of Life Rating | 75 |
|---|---|
| Type of school | private |
| Affiliation | United Church of Christ |
| Environment | suburban |

### STUDENTS

| Total undergrad enrollment | 1,195 |
|---|---|
| % male/female | 50/50 |
| % from out of state | 39 |
| % live on campus | 55 |
| % African American | 14 |
| % Asian | 1 |
| % Caucasian | 83 |
| % Hispanic | 1 |
| % international | 2 |

### SURVEY SAYS . . .
Theater is hot
Student publications are ignored
Everyone loves the Indians
Classes are small
Lousy food on campus
Political activism is (almost) nonexistent
Library needs improving

## ACADEMICS

| Academic Rating | 74 |
|---|---|
| Calendar | semester |
| Student/faculty ratio | 15:1 |
| Profs interesting rating | 94 |
| Profs accessible rating | 89 |
| % profs teaching UG courses | 100 |
| Avg lab size | 10-19 students |
| Avg reg class size | 10-19 students |

### MOST POPULAR MAJORS
Acting
Sports and fitness administration/management
Business administration/management

## STUDENTS SPEAK OUT

### Academics

Catawba College students agree that "the professors are the heartbeat of this school. They keep people motivated and loving the learning experience." With a small, cozy academic atmosphere, students are guaranteed "a lot of attention from [their] professors." Smallness does have its drawbacks, though: "The number of faculty is not that big for each department. This is not good when it comes to offering courses . . . in some departments, some courses are only offered every other semester," explains one student. And while the professors are universally hailed, "the administration is not as impressive." Apparently, many feel that "the financial end of things could be improved by giving more aid to the students and keeping the numbers consistent." In academic terms "English and education are excellent departments, as is psychology." With a 189-acre ecological preserve, plus a 300-acre wildlife refuge, the college's Center for the Environment is one of the "leading conservation efforts in the region." For those considering post-Catawba studies, be not afraid because "Catawba is great at giving you a great base of information to continue your education."

### Life

As one student told us, a certain high-ranking school administrator "seems to not believe in letting students have fun. He opposes having things like ping pong or pool tables on campus." But if your idea of sporting fun goes beyond cue balls and little paddles, you should be okay. With 17 NCAA Division II sports teams, "athletics is so important at Catawba that little else takes precedence over it. During football season, everyone is at the football games." Another student writes that since "the school doesn't have a Greek system, the sports teams" pretty much take its place. If, rather than the ole pigskin, you'd like to throw around Shakespearean verses, not to worry: "The theatre program is excellent, and most of the student body goes to see the plays." And, hey, if you want to do both, one student is happy to note that "all the students get along great; the athletes and theatre majors all get along and hang out together." Also, most agree that the student programming board, Wigwam, "has great events on the weekends, so there is always something to do." Another student adds, "Sometimes on the weekends you have to look a little harder to find something on campus but . . . if worse comes to worse, there is Charlotte right around the corner." This big-city proximity is good since hometown Salisbury doesn't receive hopping reviews. And the "nice restaurants" are important, too, as many students feel the school "could definitely improve its food."

### Student Body

If you're seriously considering Catawba College, you may as well begin practicing your "Go Indians!" cheers. Most students agree that one of the greatest aspects of Catawba is its school spirit. According to many, the student body is extremely "close-knit and friendly." One belle appreciates the "southern hospitality among the guys . . . doors are opened for you as you walk into buildings." Despite the great involvement of all the students in "either sports, music, or drama," there are some who feel that "each of these cliques gather in little groups and put huge electrified fences around them. The few remaining that aren't athletes or theatre majors tend to either hang out with themselves or subdivide into their little majors." Another student, however, is quick to point out "you can find someone on this campus that totally clicks with you no matter what." Most students are content with the diversity at Catawba: "There are people here from all different backgrounds and from many different places." And although many students state that their lives "at school are jam packed . . . with school work, organizations, work study, and other responsibilities," they still know how to take time out for each other: "Catawba students are one big family. We know how to help each other out in times of need."

# CATAWBA COLLEGE

FINANCIAL AID: 704-637-4416 • E-MAIL: ADMISSION@CATAWBA.EDU • WEBSITE: WWW.CATAWBA.EDU

## ADMISSIONS

*Very important factors considered include:* class rank, secondary school record, standardized test scores. *Important factors considered include:* character/personal qualities, essays, extracurricular activities, recommendations, talent/ability, volunteer work. *Other factors considered include:* alumni/ae relation, interview, minority status, work experience. SAT I or ACT required; SAT I preferred. TOEFL required of all international applicants. High school diploma or GED is required. *High school units required/recommended:* 16 total required; 4 English required, 2 math required, 3 math recommended, 2 science required, 3 science recommended, 3 science lab recommended, 2 foreign language recommended, 2 social studies required, 6 elective required.

### The Inside Word

Catawba's applicant pool is mainly from the Southeast, which tends to give candidates from far afield some extra appeal. There is serious competition for students among similar colleges in this neck of the woods, and the admissions staff here has to work hard to bring in the freshman class each year. They succeed because they are truly friendly and personal in their dealings with students and their families, and the college seems to have carved a worthwhile niche for itself amid the myriad choices available in the area.

## FINANCIAL AID

*Students should submit:* FAFSA. No deadline for regular filing. The Princeton Review suggests that all financial aid forms be submitted as soon as possible after January 1. *Need-based scholarships/grants offered:* Pell, SEOG, state scholarships/grants, private scholarships, the school's own gift aid. *Loan aid offered:* Direct Subsidized Stafford, Direct Unsubsidized Stafford, Direct PLUS, FFEL Subsidized Stafford, FFEL Unsubsidized Stafford, FFEL PLUS, Federal Perkins, college/university loans from institutional funds. Federal Work-Study Program available. Institutional employment available. Applicants will be notified of awards on a rolling basis beginning on or about February 15. Off-campus job opportunities are excellent.

## FROM THE ADMISSIONS OFFICE

"Perhaps one of Catawba's greatest assets is location, location, location. The town of Salisbury (www.ol.salisbury.no.us) is a small city of 26,000 people, a leader in the historic preservation movement, and a place with a rare wealth of opportunities in the arts. The town embraces the college, and vice versa. Catawba College has just significantly upgraded the computer technology made available to students. A fiber-optic loop has been completed, and our three computer labs are equipped with 486 and Pentium chip computers, many of which have sound cards and 10-watt speakers. The library has also been electronically upgraded with the addition of the same online system used by the Museum of Natural History."

---

### SELECTIVITY

| | |
|---|---:|
| Admissions Rating | 70 |
| # of applicants | 1,179 |
| % of applicants accepted | 78 |
| % of acceptees attending | 30 |
| # of early decision applicants | 20 |
| % accepted early decision | 75 |

### FRESHMAN PROFILE

| | |
|---|---:|
| Range SAT Verbal | 423-583 |
| Average SAT Verbal | 488 |
| Range SAT Math | 420-585 |
| Average SAT Math | 494 |
| Average ACT Composite | 20 |
| Minimum TOEFL | 525 |
| Average HS GPA | 3.0 |
| % graduated top 10% of class | 7 |
| % graduated top 25% of class | 24 |
| % graduated top 50% of class | 54 |

### DEADLINES

| | |
|---|---:|
| Early decision | 12/1 |
| Early decision notification | 2/16 |
| Nonfall registration? | yes |

### APPLICANTS ALSO LOOK AT AND SOMETIMES PREFER

Appalachian State
UNC Chapel Hill
UNC Charlotte

**AND RARELY PREFER**
UNC Wilmington
UNC Greensboro
North Carolina State
Elon

### FINANCIAL FACTS

| | |
|---|---:|
| Financial Aid Rating | 95 |
| Tuition | $16,400 |
| Room and board | $5,600 |
| Books and supplies | $750 |
| % frosh receiving aid | 82 |
| % undergrads receiving aid | 84 |
| Avg frosh grant | $5,100 |
| Avg frosh loan | $2,634 |

# CATHOLIC UNIVERSITY OF AMERICA

CARDINAL STATION, WASHINGTON, DC 20064 • ADMISSIONS: 202-319-5305 • FAX: 202-319-6533

## CAMPUS LIFE

| | |
|---|---|
| Quality of Life Rating | 80 |
| Type of school | private |
| Affiliation | Roman Catholic |
| Environment | urban |

### STUDENTS
| | |
|---|---|
| Total undergrad enrollment | 2,668 |
| % male/female | 45/55 |
| % from out of state | 96 |
| % from public high school | 39 |
| % live on campus | 75 |
| % in (# of) fraternities | 1 (2) |
| % in (# of) sororities | 1 (2) |
| % African American | 6 |
| % Asian | 3 |
| % Caucasian | 79 |
| % Hispanic | 3 |
| % international | 2 |
| # of countries represented | 31 |

### SURVEY SAYS . . .
Very little drug use
Classes are small
Diversity lacking on campus
Registration is a breeze
Very small frat/sorority scene
Library needs improving
Lousy food on campus
No one plays intramural sports
Dorms are like dungeons

## ACADEMICS

| | |
|---|---|
| Academic Rating | 82 |
| Calendar | semester |
| Student/faculty ratio | 8:1 |
| Profs interesting rating | 94 |
| Profs accessible rating | 92 |
| % profs teaching UG courses | 74 |
| % classes taught by TAs | 8 |
| Avg lab size | 10-19 students |
| Avg reg class size | 10-19 students |

## STUDENTS SPEAK OUT

### Academics

In Washington, D.C., a city known for its prestigious academic institutions, students seeking a quality education sometimes overlook The Catholic University of America. Some might be discouraged by the fact that the university is—surprise!—overwhelmingly populated by students who have Catholic backgrounds and are politically conservative to boot. Those who eliminate Catholic from their list of potential schools might miss out on a place where "professors know [students] by name" and the "faculty is extremely accessible." Catholic students praise the "great and available professors truly committed to a student's learning." The only university in the United States with a papal charter, it isn't surprising that the religion department earns high marks from many students, one senior writing, "My experience as a religion major has convinced me that this department is the best in the country. Where else can students have [this kind of] access to faculty members . . . even for an e-mail discussion at 3 A.M.?" The theater, nursing, and biology departments are touted by undergraduates, and many cite the quality of the music department as the primary reason they decided to attend Catholic. Meanwhile, the modern language departments need improvement, and many students wish that more classes were offered each semester and complain that the library could stand some improvement. Also, students are just plain unhappy with the university's administrators. One junior grumbles that "the administration treats us as if we cannot think for ourselves. Unless our parents call or are people of the cloth, we are not taken seriously." Despite students' dislike of the administration, most describe Catholic in a very positive light. "An education at Catholic University will last a lifetime," writes one student. "The doors opened by the professors here are amazing."

### Life

Though they cite Catholic as having "perhaps the most boring campus life this side of a veterans' hospital," most students agree that the university's proximity to the center of town (eight minutes by Metro) was a deciding factor in their decision to attend Catholic because "D.C. is full of things to do." The world-famous museums, shops, and clubs easily counterbalanced a "slow" campus life. One student explains, "The city offers a great club scene, and there's always something going on downtown." The school's strict alcohol policies cause most students to "depend on the city for night fun." One student points out that age is rarely a factor for those looking for a good time in the immediate neighborhood surrounding Catholic: "If you have a good fake ID, your weekends will be rockin'." Undergrads also mention that the food, housing, and athletic facilities need significant improvement. "We're working out on ancient machines," writes one student. Though many students point out that there are not enough on-campus activities, most agree that Catholic's campus ministry, which sponsors some events, is "very strong and growing," and "provides great support." Overall, the unique opportunities provided by living in Washington, D.C., and the "beautiful" campus more than outweigh the concerns that most students have about the lack of on-campus social activities.

### Student Body

Most students agree that homogeny in the student body is Catholic's biggest weakness. However, most say that while "the lack of diversity here is very disappointing," the majority of the students are "friendly and approachable." Many also point to a lack of school spirit as another shortcoming." Despite the religious affiliation of the university, students do not feel smothered by religion. While many students speak of an abundance of cliques, most say "people here generally get along. There is a fairly friendly atmosphere on campus."

# CATHOLIC UNIVERSITY OF AMERICA

FINANCIAL AID: 202-319-5307 • E-MAIL: CUA-ADMISSIONS@CUA.EDU • WEBSITE: WWW.CUA.EDU

## ADMISSIONS

*Very important factors considered include:* character/personal qualities, essays, recommendations, secondary school record, standardized test scores, volunteer work. *Important factors considered include:* extracurricular activities, interview, talent/ability. *Other factors considered include:* alumni/ae relation, class rank, minority status, work experience. SAT I or ACT required. TOEFL required of all international applicants. High school diploma or GED is required. *High school units required/recommended:* 17 total recommended; 4 English recommended, 3 math recommended, 3 science recommended, 1 science lab recommended, 2 foreign language recommended, 4 social studies recommended, 1 history recommended.

### The Inside Word

This is not the place to try radical approaches to completing your admissions application: smooth sailing for solid students and even friendlier for candidates from distant states or unique high schools.

## FINANCIAL AID

*Students should submit:* FAFSA. Regular filing deadline is February 1. The Princeton Review suggests that all financial aid forms be submitted as soon as possible after January 1. *Need-based scholarships/grants offered:* Pell, SEOG, state scholarships/grants, private scholarships, the school's own gift aid, Federal Nursing. *Loan aid offered:* FFEL Subsidized Stafford, FFEL Unsubsidized Stafford, FFEL PLUS, Federal Perkins, Federal Nursing. Federal Work-Study Program available. Institutional employment available. Applicants will be notified of awards on a rolling basis beginning on or about April 1. Off-campus job opportunities are excellent.

## FROM THE ADMISSIONS OFFICE

"The Catholic University of America's friendly atmosphere, rigorous academic programs, and emphasis on time-honored values attract students from most states and more than 100 foreign countries. Its 144-acre, tree-lined campus is only 10 minutes from the nation's capital. Distinguished as the national university of the Catholic Church in the United States, CUA is the only institution of higher education established by the U.S. Catholic bishops; however, students from all religious traditions are welcome.

"CUA offers undergraduate degrees in more than 60 major areas in 6 schools of study. Students enroll into the School of Arts and Sciences, Architecture, Nursing, Engineering, Music, or Philosophy. Additionally, CUA students can concentrate in areas of pre-professional study including law, dental, medicine, or veterinary.

"With Capitol Hill, the Smithsonian Institution, NASA, the Kennedy Center, and the National Institutes of Health among the places students obtain internships, first-hand experience is a valuable piece of the experience that CUA offers. Numerous students also take the opportunity in their junior year to study abroad at one of Catholic's 17 country program sites. Political science majors even have the opportunity to do a Parliamentary Internship in either England or Ireland. With the campus just minutes away from downtown via the Metrorail rapid transit system, students enjoy a residential campus in an exciting city of historical monuments, theaters, festivals, ethnic restaurants, and parks."

## SELECTIVITY

| | |
|---|---:|
| Admissions Rating | 86 |
| # of applicants | 2,708 |
| % of applicants accepted | 82 |
| % of acceptees attending | 32 |

### FRESHMAN PROFILE

| | |
|---|---:|
| Range SAT Verbal | 530-640 |
| Range SAT Math | 520-640 |
| Range ACT Composite | 21-28 |
| Minimum TOEFL | 550 |
| Average HS GPA | 3.4 |
| % graduated top 10% of class | 33 |
| % graduated top 25% of class | 62 |
| % graduated top 50% of class | 87 |

### DEADLINES

| | |
|---|---:|
| Early decision | 12/1 |
| Early decision notification | 1/15 |
| Regular admission | 2/15 |
| Regular notification | 3/20 |
| Nonfall registration? | yes |

### APPLICANTS ALSO LOOK AT AND OFTEN PREFER
Notre Dame
U. Virginia
Boston Coll.
Georgetown U.

### AND SOMETIMES PREFER
Holy Cross
William and Mary
Villanova
Loyola Coll. (MD)
U. Scranton

### AND RARELY PREFER
American
Fordham
LaSalle U.
George Washington

## FINANCIAL FACTS

| | |
|---|---:|
| Financial Aid Rating | 85 |
| Tuition | $22,200 |
| Room and board | $9,002 |
| Books and supplies | $925 |
| Required fees | $1,050 |
| % frosh receiving aid | 78 |
| % undergrads receiving aid | 78 |
| Avg frosh grant | $13,573 |
| Avg frosh loan | $3,460 |

THE BEST 351 COLLEGES ■ 121

# CENTENARY COLLEGE OF LOUISIANA

PO Box 41188, Shreveport, LA 71134-1188 • Admissions: 318-869-5131 • Fax: 318-869-5005

## CAMPUS LIFE

| Quality of Life Rating | 80 |
|---|---|
| Type of school | private |
| Affiliation | Methodist |
| Environment | suburban |

### STUDENTS

| Total undergrad enrollment | 897 |
|---|---|
| % male/female | 39/61 |
| % from out of state | 39 |
| % live on campus | 66 |
| % in (# of) fraternities | 12 (4) |
| % in (# of) sororities | 18 (2) |
| % African American | 7 |
| % Asian | 2 |
| % Caucasian | 88 |
| % Hispanic | 2 |
| % international | 3 |
| # of countries represented | 18 |

### SURVEY SAYS . . .

Students love Shreveport, LA
Great library
Great computer facilities
Intercollegiate sports unpopular or nonexistent
Registration is a pain
Campus difficult to get around
Unattractive campus
Students don't get along with local community

## ACADEMICS

| Academic Rating | 84 |
|---|---|
| Calendar | other |
| Student/faculty ratio | 12:1 |
| Profs interesting rating | 96 |
| Profs accessible rating | 98 |
| % profs teaching UG courses | 100 |
| Avg reg class size | 10-19 students |

### MOST POPULAR MAJORS
Business administration/management
Biology/biological sciences
Communications and related fields

## STUDENTS SPEAK OUT

### Academics

Size matters at Centenary College, where the school's small student population allows for "an incredible amount of personal attention, if you want it." Writes one student, "It's hard to get lost in the crowd on this campus, unless you really want to. I consider this to be a great strength, because professors can get to know your individual strengths, weaknesses, and particular needs during your time with them." Professors here "are willing to have study sessions and homework sessions with the class, if the class requests one. Also, they are willing to help you with research, finding a job, and graduate school. It's really great to know that your teachers care that you are coming to class and learning." Gushes one undergrad, "Professors develop and revise programs and classes to accommodate the wishes of students. That includes anything from class times to term materials." Similarly, the administration is "very open and understanding . . . . It's nice to see the president/dean at least once a day, and for him to know your name." A "high rate of acceptance into medical school," exceptional classroom facilities, and "an incredible music faculty" draw further praise from students.

### Life

Greek life is big on the Centenary campus, "which can be somewhat irksome to those of us who aren't involved in fraternities/sororities." Many point out, on the other hand, that "the Greeks on campus are pretty cool about how they treat the rest of the students, and they are very involved in various aspects of student life." Those outside the Greek system report satisfaction with "a rich arts culture, with the film society, Pandora fine arts/literature publication, the theatre, choir, and various little music groups." The school's diminutive student body is a definite social asset, according to some; points out one student, "I love the small size. When organizing a large event (homecoming, theme weeks, or any other multiple-organization events) all of the heads of the organizations can call each other up or run into each other easily because everyone knows everyone." Students agree that hometown Shreveport could be more student-friendly. "The only problem with this school is the lack of things to do in Shreveport for people who are under 21. I think a lot of people end up drinking at the frat houses because they can't find a better way to spend their free time, at least in terms of recreational activities." Partiers appreciate the fact that "Centenary SGA has set up a program with a local taxi service for us to be able to get a ride home for free should we drink too much while out. The best part is that people actually utilize this program." Undergrads are less sanguine about the dorms, which "need some work. More specifically, we need a new one (an extra, not a renovation) and all of the others could use some renovation." They also gripe that "the cafeteria can be really horrendous. It's almost unbelievable how bad it can be, really."

### Student Body

This year's survey responses showed a definite upgrade in campus harmony at Centenary, with fewer reports of cliquishness and far more comments along the lines of the following: "Most of the time, Centenary is just one big happy family. Well, that sounded like an admissions brochure, didn't it? But it's really true. I know damn near everyone on campus, at least by first name, and I greet them when I see them between classes." Notes one student, "This campus is the most calm thing I've ever seen. I don't believe it sometimes." Some students self-segregate, "not according to race or class, but according to involvement. The groups on campus are organizational: media, Greeks, athletic teams, etc.," but according to most, the vibe remains copasetic among different groups. Although the school maintains strong ties to the Methodist Church, "there is not a large population of religious students. There are diverse groups of personalities among students, but not diverse as far as ethnicity goes."

# CENTENARY COLLEGE OF LOUISIANA

FINANCIAL AID: 318-869-5137 • E-MAIL: ADMISSIONS@CENTENARY.EDU • WEBSITE: WWW.CENTENARY.EDU

## ADMISSIONS

*Very important factors considered include:* secondary school record. *Important factors considered include:* alumni/ae relation, character/personal qualities, extracurricular activities, interview, standardized test scores, talent/ability, volunteer work. *Other factors considered include:* class rank, essays, geographical residence, minority status, recommendations, religious affiliation/commitment, work experience. SAT I or ACT required. TOEFL required of all international applicants. High school diploma or GED is required. *High school units required/recommended:* 15 total recommended; 4 English recommended, 3 math recommended, 3 science recommended, 2 science lab recommended, 2 foreign language recommended, 3 social studies recommended.

## The Inside Word

Centenary has historically had a small applicant pool, and thus has had to admit the majority in order to meet its freshman enrollment goals. Currently, the school has attracted a larger applicant pool and become noticeably more strict in its admit rate. Its reputation, though regional, is quite solid, and the college does a good job of enrolling its admits. A very friendly and efficient admissions office no doubt contributes to such success.

## FINANCIAL AID

*Students should submit:* FAFSA. Priority filing deadline is February 15. The Princeton Review suggests that all financial aid forms be submitted as soon as possible after January 1. *Need-based scholarships/grants offered:* Pell, SEOG, state scholarships/grants, private scholarships, the school's own gift aid. *Loan aid offered:* FFEL Subsidized Stafford, FFEL Unsubsidized Stafford, FFEL PLUS, Federal Perkins. Federal Work-Study Program available. Institutional employment available. Applicants will be notified of awards on or about March 15. Off-campus job opportunities are excellent.

## FROM THE ADMISSIONS OFFICE

"Centenary students work closely with a gifted faculty and inquisitive peers. Small classes and interactive learning keep our students coming back after class to ask that extra question . . . or working a little longer to produce their very best. Our students were the leaders of their schools and communities. We know college should not be an end to their activities, but a furthering of their experiences. Centenary College provides ample and varied opportunities to further leadership experiences in an atmosphere of integrity and honesty encouraged by the Honor Code. Our students come for experiential learning through our service-learning program. They participate in a global classroom through our intercultural and study abroad programs. They develop their career paths with the help of dedicated faculty, staff, and internship mentors. Come visit Centenary College, get the facts, and find out if we are best for you."

## SELECTIVITY

| | |
|---|---|
| Admissions Rating | 76 |
| # of applicants | 936 |
| % of applicants accepted | 65 |
| % of acceptees attending | 45 |

### FRESHMAN PROFILE

| | |
|---|---|
| Range SAT Verbal | 530-650 |
| Range SAT Math | 550-650 |
| Range ACT Composite | 23-28 |
| Average ACT Composite | 25 |
| Minimum TOEFL | 600 |
| % graduated top 10% of class | 30 |
| % graduated top 25% of class | 60 |
| % graduated top 50% of class | 87 |

### DEADLINES

| | |
|---|---|
| Early decision | 12/1 |
| Early decision notification | 1/1 |
| Priority admission | 2/15 |
| Regular notification | 3/15 |
| Nonfall registration? | yes |

### APPLICANTS ALSO LOOK AT
**AND OFTEN PREFER**
Rhodes
**AND SOMETIMES PREFER**
Millsaps
LSU
**AND RARELY PREFER**
Northwestern State U

## FINANCIAL FACTS

| | |
|---|---|
| Financial Aid Rating | 90 |
| Tuition | $16,750 |
| Room and board | $5,850 |
| Books and supplies | $1,000 |
| Required fees | $500 |
| % frosh receiving aid | 67 |
| % undergrads receiving aid | 63 |

# CENTRE COLLEGE

600 WEST WALNUT STREET, DANVILLE, KY 40422 • ADMISSIONS: 800-423-6236 • FAX: 859-238-5373

## CAMPUS LIFE

| | |
|---|---|
| Quality of Life Rating | 77 |
| Type of school | private |
| Affiliation | Presbyterian |
| Environment | suburban |

### STUDENTS

| | |
|---|---|
| Total undergrad enrollment | 1,055 |
| % male/female | 47/53 |
| % from out of state | 29 |
| % from public high school | 79 |
| % live on campus | 94 |
| % in (# of) fraternities | 55 (6) |
| % in (# of) sororities | 59 (4) |
| % African American | 2 |
| % Asian | 2 |
| % Caucasian | 95 |
| % international | 1 |
| # of countries represented | 12 |

### SURVEY SAYS . . .
Campus feels safe
Low cost of living
No one cheats
Lousy off-campus food
Frats and sororities dominate social scene
Diversity lacking on campus
Athletic facilities need improving
Campus easy to get around

## ACADEMICS

| | |
|---|---|
| Academic Rating | 84 |
| Calendar | 4-1-4 |
| Student/faculty ratio | 11:1 |
| Profs interesting rating | 69 |
| Profs accessible rating | 74 |
| % profs teaching UG courses | 100 |
| Avg lab size | 10-19 students |
| Avg reg class size | 10-19 students |

### MOST POPULAR MAJORS
Economics
English language and literature
History

## STUDENTS SPEAK OUT

### Academics

Centre College may not yet have the academic reputation of, say, Harvard, but that doesn't stop its students from singing the school's praises or referring to it as "the Harvard of the South." Students love the fact that Centre's core curriculum "teaches the skills of critical thinking, public speaking, and thoughtful writing" and describe requirements as "rigorous." Writes one, "Centre is so strong academically because we are given a great deal of work and responsibility. We write papers and give presentations in every class, no matter what the subject. You are expected to be prepared, and you will be asked questions in class." Faculty and staff provide extensive support to students; explains one undergrad, "People here are committed to our undergraduate studies. They are eager for us to succeed, so they make themselves available to us all of the time. They even give us their home telephone numbers and invite us into their homes for Christmas parties and stuff." Reports another, "Skipping a class here will result in a phone call or e-mail by your prof just to make sure everything is okay. They are genuinely concerned with your progress as a student." Professors, who "live to teach," "tend to be more liberal than the student body and often encourage us to do 'radical' things." Students also note that "study abroad programs are highly recommended (there's a scholarship available for seniors that haven't done one)."

### Life

Centre students enjoy a balanced mix of academics and social life, according to most. As one explains, "Due to the intense nature of the academics, students can't afford to waste all their time partying. This doesn't mean we don't know how to have fun. If you don't believe me, go to the Phi Delta Air Guitar Party, or to an acoustic jam session, or one of Buddha's infamous 'Hooch Parties.'" While "some people complain [that] most of Centre's party life is centered on Greek Row," others commend "a very active student activities council that has been planning more activities each term. We've had several campus-wide dances, which were extremely successful and lots of fun!" Besides, "every fraternity party is open to whomever wishes to attend—there are no closed parties," meaning the Greeks play a less divisive role here than they do at many other schools. It's also "very common for a large portion of the student body to attend sporting events and other campus activities." When they're not spending time in hometown Danville, students head "to Lexington or Louisville, but not as often as you would think. Sometimes there is a trip to Eastern Kentucky University to party." Students happily report that "there are a lot of people on Centre's campus who don't drink, and the cool thing about Centre is that no one pressures them to drink, and they're usually happy to help someone who may have had a little too much."

### Student Body

Centre undergrads describe a peaceful, near-idyllic campus community. Writes one, "At Centre everyone on campus either is going to school there, teaching there, working there, or lives there in town, and everyone says 'hi' to each other when they pass on the sidewalks. Even our separate Greek organizations do collaborative projects and get along pretty well." Students here "are cultured, but not snobby. It's a nice mix between southern hospitality and northern academics." Nearly all "have high standards and strong work ethics. They know how to study hard during the week, as well as have a great time on the weekends." Students do concede, however, that "there is not much ethnic or racial diversity at Centre."

# CENTRE COLLEGE

FINANCIAL AID: 859-238-5365 • E-MAIL: ADMISSION@CENTRE.EDU • WEBSITE: WWW.CENTRE.EDU

## ADMISSIONS

*Very important factors considered include:* class rank, secondary school record. *Important factors considered include:* essays, standardized test scores. *Other factors considered include:* alumni/ae relation, character/personal qualities, extracurricular activities, interview, recommendations, talent/ability. SAT I or ACT required. TOEFL required of all international applicants. *High school units required/recommended:* 13 total required; 4 English required, 4 math required, 2 science required, 3 science recommended, 2 science lab required, 2 foreign language required, 2 history required.

### *The Inside Word*

Centre's small but very capable student body reflects solid academic preparation from high school, and it's no surprise that this is exactly what the admissions committee expects from applicants. If you're ranked in the top quarter of your graduating class and have taken challenging courses throughout your high school career, you should have smooth sailing through the admissions process. Those who rank below the top quarter or who have inconsistent academic backgrounds will find entrance here more difficult, and may benefit from an interview.

## FINANCIAL AID

*Students should submit:* FAFSA, institution's own financial aid form. Regular filing deadline is March 1. The Princeton Review suggests that all financial aid forms be submitted as soon as possible after January 1. *Need-based scholarships/grants offered:* Pell, SEOG, state scholarships/grants, private scholarships, the school's own gift aid. *Loan aid offered:* FFEL Subsidized Stafford, FFEL Unsubsidized Stafford, FFEL PLUS, Federal Perkins, college/university loans from institutional funds. Federal Work-Study Program available. Institutional employment available. Applicants will be notified of awards on or about April 1. Off-campus job opportunities are fair.

## FROM THE ADMISSIONS OFFICE

"Centre's personal approach to education produces extraordinary advantages for students. First, we demonstrate our dedication to globally focused career-relevant education with the 'Centre Commitment': all students who meet our academic and social expectations are guaranteed an internship, study abroad, and graduation in four years—or we provide up to an additional year of study, tuition-free.

"Other advantages: National top 50 academic reputation, 'majors' advantages (complete two/design your own), exposure to the world's best and most interesting (internationally known artists and scholars, Vice Presidential Debate on campus). Benefits like these produce extraordinary results. For example: entrance to top graduate and professional schools; the most prestigious postgraduate scholarships (Rhodes, Fulbright, Goldwater); interesting, rewarding jobs (within nine months of graduation, 95 percent of graduates are either employed or engaged in advance study).

"How do alumni respond? They express their customer satisfaction by leading the U.S. in their percentage of annual financial support. How much does all this cost? Because of our nation-leading alumni support, *Centre is the most affordable of America's top 50 national liberal arts colleges.*"

## SELECTIVITY

| | |
|---|---:|
| Admissions Rating | 77 |
| # of applicants | 1,345 |
| % of applicants accepted | 78 |
| % of acceptees attending | 28 |
| # accepting a place on wait list | 50 |
| % admitted from wait list | 18 |

### FRESHMAN PROFILE

| | |
|---|---:|
| Range SAT Verbal | 550-650 |
| Average SAT Verbal | 612 |
| Range SAT Math | 560-650 |
| Average SAT Math | 603 |
| Range ACT Composite | 25-29 |
| Average ACT Composite | 27 |
| Minimum TOEFL | 580 |
| Average HS GPA | 3.9 |
| % graduated top 10% of class | 53 |
| % graduated top 25% of class | 80 |
| % graduated top 50% of class | 99 |

### DEADLINES

| | |
|---|---:|
| Early action | 12/1 |
| Regular admission | 2/1 |
| Regular notification | 3/1 |

### APPLICANTS ALSO LOOK AT
### AND OFTEN PREFER
Davidson
Washington & Lee
### AND SOMETIMES PREFER
Rhodes
Kenyon
Furman
Sewanee
### AND RARELY PREFER
Kentucky
Louisville
Transylvania

## FINANCIAL FACTS

| | |
|---|---:|
| Financial Aid Rating | 84 |
| Tuition | $20,400 |
| Room and board | $6,900 |
| Books and supplies | $700 |
| % frosh receiving aid | 70 |
| % undergrads receiving aid | 66 |
| Avg frosh grant | $14,000 |
| Avg frosh loan | $2,600 |

# CITY UNIV. OF NY—BROOKLYN COLLEGE

2900 BEDFORD AVENUE, BROOKLYN, NY 11210 • ADMISSIONS: 718-951-5001

## CAMPUS LIFE

| | |
|---|---|
| Quality of Life Rating | 90 |
| Type of school | public |
| Environment | urban |

### STUDENTS

| | |
|---|---|
| Total undergrad enrollment | 10,767 |
| % male/female | 39/61 |
| % from out of state | 2 |
| % from public high school | 71 |
| % in (# of) fraternities | 2 (5) |
| % in (# of) sororities | 2 (4) |
| % African American | 30 |
| % Asian | 10 |
| % Caucasian | 48 |
| % Hispanic | 11 |
| % international | 5 |

### SURVEY SAYS . . .
Ethnic diversity on campus
Beautiful campus
Campus easy to get around
Great computer facilities
Student publications are ignored
Theater is unpopular
Student government is unpopular
Very little beer drinking

## ACADEMICS

| | |
|---|---|
| Academic Rating | 83 |
| Calendar | semester |
| Student/faculty ratio | 16:1 |
| Profs interesting rating | 90 |
| Profs accessible rating | 87 |
| % classes taught by TAs | 8 |
| Avg reg class size | 20-29 students |

### MOST POPULAR MAJORS
Business administration/management
Computer and information sciences
Education

## STUDENTS SPEAK OUT

### Academics

Students love that "there are a great deal of choices at Brooklyn College," a City University of New York campus located deep within the city's most populous borough. Undergraduates may choose from among 125 different majors; business, computer science, education, accounting, psychology, film and television, and speech pathology are among the most popular here. Students also praise the science departments. Film students note that the school's proximity to a major entertainment capital provides them teachers with broad industry experience. Reports one senior, "My overall academic experience has been great, and though some of my professors have been a little crazy, they are quite knowledgeable." Students' complaints are typical of those lodged by their peers at low-tuition public schools. The primary focus of their discontent is the bureaucracy that rules Brooklyn: "Every little thing requires a form to be filled out," and "the administration is kind of difficult to deal with, so if you wind up at BC, don't expect a ton of help." Instructors, many feel, "are distant. They teach, you learn, there is very little personal interaction." Many students dislike the 10-course core requirement, which obliges students to study a broad range of disciplines. "The requirements are outrageous," grouses one undergrad. "It's supposed to expose you to many different disciplines, which I think is great, but 10 is just too much to me." But, hey BC's students will be renaissance people before they graduate, whether they like it or not! Compounding problems is the fact that "there are not enough classes given in most fields of study for working adults. Most of the important classes that are needed to fulfill degree requirements are given during the day, when most adults are at a full-time job." Even so, most undergrads would agree that "the overall experience is positive" at BC.

### Life

With no dormitories and relatively few students living in the area immediately surrounding the campus, Brooklyn College lacks the standard components of an active campus social life, and unsurprisingly, it is relatively quiet when classes end. "Most students are busy, working, raising families, and studying," explains one student. "There is time for student events, but it is hard." Those who get involved tell us that "life at Brooklyn College is a wonderful experience, so long as one takes advantage of all the college has to offer. We have on-campus jazz concerts, dance festivals, plays, lectures from well-known scholars, and a beautiful campus that you can walk through and enjoy." Academic clubs, student organizations, and the Greeks "usually help you meet people quickly, and even though the Greek life on campus isn't really that big, there are often fun fraternity and sorority parties going on at local bars and clubs." Conveniently, "club hours—designated times that all clubs meet and no classes are scheduled—make it easy to join things." Otherwise, campus life is pretty sedate. Located in the Midwood section of Brooklyn, the college "is in a very urban environment," albeit one that has surprisingly few good eateries near campus; warns one student, "The food on campus is absolutely awful . . . . Food off campus is just as bad." Students observe that "what's cool about Brooklyn is it's easy to get places, thanks to the buses and trains, and you can usually find something going on." A subway ride from campus to midtown Manhattan takes approximately 30 minutes.

### Student Body

The student body of Brooklyn College "is extremely diverse. Many students have come from foreign countries. You'll meet every nationality you could think of (or maybe didn't) at Brooklyn College. Amazingly, everyone pretty much gets along all right despite the many differences of the diverse student body." Most appreciate the diversity, telling us they "love interacting with people of different cultural groups and learning about foreign cultures." A number of undergrads here are first-generation college students "from a lower economic status. They are working to support their own educations" and, accordingly, are busier and more serious than typical college students.

# CITY UNIVERSITY OF NEW YORK—BROOKLYN COLLEGE

FINANCIAL AID: 718-951-5051 • E-MAIL: ADMINGRY@BROOKLYN.CUNY.EDU • WEBSITE: WWW.BROOKLYN.CUNY.EDU

## ADMISSIONS

*Very important factors considered include:* secondary school record, standardized test scores. *Other factors considered include:* extracurricular activities, interview, recommendations, talent/ability. SAT I or ACT required; SAT II recommended. TOEFL required of all international applicants. High school diploma or GED is required. *High school units required/recommended:* 4 English recommended, 3 math recommended, 3 science recommended, 3 foreign language recommended, 4 social studies recommended, 4 elective recommended.

### The Inside Word

Like other City University of New York (CUNY) schools, Brooklyn College provides easy access to a college education for students who want one. Brooklyn raises the bar, however, with superior offerings in the arts and sciences. You don't have to have a spotless academic record to get into Brooklyn College, but once there you will receive a solid and respected education.

## FINANCIAL AID

*Students should submit:* FAFSA, state aid form. No deadline for regular filing. The Princeton Review suggests that all financial aid forms be submitted as soon as possible after January 1. *Need-based scholarships/grants offered:* Pell, SEOG, state scholarships/grants, private scholarships, the school's own gift aid. *Loan aid offered:* Direct Subsidized Stafford, Direct Unsubsidized Stafford, Direct PLUS, Federal Perkins. Federal Work-Study Program available. Institutional employment available. Applicants will be notified of awards on a rolling basis beginning on or about June 1. Off-campus job opportunities are excellent.

## FROM THE ADMISSIONS OFFICE

"Brooklyn College, founded in 1930, ranked first last year in The Princeton Review's *The Best 345 Colleges* as the most 'Beautiful Campus' in the country. It was also ranked fifth in the country for providing the 'Best Academic Bang for Your Buck' and for its friendly diversity on the 'Students from Different Backgrounds Interact' list.

"The College, a premiere public liberal arts college, is easily reached by subway or bus, and its accessibility to Manhattan allows students to enrich their educational experience through the city's myriad cultural events and institutions. Brooklyn College's 15,000 undergraduate and graduate students represent the ethnic and cultural diversity of the borough.

"The College continues on an ambitious drive of expansion and renewal. A dazzling new library opened on campus a year ago. It is the most technologically advanced educational and research library in the CUNY system.

"Respected nationally for its rigorous academic standards, the College takes pride in such innovative programs as its award-winning Freshman Year College and the core curriculum. The acclaimed Honors Academy houses nine programs for high achievers, including the Mellon Fellowship, which supports minority students, and the BA-MD Program in coordination with SUNY Downstate College of Medicine. Brooklyn College's strong academic reputation has attracted an outstanding faculty of nationally recognized teachers and renowned scholars. Among the awards they have won are Pulitzers, Guggenheims, Fulbrights, and National Institutes of Health grants. Brooklyn College students also receive such prestigious honors as the coveted Beinecke Memorial Scholarship, which pays for a substantial portion of graduate study; the Tow and the Furman Undergraduate Travel Stipends; and the Paul and Daisy Soros Fellowships for New Americans."

---

## ADMISSIONS

| | |
|---|---:|
| Admissions Rating | 75 |
| # of applicants | 6,184 |
| % of applicants accepted | 36 |
| % of acceptees attending | 55 |

### FRESHMAN PROFILE

| | |
|---|---:|
| Range SAT Verbal | 440-550 |
| Average SAT Verbal | 497 |
| Range SAT Math | 470-570 |
| Average SAT Math | 523 |
| Minimum TOEFL | 500 |
| Average HS GPA | 3.0 |

### DEADLINES

| | |
|---|---:|
| Priority admission | 12/15 |
| Regular admission | rolling |
| Nonfall registration? | yes |

### APPLICANTS ALSO LOOK AT
**AND OFTEN PREFER**
NYU
**AND SOMETIMES PREFER**
SUNY Binghamton
SUNY Stony Brook
**AND RARELY PREFER**
Long Island U
St. Francis College

## FINANCIAL FACTS

| | |
|---|---:|
| Financial Aid Rating | 90 |
| In-state tuition | $3,200 |
| Out-of-state tuition | $6,800 |
| Room and board | $4,200 |
| Required fees | $353 |
| % frosh receiving aid | 59 |
| % undergrads receiving aid | 75 |

# CITY UNIV. OF NY—HUNTER COLLEGE

695 PARK AVENUE, NEW YORK, NY 10021 • ADMISSIONS: 212-772-4000 • FAX: 212-650-3336

## CAMPUS LIFE

★ ★ ☆ ☆

| | |
|---|---|
| **Quality of Life Rating** | **71** |
| Type of school | public |
| Environment | urban |

### STUDENTS
| | |
|---|---|
| Total undergrad enrollment | 15,494 |
| % male/female | 30/70 |
| % from out of state | 2 |
| % from public high school | 74 |
| % in (# of) fraternities | 1 (2) |
| % in (# of) sororities | 1 (2) |
| % African American | 18 |
| % Asian | 14 |
| % Caucasian | 40 |
| % Hispanic | 21 |
| % international | 6 |

### SURVEY SAYS . . .
Ethnic diversity on campus
Political activism is hot
Everyone loves New York, NY
Different students interact
Lots of classroom discussion
Very little beer drinking
Very little hard liquor

## ACADEMICS

| | |
|---|---|
| **Academic Rating** | **73** |
| Calendar | semester |
| Profs interesting rating | 84 |
| Profs accessible rating | 86 |

## STUDENTS SPEAK OUT

### Academics
For many New York residents, Hunter College is the answer to the nagging question, "How in the world can I afford a college education?" With a solid reputation in the natural sciences, health sciences, social work, and English, Hunter offers not only a college degree but also one well regarded in academic circles, all at a price that's relatively easy on the bank account. Of course, because the school places a strong emphasis on keeping tuition and fees low, students enjoy few frills along with their learning experience. One student explains that as "with all city schools there are so many students, and sometimes getting exactly what you want is tough, but I think Hunter College does a good job trying to help students in times of need." Administrative issues are the most frustrating here. Another writes, "Classes are at times crowded and hard to get into. Nevertheless, it is possible to speak to professors and get individual attention if you are really interested." While "some profs are really good," others "need more training, and they need to be encouraged to spend time outside the classroom with their students." The honors program here is reportedly "very good."

### Life
Hunter is almost exclusively a commuter college. Even the school's few residents live away from campus, in a dormitory two miles south of the school. All others live in apartments scattered across New York's five boroughs, to which they return immediately after classes let out. Accordingly, there is "very little social life at Hunter. Everyone works and studies." Says one student, "Nothing active goes on. I try to get around and hear about social events, but it is usually a drag." Student organizations, intercollegiate and intramural sports, and campus theater help fill the void somewhat, but for most students extracurriculars take place off campus in the city that never sleeps. "New York is the best! The activities don't stop!" explains one enthusiastic student. Hunter's East Side location is close to art galleries, high-end fashion shops, and Central Park ("great for warm weather") and not nearly as dangerous as the movies make it out to be) and also provides easy subway access to Wall Street, Greenwich Village, Yankee Stadium, the Bronx Zoo, and any of a thousand other fabulous destinations. The campus itself, however, a four-building complex between Lexington and Park Avenues, "needs some serious updating."

### Student Body
Hunter's student body is among the nation's most racially varied, with African American, Asian, Latino, and Caucasian populations nearly in parity. "It would be impossible to have a more diverse student body," sums up one student. Diversity also manifests itself in students' attitudes. "Hunter is a melting pot of the highly intelligent and the extreme slacker," writes one undergrad. And another notes, "There is a scene here for any type, whether it be religious, studious, political, or stoned." Politically, student opinion ranges from the middle-of-the-road to the left, with very few students admitting to conservatism. Students are also "acutely aware of social, political, and cultural situations in general." With a large nontraditional population and little campus housing, students rarely see each other except in classes or at the library. Explains one, "Hunter students work. They are not, in the usual sense, college students. They live in the real world, not in an isolated, artificial social environment."

# CITY UNIVERSITY OF NEW YORK—HUNTER COLLEGE

FINANCIAL AID: 212-772-4820 • E-MAIL: ADMISSIONS@HUNTER.CUNY.EDU • WEBSITE: WWW.HUNTER.CUNY.EDU

## ADMISSIONS

*Very important factors considered include:* secondary school record, standardized test scores. *Other factors considered include:* essays, recommendations. SAT I or ACT required. TOEFL required of all international applicants. High school diploma or GED is required. *High school units required/recommended:* 14 total required; 16 total recommended; 2 English required, 4 English recommended, 2 math required, 3 math recommended, 1 science required, 2 science recommended, 1 science lab required, 2 science lab recommended, 2 foreign language recommended, 4 social studies recommended, 1 elective recommended.

## The Inside Word

Nothing personal here; applications are processed through CUNY's enormous central processing center. Follow the numbers—and be sure to have followed the updated high school curriculum requirements—and gain admission. Looking ahead, expect admissions requirements throughout CUNY to continue to reflect heightened concern with academic preparedness. Hunter will no doubt continue to be among the most demanding CUNY units.

## FINANCIAL AID

*Students should submit:* FAFSA, state aid form. No deadline for regular filing. The Princeton Review suggests that all financial aid forms be submitted as soon as possible after January 1. *Need-based scholarships/grants offered:* Pell, SEOG, state scholarships/grants, private scholarships, the school's own gift aid. *Loan aid offered:* Direct Subsidized Stafford, Direct Unsubsidized Stafford, Direct PLUS, Federal Perkins. Federal Work-Study Program available. Institutional employment available. Applicants will be notified of awards on a rolling basis. Off-campus job opportunities are good.

## FROM THE ADMISSIONS OFFICE

"Located in the heart of Manhattan, Hunter offers students the stimulating learning environment and career-building opportunities you might expect from a college that's been a part of the world's most exciting city since 1870. The largest college in the City University of New York, Hunter pulses with energy. Hunter's vitality stems from a large, highly diverse faculty and student body. Its schools—Arts and Sciences, Education, the Health Professions, and Social Work—provide an affordable first-rate education. Undergraduates have extraordinary opportunities to conduct high-level research under renowned faculty, and many opt for credit-bearing internships in such exciting fields as media, the arts, and government. The College's high standards and special programs ensure a challenging education. The Block Program for first-year students keeps classmates together as they pursue courses in the liberal arts, pre–health science, pre-nursing, pre-med, or honors. A range of honors programs is available for students with strong academic records, including the highly competitive tuition-free Hunter CUNY Honors College for entering freshmen and the Thomas Hunter Honors Program, which emphasizes small classes with personalized mentoring by the most outstanding faculty. Qualified students also benefit from Hunter's participation in minority science research and training programs, the prestigious Andrew W. Mellon Minority Undergraduate Program, and many other passports to professional success."

## SELECTIVITY

| Admissions Rating | 79 |
|---|---|
| # of applicants | 10,550 |
| % of applicants accepted | 29 |
| % of acceptees attending | 49 |

### FRESHMAN PROFILE

| Range SAT Verbal | 470-570 |
|---|---|
| Average SAT Verbal | 523 |
| Range SAT Math | 480-580 |
| Average SAT Math | 534 |
| Minimum TOEFL | 500 |

### DEADLINES

| Priority admission | 1/2 |
|---|---|
| Nonfall registration? | yes |

### APPLICANTS ALSO LOOK AT AND OFTEN PREFER
CUNY Queens
NYU
### AND SOMETIMES PREFER
Fordham
SUNY Stony Brook
### AND RARELY PREFER
SUNY Binghamton

## FINANCIAL FACTS

| Financial Aid Rating | 80 |
|---|---|
| In-state tuition | $3,200 |
| Out-of-state tuition | $6,800 |
| Books and supplies | $759 |
| Required fees | $329 |
| % frosh receiving aid | 60 |
| % undergrads receiving aid | 60 |
| Avg frosh grant | $4,250 |
| Avg frosh loan | $2,600 |

# CITY UNIV. OF NY—QUEENS COLLEGE

65-30 KISSENA BOULEVARD, FLUSHING, NY 11367 • ADMISSIONS: 718-997-5000 • FAX: 718-997-5617

## CAMPUS LIFE

| Quality of Life Rating | 67 |
|---|---|
| Type of school | public |
| Environment | urban |

### STUDENTS

| Total undergrad enrollment | 12,012 |
|---|---|
| % male/female | 37/63 |
| % from out of state | 1 |
| % from public high school | 67 |
| % in (# of) fraternities | 1 (3) |
| % in (# of) sororities | 1 (2) |
| % African American | 10 |
| % Asian | 20 |
| % Caucasian | 53 |
| % Hispanic | 16 |
| % international | 5 |

### SURVEY SAYS . . .
Ethnic diversity on campus
Political activism is hot
Different students interact
Students love Flushing, NY
Lots of classroom discussion
Campus difficult to get around
Very little drug use
Unattractive campus
Lousy food on campus
Students are cliquish

## ACADEMICS

| Academic Rating | 74 |
|---|---|
| Calendar | semester |
| Student/faculty ratio | 17:1 |
| Profs interesting rating | 90 |
| Profs accessible rating | 87 |
| % profs teaching UG courses | 90 |
| % classes taught by TAs | 2 |
| Avg reg class size | 20-29 students |

### MOST POPULAR MAJORS
Psychology
Sociology
Accounting

## STUDENTS SPEAK OUT

### Academics
For many New York residents, Queens College offers the best opportunity for an excellent education at cut-rate prices. Explains one student, "The realities of academic life here are top-notch. I have studied and conducted independent research with world-class professors who are eager to devote much time to helping outstanding students achieve their fullest potential. Scholarships and study abroad opportunities abound here." Queens offers honors programs in the humanities, business, and the liberal arts, and the mathematical and natural sciences, which provide enhanced learning opportunities for excellent students." Many expressed frustration over CUNY's financial status, complaining that "continuous budget cuts are destroying the CUNY system." This, however, is the trade-off students make for an affordable education. For most, it is a worthwhile tradeoff because it nets them an education that is "very good overall."

### Life
Because Queens College is a commuter school (QC has no dorms at all), campus life pretty much begins and ends during the day. Writes one student, "This is not a social campus because everyone commutes. You generally become friendly with those in your major, people you constantly have classes with." A few students do take apartments in Flushing; those that do enjoy the nearby Italian, Chinese, and Korean shopping and dining. Extracurricular activities here revolve around "lots of student organizations." Explains one student, "Campus clubs have a lot of activities." Adds another, "The doors to club offices are always open, so people make the rounds of the Student Union, visiting friends as they please. There are always free concerts at the music school during free hour." Students enjoy the fact that "professors like 'doing lunch' with their students; it alleviates a lot of the academic pressure for us." Unlike other CUNY schools such as Hunter and Baruch, Queens has an actual campus, which is "very safe" and "nice and pretty" despite an odd, sometimes clashing variety of architectural styles.

### Student Body
The borough of Queens is the residence of choice for many of New York City's immigrant groups. The Queens College student body reflects the international flavor of its home; the school's promotional material boasts that 67 different native languages are spoken on campus. The student body also accurately mirrors New York's demographics, with minority students constituting nearly half the student body. Many students work their way through school here; they are "a hard-working bunch. Most are not well-off financially but are determined to better their lives through education."

# CITY UNIVERSITY OF NEW YORK—QUEENS COLLEGE

FINANCIAL AID: 718-997-5101 • E-MAIL: ADMISSIONS@QC.EDU • WEBSITE: WWW.QC.EDU

## ADMISSIONS

*Very important factors considered include:* secondary school record. *Important factors considered include:* standardized test scores, talent/ability. *Other factors considered include:* essays, recommendations. SAT I required; SAT II recommended. TOEFL required of all international applicants. High school diploma or GED is required. *High school units required/recommended:* 16 total required; 18 total recommended; 4 English required, 3 math required, 4 math recommended, 2 science required, 3 science recommended, 2 science lab required, 3 foreign language required, 4 social studies required.

### The Inside Word

Applicants to Queens follow the usual CUNY application procedures, which have gotten tougher with the implementation of updated high school curriculum requirements. Candidates for the Aaron Copeland School of Music must also successfully pass through a rigorous audition process. CUNY admissions requirements are currently undergoing close scrutiny; beware of the possibility of further changes.

## FINANCIAL AID

*Students should submit:* FAFSA, state aid form. No deadline for regular filing. The Princeton Review suggests that all financial aid forms be submitted as soon as possible after January 1. *Need-based scholarships/grants offered:* Pell, SEOG, state scholarships/grants, private scholarships, the school's own gift aid. *Loan aid offered:* Direct Subsidized Stafford, Direct Unsubsidized Stafford, Direct PLUS, Federal Perkins. Federal Work-Study Program available. Institutional employment available. Applicants will be notified of awards on a rolling basis beginning on or about March 1. Off-campus job opportunities are good.

## FROM THE ADMISSIONS OFFICE

"New York State Governor George Pataki calls Queens College 'the jewel of the City University of New York system' for two good reasons: its faculty and its students. Queens College faculty members are renowned for their commitment to scholarship and teaching. Also major contributors to the dynamic learning environment of Queens College are the students, who come from 120 nations. The Queens College curriculum is just as diverse, with nationally recognized programs in many fields, including the Aaron Copland School of Music. In fall 2003, a new Bachelor of Business Administration will offer solid preparation for a business career that is also grounded in the liberal arts and sciences. Aspiring teachers benefit from the Education Division's strength and innovative programs (Queens College educated more teachers than any college in the tri-state area). Located in the most ethnically diverse county in America, the College is a vibrant microcosm of the world, where students interact with peers representing a range of backgrounds and viewpoints. A Queens College education, which is guided by the principal, 'We Learn in Order to Serve,' is the best possible preparation for leadership in today's global village."

### SELECTIVITY

| | |
|---|---|
| Admissions Rating | 75 |
| # of applicants | 6,280 |
| % of applicants accepted | 41 |
| % of acceptees attending | 48 |

#### FRESHMAN PROFILE

| | |
|---|---|
| Range SAT Verbal | 440-550 |
| Average SAT Verbal | 504 |
| Range SAT Math | 480-590 |
| Average SAT Math | 537 |
| Minimum TOEFL | 500 |
| Average HS GPA | 3.1 |

#### DEADLINES

| | |
|---|---|
| Priority admission | 10/15 |
| Nonfall registration? | yes |

#### APPLICANTS ALSO LOOK AT AND OFTEN PREFER
St. John's University
#### AND SOMETIMES PREFER
SUNY Stony Brook

### FINANCIAL FACTS

| | |
|---|---|
| Financial Aid Rating | 82 |
| In-state tuition | $3,200 |
| Out-of-state tuition | $6,800 |
| Required fees | $203 |
| % frosh receiving aid | 83 |
| % undergrads receiving aid | 61 |
| Avg frosh grant | $3,500 |
| Avg frosh loan | $2,500 |

# CLAREMONT McKENNA COLLEGE

890 COLUMBIA AVENUE, CLAREMONT, CA 91711 • ADMISSION: 909-621-8088 • FAX: 909-621-8516

## CAMPUS LIFE

| Quality of Life Rating | 93 |
| --- | --- |
| Type of school | private |
| Environment | suburban |

### STUDENTS
| | |
| --- | --- |
| Total undergrad enrollment | 1,024 |
| % from out of state | 51 |
| % from public high school | 70 |
| % live on campus | 96 |
| % African American | 4 |
| % Asian | 16 |
| % Caucasian | 64 |
| % Hispanic | 10 |
| % international | 3 |

### SURVEY SAYS . . .
*Dorms are like palaces*
*Political activism is hot*
*Student government is popular*
*Lab facilities need improving*
*School is well run*
*(Almost) no one smokes*
*Diverse students interact*
*Student publications are popular*

## ACADEMICS

| Academic Rating | 94 |
| --- | --- |
| Calendar | semester |
| Student/faculty ratio | 8:1 |
| Profs interesting rating | 96 |
| Profs accessible rating | 99 |
| % profs teaching UG courses | 100 |

### MOST POPULAR MAJORS
Economics
International relations and affairs
Political science and government

## STUDENTS SPEAK OUT
### Academics
Located in sunny and warm southern California, Claremont McKenna competes with the nation's most prestigious liberal arts colleges for the nation's brightest students. Money and power are on students' minds, but in a good way, at least according to one student who declares, "Economics, accounting, and government are CMC's strong suits, and they're STRONG strong suits." One can expect to "meet some serious competition" in the classroom, but this hardly ever turns nasty, as "there is a lot of academic cooperation" among students. Survey respondents cite small class sizes and dedicated faculty members (there are no TAs teaching courses here) as the primary ingredients of Claremont's terrific academic milieu. "Professors here are excellent and completely accessible," gushes one student. "They will send personalized e-mails about class questions or other concerns [and] are excited when students visit them [during] office hours." At every turn Claremont's administration is waiting in the wings to provide counsel and aid. "Students see administrators walking around campus almost everyday. It's not uncommon to randomly run into the president."

### Life
Claremont's administration goes above and beyond the call of duty to entertain students, whether it's bringing renowned speakers and events to campus through the Athenaeum Symposium or offering free late night snacks in the cafeteria. This is good, according to most students, since hometown Claremont is "pretty boring." There's all manner of ways to while some time away—"movies, parties, intramural sports, parties, student plays, parties, musical and cultural events . . . did I mention parties?"—though most of it is campus-centered. Sure, L.A. is relatively close, but if you want to venture into it, "a car is a priority." As one of The Claremont Colleges, along with Pomona, Pitzer, Harvey Mudd, and Scripps, if the Claremont scene is dead on any given night, "there is always another campus to visit right across the street." Reflecting the laid-back mentality pervasive on campus, one student summarizes the social scene this way: "In general, CMC doesn't offer a fast-paced jam-packed social life, but it leaves time to study plenty, get to know most the other students, get a tan, and have a good time."

### Student Body
The students at Claremont worked hard to get here, and you can bet that they don't lose any of their motivation: "CMC students are driven and focused," writes one student. "Most work very hard and don't do things like skip most of their classes." This is not to say that the students here don't know how to have fun. This is California, where a balanced sensibility about life is the norm. "CMC's motto could just as well be 'work hard, play hard.' CMC kids will break out the Slip 'n Slide in May, sit in the sun to study, climb the trees on campus—and drink plenty." And though the numbers state otherwise, students don't see their student body as very heterogeneous. "I would have to say the student body is very mainstream," is one typical student comment on the subject. Students are politically aware, but this is no bastion of liberalism like another, bigger, big-name school upstate. In fact, many students describe most of their peers as conservative.

132 ■ THE BEST 351 COLLEGES

# CLAREMONT MCKENNA COLLEGE

FINANCIAL AID: 909-621-8356 • E-MAIL: ADMISSION@CLAREMONTMCKENNA.EDU • WEBSITE: WWW.CLAREMONTMCKENNA.EDU

## ADMISSIONS

*Very important factors considered include:* character/personal qualities, essays, extracurricular activities, secondary school record, standardized test scores. *Important factors considered include:* recommendations, talent/ability. *Other factors considered include:* alumni/ae relation, class rank, geographical residence, interview, minority status, state residency, volunteer work, work experience. SAT I or ACT required. TOEFL required of all international applicants. High school diploma or GED is required. *High school units required/recommended:* 15 total required; 18 total recommended; 4 English required, 3 math required, 4 math recommended, 2 science required, 3 science recommended, 3 foreign language required, 2 social studies required, 1 history required, 2 history recommended.

### The Inside Word

Although applicants have to possess solid academic qualifications in order to gain admission to Claremont McKenna, the importance of making a good match should not be underestimated. Colleges of such small size and selectivity devote much more energy to determining whether the candidate as an individual fits than they do to whether a candidate has the appropriate test scores.

## FINANCIAL AID

*Students should submit:* FAFSA, CSS/Financial Aid PROFILE. Regular filing deadline is February 1. The Princeton Review suggests that all financial aid forms be submitted as soon as possible after January 1. *Need-based scholarships/grants offered:* Pell, SEOG, state scholarships/grants, private scholarships, the school's own gift aid. *Loan aid offered:* Direct Subsidized Stafford, Direct Unsubsidized Stafford, Direct PLUS, Federal Perkins, college/university loans from institutional funds. Federal Work-Study Program available. Institutional employment available. Applicants will be notified of awards on or about April 1. Off-campus job opportunities are excellent.

## FROM THE ADMISSIONS OFFICE

"CMC's mission is clear: to educate students for meaningful lives and responsible leadership in business, government, and the professions. While many other colleges champion either a traditional liberal arts education with emphasis on intellectual breadth or training that stresses acquisition of technical skills, CMC offers a clear alternative. Instead of dividing the liberal arts and working world into separate realms, education at CMC is rooted in the interplay between the world of ideas and the world of events. By combining the intellectual breadth of liberal arts with the more pragmatic concerns of public affairs, CMC students gain the vision, skills, and values necessary for leadership in all sectors of society."

## SELECTIVITY

| | |
|---|---:|
| Admissions Rating | 97 |
| # of applicants | 2,918 |
| % of applicants accepted | 28 |
| % of acceptees attending | 31 |
| # accepting a place on wait list | 155 |
| % admitted from wait list | 3 |
| # of early decision applicants | 216 |
| % accepted early decision | 31 |

### FRESHMAN PROFILE

| | |
|---|---:|
| Range SAT Verbal | 630-730 |
| Average SAT Verbal | 690 |
| Range SAT Math | 650-730 |
| Average SAT Math | 700 |
| Range ACT Composite | 28-32 |
| Average ACT Composite | 30 |
| Minimum TOEFL | 600 |
| % graduated top 10% of class | 82 |
| % graduated top 25% of class | 94 |
| % graduated top 50% of class | 100 |

### DEADLINES

| | |
|---|---:|
| Early decision | 11/15 |
| Early decision notification | 12/15 |
| Regular admission | 1/2 |
| Regular notification | 4/1 |
| Nonfall registration? | yes |

### APPLICANTS ALSO LOOK AT AND OFTEN PREFER
Stanford
Harvard
### AND SOMETIMES PREFER
Georgetown
Pomona
Princeton
### AND RARELY PREFER
Occidental
U of Chicago
Berkeley

## FINANCIAL FACTS

| | |
|---|---:|
| Financial Aid Rating | 87 |
| Tuition | $27,500 |
| Room and board | $9,180 |
| Books and supplies | $850 |
| Required fees | $200 |
| % frosh receiving aid | 60 |
| % undergrads receiving aid | 62 |
| Avg frosh grant | $26,000 |
| Avg frosh loan | $3,500 |

THE BEST 351 COLLEGES ■ 133

# CLARK UNIVERSITY

950 MAIN STREET, WORCESTER, MA 01610 • ADMISSIONS: 508-793-7431 • FAX: 508-793-8821

## CAMPUS LIFE

| Quality of Life Rating | 71 |
|---|---|
| Type of school | private |
| Environment | urban |

### STUDENTS
| Total undergrad enrollment | 1,947 |
|---|---|
| % male/female | 39/61 |
| % from out of state | 62 |
| % from public high school | 70 |
| % live on campus | 76 |
| % African American | 3 |
| % Asian | 4 |
| % Caucasian | 66 |
| % Hispanic | 3 |
| % international | 8 |
| # of countries represented | 57 |

### SURVEY SAYS . . .
Students don't like Worcester, MA
Students aren't religious
(Almost) everyone smokes
Lousy food on campus
Ethnic diversity on campus
Theater is hot
(Almost) everyone plays intramural sports

## ACADEMICS

| Academic Rating | 79 |
|---|---|
| Calendar | semester |
| Student/faculty ratio | 10:1 |
| Profs interesting rating | 94 |
| Profs accessible rating | 89 |
| % profs teaching UG courses | 100 |
| Avg lab size | 10-19 students |
| Avg reg class size | 10-19 students |

### MOST POPULAR MAJORS
Psychology
Government and international relations
Business management

## STUDENTS SPEAK OUT

### Academics
Clark University undergraduates agree that their school's "size is the greatest strength; it allows for personal contact with faculty and administration, as well as fellow students. It feels much like a small community or large family." Explains one student, "Clark is so great because of the student-teacher ratio. I know all of my professors and am basically on a first name basis with them. It feels good to know that I can go to them and talk about almost anything. That's the one thing I love most about my school." Professors "are almost always accessible and really care about informing students about their area of expertise." Students agree that Clark's administration is "primarily concerned about academics. In the psychology, geography, international business, and Holocaust studies departments, we have some of the world's best experts, [and] all departments have very intelligent, informative, and open professors in them." Clark is also a "world-class" research university in many ways (rare for such a small, private school). Undergrads here are able to participate to an unusually large degree in "interesting research." Ambitious undergrads can take advantage of the "Fifth-Year Free Program," which allows "qualified students" to attend for five years for the price of four and "receive a bachelor's and master's degree," quite a bargain in today's credential-crazed world.

### Life
Clark social life is somewhat hampered by the fact that "whereas most schools have one center of campus activities, Clark has two buildings, which really hinders the ability of either to act as a truly central hub. The school needs to become more cohesive in what it offers students socially, because right now the students can't rely on the school for much in that arena." Despite this handicap, "students here are very active. Most belong to at least one group on campus." And "for a population of 2,000," there are "almost 90 different groups" to choose from. Students also enjoy the "frequent concerts held on campus. They are not exactly national bands, but it gives you something to do on the weekend. There are parties, but not many people hold small social events." Hometown Worcester "offers many sources of entertainment but few reliable forms of transportation to get you" to where the action's happening. "Many students, including freshmen, have cars on campus but choose to stay in the general area." That's too bad because "if you are willing to explore and keep an open mind you will find many treasures, like the soul food restaurant not half a mile away, a truly authentic pupuseria, wonderful botanical gardens, decent theatre, and good concerts in the area." Boston is only 40 miles away and is easily accessible by bus and train.

### Student Body
"Diversity is a huge strength" at Clark. Observes one student, "It's nice to go from white, suburban America" to a place where you can "learn about so many countries and so many races." The student body "contains all types of people, all of whom live in general harmony with each other: jocks, punks, skaters, indie-rockers, preps, etc." Agrees one undergrad, "Students are the reason Clark has the personality it does. A little offbeat, a little quirky, a little into weird and wonderful things, and all into questioning the status quo, working for positive changes in their world, and asking questions about what is good and right and necessary to make life better. [T]he students here are a great group of people." Students "are very politically active and take part in many different social movements, from animal rights to water quality." A conservative student warns that those "who aren't liberal have a hard time being heard." The international population is large; offers one student, "Sometimes I think the university is better known outside of the U.S." than within it.

# CLARK UNIVERSITY

FINANCIAL AID: 508-793-7478 • E-MAIL: ADMISSIONS@CLARKU.EDU • WEBSITE: WWW.CLARKU.EDU

## ADMISSIONS

*Very important factors considered include:* character/personal qualities, recommendations, secondary school record, standardized test scores. *Important factors considered include:* essays, extracurricular activities, talent/ability, volunteer work. *Other factors considered include:* alumni/ae relation, class rank, geographical residence, interview, minority status, work experience. SAT I or ACT required. TOEFL required of all international applicants. High school diploma or GED is required. *High school units required/recommended:* 16 total recommended; 4 English recommended, 3 math recommended, 3 science recommended, 2 science lab recommended, 2 foreign language recommended, 2 social studies recommended, 2 history recommended.

## The Inside Word

Clark is surrounded by formidable competitors, and its selectivity suffers because of it. Most "B" students will encounter little difficulty gaining admission. Given the university's solid academic environment and access to other member colleges in the Worcester Consortium, it can be a terrific choice for students who are not up to the ultra-competitive admission expectations of "top-tier" universities.

## FINANCIAL AID

*Students should submit:* FAFSA, CSS/Financial Aid PROFILE. The Princeton Review suggests that all financial aid forms be submitted as soon as possible after January 1. *Need-based scholarships/grants offered:* Pell, SEOG, state scholarships/grants, the school's own gift aid. *Loan aid offered:* FFEL Subsidized Stafford, FFEL Unsubsidized Stafford, FFEL PLUS, Federal Perkins, state loans, college/university loans from institutional funds. Federal Work-Study Program available. Applicants will be notified of awards on or about March 31. Off-campus job opportunities are good.

## FROM THE ADMISSIONS OFFICE

"At Clark University, you are respected for challenging convention, for trying out new ideas and skills, and for inspiring new ways of thinking. You learn how social change is made, and you get to be a part of it. Individual development is nurtured by a dedicated faculty who encourages hands-on learning. Founded in 1887, Clark is home to students from more than 57 countries and 44 states."

---

### SELECTIVITY
★ ★ ★ ☆

| | |
|---|---:|
| Admissions Rating | 82 |
| # of applicants | 3,694 |
| % of applicants accepted | 68 |
| % of acceptees attending | 23 |
| # accepting a place on wait list | 28 |
| % admitted from wait list | 4 |
| # of early decision applicants | 85 |
| % accepted early decision | 85 |

### FRESHMAN PROFILE

| | |
|---|---:|
| Range SAT Verbal | 540-650 |
| Average SAT Verbal | 589 |
| Range SAT Math | 540-640 |
| Average SAT Math | 586 |
| Range ACT Composite | 22-27 |
| Average ACT Composite | 25 |
| Minimum TOEFL | 550 |
| Average HS GPA | 3.4 |
| % graduated top 10% of class | 29 |
| % graduated top 25% of class | 67 |
| % graduated top 50% of class | 93 |

### DEADLINES

| | |
|---|---:|
| Early decision | 11/15 |
| Early decision notification | 12/15 |
| Regular admission | 2/1 |
| Regular notification | 4/1 |
| Nonfall registration? | yes |

### APPLICANTS ALSO LOOK AT
**AND OFTEN PREFER**
Tufts, Vassar, Brandeis
Boston College, Boston U
**AND SOMETIMES PREFER**
Ithaca College
Northeastern U
Connecticut College, Syracuse
U of New Hampshire, Skidmore
**AND RARELY PREFER**
Wheaton College (IL), UMass at Amherst, U of Vermont, UConn
Goucher College

### FINANCIAL FACTS
★ ★ ★ ☆

| | |
|---|---:|
| Financial Aid Rating | 83 |
| Tuition | $26,700 |
| Room and board | $5,150 |
| Books and supplies | $800 |
| Required fees | $265 |
| % frosh receiving aid | 84 |
| % undergrads receiving aid | 84 |
| Avg frosh grant | $13,957 |
| Avg frosh loan | $3,717 |

THE BEST 351 COLLEGES ■ 135

# CLARKSON UNIVERSITY

Box 5605, Potsdam, NY 13699 • Admissions: 315-268-6479 • Fax: 315-268-7647

## CAMPUS LIFE

★ ★ ☆ ☆

| | |
|---|---|
| Quality of Life Rating | 73 |
| Type of school | private |
| Environment | rural |

### STUDENTS

| | |
|---|---|
| Total undergrad enrollment | 2,756 |
| % male/female | 75/25 |
| % from out of state | 23 |
| % from public high school | 87 |
| % live on campus | 75 |
| % in (# of) fraternities | 15 (10) |
| % in (# of) sororities | 12 (2) |
| % African American | 2 |
| % Asian | 3 |
| % Caucasian | 93 |
| % Hispanic | 2 |
| % international | 3 |
| # of countries represented | 46 |

### SURVEY SAYS . . .
Library needs improving
Class discussions are rare
Diversity lacking on campus
Student publications are ignored
Large classes
Musical organizations aren't popular
Students aren't religious

## ACADEMICS

| | |
|---|---|
| Academic Rating | 76 |
| Calendar | semester |
| Student/faculty ratio | 17:1 |
| Profs interesting rating | 89 |
| Profs accessible rating | 93 |
| % profs teaching UG courses | 95 |
| % classes taught by TAs | 1 |
| Avg lab size | 20-29 students |
| Avg reg class size | 20-29 students |

### MOST POPULAR MAJORS
Mechanical engineering/mechanical technology/technician
Multi/interdisciplinary studies
Civil engineering technologies/technicians

## STUDENTS SPEAK OUT

### Academics

Clarkson University offers students little in the way of bells and whistles (see "Life," below), but it excels in the one area that counts most: academics. Students proudly report that Clarkson "is academically sound. The professors are good and the facilities are even better." Engineering programs are the long-time stalwarts here; business is the rising star. Students appreciate a faculty of educators that "care so much about their students. Your teachers are more like your friends, everyone knows everyone, and teachers are even seen hanging out with students out of class." Writes one student, "My professors show such an enthusiasm for their field of teaching," which makes it hardly surprising that "they are inspirational." It's not all one big engineering love fest, though. Work here is tough ("Everybody who doesn't belong disappears miraculously after their first semester"), but the rewards can be great ("The Career Development Center does an excellent job of getting people work after college") for those who cut the grade.

### Life

Like most engineering schools, Clarkson piles the work on its students, providing students with an ideal setting in which to attack it enthusiastically, since "there is not much of anything to do" on or off campus. Writes one typical student, "The common perception around campus is that there is nothing to do but get drunk or high. When people want to do something fun, they go home or visit a high school friend at another university." The Division I powerhouse hockey team is pretty much the only show in town, and students attend the "awesome" games—which are free—enthusiastically. Otherwise they work, gripe about parking ("There is never enough parking, and campus security tickets people who resort to parking on lawns, etc."), campus facilities ("The student union is not a student union. It is a hockey arena with a hockey apparel store that happens to sell candy bars. A true student union would do the campus wonders."), and, of course, the sense that there is nothing to do besides study. Hometown Potsdam, unfortunately, "is the most uneventful town in the U.S." Brutal winters further dampen activity. Is it really all that bad? Not according to at least one dissenter, who writes, "Many students will say . . . well, there's nothing to do here. I tell them they're not looking hard enough. . . . If what you want isn't here, then start it yourself. We have over 100 different clubs and organizations with new clubs being formed every year. The Adirondacks are within a half-hour drive south and Canada is a 45-minute drive north. There are always bands, comedians, and other acts . . . at MidKnights or Club 99. Get away from the computer and you'll find what you're looking for."

### Student Body

Clarkson students admit that theirs is not a diverse demographic. But they think you should know that "while diversity here tends to be of the 'What kind of white middle-class male are you?' sort, we really do run the gamut in personality types. Almost everybody finds enough people like them to feel comfortable." Says one engineer, "Though the ratio[s] of females to males and minorities to majorities do not reflect much diversity, the diversity of thought and opinion here is many times greater than at a school whose numbers may reflect extreme diversity." Students here are a "good bunch of people, not cutthroat. Everyone helps each other with work and projects all the time, which is why I like it here. It's a 'we are all here together' attitude instead of 'we are all here, but I want to be the best' attitude." The dearth of women is a problem for most men; wrote one student, "The ratio [of] men to women at my school for my graduating class is 7:1. Sometimes it's hard to get over that, but since I am female, it is quite nice."

# CLARKSON UNIVERSITY

FINANCIAL AID: 315-268-7699 • E-MAIL: ADMISSION@CLARKSON.EDU • WEBSITE: WWW.CLARKSON.EDU

## ADMISSIONS
*Very important factors considered include:* interview, secondary school record. *Important factors considered include:* class rank, extracurricular activities, recommendations, standardized test scores, volunteer work. *Other factors considered include:* alumni/ae relation, character/personal qualities, essays, talent/ability, work experience. SAT I or ACT required. TOEFL required of all international applicants. High school diploma or GED is required. *High school units required/recommended:* 16 total required; 4 English required, 3 math required, 4 math recommended, 2 science required, 3 science recommended.

### The Inside Word
Clarkson's acceptance rate is too high for solid applicants to lose much sleep about gaining admission. Serious candidates should interview anyway. If you are particularly solid and really want to come here, it could help you get some scholarship money. Women and minorities will encounter an especially friendly admissions committee.

## FINANCIAL AID
*Students should submit:* FAFSA, institution's own financial aid form, state aid form. The Princeton Review suggests that all financial aid forms be submitted as soon as possible after January 1. *Need-based scholarships/grants offered:* Pell, SEOG, state scholarships/grants, private scholarships, the school's own gift aid, HEOP. *Loan aid offered:* Direct Subsidized Stafford, Direct Unsubsidized Stafford, Direct PLUS, Federal Perkins, college/university loans from institutional funds, GATE Loans. Federal Work-Study Program available. Institutional employment available. Applicants will be notified of awards on or about March 23. Off-campus job opportunities are fair.

## FROM THE ADMISSIONS OFFICE
"Clarkson is a blend of vivid contrasts—high-powered academics in a cooperative, friendly community; technically oriented students who enjoy people; a unique location that serves as gateway to all kinds of outdoor recreation and to social and cultural activities of four colleges within a 10-mile radius. Our students are described as smart, hardworking, outgoing, energized, fun-loving, and team players. Our academic programs are rigorous, relevant, flexible, and nationally respected. Our teachers are demanding, approachable, concerned, accomplished, and inspiring. Clarkson alumni, students, and faculty share an exceptionally solid bond and the lifetime benefits that come from an active, global network of personal and professional ties."

---

### SELECTIVITY

| | |
|---|---:|
| Admissions Rating | 82 |
| # of applicants | 2,556 |
| % of applicants accepted | 82 |
| % of acceptees attending | 35 |
| # accepting a place on wait list | 4 |
| # of early decision applicants | 221 |
| % accepted early decision | 89 |

### FRESHMAN PROFILE
| | |
|---|---:|
| Range SAT Verbal | 520-620 |
| Average SAT Verbal | 570 |
| Range SAT Math | 580-670 |
| Average SAT Math | 621 |
| Minimum TOEFL | 500 |
| Average HS GPA | 3.5 |
| % graduated top 10% of class | 36 |
| % graduated top 25% of class | 72 |
| % graduated top 50% of class | 95 |

### DEADLINES
| | |
|---|---:|
| Early decision | 12/1 |
| Early decision notification | 12/30 |
| Priority admission | 2/1 |
| Regular admission | 3/1 |
| Nonfall registration? | yes |

### APPLICANTS ALSO LOOK AT
**AND OFTEN PREFER**
Rochester Institute of Technology
SUNY Buffalo
Rensselaer Polytechnic Institute
U of Vermont
Penn State at University Park
**AND SOMETIMES PREFER**
Worcester Polytechnic Institute
UConn
U of Rochester
Alfred
Lehigh
**AND RARELY PREFER**
Syracuse

### FINANCIAL FACTS

| | |
|---|---:|
| Financial Aid Rating | 86 |
| Tuition | $23,100 |
| Room and board | $8,726 |
| Books and supplies | $900 |
| Required fees | $400 |
| % frosh receiving aid | 80 |
| % undergrads receiving aid | 81 |
| Avg frosh grant | $10,662 |
| Avg frosh loan | $5,388 |

# CLEMSON UNIVERSITY

105 SIKES HALL, BOX 345124, CLEMSON, SC 29634-5124 • ADMISSIONS: 864-656-2287 • FAX: 864-656-2464

## CAMPUS LIFE

| | |
|---|---|
| Quality of Life Rating | 79 |
| Type of school | public |
| Environment | rural |

### STUDENTS

| | |
|---|---|
| Total undergrad enrollment | 13,734 |
| % male/female | 55/45 |
| % from out of state | 30 |
| % from public high school | 89 |
| % live on campus | 46 |
| % in (# of) fraternities | 13 (25) |
| % in (# of) sororities | 23 (15) |
| % African American | 7 |
| % Asian | 2 |
| % Caucasian | 85 |
| % Hispanic | 1 |
| % international | 1 |
| # of countries represented | 84 |

### SURVEY SAYS . . .
Everyone loves the Tigers
Campus is beautiful
Lots of beer drinking
(Almost) everyone smokes
Frats and sororities dominate social scene
Hard liquor is popular
Students are happy
Great computer facilities

## ACADEMICS

| | |
|---|---|
| Academic Rating | 77 |
| Calendar | semester |
| Student/faculty ratio | 15:1 |
| % profs teaching UG courses | 95 |
| % classes taught by TAs | 7 |
| Avg lab size | 20-29 students |
| Avg reg class size | 20-29 students |

### MOST POPULAR MAJORS
Business, management, marketing, and related support services
Engineering

## STUDENTS SPEAK OUT

### Academics

One of the top public universities in the country, Clemson University offers the caliber of academics that prompts its students to declare, "If I didn't know better, I would think I were at a private Ivy League school." The university's president, who is "determined to get things accomplished and change some things here," receives serious kudos from undergraduates. Writes one satisfied student, "I am currently enrolled in a Presidential Seminar Class, and I think that it is amazing that he takes time out to do this. On a campus with over 17,000 students, it is unreal that the president knows my name." Students report that the "extremely attentive" administration "makes a daily effort to be approachable." Students also praise professors, calling them "enthusiastic, knowledgeable, caring, genuine, and passionate about teaching." One undergraduate gushes, "The students are treated respectfully, and most professors will go above and beyond to help any student who truly desires to excel." The coursework is typically "challenging, but interesting and very fair." Respondents single out the engineering, biology, and math departments as some of the strongest. Several students note problems with the registration system, while others gripe about many professors' attendance policies that "remind us of middle school." The recent tuition hike doesn't sit well with students, either. But generally, undergraduates agree, "Clemson is bliss because the school is focused on teaching the students the skills they need to succeed in the job market."

### Life

If you want the short version, it's that "Clemson is a great academic school with [an] even better social life." When they are not studying, Clemson undergraduates can most often be found at football and baseball games or Greek events. During the season, "Clemson football becomes everything. An entire culture revolves around it." While certain contrarians consider such behavior "an annoying abundance of school spirit," the vast majority of students faithfully don orange on game days and fill Death Valley (Clemson's stadium, so called because opposing teams enter it to get killed) to capacity. Tailgaters convene well before kick-off, but several students assert, "Clemson students are not the hardcore partiers that our reputation has deemed us." Some undergrads wish for "more alcohol-free options" amid the sorority- and fraternity-dominated social scene, but others focus on the "billions of ways to get involved," including popular community service programs. The town of Clemson, set amid "the beauty of the South Carolina foothills," is so small and quiet that "you can even see a tumbleweed roll through the streets of 'downtown.'" On school grounds, "We have a bowling alley and pool bar that really keeps the campus connected." In general, comments abound describing the "wonderful feel of the campus" and the "laid-back southern fun" the students create for themselves. Bottom line: "Everyone here seems to be having the time of [his] life."

### Student Body

Clemson students describe their peers as generally southern, Christian, white, middle class, and conservative. "There are, however, other valuable members of the student body who do not fit this description and contribute greatly to the Clemson experience." At first glance, the population may appear to be a "cookie cutter" group of "preppy dressers." But upon closer inspection, you'll find that even "atypical students can always find someone to get along with here." Perhaps this welcoming atmosphere has something to do with the fact that most Clemson students are "just damn funny and likable." But don't be fooled by the southern savoir faire: though students "may not seem like they're working hard all the time, they are." Several survey respondents also observe, "Though it is not the most diverse school around, Clemson has a commitment to increasing diversity and a president who is very dedicated to fulfilling that commitment." Many students emphasize the "caring community" of the "Clemson family" that fosters "a pride in treating others as you would want to be treated."

# CLEMSON UNIVERSITY

FINANCIAL AID: 864-656-2280 • E-MAIL: CUADMISSIONS@CLEMSON.EDU • WEBSITE: WWW.CLEMSON.EDU

## ADMISSIONS

*Very important factors considered include:* class rank, secondary school record, standardized test scores, state residency. *Important factors considered include:* alumni/ae relation. *Other factors considered include:* essays, geographical residence, recommendations, talent/ability. SAT I or ACT required, SAT I preferred. TOEFL required of all international applicants. High school diploma or GED is required. *High school units required/recommended:* 19 total required; 4 English required, 3 math required, 4 math recommended, 3 science required, 3 science lab required, 4 science lab recommended, 3 foreign language required, 3 social studies required, 1 history required, 2 elective required.

### The Inside Word

Admission by formula. Out-of-state students are in abundance; such applicants will find little difference in admissions standards from those for state residents.

## FINANCIAL AID

*Students should submit:* FAFSA. The Princeton Review suggests that all financial aid forms be submitted as soon as possible after January 1. *Need-based scholarships/grants offered:* Pell, SEOG, state scholarships/grants, private scholarships, the school's own gift aid. *Loan aid offered:* FFEL Subsidized Stafford, FFEL Unsubsidized Stafford, FFEL PLUS, Federal Perkins, state loans, private loans. Federal Work-Study Program available. Institutional employment available. Applicants will be notified of awards on a rolling basis beginning on or about April 1. Off-campus job opportunities are good. Institutional payment plan available.

## FROM THE ADMISSIONS OFFICE

"Clemson University is a comprehensive land-grant university with approximately 17,000 students. Noted for its academic excellence, Clemson offers over 70 undergraduate degree programs in five academic colleges. Programs such as Calhoun College, the Honors Program, and study abroad are available to outstanding students. The campus is situated in the foothills of the Blue Ridge Mountains, with numerous outdoor opportunities available for students. Clemson has over 250 clubs and organizations, and the spirit that our students show for the university is unparalleled. Students should apply early in the fall, as the entering class closes earlier each year."

---

### SELECTIVITY
★ ★ ★ ☆

| | |
|---|---|
| Admissions Rating | 83 |
| # of applicants | 11,315 |
| % of applicants accepted | 52 |
| % of acceptees attending | 42 |
| # accepting a place on wait list | 650 |
| % admitted from wait list | 43 |

### FRESHMAN PROFILE

| | |
|---|---|
| Range SAT Verbal | 540-640 |
| Average SAT Verbal | 587 |
| Range SAT Math | 570-670 |
| Average SAT Math | 618 |
| Range ACT Composite | 23-28 |
| Average ACT Composite | 26 |
| Minimum TOEFL | 550 |
| Average HS GPA | 3.9 |
| % graduated top 10% of class | 45 |
| % graduated top 25% of class | 80 |
| % graduated top 50% of class | 97 |

### DEADLINES

| | |
|---|---|
| Regular admission | 5/1 |
| Regular notification | 5/1 |
| Nonfall registration? | yes |

### APPLICANTS ALSO LOOK AT
**AND OFTEN PREFER**
UNC—Chapel Hill
Duke
U. Georgia
**AND SOMETIMES PREFER**
Furman
James Madison
U. South Carolina—Columbia
Wake Forest
Vanderbilt
**AND RARELY PREFER**
U. Florida
Auburn U.

### FINANCIAL FACTS
★ ★ ★ ☆

| | |
|---|---|
| Financial Aid Rating | 83 |
| In-state tuition | $5,834 |
| Out-of-state tuition | $12,932 |
| Room and board | $4,454 |
| Books and supplies | $768 |
| Required fees | $210 |
| % frosh receiving aid | 88 |
| % undergrads receiving aid | 78 |
| Avg frosh grant | $7,134 |
| Avg frosh loan | $3,115 |

THE BEST 351 COLLEGES

# COE COLLEGE

1220 First Avenue NE, Cedar Rapids, IA 52402 • Admissions: 319-399-8500 • Fax: 319-399-8816

## CAMPUS LIFE

| | |
|---|---|
| Quality of Life Rating | 74 |
| Type of school | private |
| Affiliation | Presbyterian |
| Environment | urban |

### STUDENTS

| | |
|---|---|
| Total undergrad enrollment | 1,300 |
| % male/female | 43/57 |
| % from out of state | 34 |
| % from public high school | 92 |
| % live on campus | 84 |
| % in (# of) fraternities | 27 (4) |
| % in (# of) sororities | 21 (3) |
| % African American | 2 |
| % Asian | 1 |
| % Caucasian | 95 |
| % Hispanic | 1 |
| % international | 3 |
| # of countries represented | 15 |

### SURVEY SAYS . . .
Classes are small
Athletic facilities are great
Great library
Registration is a breeze
Everyone loves the Kohawks
Musical organizations are hot
Student publications are popular
Diverse students interact
(Almost) no one listens to college radio

## ACADEMICS

| | |
|---|---|
| Academic Rating | 80 |
| Calendar | semester |
| Student/faculty ratio | 12:1 |
| Profs interesting rating | 81 |
| Profs accessible rating | 82 |
| % profs teaching UG courses | 100 |
| Avg lab size | 10-19 students |
| Avg reg class size | 10-19 students |

### MOST POPULAR MAJORS
Business administration/management
Psychology
Biology/biological sciences

## STUDENTS SPEAK OUT

### Academics
In the minds of many of Coe students, the powers-that-be are divided into two distinct factions: the "excellent" faculty and the "approachable" administrators. Important to note: The administration and students do not always see eye to eye; however, students are quick to credit the administration with an ability to internalize feedback—no matter if it's good or bad. One student notes, "If there's one thing I love about my school, it's how willing the faculty and administration are to work with you." And most students hold warm and venerable feelings for the college's president, who's "always smoking a cigar and waving at students." As for the "outstanding" professors, they "are very friendly" and "easily accessible outside of the classroom." As you're likely to find at many small colleges, at Coe you may discover that "access to specifics within" your field is "limited to what the two or three professors in your department specialize in. If you want a very specific field, think hard before coming to Coe." "All in all, you make the academic experience what you want it to be, mediocre, satisfying, or challenging." The choice is yours.

### Life
"Life at Coe is fun!" exclaims one underclassman. While there are definitely a handful of students who "frickin' study for fun," you'll find that the most popular pastime at this "partying school" is to "drink, and drink heavily." However, there are "tons of activities to get involved in." "Greek life is rampant" and provides its fair share of social outlets. Whether in a frat or not, students here "like to get together in big groups and party til you can't party anymore." Students will tell you that "student clubs and organizations" run a close second to these wild parties when it comes to "what people do for fun." Coe offers "everything from social and academic fraternities and sororities to music and theater to outdoor activities clubs to sports and intramurals to volunteering." And let's not forget the "campuswide" events like "Block Party, Homecoming, Presidential Ball, Flunk Day"—"an official cutting-class and beer-drinking day"—and "Winter Games." Students believe that Cedar Rapids is an agreeable place, even if it does feel like "one of those mid-size midwestern towns that all seem much the same." "Iowa City, the home of the University of Iowa" is only "20 minutes south," and this offers a world of social opportunities to antsy Coe undergrads. And when students feel especially eager to escape "the Coe bubble," they know that it's only "four hours to Chicago, St. Louis, [and] the Twin Cities."

### Student Body
Because "lots of juniors and seniors live on campus," students feel that the entire "community" exists within what they call "the Coe bubble." Inside this bubble, you'll find "a somewhat polar" group of students "made of up of segments, each with [its] own concerns and interests." "We have every clique," explains one student. There are "the jocks, the ditzies [sic], the band geeks, the volunteer people, the incredibly cute smart men, the loud and proud GLBT community, the incredibly cute, incredibly smart women, the small-town farm kids, the city-slickers, the gangsta wannabes, the playas, the chicks that absolutely hate the world and every man in it, and the Greeks, the cheerleaders, the 'fresh meat' girls, the Weezer-lovin' dudes, and probably every other stereotypical group you can think of shaking a stick at." There are also "quite a few foreign students," though "the American minority students are few and far between." Whether you like them or not, you'll be sure to get to know your classmates at Coe. "It's a close-knit community and just about everybody knows everyone else in some way."

# COE COLLEGE

FINANCIAL AID: 319-399-8540 • E-MAIL: ADMISSION@COE.EDU • WEBSITE: WWW.COE.EDU

## ADMISSIONS
*Very important factors considered include:* secondary school record. *Important factors considered include:* class rank, essays, recommendations, standardized test scores. *Other factors considered include:* alumni/ae relation, character/personal qualities, extracurricular activities, interview, minority status, talent/ability, volunteer work. SAT I or ACT required. TOEFL required of all international applicants. High school diploma or GED is required. *High school units required/recommended:* 18 total recommended; 4 English recommended, 3 math recommended, 3 science recommended, 1 science lab recommended, 2 foreign language recommended, 3 social studies recommended, 2 elective recommended.

### The Inside Word
Coe's admissions process places a very high level of importance on your numbers. Candidates who don't have at least a 2.75 high school GPA and at least a 22 on the ACT may find tough going with the admissions committee. As is true of nearly all small liberal arts colleges, Coe conducts a thorough application review that also considers your personal background and involvements, but an emerging national reputation enables them to keep their focus upon academic achievement as the primary gatekeeper.

## FINANCIAL AID
*Students should submit:* FAFSA. Regular filing deadline is April 30. The Princeton Review suggests that all financial aid forms be submitted as soon as possible after January 1. *Need-based scholarships/grants offered:* Pell, SEOG, state scholarships/grants, private scholarships, the school's own gift aid. *Loan aid offered:* Direct Subsidized Stafford, Direct Unsubsidized Stafford, Direct PLUS, Federal Perkins, college/university loans from institutional funds. Federal Work-Study Program available. Institutional employment available. Applicants will be notified of awards on a rolling basis beginning on or about March 1. Off-campus job opportunities are excellent.

## FROM THE ADMISSIONS OFFICE
"A Coe education begins to pay off right away. In fact, 98 percent of last year's graduating class was either working or in graduate school within six months of graduation. One reason our graduates do so well is the Coe Plan—a step-by-step sequence of activities designed to prepare our students for life after Coe. This required sequence stretches from the first-year seminar to community service, issue dinners, career planning seminars, and the required hands-on experience. The hands-on component may be satisfied through an internship, research, practicum, or study abroad. One student lived with a Costa Rican family while she studied the effects of selective logging on rain forest organisms. Others have interned at places like Warner Brothers in Los Angeles and the Chicago Board of Trade. Still others combine travel with an internship or student teaching for an unforgettable off-campus experience. Coe College is one of the few liberal arts institutions in the country to require hands-on learning for graduation."

### SELECTIVITY

| | |
|---|---|
| Admissions Rating | 83 |
| # of applicants | 1,285 |
| % of applicants accepted | 77 |
| % of acceptees attending | 30 |

### FRESHMAN PROFILE
| | |
|---|---|
| Range SAT Verbal | 520-640 |
| Average SAT Verbal | 577 |
| Range SAT Math | 520-640 |
| Average SAT Math | 572 |
| Range ACT Composite | 22-27 |
| Average ACT Composite | 25 |
| Minimum TOEFL | 500 |
| Average HS GPA | 3.6 |
| % graduated top 10% of class | 30 |
| % graduated top 25% of class | 65 |
| % graduated top 50% of class | 92 |

### DEADLINES
| | |
|---|---|
| Priority admission | 12/15 |
| Regular admission | 3/1 |
| Regular notification | 3/15 |
| Nonfall registration? | yes |

### APPLICANTS ALSO LOOK AT AND SOMETIMES PREFER
Macalester
Beloit
Grinnell
Cornell College
U. Iowa

### FINANCIAL FACTS

| | |
|---|---|
| Financial Aid Rating | 80 |
| Tuition | $20,280 |
| Room and board | $5,610 |
| Books and supplies | $600 |
| Required fees | $260 |
| % frosh receiving aid | 83 |
| % undergrads receiving aid | 80 |
| Avg frosh grant | $13,493 |
| Avg frosh loan | $4,000 |

# COLBY COLLEGE

4800 MAYFLOWER HILL, WATERVILLE, ME 04901-8848 • ADMISSIONS: 207-872-3168 • FAX: 207-872-3474

## CAMPUS LIFE

| Quality of Life Rating | 90 |
| --- | --- |
| Type of school | private |
| Environment | urban |

### STUDENTS
| | |
| --- | --- |
| Total undergrad enrollment | 1,830 |
| % from out of state | 84 |
| % from public high school | 58 |
| % live on campus | 94 |
| % African American | 3 |
| % Asian | 6 |
| % Caucasian | 89 |
| % Hispanic | 2 |
| % international | 6 |
| # of countries represented | 63 |

### SURVEY SAYS . . .
Great food on campus
Diversity lacking on campus
Athletic facilities are great
Everyone loves the Mules
(Almost) no one smokes
Students don't like Waterville, ME
Class discussions encouraged

## ACADEMICS

| Academic Rating | 94 |
| --- | --- |
| Calendar | 4-1-4 |
| Student/faculty ratio | 11:1 |
| Profs interesting rating | 96 |
| Profs accessible rating | 98 |
| % profs teaching UG courses | 100 |
| Avg lab size | 10-19 students |
| Avg reg class size | 10-19 students |

### MOST POPULAR MAJORS
English language and literature
Biology/biological sciences
Political science and government

## STUDENTS SPEAK OUT

### Academics

An intimate, prestigious, liberal arts college tucked away in a "superb location in the Maine woods not far from civilization," Colby College offers a challenging but manageable undergraduate experience to its small student population. Undergrads report that all the support mechanisms necessary for success in college are in place here. Writes one, "I was intimidated at first by the whole idea of college, but after my first day of classes freshman year, my fears were soon assuaged. My professors were real pros and made otherwise very complex and involved material accessible to the students. At the end of my first semester, I was even asked to be a professor's research assistant." Another explains, "It is a very intimate, personal, inspiring, and wonderful relationship between professors and students. They're always there for you, ready and willing to ease any personal or academic stresses you are under." Not surprisingly, students grow attached to this friendly place. "I consider Colby my home and cannot imagine leaving this community behind," reflects a senior. "Colby has honestly been the most wonderful academic and social experience that I have ever experienced." Unique programs here include "Jan Plan," a short semester that allows students to study nontraditional subjects or intern during the month of January.

### Life

Combine a large group of college-age kids and a beautiful, remote, bucolic location and what you get is "summer camp with alcohol. Camp Colby is totally awesome." Students here love the beauty, food, and facilities and are no less than gushy about other kids and professors. Although many students "drink for fun," those who opt for a substance-free social life say "chem-free fun" is readily available as well, especially in the "chem-free" dorms. In addition, "the range of theatre productions, concerts, lectures, and sporting events is incredible." Colby is "a very athletic school" where there are "opportunities for every level of athlete." Outdoor sports are popular year-round, particularly throughout the winter. "Lots of snow. Need I say more?" writes one student. "It's fun, though, [since] the weather provides lots of outdoor activities." As for the school's location, one student let us in on "the best thing about Waterville, Maine—local Karaoke night at the pub in town." Not surprisingly, then, students tend to stay on campus. Fortunately, "life can easily be contained entirely on campus and you will never be bored. There is always something fun going on." Even so, there are those who feel that "we need to integrate students into the surrounding community more, i.e. with more community service projects. We don't have enough contact with locals."

### Student Body

Colby undergrads report that the college works hard to increase diversity on campus and should not stop its efforts. "We need to attract kids from a wider range of economic backgrounds," notes one undergrad. However, a sophomore is quick to point out that while "a portion [of the students] are rich, religious, white snobs, the rest are wonderfully adjusting, friendly, and diverse in ideas and beliefs." Students can be "a little too cliquey, but if you catch people on an individual basis, they are usually friendly." Another student agrees, writing, "Everyone here is very approachable. We pride ourselves on it." Students describe their peers as "outgoing and always looking for a good time," though they do admit to being "focused on what is important to them only." As a result, "20 percent of the students here participate in 80 percent of the activities."

142 ■ THE BEST 351 COLLEGES

# COLBY COLLEGE

FINANCIAL AID: 207-872-3168 • E-MAIL: ADMISSIONS@COLBY.EDU • WEBSITE: WWW.COLBY.EDU

## ADMISSIONS

*Very important factors considered include:* character/personal qualities, secondary school record. *Important factors considered include:* class rank, essays, extracurricular activities, interview, minority status, recommendations, standardized test scores, talent/ability. *Other factors considered include:* alumni/ae relation, geographical residence, state residency, volunteer work, work experience. SAT I or ACT required. TOEFL required of all international applicants. *High school units required/recommended:* 16 total recommended; 4 English recommended, 3 math recommended, 2 science recommended, 2 science lab recommended, 3 foreign language recommended, 2 social studies recommended, 2 elective recommended.

### The Inside Word

Colby continues to be both very selective and successful in converting admits to enrollees, which makes for a perpetually challenging admissions process.

## FINANCIAL AID

*Students should submit:* FAFSA and either institutional application or CSS/Financial Aid PROFILE with institutional supplement. Regular filing deadline is February 1. The Princeton Review suggests that all financial aid forms be submitted as soon as possible after January 1. *Need-based scholarships/grants offered:* Pell, SEOG, state scholarships/grants, private scholarships, the school's own gift aid. *Loan aid offered:* Direct Subsidized Stafford, Direct Unsubsidized Stafford, Direct PLUS, FFEL Subsidized Stafford, FFEL Unsubsidized Stafford, FFEL PLUS, Federal Perkins, state loans, college/university loans from institutional funds, alternative loans. Federal Work-Study Program available. Institutional employment available. Applicants will be notified of awards on or about April 1. Off-campus job opportunities are fair.

## FROM THE ADMISSIONS OFFICE

"Founded in 1813, Colby is one of the nation's oldest and most prestigious independent liberal arts colleges. Colby is known for its diverse and challenging intellectual life, friendly atmosphere, and global reach. On campus, 1,800 students from many different backgrounds and from more than 60 countries live and study together in a vibrant and supportive community. Graduates are well prepared for a broad range of careers or graduate study programs. Colby is recognized as a national leader in undergraduate research and project-based learning, and the quality of the faculty is recognized as the College's greatest asset. The depth of student-faculty interaction and collaboration consistently wins praise from students and alumni. Colby has one of the most ambitious international study programs, with two-thirds of the student body studying abroad at some point in their undergraduate career, and the College maintains an international focus in many of its academic programs. There is a lively interest in political and social activism and volunteer work at Colby, and students get involved in college governance on official boards and committees, including the board of trustees. Colby's 714-acre campus is often cited as one of the nation's most beautiful, and Maine's environment is an ideal setting for the four-year residential college."

## SELECTIVITY

| | |
|---|---|
| Admissions Rating | 96 |
| # of applicants | 3,873 |
| % of applicants accepted | 33 |
| % of acceptees attending | 37 |
| # accepting a place on wait list | 308 |
| % admitted from wait list | 11 |
| # of early decision applicants | 512 |
| % accepted early decision | 42 |

### FRESHMAN PROFILE

| | |
|---|---|
| Range SAT Verbal | 620-700 |
| Average SAT Verbal | 660 |
| Range SAT Math | 640-710 |
| Average SAT Math | 670 |
| Range ACT Composite | 27-30 |
| Average ACT Composite | 28 |
| Minimum TOEFL | 600 |
| % graduated top 10% of class | 64 |
| % graduated top 25% of class | 90 |
| % graduated top 50% of class | 99 |

### DEADLINES

| | |
|---|---|
| Early decision | 11/15 |
| Early decision notification | 12/15 |
| Regular admission | 1/1 |
| Regular notification | 4/1 |
| Nonfall registration? | yes |

### APPLICANTS ALSO LOOK AT

**AND OFTEN PREFER**
Amherst College
Brown University
Middlebury College
Williams College
Dartmouth College

**AND SOMETIMES PREFER**
Bowdoin College
Tufts University
Colgate University

**AND RARELY PREFER**
Bates College
Trinity College
Wellesley College
Connecticut College, Hamilton College

## FINANCIAL FACTS

| | |
|---|---|
| Financial Aid Rating | 79 |
| Comprehensive tuition | $35,800 |
| Books and supplies | $650 |
| % frosh receiving aid | 43 |
| % undergrads receiving aid | 38 |
| Avg frosh grant | $21,966 |
| Avg frosh loan | $3,243 |

# COLGATE UNIVERSITY

13 OAK DRIVE, HAMILTON, NY 13346 • ADMISSIONS: 315-228-7401 • FAX: 315-228-7544

## CAMPUS LIFE

| | |
|---|---|
| Quality of Life Rating | 88 |
| Type of school | private |
| Environment | rural |

### STUDENTS
| | |
|---|---|
| Total undergrad enrollment | 2,827 |
| % male/female | 49/51 |
| % from out of state | 67 |
| % from public high school | 70 |
| % live on campus | 87 |
| % in (# of) fraternities | 35 (8) |
| % in (# of) sororities | 32 (4) |
| % African American | 4 |
| % Asian | 5 |
| % Caucasian | 85 |
| % Hispanic | 3 |
| % international | 5 |
| # of countries represented | 32 |

### SURVEY SAYS . . .
Frats and sororities dominate social scene
Everyone loves the Red Raiders
Diversity lacking on campus
(Almost) everyone plays intramural sports
Athletic facilities are great
Students don't like Hamilton, NY
Lousy off-campus food
Theater is unpopular
Class discussions encouraged

## ACADEMICS

| | |
|---|---|
| Academic Rating | 92 |
| Calendar | semester |
| Student/faculty ratio | 10:1 |
| Profs interesting rating | 95 |
| Profs accessible rating | 99 |
| % profs teaching UG courses | 100 |
| Avg lab size | 10-19 students |
| Avg reg class size | 10-19 students |

### MOST POPULAR MAJORS
History
English language and literature
Economics

## STUDENTS SPEAK OUT

### Academics
Colgate University offers a first-rate undergraduate experience—and with it a well-regarded degree—to its highly intelligent but business-like student body. As one student puts it, "Students here tend to look down on intellectual curiosity." Undergrads here appreciate the value of a good education and realize that they are getting one, praising the "incredible facilities: from classrooms to athletic facilities to the buildings and grounds, this campus is decked out" and professors who "are always more than willing to give extra help, read papers before you turn them in, and offer advice." They also speak highly of the freshman seminar program ("especially great for getting to know your advisor") and the "great abroad program." All Colgate students must complete core courses, "and even these are, for the most part, stimulating." For ambitious students, many opportunities for independent study are available. Sums up one undergrad, "It has the best of two worlds. It has the Greek life [although perhaps not for long; see "Life," below], alumni funding, and academic possibilities of a university, with the charm and community of a small liberal arts school. As scripted as that sounds, it's true."

### Life
Colgate's status as one of the nation's most prestigious party schools ended, perhaps permanently, in the autumn of 2000, when a tragic, alcohol-related automobile accident claimed the lives of four students. Since then, the Colgate administration has aggressively sought to curtail underage drinking and to deter student drunkenness. In an effort to replace the wild parties of the past, "the campus activities staff, the administration, the faculty, etc., are working so hard to try and find alternatives for us. So far this year, we have had speakers come like The Hurricane (Rubin Carter) and Ralph Nader. Tonight we had a comedy group from Chicago. Last weekend, the band Dispatch was here. Although we are in a rural setting, every weekend, there is a concert or other event of some sort taking place." Some warn that "these [events] really aren't attended. These days there is very little for underage students to do on the weekends." Tiny hometown Hamilton offers little ("Well Hamilton, New York, is not quite a bustling town . . . in fact it's not really a town at all") to the chronically bored. Many students occupy their free time with athletics; notes one student, "The fact that students are involved [with] a sport brings everybody together. We all [have to] deal with [balancing] practices and classes."

### Student Body
There is most definitely a "Colgate type": explains one of the horde, "Initially, I liked Colgate because I saw so many people who looked a lot like me. However, after three years of attending Colgate, that has come to be one of the aspects about the school that I loathe most. It's a preppy, white-kids-from-New-England kind of place. Khaki pants, white game hats, Jeep Grand Cherokees . . . . Individually, the students at Colgate are great people for the most part. However, all together they are an intimidating crowd." Elaborates another student, "If you are from Long Island, North Jersey, Westchester County [New York], Fairfield County [Connecticut], and like it there, you are in business at Colgate." Students tend to be mostly attractive ("A visiting friend of mine once asked me if Colgate only admits beautiful people. It is true that the vast majority of the students at Colgate are beauty-, health-, and fashion-conscious") and largely monochromatic ("We have black students. Not many though").

# COLGATE UNIVERSITY

FINANCIAL AID: 315-228-7431 • E-MAIL: ADMISSION@MAIL.COLGATE.EDU • WEBSITE: WWW.COLGATE.EDU

## ADMISSIONS

*Very important factors considered include:* class rank, secondary school record. *Important factors considered include:* character/personal qualities, essays, extracurricular activities, recommendations, standardized test scores, talent/ability, volunteer work, work experience. *Other factors considered include:* alumni/ae relation, geographical residence, minority status. TOEFL required of all international applicants. High school diploma or GED is required. *High school units required/recommended:* 16 total required; 20 total recommended; 4 English required, 3 math required, 4 math recommended, 3 science required, 4 science recommended, 2 science lab required, 3 science lab recommended, 3 foreign language required, 4 foreign language recommended, 2 social studies required, 1 history required, 3 history recommended.

### The Inside Word

Like many colleges, Colgate caters to some well-developed special interests. Athletes, minorities, and legacies (the children of alums) are among the most special of interests and benefit from more favorable consideration than applicants without particular distinction. Students without a solid, consistent academic record, beware—the University's wait list leans toward jumbo size.

## FINANCIAL AID

*Students should submit:* FAFSA, CSS/Financial Aid PROFILE, noncustodial (divorced/separated) parent's statement, business/farm supplement. Regular filing deadline is February 1. The Princeton Review suggests that all financial aid forms be submitted as soon as possible after January 1. *Need-based scholarships/grants offered:* Pell, SEOG, state scholarships/grants, private scholarships, the school's own gift aid. *Loan aid offered:* FFEL Subsidized Stafford, FFEL Unsubsidized Stafford, FFEL PLUS, Federal Perkins. Federal Work-Study Program available. Institutional employment available. Applicants will be notified of awards on or about April 1. Off-campus job opportunities are good.

## FROM THE ADMISSIONS OFFICE

"Students and faculty alike are drawn to Colgate by the quality of its academic programs. Faculty initiative has given the college a rich mix of learning opportunities that includes a liberal arts core, 50 academic concentrations, and a wealth of Colgate faculty-led, off-campus study programs in the United States and abroad. But there is more to Colgate than academic life, including more than 100 student organizations, athletics and recreation at all levels, and a full complement of living options set within a campus described as one of the most beautiful in the country. A new center for community service builds upon the tradition of Colgate students interacting with the surrounding community in meaningful ways, and an initiative to improve campus culture and social options features a brand-new, state-of-the-art dance club in the heart of downtown Hamilton. For students in search of a busy and varied campus life, Colgate is a place to learn and grow."

## SELECTIVITY

| | |
|---|---:|
| Admissions Rating | 95 |
| # of applicants | 6,268 |
| % of applicants accepted | 34 |
| % of acceptees attending | 35 |
| # accepting a place on wait list | 427 |
| % admitted from wait list | 2 |
| # of early decision applicants | 613 |
| % accepted early decision | 49 |

### FRESHMAN PROFILE

| | |
|---|---:|
| Range SAT Verbal | 610-700 |
| Average SAT Verbal | 652 |
| Range SAT Math | 630-710 |
| Average SAT Math | 665 |
| Range ACT Composite | 27-31 |
| Average ACT Composite | 29 |
| Minimum TOEFL | 600 |
| Average HS GPA | 3.6 |
| % graduated top 10% of class | 68 |
| % graduated top 25% of class | 92 |
| % graduated top 50% of class | 100 |

### DEADLINES

| | |
|---|---:|
| Early decision | 11/15 |
| Early decision notification | 12/15 |
| Regular admission | 1/15 |
| Regular notification | 4/1 |

### APPLICANTS ALSO LOOK AT AND OFTEN PREFER
Brown, Duke
Middlebury, Cornell U
Dartmouth

### AND SOMETIMES PREFER
Wesleyan, Davidson
Georgetown, Boston College

### AND RARELY PREFER
Bucknell
Vassar
Lehigh
Lafayette

## FINANCIAL FACTS

| | |
|---|---:|
| Financial Aid Rating | 82 |
| Tuition | $26,845 |
| Room and board | $6,455 |
| Books and supplies | $620 |
| Required fees | $180 |
| % frosh receiving aid | 49 |
| % undergrads receiving aid | 45 |
| Avg frosh grant | $25,261 |
| Avg frosh loan | $2,625 |

# COLLEGE OF CHARLESTON

66 George Street, Charleston, SC 29424 • Admissions: 843-953-5670 • Fax: 843-953-6322

## CAMPUS LIFE

★★★☆

| | |
|---|---|
| Quality of Life Rating | 84 |
| Type of school | public |
| Environment | urban |

### STUDENTS

| | |
|---|---|
| Total undergrad enrollment | 10,044 |
| % male/female | 37/63 |
| % from out of state | 35 |
| % from public high school | 83 |
| % live on campus | 25 |
| % in (# of) fraternities | 13 (12) |
| % in (# of) sororities | 18 (10) |
| % African American | 9 |
| % Asian | 1 |
| % Caucasian | 87 |
| % Hispanic | 1 |
| % international | 2 |

### SURVEY SAYS . . .
Campus is beautiful
Classes are small
Ethnic diversity lacking on campus
Everyone loves the Cougars
Great computer facilities
Lots of conservatives
Musical organizations aren't popular

## ACADEMICS

| | |
|---|---|
| Academic Rating | 82 |
| Calendar | semester |
| Student/faculty ratio | 14:1 |
| Profs interesting rating | 76 |
| Profs accessible rating | 84 |
| % classes taught by TAs | 2 |
| Avg lab size | 20-29 students |
| Avg reg class size | 20-29 students |

### MOST POPULAR MAJORS
Business administration/management
Communications studies/speech communication and rhetoric
Biology/biological sciences

## STUDENTS SPEAK OUT

### Academics
"For those students who prefer smaller, more intimate classes where there can be a lot of discussion, group activities, and a better professor/student relationship, then this is the school for them" is one student's advertisement for the College of Charleston. Students agree that two of its greatest strengths are the small class sizes and accessibility of its professors. One student notes that it's "easy to get to know one's teachers and the other students in" one's classes. The professors at Charleston "honestly pour their soul into teaching their students" and "are dynamic and animated in class." One adds that the professors "are well prepared and provide excellent learning experiences" for the classes of 15 to 30 students. Most students do stress, however, a need for "more teachers and more classrooms," and gripe that "registration is a pain because there are too many students and never enough course sections available." The College of Charleston offers an honors program that provides its students luxuries like early registration and access to classes that would otherwise be unavailable. In a few words, one student sums up the way many students feel about the academic experience at Charleston: "I am not a number."

### Life
Downtown Charleston seems to have a little bit of everything for everyone. According to one student, "I have never had a lack of things to do at school in Charleston." The quaint town offers "comedy improv and . . . theater shows and the Battery." The warm climate is particularly pleasing to the students. Ah, yes . . . the beach. The proximity to Hilton Head and Myrtle Beach (with Folly Beach 10 minutes away) means students can soak up the rays with the theories from the classroom. "In one day I can go to class, go to the beach, and then go to some of the best bars around," waxes one undergrad. If you're one of the pale kind who burns easily, Waterfront Park could be your choice to "hang out, play Frisbee, read, etc." A night out in Charleston will show you that "live music is everywhere, and the little restaurants are fantastic for cheap food." Athletically, Charleston is "well known for its Cougar basketball team," and for other social kicks, students turn to "Cougar Productions, which organizes student events almost daily." Although the administration has responded to the serious shortage of student housing by building new dorms, many students still have to commute, leaving the student body feeling fractured. Charleston, argue some students, could "benefit from events to create a more cohesive student body." Despite this minor complaint, most Charleston students are content with the warm weather, the downtown atmosphere of Charleston, and the fact that a student can find "everything from aerobics to yoga, Buddhist to Presbyterian organizations, [and] rowing, intramural basketball, football, volleyball" among others. Simply put, "if you're bored, you aren't trying at all."

### Student Body
The students at Charleston describe each other as "laid-back" and "really friendly." Though two-thirds of the student body are residents of South Carolina, the college still attracts students from outside the state and region. For some, Charleston is the United Nations of the South since "there is such a diverse group of people at Charleston that you are bound to fit in somewhere!" Fellas, listen up: males don't seem to mind that they are outnumbered by the females by about two to one. Some students believe that "people find cliques quickly and stick with them for four years" and yet others tend to think that "this isn't high school. Cliques tend to intermingle, and friends are easily made." Though some notice that the student population is "still predominantly white" with "not necessarily much interaction between the various ethnic groups," the campus community still works well together. "There is a spirit of cooperation among the students here, and we all work side-by-side in our mission to serve the city that educates us."

# COLLEGE OF CHARLESTON

FINANCIAL AID: 843-953-5540 • E-MAIL: ADMISSIONS@COFC.EDU • WEBSITE: WWW.COFC.EDU

## ADMISSIONS

*Very important factors considered include:* class rank, secondary school record, standardized test scores, state residency. *Important factors considered include:* essays, and recommendations. *Other factors considered include:* character/personal qualities, extracurricular activities, geographical residence, talent/ability, volunteer work, work experience. SAT I or ACT required. TOEFL required of all international applicants. High school diploma or GED is required. *High school units required/recommended:* 20 total required; 4 English required, 3 math required, 4 math recommended, 3 science required, 4 science recommended, 3 science lab required, 2 foreign language required, 3 foreign language recommended, 3 social studies required, 2 history recommended, 4 elective required.

## The Inside Word

Although the admissions process is pretty straightforward at the College of Charleston—solid grades and test scores, as at most state schools, will serve you well—it's important to know that the college reviews applications with a private-school touch. Charleston's programs in the sciences, math, languages, and the classics are particularly competitive.

## FINANCIAL AID

*Students should submit:* FAFSA. Priority deadline is March 1. The Princeton Review suggests that all financial aid forms be submitted as soon as possible after January 1. *Need-based scholarships/grants offered:* Pell, SEOG, state scholarships/grants, private scholarships, the school's own gift aid. *Loan aid offered:* Direct Subsidized Stafford, Direct Unsubsidized Stafford, Direct PLUS, Federal Perkins. Federal Work-Study Program available. Institutional employment available. Applicants will be notified of awards on a rolling basis beginning on or about April 10. Off-campus job opportunities are good.

## FROM THE ADMISSIONS OFFICE

"The College of Charleston is a student-centered public liberal arts and sciences university located in South Carolina's beautiful Lowcountry. The oldest institution of higher learning in the state, the College offers an exceptional undergraduate experience—one that emphasizes intellectual growth through a combination of challenging course work, research opportunities, co-curricular activities, and study abroad. The College also provides its students the opportunity to work closely with nationally recognized faculty and treats its students as valued participants of the College's close-knit community of scholars.

"Students are encouraged to attend the many events on campus—from dramatic performances to thought-provoking guest lectures—as well as to participate in the diverse student organizations, volunteer groups, and academic clubs. Music, art, and culture thrive both within the confines of campus and throughout the greater Charleston community. Students also enjoy traditional campus events such as convocation, senior week, Oozeball, and NCAA Division I athletics.

"The College's residential learning communities bring together students who share a common experience, students who wish to focus on a specialized theme such as leadership or wellness, or students who want to immerse themselves in Spanish or French culture and language.

"Whether inside or outside the classroom, on or off the historic campus, students of the College of Charleston receive valuable preparation for further academic study or entry into the professional world. Students, faculty, and alumni agree that the College furnishes a learning experience without equal—a creative and intellectually stimulating environment led by a committed and caring faculty within a superb setting and at an incredible value."

## SELECTIVITY

| | |
|---|---|
| Admissions Rating | 82 |
| # of applicants | 8,635 |
| % of applicants accepted | 60 |
| % of acceptees attending | 39 |

### FRESHMAN PROFILE

| | |
|---|---|
| Range SAT Verbal | 550-640 |
| Average SAT Verbal | 595 |
| Range SAT Math | 550-630 |
| Average SAT Math | 590 |
| Range ACT Composite | 22-26 |
| Average ACT Composite | 24 |
| Minimum TOEFL | 550 |
| Average HS GPA | 3.6 |
| % graduated top 10% of class | 25 |
| % graduated top 25% of class | 58 |
| % graduated top 50% of class | 91 |

### DEADLINES

| | |
|---|---|
| Early action admission | 11/15 |
| Regular admission | 4/1 |
| Regular notification | rolling |
| Nonfall registration? | yes |

### APPLICANTS ALSO LOOK AT AND OFTEN PREFER
UNC Chapel Hill
U of Georgia

### AND SOMETIMES PREFER
Furman
Clemson
USC
James Madison

### AND RARELY PREFER
Coastal Carolina
Winthrop
Wofford
Appalachian State

## FINANCIAL FACTS

| | |
|---|---|
| Financial Aid Rating | 88 |
| In-state tuition | $4,556 |
| Out-of-state tuition | $10,290 |
| Room and board | $5,668 |
| Books and supplies | $851 |
| % frosh receiving aid | 36 |
| % undergrads receiving aid | 34 |
| Avg frosh grant | $1,500 |
| Avg frosh loan | $2,625 |

THE BEST 351 COLLEGES ■ 147

# THE COLLEGE OF NEW JERSEY

PO BOX 7718, EWING, NJ 08628-0718 • ADMISSIONS: 609-771-2131 • FAX: 609-637-5174

## CAMPUS LIFE

| | |
|---|---|
| Quality of Life Rating | 84 |
| Type of school | public |
| Environment | suburban |

### STUDENTS

| | |
|---|---|
| Total undergrad enrollment | 5,961 |
| % male/female | 41/59 |
| % from out of state | 5 |
| % from public high school | 65 |
| % live on campus | 61 |
| % in (# of) fraternities | 6 (13) |
| % in (# of) sororities | 8 (11) |
| % African American | 6 |
| % Asian | 5 |
| % Caucasian | 77 |
| % Hispanic | 6 |
| # of countries represented | 17 |

### SURVEY SAYS . . .
Lots of beer drinking
Campus easy to get around
Campus is beautiful
(Almost) everyone smokes
Hard liquor is popular
Students are happy
Frats and sororities dominate social scene
Great computer facilities
Students don't like Ewing, NJ
Students don't get along with local community

## ACADEMICS

| | |
|---|---|
| Academic Rating | 84 |
| Calendar | semester |
| Student/faculty ratio | 13:1 |
| % profs teaching UG courses | 95 |
| Avg lab size | 20-29 students |
| Avg reg class size | 20-29 students |

### MOST POPULAR MAJORS
Elementary education and teaching
English language and literature
Biology/biological sciences

## STUDENTS SPEAK OUT

### Academics

For "a price-is-right education with good professors, small class sizes, and extracurricular activities," many are turning to The College of New Jersey, a state liberal arts school "with a lot of potential" that "is just now really starting to expand." While still developing—one manifestation of which is the nonstop construction on campus—the school is already well on its way to "giving the typical college life that one has always dreamed about." All the key elements of a great education are here. Classes are "small enough for close attention by professors in class, large enough to constantly meet new people." The school offers "wonderful resources, if you are aware of them. For example, TCNJ has a lot of academic and job placement services that are there, just never utilized by the students." Most important, TCNJ is home to "a lot of smart students" and a faculty who, "on the whole, are available for guidance and help outside of class." Academics are demanding but satisfying here; as one student reported, "I have found that many of my classes have been a lot of work, but that I have come out of them with more knowledge than I would have expected." Students report that "the administration is surprisingly open-minded and constantly exploring new directions for the institution," but warn that day-to-day administrative tasks "often seem very unorganized. . . . You may be sent to a few different departments for the answer to one question."

### Life

Most at TCNJ agree that "social life is not as great as you will find in a big college town or a larger school. This is a suitcase college." While "there are parties many weekends at either a fraternity/sorority or sports team house, the scene gets pretty boring pretty quickly," according to many. The biggest party night here, surprisingly, is Tuesday, "because many people don't have any classes on Wednesday until late in the day (12:30–5 is reserved for club meetings, and also sometimes lecturers and things of that nature)." Weekends, in contrast, "can seem kinda desolate." Those who are satisfied with campus life are usually those deeply involved in the Greek scene and student clubs and organizations; as one such student put it, "There are so many great opportunities to take advantage of in terms of organizations and internships!" Sporting events occasionally mobilize the campus, with the annual football game against archrival Rowan the unquestioned highlight of the athletic schedule. "Tailgating for the Rowan game is a must for any fan of football or beer," reports one sports enthusiast. "I know it's not Penn State or anything like that, but it's still a great time." TCNJ's campus is "beautiful, except for the persistent construction." Hometown Ewing, on the other hand, is "lame. It requires some effort to find stuff to do off campus." One suggestion for spicing things up here: "TCNJ should also promote more interaction with other schools such as Rider, which is five miles away, yet I do not know one student from there."

### Student Body

The undergrads of TCNJ are "very hardworking and dedicated to academics," but also know how to "maintain a balance between schoolwork and social life." They are an active bunch; explains one undergrad, "Most TCNJ students were involved in high school in something, often a high school sport. So, while the average TCNJ student had a good GPA and SAT score, she was also involved in extracurricular activities." Upon arriving at TCNJ, this student "becomes affiliated with some organization, whether a sorority or fraternity or a student group like government. This student likely wears Abercrombie & Fitch/American Eagle/Gap/Express clothing, [and] is Caucasian and Catholic with a middle- to upper-middle-class background and permanent residence in New Jersey." While the college is "trying to bring kids in from other states and add to the diversity," currently "diversity among the student population is not as great as I think the college would like to brag it is."

148 ■ THE BEST 351 COLLEGES

# THE COLLEGE OF NEW JERSEY

FINANCIAL AID: 609-771-2211 • E-MAIL: ADMISS@VM.TCNJ.EDU • WEBSITE: WWW.TCNJ.EDU

## ADMISSIONS

*Very important factors considered include:* class rank, secondary school record, standardized test scores. *Important factors considered include:* character/personal qualities, essays, talent/ability. *Other factors considered include:* extracurricular activities, minority status, recommendations. SAT I or ACT required; SAT I preferred. TOEFL required of all international applicants. High school diploma or GED is required. *High school units required/recommended:* 18 total required; 4 English required, 3 math required, 3 science required, 4 science recommended, 2 science lab required, 2 foreign language recommended, 2 social studies required, 3 social studies recommended.

### The Inside Word

A new name and new-found visibility have given a boost to the applicant pool at The College of New Jersey, but selectivity remains at about the level it has been for the past few years. Since the pool is somewhat better than in prior years, this still translates into a stronger entering class.

## FINANCIAL AID

*Students should submit:* FAFSA. No deadline for regular filing. The Princeton Review suggests that all financial aid forms be submitted as soon as possible after January 1. *Need-based scholarships/grants offered:* Pell, SEOG, state scholarships/grants, private scholarships, the school's own gift aid, Federal Nursing. *Loan aid offered:* Direct Subsidized Stafford, Direct Unsubsidized Stafford, Direct PLUS, Federal Perkins, Federal Nursing, state loans. Federal Work-Study Program available. Institutional employment available. Applicants will be notified of awards on a rolling basis beginning on or about April 1. Off-campus job opportunities are good.

## FROM THE ADMISSIONS OFFICE

"Twin lakes form the border of the The College of New Jersey campus, which is set on 289 acres of wooded and landscaped grounds in suburban Ewing Township, New Jersey. TCNJ offers more than 40 baccalaureate degree programs in seven schools: art, media, and music; culture and society; business; education; engineering; nursing; and science. The campus is residential, with nearly two-thirds of the full-time students housed on campus. Classes are small and are all taught by faculty members: there are no graduate teaching assistants. The college is strongly committed to retaining and graduating the students it enrolls. This commitment is reflected in the high return rate of entering students, which has consistently been over 90 percent for the past five years."

### SELECTIVITY

| | |
|---|---|
| Admissions Rating | 91 |
| # of applicants | 6,323 |
| % of applicants accepted | 48 |
| % of acceptees attending | 41 |
| # accepting a place on wait list | 300 |
| % admitted from wait list | 3 |
| # of early decision applicants | 510 |
| % accepted early decision | 39 |

### FRESHMAN PROFILE

| | |
|---|---|
| Range SAT Verbal | 570-660 |
| Average SAT Verbal | 610 |
| Range SAT Math | 590-690 |
| Average SAT Math | 630 |
| Minimum TOEFL | 550 |
| % graduated top 10% of class | 61 |
| % graduated top 25% of class | 89 |
| % graduated top 50% of class | 98 |

### DEADLINES

| | |
|---|---|
| Early decision | 11/15 |
| Early decision notification | 12/15 |
| Regular admission | 2/15 |
| Nonfall registration? | yes |

### APPLICANTS ALSO LOOK AT
**AND OFTEN PREFER**
Rutgers U.
**AND SOMETIMES PREFER**
Villanova
U. Delaware
Boston Coll.
Drew
Seton Hall
**AND RARELY PREFER**
Rider
Syracuse
Muhlenberg
Monmouth U. (NJ)

### FINANCIAL FACTS

| | |
|---|---|
| Financial Aid Rating | 80 |
| Out-of-state tuition | $9,822 |
| Room and board | $7,416 |
| Books and supplies | $736 |
| Required fees | $1,891 |
| Avg frosh grant | $3,500 |
| Avg frosh loan | $3,000 |

# COLLEGE OF SAINT BENEDICT/SAINT JOHN'S UNIVERSITY

PO Box 7155, Collegeville, MN 56321-7155 • Admissions: 320-363-2196 • Fax: 320-363-3206

## CAMPUS LIFE

| Quality of Life Rating | 79 |
|---|---|
| Type of school | private |
| Affiliation | Roman Catholic |
| Environment | rural |

### STUDENTS
| | |
|---|---|
| Total undergrad enrollment | 3,969 |
| % male/female | 48/52 |
| % from out of state | 14 |
| % from public high school | 77 |
| % live on campus | 84 |
| % Asian | 2 |
| % Caucasian | 96 |
| % Hispanic | 1 |
| % international | 3 |
| # of countries represented | 35 |

### SURVEY SAYS . . .
Great food on campus
Athletic facilities are great
Ethnic diversity lacking on campus
(Almost) everyone plays intramural sports
Students pack the stadium
Theater is unpopular
Students are very religious
Students get along with local community
Low cost of living

## ACADEMICS

| Academic Rating | 76 |
|---|---|
| Calendar | semester |
| Student/faculty ratio | 13:1 |
| Profs interesting rating | 79 |
| Profs accessible rating | 82 |
| % profs teaching UG courses | 100 |
| Avg lab size | 10-19 students |
| Avg reg class size | 20-29 students |

### MOST POPULAR MAJORS
Nursing/registered nurse training (RN, ASN, BSN, MSN)
Business administration/management
Biology/biological sciences

## STUDENTS SPEAK OUT

### Academics
Ninety miles northwest of Minnesota's Twin Cities lay the twin campuses of the all-women's College of Saint Benedict and the all-men's Saint John's University. The two schools forged their partnership in 1964 in an effort to "take the best of what women's, men's, and co-ed colleges offer and combine them in a way you won't find at another pair of colleges in the nation." According to students, CSB/SJU more than meets the challenge it initially set for itself. Writes one, "Our school is more than a school. It's tradition, family, beauty, and presence all rolled into a tiny backwoods campus. You can't help but fall in love with the place, everything from the people to the profs." Agrees another, "Community is the greatest strength" of CSB/SJU. Students are particularly pleased at the way in which the curriculum here stresses critical thinking. Writes one, "Not only do you learn about skills for a major, you learn a better, open, and more knowledgeable way of thinking and applying it to real-life situations." Professors receive rave reviews, with undergrads gushing that "some of the profs are real gems. They're great teachers, some even friends, who would bend over backwards to make sure you learn what you have to know, and do their best to let you enjoy it." Adds another, "Several of my professors have become close friends of mine. They really get involved with the students on a personal level. CSB/SJU has great academics, and I feel it comes directly from the attitudes of the professors."

### Life
The gorgeous natural setting of CSB/SJU sets the tone for many student pastimes. Writes one student, "Saint John's is nestled on 2,400 acres of woodland that's surrounded by five lakes. The outdoor activities available are virtually unrivaled by any other college." To facilitate students' passion for the outdoors, the school has "a place on campus called the Outdoor Leadership Center, which rents out equipment to students (e.g., camping equipment, cross-country skis, rollerblades, and snowshoes)." Students also participate in "a wide range of athletics and intramural activities." For entertainment, "the school brings many things onto campus for us to do, such as musical performers, movies, and dances. Since these are all free, there are many great, cheap ways to have fun." Writes one student, "There is truly something for everyone. For those who like to party, you can find one just about every night of the week. For those who like to sit back and relax all week, you can do that too—it's really nice to do by Lake Sagatagan at St. John's." The fact that the two campuses are about five miles apart seems to have little effect on social life; the two schools coordinate events through the Joint Events Council. And, "when there isn't anything going on here, Minneapolis is only an hour away. . . . When the serenity gets [to be] too much for you, the hustle and bustle of big city life is in reach. I have yet to be bored here."

### Student Body
The student body of CSB/SJU "is basically a bunch of white suburban kids from Minnesota and a bunch of white farm kids from Minnesota mixed together, and a few international students mainly from the Bahamas and a few out-of-state students thrown in to spice things up a bit." Students are "friendly, motivated, and courteous. Most people get along and socialize with many people." Reports one student, "It's not uncommon to say 'hello' to people you don't even know." Another points out that "there are a number of students here that do come from wealthy backgrounds, so sometimes it's tough for myself and others from not-so-wealthy backgrounds to see so many nice cars and people wearing Abercrombie. The students are in no way separated by money or what they wear, though. Everyone gets along very well."

150 ■ THE BEST 351 COLLEGES

# COLLEGE OF SAINT BENEDICT/SAINT JOHN'S UNIVERSITY

FINANCIAL AID: 320-363-3664 • E-MAIL: ADMISSIONS@CSBSJU.EDU • WEBSITE: WWW.CSBSJU.EDU

## ADMISSIONS

*Very important factors considered include:* class rank, essays, secondary school record, standardized test scores. *Important factors considered include:* alumni/ae relation, character/personal qualities, extracurricular activities, geographical residence, minority status, recommendations, religious affiliation/commitment, state residency, talent/ability, volunteer work, work experience. *Other factors considered include:* interview. SAT I or ACT required. TOEFL required of all international applicants. High school diploma or GED is required. *High school units required/recommended:* 17 total recommended; 4 English recommended, 3 math recommended, 2 science recommended, 2 science lab recommended, 2 foreign language recommended, 2 social studies recommended, 4 elective recommended.

### The Inside Word

Though Saint John's University and the College of Saint Benedict have combined most of their efforts and operations on campus, admission remains distinct. Women must apply to the College of Saint Benedict and men to Saint John's. Since it is a joint admissions office, both are seeking exactly the same qualities in their students; in addition to solid academic records from high school, much attention is paid to the match a student makes with the schools. Candidates can expect their personal side to receive thorough evaluation within the admissions processes here.

## FINANCIAL AID

*Students should submit:* FAFSA, institution's own financial aid form, federal tax forms and W-2s. The Princeton Review suggests that all financial aid forms be submitted as soon as possible after January 1. *Need-based scholarships/grants offered:* Pell, SEOG, state scholarships/grants, private scholarships, the school's own gift aid. *Loan aid offered:* FFEL Subsidized Stafford, FFEL Unsubsidized Stafford, FFEL PLUS, Federal Perkins, state loans, various private loans. Federal Work-Study Program available. Institutional employment available. Applicants will be notified of awards on a rolling basis beginning on or about March 15. Off-campus job opportunities are good.

## FROM THE ADMISSIONS OFFICE

"CSB/SJU believes that a student's hard work in high school deserves recognition—that's why renewable scholarships such as the Regents'/Trustees' (worth $38,000 over four years); the President's (worth from $22,000 to $32,000 over four years); and the Dean's (worth from $12,000 to $20,000 over four years) are awarded competitively based on the student's past academic achievement, college entrance test scores, and demonstrated leadership and service. Diversity Leadership Scholarships (worth up to $20,000 over four years) are awarded to students who have promoted diversity in their leadership and service work. Performing and Fine Arts Scholarships (worth up to $8,000 over four years) are awarded to students who have participated in and excelled in art, music, or theater in high school. Approximately 90 percent of the students currently attending the colleges receive financial assistance; many receive both scholarship and need-based assistance."

---

### SELECTIVITY

| | |
|---|---|
| Admissions Rating | 81 |
| # of applicants | 2,375 |
| % of applicants accepted | 86 |
| % of acceptees attending | 48 |
| # accepting a place on wait list | 45 |

#### FRESHMAN PROFILE

| | |
|---|---|
| Range SAT Verbal | 530-650 |
| Average SAT Verbal | 585 |
| Range SAT Math | 560-660 |
| Average SAT Math | 605 |
| Range ACT Composite | 22-28 |
| Average ACT Composite | 25 |
| Minimum TOEFL | 500 |
| Average HS GPA | 3.7 |
| % graduated top 10% of class | 30 |
| % graduated top 25% of class | 66 |
| % graduated top 50% of class | 93 |

#### DEADLINES

| | |
|---|---|
| Priority admission | 2/1 |
| Nonfall registration? | yes |

#### APPLICANTS ALSO LOOK AT
#### AND SOMETIMES PREFER
University of Saint Thomas (MN)
Gustavus Adolphus College
St. Olaf College
#### AND RARELY PREFER
Saint Cloud State University
University of Minnesota—Twin Cities

### FINANCIAL FACTS

| | |
|---|---|
| Financial Aid Rating | 88 |
| Tuition | $18,916 |
| Room and board | $5,789 |
| Books and supplies | $600 |
| Required fees | $310 |
| % frosh receiving aid | 67 |
| % undergrads receiving aid | 63 |
| Avg frosh grant | $11,656 |
| Avg frosh loan | $4,365 |

# COLLEGE OF THE ATLANTIC

105 EDEN STREET, BAR HARBOR, ME 04609 • ADMISSIONS: 800-528-0025 • FAX: 207-288-4126

## CAMPUS LIFE

| Quality of Life Rating | 94 |
| --- | --- |
| Type of school | private |
| Environment | rural |

### STUDENTS

| Total undergrad enrollment | 278 |
| --- | --- |
| % male/female | 36/64 |
| % from out of state | 70 |
| % from public high school | 67 |
| % live on campus | 40 |
| % Caucasian | 83 |
| % international | 14 |
| # of countries represented | 23 |

### SURVEY SAYS . . .
Students are cliquish
Very little hard liquor
(Almost) no one smokes
Very little beer drinking
Very little drug use
Students don't get along with local community
Musical organizations aren't popular

## ACADEMICS

| Academic Rating | 93 |
| --- | --- |
| Calendar | trimester |
| Student/faculty ratio | 10:1 |
| % profs teaching UG courses | 100 |

## STUDENTS SPEAK OUT

### Academics

"It is all about being a better citizen in the world," say the environmentally and politically conscious undergrads of College of the Atlantic, a tiny college whose "strengths include environmental sciences, biology, social sciences, philosophy, and psychology, as well as a tight community [that promotes] intellectual stimulation." COA fosters community spirit and responsibility through its administration, which "is mainly done by committees consisting of students, faculty, and staff, where everyone's opinion counts in decision making." Students love feeling plugged in to the deliberative process and say that the one-for-all approach here also engenders a pervasive feeling of "trust—we don't have locks on our mailboxes, and you can leave your laptop unattended for hours, and it will still be there when you get back." The school allows students "lots of freedom—freedom to take the classes we want, and freedom in those classes to direct our own studies." As one student tells us, "There is so much flexibility here . . . . COA has very few requirements, and they really aren't a big deal." Students praise profs as "energetic and enthusiastic and constantly involved in the students' lives and their learning." Reports one undergrad, "There are posters by each phone on campus, which list the on-campus extension as well as the home phone number of each faculty and staff member. We can call them whenever we need to regarding school, campus committees, and/or personal matters."

### Life

Bar Harbor, COA's hometown, may be the perfect antithesis of a college town; during the summer it's a hopping vacation resort, but during the school year "almost all the stores close up" and students "need to find their own entertainment." Bar Harbor is famous for its bracing winters: "It has been below zero for most of the trimester. It is gray and miserable," notes one undergrad who wishes she were somewhere else. Many here, though, are winter-philes who tout the range of available snow-related activities, which include "skating, cross-country skiing, and snowshoeing." The dearth of in-town options and the small student body combine to create a very subdued campus social scene; "this is not the place for those looking to party, drink, or do lots of drugs (or slack off, for that matter)," explains one student. For fun, "people like cooking together, playing cards, hanging out, going to contra dances, watching movies," and spending as much time outside as they can. Everyone here praises nearby Acadia National Park, "the best backyard a college student could ask for. Finding favorite beautiful hikes, walks, or study spots has become a four-year goal," reports one student. Students party on Tuesdays ("There are no classes on Wednesdays, so Tuesday night is the big social period," explains one student) and on weekends. "Parties are never big, but often fun." Students also want the world to know that "the food is SOOOOO good here! There's no corporate 'food service'—it's just people that work in the kitchen and concoct really tasty (and healthy) food."

### Student Body

"Some people think this school is a bunch of granola-eating, flower-child, pot-smoking hippies, but that's not the way it is," reports one COA undergrad. "The typical COA student has a lot of individuality. We're not all cookie-cutter Rastafarians. We're all atypical." Agrees another student, "The COA student tries to be different . . . just like everyone else. There is no 'in' to fit into, just a lot of cliques." Those cliques, students tell us, include "hippies, lobstermen, city kids, trendy people . . . just about every category one could imagine." Students do, on the whole, tend to be "environmentally and socially sensitive" and "liberal in political thought," the type who attend "protests and drive an ancient Volvo or VW with a political bumper sticker and a Darwin fish." "There are quite a few international students, especially from Europe and Asia," at COA, and "they get along well with the rest of the students, but most tend to hang out [primarily] with each other."

# COLLEGE OF THE ATLANTIC

FINANCIAL AID: 207-288-5015 • E-MAIL: INQUIRY@ECOLOGY.COA.EDU • WEBSITE: WWW.COA.EDU

## ADMISSIONS
*Very important factors considered include:* essays, extracurricular activities, interview, recommendations, secondary school record, volunteer work. *Important factors considered include:* character/personal qualities, talent/ability. *Other factors considered include:* alumni/ae relation, class rank, minority status, standardized test scores, work experience. TOEFL required of all international applicants. High school diploma or GED is required. *High school units required/recommended:* 15 total required; 19 total recommended; 4 English required, 4 math required, 2 science required, 3 science recommended, 2 science lab required, 2 foreign language recommended, 2 social studies required, 2 history recommended, 1 elective recommended.

### The Inside Word
COA's academic emphasis results in a highly self-selected applicant pool. Fortunately for the college, its focus on human ecology strikes a chord that is timely in its appeal to students. Enrolling here is definitely opting to take an atypical path to higher education. Admissions evaluations emphasize what's on your mind over what's on your transcript, which makes thoughtful essays and an interview musts for serious candidates. It also makes the admissions process a refreshing experience in the relatively uniform world of college admission. The admissions committee includes a few current students who have full voting rights as members.

## FINANCIAL AID
*Students should submit:* FAFSA, institution's own financial aid form, noncustodial (divorced/separated) parent's statement, business/farm supplement. Regular filing deadline is February 15. The Princeton Review suggests that all financial aid forms be submitted as soon as possible after January 1. *Need-based scholarships/grants offered:* Pell, SEOG, private scholarships, the school's own gift aid. *Loan aid offered:* Direct Subsidized Stafford, Direct Unsubsidized Stafford, Direct PLUS, Federal Perkins. Federal Work-Study Program available. Institutional employment available. Applicants will be notified of awards on or about April 1. Off-campus job opportunities are good.

## FROM THE ADMISSIONS OFFICE
"College of the Atlantic was created three decades ago at a time when it was becoming evident that conventional education was inadequate for citizenship in our increasingly complex and technical society. The growing interdependence of environmental and social issues and the limitations of academic specialization demanded a wider vision. COA's founders created a pioneering institution dedicated to the interdisciplinary study of human ecology, a college in which students overcome narrow points of view and integrate knowledge across traditional academic lines."

---

### SELECTIVITY

| | |
|---|---:|
| Admissions Rating | 85 |
| # of applicants | 282 |
| % of applicants accepted | 71 |
| % of acceptees attending | 34 |
| # accepting a place on wait list | 3 |
| % admitted from wait list | 33 |
| # of early decision applicants | 38 |
| % accepted early decision | 87 |

### FRESHMAN PROFILE
| | |
|---|---:|
| Range SAT Verbal | 570-670 |
| Average SAT Verbal | 624 |
| Range SAT Math | 550-640 |
| Average SAT Math | 586 |
| Range ACT Composite | 25-29 |
| Average ACT Composite | 28 |
| Minimum TOEFL | 550 |
| % graduated top 10% of class | 34 |
| % graduated top 25% of class | 73 |
| % graduated top 50% of class | 93 |

### DEADLINES
| | |
|---|---:|
| Early decision | 12/1 |
| Early decision notification | 12/15 |
| Priority admission | 2/15 |
| Regular admission | 2/15 |
| Regular notification | 4/1 |
| Nonfall registration? | yes |

### APPLICANTS ALSO LOOK AT
**AND OFTEN PREFER**
Bowdoin, Colby, Reed
**AND SOMETIMES PREFER**
Bates, U of Vermont
Marlboro, Hampshire
Cornell U
**AND RARELY PREFER**
Oberlin
U Maine at Orono
Warren Wilson
Eckerd

### FINANCIAL FACTS

| | |
|---|---:|
| Financial Aid Rating | 89 |
| Tuition | $23,601 |
| Room and board | $6,543 |
| Books and supplies | $500 |
| Required fees | $360 |
| % frosh receiving aid | 90 |
| % undergrads receiving aid | 77 |
| Avg frosh grant | $11,000 |
| Avg frosh loan | $2,625 |

# COLLEGE OF THE HOLY CROSS

ADMISSIONS OFFICE, 1 COLLEGE STREET, WORCESTER, MA 01610-2395 • ADMISSIONS: 508-793-2443 • FAX: 508-793-3888

## CAMPUS LIFE

| Quality of Life Rating | 83 |
|---|---|
| Type of school | private |
| Affiliation | Roman Catholic |
| Environment | suburban |

### STUDENTS

| Total undergrad enrollment | 2,801 |
|---|---|
| % male/female | 47/53 |
| % from out of state | 66 |
| % from public high school | 42 |
| % live on campus | 79 |
| % African American | 3 |
| % Asian | 4 |
| % Caucasian | 79 |
| % Hispanic | 5 |
| % international | 1 |
| # of countries represented | 17 |

### SURVEY SAYS . . .
Frats and sororities dominate social scene
Beautiful campus
Great library
Diverse students interact
Theater is unpopular
Computer facilities need improving

## ACADEMICS

| Academic Rating | 94 |
|---|---|
| Calendar | semester |
| Student/faculty ratio | 11:1 |
| Profs interesting rating | 75 |
| Profs accessible rating | 72 |
| % profs teaching UG courses | 100 |
| Avg lab size | under 10 students |
| Avg reg class size | 10-19 students |

### MOST POPULAR MAJORS
English language and literature
Psychology
Political science and government

## STUDENTS SPEAK OUT

### Academics
"Academics are very difficult, but very worth the effort" at College of the Holy Cross, a small liberal arts school with "a total sense of community—almost family—just like the admissions propaganda claims." Professors pile on so much work that the school allows students to take only four classes per semester. Even with this limit, "the work is by all means tough. There's a lot of studying, but it really pays off in the real world." The grading system is equally demanding. Fortunately, HC's stringent standards are well known to the outside world. "A hiring manager from one of the big accounting firms told me the company considers a 3.0 at Holy Cross [equal to] a 3.5 at other schools," explained one student. Students gripe, but they appreciate the results. Wrote one, "I may hate actually being at school, but having Holy Cross on my resume has gotten me a great summer internship, is allowing me to intern in D.C. for the spring semester, and will even indirectly lead into being accepted [by] a reputable law school." They also appreciate the "close personal attention you can receive from professors. I have never had a problem getting extra help from a professor on papers or assignments." This is due in part to the "exclusively undergraduate environment. There are no grad students teaching the classes, and the 'good' professors are also available to everyone, not just upper-level or graduate students." "Active alumni support" further sweetens the deal.

### Life
At HC, "everyone works their butt off, but also needs to let off steam. It's a really hard school with very high expectations. The stress can be too much at times." Students "work like mad Sunday through Wednesday" and then start letting off that steam on "Thirsty Thursday," usually at a kegger ("HC is a keg school," students tell us). Alternatives are few. "While the student programming people may put on events that try to bring students together, these events rarely draw many (Spring Weekend and the Opportunity Knocks dance are the exceptions)." Hometown Worcester "does not offer a lot despite the high number of colleges in the area. The city is also not very fond of college students." Nonetheless, a few intrepid souls venture out into the city and report that "dining in Worcester is amazing—many great restaurants. There are usually many choices of things to do here between film series, music performances, theatre, and varsity sports." They warn those who'd follow in their footsteps not to reveal their status as HC students. Undergrads praise their "absolutely gorgeous" campus but warn that its famous picturesque hill "is a real pain in the ass, especially in winter." Intercollegiate athletics, "especially men's and women's basketball teams, are hugely popular," as are intramurals. When escape is essential, students head to Boston or Providence.

### Student Body
"There are no surprises" in the Holy Cross student body. "It is a small, private, liberal arts college with a Jesuit identity in New England. Therefore, the population is mostly white, middle class, Irish or Italian Catholics." As one student put it, "A certain type of person, I believe, looks at Holy Cross. This type of person wants a small school in a suburb, with preppy students, small classes, and religion. I am not sure why minorities don't choose Holy Cross; I believe it is because this school just isn't what they want. . . . It is nobody's fault." HC has made some inroads into minority populations through its outreach programs, students here report. The typical HC undergrad is "friendly and outgoing" and conservative. "Religion is big, sports are bigger, and drinking is the biggest." Students like that fact that HC "is a small community, which is nice because you can generally say 'Hi' to anyone and you know them."

# COLLEGE OF THE HOLY CROSS

FINANCIAL AID: 508-793-2265 • E-MAIL: ADMISSIONS@HOLYCROSS.EDU • WEBSITE: WWW.HOLYCROSS.EDU

## ADMISSIONS

*Very important factors considered include:* class rank, secondary school record, standardized test scores. *Important factors considered include:* alumni/ae relation, character/personal qualities, essays, extracurricular activities, interview, recommendations. *Other factors considered include:* geographical residence, minority status, talent/ability, volunteer work, work experience. SAT I or ACT required; SAT II also required. TOEFL required of all international applicants. High school diploma or GED is required. *High school units required/recommended:* 20 total recommended; 4 English recommended, 4 math recommended, 4 science recommended, 3 foreign language recommended, 2 social studies recommended, 2 history recommended, 1 elective recommended.

### The Inside Word

The applicant pool at Holy Cross is strong; students are well advised to take the most challenging courses available to them in secondary school. Everyone faces fairly close scrutiny here, but as is the case virtually everywhere, the College does have its particular interests. The admissions committee takes good care of candidates from the many Catholic high schools that are the source of dozens of solid applicants each year.

## FINANCIAL AID

*Students should submit:* FAFSA, CSS/Financial Aid PROFILE, noncustodial (divorced/separated) parent's statement, business/farm supplement, parent and student federal tax returns. Regular filing deadline is February 1. The Princeton Review suggests that all financial aid forms be submitted as soon as possible after January 1. *Need-based scholarships/grants offered:* Pell, SEOG, state scholarships/grants, private scholarships, the school's own gift aid. *Loan aid offered:* FFEL Subsidized Stafford, FFEL Unsubsidized Stafford, FFEL PLUS, Federal Perkins, MEFA. Federal Work-Study Program available. Institutional employment available. Applicants will be notified of awards on or about April 3. Off-campus job opportunities are good.

## FROM THE ADMISSIONS OFFICE

"When applying to Holy Cross, two areas deserve particular attention. First, the essay should be developed thoughtfully, with correct language and syntax in mind. That essay reflects for the Board of Admissions how you think and how you can express yourself. Second, activity beyond the classroom should be clearly defined. Since Holy Cross is 2,800 students, the chance for involvement/participation is exceptional. The Board reviews many applications for academically qualified students. A key difference in being accepted is the extent to which a candidate participates in-depth beyond the classroom—don't be modest; define who you are."

### SELECTIVITY

| | |
|---|---|
| Admissions Rating | 92 |
| # of applicants | 4,884 |
| % of applicants accepted | 43 |
| % of acceptees attending | 34 |
| # accepting a place on wait list | 412 |
| % admitted from wait list | 9 |
| # of early decision applicants | 357 |
| % accepted early decision | 68 |

### FRESHMAN PROFILE

| | |
|---|---|
| Range SAT Verbal | 570-650 |
| Average SAT Verbal | 627 |
| Range SAT Math | 590-670 |
| Average SAT Math | 630 |
| Minimum TOEFL | 550 |
| % graduated top 10% of class | 59 |
| % graduated top 50% of class | 100 |

### DEADLINES

| | |
|---|---|
| Early decision | 12/15 |
| Early decision notification | 2/15 |
| Regular admission | 1/15 |
| Regular notification | 4/1 |
| Nonfall registration? | yes |

### APPLICANTS ALSO LOOK AT
**AND OFTEN PREFER**
Dartmouth
Georgetown U.
Notre Dame
Boston Coll.
Tufts
**AND SOMETIMES PREFER**
Bowdoin
Colgate
Villanova
Providence
U. Mass—Amherst
**AND RARELY PREFER**
Fairfield

### FINANCIAL FACTS

| | |
|---|---|
| Financial Aid Rating | 81 |
| Tuition | $27,560 |
| Room and board | $8,440 |
| Books and supplies | $400 |
| Required fees | $451 |
| % frosh receiving aid | 53 |
| % undergrads receiving aid | 50 |
| Avg frosh grant | $13,433 |
| Avg frosh loan | $3,904 |

THE BEST 351 COLLEGES ■ 155

# COLLEGE OF THE OZARKS

OFFICE OF ADMISSIONS, POINT LOOKOUT, MO 65726 • ADMISSIONS: 417-334-6411 • FAX: 417-335-2618

## CAMPUS LIFE

| | |
|---|---|
| **Quality of Life Rating** | **79** |
| Type of school | private |
| Affiliation | Presbyterian |
| Environment | rural |

### STUDENTS

| | |
|---|---|
| Total undergrad enrollment | 1,348 |
| % male/female | 43/57 |
| % from out of state | 33 |
| % live on campus | 84 |
| % Caucasian | 89 |
| % Hispanic | 1 |
| % international | 2 |

### SURVEY SAYS . . .
Very little drug use
Lots of conservatives on campus
Classes are small
Students love Point Lookout, MO
Beautiful campus
Very little beer drinking
Very little hard liquor
(Almost) no one smokes
Political activism is (almost) nonexistent

## ACADEMICS

| | |
|---|---|
| **Academic Rating** | **84** |
| Calendar | semester |
| Student/faculty ratio | 14:1 |
| Profs interesting rating | 76 |
| Profs accessible rating | 80 |
| % profs teaching UG courses | 100 |
| Avg lab size | 10-19 students |
| Avg reg class size | under 10 students |

### MOST POPULAR MAJORS
Agricultural business and management
English/language arts teacher education
Criminal justice/police science

## STUDENTS SPEAK OUT

### Academics

Many students at the College of the Ozarks feel that their school is "the best place to get an affordable education in a Christian setting." The school, one of six in the country that widely offer educational opportunities to needy students in exchange for work in on-campus jobs, "provides a unique experience that cannot be found at other colleges," according to undergrads. "The college seeks to fulfill a student's needs in academic, vocational, spiritual, cultural, and patriotic areas." Students caution that "it is easier to attend because of the financial support you receive, but it is not 'free' by any means"; many students work a second, off-campus job in addition to their on-campus work in order to cover expenses. In return for their labors, students here enjoy professors who "take you in under their wing and follow you throughout college and into career placement" and an administration that "actually wants to listen if you have a concern. They don't just lock themselves in their offices; they get out and get familiar with the student body." Academic offerings at this small school cover most of the liberal arts, as well as agriculturally oriented programs, aviation, and hotel and restaurant management. Some here complain that "the academics are slightly watered down"; others, conversely, refer to their school as "Hard Work U."

### Life

The academic workload, along with an average 15-hour-per-week work commitment to the school, means that C of O students "don't have a lot of free time. For the most part, however, students here find time to hang out with their friends." Many students take a second job in nearby Branson: "People work to pay for what school doesn't cover," explains one student. Students point out that "since we live in a tourist town, it's easy for everyone to be employed off-campus earning $7 an hour." As an added benefit, "being a C of O student means we get discounts on a lot of things in Branson, including movies and shows." There's a downside to living near a tourism mecca, though: "Life in Branson [occurs] among hundreds of tourists you can never escape. As students we have to learn all of the back roads." On campus, "the rules keep the school clean-cut and enjoyable for everyone." What are the rules, you ask? Reports one undergrad, "Campus gates close at 1:00 every night; opposite sexes are allowed in campus dorms for only three hours on four nights a semester; smoking is allowed only in designated areas; if you are caught drunk by a school official outside of school (even if you are over 21) you will be put on probation . . . and many [administrators] are very discriminative against the students who dress alternative or portray themselves in their own ways." Not surprisingly, "there are people who choose to take more liberties with the rules, just like everywhere. They go off campus to have fun, mostly to drink." Most, however, happily toe the line, enjoying more wholesome pursuits. Notes one, "I love the clean atmosphere: socially, environmentally, and spiritually."

### Student Body

The "mostly conservative" students of College of the Ozarks pride themselves on their "outstanding moral values" (which lead at least a few to observe that "some here are really 'holier than thou.' "). Students agree that their classmates are both affable and genuinely accommodating; writes one, "People who visit here comment on how friendly and helpful we are. Maybe it's because we are in the South, but we are really, really friendly." Adds another, "I'll just put it this way: if my car broke down on campus, at least 10 people would show up to help." Students report that "This is a pretty diverse campus . . . [and] I'm glad to say that we all pretty much get along." Though they hail from far and wide, most have roots in rural America.

# COLLEGE OF THE OZARKS

FINANCIAL AID: 417-334-6411 EXT. 4290 • E-MAIL: ADMISS4@COFO.EDU • WEBSITE: WWW.COFO.EDU

## ADMISSIONS
*Very important factors considered include:* character/personal qualities, class rank, essays, extracurricular activities, interview, secondary school record. *Important factors considered include:* alumni/ae relation, recommendations, standardized test scores, talent/ability, volunteer work, work experience. *Other factors considered include:* geographical residence, minority status, religious affiliation/commitment, state residency. ACT required. TOEFL required of all international applicants. High school diploma or GED is required. *High school units required/recommended:* 24 total recommended; 4 English recommended, 3 math recommended, 2 science recommended, 1 science lab recommended, 2 foreign language recommended, 3 social studies recommended.

### The Inside Word
The highly unusual nature of the College of the Ozarks translates directly into its admissions process. Because of the school's very purpose, providing educational opportunities to those with great financial need, one of the main qualifiers for admission is exactly that—demonstrated financial need. Despite not being a household word, Ozarks attracts enough interest to keep its admit rate consistently low from year to year. To be sure, the admissions process is competitive, but it's more important to be a good fit for the college philosophically and financially than it is to be an academic wizard. If you're a hard worker all around, you're just what they're looking for.

## FINANCIAL AID
*Students should submit:* FAFSA. The Princeton Review suggests that all financial aid forms be submitted as soon as possible after January 1. *Need-based scholarships/grants offered:* Pell, SEOG, state scholarships/grants, private scholarships, the school's own gift aid. Federal Work-Study Program available. Applicants will be notified of awards on or about July 1. Off-campus job opportunities are excellent.

## FROM THE ADMISSIONS OFFICE
"College of the Ozarks is unique because of its no-tuition, work-study program, but also because it strives to educate the head, the heart, and the hands. At C of O, there are high expectations of students—the College stresses character development as well as study and work. An education from 'Hard Work U.' offers many opportunities, not the least of which is the chance to graduate debt-free. Life at C of O isn't all hard work and no play, however. There are many opportunities for fun. The nearby resort town of Branson, Missouri, offers ample opportunities for recreation and summer employment, and Table Rock Lake, only a few miles away, is a terrific spot to swim, sun, and relax. Numerous on-campus activities such as Mudfest, Luau Night, dances, and holiday parties give students lots of chances for fun without leaving the college. At 'Hard Work U.,' we work hard, but we know how to have fun, too."

## SELECTIVITY

| | |
|---|---|
| Admissions Rating | 85 |
| # of applicants | 2,417 |
| % of applicants accepted | 12 |
| % of acceptees attending | 89 |

### FRESHMAN PROFILE
| | |
|---|---|
| Range ACT Composite | 17-26 |
| Average ACT Composite | 22 |
| Minimum TOEFL | 550 |
| Average HS GPA | 3.4 |
| % graduated top 10% of class | 11 |
| % graduated top 25% of class | 39 |
| % graduated top 50% of class | 82 |

### DEADLINES
| | |
|---|---|
| Priority admission | 2/15 |
| Regular admission | 8/20 |
| Regular notification | rolling |
| Nonfall registration? | yes |

### APPLICANTS ALSO LOOK AT AND OFTEN PREFER
Southwest Missouri State U
### AND SOMETIMES PREFER
Southwest Baptist U

## FINANCIAL FACTS

| | |
|---|---|
| Financial Aid Rating | 93 |
| Room and board | $3,250 |
| Books and supplies | $600 |
| Required fees | $250 |
| % frosh receiving aid | 90 |
| % undergrads receiving aid | 90 |
| Avg frosh grant | $12,467 |

# COLLEGE OF WILLIAM AND MARY

PO Box 8795, Williamsburg, VA 23187-8795 • Admissions: 757-221-4223 • Fax: 757-221-1242

## CAMPUS LIFE

| Quality of Life Rating | 84 |
|---|---|
| Type of school | public |
| Environment | suburban |

### STUDENTS

| Total undergrad enrollment | 5,694 |
|---|---|
| % male/female | 44/56 |
| % from out of state | 34 |
| % live on campus | 75 |
| % in (# of) fraternities | 31 (15) |
| % in (# of) sororities | 33 (12) |
| % African American | 5 |
| % Asian | 7 |
| % Caucasian | 84 |
| % Hispanic | 3 |
| % international | 1 |
| # of countries represented | 73 |

### SURVEY SAYS . . .
Frats and sororities dominate social scene
Beautiful campus
No one cheats
(Almost) everyone plays intramural sports
Campus feels safe
Students are very religious
Musical organizations are hot
(Almost) no one listens to college radio
Students get along with local community

## ACADEMICS

| Academic Rating | 92 |
|---|---|
| Calendar | semester |
| Student/faculty ratio | 12:1 |
| Profs interesting rating | 95 |
| Profs accessible rating | 98 |
| % profs teaching UG courses | 63 |
| % classes taught by TAs | 1 |
| Avg reg class size | 10-19 students |

### MOST POPULAR MAJORS
Business administration/management
English language and literature
Psychology

## STUDENTS SPEAK OUT

### Academics
Looking for a small public university with a big reputation (considered by some to be the most "prestigious" and "competitive" in the country), excellent location, and a down-to-earth attitude? William and Mary might just be your answer. Its students are certainly aware of this traditional liberal arts college's strengths and express them with intelligence and ease: "William and Mary is an undiscovered gem," writes one student. "It is an excellent undergraduate institution: small, but big enough to not limit you." Adds another, "At William and Mary, you get out of a class exactly what you put in. It's called self-determination. So, really, the school itself doesn't set the standards; we do." Listing the honor code, small class size, and rigorous academic standards as being among the college's greatest assets, students also appreciate its accessible, student-focused faculty, noting that at William and Mary, "we have professors who can make classes of 50 and more feel personal." One sophomore likes the fact that teachers "reward excellence and not competency with A's," while another appreciates "the option of being able to get to know the professors on a personal level." And though "the administration is a tad clueless," they also "listen to students the best that they can"—which presumably includes the issues surrounding financial aid, a popular gripe among William and Mary undergrads. "It's the best school for the money," comments a junior—with one caveat: You have to be a Virginia resident to take advantage of its state-school price tag. Basically, it comes down to one's feeling about a place, and the zeitgeist at William and Mary seems to be summed up best by a freshman: "Good times, guys. Good times."

### Life
"Intimate," "warm," and "tightly knit" are words often used to describe William and Mary's fairly well-developed social scene. According to a sophomore, it's the "size of the school" that "permits students to get involved in campus life." Writes another, "There is always something going on at William and Mary. It's easy to make friends and easy to be involved in activities. You can be as active as you want—there are a lot of opportunities." Some students might say that social life is somewhat skewed toward "fraternity parties and the brotherhood," however. There are lots of parties on weekends, and "delis [basically bars across the street from campus] are very fun to go to and hang out at." Williamsburg doesn't receive rave reviews. Writes one student, "Being far-ish from any major metropolitan area, cultural activities (concerts, museums, etc.) are rather rare." Still, while Williamsburg "doesn't have much," a trip to D.C. is worth the drive. Athletics are also a big draw; by one student's reckoning, "About 80 percent of the students participate in some kind of sport." Alas, "the meal plan is a rip-off," and while the colonial-style campus is scenic and lovely, parking seems to be a huge hassle (and impossible for first and second years). But hey—when the biggest complaint about a school is "more parking, better food, more hot boys," it can't be that bad.

### Student Body
In keeping with William and Mary's down-to-earth vibe, students at the school characterize their peers as "real" and "friendly," with "no fake attitudes and phoniness." Writes a sophomore, "Most everyone is approachable and genuinely concerned for others." Adds another, "Students are interesting and have neat stories—basically the same socioeconomic status but different life experiences." Of course not everyone is down with the group thing; a sophomore points out that "most students come from middle-class white backgrounds so the student body is too homogenous in attitudes/perspectives. Many are therefore unoriginal and boring." Still, a strong sense of community seems to be one of W&M's greatest strengths, even if it means getting through the hard times together. Jokes a junior, "Though half of the students are probably depressed, there exists an undeniable spirit of solidarity among them."

158 ■ THE BEST 351 COLLEGES

# COLLEGE OF WILLIAM AND MARY

FINANCIAL AID: 757-221-2420 EXT. 4290 • E-MAIL: ADMISS@FACSTAFF.WM.EDU • WEBSITE: WWW.WM.EDU

## ADMISSIONS
*Very important factors considered include:* secondary school record, state residency. *Important factors considered include:* alumni/ae relation, class rank, essays, extracurricular activities, standardized test scores. *Other factors considered include:* character/personal qualities, geographical residence, minority status, recommendations, talent/ability, volunteer work, work experience. SAT I or ACT required; SAT II optional. TOEFL required of all international applicants. *High school units required/recommended:* 4 English recommended, 4 math recommended, 4 science recommended, 3 science lab recommended, 4 foreign language recommended, 4 social studies recommended.

### The Inside Word
The volume of applications at William and Mary is extremely high; thus admission is ultra-competitive. Only very strong students from out of state should apply. The large applicant pool necessitates a rapid-fire candidate evaluation process; each admissions officer reads roughly 100 application folders per day during the peak review season. But this is one admissions committee that moves fast without sacrificing a thorough review. There probably isn't a tougher public college admissions committee in the country.

## FINANCIAL AID
*Students should submit:* FAFSA. Regular filing deadline is March 15. The Princeton Review suggests that all financial aid forms be submitted as soon as possible after January 1. *Need-based scholarships/grants offered:* Pell, SEOG, state scholarships/grants, private scholarships, the school's own gift aid. *Loan aid offered:* FFEL Subsidized Stafford, FFEL Unsubsidized Stafford, FFEL PLUS, Federal Perkins. Federal Work-Study Program available. Institutional employment available. Applicants will be notified of awards on or about April 1. Off-campus job opportunities are good.

## FROM THE ADMISSIONS OFFICE
"If you are an academicaly strong, involved student looking for a challenge in a great campus community, William and Mary may well be the place for you. Every year, students are drawn from all parts of the United States and dozens of foreign countries by the excellence of the undergraduate experience, the beauty of the campus and its surroundings, the size and residential character of the student body, and the history and traditions of the country's second oldest college."

### SELECTIVITY

| | |
|---|---|
| Admissions Rating | 94 |
| # of applicants | 8,917 |
| % of applicants accepted | 35 |
| % of acceptees attending | 43 |
| # accepting place on wait list | 1,278 |
| % admitted from wait list | 3 |
| # of early decision applicants | 889 |
| % accepted early decision | 54 |

### FRESHMAN PROFILE
| | |
|---|---|
| Range SAT Verbal | 620-730 |
| Average SAT Verbal | 669 |
| Range SAT Math | 630-710 |
| Average SAT Math | 666 |
| Range ACT Composite | 27-31 |
| Average ACT Composite | 29 |
| Minimum TOEFL | 600 |
| % graduated top 10% of class | 90 |
| % graduated top 25% of class | 99 |
| % graduated top 50% of class | 100 |

### DEADLINES
| | |
|---|---|
| Early decision | 11/1 |
| Early decision notification | 12/1 |
| Regular admission | 1/15 |
| Regular notification | 4/1 |
| Nonfall registration? | yes |

### APPLICANTS ALSO LOOK AT
**AND OFTEN PREFER**
U. Virginia
Georgetown U.
Williams
Duke, Dartmouth
**AND SOMETIMES PREFER**
Wake Forest
Randolph-Macon Woman's
Washington and Lee
Johns Hopkins, Rice
**AND RARELY PREFER**
James Madison
U. Richmond
George Mason

### FINANCIAL FACTS

| | |
|---|---|
| Financial Aid Rating | 81 |
| In-state tuition | $1,880 |
| Out-of-state tuition | $9,230 |
| % frosh receiving aid | 26 |
| % undergrads receiving aid | 26 |
| Avg frosh grant | $8,626 |
| Avg frosh loan | $3,202 |

# COLLEGE OF WOOSTER

1189 BEALL AVENUE, WOOSTER, OH 44691 • ADMISSIONS: 800-877-9905 • FAX: 330-263-2621

## CAMPUS LIFE

| Quality of Life Rating | 88 |
|---|---|
| Type of school | private |
| Affiliation | other |
| Environment | suburban |

### STUDENTS

| Total undergrad enrollment | 1,856 |
|---|---|
| % male/female | 47/53 |
| % from out of state | 44 |
| % from public high school | 73 |
| % live on campus | 97 |
| % in (# of) fraternities | 7 (4) |
| % in (# of) sororities | 8 (6) |
| % African American | 5 |
| % Asian | 2 |
| % Caucasian | 88 |
| % Hispanic | 1 |
| % international | 7 |
| # of countries represented | 21 |

### SURVEY SAYS . . .
Great computer facilities
Great library
Lots of beer drinking
Low cost of living
Students don't get along with local community
Registration is a pain
Student government is unpopular
Theater is unpopular
Lousy food on campus

## ACADEMICS

| Academic Rating | 88 |
|---|---|
| Calendar | semester |
| Student/faculty ratio | 13:1 |
| Profs interesting rating | 94 |
| Profs accessible rating | 97 |
| % profs teaching UG courses | 100 |
| Avg lab size | 10-19 students |
| Avg reg class size | under 10 students |

### MOST POPULAR MAJORS
History
English language and literature
Communications studies/speech communication and rhetoric

## STUDENTS SPEAK OUT

### Academics

Like the hallmark of its curriculum—the independent study program—the College of Wooster seems intent on nurturing students into self-reliance. From the initial freshman seminar designed to foster critical thinking and writing skills, the Wooster curriculum is geared toward preparing students for their senior-year independent project. Fully integrated major requirements force students to master both content and methodology in their chosen fields of study before confronting the difficult but rewarding Independent Study (referred to by all on campus simply as "I.S."). Students approve, adding that Wooster's faculty is uniquely suited to the task of teaching the curriculum. "Since the school requires a two-semester independent study project of all of its seniors, the professors who choose to teach here have to (and seem to like to) put their students' research interests before their own," explains one student. Undergrads advise that "grades at Wooster are definitely earned, as classes are very challenging and involve a great deal of work." Fortunately, professors are inspiring; notes one student, "The best thing about the professors at Wooster is that you can always tell that they love what they do. When they are discussing a project of theirs, you can just see in their eyes the level of commitment [to it] that they have." Administrators are "open to suggestions and criticisms from students" although they sometimes "act too much like parents, rather than allowing us to make the mistakes that all 20-somethings need to make."

### Life

Students at Wooster appreciate the wide array of activities available to them. Writes one, "There is always something going on during the week (like concerts and comedians), and there are plenty of parties on the weekends. The parties at Wooster—even the big frat parties—are open to anyone. This allows everyone to get together and have a fun time." Adds another, "People at Wooster definitely know how to have a good time. Something is always happening. We have a bar on campus, and 50-cent drafts at happy hour make Friday nights fun." Chem-free offerings? "There are always movies (either free or $1) on the weekends; we have a bowling alley (with pool and ping pong tables), and there are always plays, concerts, or dances to attend. There is never a lack of entertainment at Wooster." The campus is also host to "a million clubs and organizations, depending upon one's preferences as far as hobbies or religion." Off-campus is a different story, as "there really isn't that much to do [in town]. Until you come to Wooster you never realize how truly exciting a 24-hour Super WalMart can be!" Agrees another undergrad, "We are kind of out in the middle of a pasture, and while we don't spend our time cow tipping, we don't have as much access to museums, clubs, and good restaurants as we might were we in the middle of a big city. On the other hand, Cleveland is only an hour away, and it does have all those things."

### Student Body

"Thanks to the great financial aid packages that are awarded," Wooster students "come from all different backgrounds." A large international contingent arrives primarily from Pakistan and India; international students "live mostly in one dorm, and black students live in their own sections. Wooster says it is incredibly diverse, but it is rare to see black and white students sitting together" in, say, a dining hall. Undergrads "are very active in all sorts of volunteer groups, and they actually care about the community." Observes one student, "This seems to me like a very liberal school.

# COLLEGE OF WOOSTER

FINANCIAL AID: 800-877-3688 • E-MAIL: ADMISSIONS@WOOSTER.EDU • WEBSITE: WWW.WOOSTER.EDU

## ADMISSIONS

*Very important factors considered include:* class rank, secondary school record. *Important factors considered include:* character/personal qualities, essays, recommendations, standardized test scores, talent/ability. *Other factors considered include:* alumni/ae relation, extracurricular activities, geographical residence, interview, minority status, state residency, volunteer work, work experience. SAT I or ACT required. TOEFL required of all international applicants. High school diploma or GED is required. *High school units required/recommended:* 4 English required, 3 math required, 4 math recommended, 3 science required, 4 science recommended, 2 foreign language required, 3 foreign language recommended, 3 social studies required, 4 social studies recommended, 2 elective required.

### The Inside Word

Wooster has a solid academic reputation and holds its own against formidable competition for students with many national-caliber liberal arts colleges. Applicants should not take the admissions process lightly because candidate evaluations are very thorough and personal.

## FINANCIAL AID

*Students should submit:* FAFSA, institution's own financial aid form, CSS/Financial Aid PROFILE. No deadline for regular filing. The Princeton Review suggests that all financial aid forms be submitted as soon as possible after January 1. *Need-based scholarships/grants offered:* Pell, SEOG, state scholarships/grants, private scholarships, the school's own gift aid. *Loan aid offered:* Direct Subsidized Stafford, Direct Unsubsidized Stafford, Direct PLUS, Federal Perkins, college/university loans from institutional funds. Federal Work-Study Program available. Institutional employment available. Applicants will be notified of awards on or about April 1. Off-campus job opportunities are good.

## FROM THE ADMISSIONS OFFICE

"At The College of Wooster, our mission is to graduate educated, not merely trained, people; to produce responsible, independent thinkers, rather than specialists in any given field. Our commitment to independence is especially evident in I.S., the college's distinctive program in which every senior works one-to-one with a faculty mentor to complete a project in the major. I.S. comes from 'independent study,' but, in reality, it is an intellectual collaboration of the highest order and permits every student the freedom to pursue something in which he or she is passionately interested. I.S. is the centerpiece of an innovative curriculum. More than just the project itself, the culture that sustains I.S.—and, in turn, is sustained by I.S.—is an extraordinary college culture. The same attitudes of student initiative, openness, flexibility, and individual support enrich every aspect of Wooster's vital residential college life."

## SELECTIVITY

| | |
|---|---|
| Admissions Rating | 80 |
| # of applicants | 2,392 |
| % of applicants accepted | 72 |
| % of acceptees attending | 30 |
| # accepting a place on wait list | 31 |
| # of early decision applicants | 83 |
| % accepted early decision | 84 |

### FRESHMAN PROFILE

| | |
|---|---|
| Range SAT Verbal | 550-650 |
| Average SAT Verbal | 595 |
| Range SAT Math | 550-650 |
| Average SAT Math | 598 |
| Range ACT Composite | 23-29 |
| Average ACT Composite | 26 |
| Minimum TOEFL | 550 |
| Average HS GPA | 3.5 |
| % graduated top 10% of class | 46 |
| % graduated top 25% of class | 71 |
| % graduated top 50% of class | 93 |

### DEADLINES

| | |
|---|---|
| Early decision | 12/1 |
| Early decision notification | 12/15 |
| Regular admission | 2/15 |
| Regular notification | 4/1 |
| Nonfall registration? | yes |

### APPLICANTS ALSO LOOK AT
**AND OFTEN PREFER**
St. Olaf
Denison
Sidmore
DePauw
**AND SOMETIMES PREFER**
Kenyon
Ohio Wesleyan, Beloit
Miami of Ohio
**AND RARELY PREFER**
Ohio U, Allegheny
Wittenberg, Dickinson

## FINANCIAL FACTS

| | |
|---|---|
| Financial Aid Rating | 92 |
| Tuition | $23,687 |
| Room and board | $5,960 |
| Books and supplies | $700 |
| Required fees | $153 |
| % frosh receiving aid | 65 |
| % undergrads receiving aid | 63 |
| Avg frosh grant | $13,225 |
| Avg frosh loan | $3,291 |

# COLORADO COLLEGE

14 East Cache La Poudre Street, Colorado Springs, CO 80903 • Admissions: 719-389-6344 • Fax: 719-389-6816

## CAMPUS LIFE

| | |
|---|---|
| Quality of Life Rating | 86 |
| Type of school | private |
| Environment | urban |

### STUDENTS

| | |
|---|---|
| Total undergrad enrollment | 1,902 |
| % male/female | 45/55 |
| % from out of state | 71 |
| % from public high school | 70 |
| % live on campus | 79 |
| % in (# of) fraternities | 13 (3) |
| % in (# of) sororities | 13 (3) |
| % African American | 2 |
| % Asian | 5 |
| % Caucasian | 79 |
| % Hispanic | 8 |
| % international | 3 |
| # of countries represented | 26 |

### SURVEY SAYS . . .
Students aren't religious
Political activism is hot
Great food on campus
Great off-campus food
(Almost) everyone plays intramural sports
Campus difficult to get around
Theater is unpopular
Diversity lacking on campus

## ACADEMICS

| | |
|---|---|
| Academic Rating | 88 |
| Calendar | other |
| Student/faculty ratio | 9:1 |
| Profs interesting rating | 74 |
| Profs accessible rating | 71 |
| % profs teaching UG courses | 100 |
| Avg reg class size | 10-19 students |

### MOST POPULAR MAJORS
English language and literature
Biology/biological sciences
Economics

## STUDENTS SPEAK OUT

### Academics

The Block Plan stands as the hallmark of a Colorado College education. Students take just one course at a time in three-and-a-half-week blocks, allowing them to be "completely focused on one subject" to the point where many people are "living, breathing, and dreaming about their classes." The small class sizes facilitate discussion, and "if there's a raging debate going on, no one has another class they have to go to, so we can just continue." A content biology major writes, "The block plan allows classes to be as lab intensive as they want (a VERY good thing). I'm doing research now and can devote my time and energy to that without being distracted by tests, papers, and obligations from other courses." Instructors put as much into classes as students do. "Professors have a lot of time to spend with you if you have problems or need academic advice," report most undergrads. Students appreciate that "we call our professors by their first names and use their home phone numbers." While certain students observe "major weaknesses in facilities, research capabilities, and technology" at CC, others are quick to point out that they "got a new, state-of-the-art environmental sciences building this year." From the mixed student comments on the administration, it's tough to discern if they are "extremely accessible and willing to listen to student interests" or "entirely separate from the student body." Most people agree, however, that the "new president, though a former politician, cuts through the bureaucratic red tape and administrative obstacles and is an incredibly cool guy."

### Life

Aside from the academics, Colorado College's paradisiacal setting draws students primed to fill their nonclass hours with "mountain biking, rock climbing, skiing, hiking, and general outdoorsings (a term coined here at CC)." Though Colorado Springs sits more than two hours from the actual slopes, most students spend winter weekends and block breaks frolicking in fresh Rocky Mountain powder. When night falls, parkas are stashed and students earn their reputation for "partying hard any chance we get." Students have permission to "do pretty much whatever they want, whether that be starting an organization or drinking massive amounts of alcohol." The hockey and women's soccer teams, the only two Division I squads the school fields, enjoy an enthusiastic following, and students participate in a variety of community service activities and on-campus organizations. One student recounts, "One day I decided that I wanted to write for the student newspaper, and the next day they gave me two writing assignments. Where else does that happen?" With so much at their fingertips, CC students express contentment. The few gripes concern the leftist-beatnik–world music bent of student activities: "I wish they'd stop playing their stupid African drums outside my window all the time!"

### Student Body

Some would tell you that Colorado College is home to a hefty population of "really smart, athletic hippies" who tend to be "left-wing, artistic social activists with a sense of humor." Others harbor less generous perceptions of their classmates: "Students at CC are generally either yuppies or neo-hippie trustafarians who pretend they aren't yuppies." Lest the population seem homogenous, surveys aver the existence of "a lot of atypical students, myself included, who only enhance the College." Though "very few minorities" attend CC, "people come from all different parts of the country and the world to form an amazing mixture of cultures, beliefs, and ideas." One student relates a heartwarming example: "I love being able to see a 'Goth' and a 'hippie' both play next to each other on an IM hockey team, and have the captain of the soccer team listen to some girl freestyle on her guitar." The school's "large lesbian and gay community" is reportedly "supported by the rest of the school." In the end, this eccentric crew falls under the collective umbrella of "intense people, people who want to do everything at full volume, from academics to sports to outdoor activities to political and social pursuits."

# COLORADO COLLEGE

FINANCIAL AID: 719-389-6651 • E-MAIL: ADMISSION@COLORADOCOLLEGE.EDU • WEBSITE: WWW.COLORADOCOLLEGE.EDU

## ADMISSIONS

*Very important factors considered include:* secondary school record, standardized test scores. *Important factors considered include:* extracurricular activities, recommendations. *Other factors considered include:* alumni/ae relation, character/personal qualities, class rank, essays, geographical residence, interview, minority status, talent/ability, volunteer work, work experience. SAT I or ACT required. TOEFL required of all international applicants. *High school units required/recommended:* 16 total required; 18–20 total recommended.

### The Inside Word

Colorado is seeking thinkers with personality. This makes for an admissions process that gives more credit to the match a candidate makes than simply to good numbers. Tough high school courses are nonetheless a strong factor in admission. Minority recruitment is improving, but needs to play an even bigger part. Students who view Colorado College as a safety, beware—the admissions committee employs a policy of denying candidates who, though strong academically, demonstrate little real interest in attending.

## FINANCIAL AID

*Students should submit:* FAFSA, CSS/Financial Aid PROFILE, noncustodial (divorced/separated) parent's statement. Regular filing deadline is February 15. The Princeton Review suggests that all financial aid forms be submitted as soon as possible after January 1. *Need-based scholarships/grants offered:* Pell, SEOG, state scholarships/grants, private scholarships, the school's own gift aid. *Loan aid offered:* FFEL Subsidized Stafford, FFEL Unsubsidized Stafford, FFEL PLUS, Federal Perkins. Federal Work-Study Program available. Institutional employment available. Applicants will be notified of awards on or about March 25. Off-campus job opportunities are good.

## FROM THE ADMISSIONS OFFICE

"Students enter Colorado College for the opportunity to study intensely in small learning communities. Groups of students work closely with one another and faculty in discussion-based classes and hands-on labs. CC encourages a well-rounded education, combining the academic rigor of an honors college with rich programs in athletics, community service, student government, the arts, and more. The college encourages students to push themselves academically, and many continue their studies at the best graduate and professional schools in the nation. CC is a great choice for field study and for international study (CC ranks fourth nationally in the number of students studying abroad). CC also takes advantage of its location, using it's Baca campus in the San Luis Valley and the mountain cabin for a variety of classes. Its location at the base of the Rockies makes CC a great choice for students who enjoy backpacking, hiking, climbing, and skiing."

### SELECTIVITY

| | |
|---|---|
| Admissions Rating | 91 |
| # of applicants | 3,411 |
| % of applicants accepted | 53 |
| % of acceptees attending | 27 |
| # accepting a place on wait list | 111 |
| % admitted from wait list | 18 |

### FRESHMAN PROFILE

| | |
|---|---|
| Range SAT Verbal | 590-670 |
| Average SAT Verbal | 622 |
| Range SAT Math | 590-670 |
| Average SAT Math | 625 |
| Range ACT Composite | 26-30 |
| Average ACT Composite | 27 |
| Minimum TOEFL | 550 |
| % graduated top 10% of class | 42 |
| % graduated top 25% of class | 81 |
| % graduated top 50% of class | 96 |

### DEADLINES

| | |
|---|---|
| Early action | 11/15 |
| Early action notification | 12/15 |
| Regular admission | 1/15 |
| Regular notification | 4/1 |
| Nonfall registration? | yes |

### APPLICANTS ALSO LOOK AT
**AND OFTEN PREFER**
Stanford
Dartmouth
Carleton
Middlebury

**AND SOMETIMES PREFER**
Macalester
Reed
Occidental
Grinnell
U. Colorado—Boulder

**AND RARELY PREFER**
U. Vermont, Kenyon
Lewis & Clark Coll.

### FINANCIAL FACTS

| | |
|---|---|
| Financial Aid Rating | 85 |
| Tuition | $25,968 |
| Room and board | $6,480 |
| Books and supplies | $766 |
| Required fees | $175 |
| % frosh receiving aid | 41 |
| % undergrads receiving aid | 43 |
| Avg frosh grant | $17,550 |
| Avg frosh loan | $3,035 |

THE BEST 351 COLLEGES ■ 163

# COLORADO SCHOOL OF MINES

WEAVER TOWERS, 1811 ELM STREET, GOLDEN, CO 80401-1842 • ADMISSIONS: 303-273-3220 • FAX: 303-273-3509

## CAMPUS LIFE

| | |
|---|---|
| Quality of Life Rating | 86 |
| Type of school | public |
| Environment | suburban |

### STUDENTS
| | |
|---|---|
| Total undergrad enrollment | 2,504 |
| % male/female | 76/24 |
| % from out of state | 22 |
| % from public high school | 90 |
| % live on campus | 30 |
| % in (# of) fraternities | 20 (7) |
| % in (# of) sororities | 20 (4) |
| % African American | 1 |
| % Asian | 5 |
| % Caucasian | 81 |
| % Hispanic | 7 |
| % international | 4 |
| # of countries represented | 66 |

### SURVEY SAYS . . .
Campus easy to get around
Class discussions encouraged
Lots of beer drinking
Great computer facilities
Campus is beautiful
Campus feels safe
Hard liquor is popular
Students get along with local community

## ACADEMICS

| | |
|---|---|
| Academic Rating | 81 |
| Calendar | semester |
| Student/faculty ratio | 12:1 |
| % profs teaching UG courses | 86 |
| Avg lab size | 20-29 students |
| Avg reg class size | 30-39 students |

### MOST POPULAR MAJORS
Chemical engineering
Mechanical engineering
Mathematics

## STUDENTS SPEAK OUT

### Academics
The Colorado School of Mines focus on math, science, and engineering means that "you come here to be an engineer and make money. You don't come here to party or meet girls." By all accounts, it's a grueling process; as one undergrad put it, "Especially in the lower-level classes, professors make tests and homework as hard and time-consuming as they can." Students report that "CSM's professors are very knowledgeable in their fields," though they also cite problems with the administration's putting "a huge focus on research at the expense of teaching" and some old-school "teachers that have passed their expiration date." This leaves many undergrads with the impression that CSM "is a research facility with unachievable course work assignments." The administration as a whole receives mixed reviews, with complaints centering around "a lack of communication between different departments."

### Life
Just how much of an extracurricular life a Mines student has depends largely on his time-management abilities. Some tell us that "between a full course load, doing homework, and taking an hour or so to mellow out, there is not very much time for anything else." Others tell us that it is possible to have fun here, although it's definitely a challenge. "There is usually a party on the weekends, either at fraternity houses or off-campus," and plenty here have figured out how to "make our own fun. Some examples include snow street luge, sledding on cafeteria trays, and pick-up games of ultimate Frisbee. Because of CSM's location, "Great skiing, backpacking, and mountaineering are in the backyard, not too far from here." Furthermore, "Denver's not too far, either, and it can take as little as 20 minutes to get to clubs." Although "there isn't a whole lot to do in Golden," CSM's hometown, the burg does boast one notable feature: the Coors Brewery, which the engineers here have endearingly dubbed "Coors Lab." Reports one student, "Coors Lab kicks ass! You can't go wrong with free beer!" Even when they're partying, though, class work is never far from these engineers' thoughts: "It is a rare thing when Mines students gather that some form of schoolwork is not discussed," writes one student.

### Student Body
Quintessential Mines students are "very focused on school and obsessed with their grades and academic achievement." Notes one engineer here, "There are lots of valedictorians from high school who have to get a 4.0 or go crazy. No one smiles when walking down the sidewalk." While most are "really willing to work together to learn," they are otherwise "mostly introverts: friendly, but not outgoing." "There are a lot of international students that fit in pretty well" but "not very many ladies." Reports one student, "There is also a strong religious presence at Mines, more than I had expected."

# COLORADO SCHOOL OF MINES

FINANCIAL AID: 303-273-3301 • E-MAIL: ADMIT@MINES.EDU • WEBSITE: WWW.MINES.EDU

## ADMISSIONS
*Very important factors considered include:* class rank, secondary school record. *Important factors considered include:* standardized test scores. *Other factors considered include:* essays, extracurricular activities, interview, recommendations, talent/ability. SAT I or ACT required. TOEFL required of all international applicants. High school diploma or GED is required. *High school units required/recommended:* 16 total required; 4 English required, 4 math required, 3 science required, 3 science lab required, 2 foreign language recommended, 2 social studies required, 2 history recommended, 3 elective required.

### The Inside Word
Although the admissions process is rigorous and straightforward in its focus on the academic, the admissions staff is more personable than at most technically oriented schools. Minorities and women are in demand.

## FINANCIAL AID
*Students should submit:* FAFSA. The Princeton Review suggests that all financial aid forms be submitted as soon as possible after January 1. *Need-based scholarships/grants offered:* Pell, SEOG, state scholarships/grants, private scholarships, the school's own gift aid. *Loan aid offered:* FFEL Subsidized Stafford, FFEL Unsubsidized Stafford, FFEL PLUS, Federal Perkins, college/university loans from institutional funds. Federal Work-Study Program available. Institutional employment available. Applicants will be notified of awards on a rolling basis beginning on or about March 15. Off-campus job opportunities are good.

## FROM THE ADMISSIONS OFFICE
"CSM is a school focused on math, science, economics, and engineering. The academic environment is competitive but not cut-throat, and the social environment is informal and friendly. Campus facilities are excellent, with several new facilities having been constructed in the last several years and continued renovation and construction planned for the cafeteria, residence halls, and other Student Life areas in the next two years. The McBride Honors Program in the Humanities and the Study Abroad Program offer motivated students the chance to expand their experience at CSM, and career and graduate school opportunities for graduates have always been good. And of course, CSM's location in Golden, with all that Colorado has to offer, is an added bonus. All in all, CSM offers a combination of size, programs, facilities, and location that's hard to beat."

## SELECTIVITY

| | |
|---|---|
| Admissions Rating | 87 |
| # of applicants | 2,720 |
| % of applicants accepted | 67 |
| % of acceptees attending | 32 |

### FRESHMAN PROFILE
| | |
|---|---|
| Range SAT Verbal | 540-640 |
| Average SAT Verbal | 590 |
| Range SAT Math | 610-700 |
| Average SAT Math | 650 |
| Range ACT Composite | 25-29 |
| Average ACT Composite | 28 |
| Minimum TOEFL | 550 |
| Average HS GPA | 3.7 |
| % graduated top 10% of class | 47 |
| % graduated top 25% of class | 86 |
| % graduated top 50% of class | 100 |

### DEADLINES
| | |
|---|---|
| Priority admission | 4/15 |
| Regular admission | 6/1 |
| Nonfall registration? | yes |

### APPLICANTS ALSO LOOK AT AND OFTEN PREFER
MIT
Texas A&M
UT Austin
Stanford
Caltech

### AND SOMETIMES PREFER
U Colorado at Boulder
Colorado State
Air Force Academy

### AND RARELY PREFER
U Denver
Colorado College
U Northern Colorado

## FINANCIAL FACTS

| | |
|---|---|
| Financial Aid Rating | 82 |
| In-state tuition | $5,640 |
| Out-of-state tuition | $18,830 |
| Room and board | $6,100 |
| Books and supplies | $1,300 |
| Required fees | $740 |
| % frosh receiving aid | 60 |
| % undergrads receiving aid | 60 |
| Avg frosh grant | $4,500 |
| Avg frosh loan | $4,300 |

# COLUMBIA UNIVERSITY

535 WEST 116TH STREET, NEW YORK, NY 10027 • ADMISSIONS: 212-854-2521 • FAX: 212-894-1209

## CAMPUS LIFE

★ ★ ★ ☆

| Quality of Life Rating | 84 |
| --- | --- |
| Type of school | private |
| Environment | urban |

### STUDENTS

| Total undergrad enrollment | 4,109 |
| --- | --- |
| % from out of state | 75 |
| % live on campus | 98 |
| % African American | 9 |
| % Asian | 13 |
| % Caucasian | 55 |
| % Hispanic | 8 |
| % international | 5 |

### SURVEY SAYS . . .
Students love New York, NY
Campus easy to get around
Great library
Great off-campus food
Ethnic diversity on campus
Campus is beautiful
Campus feels safe
(Almost) everyone smokes
Student newspaper is popular
Political activism is hot

## ACADEMICS

★ ★ ★ ★

| Academic Rating | 98 |
| --- | --- |
| Calendar | semester |
| Avg reg class size | 10-19 students |

## STUDENTS SPEAK OUT

### Academics

"Academic powerhouse" Columbia University boasts offerings in a staggering array of disciplines, a faculty that includes five Nobel laureates, and one of the nation's few core curricula that students actually love. Even so, "how many schools can boast world-class education and location in the greatest city in the world? One: Columbia." Students here warn that "Columbia truly is hands-off. It's sink or swim, and you are the only person who can help yourself. Advising is minimal and the administration is a celebration of red tape." However, "for the independent-minded student, Columbia is the perfect environment." Central to the CU experience is the Core Curriculum, a sequence that immerses students in western philosophy, literature, and the fine arts. Many here will tell you that the Core "changed my life. It's a great feeling to read something junior year for another class and realize that I know where the ideas originated, and how they progressed." Profs here "are all extremely talented. That doesn't mean they can transmit the material well; in fact, some of them are actually horrible teachers. The exceptions, though, make it all worthwhile." Sums up one undergrad, "You will not have a laid-back, happy-go-lucky type of life at Columbia. Instead of spending your time on sculptured lawns with faculty mapping out the way to go, you will get on a crowded subway, push your way into a door, step over a homeless person, and even if you get tired, you won't be able to rest. Some may think this kind of college experience is terrible. Columbia students are those who think it's the only way to go."

### Life

Columbia's campus, a six-block-square plot in the middle of New York's Morningside Heights neighborhood (Harlem is just to the north), includes a surprising amount of open, grassy space for sunbathers and ultimate Frisbee fanatics. Few students linger long on campus when classes and studying are done, however; instead, they set off to explore the overstuffed metropolis that is their home. "One night on the weekends, you might go to a party with friends, a concert on campus, a Columbia-sponsored event; another night, you might go to a Broadway show, a club downtown, a Yankees game." The city provides access to "so many resources and opportunities off-campus. It's wonderful. I found a great internship this summer and since I am only a subway ride away, I can continue to work part-time during the school year." As one student put it, "In my New York City history class, we (150 students) take a bike ride through New York City, leaving campus at 11:00 P.M and returning at 7 in the morning. In my art history class, we go to the Me; in my music class we go to Lincoln Center. Can you easily do this kind of thing at Yale or Harvard? No, you cannot. Yale has New Haven, Harvard has Boston, and Columbia has New York City. Make your choice."

### Student Body

Columbia students are "stalwart NYC fans, and support hasn't flagged since 9/11. Students thrive on the city. They don't fear it." Some are from the Big Apple, while many others have merely adopted its mien; they are "very New York: they are not exceedingly polite, but can be; they mind their own business and don't butt into yours; and many are uptight and constantly on the go." These "extremely independent" students can be "hyper-intellectual, high-stress, and snobby"; as one undergrad told us, "Columbia students love being urbane, tortured intellectuals. Superiority complexes run rampant, but most students are like this and thus get along." Diversity is a bragging point for CU. Some here, however, caution that "in terms of a demographic breakdown, Columbia is diverse, but there is far less interaction than one might expect." Conservatives warn that CU "is downright über-liberal . . . . 'Left-wing' is probably an understatement." Agrees one of the pinko masses, "The two Republicans that attend here are burned in effigy fairly frequently."

# COLUMBIA UNIVERSITY

FINANCIAL AID: 212-854-3711 • E-MAIL: UGRAD-ADMISS@COLUMBIA.EDU • WEBSITE: WWW.COLUMBIA.EDU

## ADMISSIONS

*Very important factors considered include:* character/personal qualities, class rank, essays, recommendations, secondary school record, standardized test scores. *Important factors considered include:* extracurricular activities, talent/ability. *Other factors considered include:* alumni/ae relation, geographical residence, interview, minority status. SAT I or ACT required; SAT II also required. TOEFL required of all international applicants. High school diploma or GED is required. *High school units required/recommended:* 4 math recommended, 4 science recommended, 4 science lab recommended, 4 social studies recommended, 3 elective recommended.

## The Inside Word

Columbia's application increases continue to outpace the rest of the Ivy League, and as a result the University keeps moving higher up in the Ivy pecking order. Crime is down in New York City, the football team wins (while still in baby-blue uniforms, no less!), and Columbia has become even more appealing. It's less selective than the absolute cream of the Ivy crop, but offers the advantage of being a bit more open and frank in discussing the admissions process with students, parents, and counselors—refreshing amid the typical shrouds of Ivy mystique.

## FINANCIAL AID

*Students should submit:* FAFSA, institution's own financial aid form, CSS/Financial Aid PROFILE, noncustodial (divorced/separated) parent's statement, business/farm supplement, parent and student income tax returns. Regular filing deadline is February 10. The Princeton Review suggests that all financial aid forms be submitted as soon as possible after January 1. *Need-based scholarships/grants offered:* Pell, SEOG, state scholarships/grants, private scholarships, the school's own gift aid. *Loan aid offered:* FFEL Subsidized Stafford, FFEL Unsubsidized Stafford, FFEL PLUS, Federal Perkins, state loans, college/university loans from institutional funds, alternative loans. Federal Work-Study Program available. Institutional employment available. Applicants will be notified of awards on or about April 1. Off-campus job opportunities are excellent.

## FROM THE ADMISSIONS OFFICE

"Located in the world's most international city, Columbia University offers a diverse student body a solid and broad liberal arts curriculum foundation coupled with more advanced study in specific departments."

## SELECTIVITY

| | |
|---|---|
| Admissions Rating | 99 |
| # of applicants | 14,129 |
| % of applicants accepted | 12 |
| % of acceptees attending | 63 |
| # accepting a place on wait list | 600 |
| % admitted from wait list | 1 |
| # of early decision applicants | 1,611 |
| % accepted early decision | 31 |

### FRESHMAN PROFILE

| | |
|---|---|
| Range SAT Verbal | 660-760 |
| Average SAT Verbal | 701 |
| Range SAT Math | 660-750 |
| Average SAT Math | 693 |
| Range ACT Composite | 27-33 |
| Minimum TOEFL | 600 |
| Average HS GPA | 3.8 |
| % graduated top 10% of class | 84 |
| % graduated top 25% of class | 95 |
| % graduated top 50% of class | 100 |

### DEADLINES

| | |
|---|---|
| Early decision | 11/1 |
| Early decision notification | 12/15 |
| Regular admission | 1/1 |
| Regular notification | 4/4 |

### APPLICANTS ALSO LOOK AT AND OFTEN PREFER
Harvard
Yale
Princeton
Stanford
Duke

### AND SOMETIMES PREFER
Brown
U. Penn
Dartmouth, Tufts

### AND RARELY PREFER
Wesleyan U.
Binghamton U.
Vassar, Barnard

## FINANCIAL FACTS

| | |
|---|---|
| Financial Aid Rating | 85 |
| Tuition | $27,190 |
| Room and board | $8,546 |
| Required fees | $1,016 |
| % frosh receiving aid | 44 |
| % undergrads receiving aid | 41 |
| Avg frosh grant | $18,662 |
| Avg frosh loan | $2,445 |

THE BEST 351 COLLEGES ■ 167

# CONNECTICUT COLLEGE

270 MOHEGAN AVENUE, NEW LONDON, CT 06320 • ADMISSIONS: 860-439-2200 • FAX: 860-439-4301

## CAMPUS LIFE

| Quality of Life Rating | 78 |
|---|---|
| Type of school | private |
| Environment | suburban |

### STUDENTS

| Total undergrad enrollment | 1,890 |
|---|---|
| % male/female | 40/60 |
| % from out of state | 81 |
| % from public high school | 49 |
| % live on campus | 96 |
| % African American | 3 |
| % Asian | 3 |
| % Caucasian | 76 |
| % Hispanic | 4 |
| % international | 8 |
| # of countries represented | 56 |

### SURVEY SAYS . . .
Campus is beautiful
Campus easy to get around
Lots of beer drinking
Hard liquor is popular
Lab facilities are great
(Almost) everyone smokes
Students are happy
Dorms are like palaces

## ACADEMICS

| Academic Rating | 82 |
|---|---|
| Calendar | semester |
| Student/faculty ratio | 11:1 |
| % profs teaching UG courses | 100 |
| Avg lab size | 10-19 students |
| Avg reg class size | 10-19 students |

### MOST POPULAR MAJORS
English language and literature
Psychology
Political science and government

## STUDENTS SPEAK OUT

### Academics
Students at Connecticut College assert that their professors have "done cool things and they bring those experiences to the classroom." Instructors are approachable and "truly are concerned with our education," and this dedication is complemented by the deans, "who are excellent, understanding people." The small academic setting affords undergraduates very personal attention. "In one class, the professor, one of the associate Deans of the college, scheduled a meeting with every student in our 100-plus person class to talk about the take home exam." Another student writes, "Some of my professors are now my personal confidants, and I can go to them for my academic or personal needs." This type of nurturing means that "even though I'm not an exceptional student, [I'm able] to do independent research during my freshman year." Top programs include dance, chemistry, biological sciences, religion, and psychology, and many students also laud the well-organized study abroad programs. In terms of the administration, students comment, "There is supposed to be 'shared governance,' and this is true to a point, but frequently the administration does not consult students on major issues that affect us." The career center receives solid praise, particularly for the variety of "internships that focus on community action, international issues, and the environment."

### Life
In general, students at "Conn" feel "pretty pampered" in their "playground for trust-fund babies." The weekend social scene centers largely on alcohol, and several students believe "sometimes it's hard to take part in college activities without being a part of the drinking scene." Those who do indulge "look forward to the huge campus-wide parties, like Festivus or Floralia, which are reason alone to come here—think Woodstock but less hippie." The school organizes Thursday Night Events (TNE's) that draw large numbers of freshmen and sophomores. And an organization called MOBROC (Musicians Organized for Band Rights On Campus), which sets up practice space and a performance venue for campus bands, provides another mainstay of nightlife. ("It's a big deal, but almost underground scene. No other East Coast school has an organization like it.") Alternatives to drinking include "playing out on Harkness Green," attending the "very popular a capella concerts," watching the "amazing student theater productions," "cheering for mediocre sports teams," or venturing in to New London, a town that "takes some time to learn to love."

### Student Body
The stereotypical Conn student attended a "fancy boarding school," grew up "just outside Boston," (or somewhere else in New England, New Jersey, or New York) helps to "keep J.Crew in business," "gets Tiffany's for Christmas," and "drives a Volkswagen with a ski rack on top." Even in this land of self-described WASPs, a few deviants manage to survive, including "our fair share of hippies, punks, straight edge, and D and D magic kids." Reportedly, these atypical students "flock together, just like the rest of the minorities on campus." Many students lament the lack of diversity at Conn, crying, "This is not the real world!" Surveys do point out however, that "a great deal is being done on administrative and student levels to deal with issues of diversity on campus." In the meantime, they content themselves with a "substantial international student population." Some people say the student body is "very supportive of students with differing sexual orientations," while others claim "gays and minorities are segregated." In the end, most students agree, "You basically know everyone on campus, at least by association, [which] makes for a very comfortable, caring environment."

# CONNECTICUT COLLEGE

FINANCIAL AID: 860-439-2200 • E-MAIL: ADMIT@CONNCOLL.EDU • WEBSITE: WWW.CONNCOLL.EDU

## ADMISSIONS

*Very important factors considered include:* character/personal qualities, essays, minority status, recommendations, secondary school record. *Important factors considered include:* alumni/ae relation, class rank, standardized test scores, talent/ability. *Other factors considered include:* geographical residence, interview, volunteer work, work experience. SAT II required. TOEFL required of all international applicants. High school diploma or GED is required. *High school units required/recommended:* 4 English recommended, 4 math recommended, 4 science recommended, 2 foreign language recommended, 2 social studies recommended, 3 history recommended, 3 elective recommended.

### The Inside Word

Late in 1994, Connecticut became the most recent college to drop the SAT I as a requirement for admission, citing the overemphasis that the test receives from the media and, in turn, students. The college is judicious about keeping their acceptance rate as low as possible. Candidates undergo a rigorous review of their credentials, and should be strong students in order to be competitive. Still, the college's competition for students is formidable.

## FINANCIAL AID

*Students should submit:* FAFSA, CSS/Financial Aid PROFILE, noncustodial (divorced/separated) parent's statement, business/farm supplement, federal tax returns, personal and partnership federal W-2 statements. Regular filing deadline is January 15. The Princeton Review suggests that all financial aid forms be submitted as soon as possible after January 1. *Need-based scholarships/grants offered:* Pell, SEOG, state scholarships/grants, the school's own gift aid. *Loan aid offered:* FFEL Subsidized Stafford, FFEL Unsubsidized Stafford, FFEL PLUS, Federal Perkins. Federal Work-Study Program available. Institutional employment available. Applicants will be notified of awards on or about April 1. Off-campus job opportunities are good.

## FROM THE ADMISSIONS OFFICE

"Distinguishing characteristics of the diverse student body at this small, highly selective college are honor and tolerance. Student leadership is pronounced in all aspects of the college's administration from exclusive jurisdiction of the honor code and dorm life to active representation on the president's academic and administrative cabinets. Differences of opinion are respected and celebrated as legitimate avenues to new understanding. Students come to Connecticut College seeking opportunities for independence and initiative and find them in abundance."

### SELECTIVITY

| | |
|---|---|
| **Admissions Rating** | 93 |
| # of applicants | 4,395 |
| % of applicants accepted | 35 |
| % of acceptees attending | 35 |
| # accepting a place on wait list | 275 |
| # of early decision applicants | 329 |
| % accepted early decision | 63 |

### FRESHMAN PROFILE

| | |
|---|---|
| Average SAT Verbal | 660 |
| Average SAT Math | 650 |
| Average ACT Composite | 27 |
| % graduated top 10% of class | 47 |
| % graduated top 50% of class | 98 |

### DEADLINES

| | |
|---|---|
| Early decision | 11/15 |
| Early decision notification | 12/15 |
| Regular admission | 1/1 |
| Regular notification | 4/1 |
| Nonfall registration? | yes |

### APPLICANTS ALSO LOOK AT
**AND OFTEN PREFER**
Middlebury
Tufts
Bowdoin
Brown
**AND SOMETIMES PREFER**
Colby
Bates
Trinity
Haverford
**AND RARELY PREFER**
Skidmore
Mount Holyoke
Hamilton

### FINANCIAL FACTS

| | |
|---|---|
| **Financial Aid Rating** | 83 |
| Comprehensive tuition | $37,900 |
| % frosh receiving aid | 41 |
| % undergrads receiving aid | 44 |
| Avg frosh grant | $21,509 |
| Avg frosh loan | $2,708 |

# COOPER UNION

30 COOPER SQUARE, NEW YORK, NY 10003 • ADMISSIONS: 212-353-4120 • FAX: 212-353-4342

## CAMPUS LIFE

| | |
|---|---|
| Quality of Life Rating | 80 |
| Type of school | private |
| Environment | urban |

### STUDENTS

| | |
|---|---|
| Total undergrad enrollment | 896 |
| % male/female | 66/34 |
| % from out of state | 44 |
| % from public high school | 65 |
| % live on campus | 20 |
| % in (# of) fraternities | 10 (2) |
| % in (# of) sororities | 5 (1) |
| % African American | 4 |
| % Asian | 23 |
| % Caucasian | 56 |
| % Hispanic | 8 |
| % international | 8 |

### SURVEY SAYS . . .

Students love New York, NY
Great off-campus food
Dorms are like palaces
Musical organizations aren't popular
Hard liquor is popular
Ethnic diversity on campus
High cost of living
Intercollegiate sports unpopular or nonexistent
Athletic facilities need improving
No one plays intramural sports
Very little beer drinking

## ACADEMICS

| | |
|---|---|
| Academic Rating | 97 |
| Calendar | semester |
| Student/faculty ratio | 7:1 |
| Profs interesting rating | 93 |
| Profs accessible rating | 89 |
| % profs teaching UG courses | 100 |
| Avg reg class size | 10-19 students |

## STUDENTS SPEAK OUT

### Academics

Every student at The Cooper Union for the Advancement of Science and Art gets a full tuition scholarship, undeniably one of the best deals for higher education. Academically, students don't mince words: it's really, really hard. The students of art, architecture, and engineering—Cooper Union offers majors in these three areas only—must survive an "incredibly intense academic atmosphere" in which sleep is rare and good grades rarer. Warns one student, "The trick to surviving is knowing what subjects to study and not study for—there simply isn't time to do everything. That and being willing to get a C or even D and accepting that that's just how Cooper is." Notes one engineer, "If you can graduate from this school you can survive anything." Just fulfilling requirements here can be stressful; writes one undergrad, "There is a curriculum for each major, and it's difficult to take electives during the first two years because you have to take the core curriculum first." On the plus side, "the professors at Cooper are excellent and are always ready to give extra help when needed. They are also very fair. The classes are difficult, but everybody struggles together." Students endure, knowing that their programs are "very helpful in terms of finding jobs" and appreciating the fact that "the location in NYC allows many students to hold internships or real jobs during the semester."

### Life

Smack dab in the middle of what is arguably America's most exciting and fun city, Cooper Union students struggle to find any time in which to enjoy their surroundings. "Every time a Cooper student plays a game or whatever, he knows he should be studying for a test or doing his calc homework or working on his lab project." Reports another student, "[There are] two kinds of Cooper students: those who go out and those who don't. I would say one out of every four students is interested in a social life. . . . Few actually go out and experience New York City." The tiny campus—actually four buildings in the middle of a busy intersection—"is in the heart of the East Village in New York City. Our campus is our buildings, the streets, traffic lights, crosswalks, and everyone from pointy-haired punks to suit-adorning businesswomen who happen to be walking or sitting or sleeping there." Students feel their extracurricular lives would improve somewhat if Cooper would "offer school housing beyond freshman year since finding an apartment in Manhattan is close to impossible." They also wish the school would "improve its facilities—the buildings are old and dirty"—and add a workout facility.

### Student Body

Students report that "The schools of engineering, architecture, and art are VERY separated, each focusing on its own field. Naively speaking, the engineers are dorky, the artists are obtuse, and the architects are recluse. However, there exists a wide range of personalities within each discipline and everyone gets along." Students have a reputation for eccentricity, which some feel is over-hyped; writes one, "There are some really weird people at this school, but overall I think we get a bad wrap. Most of us are normal around here and we mostly get along." Then again, there are also characters like the one this student describes: "One day we discovered that one guy that we all thought was an average Joe was, in fact, a chess prodigy who bet money that he could beat anyone in the school blindfolded and did it with ease. There are lots of people like that at Cooper, people who work hard on what they're studying but have hidden talents or ideas that are fascinating." Notes one of the relatively few women here, "Due to our extremely large male-female ratio, there is a saying among the girls at Cooper that sums up the student population: The odds are good, but the goods are odd."

# COOPER UNION

FINANCIAL AID: 212-353-4130 • E-MAIL: ADMISSIONS@COOPER.EDU • WEBSITE: WWW.COOPER.EDU

## ADMISSIONS

*Very important factors considered include:* secondary school record, standardized test scores, talent/ability. *Important factors considered include:* essays. *Other factors considered include:* character/personal qualities, extracurricular activities, recommendations, volunteer work, work experience. SAT I or ACT required; SAT I preferred. TOEFL required of all international applicants. High school diploma or GED is required. *High school units required/recommended:* 16 total required; 18 total recommended; 4 English required, 1 math required, 1 science required, 1 social studies required, 1 history required, 8 elective required.

### The Inside Word

It is ultra-tough to gain admission to Cooper Union, and will only get tougher. Loads of people apply here, and national publicity and the addition of dorms have brought even more candidates to the pool. Not only do students need to have top academic accomplishments but they also need to be a good fit for Cooper's offbeat milieu.

## FINANCIAL AID

*Students should submit:* FAFSA, CSS/Financial Aid PROFILE, state aid form. Regular filing deadline is May 1. The Princeton Review suggests that all financial aid forms be submitted as soon as possible after January 1. *Need-based scholarships/grants offered:* Pell, SEOG, state scholarships/grants, private scholarships, the school's own gift aid. *Loan aid offered:* FFEL Subsidized Stafford, FFEL Unsubsidized Stafford, FFEL PLUS, Federal Perkins, college/university loans from institutional funds. Federal Work-Study Program available. Institutional employment available. Applicants will be notified of awards on or about June 1. Off-campus job opportunities are excellent.

## FROM THE ADMISSIONS OFFICE

"Each of the three schools, architecture, art, and engineering, adheres strongly to preparation for its profession and is committed to a problem-solving philosophy of education in a unique, scholarship environment. A rigorous curriculum and group projects reinforce this unique atmosphere in higher education and contribute to a strong sense of community and identity in each school. With McSorley's Ale House and the Joseph Papp Public Theater nearby, Cooper Union remains at the heart of the city's tradition of free speech, enlightenment, and entertainment. Cooper's Great Hall has hosted national leaders, from Abraham Lincoln to Booker T. Washington, from Mark Twain to Samuel Gompers, from Susan B. Anthony to Betty Friedan, and more recently, President Bill Clinton."

## SELECTIVITY

| | |
|---|---|
| Admissions Rating | 99 |
| # of applicants | 2,041 |
| % of applicants accepted | 14 |
| % of acceptees attending | 70 |
| # accepting a place on wait list | 100 |
| # of early decision applicants | 223 |
| % accepted early decision | 61 |

### FRESHMAN PROFILE

| | |
|---|---|
| Range SAT Verbal | 600-720 |
| Average SAT Verbal | 680 |
| Range SAT Math | 670-750 |
| Average SAT Math | 710 |
| Minimum TOEFL | 600 |
| Average HS GPA | 3.2 |
| % graduated top 10% of class | 80 |
| % graduated top 25% of class | 100 |

### DEADLINES

| | |
|---|---|
| Early decision | 12/1 |
| Early decision notification | 12/23 |
| Regular admission | 1/1 |
| Regular notification | 4/1 |

### APPLICANTS ALSO LOOK AT AND OFTEN PREFER
Cornell U
UC Berkeley
NYU
Columbia
MIT

### AND SOMETIMES PREFER
Harvey Mudd
Georgia Tech
Rochester Institute of Technology

## FINANCIAL FACTS

| | |
|---|---|
| Financial Aid Rating | 83 |
| Room and board | $10,000 |
| Books and supplies | $1,350 |
| Required fees | $500 |
| % frosh receiving aid | 100 |
| % undergrads receiving aid | 100 |
| Avg frosh grant | $12,247 |
| Avg frosh loan | $2,519 |

# CORNELL COLLEGE

600 FIRST STREET WEST, MOUNT VERNON, IA 52314-1098 • ADMISSIONS: 319-895-4477 • FAX: 319-895-4451

## CAMPUS LIFE

| Quality of Life Rating | 77 |
|---|---|
| Type of school | private |
| Affiliation | Methodist |
| Environment | rural |

### STUDENTS

| Total undergrad enrollment | 1,001 |
|---|---|
| % male/female | 40/60 |
| % from out of state | 68 |
| % from public high school | 93 |
| % live on campus | 92 |
| % in (# of) fraternities | 30 (7) |
| % in (# of) sororities | 32 (7) |
| % African American | 3 |
| % Asian | 1 |
| % Caucasian | 90 |
| % Hispanic | 2 |
| % international | 1 |
| # of countries represented | 5 |

### SURVEY SAYS . . .
Classes are small
Registration is a breeze
Students aren't religious
Campus easy to get around
Lousy off-campus food
Class discussions encouraged

## ACADEMICS

| Academic Rating | 80 |
|---|---|
| Calendar | other |
| Student/faculty ratio | 11:1 |
| Profs interesting rating | 65 |
| Profs accessible rating | 80 |
| % profs teaching UG courses | 100 |
| Avg reg class size | 10-19 students |

### MOST POPULAR MAJORS
Education
Psychology
Economics and business

## STUDENTS SPEAK OUT

### Academics

Most students at Cornell College chose to attend because its unique academic calendar, called "One-Course-At-A-Time" (students refer to it by its acronym, OCAAT), made intuitive sense to them. Under the system, students immerse themselves in a single course for three and a half weeks, complete a final exam, take a few days' breather, then start the whole process over again. Nearly all students find OCAAT to their liking; "The Block Plan makes learning easy, class sizes small, and one-on-one time with a professor easy. I love it here," writes a typical student. With "average class size at 14 students and classes capped off at 25," students get a "very personal teaching environment" that is heavy on discussion. Students "really get to know the professors because you're in class with them about four hours a day, three and a half weeks straight, and it's the only course they're teaching." More than a few professors are "'rent-a-profs,' which are faculty who visit for one or more blocks in a year." Students appreciate the expertise these outsiders bring to campus but warn that "it is difficult for these professors to adjust to the quick pace of class." Summing up the Cornell experience, one student tells us that "Cornell College provides a community for a small group of students to learn, socialize, and develop. Overall, the individual makes Cornell what they want it to be."

### Life

Students warn that hometown Mount Vernon sets the tone for campus life at Cornell, and note that the town is quaint but hardly a hub of activity. "Mount Vernon is very small," explains one student. "There is a grocery store, a subway, a Hardee's, and a couple of gas stations, all on the same corner. There are also four bars downtown that are hopping every weekend. I am from the suburbs of Chicago, so this atmosphere is really different." Many see an upside, concluding that the lack of action in town "helps our campus to become the center of activities." Students get into sports, community service, clubs, student government, and "social clubs," which are like fraternities and sororities but "are not nationally affiliated, which makes it less expensive to join one." The school "brings in so many speakers and musical groups that I never have to leave to get some entertainment. The arts are very popular here; there is always a concert or a play happening." Cornell undergrads often travel to Cedar Rapids (for "a midnight run to Perkins, a movie, or a shopping trip") or Iowa City ("where there are lots of clubs"), both within relatively short driving distance. Students caution prospectives to bring plenty of warm clothing to Mount Vernon, telling us that "the Cornell campus is beautiful in the snow. And it usually snows a lot!"

### Student Body

Students consider their peers extremely friendly; writes one, "I love that most people will smile and say hi to you regardless of if you know them or not. It is general Iowa hospitality!" They see another benefit of their small size; explains one student, "I think the small student body makes people much more accountable for their actions. At big schools I see people shout rude comments at women as they drive down the street. At Cornell you can't do that as easily because people will recognize and judge you because of it." Although "not very racially and ethnically diverse," Cornell has "our jocks, our preps, our punks, our Goths, our girlie-girls, our tom-boys, our hippies . . . whatever 'type' is out there, we have it. And no one cares what you wear or what 'group' you're in—people just love you for you." Students note that "Cornell has a strong exchange program with Korea and Japan, so a very high percentage of our exchange students are Asian."

# CORNELL COLLEGE

FINANCIAL AID: 319-895-4216 • E-MAIL: ADMISSIONS@CORNELLCOLLEGE.EDU • WEBSITE: WWW.CORNELLCOLLEGE.EDU

## ADMISSIONS

*Very important factors considered include:* class rank, essays, recommendations, secondary school record, standardized test scores, talent/ability. *Important factors considered include:* character/personal qualities, extracurricular activities, interview, minority status, volunteer work, work experience. SAT I or ACT required. TOEFL required of all international applicants. High school diploma or GED is required. *High school units required/recommended:* 16 total recommended; 4 English recommended, 3–4 math recommended, 3–4 science recommended, 2–4 foreign language recommended, 3–4 social studies recommended.

### The Inside Word

Given Cornell's relatively unique approach to study, it's no surprise that the admissions committee here focuses attention on both academic and personal strengths. Cornell's small, highly self-selected applicant pool is chock-full of students with solid self-awareness, motivation, and discipline. Pay particular attention to offering evidence of challenging academic course work and solid achievement on your high school record. Strong writers can do much for themselves under admissions circumstances such as these.

## FINANCIAL AID

*Students should submit:* FAFSA, institution's own financial aid form, noncustodial (divorced/separated) parent's statement. The Princeton Review suggests that all financial aid forms be submitted as soon as possible after January 1. *Need-based scholarships/grants offered:* Pell, SEOG, state scholarships/grants, private scholarships, the school's own gift aid. *Loan aid offered:* FFEL Subsidized Stafford, FFEL Unsubsidized Stafford, FFEL PLUS, Federal Perkins, college/university loans from institutional funds, McElroy Loan, Sherman Loan, United Methodist Loan. Federal Work-Study Program available. Institutional employment available. Applicants will be notified of awards on a rolling basis beginning on or about October 1. Off-campus job opportunities are fair.

## FROM THE ADMISSIONS OFFICE

"Very few colleges are truly distinctive like Cornell College. Founded in 1853, Cornell is recognized as one of the nation's finest colleges of the liberal arts and sciences. It is Cornell's combination of special features, however, that distinguishes it. An attractively diverse, caring residential college, Cornell places special emphasis on service and leadership. Foremost, it is a place where theory and practice are brought together in exciting ways through the College's One-Course-At-A-Time academic Calendar. Here, students enjoy learning as they immerse themselves in a single subject for a three-and-a-half-week term. They and their professor devote all of their efforts to that course in an engagingly interactive learning environment. This academic system also offers wonderful enrichment experiences through field-based-study, travel abroad, student research, and meaningful internship opportunities. Nine terms are offered each year; 32 course credits are required for graduation with each course equal to four credit hours. Since all classes are on a standard schedule, students are able to pursue their extracurricular interests, whether in the performing arts, athletics, or interest groups, with the same passion with which they pursue their course work. Typically, each year applicants from all 50 states and more than 40 countries apply for admission. Cornell graduates are in demand, with more than two-thirds eventually earning advanced degrees. The College's beautiful hilltop campus is one of only two campuses nationwide listed on the National register of Historic Places. Located in the charming town of Mount Vernon, Cornell is also within commuting distance of Iowa City (home of the University of Iowa) and Cedar Rapids (the second largest city in the state)."

## SELECTIVITY

| | |
|---|---:|
| Admissions Rating | 80 |
| # of applicants | 1,625 |
| % of applicants accepted | 62 |
| % of acceptees attending | 31 |

### FRESHMAN PROFILE

| | |
|---|---:|
| Range SAT Verbal | 540-660 |
| Average SAT Verbal | 599 |
| Range SAT Math | 540-640 |
| Average SAT Math | 590 |
| Range ACT Composite | 23-28 |
| Average ACT Composite | 26 |
| Minimum TOEFL | 500 |
| Average HS GPA | 3.5 |
| % graduated top 10% of class | 26 |
| % graduated top 25% of class | 59 |
| % graduated top 50% of class | 91 |

### DEADLINES

| | |
|---|---:|
| Priority admission | 3/1 |
| Nonfall registration? | yes |

### APPLICANTS ALSO LOOK AT AND OFTEN PREFER
Coe
Luther
U of Iowa
### AND SOMETIMES PREFER
Wartbug
U of Northern Iowa
Colorado College
### AND RARELY PREFER
Central College
Simpson College (IA)
Colorado State U

## FINANCIAL FACTS

| | |
|---|---:|
| Financial Aid Rating | 85 |
| Tuition | $20,795 |
| Room and board | $6,032 |
| Books and supplies | $920 |
| Required fees | $160 |
| % frosh receiving aid | 83 |
| % undergrads receiving aid | 80 |
| Avg frosh grant | $16,750 |
| Avg frosh loan | $3,745 |

THE BEST 351 COLLEGES ■ 173

# CORNELL UNIVERSITY

410 THURSTON AVENUE, ITHACA, NY 14850 • ADMISSIONS: 607-255-5241 • FAX: 607-255-0659

## CAMPUS LIFE

| Quality of Life Rating | 80 |
|---|---|
| Type of school | private |
| Environment | rural |

### STUDENTS
| | |
|---|---|
| Total undergrad enrollment | 13,725 |
| % from out of state | 66 |
| % live on campus | 51 |
| % in (# of) fraternities | 25 (44) |
| % in (# of) sororities | 24 (21) |
| % African American | 5 |
| % Asian | 15 |
| % Caucasian | 54 |
| % Hispanic | 5 |
| % international | 8 |
| # of countries represented | 79 |

### SURVEY SAYS . . .
Great food on campus
Frats and sororities dominate social scene
Great library
Class discussions are rare
Beautiful campus
Large classes
Campus difficult to get around
Ethnic diversity on campus
Student publications are popular
Musical organizations are hot

## ACADEMICS

| Academic Rating | 94 |
|---|---|
| Calendar | semester |
| Student/faculty ratio | 9:1 |
| Profs interesting rating | 91 |
| Profs accessible rating | 94 |
| % profs teaching UG courses | 100 |
| Avg lab size | 10-19 students |
| Avg reg class size | 10-19 students |

### MOST POPULAR MAJORS
History
Engineering
Biology/biological sciences

## STUDENTS SPEAK OUT

### Academics

Ivy League member Cornell boasts a catalog of over 4,000 undergraduate courses, and a top notch faculty to boot. One student boasts "Profs are friendly and approachable." Classes at Cornell are a combination of lectures and sections. Professors teach lectures, and TAs teach sections. And "it's always a pleasant surprise when a TA can speak English." Professor accessibility is also good; as one student notes, "most will give you their home number for extra assistance." Most students agree with this sentiment. The hotel school earns high marks from students. And while students have positive feelings about their professors, their opinion of the administration is nearly unanimous. Cornell is "not called 'The Big Red Tape' for nothing." Bear Access, Cornell's computer-based class registration system, "is a nightmare the day classes go open for registration." Switching courses is also a difficult process, and students who attempt to do so find themselves "run[ning] all over campus to accomplish anything." Students complain that the advising system is weak, and "advisors really have no idea what their advisees need to have accomplished for graduation." Supplemental costs are a major sticking point. "Cornell loves to charge fees for whatever it can—Internet, using the gym, buses, parking, cable, many gym classes, printing. You name it, it ain't free." "The general feeling at Cornell is that the undergrads pay for the grad students."

### Life

Cornell students work hard all week and "party hard on the weekends." Ithaca is a small but cool town; however, the Greek system corners "the Saturday night entertainment market." The university's mandatory catering rules require all frat parties to be catered by companies "who card people as they come in and give them drinking or nondrinking color-coded wristbands." However, for every "sanctioned" party, there are other unsanctioned parties that "have no qualms about serving alcohol to minors." Some students say that those who don't drink "feel a little bit left out in the cold at times." One student shrugs, "So far, the assumption that students at Ivy League schools drink heavily to ease the pressure of the academic load has proven true." Students enjoy "swimming in the gorges during the summer, traying (on dining hall trays) down the slope during the winter, and going to the mega-grocery store at 2 A.M." Collegetown, which adjoins the campus, "is full of bars, clubs, and cheap eateries with great food." Students also go to the movies in town and take advantage of the many skiing and snowboarding opportunities. Cornell hockey is also extremely popular, and the rink is sold out every year.

### Student Body

Cornell's population is "friendly" and "very diverse, not only ethnically, but also in terms of individual personalities, activities, and goals." One student describes his peers as "typical Ivy League students mostly: upper-middle-class suburban kids who have probably never worked in their lives." Different groups of students "tend to interact mostly with members of their own groups." Still, "students for the most part are friendly and open-minded. Pretty much anything goes here." Some complain that their classmates are "cut-throat," especially in the hard sciences, and that engineering students "are hard to get along with."

# CORNELL UNIVERSITY

FINANCIAL AID: 607-255-5145 • E-MAIL: ADMISSIONS@CORNELL.EDU • WEBSITE: WWW.CORNELL.EDU

## ADMISSIONS

*Very important factors considered include:* essays, extracurricular activities, recommendations, secondary school record, standardized test scores, talent/ability. *Important factors considered include:* class rank. *Other factors considered include:* alumni/ae relation, character/personal qualities, geographical residence, interview, minority status, state residency, volunteer work, work experience. SAT I or ACT required. TOEFL required of all international applicants. *High school units required/recommended:* 16 total required; 4 English required, 3 math required, 3 science recommended, 3 science lab recommended, 3 foreign language recommended, 3 social studies recommended, 3 history recommended.

### The Inside Word

Cornell is the largest of the Ivies, and its admissions operation is a reflection of the fairly grand scale of the institution: complex and somewhat intimidating. Candidates should not expect contact with admissions to reveal much in the way of helpful insights on the admissions process, as the university seems to prefer to keep things close to the vest. Only applicants with top accomplishments, academic or otherwise, will be viable candidates. The university is a very positive place for minorities, and the public status presents a value that's hard to beat.

## FINANCIAL AID

*Students should submit:* FAFSA, CSS/Financial Aid PROFILE, noncustodial (divorced/separated) parent's statement, business/farm supplement, prior year's tax forms. Regular filing deadline is February 11. The Princeton Review suggests that all financial aid forms be submitted as soon as possible after January 1. *Need-based scholarships/grants offered:* Pell, SEOG, state scholarships/grants, private scholarships, the school's own gift aid. *Loan aid offered:* Direct Subsidized Stafford, Direct Unsubsidized Stafford, Direct PLUS, FFEL Subsidized Stafford, FFEL Unsubsidized Stafford, FFEL PLUS, Federal Perkins, college/university loans from institutional funds, Key Bank alternative loan. Federal Work-Study Program available. Institutional employment available. Applicants will be notified of awards on or about April 1. Off-campus job opportunities are good.

## FROM THE ADMISSIONS OFFICE

"The admissions process at Cornell University reflects the personality of the institution. When students apply to Cornell, they must apply to one of the seven undergraduate colleges. Applications are reviewed within each undergraduate college by individuals who know the college well. Life at Cornell is a blend of college-focused and University activities, and Cornell students participate at both the college and University level. Cornell students can take classes in any of the seven undergraduate colleges and they participate in one of the largest extracurricular/athletics programs in the Ivy League. Prospective students are encouraged to examine the range of opportunities, both academic and extracurricular, at Cornell. Within this great institution, there is a wealth of possibilities."

### SELECTIVITY

| | |
|---|---|
| Admissions Rating | 98 |
| # of applicants | 21,502 |
| % of applicants accepted | 29 |
| % of acceptees attending | 49 |
| # accepting a place on wait list | 1,942 |
| % admitted from wait list | 6 |
| # of early decision applicants | 2,679 |
| % accepted early decision | 43 |

### FRESHMAN PROFILE

| | |
|---|---|
| Range SAT Verbal | 620-720 |
| Average SAT Verbal | 667 |
| Range SAT Math | 660-750 |
| Average SAT Math | 700 |
| Range ACT Composite | 25-30 |
| Average ACT Composite | 27 |
| Minimum TOEFL | 550 |
| % graduated top 10% of class | 83 |
| % graduated top 25% of class | 95 |
| % graduated top 50% of class | 100 |

### DEADLINES

| | |
|---|---|
| Early decision | 11/10 |
| Early decision notification | 12/15 |
| Regular admission | 1/1 |
| Regular notification | 4/1 |
| Nonfall registration? | yes |

### APPLICANTS ALSO LOOK AT AND OFTEN PREFER
Harvard
Yale, Princeton
MIT, Stanford
**AND SOMETIMES PREFER**
Penn, Columbia
UC Berkeley, Duke
**AND RARELY PREFER**
NYU, Carnegie Mellon
U of Michigan
Boston U, Johns Hopkins
Northwestern

### FINANCIAL FACTS

| | |
|---|---|
| Financial Aid Rating | 86 |
| Tuition | $28,630 |
| Room and board | $9,580 |
| Books and supplies | $640 |
| Required fees | $124 |
| % frosh receiving aid | 49 |
| % undergrads receiving aid | 47 |
| Avg frosh grant | $17,021 |
| Avg frosh loan | $5,811 |

# CREIGHTON UNIVERSITY

2500 CALIFORNIA PLAZA, OMAHA, NE 68178 • ADMISSIONS: 402-280-2703 • FAX: 402-280-2685

## CAMPUS LIFE

| | |
|---|---|
| Quality of Life Rating | 87 |
| Type of school | private |
| Affiliation | Roman Catholic |
| Environment | urban |

### STUDENTS

| | |
|---|---|
| Total undergrad enrollment | 3,607 |
| % male/female | 40/60 |
| % from out of state | 50 |
| % from public high school | 64 |
| % live on campus | 44 |
| % in (# of) fraternities | 26 (5) |
| % in (# of) sororities | 25 (5) |
| % African American | 3 |
| % Asian | 8 |
| % Caucasian | 85 |
| % Hispanic | 3 |
| % international | 2 |

### SURVEY SAYS . . .
Theater is hot
Frats and sororities dominate social scene
Very little drug use
Popular college radio
Students are very religious
Students get along with local community
Diverse students interact
Lousy food on campus

## ACADEMICS

| | |
|---|---|
| Academic Rating | 82 |
| Calendar | semester |
| Student/faculty ratio | 14:1 |
| Profs interesting rating | 94 |
| Profs accessible rating | 92 |
| % profs teaching UG courses | 100 |
| Avg lab size | 10-19 students |
| Avg reg class size | 10-19 students |

### MOST POPULAR MAJORS
Biomedical sciences
Business administration
Psychology

## STUDENTS SPEAK OUT

### Academics
Students can pick from more than 50 majors in three schools—the College of the Arts and Sciences, the College of Business and Administration, and the School of Nursing—at Creighton. Despite the university feel here, Creighton maintains a devotion to liberal arts education that's often found at smaller schools. "Some students don't like the liberal arts core curriculum," especially the "18 hours of theology/philosophy" they have to take "in order to graduate." But they do appreciate the attention they receive from their "absolutely phenomenal" profs. "The first thing I noticed about Creighton's professors," writes an undergrad, was "their availability." While the nursing and health sciences programs remain some of the most popular at Creighton, some students wish that the university would put "less emphasis on the medical fields." With a new science building, it's clear that science and technology will remain a strong part of this campus's academic life. Whether their sights are set on becoming scientists or literary critics, most students view Creighton as their ticket to the future. Declares one, "The students at Creighton are highly motivated intellectuals that always get into the top law, medical, and graduate schools."

### Life
Creighton's home turf is Omaha, Nebraska's largest city, with about 700,000 residents. Students regularly venture into the city for entertainment—especially to the city's "Old Market area," which has a "cool bar scene," "a lot of unique specialty shops, and excellent eats." While there's definitely some students who say that "if it were possible to change" the university's "location, say out of Omaha, then it would be perfect," others will tell you that Omaha "has a lot to offer for a midwestern city if you just get out there and look." Many students try to "balance" their social lives between on-campus and off-campus activities. While frat houses hold the majority of the parties at Creighton, students over 21 often opt for the "pretty popular" music and bar scene. Students also divvy up some of their spare hours among campus organizations, like the Speech and Debate Club or the Gay-Straight Alliance. And "the Creighton population does everything in terms of volunteerism that you could name. The Jesuit tradition promotes the idea of going out into the community and helping others." There's another thing that the Jesuit tradition promotes that students aren't so keen on: rules. "Because this is a Catholic university, the housing regulations are rather strict." In other words, during those first two years when students live in the campus dorms, they're subject to "rules about [not] having someone of a different sex in your room past 2 A.M." Fortunately, there are over 10,000 hotel rooms in Omaha.

### Student Body
Not many students will dispute the notion that their classmates are "extremely friendly," but some will tell you that, all in all, Creighton's 3,700 undergrads are too similar. "The majority of the students here could be poster children for Abercrombie and Fitch," whines one student. "A very conservative bunch," according to another. While many students are religious at this Jesuit institution, "actually less than 50 percent of the population is Catholic. . . . There is no religious pressure here whatsoever." And "no matter where people are from, what languages they speak, what color of skin they have, or what sexual orientation they practice, all people here are friendly to each other." Some Creighton students find "a division between students who only see each other during the day and those who live in the dorms during freshman and sophomore years." (First- and second-year students are required to live on campus.) Regardless of where they live, many Creighton students spend a fair amount of time with their noses in the books, as they tend to stress "out way too much about tests and grades and papers."

176 ■ THE BEST 351 COLLEGES

# CREIGHTON UNIVERSITY

FINANCIAL AID: 402-280-2731 • E-MAIL: ADMISSIONS@CREIGHTON.EDU • WEBSITE: WWW.ADMISSION.CREIGHTON.EDU

## ADMISSIONS

*Very important factors considered include:* secondary school record. *Important factors considered include:* recommendations, standardized test scores. *Other factors considered include:* character/personal qualities, class rank, essays, extracurricular activities, minority status, talent/ability, volunteer work. SAT I or ACT required. TOEFL required of all international applicants. High school diploma or GED is required. *High school units required/recommended:* 16 total recommended; 4 English recommended, 3 math recommended, 2 science recommended, 2 foreign language recommended, 1 social studies recommended, 1 history recommended, 3 elective recommended.

### The Inside Word

In this world of literal translation, even colleges and universities with admit rates that are higher than Creighton's refer to themselves as selective. While it should not be particularly difficult to get in, some applicants don't.

## FINANCIAL AID

*Students should submit:* FAFSA, institution's own financial aid form. No deadline for regular filing. The Princeton Review suggests that all financial aid forms be submitted as soon as possible after January 1. *Need-based scholarships/grants offered:* Pell, SEOG, state scholarships/grants, private scholarships, the school's own gift aid. *Loan aid offered:* FFEL Subsidized Stafford, FFEL Unsubsidized Stafford, FFEL PLUS, Federal Perkins, Federal Nursing, college/university loans from institutional funds. Federal Work-Study Program available. Institutional employment available. Applicants will be notified of awards on a rolling basis beginning on or about March 15. Off-campus job opportunities are excellent.

## FROM THE ADMISSIONS OFFICE

"Students come to Creighton to become experts in their chosen fields . . . even if they haven't already chosen a field of study! About 40 percent of the graduating seniors from Creighton go immediately into medical, dentistry, pharmacy, law, and physical and occupational therapy professional graduate programs—this is the highest rate of any midwestern university. We also produce exceptional teachers, business professionals, scientists, journalists and writers, and community service advocates. Our size is ideal. With 3,700 undergraduates and, including professional school enrollment, a total of 6,300 attendees, our students feel they have the best of both worlds—first-rate academic programs and facilities but also a more intimate relationship with our faculty that often leads to involvement in research projects and internships. Creighton students tend to have a deeper focus on their careers and lifestyle choices. As students at a leading, national, Jesuit, liberal arts university our students are encouraged to examine the moral as well as factual dimension of issues. Most students also get involved in our leadership training programs and community service and/or campus ministry organizations. The campus has its own comfortable and safe sense of space, and the downtown corporate headquarters, restaurants, and music spots are just a five-minute walk away."

## SELECTIVITY

| | |
|---|---|
| Admissions Rating | 79 |
| # of applicants | 3,306 |
| % of applicants accepted | 85 |
| % of acceptees attending | 33 |

### FRESHMAN PROFILE

| | |
|---|---|
| Range SAT Verbal | 550-640 |
| Average SAT Verbal | 590 |
| Range SAT Math | 550-660 |
| Average SAT Math | 599 |
| Range ACT Composite | 23-30 |
| Average ACT Composite | 26 |
| Minimum TOEFL | 550 |
| Average HS GPA | 3.7 |
| % graduated top 10% of class | 40 |
| % graduated top 25% of class | 70 |
| % graduated top 50% of class | 93 |

### DEADLINES

| | |
|---|---|
| Priority admission | 1/1 |
| Regular admission | 8/1 |
| Nonfall registration? | yes |

### APPLICANTS ALSO LOOK AT AND OFTEN PREFER
Notre Dame
### AND SOMETIMES PREFER
Marquette
St. Louis U
Washington U in St. Louis
Santa Clara
### AND RARELY PREFER
Loyola U Chicago
Regis
U of Nebraska at Lincoln
U of Iowa

## FINANCIAL FACTS

| | |
|---|---|
| Financial Aid Rating | 81 |
| Tuition | $19,202 |
| Room and board | $6,826 |
| Books and supplies | $900 |
| Required fees | $720 |
| Avg frosh grant | $13,052 |
| Avg frosh loan | $4,890 |

# DARTMOUTH COLLEGE

6016 MCNUTT HALL, HANOVER, NH 03755 • ADMISSIONS: 603-646-2875 • FAX: 603-646-1216

## CAMPUS LIFE

| Quality of Life Rating | 95 |
|---|---|
| Type of school | private |
| Environment | rural |

### STUDENTS
| | |
|---|---|
| Total undergrad enrollment | 4,118 |
| % male/female | 51/49 |
| % from out of state | 98 |
| % from public high school | 62 |
| % live on campus | 87 |
| % in (# of) fraternities | 23 (14) |
| % in (# of) sororities | 21 (8) |
| % African American | 7 |
| % Asian | 12 |
| % Caucasian | 61 |
| % Hispanic | 7 |
| % international | 5 |

### SURVEY SAYS . . .
Frats and sororities dominate social scene
Great food on campus
Everyone loves the Big Green
Great computer facilities
Campus feels safe
(Almost) no one smokes
Musical organizations are hot
Theater is unpopular
Student publications are popular
(Almost) no one listens to college radio

## ACADEMICS

| Academic Rating | 98 |
|---|---|
| Calendar | quarter |
| Student/faculty ratio | 8:1 |
| Profs interesting rating | 94 |
| Profs accessible rating | 98 |
| % profs teaching UG courses | 100 |
| Avg reg class size | 10-19 students |

## STUDENTS SPEAK OUT

### Academics
There are few schools in North America that can boast the combination of world-class academics and beautiful location that Dartmouth College offers its students. This Ivy-League institution, tucked away in Hanover, New Hampshire, is the home of wonderful, caring professors, who are committed to the academic needs of their students. A sophomore German major speaks for the majority of students when he writes, "I love Dartmouth because it offers world-class professors who are there because they love to teach." Professors are always accessible, thanks to the Blitz—the campus Internet network—and many students note that they have been invited to their professors' houses for dinner. Students would like too see more study space on campus, though. While the professors are beloved, students don't feel quite the same way about the "draconian" administration. One student writes that the administration "thinks of this school as an advanced placement version of Disney World. You pay, and we hold your hand and kick you out when the park closes." A disheartened senior adds, "Dartmouth's administration has made every effort to destroy a wonderful school. They are attempting to turn Dartmouth into another cookie cutter example of a bland, lifeless university." A more glass-half-full type sophomore provides a little better marketing copy: "Dartmouth's academic experience is unbeatable because it unites a small liberal arts school with all the resources of a top university."

### Life
A senior government major reports the concerns of many students: "Students aren't particularly happy with the current administration's attempt to change social life on campus." A history major adds, "The administration likes establishing social guidelines for students even when they [the guidelines] are most often counter to desires or needs." The source of the administration's concerns is the active Greek life, since "frats are the entire social scene." Still, one first-year teetotaler points out, "I was pleasantly surprised to find that [my being such] was not a problem at Dartmouth." Beer pong is one of the most popular intramural sports. A sophomore summarizes campus life: "Dartmouth is the only school that can provide an Ivy League education, the benefits of a small college town, and the cultural and social aspects of a large city without big-city problems." A senior government major asks, "Where else could you attend classes in the morning, spend your afternoons fencing, hiking, or building a snowman, and spend your evenings relaxing with your friends at a coffee house?" While fraternities play a big role in having fun, there are fair amounts of other weekend options. Outdoor activities are a popular recreational alternative in this "beautiful, intimate, and friendly environment." Students hike the Appalachian Trail, play golf, ice skate on local ponds, and ski. One senior engineering major quips, "Sometimes I think Dartmouth has a double role of college and country club."

### Student Body
Students genuinely appreciate and respect their peers. Though Dartmouth students work hard, they aren't "cut-throat," as some believe all Ivy Leaguers are. A sophomore beams, "I am continuously surprised at how accomplished, mature, friendly, and fascinating my fellow students are." Despite administration efforts to diversify the student population, it consists of "a standard mix of marginal, pretentious, and extremely intelligent students." A disappointed senior psychology major writes, "There is not very much mixing of racial groups on this campus," and an Asian student adds, "People of different races sit apart from [each] other in [the] food court." Also, a senior computer science major says, "This school is very apathetic in terms of activism and politics. People here come from very privileged backgrounds and so they don't really care about much, except for drinking, academics, and athletics." All in all, students are "cheerful," and "the college is fun, vibrant, and beautiful."

# DARTMOUTH COLLEGE

FINANCIAL AID: 603-646-2451 • E-MAIL: ADMISSIONS.OFFICE@DARTMOUTH.EDU • WEBSITE: WWW.DARTMOUTH.EDU

## ADMISSIONS

*Very important factors considered include:* character/personal qualities, class rank, essays, extracurricular activities, recommendations, secondary school record, standardized test scores. *Important factors considered include:* talent/ability. *Other factors considered include:* alumni/ae relation, geographical residence, interview, minority status, volunteer work, work experience. SAT I or ACT required; SAT II also required. TOEFL required of all international applicants. *High school units required/recommended:* 4 English recommended, 4 math recommended, 4 science recommended, 3 foreign language recommended, 3 social studies recommended.

### The Inside Word

Applications for the class of 2006 were up 5 percent from the previous year's totals, making this small-town Ivy more selective in choosing who gets offered a coveted spot in the class. As is the case with those who apply to any of the Ivies or other highly selective colleges, candidates to Dartmouth are up against (or benefit from) many institutional interests that go unmentioned in discussions of appropriate qualifications for admission. This makes an already stressful process even more so for most candidates.

## FINANCIAL AID

*Students should submit:* FAFSA, CSS/Financial Aid PROFILE, noncustodial (divorced/separated) parent's statement, business/farm supplement. The Princeton Review suggests that all financial aid forms be submitted as soon as possible after January 1. *Need-based scholarships/grants offered:* Pell, SEOG, state scholarships/grants, the school's own gift aid. *Loan aid offered:* FFEL Subsidized Stafford, FFEL Unsubsidized Stafford, FFEL PLUS, Federal Perkins, college/university loans from institutional funds. Federal Work-Study Program available. Institutional employment available. Applicants will be notified of awards on or about April 15. Off-campus job opportunities are excellent.

## FROM THE ADMISSIONS OFFICE

"Today Dartmouth's mission is to endow its students with the knowledge and wisdom needed to make creative and positive contributions to society. The college brings together a breadth of cultures, traditions, and ideas to create a campus that is alive with ongoing debate and exploration. The educational value of such discourse cannot be underestimated. From student-initiated round-table discussions that attempt to make sense of world events to the late-night philosophizing in a dormitory lounge, Dartmouth students take advantage of their opportunities to learn from each other. The unique benefits of sharing in this interchange are accompanied by a great sense of responsibility. Each individual's commitment to the Principles of Community ensures the vitality of this learning environment."

### SELECTIVITY

| | |
|---|---|
| Admissions Rating | 99 |
| # of applicants | 11,853 |
| % of applicants accepted | 18 |
| % of acceptees attending | 51 |
| # accepting a place on wait list | 250 |
| % admitted from wait list | 5 |
| # of early decision applicants | 1,216 |
| % accepted early decision | 33 |

### FRESHMAN PROFILE

| | |
|---|---|
| Range SAT Verbal | 650-750 |
| Average SAT Verbal | 702 |
| Range SAT Math | 680-770 |
| Average SAT Math | 713 |
| Range ACT Composite | 28-33 |
| Average ACT Composite | 31 |
| Minimum TOEFL | 580 |
| % graduated top 10% of class | 87 |
| % graduated top 50% of class | 100 |

### DEADLINES

| | |
|---|---|
| Early decision | 11/1 |
| Early decision notification | 12/15 |
| Regular admission | 1/1 |
| Regular notification | 4/10 |

### APPLICANTS ALSO LOOK AT AND OFTEN PREFER
Harvard
Princeton
Yale
Stanford

### AND SOMETIMES PREFER
Brown
MIT
Amherst
Williams

### AND RARELY PREFER
U. Penn, Cornell U.
Northwestern U.
Middlebury

### FINANCIAL FACTS

| | |
|---|---|
| Financial Aid Rating | 87 |
| Tuition | $28,965 |
| Room and board | $8,740 |
| Books and supplies | $810 |
| Required fees | $162 |
| % frosh receiving aid | 51 |
| % undergrads receiving aid | 47 |
| Avg frosh grant | $22,900 |
| Avg frosh loan | $2,050 |

# DAVIDSON COLLEGE

PO Box 1737, Davidson, NC 28036-1719 • Admissions: 704-894-2230 • Fax: 704-894-2016

## CAMPUS LIFE

| | |
|---|---|
| Quality of Life Rating | 88 |
| Type of school | private |
| Affiliation | Presbyterian |
| Environment | suburban |

### STUDENTS
| | |
|---|---|
| Total undergrad enrollment | 1,673 |
| % from out of state | 86 |
| % from public high school | 48 |
| % live on campus | 91 |
| % in (# of) fraternities | 48 (7) |
| % African American | 8 |
| % Asian | 3 |
| % Caucasian | 87 |
| % Hispanic | 5 |
| % international | 3 |
| # of countries represented | 32 |

### SURVEY SAYS . . .
Political activism is hot
Ethnic diversity on campus
Diverse students interact
Student government
Lots of classroom discussion
Classes are small
Athletic facilities need improving
Unattractive campus

## ACADEMICS

| | |
|---|---|
| Academic Rating | 97 |
| Calendar | semester |
| Student/faculty ratio | 11:1 |
| Profs interesting rating | 71 |
| Profs accessible rating | 73 |
| % profs teaching UG courses | 100 |
| Avg lab size | 10-19 students |
| Avg reg class size | under 10 students |

### MOST POPULAR MAJORS
English language and literature
Biology/biological sciences
Political science and government

## STUDENTS SPEAK OUT

### Academics
At Davidson the "boundaries between students and professors are set aside," affording undergraduates the respect due to "a person with a mind who is going to influence the world." Professors display a high level of sensitivity to student needs: "I wasn't even the one that brought up the fact that I needed help. My professor came to me, and I am so glad he did." Instructors make themselves easily available, even "coming in on weekends to give study sessions before tests or helping with personal problems." They keep students engaged by "stimulating class discussion and organizing curriculum-enriching events out of class." Unlike at most schools, Davidson students seem to approve of their required courses. "Because of our core curriculum, I have had to stretch myself in areas outside of my comfort zone, but that ultimately resulted in my current major." Many students single out the "strict honor code," which allows for self-scheduled and unproctored exams, as one of the best aspects of a Davidson education. "People don't come to Davidson unless they want to be part of an honor-bound community." Davidson's president "is probably one of the people we see the most around campus. Whether he's running, attending social events, or just hanging out with students, his vibrant personality and friendliness are representative of the entire school." On the small campus, "you know all the administration and most of them know you," leading to an academic atmosphere where "the professors and administrative staff seem like family."

### Life
Undergraduates at Davidson choose from a variety of social scenes, ranging from Patterson Court, where "there's always some sort of party going on," to religious groups that reflect the school's "strong connections to the Presbyterian church." Some students complain that "they need more things to do on the weekend that don't necessarily involve alcohol." Others point to additional events that round out the options, including "midnight movies, live bands, and theme events on Saturday nights." Overall, "Davidson goes to great lengths to make sure there is always some type of activity to go to no matter what your interests are." One student points out, "If there is ever something that you want to have on campus, it is easy enough to start it up yourself—with school funding." In Davidson's overachieving environment, students "focus on as many extracurriculars as they can cram into their schedule." A junior tells us, "Any one student can be involved in enough sports, activities, jobs, and volunteering that it is a miracle they finish their schoolwork and still have time to socialize and sleep." When campus life gets at all boring, "a little weekend trip to the beach or the mountains is in order." A short ride gets students to Charlotte, "a wellspring of culture, arts, clubs, bars, restaurants, [and] shopping."

### Student Body
A Davidson student is "hardworking," sometimes "to the point of chronic fatigue." Other commonly used adjectives include "very bright," "type A," "studious," and "fairly religious." Several students agree, however, that the stereotypes of "conservative and always studying" don't convey the variety of the population. "Although Davidson has many students with a conservative viewpoint," writes one undergraduate, most "students are accepting and respectful of other opinions." Several people do point out a "definite line between the churchgoers and the people who sleep in on Sundays." One respondent, however, summarizes his view of the student body optimistically: "Though we disagree, though we argue, though we truly are different people, something amazing happens when we are all together."

# DAVIDSON COLLEGE

FINANCIAL AID: 704-892-2232 • E-MAIL: ADMISSION@DAVIDSON.EDU • WEBSITE: WWW.DAVIDSON.EDU

## ADMISSIONS

*Very important factors considered include:* character/personal qualities, secondary school record, volunteer work. *Important factors considered include:* essays, extracurricular activities, recommendations, talent/ability. *Other factors considered include:* alumni/ae relation, class rank, geographical residence, standardized test scores, work experience. SAT I or ACT required; SAT II recommended. TOEFL required of all international applicants. High school diploma is required and GED is not accepted. *High school units required/recommended:* 16 total required; 4 English required, 3 math required, 4 math recommended, 2 science required, 4 science recommended, 2 foreign language required, 4 foreign language recommended.

### The Inside Word

Harbor no illusions regarding ease of admission here. Getting in is every bit as tough as staying in, because an amazingly high percentage of those who are admitted choose to attend. Look for admission to become even more difficult as the college's name recognition increases.

## FINANCIAL AID

*Students should submit:* FAFSA, CSS/Financial Aid PROFILE, noncustodial (divorced/separated) parent's statement, business/farm supplement. Regular filing deadline is February 15. The Princeton Review suggests that all financial aid forms be submitted as soon as possible after January 1. *Need-based scholarships/grants offered:* Pell, SEOG, state scholarships/grants, private scholarships, the school's own gift aid, need-linked special talent scholarship. *Loan aid offered:* FFEL Subsidized Stafford, FFEL Unsubsidized Stafford, FFEL PLUS, Federal Perkins, alternative loans. Federal Work-Study Program available. Institutional employment available. Applicants will be notified of awards on or about April 1. Off-campus job opportunities are excellent.

## FROM THE ADMISSIONS OFFICE

"Davidson College is one of the nation's premier academic institutions, a college of the liberal arts and sciences respected for its intellectual vigor, the high quality of its faculty and students, and the achievements of its alumni. It is distinguished by its strong honor system, close interaction between professors and students, an environment that encourages both intellectual growth and community service, and a commitment to international education. Davidson places great value on student participation in extracurricular activities, intercollegiate athletics, and intramural sports. The college has a strong regional identity, which includes traditions of civility and mutual respect, and has historic ties to the Presbyterian Church."

### SELECTIVITY
★★★★

| | |
|---|---|
| Admissions Rating | 99 |
| # of applicants | 3,926 |
| % of applicants accepted | 32 |
| % of acceptees attending | 40 |
| # of early decision applicants | 375 |
| % accepted early decision | 46 |

### FRESHMAN PROFILE

| | |
|---|---|
| Range SAT Verbal | 640-720 |
| Average SAT Verbal | 659 |
| Range SAT Math | 640-720 |
| Average SAT Math | 656 |
| Range ACT Composite | 27-31 |
| Average ACT Composite | 28 |
| Minimum TOEFL | 600 |
| % graduated top 10% of class | 77 |
| % graduated top 25% of class | 93 |
| % graduated top 50% of class | 99 |

### DEADLINES

| | |
|---|---|
| Early decision | 11/15 |
| Early decision notification | 12/15 |
| Regular admission | 1/2 |
| Regular notification | 4/1 |

### APPLICANTS ALSO LOOK AT AND OFTEN PREFER
Duke, Princeton
Dartmouth
Stanford
Swarthmore
Williams

### AND SOMETIMES PREFER
UNC Chapel Hill
U Virginia
Washington U
Vanderbilt

### AND RARELY PREFER
Wake Forest U
Emory, Furman
U Richmond
Colgate

### FINANCIAL FACTS

| | |
|---|---|
| Financial Aid Rating | 87 |
| Tuition | $25,903 |
| Room and board | $7,369 |
| Books and supplies | $950 |
| Required fees | $881 |
| % frosh receiving aid | 31 |
| % undergrads receiving aid | 33 |
| Avg frosh grant | $17,900 |
| Avg frosh loan | $2,314 |

# DEEP SPRINGS COLLEGE

APPLICATION COMMITTEE, BOX 45001, DYER, NV 89010 • ADMISSIONS: 760-872-2000 • FAX: 760-872-4466

### CAMPUS LIFE

| | |
|---|---|
| **Quality of Life Rating** | **93** |
| Type of school | private |
| Environment | rural |

### STUDENTS

| | |
|---|---|
| Total undergrad enrollment | 26 |
| % from out of state | 92 |
| % live on campus | 100 |

### SURVEY SAYS . . .
Great on-campus food
Registration is a breeze
(Almost) no one smokes
(Almost) no one listens to college radio
Very little hard liquor
Very little beer drinking
Very little drug use
Intercollegiate sports unpopular or nonexistent
Class discussions encouraged

### ACADEMICS

| | |
|---|---|
| **Academic Rating** | **99** |
| Calendar | continuous |
| Student/faculty ratio | 4:1 |
| % profs teaching UG courses | 100 |
| Avg reg class size | under 10 students |

## STUDENTS SPEAK OUT

### Academics

Deep Springs is more than a college, it's a way of life, one that makes exceptional mental, physical, and ethical demands of the two-baker's-dozen men who attend. Undergraduates are responsible not only for demanding academic work but also for 20-plus hours per week of manual labor on the school ranch and the administration of the school. Yes, you read correctly: "For the most part at Deep Springs, the students are the administration," explains one student. "Eight-hour meetings to discuss the fate of a fellow student [are] never something someone looks forward to. But none of us would rather have it any other way." Adds another, "I can't complain [about anything here] without blaming myself. All the faculty is here because we . . . hired them. If we wanted the president fired, it would take some convincing, but the trustees would listen to us if we had a just cause." The net result of the Deep Springs experience is a serious, tight community, one in which students "eat, study, work, and live together every single day, making you wish that for once you could sit in the reading room without falling into a three-hour conversation with a friend about the '80s, Heidegger, or what's for dinner tomorrow. You think by attending Deep Springs you'll never lack for a conversation topic again, until you go home for the first time." Students warn, "Ideally, we would have a larger selection of courses," but most agree that "nothing at Deep Springs could be improved without seriously changing the nature of the school."

### Life

Life at Deep Springs, students agree, "is all about balancing its three pillars—labor, academics, and self-governance—and letting them facilitate the growth of virtue." Most agree the experience is worth both the concomitant stress and the hard work. As one student recounts, "Being dairy boy these past two terms has taught me about responsibility, manure, and fatherhood. Walking out into the corral a few weeks ago to find a trembling baby Holstein being licked by one of our dairy cows changed my life forever." In their rare spare moments, students here must make their own fun; the ranch is in just about the middle of nowhere and offers no Greek life, no intercollegiate sports, and no drugs or alcohol (this policy is strictly enforced, all here assure us). Recreation includes "BB gun gentlemen's duels, air guitar contests, hiking, swimming in the Upper Reservoir, sensory deprivation experiments, late-night cooking . . . you know, college stuff." Movies are popular; they're the only thing students here can watch on the school television, since "we have a TV and VCR, but no TV reception." Mostly, though, students amuse themselves with "late-night conversations in the library and the BH (Boarding House), mostly when we're trying to put off the paper(s) we have to write." Ask them what they'd like most to add to the Deep Springs experience, and most will reply without hesitation: "It would be nice to see a girl from time to time. . . . We should start admitting women."

### Student Body

The young men of Deep Springs are all "stubborn, smart, eccentric, and determined. Beyond those qualities, there are very few consistencies." The tiny population includes "artists, intellectuals, country bumpkins, Canadians, gay yogis, and snobs. . . . Despite our small student body, there's a greater diversity of musical tastes here than in most HMVs." All students are extraordinary in some way. Notes one about his classmates, "They are more well traveled, well read, and well mannered than any people I have ever encountered in these numbers. It seems like between the 26 of us, we have been everywhere and seen everything." In their spare time, students "think about Martin Heidegger and Winona Ryder," but they rarely have spare time; as one undergrad cautioned, "We are an all-male college out in the middle of the desert whose students run the college and do a minimum of 20 hours of labor per week. No one sane applies, let alone gets in."

# DEEP SPRINGS COLLEGE

FINANCIAL AID: 760-872-2000 • E-MAIL: APCOM@DEEPSPRINGS.EDU • WEBSITE: WWW.DEEPSPRINGS.EDU

## ADMISSIONS

*Very important factors considered include:* character/personal qualities, essays, interview. *Important factors considered include:* class rank, extracurricular activities, secondary school record, volunteer work, work experience. *Other factors considered include:* minority status, recommendations, religious affiliation/commitment, standardized test scores, talent/ability. SAT I or ACT required.

### The Inside Word

There is no admissions staff at Deep Springs. Along with faculty, students make up the admissions committee. Finalists write seven essays and travel to the valley for a several-day visit and a two-hour interview with the admissions committee. There is likely to be no more rigorous, personal, or refreshing an admissions process to be found in U.S. higher education. This place requires serious commitment, and only the strong survive. Thorough self-assessment is a must before applying.

## FINANCIAL AID

Deep Springs does not require financial aid forms to be submitted. All admitted students receive full tuition and room and board, regardless of need. Off-campus job opportunities are poor.

## FROM THE ADMISSIONS OFFICE

"Founded in 1917, Deep Springs College lies isolated in a high desert valley of eastern California, 30 miles from the nearest town. Its enrollment is limited to 26 students, each of whom receives a full scholarship that covers tuition, room, and board and is valued at more than $50,000 per year. Students engage in rigorous academics, govern themselves, and participate in the operation of our cattle and alfalfa ranch. After two years, students generally transfer to other schools to complete their studies. Students regularly transfer to Harvard, the University of Chicago, and Brown, but also choose Cornell, Columbia, Stanford, Swarthmore, UC Berkeley, and Yale.

"In 2002, Deep Springs students garnered four major national scholarship awards: three Truman Scholarships for public service careers—more than any other school in the country—and one Udall Scholarship for careers in environmental studies and ecology."

### SELECTIVITY
★ ★ ★ ★

| | |
|---|---|
| Admissions Rating | 99 |
| # of applicants | 128 |
| % of applicants accepted | 12 |
| % of acceptees attending | 93 |
| # accepting a place on wait list | 1 |
| % admitted from wait list | 100 |

### FRESHMAN PROFILE

| | |
|---|---|
| Average SAT Verbal | 745 |
| Average SAT Math | 715 |
| Average HS GPA | 3.9 |
| % graduated top 10% of class | 90 |
| % graduated top 50% of class | 100 |

### DEADLINES

| | |
|---|---|
| Regular admission | 11/15 |
| Regular notification | 4/7 |

### AAPPLICANTS ALSO LOOK AT AND RARELY PREFER

Harvard
U of Chicago
Cornell
UC Berkeley
Swarthmore
Brown
Stanford
Columbia
Yale

### FINANCIAL FACTS
★ ★ ★ ★

| | |
|---|---|
| Financial Aid Rating | 99 |
| Books and supplies | $1,200 |
| Avg frosh grant | $52,000 |
| % frosh receiving aid | 100 |

# DENISON UNIVERSITY

Box H, Granville, OH 43023 • Admissions: 740-587-6276 • Fax: 740-587-6306

## CAMPUS LIFE

| | |
|---|---|
| **Quality of Life Rating** | **77** |
| Type of school | private |
| Environment | suburban |

### STUDENTS

| | |
|---|---|
| Total undergrad enrollment | 2,081 |
| % male/female | 46/54 |
| % from out of state | 63 |
| % from public high school | 71 |
| % live on campus | 99 |
| % in (# of) fraternities | 29 (8) |
| % in (# of) sororities | 41 (8) |
| % African American | 6 |
| % Asian | 3 |
| % Caucasian | 84 |
| % Hispanic | 3 |
| % international | 5 |
| # of countries represented | 34 |

### SURVEY SAYS . . .
Frats and sororities dominate social scene
Diversity lacking on campus
Athletic facilities are great
Students are cliquish
Classes are small
Theater is unpopular
Lousy off-campus food
Class discussions encouraged
Low cost of living

## ACADEMICS

| | |
|---|---|
| **Academic Rating** | **81** |
| Calendar | semester |
| Student/faculty ratio | 11:1 |
| Profs interesting rating | 94 |
| Profs accessible rating | 98 |
| % profs teaching UG courses | 100 |
| Avg lab size | 10-19 students |
| Avg reg class size | 10-19 students |

### MOST POPULAR MAJORS
Communications
Economics
English language and literature

## STUDENTS SPEAK OUT

### Academics

No, this is not your father's Denison, as students frequently made us aware. "It's more challenging and more fulfilling than I would have ever dreamed," writes one student. "It's a love/hate relationship because I know I could have gone somewhere easier and got all A's and made it to med school coasting, but then I would have missed out on the great academic experience Denison offers." Agrees another, "Academically, it has become more challenging each year due to the school's increasing population of strongly academic students. The rise in standards for Denison students has motivated and made my friends and me proud." Students appreciate the attentiveness and dedication of the DU faculty; writes one undergrad, "Although I have had my doubts about attending Denison, I cannot discount the superior education I have received. The faculty is engaging, interesting, and concerned about their students. Feedback flows, and help is almost always obtainable. The professors expect a lot of you, and you work hard trying not to disappoint them." Another praises the teaching methods here, explaining that "through classes based more on discussion than lecture, I have witnessed students growing not just objectively, but becoming better thinkers, and therefore better people." The administration is similarly "top notch. Not only are they accessible, but they have given me the impression that they are very interested in the well-being of students at this institution." Popular majors at Denison include English, economics, psychology, and biology. For those studying the latter, Denison offers The Polly Anderson Field Station at the Biological Reserve, and has its own planetarium for stargazers in Olin Science Hall.

### Life

Life at Denison "is pretty relaxed. Most people seem to get their work done before having fun." Writes one student, "Movies are the staple entertainment. But backing that up is the occasional spur-of-the-moment shopping trip. In general my free time is spent sitting in a friend's room laughing the day away." Students also enjoy a wide assortment of campus organizations and "activities, concerts, comedians, etc." Hometown Granville "is very small, not conducive to college students, and does not have much activity. It is a nice town though, with a few good places to eat. You have to make your own fun at Denison." Adds another student, "There is little to do off campus. Granville is not very welcoming to university students, and there is no off-campus housing allowed. The occasional house party is a big deal." Despite efforts to curb partying, "drinking is one of the most popular activities." On weekends "a lot of students make the short 30-minute commute to Columbus to enjoy the city's night-life."

### Student Body

As in previous surveys, Denison undergrads note an incremental improvement in the school's demographic makeup this year. "Although our student body is predominantly white, our minority population is growing each and every year, heightening Denison's diversity. I notice on campus that most people interact with each other regardless of gender or other minority status. I feel that the campus is gradually—but surely—becoming more diverse and open-minded." Students regard classmates as "generally very friendly" and appreciate the fact that "although Denison is a small school with approximately 2,100 undergrad[s], there seems to be a group for everyone." They also note that "there is a strong separation between people who like to party and people who don't party at all, and due to [more demanding] admission standards, the latter is becoming dominant."

184 ■ THE BEST 351 COLLEGES

# DENISON UNIVERSITY

FINANCIAL AID: 740-587-6279 • E-MAIL: ADMISSIONS@DENISON.EDU • WEBSITE: WWW.DENISON.EDU

## ADMISSIONS
*Very important factors considered include:* essays, recommendations, secondary school record, standardized test scores. *Important factors considered include:* alumni/ae relation, character/personal qualities, extracurricular activities, interview, talent/ability. *Other factors considered include:* geographical residence, religious affiliation/commitment, state residency, volunteer work, work experience. SAT I or ACT required. TOEFL required of all international applicants. High school diploma or GED is required. *High school units required/recommended:* 16 total recommended; 4 English recommended, 3 math recommended, 3 science recommended, 3 foreign language recommended, 2 social studies recommended, 1 history recommended.

### The Inside Word
Applicants who are statistically below Denison's freshman profile should proceed with caution. One of the simplest ways for a university to promote a reputation as an increasingly selective institution is to begin to cut off the bottom of the applicant pool. Only lack of success against heavy competition for students prevents Denison from being more aggressive in this regard.

## FINANCIAL AID
*Students should submit:* FAFSA. No deadline for regular filing. The Princeton Review suggests that all financial aid forms be submitted as soon as possible after January 1. *Need-based scholarships/grants offered:* Pell, SEOG, state scholarships/grants, private scholarships, the school's own gift aid. *Loan aid offered:* Direct Subsidized Stafford, Direct Unsubsidized Stafford, Direct PLUS, Federal Perkins, college/university loans from institutional funds. Federal Work-Study Program available. Institutional employment available. Applicants will be notified of awards on a rolling basis beginning on or about April 1. Off-campus job opportunities are fair.

## FROM THE ADMISSIONS OFFICE
"Denison is a college that can point with pride to its success in enrolling and retaining intellectually motivated, diverse, and well-balanced students who are being taught to become effective leaders in the 21st century. This year, nearly 50 percent of our first-year students were in the top 10 percent of their high school graduating class, their average SAT scores have risen above 1200—an increase of some 40 points over the last five years—18 percent of the class is multicultural, and 95 percent of our student body is receiving some type of financial assistance. Our First-Year Program focuses on helping students make a successful transition from high school to college, and the small classes and accessibility of faculty assure students the opportunity to interact closely with their professors and fellow students. We care about our students, and the loyalty of our 27,000 alumni proves that the Denison experience is one that lasts for a lifetime."

### SELECTIVITY

| | |
|---|---|
| Admissions Rating | 82 |
| # of applicants | 3,289 |
| % of applicants accepted | 61 |
| % of acceptees attending | 31 |
| # accepting a place on wait list | 350 |
| % admitted from wait list | 8 |
| # of early decision applicants | 150 |
| % accepted early decision | 70 |

### FRESHMAN PROFILE
| | |
|---|---|
| Range SAT Verbal | 550-650 |
| Average SAT Verbal | 602 |
| Range SAT Math | 560-670 |
| Average SAT Math | 615 |
| Range ACT Composite | 24-29 |
| Average ACT Composite | 26 |
| Minimum TOEFL | 550 |
| Average HS GPA | 3.5 |
| % graduated top 10% of class | 48 |
| % graduated top 25% of class | 82 |
| % graduated top 50% of class | 100 |

### DEADLINES
| | |
|---|---|
| Early decision I | 11/15 |
| Early decision I notification | 12/1 |
| Early decision II | 1/15 |
| Early decision II notification | 2/15 |
| Priority admission | 1/1 |
| Regular admission | 2/1 |
| Regular notification | 4/1 |

### APPLICANTS ALSO LOOK AT
**AND OFTEN PREFER**
U of Richmond, Bucknell U
Washington U, Vanderbilt U
**AND SOMETIMES PREFER**
Miami of Ohio, Kenyon College
College of Wooster, DePauw U
**AND RARELY PREFER**
Ohio U, Ohio State U
Allegheny College
Hobart and William Smith Colleges

### FINANCIAL FACTS

| | |
|---|---|
| Financial Aid Rating | 84 |
| Tuition | $25,090 |
| Room and board | $7,290 |
| Books and supplies | $600 |
| Required fees | $670 |
| % frosh receiving aid | 97 |
| % undergrads receiving aid | 98 |
| Avg frosh grant | $12,122 |
| Avg frosh loan | $4,625 |

THE BEST 351 COLLEGES ■ 185

# DePaul University

1 East Jackson Boulevard, Chicago, IL 60604-2287 • Admissions: 312-362-8300 • Fax: 312-362-5749

## CAMPUS LIFE

| | |
|---|---|
| **Quality of Life Rating** | **80** |
| Type of school | private |
| Affiliation | Roman Catholic |
| Environment | urban |

### STUDENTS
| | |
|---|---|
| Total undergrad enrollment | 14,343 |
| % male/female | 45/55 |
| % from out of state | 13 |
| % from public high school | 68 |
| % African American | 12 |
| % Asian | 10 |
| % Caucasian | 57 |
| % Hispanic | 13 |
| % international | 5 |
| # of countries represented | 85 |

### SURVEY SAYS . . .
Students love Chicago, IL
Dorms are like palaces
Great food on campus
Campus feels safe
Great off-campus food
Ethnic diversity on campus
Students get along with local community
Diverse students interact
Very little beer drinking
Very little hard liquor

## ACADEMICS

| | |
|---|---|
| **Academic Rating** | **73** |
| Calendar | differs by program |
| Student/faculty ratio | 14:1 |
| Profs interesting rating | 91 |
| Profs accessible rating | 93 |
| Avg reg class size | 20-29 students |

### MOST POPULAR MAJORS
Business
Accounting
Computer science

## STUDENTS SPEAK OUT

### Academics
A Catholic university with strengths in business, computer science, and pre-professional programs, DePaul University is the choice of many who crave the prestige and one-on-one interaction of a top private school but don't want to pay for a super-elite institution. DePaul is divided into three campuses. The downtown Loop campus caters to business and computer science students, while uptown Lincoln Park is home to the liberal arts, music, education, and DePaul's world-renowned drama department. Students get plenty of bang for their buck at any campus, which explains why most are so sanguine about their school. According to our respondents, "Professors are overflowing with knowledge and always extremely accessible. I would have no qualms about placing my academic experience at DePaul in the same league as our nation's most prestigious universities." Adds another, "Professors are great. They even know you outside of class on a first-name basis. There are 25 or less students in each class." Similarly, the administration "is near flawless, establishing DePaul as a well-oiled machine," according to one political science major.

### Life
With its large commuter population, DePaul lacks the community base on which most schools build their extracurricular life. Add the lure of Chicago, one of the nation's top urban centers, and you begin to understand why there's not a whole lot happening on the DePaul campus once classes end. Students don't seem to mind, explaining that "the best part of DePaul is not the school itself, but rather the area surrounding the school. Anything you want to do is a block or two away." Adds another student, "Life in Chicago is great. The city has so much to offer: museums, theaters, and restaurants. In the summertime, going to the lake is the best." DePaul's few residents are housed on the Lincoln Park campus in a young, fun Chicago neighborhood. They supplement their off-campus activities with clubs, internships, and Greek life. Notes one student, "There is a club here for everyone," including ethnic, race-, and gender-based support groups, sports and games clubs, community service organizations, campus government, and hobby groups.

### Student Body
Like many Catholic schools, DePaul does a good job of keeping tuition and fees down, and as a result attracts a wider variety of low- and middle-income students, among them many minorities. Students "get along" but don't see much of each other, since "most are commuter students who care little about social interaction within the student body." Among residents, "you have the jocks, the theater majors, and the Greeks," explains one undergraduate. Politically the DePaul campus is sedate: "Life at this school is far detached from important worldly issues," explains one undergrad. "Students are generally more concerned about their clothes or the party they are going to than political or social issues."

186 ■ THE BEST 351 COLLEGES

# DePaul University

FINANCIAL AID: 312-362-8091 • E-MAIL: ADMITDPU@WPPOST.DEPAUL.EDU • WEBSITE: WWW.DEPAUL.EDU

## ADMISSIONS

*Very important factors considered include:* character/personal qualities, secondary school record, volunteer work. *Important factors considered include:* class rank, extracurricular activities, minority status, recommendations, standardized test scores, work experience. *Other factors considered include:* alumni/ae relation, essays, geographical residence, interview, religious affiliation/commitment, state residency, talent/ability. SAT I or ACT required. TOEFL required of all international applicants. High school diploma or GED is required. *High school units required/recommended:* 16 total required; 4 English required, 2 math required, 2 science required, 2 science lab required, 2 social studies required, 4 elective required.

### The Inside Word

Applicants to DePaul will find the admissions staff is genuinely committed to helping students. Candidates whose academic qualifications fall below normally acceptable levels are reviewed for other evidence of potential for success. The Latino student presence on campus has begun to increase significantly, due in large part to the university's major commitment to active involvement in the National Hispanic Institute, an organization that works with top Hispanic students from junior high through college.

## FINANCIAL AID

*Students should submit:* FAFSA. Regular filing deadline is May 1. The Princeton Review suggests that all financial aid forms be submitted as soon as possible after January 1. *Need-based scholarships/grants offered:* Pell, SEOG, state scholarships/grants, private scholarships, the school's own gift aid. *Loan aid offered:* Direct Subsidized Stafford, Direct Unsubsidized Stafford, Direct PLUS, Federal Perkins. Federal Work-Study Program available. Institutional employment available. Applicants will be notified of awards on a rolling basis beginning on or about February 15. Off-campus job opportunities are excellent.

## FROM THE ADMISSIONS OFFICE

"The nation's largest Catholic university, DePaul University is nationally recognized for its innovative academic programs that embrace a comprehensive 'learn by doing' approach. DePaul has three residential campuses and four commuter campuses in the suburbs. The Lincoln Park campus is located in one of Chicago's most exciting neighborhoods, filled with theaters, cafés, clubs, and shops. It is home to DePaul's College of Liberal Arts & Sciences, the School of Education, The Theater School, and the School of Music. New buildings on the 36-acre campus include residence halls, a science building, a student recreational facility, and the student center, which features a cyber café where students can surf the Web or gather with friends. The Loop campus, located in Chicago's downtown—a world-class center for business, government, law and culture—is home to DePaul's College of Commerce; College of Law; School of Computer Science, Telecommunications, and Information Systems; School for New Learning; and School of Accountancy and Management Information Systems. The Barat campus is located on 30 wooded acres in Lake Forest, Illinois, 35 miles north of downtown Chicago. Home to the interdisciplinary Barat College, it offers the feel of an intimate liberal arts college backed by the reputation and resources of a major urban teaching university."

### SELECTIVITY

| | |
|---|---|
| Admissions Rating | 78 |
| # of applicants | 8,932 |
| % of applicants accepted | 77 |
| % of acceptees attending | 34 |

### FRESHMAN PROFILE

| | |
|---|---|
| Range SAT Verbal | 510-610 |
| Average SAT Verbal | 556 |
| Range SAT Math | 500-610 |
| Average SAT Math | 551 |
| Range ACT Composite | 21-26 |
| Average ACT Composite | 23 |
| Minimum TOEFL | 550 |
| Average HS GPA | 3.3 |
| % graduated top 10% of class | 16 |
| % graduated top 25% of class | 41 |
| % graduated top 50% of class | 75 |

### DEADLINES

| | |
|---|---|
| Priority admission | 2/1 |
| Nonfall registration? | yes |

### APPLICANTS ALSO LOOK AT
**AND OFTEN PREFER**
Northwestern U
U of Chicago
U of Illinois at Urbana-Champaign
Notre Dame
**AND SOMETIMES PREFER**
Loyola U Chicago
Marquette
U of Indiana at Bloomington
U of Illinois at Chicago
Illinois State
Northern Illinois U
**AND RARELY PREFER**
Purdue U at West Lafayette

### FINANCIAL FACTS

| | |
|---|---|
| Financial Aid Rating | 86 |
| Tuition | $18,750 |
| Room and board | $8,370 |
| Books and supplies | $750 |
| Required fees | $100 |
| % frosh receiving aid | 77 |
| % undergrads receiving aid | 67 |

# DePauw University

101 E. Seminary, Greencastle, IN 46135 • Admissions: 765-658-4006 • Fax: 765-658-4007

## CAMPUS LIFE

★ ★ ★ ☆

| | |
|---|---|
| Quality of Life Rating | 82 |
| Type of school | private |
| Affiliation | Methodist |
| Environment | rural |

### STUDENTS

| | |
|---|---|
| Total undergrad enrollment | 2,338 |
| % male/female | 44/56 |
| % from out of state | 53 |
| % from public high school | 85 |
| % live on campus | 92 |
| % in (# of) fraternities | 77 (12) |
| % in (# of) sororities | 69 (10) |
| % African American | 5 |
| % Asian | 2 |
| % Caucasian | 88 |
| % Hispanic | 3 |
| % international | 1 |
| # of countries represented | 16 |

### SURVEY SAYS . . .
Campus easy to get around
Beautiful campus
No one cheats
Great computer facilities
Great library
Student government is unpopular
Very little beer drinking
(Almost) no one listens to college radio
Diversity lacking on campus

## ACADEMICS

| | |
|---|---|
| Academic Rating | 89 |
| Calendar | 4-1-4 |
| Student/faculty ratio | 10:1 |
| % profs teaching UG courses | 100 |
| Avg reg class size | 10-19 students |

### MOST POPULAR MAJORS
Communications
Creative writing
Economics

## STUDENTS SPEAK OUT

### Academics

Students come to DePauw seeking a creative yet conservative approach to undergraduate education, presented by a capable and supportive faculty. By and large, most find what they come looking for, especially in the "great school of music," social sciences, media studies, and literature. Chief among DePauw's innovations is the Winter Term, a month-long session during which students can pursue "many outstanding opportunities to do things you can't do in the classroom." Winter Term allows students to undertake "internships and undergraduate research opportunities that are unparalleled." Dedicated instructors greatly enhance the Winter Term experience. Recounts one undergrad, "Professors are awesome, so accessible. I went on a trip for Winter Term with my Latin professor and had a blast. Professors here are your friends as well as teachers." Students also appreciate the fact that "class sizes are very small, yielding great personal relationships with the professors." The administration, however, is not well regarded, with many students complaining that "administrators just seem concerned with the image DePauw projects to the outside world."

### Life

How students feel about social life at DePauw depends primarily on how they feel about the Greek system, which "definitely dominates the social scene." Warns one student, "If you're not into Greek life, don't come here! That's where everything is at here!" For some, "It's fine because it's free beer and a nice place to party. The majority of students stay on campus and hit the four local bars on weekends." Others find it oppressive and divisive. Making matters worse is the lack of alternative activities in hometown Greencastle, "the armpit of the earth. There is NOTHING to do here!" Given the situation, it is unsurprising that drinking "is a major pastime, perpetuated by the exclusive, gender-discriminatory Greek system." "For fun," one independent admits, "we leave town." Not all students paint such a bleak picture, though; writes one, "As an independent, I have no problem staying entertained. DePauw offers a lot of opportunities. Since it is a small school, it is very easy to become involved in all the different activities." Many participate in community service, either "through their church or through the campus ministries center." According to students, "The level of volunteer involvement with the community is amazing."

### Student Body

DePauw undergrads describe a Balkanized student body, one "divided ethnically, socially, and financially." Some blame the situation on the Greeks; writes one student, "The Greek system categorizes students into a fixed mold. Often, the Greek students only converse with and befriend students in their house." Others see it as a class issue, noting that "most students here are very uppercrust. They have very definite opinions and stereotypes about our classes, and therefore tend not to mix well with others." To others still, it's racial: "The African Americans hang out with the African Americans, Hispanics with Hispanics, international students with other international students, and everyone else in whatever fraternity or sorority they joined." Politically and socially conservative, students draw such vitriolic epithets as "uncreative" and "pompous" from classmates. Is there an upside? Notes one student, "A lot of people have a 'face' they put on, but once you get to know them, they shed it."

188 ■ THE BEST 351 COLLEGES

# DePauw University

FINANCIAL AID: 765-658-4030 • E-MAIL: ADMISSIONS@DEPAUW.EDU • WEBSITE: WWW.DEPAUW.EDU

## ADMISSIONS

*Very important factors considered include:* class rank, essays, secondary school record, standardized test scores. *Important factors considered include:* alumni/ae relation, character/personal qualities, extracurricular activities, interview, minority status, recommendations, talent/ability, volunteer work. *Other factors considered include:* geographical residence, work experience. SAT I or ACT required; SAT I preferred. TOEFL required of all international applicants. High school diploma or GED is required. *High school units required/recommended:* 4 English recommended, 4 math recommended, 4 science recommended, 2 science lab recommended, 4 foreign language recommended, 4 social studies recommended, 3 history recommended, 10 elective recommended.

### The Inside Word

Students considering DePauw should not be deceived by the university's high acceptance rate. The impressive freshman profile indicates a high level of self-selection in the applicant pool.

## FINANCIAL AID

*Students should submit:* FAFSA, institution's own financial aid form. Regular filing deadline is February 15. The Princeton Review suggests that all financial aid forms be submitted as soon as possible after January 1. *Need-based scholarships/grants offered:* Pell, SEOG, state scholarships/grants, private scholarships, the school's own gift aid. *Loan aid offered:* FFEL Subsidized Stafford, FFEL Unsubsidized Stafford, FFEL PLUS, Federal Perkins, college/university loans from institutional funds, alternative loans. Federal Work-Study Program available. Institutional employment available. Applicants will be notified of awards on or about March 31. Off-campus job opportunities are fair.

## FROM THE ADMISSIONS OFFICE

"DePauw University is nationally recognized for intellectual and experiential challenge that links liberal arts education with life's work, preparing graduates for uncommon professional success, service to others, and personal fulfillment. DePauw graduates count among their ranks a Nobel laureate, a vice president and U.S. Congressman, Pulitzer Prize and Newberry Award authors, and a number of CEOs and humanitarian leaders. Our students demonstrate a love for learning, a willingness to serve others, the reason and judgement to lead, an interest in engaging worlds and cultures unknown to them, the courage to question their assumptions, and a strong commitment to community. Pre-professional and career exploration are encouraged through Winter Term, when more than 700 students pursue their own off-campus internships. This represents more students in experiential learning opportunities than at any other liberal arts college in the nation. Other innovative programs include Honor Scholars, Information Technology Associates Program, Management Fellows, Media Fellows, and Science Research Fellows, affording selected students additional seminar and internship opportunities."

### SELECTIVITY
★ ★ ★ ☆

| | |
|---|---|
| Admissions Rating | 86 |
| # of applicants | 3,682 |
| % of applicants accepted | 61 |
| % of acceptees attending | 30 |
| # accepting a place on wait list | 64 |
| # of early decision applicants | 33 |
| % accepted early decision | 76 |

### FRESHMAN PROFILE

| | |
|---|---|
| Range SAT Verbal | 560-650 |
| Average SAT Verbal | 610 |
| Range SAT Math | 570-670 |
| Average SAT Math | 620 |
| Range ACT Composite | 25-29 |
| Average ACT Composite | 27 |
| Minimum TOEFL | 560 |
| Average HS GPA | 3.7 |
| % graduated top 10% of class | 56 |
| % graduated top 25% of class | 89 |
| % graduated top 50% of class | 99 |

### DEADLINES

| | |
|---|---|
| Early decision | 11/1 |
| Early decision notification | 1/1 |
| Priority admission | 12/1 |
| Regular admission | 2/1 |
| Regular notification | 4/1 |
| Nonfall registration? | yes |

### APPLICANTS ALSO LOOK AT AND OFTEN PREFER
Indiana University—Bloomington
Vanderbilt University
Washington University in St. Louis
University of Notre Dame
Northwestern University

### AND SOMETIMES PREFER
Miami University, Denison University
Rhodes College
Purdue University—West Lafayette

### AND RARELY PREFER
Centre College

### FINANCIAL FACTS

| | |
|---|---|
| Financial Aid Rating | 92 |
| Tuition | $24,000 |
| Room and board | $7,050 |
| Books and supplies | $600 |
| Required fees | $530 |
| % frosh receiving aid | 52 |
| % undergrads receiving aid | 53 |
| Avg frosh grant | $16,121 |
| Avg frosh loan | $3,141 |

# DICKINSON COLLEGE

PO Box 1773, Carlisle, PA 17013-2896 • Admissions: 717-245-1231 • Fax: 717-245-1442

## CAMPUS LIFE

| Quality of Life Rating | 83 |
|---|---|
| Type of school | private |
| Environment | suburban |

### STUDENTS

| Total undergrad enrollment | 2,208 |
|---|---|
| % male/female | 42/58 |
| % from out of state | 59 |
| % from public high school | 69 |
| % live on campus | 92 |
| % in (# of) fraternities | 25 (8) |
| % in (# of) sororities | 26 (4) |
| % African American | 2 |
| % Asian | 2 |
| % Caucasian | 92 |
| % Hispanic | 2 |
| % international | 2 |

### SURVEY SAYS . . .
Frats and sororities dominate social scene
Great food on campus
Diversity lacking on campus
Students don't get along with local community
Campus easy to get around
Students don't like Carlisle, PA
Low cost of living
Class discussions encouraged

## ACADEMICS

| Academic Rating | 88 |
|---|---|
| Calendar | semester |
| Student/faculty ratio | 12:1 |
| Profs interesting rating | 95 |
| Profs accessible rating | 98 |
| % profs teaching UG courses | 100 |
| Avg lab size | 20-29 students |
| Avg reg class size | 10-19 students |

### MOST POPULAR MAJORS
English language and literature
Biology/biological sciences
Political science and government

## STUDENTS SPEAK OUT

### Academics

Dickinson College is a small school with about one professor for every 12 students. And while this has its benefits, one students jokes, "Be careful . . . if you skip or slack off, your professors will see you at the hockey game or the local bars and give you a piece of their minds." Students have plenty of opportunity to interact with the "well-read, super intelligent" profs in class, too, because "all courses are taught by professors," rather than TAs. Administrators are also easily accessible. In fact, around suppertime you're likely to "see the president and his wife eating in the cafeteria." Plenty of distribution requirements ensure that students get a broad taste of the academic spectrum. Once in class, you'll find that you're "expected to read heavy amounts, do independent research . . . presentations, group work, and lead discussions." With the Trout Gallery, the national headquarters of the Oral History Association, a recently renovated library, and a new science building on campus, students have an abundance of resources to help them on their journey on the academic high road.

### Life

Life "in a small town in central PA" isn't always exciting. According to one student, in hometown Carlisle, you'll find "a few bars, one movie theater, a handful of small parks, minimal shopping, lots of rednecks!" When students need a taste of city life, they "can get to Philly in under two hours, to Baltimore in an hour and a half, and to Harrisburg in about 20 minutes." But when they really want to get away, they go overseas. "Eighty-five percent of the student body studies abroad once in their four years, whether it be [for a] semester, year-long, summer, or winter program." Student sentiment about life on campus varies. While one complains that "there are not many things to do besides sit and drink in one's room," another counters that "there are lots of things to do socially here, 90 percent of them student-organized and run, but the students who complain can't see that." Aside from the fraternity or off-campus house parties, students can find "plays, intramural and intercollegiate sports to watch or play, movies, comedy clubs, dances, free food, Monday night football, lectures, and much, much more." Outdoorsy types enjoy "hiking, biking, caving, canoeing," or wandering around on the Appalachian Trail, which "runs pretty close to campus." Interestingly enough, some students would like to see a little more partying. "We still hear about 'Drinkinson,'" laments one student, referring to a nickname from several years ago, "but we're all wondering where the hell it went."

### Student Body

Students are the first to acknowledge the rich kid stigma they bear. "Dickinson definitely has a J.Crew image," one student admits. "However, the socioeconomic backgrounds of all students that attend the school are as diverse as you'll find anywhere in America." In fact, in recent years, "more and more public-school graduates and middle or lower [income] students are coming here and getting involved." Dickinson's diversity is improving, but many students tell us that "Dickinson could be a lot more diverse than it is." Nevertheless, the student body doesn't lack in "friendliness." According to one upperclassman, "I like being able to walk from my apartment to class, to lunch, to class, to work, and back and see/say 'hi' to 50 people I know." It's also the place for you if you like to study, as students often spend many of their night and weekend hours in the library's study rooms. But they're not simply a herd of nerds: "The students at Dickinson are smart as hell and love to party like rock stars."

# DICKINSON COLLEGE

FINANCIAL AID: 717-245-1308 • E-MAIL: ADMIT@DICKINSON.EDU • WEBSITE: WWW.DICKINSON.EDU

## ADMISSIONS

*Very important factors considered include:* extracurricular activities, minority status, secondary school record, talent/ability, volunteer work. *Important factors considered include:* alumni/ae relation, class rank, recommendations, standardized test scores, work experience. *Other factors considered include:* character/personal qualities, essays, geographical residence, interview, state residency. The SAT I recommended. TOEFL required of all international applicants. High school diploma or GED is required. *High school units required/recommended:* 16 total required; 4 English required, 3 math required, 3 science required, 2 science lab required, 2 foreign language required, 3 foreign language recommended, 2 social studies required, 2 elective required.

### The Inside Word

Dickinson's admissions process is typical of most small liberal arts colleges. The best candidates for such a place are those with solid grades and broad extracurricular involvement—the stereotypical "well-rounded student." Admissions selectivity is kept in check by a strong group of competitor colleges that fight tooth and nail for their cross-applicants.

## FINANCIAL AID

*Students should submit:* FAFSA, CSS/Financial Aid PROFILE, state aid form, noncustodial (divorced/separated) parent's statement, business/farm supplement. Regular filing deadline is February 1. The Princeton Review suggests that all financial aid forms be submitted as soon as possible after January 1. *Need-based scholarships/grants offered:* Pell, SEOG, state scholarships/grants, private scholarships, the school's own gift aid. *Loan aid offered:* FFEL Subsidized Stafford, FFEL Unsubsidized Stafford, FFEL PLUS, Federal Perkins, college/university loans from institutional funds. Federal Work-Study Program available. Institutional employment available. Applicants will be notified of awards on or about March 1. Off-campus job opportunities are good.

## FROM THE ADMISSIONS OFFICE

"College is more than a collection of courses. It is about crossing traditional boundaries, about seeing the interrelationships among different subjects, about learning a paradigm for solving problems, about developing critical thinking and communication skills, and about speaking out on issues that matter. Dickinson was founded to be different from the 15 colleges that existed in our nation before it: to provide a "useful" education, where students would learn by doing, through hands-on experiences and engagement with the community the region, the nation and the world. And this is truer today than ever, with workshop science courses replacing traditional lectures, fieldwork experiences in community studies where students take oral histories, and 12 study centers abroad in nontourist cities where students, under the guidance of a Dickinson faculty director, experience a true international culture. Almost 80 percent of the student body studies abroad, preparing them to compete and succeed in a complex global world."

## SELECTIVITY

| | |
|---|---|
| **Admissions Rating** | 82 |
| # of applicants | 3,820 |
| % of applicants accepted | 64 |
| % of acceptees attending | 25 |
| # accepting a place on wait list | 190 |
| % admitted from wait list | 2 |
| # of early decision applicants | 179 |
| % accepted early decision | 74 |

### FRESHMAN PROFILE

| | |
|---|---|
| Range SAT Verbal | 580-670 |
| Average SAT Verbal | 623 |
| Range SAT Math | 570-650 |
| Average SAT Math | 612 |
| Average ACT Composite | 27 |
| Minimum TOEFL | 550 |
| % graduated top 10% of class | 47 |
| % graduated top 25% of class | 79 |
| % graduated top 50% of class | 97 |

### DEADLINES

| | |
|---|---|
| Early decision | 11/15 |
| Early decision notification | 12/15 |
| Regular admission | 2/1 |
| Regular notification | 3/31 |
| Nonfall registration? | yes |

### APPLICANTS ALSO LOOK AT
**AND OFTEN PREFER**
Lehigh University
Connecticut College
Hamilton College
College of William and Mary
**AND SOMETIMES PREFER**
Bates College, Bucknell University
Franklin & Marshall College
**AND RARELY PREFER**
Pennsylvania State University—
University Park
Gettysburg College
George Washington University

## FINANCIAL FACTS

| | |
|---|---|
| **Financial Aid Rating** | 87 |
| Tuition | $28,380 |
| Room and board | $7,210 |
| Books and supplies | $750 |
| Required fees | $260 |
| % frosh receiving aid | 55 |
| % undergrads receiving aid | 59 |
| Avg frosh grant | $14,238 |
| Avg frosh loan | $3,405 |

# DREW UNIVERSITY

36 MADISON AVENUE, MADISON, NJ 07940-1493 • ADMISSIONS: 973-408-3739 • FAX: 973-408-3068

## CAMPUS LIFE

| | |
|---|---|
| Quality of Life Rating | 87 |
| Type of school | private |
| Affiliation | Methodist |
| Environment | suburban |

### STUDENTS

| | |
|---|---|
| Total undergrad enrollment | 1,558 |
| % male/female | 39/61 |
| % from out of state | 44 |
| % from public high school | 65 |
| % live on campus | 89 |
| % African American | 4 |
| % Asian | 6 |
| % Caucasian | 62 |
| % Hispanic | 5 |
| % international | 1 |

### SURVEY SAYS . . .
Beautiful campus
Students aren't religious
Class discussions encouraged
Athletic facilities are great
Classes are small
Great computer facilities
Diversity lacking on campus

## ACADEMICS

| | |
|---|---|
| Academic Rating | 90 |
| Calendar | semester |
| Student/faculty ratio | 12:1 |
| Profs interesting rating | 95 |
| Profs accessible rating | 98 |
| % profs teaching UG courses | 100 |
| Avg lab size | 10-19 students |
| Avg reg class size | 10-19 students |

### MOST POPULAR MAJORS
Political science and government
Psychology
English language and literature

## STUDENTS SPEAK OUT

### Academics

Exciting opportunities abound for undergraduates at Drew University, a small, pretty campus located just 35 miles from midtown Manhattan. Enthuses one student, "The greatest strengths of Drew are the opportunities. We have access to a number of study abroad programs that are both short- and long-term." Another elaborates: "Drew really makes an effort to make sure every student has a study abroad experience, whether it is through a Drew International Seminar that lasts one month, to a semester or year. Drew also has good connections. Because of the close proximity to New York, they are able to offer the 'Wall Street Semester' and the 'Art Semester.' You can also take advantage of the 'U.N. Semester in D.C.' I have never heard a bad review of any of these programs." An "astounding amount of varied internships and job-placement opportunities after graduation" please Drew's largely career-minded student population. Students also appreciate the "phenomenal attention and level of education. The majority of the classes here at Drew are 15 people, so you are constantly interacting with your professor. Basically, you are on a one-on-one basis with people that are experts in the things that they teach. As long as you do your part and exert some effort, it is impossible to do poorly at Drew University." Administrators earn similarly high marks: reports one undergrad, "It is very easy to get an appointment with most of the deans and professors at Drew. The administration is very lenient about things such as academic probation and required leave."

### Life

Drew undergrads agree that "Drew doesn't provide enough interesting activities that kids actually want to go to." Explains one undergrad, "Although the student activities board does a great job of planning on-campus events for the week, the weekends can be dead. So many people live close enough that Drew can be called a 'suitcase school'—people are packing up and going home" on the weekends. Hometown Madison doesn't offer much in the way of diversion: the town "isn't right outside your door, and most students don't have cars. There's not much going on in town anyway; it's not really centered on college life." Agrees one student, "The town does not encourage the students to visit their restaurants, stores, and theaters." Fortunately, "New York City is the savior. You cannot complain that there is nothing to do as long as you have ten bucks for train fare." On the upside, students appreciate that "the beauty of the school is incredible. When I first saw campus pictures I was a skeptic, but it is even better than the brochures." Campus speakers, the quality and diversity of whom result from Drew's proximity to a large, international city, are quite popular; notes one student, "Sometimes Drew has speakers on campus that discuss various things, like Buddhism in Japan or African art in Mozambique—stuff like that. Those are popular things to go to and the students enjoy them." Students also like the fact that "there or no frats or sororities, which is wonderful because parties and social gatherings are open to everyone."

### Student Body

The "intelligent and hard-working" students of Drew include "a lot of theater students" among the many pre-professionals. Most are Jerseyites "from very rich families, and they act like it." Reports one student, "They all look the same!!! GAP, J.Crew, L.L. Bean. White, white, white. Diversity? Ummm, no! Students are very cliquish." Adds another, "Students here segregate themselves in every way possible. It is amazing how homogeneous the cliques can be . . . . For such a small school, you would think it would force people to interact more." Even so, "there are a lot of nice people here; you just have to really look for them."

# DREW UNIVERSITY

FINANCIAL AID: 973-408-3112 • E-MAIL: CADM@DREW.EDU • WEBSITE: WWW.DREW.EDU

## ADMISSIONS
*Very important factors considered include:* secondary school record. *Important factors considered include:* class rank, standardized test scores. *Other factors considered include:* alumni/ae relation, character/personal qualities, essays, extracurricular activities, interview, minority status, recommendations, talent/ability, volunteer work, work experience. SAT I or ACT required; SAT I preferred. TOEFL required of all international applicants. *High school units required/recommended:* 4 English recommended, 3 math recommended, 2 science recommended, 2 foreign language recommended, 2 social studies recommended, 2 history recommended, 3 elective recommended.

### The Inside Word
Drew suffers greatly from the annual mass exodus of New Jersey's college-age residents and a lack of recognition by others. Application totals have increased slightly, but the university must begin to enroll more of its admitted students before any significant change in selectivity will occur. This makes Drew a great choice for solid students, and easier to get into than it should be given its quality.

## FINANCIAL AID
*Students should submit:* FAFSA, CSS/Financial Aid PROFILE. Regular filing deadline is February 15. The Princeton Review suggests that all financial aid forms be submitted as soon as possible after January 1. *Need-based scholarships/grants offered:* Pell, SEOG, state scholarships/grants, private scholarships, the school's own gift aid. *Loan aid offered:* FFEL Subsidized Stafford, FFEL Unsubsidized Stafford, FFEL PLUS, Federal Perkins, state loans. Federal Work-Study Program available. Institutional employment available. Applicants will be notified of awards on or about March 31. Off-campus job opportunities are excellent.

## FROM THE ADMISSIONS OFFICE
"At Drew, great teachers are transforming the undergraduate learning experience. With a commitment to teaching, Drew professors have made educating undergraduates their top priority. With a spirit of innovation, they have brought the most advanced technology and distinctive modes of experiential learning into the Drew classroom. The result is a stimulating and challenging education that connects the traditional liberal arts and sciences to the workplace and to the world."

## SELECTIVITY

| | |
|---|---:|
| **Admissions Rating** | 89 |
| # of applicants | 2,587 |
| % of applicants accepted | 72 |
| % of acceptees attending | 21 |
| # of early decision applicants | 75 |
| % accepted early decision | 97 |

### FRESHMAN PROFILE
| | |
|---|---:|
| Range SAT Verbal | 560-670 |
| Average SAT Verbal | 620 |
| Range SAT Math | 540-640 |
| Average SAT Math | 590 |
| Minimum TOEFL | 550 |
| % graduated top 10% of class | 33 |
| % graduated top 25% of class | 71 |
| % graduated top 50% of class | 92 |

### DEADLINES
| | |
|---|---:|
| Early decision | 12/1 |
| Early decision notification | 12/24 |
| Regular admission | 2/15 |
| Regular notification | 3/20 |
| Nonfall registration? | yes |

### APPLICANTS ALSO LOOK AT AND SOMETIMES PREFER
NYU
Muhlenberg
Skidmore
Connecticut College
Franklin and Marshall
Dickinson
College of New Jersey
Rutgers

## FINANCIAL FACTS

| | |
|---|---:|
| **Financial Aid Rating** | 84 |
| Tuition | $27,360 |
| Room and board | $7,644 |
| Books and supplies | $821 |
| Required fees | $546 |
| % undergrads receiving aid | 48 |
| Avg frosh grant | $13,986 |
| Avg frosh loan | $3,490 |

# DREXEL UNIVERSITY

3141 CHESTNUT STREET, PHILADELPHIA, PA 19104 • ADMISSIONS: 215-895-2400 • FAX: 215-895-5939

## CAMPUS LIFE

| Quality of Life Rating | 68 |
| --- | --- |
| Type of school | private |
| Environment | urban |

### STUDENTS
| | |
| --- | --- |
| Total undergrad enrollment | 11,584 |
| % male/female | 61/39 |
| % from out of state | 36 |
| % from public high school | 70 |
| % live on campus | 25 |
| % in (# of) fraternities | 12 (16) |
| % in (# of) sororities | 8 (6) |
| % African American | 10 |
| % Asian | 15 |
| % Caucasian | 63 |
| % Hispanic | 2 |
| % international | 5 |

### SURVEY SAYS...
Popular college radio
Musical organizations aren't popular
High cost of living
Students aren't religious
Class discussions are rare
Campus difficult to get around
Ethnic diversity on campus
Lots of long lines and red tape
Political activism is (almost) nonexistent

## ACADEMICS

| Academic Rating | 73 |
| --- | --- |
| Calendar | differs by program |
| Student/faculty ratio | 14:1 |
| Profs interesting rating | 90 |
| Profs accessible rating | 89 |
| % profs teaching UG courses | 100 |
| Avg lab size | 20-29 students |
| Avg reg class size | 10-19 students |

### MOST POPULAR MAJORS
Computer science
Electrical, electronics, and communications engineering
Mechanical engineering

## STUDENTS SPEAK OUT

### Academics

Drexel University is known for its co-op program, which adds an extra year to an undergraduate education, and provides three half-year internships with companies in and around the Philadelphia area. The co-op program "is the best part of Drexel." Some students complain that the course work is "unchallenging," and that while some of the professors are good, others are not. The university employs some foreign professors, and students grumble about the difficulty understanding many of them. Classes often get canceled, and students find that it is difficult to get into required classes because not enough sections are offered.

Students gush about the wireless system that enables a student anywhere on campus to connect to the Internet via a T1 connection. They note, however, that the $5 million system allows faculty to post "assignments, study guides, notes, and exam times and locations for each class." Many believe that the engineering and hotel management departments are among the university's best. While students have mixed feelings about the quality of a Drexel education, they agree that "the Drexel Shaft," perpetrated by the administration, "is running the school into the ground." Students believe that "they accept too many students, have no place to house them, and spend too much time recruiting new students and not enough time keeping current students satisfied." The prevailing attitude amongst the administration is that the students are "customers." Administrative offices "are not coordinated with each other, and if you want something done, you have to do it yourself." The administrative problems begin at the top levels; student issues are "only cared about . . . if they were going to do it anyway."

### Life

Students love the fact that Drexel is located only five blocks away from Center City, Philadelphia. The City of Brotherly Love offers numerous cultural opportunities, from the museums and art galleries, to the city's four professional sports franchises, to the fantastic zoo. National music acts perform in town every night in venues of varying size. "It may be because we have an inner-city campus, but this whole East Coast urban feeling kind of creates this feeling of a hectic, nonstop lifestyle," writes one student. "Everyone is either working hard or playing hard. There's no such thing as relaxing and doing nothing." There are plenty of nightclubs and bars in the area, and students often attend frat parties and visit the neighboring University of Pennsylvania. Undergrads spend much of their time studying and praise the quality of the school newspaper. A significant number of students work off campus, and their prolonged absence diminishes school spirit.

### Student Body

Drexel students describe their peers as "apathetic" but "friendly and diverse," claiming "everyone gets along because there is a common bitterness against the school's administration." International students are valued for the different views that they bring to the university. Though certain groups "tend to stick together, I don't think they try to discriminate." Still, the "Drexel Shaft" is a "bond that ties us together." Another student adds, "We bond in our utter hatred of the Drexel empire." The Greek system also brings students together.

# DREXEL UNIVERSITY

FINANCIAL AID: 215-895-2535 • E-MAIL: ENROLL@DREXEL.EDU • WEBSITE: WWW.DREXEL.EDU

## ADMISSIONS

*Very important factors considered include:* class rank, essays, secondary school record, standardized test scores. *Important factors considered include:* character/personal qualities, extracurricular activities, interview, recommendations, talent/ability. *Other factors considered include:* alumni/ae relation, minority status, volunteer work, work experience. SAT I or ACT required; SAT I preferred. TOEFL required of all international applicants. High school diploma or GED is required. *High school units required/recommended:* 3 math required, 1 science required, 1 science lab required, 1 foreign language recommended.

### *The Inside Word*

Drexel's distinct nature creates a high level of self-selection in the applicant pool, and most decent students are admitted.

## FINANCIAL AID

*Students should submit:* FAFSA. The Princeton Review suggests that all financial aid forms be submitted as soon as possible after January 1. *Need-based scholarships/grants offered:* Pell, SEOG, state scholarships/grants, private scholarships, the school's own gift aid, United Negro College Fund. *Loan aid offered:* FFEL Subsidized Stafford, FFEL Unsubsidized Stafford, FFEL PLUS, Federal Perkins, college/university loans from institutional funds. Federal Work-Study Program available. Institutional employment available. Applicants will be notified of awards on a rolling basis beginning on or about April 1. Off-campus job opportunities are excellent.

## FROM THE ADMISSIONS OFFICE

"Since its inception in 1891, Drexel University has gained national recognition among colleges and universities for its academic excellence, experiential education program (Drexel Co-op), technological expertise, and curricular innovation. In 1998, Drexel began operating one of the Philadelphia region's premier medical and health sciences schools, MCP Hahnemann University. In April, Drexel's Board of Trustees unanimously voted to approve merging MCP Hahnemann into Drexel University.

"With the addition of the nation's largest private medical school, an outstanding college of nursing and health professions, and one of only two schools of public health in Pennsylvania, Drexel University now comprises 12 academic colleges and schools. By this summer, we will offer 175 degree programs to some 11,500 undergraduates and 4,200 graduate students. Alumni will number 90,000, and the size of the full-time faculty will exceed 1,000.

"The post-merger Drexel will join the fewer than 50 private universities classified by the Carnegie Foundation as Doctoral/Research Universities-Extensive, which include Carnegie Mellon, MIT, Caltech, and Penn. Drexel also joins the top 100 U.S. universities in federal research expenditures and market value of endowment. Another benefit of this merger is that qualified Drexel applicants can now pursue four new accelerated dual-degree programs in the health sciences: the Bachelor's/MD in Medicine; Bachelor's/Master's in Nursing; Bachelor's/Doctor of Physical Therapy; and Bachelor's/Master's for Physician Assistants.

"By combining our expertise in advanced technology and cooperative education with academic programs in medicine and health-related fields, we can now offer our students a unique set of skills with which to succeed in today's ever-changing world."

## SELECTIVITY

| | |
|---|---|
| Admissions Rating | 79 |
| # of applicants | 11,981 |
| % of applicants accepted | 61 |
| % of acceptees attending | 29 |
| # accepting a place on wait list | 66 |
| % admitted from wait list | 23 |

### FRESHMAN PROFILE

| | |
|---|---|
| Range SAT Verbal | 520-620 |
| Average SAT Verbal | 570 |
| Range SAT Math | 550-660 |
| Average SAT Math | 600 |
| Minimum TOEFL | 550 |
| Average HS GPA | 3.3 |
| % graduated top 10% of class | 23 |
| % graduated top 25% of class | 55 |
| % graduated top 50% of class | 88 |

### DEADLINES

| | |
|---|---|
| Regular admission | 3/1 |
| Nonfall registration? | yes |

### APPLICANTS ALSO LOOK AT AND OFTEN PREFER
American
Boston U.
U. Delaware

### AND SOMETIMES PREFER
U. Maryland—Coll. Park
Temple
LaSalle
Lehigh
Penn State—Univ. Park
Villanova

## FINANCIAL FACTS

| | |
|---|---|
| Financial Aid Rating | 78 |
| Tuition | $17,393 |
| Room and board | $9,090 |
| Books and supplies | $650 |
| Required fees | $1,020 |
| % frosh receiving aid | 73 |
| % undergrads receiving aid | 69 |

# DUKE UNIVERSITY

2138 CAMPUS DRIVE, DURHAM, NC 27708 • ADMISSIONS: 919-684-3214 • FAX: 919-681-8941

## CAMPUS LIFE

| | |
|---|---|
| Quality of Life Rating | 84 |
| Type of school | private |
| Affiliation | Methodist |
| Environment | urban |

### STUDENTS

| | |
|---|---|
| Total undergrad enrollment | 6,033 |
| % male/female | 52/48 |
| % from out of state | 85 |
| % from public high school | 66 |
| % live on campus | 82 |
| % in (# of) fraternities | 29 (19) |
| % in (# of) sororities | 42 (12) |
| % African American | 10 |
| % Asian | 15 |
| % Caucasian | 61 |
| % Hispanic | 7 |
| % international | 7 |

### SURVEY SAYS . . .
Everyone loves the Blue Devils
Great off-campus food
Great library
Great computer facilities
Students love Durham, NC
Diversity lacking on campus
(Almost) no one listens to college radio
(Almost) everyone smokes
Lots of conservatives

## ACADEMICS

| | |
|---|---|
| Academic Rating | 99 |
| Calendar | semester |
| Student/faculty ratio | 11:1 |
| Profs interesting rating | 92 |
| Profs accessible rating | 95 |
| % classes taught by TAs | 22 |
| Avg lab size | 10-19 students |
| Avg reg class size | 10-19 students |

### MOST POPULAR MAJORS
Psychology
Economics
Biology/biological sciences

## STUDENTS SPEAK OUT

### Academics
Duke undergraduates express themselves with the pride and confidence that comes with national basketball championships AND a stellar academic reputation. As one typical student put it, "Duke's academics and beauty remind us that Harvard is the Duke of the North." Explains another, "The academics here are top notch. It doesn't matter what field you go into, you are going to learn about the field, and more importantly, how to think about and analyze issues and events. I learned how to learn here." At the undergraduate level, Duke has two divisions: Trinity College of Arts and Sciences and the Pratt School of Engineering. Political science, economics, history, and engineering are favorite majors of this largely pre-professional student body. Though Duke is a major research university with world-class graduate programs, students report that their professors are "fantastic. This is why I came to Duke. In virtually all departments, the teaching faculty is superb. They do research, publish, and teach: a rare combination." Adds another, "I've only had one bad teacher experience out of the 16 classes I've taken! If you don't like the class you can always switch around your schedule during the first week. You're most likely to get into a class you want." Students appreciate the fact that they "do not receive an overload of work to do; we have a lot, but it is never anything that we can't handle."

### Life
When your school's men's basketball team is a perennial Division I frontrunner, it stands to reason that students will be somewhat obsessed with hoops. Duke undergrads are. They sleep outside the stadium to procure game tickets (an activity known as "tenting out in K-ville," and if you don't know what the "K" stands for then you probably don't belong at Duke), then "go crazy" during and after games. Notes one student, "Obviously, the athletic program is exceptional, and all Duke students are very supportive of athletics. You can tell walking around that a majority of people on campus are wearing Duke gear." Otherwise, unity on Duke's dual campuses (one drop-dead gorgeous where upperclassmen live, and one considerably less so where freshmen live) is somewhat disrupted by a strong Greek scene that "makes the social scene very elite." Students agree that "campus parties are always popular, and I think we have done a good job keeping them alive despite the stricter national alcohol rules within Greek life. Compared to my friends at other schools, Dukies seem to still party a lot more." They also agree that "Durham isn't the greatest city" and note happily that Chapel Hill, a mere 15 minutes down the road, is the quintessential college town. Students praise the West Campus ("It's so beautiful! I can't imagine being somewhere where the school was ugly to look at because a large part of Duke's appeal is the lovely grounds.") and the Doris Duke Gardens across the street ("The gardens are exquisite, and when the weather is nice, students flock to the lawns there to relax.").

### Student Body
The public perception of Duke's student body generally focuses on its "visible minority of social elitists who go out for cocktails and have the connections to get themselves out of any kind of trouble—white prep school types. I always know which handbag is 'in,' because 85 percent of the girls in this 'caste' strut around with it slung over their anorexic shoulders." However, students note that "there are definitely a wide range of people at Duke. You have your stereotypical 'Daddy's little girl' and frat-boy types, but you also have lots of individuals not afraid to stir things up." Students agree that "Duke tends to be slightly cliquish because of the Greek system or even because of racial differences. Everyone gets along with one another, but there's still this 'high-schoolish' superficiality that pervades the Duke campus." They also agree that "basketball brings everyone together, and second semester is an absolute madhouse every night there's a game on."

196 ■ THE BEST 351 COLLEGES

# DUKE UNIVERSITY

FINANCIAL AID: 919-684-6225 • E-MAIL: UNDERGRAD-ADMISSIONS@DUKE.EDU • WEBSITE: WWW.DUKE.EDU

## ADMISSIONS
*Very important factors considered include:* recommendations, secondary school record, standardized test scores, extracurricular activities, talent/ability. *Important factors considered include:* character/personal qualities, class rank, essays. *Other factors considered include:* alumni/ae relation, interview, minority status, state residency, volunteer work, work experience. SAT I or ACT required. High school diploma is required and GED is not accepted. *High school units required/recommended:* 20 total recommended; 4 English recommended, 3 math recommended, 3 science recommended, 3 foreign language recommended, 3 social studies recommended. Engineering applicants should have 4 math and 4 science.

### The Inside Word
The way in which Duke discusses its candidate-review process should be a basic model for all schools to use in their literature. Just about all highly selective admissions committees use rating systems similar to the one described above, but few are willing to publicly discuss them.

## FINANCIAL AID
*Students should submit:* FAFSA, CSS/Financial Aid PROFILE, noncustodial (divorced/separated) parent's statement, business/farm supplement, parent and student income tax returns. Regular filing deadline is February 1. The Princeton Review suggests that all financial aid forms be submitted as soon as possible after January 1. *Need-based scholarships/grants offered:* Pell, SEOG, state scholarships/grants, private scholarships, the school's own gift aid, ROTC. *Loan aid offered:* FFEL Subsidized Stafford, FFEL Unsubsidized Stafford, FFEL PLUS, Federal Perkins, college/university loans from institutional funds, private loans. Federal Work-Study Program available. Institutional employment available. Applicants will be notified of awards on or about April 1. Off-campus job opportunities are good.

## FROM THE ADMISSIONS OFFICE
"Duke University offers an interesting mix of tradition and innovation, undergraduate college and major research university, southern hospitality and international presence, and athletic prowess and academic excellence. Students come to Duke from all over the United States and the world and from a range of racial, ethnic, and socioeconomic backgrounds. They enjoy contact with a world-class faculty through small classes and independent study. More than 40 majors are available in the arts and sciences and engineering; arts and sciences students may also design their own curriculum through Program II. Certificate programs are available in a number of interdisciplinary areas. Special academic opportunities include FOCUS programs and seminars for first-year students, study abroad, study at the Duke Marine Laboratory and Duke Primate Center, the Duke in New York and Duke in Los Angeles arts programs, and an exchange program with Howard University. While admission to Duke is highly selective, applications of U.S. citizens and permanent residents are evaluated without regard to financial need and the university pledges to meet 100 percent of the demonstrated need of all admitted U.S. students and permanent residents. A limited amount of financial aid is also available for foreign citizens, and the university will meet the full demonstrated financial need for those admitted students as well."

## SELECTIVITY

| | |
|---|---|
| Admissions Rating | 99 |
| # of applicants | 15,884 |
| % of applicants accepted | 23 |
| % of acceptees attending | 45 |
| # accepting a place on wait list | N/A |
| % admitted from wait list | N/A |
| # of early decision applicants | 1,581 |
| % accepted early decision | 32 |

### FRESHMAN PROFILE
| | |
|---|---|
| Range SAT Verbal | 650-740 |
| Range SAT Math | 670-770 |
| Range ACT Composite | 29-33 |
| Average ACT Composite | 30 |
| Average HS GPA | 3.9 |
| % graduated top 10% of class | 89 |
| % graduated top 25% of class | 98 |
| % graduated top 50% of class | 100 |

### DEADLINES
| | |
|---|---|
| Early decision | 11/1 |
| Early decision notification | 12/15 |
| Regular admission | 1/2 |
| Regular notification | 4/1 |

### APPLICANTS ALSO LOOK AT AND OFTEN PREFER
Princeton
Harvard
Stanford, Yale

### AND SOMETIMES PREFER
Brown
Columbia
Dartmouth
Cornell
Penn

### AND RARELY PREFER
UNC Chapel Hill
U of Virginia
Northwestern U
Georgetown U

## FINANCIAL FACTS

| | |
|---|---|
| Financial Aid Rating | 85 |
| Tuition | $27,050 |
| Room and board | $7,921 |
| Books and supplies | $875 |
| Required fees | $794 |
| % frosh receiving aid | 39 |
| % undergrads receiving aid | 36 |
| Avg frosh grant | $7,190 |
| Avg frosh loan | $3,522 |

# DUQUESNE UNIVERSITY

600 FORBES AVENUE, PITTSBURGH, PA 15282 • ADMISSIONS: 412-396-5000 • FAX: 412-396-5644

## CAMPUS LIFE

| | |
|---|---|
| Quality of Life Rating | 70 |
| Type of school | private |
| Affiliation | Roman Catholic |
| Environment | urban |

### STUDENTS

| | |
|---|---|
| Total undergrad enrollment | 5,556 |
| % male/female | 42/58 |
| % from out of state | 19 |
| % from public high school | 79 |
| % live on campus | 48 |
| % in (# of) fraternities | 21 (10) |
| % in (# of) sororities | 15 (9) |
| % African American | 4 |
| % Asian | 1 |
| % Caucasian | 83 |
| % Hispanic | 2 |
| % international | 3 |
| # of countries represented | 73 |

### SURVEY SAYS . . .
Students love Pittsburgh, PA
Very little drug use
Great off-campus food
Student publications are ignored
High cost of living
Political activism is (almost)
nonexistent
Student government is unpopular
Dorms are like dungeons
Students get along with local
community

## ACADEMICS

| | |
|---|---|
| Academic Rating | 72 |
| Calendar | semester |
| Student/faculty ratio | 15:1 |
| Profs interesting rating | 92 |
| Profs accessible rating | 91 |
| Avg lab size | 10-19 students |
| Avg reg class size | 20-29 students |

### MOST POPULAR MAJORS
Pre-professional doctor of pharmacy
Information technology
Elementary education

## STUDENTS SPEAK OUT

### Academics
Duquesne University students are satisfied with the education they receive. They are very career-oriented and believe that a Duquesne education prepares them for life after college. Students adore their instructors, and few classes—if any—are taught by TAs. A secondary education major writes, "I believe Duquesne University has an excellent staff who are always willing to assist the students as much as they can." A sophomore accounting major adds, "All of [my professors] have been willing to help outside of class." Professors keep classes interesting, comments one psychology major. Another student declares, "When I first came to college, I thought everything was going to be up to me. I was very surprised at how much my professors at Duquesne University are willing to help me." The administration fares just as well with Duquesne's students. "This school's administration [is] very thoughtful and caring. They will always be there when you need them," an athletic training major says. The administration is "available at convenient times to help answer any questions we may have," a special education major says. This wouldn't be The Best 345 Colleges without at least one student gripe, and for Duquesne students it's that Duquesne is too expensive. Also, while the university "offers great learning and research opportunities, even for undergrads," students believe that the library and research centers need improvement.

### Life
Duquesne is located in Pittsburgh, and students take advantage of the city's many cultural diversions. Students enjoy "both the benefits of a small campus and the opportunities of city life." Many of the university's students are commuters, and many residential students often go home on the weekend. Those who remain on campus tell us that campus life is only "satisfactory" because the place is a seeming ghostown from Friday through Sunday. Those who live on campus spend their weeknights studying and going to downtown clubs and enjoying late-night, on-campus movies on the weekends. "Life at school is fun. I feel very safe and comfortable on campus, despite the fact that we are located in the city," one biology major comments. Commuting students rave about the commuter center, where many activities go down. Parties at neighboring universities, such as the University of Pittsburgh and Carnegie Mellon, offer extra-campus amusement. The symphony is another popular distraction, as are the numerous coffee shops on the city's south side. Students say that the food and dorms need improvement ("fix the heating and cooling systems"), and they complain about the dorm policies that are "way too strict about visitors."

### Student Body
Duquesne is a Roman Catholic institution, one where students are extremely committed to volunteer work and to helping their fellow students. "You can always find someone willing to lend a helping hand," writes one biology major. Though some students mention that the campus lacks diversity, most agree that "everyone here is friendly and they seem to get along." Students mention that cliques are prevalent on campus. Nevertheless, you'll hear many students say, "I've met the best friends of my life at this campus." Oh yeah, and "everyone smokes except about 5 percent of the students." Commuter students have little interaction with those who live on campus full-time.

198 ■ THE BEST 351 COLLEGES

# DUQUESNE UNIVERSITY

FINANCIAL AID: 412-396-6607 • E-MAIL: ADMISSIONS@DUQ.EDU • WEBSITE: WWW.DUQ.EDU

## ADMISSIONS

*Very important factors considered include:* secondary school record. *Important factors considered include:* character/personal qualities, essays, extracurricular activities, recommendations, standardized test scores, talent/ability. *Other factors considered include:* alumni/ae relation, class rank, interview, volunteer work, work experience. SAT I or ACT required. High school diploma or GED is required. *High school units required/recommended:* 16 total recommended; 4 English recommended, 2 math recommended, 2 science recommended, 2 foreign language recommended, 2 social studies recommended.

### The Inside Word

With such a high admit rate, the admissions process should create little anxiety in all but the weakest candidates.

## FINANCIAL AID

*Students should submit:* FAFSA, institution's own financial aid form. Regular filing deadline is May 1. The Princeton Review suggests that all financial aid forms be submitted as soon as possible after January 1. *Need-based scholarships/grants offered:* Pell, SEOG, state scholarships/grants, private scholarships, the school's own gift aid. *Loan aid offered:* FFEL Subsidized Stafford, FFEL Unsubsidized Stafford, FFEL PLUS, Federal Perkins, Federal Nursing, college/university loans from institutional funds, health profession loans. Federal Work-Study Program available. Institutional employment available. Applicants will be notified of awards on a rolling basis beginning on or about March 15. Off-campus job opportunities are excellent.

## FROM THE ADMISSIONS OFFICE

"Duquesne University was founded in 1878 by the Holy Ghost Fathers. Although it is a private, Roman Catholic institution, Duquesne is proud of its ecumenical reputation. The total University enrollment is 9,595. Duquesne University's attractive and secluded campus is set on a 43-acre hilltop ('the bluff') overlooking the large corporate metropolis of Pittsburgh's Golden Triangle. It offers a wide variety of educational opportunities, from the liberal arts to modern professional training. Duquesne is a medium-size university striving to offer personal attention to its students while having the versatility and opportunities of a true university. A deep sense of tradition is combined with innovation and flexibility to make the Duquesne experience both challenging and rewarding. The Palumbo Convocation/Recreation Complex features a 6,300-seat arena, home court to the University's Division I basketball teams; racquetball and handball courts; weight rooms; and saunas. Extracurricular activities are recognized as an essential part of college life, complementing academics in the process of total student development. Students are involved in nearly 100 university-sponsored activities, and Duquesne's location gives students the opportunity to enjoy sports and cultural events both on campus and citywide. There are five residence halls with the capacity to house 2,777 students."

### SELECTIVITY

| | |
|---|---|
| Admissions Rating | 76 |
| # of applicants | 3,879 |
| % of applicants accepted | 91 |
| % of acceptees attending | 40 |
| # accepting a place on wait list | 22 |
| % admitted from wait list | 82 |
| # of early decision applicants | 184 |
| % accepted early decision | 98 |

### FRESHMAN PROFILE

| | |
|---|---|
| Range SAT Verbal | 490-590 |
| Average SAT Verbal | 545 |
| Range SAT Math | 490-600 |
| Average SAT Math | 545 |
| Range ACT Composite | 21-26 |
| Average ACT Composite | 24 |
| Average HS GPA | 3.5 |
| % graduated top 10% of class | 22 |
| % graduated top 25% of class | 51 |
| % graduated top 50% of class | 83 |

### DEADLINES

| | |
|---|---|
| Early decision | 11/1 |
| Early decision notification | 12/15 |
| Priority admission | 11/1 |
| Regular admission | 7/1 |
| Nonfall registration? | yes |

### APPLICANTS ALSO LOOK AT AND OFTEN PREFER
Pittsburgh State
Penn State
Carnegie Mellon

### AND SOMETIMES PREFER
Indiana U of Pennsylvania
Allegheny College
Washington & Jefferson

### AND RARELY PREFER
St. Bonaventure
Marquette

### FINANCIAL FACTS

| | |
|---|---|
| Financial Aid Rating | 82 |
| Tuition | $17,012 |
| Room and board | $7,170 |
| Books and supplies | $600 |
| Required fees | $1,515 |
| % frosh receiving aid | 67 |
| % undergrads receiving aid | 64 |
| Avg frosh grant | $8,960 |
| Avg frosh loan | $5,590 |

# EARLHAM COLLEGE

801 NATIONAL ROAD WEST, RICHMOND, IN 47374 • ADMISSIONS: 765-983-1600 • FAX: 765-983-1560

## CAMPUS LIFE

| | |
|---|---|
| Quality of Life Rating | 81 |
| Type of school | private |
| Affiliation | Quaker |
| Environment | suburban |

### STUDENTS

| | |
|---|---|
| Total undergrad enrollment | 1,080 |
| % male/female | 44/56 |
| % from out of state | 75 |
| % from public high school | 65 |
| % live on campus | 87 |
| % African American | 8 |
| % Asian | 3 |
| % Caucasian | 77 |
| % Hispanic | 2 |
| % international | 7 |
| # of countries represented | 35 |

### SURVEY SAYS . . .
Campus easy to get around
Athletic facilities are great
Political activism is hot
Great library
No one cheats
Diverse students interact
Students don't get along with local community
Students don't like Richmond, IN
Low cost of living

## ACADEMICS

| | |
|---|---|
| Academic Rating | 91 |
| Calendar | semester |
| Student/faculty ratio | 11:1 |
| % profs teaching UG courses | 100 |
| Avg lab size | 20-29 students |
| Avg reg class size | 10-19 students |

### MOST POPULAR MAJORS
History
Biology/biological sciences
Psychology

## STUDENTS SPEAK OUT

### Academics
The undergraduates of Earlham College agree that "the underlying Quaker values are what make this school so great . . . . It has nothing to do with religion and everything to do with community." Indeed, the "community, [and] noncompetitive atmosphere" at Earlham are what students appreciate most. Nurturing this unique environment is "Earlham's principle of according equal respect to all people." This code means that "everyone, up to and including the school president, operates on a first-name basis, which really underscores the personal level of interaction." The result is a free flow of ideas and opinions; explains one undergraduate, "We are encouraged to discuss difficult issues, such as issues of diversity of religion, political views, cultural identities, etc., and people don't have to be afraid to disagree." Professors excel in the classroom. The profs here "have a lot of knowledge about and a huge passion for what they are teaching." Some students warn, "Professors in smaller majors here leave occasionally because they are not getting the support they need. It is hard to attract some newer professors because we don't pay our professors here like many competing schools." Also, because "classes are often only offered every other semester or once every two or four years, class conflicts often occur between two classes you deem necessary," cautioned one student, who proceeds to point out the benefits of attending a tiny school: "The small classes and closeness to professors allow for individual planning and independent study opportunities."

### Life
Students agree that Earlham is "a place where you make your own fun," primarily because hometown Richmond "offers nothing [socially]. It is a tomb, a void of nothingness." For many, "The fun here comes from those late-night talks that last until the next morning and cost you an entire pack of cigarettes. The intellectual part of this school never stops and is so cool that the fun in daily life is many times derived from being enlightened by one of your peers." Undergrads also report, "The events (speakers, poets, musicians) that are brought to campus are usually pretty good. The movies shown on campus are often worth checking out, too." Clubs and organizations claim a good portion of students' leisure time; writes one undergrad, "The thing that I like about extracurriculars here is that they aren't really 'extra' at all. Most students are involved in activities outside of class that are also somehow related to their academic interests." The party scene here is subdued; "You won't find big frat-like parties here (no frats). Every so often there's a rowdy party, but parties usually suck or are pretty mellow (the farm party and the Hash Run are usually pretty good). Just hanging out with a group of friends is usually your best bet for a 'party.'" Those seeking more excitement suggest road-tripping, noting that "Oxford [Ohio] (Miami University), Indianapolis, and Dayton are not far, so we can go hang out there."

### Student Body
The typical Earlham student is "somewhat crunchy (but post-modern intellectual, too), politically left, could be barefoot, could be smoking a cigarette, and is likely to [have] a piercing that is not in the ear." All the while any of them could be members or patrons of the college's "Hugging Club." Reports one student, "The best way to describe an Earlham student might be the absence of showering. It is probably that almighty funk that in its sticky, smelly way binds us together." Students are "politically and environmentally conscious," and "everyone seems to have practically the same views. Just about all of us are left-wing pacifists." Warns one undergrad, "We are not accepting of right-wing views." Adds one of the school's few social and political conservatives, "The school accepts everything that society apparently does not (homosexuals, alternative religions, drug use, alternative medicine, vegans . . .)". Another adds that, "Overall, Earlham is a very tolerant place where students never have to be afraid to disagree." Several students noted that Earlham could benefit from a healthy dose of "non-liberals" to offer some balance.

# EARLHAM COLLEGE

FINANCIAL AID: 765-983-1217 • E-MAIL: ADMISSION@EARLHAM.EDU • WEBSITE: WWW.EARLHAM.EDU

## ADMISSIONS

*Very important factors considered include:* character/personal qualities, essays, minority status, recommendations, secondary school record. *Important factors considered include:* extracurricular activities, interview, standardized test scores, talent/ability, volunteer work. *Other factors considered include:* alumni/ae relation, class rank, geographical residence, religious affiliation/commitment, state residency, work experience. SAT I or ACT required; SAT I preferred. TOEFL required of all international applicants. High school diploma or GED is required. *High school units required/recommended:* 15 total required; 4 English required, 3 math required, 4 math recommended, 2 science required, 3 science recommended, 2 foreign language required, 3 foreign language recommended, 1 social studies required, 1 history required, 2 elective required, 8 elective recommended.

### The Inside Word

Like most colleges with a Friends affiliation, Earlham has a sincere interest in the person it admits. Essays and interviews carry virtually as much weight as the numbers. Quakers, minorities, legacies, and state residents receive special consideration in the admissions process, but special consideration is what this place is really all about. Earlham deserves a much higher national public awareness level than it has. Hopefully, this entry will help.

## FINANCIAL AID

*Students should submit:* FAFSA, institution's own financial aid form. The Princeton Review suggests that all financial aid forms be submitted as soon as possible after January 1. *Need-based scholarships/grants offered:* Pell, SEOG, state scholarships/grants, private scholarships, the school's own gift aid. *Loan aid offered:* Direct Subsidized Stafford, Direct Unsubsidized Stafford, Direct PLUS, Federal Perkins, college/university loans from institutional funds. Federal Work-Study Program available. Institutional employment available. Applicants will be notified of awards on a rolling basis beginning on or about March 30. Off-campus job opportunities are good.

## FROM THE ADMISSIONS OFFICE

"The world is full of people with good intentions. What it needs is people with the intellect, the vision, the skills, and the energy to back up their good intentions. It needs people who are able to make a difference. Although only a few students identify themselves as Quakers, Earlham retains those humanistic values of its tradition that have relevance to students of all backgrounds."

---

### SELECTIVITY

| | |
|---|---|
| Admissions Rating | 80 |
| # of applicants | 1,269 |
| % of applicants accepted | 78 |
| % of acceptees attending | 29 |
| # accepting a place on wait list | 11 |
| % admitted from wait list | 91 |
| # of early decision applicants | 45 |
| % accepted early decision | 93 |

#### FRESHMAN PROFILE

| | |
|---|---|
| Range SAT Verbal | 550-690 |
| Average SAT Verbal | 620 |
| Range SAT Math | 530-650 |
| Average SAT Math | 590 |
| Range ACT Composite | 23-29 |
| Average ACT Composite | 26 |
| Minimum TOEFL | 550 |
| Average HS GPA | 3.4 |
| % graduated top 10% of class | 28 |
| % graduated top 25% of class | 56 |
| % graduated top 50% of class | 84 |

#### DEADLINES

| | |
|---|---|
| Early decision | 12/1 |
| Early decision notification | 12/15 |
| Regular admission | 2/15 |
| Regular notification | 3/15 |
| Nonfall registration? | yes |

#### APPLICANTS ALSO LOOK AT AND OFTEN PREFER
Oberlin
Macalester

**AND SOMETIMES PREFER**
Grinnell
Wooster

**AND RARELY PREFER**
Kalamazoo
Beloit

### FINANCIAL FACTS

| | |
|---|---|
| Financial Aid Rating | 89 |
| Tuition | $23,920 |
| Room and board | $5,416 |
| Books and supplies | $550 |
| Required fees | $640 |
| % frosh receiving aid | 65 |
| % undergrads receiving aid | 65 |
| Avg frosh grant | $12,651 |
| Avg frosh loan | $3,168 |

# ECKERD COLLEGE

4200 54TH AVENUE SOUTH, ST. PETERSBURG, FL 33711 • ADMISSIONS: 727-864-8331 • FAX: 727-866-2304

## CAMPUS LIFE

| | |
|---|---|
| Quality of Life Rating | 89 |
| Type of school | private |
| Affiliation | Presbyterian |
| Environment | suburban |

### STUDENTS

| | |
|---|---|
| Total undergrad enrollment | 1,608 |
| % male/female | 46/54 |
| % from out of state | 70 |
| % from public high school | 80 |
| % live on campus | 69 |
| % African American | 3 |
| % Asian | 2 |
| % Caucasian | 83 |
| % Hispanic | 5 |
| % international | 6 |
| # of countries represented | 49 |

### SURVEY SAYS . . .
Students are happy
Different students interact
Registration is a breeze
Lots of beer drinking
(Almost) everyone smokes
Library needs improving
Lousy food on campus
Very small frat/sorority scene
Student publications are ignored
Very little drug use

## ACADEMICS

| | |
|---|---|
| Academic Rating | 84 |
| Calendar | 4-1-4 |
| Student/faculty ratio | 14:1 |
| Profs interesting rating | 94 |
| Profs accessible rating | 93 |
| % profs teaching UG courses | 100 |
| Avg reg class size | 20-29 students |

### MOST POPULAR MAJORS
Business administration/management
Marine science
Psychology

## STUDENTS SPEAK OUT

### Academics

Adding an entirely new meaning to the phrase "good learning environment," Eckerd College offers a solid liberal arts education in the idyllic setting of Florida's Gulf Coast. Given the easy access to water in almost any direction, it's no surprise that the marine and environmental sciences are Eckerd's strongest academic offerings. Students come from all over the nation and abroad to take advantage of the college's superb marine facilities and programs, often choosing Eckerd over better-known and more selective colleges and universities. Other academic strengths are in pre-professional studies, most notably business and management. Perhaps due to these strengths, "the opportunities for student research are phenomenal for an undergraduate institution." Though not as popular with students as the college would like it to be, the innovative Academy of Senior Professionals also presents outstanding opportunities for learning that are atypical of the college experience. The Academy brings retired professionals of varied persuasions to campus to serve as "mentors in residence" for an extended stay. Students speak highly of their faculty and visiting teachers, reporting that "the professors here really know their subjects and most have worked in their fields before coming to teach. . . . They are very helpful in and out of the classroom, always available for questions." Student satisfaction with the EC experience is tempered only in feelings expressed about the administration, which range from quite favorable to very critical—about normal for college students.

### Life

Campus life at Eckerd has quieted considerably since the school recently began aggressively enforcing the law against underage drinking. Reports a typical undergrad, "People complain about the social life on campus a lot. It's a really small campus and there are no fraternities or sororities, so there's really not much to do here on the weekends. Also, the drinking policies are pretty harsh, although the student government is working on changing this." Another adds, "Campus social life is nonexistent because of the new alcohol policy. It sucks! I only go off campus to hang out. It used to be really fun, one of the reasons I actually came here. Now we can't even have a beer at a barbecue!" For those who lament the current policy toward alcohol, please know that it is under review by a refreshed administration. Quite a few students point out, however, that "the beach is nearby, and a major city (Tampa) is within a half an hour." Students give a big thumbs-up to the beach and everything that goes with it: "I love this school because of the waterfront program. We can go sailing, canoeing, or swimming whenever we want for free." No doubt the beach contributes to the feeling of some that "life at Eckerd is pretty laid back," and "students are typically detached from reality. They live in their own country-club style. We rarely have student rallies in reaction to current events." Furthermore, Eckerd's small size makes it easy to get involved. It's "a great place for student leadership possibilities." Sports are very popular, as Eckerd has been quite successful in NCAA Division II basketball, baseball, tennis, and women's cross-country.

### Student Body

The EC student body includes a "strange mix, quite a few hippie types mixed with jock types and a sprinkling of hardworking overachievers." Many feel that "the size of the EC community, coupled with the fact that we don't have a Greek system, lends a real sense of community bonding and social strength." Some, however, point out that "there are a lot of students from families with a lot of money, so at times they can seem in general to be a bit close-minded and unaccepting of other types of people. Of course, not the entire school is like this, and there are a lot of really great smart people here." Another adds that "even though there is a good deal of ethnic diversity, there seems to be very little socioeconomic diversity." Ethnic diversity comes primarily in the form of a large international student body.

# ECKERD COLLEGE

FINANCIAL AID: 727-864-8334 • E-MAIL: ADMISSIONS@ECKERD.EDU • WEBSITE: WWW.ECKERD.EDU

## ADMISSIONS

*Very important factors considered include:* character/personal qualities, extracurricular activities, secondary school record. *Important factors considered include:* essays, interview, recommendations, standardized test scores, talent/ability, volunteer work, work experience. *Other factors considered include:* class rank. SAT I or ACT required; SAT II recommended. TOEFL required of all international applicants. High school diploma or GED is required. *High school units required/recommended:* 18 total required; 22 total recommended; 4 English required, 3 math required, 4 math recommended, 3 science required, 4 science recommended, 2 science lab required, 3 science lab recommended, 2 foreign language required, 3 foreign language recommended, 2 social studies required, 1 history required, 2 history recommended, 3 elective required.

### *The Inside Word*

Budding marine biologists are by far the strongest students at Eckerd. They make up a significant percentage of the college's total applicant pool and do much to provide for a more impressive freshman profile. Applications totals have made significant strides over the past two years.

## FINANCIAL AID

*Students should submit:* FAFSA. The Princeton Review suggests that all financial aid forms be submitted as soon as possible after January 1. *Need-based scholarships/grants offered:* Pell, SEOG, state scholarships/grants, private scholarships, the school's own gift aid. *Loan aid offered:* FFEL Subsidized Stafford, FFEL Unsubsidized Stafford, FFEL PLUS, Federal Perkins, college/university loans from institutional funds. Federal Work-Study Program available. Institutional employment available. Applicants will be notified of awards on a rolling basis beginning on or about February 1. Off-campus job opportunities are excellent.

## FROM THE ADMISSIONS OFFICE

"Eckerd's diverse student body comes from 49 states and 67 countries. In this international setting, the majors of international relations and international business are very popular. Close to 70 percent of our graduates spend at least one term studying abroad. The beautiful, waterfront campus is a perfect location for the study of marine science and environmental studies. We characterize Eckerd students as competent givers because of their extensive involvement in the life of the campus and their many volunteer service contributions to the local environment and the St. Petersburg community. The Academy of Senior Professionals draws to campus distinguished persons who have retired from fields our students aspire to enter. Academy members, such as the late novelist James Michener, Nobel Prize winner Elie Wiesel, and noted Black historian John Hope Franklin enrich classes and offer valuable counsel for career and life planning."

## SELECTIVITY

| | |
|---|---|
| Admissions Rating | 79 |
| # of applicants | 1,943 |
| % of applicants accepted | 79 |
| % of acceptees attending | 29 |
| # accepting a place on wait list | 57 |
| % admitted from wait list | 21 |

### FRESHMAN PROFILE

| | |
|---|---|
| Range SAT Verbal | 510-620 |
| Average SAT Verbal | 564 |
| Range SAT Math | 500-620 |
| Average SAT Math | 564 |
| Range ACT Composite | 20-26 |
| Average ACT Composite | 25 |
| Minimum TOEFL | 550 |
| Average HS GPA | 3.2 |
| % graduated top 10% of class | 16 |
| % graduated top 25% of class | 45 |
| % graduated top 50% of class | 81 |

### DEADLINES

| | |
|---|---|
| Priority admission | 2/15 |
| Nonfall registration? | yes |

### APPLICANTS ALSO LOOK AT AND OFTEN PREFER
Rollins College
College of Charleston
U of Central Florida

### AND SOMETIMES PREFER
U of Miami
Stetson U
U of Tampa

### AND RARELY PREFER
U of South Florida
Florida Southern College
Florida Atlantic U

## FINANCIAL FACTS

| | |
|---|---|
| Financial Aid Rating | 89 |
| Tuition | $22,538 |
| Room and board | $5,970 |
| Books and supplies | $1,000 |
| Required fees | $236 |
| % frosh receiving aid | 60 |
| % undergrads receiving aid | 57 |
| Avg frosh grant | $11,000 |
| Avg frosh loan | $3,500 |

# ELON UNIVERSITY

OFFICE OF ADMISSIONS, 2700 CAMPUS BOX, ELON, NC 27244-2010 • ADMISSIONS: 800-334-8448 • FAX: 336-278-7699

## CAMPUS LIFE

| | |
|---|---|
| Quality of Life Rating | 82 |
| Type of school | private |
| Affiliation | United Church of Christ |
| Environment | suburban |

### STUDENTS

| | |
|---|---|
| Total undergrad enrollment | 4,270 |
| % male/female | 39/61 |
| % from out of state | 72 |
| % from public high school | 79 |
| % live on campus | 63 |
| % in (# of) fraternities | 29 (9) |
| % in (# of) sororities | 39 (11) |
| % African American | 6 |
| % Asian | 1 |
| % Caucasian | 88 |
| % Hispanic | 1 |
| % international | 2 |
| # of countries represented | 41 |

### SURVEY SAYS . . .
Campus is beautiful
Classes are small
Students are happy
Campus easy to get around
Musical organizations are hot
Theater is hot
Athletic facilities are great

## ACADEMICS

| | |
|---|---|
| Academic Rating | 77 |
| Calendar | 4-1-4 |
| Student/faculty ratio | 15:1 |
| Profs interesting rating | 80 |
| Profs accessible rating | 85 |
| % profs teaching UG courses | 100 |
| Avg lab size | 20-29 students |
| Avg reg class size | 20-29 students |

### MOST POPULAR MAJORS
Business administration/management
Mass communications/media studies
Education

## STUDENTS SPEAK OUT

### Academics

Situated in a region of the country noted for quality private and public higher education, Elon University toes a tough academic line. Because of its relatively small size, Elon can boast a learning environment in which professors "all give the students their phone numbers and e-mail addresses" and "are readily available outside of the classroom." "It's nice to know that your professors actually know your name," comments one student. Elon's professors tend to focus on hands-on and interactive learning, which means that "in the classroom, many professors do not lecture, but pose questions for the class to respond to." Students are balanced in their evaluation of these discussion-oriented profs: "I have had professors that have changed my life," writes one student, "and professors that really shouldn't be teaching at all." A unique feature of Elon academic offerings is a program in engineering it offers in conjunction with North Carolina State University, Virginia Tech, Columbia University, Washington University in St. Louis, and North Carolina A&T. Students completing the program receive degrees from both institutions. While Elon offers 49 majors from which students can choose, some find that "there are limitations on the classes offered, [especially when] compared to a larger school." "Despite the aspects of Elon that I would change," concludes one undergraduate, "I feel that it is a good school and would recommend it to anyone looking for a personal learning environment in a beautiful setting."

### Life

Ever hear of former President George H.W. Bush? How about Queen Noor of Jordan, Nobel Peace Prize winner Desmond Tutu . . . did we mention broadcasting legend Walter Cronkite, historian David McCullough, or conservationist Jane Goodall? These are just a handful of the speakers who have appeared on campus recently. While students will admit that "there isn't a lot to do compared to a large school," they applaud the university for providing some impressive outlets—like these talks by headlining personalities. There are also "more than 125 student organizations," not to mention "events in The Zone, our student center, such as Monday night football, or Midnight Meals every Thursday, which always include food and features anything from a movie to a comedian to 'The Art of Kissing.' " Students can also hit the Greek parties that dominate the late-night social scene in the "very small" town of Elon. If students want to escape campus for a few hours, they're able to find some appealing options in the vicinity. "We're an hour's drive from Raleigh [and Winston-Salem], 30 minutes from Durham." Nearby Burlington offers a little diversion in the form of bowling and restaurants. The university's emphasis on internships, volunteering, and studying abroad also encourages students to explore the world beyond campus. Overall, Elon students believe they live the good life in "a very country- club kind of place."

### Student Body

"The Elon 'bubble' is a bit like *Beverly Hills: 90210*, only in North Carolina," jokes one student. "It's not uncommon to see kids driving around in BMWs and Lexuses" or donning wardrobes that leave some feeling that they are "living in an Abercrombie and Fitch" catalogue. While "diversity may be lacking" here, there's a "feeling of camaraderie" at Elon that everyone notices "when they visit for the first time." "I guess it's just that good southern hospitality kicking in!" exclaims an undergrad. Much of Elon's student body hails from mid-atlantic and southern states, though some come from "as far away as Japan and Yugoslavia." Students describe their peers in a variety of ways, ranging from "very religious" to "liberally biased." "Most are also smart and come from good families," according to one student, while another adds, "courteous, intelligent, caring, and generous" to the list of appropriate adjectives of his classmates. And, without question, the student population is "very Greek oriented."

# ELON UNIVERSITY

E-MAIL: ADMISSIONS@ELON.EDU • WEBSITE: WWW.ELON.EDU

## ADMISSIONS

*Very important factors considered include:* secondary school record, standardized test scores. *Important factors considered include:* class rank, essays. *Other factors considered include:* alumni/ae relation, character/personal qualities, extracurricular activities, minority status, recommendations, talent/ability, volunteer work, work experience. SAT I or ACT required. TOEFL required of all international applicants. High school diploma or GED is required. *High school units required/recommended:* 4 English required, 3 math required, 4 math recommended, 2 science required, 3 science recommended, 1 science lab required, 2 foreign language required, 2 social studies required, 1 history required.

### The Inside Word

Applicants with solid GPAs and test scores will have little trouble getting into Elon. To those who earn admission go the spoils! Elon has a standard liberal arts core curriculum, but goes above and beyond the call of duty in its commitment to provide each student with leadership training, internships, and study abroad opportunities. There are no flies on Elon kids.

## FINANCIAL AID

*Students should submit:* FAFSA, institution's own financial aid form, CSS/Financial Aid PROFILE. The Princeton Review suggests that all financial aid forms be submitted as soon as possible after January 1. *Need-based scholarships/grants offered:* Pell, SEOG, state scholarships/grants, private scholarships, the school's own gift aid. *Loan aid offered:* FFEL Subsidized Stafford, FFEL Unsubsidized Stafford, FFEL PLUS, Federal Perkins, state loans, college/university loans from institutional funds, privately funded alternative loans. Federal Work-Study Program available. Institutional employment available. Applicants will be notified of awards on a rolling basis beginning on or about March 30. Off-campus job opportunities are excellent.

## FROM THE ADMISSIONS OFFICE

"With an enrollment of about 4,400, Elon is the ideal size, with the resources of a university in a close-knit community atmosphere. Elon is recognized by the National Survey of Student Engagement as one of the most effective universities in the nation in actively engaging students in learning. They are challenged intellectually and supported as they develop an understanding of their roles as global citizens and put their knowledge into practice. Professors are mentors in a student-centered environment that blends academic and co-curricular activities, especially in flagship programs known as the Elon Experiences. Seventy-eight percent of students complete an internship (more than twice the national average), 85 percent participate in volunteer service projects, 54 percent hold leadership positions in 142 student organizations, and 58 percent study abroad, distinguishing Elon as the nation's top master's-level university in the percentage of students studying internationally. A 4-1-4 academic calendar allows students to devote January to travel abroad or to innovative on-campus courses such as the Holocaust in film and Literature, Globalization of Science, The Business of Nascar, Sport Psychology, and Contemporary Nature Writers. Each April, students present their research findings at the Student Undergraduate Research Forum. Elon also has one of the most beautiful campuses in the nation. Recent additions include new residence halls, Carol Grotnes Belk Library, Dalton McMichael Sr. Science Center, Belk Track, and Rhodes Stadium, home of the NCAA Division I-AA Phoenix football team. The newly renovated School of Communications building features the latest digital communications technologies and two television studios."

## SELECTIVITY

| | |
|---|---|
| Admissions Rating | 76 |
| # of applicants | 6,504 |
| % of applicants accepted | 50 |
| % of acceptees attending | 37 |
| # accepting a place on wait list | 954 |
| % admitted from wait list | 3 |
| # of early decision applicants | 447 |
| % accepted early decision | 72 |

### FRESHMAN PROFILE

| | |
|---|---|
| Range SAT Verbal | 520-610 |
| Average SAT Verbal | 567 |
| Range SAT Math | 530-620 |
| Average SAT Math | 578 |
| Average ACT Composite | 25 |
| Minimum TOEFL | 500 |
| Average HS GPA | 3.6 |
| % graduated top 10% of class | 22 |
| % graduated top 25% of class | 56 |
| % graduated top 50% of class | 92 |

### DEADLINES

| | |
|---|---|
| Early decision | 11/15 |
| Priority admission | 1/10 |

**APPLICANTS ALSO LOOK AT AND OFTEN PREFER**
UNC Chapel Hill
James Madison
**AND SOMETIMES PREFER**
Wake Forest U
North Carolina State U
**AND RARELY PREFER**
Furman U
College of Charleston

## FINANCIAL FACTS

| | |
|---|---|
| Financial Aid Rating | 86 |
| Tuition | $15,280 |
| Room and board | $5,090 |
| Books and supplies | $800 |
| Required fees | $225 |
| % frosh receiving aid | 37 |
| % undergrads receiving aid | 36 |
| Avg frosh grant | $4,693 |
| Avg frosh loan | $2,778 |

# EMERSON COLLEGE

120 BOYLSTON STREET, BOSTON, MA 02116-4624 • ADMISSIONS: 617-824-8600 • FAX: 617-824-8609

## CAMPUS LIFE

| | |
|---|---|
| Quality of Life Rating | 79 |
| Type of school | private |
| Environment | urban |

### STUDENTS
| | |
|---|---|
| Total undergrad enrollment | 3,518 |
| % male/female | 38/62 |
| % from out of state | 65 |
| % from public high school | 76 |
| % live on campus | 48 |
| % in (# of) fraternities | 5 (5) |
| % in (# of) sororities | 4 (4) |
| % African American | 2 |
| % Asian | 3 |
| % Caucasian | 86 |
| % Hispanic | 5 |
| % international | 4 |
| # of countries represented | 62 |

### SURVEY SAYS . . .
Great food on campus
Great library
Lab facilities are great
Great computer facilities
Beautiful campus
Theater is hot
Student government is unpopular
Student publications are ignored
Everyone listens to college radio
Very little beer drinking

## ACADEMICS

| | |
|---|---|
| Academic Rating | 75 |
| Calendar | semester |
| Student/faculty ratio | 15:1 |
| Profs interesting rating | 82 |
| Profs accessible rating | 89 |
| % profs teaching UG courses | 97 |
| % classes taught by TAs | 3 |
| Avg lab size | 10-19 students |
| Avg reg class size | 10-19 students |

### MOST POPULAR MAJORS
Visual and performing arts
Cinematography and film/video production
Communications, journalism, and related fields

## STUDENTS SPEAK OUT

### Academics
"The resources are vast and available" at "funky, offbeat" Emerson College, one of the nation's only four-year colleges devoted exclusively to the study of communications and performing arts. Emersonians tell us they have access to "excellent" computers, "good facilities," and a tremendous internship program, with hundreds of positions in Boston, Los Angeles, and other locations across the country and in Europe. Emerson also boasts "great, knowledgeable professors who don't drag on with theory" and who are "always available and willing to go the extra mile" for their passionate students. "Our teachers are, for the most part, struggling artists and writers themselves," notes a writing major. "This makes them especially sympathetic." However, there are also "teachers who don't know how to teach," and "some of the classes are a waste of time." And "there's too much work." Though Emerson is "not a study school" and "there isn't much book work," the "mostly hands-on" academic life here nevertheless "gets stressful," what with the massive amounts of time consumed by projects and internships. Emerson's administration is "good about allowing for creativity in planning a curriculum" but bad about a lot of other things. "Red tape is," unfortunately, "everywhere" and "communication among offices is poor for a communications school." Overall, though, "school is fun," according to a satisfied senior. "You come to Emerson to prepare for a career in something you love to do."

### Life
In "one word," life at Emerson is "busy." What with "10 billion opportunities," students tell us "the danger here isn't boredom; it's doing too much." Emersonians "may not spend as many hours as a Harvard student hitting the books," but they "get a level of hands-on experience not matched by any other school" and spend a great deal of time "in the video lab editing projects or in rehearsals." "Kids here work 30 to 40 hours per week at real jobs," emphasizes a junior. "Emerson will give you the opportunity to graduate not only with a degree but with a resume." Students are also able to establish "lots of professional contacts" by the time they get their diplomas. Not surprisingly, "social life centers around the arts" and around Boston, America's Great College Town. Emerson is "located in the heart of" Beantown, near Fenway Park, the theater district, and Copley Square. "Living across from Boston Common and the Public Garden is great," and the backdrop provides "a cool, mellow city scene." For the most part, "there's no real campus life. Students go out and do their own thing." Theaters, concerts, clubs, museums, "fabulous restaurants," "pubs," and unparalleled "cultural opportunities" abound. Drug use is more prevalent than drinking here, with marijuana as the opiate of choice, and "everyone—I mean everyone—parties," asserts one student. "That's the reality of college life in Boston." On campus, Emerson has one of the premier college radio stations on the planet.

### Student Body
"Picture the strange kid in high school who was really artsy, a little edgy, and had a strange fashion sense. Imagine an entire campus of them and you've got Emerson," says a sophomore. "If you are homosexual, have dyed hair, multiple piercings, and [/or] a creative side, it is the perfect place." Students here range from merely "fairly strange" to "fruity, artsy, atheist, freaky people." You'll find the "brooding, chain-smoking" crowd, "obnoxious theater majors," "zany, artsy types, crazy individualists," and "every color of hair." In fact, "if you don't have your eyebrow pierced, you're in the minority." Though some students here are "sickeningly pretentious," and "everyone wants to be seen in lights," students say theirs is a "very friendly, open environment," "full of creative energy and a solid work ethic." Emersonians are also "very career-oriented" and "enthusiastic about what they are doing." Most "spend every free second rehearsing a monologue, shooting a film, or writing the next Great American Novel." As far as ethnic diversity, "the school prides itself on cultural diversity and a diverse student body but it's 90 percent white," according to a perceptive first-year student.

# EMERSON COLLEGE

FINANCIAL AID: 617-824-8655 • E-MAIL: ADMISSION@EMERSON.EDU • WEBSITE: WWW.EMERSON.EDU

## ADMISSIONS

*Very important factors considered include:* secondary school record, standardized test scores. *Important factors considered include:* character/personal qualities, essays, extracurricular activities, recommendations, talent/ability. *Other factors considered include:* alumni/ae relation, class rank, interview, minority status, volunteer work, work experience. SAT I or ACT required. TOEFL required of all international applicants. High school diploma or GED is required. *High school units required/recommended:* 16 total required; 20 total recommended; 4 English required, 3 math required, 3 science required, 3 foreign language required, 3 social studies required, 4 elective recommended.

### The Inside Word
Being in Boston does more for Emerson's selectivity than do rigorous admissions standards.

## FINANCIAL AID
*Students should submit:* FAFSA, institution's own financial aid form, CSS/Financial Aid PROFILE, noncustodial (divorced/separated) parent's statement, business/farm supplement, tax returns. The Princeton Review suggests that all financial aid forms be submitted as soon as possible after January 1. *Need-based scholarships/grants offered:* Pell, SEOG, state scholarships/grants, private scholarships, the school's own gift aid. *Loan aid offered:* FFEL Subsidized Stafford, FFEL Unsubsidized Stafford, FFEL PLUS, Federal Perkins, state loans. Federal Work-Study Program available. Institutional employment available. Applicants will be notified of awards on or about April 1. Off-campus job opportunities are excellent.

## FROM THE ADMISSIONS OFFICE
"Founded in 1880, Emerson is one of the premier colleges in the United States for the study of communication and the performing arts. Students may choose from over 20 undergraduate majors and 12 graduate programs supported by state-of-the-art facilities and a nationally renowned faculty. The campus is home to WERS 88.9 FM, the oldest noncommercial radio station in New England; the 1,200-seat Emerson Majestic Theatre; and *Ploughshares*, the award-winning literary journal for new writing. A new 11-story performance and production center houses expanded performance and rehearsal space, a theatre design/technology center, makeup lab, and television studios with editing and control rooms.

"Located on Boston Common in the heart of the city's Theatre District, the Emerson campus is walking distance from the Massachusetts State House, historic Freedom Trial, Newbury Street shops, financial district, and numerous restaraunts and museums. Emerson's 2,800 undergraduate and 900 graduate students come from over 60 countries and 45 states and territories. There are more than 60 student orginizations and performance groups, 12 NCAA Division III intercollegiate teams, student publications, and honor societies. The college also sponsors programs in Los Angeles, Kasteel Well (The Netherlands), summer film study in Prague, and course cross registration with the six-member Boston ProArts Consortium."

### SELECTIVITY

| | |
|---|---|
| Admissions Rating | 82 |
| # of applicants | 3,805 |
| % of applicants accepted | 52 |
| % of acceptees attending | 33 |
| # accepting a place on wait list | 305 |
| % admitted from wait list | 4 |

### FRESHMAN PROFILE
| | |
|---|---|
| Range SAT Verbal | 570-660 |
| Average SAT Verbal | 619 |
| Range SAT Math | 540-630 |
| Average SAT Math | 584 |
| Range ACT Composite | 24-28 |
| Average ACT Composite | 27 |
| Minimum TOEFL | 550 |
| Average HS GPA | 3.5 |
| % graduated top 10% of class | 29 |
| % graduated top 25% of class | 71 |
| % graduated top 50% of class | 98 |

### DEADLINES
| | |
|---|---|
| Regular admission | 2/1 |
| Regular notification | 4/1 |
| Nonfall registration? | yes |

### APPLICANTS ALSO LOOK AT AND SOMETIMES PREFER
Ithaca College
University of Southern California
New York University

**AND RARELY PREFER**
Syracuse University
Boston University

### FINANCIAL FACTS

| | |
|---|---|
| Financial Aid Rating | 84 |
| Tuition | $21,120 |
| Room and board | $9,542 |
| Books and supplies | $680 |
| Required fees | $504 |
| % frosh receiving aid | 70 |
| % undergrads receiving aid | 61 |
| Avg frosh grant | $13,000 |
| Avg frosh loan | $3,000 |

# EMORY UNIVERSITY

BOISFEUILLET JONES CENTER, ATLANTA, GA 30322 • ADMISSIONS: 404-727-6036 • FAX: 404-727-4303

## CAMPUS LIFE

| Quality of Life Rating | 77 |
| --- | --- |
| Type of school | private |
| Affiliation | Methodist |
| Environment | suburban |

### STUDENTS

| Total undergrad enrollment | 5,630 |
| --- | --- |
| % male/female | 45/55 |
| % from out of state | 80 |
| % from public high school | 65 |
| % live on campus | 64 |
| % in (# of) fraternities | 30 (14) |
| % in (# of) sororities | 30 (10) |
| % African American | 10 |
| % Asian | 15 |
| % Caucasian | 65 |
| % Hispanic | 3 |
| % international | 4 |

### SURVEY SAYS . . .
Students love Atlanta, GA
Frats and sororities dominate social scene
Great library
Athletic facilities are great
Great off-campus food
Student publications are popular

## ACADEMICS

| Academic Rating | 79 |
| --- | --- |
| Calendar | semester |
| Student/faculty ratio | 6:1 |
| Profs interesting rating | 94 |
| Profs accessible rating | 91 |
| % profs teaching UG courses | 90 |
| % classes taught by TAs | 10 |
| Avg lab size | under 10 students |
| Avg reg class size | 10-19 students |

### MOST POPULAR MAJORS
Psychology
Economics
Political science and government

## STUDENTS SPEAK OUT

### Academics

It's the "combination of academics, social life, and real-world experience" that draws students to Emory University, "little brother to the Ivies" located in booming Atlanta, Georgia. In truth, Emory holds its own against venerable "big brothers" like Harvard and Yale. With a "big endowment" and "huge potential for growth," Emory's future—and the future of its academically oriented, competitive student body—looks bright. Notes a first-year, "Students here are smart. Everyone at Emory will go far." Nor is this excellence limited to attendees. "Professors here are leaders in their field[s]," notes a junior. "They wrote the book—literally." Fortunately for Emory undergrads, faculty is accessible and student-focused, as well. Adds another first-year, "My professors have been very good in giving me freedom to learn things in a way that's best for me. Also, professors are always free to help out even when not during office hours. All of my professors have actually cared about my success." A diverse curriculum (especially good in the sciences, say students), "amazing" classroom technology, and "awesome" research facilities and resources complement solid teaching. The administration, too, "works with students" and "doesn't try to weed us out," says a senior. (Though one first-year wonders, "Does all our tuition money go to planting new tulips in the quad every week or is it just me?") And while there is some sentiment that, with such a reputation-conscious administration, "the name associated with the school is its greatest strength," most students would probably say that Emory's reputation is well deserved. A sophomore sums up: "Emory is the embodiment of a great college experience. It has more than lived up to my expectations."

### Life

"Life at Emory has many different possibilities," explains a first-year. "The greatest strength of the school is the balance between a great academic school and a place to explore and have fun." The school's proximity to downtown Atlanta certainly helps—students can do the usual around campus ("hang out with friends, frat parties, bowl, play Frisbee, watch movies"), or they can "head into Atlanta," with its big-city restaurants, plays, films, and other cultural events. Unfortunately, the school is located some distance from the epicenter of activity, so, as a first-year points out, "As a freshman without a car, life is Emory." She continues: "We go to the mall on the free shuttle and take cabs everywhere else. City transport is great, but if you want to get out, you need friends with cars." With many upperclassmen living off campus, students say the school lacks a sense of "community" and "school spirit." They also complain that it's a fairly "materialistic" school. With a beautiful campus, Atlanta at an arm's reach, and a fairly sociable student body, "life is fun—just don't leave home without your Prada bag."

### Student Body

While there might be more than your average amount of "skinny brunettes with capri pants and cell phones," at Emory, there are also a lot of "really nice, down-to-earth people" who get along well—especially in the freshman residence halls. Granted, some of this cohesion is bound to disappear as students move away from campus. A sophomore notes that folks "seemed more friendly at the beginning of school; this has progressively decreased, however, and become somewhat cliquish." But for the most part, Emory's "diverse student body" blends well. We like this junior's take on Emory's student population: "It's a mixed lot."

# EMORY UNIVERSITY

FINANCIAL AID: 800-727-6039 • E-MAIL: ADMISS@UNIX.CC.EMORY.EDU • WEBSITE: WWW.EMORY.EDU

## ADMISSIONS
*Very important factors considered include:* recommendations, secondary school record. *Important factors considered include:* alumni/ae relation, character/personal qualities, essays, extracurricular activities, geographical residence, minority status, standardized test scores, state residency, talent/ability, volunteer work, work experience. *Other factors considered include:* class rank. SAT I or ACT required; SAT II recommended. High school diploma is required and GED is not accepted. *High school units required/recommended:* 16 total required; 4 English required, 3 math required, 2 science required, 2 science lab required, 2 foreign language required, 2 social studies required, 2 history required, 3 elective required.

### The Inside Word
Applications to Emory have doubled in the last six years. At the same time, the quality of the entering class has risen to record levels. As the South continues to increase its population and presence on the national scene, Emory will continue to increase its selectivity and prestige.

## FINANCIAL AID
*Students should submit:* FAFSA, CSS/Financial Aid PROFILE. Regular filing deadline is April 1. The Princeton Review suggests that all financial aid forms be submitted as soon as possible after January 1. *Need-based scholarships/grants offered:* Pell, SEOG, state scholarships/grants, private scholarships, the school's own gift aid. *Loan aid offered:* FFEL Subsidized Stafford, FFEL Unsubsidized Stafford, FFEL PLUS, Federal Perkins, Federal Nursing, state loans, college/university loans from institutional funds. Federal Work-Study Program available. Institutional employment available. Applicants will be notified of awards on or about April 15. Off-campus job opportunities are excellent.

## FROM THE ADMISSIONS OFFICE
"The combination Emory offers you is really a rarity in today's college marketplace. As an Emory student, you can still have the benefits of a small liberal arts college while enjoying the wider opportunities found in a major university. Emory College is the four-year undergraduate division of the university and provides a broad, rigorous liberal arts curriculum. At the same time, Emory University, with its nine major divisions, numerous centers for advanced study, and a host of prestigious affiliated institutions, provides the larger context, thus enriching your total college experience."

### SELECTIVITY

| | |
|---|---|
| Admissions Rating | 93 |
| # of applicants | 9,789 |
| % of applicants accepted | 42 |
| % of acceptees attending | 32 |
| # accepting a place on wait list | 400 |
| % admitted from wait list | 18 |
| # of early decision applicants | 864 |
| % accepted early decision | 61 |

### FRESHMAN PROFILE
| | |
|---|---|
| Range SAT Verbal | 640-720 |
| Range SAT Math | 660-740 |
| Range ACT Composite | 29-33 |
| Average HS GPA | 3.8 |
| % graduated top 10% of class | 90 |
| % graduated top 25% of class | 99 |
| % graduated top 50% of class | 100 |

### DEADLINES
| | |
|---|---|
| Early decision | 11/1 |
| Early decision notification | 12/15 |
| Regular admission | 1/15 |
| Regular notification | 4/1 |

### APPLICANTS ALSO LOOK AT AND OFTEN PREFER
Stanford
Northwestern U
Duke

**AND SOMETIMES PREFER**
Georgetown
Washington U
U of Pennsylvania

**AND RARELY PREFER**
George Washington U
Tufts
Tulane

### FINANCIAL FACTS

| | |
|---|---|
| Financial Aid Rating | 80 |
| Tuition | $26,600 |
| Room and board | $9,198 |
| Books and supplies | $700 |
| Required fees | $332 |
| % frosh receiving aid | 36 |
| % undergrads receiving aid | 37 |
| Avg frosh grant | $20,208 |
| Avg frosh loan | $3,478 |

# EUGENE LANG COLLEGE

65 WEST 11TH STREET, NEW YORK, NY 10011 • ADMISSIONS: 212-229-5665 • FAX: 212-229-5355

## CAMPUS LIFE

| | |
|---|---|
| Quality of Life Rating | 87 |
| Type of school | private |
| Environment | urban |

### STUDENTS
| | |
|---|---|
| Total undergrad enrollment | 637 |
| % male/female | 32/68 |
| % from out of state | 57 |
| % from public high school | 64 |
| % live on campus | 39 |
| % African American | 5 |
| % Asian | 4 |
| % Caucasian | 55 |
| % Hispanic | 4 |
| % international | 3 |

### SURVEY SAYS . . .
Theater is hot
Students love New York, NY
High cost of living
Student publications are ignored
Great off-campus food
Intercollegiate sports unpopular or nonexistent
No one plays intramural sports
Class discussions encouraged

## ACADEMICS

| | |
|---|---|
| Academic Rating | 85 |
| Calendar | semester |
| Student/faculty ratio | 11:1 |
| Profs interesting rating | 95 |
| Profs accessible rating | 96 |
| % profs teaching UG courses | 100 |
| % classes taught by TAs | 25 |
| Avg reg class size | 10-19 students |

### MOST POPULAR MAJORS
Creative writing
Area, ethnic, cultural, and gender studies
Social sciences

## STUDENTS SPEAK OUT

### Academics
Like its parent institution, New School University (formerly known as the New School for Social Research), Eugene Lang College has an air of experimentalism about it. Lang was founded in 1978 to extend the New School's tradition as a bastion of free academic inquiry to the undergraduate level. The school demands a large degree of self-sufficiency from its students, imposing only minimal curricular requirements. As one student explains, "Students are treated with respect; there is almost no supervision, so one must take total responsibility for success." Lang's faculty size is necessarily limited by the small student body, but undergraduates can supplement their curricula with courses at other divisions of New School University, including Parsons School of Design, the Adult Division, and the Graduate Faculty for Social and Political Science. They can also cross register at Cooper Union. Sophomores, juniors, and seniors may also take graduate courses at the New School. Students report that "professors are all available for outside help, and small classes are great." Students are less sanguine about the administration, complaining that registration is unduly difficult and that administrators are hard to reach; as one frustrated student put it, "I would think that since we are paying all this money and there are only 500 students in this college that registration and the administration would know what they are doing."

### Life
Lang has no campus to speak of: classrooms are crammed into a single building off the Avenue of the Americas, just above the heart of Greenwich Village in Manhattan. The lack of a true campus, coupled with the seemingly infinite opportunities offered by the city, translate into "no campus life, but that is to be expected because we're in the city." "Our campus is New York City," explains one student, adding that "there is always something to do, museums, galleries, clubs, world-famous restaurants, the greatest shopping, the list is endless." Students enjoy "discounts at almost all museums, opera, and ballet" as well as "incredible access to internships, political organizations, and cultural activities." The downside of all this, of course, is that "it is hard to meet people actually at the school. People go to class and then go home. The school needs to make more programs that make the students interact with classmates." As you might expect, school spirit is practically nonexistent among the student body. Students have no big festivals, no major sporting events to rally around. Even so, most appreciate the situation for what it is; as one student told us, "Hey, we may not have any official sports teams, but we do have the Anarchist Soccer League, which meets once a week in Brooklyn! Now what other college has that?"

### Student Body
Lang students "are all very interesting, but that's the biggest problem. Each student represents one of the 'weirdo-individualist' students from their high school. Put a bunch of these students together and you get a lot of social competition to be the 'most' different. Often, it just works out the opposite: the harder they try, the more similar they become." Undergrads share in common "a passion for ideas and the ability to think for ourselves. Students are very articulate and are great people with whom to engage in an impromptu discussion. Lang students are independent and question the status quo (though we might not all agree on what the status quo is and why it should be questioned)." Students are "almost exclusively politically liberal, which gets a little boring after awhile—too much preaching to the choir." Lang students are proud of the diversity of their student body, which ranges over ethnicity, race, gender, and lifestyle.

# EUGENE LANG COLLEGE

FINANCIAL AID: 212-229-8930 • E-MAIL: LANG@NEWSCHOOL.EDU • WEBSITE: WWW.LANG.EDU

## ADMISSIONS

*Very important factors considered include:* essays, recommendations, secondary school record. *Important factors considered include:* character/personal qualities, interview, standardized test scores, talent/ability, volunteer work. *Other factors considered include:* alumni/ae relation, class rank, extracurricular activities, geographical residence, minority status, work experience. SAT I or ACT required. TOEFL required of all international applicants. High school diploma or GED is required. *High school units required/recommended:* 16 total required; 18 total recommended; 4 English required, 3 math recommended, 3 science recommended, 2 foreign language recommended, 3 social studies recommended, 2 history recommended.

### The Inside Word

The college draws a very self-selected and intellectually curious pool, and applications are up. Those who demonstrate little self-motivation will find themselves denied.

## FINANCIAL AID

*Students should submit:* FAFSA, state aid form. No deadline for regular filing. The Princeton Review suggests that all financial aid forms be submitted as soon as possible after January 1. *Need-based scholarships/grants offered:* Pell, SEOG, state scholarships/grants, private scholarships, the school's own gift aid. *Loan aid offered:* FFEL Subsidized Stafford, FFEL Unsubsidized Stafford, FFEL PLUS, Federal Perkins, college/university loans from institutional funds. Federal Work-Study Program available. Institutional employment available. Applicants will be notified of awards on a rolling basis beginning on or about March 1. Off-campus job opportunities are good.

## FROM THE ADMISSIONS OFFICE

"Eugene Lang College offers students of diverse backgrounds an innovative and creative approach to a liberal arts education, combining stimulating classroom activity of a small, intimate college with rich resources of a dynamic, urban university—New School University. The curriculum at Lang College is challenging and flexible. Class size, limited to fifteen students, promotes energetic and thoughtful discussions and writing is an essential component of all classes. Students design their own program of study within one of five interdisciplinary concentrations in the Social Sciences and Humanities. They also have the opportunity to pursue a five-year BA/BFA, BA/MA, or BA/MST at one of the university's six other divisions. Our Greenwich Village location means that all the cultural treasures of the city—museums, libraries, music, theater—are literally at your doorstep."

### SELECTIVITY

| | |
|---|---|
| Admissions Rating | 77 |
| # of applicants | 696 |
| % of applicants accepted | 67 |
| % of acceptees attending | 37 |
| # accepting a place on wait list | 12 |
| % admitted from wait list | 25 |
| # of early decision applicants | 34 |
| % accepted early decision | 76 |

### FRESHMAN PROFILE

| | |
|---|---|
| Range SAT Verbal | 580-690 |
| Average SAT Verbal | 610 |
| Range SAT Math | 510-610 |
| Average SAT Math | 570 |
| Range ACT Composite | 21-27 |
| Average ACT Composite | 27 |
| Minimum TOEFL | 550 |
| Average HS GPA | 3.2 |
| % graduated top 10% of class | 18 |
| % graduated top 25% of class | 50 |
| % graduated top 50% of class | 87 |

### DEADLINES

| | |
|---|---|
| Early decision | 11/15 |
| Early decision notification | 12/15 |
| Regular admission | 2/1 |
| Nonfall registration? | yes |

### APPLICANTS ALSO LOOK AT AND OFTEN PREFER
Bard
NYU
Sarah Lawrence

### AND SOMETIMES PREFER
Hampshire
Reed

### AND RARELY PREFER
St. John's College
Bennington

### FINANCIAL FACTS

| | |
|---|---|
| Financial Aid Rating | 83 |
| Tuition | $22,500 |
| Room and board | $9,896 |
| Books and supplies | $918 |
| Required fees | $490 |
| % frosh receiving aid | 69 |
| % undergrads receiving aid | 64 |
| Avg frosh grant | $10,906 |
| Avg frosh loan | $3,125 |

# THE EVERGREEN STATE COLLEGE

OFFICE OF ADMISSIONS, OLYMPIA, WA 98505 • ADMISSIONS: 360-867-6170 • FAX: 360-867-6546

## CAMPUS LIFE

★ ★ ★ ☆

| | |
|---|---|
| Quality of Life Rating | 83 |
| Type of school | public |
| Environment | rural |

### STUDENTS
| | |
|---|---|
| Total undergrad enrollment | 4,081 |
| % male/female | 44/56 |
| % from out of state | 23 |
| % live on campus | 21 |
| % African American | 5 |
| % Asian | 4 |
| % Caucasian | 69 |
| % Hispanic | 4 |

### SURVEY SAYS . . .
School is well run
Campus easy to get around
Great library
Students love Olympia, WA
Beautiful campus
Diverse students interact
(Almost) no one smokes
(Almost) no one listens to college radio

## ACADEMICS

| | |
|---|---|
| Academic Rating | 88 |
| Calendar | quarter |
| Student/faculty ratio | 22:1 |
| Profs interesting rating | 75 |
| Profs accessible rating | 72 |
| % profs teaching UG courses | 100 |

## STUDENTS SPEAK OUT

### Academics

You want academic freedom? How much can you handle? If your answer to these questions is "How much have you got?" Evergreen State College may be the school for you. With "no prerequisites to classes," "few tests given," and no letter grades assigned, ESC stresses education for its own sake, an ideal situation for the disciplined scholar who eschews competitive grade-grubbing. Most who choose ESC end up loving it; explains one student, "The freedom the school allows in choosing programs, classes, and 'majors' is a huge strength. Majors don't really exist at Evergreen, and there are no requirements to take. You take what interests you, and you develop your own education." Evaluation ("an in-depth evaluation written by the professor" rather than a letter grade) is done through "seminar, papers, and projects" rather than tests, "making learning less a 'memorization' thing and more real and important." The net result is that students are "constantly being challenged by their peers and faculty to look beyond the surface—we all expect to have an analytical dialogue regarding the material." In other words, "the atmosphere is casual and non-competitive, but more intellectually demanding than any public institution this side of the Mississippi, perhaps in the entire U.S." As you might expect at such a school, "Professors aren't your typical 'I talk, you listen' professors; they're regular people who really know what they're teaching and are willing to help you learn it if what they do in the classroom is not enough." Adds one student, "The good and bad thing about Evergreen is that you are solely responsible for your education."

### Life

Life at Evergreen State is "relaxed" and "low-key," students agree. "Generally things are much slower here in Olympia," reports one student. "When you come from a larger city like Seattle, you should set your watch back two minutes and 'go with the flow.'" Many here "are perfectly content to just sit out in Red Square and meditate, play drums, or watch the clouds." Others relish the long discussions with other students, nature walks, and just plain hanging out. Parties "are chill, no big keggers"; as one student told us, they "are typically laid-back gatherings of friends." Unsurprisingly, the campus "is a politically charged environment, but not in an intimidating way." The more aesthetically inclined should be pleased to learn that the area is home to an active arts scene, and that "there are always things going on downtown: plays, music, art openings, etc. There is a volunteer-run indie film theater and a great co-op. Because of the local independent music scene, there are a lot of shows to see for dirt cheap prices." Nature lovers extol the many virtues of the nearby Capitol Forest.

### Student Body

"Trustafarian" is a term that came up often in Evergreen students' descriptions of one another. Some students describe the Evergreen students in terms of the typical "hippie": "leftist, politically motivated (to the point of extreme, at times), environmentally aware, if not active [and] free-thinking." Most, however, stress the "atypical" nature of the student body: "There is no typical Evergreen student. Greeners are friendly, open-minded and motivated." While students would like to see even more diversity on campus, they claim "everyone is pretty chill and easy to get along with." Most here immerse themselves in politics, art, community projects, and weed, not necessarily in that order. Undergrads happily report that "because this is a small school in a small but eccentric town, there is literally a little bit of everything that coexists in a happy academic environment."

212 ■ THE BEST 351 COLLEGES

# THE EVERGREEN STATE COLLEGE

FINANCIAL AID: 360-867-6205 • E-MAIL: ADMISSIONS@EVERGREEN.EDU • WEBSITE: WWW.EVERGREEN.EDU

## ADMISSIONS

*Very important factors considered include:* secondary school record, standardized test scores. *Important factors considered include:* essays. *Other factors considered include:* extracurricular activities, recommendations, talent/ability, volunteer work, work experience. SAT I or ACT required. TOEFL required of all international applicants. High school diploma or GED is required. *High school units required/recommended:* 16 total required; 4 English required, 3 math required, 2 science required, 1 science lab required, 2 foreign language required, 3 social studies required, 1 elective required.

### The Inside Word

Evergreen is one of the rare breed of "alternative" colleges—places where intellectual curiosity is a critical factor in the admissions process. Still, candidates must meet minimum academic standards in order to get a closer look from the admissions committee, and those with GPAs below 2.0 won't have a chance. A visit is a good idea for all candidates.

## FINANCIAL AID

*Students should submit:* FAFSA, institution's own financial aid form. Regular filing deadline is March 15. The Princeton Review suggests that all financial aid forms be submitted as soon as possible after January 1. *Need-based scholarships/grants offered:* Pell, SEOG, state scholarships/grants, private scholarships, the school's own gift aid. *Loan aid offered:* FFEL Subsidized Stafford, FFEL Unsubsidized Stafford, FFEL PLUS, Federal Perkins, college/university loans from institutional funds. Federal Work-Study Program available. Institutional employment available. Applicants will be notified of awards on a rolling basis beginning on or about April 15. Off-campus job opportunities are good.

## FROM THE ADMISSIONS OFFICE

"Evergreen, a public college of arts and sciences, is a national leader in developing full-time interdisciplinary studies programs. Students work closely with faculty (there are no teaching assistants) to study an issue or theme from the perspective of several academic disciplines. They apply what's learned to real-world issues, complete projects in groups and discuss concepts in seminars that typically involve a faculty member and 22 students. The emphasis on seminars, interdisciplinary problem-solving and collaboration means students are well prepared for graduate school and the world of work. Our students tend to be politically active, environmentally savvy and more concerned about social justice than competition and personal gain."

## SELECTIVITY

| | |
|---|---:|
| Admissions Rating | 78 |
| # of applicants | 1,399 |
| % of applicants accepted | 94 |
| % of acceptees attending | 37 |

### FRESHMAN PROFILE

| | |
|---|---:|
| Range SAT Verbal | 520-650 |
| Average SAT Verbal | 583 |
| Range SAT Math | 480-590 |
| Average SAT Math | 536 |
| Range ACT Composite | 20-26 |
| Average ACT Composite | 23 |
| Minimum TOEFL | 600 |
| Average HS GPA | 3.1 |
| % graduated top 10% of class | 14 |
| % graduated top 25% of class | 32 |
| % graduated top 50% of class | 67 |

### DEADLINES

| | |
|---|---:|
| Priority admission | 3/1 |
| Nonfall registration? | yes |

### APPLICANTS ALSO LOOK AT
**AND OFTEN PREFER**
U of Washington
Western Washington U
UC Santa Cruz
Reed
**AND SOMETIMES PREFER**
U of Oregon
Lewis & Clark
Hampshire
**AND RARELY PREFER**
U of Puget Sound
Central Washington U
Eastern Washington U

## FINANCIAL FACTS

| | |
|---|---:|
| Financial Aid Rating | 78 |
| In-state tuition | $3,441 |
| Out-of-state tuition | $12,264 |
| Room and board | $5,610 |
| Books and supplies | $780 |
| Required fees | $149 |
| % frosh receiving aid | 36 |
| % undergrads receiving aid | 52 |
| Avg frosh grant | $3,463 |
| Avg frosh loan | $3,586 |

# FAIRFIELD UNIVERSITY

1073 NORTH BENSON ROAD, FAIRFIELD, CT 06824 • ADMISSIONS: 203-254-4100 • FAX: 203-254-4199

## CAMPUS LIFE

| | |
|---|---|
| Quality of Life Rating | 89 |
| Type of school | private |
| Affiliation | Roman Catholic–Jesuit |
| Environment | suburban |

### STUDENTS

| | |
|---|---|
| Total undergrad enrollment | 4,073 |
| % male/female | 44/56 |
| % from out of state | 76 |
| % live on campus | 80 |
| % African American | 2 |
| % Asian | 3 |
| % Caucasian | 90 |
| % Hispanic | 5 |
| % international | 1 |
| # of countries represented | 43 |

### SURVEY SAYS . . .
Lots of beer drinking
Classes are small
Student government is popular
Beautiful campus
Campus easy to get around
Registration is a pain
Diversity lacking on campus
Students don't get along with local community

## ACADEMICS

| | |
|---|---|
| Academic Rating | 79 |
| Calendar | semester |
| Student/faculty ratio | 13:1 |
| Profs interesting rating | 93 |
| Profs accessible rating | 94 |
| % profs teaching UG courses | 100 |
| Avg lab size | 10-19 students |
| Avg reg class size | 20-29 students |

## STUDENTS SPEAK OUT

### Academics

With five undergraduate divisions, Fairfield University offers an unusually wide range of academic options to its small student body, and like many Jesuit schools, it manages to do so at a price that nonaffiliated private schools rarely match. Explains one student, "This school has a tremendous amount of academic resources . . . many programs, speakers, and events that are very interesting and intellectual." Another students waxes that "for business students—everything is there," including "great internships." The same student extols the science program, declaring simply that its "professors are awesome." Students report that the workload here is tough but manageable; writes one, "The academic programs are hard enough to be worthwhile, but they don't require a person to study 24/7 to keep a high GPA. It's fair." Professors receive high marks; notes one student, "I never would have imagined a faculty with more diverse thinking and teaching styles." Agrees another, "I have been most impressed with the accessibility and helpfulness of my professors. They are always helpful." The administration "is very accessible, but tends to bounce you around when you have a question—no one knows who has the final say!" Asked to name their school's single strongest suit, most students would agree that "the Jesuit ideals are our strongest points. They are taken seriously, and the quality of education demanded by that tradition is as well."

### Life

Fairfield students "try to balance working hard with playing hard, although the scale is usually tipped a little more" toward the former. Students particularly enjoy recreating at the nearby beach sweeping up from the Long Island Sound, where about 12 percent of students reside in off-campus housing. "We party at the beach! What could be better?" asks one student. Well, town-gown relations, for one. Students agree that "the relationship between the student beach residents and the full-time residents is not good." In response to complaints from the town, the university has stepped up efforts to curtail excessive drinking and unruly behavior. The school "sponsors non-alcoholic events," but most are attended by freshmen. "There is a big emphasis on doing what is 'cool,' and campus events aren't usually considered cool," reports one student. Many students "take the train in to New York City often to see shows or spend time just window shopping." Others "go into New Haven or Norwalk. There's not much to do in the town of Fairfield." Many students are active in community service; writes one, "Fairfield's community service opportunities are unparalleled. If you want to help, Fairfield's the place for you."

### Student Body

Students explain that "for years there has been this constant stigma surrounding the typical Fairfield student: the bleach-blonde, Saab-driving, beach-living, Abercrombie-wearing, parent-supported, business major, suburban specimen with his or her nose generally pointed in a skywards direction. While I will not deny that this is a definite type that we have floating about here on this campus, I will say that there are absolutely wonderful students who attend this school. [The] challenge, and this is really not so hard, is to find them." Adds one undergrad, "Some people complain that the student body is rich and spoiled, and much of it is, but that doesn't make us/them bad people." There are "lots of students from New England, especially Massachusetts" and, of course, Fairfield's home state of Connecticut and their border neighbor, New York.

# FAIRFIELD UNIVERSITY

FINANCIAL AID: 203-254-4125 • E-MAIL: ADMIS@MAIL.FAIRFIELD.EDU • WEBSITE: WWW.FAIRFIELD.EDU

## ADMISSIONS

*Very important factors considered include:* secondary school record, standardized test scores. *Important factors considered include:* class rank, essays, extracurricular activities, recommendations. *Other factors considered include:* alumni/ae relation, character/personal qualities, geographical residence, interview, minority status, talent/ability, volunteer work, work experience. SAT I or ACT required. TOEFL required of all international applicants. High school diploma is required and GED is not accepted. *High school units required/recommended:* 15 total required; 18 total recommended; 4 English required, 3 math required, 4 math recommended, 3 science required, 4 science recommended, 2 science lab required, 2 foreign language required, 4 foreign language recommended, 3 history required, 4 history recommended, 1 elective required.

### The Inside Word

Solid support from Catholic high schools goes a long way toward stocking the applicant pool. Important to note: Steady increases in the number of admission applications has nicely increased selectivity in recent years. Fairfield's campus and central location combined with improvements to the library, campus center, classrooms, athletic facilities, and campus residences, make this a campus worth seeing.

## FINANCIAL AID

*Students should submit:* FAFSA, CSS/Financial Aid PROFILE. Regular filing deadline is February 15. The Princeton Review suggests that all financial aid forms be submitted as soon as possible after January 1. *Need-based scholarships/grants offered:* Pell, SEOG, state scholarships/grants, private scholarships, the school's own gift aid. *Loan aid offered:* FFEL Subsidized Stafford, FFEL Unsubsidized Stafford, FFEL PLUS, Federal Perkins, Federal Nursing, state loans, alternative loans. Federal Work-Study Program available. Institutional employment available. Applicants will be notified of awards on or about April 5. Off-campus job opportunities are good.

## FROM THE ADMISSIONS OFFICE

"Fairfield University's primary objectives are to develop the creative intellectual potential of its students and to foster in them ethical and religious values and a sense of social responsibility. It also seeks to foster in its students a continuing intellectual curiosity and to develop leaders. As the key to the lifelong process of learning, Fairfield has developed a core curriculum (60 credits) to introduce all students to the broad range of liberal learning. Students choose from 32 majors and 19 interdisciplinary minors. They also have outstanding internship opportunities in Fairfield County and New York City. Fairfield grads wishing to continue their education are highly successful in gaining graduate and professional school admission, while others pursue extensive job opportunities throughout the region. Eighteen Fairfield students have been tapped as Fulbright Scholars in just the past five years."

### SELECTIVITY

| | |
|---|---|
| Admissions Rating | 80 |
| # of applicants | 6,974 |
| % of applicants accepted | 50 |
| % of acceptees attending | 24 |
| # accepting a place on wait list | 973 |
| % admitted from wait list | 9 |
| # of early decision applicants | 172 |
| % accepted early decision | 67 |

### FRESHMAN PROFILE

| | |
|---|---|
| Range SAT Verbal | 540-630 |
| Average SAT Verbal | 585 |
| Range SAT Math | 570-650 |
| Average SAT Math | 610 |
| Average ACT Composite | 28 |
| Minimum TOEFL | 550 |
| Average HS GPA | 3.6 |
| % graduated top 10% of class | 33 |
| % graduated top 25% of class | 70 |
| % graduated top 50% of class | 97 |

### DEADLINES

| | |
|---|---|
| Early decision | 11/15 |
| Early decision notification | 12/15 |
| Regular admission | 1/15 |
| Regular notification | 4/1 |

### APPLICANTS ALSO LOOK AT
**AND OFTEN PREFER**
Georgetown University
University of Notre Dame
**AND SOMETIMES PREFER**
Providence College
Boston College
Villanova University
College of the Holy Cross
Loyola College in Maryland
**AND RARELY PREFER**
Boston University
University of Connecticut

### FINANCIAL FACTS

| | |
|---|---|
| Financial Aid Rating | 84 |
| Tuition | $24,100 |
| Room and board | $8,560 |
| Books and supplies | $800 |
| Required fees | $455 |
| % frosh receiving aid | 52 |
| % undergrads receiving aid | 52 |
| Avg frosh grant | $11,683 |
| Avg frosh loan | $3,556 |

# FISK UNIVERSITY

1000 17TH AVENUE NORTH, NASHVILLE, TN 37208-3051 • ADMISSIONS: 615-329-8666 • FAX: 615-329-8774

## CAMPUS LIFE

| Quality of Life Rating | 68 |
|---|---|
| Type of school | private |
| Environment | urban |

### STUDENTS

| Total undergrad enrollment | 812 |
|---|---|
| % male/female | 28/72 |
| % from out of state | 71 |
| % from public high school | 85 |
| % live on campus | 56 |
| % African American | 100 |
| % international | 2 |
| # of countries represented | 5 |

### SURVEY SAYS . . .
*Frats and sororities dominate social scene*
*Diversity lacking on campus*
*Classes are small*
*Very little drug use*
*Athletic facilities need improving*
*Very little beer drinking*
*Lousy food on campus*
*Lab facilities are great*
*Library needs improving*

## ACADEMICS

| Academic Rating | 76 |
|---|---|
| Calendar | semester |
| Student/faculty ratio | 11:1 |
| Profs interesting rating | 93 |
| Profs accessible rating | 88 |
| % profs teaching UG courses | 100 |

## STUDENTS SPEAK OUT

### Academics

Ask Fisk students what they love about their school and they invariably mention the school's history. W. E. B. DuBois' alma mater was founded in 1866; its first classes convened in a Union army barracks mere months after the conclusion of the Civil War. Notes one student, "It is the history of this school that is its great strength. Most students leave Fisk with a great understanding of the struggle of the black university as a whole and are determined to do their best." From day one Fisk has striven to achieve "the highest standards, not of Negro education, but of American education at its best," succeeding despite a funding crisis and, until relatively recently, a hostile southern environment. Today, Fisk is "a wonderful place to learn" at which "individuals are definitely allowed to excel." Students here appreciate an intimate classroom setting. Explains one, "Since the student population is small, you develop a rapport with your professors. The professors are usually willing to help you with anything you need. Most teachers are challenging. They are very open-minded and caring of students' opinions." Departments in the hard sciences are popular and well respected here, as are pre-business studies and the music school. Students love the "cordial, accessible administration" but "wish Fisk was better funded," complaining that the facilities need a major upgrade. Explains one, "Despite my love for my school, I can't help but feel cheated because of the lack of organization and the lack of educational necessities (e.g. lab equipment, diversity of majors)." Sums up one student, "Fisk is unique. Despite the lack of funding and technology and advances, it produces 'top flight' students. The professors range from terrible to tremendous, but the overall experience creates well-rounded individuals with the ability to compete and succeed ultimately in any environment."

### Life

Students report that "Fisk is a very academic school. Many activities focus around academically oriented activities, like lectures and speakers." Although they enjoy the fact that Fisk is a "very historic, beautiful, and family-oriented school" with a "very peaceful" campus, they also "wish that there were more things to do on campus." Because Fisk is relatively small, "there are very few activities for the average student to partake in. Greek organizations play a big role in providing activities, whether it be a party or some type of community service. Other than that, many students are not as active as they need to be." Campus social life, many say, is also dampened by a paternalistic administration; explains one student, "The university treats students like children and not like young adults. The dorm life for freshmen ladies is awful." Most students end up learning to be satisfied with a quiet lifestyle. Writes one, "For me, a few parties, a good movie, and a seminar or two make up a fun-filled social week. School is what you make it." Food on campus is "awful," but several cheap southern-style restaurants and food stands are close by, including Mary's Bar-B-Q, perhaps Nashville's best. South Nashville, the neighborhood surrounding Fisk, is "a bad area" but one that is gradually improving.

### Student Body

Over and over, the word "family" pops up in students' descriptions of the Fisk community. Writes one, "The weird thing here is people really get along. We are really a family because we are so small. You know people by name." Another offers a slightly different perspective, observing that "because our campus is small, we all tend to feel like a family. Like most family, there are people you love and those whom you despise. But when you are off campus and see someone from Fisk, you look out for them." The typical Fiskite is politically liberal, religious, serious about study, and adamant in the belief that African American students are best served at a predominantly black university.

# FISK UNIVERSITY

FINANCIAL AID: 615-329-8735 • E-MAIL: ADMISSIONS@FISK.EDU • WEBSITE: WWW.FISK.EDU

## ADMISSIONS

*Very important factors considered include:* class rank. *Important factors considered include:* alumni/ae relation, character/personal qualities, essays, extracurricular activities, recommendations, secondary school record. *Other factors considered include:* standardized test scores, talent/ability. TOEFL required of all international applicants. High school diploma or GED is required. *High school units required/recommended:* 3 math recommended, 3 science recommended, 2 foreign language recommended.

### The Inside Word

While a solid academic record is central to getting in, applicants to Fisk should not underestimate the personal side of admissions criteria. A high level of motivation and involvement in your school, church, and/or community goes a long way toward a successful candidacy here.

## FINANCIAL AID

The Princeton Review suggests that all financial aid forms be submitted as soon as possible after January 1. *Need-based scholarships/grants offered:* Pell, SEOG, state scholarships/grants, the school's own gift aid, United Negro College Fund. *Loan aid offered:* Direct Subsidized Stafford, Direct Unsubsidized Stafford, Direct PLUS, Federal Perkins. Federal Work-Study Program available. Off-campus job opportunities are good.

## FROM THE ADMISSIONS OFFICE

"Founded in 1866, the university is coeducational, private, and one of America's premier historically black universities. The first black college to be granted a chapter of Phi Beta Kappa Honor Society, Fisk serves a national student body, with an enrollment of 900 students. There are residence halls for men and women. The focal point of the 40-acre campus and architectural symbol of the university is Jubilee Hall, the first permanent building for the education of blacks in the South, and named for the internationally renowned Fisk Jubilee Singers, who continue their tradition of singing the Negro spiritual. From its earliest days, Fisk has played a leadership role in the education of African Americans. Faculty and alumni have been among America's intellectual leaders. Among them include Fisk graduates Nikki Giovanni, poet/writer; John Hope Franklin, historian/scholar; David Lewis, professor/recipient of the prestigious Pulitzer Prize; Hazel O'Leary, U.S. Secretary of Energy; John Lewis, U.S. Representative–GA; and W. E. B. DuBois, the great social critic and cofounder of the NAACP. Former Fisk students whose distinguished careers bring color to American culture include Judith Jamison, director of the Alvin Ailey Dance Company, and Johnetta B. Cole, president of Spelman College. In proportion to its size, Fisk continues to contribute more alumni to the ranks of scholars pursuing doctoral degrees than any other institution in the United States."

## SELECTIVITY

| | |
|---|---|
| Admissions Rating | 76 |
| # of applicants | 683 |
| % of applicants accepted | 97 |
| % of acceptees attending | 37 |

### FRESHMAN PROFILE

| | |
|---|---|
| Range SAT Verbal | 395-545 |
| Average SAT Verbal | 448 |
| Range SAT Math | 365-540 |
| Average SAT Math | 441 |
| Range ACT Composite | 17-22 |
| Average ACT Composite | 19 |
| Minimum TOEFL | 500 |
| Average HS GPA | 3.0 |
| % graduated top 10% of class | 35 |
| % graduated top 25% of class | 48 |
| % graduated top 50% of class | 73 |

### DEADLINES

| | |
|---|---|
| Regular admission | 6/15 |
| Nonfall registration? | yes |

### APPLICANTS ALSO LOOK AT AND OFTEN PREFER
Howard
Morehouse
Spelman

### AND SOMETIMES PREFER
Vanderbilt
Penn State—Univ. Park

### AND RARELY PREFER
Clark Atlanta

## FINANCIAL FACTS

| | |
|---|---|
| Financial Aid Rating | 81 |
| Tuition | $8,480 |
| Room and board | $4,930 |
| Books and supplies | $800 |
| Required fees | $290 |
| % frosh receiving aid | 90 |
| % undergrads receiving aid | 90 |
| Avg frosh grant | $2,200 |
| Avg frosh loan | $6,700 |

THE BEST 351 COLLEGES ■ 217

# FLAGLER COLLEGE

74 KING STREET, PO BOX 1027, ST. AUGUSTINE, FL 32085-1027 • ADMISSIONS: 800-304-4208

## CAMPUS LIFE

| Quality of Life Rating | 75 |
|---|---|
| Type of school | private |
| Affiliation | none |
| Environment | suburban |

### STUDENTS

| Total undergrad enrollment | 1,921 |
|---|---|
| % male/female | 37/63 |
| % from out of state | 36 |
| % from public high school | 83 |
| % live on campus | 45 |
| % African American | 1 |
| % Asian | 1 |
| % Caucasian | 93 |
| % Hispanic | 3 |
| % international | 2 |
| # of countries represented | 21 |

### SURVEY SAYS . . .
Lots of beer drinking
Classes are small
Diversity lacking on campus
Student publications are popular
Theater is hot
Intercollegiate sports are popular
(Almost) everyone plays intramural sports
Popular college radio

## ACADEMICS

| Academic Rating | 77 |
|---|---|
| Calendar | semester |
| Student/faculty ratio | 22:1 |
| Profs interesting rating | 82 |
| Profs accessible rating | 83 |
| % profs teaching UG courses | 100 |
| % classes taught by TAs | 0 |
| Avg reg class size | 20-29 students |

### MOST POPULAR MAJORS
elementary education
business administration
communication

## STUDENTS SPEAK OUT

### Academics
In a setting where professors "wear floral shirts and shorts to class," Flagler students emphasize that the school's academics are "harder than they appear." Students regard their instructors as "extremely brilliant people who want to inspire rather than dictate what we should think and know." Another student confirms that opinion, commenting, "They foster and encourage your opinions, no matter how alike or different they are from their own." These "angels" are said to "really love their jobs and be totally accessible outside of the classroom." Flagler offers an innovative program in deaf education, "one of very few in the country," and classes in all areas are kept very small. Many respondents point out, "Both professors and members of the administration are actively involved in campus activities"; students can even "sit down with the president for an hour and talk." The administration, however, reportedly "plays parent too much," giving rise to the feeling that "it's Flagler's way or no way." Students also gripe about class attendance policies "reminiscent of ninth grade" and the school's "need to up admissions standards." But overall most students agree that "the tuition for a private school is relatively cheap," claiming the cost is "one-half of what it would be elsewhere." In summary, one senior remarks, "I have received a first-rate education through personal and nurturing means."

### Life
Students commonly express the sentiment that life at Flagler "resembles high school, which can be a good or bad thing." While "community service projects to karaoke to bachelor bids" count among popular activities, surfing is by far the most widely enjoyed pastime. The beach and surrounding area also offer "parasailing, swimming, skydiving, horseback riding, and museum cruising." Regarding the prevalence of "studying at the beach," students challenge, "Beat that, Harvard, Yale, or Princeton!" Flagler's location in the "tourist trap" of St. Augustine, the oldest town in the U.S., means plenty of "cool shops and neat little pubs," though some students feel there's "not much to do here unless you're 80 years old or a tourist." On campus, rules prohibiting visitation between the male and female dorms are regarded as "unbearable" by most students, with one woman lamenting, "I have a lot of guy friends I can barely hang out with." Other students consider the policies "fair": "This is just a conservative school, so if you don't like that, don't come." Though no boys are allowed, the girls adore their dorm, located in the former famous Ponce de Leon Hotel, where each room is different.

### Students
The 1,900-student Flagler population, featuring a 3-to-2 female-to-male ratio, is made up of "exceptionally friendly and welcoming" people. Though the environment is "fairly conservative," students note that "even the more radical and liberal among us get along pretty well." One undergraduate tells us, "The majority of the students are of an upper-middle-class, white background, and that makes the student body a bit one-dimensional." A minority student writes, "As a Hispanic, I have felt deprived of my culture at this school." As far as the LGBT community, one woman reports, "I'm a lesbian, and my school seems to have the 'don't ask, don't tell' policy." Amid this largely homogenous group, where "the most diversity comes from foreign students," students claim, "Those of minority groups that we do have are not discriminated against and most are actually very popular." The overall "close-knit atmosphere" is furthered by a collective willingness to "accept each others' differences."

# FLAGLER COLLEGE

Fax: 904-826-0094 • E-mail: admiss@flagler.edu • Website: www.flagler.edu

## ADMISSIONS

*Very important factors considered by the admissions committee include:* character/personal qualities, secondary school record, and standardized test scores. *Important factors considered include:* alumni/ae relation, class rank, essays, geographical residence, interview, and state residency. *Other factors considered include:* extracurricular activities, recommendations, talent/ability, volunteer work, and work experience. SAT I or ACT required. TOEFL required of all international applicants. High school diploma or GED is required. *High school units required/recommended:* 16 total required; 21 total recommended; 4 English required, 3 math required, 2 science required, 3 science recommended, 1 science lab required, 2 science lab recommended, 2 foreign language recommended, 3 social studies required, 4 social studies recommended, 2 history required, 3 history recommended, 1 elective required, 2 elective recommended.

## The Inside Word

Flagler sets no bare minimums for most applicants, but does require of its education candidates a minimum combined 1010 SAT I score or a composite 21 on the ACT. An on-campus interview is highly recommended. Use it as an excuse to visit St. Augustine in the winter; you'll be glad you did.

## FINANCIAL AID

Students should submit: FAFSA, institution's own financial aid form, and state aid form. The Princeton Review suggests that all financial aid forms be submitted as soon as possible after January 1. Federal Work-Study Program available. Institutional employment available. Applicants will be notified of awards on a rolling basis beginning on or about March 1. Off-campus job opportunities are good.

## FROM THE ADMISSIONS OFFICE

"Flagler College is an independent, four-year, co-educational, residential institution located in picturesque St. Augustine. A famous historic tourist center in northeast Florida, it is located to the south of Jacksonville and north of Daytona Beach. Flagler students have ample opportunity to explore the rich cultural heritage and international flavor of St. Augustine, and there's always time for a relaxing day at the beach, about four miles from campus. Flagler is one of the least expensive private colleges in the nation and is recognized in MoneyGuide, U.S. News & World Report, and America's Best 100 Buys as a top value in education at an affordable cost. The annual cost for tuition, room, and board at Flagler is about the same as state universities. The small student body helps to keep one from becoming 'just a number.' Flagler serves a predominately full-time student body and seeks to enroll students who can benefit from the type of educational experience the college offers. Because of the college's unique mission and distinctive characteristics, some students may benefit more from an educational experience at Flagler than others. The college's admission standards and procedures are designed to select from among the applicants those students most likely to succeed academically, to contribute significantly to the student life program at Flagler, and to become graduates of the College. Flagler College provides an exceptional opportunity for a private education at an extremely affordable cost."

### SELECTIVITY

| | |
|---|---|
| Admissions Rating | 75 |
| # of applicants | 1,994 |
| % of applicants accepted | 30 |
| % of acceptees attending | 82 |
| # accepting a place on wait list | 385 |
| % admitted from wait list | 1 |
| # of early decision applicants | 661 |
| % accepted early decision | 63 |

### FRESHMAN PROFILE

| | |
|---|---|
| Range SAT Verbal | 530-620 |
| Average SAT Verbal | 571 |
| Range SAT Math | 510-600 |
| Average SAT Math | 551 |
| Range ACT Composite | 22-26 |
| Average ACT Composite | 24 |
| Minimum TOEFL | 550 |
| Average HS GPA | 3.22 |
| % graduated top 10% of class | 18 |
| % graduated top 25% of class | 51 |
| % graduated top 50% of class | 87 |

### DEADLINES

| | |
|---|---|
| Early decision | 12/1 |
| Regular admission | 3/1 |
| Regular notification | 3/15 |
| Nonfall registration? | yes |

### APPLICANTS ALSO LOOK AT AND OFTEN PREFER
U of Central Florida
Florida State U
U of Florida
U of North Florida
U of South Florida

### AND SOMETIMES PREFER
Florida Atlantic U
Stetson U
U of Miami, U of Tampa
Jacksonville U

### AND RARELY PREFER
Florida Southern College
Rollins College, U of West Florida
Florida International U
Florida Gulf Coast U

### FINANCIAL FACTS

| | |
|---|---|
| Financial Aid Rating | 79 |
| Tuition | $7,410 |
| Room and board | $4,450 |
| Books and supplies | $700 |

# FLORIDA A&M UNIVERSITY

SUITE G-9, FOOTE-HILYER ADMINISTRATION CENTER, TALLAHASSEE, FL 32307 • ADMISSIONS: 850-599-3796 • FAX: 850-599-3069

## CAMPUS LIFE

| | |
|---|---|
| Quality of Life Rating | 71 |
| Type of school | public |
| Environment | urban |

### STUDENTS

| | |
|---|---|
| Total undergrad enrollment | 10,803 |
| % male/female | 43/57 |
| % from out of state | 21 |
| % from public high school | 85 |
| % live on campus | 77 |
| % African American | 96 |
| % Caucasian | 3 |
| % Hispanic | 1 |
| % international | 1 |

### SURVEY SAYS . . .
*Frats and sororities dominate social scene*
*Student government is popular*
*Very little drug use*
*Everyone loves the Rattlers*
*Diversity lacking on campus*
*Library needs improving*
*Musical organizations are hot*
*(Almost) no one smokes*
*Dorms are like dungeons*

## ACADEMICS

| | |
|---|---|
| Academic Rating | 72 |
| Calendar | semester |
| Student/faculty ratio | 20:1 |
| Profs interesting rating | 92 |
| Profs accessible rating | 89 |

## STUDENTS SPEAK OUT

### Academics
Students at Florida A&M University—FAMU, for short—laud their school's "top-notch programs in business, pharmacy, architecture, health sciences, journalism, political science, engineering, computer information systems, music, theatre, and education." Especially noteworthy, many agree, are the School of Business and Industry program, "which offers an excellent program for those who are entering the world of business, and the School of Pharmacy, which is also one of the best in the country." Brags one student, "The way companies come here and give millions of dollars during halftime of the football games for access to us really speaks volumes for the quality of the school." Students also appreciate the school's high-tech flourishes, such as a wireless Internet system that is "lightning fast. You can literally walk from one end of the Hill to the other with your laptop and surf the 'net." Students agree that professors here "are excellent. They genuinely care about students and are more than happy to help outside of class." The administration, however, is looked upon less kindly by most. "Upper administrators, like the university president, genuinely care about students. The mid- and lower-level admins, however, seem to often be indifferent to student concerns. There are very long lines for everything."

### Life
Football is king at Florida A&M, and the Marching 100—the school's famous band—runs a close second. Students tell us that "during the fall, FAMU is off the chain fun! Football and the band dominate the social scene." Otherwise, "there are many extracurriculars to get involved in year-round," including an active Greek system. Raves one student, "There are parties galore. We have our own rendition of the Apollo, called the 'Stoop,' for fun." Adds another, "There are a lot of clubs to go to on the weekends and during the week, so that's what usually happens." Popular student events include Greek Week, Homecoming, and Harambee. Religious and community service events also draw large turnouts. Students complain that their hometown of Tallahasse "doesn't give you many options" and that "Tallahassee is in love with Florida State University, which sucks when you attend FAMU." They also point out, however, that "if you have a car, you will have fun outside of Tallahassee. If you don't, find someone that does, especially if you live in the dorms, because it can get pretty boring." Parking is a definite problem on this small campus, although a few optimists see a silver lining to this gray cloud; writes one, "The compactness of the campus is good because no matter where you park you have access to virtually all of the buildings."

### Student Body
Unity is the watchword among the "very friendly" students at FAMU, who boast that "attending a historically black college, you do get the sense of family amongst not only the students but the school as well." Writes one undergrad, "One thing I especially want to mention is how we came together when we were bombed last year. A racist planted several bombs on our campus and two managed to do some damage. Many were frightened and security was very heavy. But we came together and kept living our lives as normal Rattlers until the criminal was caught." Many here "are from [the South] and/or Florida." On the topic of diversity, one student notes that "people have the fallacy that all black people at a predominately black school are the same, but that's not true at all. We have the same differences that could be found at a multiracial school, you just have to look deeper than skin tone. You have the athletes, Greeks, partiers, nerds, intellectuals, and so forth, just like every other school."

# FLORIDA A&M UNIVERSITY

FINANCIAL AID: 850-599-3730 • E-MAIL: BCOX2@FAMU.EDU • WEBSITE: WWW.FAMU.EDU

## ADMISSIONS
*Very important factors considered include:* secondary school record, standardized test scores. *Other factors considered include:* alumni/ae relation, character/personal qualities, essays, extracurricular activities, geographical residence, minority status, recommendations, state residency, talent/ability, volunteer work, work experience. SAT I or ACT required. TOEFL required of all international applicants. High school diploma or GED is required. *High school units required/recommended:* 19 total required; 4 English required, 3 math required, 3 science required, 1 science lab required, 2 foreign language required, 3 social studies required, 4 elective required.

### The Inside Word
FAMU's admissions staff does a terrific job. Collectively, they are warm, compassionate, and skilled counselors. This goes a long way toward explaining why the University has enrolled the highest number of National Achievement Scholars of any school in the country. There's a lot to like about the way these guys do business—they never lose sight of the notion that they are educators first and marketers second. Other colleges would do well to study FAMU's approach.

## FINANCIAL AID
*Students should submit:* FAFSA. Regular filing deadline is June 30. The Princeton Review suggests that all financial aid forms be submitted as soon as possible after January 1. *Need-based scholarships/grants offered:* Pell, SEOG, state scholarships/grants, private scholarships, the school's own gift aid, United Negro College Fund, Federal Nursing. *Loan aid offered:* Direct Subsidized Stafford, Direct Unsubsidized Stafford, Direct PLUS, Federal Perkins. Federal Work-Study Program available. Applicants will be notified of awards on a rolling basis beginning on or about March 1. Off-campus job opportunities are good.

## FROM THE ADMISSIONS OFFICE
"FAMU encourages applications for admission from qualified applicants regardless of sex, culture, race, religion, ethnic background, age, or disability. We are committed to enrolling the best possible students and we are interested in applicants who have demonstrated superior academic ability and outstanding personal qualities. For more than a century, the primary goals of FAMU have been to promote academic excellence and to improve the quality of life for those individuals it serves and their society. FAMU is located in the capital city of Florida (Tallahassee) and is a four-year public, general purpose, land-grant institution. It offers undergraduate and graduate programs designed to meet the needs of a diverse student population."

## SELECTIVITY

| | |
|---|---|
| Admissions Rating | 80 |
| # of applicants | 4,819 |
| % of applicants accepted | 78 |
| % of acceptees attending | 51 |

### FRESHMAN PROFILE
| | |
|---|---|
| Range SAT Verbal | 450-550 |
| Range SAT Math | 450-560 |
| Range ACT Composite | 18-22 |
| Average ACT Composite | 20 |
| Minimum TOEFL | 500 |
| Average HS GPA | 3.2 |

### DEADLINES
| | |
|---|---|
| Regular admission | 5/9 |
| Regular notification | rolling |
| Nonfall registration? | yes |

### APPLICANTS ALSO LOOK AT AND SOMETIMES PREFER
Tuskegee
Spelman
Morehouse
Florida State
Howard

### AND RARELY PREFER
U. South Florida
U. Florida
Hampton

## FINANCIAL FACTS

| | |
|---|---|
| Financial Aid Rating | 82 |
| In-state tuition | $1,777 |
| Out-of-state tuition | $7,368 |
| Room and board | $3,896 |
| Books and supplies | $600 |
| Required fees | $129 |
| % frosh receiving aid | 75 |
| % undergrads receiving aid | 78 |
| Avg frosh grant | $3,031 |

# FLORIDA STATE UNIVERSITY

2500 UNIVERSITY CENTER, TALLAHASSEE, FL 32306-2400 • ADMISSIONS: 850-644-6200 • FAX: 850-644-0197

## CAMPUS LIFE

| | |
|---|---|
| Quality of Life Rating | 81 |
| Type of school | public |
| Environment | suburban |

### STUDENTS

| | |
|---|---|
| Total undergrad enrollment | 29,195 |
| % male/female | 44/56 |
| % from out of state | 15 |
| % from public high school | 89 |
| % live on campus | 16 |
| % in (# of) fraternities | 14 (25) |
| % in (# of) sororities | 13 (22) |
| % African American | 12 |
| % Asian | 3 |
| % Caucasian | 74 |
| % Hispanic | 9 |
| % international | 1 |
| # of countries represented | 135 |

### SURVEY SAYS . . .
Everyone loves the Seminoles
Athletic facilities are great
Lots of beer drinking
Hard liquor is popular
Frats and sororities dominate social scene
Great computer facilities
Great library
(Almost) everyone plays intramural sports
Student newspaper is popular

## ACADEMICS

| | |
|---|---|
| Academic Rating | 81 |
| Calendar | semester |
| Student/faculty ratio | 23:1 |
| % profs teaching UG courses | 95 |
| % classes taught by TAs | 32 |
| Avg reg class size | 20-29 students |

### MOST POPULAR MAJORS
Biological sciences
Criminology
Psychology

## STUDENTS SPEAK OUT

### Academics

With its terrific climate and perennially excellent football team, one could excuse Florida State University if its academic reputation was not a strong selling point. Fortunately, it is. Along with an extremely affordable tuition, Florida State is a world-class research institution that offers an excellent education if one can ignore all of the outside distractions. While entry-level classes are extremely large, students laud their "caring" professors for both their quality and accessibility. "Teachers make it as easy as possible for a student to access them," an electrical engineering major comments. And the upper-level professors are considered "enthusiastic and motivated." A junior child development major adds that her professors "are here for us and try to help us to the best of their ability." Because of its auspicious location in Florida's capital, students can take the skills they learn on campus and apply them in a host of internships at federal and state agencies. According to students, the administration is disorganized, and a sophomore international affairs major describes the it as "more bureaucratic than Nixon's." That's just the bigwigs, though, as the campus staff is "extremely friendly" and financial aid is "the bomb." An overjoyed first-year biology major describes FSU as "an excellent school that . . . has made me realize that I made the right decision."

### Life

Students at Florida State aren't fanatical about their studying. An English major tattles that many students skip classes and that the party scene is considered by many to be as important as the academic one. Students note that there's a "glut of affordable off-campus housing within walking distance." Tallahassee clubs are "decent," and there are always parties to crash, both at private off-campus houses and at fraternities and sororities. Greek organizations are extremely popular and are known as much for their charitable endeavors as for the parties that they host. Campus organizations are active and plentiful. Students praise the top-notch recreation center and take advantage of the temperate climate to go hiking, camping, and biking. "There are all kinds of things to do for fun," a senior social sciences major explains. "You just have to be creative." The football team is a perennial national championship contender, and students take a great deal of pride ("Seminole Spirit") in their clubs. Students give the food a thumbs-down and say that the university needs to increase the number of available parking spaces because "you have to get to campus by 7:30 [or] 8 A.M. to get a spot."

### Student Body

Though most FSU students are united by their common desire to have fun, they tend to "separate themselves into groups." Consequently, "minorities hang out with minorities and whites hang out with whites," muses one junior. "They all get along, but it's still segregated." Students note that diversity is always a sensitive issue on campus and something that needs constant attention. Accordingly, some students believe that there is a limited sense of community. Nevertheless, most students describe their peers as "outgoing" and "friendly" as well as "approachable" and "helpful."

# FLORIDA STATE UNIVERSITY

FINANCIAL AID: 850-644-5871 • E-MAIL: ADMISSIONS@ADMIN.FSU.EDU • WEBSITE: WWW.FSU.EDU

## ADMISSIONS

*Very important factors considered include:* secondary school record. *Important factors considered include:* class rank, standardized test scores, state residency, talent/ability. *Other factors considered include:* alumni/ae relation, character/personal qualities, essays, extracurricular activities, recommendations, volunteer work, work experience. SAT I or ACT required. TOEFL required of all international applicants. High school diploma or GED is required. *High school units required/recommended:* 19 total required; 4 English required, 3 math required, 4 math recommended, 3 science required, 4 science recommended, 2 science lab required, 2 foreign language required, 4 elective required.

## The Inside Word

The high volume of applicants has everything to do with Florida State's selectivity, which continues to increase as budgets hold enrollment fairly level. Non-Floridians will find FSU's selection process to be a bit more welcoming than UF's, but just as impersonal. Performing arts auditions are quite competitive.

## FINANCIAL AID

*Students should submit:* FAFSA. The Princeton Review suggests that all financial aid forms be submitted as soon as possible after January 1. *Need-based scholarships/grants offered:* Pell, SEOG, state scholarships/grants, private scholarships, the school's own gift aid. *Loan aid offered:* FFEL Subsidized Stafford, FFEL Unsubsidized Stafford, FFEL PLUS, Federal Perkins. Federal Work-Study Program available. Institutional employment available. Applicants will be notified of awards on a rolling basis beginning on or about March 15. Off-campus job opportunities are excellent.

## FROM THE ADMISSIONS OFFICE

"Established in 1851, Florida State University is seated on the oldest continuous site of higher education in Florida and holds the state's first chapter of Phi Beta Kappa. It enjoys an outstanding reputation for offering a wide range of innovative academic achievements, like our College of Medicine, the first in the nation in 20 years; conducting groundbreaking research; attracting renowned faculty; being one of the "most wired" universities in the U.S.; housing an exceptional Career Center; and producing successful graduates. Seventeen colleges and schools offer nearly 200 undergraduate majors, 198 graduate degrees, and professional degrees in law and medicine. A diverse student body has access to student services that include the University Honors Program, the Center for Academic Retention and Enhancement, Disabled Student Services, the International Center, the Center for Civic Education and Service, and the Undergraduate Academic Advising Center. FSU leads the way in global education with international programs in Costa Rica, the Czech Republic, England, France, Italy, Panama, Russia, Spain, Switzerland, Vietnam, and the West Indies."

## SELECTIVITY

| | |
|---|---|
| Admissions Rating | 84 |
| # of applicants | 21,046 |
| % of applicants accepted | 70 |
| % of acceptees attending | 43 |

### FRESHMAN PROFILE

| | |
|---|---|
| Range SAT Verbal | 520-620 |
| Average SAT Verbal | 569 |
| Range SAT Math | 520-620 |
| Average SAT Math | 577 |
| Range ACT Composite | 22-26 |
| Average ACT Composite | 24 |
| Minimum TOEFL | 550 |
| Average HS GPA | 3.8 |
| % graduated top 10% of class | 58 |
| % graduated top 25% of class | 85 |
| % graduated top 50% of class | 100 |

### DEADLINES

| | |
|---|---|
| Priority admission | 12/31 |
| Regular admission | 3/1 |
| Nonfall registration? | yes |

### APPLICANTS ALSO LOOK AT

**AND OFTEN PREFER**
U of Florida
**AND SOMETIMES PREFER**
U of Central Florida
U of Miami
U of South Florida
**AND RARELY PREFER**
Florida International U

## FINANCIAL FACTS

| | |
|---|---|
| Financial Aid Rating | 83 |
| In-state tuition | $1,984 |
| Out-of-state tuition | $11,528 |
| Room and board | $5,740 |
| Books and supplies | $702 |
| Required fees | $701 |
| % frosh receiving aid | 38 |
| % undergrads receiving aid | 42 |
| Avg frosh grant | $4,033 |
| Avg frosh loan | $2,511 |

# FORDHAM UNIVERSITY

441 EAST FORDHAM ROAD, THEBAUD HALL, NEW YORK, NY 10458 • ADMISSIONS: 718-817-4000 • FAX: 718-367-9404

## CAMPUS LIFE

| | |
|---|---|
| Quality of Life Rating | 81 |
| Type of school | private |
| Affiliation | Roman Catholic |
| Environment | urban |

### STUDENTS

| | |
|---|---|
| Total undergrad enrollment | 7,228 |
| % male/female | 41/59 |
| % from out of state | 39 |
| % from public high school | 40 |
| % live on campus | 58 |
| % African American | 6 |
| % Asian | 6 |
| % Caucasian | 60 |
| % Hispanic | 11 |
| % international | 1 |
| # of countries represented | 38 |

### SURVEY SAYS . . .
Students love New York, NY
Musical organizations aren't popular
Theater is hot
Classes are small
Dorms are like palaces
Intercollegiate sports unpopular or nonexistent
Athletic facilities need improving
Lousy food on campus

## ACADEMICS

| | |
|---|---|
| Academic Rating | 76 |
| Calendar | semester |
| Student/faculty ratio | 11:1 |
| Profs interesting rating | 93 |
| Profs accessible rating | 88 |
| % profs teaching UG courses | 77 |
| Avg lab size | 10-19 students |
| Avg reg class size | 10-19 students |

## STUDENTS SPEAK OUT

### Academics
Fordham University has two campuses: Rose Hill in the Bronx and Lincoln Center in Manhattan. Rose Hill remains a traditional liberal arts and sciences program on a traditional "green lawns and Gothic architecture" campus. Lincoln Center, a "concrete campus," offers a wide range of courses but focuses on media studies, visual arts, and theater. At both campuses, students must complete a "great core curriculum" heavy in the liberal arts before proceeding to their major studies. Students appreciate the benefits of their location, explaining that "Fordham University offers a lot because of its diverse surroundings (the Bronx, New York City). Just by living here you are educated by meeting and seeing new places and things." Professors, who earn high marks, are "strict and difficult but good teachers" and also "humorous and easily accessible. Many are jolly ol' Jesuits who never fail to be passionate about what they teach." The administration is a different story: deans and upper administration receive good grades for being "very involved in the students' lives," but lower-level staff, with whom students more regularly interact, "don't answer student questions or lead you [to] where you can get help. Perhaps they don't know themselves." Still, students feel that the occasional administrative hassle is more than offset by small classes, an excellent library, and overall satisfaction with their academic experience here.

### Life
Fordham's two campuses tell a tale of two cities. Rose Hill is located in a working-class Bronx neighborhood. "The boogie-down Bronx is the best," offers one student. "It's a real culture shock for the majority of us who grew up in suburbia." Students are quick to note that both the campus and the immediate area are safe. Among Rose Hill's assets are "a beautiful green campus"; a nearby Little Italy with "great, cheap Italian food"; and easy access to the Botanical Gardens and the Bronx Zoo. Also, the Bronx campus "offers a lot of extracurriculars," writes one student. Reports another, "We have a lot of comedy and music get-togethers. There is always something going on around here." Plus, Rose Hill is only a short subway or bus ride away from Manhattan; many students take advantage of the University Shuttle Service to go between campuses. The other campus is at Lincoln Center, an exclusive area at the heart of Manhattan's West Side. Lincoln Center students have "no real campus." All residential students at Lincoln Center live in a connected campus high-rise and are almost certainly the lowest-income residents of their neighborhood. They report that "New York City provides amazing possibilities. I love to explore Central Park and the Village. Also, the museums are great." The school sits on the south end of the Lincoln Center complex, home to the New York City Opera and the Metropolitan Opera. Nearby Columbus Avenue provides high-end shopping and many restaurants, some of which, pricewise, are very reasonable.

### Student Body
Fordham students "are smart, but they also like to party. Because of the balance most students have, there is a relatively calm atmosphere on campus. Not too much partying, yet not too much stressing over the next exam or paper." Those who choose Fordham "want both a campus community and an independent city life. We all come together for big events, but there can be lulls where nothing seems to be going on." Students are "warm and friendly, but too apathetic" for some, as politics is not a preoccupation of most students here. The student body is "representative of the surrounding population, i.e. Long Island, northern Jersey, and Connecticut." Writes one student, "I feel like the entire population of Long Island goes to school here at times. It's hard to find someone who isn't from New York."

# FORDHAM UNIVERSITY

FINANCIAL AID: 718-817-3800 • E-MAIL: ENROLL@FORDHAM.EDU • WEBSITE: WWW.FORDHAM.EDU

## ADMISSIONS

*Very important factors considered include:* class rank, secondary school record, standardized test scores. *Important factors considered include:* alumni/ae relation, character/personal qualities, essays, extracurricular activities, interview, recommendations, talent/ability. *Other factors considered include:* geographical residence, minority status, volunteer work, work experience. SAT I or ACT required; SAT II recommended. TOEFL required of all international applicants. High school diploma or GED is required. *High school units required/recommended:* 22 total required; 25 total recommended; 4 English required, 3 math required, 4 math recommended, 3 science required, 4 science recommended, 2 foreign language required, 3 foreign language recommended, 2 social studies required, 3 social studies recommended, 6 elective required.

### The Inside Word

Candidates are reviewed by a committee made up of admissions officers, faculty, administrators, and deans. Admission to Fordham is quite competitive and a solid flow of applicants from metropolitan-area Catholic schools keeps their student profile sound.

## FINANCIAL AID

*Students should submit:* FAFSA, CSS/Financial Aid PROFILE, state aid form, noncustodial (divorced/separated) parent's statement, business/farm supplement. The Princeton Review suggests that all financial aid forms be submitted as soon as possible after January 1. *Need-based scholarships/grants offered:* Pell, SEOG, state scholarships/grants. *Loan aid offered:* FFEL Subsidized Stafford, FFEL Unsubsidized Stafford, FFEL PLUS, Federal Perkins. Federal Work-Study Program available. Applicants will be notified of awards on or about April 1. Off-campus job opportunities are excellent.

## FROM THE ADMISSIONS OFFICE

"Fordham, an independent institution offering an education in the Jesuit tradition, has three major campuses in the metropolitan New York area. The Rose Hill campus, the largest "green" campus in New York City, is a beautiful 85 acres located next to the New York Botanical Garden and the Bronx Zoo. The Lincoln Center campus is located in the middle of Manhattan across from one of the world's greatest cultural centers, Lincoln Center for the Performing Arts. And in July of 2002, Marymount College in Tarrytown, New York, a women's liberal arts college, will become the 11th school of Fordham. Fordham offers its students a variety of majors, concentrations, and programs that can be combined with an extensive internship program. Fordham works with more than 2,000 organizations in the New York metropolitan area to arrange internships for students in fields such as business, communications, medicine, law and education."

---

### SELECTIVITY

| | |
|---|---|
| Admissions Rating | 83 |
| # of applicants | 11,380 |
| % of applicants accepted | 57 |
| % of acceptees attending | 27 |
| # accepting a place on wait list | 441 |
| % admitted from wait list | 6 |

### FRESHMAN PROFILE

| | |
|---|---|
| Range SAT Verbal | 530-630 |
| Average SAT Verbal | 606 |
| Range SAT Math | 530-630 |
| Average SAT Math | 606 |
| Range ACT Composite | 23-27 |
| Average ACT Composite | 26 |
| Minimum TOEFL | 550 |
| Average HS GPA | 3.6 |
| % graduated top 10% of class | 30 |
| % graduated top 25% of class | 68 |
| % graduated top 50% of class | 94 |

### DEADLINES

| | |
|---|---|
| Priority admission | 2/1 |
| Regular admission | 2/1 |
| Regular notification | 4/1 |
| Nonfall registration? | yes |

### APPLICANTS ALSO LOOK AT

**AND OFTEN PREFER**
NYU
Binghamton U.
Columbia
Boston U., Villanova

**AND SOMETIMES PREFER**
SUNY—Albany
SUNY—Stony Brook
George Washington
Boston Coll., Siena

**AND RARELY PREFER**
St. John's U. (NY)
Iona, Hofstra

### FINANCIAL FACTS

| | |
|---|---|
| Financial Aid Rating | 83 |
| Tuition | $21,210 |
| Room and board | $8,745 |
| Books and supplies | $660 |
| Required fees | $460 |
| % frosh receiving aid | 73 |
| % undergrads receiving aid | 73 |

# FRANKLIN & MARSHALL COLLEGE

PO Box 3003, Lancaster, PA 17604-3003 • Admissions: 717-291-3953 • Fax: 717-291-4381

## CAMPUS LIFE

| | |
|---|---|
| Quality of Life Rating | 80 |
| Type of school | private |
| Environment | suburban |

### STUDENTS

| | |
|---|---|
| Total undergrad enrollment | 1,926 |
| % male/female | 52/48 |
| % from out of state | 65 |
| % from public high school | 55 |
| % live on campus | 67 |
| % African American | 3 |
| % Asian | 4 |
| % Caucasian | 81 |
| % Hispanic | 2 |
| % international | 7 |

### SURVEY SAYS . . .
Popular college radio
Frats and sororities dominate social scene
Campus easy to get around
Profs teach upper-levels
Classes are small
Students are cliquish
Students don't like Lancaster, PA
Lousy food on campus
Very little drug use
Student publications are ignored

## ACADEMICS

| | |
|---|---|
| Academic Rating | 92 |
| Calendar | semester |
| Student/faculty ratio | 11:1 |
| Profs interesting rating | 94 |
| Profs accessible rating | 99 |
| % profs teaching UG courses | 100 |
| Avg lab size | 10-19 students |
| Avg reg class size | 10-19 students |

### MOST POPULAR MAJORS
Business administration/management
English language and literature
Political science and government

## STUDENTS SPEAK OUT

### Academics
Academics at Franklin & Marshall are "very challenging no matter what your major. We don't get a good enough reputation for the amount of work we do. Expect to work long, hard hours for a B." Reason for disappointment? No, because "in the end, you end up getting a better education for it." Students appreciate professors who "are great, for the most part, and really like interaction with students in and out of class." Explains one student, "The professors are always around to help with anything. I'm on a first-name basis with the professors in my major department, and I only just finished my first year. I hear most departments are like that." Similarly, the administration "is surely unique. The president and vice president of the college even co-teach a course. The president holds luncheons at which any student may eat and discuss issues. I was even invited to a dean's house for dinner on one occasion." So it's not too hard to see why so many students put up with the demands at Franklin & Marshall; most of them feel like they've got a good support group behind them. And with F&M's solid reputation, many students feel as if they are bound to succeed after graduation. As one student points out, "Not a liberal arts college, really, but a pre-professional school."

### Life
Students caution prospects that F&M "is an extremely hard school." Many find the academic pressure stressful, which may help explain why "alcohol is a big part of campus life, whether it's beer in frat parties, or hard liquor in apartment parties, or just sitting in your room, watching TV and swigging Smirnoff." The Greeks "are the main social activity on weekends." Some feel that "there is nothing to do besides fraternity parties, which are very snobbish." Others disagree, reporting that "fraternities do dominate the social scene on Friday and Saturday nights. However, there has been an increase in late night activities, such as off-campus trips, comedians, and other forms of entertainment. The College Entertainment Committee is wonderful for setting up events both on and off campus. There are weekly movies that cost $1 for students, which are great. There have been trips to Philadelphia, Washington D.C., and New York City." Students particularly enjoy the Spring Arts Festival, "the craziest time of the year. It's a week of celebrating like you wouldn't believe. The administration sets up a beer tent for those who are 21, and the main street in town is closed so we can party in it. We bring in bands and chill with everyone."

### Student Body
F&M students derive largely "from the same background: Mid-Atlantic state, white, suburban, and upper middle-class. It gets boring." Complains one city dweller, "I've only met two other people that actually live in a city. There are four black students in the class of 2005, and yet we're the 'most diverse class ever.' " It's pretty much agreed among students that they "are rather conservative and conformist. Most people will be sporting new clothes from J.Crew or Abercrombie and Fitch." Some point out that "while we do have our stereotypical frat boys and sorority girls, there are certainly places where those for whom that is not the crowd can fit in. I have made friends [of students who hail] from France, Scotland, and England" and of students from "various economic and religious backgrounds, sexual orientations, and in academic years."

226 ■ THE BEST 351 COLLEGES

# FRANKLIN & MARSHALL COLLEGE

FINANCIAL AID: 717-291-3991 • E-MAIL: ADMISSION@FANDM.EDU • WEBSITE: WWW.FANDM.EDU

## ADMISSIONS
*Very important factors considered include:* character/personal qualities, class rank, secondary school record. *Important factors considered include:* essays, extracurricular activities, interview, minority status, recommendations, standardized test scores, talent/ability, volunteer work. *Other factors considered include:* alumni/ae relation, geographical residence, work experience. TOEFL required of all international applicants. High school diploma or GED is required. *High school units required/recommended:* 4 English required, 3 math required, 4 math recommended, 2 science required, 3 science recommended, 2 science lab required, 3 science lab recommended, 2 foreign language required, 4 foreign language recommended, 1 social studies required, 3 social studies recommended, 2 history required, 3 history recommended.

## The Inside Word
Applicants who are serious about attending the college should definitely interview; it will also help to make it known that F & M is one of your top choices. The college loses a lot of its admits to competitor colleges and will take notice of a candidate who is likely to enroll.

## FINANCIAL AID
*Students should submit:* FAFSA, CSS/Financial Aid PROFILE, state aid form, noncustodial (divorced/separated) parent's statement, business/farm supplement, previous year's federal taxes and W-2s. Regular filing deadline is February 1. The Princeton Review suggests that all financial aid forms be submitted as soon as possible after January 1. *Need-based scholarships/grants offered:* Pell, SEOG, state scholarships/grants, private scholarships, the school's own gift aid. *Loan aid offered:* FFEL Subsidized Stafford, FFEL Unsubsidized Stafford, FFEL PLUS, Federal Perkins, college/university loans from institutional funds. Federal Work-Study Program available. Institutional employment available. Applicants will be notified of awards on or about April 1. Off-campus job opportunities are excellent.

## FROM THE ADMISSIONS OFFICE
"Franklin & Marshall students choose from a variety of fields of study, traditional and interdisciplinary, that typify liberal learning. Professors in all of these fields are committed to a common purpose, which is to teach students to think, speak, and write with clarity and confidence. Whether the course is in theater or in physics, the class will be small, engagement will be high, and discussion will dominate over lecture. Thus throughout his or her four years, beginning with the First Year Seminar, a student at Franklin & Marshall is repeatedly invited to active participation in intellectual play at a high level. Our graduates consistently testify to the high quality of an F & M education as a mental preparation for life."

### SELECTIVITY
★ ★ ★ ☆

| | |
|---|---|
| Admissions Rating | 89 |
| # of applicants | 3,425 |
| % of applicants accepted | 62 |
| % of acceptees attending | 25 |
| # accepting a place on wait list | 592 |
| % admitted from wait list | 11 |
| # of early decision applicants | 279 |
| % accepted early decision | 70 |

### FRESHMAN PROFILE
| | |
|---|---|
| Range SAT Verbal | 570-660 |
| Average SAT Verbal | 615 |
| Range SAT Math | 590-680 |
| Average SAT Math | 633 |
| Minimum TOEFL | 600 |
| % graduated top 10% of class | 46 |
| % graduated top 25% of class | 70 |
| % graduated top 50% of class | 92 |

### DEADLINES
| | |
|---|---|
| Early decision | 11/15 |
| Early decision notification | 12/15 |
| Regular admission | 2/1 |
| Regular notification | 4/1 |
| Nonfall registration? | yes |

### APPLICANTS ALSO LOOK AT
**AND OFTEN PREFER**
U of Pennsylvania
Hamilton
Cornell
Haverford
**AND SOMETIMES PREFER**
Lafayette, Lehigh
Bucknell, Dickinson
Colgate, Skidmore
**AND RARELY PREFER**
Gettysburg, Boston U, Tufts

### FINANCIAL FACTS
★ ★ ★ ☆

| | |
|---|---|
| Financial Aid Rating | 81 |
| Tuition | $27,230 |
| Room and board | $6,580 |
| Books and supplies | $650 |
| Required fees | $50 |
| % frosh receiving aid | 65 |
| % undergrads receiving aid | 64 |
| Avg frosh grant | $15,913 |
| Avg frosh loan | $3,879 |

THE BEST 351 COLLEGES ■ 227

# FURMAN UNIVERSITY

OFFICE OF ADMISSIONS, 3300 POINSETT HIGHWAY, GREENVILLE, SC 29613 • ADMISSIONS: 864-294-2034 • FAX: 864-294-3127

## CAMPUS LIFE

| | |
|---|---|
| **Quality of Life Rating** | **86** |
| Type of school | private |
| Environment | suburban |

### STUDENTS

| | |
|---|---|
| Total undergrad enrollment | 2,772 |
| % male/female | 44/56 |
| % from out of state | 69 |
| % from public high school | 68 |
| % live on campus | 95 |
| % in (# of) fraternities | 30 (8) |
| % in (# of) sororities | 35 (8) |
| % African American | 6 |
| % Asian | 1 |
| % Caucasian | 89 |
| % Hispanic | 1 |
| % international | 1 |
| # of countries represented | 27 |

### SURVEY SAYS . . .
Very little drug use
Frats and sororities dominate social scene
Diversity lacking on campus
(Almost) everyone plays intramural sports
Beautiful campus
Students are very religious
Musical organizations are hot
Students get along with local community
Library needs improving
(Almost) no one smokes

## ACADEMICS

| | |
|---|---|
| **Academic Rating** | **90** |
| Calendar | other |
| Student/faculty ratio | 11:1 |
| Profs interesting rating | 96 |
| Profs accessible rating | 98 |
| % profs teaching UG courses | 100 |
| Avg reg class size | 20-29 students |

### MOST POPULAR MAJORS
Political science and government
Business administration/management
History

## STUDENTS SPEAK OUT

### Academics
"Furman is the best secret in the nation," writes a sophomore at this conservative, traditional liberal arts school located near the mountains in "beautiful" Greenville, South Carolina." Furman's special brand of "engaged learning" as well as its small size (under 3,000) makes for "rigorous classes and good teachers." During their first two years, students fulfill their general education requirements in humanities, social sciences, natural sciences, math, foreign language, health and exercise science, and nonwestern studies before moving on to complete their major. Music, biology, chemistry, business administration, health and exercise science, and political science are among the most popular. It's a "well-balanced and strong" curriculum that yields a "well-balanced individual," notes a senior. Professors are "generally the best part of Furman" since they're "almost always well prepared and challenging." And while "a school whose professors are more liberal than their students is odd, surely, there's a general camaraderie because we—students and teachers—feel in league together against the administration," which is "more in touch with the dead (and Furman's rich Baptist alumni) than with current students." Still, "this campus is not as conservative as people may think," according to a feisty sophomore. "There are protests and demonstrations. . . . Some of my professors influence controversy. We actually discuss issues that affect the world."

### Life
"Life at Furman is definitely privileged," writes a junior; with its "beautiful campus close to mountains and beach, amazing students, great facilities, wonderful education, and solid combination of Greeks, independents, and great student activities," who could ask for more? Not many. Furman students seem, on the whole, genuinely happy with their college experience, noting that "people at Furman are incredibly supportive. Because academics are so strenuous and students are very involved after class, people are busy but willing to be available." One senior admits that "life at Furman is like a Brady Bunch episode; everyone is smiling and friendly, and the problems are solved at the end of each episode." Chalk it up to the "Furman Bubble," says a junior, who wishes that "campus was not so far away from downtown Greenville," with its many restaurants, bars, and small-city cultural scene. Party-wise, Furman is officially a dry campus, though a senior jokes that this is "because all the bottles you see are empty." (It's "damp" rather than dry, argues a second-year. "Administrators just look the other way.") And while the larger-than-average religious population does make for something of a schizophrenic social situation, a senior declares, "Fun is either praise songs or pounding beers. . . . There is no middle ground."

### Student Body
A sophomore sums up: At FU, "regardless of race, ethnicity, and status, everyone gets along." While most students would agree with this assessment, there's also the sense that tolerance and true diversity of opinion often take a backseat to good old-fashioned southern gentility. "Students at Furman are generally friendly and intelligent; however, the lack of diversity and overwhelming presence of Betty BMW and Johnny SUV is a little disconcerting." Still, "we're not all Christians who sit around and pray together," argues a senior, calling Furman's reputation for ultraconservatism "a big misconception."

# FURMAN UNIVERSITY

FINANCIAL AID: 864-294-2204 • E-MAIL: ADMISSIONS@FURMAN.EDU • WEBSITE: WWW.FURMAN.EDU

## ADMISSIONS
*Very important factors considered include:* secondary school record. *Important factors considered include:* character/personal qualities, class rank, essays, extracurricular activities, standardized test scores. *Other factors considered include:* alumni/ae relation, minority status, recommendations, talent/ability, volunteer work, work experience. SAT I or ACT required. TOEFL required of all international applicants. High school diploma or GED is required. *High school units required/recommended:* 14 total required; 18 total recommended; 4 English required, 3 math required, 4 math recommended, 2 science required, 3 science recommended, 2 science lab required, 3 science lab recommended, 2 foreign language required, 3 foreign language recommended, 3 social studies required, 4 social studies recommended.

### The Inside Word
While Furman is selective academically, there is a high level of self-selection on the part of its applicants. Good students who truly want to be here will encounter little resistance from the admissions committee.

## FINANCIAL AID
*Students should submit:* FAFSA, institution's own financial aid form. South Carolina residents must complete required state forms when noted. Regular filing deadline is January 15. The Princeton Review suggests that all financial aid forms be submitted as soon as possible after January 1. *Need-based scholarships/grants offered:* Pell, SEOG, state scholarships/grants, private scholarships, the school's own gift aid. *Loan aid offered:* FFEL Subsidized Stafford, FFEL Unsubsidized Stafford, FFEL PLUS, Federal Perkins, state loans, donor-sponsored loans for study abroad. Federal Work-Study Program available. Institutional employment available. Applicants will be notified of awards on or about March 5. Off-campus job opportunities are excellent.

## FROM THE ADMISSIONS OFFICE
"Furman University offers an excellent liberal arts education and quality of life. Outside the classroom, the University places a high value on community service. Furman is regularly recognized as one of the nation's top educational values. On campus, Furman is currently expanding—in fact tripling—the size of the library to make way for increasing journal and book storage as well as expanding facilities for the Center for Collaborative Learning & Communication. In addition, Furman recently completed a new academic building for the Economics and Business Administrations departments and will break ground on a renovation of Furman Hall, the academic building for the humanities, beginning in the summer of 2003."

### SELECTIVITY
★ ★ ★ ☆

| | |
|---|---|
| Admissions Rating | 84 |
| # of applicants | 3,866 |
| % of applicants accepted | 58 |
| % of acceptees attending | 33 |
| # accepting a place on wait list | 582 |
| # of early decision applicants | 651 |
| % accepted early decision | 77 |

### FRESHMAN PROFILE
| | |
|---|---|
| Range SAT Verbal | 590-690 |
| Range SAT Math | 590-680 |
| Range ACT Composite | 24-29 |
| Minimum TOEFL | 570 |
| Average HS GPA | 3.9 |
| % graduated top 10% of class | 61 |
| % graduated top 25% of class | 81 |
| % graduated top 50% of class | 99 |

### DEADLINES
| | |
|---|---|
| Early decision | 11/15 |
| Early decision notification | 12/15 |
| Regular admission | 1/15 |
| Regular notification | 3/15 |

### APPLICANTS ALSO LOOK AT
**AND OFTEN PREFER**
Wake Forest
Duke
UNC—Chapel Hill
Washington and Lee
Vanderbilt

**AND SOMETIMES PREFER**
Emory
Davidson
U South Carolina—Columbia
Georgia Tech.
Wofford

**AND RARELY PREFER**
Clemson
Auburn U

### FINANCIAL FACTS
★ ★ ★ ☆

| | |
|---|---|
| Financial Aid Rating | 84 |
| Tuition | $20,856 |
| Room and board | $5,664 |
| % frosh receiving aid | 48 |
| % undergrads receiving aid | 42 |
| Avg frosh grant | $13,350 |
| Avg frosh loan | $3,750 |

# GEORGE MASON UNIVERSITY

UNDERGRADUATE ADMISSIONS OFFICE, 4400 UNIV. DRIVE MSN 3A4, FAIRFAX, VA 22030-4444 • ADMISSIONS: 703-993-2400

## CAMPUS LIFE

| | |
|---|---|
| Quality of Life Rating | 74 |
| Type of school | public |
| Environment | suburban |

### STUDENTS

| | |
|---|---|
| Total undergrad enrollment | 15,802 |
| % male/female | 44/56 |
| % from out of state | 10 |
| % live on campus | 19 |
| % in (# of) fraternities | 3 (18) |
| % in (# of) sororities | 3 (10) |
| % African American | 10 |
| % Asian | 17 |
| % Caucasian | 65 |
| % Hispanic | 8 |
| % international | 4 |

### SURVEY SAYS . . .
Students love Fairfax, VA
(Almost) everyone smokes
Popular college radio
Ethnic diversity on campus
Large classes
Athletic facilities need improving
Campus difficult to get around
Musical organizations aren't popular

## ACADEMICS

| | |
|---|---|
| Academic Rating | 79 |
| Calendar | semester |
| Student/faculty ratio | 16:1 |
| Profs interesting rating | 91 |
| Profs accessible rating | 89 |
| % profs teaching UG courses | 82 |
| % classes taught by TAs | 18 |
| Avg lab size | 10-19 students |
| Avg reg class size | 20-29 students |

### MOST POPULAR MAJORS
Business, management, marketing, and related support services
Political science and government
Computer science

## STUDENTS SPEAK OUT

### Academics
Despite its regular inclusion in this guide, "GMU has a reputation of almost being a joke university because it's mostly a commuter school. GMU deserves a lot more credit than it is given, and many people should not look at it as a 'back-up' school." We agree. At state university prices, GMU is a great bargain for Virginia residents, providing "an easygoing and helpful atmosphere and a spirit of innovation." Like many large schools, "Mason offers the best and the worst to its students. We have greatly talented administrators and professors who generally care about the students and are great educators. [Yet] there are also administrators and professors that should be teaching preschool." The most highly praised academic offerings include those of the School of Management ("getting in takes a lot of hard work") and the government studies department, which benefit from the proximity of Washington, D.C.; writes one student, "It's very cool to have a professor tell you about an encounter that he had with the secretary of defense or to hear another tell you that he will be on NPR later that evening discussing the Middle East peace process." Best of all is the Honors Program, which offers smaller classes and a strong emphasis on writing skills.

### Life
Because so many of GMU's students commute, many here feel that "life at school ends at Thursday after class. Over the weekend this place is like a ghost town; even people who live on campus leave. Typical on-campus life is attending class, hanging out at Johnson [the student center], or playing pool at the game room. Anything else is done off campus." Off campus often means Washington, D.C., accessible by the D.C. Metro, which is itself accessible from campus via a school shuttle bus. "Being only about 45 minutes from Washington, D.C., there's plenty to do in regards to social activities if one is motivated enough. You can go to a club, get a really good dinner, see some great museums, and check out the government buildings." There is less to do in hometown Fairfax, "the richest county in the U.S. The average rent is WAY over $1,000 per month. It's ridiculous." The lack of off-campus housing has led to a severe shortage of dorm space. One student warns, "There is such a housing problem that all the two-, three- and four-person rooms are now three-, four-, and five- people . . . . Don't be the last man in on move-in day because then you are fighting with three people for the two available desks." On a positive note, "drama club performances are really popular," as are GMU men's basketball games. Students also report that "the school itself is extremely aesthetically pleasing."

### Student Body
GMU is "a very diverse school, right near the heart of the nation's capital. There are students from all over the world, which really adds to the atmosphere." Some students write that "different groups do not usually interact"; more often, however, people complain that the lack of interaction is mostly caused by the fact that there are "lots of commuters" here, making students feel isolated from one another. Writes one student, "Unfortunately, the school is not very social at all. To get involved you pretty much need to go Greek. If you aren't in a fraternity or sorority you don't have the opportunity to meet many people outside of your classes." Academically, students feel there is an "excellent mix" here. "We have some of the most serious academic scholars and others who are more geared toward learning what they need to know to succeed in the real world, such as business or technology skills," writes one student.

# GEORGE MASON UNIVERSITY

Fax: 703-993-2392 • Financial Aid: 703-993-2353 • E-mail: admissions@gmu.edu • Website: www.gmu.edu

## ADMISSIONS

*Very important factors considered include:* secondary school record. *Important factors considered include:* character/personal qualities, essays, recommendations, standardized test scores, talent/ability. *Other factors considered include:* alumni/ae relation, class rank, extracurricular activities, geographical residence, interview, minority status, state residency, volunteer work, work experience. SAT I or ACT required; SAT II recommended. TOEFL required of all international applicants. High school diploma or GED is required. *High school units required/recommended:* 18 total required; 24 total recommended; 4 English required, 3 math required, 4 math recommended, 3 science required, 4 science recommended, 3 science lab required, 4 science lab recommended, 2 foreign language required, 3 foreign language recommended, 3 social studies required, 4 social studies recommended, 3 elective required, 5 elective recommended.

### *The Inside Word*

George Mason is a popular destination for college for two key reasons: its proximity to Washington, D.C., and the fact that it is not nearly as difficult to gain admission at Mason as it is at UVA or William and Mary, the two flagships of the Virginia state system. The university's quality faculty and impressive facilities make it worth taking a look if low-cost, solid programs in the D.C. area are high on your list.

## FINANCIAL AID

*Students should submit:* FAFSA. The Princeton Review suggests that all financial aid forms be submitted as soon as possible after January 1. *Need-based scholarships/grants offered:* Pell, SEOG, state scholarships/grants, private scholarships, the school's own gift aid. *Loan aid offered:* Direct Subsidized Stafford, Direct Unsubsidized Stafford, Direct PLUS, Federal Perkins. Federal Work-Study Program available. Institutional employment available. Applicants will be notified of awards on a rolling basis beginning on or about April 1. Off-campus job opportunities are excellent.

## FROM THE ADMISSIONS OFFICE

"Great minds don't think alike, and at George Mason University, we don't expect them to. From creative writing to systems engineering, Mason programs offer cutting-edge curricula and facilities along with the best that technology has to offer. Our visionary outlook has attracted a faculty of renowned scholars and teachers, while our business and community partnerships provide students with practical experience and career opportunities."

## SELECTIVITY

| | |
|---|---:|
| Admissions Rating | 85 |
| # of applicants | 8,106 |
| % of applicants accepted | 68 |
| % of acceptees attending | 39 |
| # accepting a place on wait list | 377 |
| % admitted from wait list | 36 |

### FRESHMAN PROFILE

| | |
|---|---:|
| Range SAT Verbal | 480-580 |
| Average SAT Verbal | 534 |
| Range SAT Math | 490-590 |
| Average SAT Math | 542 |
| Range ACT Composite | 19-23 |
| Minimum TOEFL | 570 |
| Average HS GPA | 3.2 |

### DEADLINES

| | |
|---|---:|
| Regular admission | 2/1 |
| Regular notification | 4/1 |
| Nonfall registration? | yes |

### APPLICANTS ALSO LOOK AT AND OFTEN PREFER

U. Virginia
Georgetown U.
William and Mary
James Madison
Virginia Tech

**AND SOMETIMES PREFER**
George Washington

## FINANCIAL FACTS

| | |
|---|---:|
| Financial Aid Rating | 77 |
| In-state tuition | $2,376 |
| Out-of-state tuition | $11,220 |
| Room and board | $5,400 |
| Books and supplies | $750 |
| Required fees | $1,416 |
| % frosh receiving aid | 37 |
| % undergrads receiving aid | 40 |
| Avg frosh grant | $3,756 |
| Avg frosh loan | $6,222 |

# GEORGE WASHINGTON UNIVERSITY

2121 I STREET NW, SUITE 201, WASHINGTON, DC 20052 • ADMISSIONS: 202-994-6040 • FAX: 202-994-0325

## CAMPUS LIFE

| Quality of Life Rating | 88 |
| --- | --- |
| Type of school | private |
| Environment | urban |

### STUDENTS
| | |
| --- | --- |
| Total undergrad enrollment | 10,063 |
| % male/female | 44/56 |
| % from out of state | 94 |
| % from public high school | 70 |
| % live on campus | 62 |
| % in (# of) fraternities | 14 (12) |
| % in (# of) sororities | 11 (9) |
| % African American | 6 |
| % Asian | 11 |
| % Caucasian | 68 |
| % Hispanic | 5 |
| % international | 5 |
| # of countries represented | 101 |

### SURVEY SAYS . . .
Students love Washington, D.C.
Political activism is hot
Dorms are like palaces
Students don't get along with local community
High cost of living
Unattractive campus
Ethnic diversity on campus
Lots of long lines and red tape
Athletic facilities need improving
No one plays intramural sports

## ACADEMICS

| Academic Rating | 88 |
| --- | --- |
| Calendar | semester |
| Student/faculty ratio | 14:1 |
| Profs interesting rating | 91 |
| Profs accessible rating | 92 |
| % profs teaching UG courses | 67 |
| % classes taught by TAs | 3 |
| Avg lab size | 20-29 students |
| Avg reg class size | 10-19 students |

## STUDENTS SPEAK OUT

### Academics
Few schools exploit their location as fully as George Washington University, a school whose faculty and programs are deeply entrenched in the goings-on of Washington, D.C. "Being in D.C., GW takes advantage of the resources and personnel found here," notes one approving student. "Much of the faculty are experts in political science and criminal justice." Writes another, "It's all about location. Whatever teachers can't give you in the classroom, they send you out to get." A few caution that "GW's profs are part of D.C., not GW. That has benefits and drawbacks," but most agree that the pluses outweigh the minuses. Nearly one-quarter of the students here are engaged in international studies, and many others pursue such government-related majors as political science, political communication, and criminal justice. Other strong programs include biology, psychology, and English. Professors here "are what make or break the course. Some are excellent and some are horrible." Lecture courses, especially those at the intro level, "can be rather large," and some suggest that "there is never a need to attend large lecture classes. By attending only the discussion sections you gain all the information necessary for the course plus a couple of extra hours sleep." However, things improve with upper-level courses. GW's administration earns low marks, with students complaining that "there's a lot of administrative bureaucratic red tape to get through for certain things" and that "the administration tends not to listen to students until they raise a big public ruckus. Making appointments to meet with upper-level administrators can be very difficult." Students give props to the Honors Program and excellent marks to the library.

### Life
GW, like New York University and Boston University, lacks a traditional campus, instead occupying buildings scattered throughout an urban neighborhood. As at other such schools, the sense of community here is weak and the social scene is fragmented. Fortunately, D.C. picks up the slack, offering students some of the nation's finest museums and monuments, beautiful public spaces, limitless shopping, a thriving nightlife, and a boatload of internship and networking opportunities. "D.C. rocks!" writes one student. "There is so much to do here, you literally could do something different every night of the week. A lot of bars and clubs turn into GW parties, which is cool." Also, "we do a lot of shopping because Georgetown is so close," explains another. On-campus activity centers on "over 300 student organizations on campus, so whatever your lifestyle is, there should be a group for you." Students complain that, due to an increase in admissions, classrooms and dining halls are growing uncomfortably overcrowded. Greek life is slight but students feel it "could be an important and positive part of this school except for the administration's vendetta against it."

### Student Body
Students come to GW to be in the nation's capital, and accordingly "it's not a school for someone who isn't into politics. Everyone here is glued to CNN." On the political spectrum, "it's a very Democratic and liberal school," writes one student. "If you want to protest, this school's for you!" Students also tend to be reformed slackers. Explains one, "This school is for everyone who could have been accepted to an Ivy League school and could have afforded it, but never applied themselves to that extent." A huge international contingent contributes to "the diversity—ethnically, politically, geographically, and intellectually—that breeds so many wonderful relationships."

232 ■ THE BEST 351 COLLEGES

# GEORGE WASHINGTON UNIVERSITY

FINANCIAL AID: 202-994-6620 • E-MAIL: GWADM@GWIS2.CIRC.GWU.EDU • WEBSITE: WWW.GWU.EDU

## ADMISSIONS

*Very important factors considered include:* secondary school record. *Important factors considered include:* class rank, essays, extracurricular activities, interview, recommendations, standardized test scores, talent/ability, volunteer work. *Other factors considered include:* alumni/ae relation, character/personal qualities, geographical residence, minority status, work experience. SAT I or ACT required; SAT I preferred. TOEFL required of all international applicants. High school diploma is required and GED is not accepted. *High school units required/recommended:* 4 English required, 2 math required, 4 math recommended, 2 science required, 4 science recommended, 1 science lab required, 2 foreign language required, 4 foreign language recommended, 2 social studies required, 4 social studies recommended.

### The Inside Word

The low percentage of admitted students who enroll at GW works to keep the admit rate relatively high. For strong students, this is definitely a low-stress admissions process. The university's location and access to faculty with impressive credentials are the main reasons for GW's sound freshman profile.

## FINANCIAL AID

*Students should submit:* FAFSA, CSS/Financial Aid PROFILE. The Princeton Review suggests that all financial aid forms be submitted as soon as possible after January 1. *Need-based scholarships/grants offered:* Pell, SEOG, state scholarships/grants, the school's own gift aid. *Loan aid offered:* FFEL Subsidized Stafford, FFEL Unsubsidized Stafford, FFEL PLUS, Federal Perkins. Federal Work-Study Program available. Institutional employment available. Applicants will be notified of awards on or about March 20. Off-campus job opportunities are excellent.

## FROM THE ADMISSIONS OFFICE

"At GW, we welcome students who show a measure of impatience with the limitations of traditional education. At many universities, the edge of campus is the real world, but not at GW, where our campus and Washington, D.C., are seamless. We look for bold, bright students who are ambitious, energetic, and self-motivated. Here, where we are so close to the centers of thought and action in every field we offer, we easily integrate our outstanding academic tradition and faculty connections with the best internship and job opportunities of Washington, D.C. A generous scholarship and financial assistance program attracts top students from all parts of the country and the world."

---

### SELECTIVITY

| | |
|---|---|
| Admissions Rating | 91 |
| # of applicants | 15,960 |
| % of applicants accepted | 48 |
| % of acceptees attending | 33 |
| # accepting a place on wait list | 709 |
| % admitted from wait list | 26 |
| # of early decision applicants | 695 |
| % accepted early decision | 61 |

### FRESHMAN PROFILE

| | |
|---|---|
| Range SAT Verbal | 570-660 |
| Average SAT Verbal | 620 |
| Range SAT Math | 580-670 |
| Average SAT Math | 620 |
| Range ACT Composite | 24-29 |
| Average ACT Composite | 26 |
| Minimum TOEFL | 550 |
| % graduated top 10% of class | 46 |
| % graduated top 25% of class | 83 |
| % graduated top 50% of class | 99 |

### DEADLINES

| | |
|---|---|
| Early decision | 12/1 |
| Early decision notification | 12/15 |
| Priority admission | 12/1 |
| Regular admission | 1/15 |
| Regular notification | 3/15 |
| Nonfall registration? | yes |

### APPLICANTS ALSO LOOK AT AND OFTEN PREFER
Georgetown U.
U. Virginia
Boston U.
Emory, NYU

### AND SOMETIMES PREFER
Tufts
U. Vermont
U. Maryland—Coll. Park
American
Catholic

### FINANCIAL FACTS

| | |
|---|---|
| Financial Aid Rating | 84 |
| Tuition | $27,790 |
| Room and board | $9,110 |
| Books and supplies | $850 |
| Required fees | $30 |
| % frosh receiving aid | 41 |
| % undergrads receiving aid | 38 |
| Avg frosh grant | $11,800 |
| Avg frosh loan | $3,000 |

THE BEST 351 COLLEGES ■ 233

# GEORGETOWN UNIVERSITY

37TH AND P STREETS, NW, WASHINGTON, DC 20057 • ADMISSIONS: 202-687-3600 • FAX: 202-687-5084

## CAMPUS LIFE

| | |
|---|---|
| Quality of Life Rating | 89 |
| Type of school | private |
| Affiliation | Roman Catholic |
| Environment | urban |

### STUDENTS

| | |
|---|---|
| Total undergrad enrollment | 6,332 |
| % male/female | 47/53 |
| % from out of state | 98 |
| % from public high school | 46 |
| % live on campus | 69 |
| % African American | 7 |
| % Asian | 10 |
| % Caucasian | 74 |
| % Hispanic | 5 |
| % international | 4 |

### SURVEY SAYS . . .
Students love Washington, DC
Everyone loves the Hoyas
Lots of classroom discussion
No one cheats
Campus feels safe
Classes are small
Political activism is hot
No one plays intramural sports
Very little beer drinking
Students are cliquish

## ACADEMICS

| | |
|---|---|
| Academic Rating | 96 |
| Calendar | semester |
| Student/faculty ratio | 11:1 |
| Profs interesting rating | 94 |
| Profs accessible rating | 92 |
| % profs teaching UG courses | 100 |
| Avg lab size | 10-19 students |
| Avg reg class size | 10-19 students |

### MOST POPULAR MAJORS
Finance
English language and literature
International relations and affairs

## STUDENTS SPEAK OUT

### Academics
Because of its location in the nation's capital, Georgetown University is uniquely positioned to offer advanced studies in government and foreign relations. The undergraduate student body is divided into four distinct schools: Arts and Sciences, Business Administration, Foreign Service, and Nursing and Health Studies. Writes one student, "The schools are definitely divided: students in each have their own stereotype. E.g., 'Oh, you're in the SFS, you must be really smart,' or 'You're in the business school, so you're a slacker.' " In all schools, students report that "classes at Georgetown are qualitatively challenging, but the workload is very manageable" and that "professors pride themselves on making time for students outside of the classroom." The school is not without its administrative difficulties, though. Some undergrads complain that "you are a number at Georgetown" and that "the quality of academic assistance is not the best. As a School of Foreign Service student I don't even have an academic advisor until my junior year"—but most agree that the benefits of a Georgetown education make up for the drawbacks many times over. Students are particularly sanguine about the university's adjunct faculty, "highly respected professionals, often working in government (or in conjunction with the government) in Washington. Calling on their 'real life' experience, they make excellent teachers."

### Life
Washington D.C., and the many career and social opportunities it presents, is one of the primary reasons students choose Georgetown. Few leave the city disappointed. "There is no better city than D.C. for internships and off-campus activities," explains one student. Points out another, "Because you are in Washington, there are countless other options if you don't feel like going to parties or don't drink (movies, theater, sports, sightseeing, every kind of restaurant imaginable . . .)." Because of the school's close connections with the government, undergrads "rub shoulders with senators and politicians. The White House is down the road, Madeline Albright lives a stone's throw away [she's also a professor], the Clintons just bought a house, there's constantly celebrities down here for filming. Students sometimes go down to the Capitol to be extras in The West Wing." On campus, students praise the absence of a Greek system and love the fact that "all clubs are student-run at GU, as are most other endeavors." They also love their men's basketball team, noting that "when there is a basketball game . . . we all stand together and celebrate." Their chief complaint concerns the university's neighbors, who have pressured the school to clamp down on rowdy off-campus activities. Offers one undergrad, "The silliest thing this year is that this man and his wife moved [into a house] a block away from the school years ago and now they are suing for TOO MUCH NOISE! Did they ever GO to college? I mean, what are they thinking?"

### Student Body
Is there a 'typical' Georgetown undergrad? It depends who you ask. Writes one student, "I always hate the stereotype that Georgetown is a bunch of Roman Catholic prep students from Connecticut who work all day. That's BS. One of my best friends is a non-practicing Jew and an atheist, and another friend is Polish and Catholic, and another friend is British and Muslim. We all get along like a house on fire." Cautions another, "Catholic students make up approximately 50 percent of the student body. I am not Catholic and do, at times, feel overrun by all the Catholics. This has improved greatly since first semester though, as I am getting to know more people." All agree that Georgetown undergrads are "smart, driven, social, and vivacious. We are all from different parts of the country and the world, but we all have in common those characteristics." Due to a large international contingent, one student notes that "nowhere else have I heard so many different languages and met individuals from such diverse backgrounds."

# GEORGETOWN UNIVERSITY

FINANCIAL AID: 202-687-4547 • WEBSITE: WWW.GEORGETOWN.EDU

## ADMISSIONS

*Very important factors considered include:* character/personal qualities, class rank, essays, recommendations, secondary school record, standardized test scores, talent/ability. *Important factors considered include:* extracurricular activities, interview, volunteer work. *Other factors considered include:* alumni/ae relation, geographical residence, minority status, state residency, work experience. SAT I or ACT required; SAT II recommended. TOEFL required of all international applicants. High school diploma or GED is required. *High school units required/recommended:* 4 English required, 2 math required, 4 math recommended, 2 science required, 4 science recommended, 1 science lab recommended, 2 foreign language required, 4 foreign language recommended, 2 social studies required, 4 social studies recommended.

### The Inside Word

It was always tough to get admitted to Georgetown, but in the early 1980s Patrick Ewing and the Hoyas created a basketball sensation that catapulted the place into position as one of the most selective universities in the nation. There has been no turning back since. GU gets almost 10 applications for every space in the entering class, and the academic strength of the pool is impressive. Virtually 50 percent of the entire student body took AP courses in high school. Candidates who are waitlisted here should hold little hope for an offer of admission; over the past several years Georgetown has taken very few off their lists.

## FINANCIAL AID

*Students should submit:* FAFSA, CSS/Financial Aid PROFILE, state aid form, noncustodial (divorced/separated) parent's statement, business/farm supplement. The Princeton Review suggests that all financial aid forms be submitted as soon as possible after January 1. *Need-based scholarships/grants offered:* Pell, SEOG, state scholarships/grants, private scholarships, the school's own gift aid, ROTC. *Loan aid offered:* FFEL Subsidized Stafford, FFEL Unsubsidized Stafford, FFEL PLUS, Federal Perkins, Federal Nursing. Federal Work-Study Program available. Institutional employment available. Applicants will be notified of awards on or about April 1. Off-campus job opportunities are excellent.

## FROM THE ADMISSIONS OFFICE

"Georgetown was founded in 1789 by John Carroll, who concurred with his contemporaries Benjamin Franklin and Thomas Jefferson in believing that the success of the young democracy depended upon an educated and virtuous citizenry. Carroll founded the school with the dynamic, Jesuit tradition of education, characterized by humanism and committed to the assumption of responsibility and action. Georgetown is a national and international university, enrolling students from all 50 states and over 100 foreign countries. Undergraduate students are enrolled in one of four undergraduate schools: the College of Arts and Sciences, School of Foreign Service, Georgetown School of Business, and Georgetown School of Nursing and Health Studies. All students share a common liberal arts core and have access to the entire university curriculum."

## SELECTIVITY

| | |
|---|---|
| Admissions Rating | 99 |
| # of applicants | 15,536 |
| % of applicants accepted | 21 |
| % of acceptees attending | 46 |
| # accepting a place on wait list | 822 |
| % admitted from wait list | 28 |

### FRESHMAN PROFILE

| | |
|---|---|
| Range SAT Verbal | 640-730 |
| Range SAT Math | 640-730 |
| Range ACT Composite | 27-32 |
| Minimum TOEFL | 550 |
| % graduated top 10% of class | 80 |
| % graduated top 25% of class | 94 |
| % graduated top 50% of class | 99 |

### DEADLINES

| | |
|---|---|
| Regular admission | 1/10 |
| Regular notification | 4/1 |

### APPLICANTS ALSO LOOK AT AND OFTEN PREFER
University of Pennsylvania
Harvard College

### AND SOMETIMES PREFER
Duke University
University of Virginia
University of Notre Dame
Northwestern University

### AND RARELY PREFER
Boston College
Tufts University
New York University
George Washington University

## FINANCIAL FACTS

| | |
|---|---|
| Financial Aid Rating | 84 |
| Tuition | $26,544 |
| Room and board | $9,692 |
| Books and supplies | $940 |
| Required fees | $309 |
| % frosh receiving aid | 41 |
| % undergrads receiving aid | 41 |
| Avg frosh grant | $16,300 |
| Avg frosh loan | $2,250 |

# GEORGIA INSTITUTE OF TECHNOLOGY

225 NORTH AVENUE, ATLANTA, GA 30332-0320 • ADMISSIONS: 404-894-4154 • FAX: 404-894-9511

## CAMPUS LIFE

| | |
|---|---|
| Quality of Life Rating | 91 |
| Type of school | public |
| Environment | urban |

### STUDENTS

| | |
|---|---|
| Total undergrad enrollment | 11,456 |
| % male/female | 72/28 |
| % from out of state | 32 |
| % from public high school | 82 |
| % live on campus | 60 |
| % in (# of) fraternities | 23 (32) |
| % in (# of) sororities | 25 (9) |
| % African American | 8 |
| % Asian | 15 |
| % Caucasian | 74 |
| % Hispanic | 3 |
| % international | 5 |

### SURVEY SAYS . . .
Students love Atlanta, GA
Everyone loves the Yellow Jackets
Students are happy
Students are religious
Great off-campus food
Frats and sororities dominate social scene
Classes are small
Unattractive campus
Ethnic diversity on campus
Campus difficult to get around

## ACADEMICS

| | |
|---|---|
| Academic Rating | 80 |
| Calendar | semester |
| Student/faculty ratio | 14:1 |
| Profs interesting rating | 87 |
| Profs accessible rating | 70 |
| % profs teaching UG courses | 100 |
| Avg lab size | 10-19 students |
| Avg reg class size | 20-29 students |

### MOST POPULAR MAJORS
Mechanical engineering
Electrical, electronics, and communications engineering
Computer science

## STUDENTS SPEAK OUT

### Academics

Georgia Tech is not for the faint of heart. At this math, science, and engineering powerhouse, "professors use a savagely overwhelming number of assignments to weed out the weak." Reports one disillusioned undergrad, "It is difficult to learn or enjoy school when half the people in a class get D's and F's. This fact is evident from the posted grade distributions." For those who can weather GT's challenges, however, the opportunities are phenomenal. As one go-getter tells us, "Academically this place is great. I've had an explosion of original ideas in physics and math since I've been here, and the professors have been nothing but encouraging [in] nurturing these pursuits. If you're not lazy, this place is the place to be." Agrees another student, "The overall academic experience, once you get comfortable, is accommodating. There are plenty of academic workshops with good tutors, an extensive library system connected with surrounding schools like Georgia State and Emory, a great co-op/internship program, and—my favorite—[scads] of undergrad research opportunities and funding." Students also brag that "the computers on-campus are extremely fast and many professors put the readings for class online, so I love being at a technology school with super-fast access." As at most tech schools, "Profs are researchers first and teachers second," TAs "often do not speak English very well," and "classes do not slow down for anyone, even if no one is getting it."

### Life

"Life at GT can be tough because school is so tough," students tell us. The demanding curriculum keeps students busy enough that "the majority of the social life falls on the weekend, as not much can be done during the week except studying." And "since many people are in state, lots of people leave campus on the weekends, which sometimes can give it an empty feeling." As a result, "fraternity parties are the only thing normally going on on-campus during the weekend." Fortunately, GT is located in the South's great city, Atlanta, so there are numerous options available to those who stick around after classes end—provided, of course, that they can spare the time away from their books. Students love Atlanta, telling us that "there are a lot of shows, movies, and festivals going on in the city at any given time." For fun and hooking up, students head to Buckhead, "the famous nightlife district of Atlanta." Atlanta is also conveniently located; observes one student, "The nice thing about Atlanta is it's in a very central location. It's only a few hours drive to either the beach or the mountains, and then, of course, with the international airport just a few minutes down the MARTA (Metropolitan Atlanta Rapid Transit Authority) line, you are connected with the rest of the world." Many never make it off campus, however: "Too many people are stuck playing computer games in their dorms" during their few leisure hours.

### Student Body

Because of the heavy workload at Georgia Tech, most students are "overly stressed, worried about tomorrow's test, and driven by the desire for the degree. This student has only minimal time for social functions." Which is just as well, since "many lack basic social skills." They go by a variety of labels: nerd, geek, square, freak, dork, poindexter—take your pick. They're the type of folks who "make fun of TV shows or movies that violate basic rules of physics. It's sort of dweeby. But in a good way." Observes one engineer, "There is a sizable population of people who are so weird that you can tell their major by the way they walk (e.g., CS [computer science] majors walk like they are uncoordinated)." Tech is home to "large populations of foreign students, especially from India and China." There is also a recognizable contingent of "'normal' white fraternity middle-class guys."

# GEORGIA INSTITUTE OF TECHNOLOGY

FINANCIAL AID: 404-894-4160 • E-MAIL: ADMISSIONS@SUCCESS.GATECH.EDU • WEBSITE: WWW.GATECH.EDU

## ADMISSIONS

*Very important factors considered include:* secondary school record. *Important factors considered include:* essays, extracurricular activities, standardized test scores, volunteer work, work experience. *Other factors considered include:* alumni/ae relation, state residency, talent/ability. SAT I or ACT required; SAT I preferred. TOEFL required of all international applicants. High school diploma or GED is required. *High school units required/recommended:* 20 total required; 4 English required, 4 math required, 3 science required, 4 science recommended, 2 science lab required, 2 foreign language required, 3 social studies required, 4 elective required.

### The Inside Word

Tech has made significant changes in its admissions requirements over the past six years, which by their nature have resulted in a somewhat more personal and well-rounded approach to selecting the entering class. Still, candidates must have solid grades and test scores in order to be competitive.

## FINANCIAL AID

*Students should submit:* FAFSA, institution's own financial aid form. The Princeton Review suggests that all financial aid forms be submitted as soon as possible after January 1. *Need-based scholarships/grants offered:* Pell, SEOG, state scholarships/grants, private scholarships, the school's own gift aid. *Loan aid offered:* FFEL Subsidized Stafford, FFEL Unsubsidized Stafford, FFEL PLUS, Federal Perkins, college/university loans from institutional funds, CitiAssist alternative loan. Federal Work-Study Program available. Institutional employment available. Applicants will be notified of awards on or about April 1. Off-campus job opportunities are excellent.

## FROM THE ADMISSIONS OFFICE

"Georgia Tech consistently ranks among the nation's leaders in engineering, computing, management, architecture, and the sciences while remaining one of the best college buys in the country. The 330-acre campus of red brick buildings and green rolling hills is nestled in the heart of the fun, dynamic, and progressive city of Atlanta in the shadows of a majestic skyline dominated by the work of Georgia Tech-trained architects and designers. During the past decade, over $400 million invested in campus improvements has yielded new state-of-the-art academic and research buildings, apartment-style housing, enhanced social and recreational facilities, and the most extensive fiber-optic cable system on any college campus. Georgia Tech's combined commitment to technologically focused hands-on educational experiences, teamwork, great teaching, innovation, leadership development, and community service make it unique. Great things are happening at Georgia Tech. We hope you will join us, become a part of our community, and help us create the future."

## SELECTIVITY

| | |
|---|---|
| Admissions Rating | 92 |
| # of applicants | 8,953 |
| % of applicants accepted | 59 |
| % of acceptees attending | 43 |

### FRESHMAN PROFILE

| | |
|---|---|
| Range SAT Verbal | 600-690 |
| Average SAT Verbal | 642 |
| Range SAT Math | 650-740 |
| Average SAT Math | 689 |
| Minimum TOEFL | 600 |
| Average HS GPA | 3.7 |

### DEADLINES

| | |
|---|---|
| Regular admission | 1/15 |
| Regular notification | 3/15 |
| Nonfall registration? | yes |

### APPLICANTS ALSO LOOK AT AND OFTEN PREFER
MIT
Duke
UNC Chapel Hill
Stanford
U of Virginia

### AND SOMETIMES PREFER
U of Illinois
Emory
U of Georgia
Clemson

### AND RARELY PREFER
U of Florida
Virginia Tech
Vanderbilt
North Carolina State

## FINANCIAL FACTS

| | |
|---|---|
| Financial Aid Rating | 91 |
| In-state tuition | $2,780 |
| Out-of-state tuition | $13,160 |
| Room and board | $5,922 |
| Books and supplies | $1,278 |
| Required fees | $826 |
| % frosh receiving aid | 30 |
| % undergrads receiving aid | 29 |
| Avg frosh grant | $9,876 |
| Avg frosh loan | $3,395 |

# GETTYSBURG COLLEGE

ADMISSIONS OFFICE, EISENHOWER HOUSE, GETTYSBURG, PA 17325-1484 • ADMISSIONS: 717-337-6100

## CAMPUS LIFE

| | |
|---|---|
| Quality of Life Rating | 84 |
| Type of school | private |
| Affiliation | Lutheran |
| Environment | suburban |

### STUDENTS

| | |
|---|---|
| Total undergrad enrollment | 2,495 |
| % male/female | 50/50 |
| % from out of state | 72 |
| % from public high school | 70 |
| % live on campus | 91 |
| % in (# of) fraternities | 44 (10) |
| % in (# of) sororities | 26 (5) |
| % African American | 3 |
| % Asian | 1 |
| % Caucasian | 94 |
| % Hispanic | 1 |
| % international | 2 |

### SURVEY SAYS...
Great food on campus
Frats and sororities dominate social scene
Diversity lacking on campus
Beautiful campus
Campus easy to get around
Theater is unpopular
Low cost of living

## ACADEMICS

| | |
|---|---|
| Academic Rating | 90 |
| Calendar | semester |
| Student/faculty ratio | 11:1 |
| Profs interesting rating | 95 |
| Profs accessible rating | 99 |
| % profs teaching UG courses | 100 |
| Avg reg class size | 10-19 students |

### MOST POPULAR MAJORS
Psychology
Business/management
Biology

## STUDENTS SPEAK OUT

### Academics

At Gettysburg, "academics are challenging and stimulating without being overbearingly stressful," a situation appreciated by most undergraduates. "The work is difficult," warns one student, "but with concentration, balance, and help from a great faculty, anyone can succeed." The small campus allows for plenty of personal attention. Writes one respondent, "At Gettysburg, I am pushed to do my best because professors will not let you slip through the cracks. We have to attend classes because they are so small. If you don't show up, you can expect a phone call." Faculty members earn high praise for being "friendly and acting as equals rather than authority figures" and for their helpfulness. They are "always willing to meet with students, [and] they offer help in obtaining internships and expose us to experiences outside the classroom." A "good advising system [that's] very personalized" helps students navigate curricular requirements, including a liberal arts core curriculum (really a set of distribution requirements covering the humanities, natural and social sciences, mathematics, foreign language, writing skills, and nonwestern civilization) geared toward introducing underclassmen to a broad spectrum of academics. Upperclassmen focus on their majors, among which history, political science, and the hard sciences are generally regarded as "top-notch." Students also applaud the computer facilities and the Honor Code, the latter "an undeniable part of campus. You're truly treated like an adult."

### Life

Greek life, most undergrads concede, holds center court at Gettysburg College. Warns one student, "The administration wants prospectives to think that Greek life isn't essential, but don't let them fool you. A lot of people end up unhappy when they are left out." Says another, "Gettysburg does offer a lot of activities; it's just that so many of them are geared toward the Greek system. There's something for most people, but a lot of times the good events aren't publicized." Drinking, not surprisingly, is big here. Writes one student, "Beer is life. Even if you don't know what Natty Ice is before you get here, your fridge will be stocked by the second week." There are other options, among them intramural sports, community service, and events organized by the Student Activities Council and the Student Senate, but many still see the 'Burg as a one-horse town. As one student puts it, "Good luck if you aren't in Greek life. The frat doormen look you up and down and decide whether you are 'good enough' to enter their frat. If you are a girl in a skirt you can get in. If you're a guy, bring a girl in a skirt." Students speak highly of the Center for Public Service, which provides opportunities for "tutoring, clean-ups, and service-related trips all over the world." The campus is "beautiful and comfortable," and the food is "among the school's greatest strengths." Students give the "lame" town of Gettysburg a thumb's-down: "It's isolated, and there are no buses to other towns," gripes one. Students list a local diner, Wal-Mart, an outlet mall, and the tour of the famous local battlefield as the best off-campus attractions.

### Student Body

Gettysburg undergrads are "very homogeneous, mostly upper- and middle-class white students." However, "although there is diversity lacking," reports one student, "the college has been doing better in recent years to change that." Politically, "many kids are very conservative. You have to search for liberals." The same goes for intellectuals; while kids here are bright, they are not bookish. Points out one frustrated egghead, "The classic term for girls here is 'eye candy,' and it goes for a lot of the guys too. They're fun to look at but don't talk about anything past next Friday night. My solution is to travel a lot and keep in touch with friends from home."

# GETTYSBURG COLLEGE

Fax: 717-337-6145 • Financial Aid: 717-337-6611 • E-mail: admiss@gettysburg.edu • Website: www.gettysburg.edu

## ADMISSIONS

*Very important factors considered include:* class rank, recommendations, secondary school record. *Important factors considered include:* character/personal qualities, essays, extracurricular activities, interview, standardized test scores, talent/ability, volunteer work. *Other factors considered include:* alumni/ae relation, geographical residence, minority status, work experience. SAT I or ACT required. TOEFL required of all international applicants. High school diploma or GED is required. *High school units required/recommended:* 4 English required, 3 math required, 4 math recommended, 3 science required, 4 science recommended, 3 science lab required, 4 science lab recommended, 3 foreign language required, 4 foreign language recommended, 3 social studies required, 4 social studies recommended, 3 history required, 4 history recommended.

### The Inside Word

Gettysburg's small size definitely allows for a more personal approach to admission. The admissions committee puts a lot of energy into matchmaking, and last year it paid off with its largest freshman class in its history. Most Gettysburg types are good students and also match up well with competitor colleges, which makes this accomplishment even more laudable. Look for a somewhat more selective profile as a result.

## FINANCIAL AID

*Students should submit:* FAFSA, CSS/Financial Aid PROFILE, noncustodial (divorced/separated) parent's statement, business/farm supplement. Regular filing deadline is March 15. The Princeton Review suggests that all financial aid forms be submitted as soon as possible after January 1. *Need-based scholarships/grants offered:* Pell, SEOG, state scholarships/grants, private scholarships, the school's own gift aid. *Loan aid offered:* FFEL Subsidized Stafford, FFEL Unsubsidized Stafford, FFEL PLUS, Federal Perkins, college/university loans from institutional funds. Federal Work-Study Program available. Institutional employment available. Applicants will be notified of awards on or about March 30. Off-campus job opportunities are good.

## FROM THE ADMISSIONS OFFICE

"Four major goals of Gettysburg College, to best prepare students to enter the 21st century, include: first, to accelerate the intellectual development of our first-year students by integrating them more quickly into the intellectual life of the campus; second, to use interdisciplinary courses combining the intellectual approaches of various fields; third, to encourage students to develop an international perspective through course work, study abroad, association with international faculty, and a variety of extracurricular activities; and fourth, to encourage students to develop (1) a capacity for independent study by ensuring that all students work closely with individual faculty members on an extensive project during their undergraduate years and (2) the ability to work with their peers by making the small group a central feature in college life."

### SELECTIVITY

| | |
|---|---:|
| Admissions Rating | 87 |
| # of applicants | 4,573 |
| % of applicants accepted | 50 |
| % of acceptees attending | 30 |
| # of early decision applicants | 210 |
| % accepted early decision | 93 |

### FRESHMAN PROFILE

| | |
|---|---:|
| Range SAT Verbal | 580-650 |
| Range SAT Math | 590-660 |
| Average ACT Composite | 28 |
| Minimum TOEFL | 550 |
| % graduated top 10% of class | 62 |
| % graduated top 25% of class | 80 |
| % graduated top 50% of class | 99 |

### DEADLINES

| | |
|---|---:|
| Early decision | 2/1 |
| Early decision notification | 2/15 |
| Priority admission | 2/15 |
| Regular notification | 4/1 |
| Nonfall registration? | yes |

### APPLICANTS ALSO LOOK AT
**AND OFTEN PREFER**
Colgate University
**AND SOMETIMES PREFER**
Bucknell University
**AND RARELY PREFER**
Muhlenberg College

### FINANCIAL FACTS

| | |
|---|---:|
| Financial Aid Rating | 87 |
| Tuition | $28,424 |
| Room and board | $6,972 |
| Books and supplies | $500 |
| Required fees | $250 |
| % frosh receiving aid | 53 |
| % undergrads receiving aid | 56 |
| Avg frosh grant | $18,600 |
| Avg frosh loan | $3,500 |

# GODDARD COLLEGE

123 PITKIN ROAD, PLAINFIELD, VT 05667 • ADMISSIONS: 802-454-8311 • FAX: 802-454-1029

## CAMPUS LIFE

| Quality of Life Rating | 94 |
|---|---|
| Type of school | private |
| Environment | rural |

### STUDENTS

| Total undergrad enrollment | 319 |
|---|---|
| % from out of state | 87 |
| % from public high school | 93 |
| % live on campus | 87 |
| % African American | 3 |
| % Asian | 2 |
| % Caucasian | 87 |
| % Hispanic | 2 |
| % international | 2 |
| # of countries represented | 2 |

### SURVEY SAYS . . .
Political activism is hot
No one cheats
(Almost) everyone smokes
Classes are small
Intercollegiate sports unpopular or nonexistent
No one plays intramural sports
Very small frat/sorority scene
Class discussions encouraged
Theater is hot

## ACADEMICS

| Academic Rating | 88 |
|---|---|
| Calendar | semester |
| Student/faculty ratio | 11:1 |
| Profs interesting rating | 97 |
| Profs accessible rating | 97 |
| % profs teaching UG courses | 100 |
| Avg reg class size | under 10 students |

### MOST POPULAR MAJORS
Liberal arts and sciences/liberal studies
Education
Psychology

## STUDENTS SPEAK OUT

### Academics

If you loathe the idea of a "traditional school," check out Goddard College, an "artsy, eccentric," "alternative, progressive" school located in rural Vermont where "academic freedom" reigns supreme. At Goddard you can "design" an individual curriculum—"a self-directed, experimental education" if you will—tailored to your own "specific needs." But be warned: "There's no handholding here." The program is "independent, self-directed, and focused." Essentially, "your education is all on you." Classes (called "group studies" in Goddard-speak) are "intriguing and thought-provoking" discussion sessions with "hardly ever more than 10 people." The "open-minded, hip, intellectual" "facilitators"—translation: professors—are "warm and caring and very much a part of the community." There are "no grades or exams, as they interfere with the business of learning." Instead, students receive written evaluations. Also, all students "are a part of the decision making and governance here" and attend "community-based meetings with students/faculty/staff." Suffice it to say, "Goddard is not for everyone" and it has its flaws even for students who thrive in this kind of environment. "The facilities blow," for example, and "the administration is a joke." Nevertheless, students happily declare that Goddard provides a "wonderful, creative, free" atmosphere. "My academic experience has been nothing short of incredible, " boasts a satisfied junior. "I truly love this school."

### Life

"Activism, art, punk rock, philosophy, and sex" are all the rage on this tiny campus. Because Goddard is so small, each student has a "tremendous opportunity" to get involved in various activities, including the popular school newspaper, radio station, and Women's Center. Students "go to musical events on campus, hang out in dorms, and spend a lot of time in discussion and debate" as well. Not surprisingly, religious activity is not popular here, although "spiritual" and "pagan clubs" are widely embraced. Community action is vital as well, and each student must work for the college in some constructive way several hours per week. Much campus life is of the "spontaneous" variety. "We held our own Olympics which included streaking, an egg toss, a three-legged race, and other events, followed after dinner by a drag show and lip synch," relates a first-year student. "Parties at Goddard consist of everyone on campus gathering together and getting really drunk." Drug use (especially pot) is profoundly high as well. Skiing trails and plenty of places to hike are nearby, and the quiet and secluded campus feels somewhat disconnected from reality—perhaps too disconnected. Goddard students report that when they "go back to the real world," they have a difficult time assimilating.

### Student Body

"The student body consists of all the kids in high school who were alienated because they were weird," making Goddard a leftist paradise which is no doubt "an uncomfortable place for a person with a conservative background." While students at Goddard admit they're "not rocket scientists," they say their campus "is filled with creative, intelligent, and artistic" students "who love life on this planet too much to abandon themselves to the materialism of the modern world." Students call themselves "amazingly unique and creative" and they swear there "is always the potential for enlightening conversations, and connections." The "eclectic" students also say there is "intense diversity of thought" here, as well as "collective ecstasy and depression," but the limited outward diversity ranges "from dirty hippies to even dirtier hippies," as a junior quips.

# GODDARD COLLEGE

FINANCIAL AID: 802-454-8311 • E-MAIL: ADMISSIONS@EARTH.GODDARD.EDU • WEBSITE: WWW.GODDARD.EDU

## ADMISSIONS

*Very important factors considered include:* character/personal qualities, essays, interview. *Important factors considered include:* talent/ability, volunteer work, work experience. *Other factors considered include:* class rank, extracurricular activities, recommendations, secondary school record, standardized test scores. TOEFL required of all international applicants. High school diploma or GED is required.

### The Inside Word

A small applicant pool, the need to have an entering class each year, and a high level of self-selection among candidates makes for Goddard's high acceptance rate. Even though students are not banging down the doors to get into the college, applicants should prepare themselves for a fairly demanding experience. The committee here wants to know a lot about the people who apply, none of which can be supplied in the clean and neat form of transcripts or score reports. This place is not for everyone, and careful self-assessment is the toughest part of the admissions process.

## FINANCIAL AID

*Students should submit:* FAFSA. No deadline for regular filing. The Princeton Review suggests that all financial aid forms be submitted as soon as possible after January 1. *Need-based scholarships/grants offered:* Pell, SEOG, state scholarships/grants, private scholarships, the school's own gift aid. *Loan aid offered:* FFEL Subsidized Stafford, FFEL Unsubsidized Stafford, FFEL PLUS, Federal Perkins, college/university loans from institutional funds. Federal Work-Study Program available. Applicants will be notified of awards on a rolling basis. Off-campus job opportunities are fair.

## FROM THE ADMISSIONS OFFICE

"Goddard is a small, coeducational liberal arts college that has an international reputation for appealing to the creative, independent student. Its commitment is to adventurous, capable persons who want to make their own educational decisions and work closely with the faculty. Individually designed programs can be pursued on or off campus."

### SELECTIVITY

★ ★ ☆ ☆

| | |
|---|---|
| Admissions Rating | 73 |
| # of applicants | 128 |
| % of applicants accepted | 93 |
| % of acceptees attending | 40 |

### FRESHMAN PROFILE

| | |
|---|---|
| Range SAT Verbal | 550-680 |
| Average SAT Verbal | 609 |
| Range SAT Math | 480-590 |
| Average SAT Math | 541 |
| Range ACT Composite | 19-27 |
| Minimum TOEFL | 550 |
| Average HS GPA | 2.5 |
| % graduated top 10% of class | 7 |
| % graduated top 25% of class | 27 |
| % graduated top 50% of class | 63 |

### DEADLINES

| | |
|---|---|
| Regular notification | rolling |
| Nonfall registration? | yes |

### APPLICANTS ALSO LOOK AT AND OFTEN PREFER
New College
Reed
Oberlin
Hampshire
Bennington

### AND SOMETIMES PREFER
Antioch
Marlboro
Coll. of the Atlantic

### FINANCIAL FACTS

| | |
|---|---|
| Financial Aid Rating | 89 |
| Tuition | $17,840 |
| Room and board | $2,964 |
| Books and supplies | $508 |
| Required fees | $252 |
| % frosh receiving aid | 90 |
| % undergrads receiving aid | 88 |
| Avg frosh grant | $2,000 |
| Avg frosh loan | $6,189 |

THE BEST 351 COLLEGES ■ 241

# GOLDEN GATE UNIVERSITY

536 MISSION STREET, SAN FRANCISCO, CA 94105 • ADMISSIONS: 415-442-7800 • FAX: 415-442-7807

## CAMPUS LIFE

| | |
|---|---|
| Quality of Life Rating | 71 |
| Type of school | private |
| Environment | urban |

### STUDENTS

| | |
|---|---|
| Total undergrad enrollment | 1,445 |
| % male/female | 44/56 |
| % from out of state | 5 |
| % African American | 8 |
| % Asian | 10 |
| % Caucasian | 39 |
| % Hispanic | 8 |
| % international | 15 |
| # of countries represented | 80 |

### SURVEY SAYS . . .
Musical organizations aren't popular
Theater is hot
High cost of living
Students love San Francisco, CA
Very little hard liquor
No one plays intramural sports
Intercollegiate sports unpopular or nonexistent

## ACADEMICS

| | |
|---|---|
| Academic Rating | 71 |
| Calendar | trimester |
| Student/faculty ratio | 6:1 |
| Profs interesting rating | 90 |
| Profs accessible rating | 89 |
| % profs teaching UG courses | 100 |
| Avg reg class size | 10-19 students |

## STUDENTS SPEAK OUT

### Academics

Golden Gate University "offers its students a unique experience that most universities don't. It's practical, up-to-date, and has a very rich and diverse culture as a community." In nearly every respect, GGU is atypical. Most of its undergraduates study part time, and many were out of high school for several years before entering college. It has no real campus or campus life to speak of, and it is decidedly orientated toward graduate, not undergraduate, study. Still, GGU has many excellent qualities. The university offers fine undergraduate business programs and attracts a bright, motivated, and unusually diverse student body. And it is located in downtown San Francisco, an exceptional place to spend one's college years. "Class size is small"—the vast majority of students indicate that their lectures have fewer than 50 students— "and most instructors are accessible." Students praise their "small classes and the opportunity to be taught by business professionals rather than professional teachers" whose "frequent use of case studies . . . will be very useful when we graduate and start our careers." Students also laud the fact that "the school allows the motivated student to get a good degree quickly." Another bonus is that there are "no student teachers." GGU cooperative education and internship programs allow students to study and work concurrently in the San Francisco business community.

### Life

If you're bound to get an education at a university where "extracurricular activities are nonexistent," it might as well be in San Francisco. The city gets raves from students at GGU. Not surprisingly, town/gown relations are solid between the City by the Bay and these "focused students." Most of the mainstays of typical college life—dormitories, parties, drinking, sports, and clubs—simply aren't to be found. As one student puts it: "Don't come here for the football team because we don't have one. We come here to learn and eventually to become prominent figures in our society." Efforts to boost extracurricular options have been undertaken, and "the club/organization activities are improving, especially student government." A "new student newspaper is doing well," although most students would like to see an improvement in recreational facilities. Given the low-key free time options afforded by the University, most students "gather their coworkers and classmates for private activities" on their own. Students only gripe: "Food is cheap in San Francisco, but rent is too expensive. We need dorms!"

### Student Body

Golden Gate University boasts a high level of diversity among its student body, including a large number of international students. Students report that interaction among undergraduates of different ethnicity and backgrounds is frequent, despite the rarity of university-supported venues in which students can congregate. GGU students report themselves to be moderate politically, but not particularly aware of political issues. Perhaps that's because while they're "very friendly," they are also "focused." They clearly admire one another for their tenacity: "My fellow students are good people, hardworking, and ambitious," says one. In general, they're pretty happy, too.

# GOLDEN GATE UNIVERSITY

FINANCIAL AID: 415-442-7270 • E-MAIL: INFO@GGU.EDU • WEBSITE: WWW.GGU.EDU

## ADMISSIONS

*Very important factors considered include:* secondary school record. *Other factors considered include:* class rank, essays, minority status, recommendations, standardized test scores, volunteer work, work experience. SAT I recommended. TOEFL required of all international applicants. High school diploma or GED is required. *High school units required/recommended:* 14 total recommended; 4 English recommended, 3 math recommended, 2 science recommended, 1 science lab recommended, 2 foreign language recommended, 1 social studies recommended, 1 history recommended.

### The Inside Word

Golden Gate's focus is unique and requires a high level of independence, self-discipline, and motivation. Grades may be the most important factor in admission, but candidates who are lacking in the aforementioned personal qualities stand the greatest likelihood of denial.

## FINANCIAL AID

The Princeton Review suggests that all financial aid forms be submitted as soon as possible after January 1. Federal Work-Study Program available. Institutional employment available. Off-campus job opportunities are good.

## FROM THE ADMISSIONS OFFICE

"Golden Gate University remains one of the most affordable private universities in Northern California. It is an ideal choice for men and women who are serious about their careers. Students work together with faculty who are leaders in their fields to build foundations for achievement in the world today and in the years ahead. Convenience, practical education, and personalized education are the norm. The average class size is 14—small enough to provide individual attention to each student. A full range of undergraduate and graduate degrees and certificates are offered days, evenings, weekends, and online via GGU's nationally recognized Cyber-Campus to accommodate the needs of working adults as well as full-time students. Located in the financial district of San Francisco, the University has just completed major renovations of its classrooms. GGU also has locations throughout the Bay Area and in Los Angeles and Seattle. A full range of financial aid and scholarship options are available for those who need financial assistance to pursue their studies. The University is a multicultural institution and celebrates its diverse student body, staff, and faculty."

---

### SELECTIVITY

★★☆☆

| | |
|---|---|
| Admissions Rating | 72 |

#### FRESHMAN PROFILE

| | |
|---|---|
| Minimum TOEFL | 525 |
| Average HS GPA | 2.7 |

#### DEADLINES

| | |
|---|---|
| Priority admission | 7/1 |
| Nonfall registration? | yes |

#### APPLICANTS ALSO LOOK AT AND SOMETIMES PREFER
San Francisco State

### FINANCIAL FACTS

★★★☆

| | |
|---|---|
| Financial Aid Rating | 81 |
| Tuition | $9,600 |
| Books and supplies | $1,000 |
| Avg frosh grant | $5,233 |
| Avg frosh loan | $7,048 |

# GONZAGA UNIVERSITY

502 E. BOONE AVENUE, SPOKANE, WA 99258 • ADMISSIONS: 509-323-6572 • FAX: 509-324-5780

## CAMPUS LIFE

| Quality of Life Rating | 89 |
|---|---|
| Type of school | private |
| Affiliation | Roman Catholic |
| Environment | urban |

### STUDENTS

| Total undergrad enrollment | 3,814 |
|---|---|
| % male/female | 46/54 |
| % from out of state | 47 |
| % from public high school | 65 |
| % live on campus | 53 |
| % African American | 1 |
| % Asian | 6 |
| % Caucasian | 81 |
| % Hispanic | 3 |
| % international | 2 |
| # of countries represented | 42 |

### SURVEY SAYS...
Theater is hot
Classes are small
Everyone loves the Bulldogs
Very little drug use
(Almost) no one smokes
Students are very religious
Students get along with local community

## ACADEMICS

| Academic Rating | 84 |
|---|---|
| Calendar | semester |
| Student/faculty ratio | 13:1 |
| Profs interesting rating | 95 |
| Profs accessible rating | 97 |
| % profs teaching UG courses | 100 |
| Avg lab size | 10-19 students |
| Avg reg class size | 20-29 students |

### MOST POPULAR MAJORS
Biology/biological sciences
Political science and government
Business/commerce

## STUDENTS SPEAK OUT

### Academics

Jesuit-run Gonzaga University, "a tough school academically," is in transition. Over the past decade, Gonzaga has increased its undergraduate enrollment by more than 20 percent: results include an increase in class sizes, additional adjunct faculty, and a housing shortage. Some students worry that, in growing so quickly, Gonzaga is losing the personal touches that make it special. "The administration has once again allowed an excess of students to enter with this freshman class. We do not have the services to support this expanding student population," complains one undergrad. Others disagree, noting that "Gonzaga is in a huge process of change.... But the administration is working hard on keeping the close, small-school environment feel at Gonzaga." Indeed, students report that "accessible" professors still devote copious amounts of time to students' work; writes one undergrad, "I get papers back with more written about my paper than I actually wrote in the paper." Students appreciate the school's wide-ranging integrated core curriculum ("It makes all of the students well rounded and makes us think in ways we usually don't"), including "required religion and philosophy classes, which is great; I would have never taken them, but I am happy that I kind of had to." Students report that "there [is] a certain bent toward the views of the Church here, but they are in no way forced upon the students in classes."

### Life

"Life is good" on the Gonzaga campus, where students report that "there are always a million things to do. For example, on an average Thursday night, you might find our student musical worship group (Thirst), a lecture on physical chemistry, a hall program on yoga, a local campus band playing in the student center, a slide show on extreme skiing, and a discussion on sexual assault." Adds one undergrad, "There is a free movie every Friday, an informal coffeehouse concert every Wednesday, and you can't forget the basketball games, which draw in hundreds of students, faculty, and people from the community." GU's Division I men's basketball team is a perennial "mouse that roared," often appearing in the nation's top 20 list amongst schools 10 times GU's size. No wonder "students long for basketball season to start every year." Undergrads report that "if you want to party, you can, but there is no pressure to. The people here are all relaxed; it's a very easy place to be yourself." Hometown Spokane offers plenty; reports one student, "The Opera House is a 10-minute walk from campus," showing concerts, ballet, and musicals, as well as the downtown mall. In addition, "Riverfront Park, a five-minute walk from campus, has an IMAX theater, a carousel, vendors, an ice-skating rink in the winters, and a huge park to play in, along with many other fun things to do. Downtown is less than 10 minutes away, so there is always lots of shopping and restaurants galore." Students also enjoy "jumping in the car and driving up to the ski hills when it gets snowy." Because of GU's rapid growth, "The housing situation is out of control.... They now put two people in rooms meant for one. It's ridiculous."

### Student Body

Most Gonzaga undergrads "are typical Northwest, Abercrombie-and-Fitch-wearing people, but they are all cool, and there really is quite a bit of diversity among the students considering we are in Spokane." Students are generally well off; reports one, "Coming to a school like Gonzaga, which mostly consists of affluent people, I figured everyone would be snobby and stuck on themselves. Surprisingly, everyone is so nice, and I've made many new friendships." Many are from the area and "are quick to leave campus on three-day weekends." Political engagement is minimal here; notes one student, "If someone is looking for a college experience where political issues are seriously focused on, Gonzaga perhaps is not the place. People are actually surprised that I watch CNN!"

244 ■ THE BEST 351 COLLEGES

# GONZAGA UNIVERSITY

FINANCIAL AID: 800-793-1716 • E-MAIL: BALLINGER@GU.GONZAGA.EDU • WEBSITE: WWW.GONZAGA.EDU

## ADMISSIONS

*Very important factors considered include:* character/personal qualities, secondary school record. *Important factors considered include:* extracurricular activities, recommendations, standardized test scores, talent/ability. *Other factors considered include:* alumni/ae relation, class rank, essays, interview, minority status, volunteer work, work experience. SAT I or ACT required. TOEFL required of all international applicants. High school diploma or GED is required. *High school units required/recommended:* 4 English recommended, 4 math recommended, 4 science recommended, 3 foreign language recommended, 3 history/social studies recommended.

## The Inside Word

As with many religiously affiliated universities, getting into Gonzaga is largely a matter of making a good match philosophically. However, keep an eye on the steadily rising SAT/ACT requirements. As always, an above-average academic record is a given for admission.

## FINANCIAL AID

*Students should submit:* FAFSA. The Princeton Review suggests that all financial aid forms be submitted as soon as possible after January 1. *Need-based scholarships/grants offered:* Pell, SEOG, state scholarships/grants, private scholarships, the school's own gift aid, United Negro College Fund, Federal Nursing. *Loan aid offered:* FFEL Subsidized Stafford, FFEL Unsubsidized Stafford, FFEL PLUS, Federal Perkins, Federal Nursing, state loans, college/university loans from institutional funds, private educational loans. Federal Work-Study Program available. Institutional employment available. Applicants will be notified of awards on or about March 21. Off-campus job opportunities are good.

## FROM THE ADMISSIONS OFFICE

"Education at Gonzaga is not comparable to an academic 'assembly line,' rather, it is person-to-person and face-to-face. This personal quality is also true of our admission and financial aid processes. Therefore, allow us to know you beyond the boundaries of your college application. Visit campus, phone us, e-mail us—let us see the person behind the data. Good luck with your college search and your applications. Go Zags!"

### SELECTIVITY

| | |
|---|---:|
| Admissions Rating | 80 |
| # of applicants | 3,339 |
| % of applicants accepted | 76 |
| % of acceptees attending | 36 |
| # accepting a place on wait list | 166 |
| % admitted from wait list | 95 |

#### FRESHMAN PROFILE

| | |
|---|---:|
| Range SAT Verbal | 530-620 |
| Average SAT Verbal | 578 |
| Range SAT Math | 540-640 |
| Average SAT Math | 593 |
| Range ACT Composite | 24-28 |
| Average ACT Composite | 26 |
| Minimum TOEFL | 550 |
| Average HS GPA | 3.6 |
| % graduated top 10% of class | 37 |
| % graduated top 25% of class | 74 |
| % graduated top 50% of class | 95 |

#### DEADLINES

| | |
|---|---:|
| Priority admission | 2/1 |
| Regular admission | 2/1 |
| Regular notification | 3/15 |
| Nonfall registration? | yes |

**APPLICANTS ALSO LOOK AT AND OFTEN PREFER**
Notre Dame
**AND SOMETIMES PREFER**
Santa Clara
U of Washington
Loyola Marymount U
**AND RARELY PREFER**
U of San Francisco
Washington State U

### FINANCIAL FACTS

| | |
|---|---:|
| Financial Aid Rating | 86 |
| Tuition | $20,510 |
| Room and board | $5,960 |
| Books and supplies | $750 |
| Required fees | $175 |
| % frosh receiving aid | 63 |
| % undergrads receiving aid | 63 |

# GOUCHER COLLEGE

1021 DULANEY VALLEY ROAD, BALTIMORE, MD 21204-2794 • ADMISSIONS: 410-337-6100 • FAX: 410-337-6354

## CAMPUS LIFE

| Quality of Life Rating | 80 |
|---|---|
| Type of school | private |
| Environment | suburban |

### STUDENTS

| Total undergrad enrollment | 1,270 |
|---|---|
| % male/female | 30/70 |
| % from out of state | 62 |
| % from public high school | 66 |
| % live on campus | 62 |
| % African American | 6 |
| % Asian | 3 |
| % Caucasian | 62 |
| % Hispanic | 2 |
| % international | 2 |

### SURVEY SAYS . . .
Theater is hot
Students love Baltimore, MD
Great off-campus food
(Almost) everyone smokes
Student government is popular
Class discussions encouraged
Library needs improving

## ACADEMICS

| Academic Rating | 81 |
|---|---|
| Calendar | semester |
| Student/faculty ratio | 10:1 |
| Profs interesting rating | 94 |
| Profs accessible rating | 94 |
| % profs teaching UG courses | 100 |
| Avg reg class size | 10-19 students |

## STUDENTS SPEAK OUT

### Academics

"Many opportunities in a little school" makes the academically challenging Goucher College a popular choice for students looking for personal attention, top-quality professors, and a left-of-center social and political environment. With both a strong science program and a solid emphasis on writing proficiency, Goucher manages to offer "creative and exceptional" classes in many disciplines, with professors who "go out of their way" to help students succeed. A first-year provides an example: "When teachers know what mode of transportation you use in coming to class (i.e., scooter), and they draw a 'scooter parking meter' on the board of the classroom, you know you're at a place where people care about your well-being and academic achievement." And though you wouldn't expect it from such a tiny school, it's Goucher's bureaucracy that gets the thumbs-down from students: "The administration process is lengthy and tedious at best," says a sophomore. Perhaps too much attention can be a bad thing? A junior notes that "student input is really used in the selection and hiring of professors. They're willing to do independent studies with you for whatever topic you want. Lots of paperwork, red tape, hoops to jump through, though." Still, with a "good reputation, great location, and generous scholarships" (the average frosh grant is about $13,500), a little paper pushing might not be such a bad thing. And though Goucher could "clean up their dorms," improve the library, and "get a T3," major renovation during the last few years should put Goucher back on track facilities-wise.

### Life

Situated in an upscale suburb a few miles north of Baltimore, Goucher's "beautiful" campus is "close to D.C. and Baltimore but outside of the city"—important for students who consider themselves "politically aware" and "care about what's going on in the world," and also for those who like to go to Baltimore's "movies, concerts, clubs, and bars." Though Goucher's "warm environment," small size, and "active students" guarantee the "opportunity to get involved in the campus community," some students complain that "there needs to be more to do on campus. It's dead on the weekends." Some of it may have to do with Goucher's men-to-women ratio (about 70 percent of the former women's college are female). What does Goucher College need? A senior jokes, "cuter, smarter boys with better bodies who are sensitive to my needs." Or, as a first-year puts it, "The odds are good but the goods are odd." Baltimore, however, "is a 'college town,' so the lack of men is compensated by the large amount of Johns Hopkins boys." In terms of partying, although one sophomore claims that "we are all pot-smoking, fun-loving, intellectually curious, caring people," a been-there-done-that senior argues that "Goucher's once easy-going social atmosphere has been threatened by a heightened presence of policing/weekly pot busts and a new lockdown policy aimed to keep everyone in their respective houses." Maybe she's just tired of Goucher's "incredible one-on-one attention: professors, administration . . . even security."

### Student Body

While "men are somewhat fishbowled at Goucher," notes a first-year, "everyone is really relaxed, and there is no real campus strife—except maybe the parking tickets." Adds a senior, "People here are politically aware, intelligent, and love class discussion. There are lots of weirdos but I love them anyway, and I know I'm one of them." Love—and lots of it—seems to be a theme at Goucher. Writes another freshman: "I love the majority of our students. They are very caring, loving, curious, optimistic, and out-to-get-the-world people, more conscious than most of our peers." And though there are your "superficial" types ("dancers & equestrians = snobs," writes a junior), a sophomore points out that "there are a lot of interesting people at Goucher. You just have to take the time to get to know them, which isn't hard at such a small school. I can't go anywhere on campus without seeing someone I can smile at."

# GOUCHER COLLEGE

FINANCIAL AID: 410-337-6141 • E-MAIL: ADMISSIONS@GOUCHER.EDU • WEBSITE: WWW.GOUCHER.EDU

## ADMISSIONS
*Very important factors considered include:* recommendations, secondary school record. *Important factors considered include:* essays, extracurricular activities, standardized test scores, talent/ability. *Other factors considered include:* alumni/ae relation, character/personal qualities, class rank, interview, volunteer work, work experience. SAT I or ACT required. TOEFL required of all international applicants. High school diploma is required and GED is not accepted. *High school units required/recommended:* 16 total required; 4 English required, 3 math required, 2 science required, 2 science lab required, 2 foreign language required, 2 social studies required, 3 social studies recommended.

### The Inside Word
Goucher is in serious battle for the students to which it is best-suited, and often fills the role of safety to some of the region's strongest colleges. Though the College is a solid choice in its own right, its admissions profile reflects modest competitiveness as a result of these circumstances.

## FINANCIAL AID
*Students should submit:* FAFSA, CSS/Financial Aid PROFILE. Regular filing deadline is February 15. The Princeton Review suggests that all financial aid forms be submitted as soon as possible after January 1. *Need-based scholarships/grants offered:* Pell, SEOG, state scholarships/grants, private scholarships, the school's own gift aid. *Loan aid offered:* Direct Subsidized Stafford, Direct Unsubsidized Stafford, Federal Perkins, state loans, college/university loans from institutional funds. Federal Work-Study Program available. Institutional employment available. Applicants will be notified of awards on or about April 1. Off-campus job opportunities are good.

## FROM THE ADMISSIONS OFFICE
"A Goucher liberal arts education aims to prepare students for the real world. The college integrates thought and action, combining a strong liberal arts curriculum with hands-on learning in off-campus settings through internships, field work, study abroad, and independent projects. Students can choose majors in 18 departments and four interdisciplinary areas, or they may design their own individualized program of study. Small classes taught by skilled faculty, strong international studies programs, and research with faculty are other key characteristics. Goucher has impressive resources in technology, including a campus fully wired for access to the Internet and the World Wide Web. Goucher's merit scholarship program is one of the top programs in the nation, offering strong students awards ranging from partial tuition to full tuition plus room and board."

## SELECTIVITY

| | |
|---|---|
| Admissions Rating | 80 |
| # of applicants | 2,596 |
| % of applicants accepted | 68 |
| % of acceptees attending | 21 |
| # of early decision applicants | 531 |
| % accepted early decision | 84 |

### FRESHMAN PROFILE
| | |
|---|---|
| Range SAT Verbal | 540-650 |
| Average SAT Verbal | 605 |
| Range SAT Math | 520-640 |
| Average SAT Math | 575 |
| Range ACT Composite | 22-28 |
| Average ACT Composite | 26 |
| Minimum TOEFL | 550 |
| Average HS GPA | 3.2 |
| % graduated top 10% of class | 19 |
| % graduated top 25% of class | 63 |
| % graduated top 50% of class | 75 |

### DEADLINES
| | |
|---|---|
| Early decision | 11/15 |
| Early decision notification | 12/15 |
| Regular admission | 2/1 |
| Regular notification | 4/1 |
| Nonfall registration? | yes |

### APPLICANTS ALSO LOOK AT
**AND OFTEN PREFER**
Skidmore
U of Maryland at College Park
Dickinson
NYU, Mount Holyoke
Boston U

**AND SOMETIMES PREFER**
Trinity College
Loyola (MD), American
Franklin & Marshall
George Washington

**AND RARELY PREFER**
Mary Washington, Towson

## FINANCIAL FACTS

| | |
|---|---|
| Financial Aid Rating | 88 |
| Tuition | $24,150 |
| Room and board | $8,200 |
| Books and supplies | $800 |
| Required fees | $300 |
| % frosh receiving aid | 69 |
| % undergrads receiving aid | 57 |
| Avg frosh grant | $13,500 |
| Avg frosh loan | $3,500 |

# GRINNELL COLLEGE

GRINNELL, IA 50112-1690 • ADMISSIONS: 800-247-0113 • FAX: 641-269-4800

## CAMPUS LIFE

| | |
|---|---|
| Quality of Life Rating | 82 |
| Type of school | private |
| Environment | rural |

### STUDENTS
| | |
|---|---|
| Total undergrad enrollment | 1,485 |
| % male/female | 45/55 |
| % from out of state | 85 |
| % from public high school | 78 |
| % live on campus | 85 |
| % African American | 4 |
| % Asian | 5 |
| % Caucasian | 76 |
| % Hispanic | 4 |
| % international | 10 |
| # of countries represented | 52 |

### SURVEY SAYS . . .
Campus easy to get around
Campus feels safe
Lab facilities are great
Lots of beer drinking
Political activism is hot
Great library
Students are happy
No one cheats
Campus is beautiful
Great computer facilities

## ACADEMICS

| | |
|---|---|
| Academic Rating | 94 |
| Calendar | semester |
| Student/faculty ratio | 10:1 |
| % profs teaching UG courses | 100 |
| Avg lab size | 10-19 students |
| Avg reg class size | 10-19 students |

### MOST POPULAR MAJORS
English
Biology
Anthropology

## STUDENTS SPEAK OUT

### Academics
Rural Iowa's Grinnell College, true to its long-held reputation, remains "a rigorous liberal arts institution in a somewhat remote location, offering a total immersion in campus life and academia." Students here praise faculty, reporting that profs are "top-notch; the number of incredible teachers is staggering, and they are all readily available and in fact eager to assist students outside of class. They are all extremely intelligent and take an active interest in their students' lives." Students also caution that the workload is "intense." Recently, however, a mood of uneasiness has descended on students, caused by the direction in which they perceive Grinnell is headed. Explains one student, "The goal seems to be to [become] 'more competitive' with our 'peer institutions,' which translates to charging students a little more every year for a little less, and putting the difference into long-term projects, such as construction." Students dislike the accompanying hassles (e.g., the attendant noise of building).

### Life
Grinnell, students agree, is "in the middle of nowhere in Iowa. Which is good because everyone really wants to be at the school because they like it, not because they spent their entire time in high school daydreaming about the utopian lifestyle of a college in a small farm town in Iowa." The location naturally means that "we're sometimes short on things to go out and do" and that students must "make our own fun." Fortunately, the Grinnell campus is a fairly active one. "Throughout the week, the campus attempts to keep us entertained with music/theatre events, movies, multicultural events, and colloquia," students report. When the weekend rolls around, there are "parties ranging from about four or five people in a dorm room to hundreds of people in a lounge or the Harris Center." There is no Greek system here, so "parties are almost always open to anyone who happens to walk by, and at such a small school that really helps build a sense of community." Students have mixed feelings about their hometown of Grinnell; some describe it as "small and cozy and a great place to 'escape to' within a ten-minute walk. There's a fabulous coffee shop downtown, Saint's Rest, as well as a one-screen movie theater and a bowling alley." Life here "is more enjoyable if you have a car," since "Iowa City and Des Moines are only 45 minutes to an hour away."

### Student Body
"In one of the publications on campus, both prospective students and seniors were asked how popular they thought the average Grinnell student was in high school, on a scale of one to ten," reports one Grinnell undergrad. "Both agreed on the number 4." Conclusion: "Most of the students at Grinnell are the people who did not fit into a single social group in high school." Nearly all feel they have found a comfortable home at Grinnell although more than a few admit to being somewhat cowed by their peers. Writes one, "One thing I will say about the students here is that almost everyone is brilliant. I was at the top of my class in high school and was quickly humbled when I arrived as a first-year." Most students lean well to the left politically; notes one, "Part of the appeal about Grinnell is its legendary social consciousness and socio-political activism." Grinnell students are not immune to self-segregation, however: "On the north side of [campus], students are sportily clad with some kind of personal touch. On the south side: hippie styling, dreads, and barefoot."

# GRINNELL COLLEGE

FINANCIAL AID: 515-269-3250 • E-MAIL: ASKGRIN@GRINNELL.EDU • WEBSITE: WWW.GRINNELL.EDU

## ADMISSIONS
*Very important factors considered include:* character/personal qualities, class rank, essays, extracurricular activities, recommendations, secondary school record, standardized test scores, talent/ability. *Important factors considered include:* interview. *Other factors considered include:* alumni/ae relation, ethnicity, volunteer work, work experience. SAT I or ACT required. TOEFL required of all international applicants. High school diploma or GED is required. *High school units required/recommended:* 17 total recommended; 4 English recommended, 4 math recommended, 3 science recommended, 3 science lab recommended, 3 foreign language recommended, 3 social studies/history recommended.

### The Inside Word
Grinnell has plenty of academically talented applicants. This enables the admissions committee to put a lot of energy into matchmaking, and gives candidates who have devoted time and energy to thought about themselves, their future, and Grinnell the opportunity to rise to the top. All applicants should consider interviewing; you're likely to leave with a positive impression.

## FINANCIAL AID
*Students should submit:* FAFSA, institution's own financial aid form, noncustodial (divorced/separated) parent's statement. Regular filing deadline is February 1. The Princeton Review suggests that all financial aid forms be submitted as soon as possible after January 1. *Need-based grants offered:* Pell, SEOG, state scholarships/grants, private scholarships, the school's own gift aid. *Loan aid offered:* FFEL Subsidized Stafford, FFEL Unsubsidized Stafford, FFEL PLUS, Federal Perkins, college/university loans from institutional funds. Federal Work-Study Program available. Institutional employment available. Applicants will be notified of awards by April 1. Off-campus job opportunities are fair.

## FROM THE ADMISSIONS OFFICE
"Grinnell students are involved and committed to academic work and involved in community and volunteer service. Students are independent and can exercise that independence in Grinnell's open curriculum. Grinnell hopes to produce individualism, social commitment, and intellectual self-awareness in its graduates."

### SELECTIVITY

| | |
|---|---|
| Admissions Rating | 92 |
| # of applicants | 3,031 |
| % of applicants accepted | 48 |
| % of acceptees attending | 28 |
| # accepting a place on wait list | 71 |
| % admitted from wait list | 39 |
| # of early decision applicants | 119 |
| % accepted early decision | 79 |

### FRESHMAN PROFILE
| | |
|---|---|
| Range SAT Verbal | 630-730 |
| Average SAT Verbal | 682 |
| Range SAT Math | 620-710 |
| Average SAT Math | 670 |
| Range ACT Composite | 28-31 |
| Average ACT Composite | 30 |
| Minimum TOEFL | 550 |
| % graduated top 10% of class | 59 |
| % graduated top 25% of class | 91 |
| % graduated top 50% of class | 99 |

### DEADLINES
| | |
|---|---|
| Early decision I | 11/20 |
| Early decision I notification | 12/20 |
| Early decision II | 1/1 |
| Early decision II notification | 2/1 |
| Regular admission | 1/20 |
| Regular notification | 4/1 |

### APPLICANTS ALSO LOOK AT AND SOMETIMES PREFER
Carleton
Macalester
Washington U
Oberlin
Swarthmore
Brown

### AND RARELY PREFER
Kenyon
Colorado College
Denison

### FINANCIAL FACTS

| | |
|---|---|
| Financial Aid Rating | 94 |
| Tuition | $22,960 |
| Room and board | $6,330 |
| Books and supplies | $400 |
| Required fees | $570 |
| % frosh receiving aid | 58 |
| % undergrads receiving aid | 58 |
| Avg frosh grant | $12,927 |
| Avg frosh loan | $4,211 |

# GROVE CITY COLLEGE

100 CAMPUS DRIVE, GROVE CITY, PA 16127-2104 • ADMISSIONS: 724-458-2100 • FAX: 724-458-3395

## CAMPUS LIFE

| | |
|---|---:|
| Quality of Life Rating | 79 |
| Type of school | private |
| Affiliation | Presbyterian |
| Environment | rural |

### STUDENTS
| | |
|---|---:|
| Total undergrad enrollment | 2,288 |
| % male/female | 49/51 |
| % from out of state | 46 |
| % from public high school | 88 |
| % live on campus | 91 |
| % in (# of) fraternities | 9 (10) |
| % in (# of) sororities | 12 (8) |
| % Asian | 1 |
| % Caucasian | 98 |
| % international | 1 |
| # of countries represented | 11 |

### SURVEY SAYS . . .
Campus is beautiful
Campus easy to get around
Students are religious
Campus feels safe
(Almost) everyone plays intramural sports
No one cheats
Great computer facilities
Students get along with local community

## ACADEMICS

| | |
|---|---:|
| Academic Rating | 86 |
| Calendar | semester |
| Student/faculty ratio | 19:1 |
| % profs teaching UG courses | 100 |
| Avg lab size | 10-19 students |
| Avg reg class size | 20-29 students |

### MOST POPULAR MAJORS
Business administration/management
Elementary education and teaching
English/language arts teacher education

## STUDENTS SPEAK OUT

### Academics
The Grove City College environment allows students to be "continually challenged to learn more—more about my field of studies, more about the world around me, more about my faith, and more about myself." This "Ivy League school in disguise" runs according to a "Christian viewpoint that is refreshing and open-minded." Some students feel that the religious bent makes "almost every course become in some way, shape, or form a theology course." One respondent feels that the school's "pride in a 'rigorous curriculum' translates into standards that sometimes border on the ridiculous." Amid the challenging course work, students work with professors who are "inconceivably intelligent and brilliant in their fields" and "not afraid to stand up for liberty and truth." Undergraduates feel personally supported by the faculty, noting that instructors "go out of their way to help students understand material without robbing them of the learning experience." Students embrace their core curriculum, eager to "dabble in everything from physics to Spanish to philosophy, no matter what your major." Several students think "it seems that faculty and students mesh well, while the administration isolates itself." Reportedly, students and professors alike "voice their displeasure concerning administrative direction." A common sentiment goes, "Administration needs to get with the times and realize we're big boys and big girls and we can handle ourselves." On the other hand, one student writes, "Where else can you watch the president of the college team up with faculty members for a basketball game against students?" In the end, the school succeeds in "giving support to students in many ways, which lightens the academic load."

### Life
A defining factor of Grove is the "definite focus on God." That means "Calvin and Luther are generally on the tip of the tongue here" and "we do have parties, just minus the alcohol." Employing a well-used double negative, one student writes "the party scene isn't nonexistent," but typically, students partake in "snowball fights, movie nights, Bible study, IM bowling, ice cream socials, square dancing, lots of long conversations," and other activities that "don't involve breaking the law." Some students think that Greeks don't do much besides "wear matching sweatshirts," but others say, "Greek life gives variety, friendship, and fun that the campus does not offer." The anti-Greek faction goes so far as to say that fraternities and sororities are "the cause of all drinking and sex that goes on." "Intervisitation," that fated time when men and women are allowed to be in the same residences at the same time, means that "the freshmen dorms get loud, and stay loud until 12:45." That early collegiate bedtime hints at the "atmosphere bordering on repressive at times." All told, certain students remark suggestively, "Don't let the Norman Rockwell facade fool you."

### Student Body
Students offer three basic descriptions of TGs, or "typical Grovers." The first camp, "the home-schooled, very sheltered kids who go home every weekend and are engaged by sophomore year," give the campus its reputation, but many students will tell you that students are not as marriage-obsessed as outsiders believe. These kids are the ones "who would ask, 'What are hallucinogens?'" one student explains. Another group comprises "the normal, Nalgene bottle–carrying, Christian summer camp–working, service-oriented students." The leftovers are those who "slack off, drink, and get off campus." In general, most undergrads are "white, suburban, Christian Republicans." Many students point out, "We're diverse in our Christian denominations, but not our ethnicities," to the degree that "there are more amputees than minorities on this campus." In this "homogenous group," "there are a few gays/lesbians, and they probably don't fit in well since this is a Christian school and the Bible is against homosexuality." Reportedly, atypical students are "acknowledged as individuals and accepted for [whom] they are." The cumulative effect is "so many people who enjoy being around each other so much."

250 ■ THE BEST 351 COLLEGES

# GROVE CITY COLLEGE

FINANCIAL AID: 724-458-2163 • E-MAIL: ADMISSIONS@GCC.EDU • WEBSITE: WWW.GCC.EDU

## ADMISSIONS

*Very important factors considered include:* character/personal qualities, interview, secondary school record. *Important factors considered include:* essays, extracurricular activities, recommendations, standardized test scores, talent/ability. *Other factors considered include:* alumni/ae relation, class rank, geographical residence, minority status, religious affiliation/commitment, state residency, volunteer work, work experience. SAT I or ACT required. TOEFL required of all international applicants. High school diploma or GED is required. *High school units required/recommended:* 16 total recommended; 4 English recommended, 3 math recommended, 3 science recommended, 3 foreign language recommended, 2 social studies recommended, 1 history recommended.

### The Inside Word

If you're looking for a northeastern college with a Christian orientation, Grove City is a pretty good choice, but it's getting tougher to get in as we speak. Applications and standards are on the rise, and the college is fast becoming the newest addition to the lofty realm of the highly selective. Minorities are in short supply, and will encounter a somewhat friendlier admissions process. All students should definitely follow the college's recommendation and interview.

## FINANCIAL AID

*Students should submit:* institution's own financial aid form. Regular filing deadline is April 15. The Princeton Review suggests that all financial aid forms be submitted as soon as possible after January 1. *Need-based scholarships/grants offered:* private scholarships, the school's own gift aid. *Loan aid offered:* College Loan Program funded by PNC Bank. Institutional employment available. Applicants will be notified of awards on a rolling basis beginning on or about March 15. Off-campus job opportunities are good.

## FROM THE ADMISSIONS OFFICE

"A good college education doesn't have to cost a fortune. For decades, Grove City College has offered a quality education at costs among the lowest nationally. Since the 1990s, increased national academic acclaim has come to Grove City College. Grove City College is a place where professors teach. You will not see graduate assistants or teacher's aides in the classroom. Our professors are also active in the total life of the campus. More than 100 student organizations on campus afford opportunity for a wide variety of co-curricular activities. Outstanding scholars and leaders in education, science, and international affairs visit the campus each year. The environment at GCC is friendly, secure, and dedicated to high standards. Character-building is emphasized and traditional Christian values are supported."

## SELECTIVITY

| | |
|---|---|
| Admissions Rating | 91 |
| # of applicants | 2,001 |
| % of applicants accepted | 47 |
| % of acceptees attending | 62 |
| # accepting a place on wait list | 157 |
| % admitted from wait list | 15 |
| # of early decision applicants | 683 |
| % accepted early decision | 48 |

### FRESHMAN PROFILE

| | |
|---|---|
| Range SAT Verbal | 570-692 |
| Average SAT Verbal | 633 |
| Range SAT Math | 574-690 |
| Average SAT Math | 639 |
| Range ACT Composite | 24-30 |
| Average ACT Composite | 28 |
| Minimum TOEFL | 550 |
| Average HS GPA | 3.7 |
| % graduated top 10% of class | 60 |
| % graduated top 25% of class | 87 |
| % graduated top 50% of class | 98 |

### DEADLINES

| | |
|---|---|
| Early decision | 11/15 |
| Early decision notification | 12/15 |
| Priority admission | 11/15 |
| Regular admission | 2/1 |
| Regular notification | 3/15 |
| Nonfall registration? | yes |

### APPLICANTS ALSO LOOK AT AND OFTEN PREFER
Penn State at U Park
Wheaton (IL)
Hillsdale

### AND RARELY PREFER
Slippery Rock U
Thiel

## FINANCIAL FACTS

| | |
|---|---|
| Financial Aid Rating | 88 |
| Tuition | $9,376 |
| Room and board | $4,852 |
| Books and supplies | $900 |
| % frosh receiving aid | 62 |
| % undergrads receiving aid | 37 |
| Avg frosh grant | $4,623 |
| Avg frosh loan | $6,055 |

# GUILFORD COLLEGE

5800 WEST FRIENDLY AVENUE, GREENSBORO, NC 27410 • ADMISSIONS: 800-992-7759 • FAX: 336-316-2954

## CAMPUS LIFE

| Quality of Life Rating | 88 |
|---|---|
| Type of school | private |
| Affiliation | Quaker |
| Environment | suburban |

### STUDENTS

| Total undergrad enrollment | 1,801 |
|---|---|
| % male/female | 42/58 |
| % from out of state | 39 |
| % from public high school | 67 |
| % live on campus | 47 |
| % African American | 16 |
| % Asian | 1 |
| % Caucasian | 70 |
| % Hispanic | 2 |
| % international | 2 |
| # of countries represented | 21 |

### SURVEY SAYS . . .
Campus easy to get around
Campus is beautiful
Great computer facilities
(Almost) everyone smokes
Lab facilities are great
Political activism is hot
Popular college radio
Lots of beer drinking
Campus feels safe

## ACADEMICS

| Academic Rating | 87 |
|---|---|
| Calendar | semester |
| Student/faculty ratio | 15:1 |
| % profs teaching UG courses | 100 |
| Avg lab size | 20-29 students |
| Avg reg class size | 10-19 students |

### MOST POPULAR MAJORS
Business administration/management
English language and literature
Psychology

## STUDENTS SPEAK OUT

### Academics
Students at Guilford College laud their school's Quaker values of "friendliness, simplicity, and equality," telling us that the Quaker spirit makes Guilford "a great place to build one's confidence. Teachers and peers are supportive and friendly." Explains one undergrad, "Because the school was founded by the Society of Friends, Quakers, we believe in the equality of everyone. One way this manifests itself is that we refer to our professors by their first names rather than titles. This puts us all on much more equal footing, which I think enhances the learning process." Classes at Guilford "are primarily discussion-based; teachers want to learn from the students, as well as share what knowledge they have with them. Courses are also writing- and reading-intensive." Students here warn that "Guilford has some classes that will kick your butt . . . in a good way. They get you thinking. You are forced to deal with things from outside the ordinary perspective." The profs, as at many small, teaching-oriented colleges, "are wonderful, and it's very refreshing to know that you have teachers that genuinely care about you and how you are doing. There is almost no way to slip through the cracks." Students especially appreciate how professors "will always help you until you understand the concept, and if you are not being challenged enough, they will make sure you get the challenges you need. It's also nice that at the end of the semester your professor has the class over for dinner at his house."

### Life
Students love this "beautiful campus" in northwest Greensboro, one of three cities that constitute North Carolina's Triad (Winston-Salem and High Point are the other two). Students tell us that "Greensboro is a mecca for good underground music" and that the small city (pop. 230,000) offers up some good eats as well as the expected array of movies, bars, and shopping. Chapel Hill, a quintessential college town an hour to the east, offers even more options. Many here are content to remain within the confines of the school, however, since "there is always something going on on campus: live music (tonight Holly Near is playing), concerts, movies . . . discussions (about peace in the Middle East, God and gender, art and social action, etc.), clubs, sports (ultimate Frisbee, rugby, etc.), special events put on by the Student Union (Mardi Gras ball, etc.), meditation groups, drum circle, art workshops, contra dancing, you name it." Campus theater productions "are always outstanding," while "the *Guilfordian* newspaper and Guilford radio station are [also] great." A number of students take advantage of the mild weather during the school year to enjoy "outdoor club trips, which have included skiing (in the mountains to the west), hiking/backpacking, and rafting." "Community service is popular" among many here as well. Small parties are the choice of most on the weekends despite the school's recent vigilance in enforcing its alcohol policies.

### Student Body
"In high school there were always ways you could categorize people and pigeonhole them," notes one Guilford undergrad, continuing, "but there were always a few that didn't quite fit into these categories. Guilford is full of these kinds of people." Or, as another student here put it, "We're all unique . . . just like everyone else." Students tell us that "most of the campus is a very liberal, 'hippie' kind of place. There are the athletes, conservatives, and whatnot, although their numbers are small." Much of the student body leans hard left politically, actively demonstrating "a strong sense of social responsibility." Many here report a clear divide between athletes and the rest of the student body, but report that otherwise students mostly get along.

# GUILFORD COLLEGE

FINANCIAL AID: 336-316-2354 • E-MAIL: ADMISSION@GUILFORD.EDU • WEBSITE: WWW.GUILFORD.EDU

## ADMISSIONS

*Very important factors considered include:* character/personal qualities, essays, secondary school record. *Important factors considered include:* alumni/ae relation, interview, recommendations, standardized test scores, talent/ability, volunteer work, work experience. *Other factors considered include:* class rank, extracurricular activities, geographical residence, minority status, state residency. SAT I or ACT required. TOEFL required of all international applicants. High school diploma or GED is required. *High school units required/recommended:* 18 total required; 4 English required, 3 math required, 4 math recommended, 2 science required, 2 science lab required, 2 foreign language required, 2 social studies required, 1 history required, 2 elective required.

### The Inside Word

Guilford is indeed a sleeper, and is likely to become more selective as it becomes better known. Its current acceptance rate is high mainly because the competition includes many of the best colleges and universities east of the Mississippi.

## FINANCIAL AID

*Students should submit:* FAFSA, noncustodial (divorced/separated) parent's statement, business/farm supplement. The Princeton Review suggests that all financial aid forms be submitted as soon as possible after January 1. *Need-based scholarships/grants offered:* Pell, SEOG, state scholarships/grants, private scholarships, the school's own gift aid. *Loan aid offered:* FFEL Subsidized Stafford, FFEL Unsubsidized Stafford, FFEL PLUS, Federal Perkins, college/university loans from institutional funds. Federal Work-Study Program available. Institutional employment available. Applicants will be notified of awards on a rolling basis beginning on or about February 15. Off-campus job opportunities are good.

---

## FROM THE ADMISSIONS OFFICE

"We want you to know this about Guilford:

1) Guilford is difficult. Not only will you have to adapt to the diversity at Guilford (we have students from 44 states and 21 countries) but the academic expectations are significant. With an average class size of 18 students, our full-time professors (no graduate assistants) will see you often in class and expect daily contributions from you. Class participation is critical.

2) Our Quaker values of integrity, respect for difference, social justice, and responsibility are sure to challenge all students. You need to be a mature student to enroll at Guilford. No matter your background, academic preparation, values, thoughts, and beliefs you will be challenged here. We admit that our mission is idealistic; however, we expect our students to deal with very difficult issues. An education from Guilford prepares you for life in a rapidly changing world.

3) Community service and volunteerism is a hallmark of Guilford. Our Project Community (run by students) contributes more than 50,000 hours of community service to the Greensboro, North Carolina, community each year. Service is a true part of the daily experience at Guilford.

For more information on Guilford, create your individualized online brochure at: www.guilford.edu/myguilford."

---

### SELECTIVITY

| | |
|---|---:|
| Admissions Rating | 74 |
| # of applicants | 1,339 |
| % of applicants accepted | 75 |
| % of acceptees attending | 31 |
| # of early decision applicants | 38 |
| % accepted early decision | 87 |

### FRESHMAN PROFILE

| | |
|---|---:|
| Range SAT Verbal | 500-640 |
| Average SAT Verbal | 570 |
| Range SAT Math | 490-620 |
| Average SAT Math | 550 |
| Range ACT Composite | 20-27 |
| Average ACT Composite | 25 |
| Minimum TOEFL | 550 |
| Average HS GPA | 3.0 |
| % graduated top 10% of class | 14 |
| % graduated top 25% of class | 37 |
| % graduated top 50% of class | 77 |

### DEADLINES

| | |
|---|---:|
| Priority admission | 1/15 |
| Regular admission | 2/15 |
| Regular notification | 4/1 |
| Nonfall registration? | yes |

### APPLICANTS ALSO LOOK AT
#### AND OFTEN PREFER
Oberlin College
Hampshire College
Warren Wilson

#### AND SOMETIMES PREFER
Earlham College
University of North Carolina—Chapel Hill
Goucher College
Elon University

### FINANCIAL FACTS

| | |
|---|---:|
| Financial Aid Rating | 90 |
| Tuition | $18,700 |
| Room and board | $6,260 |
| Books and supplies | $700 |
| Required fees | $425 |
| % frosh receiving aid | 59 |
| % undergrads receiving aid | 39 |
| Avg frosh grant | $10,240 |
| Avg frosh loan | $4,725 |

# GUSTAVUS ADOLPHUS COLLEGE

800 WEST COLLEGE AVENUE, SAINT PETER, MN 56082 • ADMISSIONS: 507-933-7676 • FAX: 507-933-7474

## CAMPUS LIFE

| Quality of Life Rating | 81 |
|---|---|
| Type of school | private |
| Affiliation | Lutheran |
| Environment | suburban |

### STUDENTS

| Total undergrad enrollment | 2,536 |
|---|---|
| % male/female | 42/58 |
| % from out of state | 18 |
| % from public high school | 92 |
| % live on campus | 85 |
| % in (# of) fraternities | 27 (7) |
| % in (# of) sororities | 22 (5) |
| % African American | 1 |
| % Asian | 3 |
| % Caucasian | 95 |
| % Hispanic | 1 |
| % international | 1 |
| # of countries represented | 17 |

### SURVEY SAYS . . .
Campus easy to get around
Musical organizations are hot
Great computer facilities
Students are happy
Athletic facilities are great
Campus feels safe
Campus is beautiful
Lots of beer drinking

## ACADEMICS

| Academic Rating | 82 |
|---|---|
| Calendar | 4-1-4 |
| Student/faculty ratio | 13:1 |
| % profs teaching UG courses | 100 |
| Avg lab size | 10-19 students |
| Avg reg class size | 10-19 students |

### MOST POPULAR MAJORS
Communications studies/speech
communication and rhetoric
Biology/biological sciences
Psychology

## STUDENTS SPEAK OUT
### Academics
At Gustavus Adophus College, a small Lutheran school in rural Minnesota, students enjoy "many opportunities to make the most out of [their] education through research, independent study, or simply the awesome, enthusiastic professors who care about what they teach." Reports one busy student, "As a sophomore, I am already involved with two research projects on campus and have come to know all three of the professors I am working with very well. The professors are really approachable and are passionate about what they teach." Business, biology, and music are among Gustavus' top departments; of the last, students crow that "the music program at Gustavus is phenomenal. Band, orchestra, or choir—the groups are just amazing, and the students are really talented. The top choir just returned from a tour of Italy, singing in places like the Duomo in Florence and the Basilica of St. Francis in Assisi." While "classes are challenging" and "professors often grade super-hard," students do not feel overburdened by their academic chores because "the school has a number of resources to help you out if you get overwhelmed," and profs "will bend over backward to help us learn." Despite the rigors of the curriculum, students find time to enjoy themselves. "The school stresses a balance between academics and extracurriculars," writes one student. Gustavus offers a short January term, during which "students try an entirely new subject for a month. It also provides a study-abroad opportunity for those that can't go abroad for an entire semester."

### Life
Most students indicate a subdued but agreeable pace of life at Gustavus Adolphus: "As with all colleges, drinking is a social activity in which many students partake." Freshmen and sophomores often visit The Dive, "the on-campus dance club that has something going on every Friday and Saturday," while upperclassmen sometimes head for nearby bars. Those who abjure alcohol report that "the school does have a nice selection of on-campus, substance-free events, most of which are fun. These would include currently running movies, concerts, comedians, speakers, dancing, and other mingling events." Students also tell us that "community service organizations seem to involve a large majority of the students" and that "athletic events, both intercollegiate and intramural, are a favorite." Hometown Saint Peter is "friendly" and Mankato, home to Minnesota State University, is only 15 miles to the south. While many at this Lutheran school are religious, "religion here is what you make of it; those who want to be highly involved will find numerous opportunities to do so, but those who don't want to be involved are not hit over the head with it."

### Student Body
The students of Gustavus are typically "Scandinavian, tall, blonde, attractive, intelligent, and especially nice," with "about half coming from large cities and the other half from farm areas." Most are midwestern and Lutheran, which helps explain their similarities in appearance. Despite their outward similitude, however, "there is a variety of different personality types at Gustavus," so "it is not too difficult for people to find a niche." The school also has "lots of international students that fit in with everyone." Music and athletics are the two most popular extracurricular activities. Athletes tend to live on the North Side of campus, near the athletic facilities. Reports one student, "The school has a North Side/South Side division, where the students on the North Side drink more and tend to be involved in sports, [and those] living on the South Side are more likely to be involved in the fine arts and are more serious about academics."

# GUSTAVUS ADOLPHUS COLLEGE

FINANCIAL AID: 507-933-7527 • E-MAIL: ADMISSION@GUSTAVUS.EDU • WEBSITE: WWW.GUSTAVUS.EDU

## ADMISSIONS

*Very important factors considered include:* essays, secondary school record, standardized test scores. *Important factors considered include:* character/personal qualities, class rank, extracurricular activities, interview, recommendations, religious affiliation/commitment, talent/ability. *Other factors considered include:* alumni/ae relation, geographical residence, minority status, volunteer work, work experience. SAT I or ACT required. TOEFL required of all international applicants. High school diploma or GED is required. *High school units required/recommended:* 17 total required; 22 total recommended; 4 English required, 3 math required, 4 math recommended, 2 science required, 3 science recommended, 2 science lab required, 3 science lab recommended, 2 foreign language required, 3 foreign language recommended, 2 social studies required, 2 history required, 2 elective recommended.

## The Inside Word

While the college refers to itself as a national liberal arts college, the applicant pool is decidedly regional and mostly from Minnesota. The pool is also small and highly self-selected, which explains the high acceptance rate and solid freshman profile. Minorities and those who hail from far afield will find their applications met with enthusiasm by the admissions committee.

## FINANCIAL AID

*Students should submit:* FAFSA, institution's own financial aid form. Students who want to receive an award by March 1 must file the CSS/Financial Aid PROFILE. Regular filing deadline is June 15. The Princeton Review suggests that all financial aid forms be submitted as soon as possible after January 1. *Need-based scholarships/grants offered:* Pell, SEOG, state scholarships/grants, private scholarships, the school's own gift aid. *Loan aid offered:* Direct Subsidized Stafford, Direct Unsubsidized Stafford, Direct PLUS, Federal Perkins, state loans, college/university loans from institutional funds, alternative loans from private lenders. Federal Work-Study Program available. Institutional employment available. Applicants will be notified of awards on a rolling basis beginning on or about March 1. Off-campus job opportunities are good.

## FROM THE ADMISSIONS OFFICE

"Gustavus Adolphus, a national liberal arts college with a strong tradition of quality teaching, is committed to the liberal arts and sciences; to its Lutheran history; to innovation as evidenced by the 4-1-4 calendar, Curriculum I and II, and the writing program; and to affordable costs with its unique Guaranteed Cost Plan and Partners in Scholarship Program. The most recent additions to its excellent facilities are Olin Hall for physics and mathematics; Confer Hall for the humanities; Lund Center for physical education, athletics, and health; International Center for residential living and international education; and Jackson Campus Center."

### SELECTIVITY

| | |
|---|---|
| Admissions Rating | 84 |
| # of applicants | 2,203 |
| % of applicants accepted | 77 |
| % of acceptees attending | 39 |
| # accepting a place on wait list | 70 |
| % admitted from wait list | 7 |
| # of early decision applicants | 146 |
| % accepted early decision | 97 |

### FRESHMAN PROFILE

| | |
|---|---|
| Range SAT Verbal | 550-660 |
| Average SAT Verbal | 610 |
| Range SAT Math | 540-670 |
| Average SAT Math | 620 |
| Range ACT Composite | 23-28 |
| Average ACT Composite | 26 |
| Minimum TOEFL | 550 |
| Average HS GPA | 3.6 |
| % graduated top 10% of class | 36 |
| % graduated top 25% of class | 69 |
| % graduated top 50% of class | 94 |

### DEADLINES

| | |
|---|---|
| Early decision | 11/15 |
| Early decision notification | 12/1 |
| Priority admission | 2/15 |
| Regular admission | 4/1 |
| Nonfall registration? | yes |

### APPLICANTS ALSO LOOK AT AND OFTEN PREFER
U of Wisconsin at Madison
Carleton

### AND SOMETIMES PREFER
U of Minnesota
St. Olaf

### FINANCIAL FACTS

| | |
|---|---|
| Financial Aid Rating | 90 |
| Tuition | $21,330 |
| Room and board | $5,460 |
| Books and supplies | $700 |
| Required fees | $320 |
| % frosh receiving aid | 65 |
| % undergrads receiving aid | 65 |
| Avg frosh grant | $7,400 |
| Avg frosh loan | $4,500 |

# HAMILTON COLLEGE
198 COLLEGE HILL ROAD, CLINTON, NY 13323 • ADMISSIONS: 800-843-2655 • FAX: 315-859-4457

## CAMPUS LIFE

| | |
|---|---|
| Quality of Life Rating | 89 |
| Type of school | private |
| Environment | rural |

### STUDENTS
| | |
|---|---|
| Total undergrad enrollment | 1,760 |
| % from out of state | 61 |
| % from public high school | 63 |
| % live on campus | 96 |
| % in (# of) fraternities | 34 (7) |
| % in (# of) sororities | 20 (3) |
| % African American | 4 |
| % Asian | 5 |
| % Caucasian | 87 |
| % Hispanic | 4 |
| % international | 3 |
| # of countries represented | 31 |

### SURVEY SAYS . . .
Registration is a breeze
athletic facilities are great
Classes are small
lots of beer drinking
Students are religious
Political activism is hot
Lots of classroom discussion

## ACADEMICS

| | |
|---|---|
| Academic Rating | 94 |
| Calendar | semester |
| Student/faculty ratio | 10:1 |
| Profs interesting rating | 76 |
| Profs accessible rating | 74 |
| % profs teaching UG courses | 100 |
| Avg lab size | 10-19 students |
| Avg reg class size | 10-19 students |

### MOST POPULAR MAJORS
Psychology
Economics
Political science and government

## STUDENTS SPEAK OUT

### Academics
According to a studious junior, Hamilton affords a "grueling but fulfilling education" in a "rigorous yet nurturing" environment. The college "really produces great writers and great thinkers," another student comments, and several respondents highlight the strength of the school's writing program, designed to ensure that graduates can wield the pen as effectively as the institution's namesake, Alexander Hamilton. The college's "very helpful and available" professors conduct classes in a "hands-on" manner and hold students to "very high standards." Luckily, instructors "really communicate the material well" and are always "there for you if you have a problem." The faculty has a reputation for being "eager to meet with students to help prepare for exams or write papers." They also develop camaraderie with their wards: "Only at Hamilton can you go to the pub and have a beer with your professor." Other students concur: "Your teacher is your best friend," and "professors are constantly having entire classes over for dinner." The small classes "concentrate on discussion," which means "you are expected to participate." A music major waxes, "I adore the fact that we call all the professors in our department by their first names." The administration is said to be "exceedingly accessible" as well as "concerned with student opinion and open to suggestions." Hamilton's president holds a weekly "open hour" to meet with students, and most "administrators know student names." In this supportive atmosphere, students aver that "if you have a vision, Hamilton will provide the funding and assistance to [help you] achieve your goals."

### Life
For students sometimes it seems that life at Hamilton consists of "nothing but work and alcohol." Students attribute the drinking culture on campus to the fact that "it is always ass-cold winter" in central New York. Although "beer is readily available" and many students say they "drink for fun," a sophomore wants you to know that "drinking isn't compulsory, just common" in Clinton. While some students wish for "more things for people who don't drink to do," others point out "alternatives like movies, dance, theater, comedy, and other low-key activities." Fraternities and sororities are considered "integral" to Hamilton social life, and many students agree that things "would be better if the Greeks still had houses." Others feel that "Greek life is too important," but rest assured, "you can find a party whether you're Greek or not." Students also venture off campus in search of a colder beer. "Three words: The Village Tavern," a senior writes, referring to one of the two bars in town and the scene of many a Hamilton student's fond college memories. Students report that their adopted hometown of Clinton "is the textbook definition of boring," but nonetheless wish for improved town-gown relations. One student notes, "Being isolated on 'the Hill' can sometimes warp students' perception of the real world."

### Student Body
A large number of respondents share the sentiment that "a small percentage of the students account for the Hamilton image of rich, white, and preppy." While the Greek population may be the most visible and "sometimes it seems like everyone is from old-money Greenwich," students emphasize that other types do coexist in Clinton. In general, "the majority of people are friendly, open-minded, and intelligent," and "most people smile, even if they don't know you," contributing to a "nice sense of community." Currently, students note the decidedly "homogeneous population" when it comes to race and ethnicity. One junior tells us, "I'm not sure that minorities feel welcome." But other students observe, "Hamilton's diversity is increasing. It has come a long way in a few years." According to a senior, "Even though Hamilton is sort of über-whitey land, it's clear that admissions and the administration are trying very hard to diversify the campus."

# HAMILTON COLLEGE

FINANCIAL AID: 800-859-4413 • E-MAIL: ADMISSION@HAMILTON.EDU • WEBSITE: WWW.HAMILTON.EDU

## ADMISSIONS

*Very important factors considered include:* class rank, recommendations, secondary school record. *Important factors considered include:* alumni/ae relation, character/personal qualities, essays, extracurricular activities, interview, minority status, standardized test scores. *Other factors considered include:* talent/ability. TOEFL required of all international applicants. *High school units required/recommended:* 16 total recommended; 4 English recommended, 3 math recommended, 3 science recommended, 3 foreign language recommended, 3 social studies recommended.

### The Inside Word

Gaining admission to Hamilton is difficult, and would be more so if the college didn't lose many of its shared applicants to competitor schools. The college's position as a popular safety for the top tier of northeastern colleges has always benefited the quality of its applicant pool, but it translates into a tough fight when it comes to getting admits to enroll. Although selectivity has risen significantly of late, Hamilton remains in the position of losing many of its best candidates to other, more prestigious schools. Students who view Hamilton as their first-choice college should definitely make it plain to the admissions committee—such news can often be influential, especially under circumstances like those mentioned here.

## FINANCIAL AID

*Students should submit:* FAFSA, institution's own financial aid form, CSS/Financial Aid PROFILE, state aid form, noncustodial (divorced/separated) parent's statement, business/farm supplement, parent and student federal tax returns. Regular filing deadline is February 1. The Princeton Review suggests that all financial aid forms be submitted as soon as possible after January 1. *Need-based scholarships/grants offered:* Pell, SEOG, state scholarships/grants, private scholarships, the school's own gift aid. *Loan aid offered:* FFEL Subsidized Stafford, FFEL Unsubsidized Stafford, FFEL PLUS, Federal Perkins, college/university loans from institutional funds. Federal Work-Study Program available. Institutional employment available. Applicants will be notified of awards on or about April 1. Off-campus job opportunities are fair.

## FROM THE ADMISSIONS OFFICE

"One of Hamilton's most important characteristics is the exceptional interaction that takes place between students and faculty members. Whether in class or out, they work together, challenging one another to excel. Academic life at Hamilton is rigorous, and emerging from that rigor is a community spirit based on common commitment. It binds together student and teacher, and stimulates self-motivation, thus making the learning process not only more productive but also more enjoyable and satisfying. Hamilton's Bristol Scholars program is merit-based, offering ten half-tuition scholarships. Both the Bristol and the need-based Schambach Scholars program also offer special research opportunities with faculty on campus. National merit finalists also receive $2,000 a year."

---

### SELECTIVITY

★ ★ ★ ★

| | |
|---|---:|
| Admissions Rating | 92 |
| # of applicants | 4,395 |
| % of applicants accepted | 33 |
| % of acceptees attending | 31 |
| # accepting a place on wait list | 455 |
| % admitted from wait list | 2 |
| # of early decision applicants | 434 |
| % accepted early decision | 45 |

### FRESHMAN PROFILE

| | |
|---|---:|
| Range SAT Verbal | 600-700 |
| Range SAT Math | 610-700 |
| Minimum TOEFL | 600 |
| % graduated top 10% of class | 60 |
| % graduated top 25% of class | 92 |
| % graduated top 50% of class | 99 |

### DEADLINES

| | |
|---|---:|
| Early decision | 11/15 |
| Early decision notification | 12/15 |
| Regular admission | 1/1 |
| Regular notification | 4/1 |
| Nonfall registration? | yes |

### APPLICANTS ALSO LOOK AT AND OFTEN PREFER
Middlebury
Williams
Amherst

### AND SOMETIMES PREFER
Colgate
Bowdoin
Colby

### AND RARELY PREFER
Union
Skidmore
Dickinson

### FINANCIAL FACTS

★ ★ ★ ☆

| | |
|---|---:|
| Financial Aid Rating | 85 |
| Tuition | $28,610 |
| Room and board | $7,040 |
| Required fees | $150 |
| % frosh receiving aid | 51 |
| % undergrads receiving aid | 54 |
| Avg frosh grant | $21,520 |
| Avg frosh loan | $2,531 |

# HAMPDEN-SYDNEY COLLEGE

PO Box 667, Hampden-Sydney, VA 23943 • Admissions: 804-223-6120 • Fax: 804-223-6346

## CAMPUS LIFE

| | |
|---|---|
| Quality of Life Rating | 84 |
| Type of school | private |
| Affiliation | Presbyterian |
| Environment | rural |

### STUDENTS

| | |
|---|---|
| Total undergrad enrollment | 1,026 |
| % from out of state | 37 |
| % from public high school | 62 |
| % live on campus | 94 |
| % in (# of) fraternities | 37 (11) |
| % African American | 4 |
| % Asian | 1 |
| % Caucasian | 88 |
| % Hispanic | 1 |
| # of countries represented | 3 |

### SURVEY SAYS . . .
Lots of conservatives on campus
Students don't like
Hampden-Sydney, VA
Diversity lacking on campus
Frats dominate social scene
No one cheats
Great library
Beautiful campus
Musical organizations aren't popular
Students get along with local community
Class discussions encouraged
Computer facilities need improving

## ACADEMICS

| | |
|---|---|
| Academic Rating | 85 |
| Calendar | semester |
| Student/faculty ratio | 10:1 |
| Profs interesting rating | 96 |
| Profs accessible rating | 97 |
| % profs teaching UG courses | 100 |
| Avg reg class size | 10-19 students |

### MOST POPULAR MAJORS
Economics
History
Political science and government

## STUDENTS SPEAK OUT

### Academics

Who says the Old South is dead? The students of Virginia's all-male Hampden-Sydney College, founded in 1775, continue the region's genteel traditions at an institution defined by its rigid honor code, a solid core curriculum emphasizing those things a gentleman needs to know, a great "'old boy network' of alumni," and professors who "are more enjoyable than a glass of sweet ice tea and a plate of Mom's homestyle." For the right type of student—namely, one comfortable in so arguably archaic an atmosphere—H-SC is a slice of southern heaven on Earth. Students revere H-SC's age-old honor code, under which "no person who lies, cheats, [or] steals will be tolerated. There is a very strict honor code that all people should obey, not just inside the walls of Hampden-Sydney, but in society as a whole. A good system to live by." Work is hard and grades difficult to come by—"Don't expect an A in any class, even if you have the highest grade in the class, because H-SC doesn't have grade inflation," points out one student. Even so, students remain upbeat in assessing their academic experience. They brag that "small class sizes offer a great atmosphere for discussion among class members and faculty" and greatly appreciate how "everyone here at Hampden-Sydney is very accessible. All you have to do is ask for an appointment, and chances are you'll get one for the time requested." (It's even possible to "get a free meal or something like it out of the deal. Every effort is made to assure a good experience.") Many students think highly of the rhetoric requirement, which students feel "makes graduates competitive with grads from other schools. We may not have a diploma from one of the most recognized schools in the country, but thanks to Rhetoric, we can write and edit."

### Life

Students report that "life at Hampden-Sydney is extremely academically oriented from Sunday through Thursday, but from Thursday night through Saturday night, the focus turns to social interaction." H-SC's all-male status is not a problem, most students agree, because there are "so many all-female schools around the area [that] the college basically turns coeducational on the weekends," which means that "a good time is had by all." Because of the school's rural setting, "some people have a hard time adjusting to life [here]. Hampden-Sydney is what you make of it, though. Social acceptance is sometimes hard to achieve at first, but once you start to meet people, it seems too easy. Fraternities are a very large part of the social scene." All students agree that "for fun, people go to fraternity parties and go out of town to the girls' schools." Otherwise, H-SC men love "play[ing] a lot of sports; hunting, fishing, and golf[ing] seem to be the most popular." Students note that "there are about 45 different student-operated clubs/societies/organizations that cater to just about every idea imaginable" and that "most of the student body is interested in politics and public service in [the] community."

### Student Body

The student body at H-SC "is not very diverse, but everyone gets along amazingly well. People here don't care where you came from. This is because of the brotherhood at Hampden-Sydney. People, for the most part, are very friendly, and they are always willing to help you out." Undergraduates generally "come from upper-class, white backgrounds from throughout the South. . . . Many are the fraternity type. The remainder of the school, about 65 percent of us, fills in other groups on campus: football, basketball, lacrosse, rugby, rescue squad, stoners, and, of course, the dorks." Students are overwhelmingly "Christian in their beliefs" and generally quite conservative; warns one, "Only one group is isolated by the students: homosexuals. Not a good school for gay men at all."

# HAMPDEN-SYDNEY COLLEGE

FINANCIAL AID: 804-223-6119 • E-MAIL: HSAPP@TIGER.HSC.EDU • WEBSITE: WWW.HSC.EDU

## ADMISSIONS

*Very important factors considered include:* character/personal qualities, essays, recommendations, secondary school record, standardized test scores. *Important factors considered include:* class rank, extracurricular activities. *Other factors considered include:* alumni/ae relation, interview, minority status, talent/ability, volunteer work, work experience. SAT I or ACT required; SAT II recommended. TOEFL required of all international applicants. High school diploma or GED is required. *High school units required/recommended:* 16 total required; 4 English required, 3 math required, 4 math recommended, 2 science required, 3 science recommended, 1 science lab required, 2 foreign language required, 3 foreign language recommended, 1 social studies required, 3 elective required.

### The Inside Word

Hampden-Sydney is one of the last of its kind. Understandably, the applicant pool is heavily self-selected, and a fairly significant percentage of those who are admitted choose to enroll. This enables the admissions committee to be more selective, which in turn requires candidates to take the process more seriously than might otherwise be necessary. Students with consistently sound academic records should have little to worry about nonetheless.

## FINANCIAL AID

*Students should submit:* FAFSA, CSS/Financial Aid PROFILE, state aid form. Regular filing deadline is May 1. The Princeton Review suggests that all financial aid forms be submitted as soon as possible after January 1. *Need-based scholarships/grants offered:* Pell, SEOG, state scholarships/grants, private scholarships, the school's own gift aid. *Loan aid offered:* FFEL Subsidized Stafford, FFEL Unsubsidized Stafford, FFEL PLUS, Federal Perkins, college/university loans from institutional funds, private loans. Federal Work-Study Program available. Institutional employment available. Applicants will be notified of awards on or about March 1. Off-campus job opportunities are fair.

## FROM THE ADMISSIONS OFFICE

"The spirit of Hampden-Sydney is its sense of community. As one of only 1,026 students, you will be in small classes and find it easy to get extra help or inspiration from professors when you want it. Many of our professors live on campus and enjoy being with students in the snack bar as well as in the classroom. They give you the best, most personal education as possible. A big bonus of small-college life is that everybody is invited to go out for everything, and you can be as much of a leader as you want to be. From athletics to debating to publications to fraternity life, this is part of the process that produces a well-rounded Hampden-Sydney graduate."

## SELECTIVITY

| | |
|---|---|
| Admissions Rating | 78 |
| # of applicants | 925 |
| % of applicants accepted | 77 |
| % of acceptees attending | 46 |
| # accepting a place on wait list | 26 |
| % admitted from wait list | 73 |
| # of early decision applicants | 122 |
| % accepted early decision | 84 |

### FRESHMAN PROFILE

| | |
|---|---|
| Range SAT Verbal | 500-620 |
| Average SAT Verbal | 561 |
| Range SAT Math | 510-610 |
| Average SAT Math | 562 |
| Range ACT Composite | 20-25 |
| Average ACT Composite | 22 |
| Minimum TOEFL | 570 |
| Average HS GPA | 3.1 |
| % graduated top 10% of class | 13 |
| % graduated top 25% of class | 32 |
| % graduated top 50% of class | 69 |

### DEADLINES

| | |
|---|---|
| Early decision | 11/15 |
| Early decision notification | 12/15 |
| Regular admission | 3/1 |
| Regular notification | 4/15 |
| Nonfall registration? | yes |

### APPLICANTS ALSO LOOK AT AND OFTEN PREFER
U of Virginia
Virginia Tech

### AND SOMETIMES PREFER
James Madison U
U of Georgia
U of the South
UNC Chapel Hill
U of Mississippi

### AND RARELY PREFER
Randolph-Macon College

## FINANCIAL FACTS

| | |
|---|---|
| Financial Aid Rating | 87 |
| Tuition | $20,446 |
| Room and board | $7,020 |
| Books and supplies | $800 |
| Required fees | $891 |
| % frosh receiving aid | 50 |
| % undergrads receiving aid | 46 |
| Avg frosh grant | $11,589 |
| Avg frosh loan | $3,294 |

THE BEST 351 COLLEGES ■ 259

# HAMPSHIRE COLLEGE

ADMISSIONS OFFICE, 893 WEST STREET, AMHERST, MA 01002 • ADMISSIONS: 413-559-5471 • FAX: 413-559-5631

## CAMPUS LIFE

| | |
|---|---|
| Quality of Life Rating | 85 |
| Type of school | private |
| Environment | rural |

### STUDENTS
| | |
|---|---|
| Total undergrad enrollment | 1,267 |
| % from out of state | 81 |
| % from public high school | 65 |
| % live on campus | 89 |
| % African American | 3 |
| % Asian | 4 |
| % Caucasian | 79 |
| % Hispanic | 5 |
| % international | 3 |

### SURVEY SAYS . . .
Political activism is hot
(Almost) everyone smokes
No one cheats
Campus easy to get around
Great off-campus food
Campus feels safe
Students love Amherst, MA
Lots of beer drinking

## ACADEMICS

| | |
|---|---|
| Academic Rating | 87 |
| Calendar | 4-1-4 |
| Student/faculty ratio | 11:1 |
| % profs teaching UG courses | 100 |
| Avg reg class size | 10-19 students |

## STUDENTS SPEAK OUT

### Academics

Independent study and self-designed majors are the norm at Hampshire College, a small Pioneer Valley liberal arts school that "takes you up on your wager that all you need is academic freedom." Hampshire freshmen must complete the recently added First Year Program. ("Actual academic requirements for this year's freshman class have turned Hampshire mainstream," gripes one old-timer.) After that, students are pretty much on their own, although they must complete a concentration and an advanced study project. Most students meet the last two requirements through curricula of their own choosing. "Academically, Hampshire is a place where you can do whatever you want, as long as you are able to find a few professors who are willing to work with you on your self-constructed major," explains one student. Although the school is small, students' options are broadened considerably by Hampshire's participation in the Five-College Consortium, which allows students to cross-register at Amherst, Smith, University of Massachusetts, and Mount Holyoke. Some here warn that "Hampshire's academic structure is not for everyone. It's very well suited for people who have a strong idea of what they would like to study, but don't want to squeeze their interests into the confines of traditional majors. It's also good for people who want to explore several interests. . . . However, if you're easily distracted and need someone to point you in a clear, well-defined direction, then Hampshire is probably not the place for you."

### Life

"There's not much centralized activity" at Hampshire College, students here agree. As one student put it, "Everything is pretty laid-back and easygoing. People are really into the work they are doing, and they spend a lot of time thinking about that and talking to others about it." While campus is usually quiet, the other four area colleges and the towns of Amherst and Northampton offer all the action most students want. "If you're bored, it's your own fault," writes one undergrad. "The Pioneer Valley is a happening little place. Amherst and Northampton are both funky little college towns with lots to do in nice weather. There's excellent shopping at numerous vintage stores. The Pearl Street nightclub has cheap concerts every week. Ani DiFranco, Carrot Top, BB King, and Sonic Youth have been to Northampton at least once, to name a few." Furthermore, "if you want to escape, you can do that too. There are miles and miles of hiking trails within walking distance of campus, as well as biking trails. I knew that I wasn't going to have a car, so the free bus system was a humongous plus." Activity reaches its lowest ebb "during the long, hard winters." "That's when we start smoking marijuana," explains one student. Campus movies—"Indie, hip-hop, action, anime, classic low camp; we tend to like movies we can laugh with (or at least at)"—are also very popular.

### Student Body

The "talented, artistic, quixotic, eccentric, and highly motivated" undergrads of Hampshire include a large group of "those kids in elementary school who were caught trying to dissect the pencil sharpener during math class. We're horrible at following rules." While students like to regard themselves as entirely unique, there is "definitely a stereotype of the pot-smoking, Phish-loving, hippie activist kid at Hampshire, and for the most part, I would say it's true." Critics might accuse these students of being self-absorbed; "I think that's true," agrees one undergrad. "We all spend a ridiculous amount of time thinking about ourselves and what we do, which makes us an incredibly self-aware (if sometimes egocentric) group of people." Politically, "Hampshire students are ultra-liberal. While many would claim that we are an open-minded community because all kinds of lifestyles and ethnic groups are accepted, just try bringing in a conservative speaker to campus and students will be there quicker than the lifespan of a Hollywood marriage to protest, disrupt, and cause mayhem." Students are proud to report that Hampshire is extremely GLBT-friendly.

# HAMPSHIRE COLLEGE

FINANCIAL AID: 413-559-5484 • E-MAIL: ADMISSIONS@HAMPSHIRE.EDU • WEBSITE: WWW.HAMPSHIRE.EDU

## ADMISSIONS
*Very important factors considered include:* essays, recommendations, secondary school record. *Important factors considered include:* character/personal qualities, extracurricular activities, talent/ability. *Other factors considered include:* alumni/ae relation, class rank, interview, minority status, standardized test scores, volunteer work, work experience. TOEFL required of all international applicants. *High school units required/recommended:* 19 total recommended; 4 English recommended, 4 math recommended, 4 science recommended, 2 science lab recommended, 3 foreign language recommended, 2 social studies recommended, 2 history recommended.

## The Inside Word
Don Quixote would be a fairly solid candidate for admission to Hampshire. The admissions committee (and it really is one, unlike at many colleges) looks to identify thinkers, dreamers, and the generally intellectually curious. It is important to have a solid record from high school, but high grades only go so far toward impressing the committee. Those who are denied usually lack self-awareness and are fairly poor communicators. Candidates should expect their essays to come under close scrutiny.

## FINANCIAL AID
*Students should submit:* FAFSA, institution's own financial aid form, CSS/Financial Aid PROFILE, noncustodial (divorced/separated) parent's statement. Regular filing deadline is February 1. The Princeton Review suggests that all financial aid forms be submitted as soon as possible after January 1. *Need-based scholarships/grants offered:* Pell, SEOG, state scholarships/grants, private scholarships, the school's own gift aid. *Loan aid offered:* Direct Subsidized Stafford, Direct Unsubsidized Stafford, FFEL PLUS, Federal Perkins. Federal Work-Study Program available. Institutional employment available. Applicants will be notified of awards on a rolling basis beginning on or about April 1. Off-campus job opportunities are fair.

## FROM THE ADMISSIONS OFFICE
"Students tell us they like our application. It is less derivative and more open-ended than most. Rather than assigning an essay topic, we ask to learn more about you as an individual and invite your ideas. Instead of just asking for lists of activities, we ask you how those activities (and academic or other endeavors) have shown some of the traits that lead to success at Hampshire (initiative, independence, persistence, for example). This approach parallels the work you will do at Hampshire, defining the questions you will ask and the courses and experiences that will help you to answer them, and integrating your interests."

### SELECTIVITY

| | |
|---|---|
| Admissions Rating | 83 |
| # of applicants | 2,094 |
| % of applicants accepted | 51 |
| % of acceptees attending | 29 |
| # accepting a place on wait list | 100 |
| % admitted from wait list | 81 |
| # of early decision applicants | 65 |
| % accepted early decision | 72 |

### FRESHMAN PROFILE
| | |
|---|---|
| Range SAT Verbal | 600-700 |
| Average SAT Verbal | 648 |
| Range SAT Math | 540-660 |
| Average SAT Math | 597 |
| Range ACT Composite | 25-29 |
| Minimum TOEFL | 577 |
| Average HS GPA | 3.4 |
| % graduated top 10% of class | 23 |
| % graduated top 25% of class | 58 |
| % graduated top 50% of class | 95 |

### DEADLINES
| | |
|---|---|
| Early decision | 11/15 |
| Early decision notification | 12/15 |
| Regular admission | 2/1 |
| Regular notification | 4/1 |
| Nonfall registration? | yes |

### APPLICANTS ALSO LOOK AT
**AND OFTEN PREFER**
Brown
Vassar, Smith
New College, Oberlin
**AND SOMETIMES PREFER**
Reed
Sarah Lawrence, Bard
Skidmore, NYU
**AND RARELY PREFER**
Antioch
Goddard, Marlboro

### FINANCIAL FACTS

| | |
|---|---|
| Financial Aid Rating | 85 |
| Tuition | $27,354 |
| Room and board | $7,294 |
| Books and supplies | $400 |
| Required fees | $516 |
| % frosh receiving aid | 53 |
| % undergrads receiving aid | 52 |
| Avg frosh grant | $14,900 |
| Avg frosh loan | $2,625 |

# HAMPTON UNIVERSITY

Office of Admissions, Hampton University, Hampton, VA 23668 • Admissions: 804-727-5328 • Fax: 757-727-5084

## CAMPUS LIFE

| Quality of Life Rating | 69 |
| --- | --- |
| Type of school | private |
| Environment | urban |

### STUDENTS
| | |
| --- | --- |
| Total undergrad enrollment | 4,981 |
| % male/female | 39/61 |
| % from out of state | 69 |
| % from public high school | 90 |
| % live on campus | 59 |
| % in (# of) fraternities | 5 (6) |
| % in (# of) sororities | 4 (3) |
| % African American | 96 |
| % Caucasian | 3 |
| # of countries represented | 33 |

### SURVEY SAYS . . .
Very little drug use
Frats and sororities dominate social scene
Diversity lacking on campus
Classes are small
Students are cliquish
Registration is a pain
Library needs improving
Lots of long lines and red tape
Athletic facilities need improving

## ACADEMICS

| Academic Rating | 72 |
| --- | --- |
| Calendar | semester |
| Student/faculty ratio | 16:1 |
| Profs interesting rating | 89 |
| Profs accessible rating | 91 |
| % profs teaching UG courses | 100 |
| Avg lab size | 10-19 students |
| Avg reg class size | under 10 students |

### MOST POPULAR MAJORS
Business administration/management
Biology/biological sciences
Psychology

## STUDENTS SPEAK OUT

### Academics
Hampton University, a historically black school founded in the wake of Reconstruction, makes no bones about its approach to undergraduate education. School promotional literature announces Hampton's commitment to "rigorous academics" that stress "scientific and professional [subjects] with a strong liberal arts undergirding" and an "emphasis on the development of character" through a strict code of conduct. In short: Get ready to work hard and toe the line if you choose Hampton. This approach yields ample benefits, according to students. Writes one, "Hampton University is a school of great educational opportunity. There is always room for academic, social, and personal growth. One must only take advantage of those opportunities." Adds a psychology/education double major, "Overall, the academic experience here is very fulfilling and educational. There are superior programs offered here at Hampton University." Professors "range from very articulate and understanding in their teachings to having a heavy accent and just lecturing the whole time, not answering students' questions." Students in business departments were most sanguine about their profs, while those in mathematics and computer science complained most about unintelligible instructors. Student opinion of the administration is more uniform—students agree it is "unorganized" because "the business office and administration do not communicate with each other."

### Life
Life at Hampton involves conforming to an unusual number of rules, including an 11 P.M. curfew for freshmen, a schoolwide dress code, and strict visitation restrictions at dormitories, all of which are single-sex. Writes one student, "The school is very strict, too strict maybe. We are all adults, aren't we?" Freshmen and sophomores are not allowed to have cars, and "without a car or friends with cars you are stuck on campus, which sucks. There is nothing on campus, not to mention anything on or off campus open after 11 P.M." Sub-par dorms and dining services further undermine on-campus life. As a result, "Life at school can be boring. On weekends there are parties, but they are wack, and you get tired of seeing the same faces and the same parties ending at 2 A.M. Sororities and fraternities are stressed too much." Explains one student, "You must go off campus or to neighboring schools to find creative, stimulating, educational, and open-minded entertainment." Campus is not totally devoid of entertainment, though, as "Greeks are involved in a lot of fun yet educational opportunities. They provide a support group not only for themselves but for every student here." Furthermore, sports teams, especially the football team, provide a rallying point for most students. Despite the shortcomings of life here, students have a great deal of school spirit. Reports one, "Before freshmen even start class, they are taught a whole bunch of cheers and dances to do at sporting events. That's why I love Hampton: I can be the cheerleader I've always wanted to be."

### Student Body
There is little racial diversity at Hampton, but there is a great deal of regional diversity. Explains one student, "We have students from all over the world. To attend a mostly black institution where I am able to learn alongside people who look and act like me is a very powerful experience." Students are generally "friendly but high maintenance." While they "always have smiles on their faces, and the upperclassmen are very helpful with orienting freshmen to campus," some complain that superficiality pervades the student body. One student comments, "My fellow students are sometimes shallow and pretentious. Although I enjoy fashion, too much emphasis is placed on it by students attending HU; there seems to be a judgment of one's character based on what one wears." Some see an upside, noting that "many of the students here are arrogant, but arrogance sparks competition and encourages students to do as well as they possibly can."

# HAMPTON UNIVERSITY

FINANCIAL AID: 800-624-3341 • E-MAIL: ADMIT@HAMPTONU.EDU • WEBSITE: WWW.HAMPTONU.EDU

## ADMISSIONS
*Very important factors considered include:* character/personal qualities, essays, secondary school record, standardized test scores. *Important factors considered include:* class rank, recommendations. *Other factors considered include:* alumni/ae relation, extracurricular activities, talent/ability, volunteer work. SAT I or ACT required. TOEFL required of all international applicants. High school diploma or GED is required. *High school units required/recommended:* 17 total required; 4 English required, 3 math required, 2 science required, 2 science lab required, 2 foreign language recommended, 2 social studies required, 6 elective required.

### The Inside Word
Hampton has less general visibility than such better-known historically black colleges as Morehouse, Spelman, and Howard, but it has just as much of a tradition of academic quality. In recent years the university's profile has been boosted by hosting national workshops on counseling minority students in the college admissions process. Candidates can expect a personal and caring experience in the admissions process.

## FINANCIAL AID
*Students should submit:* FAFSA. The Princeton Review suggests that all financial aid forms be submitted as soon as possible after January 1. *Need-based scholarships/grants offered:* Pell, SEOG, state scholarships/grants, private scholarships, the school's own gift aid, Federal Nursing. *Loan aid offered:* Direct Subsidized Stafford, Direct Unsubsidized Stafford, Direct PLUS, Federal Perkins, alternative loans. Federal Work-Study Program available. Applicants will be notified of awards on a rolling basis beginning on or about April 1. Off-campus job opportunities are excellent.

## FROM THE ADMISSIONS OFFICE
"Hampton attempts to provide the environment and structures most conducive to the intellectual, emotional, and aesthetic enlargement of the lives of its members. The university gives priority to effective teaching and scholarly research while placing the student at the center of its planning. Hampton will ask you to look inwardly at your own history and culture and examine your relationship to the aspirations and development of the world."

---

### SELECTIVITY

| | |
|---|---|
| **Admissions Rating** | 79 |
| # of applicants | 5,696 |
| % of applicants accepted | 62 |
| % of acceptees attending | 30 |

#### FRESHMAN PROFILE
| | |
|---|---|
| Range SAT Verbal | 490-590 |
| Average SAT Verbal | 526 |
| Range SAT Math | 480-580 |
| Average SAT Math | 516 |
| Range ACT Composite | 20-24 |
| Average ACT Composite | 20 |
| Minimum TOEFL | 550 |
| Average HS GPA | 3.0 |
| % graduated top 10% of class | 20 |
| % graduated top 25% of class | 45 |
| % graduated top 50% of class | 90 |

#### DEADLINES
| | |
|---|---|
| Priority admission | 3/1 |
| Nonfall registration? | yes |

#### APPLICANTS ALSO LOOK AT AND OFTEN PREFER
Florida A&M
Tuskegee
Spelman

#### AND SOMETIMES PREFER
U. Maryland—Coll. Park
Howard
Virginia Tech

### FINANCIAL FACTS

| | |
|---|---|
| **Financial Aid Rating** | 73 |
| Tuition | $10,990 |
| Room and board | $5,828 |
| Books and supplies | $730 |
| Required fees | $1,262 |
| % frosh receiving aid | 56 |
| % undergrads receiving aid | 58 |
| Avg frosh grant | $2,885 |
| Avg frosh loan | $2,254 |

THE BEST 351 COLLEGES ■ 263

# Hanover College

PO Box 108, Hanover, IN 47243-0108 • Admissions: 812-866-7021 • Fax: 812-866-7098

## CAMPUS LIFE

| | |
|---|---|
| Quality of Life Rating | 80 |
| Type of school | private |
| Affiliation | Presbyterian |
| Environment | rural |

### STUDENTS

| | |
|---|---|
| Total undergrad enrollment | 1,050 |
| % male/female | 46/54 |
| % from out of state | 30 |
| % from public high school | 85 |
| % live on campus | 92 |
| % in (# of) fraternities | 33 (4) |
| % in (# of) sororities | 47 (4) |
| % African American | 1 |
| % Asian | 3 |
| % Caucasian | 91 |
| % Hispanic | 1 |
| % international | 4 |
| # of countries represented | 18 |

### SURVEY SAYS . . .

Frats and sororities dominate social scene
Theater is hot
Very little drug use
Athletic facilities are great
Diversity lacking on campus
Library needs improving
Students don't like Hanover, IN
Political activism is (almost) nonexistent
Lousy off-campus food
Lab facilities are great

## ACADEMICS

| | |
|---|---|
| Academic Rating | 87 |
| Calendar | other |
| Student/faculty ratio | 11:1 |
| Profs interesting rating | 94 |
| Profs accessible rating | 95 |
| % profs teaching UG courses | 100 |
| Avg reg class size | 10-19 students |

### MOST POPULAR MAJORS

Business administration/management
Sociology
Chemistry

## STUDENTS SPEAK OUT

### Academics

Among small liberal arts schools, Hanover College scores high on the "quality-to-price ratio" scale. Hanover is a very affordable private school made even more so by a large endowment, which finances the school's generous aid packages. A Hanover education comes with a few caveats, however. Those attending must be comfortable in an extremely homogenous population, as the vast majority of students are white, midwestern, and Christian. Students must also be willing to live under an extremely—many say excessively—paternalistic administration. Complains one typical student, "The administration does not treat us like the adults we are. They are unreasonably strict. I feel like I'm back in kindergarten." Within those parameters, however, lies an excellent, well-rounded liberal arts education. Students here must complete a wide range of distribution requirements, including courses in philosophy, theology, literature, science, and nonwestern society. Approves one student, "This liberal arts school truly captures all that liberal arts means as far as linking completely different courses to one another." Professors, by all accounts, are top-notch. Writes one undergrad, "The professors really care that you learn and understand the concepts being taught. There is a strong emphasis on open-minded learning, in which, by discussion and research, the student draws the conclusion. The professor is more like a coach." Another reports that "the professors are very knowledgeable and . . . always open to one-on-one conversation."

### Life

Two factors strongly influence the quality of life at Hanover. The first is the administration, which strictly enforces drinking and visitation rules. Explains one student, "Our administration's social policies are up-to-date with the 90s . . . the 1890s! The campuswide prohibition on alcohol and restrictions on times males are allowed in female rooms and vice versa are oppressive and out of date." The other is the town of Hanover and the area immediately surrounding it. Says one student, "There is not much in the way of cultural attractions in southern Indiana." Students quickly resign themselves to the fact that "since we are in the sticks, there is nothing much to do except grab a movie and/or drink." Many gravitate toward the Greeks, who "run the campus socially." Reports one senior, "If you aren't in a fraternity you're kind of screwed as far as a partying social life goes. Many upperclassmen go to the local bars to get away from campus. The social life revolves around fraternities/sororities and maybe venturing to Louisville, Indy, or Cincy." Otherwise, "for fun we have fire pits, late night Wal-Mart trips, dinner at 3 A.M., Nerf wars, and . . . the occasional band." The Hanover football program has recently made a name for itself nationally, but not all students are pleased. Writes one dissident, "Our school used to be excellent academically. Then, our football team got really good, so the school seemed to think we need[ed] more football players. It's like half the freshman class is the football team."

### Student Body

The "very conservative, religious, not very open-minded, Republican majority" that makes up Hanover's student body recognize that they are "all from the same socioeconomic status. There's no diversity, and they are somewhat snobby." Writes one student, "Unless you are totally at ease living with kids from small-town Indiana, you will get an uncomfortable feeling from the total lack of diversity here." Adds another, "The administration is making extreme attempts to make the campus diverse. Hanover, Indiana, though, isn't the most appealing place for a minority because of its size and location." Students note that there are divisions among the student body and that "our differences arise from Greek affiliation rather than other factors."

# HANOVER COLLEGE

FINANCIAL AID: 812-866-7030 • E-MAIL: ADMISSIONS@HANOVER.EDU • WEBSITE: WWW.HANOVER.EDU

## ADMISSIONS
*Very important factors considered include:* class rank, secondary school record. *Important factors considered include:* character/personal qualities, essays, standardized test scores, talent/ability. *Other factors considered include:* alumni/ae relation, extracurricular activities, geographical residence, interview, minority status, recommendations, state residency, volunteer work, work experience. SAT I or ACT required. TOEFL required of all international applicants. High school diploma is required and GED is not accepted. *High school units required/recommended:* 4 English required, 3 math required, 4 math recommended, 3 science required, 2 science lab required, 2 foreign language required, 4 foreign language recommended, 2 social studies required, 2 history required.

## The Inside Word
Despite significant national publicity in recent years, Hanover still has a relatively small applicant pool. There is no doubt that these candidates are capable academically—few schools have as impressive a graduation rate or percentage of its alums going on to grad school. It pays to put some energy into the completion of the application process, especially given the sizable percentage of students awarded academic scholarships.

## FINANCIAL AID
*Students should submit:* FAFSA. The Princeton Review suggests that all financial aid forms be submitted as soon as possible after January 1. *Need-based scholarships/grants offered:* Pell, state scholarships/grants, private scholarships, the school's own gift aid. *Loan aid offered:* FFEL Subsidized Stafford, FFEL Unsubsidized Stafford, FFEL PLUS, college/university loans from institutional funds. Institutional employment available. Applicants will be notified of awards on a rolling basis beginning on or about March 10. Off-campus job opportunities are fair.

## FROM THE ADMISSIONS OFFICE
"Hanover College offers a unique community to all who live here. With 95 percent of our students and over 50 percent of our faculty and staff residing on campus, the pursuit of academic excellence extends well beyond the confines of the classroom. This is enhanced by a caring faculty, 90 percent of whom hold earned doctoral degrees. The desire to meet academic challenges and the strong sense of community may be the two greatest contributors to the 86 percent retention rate of which Hanover is quite proud. These contributions are also apparent in that over the past five years more than 65 percent of our graduates have advanced their educational degrees. Hanover's total cost qualifies the college as one of the best values in the nation, and its sizable endowment, on a dollar-per-student ratio, places it in the top 10 percent nationally."

## SELECTIVITY

| | |
|---|---:|
| Admissions Rating | 79 |
| # of applicants | 1,227 |
| % of applicants accepted | 76 |
| % of acceptees attending | 30 |
| # accepting a place on wait list | 78 |
| % admitted from wait list | 47 |

### FRESHMAN PROFILE
| | |
|---|---:|
| Range SAT Verbal | 500-620 |
| Average SAT Verbal | 559 |
| Range SAT Math | 520-630 |
| Average SAT Math | 576 |
| Range ACT Composite | 21-27 |
| Average ACT Composite | 24 |
| Minimum TOEFL | 550 |
| % graduated top 10% of class | 38 |
| % graduated top 25% of class | 72 |
| % graduated top 50% of class | 95 |

### DEADLINES
| | |
|---|---:|
| Priority admission | 3/1 |
| Regular admission | 3/1 |
| Nonfall registration? | yes |

### APPLICANTS ALSO LOOK AT AND SOMETIMES PREFER
Indiana University—Bloomington
University of Evansville
Miami University
Butler University
Depauw University
Centre College
Wabash College

## FINANCIAL FACTS

| | |
|---|---:|
| Financial Aid Rating | 88 |
| Tuition | $14,300 |
| Room and board | $5,900 |
| Books and supplies | $800 |
| Required fees | $400 |
| % frosh receiving aid | 61 |
| % undergrads receiving aid | 58 |
| Avg frosh grant | $12,313 |
| Avg frosh loan | $3,113 |

# HARVARD COLLEGE

BYERLY HALL, 8 GARDEN STREET, CAMBRIDGE, MA 02318 • ADMISSIONS: 617-495-1551 • FAX: 617-495-8821

## CAMPUS LIFE

| | |
|---|---|
| Quality of Life Rating | 94 |
| Type of school | private |
| Environment | urban |

### STUDENTS

| | |
|---|---|
| Total undergrad enrollment | 6,649 |
| % male/female | 53/47 |
| % from out of state | 84 |
| % from public high school | 65 |
| % live on campus | 96 |
| % African American | 9 |
| % Asian | 19 |
| % Caucasian | 46 |
| % Hispanic | 8 |
| % international | 7 |

### SURVEY SAYS . . .
Great library
High cost of living
Registration is a breeze
Students love Cambridge, MA
Great computer facilities
Student government is unpopular
Ethnic diversity on campus

## ACADEMICS

| | |
|---|---|
| Academic Rating | 97 |
| Calendar | semester |
| Student/faculty ratio | 8:1 |
| Profs interesting rating | 93 |
| Profs accessible rating | 86 |
| % profs teaching UG courses | 100 |
| Avg lab size | under 10 students |
| Avg reg class size | 10-19 students |

### MOST POPULAR MAJORS
Psychology
Economics
Political science and government

## STUDENTS SPEAK OUT

### Academics

Reputations like Harvard's aren't given to them; they are earned with "unparalleled resources" ("the libraries are great, and my friends who are in the sciences usually have their own desks or offices in the science buildings," writes one student), "excellent professors who definitely do very important things outside of teaching," and a "talented, motivated, unique, brilliant" student body. Students tell us that "the academic experience is amazing. Sitting in an economics class taught by Marty Feldstein . . . is not something that students get to do everywhere." They also warn that "it's humbling to rub shoulders with Nobel laureates and presidential advisors." But don't think anyone caters to your needs alone: "There's no hand-holding. You'd better be an independent, self-motivated type, or else maybe one of those liberal arts schools out in the woods is a better choice." The quality of instruction varies widely; speculates one undergrad, "Profs are an argument for free market economics: in the classes that nobody takes unless they want to they are wonderful. In required classes they go from OK to pathetic." Some advise that while "Harvard is known for the lawyers, doctors, and politicians that come out of it, I have found that if you desire small, personal classes and access to faculty, Harvard is really better for smaller concentrations (majors) since the instruction is equally phenomenal." The administration "is distant and inattentive to students' needs. They can replace you, and don't think they don't know that."

### Life

"Contrary to popular belief," students want you to know, "Harvard is actually a lot of fun." While many people—and nearly all pre-meds—do "nothing but study," others "actually take breaks from studying long enough to down a few beers and hook up." The campus is a cultural hotbed, as "there's always so much going on: plays, concerts, seminars." Parties "are less plentiful," "only occur Thursday through Saturday," and if held in the dorms "end at 1 A.M. (Harvard has a strict policy on that)." However, "it is easy to travel to one of numerous close colleges for parties," or hit the "clubs, bars, and nightlife of Cambridge or Boston." You might also join one of the social clubs (membership by invitation only) "similar to a combination of fraternities and Princeton's eating clubs" that provide some social life, though they are not affiliated with the college. Harvard's "teams are competitive, so if you're an athlete, well, you usually hang out with other athletes." Many students speak highly of campus living quarters; reports one upperclassman, "Freshman year everybody lives in the same general location, The Yard, which is really conducive to meeting people and hanging out and class. Living in the upper class 'houses' is really nice," too.

### Student Body

"Everyone here is brilliant," Harvard undergrads report, "and some are very academically competitive. Only come here if you are willing to put up with a fair share of dorks." Because many got here by burying their heads in books, "social graces are very lacking at Harvard. Most people here spent most of high school working hard, so little skills like small talk are not very well developed. However, the population is so diverse that you'll no doubt find people that you like to hang out with, and once you get your core group of friends, those are pretty much the only people you'll hang out with for four years." Many note that "there are two types of Harvard people: those who stress too much and those who know the importance of balancing work and play. It's all about that second group." Mixed in among the student body are "a handful of the blue-blooded, prep-school types," but, "on the whole, you will not find a more vibrant, diverse, exciting, and fascinating group of students anywhere in the world."

266 ■ THE BEST 351 COLLEGES

# HARVARD COLLEGE

FINANCIAL AID: 617-495-1581 • E-MAIL: COLLEGE@FAS.HARVARD.EDU • WEBSITE: WWW.FAS.HARVARD.EDU

## ADMISSIONS

*Very important factors considered include:* character/personal qualities, extracurricular activities, recommendations, secondary school record, talent/ability. *Important factors considered include:* class rank, essays, interview, standardized test scores. *Other factors considered include:* alumni/ae relation, geographical residence, minority status, volunteer work, work experience. SAT I or ACT required; SAT II also required. *High school units required/recommended:* 19 total recommended; 4 English recommended, 4 math recommended, 4 science recommended, 4 foreign language recommended.

### *The Inside Word*

It just doesn't get any tougher than this. Candidates to Harvard face dual obstacles—an awe-inspiring applicant pool and, as a result, admissions standards that defy explanation in quantifiable terms. Harvard denies admission to the vast majority, and virtually all of them are top students. It all boils down to splitting hairs, which is quite hard to explain and even harder for candidates to understand. Rather than being as detailed and direct as possible about the selection process and criteria, Harvard keeps things close to the vest—before, during, and after. They even refuse to admit that being from South Dakota is an advantage. Thus the admissions process does more to intimidate candidates than to empower them. Moving to a common application seemed to be a small step in the right direction, but with the current explosion of early decision applicants and a super-high yield of enrollees, things are not likely to change dramatically.

## FINANCIAL AID

*Students should submit:* FAFSA, CSS/Financial Aid PROFILE, noncustodial (divorced/separated) parent's statement, business/farm supplement, tax returns. No deadline for regular filing. The Princeton Review suggests that all financial aid forms be submitted as soon as possible after January 1. *Need-based scholarships/grants offered:* Pell, SEOG, state scholarships/grants, private scholarships, the school's own gift aid. *Loan aid offered:* Direct Subsidized Stafford, Direct Unsubsidized Stafford, Direct PLUS, Federal Perkins, state loans, college/university loans from institutional funds. Federal Work-Study Program available. Institutional employment available. Applicants will be notified of awards on or about April 1. Off-campus job opportunities are excellent.

## FROM THE ADMISSIONS OFFICE

"The admissions committee looks for energy, ambition, and the capacity to make the most of opportunities. Academic ability and preparation are important, and so is intellectual curiosity—but many of the strongest applicants have significant nonacademic interests and accomplishments as well. There is no formula for admission and applicants are considered carefully, with attention to future promise."

## SELECTIVITY

| | |
|---|---|
| **Admissions Rating** | 99 |
| # of applicants | 20,986 |
| % of applicants accepted | 10 |
| % of acceptees attending | 79 |

### FRESHMAN PROFILE

| | |
|---|---|
| Range SAT Verbal | 700-800 |
| Range SAT Math | 700-790 |
| Range ACT Composite | 30-34 |
| % graduated top 10% of class | 90 |
| % graduated top 25% of class | 98 |
| % graduated top 50% of class | 100 |

### DEADLINES

| | |
|---|---|
| Priority admission | 12/15 |
| Regular admission | 1/1 |
| Regular notification | 4/1 |

### APPLICANTS ALSO LOOK AT AND SOMETIMES PREFER
Princeton
Stanford
Yale
U Penn

### AND RARELY PREFER
Northwestern
Georgetown
Amherst
Williams

## FINANCIAL FACTS

| | |
|---|---|
| **Financial Aid Rating** | 88 |
| Tuition | $26,066 |
| Room and board | $8,868 |
| Books and supplies | $2,522 |
| Required fees | $2,994 |
| % frosh receiving aid | 47 |
| % undergrads receiving aid | 47 |
| Avg frosh grant | $23,750 |
| Avg frosh loan | $1,100 |

# HARVEY MUDD COLLEGE

301 East 12th Street, Claremont, CA 91711-5990 • Admissions: 909-621-8011 • Fax: 909-621-8360

## CAMPUS LIFE

| | |
|---|---|
| Quality of Life Rating | 84 |
| Type of school | private |
| Environment | suburban |

### STUDENTS

| | |
|---|---|
| Total undergrad enrollment | 703 |
| % from out of state | 59 |
| % live on campus | 96 |
| % Asian | 19 |
| % Caucasian | 63 |
| % Hispanic | 5 |
| % international | 3 |

### SURVEY SAYS . . .
Student publications are ignored
Great computer facilities
Popular college radio
No one cheats
Lab facilities need improving
Very small frat/sorority scene
Intercollegiate sports unpopular or nonexistent
Unattractive campus
Lousy food on campus

## ACADEMICS

| | |
|---|---|
| Academic Rating | 98 |
| Calendar | semester |
| Student/faculty ratio | 9:1 |
| Profs interesting rating | 96 |
| Profs accessible rating | 99 |
| % profs teaching UG courses | 100 |
| Avg lab size | 20-29 students |
| Avg reg class size | 10-19 students |

### MOST POPULAR MAJORS
Computer science
Engineering
Physics

## STUDENTS SPEAK OUT

### Academics

Harvey Mudd College, the mathematics, engineering, and science school of the Claremont Colleges is, students admit, "an incredibly hard school; the work load is huge, and the classes are just dead hard." However, most not only feel the effort is worth it, but furthermore sense that theirs is a better lot than that of their fellow overworked peers at similarly prestigious schools. The primary reason for this is that "the sense of community around Mudd is great. It's like a giant family of 700 students. You get to know the upperclassmen easily, borrow books from them, ask about profs, and seek out old midterms." Professors contribute to the communal good vibes, as they "are more than willing to help you out any time they are available, which is a good deal of the day." Writes one engineer, "The professors here, save a very, very few, are phenomenal. Besides always being accessible at any hour almost, they aren't just going to listen and tell you why you're dumb and dismiss you. They make you stay until you get it and hardly ever get frustrated." Students believe this exceptional attention stems from the fact that "there isn't any graduate program, so the focus is on undergraduate education." Mudd strives to produce well-rounded graduates by "requiring about a third of the classes you take be in the humanities. Also, all students have to take at least one class from each one of Mudd's departments, so after your sophomore year, everyone gets a feeling of what they are good at and what they aren't."

### Life

Given the academic demands of Mudd, it should come as no surprise that "homework is probably one of the most common pastimes. It turns into a social function. People gather to enjoy each other's company and have fun, as well as get work done." It's not all about studying here, though. "On the weekends there are big parties, and considering we have five colleges to choose from, there are several things going on every weekend." Students unwind in different ways. "Some people sit around and talk about science a lot, some people play lots of video games, some people like to watch cartoons, some people go out and get really drunk." Many pull pranks, limited in scope only by imagination and an honor code that "requires that pranks be reversible and non-malicious so that, in general, pranks are enjoyed rather than feared." Students "build large structures out [of] cardboard or furniture, relocate people's dorm rooms, and move rather large boulders onto the middle of campus for no particular reason. It's a major stress relief." For outdoorsy types, "Mount Baldy is 10,000 feet and less than 20 minutes away, so there is always great hiking and a bit of skiing in the winter." Los Angeles and San Diego are relatively close to the surrounding town of Claremont. Students say the town is "nice, but there is nothing of interest here."

### Student Body

Mudders, as they like to call themselves, "are mostly pretty cool. There are some dorks here, but not nearly as many as you might think." "The most striking feature of the students here," writes one engineer, "is that they're incredibly smart, and there is a surprisingly low nerdiness level for a school with an average SAT score in the upper 1400s." Students "come from all geographic regions and a variety of backgrounds; however, most are white or Asian, middle- to upper-class [and] incredibly strong in math and science. This leads to a social mindset which is more homogenous than I'd like at times." Students get along well, they say, because of "the strictly enforced and very formal Honor Code ('Each Harvey Mudd student is responsible for maintaining his or her integrity and the integrity of the college . . .') and the almost-as-strictly enforced and very informal Cardinal Rule ('Don't be a jackass')."

# HARVEY MUDD COLLEGE

FINANCIAL AID: 909-621-8055 • E-MAIL: ADMISSION@HMC.EDU • WEBSITE: WWW.HMC.EDU

## ADMISSIONS

*Very important factors considered include:* character/personal qualities, class rank, essays, recommendations, secondary school record, standardized test scores. *Important factors considered include:* alumni/ae relation, interview. *Other factors considered include:* extracurricular activities, geographical residence, minority status, talent/ability, volunteer work, work experience. SAT I required. TOEFL required of all international applicants. High school diploma or GED is required. *High school units required/recommended:* 4 English required, 4 math required, 3 science required, 3 science lab required, 2 foreign language recommended, 1 social studies recommended, 1 history recommended.

## The Inside Word

Harvey Mudd is a place for serious students, and its admissions process expects excellence from all candidates. Not to say that they don't have a sense of humor out there in Claremont. The college attracted national attention in the past by mailing recruitment literature that poked fun at the overly serious world of college admissions while at the same time showcasing the school's academic quality. Any admissions staff that contributes to the lessening of student stress in the college search and admissions process is to be commended.

## FINANCIAL AID

*Students should submit:* FAFSA, CSS/Financial Aid PROFILE, state aid form, noncustodial (divorced/separated) parent's statement, business/farm supplement. Regular filing deadline is February 1. The Princeton Review suggests that all financial aid forms be submitted as soon as possible after January 1. *Need-based scholarships/grants offered:* Pell, SEOG, state scholarships/grants, private scholarships, the school's own gift aid. *Loan aid offered:* FFEL Subsidized Stafford, FFEL Unsubsidized Stafford, FFEL PLUS, Federal Perkins, college/university loans from institutional funds. Federal Work-Study Program available. Institutional employment available. Applicants will be notified of awards on a rolling basis beginning on or about April 1. Off-campus job opportunities are fair.

## FROM THE ADMISSIONS OFFICE

"Students interested in HMC must have a talent and passion for science and mathematics. The college offers majors in mathematics, physics, engineering, chemistry, biology, and computer science. 'Mudders' have very diverse interests. Because nearly one-third of the course work at HMC is in the humanities and social sciences, HMC students also enjoy studying economics, psychology, philosophy, history, the fine arts, and literature."

## SELECTIVITY

| | |
|---|---|
| Admissions Rating | 94 |
| # of applicants | 1,669 |
| % of applicants accepted | 37 |
| % of acceptees attending | 30 |
| # accepting a place on wait list | 96 |
| % admitted from wait list | 31 |
| # of early decision applicants | 78 |
| % accepted early decision | 50 |

### FRESHMAN PROFILE

| | |
|---|---|
| Range SAT Verbal | 650-750 |
| Average SAT Verbal | 700 |
| Range SAT Math | 720-790 |
| Average SAT Math | 750 |
| Minimum TOEFL | 600 |
| Average HS GPA | 3.8 |
| % graduated top 10% of class | 83 |
| % graduated top 25% of class | 96 |
| % graduated top 50% of class | 100 |

### DEADLINES

| | |
|---|---|
| Early decision | 11/15 |
| Early decision notification | 12/15 |
| Regular admission | 1/15 |
| Regular notification | 4/1 |

**APPLICANTS ALSO LOOK AT AND OFTEN PREFER**
Stanford
MIT

**AND SOMETIMES PREFER**
Cornell U.
Rice

**AND RARELY PREFER**
Worcester Poly.
Virginia Tech

## FINANCIAL FACTS

| | |
|---|---|
| Financial Aid Rating | 83 |
| Tuition | $26,425 |
| Room and board | $8,971 |
| Books and supplies | $800 |
| Required fees | $612 |
| % frosh receiving aid | 58 |
| % undergrads receiving aid | 57 |
| Avg frosh grant | $12,141 |
| Avg frosh loan | $3,103 |

# HAVERFORD COLLEGE

370 LANCASTER AVENUE, HAVERFORD, PA 19041 • ADMISSIONS: 610-896-1350 • FAX: 610-896-1338

## CAMPUS LIFE

| | |
|---|---|
| Quality of Life Rating | 87 |
| Type of school | private |
| Environment | suburban |

### STUDENTS
| | |
|---|---|
| Total undergrad enrollment | 1,105 |
| % from out of state | 80 |
| % from public high school | 58 |
| % live on campus | 98 |
| % African American | 5 |
| % Asian | 15 |
| % Caucasian | 72 |
| % Hispanic | 7 |
| % international | 3 |
| # of countries represented | 38 |

### SURVEY SAYS . . .
Campus is beautiful
Campus easy to get around
No one cheats
Great library
Campus feels safe
Students are happy
Registration is a breeze
School is well run

## ACADEMICS

| | |
|---|---|
| Academic Rating | 98 |
| Calendar | semester |
| Student/faculty ratio | 8:1 |
| % profs teaching UG courses | 100 |
| Avg lab size | under 10 students |
| Avg reg class size | 10-19 students |

### MOST POPULAR MAJORS
History
Biology/biological sciences
Political science and government

## STUDENTS SPEAK OUT
### Academics
Haverford College "is the quintessence of the liberal arts experience: superb academics with an emphasis on teacher/student interaction." Originally a Quaker school, Haverford has "never forgotten its Quaker roots" and accordingly "is a community committed to the ideals of taking responsibility for your actions." This is a "high-pressure academic environment" but also "cooperative and nonthreatening." Students warn, "The sciences and math here are hard core; the humanities are somewhat less challenging," though "professors who are brilliant people and who truly care about their students" are there to ensure undergraduates' success. Haverford's Honor Code plays a prominent role in fostering a sense of unity; "the honor code here is amazing; it promotes a lot of trust and freedom in the community, which the students love," explains one undergrad. Students receive the red carpet treatment from the moment they arrive; "Haverford knows how to take care of freshmen," explains one undergrad. "When you come here, you get Customs People (like RAs, except cooler), Honor Code Orienteers, an Upper Class Advisor, Peer Awareness Facilitators, a faculty advisor, and a dean. So there are a million people whom you can go to for help and advisement." For those students with wanderlust, "Our study abroad office is excellent! I'm studying at the London School of Economics this year thanks to my accessible, helpful and alarmingly organized study abroad dean." Students speak in similarly glowing terms about the rest of the administration, noting also the large degree of autonomy afforded them in running the school. Explains one student, "In terms of the administrators, Haverford is mostly run by the students. We start our own organizations. We allocate where the Student Council funds go."

### Life
Haverford's rigorous curriculum means that "during the week, work pretty much dominates everything. Even if, by luck, you do not have work to do, all of your friends do, so you are pretty much bound to stay in the dorm." Students unwind on weekends, enjoying "a lot of activities, like dances, plays, concerts, and musicals. Last weekend, we had a play, a formal dance, a musical performance, and an improv group. It's pretty easy to find activities to keep you busy." While some here take advantage of nearby Philadelphia ("good history and culture, as well as a club scene and places like South Street to hang out at"), most tend to stick close to campus. And what a campus! "It's so beautiful that it's practically unbearable," gushes one undergrad. Parties here are generally low-key and usually involve alcohol and other substances; as with academics, the Honor Code applies. Reports one student, "I'm impressed by the leniency and respectfulness of Security and the administration vis-à-vis drinking and substance use. They definitely trust students to be responsible for themselves and for one another, and I think that for the most part, that trust is well placed." Students report an active intramural sports program, lots of clubs and organizations (with ample opportunities to start your own), and a fair amount of political activity, most of which leans leftward.

### Student Body
As befits an elite liberal arts school, Haverford is home to a student body "good at more things than you can count on your fingers and toes, and interested in just about everything." More than one student confided that "the typical student is a cool dork: someone with really funky interests and life experiences who loves sharing and learning, even if s/he's not amazing at performing or shmoozing a crowd." Most "probably own a pair of Birkenstocks but aren't quite as leftist as they makes themselves out to be." Complains one conservative, "Haverford is accepting of anyone . . . except for non-left-wingers." While most feel that "there is a good amount of diversity here," especially for such a small, expensive school, many also report that the school needs to make an "effort to increase the diversity."

# HAVERFORD COLLEGE

FINANCIAL AID: 610-896-1350 • E-MAIL: ADMITME@HAVERFORD.EDU • WEBSITE: WWW.HAVERFORD.EDU

## ADMISSIONS

*Very important factors considered include:* character/personal qualities, recommendations, secondary school record, standardized test scores. *Important factors considered include:* class rank, essays, extracurricular activities, volunteer work. *Other factors considered include:* alumni/ae relation, geographical residence, interview, minority status, talent/ability, work experience. SAT I or ACT required; SAT II also required. High school diploma or GED is required. *High school units required/recommended:* 12 total required; 4 English required, 3 math required, 4 math recommended, 1 science required, 2 science recommended, 1 science lab required, 3 foreign language required, 1 social studies required.

### The Inside Word

Candidate evaluation at Haverford is quite thorough, and the applicant pool is sizable and strong. Applicants who are successful through the initial academic review are then carefully considered for the match they make with the college. This part of the process is especially important at small schools like Haverford, and students should definitely spend some time assessing the reasons for their interest in attending before responding to essays and interviewing. Interviewing is a must.

## FINANCIAL AID

*Students should submit:* FAFSA, CSS/Financial Aid PROFILE, state aid form, noncustodial (divorced/separated) parent's statement, business/farm supplement. Regular filing deadline is January 31. The Princeton Review suggests that all financial aid forms be submitted as soon as possible after January 1. *Need-based scholarships/grants offered:* Pell, SEOG, state scholarships/grants, private scholarships, the school's own gift aid. *Loan aid offered:* FFEL Subsidized Stafford, FFEL Unsubsidized Stafford, FFEL PLUS, Federal Perkins. Federal Work-Study Program available. Institutional employment available. Applicants will be notified of awards on or about April 15. Off-campus job opportunities are good.

## FROM THE ADMISSIONS OFFICE

"Haverford strives to be a college in which integrity, honesty, and concern for others are dominant forces. The college does not have many formal rules; rather, it offers an opportunity for students to govern their affairs and conduct themselves with respect and concern for others. Each student is expected to adhere to the Honor Code as it is adopted each year by the Students' Association. Haverford's Quaker roots show most clearly in the relationship of faculty and students, in the emphasis on integrity, in the interaction of the individual and the community, and through the college's concern for the uses to which its students put their expanding knowledge. Haverford's 1,100 students represent a wide diversity of interests, backgrounds, and talents. They come from public, parochial, and independent schools across the United States, Puerto Rico, and 27 foreign countries. Students of color are an important part of the Haverford community. The Minority Coalition, which includes Asian, black, and Hispanic students' associations, works with faculty and administration on matters directly concerned with the quality of life at the college."

### SELECTIVITY

| | |
|---|---|
| Admissions Rating | 98 |
| # of applicants | 2,598 |
| % of applicants accepted | 32 |
| % of acceptees attending | 37 |
| # accepting a place on wait list | 208 |
| # of early decision applicants | 199 |
| % accepted early decision | 55 |

### FRESHMAN PROFILE

| | |
|---|---|
| Range SAT Verbal | 640-740 |
| Range SAT Math | 640-720 |
| % graduated top 10% of class | 80 |
| % graduated top 25% of class | 94 |
| % graduated top 50% of class | 100 |

### DEADLINES

| | |
|---|---|
| Early decision | 11/15 |
| Early decision notification | 12/15 |
| Regular admission | 1/15 |
| Regular notification | 4/15 |

### APPLICANTS ALSO LOOK AT AND OFTEN PREFER

Princeton
Harvard
Yale
Brown
Wellesley

### AND SOMETIMES PREFER

Amherst
Swarthmore
Williams
U. Penn
Bryn Mawr

### AND RARELY PREFER

Vassar
Middlebury
Earlham

### FINANCIAL FACTS

| | |
|---|---|
| Financial Aid Rating | 86 |
| Tuition | $28,612 |
| Room and board | $9,020 |
| Required fees | $268 |
| % frosh receiving aid | 42 |
| % undergrads receiving aid | 44 |
| Avg frosh grant | $22,706 |
| Avg frosh loan | $3,459 |

# HENDRIX COLLEGE

1600 WASHINGTON AVENUE, CONWAY, AR 72032 • ADMISSIONS: 501-450-1362 • FAX: 501-450-3843

## CAMPUS LIFE

| | |
|---|---|
| Quality of Life Rating | 86 |
| Type of school | private |
| Affiliation | Methodist |
| Environment | suburban |

### STUDENTS

| | |
|---|---|
| Total undergrad enrollment | 1,082 |
| % male/female | 45/55 |
| % from out of state | 34 |
| % live on campus | 80 |
| % African American | 4 |
| % Asian | 3 |
| % Caucasian | 74 |
| % Hispanic | 2 |
| % international | 1 |
| # of countries represented | 10 |

### SURVEY SAYS . . .
Political activism is hot
Student government is popular
(Almost) everyone smokes
Campus easy to get around
Great library
Diverse students interact

## ACADEMICS

| | |
|---|---|
| Academic Rating | 92 |
| Calendar | semester |
| Student/faculty ratio | 12:1 |
| Profs interesting rating | 96 |
| Profs accessible rating | 98 |
| % profs teaching UG courses | 100 |
| Avg lab size | 10-19 students |
| Avg reg class size | 10-19 students |

### MOST POPULAR MAJORS
Business/managerial economics
Biology/biological sciences
Psychology

## STUDENTS SPEAK OUT

### Academics

"Hendrix is a place where you can walk into the cafeteria and sit down beside your professor, your dean, or administrators, and they will know your name," notes one Hendrix undergrad, identifying her favorite aspect about life in this small Arkansas liberal arts college. Students here brag that "the professors are absolutely the best thing about Hendrix. They devote their lives to teaching and helping students. They're excellent teachers and excellent role models." Undergraduates heap similarly generous amounts of praise on the administration, reporting that "those making decisions here are accessible and open to suggestions." Academically, Hendrix is a lot harder than most students expect. "Kids come from their high schools in 'Podunk,' Arkansas, where they were valedictorian without ever opening a book, and are shocked to get here and actually have to work, and work hard." The curriculum includes a host of flexible but demanding general education requirements in the humanities, social sciences, natural sciences, and a foreign language. "Journey is required for all freshmen, and it's a good foundation," declares a religion major. "'Unto the whole person' is our whole motto, and I think we live up to it. This college makes you think. It makes you think about things you don't want to think about."

### Life

The hard-working undergrads of Hendrix "mostly study until they can't take it anymore," which means that "the biggest parties are always the Fridays before finals." They do enjoy their parties though: "The social events on campus are definitely a plus. Just two semesters here, and I've already seen a dozen partying traditions. The students hold a number of unofficial annual parties, and it seems like there is something to do every weekend." Reports one student, "Drinking is definitely a part of the mainstream social atmosphere here, but it's not the rule. There is always a plethora of scheduled events on campus (almost without exception free of charge to students), both of academic and entertainment natures. There are visiting lecturers, poets, musicians, bands, and an occasional hypnotist. . . . We have a social committee (with a generous budget) that takes charge of scheduling campus events." Most students approve of the lack of Greek organizations here; writes one typical undergrad, "Because there is no Greek life, I never really feel uncomfortable showing up at a party on campus—that is, pretty much everyone is welcome." Hometown Conway receives poor marks: "The worst aspect of Hendrix is definitely its location. There isn't much to do here. Going to the Super Wal-Mart is sometimes the only time-killing option." Adds another, "There is no night life in Conway. There are no clubs, little to no concerts, and no bars since this is a dry county." As a result, "weekend excursions to Little Rock (30 minutes away) for a nice dinner or shopping are common."

### Student Body

The "very liberal" students of Hendrix pride themselves on their acceptance of "those whose practices are traditionally discriminated against." The school's "very 'out' gay population," for example, enjoys a comfort level unusual for a campus in the conservative South. "There's also acceptance and respect for different religious, philosophical, and political beliefs." Well, except for conservative views, according to the few lonely Republicans. "My fellow students would like to pretend that they are the most diverse, accepting group of people in the world," observes one. "Unfortunately, they are not diverse at all; they are all liberals, environmentalists, and radical feminists." Some students complain that "there are dozens of cliques on campus, and if you're not a part of one, then having friends that are readily accessible is not an option."

# HENDRIX COLLEGE

FINANCIAL AID: 501-450-1368 • E-MAIL: ADM@HENDRIX.EDU • WEBSITE: WWW.HENDRIX.EDU

## ADMISSIONS

*Very important factors considered include:* essays, secondary school record, standardized test scores. *Important factors considered include:* character/personal qualities, class rank, extracurricular activities, interview, recommendations. *Other factors considered include:* minority status, talent/ability, volunteer work. SAT I or ACT required. TOEFL required of all international applicants. High school diploma or GED is required. *High school units required/recommended:* 14 total recommended; 4 English recommended, 3 math recommended, 2 science recommended, 2 foreign language recommended, 3 social studies recommended.

### *The Inside Word*

Hendrix has a small but well-qualified applicant pool. The college is a sleeper, and is an especially good bet for students with strong grades who lack the test scores usually necessary for admission to colleges on a higher level of selectivity. Look for Hendrix to get tougher as they continue to garner attention from national publications. This place has been making the lists, and it is solid.

## FINANCIAL AID

*Students should submit:* FAFSA. The Princeton Review suggests that all financial aid forms be submitted as soon as possible after January 1. *Need-based scholarships/grants offered:* Pell, SEOG, state scholarships/grants, private scholarships, the school's own gift aid. *Loan aid offered:* FFEL Subsidized Stafford, FFEL Unsubsidized Stafford, FFEL PLUS, Federal Perkins, Methodist Loan. Federal Work-Study Program available. Institutional employment available. Applicants will be notified of awards on a rolling basis beginning on or about March 1. Off-campus job opportunities are excellent.

## FROM THE ADMISSIONS OFFICE

"Students who choose Hendrix are bright, eager learners. They have high aspirations; many go on to pursue advanced degrees in graduate and professional schools. Each year the average ACT and College Board scores of the incoming class are in the 85th to 90th percentile range nationally. But Hendrix students expect more from the school than academic challenge. For most, there is a desire to balance their schedules with other kinds of activity—from ensemble practice to a game of intramural racquetball. Everyone fits in; the small campus engenders a sense of openness and belonging. Among the recent graduating class, 200 seniors are recipients of offers to study biochemistry at Yale, English at the University of Virginia, electrical engineering at Duke, business administration at Harvard, medicine at Johns Hopkins, theology at Claremont, and law at Georgetown."

## SELECTIVITY

| | |
|---|---|
| Admissions Rating | 83 |
| # of applicants | 1,071 |
| % of applicants accepted | 83 |
| % of acceptees attending | 35 |
| # accepting a place on wait list | 10 |
| % admitted from wait list | 40 |

### FRESHMAN PROFILE

| | |
|---|---|
| Range SAT Verbal | 570-690 |
| Average SAT Verbal | 630 |
| Range SAT Math | 550-670 |
| Average SAT Math | 610 |
| Range ACT Composite | 25-31 |
| Average ACT Composite | 27 |
| Minimum TOEFL | 550 |
| Average HS GPA | 3.7 |
| % graduated top 10% of class | 42 |
| % graduated top 25% of class | 76 |
| % graduated top 50% of class | 94 |

### DEADLINES

| | |
|---|---|
| Priority admission | 2/1 |
| Nonfall registration? | yes |

### APPLICANTS ALSO LOOK AT AND OFTEN PREFER
Tulane
Vanderbilt
Washington U
U of Tulsa

### AND SOMETIMES PREFER
Birmingham-Southern
Rhodes
U of Arkansas
Southern Methodist

## FINANCIAL FACTS

| | |
|---|---|
| Financial Aid Rating | 83 |
| Tuition | $15,630 |
| Room and board | $5,340 |
| Books and supplies | $800 |
| % frosh receiving aid | 52 |
| % undergrads receiving aid | 50 |
| Avg frosh grant | $10,209 |
| Avg frosh loan | $3,500 |

# HIRAM COLLEGE

PO Box 67, Hiram, OH 44234 • Admissions: 800-362-5280 • Fax: 330-569-5944

## CAMPUS LIFE

| | |
|---|---|
| Quality of Life Rating | 85 |
| Type of school | private |
| Affiliation | Disciples of Christ |
| Environment | rural |

### STUDENTS
| | |
|---|---|
| Total undergrad enrollment | 1,134 |
| % male/female | 41/59 |
| % from out of state | 17 |
| % from public high school | 86 |
| % live on campus | 89 |
| % African American | 10 |
| % Asian | 1 |
| % Caucasian | 86 |
| % Hispanic | 2 |
| % international | 3 |

### SURVEY SAYS . . .
Lots of beer drinking
Campus easy to get around
(Almost) everyone smokes
Hard liquor is popular
Campus is beautiful
Campus feels safe
Lab facilities are great
Students are happy

## ACADEMICS

| | |
|---|---|
| Academic Rating | 86 |
| Calendar | semester |
| Student/faculty ratio | 11:1 |
| % profs teaching UG courses | 100 |
| Avg lab size | under 10 students |
| Avg reg class size | 10-19 students |

### MOST POPULAR MAJORS
Business/commerce
Education
Biology/biological sciences

## STUDENTS SPEAK OUT

### Academics
One satisfied undergraduate tells us, "I believe that the education that most people get at Hiram is strong and often surpasses educations from larger institutions." Students at the college "want to suck the marrow out of their educational experience" and describe the course load as "challenging enough that it isn't a walk in the park, but it's not overwhelming by any means." Students feel legit calling most professors by their first names: "They want to get to know me as a person and not just another student in the classroom." Professors merit gold stars because "they are very willing to devote their time to help students, or just to talk. This goes even for professors whose classes you might not be currently attending." Most instructors are "very understanding, down-to-earth people who encourage individual thought" and even grab lunch with students and send timely e-mail help over the weekends. The administration comes in a distant second in the popularity contest among the "grownups." Students cite "a lot of miscommunication" between departments. In all fairness, one student writes, "I know of very few other places where deans know many students' names." Other respondents call the staff "helpful," "attentive," and "available to explain their decisions."

### Life
On certain desperate nights at Hiram, when "we'll be so bored that we'll just go and walk at night because that's the only thing to do," students have an eerie moment, and "the sudden realization that you are living in a cornfield begins to set in." Students quickly learn to accept the situation and make the best of it." Common weekend activities include "going from dorm to dorm drinking" and "driving to Taco Bell or Wal-Mart." Student organizations attempt to fill the activity void with events such as "toga parties, Springfest, Halloween, the Hiram version of Greek pledging, Homecoming, and athletic-related events." Students can hop the shuttle to Cleveland on Saturday nights, since "most programming is over by nine or so, and there's nothing else to do besides get into trouble." However, not everyone complains of tedium; in fact, there are "a lot of students who enjoy the peacefulness of Hiram," a place that manages to "teach you about the real world in a safe, almost surreal setting."

### Student Body
Hiram is a school that "prides itself on being culturally diverse." Students report, "We have a very diverse group of students from all ethnic and economic groups" as well as people with "all sorts of backgrounds and belief structures." Even in this Hiram salad bowl, a few people notice that the population seems "almost segregated down racial lines sometimes." One student observes "tension between minority students or international students and white students." Nonetheless, respondents express a heartening enthusiasm regarding diversity: "It has been a great pleasure learning about so many cultures!" Reportedly, aside from being humanoid, "no two people are even remotely similar," but at the same time, "there is a group of people for everyone." These posses "tend to be a little on the exclusive side," limited to people with the same "interests, major, or residence hall," according to one respondent. Other common bonds include a past as "freaks in high school" and an interest in "discussing issues on a deeper level." One student summarizes the crew as "a friendly community who cares about what goes on around them and is accepting to new thoughts and ideas."

# HIRAM COLLEGE

FINANCIAL AID: 330-569-5107 • E-MAIL: ADMISSION@HIRAM.EDU • WEBSITE: WWW.HIRAM.EDU

## ADMISSIONS

*Very important factors considered include:* secondary school record. *Important factors considered include:* character/personal qualities, class rank, essays, interview, recommendations, standardized test scores. *Other factors considered include:* alumni/ae relation, extracurricular activities, geographical residence, minority status, talent/ability, volunteer work, work experience. SAT I or ACT required. TOEFL required of all international applicants. High school diploma or GED is required. *High school units required/recommended:* 18 total required; 21 total recommended; 4 English required, 3 math required, 4 math recommended, 3 science required, 2 science lab required, 2 foreign language recommended, 3 social studies required, 1 history required, 2 elective required.

### The Inside Word

Students with consistent academic records will find little difficulty in gaining admission. The applicant pool is decidedly local; out-of-state candidates benefit from their scarcity.

## FINANCIAL AID

*Students should submit:* FAFSA. The Princeton Review suggests that all financial aid forms be submitted as soon as possible after January 1. *Need-based scholarships/grants offered:* Pell, SEOG, state scholarships/grants, private scholarships, the school's own gift aid. *Loan aid offered:* FFEL Subsidized Stafford, FFEL Unsubsidized Stafford, FFEL PLUS, Federal Perkins, college/university loans from institutional funds. Federal Work-Study Program available. Institutional employment available. Applicants will be notified of awards on a rolling basis beginning on or about February 15. Off-campus job opportunities are good.

## FROM THE ADMISSIONS OFFICE

"Hiram College offers several distinctive programs that set us apart from other small, private liberal arts colleges. Over half of Hiram's students participate in our nationally recognized study abroad program at some point during their four years here. In 2001–2002, Hiram faculty will lead trips to England, France, Costa Rica, Pakistan, Greece, and Turkey; in 2002–2003, we will visit Australia, Germany, Denmark, Zimbabwe, Israel, Guatemala, and Mexico. Because Hiram students receive credits for the courses taught by faculty on these trips, studying abroad will not impede progress in their majors or delay graduation. Another unique aspect of a Hiram education is our academic calendar, known as the Hiram Plan. Our semesters are divided into 12-week and 3-week periods. Students usually enroll in three courses during each 12-week period, and one intensive course during the 3-week periods. Many students spend the 3-week periods on study abroad trips or taking unusual courses not typically offered during the 12-week periods. In addition to numerous study abroad options and the Hiram Plan, our small classes (the average class size is 15) encourage interaction between students and their professors, both in and out of the classroom. Students can work with professors on original research projects, and often participate in musical groups and intramural sports teams alongside faculty members."

## SELECTIVITY

| | |
|---|---|
| Admissions Rating | 80 |
| # of applicants | 1,294 |
| % of applicants accepted | 69 |
| % of acceptees attending | 26 |
| # of early decision applicants | 38 |
| % accepted early decision | 84 |

### FRESHMAN PROFILE

| | |
|---|---|
| Range SAT Verbal | 510-630 |
| Average SAT Verbal | 573 |
| Range SAT Math | 480-620 |
| Average SAT Math | 566 |
| Average ACT Composite | 24 |
| Minimum TOEFL | 550 |
| Average HS GPA | 3.4 |
| % graduated top 10% of class | 39 |
| % graduated top 25% of class | 53 |
| % graduated top 50% of class | 85 |

### DEADLINES

| | |
|---|---|
| Early decision | 12/1 |
| Early decision notification | 1/1 |
| Priority admission | 2/1 |
| Regular admission | 2/1 |
| Nonfall registration? | yes |

### APPLICANTS ALSO LOOK AT
**AND OFTEN PREFER**
Kenyon College
Denison University
**AND SOMETIMES PREFER**
John Carroll University
College of Wooster
**AND RARELY PREFER**
Kent State University
University of Akron

## FINANCIAL FACTS

| | |
|---|---|
| Financial Aid Rating | 86 |
| Tuition | $19,650 |
| Room and board | $7,100 |
| Books and supplies | $600 |
| Required fees | $694 |
| % frosh receiving aid | 83 |
| % undergrads receiving aid | 83 |
| Avg frosh grant | $10,998 |
| Avg frosh loan | $5,176 |

# HOBART AND WILLIAM SMITH COLLEGES

639 SOUTH MAIN STREET, GENEVA, NY 14456 • ADMISSIONS: 315-781-3472 • FAX: 315-781-3471

## CAMPUS LIFE

| | |
|---|---|
| Quality of Life Rating | 82 |
| Type of school | private |
| Environment | rural |

### STUDENTS

| | |
|---|---|
| Total undergrad enrollment | 1,893 |
| % male/female | 45/55 |
| % from out of state | 50 |
| % from public high school | 65 |
| % live on campus | 90 |
| % in (# of) fraternities | 17 (5) |
| % African American | 4 |
| % Asian | 2 |
| % Caucasian | 86 |
| % Hispanic | 4 |
| % international | 2 |
| # of countries represented | 19 |

### SURVEY SAYS . . .
Great food on campus
Everyone loves the Statesmen
Beautiful campus
Athletic facilities are great
Students don't like Geneva, NY
Theater is unpopular
Class discussions encouraged

## ACADEMICS

| | |
|---|---|
| Academic Rating | 87 |
| Calendar | semester |
| Student/faculty ratio | 11:1 |
| Profs interesting rating | 95 |
| Profs accessible rating | 98 |
| % profs teaching UG courses | 100 |
| Avg reg class size | 10-19 students |

### MOST POPULAR MAJORS
History
English language and literature
Economics

## STUDENTS SPEAK OUT

### Academics

Hobart and William Smith Colleges are separate, single-sex institutions sharing the same campus and classes. In an effort to combine the best aspects of single-sex and coeducational instruction, the schools share classes and even a common faculty, yet maintain separate traditions and coordinate priorities. The effect of this "coordinate education" is particularly prominent at William Smith, the women's school. Acknowledging that women often take a "back seat" at "traditionally male-dominated coeducational colleges," William Smith co-opts the most successful attributes of all-women's colleges, such as self-government and an emphasis on gender studies. According to students at both schools, HWS' chief assets include "small classes and discussion groups" and professors who "are always around to help the students out, giving out e-mail addresses and even home phone numbers and encouraging us to call. They seem to care about the students and want them to do well." Writes one student, "The interaction I've had with the faculty has been extremely helpful and constructive. There is a high expectation in the courses, but the profs are very willing to meet with you [to] help you meet those expectations." Administrators are regarded more ambivalently. While one freshman gushes that "we have administrators who make sure you are adjusting to school easily. They are willing to help if you have any problems," many upperclassmen complain about the administration. Most students, however, feel it's worth enduring some rough spots to be "recognized as an individual, which to me is extremely important. At a large university, I would be recognized as merely a number."

### Life

The social scene at HWS runs the whole spectrum from "hanging down town with all the sweet townies to getting drunk or stoned." According to one respondent, "There are two bars that let everyone in. So everyone goes, which means you have to wait 20 minutes before you can get a drink. Either the school should think of better things for us to do or they should build more bars." Plenty of students offered another solution to the situation: "For myself and everyone on campus," writes a typical undergrad, "we have one word for you: fraternities!!!" To its credit, "the school has increased the number of on-campus activities." A typical weekend could include a cold one at the campus pub, taking in a movie at the Friday Flix Series with your main squeeze, or shakin' your booty at the on-campus answer to the Copa Cabana. HWS boasts a "beautiful campus, which is enjoyed by students. People really like the outdoors and will do the craziest things just to have an excuse to be outdoors, like sled downhill on trays from the dining hall." Besides traying, lots of students are involved in athletics, especially lacrosse.

### Student Body

Don't come to HWS looking for a melting pot. As one student points out, "I really like a lot of people who go here, but they are all carbon copies of one another." Writes one, "Going to class is like going to a J.Crew fashion show and the parking lot is a SAAB dealership." There is "noticeable segregation of the races, particularly in the dining hall. It's a little disturbing." Students also subdivide into "cliques structured along socioeconomic lines, but this does not mean that these groups don't interact with each other." It is clear that cliques, though friendly, are king.

# HOBART AND WILLIAM SMITH COLLEGES

FINANCIAL AID: 315-781-3315 • E-MAIL: HOADM@HWS.EDU • WEBSITE: WWW.HWS.EDU

## ADMISSIONS
*Very important factors considered include:* essays, secondary school record. *Important factors considered include:* character/personal qualities, class rank, extracurricular activities, recommendations, standardized test scores, volunteer work, work experience. *Other factors considered include:* alumni/ae relation, geographical residence, interview, minority status, talent/ability. SAT I or ACT required; SAT I preferred. TOEFL required of all international applicants. High school diploma or GED is required. *High school units required/recommended:* 19 total required; 4 English required, 3 math required, 3 science required, 2 science lab required, 3 foreign language required, 2 social studies required, 2 history required, 4 elective recommended.

### The Inside Word
Hobart and William Smith lose a lot of students to their competitors, who are many and strong. This helps open up the gates a bit for more candidates. However, the schools' location, right on Seneca Lake, offers students a great place to study.

## FINANCIAL AID
*Students should submit:* FAFSA, CSS/Financial Aid PROFILE, state aid form, noncustodial (divorced/separated) parent's statement, business/farm supplement, parent's and student's tax return. Regular filing deadline is February 15. The Princeton Review suggests that all financial aid forms be submitted as soon as possible after January 1. *Need-based scholarships/grants offered:* Pell, SEOG, state scholarships/grants, private scholarships, the school's own gift aid. *Loan aid offered:* FFEL Subsidized Stafford, FFEL Unsubsidized Stafford, FFEL PLUS, Federal Perkins. Federal Work-Study Program available. Institutional employment available. Applicants will be notified of awards on or about April 1. Off-campus job opportunities are fair.

## FROM THE ADMISSIONS OFFICE
"Hobart and William Smith Colleges seek students with a sense of adventure and a commitment to the life of the mind. Inside the classroom, students find the academic climate to be rigorous, with a faculty that is deeply involved in teaching and working with them. Outside, they discover a supportive community that helps to cultivate a balance and hopes to foster an integration among academics, extracurricular activities, and social life. Hobart and William Smith, as coordinate colleges, have an awareness of gender differences and equality and are committed to respect and a celebration of diversity."

## SELECTIVITY

| | |
|---|---|
| Admissions Rating | 86 |
| # of applicants | 3,108 |
| % of applicants accepted | 66 |
| % of acceptees attending | 26 |
| # accepting a place on wait list | 93 |
| % admitted from wait list | 19 |
| # of early decision applicants | 159 |
| % accepted early decision | 81 |

### FRESHMAN PROFILE
| | |
|---|---|
| Range SAT Verbal | 540-630 |
| Average SAT Verbal | 550 |
| Range SAT Math | 540-630 |
| Average SAT Math | 600 |
| Minimum TOEFL | 550 |
| Average HS GPA | 3.3 |
| % graduated top 10% of class | 31 |
| % graduated top 25% of class | 60 |
| % graduated top 50% of class | 93 |

### DEADLINES
| | |
|---|---|
| Early decision | 11/15 |
| Early decision notification | 12/15 |
| Regular admission | 2/1 |
| Regular notification | 4/1 |

### APPLICANTS ALSO LOOK AT AND OFTEN PREFER
Colgate
Trinity College (CT)
Connecticut College
Hamilton
Union College (NY)

### AND SOMETIMES PREFER
Skidmore
Kenyon
Gettysburg
St. Lawrence
Dickinson

## FINANCIAL FACTS

| | |
|---|---|
| Financial Aid Rating | 84 |
| Tuition | $26,818 |
| Room and board | $7,230 |
| Books and supplies | $850 |
| Required fees | $530 |
| % frosh receiving aid | 70 |
| % undergrads receiving aid | 69 |
| Avg frosh grant | $17,918 |
| Avg frosh loan | $3,420 |

# HOFSTRA UNIVERSITY

ADMISSIONS CENTER, BERNON HALL, HEMPSTEAD, NY 11549 • ADMISSIONS: 516-463-6700 • FAX: 516-463-5100

## CAMPUS LIFE

| | |
|---|---|
| Quality of Life Rating | 70 |
| Type of school | private |
| Environment | suburban |

### STUDENTS

| | |
|---|---|
| Total undergrad enrollment | 9,469 |
| % male/female | 46/54 |
| % from out of state | 22 |
| % live on campus | 41 |
| % in (# of) fraternities | 6 (21) |
| % in (# of) sororities | 7 (15) |
| % African American | 9 |
| % Asian | 4 |
| % Caucasian | 60 |
| % Hispanic | 7 |
| % international | 2 |
| # of countries represented | 67 |

### SURVEY SAYS . . .
Frats and sororities dominate social scene
High cost of living
(Almost) everyone smokes
Students don't get along with local community
Students don't like Hempstead, NY
Students not very happy
Ethnic diversity on campus

## ACADEMICS

| | |
|---|---|
| Academic Rating | 73 |
| Calendar | 4-1-4 |
| Student/faculty ratio | 15:1 |
| Profs interesting rating | 90 |
| Profs accessible rating | 90 |
| % profs teaching UG courses | 79 |
| Avg reg class size | 10-19 students |

### MOST POPULAR MAJORS
Management
Marketing
Psychology

## STUDENTS SPEAK OUT

### Academics
What draws students to Hofstra University, an up-and-coming school located just a half-hour outside New York City, is its "growing academic reputation. It seems everywhere you turn, somebody tells you what a great school Hofstra is." With "good education, law and business majors," "a fine English department," "strong music, drama, film, philosophy, chemistry, and biology departments," and "a really good astronomy observatory," Hofstra boasts a diversity of strengths that larger universities might justifiably envy. And the improvements keep coming; as one student avers, "It's a constantly growing school. It's not at a stand still. There's constantly research going on and it's constantly getting better with more students attending. The sports teams are getting better and are getting more recognition, too." Students appreciate the degree of academic freedom accorded them here; as one explains, "While most universities are very specific concerning their core requirements, Hofstra offers an overwhelming amount of core courses and electives so that students with very specific or very eclectic interests can find something satisfactory." Added bonuses: "It is close to NYC, where there is a great job market," and "alumni heavily support their alma mater." Student complaints center on "long lines for books [and] financial aid." and the perception that some core courses "are mind-numbingly easy."

### Life
Hofstra's "beautiful" campus is "an arboretum and a museum, with beautiful flowers, trees, sculptures, and statues lining the sidewalks," offering a pastoral antidote to the bustle outside the school's gates. About half of Hofstra's full-time student body live in the "nice and fun" dormitories; others scramble for off-campus apartments or commute (the school is popular among native Long Islanders). Campus life offers numerous clubs and organizations; reports one student, "The clubs on campus, such as Hofstra Concerts or Entertainment Unlimited, are also strengths of our school because they help to plan lots of events that students can attend." Athletic facilities are fine and the teams are competitive, if not especially well supported: "It would be great to see more students at games. Hardly anybody goes; even for Homecoming, only half the stadium gets filled," complains one student. The Greeks are popular even though they don't have houses; most Greek parties take place in Hofstra USA, the on-campus pub, or in one of the three bars located "just across the street from campus." Those bars are about the only popular sites in hometown Hempstead, which students describe as "a little drab." Fortunately, "the school is only 25 miles away from NYC, so a lot of people like to go there." Word to the wise: Take the nearby Long Island Railroad into the city. Do not drive. Don't say we didn't warn you.

### Student Body
While the numbers bear out one student's assertion that "there are so many different kinds of people at [Hofstra]; it's very diverse," there is still a widely held perception that "at Hofstra, you see a lot of the typical 'Long Island Kids': Gucci, Armani, stilettos in the middle of December, Beemers . . . the whole deal." Many report that the dividing line runs between the school's resident and commuter populations; as one residential student puts it, "Campus students and commuting students are like fire and ice. The campus students are fun-loving and rowdy . . . . There is always laughing and random acts of craziness going on." Undergrads on both sides of the divide agree that "if you don't have a clique, it is 10 times harder to make friends." Writes one undergrad, "Students tend to stay in their own groups, especially the Greeks. When push comes to shove, though, the students do come together."

# HOFSTRA UNIVERSITY

FINANCIAL AID: 516-463-6680 • E-MAIL: HOFSTRA@HOFSTRA.EDU • WEBSITE: WWW.HOFSTRA.EDU

## ADMISSIONS

*Very important factors considered include:* class rank, recommendations, secondary school record, standardized test scores. *Important factors considered include:* character/personal qualities, essays, extracurricular activities, interview, talent/ability. *Other factors considered include:* volunteer work, work experience. TOEFL required of all international applicants. High school diploma or GED is required. *High school units required/recommended:* 16 total required; 4 English required, 2 math required, 3 math recommended, 1 science required, 3 science recommended, 1 science lab required, 2 foreign language required, 3 social studies required, 4 social studies recommended, 4 elective required. Prospective engineering majors need at least 4 years of mathematics, 1 year of chemistry, and 1 year of physics.

## The Inside Word

Hofstra wants to be national, and has positioned itself very well with impressive facilities, appealing program offerings, solid athletic teams, and an effective national ad campaign. As a result, Hofstra's current student profile has increased dramatically. Presently, Hofstra is a solidly competitive regional university; it is a school to watch in the future.

## FINANCIAL AID

*Students should submit:* FAFSA, state aid form. The Princeton Review suggests that all financial aid forms be submitted as soon as possible after January 1. *Need-based scholarships/grants offered:* Pell, SEOG, state scholarships/grants, private scholarships, the school's own gift aid. *Loan aid offered:* FFEL Subsidized Stafford, FFEL Unsubsidized Stafford, FFEL PLUS, Federal Perkins, college/university loans from institutional funds. Federal Work-Study Program available. Institutional employment available. Applicants will be notified of awards on a rolling basis beginning on or about March 1. Off-campus job opportunities are excellent.

## FROM THE ADMISSIONS OFFICE

"Hofstra's first priority is excellence in teaching. Faculty are experts in their fields, accessible to students, and committed to providing a stimulating education. Classes are small, yet students have extensive choices, including more than 110 majors. Eligible students may enroll in Honors College, which provides additional opportunities for the most academically qualified students. Great emphasis is placed on the role of students in the life of the University. Hofstra's educational offerings are verified by prestigious national accreditations in business, law, education, journalism, and engineering among others, as well as the only chapter of Phi Beta Kappa at a private university on Long Island.

"The Hofstra libraries are computerized and contain 1.6 million volumes or equivalents. The libraries, and most of the campus, are wired to a computer network allowing immediate access to information, including the Hofstra Online Information System, which provides students quick access to their academic records. The campus has theaters, art galleries, an accredited museum, an FCC-licensed FM radio station, an on-campus television station, a variety of restaurants, an Olympic-size indoor pool, and extensive recreational facilities. Several housing options are provided in on-campus residence halls and off-campus apartments. Students have access to a beauty salon, post office, nightclub, and entertainment center on campus. Hofstra's beautiful campus, just 25 miles from Manhattan, is located on 250 acres designated as an arboretum. A new state-of-the-art facility for the School of Education and Allied Human Services will open this fall.

"Call 1-800-HOFSTRA to schedule an Admission Information session, which are available six days a week, Monday through Saturday."

## SELECTIVITY

★ ★ ☆ ☆

| | |
|---|---|
| Admissions Rating | 76 |
| # of applicants | 11,741 |
| % of applicants accepted | 72 |
| % of acceptees attending | 21 |

### FRESHMAN PROFILE

| | |
|---|---|
| Range SAT Verbal | 510-600 |
| Average SAT Verbal | 559 |
| Range SAT Math | 520-610 |
| Average SAT Math | 570 |
| Range ACT Composite | 23-27 |
| Average ACT Composite | 25 |
| Minimum TOEFL | 550 |
| Average HS GPA | 2.9 |
| % graduated top 10% of class | 16 |
| % graduated top 25% of class | 41 |
| % graduated top 50% of class | 77 |

### DEADLINES

| | |
|---|---|
| Nonfall registration? | yes |

### APPLICANTS ALSO LOOK AT AND OFTEN PREFER
NYU
Boston U
### AND SOMETIMES PREFER
St. John's U (NY)
Fordham U
Syracuse U
SUNY Binghamton
### AND RARELY PREFER
Rutgers at Camden
Long Island U at C.W. Post

## FINANCIAL FACTS

★ ★ ★ ☆

| | |
|---|---|
| Financial Aid Rating | 82 |
| Tuition | $15,740 |
| Room and board | $8,450 |
| Books and supplies | $760 |
| Required fees | $802 |
| % frosh receiving aid | 58 |
| % undergrads receiving aid | 58 |
| Avg frosh grant | $6,935 |
| Avg frosh loan | $3,026 |

# HOLLINS UNIVERSITY

PO Box 9707, Roanoke, VA 24020-1707 • Admissions: 540-362-6401 • Fax: 540-362-6218

## CAMPUS LIFE

| | |
|---|---|
| Quality of Life Rating | 98 |
| Type of school | private |
| Environment | suburban |

### STUDENTS

| | |
|---|---|
| Total undergrad enrollment | 847 |
| % from out of state | 48 |
| % from public high school | 74 |
| % live on campus | 90 |
| % African American | 7 |
| % Asian | 1 |
| % Caucasian | 83 |
| % Hispanic | 2 |
| % international | 3 |
| # of countries represented | 12 |

### SURVEY SAYS . . .
Dorms are like palaces
Student government is popular
Class discussions encouraged
Classes are small
No one cheats
Campus feels safe
Very small frat/sorority scene
No one plays intramural sports
(Almost) no one listens to college radio

## ACADEMICS

| | |
|---|---|
| Academic Rating | 90 |
| Calendar | 4-1-4 |
| Student/faculty ratio | 9:1 |
| Profs interesting rating | 97 |
| Profs accessible rating | 99 |
| % profs teaching UG courses | 100 |
| Avg lab size | under 10 students |
| Avg reg class size | 10-19 students |

### MOST POPULAR MAJORS
Creative writing
Psychology
Fine/studio arts

## STUDENTS SPEAK OUT

### Academics

Students agree that "the small size of the student body is the key factor in the greatness of academics at Hollins. The professors here are extremely accessible and get to know all their students personally, which is great motivation to work hard in classes and adds to the friendly, family atmosphere here at Hollins." This small, Virginian, all-women's school has "a great creative writing program" as well as a small but vibrant arts program that complement its more popular departments. In all areas, students proudly tell us, "The main focus of the professors is the student body. Classes are small and challenging, and the base of liberal arts is wonderful." Students also love the honor code, which allows them to take self-scheduled, unproctored exams, and the "amazing" study abroad opportunities, which send "two-thirds of the student body [to] spend at least a semester abroad. January term is well spent, too. January term is where we spend the month of January interning somewhere, or you can opt to travel with the school to other countries and learn [their] history." Students note that "while the administration tends to be more than a little clumsy and tangled in red tape at times, the friendliness and flexibility of the staff in all offices tends to make up for the mix-ups, confusion, and delays in administrative matters."

### Life

Many students are pleasantly surprised that "for a women's college a good 20 to 40 minutes away from college-age males, this school does a pretty damn good job of keeping us entertained on campus. In addition to the many, many cultural events on campus, there are at least two school-sponsored popular concerts a month, visits by comedy troupes, and themed parties that people actually go to." Adds another student, "There are tons of organizations, and it is very easy to begin an organization if you are interested. The more you get involved, the more there is to do. Aside from the planned activities, there are often parties in the apartments or in NEFA (the fine arts house). There is also a small arcade and pool area in the snack bar, and it's pretty easy to find people around to play games." What's missing, of course, are boys; some students give this as the principal reason that Hollins "is pretty much a road trip/suitcase college. There is nothing to do here, especially on weekends." Typical weekend destinations include Washington and Lee University or all-male Hampden-Sydney. Students like Roanoke, "a medium-sized town with lots of things to do, good clubs and restaurants." The campus is conveniently located "very close to downtown Roanoke, and everything (grocery stores, malls, movie theatres, restaurants) is within a 10-minute drive from campus; still it would be nice if the school provided at least occasional transportation to popular destinations like the grocery store, for the unfortunate car-less students." Hollins' campus "is as beautiful as our publicity says" it is.

### Student Body

As one student puts it, "Hollins has a reputation for being comprised of largely white upper-middle-class 'pearl girls,' and not without reason." Things are changing, though. As one undergraduate told us, "In the past, many of the students were rather wealthy, young, Southern women. Now it is composed generally of middle-class women. Most are easy to get along with, and traditions often bring us closer together." Explains another, "At our school, you're either A or you're B. We have the truly arty students who came to a liberal arts school to get a liberal arts education, and then we have these really sheltered, white, southern-belle types who sneer at anything the arts programs do." Most students agree that Hollins "could stand to improve on the diversity levels" by enrolling more "students of color and [varied] economic backgrounds." According to many we surveyed, the school's lesbian contingent has grown in number and volubility in recent years.

# HOLLINS UNIVERSITY

FINANCIAL AID: 540-362-6332 • E-MAIL: HUADM@HOLLINS.EDU • WEBSITE: WWW.HOLLINS.EDU

## ADMISSIONS
*Very important factors considered include:* recommendations, secondary school record, standardized test scores. *Important factors considered include:* class rank, essays, extracurricular activities, talent/ability. *Other factors considered include:* alumni/ae relation, character/personal qualities, interview, volunteer work, work experience. SAT I or ACT required; SAT II recommended. TOEFL required of all international applicants. High school diploma or GED is required. *High school units required/recommended:* 16 total required; 4 English recommended, 3 math recommended, 3 science recommended, 3 foreign language recommended, 3 social studies recommended.

## The Inside Word
Only candidates who overtly display their lack of compatibility with the Hollins milieu are likely to encounter difficulty in gaining admission. A high level of self-selection and its weak, but improving, freshman profile allow most candidates to relax.

## FINANCIAL AID
*Students should submit:* FAFSA, state aid form. Regular filing deadline is March 1. The Princeton Review suggests that all financial aid forms be submitted as soon as possible after January 1. *Need-based scholarships/grants offered:* Pell, SEOG, state scholarships/grants, private scholarships, the school's own gift aid, United Negro College Fund. *Loan aid offered:* Direct Subsidized Stafford, Direct Unsubsidized Stafford, Direct PLUS, Federal Perkins, state loans, Sallie Mae, OneChoice, GATE Loans, Plato. Federal Work-Study Program available. Institutional employment available. Applicants will be notified of awards on a rolling basis beginning on or about March 15. Off-campus job opportunities are good.

## FROM THE ADMISSIONS OFFICE
"As a liberal arts college dedicated to high achievement for women, Hollins celebrates and encourages the success—whether in the classroom, in the laboratory, on stage, or on the athletic field—of each student. A spirit of independent inquiry, the free exchange of ideas, and a love for learning characterize life on campus. At Hollins, creativity and imaginative thinking are applauded with the same vigor that rewards academic achievement.

"Women who are going places start at Hollins."

---

### SELECTIVITY
★ ★ ☆ ☆

| | |
|---|---|
| Admissions Rating | 79 |
| # of applicants | 686 |
| % of applicants accepted | 80 |
| % of acceptees attending | 37 |
| # accepting a place on wait list | 9 |
| % admitted from wait list | 89 |
| # of early decision applicants | 57 |
| % accepted early decision | 79 |

### FRESHMAN PROFILE
| | |
|---|---|
| Range SAT Verbal | 530-660 |
| Average SAT Verbal | 595 |
| Range SAT Math | 490-610 |
| Average SAT Math | 550 |
| Range ACT Composite | 21-28 |
| Average ACT Composite | 24 |
| Minimum TOEFL | 550 |
| Average HS GPA | 3.4 |
| % graduated top 10% of class | 30 |
| % graduated top 25% of class | 58 |
| % graduated top 50% of class | 89 |

### DEADLINES
| | |
|---|---|
| Early decision | 12/1 |
| Early decision notification | 12/15 |
| Priority admission | 2/15 |
| Nonfall registration? | yes |

### APPLICANTS ALSO LOOK AT AND OFTEN PREFER
Randolph-Macon Woman's College
Sweet Briar College
James Madison U
Mary Washington College
**AND SOMETIMES PREFER**
Roanoke College
Mary Baldwin College
U of Virginia
Virginia Tech
Virginia Commonwealth

### FINANCIAL FACTS

| | |
|---|---|
| Financial Aid Rating | 95 |
| Tuition | $18,200 |
| Room and board | $6,875 |
| Books and supplies | $600 |
| Required fees | $250 |
| % frosh receiving aid | 65 |
| % undergrads receiving aid | 59 |
| Avg frosh grant | $9,041 |
| Avg frosh loan | $3,979 |

THE BEST 351 COLLEGES ■ 281

# HOWARD UNIVERSITY

2400 SIXTH STREET NW, WASHINGTON, DC 20059 • ADMISSIONS: 202-806-2700 • FAX: 202-806-4462

## CAMPUS LIFE

★ ★ ☆ ☆

| Quality of Life Rating | 77 |
|---|---|
| Type of school | private |
| Environment | urban |

### STUDENTS

| Total undergrad enrollment | 6,892 |
|---|---|
| % male/female | 34/66 |
| % from out of state | 88 |
| % from public high school | 80 |
| % live on campus | 58 |
| % African American | 85 |
| % Asian | 1 |
| % Hispanic | 1 |
| % international | 12 |
| # of countries represented | 102 |

### SURVEY SAYS . . .
Frats and sororities dominate social scene
Political activism is hot
Student government is popular
Students don't get along with local community
Registration is a pain
Theater is unpopular
Very little beer drinking
Lots of long lines and red tape
Student publications are popular

## ACADEMICS

★ ★ ☆ ☆

| Academic Rating | 72 |
|---|---|
| Calendar | semester |
| Student/faculty ratio | 8:1 |
| Profs interesting rating | 92 |
| Profs accessible rating | 94 |
| Avg lab size | 10-19 students |
| Avg reg class size | 10-19 students |

### MOST POPULAR MAJORS
Biology
Psychology
Radio, TV, and film

## STUDENTS SPEAK OUT

### Academics

Students at Howard University appreciate the "great legacy and wonderful traditions" of their HBCU (historically black college/university). Explains one undergraduate, "Our rich history is not just history, but is relived every day. Marches, rallies, and political activism are things that stay strong and are supported by the Administration." Students here feel strong bonds not only to the school's rich past but also to minority communities around the world today. Notes one, "'Leadership for America and the Global Community' is our phrase, and we stick by it to the end. For the people of the African Diaspora and all other minorities, this is a place to appreciate your culture in every way." Many brag that "research is another strength of our university. Howard is the only HBCU ranked as a Level 1 research institution by the Carnegie Foundation, and it is very clear why. With our huge library system and Moorland-Spingarn Research Center there is no doubting Howard's greatness!" Students brag that "professors are willing to help with problems, both inside and outside of school. Many of the professors take you into their families. You become their children for the four or more years that you attend." All these assets help soften the blow of the demanding curriculum ("Not very forgiving—perform or you're out. Typical days are long and tiring.") and the hassle-filled bureaucracy that runs the school.

### Life

Washington, D.C., Howard's hometown, looms large in the extracurricular activities of most students. "Clubbing is one of the biggest weekend activities," writes one undergrad, adding that "some clubs provide shuttles from the dorms straight to the clubs." Students involve themselves in community volunteer work, internships, and the big-league politics that permeate the city. Nearly all love D.C., although most are less positive about the neighborhood surrounding the school: "It is in the middle of the ghetto. There are a bunch of crack fiends in the surrounding areas," warns one student. On campus, "there are a lot of groups, clubs, and organizations to get into, such as state clubs and religious organizations." Students also enjoy "on-campus concerts and shows." As for the party scene, students report that "unlike at most white schools, keg parties are not cool. Howard students prefer liquor and weed. Every now and then, a Greek organization will have a party, but more than likely it will be at a local club, not at a frat house." For those less inclined to party, one student sums up other possibilities, "There . . . is always something mind-stimulating that you can get into. Go to a student play on campus or visit a Shakespeare play downtown. Join NABA, NSBE, a pan-Hellenic organization, or student council. Take a walk downtown and visit the monuments, or simply gaze at the gorgeous fountains."

### Student Body

The predominantly African American student body of Howard "comes from diverse backgrounds socially and economically." Notes one student, "Coming from a small town, I would have never imagined interacting with so many people from so many places and meshing so well with all of them. Students from Howard come from all 50 states, the two U.S. territories, and over 104 countries abroad! On top of that, they don't just stick to their own; everyone is in the mix with common goals." Some students complain that their classmates are too materialistic ("Prepare to enter the fashion zone. Students at HU spend lots of money on clothing and looking good. Most women wear full makeup and high-heeled boots to strut around campus.") and are overly focused on career goals ("The pre-professionalism at this place kills me," gripes one student. "If you're one of those rare breeds who's interested in learning for the sake of learning, go to Swarthmore or Bard or somewhere and deal with their respective low levels of melanin. Howard is NOT the place for you.").

# HOWARD UNIVERSITY

FINANCIAL AID: 202-806-2800 • E-MAIL: ADMISSION@HOWARD.EDU • WEBSITE: WWW.HOWARD.EDU

## ADMISSIONS

*Very important factors considered include:* class rank, secondary school record, standardized test scores. *Important factors considered include:* character/personal qualities, recommendations. *Other factors considered include:* alumni/ae relation, essays, extracurricular activities, talent/ability, volunteer work, work experience. SAT I or ACT required. TOEFL required of all international applicants. High school diploma or GED is required. *High school units required/recommended:* 14 total required; 4 English required, 2 math required, 2 science required, 2 foreign language required, 2 social studies required, 2 history required.

### The Inside Word

A large applicant pool and solid yield of acceptees who enroll is a combination that adds up to selectivity for Howard. Pay strict attention to the formula.

## FINANCIAL AID

*Students should submit:* FAFSA, institution's own financial aid form. Regular filing deadline is April 1. The Princeton Review suggests that all financial aid forms be submitted as soon as possible after January 1. *Need-based scholarships/grants offered:* Pell, SEOG, private scholarships, the school's own gift aid, Federal Nursing. *Loan aid offered:* FFEL Subsidized Stafford, FFEL PLUS, Federal Perkins, Federal Nursing, college/university loans from institutional funds. Federal Work-Study Program available. Institutional employment available. Applicants will be notified of awards on a rolling basis. Off-campus job opportunities are excellent.

## FROM THE ADMISSIONS OFFICE

"Since its founding, Howard has stood among the few institutions of higher learning where African Americans and other minorities have participated freely in a truly comprehensive university experience. Thus, Howard has assumed a special responsibility to prepare its students to exercise leadership wherever their interest and commitments take them. Howard has issued approximately 97,214 degrees, diplomas, and certificates to men and women in the professions, the arts and sciences, and the humanities. The university has produced and continues to produce a high percentage of the nation's African American professionals in the fields of medicine, dentistry, pharmacy, engineering, nursing, architecture, religion, law, music, social work, education, and business. There are more than 8,830 students from across the nation and approximately 104 countries and territories attending the university. Their varied customs, cultures, ideas, and interests contribute to Howard's international character and vitality. More than 1,360 faculty members represent the largest concentration of African American scholars in any single institution of higher education."

## SELECTIVITY

★ ★ ★ ☆

| Admissions Rating | 80 |
|---|---|
| # of applicants | 6,664 |
| % of applicants accepted | 56 |
| % of acceptees attending | 27 |

### FRESHMAN PROFILE

| Range SAT Verbal | 440-680 |
|---|---|
| Average SAT Verbal | 545 |
| Range SAT Math | 430-680 |
| Average SAT Math | 534 |
| Range ACT Composite | 16-27 |
| Minimum TOEFL | 500 |

### DEADLINES

| Early decision | 11/1 |
|---|---|
| Early decision notification | 12/24 |
| Regular admission | 2/15 |
| Nonfall registration? | yes |

### APPLICANTS ALSO LOOK AT AND OFTEN PREFER
Morehouse
Spelman
Hampton

### AND SOMETIMES PREFER
George Washington
U. Maryland—Coll. Park
Florida A&M

### AND RARELY PREFER
Morgan State

## FINANCIAL FACTS

★ ★ ☆ ☆

| Financial Aid Rating | 76 |
|---|---|
| Tuition | $10,130 |
| Room and board | $5,570 |
| Books and supplies | $1,020 |
| Required fees | $405 |
| % frosh receiving aid | 68 |
| % undergrads receiving aid | 68 |
| Avg frosh grant | $4,475 |
| Avg frosh loan | $9,457 |

# ILLINOIS INSTITUTE OF TECHNOLOGY

10 WEST 33RD STREET, CHICAGO, IL 60616 • ADMISSIONS: 312-567-3025 • FAX: 312-567-6939

## CAMPUS LIFE

| | |
|---|---|
| Quality of Life Rating | 69 |
| Type of school | private |
| Environment | urban |

### STUDENTS

| | |
|---|---|
| Total undergrad enrollment | 1,544 |
| % male/female | 76/24 |
| % from out of state | 51 |
| % from public high school | 71 |
| % live on campus | 70 |
| % in (# of) fraternities | 19 (7) |
| % in (# of) sororities | 10 (3) |
| % African American | 6 |
| % Asian | 16 |
| % Caucasian | 47 |
| % Hispanic | 8 |
| % international | 11 |

### SURVEY SAYS . . .
Ethnic diversity on campus
Different students interact
Everyone loves Chicago, IL
Low cost of living
Great off-campus food
Unattractive campus
Very little drug use
Musical organizations aren't popular
Students are not very happy
No one plays intramural sports

## ACADEMICS

| | |
|---|---|
| Academic Rating | 77 |
| Calendar | semester |
| Student/faculty ratio | 12:1 |
| Profs interesting rating | 90 |
| Profs accessible rating | 90 |
| % profs teaching UG courses | 74 |
| Avg lab size | 10-19 students |
| Avg reg class size | 10-19 students |

### MOST POPULAR MAJORS
Architecture (BArch, BA/BS, MArch, MA/MS, PhD)
Computer science
Electrical and computer engineering

## STUDENTS SPEAK OUT

### Academics
Like most engineering institutions, Illinois Institute of Technology "is an intense school." Undergrads appreciate the fact that studies "are very good and career-oriented" and that "even though we are small and [aren't] that well known, we have a very challenging and strong engineering curriculum." Hoping to give its student body a leg up in the working world, IIT requires undergraduates to complete two Interprofessional Projects before graduation. IPROs, as they're known at IIT, bring together undergraduate and graduate students from different academic disciplines to complete a task as a team. Recent IPROs have ranged from designing a new football stadium for the Chicago Bears to improving automated patient monitoring and diagnosis systems. In its efforts to create well-rounded students, IIT requires a wide array of courses in the humanities, writing, and social and behavioral sciences. Do students appreciate these efforts on their behalf? Well, some of the students we spoke to didn't think so. Although they appreciate the value of their academic programs, students find fault with several aspects of the school. They complain that "most professors don't utilize the small class sizes for discussions—they seem to enjoy lecturing too much," and that the administration could do more to involve students and their opinions. Most of all, they gripe about the advising system: "There is no proper guidance to choose the right courses pertaining to the interest of each student," writes a typical student.

### Life
Academic demands encroach a lot on social life at IIT, to the dissatisfaction of many. Writes one typically disgruntled student: "Homework dominates our lives. We do homework all the time, including weekends." Adds another, "You really have to work in order to get involved. Classes require a lot of time and leave little left to do fun stuff." Of the campus itself, most of which was designed by legendary architect Ludwig Mies Van der Rohe, making it one of the 100 top travel destinations of the new millenium by *Travel & Leisure Magazine*. As one student explains life on campus, "Being involved in a fraternity has been pretty fun for me. There are also a lot of opportunities to participate in a variety of student organizations. IIT has attracted some big-name entertainment for its size . . . which is cool." Adds another, "Life in the dorms is quite fun. On weekends we [usually] have movies in the lounge." Most students try to get off campus as often as possible. The El, Chicago's version of a subway system, "runs through campus, so we have access to everything that Chicago has to offer."

### Student Body
The "very diverse and intelligent" students of IIT inhabit "a very international campus," prompting one student to exclaim that "I've made friends with people from all over the world!" Some students report, however, that "to some degree cultures split off into their own groups," making interaction somewhat more difficult. Exacerbating the situation is the fact that "this school doesn't have enough facilities to get together. It makes it hard to get to know other students." Men and women alike agree that "more women are needed at this school!"

# ILLINOIS INSTITUTE OF TECHNOLOGY

FINANCIAL AID: 312-567-3025 • E-MAIL: ADMISSION@IIT.EDU • WEBSITE: WWW.IIT.EDU

## ADMISSIONS
*Very important factors considered include:* secondary school record, standardized test scores. *Important factors considered include:* character/personal qualities, class rank, essays, recommendations. *Other factors considered include:* alumni/ae relation, extracurricular activities, interview, talent/ability, volunteer work, work experience. SAT I or ACT required. TOEFL required of all international applicants. High school diploma is required and GED is not accepted. *High school units required/recommended:* 4 English required, 4 math required, 3 science required, 2 science lab required, 2 social studies required.

### The Inside Word
IIT's applicant pool is small and includes a strong element of self-selection. This means the majority get in, but not without solid academic preparation. While the committee evaluates other criteria, the bottom line is that candidates need fairly solid grades and better than average test scores in order to get admitted.

## FINANCIAL AID
*Students should submit:* FAFSA. The Princeton Review suggests that all financial aid forms be submitted as soon as possible after January 1. *Need-based scholarships/grants offered:* Pell, SEOG, state scholarships/grants, private scholarships, the school's own gift aid. *Loan aid offered:* FFEL Subsidized Stafford, FFEL Unsubsidized Stafford, FFEL PLUS, Federal Perkins, college/university loans from institutional funds. Federal Work-Study Program available. Institutional employment available. Applicants will be notified of awards on a rolling basis beginning on or about March 1. Off-campus job opportunities are excellent.

## FROM THE ADMISSIONS OFFICE
"IIT is committed to providing students with the highest caliber education through dedicated teachers, small class sizes, and undergraduate research opportunities. Classes are taught by senior faculty—not teaching assistants—who bring first-hand research experience into daily class discussion. The university's diverse student population mirrors the global work environment faced by all graduates. IIT promotes a unique interdisciplinary approach to learning. Students experience team-based, creative problem solving through two required Interprofessional Projects (IPROs). Our entrepreneurship program challenges students to develop start-up technology companies. The Leadership Academy teaches leadership skills that advance students in their personal and professional development. IIT's location in one of the nation's great cities affords many opportunities for internships and employment. A new campus center and student residence hall opening in 2003 will provide exciting new living and campus life opportunities."

## SELECTIVITY

| | |
|---|---|
| Admissions Rating | 84 |
| # of applicants | 2,269 |
| % of applicants accepted | 67 |
| % of acceptees attending | 24 |

### FRESHMAN PROFILE
| | |
|---|---|
| Range SAT Verbal | 550-650 |
| Average SAT Verbal | 602 |
| Range SAT Math | 630-730 |
| Average SAT Math | 681 |
| Range ACT Composite | 26-31 |
| Average ACT Composite | 28 |
| Minimum TOEFL | 550 |
| Average HS GPA | 3.6 |
| % graduated top 10% of class | 70 |
| % graduated top 25% of class | 74 |
| % graduated top 50% of class | 94 |

### DEADLINES
| | |
|---|---|
| Nonfall registration? | yes |

### APPLICANTS ALSO LOOK AT
Purdue
U of Illinois at Urbana-Champaign
Northwestern
MIT

**AND SOMETIMES PREFER**
Georgia Tech
Case Western Reserve
Milwaukee School of Engineering
Marquette

**AND RARELY PREFER**
DePaul
U of Illinois at Chicago

## FINANCIAL FACTS

| | |
|---|---|
| Financial Aid Rating | 82 |
| Tuition | $19,775 |
| Room and board | $6,282 |
| Books and supplies | $1,000 |
| Required fees | $556 |
| % frosh receiving aid | 63 |
| % undergrads receiving aid | 54 |
| Avg frosh grant | $14,695 |
| Avg frosh loan | $7,534 |

# ILLINOIS WESLEYAN UNIVERSITY

PO Box 2900, Bloomington, IL 61720 • Admissions: 309-556-3031 • Fax: 309-556-3411

## CAMPUS LIFE

| | |
|---|---|
| Quality of Life Rating | 74 |
| Type of school | private |
| Affiliation | Methodist |
| Environment | suburban |

### STUDENTS

| | |
|---|---|
| Total undergrad enrollment | 2,107 |
| % male/female | 43/57 |
| % from out of state | 11 |
| % from public high school | 82 |
| % live on campus | 82 |
| % in (# of) fraternities | 30 (6) |
| % in (# of) sororities | 41 (5) |
| % African American | 3 |
| % Asian | 3 |
| % Caucasian | 88 |
| % Hispanic | 2 |
| % international | 2 |
| # of countries represented | 22 |

### SURVEY SAYS . . .
Athletic facilities are great
Frats and sororities dominate social scene
Very little drug use
Everyone loves the Titans
Theater is hot
Musical organizations are hot
(Almost) no one listens to college radio
Students get along with local community

## ACADEMICS

| | |
|---|---|
| Academic Rating | 84 |
| Calendar | other |
| Student/faculty ratio | 12:1 |
| Profs interesting rating | 94 |
| Profs accessible rating | 94 |
| % profs teaching UG courses | 100 |
| Avg lab size | 10-19 students |
| Avg reg class size | 10-19 students |

### MOST POPULAR MAJORS
Business administration/management
Biology/biological sciences
Music performance

## STUDENTS SPEAK OUT

### Academics
Through aggressive expansion of its facilities, the "constantly building and improving" Illinois Wesleyan has transformed itself in the last decade from a well-respected regional school to a nationally renowned university; the newest additions include a library and campus center. At the same time, IWU has remained committed to maintaining a moderate-size student body, and as a result, students here feel they get the best of both worlds. "It's just the right size: enough people but small enough that the personal attention and benefits are huge," explains one undergrad. Says another, "The reason I decided to go to this school is because I knew that I could participate in a variety of activities, and that I could work first-hand with professors." Facilities "are incredible. For a school of its size, Illinois Wesleyan has one of the best science/academic facilities in the nation." Professors "are generally really cool: interesting, knowledgeable, and real. They remember their students, even from 25 years ago. I get teased by one professor because he had my dad and recognized the name." Reports one student, "Profs have stayed past midnight in study groups when we needed help. One even came back after a tuxedo dinner and was helping us in full attire!" Students gripe that "grading is way too tough. It is extremely hard at this school to get an A," but concede that "academically, Illinois Wesleyan challenges you to be the best and does it in a way that isn't discouraging. Smaller class sizes and more attention from the professors help students become more excited about their work." Among the school's innovative offerings is May Term, which one student describes as "the best part of our academic program. It provides amazing experiential learning opportunities. Through May Term, I have traveled to eastern Europe, the Democratic National Convention, and backpacked in the Appalachians."

### Life
IWU students describe a low-key but enjoyable social scene, reporting that "people at this school are hard workers and put a lot into their studies. Naturally, however, the weekends are filled with parties and dances, mostly involving fraternities and sororities. There are a lot of really good co-curricular programs, too." Agrees one undergrad, "During the week, studying is the social life, in between trips to Denny's. It's not bad, though; everyone here wants to learn, but is laid-back enough that we can still do crazy stuff like steal someone's mattress and put it outside." Intercollegiate sports "are big here: our basketball games are always packed (we won the Division III championship a few years ago)." So too are student clubs and organizations and guest lectures. Writes one student, "There is always something going on, from speakers to workshops to athletics to parties. We know how to have fun." Because "the town of Bloomington-Normal is very boring," students soon discover that "most people stay on campus for activities and entertainment." When they leave, they "either go to Chicago or to Illinois State University, which is right down the street."

### Student Body
IWU students enjoy a "highly friendly atmosphere on campus," although students are also "very cliquey between Greek houses and theater, music, and other groups." The small minority populations here benefit from a support network that includes the Black Student Union, the Council of Latin American Student Enrichment, and an on-campus Multicultural Center. Still, minority students report that "being a minority student here is like you're always under someone's microscope." Agrees a white student, "Most of the students, myself included, are spoiled white middle-class suburbia. The real downfall is their narrow-minded prejudices due to a lack of exposure to diversity." Students' similarity in background fosters the "Wesleyan bubble," a sense that life begins and ends at the campus gates.

# ILLINOIS WESLEYAN UNIVERSITY

FINANCIAL AID: 309-556-3096 • E-MAIL: IWUADMIT@TITAN.IWU.EDU • WEBSITE: WWW.IWU.EDU

## ADMISSIONS

*Very important factors considered include:* secondary school record. *Important factors considered include:* character/personal qualities, class rank, essays, recommendations, standardized test scores, talent/ability. *Other factors considered include:* alumni/ae relation, extracurricular activities, geographical residence, interview, minority status, volunteer work, work experience. SAT I or ACT required. TOEFL required of all international applicants. High school diploma or GED is required. *High school units required/recommended:* 4 English recommended, 3 math recommended, 3 science recommended, 2 science lab recommended, 3 foreign language recommended, 2 social studies recommended.

## The Inside Word

Illinois Wesleyan is selective enough that serious candidates should exceed the suggested curriculum requirements in order to improve their chances for admission.

## FINANCIAL AID

*Students should submit:* FAFSA, institution's own financial aid form, CSS/Financial Aid PROFILE, business/farm supplement. Regular filing deadline is March 1. The Princeton Review suggests that all financial aid forms be submitted as soon as possible after January 1. *Need-based scholarships/grants offered:* Pell, SEOG, state scholarships/grants, private scholarships, the school's own gift aid. *Loan aid offered:* FFEL Subsidized Stafford, FFEL Unsubsidized Stafford, FFEL PLUS, Federal Perkins, Federal Nursing, college/university loans from institutional funds. Federal Work-Study Program available. Institutional employment available. Applicants will be notified of awards on a rolling basis beginning on or about January 1. Off-campus job opportunities are good.

## FROM THE ADMISSIONS OFFICE

"Illinois Wesleyan University attracts a wide array of multitalented students—students interested in pursuing diverse fields like vocal performance and biology, psychology and German, or physics and business administration. At IWU, students are not forced into 'either/or' choices. Rather, they are encouraged to pursue multiple interests simultaneously—a philosophy in keeping with the spirit and value of a liberal arts education. The distinctive 4-4-1 calendar allows students to follow their interests each school year in two semesters followed by an optional month-long class in May. May Term opportunities include classes on campus; research collaboration with faculty; travel and study in such places as Australia, China, South Africa, and Europe; as well as local, national, and international internships.

"At Illinois Wesleyan, we assume the mind is the key to an educated person; thus, we hope to foster during the college years the knowledge, values, and skills that will sustain a lifetime of learning. We prepare our students for responsible citizenship and leadership in a democratic society and global community. Above all, whatever their course of studies, we wish to enable Illinois Wesleyan University graduates to lead useful, creative, fully realized lives."

### SELECTIVITY

| | |
|---|---|
| Admissions Rating | 91 |
| # of applicants | 3,116 |
| % of applicants accepted | 48 |
| % of acceptees attending | 39 |
| # accepting a place on wait list | 156 |

#### FRESHMAN PROFILE
| | |
|---|---|
| Range SAT Verbal | 580-670 |
| Average SAT Verbal | 635 |
| Range SAT Math | 590-690 |
| Average SAT Math | 625 |
| Range ACT Composite | 26-30 |
| Average ACT Composite | 28 |
| Minimum TOEFL | 550 |
| % graduated top 10% of class | 47 |
| % graduated top 25% of class | 83 |
| % graduated top 50% of class | 100 |

#### DEADLINES
| | |
|---|---|
| Priority admission | 11/1 |
| Regular admission | 2/15 |
| Nonfall registration? | yes |

#### APPLICANTS ALSO LOOK AT AND OFTEN PREFER
Washington U
U of Illinois at Urbana Campaign
Northwestern
U of Chicago
Notre Dame

#### AND SOMETIMES PREFER
Indiana U at Bloomington
DePauw
Augustana
Illinois State

#### AND RARELY PREFER
Eastern Illinois
Bradley
Southern Illinois U at Edwardsville

### FINANCIAL FACTS

| | |
|---|---|
| Financial Aid Rating | 87 |
| Tuition | $24,390 |
| Room and board | $5,840 |
| Books and supplies | $650 |
| Required fees | $150 |
| % frosh receiving aid | 56 |
| % undergrads receiving aid | 54 |
| Avg frosh grant | $11,835 |
| Avg frosh loan | $2,816 |

# INDIANA UNIVERSITY—BLOOMINGTON

300 NORTH JORDAN AVENUE, BLOOMINGTON, IN 47405-1106 • ADMISSIONS: 812-855-0661 • FAX: 812-855-5102

## CAMPUS LIFE

| | |
|---|---|
| Quality of Life Rating | 85 |
| Type of school | public |
| Environment | suburban |

### STUDENTS

| | |
|---|---|
| Total undergrad enrollment | 30,752 |
| % male/female | 44/56 |
| % from out of state | 36 |
| % live on campus | 43 |
| % in (# of) fraternities | 16 (30) |
| % in (# of) sororities | 18 (25) |
| % African American | 4 |
| % Asian | 3 |
| % Caucasian | 90 |
| % Hispanic | 2 |
| % international | 4 |

### SURVEY SAYS . . .
Campus is beautiful
Lots of beer drinking
Athletic facilities are great
(Almost) everyone smokes
Everyone loves the Hoosiers
Great library
Great computer facilities
Frats and sororities dominate social scene
Hard liquor is popular
Students are happy

## ACADEMICS

| | |
|---|---|
| Academic Rating | 72 |
| Calendar | semester |
| Student/faculty ratio | 20:1 |
| Avg lab size | 20-29 students |
| Avg reg class size | 20-29 students |

### MOST POPULAR MAJORS
Business administration/management
Elementary education and teaching
Biological and biomedical sciences

## STUDENTS SPEAK OUT

### Academics
Students appreciate the near-limitless choices available at Indiana University. As one student puts it, "There's a major for everything here. You could probably major in tying your shoes if you wanted to." As at most large universities, "you really have to get into student activities or organizations and establish your community here. Otherwise, you'll get lost and become just a number." Some note encouragingly that "although IU is a very big school with some large classes, discussion classes are made to give students the opportunity to get questions answered and discuss subject matter one-on-one." Students also report that class sizes get smaller once one clears his or her intro courses; writes one, "I really like my upper-level classes the best. Just hang in there through all those 100- and 200-level classes!" Interesting note: IU is famed for having the smallest number of large lecture halls, only two classrooms that can fit 400 max; definitely a good thing! Professors here "don't really seek you out individually, but once you go to them, they are extremely open, friendly, and helpful. Use the office hours!" Students are more critical of the administration. While they acknowledge that "IU is a giant bureaucracy with over 30,000 students—there has to be some law and order," they also complain that "it's very hard when you have a problem with something that you can't fix yourself, like parking, personal computers problems, etc. The administration will transfer you here and there and put you on hold or tell you there is nothing that can be done."

### Life
At a school as large as IU, students agree that "life can be whatever you want it to be. And that's the bottom line. You can be a . . . partier, at the bars every night dancing and whoopin' it up . . . . You can go to massive house parties. . . . You can stay at home [and] watch movies with a group of friends. You can go to the mall and go out to eat. You can go to a coffee shop, smoke, and listen to music. You can study in any one of the libraries. You can join all sorts of clubs and organizations (including the Greek system). You can do whatever you want, really. And you should be able to find people to do it with." Sports are very popular here; writes one student, "One of the most exciting things to do is attend the basketball games. The fans here are the best, and IU definitely [is] basketball-oriented." Student complaints center on the town of Bloomington ("Sometimes it seems all there is to do is party because Bloomington is such a small town") and the school's alcohol policy ("ridiculous, and completely unreasonable for a college campus—we are dry, or at least are supposed to be. There is less tolerance for alcohol than for abusive coaches!").

### Student Body
"I love the students at IU because they are so diverse! IU has something like 35,000 [actually 30,000 undergraduate] students and they are all different! I have met people of all different races, from countries I've never even heard of, and with all different religious beliefs and sexual orientations. It has really made me aware of different cultures and life choices," crows one student. Others disagree, however, like one who believes that while "the majority of people here are very friendly," the population "is very divided [by] race, Greeks/non-Greeks, and majors. There is not a lot of intermixing unless you are in a leadership position, when you get to meet others and work with others." Independents observe that "there do tend to be a fair amount of rich snobby people, especially in the Greek system." As for students of different races, "there is some sort of divide made by the students. Though I notice it, it isn't a big deal. Everyone does their own thing."

# INDIANA UNIVERSITY—BLOOMINGTON

FINANCIAL AID: 812-855-0321 • E-MAIL: IUADMIT@INDIANA.EDU • WEBSITE: WWW.ADMIT.INDIANA.EDU

## ADMISSIONS

The typical freshman at Indiana successfully completed 18 to 19 year-long academic courses in high school. Students are strongly encouraged to apply for admission if they have been taking four to five academic classes each year in a balanced program and earned above-average grades in those classes. *Other factors considered include* class rank, grade trends, and SAT or ACT results. The TOEFL is required of all international School of Music applicants and non-native speakers of English who wish to be considered for limited merit scholarships and/or an invitation to the Honors College. *The admissions office says:* "Students should establish a solid foundation at the high school level in English (4 years required), laboratory sciences (minimum 1 year), social sciences (minimum 2 years), and mathematics, including algebra II and trigonometry (minimum 3 years total required) to be prepared for any academic program at Indiana University. Foreign language is strongly recommended but not required for admission."

### The Inside Word

A high volume of applicants makes Indiana's individual admissions review process relatively selective for a university of its size. Candidates to the School of Music face a highly selective audition process.

## FINANCIAL AID

*Students should submit:* FAFSA. The Princeton Review suggests that all financial aid forms be submitted as soon as possible after January 1. *Need-based scholarships/grants offered:* Pell, SEOG, state scholarships/grants, private scholarships, the school's own gift aid. *Loan aid offered:* Subsidized Stafford, Unsubsidized Stafford, PLUS, Federal Perkins. Federal Work-Study Program available. Institutional employment available. Applicants will be notified of awards on a rolling basis beginning on or about April 1. Off-campus job opportunities are excellent.

## FROM THE ADMISSIONS OFFICE

"Indiana University—Bloomington, one of America's great teaching and research universities, extends learning and teaching beyond the walls of the traditional classroom. When visiting campus, students and parents typically describe IU as 'what a college should look and feel like.' Students bring their diverse experiences, beliefs, and backgrounds from all 50 states and 136 countries, which adds a richness and diversity to life at IU—a campus often cited as one of the most beautiful in the nation. Indiana University—Bloomington truly offers a quintessential college town, campus, and overall experience. Students enjoy all of the advantages, opportunities, and resources that a larger school can offer, while still receiving personal attention and support. *Time* magazine named IU its 'College of the Year' among research universities based on the outstanding programs offered to help freshmen succeed. Because of the variety of outstanding academic and cultural resources, students at IU have the best of both worlds.

"Indiana offers more than 5,000 courses and more than 100 undergraduate programs, with many known nationally and internationally. IU—Bloomington is known worldwide for outstanding programs in the arts, sciences, humanities, and social sciences as well as for highly rated schools of business, music, education, journalism, optometry, public and environmental affairs, and health, physical education, and recreation. Students can customize academic programs with double and individualized majors, internships, and research opportunities, while utilizing state-of-the-art technology at one of *Yahoo! Internet Life* magazine's top five 'most wired colleges.' Representatives from more than 1,000 businesses, government agencies, and not-for-profit organizations come to campus each year to recruit IU students."

### SELECTIVITY

| | |
|---|---|
| Admissions Rating | 75 |
| # of applicants | 21,264 |
| % of applicants accepted | 81 |
| % of acceptees attending | 41 |

#### FRESHMAN PROFILE

| | |
|---|---|
| Range SAT Verbal | 490-600 |
| Average SAT Verbal | 543 |
| Range SAT Math | 500-610 |
| Average SAT Math | 556 |
| Range ACT Composite | 22-27 |
| Average ACT Composite | 24 |
| % graduated top 10% of class | 22 |
| % graduated top 25% of class | 52 |
| % graduated top 50% of class | 90 |

#### DEADLINES

| | |
|---|---|
| Priority admission | 2/1 |
| Nonfall registration? | yes |

#### APPLICANTS ALSO LOOK AT AND OFTEN PREFER
Notre Dame U
U of Illinois at Urbana-Champaign
U of Michigan

#### AND SOMETIMES PREFER
U of Wisconsin at Madison
Miami of Ohio
Purdue

### FINANCIAL FACTS

| | |
|---|---|
| Financial Aid Rating | 80 |
| In-state tuition | $4,573 |
| Out-of-state tuition | $15,184 |
| Room and board | $5,676 |
| Books and supplies | $740 |
| Required fees | $742 |
| % frosh receiving aid | 42 |
| % undergrads receiving aid | 37 |
| Avg frosh grant | $4,530 |
| Avg frosh loan | $5,712 |

# INDIANA UNIVERSITY OF PENNSYLVANIA

216 PRATT HALL, INDIANA, PA 15705 • ADMISSIONS: 724-357-2230 • FAX: 724-357-6281

## CAMPUS LIFE

| | |
|---|---|
| Quality of Life Rating | 80 |
| Type of school | public |
| Environment | suburban |

### STUDENTS

| | |
|---|---|
| Total undergrad enrollment | 11,834 |
| % male/female | 44/56 |
| % from out of state | 3 |
| % from public high school | 95 |
| % live on campus | 32 |
| % in (# of) fraternities | 10 (19) |
| % in (# of) sororities | 11 (14) |
| % African American | 6 |
| % Asian | 1 |
| % Caucasian | 91 |
| % Hispanic | 1 |
| % international | 2 |
| # of countries represented | 71 |

### SURVEY SAYS . . .
Lots of beer drinking
(Almost) everyone smokes
Hard liquor is popular
Frats and sororities dominate social scene
Registration is a breeze
Student newspaper is popular
Great off-campus food
Students are happy

## ACADEMICS

| | |
|---|---|
| Academic Rating | 81 |
| Calendar | semester |
| Student/faculty ratio | 17:1 |
| % profs teaching UG courses | 100 |
| Avg reg class size | 20-29 students |

### MOST POPULAR MAJORS
Communications studies/speech communication and rhetoric
Elementary education and teaching
Criminology

## STUDENTS SPEAK OUT

### Academics

The Robert E. Cook Honors College is what distinguishes Indiana University of Pennsylvania from your typical big-box state university. Reports one honors student, "The Honors College allows students to take interesting discussion-based classes instead of the standard liberal studies freshman classes. These honor classes are never lecture-based, and have made me a much better writer and thinker." Students' only complaint about the honors program concerns its limited scope; as one student told us, "My academic experience has been pretty good; however, there needs to be more honors courses and an honors program in each academic college." Beyond the Honors College, "the rest of the university is pretty much only concerned with partying." While profs "are easily accessible and encouraging," they face "a huge obstacle: a student body with too much laziness." Since the Honors College covers only some of students' course work, all students must take at least some courses outside the college. Reports one student, "Required classes are large, freakishly easy, and completely made up of lecture time. . . . My honors classes are absolutely excellent, with discussion 60 percent of the time." Even so, IUP offers plenty of challenges to those willing to step up to the plate. Sums up one undergrad, "IUP might not have ten sets of all the newest equipment, but it does train me in everything I need to know and gives me additional chances to learn outside of the school through its numerous internship and study abroad programs."

### Life

Hometown Indiana, students at IUP tell us, "is not the place for city people who like a lot of excitement and nightclubs." The town "offers a myriad of bars but very little else." it is the birthplace of film legend Jimmy Stewart, and many here feel "it could very well be named 'Jimmy Stewart-ville' for all the paraphernalia: the Jimmy Stewart Museum, the sign coming into town proclaiming that Indiana, Pennsylvania, is the birthplace of Jimmy Stewart, and the showings of *It's a Wonderful Life* during the holidays at the local theater." Irreverent IUP undergrads occasionally "steal away in the middle of the night to put a dress and hat on the Jimmy Stewart statue, which proudly stands in front of the courthouse," giving you some idea of how little else there is to do here. Students tell us IUP was once a big party school but that "life in general at IUP is changing. They have increased the police force in order to better enforce drug and alcohol laws." To fill the void, "IUP offers many student organizations and musical events . . . from an anime club to equestrian team to dance squad to sororities and fraternities. If you have an interest, IUP is a good place to pursue it." Otherwise, students seek quiet entertainment of their own devising or, more often, pack up and go home when their last class ends. Pittsburgh is only an hour's drive.

### Student Body

With over 11,000 undergraduates, "there are students from all walks of life here at IUP. . . . The majority are related by the fact that they come from a middling-income family . . . and are here to get the best education they can for their dollar." Many "are from within a 60-mile radius of the school," an area that is "very conservative Christian and not generally accepting of liberal viewpoints." IUP also has "a large population of African Americans and foreign students from all around the world, like Asia, Africa, and Europe." Students warn, however, "There is a visual segregation between the African American community and the rest of the campus." Most here "are more concerned with getting a job and money than being educated," according to their critics.

290 ■ THE BEST 351 COLLEGES

# INDIANA UNIVERSITY OF PENNSYLVANIA

FINANCIAL AID: 415-357-2218  E-MAIL: ADMISSIONS_INQUIRY@GROVE.IUP.EDU  WEBSITE: WWW.IUP.EDU

## ADMISSIONS

*Very important factors considered include:* secondary school record, talent/ability. *Important factors considered include:* class rank, standardized test scores. *Other factors considered include:* alumni/ae relation, character/personal qualities, essays, extracurricular activities, geographical residence, interview, recommendations, state residency, volunteer work, work experience. SAT I or ACT required; SAT I preferred. TOEFL required of all international applicants. High school diploma or GED is required. *High school units required/recommended:* 16 total recommended; 4 English recommended, 3 math recommended, 3 science recommended, 2 foreign language recommended, 2 social studies recommended, 1 history recommended, 1 elective recommended.

### The Inside Word

IUP is impressive in many ways and should command more attention than it does. As a state school, it provides Pennsylvania residents with a great education at a rock-bottom price. Students applying to IUP with an average academic record will have little trouble getting admitted. Once on campus, students will find an unexpectedly diverse population hailing from many states and countries.

## FINANCIAL AID

*Students should submit:* FAFSA. Regular filing deadline is April 15. The Princeton Review suggests that all financial aid forms be submitted as soon as possible after January 1. *Need-based scholarships/grants offered:* Pell, SEOG, state scholarships/grants, private scholarships, the school's own gift aid. *Loan aid offered:* FFEL Subsidized Stafford, FFEL Unsubsidized Stafford, FFEL PLUS, Federal Perkins, private alternative loans. Federal Work-Study Program available. Institutional employment available. Applicants will be notified of awards on a rolling basis beginning on or about April 15. Off-campus job opportunities are fair.

### ADMISSIONS

| | |
|---|---:|
| Admissions Rating | 78 |
| # of applicants | 8,005 |
| % of applicants accepted | 54 |
| % of acceptees attending | 64 |

### FRESHMAN PROFILE

| | |
|---|---:|
| Range SAT Verbal | 480-580 |
| Average SAT Verbal | 534 |
| Range SAT Math | 480-570 |
| Average SAT Math | 528 |
| Minimum TOEFL | 500 |
| % graduated top 10% of class | 17 |
| % graduated top 25% of class | 44 |
| % graduated top 50% of class | 77 |

### DEADLINES

| | |
|---|---:|
| Priority admission | 12/31 |
| Nonfall registration? | yes |

### APPLICANTS ALSO LOOK AT AND OFTEN PREFER
Carnegie Mellon
Amherst
Yale
Harvard
Princeton

### AND SOMETIMES PREFER
U Pittsburgh
Penn State
Junaita
Bucknell
Cornell U

### AND RARELY PREFER
Kent State
Clarion U of Pennsylvania
Duquesne U
Millersville U of Pennsylvania

### FINANCIAL FACTS

| | |
|---|---:|
| Financial Aid Rating | 82 |
| In-state tuition | $4,378 |
| Out-of-state tuition | $10,946 |
| Room and board | $4,524 |
| Books and supplies | $800 |
| Required fees | $1,163 |
| % frosh receiving aid | 64 |
| % undergrads receiving aid | 64 |
| Avg frosh grant | $3,682 |
| Avg frosh loan | $2,573 |

THE BEST 351 COLLEGES ■ 291

# IOWA STATE UNIVERSITY

100 ALUMNI HALL, AMES, IA 50011-2011 • ADMISSIONS: 515-294-5836 • FAX: 515-294-2592

## CAMPUS LIFE

| | |
|---|---|
| Quality of Life Rating | 78 |
| Type of school | public |
| Environment | urban |

### STUDENTS
| | |
|---|---|
| Total undergrad enrollment | 22,999 |
| % male/female | 56/44 |
| % from out of state | 19 |
| % from public high school | 93 |
| % live on campus | 35 |
| % in (# of) fraternities | 13 (31) |
| % in (# of) sororities | 12 (18) |
| % African American | 3 |
| % Asian | 3 |
| % Caucasian | 87 |
| % Hispanic | 2 |
| % international | 4 |
| # of countries represented | 117 |

### SURVEY SAYS . . .
Campus is beautiful
Everyone loves the Wildcats
Lots of beer drinking
Athletic facilities are great
Great library
Campus easy to get around
(Almost) everyone plays intramural sports
Great computer facilities
Student newspaper is popular
Frats and sororities dominate social scene

## ACADEMICS

| | |
|---|---|
| Academic Rating | 69 |
| Calendar | semester |
| Student/faculty ratio | 16:1 |
| % profs teaching UG courses | 86 |
| % classes taught by TAs | 17 |
| Avg lab size | 20-29 students |
| Avg reg class size | 20-29 students |

### MOST POPULAR MAJORS
Management information systems
Elementary education and teaching
Mechanical engineering

## STUDENTS SPEAK OUT
### Academics
Undergraduates are drawn to Iowa State by a number of standout programs (engineering, design, agriculture, and journalism, to name a few) and its low tuition, especially for native Iowans. Like many state schools, ISU is "trying to get by with huge budget cuts"; the school's efforts to address budget shortfalls have included substantial tuition increases. Despite the still-reasonable price of an ISU education, undergrads here are not happy about the situation. Gripes one, "Tuition has been spiraling out of control." Compounding students' financial frustration are large classes ("I have six classes this semester and four of them have over 200 students in them, plus I have only one class that is under 50. That's just too big") and registration woes. Those who seek a hand-holding atmosphere, be forewarned: "Research is the purpose of Iowa State. There are a lot of excellent extension publications and extension specialists for your reference on most any subject. However, this also means that a lot of the professors don't seem to care about teaching. They are more interested in their research." While students grouse, they also understand that the university is doing the best it can in a bad financial situation; furthermore, they are not blind to the school's many assets. "Technical majors are very heavily recruited here, which makes it easier to get a job," writes one engineer. Another student points out that the Honors Program offers "smaller sections of most classes. . . . The [Honors] professors are accessible, helpful, and seem genuinely interested in teaching."

### Life
The distinguishing trait of ISU campus life, students tell us, is "the strong sense of community. I've always been amazed at how close-knit the school manages to be with [23,000] undergraduates; it's the best of both worlds because we have the feel of a small college but the resources of a large university." Those resources mean that "there is something for everyone here. There are over 500 clubs and organizations." Undergrads love their "nationally recognized football, wrestling, hockey, and men's and women's basketball" teams, as well as "plentiful intramural opportunities [and] the largest broomball participation in the country." Campus bustles most noticeably "in the spring and fall, [when] most people hang around central campus or the yards by the dorms. In the winter, there are hockey and basketball games and stuff to do on campus sometimes. Winter is more boring than the warmer months." But when a Cyclone team isn't playing, "the big thing here is drinking." Students say, "There are plenty of bars . . . with plenty of specials during the week." Alternatives for the under-21 set include "a dollar theatre at the mall for those students that don't mind seeing old movies," "ample places to eat, a nice mall, lots of places to run and road races to participate in, and many bike paths. Also, Des Moines is only 20 minutes away." Finally, "the Greek system is really popular at ISU."

### Student Body
How diverse is the Iowa State student body? It depends on which yardstick you use. "Iowa State does have a diverse student population by Iowa standards, but to someone outside of Iowa it might not seem so very diverse," explains one student, who continued: "There is a very large and active lesbian, gay, bisexual, transgender group. [There are also] many students who tend to be somewhat close-minded about gays and tend to be more religious than students at other schools." Most here are "pretty small town–oriented, and Ames is a big town for them." They are "generally warm and friendly, appreciate the fact that they are at a great university, and respect other students." They also "don't spend a whole lot of time thinking about academics." ISU has "a large international student population who fit in well with the rest of the student body"; among these students is "a large population of East Asian students and, in the computer science department particularly, many people from India as well."

# IOWA STATE UNIVERSITY

FINANCIAL AID: 515-294-2223 • E-MAIL: ADMISSIONS@IASTATE.EDU • WEBSITE: WWW.IASTATE.EDU

## ADMISSIONS

*Very important factors considered include:* class rank, secondary school record, standardized test scores. *Other factors considered include:* character/personal qualities, essays, extracurricular activities, geographical residence, interview, recommendations, state residency, talent/ability, volunteer work, work experience. SAT I or ACT required. TOEFL required of all international applicants. High school diploma or GED is required. *High school units required/recommended:* 4 English required, 3 math required, 3 science required, 2 science lab required, 2 foreign language recommended, 2 social studies required, 3 social studies recommended.

## The Inside Word

With a decided lack of mystery in the admissions process and a super-high acceptance rate, Iowa State still attracts a solid student body. What we have here is living proof of the value of a good reputation and a little national press.

## FINANCIAL AID

*Students should submit:* FAFSA. No deadline for regular filing. The Princeton Review suggests that all financial aid forms be submitted as soon as possible after January 1. *Need-based scholarships/grants offered:* Pell, SEOG, state scholarships/grants, private scholarships, the school's own gift aid. *Loan aid offered:* Direct Subsidized Stafford, Direct Unsubsidized Stafford, Direct PLUS, Federal Perkins, state loans, college/university loans from institutional funds, private alternative loans. Federal Work-Study Program available. Institutional employment available. Applicants will be notified of awards on a rolling basis beginning on or about April 1. Off-campus job opportunities are excellent.

## FROM THE ADMISSIONS OFFICE

"Iowa State University offers all the advantages of a major university along with the friendliness and warmth of a residential campus. There are more than 100 undergraduate programs of study in the Colleges of Agriculture, Business, Design, Education, Engineering, Family and Consumer Sciences, Liberal Arts and Sciences, and Veterinary Medicine. Our 1,700 faculty members include Rhodes Scholars, Fulbright Scholars, and National Academy of Sciences and National Academy of Engineering members. Recognized for its high quality of life, Iowa State has taken practical steps to make the university a place where students feel like they belong. Iowa State has been recognized for the high quality of campus life and the exemplary out-of-class experiences offered to its students. Along with a strong academic experience, students also have opportunities for further developing their leadership skills and interpersonal relationships through any of the more than 500 student organizations, 60 intramural sports, and a multitude of arts and recreational activities. All residence hall rooms are wired for Internet connections and all students have the opportunity to create their own World Wide Web pages."

### SELECTIVITY

★ ★ ☆ ☆

| | |
|---|---|
| Admissions Rating | 76 |
| # of applicants | 10,370 |
| % of applicants accepted | 89 |
| % of acceptees attending | 46 |

### FRESHMAN PROFILE

| | |
|---|---|
| Range SAT Verbal | 510-650 |
| Average SAT Verbal | 590 |
| Range SAT Math | 550-670 |
| Average SAT Math | 620 |
| Range ACT Composite | 22-27 |
| Average ACT Composite | 24 |
| Minimum TOEFL | 500 |
| Average HS GPA | 3.5 |
| % graduated top 10% of class | 25 |
| % graduated top 25% of class | 58 |
| % graduated top 50% of class | 93 |

### DEADLINES

| | |
|---|---|
| Regular admission | 8/1 |
| Nonfall registration? | yes |

### APPLICANTS ALSO LOOK AT AND OFTEN PREFER

U. Iowa
U. Kansas
U. Northern Iowa

### AND SOMETIMES PREFER

U. Wisconsin—Madison
U. Michigan—Ann Arbor
Purdue U.—West Lafayette
U. Minnesota

### AND RARELY PREFER

Kansas State
Illinois State
Creighton

### FINANCIAL FACTS

| | |
|---|---|
| Financial Aid Rating | 83 |
| In-state tuition | $4,342 |
| Out-of-state tuition | $13,684 |
| Room and board | $5,020 |
| Books and supplies | $754 |
| Required fees | $686 |
| % frosh receiving aid | 57 |
| % undergrads receiving aid | 46 |
| Avg frosh grant | $4,260 |
| Avg frosh loan | $5,923 |

# ITHACA COLLEGE

100 JOB HALL, ITHACA, NY 14850-7020 • ADMISSIONS: 607-274-3124 • FAX: 607-274-1900

## CAMPUS LIFE

| | |
|---|---|
| Quality of Life Rating | 74 |
| Type of school | private |
| Environment | suburban |

### STUDENTS

| | |
|---|---|
| Total undergrad enrollment | 6,190 |
| % male/female | 43/57 |
| % from out of state | 51 |
| % from public high school | 85 |
| % live on campus | 70 |
| % in (# of) sororities | 2 (1) |
| % African American | 2 |
| % Asian | 3 |
| % Caucasian | 89 |
| % Hispanic | 3 |
| % international | 3 |
| # of countries represented | 76 |

### SURVEY SAYS . . .
Students love Ithaca, NY
Student government is popular
Lots of beer drinking
Great off-campus food
Student publications are popular
Great computer facilities
Very small frat/sorority scene
Musical organizations are hot
Diversity lacking on campus
Lab facilities need improving

## ACADEMICS

| | |
|---|---|
| Academic Rating | 76 |
| Calendar | semester |
| Student/faculty ratio | 12:1 |
| Profs interesting rating | 68 |
| Profs accessible rating | 77 |
| % profs teaching UG courses | 99 |
| % classes taught by TAs | 1 |
| Avg reg class size | 10-19 students |

### MOST POPULAR MAJORS
Mass communications/media studies
Music/music and performing arts studies
Business administration/management

## STUDENTS SPEAK OUT

### Academics
Students identify several standout programs at Ithaca College, the "other school" in the tiny upstate New York town. (It also happens to be home to Cornell University.) Music, theater, physical therapy, and communication (the latter of which "offers four years of hands-on experience, whereas most colleges only offer two years") are considered the finest the school has to offer. On these programs, students heap lavish praise. Writes one, "I absolutely love it here at IC. I mentioned that I was interested in becoming a drama therapist, and the school was more than helpful with arranging a double major. They even went above and beyond and helped me set up a drama therapy program, which I run at a local retirement home." Offers another, "As a music major, I am very pleased with my professors. Their knowledge in their field is impressive; they are very approachable and teach well. As for my liberal arts classes, I'm not as impressed. I've had a few excellent professors, but most seem about average." Students agree that "the professors are the best part of school. They are really here to help us learn, and the school puts value on hiring teachers that are good at teaching." They also report that "the school administration is a good one. However, there is a lot of bureaucracy to get anything done."

### Life
In a nutshell, "life at Ithaca is a college student's dream." Students proclaim that "there are plenty of things to do. Since the town houses two colleges, fun and unique bars and coffeehouses are around every hilly corner. The wine trails are always fun, and swimming and hiking around the 'gorge'ous waterfalls is practically a tradition. Lake Cayuga is fun to boat on, and certain festivals held in the Commons, like the popular Apple Harvest Festival, are sure to bring everyone (both locals and students) downtown together." Adds another undergrad, "The Ithaca Commons are an awesome place to go shopping or to find a huge array of good food, from all-American to more exotic cuisine. And the city has tons of culture (think plays, concerts, art galleries, and seminars in cooking, dancing, etc.)." Students report "a large amount of drinking that goes on here, but there are other things to do besides [that]." Students love athletics ("People are very interested in participating in sports, both intercollegiate and intramural") and outdoor activity ("The campus is located in some of the most beautiful nature to be found east of the Mississippi"). Despite IC's proximity to Cornell, "there isn't as much mingling between the two colleges as one might expect. Relations between the two are okay, but they could be better. They think of IC as the party school on the other hill; we think of them as a bunch of nerds that have no lives." Students can escape when necessary to more exotic locales, as they "are only hours away from Niagara Falls, Boston, Philadelphia, and New York City."

### Student Body
Ithaca draws its students from a relatively small demographic, according to student respondents. "If you are not from Massachusetts, Long Island, or New Jersey, you will not fit in," warns one. "Plus, if your parents make less than six figures, you are painfully made aware of the fact everyday. Many so-called 'snobs' [attend], but an okay amount of friendly people too." Students recognize that there is religious diversity here—"about one-third Jewish, one-third Catholic, and one-third Protestant"—and report that "as far as discrimination, it is not seen at Ithaca College. There is an especially large homosexual community that is very accepted by all, including a month of Gaypril to celebrate diversity." Students in the school's premier departments are considered serious and studious; others "have a social life as their primary focus instead of academics."

# ITHACA COLLEGE

FINANCIAL AID: 607-274-3131 • E-MAIL: ADMISSION@ITHACA.EDU • WEBSITE: WWW.ITHACA.EDU

## ADMISSIONS
*Very important factors considered include:* secondary school record, standardized test scores. *Important factors considered include:* character/personal qualities, class rank, essays, extracurricular activities, interview, recommendations, talent/ability. *Other factors considered include:* alumni/ae relation, volunteer work, work experience. SAT I or ACT required. TOEFL required of all international applicants. High school diploma or GED is required. *High school units required/recommended:* 16 total required; 4 English required, 3 math required, 3 science required, 2 foreign language required, 3 social studies required, 1 elective required.

### The Inside Word
Ithaca has enjoyed a renaissance of interest from prospective students of late, and its moderately competitive admissions profile has been bolstered as a result. In addition to a thorough review of academic accomplishments, candidates are always given close consideration of their personal background, talents, and achievements. Programs requiring an audition or portfolio review are among the college's most demanding for admission; the arts have always been particularly strong here.

## FINANCIAL AID
*Students should submit:* FAFSA. CSS/Financial Aid PROFILE is required of early decision applicants and must be submitted by November 1. The Princeton Review suggests that all regular financial aid forms be submitted as soon as possible after January 1. *Need-based scholarships/grants offered:* Pell, SEOG, state scholarships/grants, private scholarships, the school's own gift aid. *Loan aid offered:* FFEL Subsidized Stafford, FFEL Unsubsidized Stafford, FFEL PLUS, Federal Perkins, college/university loans from institutional funds. Federal Work-Study Program available. Institutional employment available. Applicants will be notified of awards on a rolling basis beginning on or about March 15. Off-campus job opportunities are good.

## FROM THE ADMISSIONS OFFICE
"Ithaca College was founded in 1892 as a music conservatory and today continues that commitment to performance and excellence. Its modern, residential, 750-acre campus, equipped with state-of-the-art facilities, is home to the Schools of Business, Communications, Health Sciences and Human Performance, Humanities and Sciences, and Music. With more than 100 majors—from biochemistry to business administration, journalism to jazz, philosophy to physical therapy, and with upper-division programs in Rochester, Los Angeles, and London—students get the curricular opportunities of a large university in a personalized smaller college environment. Ithaca's students benefit from an education that emphasizes hands-on learning, collaborative student-faculty research, and development of the whole student. Located in central New York's spectacular Finger Lakes region in what many consider the classic college town, Ithaca College offers 25 highly competitive varsity teams, more than 140 campus clubs, and two radio stations and a television station, as well as hundreds of concerts, recitals, and theater performances annually."

### SELECTIVITY

| | |
|---|---|
| Admissions Rating | 83 |
| # of applicants | 11,305 |
| % of applicants accepted | 56 |
| % of acceptees attending | 24 |
| # of early decision applicants | 309 |
| % accepted early decision | 50 |

### FRESHMAN PROFILE
| | |
|---|---|
| Range SAT Verbal | 540-630 |
| Average SAT Verbal | 587 |
| Range SAT Math | 550-640 |
| Average SAT Math | 595 |
| Minimum TOEFL | 550 |
| % graduated top 10% of class | 36 |
| % graduated top 25% of class | 76 |
| % graduated top 50% of class | 98 |

### DEADLINES
| | |
|---|---|
| Early decision | 11/1 |
| Early decision notification | 12/15 |
| Priority admission | 3/1 |
| Regular notification | 4/15 |
| Nonfall registration? | yes |

### APPLICANTS ALSO LOOK AT AND OFTEN PREFER
Cornell U
Boston U
NYU

### AND SOMETIMES PREFER
U of Vermont
Syracuse U
Penn State
Skidmore
Union College
U of Rochester

### AND RARELY PREFER
Binghamton U
SUNY Geneseo
U of Delaware
UMass at Amherst

### FINANCIAL FACTS

| | |
|---|---|
| Financial Aid Rating | 80 |
| Tuition | $21,102 |
| Room and board | $8,960 |
| Books and supplies | $876 |
| % frosh receiving aid | 71 |
| % undergrads receiving aid | 68 |
| Avg frosh grant | $13,111 |
| Avg frosh loan | $3,868 |

# JAMES MADISON UNIVERSITY

UNDERGRADUATE ADMISSIONS, SONNER HALL MSC 0101, HARRISONBURG, VA 22807 • ADMISSIONS: 540-568-5681

## CAMPUS LIFE

| | |
|---|---|
| Quality of Life Rating | 85 |
| Type of school | public |
| Environment | rural |

### STUDENTS

| | |
|---|---|
| Total undergrad enrollment | 14,402 |
| % male/female | 40/60 |
| % from out of state | 29 |
| % from public high school | 95 |
| % live on campus | 40 |
| % in (# of) fraternities | 5 (14) |
| % in (# of) sororities | 8 (8) |
| % African American | 4 |
| % Asian | 4 |
| % Caucasian | 84 |
| % Hispanic | 2 |
| % international | 2 |
| # of countries represented | 60 |

### SURVEY SAYS . . .
Campus feels safe
Lots of beer drinking
Very little drug use
Everyone loves the Dukes
Student publications are popular
Great food on campus
Beautiful campus
Campus easy to get around
Students are cliquish
Students don't like Harrisonburg, VA
Student government is unpopular

## ACADEMICS

| | |
|---|---|
| Academic Rating | 81 |
| Calendar | semester |
| Student/faculty ratio | 17:1 |
| Profs interesting rating | 92 |
| Profs accessible rating | 88 |
| % profs teaching UG courses | 100 |
| % classes taught by TAs | 1 |
| Avg lab size | 20-29 students |
| Avg reg class size | 20-29 students |

### MOST POPULAR MAJORS
Marketing/marketing management
Psychology
Integrated science and technology

## STUDENTS SPEAK OUT

### Academics

With "topnotch facilities," affordable tuition for both in-state and out-of-state students, and standout programs in music and business, James Madison University has a lot going for it. JMU also boasts an "innovative" Integrated Science and Technology (ISAT) program that offers degree programs in health sciences, computer science, and other technology-based fields. Writes one student, "The new ISAT buildings are equipped with excellent computers, and every ISAT major that I know has really liked the facilities." Not all students praise ISAT, however; many feel that "some areas of the university, such as the College of Integrated Science and Technology (ISAT), eat up (what seems like) more than their share of the school budget while the College of Arts and Letters remains underfunded." Students also gripe about core requirements, called General Education here; notes one, "General Education is seen as a big problem here. Students don't really care about those classes and neither do professors." Making matters worse is the perception that "Gen Ed classes are hard to get into, which can be frustrating because they're required and a lot of teachers won't give overrides into their classes." Fortunately, things get better for upperclassmen. Writes one typical student, "The first two years were pretty bad. Classes were huge; teachers couldn't put faces with names unless you contacted them on a regular basis. This past year has been a totally different story. I'm finally taking classes for my major. The teachers are great. They listen to the students, are easy to find outside of the classroom, and really seem invested in helping us to learn."

### Life

JMU's undergrads "are generally geared towards making their four years at school the most beneficial and most fun of their lives." Reports one, "For a good four days of every week the school is studious, the library is packed, and students read for pleasure on the quad and debate on picnic tables outside of the on-campus restaurants; but come Thursday night, JMU students know how to party!" Weekends here "pretty much give way to the party scene. Lots of drinking goes on. There aren't too many bars, so there are always tons of apartment parties and house parties." There are Greek organizations here, but "Greek life is not the center of the social [scene]. However, there is always some Greek event to go to if you want [to]." Student organizations are popular; writes one student, "There are a lot of kids in religious groups (Inter Varsity, YL, etc.). There are tons of clubs (sports, ethnic, academic, religious, etc.)." Also, "There are always fun activities going on. For example UPB (University Program Board) sets out to attract large-name bands, comedians, or shows to campus. Although the school is mid-sized we've had names such as Vertical Horizon, Wyclef, Third Eye Blind, Foo Fighters, and the Indigo Girls." Beyond campus lies the "boring" town of Harrisonburg, but beyond that lies the Shenandoah Valley; brags one student, "Since JMU is situated in the mountains, camping is a pretty popular activity. Tents, sleeping bags, and other gear can be rented from the rec center on campus for little money. Biking and hiking are also popular."

### Student Body

The "active, open, and friendly" students of JMU strike newcomers with an "overwhelming feeling of niceness. Everyone smiles at you and everyone holds doors. Even the cafeteria ladies seem to brighten your day a little." Students report that "it is not cutthroat competitive like other schools. People compete, but it is not at the expense of others. Groups tend to work out, with students complementing each others strengths." Since "most everyone in the student body is from Virginia," "a southern gentility" pervades the campus. Students admit that "different races and ethnicities are very separate. It's not that they don't get along with each other or hate each other—there just isn't a lot of interaction."

296 ■ THE BEST 351 COLLEGES

# JAMES MADISON UNIVERSITY

Fax: 540-568-3332 • Financial Aid: 540-568-7820 • E-mail: gotojmu@jmu.edu • Website: www.jmu.edu

## ADMISSIONS

*Very important factors considered include:* secondary school record, class rank, standardized test scores. *Important factors considered include:* essays, extracurricular activities. *Other factors considered include:* alumni/ae relation, character/personal qualities, geographical residence, minority status, recommendations, state residency, talent/ability, volunteer work, work experience. SAT I or ACT required. TOEFL required of all international applicants. High school diploma or GED is required. *High school units required/recommended:* 19 total required; 22 total recommended; 4 years in each core area: English, math, lab science, social science/history; 3 years of some foreign language.

### The Inside Word

James Madison has prospered from the applications of students faced with severe competition for admission to UVA and William and Mary. Third place on the Virginia public university totem pole is not a bad spot to be, as JMU's admissions committee will attest. Pay attention when they stress that your high school schedule should be chock-full of challenging academic courses.

## FINANCIAL AID

*Students should submit:* FAFSA. The Princeton Review suggests that all financial aid forms be submitted as soon as possible after January 1. *Need-based scholarships/grants offered:* Pell, SEOG, state scholarships/grants, private scholarships. *Loan aid offered:* FFEL Subsidized Stafford, FFEL Unsubsidized Stafford, FFEL PLUS, Federal Perkins. Federal Work-Study Program available. Institutional employment available. Applicants will be notified of awards on a rolling basis beginning on or about April 1. Off-campus job opportunities are excellent.

## FROM THE ADMISSIONS OFFICE

"James Madison University's philosophy of inclusiveness—known as 'all together one'—means that students become a part of a real community that nurtures its own to learn, grow, and succeed. Our professors, many of whom have a wealth of real-world experience, pride themselves on making teaching their top priority. We take seriously the responsibility to maintain an environment that fosters learning and encourages students to excel in and out of the classroom. Our rich variety of educational, social, and extracurricular activities include more than 100 innovative and traditional undergraduate majors and programs, a well-established study abroad program, a cutting-edge information security program, more than 280 student clubs and organizations, and a 147,000-square-foot, state-of-the-art recreation center. The university's picturesque, self-contained campus is located in the heart of the Shenandoah Valley, a four-season area that's easy to call home. Great food, fun times, exciting intercollegiate athletics, and rigorous academics all combine to create the unique James Madison experience. From the library to the residence halls and from our outstanding honors program to our highly successful career placement program, the university is committed to equipping our students with the tools they need to achieve their dreams."

## ADMISSIONS

| | |
|---|---|
| Admissions Rating | 84 |
| # of applicants | 15,639 |
| % of applicants accepted | 58 |
| % of acceptees attending | 21 |
| # accepting a place on wait list | 902 |
| % admitted from wait list | 21 |

### FRESHMAN PROFILE

| | |
|---|---|
| Range SAT Verbal | 540-620 |
| Average SAT Verbal | 578 |
| Range SAT Math | 540-630 |
| Average SAT Math | 587 |
| Minimum TOEFL | 570 |
| Average HS GPA | 3.6 |
| % graduated top 10% of class | 28 |
| % graduated top 25% of class | 85 |
| % graduated top 50% of class | 95 |

### DEADLINES

| | |
|---|---|
| Priority admission | 11/1 |
| Regular admission | 1/15 |
| Regular notification | 4/1 |

### APPLICANTS ALSO LOOK AT AND OFTEN PREFER
U of Virginia
William and Mary

### AND SOMETIMES PREFER
Virginia Tech
George Mason
U of Maryland
U of Delaware
Penn State
Villanova
Rutgers

## FINANCIAL FACTS

| | |
|---|---|
| Financial Aid Rating | 82 |
| In-state tuition | $5,058 |
| Out-of-state tuition | $13,280 |
| Room and board | $5,736 |
| Books and supplies | $750 |
| % frosh receiving aid | 28 |
| % undergrads receiving aid | 29 |
| Avg frosh grant | $3,437 |
| Avg frosh loan | $2,959 |

# JOHNS HOPKINS UNIVERSITY

3400 NORTH CHARLES STREET/140 GARLAND, BALTIMORE, MD 21218 • ADMISSIONS: 410-516-8171 • FAX: 410-516-6025

## CAMPUS LIFE

| | |
|---|---|
| Quality of Life Rating | 85 |
| Type of school | private |
| Environment | urban |

### STUDENTS

| | |
|---|---|
| Total undergrad enrollment | 5,523 |
| % male/female | 52/48 |
| % from out of state | 78 |
| % from public high school | 59 |
| % live on campus | 54 |
| % in (# of) fraternities | 18 (11) |
| % in (# of) sororities | 19 (7) |
| % African American | 6 |
| % Asian | 18 |
| % Caucasian | 72 |
| % Hispanic | 7 |
| % international | 6 |

### SURVEY SAYS . . .
Popular college radio
Political activism is hot
Students are religious
Athletic facilities are great
(Almost) everyone plays intramural sports
Student publications are popular
Unattractive campus
Library needs improving

## ACADEMICS

| | |
|---|---|
| Academic Rating | 96 |
| Calendar | 4-1-4 |
| Student/faculty ratio | 8:1 |
| Profs interesting rating | 83 |
| Profs accessible rating | 80 |
| Avg lab size | 10-19 students |
| Avg reg class size | under 10 students |

### MOST POPULAR MAJORS
Biomedical/medical engineering
Biology/biological sciences
International relations and affairs

## STUDENTS SPEAK OUT

### Academics
Johns Hopkins has earned a top reputation as an "excellent and challenging" university, with students who believe their school is "second to none." They value the "contacts you can make" with top professionals in a wide variety of fields. Professors, known to be "experts in their respective areas," take the time to "learn names, talk with students, and give them great advice," according to a student in the political science department, who adds, "Get to know them—it's worthwhile." Another student gushes, "I love the way instructors care about us," making themselves "generally available to offer help outside of class." One student in the "phenomenal" accelerated nursing program calls the course load "highly intense," which leaves "barely any time for social life." The most common complaint logged at Johns Hopkins concerns the perception that professors and administration alike prioritize research over teaching, leading some students to moan that professors think "undergraduates are peons who don't matter much." Students want to see more support for the arts at the school and say that professors in the humanities focus more on their role as teachers than their counterparts in the sciences. The administration, which "needs to be more helpful and understanding," in the words of a few respondents, "prioritizes engineering and medical research" over the needs of undergraduates. Current students remind prospective attendees that they will have to be "proactive to get the best education," but the rewards include the "immense amount of opportunity available for students with good ideas."

### Life
In the "highly educational environment" of Johns Hopkins, it may seem that "there's not a lot to do besides fraternity parties and homework." Students report, "You have to find your own fun, but it isn't hard to do." Those who have a difficult time entertaining themselves can always fall back on the "instant social life that erupts when you join a fraternity." One undergrad writes, "We generally don't go out more than once or twice a week, but when we do, we live it up." A freshman majoring in international relations appreciates that "there's enough that you can find stuff to do but not so much that it is a distraction." Though one student whines that "Baltimore is a ghetto," many students head downtown when "there isn't much to do on campus." An upperclassman reassures students, "Once you are old enough for bars, it gets better," especially for those with wheels. Many surveys note the brand-spanking-new athletic center, which entices students to play sports and attend to their cardiovascular systems during study breaks. Some students say the school could improve in terms of "clubs and anything school supported," but others offer, "If you want to build a new social outlet, the money [from the school] is available."

### Student Body
A typical student who chooses Johns Hopkins might be described as "overly ambitious," "introverted," and "hardworking." To some people, the assortment of "too many weirdos" that makes up the student body displays "little personality." A few students accuse their group of peers, in general, of being "ruled too much by their parents' wishes." On the other hand, one student tells us, "People surprise me (in a good way) every day." Even if "kids could be cooler," respondents agree that "most are good people" and "everyone tends to work together." Accusations of blandness aren't universal; some students boast that "everyone here has done interesting things." While many students say, "We all get along," the population seems to "lack of a sense of unified community," and at times "cultural barriers are very hard to break through."

# JOHNS HOPKINS UNIVERSITY

FINANCIAL AID: 410-516-8028 • E-MAIL: gotojhu@jhu.edu • WEBSITE: www.jhu.edu

## ADMISSIONS
*Very important factors considered include:* character/personal qualities, essays, recommendations, rigor of secondary school course load. *Important factors considered include:* class rank, extracurricular activities, standardized test scores, talent/ability, volunteer work. *Other factors considered include:* alumni/ae relation, geographical residence, interview, minority status, work experience. TOEFL required of all international applicants. *High school units required/recommended:* 20 total recommended; 4 English, 4 math, 2–3 lab science, 3–4 foreign language, 2–3 history and social science.

### *The Inside Word*
The admissions process at Hopkins demands to be taken seriously. Competition with the best colleges and universities in the country keeps the acceptance rate artificially high. Make certain that your personal credentials—essays, recommendations, and extracurricular activities—are impressive.

## FINANCIAL AID
*Students should submit:* FAFSA, institution's own financial aid form, noncustodial (divorced/separated) parent's statement, business/farm supplement, prior and current year's federal tax returns. Regular filing deadline is February 15. The Princeton Review suggests that all financial aid forms be submitted as soon as possible after January 1. *Need-based scholarships/grants offered:* Pell, SEOG, state scholarships/grants, private scholarships, the school's own gift aid. *Loan aid offered:* Direct Subsidized Stafford, Direct Unsubsidized Stafford, FFEL PLUS, Federal Perkins, college/university loans from institutional funds. Federal Work-Study Program available. Institutional employment available. Applicants will be notified of awards on or about April 1. Off-campus job opportunities are excellent.

## FROM THE ADMISSIONS OFFICE
"The Hopkins tradition of preeminent academic excellence naturally attracts the very best students in the nation and from around the world. The Admissions Committee carefully examines each application for evidence of compelling intellectual interest and academic performance as well as strong personal recommendations and meaningful extracurricular contributions. Every applicant who matriculates to Johns Hopkins University was found qualified by the Admissions Committee through a 'whole person' assessment, and every applicant accepted for admission is fully expected to graduate. The Admissions Committee determines whom they believe will take full advantage of the exceptional opportunities offered at Hopkins, contribute the most to the educational process of the institution, and be the most successful in using what they have learned and experienced for the benefit of society."

### SELECTIVITY

| | |
|---|---|
| Admissions Rating | 99 |
| # of applicants | 8,915 |
| % of applicants accepted | 35 |
| % of acceptees attending | 36 |
| # accepting a place on wait list | 839 |
| # of early decision applicants | 507 |
| % accepted early decision | 60 |

### FRESHMAN PROFILE
| | |
|---|---|
| Range SAT Verbal | 620-730 |
| Average SAT Verbal | 671 |
| Range SAT Math | 660-760 |
| Average SAT Math | 703 |
| Range ACT Composite | 27-31 |
| Average ACT Composite | 29 |
| Minimum TOEFL | 200 (CBT) |
| Average HS GPA | 3.7 |
| % graduated top 10% of class | 72 |
| % graduated top 25% of class | 94 |
| % graduated top 50% of class | 100 |

### DEADLINES
| | |
|---|---|
| Early decision | 11/15 |
| Early decision notification | 12/15 |
| Regular admission | 1/1 |
| Regular notification | 4/1 |

### APPLICANTS ALSO LOOK AT
**AND OFTEN PREFER**
Harvard
Princeton
Yale
MIT, U Penn
**AND SOMETIMES PREFER**
Brown
Columbia
Cornell, Duke
Georgetown
**AND RARELY PREFER**
Tufts
Carnegie Mellon, Boston U
Washington U, UC Berkeley

### FINANCIAL FACTS

| | |
|---|---|
| Financial Aid Rating | 86 |
| Tuition | $27,390 |
| Room and board | $8,829 |
| Books and supplies | $1,600 |
| % frosh receiving aid | 43 |
| % undergrads receiving aid | 40 |
| Avg frosh grant | $21,375 |
| Avg frosh loan | $2,529 |

# JUNIATA COLLEGE

ENROLLMENT OFFICE, 1700 MOORE STREET, HUNTINGDON, PA 16652 • ADMISSIONS: 877-586-4282 • FAX: 814-641-3100

## CAMPUS LIFE

| | |
|---|---|
| Quality of Life Rating | 79 |
| Type of school | private |
| Affiliation | Church of Brethren |
| Environment | rural |

### STUDENTS

| | |
|---|---|
| Total undergrad enrollment | 1,345 |
| % male/female | 42/58 |
| % from out of state | 24 |
| % from public high school | 89 |
| % live on campus | 86 |
| % African American | 1 |
| % Asian | 1 |
| % Caucasian | 97 |
| % Hispanic | 1 |
| % international | 3 |
| # of countries represented | 27 |

### SURVEY SAYS . . .
Classes are small
Great computer facilities
Dorms are like palaces
Very little drug use
Campus easy to get around
Registration is a pain
Students don't get along with local community

## ACADEMICS

| | |
|---|---|
| Academic Rating | 81 |
| Calendar | semester |
| Student/faculty ratio | 13:1 |
| Profs interesting rating | 81 |
| Profs accessible rating | 83 |
| % profs teaching UG courses | 100 |
| Avg lab size | 10-19 students |
| Avg reg class size | 10-19 students |

### MOST POPULAR MAJORS
Business administration/management
Education
Biology/biological sciences

## STUDENTS SPEAK OUT

### Academics

Located in rural Pennsylvania, Juniata College wouldn't seem to be the place to offer stellar science and competitive pre-med programs. But the rural looks can be deceiving. "If you want to be a doctor, Juniata can show you how," states one student. Indeed, Juniata prides itself on a relatively intense academic program, pre-med or not. One student warns, "Don't come here if you want to be lazy and do nothing but party. . . . The professors will challenge you until you think you can't take it anymore." The intensity may seem overwhelming, especially for incoming freshmen ("I have never done so much work"), but students at JC are pleased with the level of education and the caliber of their professors, who are "all very involved in their students' education." Each student at Juniata is assigned two advisors who "truly care about you and how you are doing. They help the students in any way that they can." Advisors and professors are accessible and will bend over backwards to help students. One pleased student marvels that she's "developed excellent relationships with professors who respect, challenge, and inspire me, inside and outside of the formal classroom."

### Life

Although students at Juniata readily admit that the small town of Huntingdon isn't the entertainment capital of the world, there's enough to do on campus that boredom is rarely an issue. JAB, "the activities board at Juniata, does a good job [in] bringing acts [like] comedians and other performers" to the campus. With more than 90 organizations to choose from, "a lot of students here are in clubs involving their academic or career interests." Students can join socially active groups like "Model U.N., Peace and Conflict, or Habitat for Humanity," or simply partake in the hiking and hanging that goes on at nearby Raystown Lake. One student loves JC "traditions [like] Lobsterfest (where everyone gets together and eats lobster and hangs out on the lawn), Mountain Day (a surprise cancellation of classes for a day [when] everyone goes and has a picnic instead), Madrigal Dinner, All Class Night, Storming of the Arch, and Pig Roast." And while partying is another JC tradition ("Juniata students work hard during the week and party hard on the weekends"), there is a strong contingent of students that doesn't feel the need to imbibe every weekend, but "the students that are not into nightlife are not frowned upon by the other students." For those who need a little break from the small town life of Huntingdon, or from the campus itself, students hop in a car and head to State College and Altoona. Overall, students at Juniata are content with life at JC: "Let's just say there is always something to do if you look hard enough. Life here is good."

### Student Body

"Amicable but homogenous" is one student's description of the students at Juniata, with many students describing themselves as "white and middle class." But what JC might be lacking in diversity, it more than makes up for in an abundance of good cheer: "Everyone here is overly nice. EVERYONE says hello and smiles when you walk by." Most feel that the small undergrad population is "incredibly friendly" and that "students are anxious to meet new people and make as many friends as they can in the short time they're all here." Such a small campus also allows "everyone to know everyone else," which could be the reason why "cliques are not very dominant on this campus." Juniata is also host to many foreign exchange students who "are fun to hang out with and make daily life interesting." Some also grumble that their peers "are narrow minded when it comes to sexual orientation." For the most part, though, "everyone is compatible, and if they're not, the campus isn't SO small that you can't avoid people."

# JUNIATA COLLEGE

FINANCIAL AID: 814-641-3142 • E-MAIL: ADMISSION@JUNIATA.EDU • WEBSITE: WWW.JUNIATA.EDU

## ADMISSIONS

*Very important factors considered include:* character/personal qualities, essays, extracurricular activities, recommendations, secondary school record, standardized test scores. *Important factors considered include:* alumni/ae relation, interview, talent/ability, volunteer work, minority status. *Other factors considered include:* class rank, work experience. SAT I or ACT required. TOEFL required of all international applicants. High school diploma or GED is required. *High school units required/recommended:* 16 total required; 4 English required, 3 math required, 3 science required, 2 foreign language required, 1 social studies required, 3 history required.

### The Inside Word

Like at many traditional liberal arts schools, the admissions process at Juniata is a personal one. The school wants students who will decide to attend Juniata, and stay for the next fours years. Among Juniata's bragging rights are that a staggering 40 percent of students graduate with a degree in science, 60 percent of undergrads design their own major, and 70 percent participate in internships.

## FINANCIAL AID

*Students should submit:* FAFSA. The Princeton Review suggests that all financial aid forms be submitted as soon as possible after January 1. *Need-based scholarships/grants offered:* Pell, SEOG, state scholarships/grants, private scholarships, the school's own gift aid. *Loan aid offered:* FFEL Subsidized Stafford, FFEL Unsubsidized Stafford, FFEL PLUS, Federal Perkins. Federal Work-Study Program available. Institutional employment available. Applicants will be notified of awards on a rolling basis beginning on or about December 1. Off-campus job opportunities are fair.

## FROM THE ADMISSIONS OFFICE

"This is a great time to be a part of the Juniata community. There is intellectual engagement and opportunity at every turn. Our museum studies program is one of only 12 in the country. Our new information technology program is producing 'fearless learners' with the support of a $4 million endowment. The just-completed von Liebig Center for Science provides increased opportunities for student/faculty research surpassing those available even at large universities. The college's expanded Environmental Studies Field Station on nearby Raystown Lake provides 365 acres for exclusive college use and a full 29,000 acres for additional study. The future Halbritter Center will be an exceptional facility to house the performing arts. More importantly, we believe the ultimate measure of quality is found in the success of our graduates. Just a few include Dr. William Phillips '70, Nobel Prize winner in Physics; Rebecca McClaine '00, USA Today Academic All American; Robert Rose '61, Nevada supreme court justice; Casey Craig '97, director of special events, Boston Celtics; Dr. Robert Biter '92, playwright and AMA Outstanding Young Medical Professional Award recipient; Tonya Grimes '90, Sallie Mae Award (100 best teachers nationally); William Boswell '83, chief technology officer, E-Markets Inc.; Dr. James Madara '71, dean, University of Chicago Medical School; Peter Marzio '65, executive director, Houston Museum of Fine Arts; Timothy Statton '72, president, Bechtel Energy; Bruce Davis '65, executive director, Academy Motion Picture Arts and Sciences; Mary White '73, CEO, Swedish Medical Center; and Sammy Buo '73, deputy director, African Division, United Nations. At Juniata you will work harder and learn more than you ever have in your life, and we will provide the supportive faculty and staff to be certain that you have every opportunity to succeed."

## SELECTIVITY

★★☆☆

| | |
|---|---|
| Admissions Rating | 76 |
| # of applicants | 1,346 |
| % of applicants accepted | 79 |
| % of acceptees attending | 35 |
| # of early decision applicants | 97 |
| % accepted early decision | 75 |

### FRESHMAN PROFILE

| | |
|---|---|
| Range SAT Verbal | 520-620 |
| Average SAT Verbal | 574 |
| Range SAT Math | 530-640 |
| Average SAT Math | 583 |
| Minimum TOEFL | 550 |
| Average HS GPA | 3.7 |
| % graduated top 10% of class | 36 |
| % graduated top 25% of class | 71 |
| % graduated top 50% of class | 98 |

### DEADLINES

| | |
|---|---|
| Early decision | 11/15 |
| Early decision notification | 12/30 |
| Priority admission | 11/15 |
| Regular admission | 3/15 |
| Regular notification | rolling |
| Nonfall registration? | yes |

### APPLICANTS ALSO LOOK AT
**AND OFTEN PREFER**
Bucknell University
**AND SOMETIMES PREFER**
Ursinus College
Muhlenberg College
Gettysburg College
Dickinson College
**AND RARELY PREFER**
Allegheny College
Susquehanna University
Elizabethtown College
Lebanon Valley College
Lycoming College

## FINANCIAL FACTS

| | |
|---|---|
| Financial Aid Rating | 83 |
| Tuition | $22,240 |
| Room and board | $6,290 |
| Books and supplies | $450 |
| Required fees | $550 |
| % frosh receiving aid | 100 |
| % undergrads receiving aid | 99 |
| Avg frosh grant | $14,651 |
| Avg frosh loan | $2,965 |

# KALAMAZOO COLLEGE

1200 ACADEMY STREET, KALAMAZOO, MI 49006 • ADMISSIONS: 616-337-7166 • FAX: 616-337-7390

## CAMPUS LIFE

| | |
|---|---|
| Quality of Life Rating | 75 |
| Type of school | private |
| Environment | suburban |

### STUDENTS

| | |
|---|---|
| Total undergrad enrollment | 1,265 |
| % from out of state | 21 |
| % from public high school | 85 |
| % live on campus | 75 |
| % African American | 2 |
| % Asian | 5 |
| % Caucasian | 83 |
| % Hispanic | 2 |
| # of countries represented | 20 |

### SURVEY SAYS . . .
Classes are small
Lab facilities need improving
Students aren't religious
Diversity lacking on campus
Campus easy to get around
Athletic facilities need improving
No one plays intramural sports
Lousy food on campus
Registration is a pain

## ACADEMICS

| | |
|---|---|
| Academic Rating | 84 |
| Calendar | quarter |
| Student/faculty ratio | 12:1 |
| Profs interesting rating | 96 |
| Profs accessible rating | 99 |
| % profs teaching UG courses | 100 |
| Avg lab size | 20-29 students |
| Avg reg class size | 20-29 students |

### MOST POPULAR MAJORS
Business/commerce
Biology/biological sciences
Psychology

## STUDENTS SPEAK OUT

### Academics

Kalamazoo College's unique K Plan provides students a well-rounded education through a combination of classroom instruction, study abroad, a senior thesis project, and internships. This "diverse, yet rigorous" plan "is geared toward preparing you for your future endeavors." The approach, one human development major explains, is that "here, education is a process." An enthusiastic sophomore gushes, "Last quarter, I had an internship at the Philadelphia District Attorney's office. . . . Next year, I'll be studying in Thailand for five months." Though the quality of professors varies from "great" to "terrible," students believe that their professors are always accessible and incredibly dedicated. "I wholeheartedly believe that some of them never leave their offices," an English major writes. Professors expect a similar level of dedication from their students. "The work can be overwhelming," warns one sophomore, and others complain about the "ridiculous amount" of "busy work assigned." Students rave about the small class sizes, even in lower-level courses. "I expected large lectures in college and found only seven other students in my class," one first-year English major explains. "I was shocked and impressed to find that such classes are the rule, not the exception." The administration is open, friendly, and "interested in helping each and every one of their students succeed." Offers a senior biology major, "I have shown up at the president's home unannounced and [was] welcomed in with open arms." Despite its small size, Kalamazoo offers students "an amazing amount of options." Writes a sophomore, "The academics are rigorous, but extremely rewarding." Students believe that the heavy academic workload prepares them well for graduate school.

### Life

Ask a student about his or her choice to attend Kalamazoo College, and a standard response might be, "I can't imagine having a more intellectually and socially stimulating environment." Students "spend way too much time studying" but still have time to participate in many extracurricular activities. Bowling and the three formal dances held every year are among students' favorite amusements. The campus improvisational group, Monkapult, is another popular diversion. Students say that the food needs to be improved. First-year students are not allowed to have cars on campus, which seriously curtails their off-campus activities. There are no fraternities on campus, and students often go to small house parties or fiestas thrown at Western Michigan University. The onerous workload means that most students restrict their partying to Friday and Saturday nights. "Study is the key word around here," a senior Spanish major advises. "Academics are by far the most important [priority]." Of course, this means that students will use words like "dull" and "boring" to describe on-campus life.

### Student Body

Kalamazoo College attracts a "disparate and not entirely meshing group of students." Which is cool. The dearth of fraternities adds to the "family atmosphere" and eliminates some of the associated cliques, but "it's easy to feel inadequate with so many overachievers." Students like their peers and believe that they are genuinely friendly, "compassionate," and always willing to help. Students agree, however, that they "do not have enough ethnic diversity." Most students come from upper-middle-class backgrounds. Still, "there are lots of different people here who are respectful and tolerant," according to one sophomore biology major. Social activism could use a jump-start, too.

# KALAMAZOO COLLEGE

FINANCIAL AID: 616-337-7192 • E-MAIL: ADMISSION@KZOO.EDU • WEBSITE: WWW.KZOO.EDU

## ADMISSIONS

*Very important factors considered include:* extracurricular activities, secondary school record, standardized test scores, talent/ability. *Important factors considered include:* character/personal qualities, class rank, essays, recommendations, volunteer work, work experience. *Other factors considered include:* alumni/ae relation, geographical residence, interview, minority status, state residency. SAT I or ACT required. TOEFL required of all international applicants. High school diploma or GED is required. *High school units required/recommended:* 17 total required; 4 English recommended, 3 math recommended, 3 science recommended, 3 foreign language recommended, 2 social studies recommended, 2 history recommended.

## The Inside Word

K-Zoo's applicant pool is small and self-selected academically, which leads to the unusual combination of a very high acceptance rate and an impressive freshman profile. The admissions committee expects candidates to show evidence of serious academic intent, suitability for the college, and a willingness to contribute to the life of the college. Those who underestimate the evaluation process risk denial.

## FINANCIAL AID

*Students should submit:* FAFSA, institution's own financial aid form. No deadline for regular filing. The Princeton Review suggests that all financial aid forms be submitted as soon as possible after January 1. *Need-based scholarships/grants offered:* Pell, SEOG, state scholarships/grants, private scholarships, the school's own gift aid. *Loan aid offered:* Direct Subsidized Stafford, Direct Unsubsidized Stafford, Direct PLUS, Federal Perkins, state loans. Federal Work-Study Program available. Institutional employment available. Applicants will be notified of awards on or about March 21. Off-campus job opportunities are good.

## FROM THE ADMISSIONS OFFICE

"The educational program offered by Kalamazoo College combines traditional classroom instruction with experiential education. During their four years, students move freely from working and learning in groups to pursuing individual academic and artistic projects. The Kalamazoo Plan, or K Plan, enables every student to participate in four different educational experiences: on-campus learning, a career development internship, overseas study, and a senior project. The Career Development internship is typically done during the sophomore year summer allowing students to 'try on' a career. Eighty percent of all Kalamazoo College students choose to participate in this valuable experience. The Senior Individualized Project provides students with the opportunity to make use of all their experiences at the college. They may choose to do research, a thesis, creative or artistic work, or other work related to their major. All students complete a Senior Individualized Project prior to graduation."

### SELECTIVITY

| | |
|---|---|
| Admissions Rating | 82 |
| # of applicants | 1,411 |
| % of applicants accepted | 73 |
| % of acceptees attending | 33 |
| # accepting a place on wait list | 64 |
| % admitted from wait list | 50 |
| # of early decision applicants | 36 |
| % accepted early decision | 81 |

### FRESHMAN PROFILE

| | |
|---|---|
| Range SAT Verbal | 590-680 |
| Average SAT Verbal | 631 |
| Range SAT Math | 580-690 |
| Average SAT Math | 630 |
| Range ACT Composite | 26-30 |
| Average ACT Composite | 28 |
| Minimum TOEFL | 550 |
| Average HS GPA | 3.6 |
| % graduated top 10% of class | 42 |
| % graduated top 25% of class | 74 |
| % graduated top 50% of class | 95 |

### DEADLINES

| | |
|---|---|
| Early decision | 11/15 |
| Early decision notification | 12/1 |
| Priority admission | 2/15 |
| Regular admission | 2/15 |
| Regular notification | 4/1 |

### APPLICANTS ALSO LOOK AT AND OFTEN PREFER
U Michigan
Northwestern
Georgetown
Dartmouth

### AND SOMETIMES PREFER
Notre Dame
Oberlin, Earlham
Macalester
Wooster, Denison

### AND RARELY PREFER
Albion, Alma
Hope, DePauw

### FINANCIAL FACTS

| | |
|---|---|
| Financial Aid Rating | 83 |
| Tuition | $21,603 |
| Room and board | $6,354 |
| % frosh receiving aid | 58 |
| % undergrads receiving aid | 50 |
| Avg frosh grant | $12,510 |
| Avg frosh loan | $4,230 |

# KANSAS STATE UNIVERSITY

119 ANDERSON HALL, MANHATTAN, KS 66506 • ADMISSIONS: 800-432-8270 • FAX: 785-532-6393

## CAMPUS LIFE

| | |
|---|---|
| Quality of Life Rating | 78 |
| Type of school | public |
| Environment | suburban |

### STUDENTS

| | |
|---|---|
| Total undergrad enrollment | 19,048 |
| % male/female | 52/48 |
| % from out of state | 9 |
| % from public high school | 90 |
| % live on campus | 33 |
| % in (# of) fraternities | 20 (28) |
| % in (# of) sororities | 20 (15) |
| % African American | 3 |
| % Asian | 1 |
| % Caucasian | 90 |
| % Hispanic | 2 |
| % international | 1 |

### SURVEY SAYS . . .

Frats and sororities dominate social scene
Everyone loves the Wildcats
Athletic facilities are great
(Almost) everyone plays intramural sports
Students love Manhattan, KS
Large classes
Students get along with local community
Student publications are popular
Students are very religious
Library needs improving

## ACADEMICS

| | |
|---|---|
| Academic Rating | 80 |
| Calendar | semester |
| Student/faculty ratio | 20:1 |
| Profs interesting rating | 85 |
| Profs accessible rating | 70 |
| % profs teaching UG courses | 74 |
| % classes taught by TAs | 17 |
| Avg reg class size | 10-19 students |

## STUDENTS SPEAK OUT

### Academics

There's no doubt about it: K-State is a big school. This means that some students end up sticking around for five or six years trying to finish their degrees. It also means lectures are common, and class sizes regularly swell into the few-hundred range. But this is all to be expected. Less expected, perhaps, are the personal bonds that many students foster with their teachers. Of her professors, one junior writes, "They want students to succeed, and this is apparent through their extra effort." A marketing/international business major concurs: "Most of my lecture professors take time to not only teach (obviously), but to tell us that they care and want us to do well." For the most part, when talk of the classroom comes up, students tell you they are "impressed with K-State and happy to be here." Undergraduates have an unusual appreciation for the People in Charge. Students report that "K-State's administration is continually being improved and constantly focused on how to provide the highest quality of education possible for the students." Regarding the academic experience, perhaps the greatest praise came in the shortest phrase. One junior wrote plainly, "I am getting my money's worth."

### Life

Kansas State shares a trait with many midwestern schools: "Everyone thinks about football—if we lose, that's everyone's low for the week." K-State is a school of more than 18,000, and it's a member of the Big 12, so the importance of sports isn't surprising. Although Manhattan is a small town in a big, sparsely populated state, students will tell you that the city is "very entertaining for its size." Oddly, one of its biggest draws is a nearby superstore. "Wal-Mart is everyone's second home," explains a student. In regards to life on campus, students boast that they "have an excellent union that is fun to spend time in." And Greek life is vibrant on campus. On the weekends, it sometimes seems "there's nothing to do if you don't drink or smoke." Reflecting on his time at K-State, a senior says, yes, "drinking is very popular here." "Most guys think about getting laid, drinking beer, smoking, not going to class," notes a freshman, "and most girls don't think about these things, but still do them." So it's fair to say that this is a school with a festive mindset. But don't fret if the beer bong isn't your instrument of choice. "It's a very laid back and comfortable campus" all around. And when campus isn't comfortable, students can always get away by taking an hour-long drive to Topeka or a two-hour trip to Wichita.

### Student Body

Steal a glance at the K-State student body, and you're likely to see a group of students that looks fairly uniform. Nine out of 10 students at this school are white, and as a whole the student body tends to be "very racially divided." One black student complains that the college needs to improve in its "treatment and acknowledgement of minority programs, accomplishments, and students." A white junior adds that "attending a university located in a rural 'college town' does not offer the diversity among students that I would have liked to [have been] immersed in, but K-State students' overwhelming hospitality makes up for that." Overall, friendliness is one thing you can come to count on in Manhattan, Kansas. "Smiles and nods are common," remarks one undergrad. Some are turned off by "the ultra-religious nature of this school," while still feeling comfortable in a place that's populated by many students from the Midwest—especially Kansas. "Very nice farm boys," comments a freshman. So, "if you can get past" the homogeneity of the student population, "you will meet a lot of great people."

# KANSAS STATE UNIVERSITY

FINANCIAL AID: 785-532-6420 • E-MAIL: KSTATE@KSU.EDU • WEBSITE: WWW.CONSIDER.K-STATE.EDU

## ADMISSIONS

*Very important factors considered include:* class rank, secondary school record, standardized test scores. *Other factors considered include:* recommendations. SAT I or ACT required. TOEFL required of all international applicants. High school diploma or GED is required. *High school units required/recommended:* 14 total required; 4 English required, 3 math required, 3 science required, 3 social studies required.

### The Inside Word

As at most public universities, the admissions process is about as straightforward as it can get. Kansas high school grads are admitted with little trouble; out-of-state students are expected to be in the top half of their graduating class and to show evidence of academic potential via ACT scores. (SAT scores are acceptable, but if you haven't taken the ACT you'll have to do so once you enroll. Ouch!) Don't be deceived by the seeming lack of rigor in admissions standards—K-State is chock full of strong students. Heightened national visibility for its athletic teams over the past few years will no doubt attract more applicants.

## FINANCIAL AID

*Students should submit:* FAFSA. No deadline for regular filing. The Princeton Review suggests that all financial aid forms be submitted as soon as possible after January 1. *Need-based scholarships/grants offered:* Pell, SEOG, state scholarships/grants. *Loan aid offered:* Direct Subsidized Stafford, Direct Unsubsidized Stafford, Direct PLUS, Federal Perkins, college/university loans from institutional funds. Federal Work-Study Program available. Institutional employment available. Applicants will be notified of awards on a rolling basis beginning on or about April 15. Off-campus job opportunities are good.

## FROM THE ADMISSIONS OFFICE

"Kansas State University offers strong academic programs, a lively intellectual atmosphere, a friendly campus community, and an environment where students achieve: K-State's total of Rhodes, Marshall, Truman, Goldwater, and Udall scholars since 1986 ranks first in the nation among state universities. In the Goldwater competition, only Princeton and Harvard have produced more winners. K-State's student government was named best in the nation in 1997 and 1995. The forensics squad finished ninth in the 2003 national tournement, and K-State was the only school in the nation with two champions in individual events. A K-State team finished in the top eight at the national debate tournament in 2003. Research facilities include the Konza Prairie, the world's largest tall grass prairie preserve, and the Macdonald Lab, the only university accelerator devoted primarily to atomic physics. Open House, held each spring, is a great way to explore K-State's more than 200 majors and options and 370 student organizations."

---

### SELECTIVITY
★ ★ ★ ☆

| | |
|---|---|
| Admissions Rating | 82 |
| # of applicants | 8,212 |
| % of applicants accepted | 58 |
| % of acceptees attending | 74 |

### FRESHMAN PROFILE

| | |
|---|---|
| Range ACT Composite | 19-25 |
| Average ACT Composite | 24 |
| Minimum TOEFL | 550 |
| % graduated top 25% of class | 59 |
| % graduated top 50% of class | 90 |

### DEADLINES

| | |
|---|---|
| Nonfall registration? | yes |

### FINANCIAL FACTS
★ ★ ★ ☆

| | |
|---|---|
| Financial Aid Rating | 84 |
| In-state tuition | $2,918 |
| Out-of-state tuition | $10,178 |
| Room and board | $4,500 |
| Books and supplies | $1,000 |
| Required fees | $526 |
| % frosh receiving aid | 55 |
| % undergrads receiving aid | 56 |
| Avg frosh grant | $2,000 |
| Avg frosh loan | $1,098 |

# KENYON COLLEGE

ADMISSIONS OFFICE, RANSOM HALL, GAMBIER, OH 43022-9623 • ADMISSIONS: 800-848-2468 • FAX: 740-427-5770

## CAMPUS LIFE

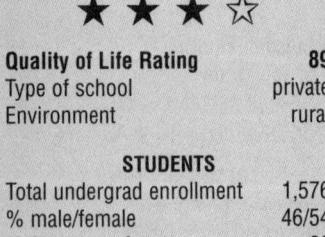

| | |
|---|---|
| Quality of Life Rating | 89 |
| Type of school | private |
| Environment | rural |

### STUDENTS
| | |
|---|---|
| Total undergrad enrollment | 1,576 |
| % male/female | 46/54 |
| % from out of state | 80 |
| % from public high school | 53 |
| % live on campus | 98 |
| % in (# of) fraternities | 23 (8) |
| % in (# of) sororities | 8 (4) |
| % African American | 4 |
| % Asian | 3 |
| % Caucasian | 85 |
| % Hispanic | 2 |
| % international | 3 |
| # of countries represented | 26 |

### SURVEY SAYS . . .
Diversity lacking on campus
Beautiful campus
Classes are small
Students aren't religious
(Almost) everyone smokes
Lousy off-campus food
(Almost) no one listens to college radio
Athletic facilities need improving
Musical organizations are hot

## ACADEMICS

| | |
|---|---|
| Academic Rating | 95 |
| Calendar | semester |
| Student/faculty ratio | 9:1 |
| Profs interesting rating | 97 |
| Profs accessible rating | 98 |
| % profs teaching UG courses | 100 |
| Avg reg class size | 10-19 students |

### MOST POPULAR MAJORS
English language and literature
History
Political science and government

## STUDENTS SPEAK OUT
### Academics
With its small classes, dedicated teachers, and sharp student body, Kenyon College is a classic example of a small liberal arts college. Perhaps most paradigmatic is the close relationship students enjoy with the faculty; writes one undergrad, "Professors are amazing. They are a huge part of the family known as Kenyon. We have dinner at their houses, babysit their kids, and look to many of them as mentors." Adds another, "Professors here are completely approachable. We often know their spouses, their children, their dogs, and their houses. As a result, it's extremely easy to find them and to ask them questions, etc." The community atmosphere helps students deal with the considerable rigors of a Kenyon education. Explains one student, "It's not easy here, but it's satisfying in every way when you do well. I feel quite lucky to be surrounded by such a select group of intelligent students and faculty." Says another, "Kenyon is very academic in atmosphere, but it doesn't have a competitive slant to it. We have lots of interesting, specialized classes and very much focus on knowing things in depth rather than simply what you need to know to get by." Students enjoy a surprisingly wide variety of courses considering the size of the school. Says one, "Often students are heard saying there are so many courses they want to take they don't know if they'll have time to take all the ones they want in the four years they have." The administration, though it is "too politically correct," receives praise as well for its willingness "to listen and discuss anything" at practically any time.

### Life
The Greek system, student organizations, and a full slate of school-sponsored events attempt to offset the relative lack of activity in Gambier, Kenyon's small hometown. Students report that "there are a TON of student organizations and activities to get involved in on campus and opportunities to create new ones each year." Writes one student, "Life at Kenyon is busy. . . . With over 90 student organizations from fencing to Zen meditation there is simply not enough time." Still, "Kenyon can be a bit boring at times. It's just such a small place that if you're not into the frat party scene, you don't have many other party environment options. But the school does try to provide other opportunities for students to have fun. There is almost always a movie showing, a musical performance, or a comedian somewhere on campus! And the college also provides shuttles to go into the little town that is near us in case we need anything. Once or twice a month there is even a shuttle that goes into Columbus." Kenyon students will soon enjoy the benefits of a much-needed new state-of-the-art fitness, recreation, and athletic facility, due to open in the fall of 2005.

### Student Body
As at many private colleges, diversity at Kenyon is primarily geographic. Writes one student, "Students come here from all over the U.S. They are some of the brightest and friendliest scholars in the country. As a freshman, I was humbled by my peers. In high school, I was the valedictorian, but at Kenyon I discovered that there are so many people that are more talented and intelligent." Students acknowledge that "Kenyon has a problem with the fact that so many of its students come from well-off, two-parent households that sent them to private school. Many people led sheltered lives and continue to do that here. But not everyone is that way, and there is diversity, just not as much as there ideally would be." Students enjoy the fact that "people generally get along," which makes the "strong" community here "more close-knit than most." Undergrads are usually so absorbed in their studies that they "tend to be somewhat apathetic politically."

# KENYON COLLEGE

FINANCIAL AID: 740-427-5430 • E-MAIL: ADMISSIONS@KENYON.EDU • WEBSITE: WWW.KENYON.EDU

## ADMISSIONS

*Very important factors considered include:* character/personal qualities, class rank, recommendations, secondary school record. *Important factors considered include:* essays, extracurricular activities, interview, standardized test scores, talent/ability. *Other factors considered include:* alumni/ae relation, geographical residence, minority status, state residency, volunteer work, work experience. SAT I or ACT required. TOEFL required of all international applicants. High school diploma or GED is required. *High school units required/recommended:* 18 total required; 23 total recommended; 4 English required, 3 math required, 4 math recommended, 3 science required, 4 science recommended, 2 science lab required, 3 science lab recommended, 3 foreign language required, 4 foreign language recommended, 2 social studies required, 3 social studies recommended, 3 elective required, 4 elective recommended.

### The Inside Word

Kenyon pays close attention to matchmaking in the course of candidate selection, and personal accomplishments are just as significant as academic ones. Applicants who rank the college high among their choices should definitely interview.

## FINANCIAL AID

*Students should submit:* FAFSA, CSS/Financial Aid PROFILE, noncustodial (divorced/separated) parent's statement, completed tax returns. Regular filing deadline is February 15. The Princeton Review suggests that all financial aid forms be submitted as soon as possible after January 1. *Need-based scholarships/grants offered:* Pell, SEOG, state scholarships/grants, private scholarships, the school's own gift aid. *Loan aid offered:* FFEL Subsidized Stafford, FFEL Unsubsidized Stafford, FFEL PLUS, Federal Perkins, college/university loans from institutional funds. Federal Work-Study Program available. Institutional employment available. Applicants will be notified of awards on or about April 1. Off-campus job opportunities are fair.

## FROM THE ADMISSIONS OFFICE

"Students and alumni alike think of Kenyon as a place that fosters 'learning in the company of friends.'. While faculty expectations are rigorous and the work challenging, the academic atmosphere is cooperative, not competitive. Indications of intellectual curiosity and passion for learning, more than just high grades and test scores, are what we look for in applications. Important as well are demonstrated interests in nonacademic pursuits, whether in athletics, the arts, writing, or another passion. Life in this small college community is fueled by the talents and enthusiasm of our students, so the admission staff seeks students who have a range of talents and interests."

## SELECTIVITY

| | |
|---|---|
| Admissions Rating | 92 |
| # of applicants | 3,356 |
| % of applicants accepted | 44 |
| % of acceptees attending | 30 |
| # accepting a place on wait list | 169 |
| % admitted from wait list | 31 |
| # of early decision applicants | 174 |
| % accepted early decision | 78 |

### FRESHMAN PROFILE

| | |
|---|---|
| Range SAT Verbal | 620-720 |
| Average SAT Verbal | 681 |
| Range SAT Math | 610-690 |
| Average SAT Math | 661 |
| Range ACT Composite | 27-32 |
| Average ACT Composite | 30 |
| Minimum TOEFL | 570 |
| Average HS GPA | 3.8 |
| % graduated top 10% of class | 51 |
| % graduated top 25% of class | 80 |
| % graduated top 50% of class | 97 |

### DEADLINES

| | |
|---|---|
| Early decision | 12/1 |
| Early decision notification | 12/15 |
| Regular admission | 2/1 |
| Regular notification | 4/1 |

### APPLICANTS ALSO LOOK AT
**AND OFTEN PREFER**
Brown
Northwestern
Williams
Middlebury, Oberlin
**AND SOMETIMES PREFER**
Bowdoin
Bates, Carleton
Colgate, Macalester
**AND RARELY PREFER**
Colby, Denison
Skidmore, Hamilton

### FINANCIAL FACTS

| | |
|---|---|
| Financial Aid Rating | 81 |
| Tuition | $27,900 |
| Room and board | $4,690 |
| Books and supplies | $950 |
| Required fees | $810 |
| % frosh receiving aid | 39 |
| % undergrads receiving aid | 45 |
| Avg frosh grant | $22,835 |
| Avg frosh loan | $3,577 |

# KNOX COLLEGE

Box K-148, Galesburg, IL 61401 • Admissions: 800-678-KNOX • Fax: 309-341-7070

## CAMPUS LIFE

★ ★ ★ ☆

| | |
|---|---|
| **Quality of Life Rating** | **87** |
| Type of school | private |
| Environment | rural |

### STUDENTS

| | |
|---|---|
| Total undergrad enrollment | 1,121 |
| % male/female | 47/53 |
| % from out of state | 44 |
| % from public high school | 88 |
| % live on campus | 96 |
| % in (# of) fraternities | 30 (5) |
| % in (# of) sororities | 10 (2) |
| % African American | 5 |
| % Asian | 5 |
| % Caucasian | 78 |
| % Hispanic | 4 |
| % international | 8 |
| # of countries represented | 32 |

### SURVEY SAYS . . .
Campus easy to get around
Great library
Great computer facilities
Lots of beer drinking
Campus is beautiful
Registration is a breeze
Lab facilities are great
Students are happy
Hard liquor is popular

## ACADEMICS

| | |
|---|---|
| **Academic Rating** | **92** |
| Calendar | other |
| Student/faculty ratio | 12:1 |
| % profs teaching UG courses | 100 |
| Avg lab size | 10-19 students |
| Avg reg class size | 10-19 students |

### MOST POPULAR MAJORS
Psychology
Economics
Biology/biological sciences

## STUDENTS SPEAK OUT

### Academics
"Freedom. Lots of freedom. Freedom to express, print, say, or do what you want." That's what tiny Knox College is all about, its students say, and that's why students praise this "extremely demanding" school. "If you're passionate and ambitious enough about something, you can make it happen at Knox," explains one undergrad. "New clubs are always starting, people get school money to fund trips to D.C. for protests, students direct their own plays, etc. The administration is supportive of just about anything." The student/faculty relationships here are "truly special, very relaxed, and very personal. Professors are more than educators. They dedicate their time to the students to ensure that everyone is getting out of the education what they put into it." The same holds true for student/administration relations; writes one student, "When I first visited Knox, I was greeted by Roger, who introduced himself as an alumnus. It wasn't until they introduced him in a speech that I knew he was the president of the college. But that's how it is at Knox: a very tight-knit community that works together." Knox is the kind of place that inspires long-term loyalty, which explains why "the amount of alumni that come back to speak to students is quite impressive." As one student summed up, "Rather than a school where one spends four years, Knox is a school that permeates your entire life."

### Life
If you've never heard of Knox's hometown of Galesburg, you aren't alone. Students here concede that "Galesburg is . . . well, Galesburg." Reported one undergrad, it "isn't exactly the center of the universe. Luckily for us, Knox is usually very conscious of this. They are very good about bringing in outside entertainment." Events include "student theatre, the choir, or sports, and while none of these events are sold out, they are fairly well attended. Outside speakers are sometimes scheduled and their talks are often crammed full." Other options include "movie night in the Round Room, Jazz Night at Cherry Street, or a band playing in The Gizmo." Despite the availability of such varied activity, many here tell us that Knox "definitely has a culture where all that 'happens' on the weekends is drinking at frat parties." As one student put it, "The weekends are weak, unless your friends consist of Keystone and Busch Light. Alcohol is a major factor at Knox. The Greek system is really strong." Despite the Greek presence, students tell us that the suite-style dorms, and not the Greek system, are the key to the school's social universe. "The suite system here is unique," explains one student. "Students usually live in a hall where all rooms open onto a common living area. This allows for interaction between everyone, not just the people that you live next to. In addition, you take a lot of classes together, so you can have a discussion on current issues or on an assignment for a class. It is very conducive to forming long-lasting friendships."

### Student Body
Students are adamant that Knox College "has a pretty broad range of students" among its small population. "This campus is so diverse ethnically, and no one comes from the same background," writes one student. "Everyone has different interests, likes, and dislikes. We're here for a common purpose—to learn—but other than that, we're all different." Although the "majority of students here are white liberals," there is also "a crowd of more conservative and religious (mostly white American) population," and students report that relations among the various groups are remarkably stress-free. Knox's "high school jock frat boys who haven't really grown up yet, rich kids that want to be hippies, kids that actually are hippies, and geeks that are happy to be left alone and play computer games" share one more common trait: they were "probably all the kind of smart, kind of strange, but not-too-weird students in high school. We all kind of fit in but were never really popular."

308 ■ THE BEST 351 COLLEGES

# KNOX COLLEGE

FINANCIAL AID: 309-341-7149 • E-MAIL: ADMISSION@KNOX.EDU • WEBSITE: WWW.KNOX.EDU

## ADMISSIONS

*Very important factors considered include:* secondary school record. *Important factors considered include:* class rank, essays, recommendations. *Other factors considered include:* alumni/ae relation, character/personal qualities, extracurricular activities, interview, minority status, standardized test scores, talent/ability, volunteer work. SAT I or ACT required. TOEFL required of all international applicants. High school diploma or GED is required. *High school units required/recommended:* 15 total required; 18 total recommended; 4 English recommended, 4 math recommended, 3 science recommended, 2 science lab recommended, 3 foreign language recommended, 2 social studies recommended, 2 history recommended.

### The Inside Word

A small applicant pool necessitates Knox's high acceptance rate. The student body is nonetheless well qualified, and candidates should show solid academic accomplishment.

## FINANCIAL AID

*Students should submit:* FAFSA, institution's own financial aid form. No deadline for regular filing. The Princeton Review suggests that all financial aid forms be submitted as soon as possible after January 1. *Need-based scholarships/grants offered:* Pell, SEOG, state scholarships/grants, private scholarships, the school's own gift aid. *Loan aid offered:* Direct Subsidized Stafford, Direct Unsubsidized Stafford, Direct PLUS, Federal Perkins, college/university loans from institutional funds. Federal Work-Study Program available. Institutional employment available. Applicants will be notified of awards on a rolling basis beginning on or about March 15. Off-campus job opportunities are fair.

## FROM THE ADMISSIONS OFFICE

"Freedom to Flourish: The idea is simple. College should be a place where you discover yourself—where your talents are nourished and your aspirations become clear. A place that prepares you to turn your dreams into reality. But this is not the only reason college is important. By helping you learn to think clearly and independently, getting you ready to face the future with confidence, college should make you free. At Knox you are challenged to think for yourself and to explain your ideas. You learn how to analyze and to write clearly. Your mind and talents are stretched by exploring new areas of knowledge. You grow, too, in unexpected ways, through the rich opportunities and challenges of life in this creative, vital community. By graduation, you have received a sound, comprehensive education and are ready for the future. You will have the skills, background, and confidence to make the future your own."

## SELECTIVITY

| | |
|---|---|
| Admissions Rating | 81 |
| # of applicants | 1,542 |
| % of applicants accepted | 72 |
| % of acceptees attending | 27 |

### FRESHMAN PROFILE

| | |
|---|---|
| Range SAT Verbal | 550-680 |
| Range SAT Math | 550-660 |
| Range ACT Composite | 23-29 |
| Minimum TOEFL | 550 |
| % graduated top 10% of class | 33 |
| % graduated top 25% of class | 67 |
| % graduated top 50% of class | 94 |

### DEADLINES

| | |
|---|---|
| Regular admission | 2/1 |
| Regular notification | 3/31 |
| Nonfall registration? | yes |

### APPLICANTS ALSO LOOK AT AND OFTEN PREFER
Northwestern U.
Grinell
U. Illinois—Urbana-Champaign

### AND SOMETIMES PREFER
Bradley
Lawrence U.
Beloit

## FINANCIAL FACTS

| | |
|---|---|
| Financial Aid Rating | 96 |
| Tuition | $24,105 |
| Room and board | $5,925 |
| Books and supplies | $600 |
| Required fees | $264 |
| % frosh receiving aid | 71 |
| % undergrads receiving aid | 75 |
| Avg frosh grant | $20,531 |
| Avg frosh loan | $4,306 |

# LAFAYETTE COLLEGE

118 MARKLE HALL, EASTON, PA 18042 • ADMISSIONS: 610-330-5100 • FAX: 610-330-5355

## CAMPUS LIFE

| Quality of Life Rating | 80 |
|---|---|
| Type of school | private |
| Affiliation | Presbyterian |
| Environment | suburban |

### STUDENTS

| Total undergrad enrollment | 2,300 |
|---|---|
| % male/female | 51/49 |
| % from out of state | 70 |
| % from public high school | 68 |
| % live on campus | 96 |
| % in (# of) fraternities | 26 (7) |
| % in (# of) sororities | 45 (6) |
| % African American | 5 |
| % Asian | 2 |
| % Caucasian | 91 |
| % Hispanic | 2 |
| % international | 5 |
| # of countries represented | 46 |

### SURVEY SAYS . . .
Frats and sororities dominate social scene
Diversity lacking on campus
Campus easy to get around
Classes are small
Students don't like Easton, PA
Theater is unpopular
Low cost of living

## ACADEMICS

| Academic Rating | 85 |
|---|---|
| Calendar | semester |
| Student/faculty ratio | 11:1 |
| Profs interesting rating | 94 |
| Profs accessible rating | 95 |
| % profs teaching UG courses | 100 |
| Avg lab size | 10-19 students |
| Avg reg class size | 10-19 students |

## STUDENTS SPEAK OUT

### Academics

With "an engineering program that is top notch for a small liberal arts school," "opportunities for research" usually available only at larger schools, and "great accessibility to professors," Lafayette College of Pennsylvania presents a superlative academic package to those interested in engineering, business, pre-law, and pre-medical studies. Students warn that "Lafayette's academic standards are very high. The courses are extremely challenging but rewarding as well. The topics are covered in detail, and the examinations require you to know the material in detail and be able to apply what you have learned, not just memorize it." The intimate atmosphere helps ease the burden of Lafayette's workload; as one student puts it, "The size is a big strength. I was amazed at the availability and enthusiasm of my professors and have had a fulfilling and challenging academic life. I wish I could afford to stay longer just so I could take all the classes that I am interested in taking. The selection is excellent." Professors here receive high marks; students report that profs "are always willing to spend extra time with you, helping you sift through schedule changes around registration time, attempting to understand what you want from Lafayette, and helping with any problems you may have with homework, tests, etc." The administration receives mixed reviews, with students complaining about the school's drinking policies and also about various administrative chores.

### Life

Undergrads report that "Lafayette's professors are demanding, so for the most part students study on weekdays and party during the weekend. Aside from academics, we spend time participating in sports, playing videogames, watching movies, and of course, partying." Students enjoy partying Wednesday through Saturday nights at the "huge" frats ("everyone goes to them and so many people join them") as well as at local bars on and around College Hill. Students report that "the administration is cracking down on the Greek system in general, and the alcohol policy has definitely affected the social life," so things may be changing here. Then again, maybe not; students here have complained of administration crackdowns in every edition of this guidebook, yet just as consistently report that drinking is big on campus. Students tell us that "LAF (Lafayette Activities Forum) brings a lot of great programs to campus," that "there are performances in the Williams Center quite frequently," and that "many students are involved in intramural sports, the choir has doubled in size in one year, and attendance at varsity sports events is a decent amount." In other words, the "absolutely beautiful" campus is a happening place. Not so for hometown Easton, which is "awful except the Crayola Factory, which is a neat place to visit." Students like to escape Easton and head to New York City, Philadelphia, or the New Jersey shore, all within reasonable driving distance.

### Student Body

Students admit that "Lafayette has the reputation of being Prep School Part II with the high percentage of upper-middle-class white students, and there are a lot of people who fit in this stereotype. If you are seeking diversity in the traditional sense of the word then Lafayette will probably disappoint you." Observes one undergrad, "We all wear our newest Abercrombie outfits and drive around in our SUVs and BMWs. I know Lafayette College is in Easton, Pennsylvania, but the area code should be 90210." Diversity has recently received a boost: "This year there were many more international students, which a lot of the student population was happy to see," writes one undergrad. Students "have great school spirit (especially against Lehigh) and are genuinely nice to one another," but also form "a lot of different cliques . . . that don't mix as much as you'd like." They are a conservative lot who are "very homophobic," according to some.

# LAFAYETTE COLLEGE

FINANCIAL AID: 610-330-5055 • E-MAIL: ADMISSIONS@LAFAYETTE.EDU • WEBSITE: WWW.LAFAYETTE.EDU

## ADMISSIONS

*Very important factors considered include:* secondary school record. *Important factors considered include:* alumni/ae relation, character/personal qualities, class rank, essays, extracurricular activities, minority status, recommendations, standardized test scores, talent/ability, volunteer work. *Other factors considered include:* geographical residence, interview, work experience. SAT I or ACT required; SAT II recommended. TOEFL required of all international applicants. *High school units required/recommended:* 16 total recommended; 4 English recommended, 3 math recommended, 2 science recommended, 2 science lab recommended, 2 foreign language recommended, 5 elective recommended.

### The Inside Word

Applications are reviewed three to five times and evaluated by as many as nine different committee members. In all cases, students who continually seek challenges and are willing to take risks academically win out over those who play it safe in order to maintain a high GPA.

## FINANCIAL AID

*Students should submit:* FAFSA, CSS/Financial Aid PROFILE, noncustodial (divorced/separated) parent's statement, business/farm supplement. Regular filing deadline is February 1. The Princeton Review suggests that all financial aid forms be submitted as soon as possible after January 1. *Need-based scholarships/grants offered:* Pell, SEOG, state scholarships/grants, private scholarships. *Loan aid offered:* FFEL Subsidized Stafford, FFEL Unsubsidized Stafford, FFEL PLUS, Federal Perkins, state loans, college/university loans from institutional funds, HELP loans to parents. Federal Work-Study Program available. Institutional employment available. Applicants will be notified of awards on or about April 1. Off-campus job opportunities are good.

## FROM THE ADMISSIONS OFFICE

"We choose students individually, one by one, and we hope that the ones we choose will approach their education the same way, as a highly individual enterprise. Our first-year seminars have enrollments limited to 15 or 16 students each in order to introduce the concept of learning not as passive receipt of information but as an active, participatory process. Our low average class size and 11:1 student/teacher ratio reflect that same philosophy. We also devote substantial resources to our Marquis Scholars Program, to one-on-one faculty-student mentoring relationships, and to other programs in engineering within a liberal arts context, giving Lafayette its distinctive character, articulated in our second-year seminars exploring values in science and technology. Lafayette provides an environment in which its students can discover their own personal capacity for learning, personal growth, and leadership."

### SELECTIVITY

| | |
|---|---|
| Admissions Rating | 86 |
| # of applicants | 5,504 |
| % of applicants accepted | 36 |
| % of acceptees attending | 30 |
| # accepting a place on wait list | 664 |
| % admitted from wait list | 4 |
| # of early decision applicants | 367 |
| % accepted early decision | 66 |

### FRESHMAN PROFILE

| | |
|---|---|
| Range SAT Verbal | 560-650 |
| Average SAT Verbal | 620 |
| Range SAT Math | 610-700 |
| Average SAT Math | 665 |
| Range ACT Composite | 25-29 |
| Average ACT Composite | 28 |
| Minimum TOEFL | 550 |
| Average HS GPA | 3.8 |
| % graduated top 10% of class | 59 |
| % graduated top 25% of class | 89 |
| % graduated top 50% of class | 100 |

### DEADLINES

| | |
|---|---|
| Early decision | 2/15 |
| Early decision notification | 12/1 |
| Priority admission | 1/1 |
| Regular admission | 1/1 |
| Regular notification | 4/1 |
| Nonfall registration? | yes |

### APPLICANTS ALSO LOOK AT
**AND OFTEN PREFER**
Princeton, Cornell, Tufts
Johns Hopkins, Boston College
**AND SOMETIMES PREFER**
Colgate, Bucknell
Villanova, Lehigh
**AND RARELY PREFER**
Trinity
Rensselaer Polytechnic Institute
Franklin & Marshall, Penn State

### FINANCIAL FACTS

| | |
|---|---|
| Financial Aid Rating | 82 |
| Tuition | $25,884 |
| Room and board | $8,069 |
| Books and supplies | $600 |
| Required fees | $98 |
| % frosh receiving aid | 57 |
| % undergrads receiving aid | 54 |
| Avg frosh grant | $20,552 |
| Avg frosh loan | $3,500 |

THE BEST 351 COLLEGES ■ 311

# LAKE FOREST COLLEGE

555 NORTH SHERIDAN ROAD, LAKE FOREST, IL 60045 • ADMISSIONS: 847-735-5000 • FAX: 847-735-6291

## CAMPUS LIFE

| | |
|---|---|
| Quality of Life Rating | 84 |
| Type of school | private |
| Affiliation | Presbyterian |
| Environment | suburban |

### STUDENTS

| | |
|---|---|
| Total undergrad enrollment | 1,319 |
| % male/female | 41/59 |
| % from out of state | 52 |
| % from public high school | 65 |
| % live on campus | 81 |
| % in (# of) fraternities | 19 (3) |
| % in (# of) sororities | 27 (4) |
| % African American | 6 |
| % Asian | 5 |
| % Caucasian | 85 |
| % Hispanic | 3 |
| % international | 8 |
| # of countries represented | 42 |

### SURVEY SAYS . . .
Great food on campus
Student publications are ignored
Classes are small
Campus feels safe
Computer facilities need improving
Lousy off-campus food
Class discussions encouraged

## ACADEMICS

| | |
|---|---|
| Academic Rating | 92 |
| Calendar | semester |
| Student/faculty ratio | 12:1 |
| Profs interesting rating | 97 |
| Profs accessible rating | 99 |
| % profs teaching UG courses | 100 |
| Avg lab size | 10-19 students |
| Avg reg class size | 10-19 students |

### MOST POPULAR MAJORS
Business/commerce
Psychology
Communications

## STUDENTS SPEAK OUT

### Academics
The 1,300 students that rub elbows at Lake Forest College believe they receive a quality education in the context of a supportive, liberal arts environment. Boasts one, "The fact that I have seen many of my professors in the cafeteria, at sporting events, and at music concerts on campus shows how concerned they are with everyone's total college experience." Not only do professors "go out of their way to make themselves accessible" both inside and outside the classroom, but the school offers free tutoring in every entry-level subject and many advanced classes. A senior sums it up, "I was challenged, but [also] given every resource I needed to succeed." Students tout not just the accessibility, but also the quality of the faculty, reporting that "Lake Forest boasts a wonderful mix of old and new professors who are second to none." Many agree that their professors "could be teaching at universities like Northwestern or University of Chicago for higher salaries," but choose LFC "because they love to teach and they believe in the liberal arts system of study." And while some call professors "nurturing," others think "overbearing" is the more appropriate word to describe them. Similarly, what some call a "supportive" environment, others describe as "a bit on the easy side."

### Life
Located 30 miles north of Chicago, in the affluent, "mansion-filled" suburb of Lake Forest, it's no surprise that students "often gripe about the town shutting down too early" and declare that the surrounding area is "not a college town at all." Most see benefit to the setup, however, explaining that "being at such a small school in a small town creates a true cohesive community." Though Chicago is "an easy train ride away," many LFC students choose to hang out on campus, where they can participate in the school's "really strong drama organization" or kill some time playing and watching sports. Enthuses one undergrad, "Everyone enjoys going to support every sport, not just the big ones like basketball and football." Agrees another, "For fun we either play sports (basketball, powder puff football), support our awesome sports teams . . . go to bars, or hang out at the quad." On the weekends, "the Campus Activities department does a lot to try and help by bringing lots of stuff to the campus." The consensus is that the plentiful "all-campus parties" are the preferred venues for blowing off steam. Students describe Lake Forest as a "wet campus" and says that a large portion of the "social life revolves around drinking beer."

### Student Body
Though some claim "Lake Forest is a very economically diverse school," others are skeptical of this description. However, it is undeniable that the school gives out a ton of need-based financial aid—to 70 percent of its students, to be exact. Indeed, it is reported that Lake Forest's undergraduate population primarily consists of "smart kids from the public and private high schools across the country" mixed with some "New England boarding school types." However, "there is a growing group of ethnic minorities on campus," and "faculty and staff [are] extremely supportive of gay students." Nonetheless, Lake Forest students say that the majority of their classmates "respect the difference of others, even if they don't agree with them," and that "for the most part, people seem to get along."

# LAKE FOREST COLLEGE

FINANCIAL AID: 847-735-5103 • E-MAIL: ADMISSIONS@LFC.EDU • WEBSITE: WWW.LAKEFOREST.EDU

## ADMISSIONS

*Very important factors considered include:* secondary school record. *Important factors considered include:* essays, extracurricular activities. *Other factors considered include:* alumni/ae relation, character/personal qualities, class rank, geographical residence, interview, recommendations, standardized test scores, talent/ability, volunteer work, work experience. SAT I or ACT required. TOEFL required of all international applicants. High school diploma or GED is required. *High school units required/recommended:* 16 total required; 19 total recommended; 4 English required, 3 math required, 4 math recommended, 2 science required, 3 science recommended, 2 science lab required, 3 science lab recommended, 2 foreign language required, 4 foreign language recommended, 1 social studies required, 2 social studies recommended, 1 history required, 2 history recommended, 3 elective required.

### The Inside Word

Candidates with a solid academic record will meet with little resistance on the road to acceptance. But remember that Lake Forest definitely has a prep-school-at-the-college-level feel. It pays to keep the admissions committee's eagerness to assess the whole person in mind when completing the application.

## FINANCIAL AID

*Students should submit:* FAFSA, CSS/Financial Aid PROFILE, federal income tax return. The Princeton Review suggests that all financial aid forms be submitted as soon as possible after January 1. *Need-based scholarships/grants offered:* Pell, SEOG, state scholarships/grants, private scholarships, the school's own gift aid. *Loan aid offered:* Direct Subsidized Stafford, Direct Unsubsidized Stafford, Direct PLUS, Federal Perkins, college/university loans from institutional funds. Federal Work-Study Program available. Institutional employment available. Applicants will be notified of awards on a rolling basis beginning on or about March 15. Off-campus job opportunities are good.

## FROM THE ADMISSIONS OFFICE

"Where you go to college can have everything to do with what you get out of college. As you think about the academic challenges and resources you seek—and the overall experience you desire—consider what Lake Forest College has to offer you.

"Lake Forest College is Chicago's national liberal arts college. Located 30 miles north of downtown Chicago, the College's proximity to the city provides Lake Forest students and faculty with unique academic, cultural, and employment resources. Through partnerships with a variety of cultural, educational, financial, research, and scientific institutions in Chicago and its environs, students are engaged in an active learning process that takes them beyond the traditional boundaries of the classroom, integrating the theoretical and the practical.

"The 1,300 students represent 43 countries and 45 states. Lake Forest College fosters interaction among a diverse community of students and faculty with a significant international and minority population. The faculty are dedicated teachers and accomplished scholars, with 98 percent holding a PhD or equivalent. The faculty do all the teaching; you will not find teaching assistants at Lake Forest. The College's Career Advancement Center (CAC) begins working with students during their first year on campus, and later provides mentoring opportunities with alumni from around the globe as well as internship assistance and job placement.

"College should be demanding, but not a relentless grind. With more than 80 student-run organizations and clubs, 17 varsity NCAA Division III teams, and a variety of intramural and club sports, students find many opportunities outside the classroom."

## SELECTIVITY

★ ★ ☆ ☆

| | |
|---|---|
| Admissions Rating | 79 |
| # of applicants | 1,666 |
| % of applicants accepted | 66 |
| % of acceptees attending | 33 |
| # accepting a place on wait list | 21 |
| % admitted from wait list | 43 |
| # of early decision applicants | 40 |
| % accepted early decision | 63 |

### FRESHMAN PROFILE

| | |
|---|---|
| Range SAT Verbal | 520-620 |
| Average SAT Verbal | 570 |
| Range SAT Math | 510-620 |
| Average SAT Math | 573 |
| Range ACT Composite | 23-28 |
| Average ACT Composite | 25 |
| Minimum TOEFL | 550 |
| Average HS GPA | 3.4 |
| % graduated top 10% of class | 25 |
| % graduated top 25% of class | 53 |
| % graduated top 50% of class | 80 |

### DEADLINES

| | |
|---|---|
| Early decision | 12/1 |
| Early decision notification | 12/15 |
| Regular admission | 3/1 |
| Regular notification | 3/15 |
| Nonfall registration? | yes |

### APPLICANTS ALSO LOOK AT AND OFTEN PREFER

Kenyon
Connecticut College
Northwestern

### AND SOMETIMES PREFER

U of Illinois at Urbana Champaign
U of Denver
Lewis & Clark
U of Wisconsin at Madison

### AND RARELY PREFER

DePaul, Loyola U Chicago

## FINANCIAL FACTS

★ ★ ★ ★

| | |
|---|---|
| Financial Aid Rating | 93 |
| Tuition | $24,096 |
| Room and board | $5,764 |
| Books and supplies | $600 |
| Required fees | $310 |
| % frosh receiving aid | 70 |
| % undergrads receiving aid | 70 |
| Avg frosh grant | $17,496 |
| Avg frosh loan | $3,599 |

# LAWRENCE UNIVERSITY

PO Box 599, Appleton, WI 54912-0599 • Admissions: 920-832-6500 • Fax: 920-832-6782

## CAMPUS LIFE

| Quality of Life Rating | 81 |
|---|---|
| Type of school | private |
| Environment | suburban |

### STUDENTS

| Total undergrad enrollment | 1,392 |
|---|---|
| % male/female | 47/53 |
| % from out of state | 59 |
| % from public high school | 81 |
| % live on campus | 98 |
| % in (# of) fraternities | 30 (5) |
| % in (# of) sororities | 15 (3) |
| % African American | 2 |
| % Asian | 2 |
| % Caucasian | 78 |
| % Hispanic | 3 |
| % international | 10 |

### SURVEY SAYS . . .
No one cheats
Student publications are ignored
Classes are small
Campus feels safe
Students aren't religious
Musical organizations are hot
Low cost of living
Diverse students interact
No one plays intramural sports

## ACADEMICS

| Academic Rating | 92 |
|---|---|
| Calendar | trimester |
| Student/faculty ratio | 11:1 |
| Profs interesting rating | 96 |
| Profs accessible rating | 98 |
| % profs teaching UG courses | 100 |
| Avg reg class size | 10-19 students |

### MOST POPULAR MAJORS
Biology/biological sciences
Psychology
Music performance

## STUDENTS SPEAK OUT

### Academics

Students at Lawrence University, a small midwestern school, brag about their "very strong" and "nationally known" biology, psychology, and music programs. Other departments are solid, too, although some students worry that the school sometimes ignores its less renowned programs in order to tout its star attractions. Across the board, "the academics at Lawrence are challenging and the class work is rigorous but fulfilling." Writes one student, "Lawrence is tough, but you do get a top-notch education for how hard you work. Because of the school's size, Lawrence's faculty expects each student to do their absolute best rather than fulfilling a general class requirement." Many departments place a strong emphasis on writing skills; students note approvingly that the school provides "facilities that assist students with their work, such as the writing lab, where students can go to check their paper before handing it in to the professors." Professors, students agree, "are amazing. They are great teachers and wonderful people. They are always available for student questions and concerns, or just to chat." Administrators are "very friendly and accessible. The president of the college can often be seen walking through the campus," and "the facilities are great."

### Life

Lawrence is home to a pretty placid social scene, according to most students. "If partying is your scene, Lawrence probably isn't the answer. Occasionally there are frat parties, and alcohol is sometimes available if you hunt it down." Usually, though, "weekends on campus are dull," reports one typical student. Hometown Appleton "is not the most exciting place to be. The movie theatres are about two miles away, as are the grocery stores and the mall. It's crucial to know someone with a car." Students appreciate the fact that "the small community makes for a safe and cozy environment" but still wish the town had more to offer in the way of diversion. Lawrence does have a very active arts scene featuring "a lot of student and faculty (and guest) concerts to go to because of the conservatory presence." There are also "several film societies that show art films or theme-related films on a regular basis," art openings, and "guest performers at the underground coffeehouse." Students enjoy "sledding down Union Hill on cafeteria trays" during the long winter months and note that "the residence halls put on activities for us, like Capture the Flag between two halls. In the fall the frat quad will have barbeques for the campus, and everybody will go have a hot dog and play Frisbee or pass around a football." Still, many students find that "for fun, we end up watching movies or hanging out to play cards or darts."

### Student Body

Lawrence's "very open-minded," "friendly" undergrads "seems to be from a specific income bracket and social background. Diversity would be nice, but it's hard to come by at a school that costs so much to attend," explains one undergrad. Students observe that "the admissions committee does a great deal to offset this homogenous group by attracting a large number of international students, which benefits the student body as a whole," although many also say that internationals tend to keep to themselves. Students also report that "conservatory students do not interact much with the other students." Despite the divisions, undergrads admire each other's "overall spunk and good humor in the face of frigid weather and snowballing homework." There is "a large homosexual population, and everyone accepts them. I've seen gay couples dancing at frat parties."

# LAWRENCE UNIVERSITY

FINANCIAL AID: 920-832-6583 • E-MAIL: EXCEL@LAWRENCE.EDU • WEBSITE: WWW.LAWRENCE.EDU

## ADMISSIONS
*Very important factors considered include:* secondary school record. *Important factors considered include:* class rank, essays, minority status, recommendations, standardized test scores, talent/ability. *Other factors considered include:* character/personal qualities, extracurricular activities, interview, volunteer work, alumni/ae relation, work experience. SAT I or ACT required. TOEFL required of all international applicants. High school diploma is required and GED is not accepted. *High school units required/recommended:* 4 English recommended, 3 math recommended, 3 science recommended, 3 foreign language recommended, 2 social studies recommended, 2 history recommended.

### The Inside Word
Although the admit rate is fairly high, getting into Lawrence demands an above-average academic record. Students who are serious about the university should stick with a very challenging high school courseload straight through senior year, put significant energy into their application essays, and definitely interview.

## FINANCIAL AID
*Students should submit:* FAFSA, institution's own financial aid form. Regular filing deadline is March 15. The Princeton Review suggests that all financial aid forms be submitted as soon as possible after January 1. *Need-based scholarships/grants offered:* Pell, SEOG, state scholarships/grants, private scholarships, the school's own gift aid. *Loan aid offered:* Direct Subsidized Stafford, Direct Unsubsidized Stafford, Direct PLUS, Federal Perkins. Federal Work-Study Program available. Institutional employment available. Applicants will be notified of awards on or about April 15. Off-campus job opportunities are excellent.

## FROM THE ADMISSIONS OFFICE
"Lawrence students are characterized by their energy, commitment to community service, respect for each other, and desire to achieve their full potential. Campus activities are abundant, off-campus study programs are popular (more than half of the students take advantage of them), small classes are the norm (65 percent of the classes have 10 or fewer students in them), and, yes, winters are for the hardy! But the diversity of interests and experiences, the drive to excel, the wealth of cultural opportunities presented by the art, theater, and music departments, the quality of research students undertake alongside PhD faculty, and the general friendly attitude of everyone at the university contribute to an excitement that more than outweighs the challenge of winter."

## SELECTIVITY

| | |
|---|---|
| Admissions Rating | 85 |
| # of applicants | 1,812 |
| % of applicants accepted | 68 |
| % of acceptees attending | 29 |
| # accepting a place on wait list | 53 |
| % admitted from wait list | 21 |
| # of early decision applicants | 17 |
| % accepted early decision | 94 |

### FRESHMAN PROFILE
| | |
|---|---|
| Range SAT Verbal | 560-690 |
| Average SAT Verbal | 620 |
| Range SAT Math | 560-670 |
| Average SAT Math | 625 |
| Range ACT Composite | 24-30 |
| Average ACT Composite | 27 |
| Minimum TOEFL | 575 |
| Average HS GPA | 3.5 |
| % graduated top 10% of class | 36 |
| % graduated top 25% of class | 73 |
| % graduated top 50% of class | 94 |

### DEADLINES
| | |
|---|---|
| Early decision | 11/15 |
| Early decision notification | 12/1 |
| Regular admission | 1/15 |
| Regular notification | 4/1 |

### APPLICANTS ALSO LOOK AT
**AND OFTEN PREFER**
Carleton University
**AND SOMETIMES PREFER**
Beloit College
Macalester College
**AND RARELY PREFER**
Ripon College

## FINANCIAL FACTS

| | |
|---|---|
| Financial Aid Rating | 91 |
| Tuition | $23,487 |
| Room and board | $5,337 |
| Books and supplies | $555 |
| Required fees | $180 |
| % frosh receiving aid | 69 |
| % undergrads receiving aid | 70 |
| Avg frosh grant | $15,569 |
| Avg frosh loan | $2,780 |

# LEHIGH UNIVERSITY

27 MEMORIAL DRIVE WEST, BETHLEHEM, PA 18015 • ADMISSIONS: 610-758-3100 • FAX: 610-758-4361

## CAMPUS LIFE

| | |
|---|---|
| Quality of Life Rating | 85 |
| Type of school | private |
| Environment | suburban |

### STUDENTS
| | |
|---|---|
| Total undergrad enrollment | 4,685 |
| % male/female | 60/40 |
| % from public high school | 69 |
| % live on campus | 65 |
| % in (# of) fraternities | 33 (23) |
| % in (# of) sororities | 43 (9) |
| % African American | 3 |
| % Asian | 6 |
| % Caucasian | 76 |
| % Hispanic | 3 |
| % international | 3 |

### SURVEY SAYS . . .
Beautiful campus
Great library
Great computer facilities
Athletic facilities are great
Frats and sororities dominate social scene
Students don't like Bethlehem, PA
Political activism is (almost) nonexistent
Lousy off-campus food

## ACADEMICS

| | |
|---|---|
| Academic Rating | 87 |
| Calendar | semester |
| Student/faculty ratio | 10:1 |
| Profs interesting rating | 77 |
| Profs accessible rating | 96 |
| % profs teaching UG courses | 100 |

## STUDENTS SPEAK OUT

### Academics
Lehigh is well known for its P.C. Rossin College of Engineering and Applied Science and College of Business and Economics. But with about 45 percent of its undergrads enrolled in the College of Arts and Sciences, the university has made recent attempts to bolster the quality of its liberal arts program. Regardless of what college the students settle into, most of them say that they've found "wonderful professors" who teach "very challenging" classes. Students are less enthusiastic about the "pretty bad" TAs and the regularity of visiting professors. As students progress, they often find that their classes become smaller. And "smaller classes are better," states an upperclassman. Opinions about the administration vary from "annoying in the way they get things done" to "superb." Regardless of dissent as to how the administration responds to them, students agree that they are "free to have an open and honest opinion" that'll be heard—in class or elsewhere.

### Life
A few students have told us that Lehigh no longer deserves its reputation as a party school, but this is a minority opinion. "There's no denying it," report most students, "drinking is huge." "Work Hard, Drink Harder," is a common refrain heard from Lehigh undergrads. While "a decent amount of off-campus parties" provide bibulous opportunities, most of the guzzling takes place on "The Hill," where the university's 23 fraternity houses lie. "Hotels" are favorite frat events, where a "different mixed drink [waits] in every room of a frat." These sorts of bacchanalian fêtes are less common today than they were a few years ago, thanks largely to campus initiatives for a healthier and safer living and learning environment. "It's not all drinking and smoking" at Lehigh. There's often a good turnout "at on-campus events like theatre shows, magicians, psychics, comedians, and sports events." A student group called University Productions works hard to make sure that the entertainment options keep coming. As for the surrounding town of Bethlehem, students complain about its "dull nature" and the fact that it's "not a very inviting town for the students." If upperclassmen have cars (freshmen aren't allowed to have them), they'll often take day trips to Philadelphia or New York, each about an hour away.

### Student Body
When making plans to attend Lehigh University, the first thing one buys is a sturdy pair of hiking boots. Clinging to the side of Bethlehem, Pennsylvania's "Old South Mountain," Lehigh's campus is an ivy-covered spread of "pretty buildings and steps." "Getting around is a chore—unless you are a mountain goat," jokes one student. Perhaps as a result of the hardy physiques students develop walking to and from class, "almost everyone participates in sports of some kind." Students here have other things in common, as well. Most of them "are from New York, New Jersey, or Pennsylvania," and many "are white, upper-middle class." On this note, one student grumbles, "Everyone wears the same clothes, the same makeup, carries the same bag, and does their hair the same way. After a while I started to wonder if I was just running into the same person over and over and over." While students will admit the campus' homogeneity, they tell us that it remains an open and tolerant community. "I am Asian and have found no problems as far as discrimination goes," assures a satisfied student. Overall, "friendliness" is the glue that holds together this undergraduate body of 4,700 students. Another thing that envelops undergrads is Greek life. About 37 percent of Lehigh students are members of fraternities or sororities. But students say there aren't many schisms between Greeks and non-Greeks, and "everyone seems to get along."

316 ■ THE BEST 351 COLLEGES

# LEHIGH UNIVERSITY

FINANCIAL AID: 610-758-3181 • E-MAIL: ADMISSIONS@LEHIGH.EDU • WEBSITE: WWW.LEHIGH.EDU

## ADMISSIONS

*Very important factors considered include:* secondary school record. *Important factors considered include:* character/personal qualities, essays, extracurricular activities, recommendations, standardized test scores, talent/ability, volunteer work. *Other factors considered include:* alumni/ae relation, class rank, geographical residence, minority status, state residency, work experience. SAT I or ACT required. TOEFL required of all international applicants. High school diploma or GED is required. *High school units required/recommended:* 16 total required; 4 English required, 3 math required, 2 science required, 2 foreign language required, 2 social studies required, 3 elective required.

### The Inside Word

Lots of work at bolstering Lehigh's public recognition for overall academic quality has paid off—liberal arts candidates will now find the admissions process to be highly selective. Students without solidly impressive academic credentials will have a rough time getting in regardless of their choice of programs. So will unenthusiastic but academically strong candidates who have clearly chosen Lehigh as a safety.

## FINANCIAL AID

*Students should submit:* FAFSA, CSS/Financial Aid PROFILE, noncustodial (divorced/separated) parent's statement, business/farm supplement. The Princeton Review suggests that all financial aid forms be submitted as soon as possible after January 1. *Need-based scholarships/grants offered:* Pell, SEOG, state scholarships/grants, private scholarships, the school's own gift aid. *Loan aid offered:* FFEL Subsidized Stafford, FFEL Unsubsidized Stafford, FFEL PLUS, Federal Perkins, college/university loans from institutional funds. Federal Work-Study Program available. Institutional employment available. Applicants will be notified of awards on or about March 30. Off-campus job opportunities are fair. Merit scholarships offered.

## FROM THE ADMISSIONS OFFICE

"Lehigh University is located 50 miles north of Philadelphia and 90 miles southwest of New York City in Bethlehem, Pennsylvania, where a cultural renaissance has taken place with the opening of more than a dozen ethnic restaurants, the addition of several boutiques and galleries, and Lehigh's new Campus Square residential/retail complex.

"Lehigh combines learning opportunities of a large research university with the personal attention of a small, private college, by offering an education that integrates courses from four colleges and dozens of fields of study. Students customize their experience to their interests by tailoring majors and academic programs from more than 2,000 courses, changing majors, carrying a double major, or taking courses outside their college or major field of study. Lehigh offers unique learning opportunities through interdisciplinary programs such as music and engineering and computer science and business (www.lehigh.edu/specialprograms). The arts are essential to the learning experience and are integrated throughout the curriculum. Students develop their imagination and creativity while acquiring skills that will complement their professional development.

"Students have access to world-class faculty who offer their time and personal attention to help students learn and succeed. Students gain hands-on, real-world experience and take part in activities that build confidence and help them develop as leaders.

"Lehigh's vibrant campus life offers many social and extracurricular activities. Choose from 130 clubs and social organizations or 24 intercollegiate sports teams or become one of the 3,500 students (75 percent) who participate in intramural and club programs."

## SELECTIVITY

| | |
|---|---|
| Admissions Rating | 88 |
| # of applicants | 8,254 |
| % of applicants accepted | 44 |
| % of acceptees attending | 31 |
| # accepting a place on wait list | 1,319 |
| % admitted from wait list | 1 |
| # of early decision applicants | 467 |
| % accepted early decision | 80 |

### FRESHMAN PROFILE

| | |
|---|---|
| Range SAT Verbal | 580-660 |
| Average SAT Verbal | 617 |
| Range SAT Math | 630-710 |
| Average SAT Math | 665 |
| Minimum TOEFL | 570 |
| % graduated top 10% of class | 55 |
| % graduated top 25% of class | 88 |
| % graduated top 50% of class | 99 |

### DEADLINES

| | |
|---|---|
| Early decision | 11/15 |
| Early decision notification | 12/15 |
| Regular admission | 1/1 |
| Regular notification | 4/1 |
| Nonfall registration? | yes |

### APPLICANTS ALSO LOOK AT

**AND OFTEN PREFER**
U of Pennsylvania
Cornell U

**AND SOMETIMES PREFER**
Penn State at University Park
Bucknell
Carnegie Mellon
Boston College

**AND RARELY PREFER**
NYU
Villanova
Lafayette
Rutgers

## FINANCIAL FACTS

| | |
|---|---|
| Financial Aid Rating | 85 |
| Tuition | $27,230 |
| Room and board | $7,880 |
| Required fees | $200 |
| % frosh receiving aid | 43 |
| % undergrads receiving aid | 46 |
| Avg frosh grant | $13,676 |
| Avg frosh loan | $4,424 |

# LEWIS & CLARK COLLEGE

0615 SW PALATINE HILL ROAD, PORTLAND, OR 97219-7899 • ADMISSIONS: 800-444-4111 • FAX: 503-768-7055

## CAMPUS LIFE

| | |
|---|---|
| Quality of Life Rating | 84 |
| Type of school | private |
| Environment | Urban |

### STUDENTS

| | |
|---|---|
| Total undergrad enrollment | 1,763 |
| % male/female | 40/60 |
| % from out of state | 87 |
| % from public high school | 66 |
| % live on campus | 63 |
| % African American | 2 |
| % Asian | 6 |
| % Caucasian | 67 |
| % Hispanic | 3 |
| % international | 5 |
| # of countries represented | 44 |

### SURVEY SAYS . . .
Students aren't religious
Great off-campus food
Students love Portland, OR
Political activism is hot
Hard liquor is popular
Great library
Theater is unpopular
Intercollegiate sports unpopular or nonexistent
Student government is unpopular

## ACADEMICS

| | |
|---|---|
| Academic Rating | 84 |
| Calendar | semester |
| Student/faculty ratio | 12:1 |
| Profs interesting rating | 94 |
| Profs accessible rating | 94 |
| % profs teaching UG courses | 100 |
| Avg lab size | 10-19 students |
| Avg reg class size | 10-19 students |

### MOST POPULAR MAJORS
English language and literature
Biology/biological sciences
Psychology

## STUDENTS SPEAK OUT

### Academics
Many Lewis and Clark faculty put the 'liberal' in 'liberal arts education,' according to many of its students. Writes one, "The professors are great people, very knowledgeable, openly left-wing, enthusiastic, and fun. They help create the radical, liberal . . . atmosphere on campus," but equally important is that they are "totally happy" to be teaching here. Agrees another, "The professors here are awesome. They are very accessible and many are involved in activist campaigns both on and off campus, which makes it easy to get to know them as people and as equals." Reports on LC's administration ran the gamut from "administration-bashing as sport" to claims that they are "totally accessible." Students note that "academics are strong at LC, but there is a lack of diversity for major choices." Students may, however, "design their own majors, and grants are awarded to students to fund research toward those majors." Some worry that the school doesn't push its students hard enough; writes one, "The folks who teach here certainly have the capacity to teach well, but they seem to believe that the students can't handle a challenge. This school can be challenging; I just wish the students wanted to be challenged. Grade inflation is a problem." Most students, however, enjoy LC and appreciate how the school "pushes people to think in new areas and mentally get out of their comfort zones."

### Life
Students describe campus life at LC as quiet except for the occasional Ultimate Frisbee match or protest rally. Most prefer to seek entertainment in hometown Portland. Explains one undergrad, "One of the main reasons I came here was for Portland, and I haven't been let down with all the opportunities to explore art, theater, music, food, and the outdoors." Among the large contingent with whom patchouli oil is popular, "jam bands" are very popular. Students explain that "it's bearable to live on campus without a car because the college runs free shuttles to Portland and a nearby grocery store." As far as on-campus activity goes, writes one senior, "the fact that . . . there are no fraternities probably attributes to the [big number] of students in the library on a Friday night." There are "a large number of student organizations on campus [that] represent the range of diversities at the school. Unfortunately, this serves to create factions among students because we are so spread out." Many students are politically active, explaining that "we like to cause trouble, in a good way."

### Student Body
LC is home to either a large hippie population or a large hippie-wannabe population, depending on whom you ask. Writes one student, "The cliché about Lewis & Clark is that everyone sits under the trees all day playing didgeridoos and smoking pot, nobody showers, and we voted for Nader. Clichés exist for a reason: they are always rooted in some truth." Counters another, "At LC, there are no real hippies. You think you're going to a hippie school, and sure, there's pot, but all the kids—with their Birkenstocks and open sexualities and political activism—are calling mom every weekend on their cell phones to see if she can wire out some more cash because they want to go to some concert." LC "tends to be very left-wing," and "most students here have a cause that they feel strongly about and are very knowledgeable about." Some complain about the 3:2 ratio of female to male students. Others would like to see more diversity: "It's awful. And everyone here has brown eyes, curly hair, and wears bandannas. Definitely needs to work on diversity . . . . I think they're trying to, but failing."

# LEWIS & CLARK COLLEGE

FINANCIAL AID: 503-768-7090 • E-MAIL: ADMISSIONS@LCLARK.EDU • WEBSITE: WWW.LCLARK.EDU

## ADMISSIONS

*Very important factors considered include:* secondary school record, class rank, standardized test scores, essays, minority status. *Important factors considered include:* character/personal qualities, extracurricular activities, interview, recommendations, alumni relation. *Other factors considered include:* geographical residence, state residency, work experience. TOEFL or equivalent required of all international applicants. High school diploma or GED is required. *High school units required/recommended:* 16 total recommended; 4 English recommended, 3–4 math recommended, 3 science recommended, 3 science lab recommended, 2–3 foreign language recommended, 3–4 social studies recommended, 1 fine arts recommended.

### The Inside Word

Admissions evaluations are thorough, and the Portfolio Path is an intriguing option that guarantees a purely personal evaluation. Few colleges of Lewis & Clark's quality are as accommodating to students.

## FINANCIAL AID

*Students should submit:* FAFSA. Regular filing deadline is March 1. The Princeton Review suggests that all financial aid forms be submitted as soon as possible after January 1. *Need-based scholarships/grants offered:* Pell, SEOG, state scholarships/grants, private scholarships, the school's own gift aid. *Loan aid offered:* FFEL Subsidized Stafford, FFEL Unsubsidized Stafford, FFEL PLUS, Federal Perkins. Federal Work-Study Program available. Institutional employment available. Applicants will be notified of awards on or about April 1. Off-campus job opportunities are fair.

## FROM THE ADMISSIONS OFFICE

"A record number of applicants in recent years cited a variety of reasons they were drawn to Lewis & Clark. Many had to do with the multiple environments experienced by our students, including (1) a small arts and sciences college with a 12:1 student/faculty ratio; (2) a location only six miles from downtown Portland (metropolitan population 1.7 million); (3) a setting in the heart of the Pacific Northwest, making more than 80 trips per year possible for our College Outdoors Program; and (4) the rest of the world—more than 55 percent of our graduates included an overseas program in their curriculum. Since 1962, more than 8,600 students and 192 faculty members have participated in 512 programs in 66 countries on 6 continents. Our international curriculum has undergone a total review to better prepare graduates going into the twenty-first century."

---

### SELECTIVITY

| | |
|---|---|
| Admissions Rating | 85 |
| # of applicants | 3,223 |
| % of applicants accepted | 68 |
| % of acceptees attending | 23 |
| # accepting a place on wait list | 143 |
| % admitted from wait list | 15 |

### FRESHMAN PROFILE

| | |
|---|---|
| Range SAT Verbal | 600-690 |
| Range SAT Math | 580-670 |
| Range ACT Composite | 25-29 |
| Minimum TOEFL | 550 |
| Average HS GPA | 3.6 |
| % graduated top 10% of class | 36 |
| % graduated top 25% of class | 73 |
| % graduated top 50% of class | 96 |

### DEADLINES

| | |
|---|---|
| Priority admission | 2/1 |
| Regular admission | 2/1 |
| Regular notification | 4/1 |
| Nonfall registration? | yes |

### APPLICANTS ALSO LOOK AT AND OFTEN PREFER

UC Berkeley
Pomona
Wesleyan

### AND SOMETIMES PREFER

U of Puget Sound
Colorado College
Whitman
Willamette

### AND RARELY PREFER

U of Oregon
U of Colorado
Pitzer

### FINANCIAL FACTS

| | |
|---|---|
| Financial Aid Rating | 85 |
| Tuition | $23,730 |
| Room and board | $6,630 |
| Books and supplies | $800 |
| Required fees | $200 |
| % frosh receiving aid | 54 |
| % undergrads receiving aid | 55 |

# LOUISIANA STATE UNIVERSITY—BATON ROUGE

110 THOMAS BOYD HALL, BATON ROUGE, LA 70803 • ADMISSIONS: 225-578-1175 • FAX: 225-578-4433

## CAMPUS LIFE

| | |
|---|---|
| Quality of Life Rating | 88 |
| Type of school | public |
| Environment | urban |

### STUDENTS

| | |
|---|---|
| Total undergrad enrollment | 26,660 |
| % male/female | 47/53 |
| % from out of state | 8 |
| % live on campus | 22 |
| % in (# of) fraternities | 10 (23) |
| % in (# of) sororities | 16 (15) |
| % African American | 10 |
| % Asian | 3 |
| % Caucasian | 80 |
| % Hispanic | 2 |
| % international | 3 |
| # of countries represented | 123 |

### SURVEY SAYS . . .
Everyone loves the Tigers
Lots of beer drinking
(Almost) everyone smokes
Hard liquor is popular
No one cheats
Frats and sororities dominate social scene
Dorms are like palaces
Great on-campus food
Students are religious

## ACADEMICS

| | |
|---|---|
| Academic Rating | 74 |
| Calendar | semester |
| Student/faculty ratio | 21:1 |
| % profs teaching UG courses | 61 |
| % classes taught by TAs | 15 |
| Avg lab size | 10-19 students |
| Avg reg class size | 10-19 students |

### MOST POPULAR MAJORS
Biological sciences
Psychology
Mass communication

## STUDENTS SPEAK OUT

### Academics

Typical of the Louisiana spirit and sense of priorities, students at LSU boast that their school "is a wonderful place to learn, meet people, and actually have fun." A "tough school in some areas, but pretty laid-back in general," LSU offers "a huge variety of subjects to study," including well-regarded programs in engineering, business and management, and basic science. Students here enjoy a more personable atmosphere than is found at most large state schools. Reports one undergrad, "At a big school like LSU, it is easy to assume that professors and other officials do not care about students, but that is not true. I will never forget my first English professor, who brought the entire class [out] for ice cream on a hot day and let us write a paper comparing the two flavors he bought for [each of] us." Another agrees, "I was genuinely surprised by the accessibility of administrators and professors at LSU. Everyone seems to want their students to both learn and perform well academically." On the whole, however, professors here receive mixed grades. "Most professors are average," says one student. "Only a few are memorable, both on the great end and the terrible end." Writes another, "Overall, most professors know what they're talking about. However, there are a few who don't and need to consult other professors about every question asked. Students appreciate the "great internships and research opportunities" the university affords them.

### Life

"Students reacted with mixed emotions to their school's ranking in 2000 as the "Number One Party School" in a certain college guide. Though the ranking was based entirely on information LSU students reported about campus life there, some students responded with skepticism. Said a sophomore accounting major, "They don't really have parties on campus or anything like that." But a freshman called the ranking "a source of pride" and a senior said it was "pretty much accurate," adding, "It doesn't have to mean it's a bad thing. I party, but I do well in school, and that goes for most of my friends." Everyone agrees, however, that this is a fun place to go to school." According to LSU's student newspaper, *The Daily Reveille*, even the school's Chancellor, Mark Emmert, agrees, saying before a group of fraternity leaders, "Being ranked the number one party school is fine with me if it means this is a fun place to study." The LSU experience is enhanced by "great school spirit," as well as "beautiful surroundings, an excellent learning environment," and a plethora of extracurricular activities that include "local bands, trips to New Orleans, community service, social gatherings at apartments, drinking games, flirting, etc." Athletic events, of course, are number one. Writes one undergrad, "Student life is great, especially during football season when the students tailgate before and after the game." Baseball and basketball also attract large crowds here, and students appreciate the "300-plus student organizations on campus, giving us many ways to get involved." Hometown Baton Rouge "is fantastic! The city also offers plenty in the way of live music and "really good restaurants (Louisiana cuisine is great!)" Students have few complaints here but do point out that "parking is pretty bad, and several buildings could stand a serious renovation."

### Student Body

The student population at LSU is composed of about 30,000 students from every state and from more than 100 countries. Students here run the gamut from "shallow sorority girls" to "righteous Catholics to everyday pot heads." Though students say their campus is a warm, "friendly," and close-knit place full of "southern hospitality," some warn that "people whose ideas and lifestyles differ from the norm stand out in the crowd." Student life at LSU is marked by "strong social distinctions between blacks and whites, gays and straights, Greeks and GDIs," says one student. About the only time all students rally together is during football games. For reasons that sociologists don't completely understand, "everyone loves each other at football games" at LSU.

# LOUISIANA STATE UNIVERSITY—BATON ROUGE

FINANCIAL AID: 225-578-3103 • E-MAIL: ADMISSIONS@LSU.EDU • WEBSITE: WWW.LSU.EDU

## ADMISSIONS
*Very important factors considered include:* secondary school record, standardized test scores. *Important factors considered include:* class rank. *Other factors considered include:* character/personal qualities, essays, extracurricular activities, recommendations, talent/ability. SAT I or ACT required. TOEFL required of all international applicants. High school diploma or GED is required. *High school units required/recommended:* 17.5 total required; 4 English required, 3 math required, 3 science required, 2 foreign language required, 3 social studies required, 2 elective required, .5 computer science required.

### The Inside Word
The university is rare among formula-driven institutions in recognizing that some good students fall through the cracks in such systems. It is commendable that LSU's admissions committee is also willing to take a closer, more personal look if circumstances warrant.

## FINANCIAL AID
*Students should submit:* FAFSA and institution's own financial aid form. The Princeton Review suggests that all financial aid forms be submitted as soon as possible after January 1. *Need-based scholarships/grants offered:* Pell, SEOG, state scholarships/grants, private scholarships, the school's own gift aid. *Loan aid offered:* FFEL Subsidized Stafford, FFEL Unsubsidized Stafford, FFEL PLUS, Federal Perkins. Federal Work-Study Program available. Institutional employment available. Applicants will be notified of awards on a rolling basis beginning on or about March 1. Off-campus job opportunities are excellent.

## FROM THE ADMISSIONS OFFICE
"LSU is the most prestigious and comprehensive public institution of higher learning in Louisiana. We are a leader in higher education with a world-renowned reputation for preparing students for future educational and professional success. Louisiana State University offers the southern hospitality of a small community while providing the benefits of a large, technologically advanced institution. Throughout its history, LSU has served the people of Louisiana, the region, the nation, and the world through extensive, multipurpose programs encompassing instruction, research, and public service."

### SELECTIVITY

| | |
|---|---|
| Admissions Rating | 63 |
| # of applicants | 10,376 |
| % of applicants accepted | 77 |
| % of acceptees attending | 66 |

#### FRESHMAN PROFILE
| | |
|---|---|
| Range ACT Composite | 22-26 |
| Average ACT Composite | 24 |
| Minimum TOEFL | 500 |
| Average HS GPA | 3.4 |
| % graduated top 10% of class | 26 |
| % graduated top 25% of class | 55 |
| % graduated top 50% of class | 86 |

#### DEADLINES
| | |
|---|---|
| Priority admission | 12/1 |
| Regular admission | 4/1 |
| Nonfall registration? | yes |

#### APPLICANTS ALSO LOOK AT
**AND OFTEN PREFER**
Air Force Academy
MIT
Harvard
**AND SOMETIMES PREFER**
UConn
Arizona State
U of Texas
**AND RARELY PREFER**
U of Florida
Texas A&M
USC

### FINANCIAL FACTS

| | |
|---|---|
| Financial Aid Rating | 87 |
| In-state tuition | $3,536 |
| Out-of-state tuition | $8,836 |
| Room and board | $4,968 |
| Books and supplies | $1,000 |
| Required fees | $0 |
| % frosh receiving aid | 43 |
| % undergrads receiving aid | 42 |
| Avg frosh grant | $3,960 |
| Avg frosh loan | $4,000 |

# LOYOLA COLLEGE IN MARYLAND

4501 NORTH CHARLES STREET, BALTIMORE, MD 21210 • ADMISSIONS: 410-617-5012 • FAX: 410-617-2176

## CAMPUS LIFE

| | |
|---|---|
| Quality of Life Rating | 89 |
| Type of school | private |
| Affiliation | Roman Catholic |
| Environment | suburban |

### STUDENTS

| | |
|---|---|
| Total undergrad enrollment | 3,488 |
| % male/female | 42/58 |
| % from out of state | 79 |
| % live on campus | 76 |
| % African American | 5 |
| % Asian | 2 |
| % Caucasian | 89 |
| % Hispanic | 2 |
| # of countries represented | 18 |

### SURVEY SAYS . . .
*Dorms are like palaces*
*Hard liquor is popular*
*Lots of beer drinking*
*Student government is popular*
*Great off-campus food*
*Students are cliquish*
*Very little drug use*
*Student publications are ignored*
*Musical organizations aren't popular*

## ACADEMICS

| | |
|---|---|
| Academic Rating | 84 |
| Calendar | semester |
| Student/faculty ratio | 12:1 |
| Profs interesting rating | 94 |
| Profs accessible rating | 94 |
| Avg reg class size | 20-29 students |

### MOST POPULAR MAJORS
Business administration/management
Communications studies/speech
communication and rhetoric
Psychology

## STUDENTS SPEAK OUT

### Academics

"Extremely accessible teachers" who "really want to help students learn and grow into intelligent, mature, and enlightened adults" are "the strongest aspect of the academic component" at Loyola College in Maryland, a small Catholic, Jesuit school just north of downtown Baltimore. Explains one student, "The main reason I chose [Loyola] was because it's a small school where professors get to know everybody by name. There aren't lectures and tutorials. There's more of a combined lecture/discussion group with no more than 25 to 30 students per class. Professors encourage classroom discussion." Psychology, communication, education, and especially business studies receive students' praise here. Students warn that academic demands—which include a rigorous core curriculum, the majority of which must be completed by the end of one's sophomore year—can be taxing. "If you are looking to coast through your classes without being challenged," writes one undergrad, "Loyola is not the place for you." Students also happily report that the variety of courses offered at Loyola is steadily increasing: "Although a great variety of new classes weren't available in the beginning," writes one senior, "the faculty is slowing expanding the course catalogue and introducing many new upcoming fields and subjects." Administrators receive low marks, with students complaining that "the red tape is ridiculous."

### Life

Loyola College, according to many we surveyed, "is a bar school, no doubt about it. No sororities or fraternities, just a block full of bars dedicated to Loyola kids. You always know where you can find people if you want to go out." Notes one student, "Don't go here if you don't have or plan on getting a fake I.D. I know there are other options, but most people go to the bars" for entertainment. Warns another, "The school is very strict with on-campus drinking and even ventures its authority off campus to the local bars that most of the student body frequents." This policy irks many students who "understand that the college must enforce the drinking age; however, it must also understand that if we are prohibited from drinking on campus then we have no choice but to move off campus. What students do off campus should be their own business." Hometown Baltimore offers a lot more than bars: there's the Inner Harbor with its shops, restaurants, and a world-class aquarium; several exceptional art museums; a symphony; the opera; two major sports franchises; numerous college campuses that host parties, concerts, and the like; and much more. In addition, Washington, D.C., offering another universe of entertainment options, is less than an hour away by car or commuter train. Students report that "club and intramural sports are popular. The new fitness center is amazing and [provides] another option for something to do . . . . From the basketball courts to the field, most spaces are occupied with various sports at all times." Greyhound fans turn out in droves to support Loyola's excellent intercollegiate lacrosse and soccer teams.

### Student Body

"Everyone looks exactly the same" at Loyola, complain many undergrads here. Some point out that "although there is undoubtedly a typical Loyola student (see any Abercrombie ad), individuals who don't fit this mold can find others like them. Overall, everyone is usually pretty friendly." Students hail primarily from "Long Island, New Jersey, and Maryland middle-upper-class backgrounds. We are all white, we all have money, and we all know it." Socially, "Loyola has the same cliques that your high school did, but all the groups interact on friendly terms. Walking across campus, you see a lot of smiles, and it seems as if students truly want to be here." There is a real commitment to public service at Loyola: "Community service is an integral part of my life and most students' lives."

# LOYOLA COLLEGE IN MARYLAND

FINANCIAL AID: 410-617-2576 • WEBSITE: WWW.LOYOLA.EDU

## ADMISSIONS
*Very important factors considered include:* secondary school record. *Important factors considered include:* standardized test scores. *Other factors considered include:* alumni/ae relation, character/personal qualities, class rank, essays, extracurricular activities, minority status, recommendations, talent/ability, volunteer work, work experience. SAT I required. TOEFL required of all international applicants. High school diploma or GED is required. *High school units required/recommended:* 16 total required; 19 total recommended; 4 English required, 3 math required, 4 math recommended, 3 science required, 4 science recommended, 3 foreign language required, 4 foreign language recommended, 2 history required, 3 history recommended.

## The Inside Word
Loyola is to be commended for notifying outstanding candidates of acceptance early in the applicant review cycle without demanding an early commitment in return. Traditional Early Decision plans are confusing, archaic, and unreasonable to students. A binding commitment is a huge price to pay to get a decision four months sooner. This is obviously one place that cares.

## FINANCIAL AID
*Students should submit:* FAFSA, CSS/Financial Aid PROFILE application, noncustodial (divorced/separated) parent's statement, business/farm supplement. Regular filing deadline is February 10. The Princeton Review suggests that all financial aid forms be submitted as soon as possible after January 1. *Need-based scholarships/grants offered:* Pell, SEOG, state scholarships/grants, private scholarships, the school's own gift aid. *Loan aid offered:* Direct Subsidized Stafford, Direct Unsubsidized Stafford, FFEL PLUS, Federal Perkins, college/university loans from institutional funds. Federal Work-Study Program available. Institutional employment available. Academic scholarship recipients are notified by March 15. Applicants for need-based aid are notified of their eligibility by April 5. Off-campus job opportunities are good.

## FROM THE ADMISSIONS OFFICE
"To make a wise choice about your college plans, you will need to find out more. We extend to you these invitations. Question-and-answer periods with an admissions counselor are helpful to prospective students. An appointment should be made in advance. Admissions office hours are 9 A.M. to 5 P.M., Monday through Friday. College day programs and Saturday information programs are scheduled during the academic year. These programs include a video about Loyola, a general information session, a discussion of various majors, a campus tour, and lunch. Summer information programs can help high school juniors to get a head start on investigating colleges. These programs feature an introductory presentation about the college and a campus tour."

---

### SELECTIVITY
★ ★ ★ ☆

| | |
|---|---|
| Admissions Rating | 83 |
| # of applicants | 6,368 |
| % of applicants accepted | 61 |
| % of acceptees attending | 23 |
| # accepting a place on wait list | 670 |
| % admitted from wait list | 21 |

### FRESHMAN PROFILE
| | |
|---|---|
| Range SAT Verbal | 560-640 |
| Range SAT Math | 570-650 |
| Minimum TOEFL | 550 |
| Average HS GPA | 3.5 |
| % graduated top 10% of class | 35 |
| % graduated top 25% of class | 76 |
| % graduated top 50% of class | 97 |

### DEADLINES
| | |
|---|---|
| Priority admission | 1/15 |
| Regular admission | 1/15 |
| Regular notification | 4/1 |

### APPLICANTS ALSO LOOK AT
**AND OFTEN PREFER**
Georgetown
U of Notre Dame
Boston College
**AND SOMETIMES PREFER**
U of Richmond
College of the Holy Cross
Villanova
**AND RARELY PREFER**
Fordham
Providence
Fairfield

### FINANCIAL FACTS
★ ★ ★ ★

| | |
|---|---|
| Financial Aid Rating | 90 |
| Tuition | $26,010 |
| Room and board | $7,800 |
| Books and supplies | $760 |
| Required fees | $900 |
| % frosh receiving aid | 61 |
| % undergrads receiving aid | 64 |

# LOYOLA MARYMOUNT UNIVERSITY

ONE LMU DRIVE, SUITE 100, LOS ANGELES, CA 90045 • ADMISSIONS: 310-338-2750 • FAX: 310-338-2797

## CAMPUS LIFE

| Quality of Life Rating | 83 |
| --- | --- |
| Type of school | private |
| Affiliation | Roman Catholic |
| Environment | suburban |

### STUDENTS

| Total undergrad enrollment | 5,358 |
| --- | --- |
| % male/female | 42/58 |
| % from out of state | 22 |
| % live on campus | 56 |
| % in (# of) fraternities | 7 (4) |
| % in (# of) sororities | 7 (3) |
| % African American | 6 |
| % Asian | 11 |
| % Caucasian | 52 |
| % Hispanic | 19 |
| % international | 2 |

### SURVEY SAYS . . .
Students love Los Angeles, CA
High cost of living
Hard liquor is popular
Campus easy to get around
Classes are small
Ethnic diversity on campus
Students get along with local community

## ACADEMICS

| Academic Rating | 84 |
| --- | --- |
| Calendar | semester |
| Student/faculty ratio | 13:1 |
| Profs interesting rating | 96 |
| Profs accessible rating | 89 |
| % profs teaching UG courses | 100 |
| Avg lab size | 10-19 students |
| Avg reg class size | 20-29 students |

### MOST POPULAR MAJORS
Business administration/management
Communications, journalism, and related fields
Psychology

## STUDENTS SPEAK OUT

### Academics
Students describe LMU as "the best kept secret in Los Angeles," largely because of the "priceless" education it offers. All students must complete a core curriculum that emphasizes humanities, sciences, math, philosophy, and theology. On top of this, students choose a major from one of five colleges: liberal arts, science and engineering, business administration, education, and film and television. Considering the available resources particular to the university's location, it's not surprising to hear that LMU is an "excellent school for communications, media, and communication arts." Other popular disciplines include film, music production, and business administration. With a little more than 5,000 schoolmates, LMU students report that "class sizes are small" and "professors are always available to talk and help with work or give advice." Though there are a few grumbles about "the typical Jesuit bureaucracy" here, most students find that the "administration is friendly." They even report that "online registration is a breeze." The most appreciated aspect of LMU's academic experience seems to be its well-roundedness. "The opportunities to learn and grow mentally, spiritually, emotionally, and physically are endless," writes one student. Another adds, "My academic experience has been stellar: truly challenging, yet in the most practical manner, because all lessons are applied to everyday life and especially to the achievement of social justice."

### Life
"If you don't like LMU, it's because you're not involved," writes a junior. Because "LMU's objective is to educate the whole person," the university offers a breadth of extracurricular options, "ranging from sports and music to student government and service groups. Ask anyone on campus about their extracurricular activities, and the majority would name at least three major commitments/activities they have outside of class." The dearth of its social options counters the strength of the university's extracurricular opportunities, especially on the weekends. There is a "visible" Greek system, but since Greek houses are barred from campus, frat parties aren't a major part of the social scene. It's not uncommon for students to venture off campus to parties. Two particularly hot party spots are the nearby campuses of USC and UCLA, the proximity of which "compensates for ANY deficits in social activity" on campus. LMU's seat in the heart of Los Angeles "provides wonderful opportunities to experience life in a major metropolis." A student brags, "In the past year, I have been to dozens of restaurants, been at the Oscars' red carpet, seen numerous sporting events, and studied at the beach." Other students mention outings to the popular "Third Street Promenade," "the new Howard Hughes Promenade," "the Hermosa Beach Pier," "Westwood," "lots of movie theaters," and "fun bars." And one final note: unlike many religiously affiliated schools, LMU lacks the "strict policies regarding men and women visiting each other's dorms."

### Student Body
Fittingly, the City of Angels is home to LMU, a university inhabited by "caring, religious, friendly people." In fact, it's not uncommon to hear students proclaim, "This is the friendliest campus in the U.S," a place where most students "smile as you pass them on your way to class." A few detractors beg to differ, however, asserting that LMU students are just "a bunch of rich sons of bitches" and "superficial, conceited, and self-absorbed." By the numbers, Loyola Marymount is a diverse school, with Caucasians making up only 50 percent of its population, but a minority student warns that "those who are of some type of ethnic background get easily whitewashed." On campus, "many of the students act and look alike, and there are several fake people." One student describes this "phoniness" as the "L.A. Attitude," something not exclusive to LMU. But "as long as you call them on it or spend time to get beyond their wall of phoniness," advises one undergrad about his peers, "they open up and you can really get to know them, and they can get to know you."

# LOYOLA MARYMOUNT UNIVERSITY

FINANCIAL AID: 310-338-2753 • E-MAIL: ADMISSIONS@LMU.EDU • WEBSITE: WWW.LMU.EDU

## ADMISSIONS

*Very important factors considered include:* secondary school record. *Important factors considered include:* class rank, standardized test scores, talent/ability. *Other factors considered include:* alumni/ae relation, character/personal qualities, essays, extracurricular activities, geographical residence, interview, recommendations, volunteer work, work experience. SAT I or ACT required. TOEFL required of all international applicants. High school diploma or GED is required. *High school units required/recommended:* 16 total recommended; 4 English recommended, 3 math recommended, 2 science recommended, 2 science lab recommended, 3 foreign language recommended, 3 social studies recommended, 1 elective recommended.

### The Inside Word

Loyola Marymount's admissions committee is particular about candidate evaluation, but a large applicant pool has more to do with the university's moderate acceptance rate than does academic selectivity. Even so, underachievers will have difficulty getting in.

## FINANCIAL AID

*Students should submit:* FAFSA, CSS/Financial Aid PROFILE, state aid form. No deadline for regular filing. The Princeton Review suggests that all financial aid forms be submitted as soon as possible after January 1. *Need-based scholarships/grants offered:* Pell, SEOG, state scholarships/grants, private scholarships, the school's own gift aid. *Loan aid offered:* FFEL Subsidized Stafford, FFEL Unsubsidized Stafford, FFEL PLUS, Federal Perkins, college/university loans from institutional funds. Federal Work-Study Program available. Institutional employment available. Applicants will be notified of awards on a rolling basis beginning on or about April 10. Off-campus job opportunities are excellent.

## FROM THE ADMISSIONS OFFICE

"Loyola Marymount University is a dynamic, student-centered university. We are medium sized (4,500 undergraduates), and we are the only Jesuit University in the southwestern United States.

"Our campus is located in Westchester, a friendly, residential neighborhood that is removed from the hustle and bustle of Los Angeles yet offers easy access to all the richnesss of our most cosmopolitan environment. One mile from the ocean, our students enjoy ocean and mountain vistas as well as the moderate climate and crisp breezes characteristic of a coastal location.

"Loyola Marymount is committed to the ideals of Jesuit and Marymount education. We are a student-centered university, dedicated to the education of the whole person and to the preparation of our students for lives of service to their families, communities, and professions. Breadth and rigor are the hallmarks of the curriculum.

"Taken together, our academic program, our Jesuit and Marymount heritage, and our terrific campus environment afford our students unparalleled opportunity to prepare for life and leadership in the 21st century."

## SELECTIVITY

| | |
|---|---|
| Admissions Rating | 74 |
| # of applicants | 7,959 |
| % of applicants accepted | 56 |
| % of acceptees attending | 27 |

### FRESHMAN PROFILE

| | |
|---|---|
| Range SAT Verbal | 510-610 |
| Average SAT Verbal | 573 |
| Range SAT Math | 530-620 |
| Average SAT Math | 581 |
| Minimum TOEFL | 550 |
| Average HS GPA | 3.4 |
| % graduated top 10% of class | 30 |
| % graduated top 25% of class | 95 |
| % graduated top 50% of class | 99 |

### DEADLINES

| | |
|---|---|
| Priority admission | 2/1 |
| Nonfall registration? | yes |

### APPLICANTS ALSO LOOK AT AND OFTEN PREFER
Stanford
UCLA

### AND SOMETIMES PREFER
UC Irvine
UC San Diego
UC Santa Barbara
USC

### AND RARELY PREFER
Santa Clara U
UC Riverside
Pepperdine

## FINANCIAL FACTS

| | |
|---|---|
| Financial Aid Rating | 86 |
| Tuition | $20,342 |
| Room and board | $7,800 |
| Books and supplies | $810 |
| Required fees | $612 |

# LOYOLA UNIVERSITY CHICAGO

820 NORTH MICHIGAN AVENUE, CHICAGO, IL 60611 • ADMISSIONS: 800-262-2373 • FAX: 312-915-6449

## CAMPUS LIFE

| | |
|---|---|
| Quality of Life Rating | 73 |
| Type of school | private |
| Affiliation | Roman Catholic |
| Environment | urban |

### STUDENTS

| | |
|---|---|
| Total undergrad enrollment | 7,533 |
| % male/female | 34/66 |
| % from out of state | 50 |
| % from public high school | 38 |
| % live on campus | 29 |
| % in (# of) fraternities | 5 (6) |
| % in (# of) sororities | 3 (6) |
| % African American | 9 |
| % Asian | 11 |
| % Caucasian | 56 |
| % Hispanic | 10 |
| % international | 3 |

### SURVEY SAYS . . .
Musical organizations aren't popular
Classes are small
Class discussions are rare
Students don't get along with local community
Unattractive campus
Students are not very happy
Ethnic diversity on campus
Intercollegiate sports unpopular or nonexistent
Lots of long lines and red tape

## ACADEMICS

| | |
|---|---|
| Academic Rating | 75 |
| Calendar | semester |
| Student/faculty ratio | 13:1 |
| Profs interesting rating | 90 |
| Profs accessible rating | 91 |
| Avg lab size | under 10 students |
| Avg reg class size | 20-29 students |

### MOST POPULAR MAJORS
Biology/biological sciences
Psychology
Business administration/management

## STUDENTS SPEAK OUT

### Academics
Top four reasons to attend this mid-sized Roman Catholic institution perched at the edge of "beautiful" Lake Michigan on Chicago's North Shore: "academic reputation, diverse student body, small class size, and great location." Many students, religious and nonreligious, still consider the school's "Jesuit character" one of its biggest draws. "Loyola's greatest strength is its commitment to providing students" with a "whole-person education," the mark of the Jesuits. Most students agree that "Loyola's professors are dedicated to their research, to their students (by being approachable), and to the Loyola mission—which is to provide a good education and guide to [becoming] a balanced, independent thinker." The historical Jesuit commitment to providing education for all has another benefit: true cultural, economic, and ethnic diversity amongst its faculty, staff, and student body. This diversity is enhanced by the school's division into several different campuses—one in downtown Chicago, another on the north side, and the medical center (Loyola has a popular pre-med program) in the western suburbs. Notes a sophomore, "The diverse atmosphere at the different campuses is great. Where else can you be a frat boy on Monday, Wednesday, Friday, and a corporate guru on Tuesday and Thursday?" And while some point out that Loyola has had some rough times in recent years with lack of funds, long-tenured professors, substandard facilities, and an out-of-touch administration ("Trying to talk to the administration is like trying to contact Elvis," writes a junior), a sophomore points out that "Loyola is in a transition period" and that the mood is very hopeful about the school's new president.

### Life
A senior sums up the scene: "Loyola isn't your 'typical' college campus. If you are looking for big frat parties or keggers this isn't the place to be. However, if you are into smaller parties, cultural events, and the fun of Chicago, this place ROCKS!" Whether it's going down to Clarke & Belmont (a nexus for the Alternation); taking in an improv show right down the street from the uptown campus; or "heading downtown to grab some famous Chicago-style pizza," the city is "just a short El ride away," as a junior puts it, "and there's never a shortage of fun things to do." Indeed, as one first-year writes, "Life at Loyola is living in Chicago with a side of school." An international student from Ireland gives the down-low: "So far the social activities organized have been as exciting as knitting with my mum." What's needed? More sports events, a better newspaper, more funding for student events, and the renovation of key facilities are high on students' wish lists. Still, proximity to the city has its upside—"social justice and volunteer opportunities" abound, and, as a senior points out, "despite the high percentage of commuters [students], attendance at on-campus events is on the rise."

### Student Body
"Choose Loyola if you're comfortable enough with yourself to handle serious diversity," writes a frank first-year, though most rave about Loyola's unique mix of people from all around the nation and the world. "I enjoy my fellow students," remarks a senior. "I have learned a lot about other cultures and religions because of them." Adds another, "If you have an open mind, you can make friends from almost every ethnic group." With such a heterogeneous community, there's bound to be cliques and divisions, which some Loyola undergrads complain can be "closed off and unapproachable."

# LOYOLA UNIVERSITY CHICAGO

FINANCIAL AID: 312-915-6639 • E-MAIL: ADMISSION@LUC.EDU • WEBSITE: WWW.LUC.EDU

## ADMISSIONS
*Very important factors considered include:* secondary school record, standardized test scores. *Important factors considered include:* character/personal qualities, essays, recommendations. *Other factors considered include:* extracurricular activities, geographical residence, interview, talent/ability, volunteer work, work experience. SAT I or ACT required. TOEFL required of all international applicants. High school diploma or GED is required. *High school units required/recommended:* 15 total required; 18 total recommended; 4 English required, 2 math required, 4 math recommended, 2 science required, 3 science recommended, 2 foreign language required, 3 foreign language recommended, 1 social studies required, 3 social studies recommended.

### The Inside Word
The admissions process is fairly formulaic, and the standards are attainable for most competitive candidates.

## FINANCIAL AID
*Students should submit:* FAFSA. Recommended filing by February 1. *Need-based scholarships/grants offered:* Pell, SEOG, state scholarships/grants, private scholarships, the school's own gift aid. *Loan aid offered:* FFEL Subsidized Stafford, FFEL Unsubsidized Stafford, FFEL PLUS, Federal Perkins, Federal Nursing. Federal Work-Study Program available. Institutional employment available. Applicants will be notified of awards on a rolling basis beginning on or about February 15. Off-campus job opportunities are excellent.

## FROM THE ADMISSIONS OFFICE
"As a national research university, Loyola University of Chicago provides a superb academic program that is distinctive because of its personal approach. Nationally and internationally renowned scholars teach introductory freshman-level courses in classes that average 21 students. A special emphasis in our curriculum is placed on the examination of ethics and values as well as a commitment to instill intensive writing skills that will benefit the student throughout his/her life. Loyola is committed to the individual student, and its programs and policies reflect the importance of community. Students from throughout the nation are attracted to Loyola for the opportunities offered by the university, our Jesuit tradition, as well as the benefits of studying in Chicago, a world-class city."

### SELECTIVITY

| | |
|---|---|
| Admissions Rating | 73 |
| # of applicants | 10,214 |
| % of applicants accepted | 71 |
| % of acceptees attending | 22 |

### FRESHMAN PROFILE
| | |
|---|---|
| Range SAT Verbal | 520-630 |
| Average SAT Verbal | 574 |
| Range SAT Math | 520-640 |
| Average SAT Math | 574 |
| Range ACT Composite | 22-27 |
| Average ACT Composite | 25 |
| Minimum TOEFL | 550 |
| % graduated top 10% of class | 29 |
| % graduated top 25% of class | 63 |
| % graduated top 50% of class | 92 |

### DEADLINES
| | |
|---|---|
| Priority admission | 2/1 |
| Regular admission | 4/1 |
| Nonfall registration? | yes |

### APPLICANTS ALSO LOOK AT AND OFTEN PREFER
De Paul
U Illinois—Urbana-Champaign
U Illinois—Chicago
Northwestern
Marquette

### AND SOMETIMES PREFER
Northern Illinois
Notre Dame
U Chicago
Indiana U—Bloomington

### AND RARELY PREFER
Saint Louis

### FINANCIAL FACTS

| | |
|---|---|
| Financial Aid Rating | 86 |
| Tuition | $20,540 |
| Room and board | $7,600 |
| Books and supplies | $1,000 |
| Required fees | $656 |
| % frosh receiving aid | 94 |
| % undergrads receiving aid | 77 |
| Avg frosh grant | $13,093 |
| Avg frosh loan | $3,958 |

# LOYOLA UNIVERSITY NEW ORLEANS

6363 ST. CHARLES AVENUE, BOX 18, NEW ORLEANS, LA 70118 • ADMISSIONS: 504-865-3240 • FAX: 504-865-3383

## CAMPUS LIFE

| Quality of Life Rating | 81 |
| --- | --- |
| Type of school | private |
| Affiliation | Roman Catholic-Jesuit |
| Environment | urban |

### STUDENTS

| Total undergrad enrollment | 3,702 |
| --- | --- |
| % male/female | 38/62 |
| % from out of state | 50 |
| % from public high school | 57 |
| % live on campus | 38 |
| % in (# of) fraternities | 21 (6) |
| % in (# of) sororities | 24 (6) |
| % African American | 11 |
| % Asian | 4 |
| % Caucasian | 68 |
| % Hispanic | 10 |
| % international | 4 |

### SURVEY SAYS . . .
Lots of beer drinking
Students love New Orleans, LA
Great off-campus food
Great library
Campus easy to get around
Hard liquor is popular
Great computer facilities
(Almost) everyone smokes
Student government is popular
Students are happy

## ACADEMICS

| Academic Rating | 76 |
| --- | --- |
| Calendar | semester |
| Student/faculty ratio | 13:1 |
| % profs teaching UG courses | 90 |
| Avg lab size | 10-19 students |
| Avg reg class size | 10-19 students |

### MOST POPULAR MAJORS
Marketing/marketing management
Communications studies/speech
communication and rhetoric
Psychology

## STUDENTS SPEAK OUT

### Academics
"It's about one-on-one contact with teachers" at Loyola University New Orleans, according to students at this "small, urban Jesuit school which for the most part upholds the Jesuit ideal of scholarship." Freshmen here brag that even the profs in intro classes are "very accessible, excellent in promoting class discussion, and most are experts in their fields. I appreciate that this is a rarity in introductory freshmen classes at other schools." Things only get better as students progress to upper-level course work; as one student in the business college told us, "I know almost all the professors and administrators. This is due to their availability to students and their genuine interest in helping out with what they can . . . . Most professors transmit their passion and seem to have fun with their teaching experience." Administrators are also "highly accessible . . . . Walking around campus, you can see the president of the school talking with students and all the teachers greeting their students by name." Students also appreciate the Jesuit focus "on educating a well-rounded person who is committed to giving back to the community." They also brag that Loyola is "a place of great diversity that allows students to gain knowledge in all areas of education as well as in matters of the world." Some here worry about the school's recent growth spurt, complaining that currently "there are not enough professors to accommodate the increasing size of the university."

### Life
Anyone who knows anything at all about New Orleans will understand why "pretty much everyone at Loyola is really happy with the school. It's hard not to be happy with living in New Orleans." New Orleans is a town that "always has something going on. There is a ton of ways to have fun: music (jazz and blues), bars and clubs to go out to, parks and places to go for the day, a cultural heritage to investigate further, etc." Because "on any given night of the week you can go out and have great time with tons of people your own age," "it's easy to get involved in really shady situations, e.g., running into a classmate at 4 A.M. on a Tuesday . . . on Bourbon Street." The university clearly isn't oblivious to its students' extracurricular activities. In fact, "the school even takes into account that we live in New Orleans when planning school holidays, which is nice. For example, we always get the day after Halloween off and the days surrounding Mardi Gras." Students who stick close to campus will also find plenty to occupy their time, as "the Student Government Association and other organizations have been taking amazing steps over the past couple of years to do more on-campus programming, so there is pretty much always something going on at Loyola." And on the rare occasion when there's not, there's certainly something cooking at Tulane University, located right across the street from Loyola. Given the irresistible pull of all these diversions, it's fortunate that "the workload isn't overwhelming."

### Student Body
Undergrads at Loyola agree that their school "attracts all kinds of students, from Louisiana natives to out-of-state students, from preppy pre-law majors to music majors with alternative tastes." Students report approvingly of "a large number of minority students, something that is immediately apparent. There are people from different parts of the world, religions, appearances, political beliefs, schools of thought, etc. This makes being a part of Loyola very enriching." Some women here complain that there are "a lot more females than males." The more eccentric students note that "it seems like many students here care more about their style of shoes than academics. But they are friendly people, and there are enough non-mainstream people here that one could find a group of people to hang out with."

328 ■ THE BEST 351 COLLEGES

# LOYOLA UNIVERSITY NEW ORLEANS

FINANCIAL AID: 504-865-3231 • E-MAIL: ADMIT@LOYNO.EDU • WEBSITE: WWW.LOYNO.EDU

## ADMISSIONS
*Very important factors considered include:* secondary school record, standardized test scores. *Important factors considered include:* character/personal qualities, essays, extracurricular activities, interview, recommendations, talent/ability, volunteer work, work experience. *Other factors considered include:* alumni/ae relation, class rank. SAT I or ACT required. TOEFL required of all international applicants. High school diploma or GED is required. *High school units required/recommended:* 10 total required; 15 total recommended; 4 English required, 2 math required, 3 math recommended, 2 science required, 3 science recommended, 2 foreign language recommended, 2 social studies required, 3 social studies recommended.

## The Inside Word
Students with a solid academic record can expect smooth sailing to admission at Loyola. The majority of the University's applicants are admitted. The admissions process is truly personal, and many of the weaker applicants benefit from Loyola's willingness to consider more than just numbers.

## FINANCIAL AID
*Students should submit:* FAFSA. Regular filing deadline is May 1. The Princeton Review suggests that all financial aid forms be submitted as soon as possible after January 1. *Need-based scholarships/grants offered:* Pell, SEOG, private scholarships, the school's own gift aid. *Loan aid offered:* FFEL Subsidized Stafford, FFEL Unsubsidized Stafford, FFEL PLUS, Federal Perkins. Federal Work-Study Program available. Institutional employment available. Applicants will be notified of awards on a rolling basis beginning on or about March 1. Off-campus job opportunities are good.

## FROM THE ADMISSIONS OFFICE
"Founded by the Jesuits in 1912, Loyola University New Orleans has had more than 35,000 graduates who have excelled in innumerable professions for more than 80 years. Loyola's rich Jesuit tradition, its commitment to academic excellence, and its ideal size set it apart from other academic institutions. The total enrollment is approximately 5,500 students, 3,500 of whom are undergraduates. Loyola has a student/faculty ratio of 13:1. Ninety-two percent of our faculty hold the highest degree in their field. Loyola offers more than 60 majors, the largest of which are communications, business, psychology, music, and pre-med. Our undergraduate students enjoy individual attention in a university that strives to educate the whole person, not only intellectually, but also spiritually, socially, and athletically. Students hail from 50 states, Puerto Rico, the District of Columbia, and 49 foreign countries."

## SELECTIVITY

| | |
|---|---|
| Admissions Rating | 77 |
| # of applicants | 3,603 |
| % of applicants accepted | 68 |
| % of acceptees attending | 36 |

### FRESHMAN PROFILE
| | |
|---|---|
| Range SAT Verbal | 540-650 |
| Average SAT Verbal | 629 |
| Range SAT Math | 520-620 |
| Average SAT Math | 605 |
| Range ACT Composite | 23-28 |
| Average ACT Composite | 27 |
| Minimum TOEFL | 550 |
| Average HS GPA | 3.76 |
| % graduated top 10% of class | 28 |
| % graduated top 25% of class | 59 |
| % graduated top 50% of class | 88 |

### DEADLINES
| | |
|---|---|
| Priority admission | 12/1 |
| Regular admission | 1/15 |
| Nonfall registration? | yes |

### APPLICANTS ALSO LOOK AT
**AND OFTEN PREFER**
Tulane University
Spring Hill College
Louisiana State University
**AND SOMETIMES PREFER**
Florida State University
Xavier University of Louisiana
Southern Methodist University
University of New Orleans
Centenary College
**AND RARELY PREFER**
Boston College
Vanderbilt University

## FINANCIAL FACTS

| | |
|---|---|
| Financial Aid Rating | 88 |
| Tuition | $21,320 |
| Room and board | $7,660 |
| Books and supplies | $1,000 |
| Required fees | $806 |
| % frosh receiving aid | 71 |
| % undergrads receiving aid | 68 |
| Avg frosh grant | $16,591 |
| Avg frosh loan | $2,696 |

THE BEST 351 COLLEGES ■ 329

# MACALESTER COLLEGE

1600 GRAND AVENUE, ST. PAUL, MN 55105 • ADMISSIONS: 651-696-6357 • FAX: 651-696-6724

## CAMPUS LIFE

| | |
|---|---|
| Quality of Life Rating | 93 |
| Type of school | private |
| Affiliation | Presbyterian |
| Environment | urban |

### STUDENTS
| | |
|---|---|
| Total undergrad enrollment | 1,840 |
| % male/female | 42/58 |
| % from out of state | 76 |
| % from public high school | 66 |
| % live on campus | 68 |
| % African American | 4 |
| % Asian | 6 |
| % Caucasian | 85 |
| % Hispanic | 3 |
| % international | 15 |
| # of countries represented | 88 |

### SURVEY SAYS . . .
Students aren't religious
Ethnic diversity on campus
Classes are small
Political activism is hot
Students love the Twin Cities
Campus easy to get around
Beautiful campus
Theater is unpopular
Athletic facilities need improving

## ACADEMICS

| | |
|---|---|
| Academic Rating | 93 |
| Calendar | semester |
| Student/faculty ratio | 10:1 |
| Profs interesting rating | 95 |
| Profs accessible rating | 96 |
| % profs teaching UG courses | 100 |
| Avg lab size | 10-19 students |
| Avg reg class size | 10-19 students |

### MOST POPULAR MAJORS
Biology/biological sciences
Psychology
Economics

## STUDENTS SPEAK OUT

### Academics
True to its liberal arts ideals, Macalester offers an academic environment with small classes and "close student-professor relationships." And while the courses are "challenging," the overall atmosphere is comfortable, not cutthroat. "Macalester is the kind of place where you can show up for class every day in your pajamas and still be taken seriously and get the respect you deserve from your profs." And these accepting and accessible professors "know their [expletive]." "Even the bad profs are better than average, and the good ones are really good—innovative, attentive, and challenging," writes an enthusiastic freshman. Mac's 1,700-plus student body is spread throughout 39 majors and 31 minors. And because Macalester, like many liberal arts schools, is ripe with distribution requirements, students often mingle under the umbrella of varied topics. Over 60 percent of the students take advantage of Macalester's renowned study-abroad opportunities. You'll be hard pressed to find a Mac student talk down the academics here, while uber-accessibility is clearly the strength of administrators and staff. This place might just be undergraduate Canaan!

### Life
It's hard to talk about student life at Macalester without talking about the area around campus. Located in St. Paul, Macalester offers its students easy access to Minnesota's Twin Cities. Nearby, students find things like the Mall of America, "dance clubs," "a local movie theater called 'Grandview,'" "lots of shops and cultural events," and "so many beautiful natural areas within the cities." Getting outdoors is important to Mac students. "I explore the Twin Cities on my bike," writes one student, while others cite "canoeing" and "Ultimate Frisbee" as other possible diversions. On the other side of the coin, students report some less-than-attractive features of the college's location, particularly when it comes to partying. "The parties are nonexistent because of the St. Paul police," complains a junior. But if partying is your thing, don't think you're entirely out of luck because "you can be a party animal" here if you want to. There's "lots of drinking" in the dorm rooms, as well as the use of "assorted substances." (Perhaps this is why "streaking is not a strange sight.") Though the campus brings in its fair share of speakers and performances, some students complain that if you don't drink "there's no place to have fun." However, every night Mac students feel that they've just put an active day behind them, with another active day ahead. "My friends and I are busy people," chirps a sophomore. "We try to schedule each other in for breakfasts, events in the cities, politics, or sleeping together."

### Student Body
"Some schools say they're diverse, and when you get there they're all white, upper-middle-class yuppies . . . NOT Mac." In fact, diversity is one of the college's big selling points. However, says one student, "Most of the ethnic diversity is because of international students." According to the college, about one in every six students on campus comes from one of 88 foreign countries. The opinions Mac students propound are "liberal and very left-wing,"a fact that prompts one freshman to note that one will "get along fine here unless you're a Republican." And politics are on students' minds. "Very proactive, very socially aware, and justice conscious," a student writes about her classmates. Another concurs, "I like the creativity, humor, and openness of the students." Unfortunately, students don't always make an effort to widen their circles. "Minnesota cold weather sometimes makes it a little harder to be social," explains a sophomore. "It's hard to meet people when you dread going outside."

330 ■ THE BEST 351 COLLEGES

# MACALESTER COLLEGE

FINANCIAL AID: 651-696-6214 • E-MAIL: ADMISSIONS@MACALESTER.EDU • WEBSITE: WWW.MACALESTER.EDU

## ADMISSIONS

*Very important factors considered include:* secondary school record. *Important factors considered include:* character/personal qualities, essays, extracurricular activities, recommendations, standardized test scores. *Other factors considered include:* alumni/ae relation, class rank, interview, minority status, talent/ability, volunteer work, work experience. SAT I or ACT required. TOEFL required of all international applicants. *High school units required/recommended:* 4 English recommended, 3 math recommended, 3 science recommended, 3 science lab recommended, 3 foreign language recommended, 3 social studies recommended.

## The Inside Word

Macalester is just a breath away from moving into the highest echelon of American colleges; a gift of *Reader's Digest* stock several years ago has recently translated into over $500 million in endowment. As the college has reaped the benefits of this generous gift, the applicant pool has grown dramatically. Macalester is already among the 25 or so most selective colleges in the country. An interview is a good idea: even though they are offered across the country, we also encourage you to visit the campus.

## FINANCIAL AID

*Students should submit:* FAFSA, CSS/Financial Aid PROFILE, noncustodial (divorced/separated) parent's statement, business/farm supplement. Regular filing deadline is April 15. The Princeton Review suggests that all financial aid forms be submitted as soon as possible after January 1. *Need-based scholarships/grants offered:* Pell, SEOG, state scholarships/grants, private scholarships, the school's own gift aid. *Loan aid offered:* FFEL Subsidized Stafford, FFEL Unsubsidized Stafford, FFEL PLUS, Federal Perkins, state loans. Federal Work-Study Program available. Institutional employment available. Applicants will be notified of awards on or about April 1. Off-campus job opportunities are excellent.

## FROM THE ADMISSIONS OFFICE

"Recent news about Macalester (Spring 2002): Macalester students come from all 50 states and 88 other countries. Before graduating, half of them will study abroad, going to more than 50 countries in any given year. For over 30 years, Macalester's debate program has been ranked among the top 10 in the nation. A Macalester team has qualified for the International Collegiate Programming Contest in four of the past seven years, and recently the team tied with Stanford, Columbia, Carnegie-Mellon, and Harvard. The women's soccer team won the 1998 NCAA Division III national championship. A new campus center opened in 2001. Each year Macalester students win an impressive number of post-graduate awards, including Fulbright Scholarships, National Science Foundation Graduate Fellowships, Truman Scholarships, Watson Fellowships, and more. Recent graduates fare well in the job market and graduate programs. One reports that she was 'accepted into top med school choices: Mayo, Stanford, UCLA and Minnesota' and another that he had a 'striking advantage over many other candidates' and is now enrolled in a PhD program in economics at Princeton University."

## SELECTIVITY

| Admissions Rating | 96 |
|---|---|
| # of applicants | 3,713 |
| % of applicants accepted | 44 |
| % of acceptees attending | 27 |
| # accepting a place on wait list | 93 |
| % admitted from wait list | 6 |
| # of early decision applicants | 201 |
| % accepted early decision | 54 |

### FRESHMAN PROFILE

| Range SAT Verbal | 630-730 |
|---|---|
| Average SAT Verbal | 690 |
| Range SAT Math | 620-710 |
| Average SAT Math | 670 |
| Range ACT Composite | 27-31 |
| Average ACT Composite | 29 |
| Minimum TOEFL | 570 |
| % graduated top 10% of class | 71 |
| % graduated top 25% of class | 96 |
| % graduated top 50% of class | 100 |

### DEADLINES

| Early decision | 11/15 |
|---|---|
| Early decision notification | 12/15 |
| Regular admission | 1/15 |
| Regular notification | 4/1 |

### APPLICANTS ALSO LOOK AT
**AND OFTEN PREFER**
Swarthmore College
Brown University, Yale University
University of Chicago
**AND SOMETIMES PREFER**
Grinnell College, Carleton College
Wesleyan College, Pomona College
Washington University in St. Louis
Oberlin College
Northwestern University
**AND RARELY PREFER**
Colorado College, Kenyon College
University of Wisconsin—Madison

## FINANCIAL FACTS

| Financial Aid Rating | 91 |
|---|---|
| Tuition | $24,902 |
| Room and board | $6,874 |
| Books and supplies | $750 |
| Required fees | $168 |
| % frosh receiving aid | 77 |
| % undergrads receiving aid | 69 |
| Avg frosh grant | $15,564 |
| Avg frosh loan | $3,113 |

THE BEST 351 COLLEGES ■ 331

# MANHATTANVILLE COLLEGE

2900 PURCHASE STREET, ADMISSIONS OFFICE, PURCHASE, NY 10577 • ADMISSIONS: 914-323-5124

## CAMPUS LIFE

| | |
|---|---|
| **Quality of Life Rating** | 77 |
| Type of school | private |
| Affiliation | none |
| Environment | suburban |

### STUDENTS

| | |
|---|---|
| Total undergrad enrollment | 1,618 |
| % male/female | 32/69 |
| % from out of state | 31 |
| % live on campus | 71 |
| % African American | 6 |
| % Asian | 3 |
| % Caucasian | 60 |
| % Hispanic | 13 |
| % international | 8 |

### SURVEY SAYS . . .
Political activism is hot
Frats and sororities dominate social scene
Student publications are popular
Lab facilities are great
Lots of classroom discussion
Student government is popular
School is well run
Campus difficult to get around

## ACADEMICS

| | |
|---|---|
| **Academic Rating** | 75 |
| Calendar | semester |
| Student/faculty ratio | 12:1 |
| % profs teaching UG courses | 100 |
| % classes taught by TAs | 0 |
| Avg reg class size | 10-19 students |

## STUDENTS SPEAK OUT

### Academics

Ask students to describe the Manhattanville experience, and they'll likely use the word "family" time and again. "Manhattanville is a family. Professors' and administrators' doors are always open," writes a typical student. Giving rise to this homey atmosphere are "small and personal classrooms that contribute to a very engaging learning experience between yourself, your professor, and your classmates, all giving and taking equally and efficiently." The success of such an approach, of course, hinges on the quality of the faculty. Fortunately, "The professors are incredible, very down-to-earth . . . . They greet you when they see you, and they give their home phone numbers so you can contact them at any time." Crowed one student, "My profs make me feel important so that I want to work harder for them." Upper-level administration is equally accessible. In fact, many students singled out President Berman as one of Manhattanville's greatest assets. "The president holds monthly dinners at his house, and many of us stay for hours to discuss various issues, both personal and school-related. He also attends most student events. How many other college students can say that they see and interact with the school's president at least once a week?" Students report that "The education department has made quite a name for itself and is helpful getting jobs for grad students," but add that the school is strong in many areas. Wrote one student, "Manhattanville offers a great liberal arts education, with strength in a variety of departments, from drama to computer science." A few warned that the small departments are very small; chemistry majors, for example, cross-register at SUNY Purchase for a few of their classes.

### Life

There's "not much to do on campus" at Manhattanville, students here agree, attributing the subdued social scene to a several factors. Many report that "Security is ridiculously tight," and "there are no Greeks on campus, so there isn't even a place to have huge parties." The most compelling reason, perhaps, is that "most people go to NYC for fun. It is only 45 minutes by train" or on the free valiant bus service provided by the school. Being "the most amazing cultural activity center in the world" students find no lack of things to do in the city. Campus fun consists of quiet activities; explains one undergrad, "There's pretty much always someone's room to go hang out in. Watching movies, playing video games, watching TV, playing guitar, drinking, playing Frisbee or lacrosse, and just talking are what people do—among a few other things—to have fun." Undergrads also tell us that "major sporting events and theater productions are lots of fun and are well attended." As one student summarizes, "Situated in a rich Westchester suburb, the campus is beautifully serene. Yet within 10 minutes of the campus is the center of Westchester County, offering plenty of great food, shopping, and night life."

### Student Body

The "smart, sociable," "athletic, easygoing" undergrads of Manhattanville generally hail from New York and Connecticut, although there is also a sizeable international student population. Wrote one local, "The greatest strengths [of] my school are the extreme levels of diversity. There are students from Europe, the Orient, the Middle East, and the Caribbean. I have never known so many international people before!" A few complain, however, that "while there is diversity, students are segregated into their own groups." Others gripe that their classmates are "highly concerned with materialistic issues." One student wryly described his peers here as "Attack of the Rich Clones: a look at the parking lot and students' attire speaks volumes."

# MANHATTANVILLE COLLEGE

Fax: 914-694-1732 • E-MAIL: ADMISSIONS@MVILLE.EDU • WEBSITE: WWW.MVILLE.EDU

## ADMISSIONS

*Very important factors considered by the admissions committee include:* secondary school record and standardized test scores. *Important factors considered include:* essays, extracurricular activities, interview, and recommendations. *Other factors considered include:* alumni/ae relation, character/personal qualities, geographical residence, talent/ability, volunteer work, and work experience. SAT I or ACT required. TOEFL required of all international applicants. High school diploma or GED required. *High school units required/recommended:* 16 total required; 4 English required, 3 math required, 2 science required, 2 social studies required, 5 elective required.

### The Inside Word

More than 30 years after going coed, this former women's college is still predominantly female and is still looking to boost its male population. The fact that the school accepts only half its male applicants speaks more to the quality of the applicant pool than to selectiveness; if male and female candidates of equal qualifications are vying for the last seat in the freshman class, it will go to the male.

## FINANCIAL AID

*Students should submit:* FAFSA and state aid form. No deadline for regular filing. The Princeton Review suggests that all financial aid forms be submitted as soon as possible after January 1. Need-based scholarships/grants offered: Pell, SEOG, state scholarships/grants, private scholarships, and the school's own gift aid. *Loan aid offered:* FFEL Subsidized Stafford, FFEL Unsubsidized Stafford, FFEL PLUS, and Federal Perkins. Federal Work-Study Program available. Institutional employment available. Applicants will be notified of awards on a rolling basis. Off-campus job opportunities are excellent.

## FROM THE ADMISSIONS OFFICE

"Manhattanville's mission—to educate ethically and socially responsible leaders for the global community—is evident throughout the College, from academics to athletics to social and extracurricular activities. With 1,500 undergraduates from 53 nations and 37 states, our diversity spans geographic, cultural, ethnic, religious, and socioeconomic backgrounds as well as academic interests. All students are free to express and share their views in this tight-knit community, where we value the personal as well as the global. Any six students with a similar interest can start a club, and most participate in community service projects, club activities, or other campuswide programs. Study abroad opportunities include not only the most desirable international locations, but also a semester-long immersion for living, studying, and working in New York City. In the true liberal arts tradition, Manhattanville students are encouraged to think for themselves and develop new skills—in music, in the studio arts, on stage, in the sciences, or on the playing field. We offer more than 50 areas of study as well as a popular self-designed major, so there is no limit to our academic scope. Our Westchester County location, just 35 miles north of New York City, gives students an edge for jobs and internships. Over the past few years, Manhattanville has been rated among the '100 Most Wired,' the '100 Most Undeservedly Under-Appreciated,' the '320 Hottest,' and *U.S. News & World Report*'s first tier."

---

### SELECTIVITY
★ ★ ☆ ☆

| | |
|---|---|
| **Admissions Rating** | 74 |
| # of applicants | 2,330 |
| % of applicants accepted | 55 |
| % of acceptees attending | 32 |
| # accepting a place on wait list | 80 |
| % admitted from wait list | 2 |
| # of early decision applicants | 50 |
| % accepted early decision | 44 |

### FRESHMAN PROFILE

| | |
|---|---|
| Average SAT Verbal | 530 |
| Average SAT Math | 530 |
| Range ACT Composite | 22-26 |
| Average ACT Composite | 24 |
| Minimum TOEFL | 550 |
| Average HS GPA | 3.0 |

### DEADLINES

| | |
|---|---|
| Early decision | 12/1 |
| Regular admission | 3/1 |
| Nonfall registration? | yes |

### APPLICANTS ALSO LOOK AT AND OFTEN PREFER
NYU
**AND SOMETIMES PREFER**
Fordham
**AND RARELY PREFER**
College of Mount St. Vincent

### FINANCIAL FACTS

★ ★ ★ ☆

| | |
|---|---|
| **Financial Aid Rating** | 83 |
| Tuition | $22,150 |
| Room and board | $9,380 |
| Books and supplies | $800 |
| Avg frosh grant | $15,322 |
| Avg frosh loan | $3,071 |

# MARIST COLLEGE

3399 NORTH ROAD, POUGHKEEPSIE, NY 12601-1387 • ADMISSIONS: 845-575-3226 • FAX: 845-575-3215

## CAMPUS LIFE

| | |
|---|---|
| **Quality of Life Rating** | **76** |
| Type of school | private |
| Affiliation | none |
| Environment | suburban |

### STUDENTS

| | |
|---|---|
| Total undergrad enrollment | 4,000 |
| % male/female | 42/58 |
| % from out of state | 50 |
| % from public high school | 77 |
| % live on campus | 68 |
| % in (# of) fraternities | 3 (5) |
| % in (# of) sororities | 4 (4) |
| % African American | 3 |
| % Asian | 2 |
| % Caucasian | 77 |
| % Hispanic | 6 |
| # of countries represented | 18 |

### SURVEY SAYS . . .
School is well run
Classes are small
Profs teach upper levels
Instructors are good teachers
Hard liquor is popular
Popular college radio
Student publications are popular

## ACADEMICS

| | |
|---|---|
| **Academic Rating** | **86** |
| Calendar | semester |
| Student/faculty ratio | 14:1 |
| Profs interesting rating | 81 |
| Profs accessible rating | 78 |
| % profs teaching UG courses | 96 |
| % classes taught by TAs | 0 |
| Avg lab size | under 10 students |
| Avg reg class size | 10-19 students |

### MOST POPULAR MAJORS
psychology
communications
business

## STUDENTS SPEAK OUT

### Academics

Marist College's "simply spectacular" library, called "one of the nicest and most modern with a very high student-to-Internet connection ratio," stands as a testament to the college's commitment to academics. The professors count among "the most devoted I have ever met" and are "active participants in their field outside of class." One of the school's "greatest strengths is the interaction between professor and student," causing one student to point out, "Getting together to watch college hoops with your professor is not something you can do at every school." Most students save their criticism for the "mediocre assistant professors." Snipes one malcontent, "Adjunct professors in foundation courses are destroying the academic continuity of the college." "I rarely get into the classes I need for my major," is a common complaint, but most agree: "I go to classes because I enjoy them." The most popular and renowned programs include communications, business, education, fashion, IT, and the Public Praxis Program, "an exceptional blend of philosophy courses and community service." The Marist administration is composed of "consummate professionals" who also happen to be "very strict. They try to act like our parents." On the positive side, students share their residence halls with "mentors who help us with any problems we have, even if it's not related to academics." The school enjoys a "good reputation with surrounding businesses" and "many connections with large companies, especially IBM." The "great internship program" ensures that Marist undergrads are "well prepared for jobs after graduation."

### Life

Many students characterize Marist as a "big bar school," as opposed to your run-of-the-mill "party school," and thus, an ID (of any degree of authenticity) is "crucial." Though the school hosts no on-campus sororities or fraternities, everybody apparently "knows how to have a good time while getting their work done." According to many, the surrounding town of Poughkeepsie is "very ghetto" and "economically challenged and in need of student involvement." Undergrads consider the school's strict guest policy, with its roots in Marist's Catholic past, "old-fashioned," making dorms "like a prison, especially for freshmen." Opines one, "We are college students, and having curfew for visiting other students is just inexplicable." A system based on "Priority Points," awarded for all types of campus involvement, dictates the on-campus housing lottery, and some students "think that this is a great thing." Others bitterly note, "This college needs to actually reward the students who spend a majority of their time going to class and studying." In terms of activities, many respondents praise the school-sponsored "bus trips to Broadway shows for only $25. You can't beat that!" The city looms only 90 minutes away, and closer to home, the "Hudson Valley has a large amount of history to explore."

### Student Body

Among the population of 4,000, "there isn't a lot of diversity, culturally or socially." Many students are "white middle-class Catholics," often from Long Island; one student notes, "Sometimes I look around campus and feel like I'm looking at a mirror." Students call for "more minority-oriented events" but still believe "the minority community mixes in very well with everyone, even though there are very few of us." "I know it's cheesy when you see kids of all different types playing Frisbee and laughing on the green outside in brochures," comments a student, "but it really does happen here." Perfect harmony is confronted by obstacles like "segregation between 'normal' students and athletes" and the perception that "commuters are generally not as valued as live-in students." Generally, though, friendliness abounds at Marist, where "everyone says 'hi' to everyone," which "makes you feel like a rock star."

# MARIST COLLEGE

E-MAIL: ADMISSIONS@MARIST.EDU • WEBSITE: WWW.MARIST.EDU

## ADMISSIONS

*Very important factors considered include:* secondary school record, recommendations, and standardized test scores. *Important factors considered include:* character/personal qualities, essays, extracurricular activities, minority status, volunteer work, and work experience. *Other factors considered include:* alumni/ae relation and talent/ability. SAT I or ACT required. TOEFL required of all international applicants. High school diploma or GED is required. *High school units required/recommended:* 16 total required; 19 total recommended; 4 English required, 3 math required, 4 math recommended, 3 science required, 4 science recommended, 2 science lab required, 3 science lab recommended, 3 foreign language recommended, 2 social studies required, 2 social studies recommended, 1 history required, 2 history recommended, 1 elective required.

## The Inside Word

As the school's housing policy indicates, Marist places a strong emphasis on civic responsibility. Candidates who show a strong record of community service and leadership activities will have a definite leg up in the admissions process here.

## FINANCIAL AID

*Students should submit:* FAFSA and institution's own financial aid form. Regular filing deadline is March 1. The Princeton Review suggests that all financial aid forms be submitted as soon as possible after January 1. *Need-based scholarships/grants offered:* Pell, SEOG, state scholarships/grants, private scholarships, and the school's own gift aid. *Loan aid offered:* FFEL Subsidized Stafford, FFEL Unsubsidized Stafford, FFEL PLUS, and Federal Perkins. Federal Work-Study Program available. Institutional employment available. Applicants will be notified of awards on a rolling basis beginning on or about March 15. Off-campus job opportunities are excellent.

## FROM THE ADMISSIONS OFFICE

"Marist is a 'hot school' among prospective students. We are seeing a record number of applications each year. But the number of seats available for the freshman class remains the same, about 950. Therefore, becoming an accepted applicant is an increasingly competitive process. Our recommendations: Keep your grades up, score well on the SAT, participate in community service both in and out of school, and exercise leadership in the classroom, athletics, extracurricular activities, and your place of worship. We encourage a campus visit. When prospective students see Marist—our beautiful location on a scenic stretch of the Hudson River, the quality of our facilities, the interaction between students and faculty, and the fact that everyone really enjoys their time here—they want to become a part of the Marist College community. We'll help you in the transition from high school to college through an innovative first-year program that provides mentors for every student. You'll also learn how to use technology in whatever field you choose. We emphasize three aspects of a true Marist experience: excellence in education, service to others, and the pursuit of higher human values. At Marist, you will get a premium education, develop your skills, have fun and make lifelong friends, be given the opportunity to gain valuable experience through our internship and study abroad programs, and be ahead of the competition for graduate school or work."

## SELECTIVITY

| | |
|---|---|
| Admissions Rating | 83 |
| # of applicants | 6,204 |
| % of applicants accepted | 54 |
| % of acceptees attending | 31 |
| # accepting a place on wait list | 334 |

### FRESHMAN PROFILE

| | |
|---|---|
| Range SAT Verbal | 500-600 |
| Average SAT Verbal | 560 |
| Range SAT Math | 510-610 |
| Average SAT Math | 565 |
| Range ACT Composite | 21-25 |
| Average ACT Composite | 24 |
| Minimum TOEFL | 550 |
| Average HS GPA | 3.2 |
| % graduated top 10% of class | 18 |
| % graduated top 25% of class | 60 |
| % graduated top 50% of class | 98 |

### DEADLINES

| | |
|---|---|
| Regular admission | 2/15 |
| Regular notification | 3/15 |
| Nonfall registration? | yes |

### APPLICANTS ALSO LOOK AT AND OFTEN PREFER

Boston College
Holy Cross
Villanova
SUNY Binghamton

### AND SOMETIMES PREFER

Fordham
Loyola College in Maryland
Providence College
SUNY Geneseo

### AND RARELY PREFER

Iona College
Hofstra
SUNY Oneonta
Rider

## FINANCIAL FACTS

| | |
|---|---|
| Financial Aid Rating | 79 |
| Tuition | $17,444 |
| Room and board | $8,332 |
| Books and supplies | $850 |
| Avg frosh grant | $6,331 |
| Avg frosh loan | $2,966 |

# MARLBORO COLLEGE

PO Box A, South Road, Marlboro, VT 05344 • Admissions: 802-258-9236 • Fax: 802-257-4154

## CAMPUS LIFE

| | |
|---|---|
| Quality of Life Rating | 94 |
| Type of school | private |
| Environment | rural |

### STUDENTS

| | |
|---|---|
| Total undergrad enrollment | 290 |
| % male/female | 41/59 |
| % from out of state | 82 |
| % from public high school | 65 |
| % live on campus | 78 |
| % African American | 1 |
| % Asian | 1 |
| % Caucasian | 87 |
| % Hispanic | 2 |
| % international | 2 |
| # of countries represented | 6 |

### SURVEY SAYS . . .
Theater is hot
Student government is popular
No one cheats
Registration is a breeze
Campus feels safe
Class discussions are encouraged
Intercollegiate sports are unpopular or nonexistent
Lab facilities are great

## ACADEMICS

| | |
|---|---|
| Academic Rating | 95 |
| Calendar | semester |
| Student/faculty ratio | 8:1 |
| Profs interesting rating | 98 |
| Profs accessible rating | 98 |
| % profs teaching UG courses | 100 |

## STUDENTS SPEAK OUT

### Academics

Like everything else at Marlboro, academics are centered around the individual student. Because students are given "freedom to design" their "own academic programs," "you can study whatever you want." In other words, students tend to believe that "the possibilities are endless." Through the system of "self-governance," students are intimately involved in the administration of their educations. One student notes that he and fellow classmates even participate in "hiring professors." A senior, however, complains that "the self-governance we advertise is a myth—student government consists only of the 'good kids.'" Other students will tell you that it's the grown-up administration that's "counterproductive to the ideals this school was founded on." (It should be mentioned, though, that the administration is so accessible that even "the president of the college plays basketball with students during lunch hour.") You won't hear any complaints about the faculty. "They're hardworking, quirky, rugged types," describes a freshman. A senior adds, "Professors . . . are here because they sincerely want to teach." While students focus on a range of topics, the school seems particularly proud of its creative endeavors, like theatre and creative writing. Regardless of what you study here, "there's no such thing as sitting in the back and twiddling your thumbs." Of course, the very fact that there's enough schoolwork to "kill an average individual" means that "a true Marlboro student thinks about dropping daily."

### Life

While Marlboro neighbors the 12,000-person town of Brattleboro, which has a "spa" and occasional "performances," students manage to find their excitement on campus. Like all college students, Marlboro students "often drink on the weekends." But more than drinking, they like talking. For fun, people regularly "engage in conversation that is usually somewhat intellectual." A freshman says, "We talk about everything from the Muppets to political and religious theories to whether vampires are ticklish." We should mention that these chat sessions often take place in the rustic dorms—one of them a converted ski chalet—where three-quarters of the student body lives. Students also take advantage of school activities, like the Outdoor Program, which loans everything from cross-country skis to kayaks and climbing gear to students at no cost. In fact, Marlboro students have a thing for skis, and outdoor activities in general. When the "cabin fever" sets in, students here start "affixing skis to the bottom of objects and riding them down hills." Thus, things like the "ski-chair" and "ski-bike" are born. But more than anything, schoolwork dominates a student's life at Marlboro. One senior writes, "Students spend a remarkable amount of time studying" at Marlboro. But they enjoy it. "It's like summer camp plus stress." And snow.

### Student Body

Marlboro was started by a bunch of young World War II vets who returned from the front and wanted a rigorous education rooted in an ideal of student independence. Their legacy sustains. Marlboro students pride themselves on their independence. Sometimes this backfires. "We tend to stick to our established friends and groups," admits one junior. "Students can get pretty self-absorbed, and it becomes irritating," writes a freshman, adding, "until, of course, you yourself become self-absorbed!" All in all, most members on "Planet Marlboro" "get along" and remain "very open to a diversity of lifestyles." This is a good thing because of "the smallness and isolation of the campus—any enemy you make you will see at every meal for four years." Naturally, though, "there are always assholes, and with only 300 people they can really make themselves known." The biggest gripe that students have with their own flock is the "lack of racial diversity." And, while we're hearing grievances, they also want to break down a stereotype that has long draped over these individualistic, outdoorsy students: "We're NOT a bunch of hippies. We're a bunch of dorks and nerds." And "far more mature than most college students," opines a junior.

# MARLBORO COLLEGE

FINANCIAL AID: 802-257-4333 • E-MAIL: ADMISSIONS@MARLBORO.EDU • WEBSITE: WWW.MARLBORO.EDU

## ADMISSIONS

*Very important factors considered include:* secondary school record. *Important factors considered include:* interview, character/personal qualities, class rank, essays, extracurricular activities, recommendations, standardized test scores, talent/ability, volunteer work. *Other factors considered include:* alumni/ae relation, geographical residence, work experience. SAT I or ACT required; SAT II recommended. TOEFL required of all non-native speakers of English. High school diploma or GED is required. *High school units required/recommended:* 4 English required, 3 math recommended, 3 science recommended, 3 foreign language recommended, 3 social studies recommended, 3 history recommended.

### The Inside Word

Don't be misled by Marlboro's high acceptance rate; the College's applicant pool consists mainly of candidates who are sincerely interested in a nontraditional path to their BA. They also possess sincere intellectual curiosity, and students who don't should not bother applying. The admissions process here is driven by matchmaking and a search for those who truly want to learn. For the right kind of person, Marlboro can be a terrific college choice.

## FINANCIAL AID

*Students should submit:* FAFSA, CSS/Financial Aid PROFILE, noncustodial (divorced/separated) parent's statement. Regular filing deadline is March 1. The Princeton Review suggests that all financial aid forms be submitted as soon as possible after January 1. *Need-based scholarships/grants offered:* Pell, SEOG, state scholarships/grants, private scholarships, the school's own gift aid. *Loan aid offered:* FFEL Subsidized Stafford, FFEL Unsubsidized Stafford, FFEL PLUS, college/university loans from institutional funds. Federal Work-Study Program available. Institutional employment available. Applicants will be notified of awards on a rolling basis beginning on or about April 1. Off-campus job opportunities are fair.

## FROM THE ADMISSIONS OFFICE

"Marlboro College is distinguished by its curriculum, praised in higher education circles as unique; it is known for its self-governing philosophy, in which each student, faculty, and staff has an equal vote on many issues affecting the community; and it is recognized for its 50-year history of offering a rigorous, exciting, self-designed course of study taught in very small classes and individual tutorials. Marlboro's size also distinguishes it from most other schools. With 300 students and a student/faculty ratio of 8 to 1, it is one of the nation's smallest liberal arts colleges. Few other schools offer a program where students have such close interaction with faculty, and where community life is inseparable from academic life. The result, the self-designed, self-directed Plan of Concentration, allows students to develop their own unique academic work by defining a problem, setting clear limits on an area of inquiry, and analyzing, evaluating, and reporting on the outcome of a significant project. A Marlboro education teaches you to think for yourself, articulate your thoughts, express your ideas, believe in yourself, and do it all with the clarity, confidence and self-reliance necessary for later success, no matter what postgraduate path you take."

### SELECTIVITY

| | |
|---|---|
| Admissions Rating | 82 |
| # of applicants | 308 |
| % of applicants accepted | 80 |
| % of acceptees attending | 40 |
| # of early decision applicants | 19 |
| % accepted early decision | 79 |

### FRESHMAN PROFILE

| | |
|---|---|
| Range SAT Verbal | 580-680 |
| Average SAT Verbal | 610 |
| Range SAT Math | 500-620 |
| Average SAT Math | 580 |
| Minimum TOEFL | 550 |
| Average HS GPA | 3.2 |
| % graduated top 10% of class | 31 |
| % graduated top 25% of class | 51 |
| % graduated top 50% of class | 79 |

### DEADLINES

| | |
|---|---|
| Early decision | 11/15 |
| Early decision notification | 12/15 |
| Priority admission | 3/1 |
| Regular admission | 3/1 |
| Nonfall registration? | yes |

### APPLICANTS ALSO LOOK AT AND OFTEN PREFER
Sarah Lawrence
Bard
Hampshire
### AND SOMETIMES PREFER
Bennington
Evergreen State
Antioch
### AND RARELY PREFER
Goddard
U of Vermont

### FINANCIAL FACTS

| | |
|---|---|
| Financial Aid Rating | 91 |
| Tuition | $20,950 |
| Room and board | $7,425 |
| Books and supplies | $600 |
| Required fees | $680 |
| % frosh receiving aid | 82 |
| % undergrads receiving aid | 76 |
| Avg frosh grant | $12,007 |
| Avg frosh loan | $2,619 |

THE BEST 351 COLLEGES ■ 337

# MARQUETTE UNIVERSITY

PO Box 1881, Milwaukee, WI 53201-1881 • Admissions: 414-288-7302 • Fax: 414-288-3764

## CAMPUS LIFE

| | |
|---|---|
| Quality of Life Rating | 80 |
| Type of school | private |
| Affiliation | Roman Catholic |
| Environment | urban |

### STUDENTS

| | |
|---|---|
| Total undergrad enrollment | 7,644 |
| % male/female | 44/56 |
| % from out of state | 53 |
| % from public high school | 55 |
| % live on campus | 54 |
| % in (# of) fraternities | 7 (10) |
| % in (# of) sororities | 8 (9) |
| % African American | 5 |
| % Asian | 5 |
| % Caucasian | 86 |
| % Hispanic | 4 |
| % international | 2 |
| # of countries represented | 80 |

### SURVEY SAYS . . .
Lots of beer drinking
Campus easy to get around
Athletic facilities are great
(Almost) everyone smokes
Students are happy
Great off-campus food
Great library
Great computer facilities
Hard liquor is popular
Everyone loves the Golden Eagles

## ACADEMICS

| | |
|---|---|
| Academic Rating | 77 |
| Calendar | semester |
| Student/faculty ratio | 15:1 |
| Avg lab size | 10-19 students |
| Avg reg class size | 20-29 students |

### MOST POPULAR MAJORS
Nursing/registered nurse training (RN, ASN, BSN, MSN)
Business administration/management
Biomedical sciences

## STUDENTS SPEAK OUT

### Academics
"There is really a lot more to Marquette than just the 'community service' opportunities and excellent basketball program that they advertise so much," notes one student at this solid, demanding Catholic school in Milwaukee. Undergrads here warn that "sometimes professors forget that we are college students and some of us work. The workloads can sometimes get out of hand." When students feel overwhelmed, however, they can take advantage of the "many opportunities to get help and ask questions." Marquette's faculty are "engaging, funny, and knowledgeable" and "encourage meeting outside of class and accessing them at all times, even at home. They have flexible office hours and truly try to get to know their students." Students single out for praise the "great chemistry department," the "extremely well-informed professors in the College of Engineering," and the b-school teachers "who have actual work experience." The core curriculum, required of all undergrads, earns students' approval. "While sometimes tedious, these classes provide a breadth of knowledge regardless of your major," notes one. Upperclassmen warn that "upper-division classes tend to have few sections and fill up quickly" and that "registration is done by a lottery, which prevents many upperclassmen from getting classes they need."

### Life
Because academics are rigorous at Marquette, students' weekdays here are largely filled with classes, study sessions, and homework. Writes one student, "It is very typical to take heavy class loads, like at least 16 or 17 credits. I've had three 19-credit semesters, and because of that, many of us graduate on time or early. It is expected that you juggle lots of things. Otherwise it seems like you're 'lazy.'" Students know where to draw the line, however, and when the weekend comes, "the general population knows how to cut loose and have fun." How do they do that? "Marquette is a bar school. There are few house parties, and as a result of the lack of Greek life here, frat parties are also rarities. Bars are the most common form of weekend entertainment." Students also love the "major league baseball, shopping, theater, concerts, excellent nightlife downtown, Lake Michigan, etc." that Milwaukee offers and report that "the safety program here at Marquette is excellent. . . . I feel safe living in the downtown area of Milwaukee, where the school is located." On campus, Marquette offers "a lot of activities every week," and of course "Division I intercollegiate sports. The men's B-ball team, in particular, rocks our world. We are the best fans and will do anything to support the Golden Eagles." As at many Jesuit schools, "most students are involved in community service. We live in an urban area, so it is quite easy to find volunteer work. A rescue mission is just one block from campus; many of us serve meals to the homeless."

### Student Body
The "studious, religious, friendly, clean-cut" students of Marquette "are typically Catholic and from Wisconsin or Illinois." As one student relates, "You will not see many ethnic differences or hippie types around the campus." Economic backgrounds vary. Wrote one undergrad, "Looking at a student, you never know their story. Some have everything paid for. Others (like me) are working their tails off to pay their own way through college." Because Catholic prep schools feed Marquette heavily, the student body does have a large preppy contingent. Students "tend to be a bit on the conservative side" and are generally very polite. As one undergrad reported, "That's the one thing that impressed me most about Marquette: the way people hold the door for each other, the way eye contact is made with strangers, and the overall inviting atmosphere of campus."

338 ■ THE BEST 351 COLLEGES

# MARQUETTE UNIVERSITY

FINANCIAL AID: 414-288-7390 • E-MAIL: ADMISSIONS@MARQUETTE.EDU • WEBSITE: WWW.MARQUETTE.EDU

## ADMISSIONS

*Very important factors considered include:* secondary school record, standardized test scores. *Important factors considered include:* class rank. *Other factors considered include:* alumni/ae relation, character/personal qualities, essays, extracurricular activities, geographical residence, interview, minority status, recommendations, religious affiliation/commitment, state residency, talent/ability, volunteer work, work experience. SAT I or ACT required; SAT I recommended. TOEFL required of all international applicants. High school diploma or GED is required. *High school units required/recommended:* 16 total recommended; 4 English recommended, 3 math recommended, 3 science recommended, 2 science lab recommended, 2 foreign language recommended, 2 social studies recommended, 2 history recommended, 3 elective recommended.

### *The Inside Word*

Class rank may be important to the admissions office as a required criterion, but not to worry—in practice, a little less than a tenth of Marquette's freshmen ranked in the bottom half of their graduating class. The university's low level of selectivity makes it a no-sweat proposition for most candidates.

## FINANCIAL AID

*Students should submit:* FAFSA. Admission application required for Marquette University Ignatius Scholarship. Regular filing deadline is March 1. The Princeton Review suggests that all financial aid forms be submitted as soon as possible after January 1. *Need-based scholarships/grants offered:* Pell, SEOG, state scholarships/grants, private scholarships, the school's own gift aid, Federal Nursing. *Loan aid offered:* Direct Subsidized Stafford, Direct Unsubsidized Stafford, Direct PLUS, Federal Perkins, Federal Nursing, state loans, college/university loans from institutional funds, alternative educational loans. Federal Work-Study Program available. Institutional employment available. Applicants will be notified of awards on a rolling basis beginning on or about March 21. Off-campus job opportunities are excellent.

## FROM THE ADMISSIONS OFFICE

"Since 1881, Marquette has been noted for its commitment to educational excellence in the 450-year-old Jesuit, Catholic tradition. Marquette embraces the philosophy that true education should be more than an acquisition of knowledge. Marquette seeks to develop your intellect as well as your moral and spiritual character. This all-encompassing education will challenge you to develop the goals and values that will shape the rest of your life. Each of Marquette's 7,500 undergraduates are admitted as freshman to one of six colleges: Arts and Sciences, Business Administration, Communication, Engineering, Health Sciences, or Nursing. Many co-enroll in the School of Education. The faculty within these colleges are prolific writers and researchers, but more important, they all teach and advise students. Marquette is nestled in the financial center of Milwaukee, the nation's eighteenth largest city, allowing you to take full advantage of the city's cultural, professional, and governmental opportunities. Marquette's urban experience is unique; an 80-acre campus (with real grass and trees), an outdoor athletic complex, and an internationally diverse student body (90 percent of which live on campus) all make Marquette a close-knit community in which you can learn and live."

## SELECTIVITY

| | |
|---|---|
| Admissions Rating | 78 |
| # of applicants | 7,593 |
| % of applicants accepted | 82 |
| % of acceptees attending | 30 |

### FRESHMAN PROFILE

| | |
|---|---|
| Range SAT Verbal | 520-640 |
| Average SAT Verbal | 560 |
| Range SAT Math | 530-650 |
| Average SAT Math | 590 |
| Range ACT Composite | 23-28 |
| Average ACT Composite | 25 |
| Minimum TOEFL | 525 |
| % graduated top 10% of class | 20 |
| % graduated top 25% of class | 40 |
| % graduated top 50% of class | 94 |

### DEADLINES

| | |
|---|---|
| Priority admission | 2/1 |
| Nonfall registration? | yes |

### APPLICANTS ALSO LOOK AT AND OFTEN PREFER

U of Wisconsin at Madison
U of Wisconsin at Milwaukee
U of Illinois at Urbana-Champaign
Notre Dame
Miami of Ohio

### AND SOMETIMES PREFER

St. Louis U
Purdue U at West Lafayette
Case Western Reserve

### AND RARELY PREFER

Vanderbilt
Villanova
U of Oklahoma

## FINANCIAL FACTS

| | |
|---|---|
| Financial Aid Rating | 82 |
| Tuition | $20,350 |
| Room and board | $7,036 |
| Books and supplies | $900 |
| Required fees | $374 |
| % frosh receiving aid | 65 |
| % undergrads receiving aid | 60 |
| Avg frosh grant | $11,640 |
| Avg frosh loan | $4,385 |

THE BEST 351 COLLEGES ■ 339

# MARY WASHINGTON COLLEGE

1301 COLLEGE AVENUE, FREDERICKSBURG, VA 22401 • ADMISSIONS: 540-654-2000 • FAX: 540-654-1857

## CAMPUS LIFE

| Quality of Life Rating | 84 |
|---|---|
| Type of school | public |
| Environment | suburban |

### STUDENTS

| Total undergrad enrollment | 4,275 |
|---|---|
| % male/female | 32/68 |
| % from out of state | 35 |
| % from public high school | 76 |
| % live on campus | 70 |
| % African American | 4 |
| % Asian | 4 |
| % Caucasian | 88 |
| % Hispanic | 3 |

### SURVEY SAYS . . .
Very little drug use
Athletic facilities need improving
Diversity lacking on campus
No one cheats
Classes are small
Campus is beautiful
Very small frat/sorority scene
Registration is a pain
Low cost of living

## ACADEMICS

| Academic Rating | 80 |
|---|---|
| Calendar | semester |
| Student/faculty ratio | 17:1 |
| Profs interesting rating | 93 |
| Profs accessible rating | 94 |
| % profs teaching UG courses | 100 |
| Avg lab size | 20-29 students |
| Avg reg class size | 20-29 students |

### MOST POPULAR MAJORS
Business administration/management
English language and literature
Psychology

## STUDENTS SPEAK OUT

### Academics

If you manage to survive the oft-tedious class registration process at Mary Washington, you're in for an academic ride that'll leave you screaming, as this one senior did: "I hate every other college, but I love my college." At Mary Washington, the combination of rigorous courses and close student/faculty relationships challenges students without leaving them feeling as though they've been stranded at sea. While the "hard" classes are an important part of the college's academic landscape, the professors are the most outstanding feature of Mary Washington. "My professors are so rad!" exclaims one senior, mentioning that her professors have "hobbies that include skydiving and motorcycle riding. And they know how to throw a great party, too!" Whether discussing a Keats poem in class or talking about the latest headlines at an "end-of-the-year dinner," professors at this liberal arts college seem to continually inspire their students. One freshman explains that she feels "like a person as well as student" in the faculty's eyes. And "they know their stuff," adds another. Most importantly, the professors are usually available to share the "stuff" they know. They "always make themselves available for extra help." So there is some hard work and some good help in Mary Washington's academic world. Or, as one freshman put it, "Mary Washington is a roller coaster ride of thrills and chills. I give it two thumbs up." Students are split on the administration, citing the increasing number of freshman it has admitted in recent years as the cause of a housing crunch.

### Life

Not more than 50 miles south of Washington, D.C., and not more than 50 miles north of Richmond, Virginia, and not more than a few miles off of Interstate 95, you'll find the city of Fredericksburg and the "prestigious" and "beautiful campus" of Mary Washington College. Despite the campus' beauty, many students venture home or into the neighboring metro areas on the weekends. (Leaving campus is a tougher task for freshman, who "cannot have cars," which means they have to "ride public transportation to Wal-Mart or Target.") "It's a small school full of life," chirps one student who's happy to stick around on the weekends. But others complain that "life" is exactly what's lacking. "The social life is pretty weak unless you're into movies and small-party drinking," writes a senior. Without frats and sororities, students usually stumble upon parties "in people's rooms instead of houses." Another student laments, "Good parties are few and far between." OK, so Mary Washington is "NOT a party school," but that's not the end of the world. "Life here is great," declares a student. "You sometimes have to go out and look for the fun, but I have enjoyed my four years here thoroughly."

### Student Body

About 30 years ago, if you took a look Mary Washington's student body, you'd notice that it was completely female. Today, that's not quite the case, with about two guys for every three girls. "A good gender ratio," comments a male student. Still, a student from New Jersey complains that Mary Washington, unlike his "ethnically diverse" hometown, seems full of "mostly white and female" students. While most students won't claim that diversity is one of the college's strong suits, few people will dispute that this is "a friendly campus." One freshman is pleased to report that "students get along, smile, and wave at each other across campus." "It's a small college so you know almost everyone," concurs another student. As in any small community, some students tend to be "cliquey"—"but there is still a lot of individuality."

# MARY WASHINGTON COLLEGE

FINANCIAL AID: 800-468-5614 • E-MAIL: ADMIT@MWC.EDU • WEBSITE: WWW.MWC.EDU

## ADMISSIONS

*Very important factors considered include:* secondary school record. *Important factors considered include:* class rank, essays, standardized test scores. *Other factors considered include:* alumni/ae relation, character/personal qualities, extracurricular activities, geographical residence, minority status, recommendations, state residency, talent/ability, volunteer work, work experience. SAT I or ACT required; SAT II recommended. TOEFL required of all international applicants. High school diploma or GED is required. *High school units required/recommended:* 4 English required, 3 math required, 4 math recommended, 3 science required, 4 science recommended, 3 science lab required, 4 science lab recommended, 2 foreign language required, 4 foreign language recommended, 2 social studies required, 1 history required, 2 history recommended.

## The Inside Word

It's hard to beat small, selective public colleges like Mary Washington for quality and cost, and more and more students are discovering this. The admissions process is very selective and, with the exception of preferential treatment for Virginia residents, functions in virtually the same manner as small private college admissions committees do. Students who are interested need to focus on putting their best into all aspects of the application.

## FINANCIAL AID

*Students should submit:* FAFSA. The Princeton Review suggests that all financial aid forms be submitted as soon as possible after January 1. *Need-based scholarships/grants offered:* Pell, SEOG, state scholarships/grants, private scholarships, the school's own gift aid. *Loan aid offered:* FFEL Subsidized Stafford, FFEL Unsubsidized Stafford, FFEL PLUS, Federal Perkins. Federal Work-Study Program available. Institutional employment available. Applicants will be notified of awards on or about April 15. Off-campus job opportunities are excellent.

## FROM THE ADMISSIONS OFFICE

"Among institutions of higher learning in Virginia, Mary Washington College stands alone. We have distinctive academic programs, a breathtakingly beautiful campus, a sharp and diverse student body, and a unique sense of friendship and camaraderie that make MWC very special. In fact, we have one of the best combinations of strong academics, personal attention, low cost, and impressive graduate school and job placement of any school in the country. Our students come from all over the country and the world, and are instructed by a faculty that considers teaching its primary objective—research and publishing come second. Committed to providing a well-rounded liberal arts and sciences education, MWC offers its students the opportunity to pursue individual or collaborative research projects. Supportive faculty and more than $60,000 in student research funds annually make ours one of the most ambitious undergraduate research programs in the country. Mary Washington College recently broke ground on a new student fitness center, and a new apartment-style housing community, which will both open in fall 2003."

## SELECTIVITY

| | |
|---|---|
| Admissions Rating | 91 |

### FRESHMAN PROFILE

| | |
|---|---|
| Range SAT Verbal | 570-660 |
| Average SAT Verbal | 613 |
| Range SAT Math | 560-640 |
| Average SAT Math | 595 |
| Range ACT Composite | 24-29 |
| Average ACT Composite | 27 |
| Minimum TOEFL | 550 |
| Average HS GPA | 3.7 |
| % graduated top 10% of class | 40 |
| % graduated top 25% of class | 85 |
| % graduated top 50% of class | 99 |

### DEADLINES

| | |
|---|---|
| Priority admission | 1/15 |
| Regular admission | 2/1 |
| Regular notification | 4/1 |
| Nonfall registration? | yes |

### APPLICANTS ALSO LOOK AT AND OFTEN PREFER
William and Mary
U of Virginia
### AND SOMETIMES PREFER
U of Richmond
James Madison
### AND RARELY PREFER
George Mason
Longwood U

## FINANCIAL FACTS

| | |
|---|---|
| Financial Aid Rating | 83 |
| In-state tuition | $4,089 |
| Out-of-state tuition | $11,122 |
| Room and board | $5,318 |
| Books and supplies | $800 |
| % frosh receiving aid | 44 |
| % undergrads receiving aid | 39 |
| Avg frosh grant | $2,753 |
| Avg frosh loan | $1,894 |

# MASSACHUSETTS INSTITUTE OF TECHNOLOGY

77 MASSACHUSETTS AVENUE, CAMBRIDGE, MA 02139 • ADMISSIONS: 617-253-4791 • FAX: 617-253-1986

## CAMPUS LIFE

★ ★ ★ ☆

| | |
|---|---|
| Quality of Life Rating | 83 |
| Type of school | private |
| Environment | urban |

### STUDENTS

| | |
|---|---|
| Total undergrad enrollment | 4,178 |
| % male/female | 57/43 |
| % from out of state | 91 |
| % from public high school | 68 |
| % live on campus | 97 |
| % in (# of) fraternities | 26 (27) |
| % in (# of) sororities | 8 (5) |
| % African American | 7 |
| % Asian | 30 |
| % Caucasian | 38 |
| % Hispanic | 13 |
| % international | 8 |
| # of countries represented | 108 |

### SURVEY SAYS . . .
Frats and sororities dominate social scene
Great computer facilities
Students love Cambridge, MA
(Almost) everyone plays intramural sports
Lab facilities need improving
Unattractive campus
Large classes
(Almost) no one smokes

## ACADEMICS

★ ★ ★ ★

| | |
|---|---|
| Academic Rating | 99 |
| Calendar | 4-1-4 |
| Student/faculty ratio | 6:1 |
| Profs interesting rating | 91 |
| Profs accessible rating | 88 |
| % profs teaching UG courses | 100 |
| Avg lab size | under 10 students |
| Avg reg class size | under 10 students |

### MOST POPULAR MAJORS
Business administration/management
Computer science
Electrical, electronics, and communications engineering

## STUDENTS SPEAK OUT

### Academics
How intense is an MIT education? "Say you like Pez candy," posits one MIT undergrad. "MIT, then, is like being forced to eat $1 \times 10^9$ Pez candies." Indeed, "the workload is heavy" here, but the crunch is mitigated by an atmosphere of teamwork and a sense that students are getting the very best education money can buy. They study directly under "Nobel Prize–winning faculty, even as freshmen" and enjoy access to "superior labs and outstanding opportunities for undergraduate research." Time management, students point out, is critical. "Tech is hell if you want to attend every lecture, read everything twice, do the homework perfectly, and ace every test," explains one student. "If you understand what does and does not help you learn, life here becomes much more manageable." Material "is taught extremely fast. It takes a few weeks to get used to, but it makes everything so much more interesting and motivating." Most classes consist of "lectures taught by a full professor and recitations taught by TAs." According to several students, "Usually, recitations by undergraduate and graduate TAs, not the classes taught by distinguished faculty, are the most helpful [in learning] the material." MIT's "world-renowned" profs are, for the most part, "excellent teachers as well as researchers. Some are not good at teaching. Many are famous and offer cutting-edge information." Students appreciate the fact that "freshman year is pass/no record, and that was awesome in helping me adjust," and also that "the administration has gone through a lot of work sorting us out and choosing whom to select. They really hate to see students flunk out or transfer."

### Life
Students at MIT warn that their studies leave little time for socializing. They also note, however, that because they are located in Cambridge with so many undergraduate institutions nearby, they are well-situated to make the most of their few free hours. Explains one undergrad, "There are always concerts and events on campus, but when we want to get off campus, Boston is a beautiful, cultural city. Walking down Newbury Street, rollerblading along the Charles River, or eating in the North End Italian district are just a few favorites." The Greek scene "is huge, especially on the weekends," and "guest lectures and movies are always available." Also, students always seem to find some time for "hacking," the time-honored school tradition one student defines as "the act of pulling off elaborate, skillful practical jokes. It requires teamwork and reflects the student body's sense of humor." Among the school's most celebrated hacks are placing a replica of a campus police cruiser atop the Great Dome; the creation of a water fountain–fire plug hybrid (because learning at MIT is "like drinking water from a fire hose"); and the distribution of "Buzzword Bingo" cards during Al Gore's 1996 commencement address. On the downside, the campus "is different shades of ugly." Reports one student, "It seems like all the green patches are being taken away because of new building projects."

### Student Body
The "very diverse" MIT student body lacks variety in one area only: brains. "People here range from the really smart to the insanely smart," writes one student, although some note that their peers have "plenty of book sense but hardly any common sense." Because "students don't compete with each other as much as with themselves, everyone is willing to help everyone else out." MIT undergrads regard each other as "awesome people, although a bit nerdy. They will go out of their way to help, but some of them don't shower enough." Some are overly introverted (warns one student, "Too many people are happy to lock themselves in their rooms and study all day. If you come to MIT do not become one of these people"), but mostly this is a happy, sociable group. Notes one student, "When you come to MIT, the real you comes out. Everyone here is unique and not afraid to show it. That's because we're all tolerant of each other's differences."

342 ■ THE BEST 351 COLLEGES

# MASSACHUSETTS INSTITUTE OF TECHNOLOGY

FINANCIAL AID: 617-253-4971 • E-MAIL: ADMISSIONS@MIT.EDU • WEBSITE: WWW.MIT.EDU

## ADMISSIONS
*Very important factors considered include:* secondary school record. *Important factors considered include:* character/personal qualities, class rank, extracurricular activities, recommendations, standardized test scores, talent/ability. *Other factors considered include:* student's context, essays, interview, minority status, volunteer work, work experience. SAT I or ACT required; SAT II also required. TOEFL required of all international applicants. *High school units recommended:* 4 English recommended, 4 math recommended, 4 science recommended, 2 foreign language recommended, 1 social studies recommended, 1 history recommended.

### The Inside Word
High academic achievement, lofty test scores, and the most rigorous high school courseload possible are prerequisites for a successful candidacy. Among the most selective institutions in the country, MIT's admissions operation is easily one of the most down-to-earth and accessible. Over the years they have shown both a sense of humor in admissions literature and an awareness that applying to such a prestigious and demanding place creates a high level of anxiety in students. Their relaxed and helpful approach does much to temper such stress.

## FINANCIAL AID
*Students should submit:* FAFSA, CSS/Financial Aid PROFILE, noncustodial (divorced/separated) parent's statement, business/farm supplement, parent's complete federal income tax returns from prior year including all schedules and W-2s. Regular filing deadline is February 1. The Princeton Review suggests that all financial aid forms be submitted as soon as possible after January 1. *Need-based scholarships/grants offered:* Pell, SEOG, state scholarships/grants, private scholarships, the school's own gift aid. *Loan aid offered:* Direct Subsidized Stafford, Direct Unsubsidized Stafford, Direct PLUS, Federal Perkins, college/university loans from institutional funds. Federal Work-Study Program available. Institutional employment available. Applicants will be notified of awards on or about March 15. Off-campus job opportunities are excellent.

## FROM THE ADMISSIONS OFFICE
"The students who come to the Massachusetts Institute of Technology are some of America's—and the world's—best and most creative. As graduates, they leave here to make real contributions—in science, technology, business, education, politics, architecture, and the arts. From any class, many will go on to do work that is historically significant. These young men and women are leaders, achievers, producers. Helping such students make the most of their talents and dreams would challenge any educational institution. MIT gives them its best advantages: a world-class faculty, unparalleled facilities, remarkable opportunities. In turn, these students help to make the Institute the vital place it is. They bring fresh viewpoints to faculty research: More than three-quarters participate in the Undergraduate Research Opportunities Program. They play on MIT's 41 intercollegiate teams as well as in its 15 musical ensembles. To their classes and to their out-of-class activities, they bring enthusiasm, energy, and individual style."

### SELECTIVITY

| | |
|---|---|
| Admissions Rating | 99 |
| # of applicants | 10,664 |
| % of applicants accepted | 16 |
| % of acceptees attending | 57 |
| # accepting a place on wait list | 296 |
| % admitted from wait list | 13 |

### FRESHMAN PROFILE
| | |
|---|---|
| Range SAT Verbal | 680-760 |
| Average SAT Verbal | 712 |
| Range SAT Math | 740-800 |
| Average SAT Math | 757 |
| Range ACT Composite | 30-34 |
| Average ACT Composite | 31 |
| Minimum TOEFL | 577 |
| % graduated top 10% of class | 99 |
| % graduated top 25% of class | 100 |

### DEADLINES
| | |
|---|---|
| Regular admission | 1/1 |
| Regular notification | 3/15 |

### APPLICANTS ALSO LOOK AT AND SOMETIMES PREFER
Harvard
Yale
Stanford
Caltech
Princeton

### AND RARELY PREFER
Penn
Berkeley
Cornell U.
Brown

### FINANCIAL FACTS

| | |
|---|---|
| Financial Aid Rating | 88 |
| Tuition | $28,030 |
| Room and board | $7,830 |
| Required fees | $1,100 |
| % frosh receiving aid | 57 |
| % undergrads receiving aid | 57 |
| Avg frosh grant | $17,267 |
| Avg frosh loan | $4,638 |

# McGill University

845 Sherbrooke Street West, Montreal, Quebec H3A 2T5, Canada • Admissions: 514-398-3910 • Fax: 514-398-8939

## CAMPUS LIFE

| | |
|---|---|
| Quality of Life Rating | 90 |
| Type of school | public |
| Environment | urban |

### STUDENTS

| | |
|---|---|
| Total undergrad enrollment | 22,915 |
| % male/female | 40/60 |
| % from out of state | 29 |
| % live on campus | 10 |
| % international | 13 |
| # of countries represented | 150 |

### SURVEY SAYS . . .
Students love Montreal
Great off-campus food
Ethnic diversity on campus
Different students interact
Computer lab facilities need improving
Very small frat/sorority scene
Student government is unpopular
Musical organizations aren't popular

## ACADEMICS

| | |
|---|---|
| Academic Rating | 93 |
| Calendar | semester |
| Student/faculty ratio | 15:1 |
| Profs interesting rating | 90 |
| Profs accessible rating | 88 |
| % profs teaching UG courses | 100 |
| Avg lab size | 20-29 students |
| Avg reg class size | 100+ students |

## STUDENTS SPEAK OUT

### Academics

Its students consider McGill the "Harvard of Canada" in part because of the "quite high" expectations of their professors and the wealth of available "research" opportunities. But they also bear the burdens of any other large-university students: "First-year classes are enormous, and students find that they are identified only by their student numbers." A concurring student laments, "All of my courses have over 500 students in them. I've never met any of my professors." Students readily acknowledge that "underfunding in recent years by the government of Quebec" is largely to blame for the lack of a larger faculty as well as shortfalls in library resources. So, "an important step to getting used to McGill life is realizing that you are in charge of most of it." When students do get together with faculty, they find that professors are "amazingly helpful, professional, and hugely entertaining." Some students report that a number of classes "have multiple lecturers, each teaching the unit in which (s)he specializes"—a feature that makes lectures exciting. Overall, the "independent" yet "challenging" nature of a McGill education "teaches you to work for what you want and that you should never just 'slide by.' " What's least inspiring about McGill is any administrative office, which many students sketch as "a terror zone of red tape."

### Life

Welcome to Montreal, "an amazing city to live in," with its "French, laid-back, sexy, hedonistic attitude." It has "something to offer every personality. There are cinemas, coffee shops, clubs of any style, bars, lounges, jazz lounges, and so many amazing restaurants." It comes as no surprise, then, that only 7 percent of McGill's student body lives on campus. Maybe students overwhelmingly choose to live beyond the campus gates because "housing in the city is not a problem and is incredibly cheap compared to any American or even other Canadian cities." Students here commonly weigh their social experience against that of American universities, and they conclude that "unlike American schools, McGill doesn't have a binge drinking problem." Some cite the Canadian drinking age of 18 as a reason for their restraint. That said, many students indicate that drinking is among their favorite pastimes and that one of McGill's "major corporate sponsors is Molson Breweries." Otherwise, "McGill has hundreds of clubs and societies," as well as "three theatres" and "various sports, ranging from football to rowing, from soccer to ultimate Frisbee, from volleyball to hockey." Winter sportspersons will be pleased to know that "Mount Royal is right behind the school and you can rent cross-country skis from the gym and go skiing there during the winter. It is also great for tobogganing, and running or biking in the summer." And in case you were wondering, "you don't have to know French to get along in Montreal," though "speaking and understanding just a little bit helps."

### Student Body

Can anybody say "diverse"? "Virtually every group of people is represented on McGill's campus," thanks particularly to "the large international population," with over 140 nations represented in this student body. "On my floor alone there are people from Egypt, Korea, Pakistan, and India," writes a member of McGill's wrestling team. A classmate boasts, "I've met people from six continents now, and most of my friends are at least bilingual, if not trilingual or more." To a large degree, it's the "sheer diversity" at McGill that gives the campus its "vibrant and stimulating atmosphere." While backgrounds may vary, McGill's populace seems to have some things in common: it's composed of "very friendly, open-minded people who are easy to talk to and easy to become close with." And according to one student, even the ones who stray from this friendly path have, "at the very least, the redeeming quality of above-average intelligence."

# MCGILL UNIVERSITY

FINANCIAL AID: 514-398-6013 • E-MAIL: ADMISSIONS@MCGILL.CA • WEBSITE: WWW.MCGILL.CA

## ADMISSIONS
*Very important factors considered include:* secondary school record, standardized test scores. *Important factors considered include:* class rank. *Other factors considered include:* recommendations. TOEFL required of all international applicants. High school diploma is required and GED is not accepted.

### The Inside Word
McGill is as tough as it comes in Canadian higher education. The university is provincially funded. As there are no geographic quotas, competition from applicants around the world is intense. The admissions process is thorough and demanding, and high SAT I and II scores just don't have the same clout across the border. Students who are serious about McGill should put extra energy into French classes. While English is the language of instruction, French is the language of Montreal, and those who speak it fare much better in everyday life than those who do not.

## FINANCIAL AID
*Students should submit:* FAFSA, institution's own financial aid form. The Princeton Review suggests that all financial aid forms be submitted as soon as possible after January 1. Institutional employment available. Applicants will be notified of awards on a rolling basis. Off-campus job opportunities are fair.

## FROM THE ADMISSIONS OFFICE
"McGill processes over 20,000 first-year and transfer applicants for the September session. Very few programs are available to non-Quebec students for January admission; consult the website for details."

---

### SELECTIVITY

| | |
|---|---|
| **Admissions Rating** | 95 |
| # of applicants | 16,952 |
| % of applicants accepted | 55 |
| % of acceptees attending | 47 |

### FRESHMAN PROFILE
| | |
|---|---|
| Minimum TOEFL | 577 |
| Average HS GPA | 3.5 |
| % graduated top 10% of class | 90 |
| % graduated top 25% of class | 100 |

### DEADLINES
| | |
|---|---|
| Regular admission | 1/15 |

### APPLICANTS ALSO LOOK AT AND SOMETIMES PREFER
Queen's University
Universite De Montreal

### FINANCIAL FACTS

| | |
|---|---|
| **Financial Aid Rating** | 84 |
| In-province tuition | $1,668 |
| Out-of-province tuition | $4,012 |
| International tuition | $9,500-$15,000 |
| Room and board | $7,500 |
| Books and supplies | $1,000 |
| Required fees | $1,200 |
| Avg frosh grant | $3,000 |
| Avg frosh loan | $2,625 |

Note: All figures in Canadian dollars

# MERCER UNIVERSITY

ADMISSIONS OFFICE, 1400 COLEMAN AVENUE, MACON, GA 31207-0001 • ADMISSIONS: 478-301-2650

## CAMPUS LIFE

| | |
|---|---|
| Quality of Life Rating | 75 |
| Type of school | private |
| Affiliation | Baptist |
| Environment | urban |

### STUDENTS

| | |
|---|---|
| Total undergrad enrollment | 3,040 |
| % male/female | 43/57 |
| % from out of state | 25 |
| % live on campus | 61 |
| % in (# of) fraternities | 24 (10) |
| % in (# of) sororities | 26 (7) |
| % African American | 18 |
| % Asian | 7 |
| % Caucasian | 70 |
| % Hispanic | 1 |
| % international | 2 |

### SURVEY SAYS . . .
School is well run
Registration is a breeze
Campus is easy to get around
Campus is beautiful
Students are religious
Student government is popular
Ethnic diversity on campus

## ACADEMICS

| | |
|---|---|
| Academic Rating | 77 |
| Calendar | semester |
| Student/faculty ratio | 15:1 |
| Profs interesting rating | 81 |
| Profs accessible rating | 79 |
| % classes taught by TAs | 0 |
| Avg lab size | 20-29 students |
| Avg regular class size | 20-29 students |

### MOST POPULAR MAJORS
biology/biological sciences
finance
Communication/theatre arts

## STUDENTS SPEAK OUT

### Academics
If you're looking for a small school with "tough" academics that is equally devoted to scholastic development and spiritual growth, then read on. According to Mercer University's website, it's a Baptist-affiliated institution that's "guided by the historic principles of religious and intellectual freedom, while affirming religious and moral values that arise from the Judeo-Christian understanding of the world." Some students tell us that the whole Baptist thing is overdone, like this nontraditional student who describes herself as having "no religious preference" and choosing Mercer because of its location: "The school . . . caters to 18- to 20-year-old, high-income Baptists." Regarding instructors, the overriding opinion is that Mercer's "professors are smart as hell" and "care a great deal about their students." Whether or not students like the profs, they'd better be prepared to interact with them. "Real professors," as opposed to TAs, "teach the classes" at Mercer, and they "make it easy to come to talk to them if you have any problems." One student reports that his current schedule consists of "two classes in which there are only four students." But he's an upperclassman. Underclassmen can expect larger classes of less academic rigor. According to students, the old forest-for-the-trees axiom applies when speaking of Mercer's administration. Though the people in charge are "constantly trying to make Mercer better," they often fail to see how the students react to different policies. Students can at least count on honesty from management, however: "The administration speaks the truth," applauds an undergrad. "If there is a matter at the school that cannot be dealt with easily, they do not try to make light of the situation."

### Life
Metaphorically, "Mercer is an island. Inside the walls, there's a feeling of protection and guidance." But when it comes to finding entertainment, many students choose to scale those walls. "For fun, people go to clubs, movies, bowling, community activities, the mall," and other places in the city of Macon, Georgia. With a population of about 125,000, Macon has attractions to suit a range of personalities. It's also the home of three other colleges and universities, each with some social options for interested students. Students with cars also take road trips to Atlanta (an hour north by car) or Athens, the home of the University of Georgia (an hour and a half northeast). The Mercer campus offers more than 100 student organizations, including the 17 Greek organizations that often take it upon themselves to serve up Mercer's local nightlife. "I love the Greek system," raves one student. When students take a break from their frat-hopping, they're often able to take advantage of the musical and theatre performances that frequent campus. For instance, the university's Grand Opera House is a regular stop for nationally touring Broadway musicals. When all else fails, some students "choose the option of going home on the weekends."

### Students
When you talk about diversity at Mercer, use music as your metaphor. Like this student, who estimates of his classmates, "They range from Christian rock to R&B to country." Music aside, most of Mercer's undergrads fit a similar mold: white, southern, financially comfortable, and Baptist. "If you would like a poorly done, southern version of Beverly Hills 90210, you'll love Mercer," cracks one student. Others use words like "snobs" and "cliques" when describing their peers. But these are the most critical voices. If you find your niche at Mercer, you'll discover "very friendly" students who "get along" in an "atmosphere of southern hospitality." If you spend a little time on campus, "it's not hard to find someone with compatible interests."

346 ■ THE BEST 351 COLLEGES

# MERCER UNIVERSITY

Fax: 478-301-2828 • E-mail: ADMISSIONS@MERCER.EDU • Website: WWW.MERCER.EDU

## ADMISSIONS

*Very important factors considered by the admissions committee include:* character/personal qualities, secondary school record, and standardized test scores. *Important factors considered include:* alumni/ae relation, extracurricular activities, talent/ability, and volunteer work. *Other factors considered include:* interview and recommendations. SAT I or ACT required. TOEFL required of all international applicants. High school diploma is required and GED is accepted. *High school units required/recommended:* 16 total are required; 4 English required, 4 math required, 3 science required, 2 science lab required, 2 foreign language required, 3 social studies required.

### The Inside Word

Busy development and renovation on campus has Mercer on track to serve a larger and more diverse student body in the near future. An applicant with a commitment to academic achievement and recognition of his or her calling as a Christian will likely thrive at Mercer.

## FINANCIAL AID

*Students should submit:* FAFSA, institution's own financial aid form, and state aid form. No deadline for regular filing. The Princeton Review suggests that all financial aid forms be submitted as soon as possible after January 1. *Need-based scholarships/grants offered:* Pell, SEOG, state scholarships/grants, the school's own gift aid, and Federal Nursing. Loan aid offered: Direct Subsidized Stafford, Direct Unsubsidized Stafford, Direct PLUS, Federal Perkins, Federal Nursing, and college/university loans from institutional funds. Federal Work-Study Program available. Institutional employment available. Applicants will be notified of awards on a rolling basis beginning on or about March 15. Off-campus job opportunities are excellent.

## FROM THE ADMISSIONS OFFICE

"The mission of the Mercer University Office of Admissions is to attract, admit, and enroll qualified and talented students who will ultimately become happy, successful alumni. We do this by becoming personally involved with each admitted student and family during the admissions process. Mercer admissions staff (98 percent of whom are Mercer graduates) takes time to know each admitted applicant on a personal level and are concerned about the family's questions regarding financial assistance, campus life, and academic affairs. High school and campus visits, regional receptions, and programs are all conducted by admissions staff who are knowledgeable about the high schools and two-year colleges in a particular region. This makes for a truly enjoyable and productive admissions experience for all involved."

### SELECTIVITY

| | |
|---|---|
| Admissions Rating | 73 |
| # of applicants | 3,200 |
| % of applicants accepted | 70 |
| % of acceptees attending | 29 |

### FRESHMAN PROFILE

| | |
|---|---|
| Range SAT Verbal | 530-630 |
| Average SAT Verbal | 578 |
| Range SAT Math | 530-630 |
| Average SAT Math | 580 |
| Range ACT Composite | 22-27 |
| Average ACT Composite | 25 |
| Minimum TOEFL | 550 |
| Average HS GPA | 3.5 |
| % graduated top 10% of class | 43 |
| % graduated top 25% of class | 72 |
| % graduated top 50% of class | 91 |

### DEADLINES

| | |
|---|---|
| Regular admission | 4/1 |
| Nonfall registration? | yes |

### APPLICANTS ALSO LOOK AT AND OFTEN PREFER
U of Georgia
Berry College
Furman U
Samford U

### AND SOMETIMES PREFER
Georgia Tech
Vanderbilt
Emory

### AND RARELY PREFER
Georgia Southern
Valdosta State
Wesleyan College

### FINANCIAL FACTS

| | |
|---|---|
| Financial Aid Rating | 79 |
| Tuition | $20,796 |
| Room and board | $6,720 |
| Books and supplies | $650 |

# MIAMI UNIVERSITY

301 SOUTH CAMPUS AVENUE BUILDING, OXFORD, OH 45056 • ADMISSIONS: 513-529-2531 • FAX: 513-529-1550

## CAMPUS LIFE

| | |
|---|---|
| **Quality of Life Rating** | 85 |
| Type of school | public |
| Environment | suburban |

### STUDENTS

| | |
|---|---|
| Total undergrad enrollment | 15,153 |
| % male/female | 45/55 |
| % from out of state | 27 |
| % live on campus | 45 |
| % in (# of) fraternities | 24 (28) |
| % in (# of) sororities | 27 (20) |
| % African American | 4 |
| % Asian | 2 |
| % Caucasian | 89 |
| % Hispanic | 2 |
| % international | 1 |
| # of countries represented | 76 |

### SURVEY SAYS . . .
Popular college radio
Students are religious
Political activism is hot
No one cheats
Students are happy
Athletic facilities need improving

## ACADEMICS

| | |
|---|---|
| **Academic Rating** | 82 |
| Calendar | semester |
| Student/faculty ratio | 17:1 |
| Profs interesting rating | 80 |
| Profs accessible rating | 77 |
| % profs teaching UG courses | 100 |
| % classes taught by TAs | 25 |
| Avg lab size | 20-29 students |
| Avg reg class size | 20-29 students |

## STUDENTS SPEAK OUT

### Academics

Students at Miami University, a highly regarded public institution, brag that their school is "very devoted to its undergraduate program." "I have to admit that in my four years at the school, I only had one or two classes with 90 students," writes one undergrad. "Most of my classes were small (approx. 20 students) and were based around discussion." But this is no small liberal arts college; Miami is a full-scale university, with a wide variety of course offerings and myriad opportunities for students to distinguish themselves. "The best part of Miami is the opportunities," reports one student. "There are internships, clubs, classes, majors, minors, or traveling abroad." Adds another, "Through Miami, I've interned at the Democratic National Convention, studied a semester at our campus in Luxembourg, and attended our Washington, D.C., Media Experience Program and got to talk with people like Sam Donaldson, Bob Dole, and Tim Russert." Be forewarned that Miami's curriculum is "challenging; you need to put serious time into your work." Fortunately, profs are "very approachable and always have convenient office hours. They love teaching and love their students." Students also tell us that "the alumni network is also amazing."

### Life

Miami offers "a pretty good balance as a party/academic school. Most people stay in Sunday through Wednesday nights and study. However, the weekend definitely starts on Thursday, and partying can be pretty intense." Oxford's remote location contributes to the spirited party scene. Students explain that "being surrounded by cornfields means there's not a whole lot to do other than party on the weekends. So, yeah, there is a lot of drinking. But it's fun! There are a ton of bars uptown. There are plenty of house parties to go to." The Greek houses are also abuzz with activity, as "Greek life is definitely huge." "If partying isn't your thing, you will probably find college life to be pretty boring here," many warn. That's because "the town of Oxford has nothing to offer. There is a Wal-Mart and a grocery store. It is miniscule and at times very claustrophobic." Students praise the Miami campus, calling it a "beautiful, easy-leaning environment. Lots of trees, pretty buildings, and red brick roads." They also tell us the school has a "great intramural program" that includes "broomball, a combination of hockey and soccer that is played on the ice. It is incredibly popular. It was the most fun I have ever had in a sport, and one of my most fond memories of my freshman year."

### Student Body

Whether they agree or disagree with the stereotype, almost all students at Miami University concede that their school has a widespread reputation as '"J.Crew U." Writes one student, "If you were to take away the rich, white, Jetta/Audi-driving frat/sorority members, and the students who are more worried about their image than anything else, you would have a student body that could fill a small auditorium." Counters another, "Students joke about the Miami image more than they strive to conform to it. I have found most of the students to be friendly and open, and I have made many friends." Those who feel the stereotype is apt call their classmates "cliquish," "superficial," and "very unfriendly. The cement in front of them is more appealing than the person walking by. Saying 'Hi' to someone on the sidewalk seems to be a chore." Nearly everyone agrees that Miami students are "very driven," "socially conservative," and "white bread." The school is trying to recruit more minority students, but many here see it as an uphill battle. "It is somewhat difficult to attract minority students to a predominantly white, rural campus, regardless of how well the university markets itself," explains one student.

348 ■ THE BEST 351 COLLEGES

# MIAMI UNIVERSITY

FINANCIAL AID: 513-529-8734 • E-MAIL: ADMISSION@MUOHIO.EDU • WEBSITE: WWW.MUOHIO.EDU

## ADMISSIONS

*Very important factors considered include:* strength of curriculum, class rank, secondary school record, standardized test scores. *Important factors considered include:* essays, recommendations. *Other factors considered include:* alumni/ae relation, character/personal qualities, extracurricular activities, minority status, talent/ability, volunteer work, work experience. SAT I or ACT required. TOEFL required of all international applicants. High school diploma or GED is required. *High school units required/recommended:* 16 total recommended; 4 English recommended, 3 math recommended, 3 science recommended, 2 foreign language recommended, 3 social studies recommended. Most students admitted to Miami exceed these minimum requirements.

### The Inside Word

Miami is one of the few selective public universities with an admissions process similar to those at highly selective private colleges. The university takes into account a variety of institutional needs as well as the qualifications of individual candidates when making admissions decisions. Don't be deceived by a high acceptance rate; the academic requirements for admission are quite high.

## FINANCIAL AID

*Students should submit:* FAFSA. No deadline for regular filing. The Princeton Review suggests that all financial aid forms be submitted as soon as possible after January 1. *Need-based scholarships/grants offered:* Pell, SEOG, state scholarships/grants, private scholarships, the school's own gift aid. *Loan aid offered:* Direct Subsidized Stafford, Direct Unsubsidized Stafford, Direct PLUS, Federal Perkins, Federal Nursing, college/university loans from institutional funds, bank alternative loans. Federal Work-Study Program available. Institutional employment available. Applicants will be notified of awards on a rolling basis beginning on or about March 31. Off-campus job opportunities are good.

## FROM THE ADMISSIONS OFFICE

"Miami's primary concern is its students. This concern is reflected in a broad array of efforts to develop the potential of each student. The university endeavors to individualize the educational experience. It provides personal and professional guidance, and it offers opportunities for its students to achieve understanding and appreciation not only of their own culture but of the cultures of others as well. Selected undergraduate, graduate, and professional programs of quality are offered with the expectation of students achieving a high level of competence and understanding and developing a personal value system. Miami University is one of only eight universities in the country to produce a Rhodes, Truman, and Goldwater scholar in 2002 and one of only two public universities with this same distinction. This recognition is directly attributed to the wonderful research opportunities that exist for our undergraduate students."

## SELECTIVITY

| | |
|---|---|
| Admissions Rating | 86 |
| # of applicants | 12,500 |
| % of applicants accepted | 74 |
| % of acceptees attending | 37 |
| # accepting a place on wait list | 205 |
| % admitted from wait list | 36 |
| # of early decision applicants | 839 |
| % accepted early decision | 73 |

### FRESHMAN PROFILE

| | |
|---|---|
| Range SAT Verbal | 550-640 |
| Average SAT Verbal | 590 |
| Range SAT Math | 580-660 |
| Average SAT Math | 610 |
| Range ACT Composite | 24-28 |
| Average ACT Composite | 26 |
| Minimum TOEFL | 530 |
| Average HS GPA | 3.7 |
| % graduated top 10% of class | 37 |
| % graduated top 25% of class | 77 |
| % graduated top 50% of class | 97 |

### DEADLINES

| | |
|---|---|
| Early decision | 11/1 |
| Early decision notification | 12/15 |
| Regular admission | 1/31 |
| Regular notification | 3/15 |
| Nonfall registration? | yes |

### APPLICANTS ALSO LOOK AT AND OFTEN PREFER
Notre Dame
Northwestern, Vanderbilt

### AND SOMETIMES PREFER
U of Michigan
U of Illinois at Urbana-Champaign
U of Wisconsin at Madison
Boston College, Penn State
Washington U

### AND RARELY PREFER
Ohio U, Ohio State
U of Dayton, Xavier, Denison, Purdue

## FINANCIAL FACTS

| | |
|---|---|
| Financial Aid Rating | 86 |
| In-state tuition | $6,386 |
| Out-of-state tuition | $15,110 |
| Room and board | $6,240 |
| Books and supplies | $803 |
| Required fees | $1,214 |
| % frosh receiving aid | 34 |
| % undergrads receiving aid | 31 |

# MICHIGAN STATE UNIVERSITY

250 Administration Building, East Lansing, MI 48824-1046 • Admissions: 517-355-8332 • Fax: 517-353-1647

## CAMPUS LIFE

| | |
|---|---|
| Quality of Life Rating | 78 |
| Type of school | public |
| Environment | suburban |

### STUDENTS

| | |
|---|---|
| Total undergrad enrollment | 35,197 |
| % male/female | 47/53 |
| % from out of state | 6 |
| % live on campus | 44 |
| % African American | 9 |
| % Asian | 5 |
| % Caucasian | 82 |
| % Hispanic | 3 |
| % international | 2 |
| # of countries represented | 100 |

### SURVEY SAYS . . .
Everyone loves the Spartans
Popular college radio
No one cheats
Students get along with local community
Great on-campus food
Musical organizations are hot
Theater is hot
Students are cliquish

## ACADEMICS

| | |
|---|---|
| Academic Rating | 68 |
| Calendar | semester |
| Student/faculty ratio | 18:1 |
| Profs interesting rating | 82 |
| Profs accessible rating | 77 |
| Avg lab size | 20-29 students |
| Avg reg class size | 20-29 students |

### MOST POPULAR MAJORS
Marketing/marketing management
Communications
Social sciences

## STUDENTS SPEAK OUT

### Academics

The fact that Michigan State is such a "mega institution" has its ups and its downs. On the downside, "you do not get the advantage of having the professor's individual attention." In many cases, you don't get the advantage of having the professor, as some lower-level classes are enormous lectures taught by TAs. Another common complaint is that "many of the classes are taught by . . . teachers that don't know a lick of English." An upside to MSU's size is the "plethora of academic resources" and the wide variety of "classes and majors available." And if you're really seeking a challenge, look into MSU's highly esteemed Honors College. To top students it offers "a small, personalized feel to a large campus," not to mention a streamlined registration process, access to certain graduate classes, and plenty of opportunities for independent studies, thesis work, and research projects. "James Madison College, the residential liberal arts school at Michigan State University," also draws praise. According to one JMC student, "It should be ranked in a different category from Michigan State University. It has great professors, none of the classes are taught by TAs, the faculty is always available, the classes are no more than 35 people, it's a competitive environment, and is very challenging." Engineering, business, marketing, and various social sciences are among the most popular paths of study here, and we've also heard rave reviews for the writing, nursing, and veterinary programs.

### Life

School spirit is alive and well in East Lansing, Michigan, which students describe as "the happiest place on earth." Students follow Big Ten sports religiously and tell us that Spartan games are "amazing and crazily fun to watch." During football season, thousands of students "get up at the butt-crack of dawn in order to get a good spot to tailgate" outside of Spartan Stadium. Greek life provides plenty of party opportunities for the underage revelers, while upperclassmen tend to make their way to off-campus parties or the "very popular" bar scene in East Lansing. Though few students will deny that MSU's "party school" reputation is deserved, they're quick to assert that drinking has been put under control of late. If MSU sounds appealing but drinking does not, "choosing a dorm with an alcohol-free option, a quiet floor, or an honors floor will make a HUGE difference in the types of people you meet." The university offers a multitude of "volunteering" opportunities and "school activities/groups" for students who want to exercise their hobbies and talents. MSU also plays host to "many famous speakers, entertainers, and scholars." Astoundingly, nearly half of the student population is involved in intramural sports. The city of East Lansing itself is a lively town, with "bars," "a good indie band scene," and "a multitude of diverse festivities . . . such as the Native American Pow Wow of Love and the International Folk Festival and the East Lansing Arts Festival." One straight-shooting students says, "If you can't find something fun to do, you have some major social skills to work on."

### Student Body

One thing's certain at Michigan State University: You're bound to run into a lot of students from Michigan. "It seems like 90 percent of our school is from Michigan," a student comments. Four-fifths of the student population is white, but there's still a mix of races and backgrounds here. "However, the different racial groups do not really socialize with each other," notes an undergrad. "Whites stick with whites, blacks stick with blacks, etc." But don't misunderstand. Most MSU students are "friendly and welcoming." One student even goes so far as to say, "I am sure that nowhere else on the planet are there 40,000+ young people [that's undergrads and grads combined] that get along as well as those attending Michigan State University."

# MICHIGAN STATE UNIVERSITY

Financial Aid: 517-353-5940 • E-mail: admis@msu.edu • Website: www.msu.edu

## ADMISSIONS

*Very important factors considered include:* secondary school record. *Important factors considered include:* standardized test scores. *Other factors considered include:* alumni/ae relation, class rank, essays, extracurricular activities, geographical residence, minority status, recommendations, talent/ability, volunteer work, work experience. SAT I or ACT required. TOEFL required of all international applicants. High school diploma or GED is required. *High school units required/recommended:* 14 total required; 4 English required, 3 math required, 2 science required, 2 foreign language required, 3 social studies required.

### The Inside Word

Gaining admission to MSU is a matter of following the formulas. Grades, tests, and rank—numbers, numbers, numbers. Solid extracurricular involvement and recommendations may help borderline candidates.

## FINANCIAL AID

*Students should submit:* FAFSA, institution's own financial aid form. Regular filing deadline is June 30. The Princeton Review suggests that all financial aid forms be submitted as soon as possible after January 1. *Need-based scholarships/grants offered:* Pell, SEOG, state scholarships/grants, private scholarships, the school's own gift aid. *Loan aid offered:* Direct Subsidized Stafford, Direct Unsubsidized Stafford, Direct PLUS, Federal Perkins, state loans, college/university loans from institutional funds. Federal Work-Study Program available. Institutional employment available. Applicants will be notified of awards on a rolling basis beginning on or about March 15. Off-campus job opportunities are excellent.

## FROM THE ADMISSIONS OFFICE

"Although Michigan State University is a graduate and research institution of international stature and acclaim, your undergraduate education is a high priority. More than 2,600 instructional faculty members (89 percent of whom hold a terminal degree) are dedicated to providing academic instruction, guidance, and assistance to our undergraduate students. Our 35,000 undergraduate students are a select group of academically motivated men and women. The diversity of ethnic, racial, religious, and socioeconomic heritage makes the student body a microcosm of the state, national, and international community."

### SELECTIVITY

| | |
|---|---|
| Admissions Rating | 74 |
| # of applicants | 25,210 |
| % of applicants accepted | 67 |
| % of acceptees attending | 41 |
| # accepting a place on wait list | 950 |
| % admitted from wait list | 29 |

### FRESHMAN PROFILE

| | |
|---|---|
| Range SAT Verbal | 490-610 |
| Average SAT Verbal | 552 |
| Range SAT Math | 520-640 |
| Average SAT Math | 579 |
| Range ACT Composite | 22-27 |
| Average ACT Composite | 24 |
| Minimum TOEFL | 550 |
| Average HS GPA | 3.6 |
| % graduated top 10% of class | 26 |
| % graduated top 25% of class | 66 |
| % graduated top 50% of class | 95 |

### DEADLINES

| | |
|---|---|
| Regular admission | 8/1 |
| Regular notification | 9/1 |
| Nonfall registration? | yes |

### APPLICANTS ALSO LOOK AT
**AND OFTEN PREFER**
U of Michigan at Ann Arbor
Kalamazoo
Eastern Michigan
Central Michigan
Western Michigan
**AND SOMETIMES PREFER**
U of Illinois at Urbana-Champaign
Indiana U at Bloomington
U of Wisconsin at Madison
Oakland U
**AND RARELY PREFER**
Wayne State U

### FINANCIAL FACTS

| | |
|---|---|
| Financial Aid Rating | 81 |
| In-state tuition | $6,015 |
| Out-of-state tuition | $14,970 |
| Room and board | $4,932 |
| Books and supplies | $790 |
| Required fees | $708 |
| % frosh receiving aid | 54 |
| % undergrads receiving aid | 40 |

# MICHIGAN TECHNOLOGICAL UNIVERSITY

1400 TOWNSEND DRIVE, HOUGHTON, MI 49931 • ADMISSIONS: 906-487-2335 • FAX: 906-487-2125

## CAMPUS LIFE

| | |
|---|---|
| Quality of Life Rating | 77 |
| Type of school | public |
| Environment | rural |

### STUDENTS
| | |
|---|---|
| Total undergrad enrollment | 5,915 |
| % male/female | 76/24 |
| % from out of state | 19 |
| % live on campus | 39 |
| % in (# of) fraternities | 9 (14) |
| % in (# of) sororities | 16 (8) |
| % African American | 2 |
| % Asian | 1 |
| % Caucasian | 85 |
| % Hispanic | 1 |
| % international | 6 |
| # of countries represented | 80 |

### SURVEY SAYS . . .
Frats and sororities dominate social scene
Popular college radio
Hard liquor is popular
Class discussions are rare
(Almost) everyone plays intramural sports
Registration is a pain
Library needs improving
Theater is unpopular
Political activism is (almost) nonexistent

## ACADEMICS

| | |
|---|---|
| Academic Rating | 74 |
| Calendar | semester |
| Student/faculty ratio | 11:1 |
| Profs interesting rating | 91 |
| Profs accessible rating | 95 |
| % profs teaching UG courses | 100 |
| % classes taught by TAs | 4 |
| Avg lab size | 10-19 students |
| Avg reg class size | 20-29 students |

### MOST POPULAR MAJORS
Civil engineering
Electrical, electronics, and communications engineering
Mechanical engineering

## STUDENTS SPEAK OUT

### Academics
More than half of MTU's 6,000 undergrads are enrolled in its College of Engineering. The four other colleges that comprise the university are the College of Sciences and Arts, the School of Technology, the School of Business and Economics, and the School of Forestry and Wood Products. A good many students take pride in the technological bent of the institution, and frown on recent administrative investments, such as "the money pit that is the Rozsa Center for Performing Arts," that threaten "to turn MTU into a more generic university rather than a technical one." Some science students tell us that they'd rather see the university spend money on improving the laboratories. "My labs are very lacking," one student gripes. "I pay extra money in my tuition for my labs and only one of them even has disk drives in the computers." In class, students often end up "trying to decipher the chopped English of some of the professors and TAs," but students at MTU still report that they're having "an excellent academic experience." Small class sizes and professor accessibility are among the aspects of the university that students love. "Tech isn't a really big school, so if you need help all you have to do is schedule a time with your professors and they will meet with you."

### Life
"If you're into winter sports, this is definitely the place to be," students tell us MTU is located on Michigan's Upper Peninsula, "right on the Portage," (a large waterway) and "only a half-hour away from Lake Superior," not to mention the nearby Ottawa National Forest and the university's own Mont Ripley ski mountain. With all of these natural resources at their fingertips, MTU students regularly go "hiking and biking," "canoeing and swimming," "cross-country skiing and downhill skiing," as well as rock climbing, fishing, and snowshoeing. Competitively, hockey and broomball rule the scene. Broomball is a sport involving protective masks, brooms, a ball, and goals—not terribly unlike hockey. MTU has a Web page, www.broomball.mtu.edu, that explains the rules. They don't, however, have a Web page for "the number-one pastime at this university": drinking, especially at frat parties. One student told us that there's a rational explanation for all of the drinking that goes on here: "It is so cold and snowy, and there is an ungodly small percentage of girls that go here. So if people didn't drink, they would go insane and EXPLODE." When students get tired of life "in the boonies" and need a spark of urban energy, they'd better pull on their driving gloves. "The nearest big city is Minneapolis," an international student told us. And that's about seven hours away.

### Student Body
The Tech student body is predominantly male, white, and both socially and politically conservative. Did we forget anything? Oh, yes . . . as one student succinctly puts it, "this is a very nerdy school. If you aren't a nerd and you come here, this school will turn you into one." Writes another, "Students seem too caught up in their technical selves. Students here who avoid eye contact are plentiful. I think this is mainly because they have too much technical attachment to attach their minds to anything but school." Agrees one engineer, "Students are either really gregarious, or lock themselves in their rooms. Very little in between." The relatively scarce female population get to "date frequently," but as for the men . . . well, as one student reports, "since MTU is all guys, all we think about is women. For fun, we talk about women, drink a lot and fantasize about women, and try to hit on women. It's tough being a guy in the UP!"

# MICHIGAN TECHNOLOGICAL UNIVERSITY

FINANCIAL AID: 906-487-2622 • E-MAIL: MTU4U@MTU.EDU • WEBSITE: WWW.MTU.EDU

## ADMISSIONS

*Very important factors considered include:* class rank, secondary school record, standardized test scores. *Other factors considered include:* alumni/ae relation, character/personal qualities, essays, extracurricular activities, interview, recommendations, talent/ability, volunteer work, work experience. SAT I or ACT required. TOEFL required of all international applicants. High school diploma or GED is required. *High school units required/recommended:* 15 total required; 3 English required, 4 English recommended, 3 math required, 4 math recommended, 2 science required, 3 science recommended, 1 foreign language recommended, 1 social studies recommended, 1 history recommended, 1 elective recommended.

### The Inside Word

Michigan Tech has a pretty good reputation and a highly self-selected applicant pool. In light of this, students who are interested should not be deceived by the high admit rate and should spend a little time on self-assessment of their ability to handle an engineering curriculum. There's nothing gained by getting yourself into a program that you can't get out of successfully.

## FINANCIAL AID

*Students should submit:* FAFSA. No deadline for regular filing. The Princeton Review suggests that all financial aid forms be submitted as soon as possible after January 1. *Need-based scholarships/grants offered:* Pell, SEOG, state scholarships/grants, private scholarships, the school's own gift aid. *Loan aid offered:* Direct Subsidized Stafford, Direct Unsubsidized Stafford, Direct PLUS, Federal Perkins, state loans, college/university loans from institutional funds, external private loans. Federal Work-Study Program available. Institutional employment available. Applicants will be notified of awards on a rolling basis beginning on or about February 28. Off-campus job opportunities are good.

## FROM THE ADMISSIONS OFFICE

"Michigan Tech is recognized as one of the nation's leading univesities for undergraduate and graduate education in science and engineering. Its state-of-the-art campus is located near Lake Superior in Michigan's beautiful Upper Peninsula. The university owns and operates a downhill ski area and 18-hole golf course.... MTU is one of Michigan's four nationally recognized research universities."

## SELECTIVITY

| | |
|---|---|
| Admissions Rating | 82 |
| # of applicants | 2,957 |
| % of applicants accepted | 92 |
| % of acceptees attending | 44 |

### FRESHMAN PROFILE

| | |
|---|---|
| Range SAT Verbal | 510-640 |
| Average SAT Verbal | 570 |
| Range SAT Math | 570-690 |
| Average SAT Math | 624 |
| Range ACT Composite | 23-28 |
| Average ACT Composite | 25 |
| Minimum TOEFL | 500 |
| Average HS GPA | 3.5 |
| % graduated top 10% of class | 31 |
| % graduated top 25% of class | 60 |
| % graduated top 50% of class | 89 |

### DEADLINES

| | |
|---|---|
| Nonfall registration? | yes |

### APPLICANTS ALSO LOOK AT AND SOMETIMES PREFER
Michigan State
U of Michigan at Ann Arbor
U of Wisconsin at Madison
### AND RARELY PREFER
Kettering U
Lawrence
Milwaukee School of Engineering

## FINANCIAL FACTS

| | |
|---|---|
| Financial Aid Rating | 87 |
| In-state tuition | $5,782 |
| Out-of-state tuition | $14,152 |
| Room and board | $5,465 |
| Books and supplies | $900 |
| Required fees | $673 |
| % frosh receiving aid | 47 |
| % undergrads receiving aid | 42 |
| Avg frosh grant | $5,303 |
| Avg frosh loan | $4,906 |

THE BEST 351 COLLEGES ■ 353

# MIDDLEBURY COLLEGE

THE EMMA WILLARD HOUSE, MIDDLEBURY, VT 05753 • ADMISSIONS: 802-443-3000 • FAX: 802-443-2056

## CAMPUS LIFE

| | |
|---|---|
| Quality of Life Rating | 81 |
| Type of school | private |
| Environment | rural |

### STUDENTS

| | |
|---|---|
| Total undergrad enrollment | 2,297 |
| % male/female | 49/51 |
| % from out of state | 94 |
| % live on campus | 96 |
| % African American | 3 |
| % Asian | 8 |
| % Caucasian | 76 |
| % Hispanic | 6 |
| % international | 8 |
| # of countries represented | 71 |

### SURVEY SAYS . . .
Everyone loves the Panthers
Athletic facilities are great
No one cheats
Diversity lacking on campus
Great food on campus
(Almost) no one smokes
(Almost) no one listens to college radio
Theater is hot
Musical organizations are hot
Political activism is (almost) nonexistent

## ACADEMICS

| | |
|---|---|
| Academic Rating | 92 |
| Calendar | 4-1-4 |
| Student/faculty ratio | 11:1 |
| Profs interesting rating | 96 |
| Profs accessible rating | 97 |
| % profs teaching UG courses | 100 |
| Avg lab size | 10-19 students |
| Avg reg class size | 10-19 students |

### MOST POPULAR MAJORS
Economics
Psychology
English language and literature

## STUDENTS SPEAK OUT

### Academics
Academically one of the most rigorous programs in the country, "top-rate" Middlebury College, tucked away in rural Vermont (about three and a half hours' drive to Boston, 45 minutes to Burlington, and two hours to Montreal) manages to offer the resources, facilities, and faculty excellence of a much larger school—while keeping enrollment for undergrads at around 2,300. Nationally recognized language, writing, and theater programs share the spotlight with a top-notch science curriculum—which has benefited in recent years from the construction of a new science center. One student is thrilled that "professors here actually teach. They manage classes, advising, and research demands seamlessly." Despite "tons of homework" and tough classes, students say there's little of the "cutthroat competition" that might characterize other schools of Middlebury's caliber. It might have something to do with the pristine location of "Club Midd," their "laid-back" atmosphere, and an excellent alumni network that makes finding a job after graduation a whole lot easier. Or it might be the result of a bit of grade inflation (some kids complain that "if you're smart, you can get A's and B's hardly doing any work"). But most likely, it's just Middlebury's special blend of a quality program, personal attention, and something a little more nebulous one student calls "attitude." In any case, Middlebury's got it. Sums up a senior, "Academically, I've been challenged, but also have had time to breathe and have fun."

### Life
You'd think that at a place that gets "so cold your nostrils freeze together" folks would be spending most of their time inside. Not so at Club Midd! "We own our own ski mountain," notes a junior, one of the reasons why, come winter, most students head outside for fun. With skiing, hiking, rock climbing, mountain biking, kayaking, and fishing right in the college's backyard, you can see why "year round people are involved in outdoor activities." "Almost everyone is athletic one way or another," adds another senior. The school's facilities say as much—students can choose between a hockey rink, fitness center, pool, golf course, and "snow bowl" for fun. It's no surprise, then, that "sports are a major preoccupation here." The "work hard, play hard" ethos extends into socializing, too. A senior explains: "As opportunities for nightlife are virtually nonexistent, we drink. While fun, this does take its toll on one's health." And though there doesn't seem to be a shortage of school-sponsored activities and clubs (social houses and a "commons"-style freshman dorm system provide social opportunities for underclassmen), some students complain that the Middlebury experience "varies between having amazing times to wanting to get the hell out of here." What's more, besides the professed lack of academic competition, "life can be very stressful," notes a junior; "everyone around is an overachiever, star athlete, talented musician, and very attractive."

### Student Body
"Students here come from every corner of the world . . . and every New England prep school," jokes a first-year on the subject of Middlebury's fairly homogenous student body (80 percent of its undergrads self-identify as "Caucasian"). A junior gives his take on the situation: "They're cool but the same. This is what I heard before I got here, and this is definitely true. . . . [M]ost are rich and white" and from somewhere "just outside of Boston." Still, it's the people that most students say make the Middlebury experience what it is. Take it from this sophomore: "The main reason I fell in love with Midd was the students. At no other school did I see so many happy, outgoing students." Concludes a classmate, "The majority of the students are really smart and really cool, which makes a small school not feel that way."

# MIDDLEBURY COLLEGE

FINANCIAL AID: 802-443-5158 • E-MAIL: ADMISSIONS@MIDDLEBURY.EDU • WEBSITE: WWW.MIDDLEBURY.EDU

## ADMISSIONS
*Very important factors considered include:* character/personal qualities, secondary school record. *Important factors considered include:* class rank, essays, extracurricular activities, recommendations, standardized test scores, talent/ability. *Other factors considered include:* alumni/ae relation, geographical residence, interview, minority status, volunteer work, work experience. *High school units required/recommended:* 4 English recommended, 4 math recommended, 4 science recommended, 4 science lab recommended, 4 foreign language recommended, 3 social studies recommended.

### The Inside Word
While Middlebury benefits tremendously from its age-old position as an Ivy League safety, it is nonetheless a very strong and demanding place in its own right. Middlebury has a broad national applicant pool and sees more ACT scores than most eastern colleges, so submitting ACT scores to Middlebury is a more comfortable option than at most eastern schools.

## FINANCIAL AID
*Students should submit:* FAFSA, CSS/Financial Aid PROFILE, federal income tax return (or statement of nonfiling). Regular filing deadline is January 1. The Princeton Review suggests that all financial aid forms be submitted as soon as possible after January 1. *Need-based scholarships/grants offered:* Pell, SEOG, state scholarships/grants, private scholarships, the school's own gift aid. *Loan aid offered:* Direct Subsidized Stafford, Direct Unsubsidized Stafford, Direct PLUS, Federal Perkins, college/university loans from institutional funds. Federal Work-Study Program available. Institutional employment available. Applicants will be notified of awards on or about April 1. Off-campus job opportunities are good.

## FROM THE ADMISSIONS OFFICE
"The successful Middlebury candidate excels in a variety of areas including academics, athletics, the arts, leadership, and service to others. These strengths and interests permit students to grow beyond their traditional 'comfort zones' and conventional limits. Our classrooms are as varied as the Green Mountains, the Metropolitan Museum of Art, or the great cities Russia and Japan. Outside the classroom, students informally interact with professors in activities such as intramural basketball games and community service. At Middlebury, students develop critical thinking skills, enduring bonds of friendship, and the ability to challenge themselves."

### SELECTIVITY

| | |
|---|---|
| Admissions Rating | 98 |
| # of applicants | 5,299 |
| % of applicants accepted | 27 |
| % of acceptees attending | 41 |
| # accepting a place on wait list | 600 |
| # of early decision applicants | 827 |
| % accepted early decision | 27 |

### FRESHMAN PROFILE
| | |
|---|---|
| Range SAT Verbal | 680-750 |
| Average SAT Verbal | 710 |
| Range SAT Math | 670-740 |
| Average SAT Math | 700 |
| Range ACT Composite | 29-32 |
| Average ACT Composite | 30 |
| % graduated top 10% of class | 74 |
| % graduated top 25% of class | 92 |
| % graduated top 50% of class | 99 |

### DEADLINES
| | |
|---|---|
| Early decision | 11/15 |
| Early decision notification | 12/15 |
| Regular admission | 12/15 |
| Regular notification | 4/1 |
| Nonfall registration? | yes |

### APPLICANTS ALSO LOOK AT AND OFTEN PREFER
Dartmouth
Harvard
Williams
Amherst
Princeton

### AND SOMETIMES PREFER
Brown
Yale

### AND RARELY PREFER
Bowdoin
Hamilton
Skidmore
St. Lawrence

### FINANCIAL FACTS

| | |
|---|---|
| Financial Aid Rating | 74 |
| Comprehensive tuition | $35,900 |
| Books and supplies | $750 |
| % frosh receiving aid | 37 |
| % undergrads receiving aid | 36 |
| Avg frosh grant | $20,161 |
| Avg frosh loan | $5,377 |

# MILLSAPS COLLEGE

1701 NORTH STATE STREET, JACKSON, MS 39210 • ADMISSIONS: 601-974-1050 • FAX: 601-974-1059

## CAMPUS LIFE

| Quality of Life Rating | 90 |
|---|---|
| Type of school | private |
| Affiliation | Methodist |
| Environment | urban |

### STUDENTS

| Total undergrad enrollment | 1,158 |
|---|---|
| % male/female | 45/55 |
| % from out of state | 52 |
| % from public high school | 61 |
| % live on campus | 85 |
| % in (# of) fraternities | 50 (6) |
| % in (# of) sororities | 50 (6) |
| % African American | 11 |
| % Asian | 3 |
| % Caucasian | 83 |
| % Hispanic | 1 |
| % international | 1 |
| # of countries represented | 8 |

### SURVEY SAYS . . .
Frats and sororities dominate social scene
Lots of beer drinking
Campus is beautiful
Hard liquor is popular
Campus easy to get around
Athletic facilities are great
(Almost) everyone smokes
No one cheats

## ACADEMICS

| Academic Rating | 84 |
|---|---|
| Calendar | semester |
| Student/faculty ratio | 13:1 |
| % profs teaching UG courses | 100 |
| Avg lab size | 20-29 students |
| Avg reg class size | 10-19 students |

### MOST POPULAR MAJORS
Business administration/management
Biology/biological sciences
English language and literature

## STUDENTS SPEAK OUT

### Academics
"You'll write more than you've ever written before" at Millsaps College. About one-third of a student's tenure here is spent fulfilling core requirements, nearly all of which include a substantial writing component. All of this writing forces students to learn to express themselves and "really think outside the box. I've enjoyed learning and enjoyed the difficulties; it's made me a better student and a better person." Agrees one undergrad, "Millsaps College is about thinking for yourself, finding out what you are passionate about, and then using that vocation to make a positive difference in your community and society as a whole." Students here enjoy a solid support network; the "knowledgeable, enthusiastic, and down-to-earth professors truly care about the students and want us to succeed" and are "always eager to help the students outside of class." Administrators are equally accessible; notes one student, "About once a month, we have a lunch with the deans in the cafeteria and students can come to them with suggestions and comments or just to hang out." Adds another, "I feel that the school really listens to the student voice and takes the student opinion into account when making decisions." Undergrads here acknowledge some of the common drawbacks of attending a small school. Reports one, "Because the college tries to keep its classroom size small to maintain a good image, many upperclass students do not get classes they want."

### Life
Millsaps is a rock-solid Greek school. "Greek life is huge," explains one undergrad. But Greeks and independents "get along well. The school is just too small to be petty over . . . a few letters." Recent administrative policy changes, however, have curtailed the once-wild parties that typified Millsaps campus life; currently, all parties must be registered with and sanctioned by the school, Thursday parties are forbidden, and alcohol regulations are more strictly enforced. The results have a lot of upperclassmen, who remember wilder days gone by, complaining that the "new dry rush rule is horrible." Non-Greek options, many complain, are few. The Jackson neighborhood in which Millsaps is located "isn't exactly one you'd want to walk through, so you have to drive a ways to go anywhere safe." Many here find greater Jackson equally forbidding, resulting in "the 'Millsaps Bubble'; once you are here, you are stuck in this bubble and oblivious to the world around you." Dorm regulations are strictly enforced; avers one undergraduate, "Any social activity in the dorm is really discouraged. I was once asked to 'Stop making so much noise!' at 4 o'clock on a Friday afternoon. My door was open and my TV was on." Students also complain that "Millsaps could use more school spirit in supporting our intercollegiate teams." Students often road-trip to New Orleans when they want to blow off steam.

### Student Body
Millsaps undergrads tell us that their school is "fairly diverse as far as the students go, for being such a small school." The typical student is an "upper-middle-class, intelligent, achieving person from a southern family, either from Louisiana, Mississippi, Alabama, or Tennessee. However, at Millsaps there is no real 'norm' for student types. . . . Students are more associated with what organization they are a part of, be that an athletic team, a sorority or fraternity, or a philanthropic organization." Undergrads "are particularly politically aware and are often very involved with political campaigns." They are also "pretty intellectual and there is always good conversation." Many agree that "the small student body definitely gives the campus a comfortable vibe." A few warn, however, that the tiny population means that "people will know who you shacked with, when you left, what you were wearing, and what type of toothpaste you used when you got home before you enter the 'caf' for lunch. . . . Everyone knows everyone. You learn to deal with it."

# MILLSAPS COLLEGE

FINANCIAL AID: 601-974-1220 • E-MAIL: ADMISSIONS@MILLSAPS.EDU • WEBSITE: WWW.MILLSAPS.EDU

## ADMISSIONS
*Very important factors considered include:* character/personal qualities, secondary school record, standardized test scores. *Important factors considered include:* class rank, essays, extracurricular activities, interview, recommendations, talent/ability, volunteer work, work experience. SAT I or ACT required. TOEFL required of all international applicants. High school diploma or GED is required. *High school units required/recommended:* 14 total required; 20 total recommended; 4 English required, 3 math required, 4 math recommended, 3 science required, 4 science recommended, 1 science lab required, 2 foreign language recommended, 2 social studies required, 2 history required, 2 elective recommended.

### The Inside Word
Despite the college's seemingly deep-probing evaluation process, candidates with a solid track record in high school encounter little resistance in gaining admission. In reality, there is little room for extensive matchmaking by the admissions staff. The high percentage of acceptees who choose to enroll, comparatively, makes getting in less than definite for candidates with weak academic credentials.

## FINANCIAL AID
*Students should submit:* FAFSA, institution's own financial aid form, state aid form. Priority deadline is March 1. The Princeton Review suggests that all financial aid forms be submitted as soon as possible after January 1. *Need-based scholarships/grants offered:* Pell, SEOG, state scholarships/grants, private scholarships, the school's own gift aid. *Loan aid offered:* FFEL Subsidized Stafford, FFEL Unsubsidized Stafford, FFEL PLUS, Federal Perkins, college/university loans from institutional funds. Federal Work-Study Program available. Institutional employment available. Applicants will be notified of awards on a rolling basis beginning on or about March 15. Off-campus job opportunities are good.

## FROM THE ADMISSIONS OFFICE
"Your academic experience at Millsaps begins with Introduction to Liberal Studies, a comprehensive freshman experience. You will be encouraged to develop critical thinking skills, analytical reasoning, and independence of thought as preparation for study in your major. The interdisciplinary Heritage Program offers a unique approach to the culture and development of society through lectures and small group discussions by a team of faculty who represent a cross-section of the humanities. Entering freshmen are primarily taught by full-time PhD professors. The close relationship between faculty and students encourages classroom participation and enables students to explore their options as they choose a major field of study. Coursework in the major may begin as early as the freshman year."

### SELECTIVITY

| | |
|---|---|
| Admissions Rating | 81 |
| # of applicants | 913 |
| % of applicants accepted | 87 |
| % of acceptees attending | 31 |

#### FRESHMAN PROFILE
| | |
|---|---|
| Range SAT Verbal | 550-640 |
| Average SAT Verbal | 590 |
| Range SAT Math | 530-650 |
| Average SAT Math | 590 |
| Range ACT Composite | 23-29 |
| Average ACT Composite | 25 |
| Minimum TOEFL | 550 |
| Average HS GPA | 3.5 |
| % graduated top 10% of class | 39 |
| % graduated top 25% of class | 68 |
| % graduated top 50% of class | 89 |

#### DEADLINES
| | |
|---|---|
| Priority admission | 12/1 |
| Regular admission | 2/1 |
| Nonfall registration? | yes |

#### APPLICANTS ALSO LOOK AT AND OFTEN PREFER
Vanderbilt
Tulane
Rhodes
U of Mississippi
Birmingham Southern

#### AND SOMETIMES PREFER
Duke
Emory
UT Austin
University of the South

#### AND RARELY PREFER
Hendrix

### FINANCIAL FACTS

| | |
|---|---|
| Financial Aid Rating | 91 |
| Tuition | $17,346 |
| Room and board | $6,768 |
| Books and supplies | $800 |
| Required fees | $1,068 |
| % frosh receiving aid | 51 |
| % undergrads receiving aid | 55 |
| Avg frosh grant | $12,880 |
| Avg frosh loan | $3,111 |

# MONTANA TECH OF THE UNIVERSITY OF MONTANA

1300 WEST PARK STREET, BUTTE, MT 59701 • ADMISSIONS: 406-496-4178 • FAX: 406-496-4710

## CAMPUS LIFE

| | |
|---|---|
| Quality of Life Rating | 84 |
| Type of school | public |
| Environment | suburban |

### STUDENTS

| | |
|---|---|
| Total undergrad enrollment | 2,065 |
| % male/female | 56/44 |
| % from out of state | 11 |
| % live on campus | 13 |
| % Asian | 1 |
| % Caucasian | 87 |
| % Hispanic | 1 |
| % international | 2 |
| # of countries represented | 13 |

### SURVEY SAYS . . .
Popular college radio
Musical organizations aren't popular
(Almost) everyone plays intramural sports
Low cost of living
Class discussions are rare
Very small frat/sorority scene
Political activism is (almost) nonexistent
(Almost) no one smokes
Students get along with local community

## ACADEMICS

| | |
|---|---|
| Academic Rating | 76 |
| Calendar | semester |
| Student/faculty ratio | 16:1 |
| Profs interesting rating | 93 |
| Profs accessible rating | 92 |
| % profs teaching UG courses | 100 |
| Avg lab size | 10-19 students |
| Avg reg class size | under 10 students |

### MOST POPULAR MAJORS
Business administration/management
Engineering
Petroleum engineering

## STUDENTS SPEAK OUT

### Academics

Students at Montana Tech appreciate what sets their school apart from other state institutions. "Unlike other schools," one engineer here observes, "the ratio of teachers to students is small and most of the professors know your name. This allows good two-way communication and ready assistance for learning problem areas." Add the bargain tuition (especially for Montana residents) and you'll understand why students' level of satisfaction with MT is high. Students here must complete a number of distribution requirements, including communications, social sciences, and the humanities. Afterward, they focus their sights on the practical applications of engineering and mining. Observes one student, "This is a great school if you are interested in real-world engineering." MT offers plenty of opportunities for cooperative education (working at a major-related job for credit during the school year). Boasts one student, "Montana Tech's co-op offices work very hard to coordinate employers' on-campus interviews. This is a major reason why I chose Montana Tech. I've interviewed with an average of five companies a year, and I've had an internship two of the four summers I've been here." Students' complaints concern recent budget cuts throughout the Montana university system. "The only real disadvantage is that funding has gone down," explains one undergrad. "This is especially apparent in the smaller departments, which are finding it a little more difficult to offer all the classes listed in the catalog."

### Life

Students warn that "Montana Tech is a very challenging school. If you want to go to school to party a lot, I wouldn't recommend coming to Tech." Writes one engineer, "Life at Montana Tech is definitely academic-oriented. Most time is spent thinking about school projects, extracurricular activities, and/or research projects." MT's setting is ideal for this lifestyle, as it offers relatively few distractions. "Butte is a pretty old mining town with not much to do," agree most students here. One elaborates, "Butte is a very small town and is limited as to night life and recreational activities. Montana Tech attempts to fill some of the void with school clubs, trips, and community activities. For example, we have about a foot of snow and we just had a softball tournament called 'Mulletfest.' It was a great opportunity to get out and meet other students, and we all had a blast." In one respect, the campus' location reigns supreme. "If you are an outdoorsman," explains one student, "this is paradise. Hunting, fishing, hiking, skiing, camping, and climbing are so close to here it is not even funny." When students crave an active, diverse nightlife, they head to Missoula "because it is more fun there and there is more to do."

### Student Body

Engineers at MT brag that "the smaller class size at Tech fosters a spirit of cooperativeness among most of the students, and there is ample opportunity for forming study groups and taking notes for each other when one student is missing from class." Even so, many students describe small rifts among the student body, especially between athletes and nonathletes ("The football players are stuck up, big surprise there") and engineers and nonengineers at the university ("The biggest and most irritating discrimination on campus is toward students who are not in engineering programs. There are a lot of stuck-up engineering students, and this is coming from an engineering student over behavior I've witnessed!"). Many "are from rural areas" and conservative in their politics. One student warns that MT students' conservative bent does not make it easy to be openly gay.

# MONTANA TECH OF THE UNIVERSITY OF MONTANA

FINANCIAL AID: 406-496-4212 • E-MAIL: ADMISSIONS@MTECH.EDU • WEBSITE: WWW.MTECH.EDU

## ADMISSIONS

*Important factors considered include:* class rank, secondary school record, standardized test scores. SAT I or ACT required; ACT preferred. TOEFL required of all international applicants. High school diploma or GED is required. *High school units required/recommended:* 14 total required; 4 English required, 3 math required, 4 math recommended, 2 science required, 4 science recommended, 2 science lab recommended, 2 foreign language recommended, 3 social studies required.

### The Inside Word

Underrecognized schools like Montana Tech can be a godsend for students who are strong academically but not likely to be offered admission to nationally renowned technical institutes. In fact, because of its small size and relatively remote location, Montana Tech is a good choice for anyone leaning toward a technical career. You'd be hard-pressed to find many other places that are as low-key and personal in this realm of academe.

## FINANCIAL AID

*Students should submit:* FAFSA. No deadline for regular filing. The Princeton Review suggests that all financial aid forms be submitted as soon as possible after January 1. *Need-based scholarships/grants offered:* Pell, SEOG, state scholarships/grants, private scholarships, the school's own gift aid. *Loan aid offered:* FFEL Subsidized Stafford, FFEL Unsubsidized Stafford, FFEL PLUS, Federal Perkins, college/university loans from institutional funds. Federal Work-Study Program available. Institutional employment available. Applicants will be notified of awards on a rolling basis beginning on or about April 1. Off-campus job opportunities are good.

## FROM THE ADMISSIONS OFFICE

"Characterize Montana Tech by listening to what employers say. They tell us Tech graduates stand out with an incredible work ethic and top-notch technical skills. Last year, 130 employers came to our small campus competing for our students and graduates. The benefactors? The students! Montana Tech has had a ten-year placement rate of over 95 percent. Learning takes place in a personalized environment, in first-class academic facilities, and in the heart of the Rocky Mountains. Student at Tech work hard and play hard. Outdoor recreation provides a great balance to the rigors of the course work at Montana Tech. It's is not a large, multifaceted university with lots of frills, but our students get a terrific education, and in the end, great jobs!"

### SELECTIVITY

| | |
|---|---|
| Admissions Rating | 74 |
| # of applicants | 395 |
| % of applicants accepted | 97 |
| % of acceptees attending | 100 |

### FRESHMAN PROFILE

| | |
|---|---|
| Range SAT Verbal | 480-590 |
| Average SAT Verbal | 530 |
| Range SAT Math | 480-610 |
| Average SAT Math | 539 |
| Range ACT Composite | 19-25 |
| Average ACT Composite | 22 |
| Minimum TOEFL | 525 |
| Average HS GPA | 3.2 |
| % graduated top 10% of class | 15 |
| % graduated top 25% of class | 36 |
| % graduated top 50% of class | 67 |

### DEADLINES

| | |
|---|---|
| Priority admission | 3/1 |
| Nonfall registration? | yes |

### APPLICANTS ALSO LOOK AT AND SOMETIMES PREFER

U. Montana
Montana State—Bozeman
Colorado Mines
U. Washington
Western Montana

**AND RARELY PREFER**
Carroll (MT)

### FINANCIAL FACTS

| | |
|---|---|
| Financial Aid Rating | 83 |
| In-state tuition | $3,350 |
| Out-of-state tuition | $8,060 |
| Room and board | $4,980 |
| Books and supplies | $700 |
| Required fees | $1,000 |
| % frosh receiving aid | 67 |
| % undergrads receiving aid | 69 |
| Avg frosh grant | $1,000 |
| Avg frosh loan | $2,000 |

# MORAVIAN COLLEGE

1200 MAIN STREET, BETHLEHEM, PA 18018 • ADMISSIONS: 800-441-3191 • FAX: 610-625-7930

## CAMPUS LIFE

| Quality of Life Rating | 79 |
|---|---|
| Type of school | private |
| Affiliation | Moravian |
| Environment | suburban |

### STUDENTS

| Total undergrad enrollment | 1,824 |
|---|---|
| % male/female | 39/61 |
| % from out of state | 39 |
| % from public high school | 86 |
| % live on campus | 73 |
| % in (# of) fraternities | 14 (2) |
| % in (# of) sororities | 22 (4) |
| % African American | 2 |
| % Asian | 1 |
| % Caucasian | 93 |
| % Hispanic | 4 |
| % international | 2 |
| # of countries represented | 21 |

### SURVEY SAYS...
Great computer facilities
Student publications are popular
Campus easy to get around

## ACADEMICS

| Academic Rating | 76 |
|---|---|
| Calendar | semester |
| Student/faculty ratio | 12:1 |
| Profs interesting rating | 80 |
| Profs accessible rating | 85 |
| % profs teaching UG courses | 100 |
| Avg lab size | under 10 students |
| Avg reg class size | 10-19 students |

### MOST POPULAR MAJORS
Psychology
Business administration/management
Fine/studio arts

## STUDENTS SPEAK OUT

### Academics

Many students here agree that "the Moravian Experience is something definitely worthwhile." But what makes it truly distinctive? Maybe it's the "professors who really care about you, whether or not it has to do with class." "Of course, there are a few bad apples, and a couple really rotten ones," but for the most part, you'd be hard pressed to find a Moravian student taking shots at the faculty or the administration at this college. Class sizes here are "small," the library is "excellent," and the music department is "very good for a small liberal arts college." (Actually, the 250-year-old department is housed on the college's slightly-set-apart Priscilla Payne Hurd Campus.) Still, when some students glance through the course booklet, they'd like to see "more choices for classes." At the head of this academic ship is a retired Air Force general, Dr. Ervin J. Rokke—and to the Moravian students he's both an icon and a best friend. "He holds regular fireside chats," explains a student, "which are open forums for students to ask questions and give suggestions to administrators." Of course, academics rarely cause complaint. More likely, students will bring up issues like the dining hall's habit of dishing out "the same thing for dinner that they serve for lunch."

### Life

Here's a tidbit of info for all potential Moravian students: "Once you get involved there are worlds of things to do and explore." If you don't get involved, however, you may find that Moravian is "nothing out of the ordinary." Alcohol and drugs definitely have a place in the campus life, and as one student says, "It's party time every night." Some students consider Moravian a suitcase school. One student estimates that "about 60 percent of the students go home on the weekend because many live close to school." For those that stick around, IMPACT (Innovative Multi-Cultural Programming Activities for Campus Togetherness), a student organization, regularly offers well attended "concerts, trips, and events," among other diversions. And Greek life is alive and well on the Moravian campus—both "social and service" organizations. While nobody here will tell you that Bethlehem is a hopping metropolis, most have a secret affection for it. "The historic part of the town is within walking distance of campus," and there you'll find "quaint little stores and coffee shops and restaurants," as well as a few bars for the 21-and-overs. The town also has events like "a Celtic festival, Musikfest, and a Christmas festival." On the campus itself, sports are a favorite pastime, from collegiate competition to intramural recreation. If this isn't enough, there are other institutions in the neighborhood worth visiting, namely Lehigh University, also in Bethlehem, and Lafayette College in nearby Easton.

### Student Body

"Friendliness" is the trademark of Moravian undergraduates. "It's like a disease," reports one student of his peers. "Generally there is an ease to the air" in Bethlehem, Pennsylvania, where Moravian has made its home since 1742. (In fact, it's the sixth oldest college in the nation.) But while Moravian has managed to survive the length of the nation's history, it hasn't quite managed to draw in the breadth of the nation's diversity. "We have barely any racial and ethnic diversity," grumbles a student. While the college reports that students hail from 25 U.S. states, many students complain that it seems like "everyone comes from the Lehigh Valley or somewhere within 30 to 40 minutes." Some cite that "the students are pretty religious" here. But as a rule, you should never stop with generalizations. "Individuals" with a range of interests can be found all over campus, and "everyone is respectful of everyone else."

# MORAVIAN COLLEGE

FINANCIAL AID: 610-861-1330 • E-MAIL: ADMISSIONS@MORAVIAN.EDU • WEBSITE: WWW.MORAVIAN.EDU

## ADMISSIONS
*Very important factors considered include:* character/personal qualities, class rank, secondary school record. *Important factors considered include:* essays, extracurricular activities, recommendations, standardized test scores. *Other factors considered include:* alumni/ae relation, geographical residence, interview, minority status, talent/ability, volunteer work, work experience. SAT I or ACT required; SAT I preferred. TOEFL required of all international applicants. High school diploma or GED is required. *High school units required/recommended:* 15 total required; 17 total recommended; 4 English required, 3 math required, 4 math recommended, 2 science required, 2 science lab required, 2 foreign language required, 3 foreign language recommended, 4 social studies required.

### The Inside Word
Moravian is a small liberal arts school with all the bells and whistles. Applicants will find a pretty straightforward admissions process—solid grades and test scores are required. Counselors will look closely to find the extras—community service, extracurricular activities—that make students stand out from the crowd. Moravian has many programs that should not be overlooked, including music, education, and the sciences.

## FINANCIAL AID
*Students should submit:* FAFSA, CSS/Financial Aid PROFILE, state aid form, noncustodial (divorced/separated) parent's statement, business/farm supplement, copies of parent's and student's W-2s and 1040s. Regular filing deadline is March 15. The Princeton Review suggests that all financial aid forms be submitted as soon as possible after January 1. *Need-based scholarships/grants offered:* Pell, SEOG, state scholarships/grants, private scholarships, the school's own gift aid. *Loan aid offered:* FFEL Subsidized Stafford, FFEL Unsubsidized Stafford, FFEL PLUS, Federal Perkins, state loans. Federal Work-Study Program available. Institutional employment available. Applicants will be notified of awards on a rolling basis beginning on or about April 1. Off-campus job opportunities are good.

## FROM THE ADMISSIONS OFFICE
"Founded in 1742, Moravian is proud of its history as one of America's oldest and most respected liberal arts colleges. The low student/faculty ratio allows for an immediate and unusually close bond. The Moravian family, comprising current students and faculty as well as alumni and emeritus professors, praises the College as a supportive environment for learning, personal exploration, and character development. The overarching emphasis of our curriculum is on scholarship enriched by self-discovery. In the last four years, Moravian has produced four Fulbright scholars, a Goldwater scholar, a Rhodes finalist, and three NCAA Postgraduate Scholars. Its robust varsity athletic program has produced All-American student athletes, Academic All-Americans, national champions, a national Player of the Year, and several Olympic hopefuls. The most important recent addition to the facilities is a $20 million academic building, completed in January 2003. At the heart of the central campus, it houses 15 new classrooms, four faculty departments, laboratories, research facilities, and 'smart' classrooms for easy technological interface. The College welcomes inquiries from students eager to participate in an environment of self-directed, life-long learning."

---

### ADMISSIONS

| | |
|---|---:|
| Admissions Rating | 78 |
| # of applicants | 1,509 |
| % of applicants accepted | 77 |
| % of acceptees attending | 32 |
| % admitted from wait list | 35 |
| # of early decision applicants | 145 |
| % accepted early decision | 77 |

#### FRESHMAN PROFILE
| | |
|---|---:|
| Range SAT Verbal | 490-610 |
| Average SAT Verbal | 553 |
| Range SAT Math | 500-610 |
| Average SAT Math | 556 |
| Minimum TOEFL | 550 |
| % graduated top 10% of class | 25 |
| % graduated top 25% of class | 56 |
| % graduated top 50% of class | 85 |

#### DEADLINES
| | |
|---|---:|
| Early decision | 2/1 |
| Early decision notification | 12/15 |
| Priority admission | 3/1 |
| Regular admission | 3/1 |
| Regular notification | 3/15 |
| Nonfall registration? | yes |

#### APPLICANTS ALSO LOOK AT AND OFTEN PREFER
Muhlenburg
Lafayette
Gettysburg
#### AND SOMETIMES PREFER
Ursinus
Susquehanna
College of New Jersey
#### AND RARELY PREFER
Elizabethtown
Lebanon Valley
Albright

### FINANCIAL FACTS

| | |
|---|---:|
| Financial Aid Rating | 83 |
| Tuition | $21,663 |
| Room and board | $7,095 |
| Books and supplies | $700 |
| Required fees | $365 |
| % frosh receiving aid | 74 |
| % undergrads receiving aid | 78 |
| Avg frosh grant | $11,536 |
| Avg frosh loan | $3,265 |

# MOREHOUSE COLLEGE

830 WESTVIEW DRIVE, SW, ATLANTA, GA 30314 • ADMISSIONS: 404-215-2632 • FAX: 404-524-5635

## CAMPUS LIFE

| Quality of Life Rating | 82 |
|---|---|
| Type of school | private |
| Environment | urban |

### STUDENTS
| | |
|---|---|
| Total undergrad enrollment | 2,738 |
| % from out of state | 65 |
| % from public high school | 80 |
| % live on campus | 45 |
| % in (# of) fraternities | 7 (6) |
| % African American | 97 |
| % international | 4 |

### SURVEY SAYS . . .
Students love Atlanta, GA
Very little drug use
Student government is popular
Class discussions are rare
Registration is a pain
Library needs improving
Students are very religious
Lab facilities are great

## ACADEMICS

| Academic Rating | 85 |
|---|---|
| Calendar | semester |
| Student/faculty ratio | 15:1 |
| Profs interesting rating | 96 |
| Profs accessible rating | 87 |
| % profs teaching UG courses | 100 |

### MOST POPULAR MAJORS
Business administration/management
Computer science
Biology/biological sciences

## STUDENTS SPEAK OUT

### Academics

Morehouse College is a star among the nation's historically black colleges and one of America's three remaining all-male institutions. The place is all about a tradition of excellence and commitment. To paraphrase one oft-expressed sentiment, "Give them a boy, they'll give you back a Morehouse man." Distinguished alumni run far and wide, including Dr. Martin Luther King, Jr., Julian Bond, Spike Lee, and Lerone Bennett, to name a few. Morehouse has been a continual source of leaders; half of all recent Morehouse graduates went on to pursue a graduate degree. The college "has excellent science, math, and business programs." Business and management, pre-medical sciences, engineering, and pre-law studies enroll well over half the students. A well-rounded liberal arts, sciences, and ethnic studies background is paramount within every major. Because Morehouse is a member of the Atlanta University Center, a consortium of six predominantly black schools, students have an even greater variety of course offerings to choose from. Students report that their professors are excellent teachers but do not always make themselves readily available outside the classroom. "This school requires a dedication on the part of the student in order to work closely with the faculty." "My overall academic experience is great because I have made it that way." Administrative chores can be difficult. One frustrated sophomore exclaims that "it seems as if the administrative faculty comes from Mars." While recognizing problems, students report satisfaction with Morehouse; the arrival of Dr. Massey as president has them even more pleased—he's been seen serving on the chow line in the cafeteria and eliminating a separate faculty dining room so that "professors now sit down and eat with us." Concludes one student, "There is a true spirit of pride that flows through here. The school's positive effects can be seen in the attitudes of students and faculty. This school teaches you to know yourself." Morehouse's endowment, nearly $95 million, is one of the largest among all such colleges and universities, and has enabled the school to make a $4.5 million investment in technology, wiring the entire campus with computer access to e-mail and the Internet. Next on tap is a new Leadership Development Center.

### Life

Atlanta consistently ranks among the most popular college towns in our annual surveys. It's chock-full of college students, and is a spring-break destination for those at HBCUs. Greek life is popular—although black Greek organizations have many of the same issues to deal with as other national frats do, they can also be very rewarding lifelong affiliations that facilitate career networking. Morehouse's participation in the Atlanta University Center is not solely academic; it gives students the opportunity for social interaction with coeds from Spelman and other member colleges. As a result, social life here is much more lively than at most single-sex institutions. The college's historic campus, while undergoing much needed renovations, still elicits the comment that "Morehouse is by no means a country club."

### Student Body

Morehouse draws students from all over the country. Outside the South, the Eastern Seaboard is the most prolific source of its undergrads. Students are politically progressive but also fairly religious, and therefore socially a little conservative. The typical Morehouse attitude is summed up by the student who writes, "Adversity builds character and the hotter the fire, the tougher the steel. If you come to Morehouse, you will either become a man or you will leave, plain and simple."

# MOREHOUSE COLLEGE

FINANCIAL AID: 404-681-2800 EXT. 2638 • E-MAIL: APATTILLO@MOREHOUSE.EDU • WEBSITE: WWW.MOREHOUSE.EDU

## ADMISSIONS

*Very important factors considered include:* secondary school record, standardized test scores. *Important factors considered include:* class rank, essays, leadership potential, recommendations. *Other factors considered include:* alumni/ae relation, character/personal qualities, extracurricular activities, geographical residence, interview, minority status, talent/ability, volunteer work. SAT I or ACT required. TOEFL required of all international applicants. High school diploma or GED is required. *High school units required/recommended:* 4 English required, 3 math required, 2 science required, 2 foreign language required, 2 social studies required.

### The Inside Word

Morehouse is one of the most selective historically black colleges in the country. Applicants should prepare themselves for a rigorous candidate review process. Much more than a solid academic profile is necessary to gain admission; expect to devote significant energy toward demonstrating that you make a good match with the college.

## FINANCIAL AID

*Students should submit:* FAFSA, institution's own financial aid form, CSS/Financial Aid PROFILE. Regular filing deadline is April 1. The Princeton Review suggests that all financial aid forms be submitted as soon as possible after January 1. *Need-based scholarships/grants offered:* Pell, SEOG, state scholarships/grants, private scholarships, the school's own gift aid, United Negro College Fund. *Loan aid offered:* Direct Subsidized Stafford, Direct Unsubsidized Stafford, Direct PLUS, Federal Perkins, state loans. Federal Work-Study Program available. Institutional employment available. Applicants will be notified of awards on or about May 1. Off-campus job opportunities are good.

## FROM THE ADMISSIONS OFFICE

"Morehouse College is the nation's only predominantly black, all-male, four-year liberal arts college. It is an independent institution located on a 61-acre campus in Atlanta, Georgia. The college was founded in 1867 as the Augusta Institute in Augusta, Georgia. The college was relocated to Atlanta in 1879 as the Atlanta Baptist College and was renamed Morehouse College in 1913. Morehouse is committed to educating and developing strong black leaders who will be dedicated to addressing the problems of society. The Morehouse education is designed to serve the three basic aspects of a well-rounded man: the personal, the social, and the professional."

## SELECTIVITY

| | |
|---|---:|
| **Admissions Rating** | 86 |
| # of applicants | 2,419 |
| % of applicants accepted | 62 |
| % of acceptees attending | 51 |

### FRESHMAN PROFILE

| | |
|---|---:|
| Range SAT Verbal | 480-590 |
| Average SAT Verbal | 530 |
| Range SAT Math | 480-600 |
| Average SAT Math | 550 |
| Range ACT Composite | 19-24 |
| Average ACT Composite | 23 |
| Minimum TOEFL | 250 |
| Average HS GPA | 3.3 |
| % graduated top 10% of class | 21 |
| % graduated top 25% of class | 44 |
| % graduated top 50% of class | 86 |

### DEADLINES

| | |
|---|---:|
| Early decision | 10/15 |
| Regular admission | 2/15 |
| Regular notification | 4/1 |

### APPLICANTS ALSO LOOK AT AND OFTEN PREFER
Georgia Tech
### AND SOMETIMES PREFER
Howard
Hampton
Washington U
U Maryland at College Park
U Georgia
Florida State
### AND RARELY PREFER
Emory

## FINANCIAL FACTS

| | |
|---|---:|
| **Financial Aid Rating** | 88 |
| Tuition | $11,786 |
| Room and board | $8,418 |
| Books and supplies | $800 |
| Required fees | $2,524 |

THE BEST 351 COLLEGES ■ 363

# MOUNT HOLYOKE COLLEGE

50 COLLEGE STREET, SOUTH HADLEY, MA 01075 • ADMISSIONS: 413-538-2023 • FAX: 413-538-2409

## CAMPUS LIFE

| | |
|---|---|
| Quality of Life Rating | 90 |
| Type of school | private |
| Environment | suburban |

### STUDENTS

| | |
|---|---|
| Total undergrad enrollment | 2,191 |
| % male/female | 0/100 |
| % from out of state | 65 |
| % from public high school | 66 |
| % live on campus | 93 |
| % African American | 5 |
| % Asian | 12 |
| % Caucasian | 67 |
| % Hispanic | 5 |
| % international | 15 |

### SURVEY SAYS . . .
Student publications are ignored
Students don't get along with local community
Students don't like Socorro, NM
Intercollegiate sports unpopular or nonexistent
Campus easy to get around
Lousy food on campus
Popular college radio

## ACADEMICS

| | |
|---|---|
| Academic Rating | 93 |
| Calendar | semester |
| Student/faculty ratio | 10:1 |
| % profs teaching UG courses | 100 |
| Avg lab size | 10-19 students |
| Avg reg class size | 10-19 students |

### MOST POPULAR MAJORS
English language and literature
Biology/biological sciences
Psychology

## STUDENTS SPEAK OUT

### Academics

Rigorous academics in a nurturing environment distinguish the Mount Holyoke undergraduate experience. As one student simply puts it, "Mount Holyoke is an extremely tough school. Students enrolled need to learn to separate their 'fun' time from their study time. If they do not, they will sink like rocks." Mount Holyoke demands a lot from its students, but the school also strives to ensure that undergrads have every chance to succeed. Explains one, "At times you feel like you are drowning in work. But there are plenty of lifeguards to help you. By the end of your first semester, not only are you learning to swim, but you're beginning to feel more confident in the water." "The courses are rigorous but not impossible," notes another. Easing the academic burden is a faculty that students universally praise. Writes one typical student, "The professors are unbelievable. I find out every day something new that they have done. They are the top of the line, the most accomplished and most understanding teachers I have ever had. They genuinely care about you and how you are doing, and will make sure that you are performing up to your potential." The administration, "although not as good as the professors, are helpful and cordial." Membership in the Five College Consortium, which also includes UMass—Amherst, Smith, Amherst, and Hampshire, provides access to top profs at other area schools. The MHC Honor Code, which every student signs during their first year and "which the campus takes very seriously," is another plus; it allows ample academic freedom, including "self-scheduled exams." About the only thing the students here really pine for is more "name recognition." As a biology major points out, "No one knows how cool we are."

### Life

Hard work means less play for the women of Mount Holyoke. "This is not the school for a stereotypical college social life," explains one undergrad. "However, if you enjoy Friday night study sessions, come on down." Adds another, "Unfortunately, although there are four other colleges in the area, it is very hard to find anything on the weekend besides the general frat parties of UMass and TAP (the Amherst party) at Amherst College." The administration, to its credit, works hard to provide activities such as "improv comedy, free dances, movie showings, and music performances." Students also point out that "if you can't find something to do on campus, hop on the free bus to the neighboring towns with diverse restaurants, fun shopping, and great bars/clubs. The school provides weekly transportation to the mall and the grocery store (one mile down the road)." But don't hang out in South Hadley. Cautions one undergrad, "Mount Holyoke College is located in a very small town called South Hadley, Massachusetts, which we refer to it as 'How Sadly.' The town hates us." Students conclude that "If you want a social life, you can get it. It's just a little more [of an] effort to find."

### Student Body

The typical Mount Holyoke woman, students report, "seems to be one that believes that she can single-handedly change the world. Most of the students are exceptionally friendly—many, however, are overly p.c." A large and vocal lesbian community makes Mount Holyoke home, prompting one student to write, "If you're gay, you've entered your heaven." Others add, "We have a few major subcultures, like the athletes, the party girls, the queer community, some religious groups, but most people have diverse groups of friends from all over campus. It is easy to make new friends in classes, in clubs, or over a meal in one of our cafeterias (there is one in every dorm). The friends you make here will last a good long time." Be forewarned, though. "There are a lot of opinionated women, which means that there tend to be arguments and debates in classes, in the dorms, in online forums, in the newspaper, etc."

# MOUNT HOLYOKE COLLEGE

FINANCIAL AID: 413-538-2291 • E-MAIL: ADMISSIONS@MTHOLYOKE.EDU • WEBSITE: WWW.MTHOLYOKE.EDU

## ADMISSIONS
*Very important factors considered include:* class rank, essays, recommendations, secondary school record. *Important factors considered include:* character/personal qualities, extracurricular activities, interview, talent/ability, volunteer work, work experience. *Other factors considered include:* alumni/ae relation, geographical residence, minority status, standardized test scores. TOEFL required of all international applicants. High school diploma or GED is required. *High school units required/recommended:* 4 English recommended, 3 math recommended, 3 science recommended, 3 science lab recommended, 3 foreign language recommended, 3 history recommended, 1 elective recommended.

## The Inside Word
Mount Holyoke has benefited well from the renaissance of interest in women's colleges; selectivity and academic quality are on the rise. Considering that the college was already fairly selective, candidates are well advised to take the admissions process seriously. Matchmaking is a significant factor here; strong academic performance, well-written essays, and an understanding of and appreciation for "the Mount Holyoke experience" will usually carry the day.

## FINANCIAL AID
*Students should submit:* FAFSA, CSS/Financial Aid PROFILE, noncustodial (divorced/separated) parent's statement, business/farm supplement, federal income tax returns and W-2 forms of parents and student. Regular filing deadline is February 1. The Princeton Review suggests that all financial aid forms be submitted as soon as possible after January 1. *Need-based scholarships/grants offered:* Pell, SEOG, state scholarships/grants, private scholarships, the school's own gift aid. *Loan aid offered:* Direct Subsidized Stafford, Direct Unsubsidized Stafford, Direct PLUS, Federal Perkins, state loans, college/university loans from institutional funds. Federal Work-Study Program available. Institutional employment available. Applicants will be notified of awards on or about March 25. Off-campus job opportunities are excellent.

## FROM THE ADMISSIONS OFFICE
"Did you know that the majority of students who choose Mount Holyoke do so simply because it is an outstanding liberal arts college? After a semester or two, they start to appreciate the fact that Mount Holyoke is a women's college, even though most Mount Holyoke students never thought they'd go to a women's college when they started their college search. Students talk of having 'space' to really figure out who they are. They speak about feeling empowered to excel in traditionally male subjects such as science and technology. They talk about the remarkable array of opportunities—for academic achievement, career exploration, and leadership—and the impressive, creative accomplishments of their peers. If you're looking for a college that will challenge you to be your best, most powerful self and to fulfill potential, Mount Holyoke should be at the top of your list."

### SELECTIVITY

| | |
|---|---|
| Admissions Rating | 87 |
| # of applicants | 2,936 |
| % of applicants accepted | 52 |
| % of acceptees attending | 38 |
| # accepting a place on wait list | 278 |
| % admitted from wait list | 9 |
| # of early decision applicants | 259 |
| % accepted early decision | 65 |

### FRESHMAN PROFILE
| | |
|---|---|
| Range SAT Verbal | 608-700 |
| Average SAT Verbal | 651 |
| Range SAT Math | 580-670 |
| Average SAT Math | 627 |
| Range ACT Composite | 26-30 |
| Average ACT Composite | 28 |
| Minimum TOEFL | 600 |
| Average HS GPA | 3.7 |
| % graduated top 10% of class | 52 |
| % graduated top 25% of class | 84 |
| % graduated top 50% of class | 98 |

### DEADLINES
| | |
|---|---|
| Early decision | 11/15 |
| Early decision notification | 1/1 |
| Regular admission | 1/15 |
| Regular notification | 4/1 |
| Nonfall registration? | yes |

### APPLICANTS ALSO LOOK AT
**AND OFTEN PREFER**
Dartmouth
Wellesley
Cornell U
**AND SOMETIMES PREFER**
Smith
Vassar
Bryn Mawr
**AND RARELY PREFER**
Skidmore
UMass at Amherst
Boston U

### FINANCIAL FACTS

| | |
|---|---|
| Financial Aid Rating | 93 |
| Tuition | $27,540 |
| Room and board | $8,100 |
| Required fees | $168 |
| % frosh receiving aid | 65 |
| % undergrads receiving aid | 67 |
| Avg frosh grant | $21,087 |
| Avg frosh loan | $2,700 |

# MUHLENBERG COLLEGE

2400 WEST CHEW STREET, ALLENTOWN, PA 18104-5596 • ADMISSIONS: 484-664-3200 • FAX: 484-664-3234

## CAMPUS LIFE

| | |
|---|---|
| Quality of Life Rating | 80 |
| Type of school | private |
| Affiliation | Lutheran |
| Environment | suburban |

### STUDENTS

| | |
|---|---|
| Total undergrad enrollment | 2,470 |
| % male/female | 44/56 |
| % from out of state | 63 |
| % from public high school | 70 |
| % live on campus | 89 |
| % in (# of) fraternities | 27 (4) |
| % in (# of) sororities | 22 (4) |
| % African American | 2 |
| % Asian | 3 |
| % Caucasian | 90 |
| % Hispanic | 3 |

### SURVEY SAYS . . .
Students are religious
Political activism is hot
Popular college radio
Students don't get along with local community
Registration is a breeze
Very little beer drinking
Very little drug use

## ACADEMICS

| | |
|---|---|
| Academic Rating | 82 |
| Calendar | semester |
| Student/faculty ratio | 13:1 |
| Profs interesting rating | 77 |
| Profs accessible rating | 74 |
| % profs teaching UG courses | 100 |
| Avg lab size | 10-19 students |
| Avg reg class size | 10-19 students |

### MOST POPULAR MAJORS
Business administration/management
Biology/biological sciences
Psychology

## STUDENTS SPEAK OUT

### Academics

Students praise the "amazing" theater and science departments at Muhlenberg College. Notes one undergrad here, "The single greatest strength [of this school] is the reputation of the science departments . . . . The rigor I have faced here as a biology major, although at times extremely tough, has been also very rewarding." Muhlenberg also boasts "excellent" departments of English and history; the business and philosophy departments here "aren't too shabby either." Indeed, Muhlenberg has a lot to offer for an institution with less than 3,000 students. Undergrads appreciate how "the small student body allows the professors to tailor the education for each student." As one student told us, "The best part about my school is its smallness—something I thought I would hate about Muhlenberg turned out to be what makes it so great." Another benefit of the school's small size: "Since we don't have a graduate school, we don't have any graduate students, so undergrads have opportunities to do research." Prospective students are forewarned that "this is a tough school to get into and to stay in, due to a heavy workload." While profs pile on the work, they are also "extremely approachable and welcome you to speak with them about anything, not just class work. They can help you succeed in school if you take the initiative to get to know them." Sums up one student here: "Muhlenberg is what you make of it; if you're ambitious, the school will be good to you; if you're not, most likely you'll get swept along for the ride."

### Life

The "beautiful and safe" Muhlenberg campus provides a serene setting to counteract students' hectic academic schedules. "Life is very busy," notes one student. "The best days are the ones where you have a spare hour or two to sit out on the lawn and read or study with some friends when the weather is nice. The front lawn is great; it always gets crowded with kids just hanging out in the spring and fall or playing in the snow in the winter." An active social scene, however, is not part of what clutters most kids' calendars here. There are school-sponsored activities offered, but "most are lame," and as far as the Greek scene goes, the frats "are now either kicked off campus or on probation, so now we are becoming a bar and house party school." Hometown Allentown offers little. Explains one undergrad, "Allentown is technically a city, but don't expect it to be like Manhattan. The college is located in the middle of the suburbs, and most people don't go downtown." Adds another, "I wish they would just pick up the whole damn school and move it out of Allentown." Students enjoy "a few sporting events, mainly men's soccer and women's rugby." Even so, most who can do so seek entertainment elsewhere, often in Philadelphia or New York City. Unfortunately, "freshmen are not allowed to have cars on campus due to major lack of parking space and the rule is pretty strictly enforced," which is why they "tend to flock to the fraternities or hang out in their dorm rooms."

### Student Body

Muhlenberg's student body is predominantly white and affluent, students here agree. Detractors describe their peers as people "who have never worked in their lives, drive BMWs and have exorbitant allowances." They "tend to be conservative" and cliquish; reports one, "I don't think anyone really goes out of their way to make new friends once they have found their clique. That's not to say people aren't friendly, though. Overall, the students all get along with each other." Theater majors tend to be the major exception to the preppy, conservative stereotype; their ranks include a disproportionate number of iconoclasts as well as gay students. Despite its Lutheran affiliation, "most kids here are Roman Catholic or Jewish."

366 ■ THE BEST 351 COLLEGES

# MUHLENBERG COLLEGE

FINANCIAL AID: 484-664-3175 • E-MAIL: ADMISSION@MUHLENBERG.EDU • WEBSITE: WWW.MUHLENBERG.EDU

## ADMISSIONS
*Very important factors considered include:* character/personal qualities, secondary school record, talent/ability. *Important factors considered include:* class rank, essays, extracurricular activities, interview, recommendations, standardized test scores, volunteer work. *Other factors considered include:* alumni/ae relation, geographical residence, minority status, work experience. TOEFL required of all international applicants. High school diploma or GED is required. *High school units required/recommended:* 16 total required; 4 English required, 3 math required, 2 science required, 3 science recommended, 2 science lab required, 2 foreign language required, 3 foreign language recommended, 2 history required, 1 elective required.

### The Inside Word
Muhlenberg's inquiries and applications continue to increase, which serves to reinforce its selectivity. Competition for students among small Pennsylvania liberal arts colleges is quite heated, and the college is among the more competitive of the lot.

## FINANCIAL AID
*Students should submit:* FAFSA, institution's own financial aid form, CSS/Financial Aid PROFILE, noncustodial (divorced/separated) parent's statement, business/farm supplement. Regular filing deadline is February 15. The Princeton Review suggests that all financial aid forms be submitted as soon as possible after January 1. *Need-based scholarships/grants offered:* Pell, SEOG, state scholarships/grants, private scholarships, the school's own gift aid. *Loan aid offered:* FFEL Subsidized Stafford, FFEL Unsubsidized Stafford, FFEL PLUS, Federal Perkins. Federal Work-Study Program available. Institutional employment available. Applicants will be notified of awards on or about April 1. Off-campus job opportunities are good.

## FROM THE ADMISSIONS OFFICE
"Listening to our own students, we've learned that most picked Muhlenberg mainly because it has a long-standing reputation for being academically demanding on one hand, but personally supportive on the other. We expect a lot from our students, but we also expect a lot from ourselves in providing the challenge and support they need to stretch, grow, and succeed. It's not unusual for professors to put their home phone numbers on the course syllabus and encourage students to call them at home with questions. Upperclassmen are helpful to underclassmen. 'We really know about collegiality here,' says an alumna who now works at Muhlenberg. 'It's that kind of place.' The supportive atmosphere and strong work ethic produce lots of successes. The pre-med and pre-law programs are very strong, as are programs in theater arts, English, psychology, the sciences, business, and accounting. 'When I was a student here,' recalls Dr. Walter Loy, now a professor emeritus of physics, 'we were encouraged to live life to its fullest, to do our best, to be honest, to deal openly with others, and to treat everyone as an individual. Those are important things, and they haven't changed at Muhlenberg.'"

## SELECTIVITY

| Admissions Rating | 82 |
|---|---|
| # of applicants | 3,822 |
| % of applicants accepted | 35 |
| % of acceptees attending | 41 |
| # accepting a place on wait list | 407 |
| % admitted from wait list | 7 |
| # of early decision applicants | 527 |
| % accepted early decision | 59 |

### FRESHMAN PROFILE
| Range SAT Verbal | 550-640 |
|---|---|
| Average SAT Verbal | 595 |
| Range SAT Math | 560-650 |
| Average SAT Math | 606 |
| Minimum TOEFL | 550 |
| Average HS GPA | 3.7 |
| % graduated top 10% of class | 39 |
| % graduated top 25% of class | 75 |
| % graduated top 50% of class | 97 |

### DEADLINES
| Early decision | 1/15 |
|---|---|
| Early decision notification | 2/1 |
| Regular admission | 2/15 |
| Regular notification | 3/15 |
| Nonfall registration? | yes |

### APPLICANTS ALSO LOOK AT AND OFTEN PREFER
Lafayette
Skidmore
NYU

### AND SOMETIMES PREFER
Gettysburg
Dickinson
Franklin & Marshall
Lehigh

### AND RARELY PREFER
Rutgers
Drew
Susquehanna

## FINANCIAL FACTS

| Financial Aid Rating | 82 |
|---|---|
| Tuition | $23,250 |
| Room and board | $6,295 |
| Books and supplies | $750 |
| Required fees | $205 |
| % frosh receiving aid | 43 |
| % undergrads receiving aid | 44 |
| Avg frosh grant | $12,819 |
| Avg frosh loan | $2,971 |

# NEW COLLEGE OF FLORIDA

5700 NORTH TAMIAMI TRAIL, SARASOTA, FL 34243-2197 • ADMISSIONS: 941-359-4269 • FAX: 941-359-4435

## CAMPUS LIFE

| | |
|---|---|
| Quality of Life Rating | 79 |
| Type of school | public |
| Environment | suburban |

### STUDENTS

| | |
|---|---|
| Total undergrad enrollment | 650 |
| % from out of state | 25 |
| % from public high school | 81 |
| % live on campus | 71 |
| % African American | 2 |
| % Asian | 3 |
| % Caucasian | 85 |
| % Hispanic | 6 |
| % international | 2 |
| # of countries represented | 8 |

### SURVEY SAYS . . .
Diversity lacking on campus
Registration is a breeze
Theater is hot
Political activism is hot
No one cheats
Lousy food on campus
No one watches intercollegiate sports
Computer facilities need improving

## ACADEMICS

| | |
|---|---|
| Academic Rating | 88 |
| Calendar | 4-1-4 |
| Student/faculty ratio | 11:1 |
| Profs interesting rating | 94 |
| Profs accessible rating | 94 |
| % profs teaching UG courses | 100 |
| Avg reg class size | 20-29 students |

## STUDENTS SPEAK OUT

### Academics

If you're a high school student who's looking for a college that's "a bacchanalian revelry for the mind," then you might just have found your place. At the core of New College's academic virtues are "freedom" and "rigorous standards." Freedom is what makes the college fairly unique on the American higher-ed landscape. Students devise their own courses of study, which gives them "freedom to study how and what" they want. And their knowledge is assessed with "written evaluations instead of grades." No grades! Don't get too excited. New College, one junior warns, "is not for the faint of heart," and though students don't get graded, they either pass or fail. At the end of four years, every student must present a thesis to a faculty committee of three. Though the coursework can be "stressful," students are encouraged and supported by "personal attention from profs." One sophomore declares, "Nowhere else could I find such dedicated, passionate professors." "Everything about this school reeks of accessibility," adds a senior. "You can go talk to the president, create a campus event, or write your thesis about male pattern baldness—all you need is the drive and a sense of humor." Another student summed up his sentiments more plainly: "This school kicks ass!"

### Life

"Everything blurs together in a mélange of inquiry and fun," at New College. With the "awesome beaches" of the Gulf Coast right in front of them and the city of Sarasota in the background, students live a life that seems like "paradise." They tend to talk about parties in class and talk about class at parties, not to mention do their homework while lying in the sand. "The biggest thing to do for fun here are walls—big weekend parties held in Palm Court." You're likely to find just about anything at these parties—from binge drinking and an array of drugs to conversations about philosophy and a swirl of dance moves. Also, students come together for a variety of "festive occasions" on campus, like "the Latino Ball" and the "Queer Ball." One thing you can count on in Sarasota is that students "spend an incredible amount of time out of doors, studying, playing sports, going to the beach, and partying." Because the campus administration is so supportive of student initiative, it's also common to find a classmate who is, say, itching to "protest Taco Bell" or pitch in to help "build wetlands." Everyone is poised to have an effect—either on the party scene, the academic scene, the community scene, or every-other-scene. "Trouble is, when you've got 400 revolutionaries,"—actually, about 650—"all in one place, egos clash and the scent of self-righteousness becomes more pervasive than the marijuana smoke."

### Student Body

If there's one way to describe the student body at New College, it's "open-minded." One student brags that her school "is one of the few places on Earth where you can truly be yourself and be embraced for it." You'll be especially embraced if you're of a liberal mind—the student body is a "motley bunch of (mainly) leftist spoiled Americans kids," as one student put it. But that doesn't mean that different views aren't tolerated. "Regardless of your race, age, creed, gender, or sexual orientation, you will fit in here." (A student even goes so far as to say that "males and straight people are the minority.") To many of the students' chagrin, racial and ethnic diversity among the small student body is lacking. But diversity of thought, on the other hand, is what glues the students together. "It's a homogeny of weirdness," writes a senior. The "weirdness" of NCF students works in tandem with their intelligence. Many students tore up acceptance letters from other prestigious institutions, like Princeton, Yale, Harvard, Columbia, Williams, and, well, the list is long, in favor of studying alongside the "wonderfully creative, intelligent" students at NCF.

# NEW COLLEGE OF FLORIDA

FINANCIAL AID: 941-359-4255 • E-MAIL: ADMISSIONS@NCF.EDU • WEBSITE: WWW.NCF.EDU

## ADMISSIONS

*Very important factors considered include:* essays, secondary school record. *Important factors considered include:* character/personal qualities, recommendations, standardized test scores. *Other factors considered include:* alumni/ae relation, class rank, extracurricular activities, geographical residence, interview, state residency, talent/ability, volunteer work, work experience. SAT I or ACT required. TOEFL required of all international applicants. High school diploma or GED is required. *High school units required/recommended:* 19 total required; 20 total recommended; 4 English required, 3 math required, 3 science required, 2 science lab required, 2 foreign language required, 3 social studies required, 4 elective required, 5 elective recommended.

### The Inside Word

Applications keep rolling in to New College like the evening tide on Sarasota Bay. Increases in the academic quality of entering students are virtually perpetual, as is recognition by the media. Perhaps the biggest drawback is a high attrition rate for a college of this caliber—just as the admissions committee strives to choose wisely, so should prospective students. Don't apply simply because it's a great buy; make sure that it's what you're seeking. In order to be successful, candidates must demonstrate a high level of intellectual curiosity, self-awareness, and maturity. It also helps to be a strong writer, given that the application process requires candidates to submit three essays, two long essays, and a graded paper from school. Did we forget to mention high grades and test scores? They'll help, too, but if you're someone with lots of "potential" as opposed to "credentials," the admissions committee might still vote you in provided you've put together some very convincing evidence that you make a match and deserve a shot.

## FINANCIAL AID

*Students should submit:* FAFSA. No deadline for regular filing. The Princeton Review suggests that all financial aid forms be submitted as soon as possible after January 1. *Need-based scholarships/grants offered:* Pell, state scholarships/grants, private scholarships, the school's own gift aid. *Loan aid offered:* FFEL Subsidized Stafford, FFEL Unsubsidized Stafford, FFEL PLUS. Institutional employment available. Applicants will be notified of awards on a rolling basis beginning on or about October 1. Off-campus job opportunities are good.

## FROM THE ADMISSIONS OFFICE

"New College provides the opportunity to obtain a very high-quality education for the very affordable cost of attending a public college. Students work in close consultation with faculty to develop individualized programs of seminars, tutorials, independent research, and off-campus experiences. The student who will do best at New College is one who is independent, broad-minded, self-confident, and capable of rigorous academic work. The very nature of New College requires one to be dedicated to education and the pursuit of individual growth."

## SELECTIVITY

| | |
|---|---|
| Admissions Rating | 97 |
| # of applicants | 494 |
| % of applicants accepted | 65 |
| % of acceptees attending | 50 |
| # accepting a place on wait list | 14 |
| % admitted from wait list | 50 |

### FRESHMAN PROFILE

| | |
|---|---|
| Range SAT Verbal | 640-730 |
| Average SAT Verbal | 693 |
| Range SAT Math | 590-680 |
| Average SAT Math | 637 |
| Range ACT Composite | 27-29 |
| Average ACT Composite | 27 |
| Minimum TOEFL | 560 |
| Average HS GPA | 3.9 |
| % graduated top 10% of class | 51 |
| % graduated top 25% of class | 91 |
| % graduated top 50% of class | 97 |

### DEADLINES

| | |
|---|---|
| Priority admission | 2/1 |
| Regular admission | 5/1 |
| Nonfall registration? | yes |

### APPLICANTS ALSO LOOK AT
**AND OFTEN PREFER**
University of Florida
**AND SOMETIMES PREFER**
Grinnell College
University of Miami
Hampshire College
University of South Florida
**AND RARELY PREFER**
Sarah Lawrence College
Reed College
Eckerd College

## FINANCIAL FACTS

| | |
|---|---|
| Financial Aid Rating | 85 |
| In-state tuition | $3,020 |
| Out-of-state tuition | $13,810 |
| Room and board | $5,394 |
| Books and supplies | $750 |
| % frosh receiving aid | 45 |
| % undergrads receiving aid | 42 |
| Avg frosh loan | $2,181 |

# NEW JERSEY INSTITUTE OF TECHNOLOGY

UNIVERSITY HEIGHTS, NEWARK, NJ 07102 • ADMISSIONS: 973-596-3300 • FAX: 973-596-3461

## CAMPUS LIFE

| | |
|---|---|
| Quality of Life Rating | 66 |
| Type of school | public |
| Environment | urban |

### STUDENTS

| | |
|---|---|
| Total undergrad enrollment | 5,730 |
| % male/female | 79/21 |
| % from out of state | 4 |
| % from public high school | 80 |
| % live on campus | 23 |
| % in (# of) fraternities | 7 (19) |
| % in (# of) sororities | 5 (8) |
| % African American | 11 |
| % Asian | 22 |
| % Caucasian | 33 |
| % Hispanic | 12 |
| % international | 6 |

### SURVEY SAYS . . .
Musical organizations aren't popular
Popular college radio
High cost of living
Very little drug use
Unattractive campus
Very little beer drinking
Very little hard liquor

## ACADEMICS

| | |
|---|---|
| Academic Rating | 79 |
| Calendar | semester |
| Student/faculty ratio | 13:1 |
| Profs interesting rating | 87 |
| Profs accessible rating | 87 |
| % profs teaching UG courses | 70 |
| % classes taught by TAs | 7 |

### MOST POPULAR MAJORS
Computer science
Computer engineering
Architecture

## STUDENTS SPEAK OUT

### Academics

Those looking for "great 'bang for the buck' " in the world of engineering would do well to consider the New Jersey Institute of Technology. While the school also maintains divisions of architecture, management, and arts and sciences, the low-cost, high-return College of Engineering is the undisputed star of the show. According to NJIT, graduates make up one-fourth of all engineers currently working in the Garden State. Important to note, the university is opening the College of Computing Sciences in fall 2001. Students warn "this school is easy to get into, but when it comes to sticking through it and getting a degree from here, life is 'hell.' The professors love to challenge you, and I can say that when I graduate I know I am going to be very well off." NJIT's curriculum is "extremely vigorous and challenging" and "helps provide you with the proper learning skills that are needed in order for you to make it in the world." Professors receive mixed reviews; some "go above and beyond for 'positive and eager-to-learn' students," while others "tend to read from slides instead of using them as aids" and "are rarely available beyond class hours." The administration "is slow to enact changes desired by students" and could use more "financial advisors and otherwise more help for registration, particularly for freshmen!" Students also gripe about the condition of lecture halls, dorms, and other facilities. Even so, most agree that the NJIT experience is an enriching one. Writes one, "It feels like you're in the United Nations school, as there are so many international students and professors. Great cultural experience if nothing else; sometimes, though, it makes it hard to understand what's going on."

### Life

Hmm . . . a tech school in Newark, New Jersey. Not exactly the formula for a swinging campus, you have to admit. NJIT has other hurdles to overcome as well. As one student explains, "Because we are so diverse and a large percentage of our students are commuters, it is really hard to form any kind of school unity, whether it be in clubs, student government, or athletics." All the same, "While our school is extremely technology-oriented, we do know how to have fun, regardless of how busy we are." As for NJIT's reputation as a dead campus, several students note that "contrary to popular belief, there is plenty to do on campus. More often than not, it is the lack of student participation that creates the perception of a nonexistent social life on campus." Many students report participating in such sports as bowling, swimming, volleyball, lifting weights, and track and field, while some insist that "pool is the biggest 'sport' on campus. Everyone owns a pool cue." Downtown Newark is enjoying a renaissance with the recent addition of a new performing arts center that draws major international artists in music, dance, and theater. And of course, New York City is only a PATH train ride away.

### Student Body

NJIT boasts "good ethnic diversity and individual acceptance," and although "students tend to self-segregate into ethnic/gender/major-related groups," most agree that the atmosphere here is congenial. Writes one student, "I actually often brag about how friendly our campus is. Maybe that's just reflecting the desperation of the male population in [light of] the male-female ratio of 10:1." Students wish there "was more interaction between residents and commuters." Commuters "often come to class and just leave. It's hard to meet non-dormers."

# NEW JERSEY INSTITUTE OF TECHNOLOGY

FINANCIAL AID: 973-596-3480 • E-MAIL: ADMISSIONS@NJIT.EDU • WEBSITE: WWW.NJIT.EDU

## ADMISSIONS

*Very important factors considered include:* class rank, secondary school record, standardized test scores. *Other factors considered include:* character/personal qualities, essays, extracurricular activities, interview, recommendations, talent/ability, volunteer work, work experience. SAT I or ACT required; SAT I preferred. TOEFL required of all international applicants. High school diploma or GED is required. *High school units required/recommended:* 16 total required; 4 English required, 4 math required, 2 science required, 2 science lab required, 2 foreign language recommended, 1 social studies recommended, 1 history recommended, 2 elective recommended.

### The Inside Word

NJIT is a great choice for students who aspire to technical careers but don't meet the requirements for better known and more selective universities. To top it off, it's a pretty good buy.

## FINANCIAL AID

*Students should submit:* FAFSA. The Princeton Review suggests that all financial aid forms be submitted as soon as possible after January 1. *Need-based scholarships/grants offered:* Pell, SEOG, state scholarships/grants, private scholarships, the school's own gift aid. *Loan aid offered:* Direct Subsidized Stafford, Direct Unsubsidized Stafford, Direct PLUS, FFEL Subsidized Stafford, FFEL Unsubsidized Stafford, FFEL PLUS, Federal Perkins, state loans, college/university loans from institutional funds. Federal Work-Study Program available. Institutional employment available. Off-campus job opportunities are good.

## FROM THE ADMISSIONS OFFICE

"Talented high school graduates from across the nation come to NJIT to prepare for leadership roles in architecture, business, engineering, medical, legal, science, and technological fields. Students experience a public research university conducting more than $50 million in research that maintains a small-college atmosphere at a modest cost. Our attractive 45-acre campus is just minutes from New York City and less than an hour from the Jersey shore. Students find an outstanding faculty and a safe, diverse, caring learning and residential community. All dormitory rooms have sprinklers. NJIT's academic environment challenges and prepares students for rewarding careers and full-time advanced study after graduation. The campus is computing-intensive. For five consecutive years, *Yahoo! Internet Life* has ranked NJIT among America's Most Wired Universities."

## SELECTIVITY

| | |
|---|---|
| Admissions Rating | 80 |
| # of applicants | 2,591 |
| % of applicants accepted | 58 |
| % of acceptees attending | 44 |

### FRESHMAN PROFILE

| | |
|---|---|
| Range SAT Verbal | 490-590 |
| Average SAT Verbal | 546 |
| Range SAT Math | 550-650 |
| Average SAT Math | 606 |
| Minimum TOEFL | 550 |
| % graduated top 10% of class | 24 |
| % graduated top 25% of class | 59 |
| % graduated top 50% of class | 90 |

### DEADLINES

| | |
|---|---|
| Priority admission | 4/1 |
| Nonfall registration? | yes |

### APPLICANTS ALSO LOOK AT AND OFTEN PREFER
Rutgers U
College of New Jersey
Stevens Institute of Technology
Rensselaer Polytechnic Institute
### AND SOMETIMES PREFER
Worcester Polytechnic
Penn State at University Park
Virginia Tech

## FINANCIAL FACTS

| | |
|---|---|
| Financial Aid Rating | 85 |
| In-state tuition | $6,758 |
| Out-of-state tuition | $11,710 |
| Room and board | $7,864 |
| Books and supplies | $1,000 |
| Required fees | $1,148 |
| % frosh receiving aid | 65 |
| % undergrads receiving aid | 57 |
| Avg frosh grant | $4,400 |
| Avg frosh loan | $2,500 |

# NEW MEXICO INSTITUTE OF MINING & TECHNOLOGY

CAMPUS STATION, 801 LEROY PLACE, SOCORRO, NM 87801 • ADMISSIONS: 505-835-5424 • FAX: 505-835-5989

## CAMPUS LIFE

| | |
|---|---|
| Quality of Life Rating | 69 |
| Type of school | public |
| Environment | rural |

### STUDENTS

| | |
|---|---|
| Total undergrad enrollment | 1,336 |
| % male/female | 65/35 |
| % from out of state | 16 |
| % from public high school | 80 |
| % live on campus | 40 |
| % African American | 1 |
| % Asian | 4 |
| % Caucasian | 71 |
| % Hispanic | 21 |
| % international | 2 |
| # of countries represented | 30 |

### SURVEY SAYS . . .
Student publications are ignored
Students don't get along with local community
Students don't like Socorro, NM
Campus easy to get around
Popular college radio

## ACADEMICS

| | |
|---|---|
| Academic Rating | 78 |
| Calendar | semester |
| Student/faculty ratio | 13:1 |
| Profs interesting rating | 93 |
| Profs accessible rating | 89 |
| % profs teaching UG courses | 85 |
| Avg lab size | 10-19 students |
| Avg reg class size | under 10 students |

### MOST POPULAR MAJORS
Computer science
Electrical, electronics, and communications engineering
Physics

## STUDENTS SPEAK OUT

### Academics
The academic benefits of New Mexico Tech are two-fold. First, for the student serious about an intensive future in science and technologies, "this school is good about receiving research money from industry sources." And nearly a third of all graduates matriculate to further training in graduate and professional schools. While some students complain that "a lot of profs are here to do research, so they do not like to teach," more students tout the school for its "immensely helpful" faculty. Because the school is so small—less than 1,300 undergrads—professors are often available to "help you not just with school but many other career and personal issues." But don't be fooled by these personal touches. The "good education" that New Mexico Tech offers comes to students who can endure "challenging" classes and plenty of homework. Take this as an enticement or a warning. "If you want to spend all of your free time doing homework," says one freshman, "this school's for you." The academic road may be a challenging one, but there's a worthy degree waiting at the finish line for the successful student. "But deep inside," sighs one senior, "you feel you'll never get there."

### Life
New Mexico Tech seems to attract the kind of students who think an ideal day consists of, say, attending classes, studying, interning, rock-climbing, and capping things off with a book, or movie, or a few beers and friendly conversation. On the other hand, it does not attract students who want endless streams of wild parties, floods of booze, and pretty good odds of pretty easy sex. In fact, as far as the gender pairing goes, one junior male called Socorro "the single most sexually frustrated three square miles on Earth." But New Mexico Tech isn't entirely without women (about 37 percent of the student body is female) or social outlets. Clubs and activities abound at the institute, including "intramural" sports, "hiking," "rock climbing," "caving," and "involvement with the school's experimental underground mine." Students also make regular trips to Albuquerque to enjoy city life. Though drugs and alcohol don't seem noticeably prevalent here—and the absence of Greek life keeps the number of big parties down—students find ways to add spice to their social lives and still manage to have some less-than-sober nights. "We shoot cows with potato guns . . . drink heavily, and play chess," reports one senior. Another senior confirms that, for fun, NMT students do "whatever comes to mind, from duck, duck goose to slamming golf balls into blast craters." The smallness of Socorro is just a simple challenge for creative minds. "People who can entertain themselves can find plenty to do," a junior from Texas says. And if you do get bored, there's one logical explanation: "You're not studying enough."

### Student Body
"Most of the students here are geeks and nerds," confirms one freshman. But in this case, words like "geeks" and "nerds" are not derogatory terms. In fact, they're uttered with a sense of pride. They indicate that New Mexico Tech is alive with a student body that not only likes things such as math and computers and the sciences, but one that also has a knack for studying them. Though many students hail from New Mexico, there's a visible diversity of races and ethnicities. Still, the students are, well, "not terribly exciting," at least not in that inflated party-school sense of the word "exciting." Students at New Mexico Tech are "very dedicated" when it comes to "being successful students" but not so hot at "having social lives." But no one can say they're not a friendly bunch—"so friendly it's scary," writes a freshman. "They rock," according to another freshman, "if you can get them away from their computers." One senior warns, "Valedictorians from high school will be humbled by the other geniuses here."

372 ■ THE BEST 351 COLLEGES

# NEW MEXICO INSTITUTE OF MINING & TECHNOLOGY

Financial Aid: 505-835-5333 • E-mail: admission@admin.nmt.edu • Website: www.nmt.edu

## ADMISSIONS
*Very important factors considered include:* secondary school record, standardized test scores. *Other factors considered include:* class rank, extracurricular activities, talent/ability. SAT I or ACT required, ACT preferred. TOEFL required of all international applicants. High school diploma or GED is required. *High school units required/recommended:* 15 total required; 18 total recommended; 4 English required, 3 math required, 4 math recommended, 2 science required, 4 science recommended, 2 science lab required, 3 science lab recommended, 2 foreign language recommended, 2 social studies required, 3 social studies recommended, 1 history required, 3 elective required.

### The Inside Word
A 2.5 GPA and a 21 ACT score is far from stringent. This is one of those situations that call for serious self-examination. Are you really ready to take on the demands of a fairly solid technical institute? If you aren't sure, you should probably pass, even if you're admissible.

## FINANCIAL AID
*Students should submit:* FAFSA, institution's own financial aid form. Regular filing deadline is June 1. The Princeton Review suggests that all financial aid forms be submitted as soon as possible after January 1. *Need-based scholarships/grants offered:* Pell, SEOG, state scholarships/grants, private scholarships, the school's own gift aid. *Loan aid offered:* FFEL Subsidized Stafford, FFEL Unsubsidized Stafford, FFEL PLUS, Federal Perkins, state loans. Federal Work-Study Program available. Institutional employment available. Applicants will be notified of awards on a rolling basis beginning on or about April 1. Off-campus job opportunities are fair.

## FROM THE ADMISSIONS OFFICE
"More than a century old, New Mexico Tech has research programs at the cutting edge of today's technology. This is exciting for students because many of them get jobs working for professors or for one of our many research divisions, learning skills they will use in graduate schools or high-tech careers. Pulsars, thunderstorms, volcanoes, lightning, quasars, earthquakes, energetic materials, and caves are just a few of the areas we study. We also teach and work in areas of computer and information security, business management, and several fields of engineering. Many of our research divisions are known worldwide in their fields, including Magdalena Ridge Observatory, the Energetic Materials Research and Testing Center, and Langmuir Laboratory for Atmospheric Research. Our 2002 graduates with engineering degrees received starting salaries averaging $51,755, those with computer science degrees averaged $55,583, and those with degrees in both computer science and electrical engineering started at $63,333."

## SELECTIVITY

| | |
|---|---|
| Admissions Rating | 83 |
| # of applicants | 1,228 |
| % of applicants accepted | 62 |
| % of acceptees attending | 47 |

### FRESHMAN PROFILE
| | |
|---|---|
| Range SAT Verbal | 540-660 |
| Average SAT Verbal | 596 |
| Range SAT Math | 540-680 |
| Average SAT Math | 612 |
| Range ACT Composite | 24-29 |
| Average ACT Composite | 26 |
| Minimum TOEFL | 540 |
| Average HS GPA | 3.6 |
| % graduated top 10% of class | 39 |
| % graduated top 25% of class | 66 |
| % graduated top 50% of class | 90 |

### DEADLINES
| | |
|---|---|
| Priority admission | 3/1 |
| Regular admission | 8/1 |
| Nonfall registration? | yes |

### APPLICANTS ALSO LOOK AT AND OFTEN PREFER
Caltech
MIT
### AND SOMETIMES PREFER
Colorado School of Mines
U of New Mexico
### AND RARELY PREFER
New Mexico State
Arizona State

## FINANCIAL FACTS

| | |
|---|---|
| Financial Aid Rating | 90 |
| In-state tuition | $2,053 |
| Out-of-state tuition | $8,264 |
| Room and board | $4,218 |
| Books and supplies | $800 |
| Required fees | $858 |
| % frosh receiving aid | 29 |
| % undergrads receiving aid | 40 |
| Avg frosh grant | $4,600 |
| Avg frosh loan | $2,412 |

# NEW YORK UNIVERSITY

22 WASHINGTON SQUARE NORTH, NEW YORK, NY 10011 • ADMISSIONS: 212-998-4500 • FAX: 212-995-4902

## CAMPUS LIFE

★★★☆

| Quality of Life Rating | 88 |
|---|---|
| Type of school | private |
| Environment | urban |

### STUDENTS

| Total undergrad enrollment | 19,490 |
|---|---|
| % male/female | 40/60 |
| % from out of state | 51 |
| % from public high school | 72 |
| % live on campus | 56 |
| % in (# of) fraternities | 4 (13) |
| % in (# of) sororities | 2 (13) |
| % African American | 6 |
| % Asian | 15 |
| % Caucasian | 45 |
| % Hispanic | 7 |
| % international | 4 |
| # of countries represented | 137 |

### SURVEY SAYS . . .
Students love New York, NY
Great off-campus food
(Almost) everyone smokes
Ethnic diversity on campus
Great library
Campus feels safe
No one plays intramural sports
Very small frat/sorority scene
No one watches intercollegiate sports

## ACADEMICS

| Academic Rating | 89 |
|---|---|
| Calendar | semester |
| Student/faculty ratio | 12:1 |
| Avg lab size | 20-29 students |
| Avg reg class size | 10-19 students |

## STUDENTS SPEAK OUT

### Academics

Most colleges would be honored to have a single world-renowned academic department. Then again, most aren't New York University. The programs at NYU's Stern School of Business and the Tisch School of the Arts are among the best undergraduate programs in the country. NYU professors are "very intelligent, informed, and open-minded." They are both "witty" and "well-prepared" and, considering that many of them live in the city, "tend to be very accessible," though some students complain that, because of the university's size, profs occasionally get "lost in the crowd." Explains one student, "They are helpful in guiding students . . . to careers, internships, grad school programs, good restaurants, movies, hairdressers, and all the best deals that New York City has to offer." Undergrads also appreciate the fact that professors are often the authors of the textbooks used in class. A senior broadcast journalism major writes that though he harbors "a lifelong hatred towards school and education, I've enjoyed learning here." Students not interested in an academic culture need not apply since, according to one junior, "as a freshman, I began doing work people don't touch until grad school." Students get practice as the vociferous liberals they are when dealing with the administration, as they must be "persistent and demanding" in order to get things done. Students rave about online registration, though some complain that upper-level classes close too quickly, "often with the speed of Japan's bullet train."

### Life

"What do we do for fun?" a senior theater major asks. "We do New York." While studies are undeniably important, NYU is located in the heart of downtown Manhattan's Greenwich Village, within shouting distance of hundreds of restaurants, theaters, clubs, and other cultural opportunities. Guess what that means. "Life here is never dull or routine," a junior politics major writes, and "no student can say that she is bored." Students who wish to commune with nature spend time bike riding or inline skating in Central Park. Sports fans not only attend college basketball games on campus (the university's Division III women's basketball team is among the best in the nation), but can also choose from any of the city's professional baseball, basketball, football, and hockey teams. Numerous museums and theaters provide more cultural stimulation than a student can possibly absorb in four years. The city's extensive concert scene assures that both local and national acts can be found somewhere every night of the year. Though there are plenty of on-campus activities, students downplay their importance because of the numerous off-campus opportunities. The lack of a defined campus allows the school to become a part of the city, which, in turn, allows students to smoothly coexist with fellow city dwellers. The tension between towns and campuses that are evident at other universities are nowhere to be found at NYU. While on-campus housing is expensive, the "apartment-style dorms" are often looked upon wistfully by those who end up in almost-as-costly off-campus housing.

### Student Body

New York is one of the most diverse cities in the world and that doesn't exclude the student body of NYU. "Everyone here is very unique—some you love, some you hate." Students are individualistic and passionate, "but somehow this manages to bond us all," and students create close friendships, writes one senior musical theater major. "People are cool and unique," adds a sophomore. Students are "tolerant and open-minded" and develop neighborly relationships. Students see their peers as adventurous and focused, which "makes for some really interesting people." A junior English major advises, "If you're looking for an accepting community, this is it." If students have any complaints, it is that their peers are sometimes apathetic about campus life, and "as a result, school spirit is negligible." Still, it's unlikely that anyone looking for a diverse educational experience will easily find one that surpasses the one found at NYU.

374 ■ THE BEST 351 COLLEGES

# NEW YORK UNIVERSITY

FINANCIAL AID: 212-998-4444 • E-MAIL: ADMISSIONS@NYU.EDU • WEBSITE: WWW.NYU.EDU

## ADMISSIONS

*Very important factors considered include:* essays, secondary school record, standardized test scores. *Important factors considered include:* character/personal qualities, class rank, extracurricular activities, recommendations, talent/ability. *Other factors considered include:* alumni/ae relation, minority status, volunteer work, work experience. SAT I or ACT required. TOEFL required of all international applicants. High school diploma or GED is required. *High school units required/recommended:* 18 total required; 4 English required, 3 math required, 4 math recommended, 3 science required, 2 science lab required, 2 foreign language required, 3 foreign language recommended, 4 history required.

### The Inside Word

NYU is more selective than most large private universities but, except for a few particularly choosy programs, no more personal in its evaluation of candidates. A solid GPA and test scores go further toward getting in than anything else. Still, the university is very serious about projecting a highly selective image and it's dangerous to take your application too lightly. Since the completion of several major dormitories in the late 1980s, NYU has turned its attention to increasing the national profile of its student body. Applications have increased by more than half over the past four years.

## FINANCIAL AID

*Students should submit:* FAFSA, state aid form. Early decision applicants may submit an institutional form for an estimated award. Regular filing deadline is February 15. The Princeton Review suggests that all financial aid forms be submitted as soon as possible after January 1. *Need-based scholarships/grants offered:* Pell, SEOG, state scholarships/grants, private scholarships, the school's own gift aid. *Loan aid offered:* FFEL Subsidized Stafford, FFEL Unsubsidized Stafford, FFEL PLUS, Federal Perkins, Federal Nursing. Federal Work-Study Program available. Institutional employment available. Applicants will be notified of awards on a rolling basis beginning on or about April 1. Off-campus job opportunities are excellent.

## FROM THE ADMISSIONS OFFICE

"NYU is distinctive both in the quality of education we provide and in the exhilarating atmosphere in which our students study and learn. As an undergraduate in one of our seven small- to medium-size colleges, you will enjoy a small faculty/student ratio and a dynamic, challenging learning environment that encourages lively interaction between students and professors. At the same time, you will have available to you all the resources of a distinguished university dedicated to research and scholarship at the highest levels, including a curriculum that offers over 2,500 courses and 160 programs of study and a faculty that includes some of the most highly regarded scholars, scientists, and artists in the country. New York University is a vital, vibrant community. There is an aura of energy and excitement here, a sense that possibilities and opportunities are limited only by the number of hours in a day. The educational experience at NYU is intense, but varied and richly satisfying. You will be actively engaged in your own education, both in the classroom and beyond."

### SELECTIVITY

| | |
|---|---:|
| Admissions Rating | 90 |
| # of applicants | 29,581 |
| % of applicants accepted | 28 |
| % of acceptees attending | 40 |
| # accepting a place on wait list | 1,430 |
| % admitted from wait list | 13 |
| # of early decision applicants | 2,935 |
| % accepted early decision | 39 |

### FRESHMAN PROFILE

| | |
|---|---:|
| Range SAT Verbal | 620-710 |
| Average SAT Verbal | 672 |
| Range SAT Math | 630-720 |
| Average SAT Math | 666 |
| Range ACT Composite | 28-32 |
| Average ACT Composite | 29 |
| Minimum TOEFL | 600 |
| Average HS GPA | 3.7 |
| % graduated top 10% of class | 70 |
| % graduated top 25% of class | 93 |
| % graduated top 50% of class | 100 |

### DEADLINES

| | |
|---|---:|
| Early decision | 11/15 |
| Early decision notification | 12/15 |
| Priority admission | 11/15 |
| Regular admission | 1/15 |
| Regular notification | 4/1 |
| Nonfall registration? | yes |

### APPLICANTS ALSO LOOK AT AND OFTEN PREFER
Columbia
Barnard, U. Penn
Cornell U., Boston U.

### AND SOMETIMES PREFER
UCLA
UC—Berkeley
U. Michigan
U. Chicago, Yale

### AND RARELY PREFER
Hofstra, Rutgers U.

### FINANCIAL FACTS

| | |
|---|---:|
| Financial Aid Rating | 83 |
| Tuition | $26,646 |
| Room and board | $10,430 |
| Books and supplies | $450 |
| % frosh receiving aid | 61 |
| % undergrads receiving aid | 55 |
| Avg frosh grant | $18,444 |
| Avg frosh loan | $4,384 |

# NORTH CAROLINA STATE UNIVERSITY

Box 7103, Raleigh, NC 27695 • Admissions: 919-515-2434 • Fax: 919-515-5039

## CAMPUS LIFE

| | |
|---|---|
| Quality of Life Rating | 83 |
| Type of school | public |
| Environment | suburban |

### STUDENTS

| | |
|---|---|
| Total undergrad enrollment | 22,780 |
| % male/female | 58/42 |
| % from out of state | 7 |
| % from public high school | 92 |
| % live on campus | 31 |
| % in (# of) fraternities | 10 (29) |
| % in (# of) sororities | 9 (12) |
| % African American | 10 |
| % Asian | 5 |
| % Caucasian | 82 |
| % Hispanic | 2 |
| % international | 1 |
| # of countries represented | 110 |

### SURVEY SAYS . . .
High cost of living
Everyone loves the Wolfpack
Students love Raleigh, NC
Class discussions are rare
Athletic facilities are great
Ethnic diversity on campus
Large classes
Dorms are like dungeons

## ACADEMICS

| | |
|---|---|
| Academic Rating | 77 |
| Calendar | semester |
| Student/faculty ratio | 16:1 |
| Profs interesting rating | 91 |
| Profs accessible rating | 93 |
| % profs teaching UG courses | 100 |
| % classes taught by TAs | 7 |
| Avg lab size | 20-29 students |
| Avg reg class size | 20-29 students |

### MOST POPULAR MAJORS
Business administration/management
Computer science
Mechanical engineering

## STUDENTS SPEAK OUT

### Academics

North Carolina State is revamping its academic image after years of media focus on the university's athletic programs. Students confirm that the university's efforts are succeeding. One sophomore biology major gushes, "NC State is a great school. The faculty and professors are well prepared and outgoing." Overall, the students hold their professors in high regard. A first-year business major tells us that the professors are "very helpful and not bothered by student e-mails." Another freshman writes, "My math professor is a genius. He was actually able to explain everything so I understand." Most students (even those who are not engineering majors) cite the strength of the engineering program. However, one junior communications major admonishes that when it comes to the administration's concern for students, "if you aren't engineering, they don't care." A number of students applaud the "first-year college," a program that helps students with undeclared majors . . . well . . . select a major. Comments one sophomore, "The first-year college offered here at State is a great thing for freshmen coming in with an undecided major. It helped me a lot." Students praise the library and the overall beauty of the campus, but complain that many of the academic buildings need improvement. A majority of NC State students live off campus, and many of these commuter students complain about a lack of on-campus parking.

### Life

NC State is a member of the Atlantic Coast Conference, one of the most renowned athletic conferences in Division I sports. Accordingly, sports are a major part of life on campus. On-campus social activities are limited, and most students go off-campus to find their fun. As one sophomore engineering major writes, "Work is tough, but we cut loose on the weekends by drinking excessive amounts of alcohol at parties and bars." Many students echo that sentiment, adding that beer and hard liquor are their drinks of choice. The bars on Hillsborough Street are very popular, and local bands play in Raleigh. Students rate the on-campus food and dormitories as poor. The majority of students, however, live off-campus, where they enjoy a respectable array of dining opportunities.

### Student Body

The student body at NC State is "very open and friendly." Students who live on campus agree that "people always make eye contact and say 'hi.' " A sophomore history major attests, "NC State students are some of the most friendly and helpful people." Those who don't live on campus agree but warn that it's harder for commuters to meet their fellow students, no matter how amiable. "I live off campus, so besides friends I've previously made, I don't really get to know people," complains one. Students who live on campus agree that the campus is "tight-knit" and "very friendly," and "everyone seems to get along." Though racial and ethnic distinctions don't impede this initial friendliness, relations between different groups don't go much deeper than that. Still, a sophomore history major succinctly summarizes students on this diverse and friendly campus: "I have only met two people I dislike, and in a school this big, that's great."

# NORTH CAROLINA STATE UNIVERSITY

FINANCIAL AID: 919-515-2421 • E-MAIL: UNDERGRAD_ADMISSIONS@NCSU.EDU • WEBSITE: WWW.NCSU.EDU

## ADMISSIONS

*Very important factors considered include:* class rank, secondary school record, standardized test scores. *Other factors considered include:* alumni/ae relation, character/personal qualities, essays, extracurricular activities, geographical residence, minority status, recommendations, state residency, talent/ability, volunteer work, work experience. SAT I or ACT required. TOEFL required of all international applicants. High school diploma is required and GED is not accepted. *High school units required/recommended:* 15 total required; 20 total recommended; 4 English required, 3 math required, 4 math recommended, 3 science required, 1 science lab required, 2 foreign language required, 1 social studies required, 1 history required, 4 elective recommended.

### The Inside Word

Prospective students should be certain to investigate additional requirements for the college they wish to enter; universities that admit students to specific programs often vary standards significantly. Nonresidents will find it dramatically easier to get into NC State than to UNC, but application totals have gone up at State and eventually selectivity will follow.

## FINANCIAL AID

*Students should submit:* FAFSA, institution's own financial aid form. No deadline for regular filing. The Princeton Review suggests that all financial aid forms be submitted as soon as possible after January 1. *Need-based scholarships/grants offered:* Pell, SEOG, state scholarships/grants, private scholarships, the school's own gift aid. *Loan aid offered:* FFEL Subsidized Stafford, FFEL Unsubsidized Stafford, FFEL PLUS, Federal Perkins, state loans, college/university loans from institutional funds. Federal Work-Study Program available. Institutional employment available. Applicants will be notified of awards on a rolling basis beginning on or about March 1. Off-campus job opportunities are good.

## FROM THE ADMISSIONS OFFICE

"NC State is arguably the most popular university in the state, with more NC students seeking admission than at any other college or university. Over 12,000 students from across the nation seek one of the 3,600 available freshman spaces. Students choose NC State for its strong and varied academic programs (approximately 90), national reputation for excellence, low cost, location in Raleigh and the Research Triangle Park area, and very friendly atmosphere. Our students like the excitement of a large campus and the many opportunities it offers, such as Cooperative Education, Study Abroad, extensive honors programming, and theme residence halls. Each year, hundreds of NC State graduates are accepted into medical or law schools or other areas of advanced professional study. More corporate and government entities recruit graduates from NC State than from any other university in the United States. In 1999, IBM hired more graduates from NC State than from any other university in the United States."

## SELECTIVITY

| | |
|---|---|
| **Admissions Rating** | 83 |
| # of applicants | 12,133 |
| % of applicants accepted | 59 |
| % of acceptees attending | 51 |
| # accepting a place on wait list | 350 |
| % admitted from wait list | 14 |

### FRESHMAN PROFILE

| | |
|---|---|
| Range SAT Verbal | 530-630 |
| Average SAT Verbal | 578 |
| Range SAT Math | 560-670 |
| Average SAT Math | 615 |
| Range ACT Composite | 23-28 |
| Average ACT Composite | 25 |
| Minimum TOEFL | 550 |
| Average HS GPA | 4.0 |
| % graduated top 10% of class | 37 |
| % graduated top 25% of class | 78 |
| % graduated top 50% of class | 98 |

### DEADLINES

| | |
|---|---|
| Priority admission | 11/1 |
| Regular admission | 2/1 |
| Nonfall registration? | yes |

### APPLICANTS ALSO LOOK AT AND OFTEN PREFER

U. Tennessee—Knoxville
UNC—Chapel Hill

### AND SOMETIMES PREFER

Wake Forest
UNC—Charlotte
Catawba

### AND RARELY PREFER

Clemson
U. South Carolina—Columbia
Auburn
Georgia Tech.
Virginia Tech.

## FINANCIAL FACTS

| | |
|---|---|
| **Financial Aid Rating** | 84 |
| In-state tuition | $2,814 |
| Out-of-state tuition | $14,098 |
| Room and board | $5,917 |
| Books and supplies | $800 |
| Required fees | $1,015 |
| % frosh receiving aid | 38 |
| % undergrads receiving aid | 36 |
| Avg frosh grant | $5,738 |
| Avg frosh loan | $2,238 |

# NORTHEASTERN UNIVERSITY

360 HUNTINGTON AVENUE, 150 RICHARDS HALL, BOSTON, MA 02115 • ADMISSIONS: 617-373-2200 • FAX: 617-373-8780

## CAMPUS LIFE

| Quality of Life Rating | 76 |
|---|---|
| Type of school | private |
| Environment | urban |

### STUDENTS
| | |
|---|---|
| Total undergrad enrollment | 14,144 |
| % from out of state | 63 |
| % in (# of) fraternities | 4 (11) |
| % in (# of) sororities | 3 (8) |
| # of countries represented | 110 |

### SURVEY SAYS . . .
Students love Boston, MA
Athletic facilities are great
High cost of living
Ethnic diversity on campus
Popular college radio
Campus feels safe
Great off-campus food

## ACADEMICS

| Academic Rating | 76 |
|---|---|
| Calendar | semester |
| Student/faculty ratio | 16:1 |
| Profs interesting rating | 91 |
| Profs accessible rating | 92 |
| % profs teaching UG courses | 100 |
| Avg reg class size | 10-19 students |

### MOST POPULAR MAJORS
Business/commerce
Engineering
Health services/allied health

## STUDENTS SPEAK OUT

### Academics
The academic calendar at Northeastern comes in an unusual shape. Northeastern runs on four "short quarter terms" each year, rather than the two-semester model used by most universities. Yes, this means four healthy breaks a year, but at the expense of one large summer break. (If this is a concern, take note that the administration plans to convert to the semester model in the fall of 2003.) With an undergraduate population the size of a small city, "students must be self-starters and self-helpers to succeed here." On this note, some students wish the university administrators and professors would offer "more guidance." While students offer unified complaints about the accessibility of professors, they garnish their thoughts with universal praise for the campus's unique "co-op" program. This program is geared toward preparing students for the global marketplace by getting them into real-world internships and linking them up with a variety of resources, including alumni contacts. This experiential program is supplemented by "a good selection of classes" in the scholastic curriculum. Add all of this up and what you get on any given weekday is what one student calls "a revolving door—in and out all the time—between classes and co-op; students are always moving around."

### Life
It's probably not surprising that student life at Northeastern revolves around Boston at least as much as it does around the university itself. "There isn't much to do on campus," admits a junior. Despite having nearly 140 student organizations and a living (if not always lively) Greek system, Northeastern constantly spews its students into Boston's "clubs," "museums," "coffee shops," "movies," "concerts," sports "games," and . . . well . . . it's Boston—"you're bound to find something you like." In fact, one student says that it's "everything around campus" that "provides you with culture and social interactions." Of course, before you dive headfirst into the rich social life of Boston, you have to "make sure you can finance yourself." Boston, remember, is not a cheap city. Whether they stay on campus or venture into the city, NU students tend to "party fairly hard on weekends." They also "work relatively hard" on the weekdays. So when all's told, most students here are able to strike "a balance between social life and academics."

### Student Body
Situated in the heart of a city that has dozens of universities and professional schools, Northeastern students are not always distinguishable from the other young faces in the Boston crowd. Like Boston itself, Northeastern is composed of "a very diverse" student body. Because the students come from a variety of backgrounds, says one student, "everyone I meet has something new to offer." Although every tax bracket is certainly represented in the NU population, a noticeable core of students comes from a background of deep pockets. "Everyone here has money," a sophomore says, "and they're not afraid to show it." Among the nearly 14,000 undergraduate students, the most interaction occurs in dorms ("The best dorms in Boston," raves one student), classrooms, or, when applicable, campus groups. Overall, though, "everyone seems to only care about their own little clique." Cliques aside, Northeastern students are "very friendly and helpful, especially to freshman." And they plan to make a dent in the world when they leave the campus halls. Declares one undergrad, "Students here are very goal-oriented and know where they want to go."

# NORTHEASTERN UNIVERSITY

FINANCIAL AID: 617-373-3190 • E-MAIL: ADMISSIONS@NEU.EDU • WEBSITE: WWW.NEU.EDU

## ADMISSIONS
*Very important factors considered include:* secondary school record. *Important factors considered include:* character/personal qualities, class rank, essays, extracurricular activities, recommendations, standardized test scores, talent/ability. *Other factors considered include:* alumni/ae relation, geographical residence, minority status, volunteer work, work experience. SAT I or ACT required; SAT I preferred. TOEFL required of all international applicants. High school diploma or GED is required. *High school units required/recommended:* 17 total recommended; 4 English recommended, 3 math recommended, 3 science recommended, 2 science lab recommended, 2 foreign language recommended, 3 social studies recommended, 2 history recommended.

### The Inside Word
Northeastern is one of the moderately selective of Boston's mélange of colleges and universities, which makes it a popular safety for students who must go to school in Beantown. This translates into a large applicant pool and a lower acceptance rate than might otherwise be the case. The source of any true selectivity in NU's admissions process is a heavy reliance on the numbers: GPA, rank, and tests.

## FINANCIAL AID
*Students should submit:* FAFSA, CSS/Financial Aid PROFILE. No deadline for regular filing. The Princeton Review suggests that all financial aid forms be submitted as soon as possible after January 1. *Need-based scholarships/grants offered:* Pell, SEOG, state scholarships/grants, private scholarships, the school's own gift aid, Federal Nursing. *Loan aid offered:* FFEL Subsidized Stafford, FFEL Unsubsidized Stafford, FFEL PLUS, Federal Perkins, Federal Nursing, state loans, MEFA, TERI, Signature, Massachusetts No Interest Loan (NIL), CitiAssist. Federal Work-Study Program available. Institutional employment available. Applicants will be notified of awards on a rolling basis beginning on or about February 15. Off-campus job opportunities are excellent.

## FROM THE ADMISSIONS OFFICE
"Northeastern University's energy comes from its bright, ambitious students and their sense of purpose. In the classroom, in campus activities, and in the city of Boston, they make things happen. Backed by the three components of a Northeastern education—a solid liberal arts foundation, professional knowledge and skills, and on-the-job experience—they're ready to take on any challenge, anywhere. Through Northeastern's cooperative education (co-op) program, students alternate classroom learning with periods of full-time paid work related to their majors or interests. Northeastern students try out different jobs, build their résumés, earn money, and understand the connection between work and classes all before they graduate. And they do it in the heart of an exciting city, where culture, commerce, civic pride, and college students from around the globe are all a part of the mix."

---

### SELECTIVITY

| | |
|---|---|
| Admissions Rating | 77 |
| # of applicants | 17,037 |
| % of applicants accepted | 61 |
| % of acceptees attending | 28 |
| # accepting a place on wait list | 472 |

#### FRESHMAN PROFILE
| | |
|---|---|
| Range SAT Verbal | 520-620 |
| Average SAT Verbal | 565 |
| Range SAT Math | 540-640 |
| Average SAT Math | 588 |
| Range ACT Composite | 22-27 |
| Average ACT Composite | 24 |
| Minimum TOEFL | 550 |
| Average HS GPA | 3.2 |
| % graduated top 10% of class | 21 |
| % graduated top 25% of class | 57 |
| % graduated top 50% of class | 88 |

#### DEADLINES
| | |
|---|---|
| Priority admission | 2/15 |
| Nonfall registration? | yes |

#### APPLICANTS ALSO LOOK AT AND OFTEN PREFER
Suffolk University
Boston College
Boston University
University of Massachusetts—Boston
Worcester Polytechnic Institute
George Washington University

#### AND SOMETIMES PREFER
American University
University of Delaware
Rutgers University—New Brunswick

#### AND RARELY PREFER
University of Rhode Island

### FINANCIAL FACTS

| | |
|---|---|
| Financial Aid Rating | 88 |
| Tuition | $24,266 |
| Room and board | $5,160 |
| Books and supplies | $900 |
| Required fees | $201 |
| % frosh receiving aid | 67 |
| % undergrads receiving aid | 63 |
| Avg frosh grant | $12,321 |
| Avg frosh loan | $3,028 |

THE BEST 351 COLLEGES ■ 379

# NORTHWESTERN UNIVERSITY

PO Box 3060, 1801 Hinman Avenue, Evanston, IL 60208-3060 • Admissions: 847-491-7271

## CAMPUS LIFE

| | |
|---|---|
| Quality of Life Rating | 89 |
| Type of school | private |
| Environment | suburban |

### STUDENTS

| | |
|---|---|
| Total undergrad enrollment | 7,946 |
| % male/female | 47/53 |
| % from out of state | 74 |
| % from public high school | 76 |
| % live on campus | 65 |
| % in (# of) fraternities | 30 (23) |
| % in (# of) sororities | 40 (17) |
| % African American | 7 |
| % Asian | 14 |
| % Caucasian | 67 |
| % Hispanic | 6 |
| % international | 5 |
| # of countries represented | 46 |

### SURVEY SAYS . . .

Frats and sororities dominate social scene
Athletic facilities are great
Class discussions are rare
Great library
Everyone loves the Wildcats
Large classes
Student publications are popular
(Almost) no one listens to college radio
Campus difficult to get around

## ACADEMICS

| | |
|---|---|
| Academic Rating | 98 |
| Calendar | quarter |
| Student/faculty ratio | 7:1 |
| Profs interesting rating | 92 |
| Profs accessible rating | 96 |
| % profs teaching UG courses | 100 |
| % classes taught by TAs | 2 |

### MOST POPULAR MAJORS
Engineering
Economics
Journalism

## STUDENTS SPEAK OUT

### Academics

Considered by many an Ivy of the Midwest, Northwestern University is unarguably "an academically rigorous school" with an "awesome reputation" that "expects hard work from its students." Students warn that "academics here are very challenging, especially with the quarter system," which "makes the pace extremely hectic." Engineering, journalism, pre-medical studies, and the liberal arts departments are all well regarded, as is the "great theater program"—which, according to many, is "essentially a pre-professional program" that is uncommonly rigorous. Students caution that most of the professors here are among the "most important researchers in their fields" and that, while many are "genuinely interested in their students' performance" and "very generous with their time," others are "very research-oriented and lack teaching skills." During a given quarter, "it's likely that you'll take a class with the most enthusiastic and interesting person you've ever met and also one with a professor far inferior to your worst high school teacher." Fortunately, "the teacher evaluation information is excellent. There are so many classes to take here. Like anywhere, there are good and bad professors, but the evaluation system makes it easy to differentiate between them, and it's all online."

### Life

There are two schools of thought about the Northwestern social scene. The first, subscribed to by those who rarely venture off campus or outside Evanston, say that life at Northwestern is pleasant but unexceptional. They report that the Greeks occupy a central position on campus. The Greek system caters to every kind of student—even the ones who would never even consider joining a fraternity or sorority." These students also enjoy the school's "great theater program.... There are shows going up all the time. People here are amazingly talented, and I've seen a really diverse range of shows—from mainstage musical productions to small, no-budget plays, all for pretty cheap." Finally, they commend NU's "gorgeous" campus. The second school of thought, championed by those who simply cannot wait to get off campus and into Chicago, holds that Northwestern offers the best of all possible worlds. Not only does the school boast all the above-mentioned benefits, explains one student, but "going into Chicago is a popular weekend activity. Public transportation (the 'EL') is only a block from campus and takes you directly to some of the best shopping in the world," as well as to excellent museums, restaurants, and night life. Adds another, "In Evanston," there are "great restaurants within walking distance but not much in the way of entertainment, which is why you need Chicago!" Both groups agree that "studying is a large part of student life" and also that "people here are very busy. Everyone I know has a TON on their plate, i.e. work, very difficult classes, one to five clubs/organizations, executive board positions, volunteering, sports (varsity, club, or intramural) . . ."

### Student Body

Northwestern students admit that they are probably not America's coolest college kids. "It's a dork school—be forewarned," writes one student. "But it's not cutthroat or pretentious like our neighbors on the East." Even so, "there is so much pressure to succeed at everything and be involved in everything, and everyone here is so good at everything already. Because we were all overachievers and at the top of our classes in high school, we're bound to be disappointed when we realize that there are so many smarter people around us here at college." Many here are "pretty upper-, middle-class conservative," "Greek-loving, country-club types, generally talented, and lots of princess and book-smart dummies, with a few intellectual giants and truly outstanding human beings thrown in the bunch." Despite their sometimes hypercritical reviews of their peers, most students ultimately concede that their classmates are "great. They are all interesting, smart, and fun to talk to."

380 ■ THE BEST 351 COLLEGES

# NORTHWESTERN UNIVERSITY

FINANCIAL AID: 847-491-7400 • E-MAIL: UG-ADMISSION@NORTHWESTERN.EDU • WEBSITE: WWW.NORTHWESTERN.EDU

## ADMISSIONS
*Very important factors considered include:* class rank, essays, secondary school record, standardized test scores. *Important factors considered include:* character/personal qualities, extracurricular activities, recommendations, talent/ability. *Other factors considered include:* alumni/ae relation, interview, minority status, volunteer work, work experience. SAT I or ACT required. TOEFL required of all international applicants. *High school units required/recommended:* 16 total recommended; 4 English recommended, 4 math recommended, 2 science recommended, 2 science lab recommended, 2 foreign language recommended, 4 social studies recommended, 3 elective recommended.

## The Inside Word
Northwestern's applicant pool is easily among the best in the country. Candidates face both a rigorous evaluation by the admissions committee and serious competition from within the pool. The best approach (besides top grades and a strong personal background) is to take the committee up on their recommendations to visit the campus or interview with an alumnus/a and submit SAT II scores. The effort it takes to get in is well worth it.

## FINANCIAL AID
*Students should submit:* FAFSA, CSS/Financial Aid PROFILE, noncustodial (divorced/separated) parent's statement, business/farm supplement, parent and student federal tax returns. The Princeton Review suggests that all financial aid forms be submitted as soon as possible after January 1. *Need-based scholarships/grants offered:* Pell, SEOG, state scholarships/grants, private scholarships, the school's own gift aid. *Loan aid offered:* FFEL Subsidized Stafford, FFEL Unsubsidized Stafford, FFEL PLUS, Federal Perkins, college/university loans from institutional funds. Federal Work-Study Program available. Institutional employment available. Applicants will be notified of awards on or about April 15. Off-campus job opportunities are excellent.

## FROM THE ADMISSIONS OFFICE
"Consistent with its dedication to excellence, Northwestern provides both an educational and an extracurricular environment that enable its undergraduate students to become accomplished individuals and informed and responsible citizens. To the students in all its undergraduate schools, Northwestern offers liberal learning and professional education to help them gain the depth of knowledge that will empower them to become leaders in their professions and communities. Furthermore, Northwestern fosters in its students a broad understanding of the world in which we live as well as excellence in the competencies that transcend any particular field of study: writing and oral communication, analytical and creative thinking and expression, quantitative and qualitative methods of thinking."

### SELECTIVITY

| | |
|---|---|
| Admissions Rating | 99 |
| # of applicants | 14,283 |
| % of applicants accepted | 33 |
| % of acceptees attending | 43 |
| # accepting a place on wait list | 350 |
| # of early decision applicants | 960 |
| % accepted early decision | 53 |

### FRESHMAN PROFILE
| | |
|---|---|
| Range SAT Verbal | 640-730 |
| Average SAT Verbal | 675 |
| Range SAT Math | 660-750 |
| Average SAT Math | 703 |
| Range ACT Composite | 28-33 |
| Average ACT Composite | 30 |
| Minimum TOEFL | 600 |
| % graduated top 10% of class | 82 |
| % graduated top 25% of class | 96 |
| % graduated top 50% of class | 99 |

### DEADLINES
| | |
|---|---|
| Early decision | 11/1 |
| Early decision notification | 12/15 |
| Regular admission | 1/1 |
| Regular notification | 4/15 |
| Nonfall registration? | yes |

### APPLICANTS ALSO LOOK AT
**AND OFTEN PREFER**
Yale
Harvard
**AND SOMETIMES PREFER**
U. Chicago
Stanford
Princeton
Columbia
**AND RARELY PREFER**
DePaul
Marquette
Purdue U.—West Lafayette

### FINANCIAL FACTS

| | |
|---|---|
| Financial Aid Rating | 85 |
| Tuition | $28,404 |
| Room and board | $8,967 |
| Books and supplies | $1,326 |
| Required fees | $120 |
| % frosh receiving aid | 45 |
| % undergrads receiving aid | 44 |
| Avg frosh grant | $22,515 |
| Avg frosh loan | $2,660 |

# OBERLIN COLLEGE

101 North Professor Street, Oberlin, OH 44074 • Admissions: 440-775-8411 • Fax: 440-775-6905

## CAMPUS LIFE

| Quality of Life Rating | 73 |
|---|---|
| Type of school | private |
| Environment | rural |

### STUDENTS

| Total undergrad enrollment | 2,848 |
|---|---|
| % male/female | 45/55 |
| % from out of state | 89 |
| % from public high school | 66 |
| % live on campus | 72 |
| % African American | 8 |
| % Asian | 6 |
| % Caucasian | 81 |
| % Hispanic | 4 |
| % international | 6 |

### SURVEY SAYS . . .
Political activism is hot
Great library
Students don't get along with local community
Students aren't religious
Musical organizations are hot
Intercollegiate sports unpopular or nonexistent
Theater is popular

## ACADEMICS

| Academic Rating | 86 |
|---|---|
| Calendar | 4-1-4 |
| Student/faculty ratio | 10:1 |
| Profs interesting rating | 94 |
| Profs accessible rating | 97 |
| % profs teaching UG courses | 100 |
| Avg lab size | 10-19 students |
| Avg reg class size | 10-19 students |

### MOST POPULAR MAJORS
History
English language and literature
Biology/biological sciences

## STUDENTS SPEAK OUT

### Academics

With a "culture unlike any other" and a "commitment to developing well-rounded, free-thinking individuals," Oberlin College consistently ranks high among college students looking for a small, politically progressive, and academically challenging liberal arts school. Its highly respected music conservatory is a major draw, as are its "great double degree program," EXCO (Experimental College, where students teach courses for credit), and strong curriculum in both the arts and sciences. In a place where "students are smart and interesting, work is challenging," and there's "no red tape," it's no wonder Oberlin undergrads are so positive about their choice of college. Notes a senior, "The learning community is great, teachers are accessible, and there are great resources." The "fantastic" and "totally available" professors who "love teaching" play a big part in creating Oberlin's reputation of academic excellence. As for administration, though some claim that "the administration hates us," a senior takes the long view: "There is a lot of administration-student interaction. Students are very much involved in the politics on campus and way into creating the environment in which we learn. The administration tries to be responsive."

### Life

At a place where "most learning takes place at formal and informal discussions outside of class," it's not surprising that Oberlin undergrads have a lot to say on the subject of life at this tiny college. Writes a junior, "People think about everything, and basically, that's what we do for fun." Students are, for the most part, "aware and involved" so, as a senior points out, there's "lots of activism and challenges to the status quo." A first-year sees the typical "Obie" philosophizing a little differently, however, noting that "people spend a lot of time dwelling in the saturation of their white liberalism and patting themselves on the back for their guilt." All that and a BA too? As for social pursuits, Cleveland's only 45 minutes away, but most students' social lives revolve around campus with its myriad free or inexpensive "films, lectures, speakers, recitals, performances, art openings, and theme parties" (The Drag Ball headlines the year). There aren't any frats at Oberlin, but the OSCA co-ops "are a great alternative for food and living." As for letting off all that steam built up discussing identity politics and "overdramatic interpersonal dramas," there is a "substantial party and drug scene but no pressure to do either."

### Student Body

The "eclectic" and "diverse" as well as "friendly" people make Oberlin what it is, say students. Notes a junior, They're amazing, aggravating, intimidating, and intimate all at the same time. They help me to grow . . . ." And while these "open-minded" and "liberal-thinking" kids are well known for their left-of-center politics, just how left is left? A first-year explains, "The political affiliation bubble on your survey is not comprehensive enough. To the left of the 'left wing' option, there should be a bubble that says either 'radically leftist' or just 'Oberlin.'" On the other hand, one student tells us, "This is a very liberal school on the outside but I think an overwhelming amount of students are more moderate. There are conservatives [too], but they aren't as vocal." Of course, all that intense political discussion can lead to a few "closed-minded people unwilling to listen to others' points of view," but still, most like it that way.

# OBERLIN COLLEGE

FINANCIAL AID: 440-775-8142 • E-MAIL: COLLEGE.ADMISSIONS@OBERLIN.EDU • WEBSITE: WWW.OBERLIN.EDU

## ADMISSIONS

*Very important factors considered include:* class rank, secondary school record, standardized test scores. *Important factors considered include:* character/personal qualities, essays, extracurricular activities, recommendations, talent/ability. *Other factors considered include:* alumni/ae relation, geographical residence, interview, minority status, state residency, volunteer work, work experience. SAT I or ACT required. TOEFL required of all international applicants. High school diploma or GED is required. *High school units required/recommended:* 4 English recommended, 4 math recommended, 3 science recommended, 3 science lab recommended, 3 foreign language recommended, 3 social studies recommended.

## The Inside Word

The admissions process at Oberlin is especially demanding for candidates to the Conservatory of Music, which seeks only the best-prepared musicians for its excellent program. All applicants to the college face a thorough and rigorous review of their credentials by the admissions committee regardless of their choice of major. Take our advice—visit the campus to interview, and put extra effort into admissions essays.

## FINANCIAL AID

*Students should submit:* FAFSA, CSS/Financial Aid PROFILE, noncustodial (divorced/separated) parent's statement, business/farm supplement. Regular filing deadline is February 15. The Princeton Review suggests that all financial aid forms be submitted as soon as possible after January 1. *Need-based scholarships/grants offered:* Pell, SEOG, state scholarships/grants, private scholarships, the school's own gift aid. *Loan aid offered:* Direct Subsidized Stafford, Direct Unsubsidized Stafford, Direct PLUS, Federal Perkins, college/university loans from institutional funds. Federal Work-Study Program available. Institutional employment available. Applicants will be notified of awards on or about April 15. Off-campus job opportunities are good.

## FROM THE ADMISSIONS OFFICE

"Oberlin College is an independent, coeducational, liberal arts college. It comprises two divisions, the College of Arts and Sciences, with roughly 2,300 students enrolled, and the Conservatory of Music, with about 500 students. Students in both divisions share one campus; they also share residence and dining halls as part of one academic community. Many students take courses in both divisions. Oberlin awards the Bachelor of Arts and the Bachelor of Music degrees; a five-year program leads to both degrees. Selected master's degrees are offered in the Conservatory. Oberlin is located 35 miles southwest of Cleveland. Founded in 1833, Oberlin College is highly selective and dedicated to recruiting students from diverse backgrounds. Oberlin was the first coeducational college in the United States, as well as a historic leader in educating black students. Oberlin's 440-acre campus provides outstanding facilities, modern scientific laboratories, a large computing center, a library unexcelled by other college libraries for the depth and range of its resources, and the Allen Memorial Art Museum."

## SELECTIVITY

| | |
|---|---:|
| Admissions Rating | 91 |
| # of applicants | 5,934 |
| % of applicants accepted | 33 |
| % of acceptees attending | 38 |
| # accepting a place on wait list | 585 |
| % admitted from wait list | 19 |
| # of early decision applicants | 341 |
| % accepted early decision | 75 |

### FRESHMAN PROFILE

| | |
|---|---:|
| Range SAT Verbal | 630-740 |
| Average SAT Verbal | 691 |
| Range SAT Math | 610-710 |
| Average SAT Math | 659 |
| Range ACT Composite | 26-31 |
| Average ACT Composite | 30 |
| Minimum TOEFL | 600 |
| Average HS GPA | 3.5 |
| % graduated top 10% of class | 63 |
| % graduated top 25% of class | 93 |
| % graduated top 50% of class | 99 |

### DEADLINES

| | |
|---|---:|
| Early decision | 11/15 |
| Early decision notification | 12/20 |
| Regular admission | 1/15 |
| Regular notification | 4/1 |

### APPLICANTS ALSO LOOK AT AND OFTEN PREFER
Yale
Swarthmore
Wesleyan
Stanford
Brown
### AND SOMETIMES PREFER
Carleton
Haverford, Tufts
Grinnell, Williams
### AND RARELY PREFER
Connecticut

## FINANCIAL FACTS

| | |
|---|---:|
| Financial Aid Rating | 83 |
| Tuition | $27,880 |
| Room and board | $6,830 |
| Books and supplies | $734 |
| Required fees | $170 |
| % frosh receiving aid | 56 |
| % undergrads receiving aid | 56 |
| Avg frosh grant | $23,700 |
| Avg frosh loan | $4,000 |

THE BEST 351 COLLEGES ■ 383

# Occidental College

1600 Campus Road, Office of Admission, Los Angeles, CA 90041 • Admissions: 323-259-2700 • Fax: 323-341-4875

## CAMPUS LIFE

| | |
|---|---|
| **Quality of Life Rating** | **84** |
| Type of school | private |
| Environment | suburban |

### STUDENTS

| | |
|---|---|
| Total undergrad enrollment | 1,802 |
| % male/female | 42/58 |
| % from out of state | 45 |
| % from public high school | 60 |
| % live on campus | 70 |
| % in (# of) fraternities | 7 (2) |
| % in (# of) sororities | 5 (2) |
| % African American | 7 |
| % Asian | 14 |
| % Caucasian | 56 |
| % Hispanic | 14 |
| % international | 4 |
| # of countries represented | 27 |

### SURVEY SAYS . . .
Theater is hot
Student publications are ignored
Classes are small
No one cheats
Political activism is hot
Ethnic diversity on campus
Athletic facilities need improving
Diverse students interact

## ACADEMICS

| | |
|---|---|
| **Academic Rating** | **94** |
| Calendar | semester |
| Student/faculty ratio | 11:1 |
| Profs interesting rating | 94 |
| Profs accessible rating | 98 |
| % profs teaching UG courses | 100 |
| Avg lab size | 10-19 students |
| Avg reg class size | 10-19 students |

## STUDENTS SPEAK OUT

### Academics

A small liberal arts college in a huge city, Occidental ("Oxy" to cognoscenti) students claim that at their school, "the academics are tops in the nation." At the heart of an Occidental education is close interaction between students and faculty. "I'm constantly amazed at how much professors—who, by and large, are incredibly intelligent, capable instructors—take a genuine interest in our progress as students," explains a student. Aside from completing classes in their majors, students are required to take part in the so-called Core Program. According to the college, this program, which is so extensive that students often need two years to wrap it up, is a collection of courses that promotes "skills such as clear and effective writing, logical argument, critical reading, and an appreciation of the evolution of world cultures." Science students tell us that while Oxy may be small and intimate, it offers many of the resources you'd expect to find only at a larger institution. "Oxy has the best undergraduate research program for schools of its size," contends one young scientist, "with over 40 students receiving funding for summer research projects." Other perks at Oxy include joint degree or exchange programs with Cal Tech, the Art Center College of Design, and the Columbia University School of Law. On the flipside, the college falls short in areas like study abroad and making "the application process so confusing and exclusive that many students are discouraged from even applying." Students have mixed opinions on the folks running the school. While some say the administration "ain't really nice to students," others counter that "the administrators are constantly working to make sure that students have a well-rounded experience here."

### Life

Oxy sits on a "hillside facing West" in the Eagle Rock section of northeast L.A. Not surprisingly, students cite the college's location as one of its prime benefits. "There's a lot to do off campus," raves a student. "Clubs, Hollywood, Universal City, Old Town Pasadena, Burbank theatres are all within half an hour from campus." Eagle Rock itself "is not the most exciting place," but campus life provides "plenty of opportunities" for students who don't feel like battling the ceaseless L.A. traffic. Aside from student organizations and events, community service is a major component of an Oxy student's out-of-class life. Almost half of all undergrads participate in the college's Center for Community-Based Learning, which reaches out to the area around campus. Though only about 10 percent belong to Greek organizations, Greek life "provides most of the social life" on campus. Sometimes students will party in their residence halls, but often they're looking for an excuse to get out of them. "Most of the dorms are 40-plus years old and really show their age," explains one student. "Only [three] have air-conditioning and it gets over 100 [degrees] for sustained periods of time at the beginning and end of each school year." Another popular destination is the library: "Classes are pretty hard here, so many students spend a lot of time studying."

### Student Body

At Occidental College, "the people are so diverse and there's so much to do in Los Angeles that there's no one thing that ties everyone together." One student declares with certainty, "I have never encountered such a diverse group of people in my life." Students here hail from a variety of backgrounds, including sizable Asian and Hispanic populations. One common thread that binds these students together is their liberal leaning. "Heaven help you if you're a Republican," writes a student. There are about 15 liberal political groups on campus, but when a pocket of conservative students tried to start a political club recently, "they were booed and publicly criticized for it." Overall, students have trouble pinning a description on their fellow classmates. "Let's just say they're all unique," concludes one. "Intelligent, articulate, laid back, supportive, and completely insane."

384 ■ THE BEST 351 COLLEGES

# OCCIDENTAL COLLEGE

FINANCIAL AID: 323-259-2548 • E-MAIL: ADMISSION@OXY.EDU • WEBSITE: WWW.OXY.EDU

## ADMISSIONS
*Very important factors considered include:* secondary school record, extracurricular activities, volunteer work, work experience. *Important factors considered include:* character/personal qualities, class rank, recommendations, standardized test scores, essay. *Other factors considered include:* alumni/ae relation, geographical residence, minority status, interview, talent/ability. SAT I or ACT required; SAT II recommended. TOEFL required of all international applicants. High school diploma or GED is required. *High school units required/recommended:* 4 English recommended, 4 math recommended, 3 science recommended, 2 science lab recommended, 3 foreign language recommended, 2 social studies recommended, 2 history recommended.

## *The Inside Word*
Students who are considering Occidental, or any other college with a rigorous core curriculum, should take five full academic courses a year straight through to graduation from high school. Such work not only gives the admissions committee solid evidence of your ability to handle Oxy's core requirements; it will make completing them much less painful as well.

## FINANCIAL AID
*Students should submit:* FAFSA, CSS/Financial Aid PROFILE, state aid form, noncustodial (divorced/separated) parent's statement, business/farm supplement. Regular filing deadline is February 1. The Princeton Review suggests that all financial aid forms be submitted as soon as possible after January 1. Federal Work-Study Program available. Institutional employment available. Applicants will be notified of awards on or about April 1. Off-campus job opportunities are good.

## FROM THE ADMISSIONS OFFICE
"The college is committed to a philosophy of total education. Intellectual capability is a dominant component, but is conceived of as one dimension in a process that includes and stresses personal, ethical, social, and political growth toward maturation as well. The high percentage of students in residence at the college work toward the achievement of this objective. Successful Occidental students are self-motivated, independent-minded, and intellectually talented people. They base their judgments upon respect for evidence, ideas, and a deep concern for values, both private and public. They are alert to the possibilities of betterment in themselves, their college, and their society."

---

### SELECTIVITY

| | |
|---|---:|
| Admissions Rating | 88 |
| # of applicants | 4,174 |
| % of applicants accepted | 43 |
| % of acceptees attending | 26 |
| # accepting a place on wait list | 252 |
| % admitted from wait list | 5 |

### FRESHMAN PROFILE
| | |
|---|---:|
| Range SAT Verbal | 580-670 |
| Average SAT Verbal | 630 |
| Range SAT Math | 590-680 |
| Average SAT Math | 630 |
| Minimum TOEFL | 600 |
| Average HS GPA | 3.8 |
| % graduated top 10% of class | 63 |
| % graduated top 25% of class | 93 |
| % graduated top 50% of class | 100 |

### DEADLINES
| | |
|---|---:|
| Early decision | 11/15 |
| Early decision notification | 12/15 |
| Regular admission | 1/15 |
| Regular notification | 4/1 |

### APPLICANTS ALSO LOOK AT AND OFTEN PREFER
Stanford
UCLA
Pomona
UC Berkeley
USC

### AND SOMETIMES PREFER
Claremont McKenna
Macalester

### FINANCIAL FACTS

| | |
|---|---:|
| Financial Aid Rating | 90 |
| Tuition | $27,734 |
| Room and board | $7,823 |
| Books and supplies | $870 |
| Required fees | $528 |
| % frosh receiving aid | 65 |
| % undergrads receiving aid | 74 |
| Avg frosh grant | $22,431 |
| Avg frosh loan | $3,225 |

# OGLETHORPE UNIVERSITY

4484 PEACHTREE ROAD, NE, ATLANTA, GA 30319 • ADMISSIONS: 404-364-8307 • FAX: 404-364-8491

## CAMPUS LIFE

| | |
|---|---|
| Quality of Life Rating | 85 |
| Type of school | private |
| Environment | suburban |

### STUDENTS

| | |
|---|---|
| Total undergrad enrollment | 1,037 |
| % male/female | 34/66 |
| % from out of state | 44 |
| % from public high school | 77 |
| % live on campus | 66 |
| % in (# of) fraternities | 30 (4) |
| % in (# of) sororities | 20 (3) |
| % African American | 21 |
| % Asian | 4 |
| % Caucasian | 70 |
| % Hispanic | 3 |
| % international | 6 |
| # of countries represented | 32 |

### SURVEY SAYS . . .
Students love Atlanta, GA
Theater is hot
Frats and sororities dominate social scene
Classes are small
Great off-campus food
Lousy food on campus
Library needs improving
Political activism is (almost) nonexistent

## ACADEMICS

| | |
|---|---|
| Academic Rating | 86 |
| Calendar | semester |
| Student/faculty ratio | 12:1 |
| Profs interesting rating | 94 |
| Profs accessible rating | 97 |
| % profs teaching UG courses | 100 |
| Avg reg class size | 10-19 students |

## STUDENTS SPEAK OUT

### Academics

Students agree that "Oglethorpe is unique because of its small size," which facilitates personal contact with and close mentoring from professors. "The class sizes are great; it's almost like it's only you and the professor. It's a better learning environment," brags one undergraduate. Of course, the school's size also has its drawbacks: "Because OU is small, you can't avoid the bad professors," complains one pre-med. Warns another student, "The course catalog is thinner than the coupon book given in the Sunday paper." Some students point out that the school has recently addressed its curricular shortcomings by allowing students to take classes at any of 18 other schools in the Atlanta Regional Consortium for Higher Education; as one put it, "Everything that Oglethorpe lacks academically has been remedied by cross registration with Tech." OU's core curriculum engenders strong feelings on both sides; those who hate it really hate it, but those who love it rave about it just as adamantly. Writes one student, "I have grown intellectually here at Oglethorpe more than I imagined I would, and much of that is due to the unique core curriculum here." Students also appreciate the fact that "every student has the option to make what they want out of their Oglethorpe experience, as the school leaves individuals to make many decisions for themselves."

### Life

Many students agree that "social life at Oglethorpe is virtually nonexistent." Reports one undergrad, "Everyone leaves during the weekend, and the atmosphere is pretty dead." The chief culprit: Atlanta, "a great place, but it sucks the life out of OU as soon as the school week ends." A glass-half-full type writes, "Students have to leave campus to really have a great time, but I think that is a good thing. We really have to learn about Atlanta to have a good time." Some students see another, equally pressing problem here. Explains one, "Oglethorpe has no school spirit because there is no rallying point." "There is no football team, and all the other sports have weak followings. Parties on campus are slowly dropping off the social scene." While "there are fraternity parties on campus that Greek students usually attend, the campus is so small that these parties are attended by the same students every time and can get quite boring." Some report that "there is a current push to improve campus activity on the weekends. . . . Steps are being taken and I see the situation improving." Whether these efforts will bear fruit, however, remains to be seen. "Greek life is very popular on [this] small campus," but students also note that "there is no pressure to join and not really any division between Greeks and non-Greeks. There are so many organizations that people can join that no one group dominates." Many students complain that "the food is the worst stuff on Earth . . . . If I could improve anything about the school, I would improve the food."

### Student Body

With a "majority made up of nice southern hospitable people," the Oglethorpe student body exudes a cordial vibe. Reports one student, "Everyone is friendly . . . . [It is, however,] hard to really get to know people because there are a lot of tight cliques." Warns one undergrad, "For the most part, students at OU are friendly, caring, and supportive. An air of snobbery can be detected at times, which only comes with the territory of a private school." Diversity remains an issue here; notes one student, "The students all seem nice and caring, but they do not represent a very diverse cross-section of races, religions, or nationality." Adds another, "As an African American female student, I often find myself providing the only minority perspective in many of my classes." Students are largely "conservative and Republican" and "are very passionate about issues here, and they have no problem expressing themselves."

386 ■ THE BEST 351 COLLEGES

# OGLETHORPE UNIVERSITY

FINANCIAL AID: 404-364-8356 • E-MAIL: ADMISSIONS@OGLETHORPE.EDU • WEBSITE: WWW.OGLETHORPE.EDU

## ADMISSIONS
*Very important factors considered include:* essays, interview, secondary school record. *Important factors considered include:* standardized test scores. *Other factors considered include:* alumni/ae relation, character/personal qualities, class rank, extracurricular activities, recommendations, talent/ability, volunteer work, work experience. SAT I or ACT required. High school diploma or GED is required. *High school units required/recommended:* 4 English required, 3 math required, 4 math recommended, 2 science required, 3 science recommended, 2 foreign language recommended, 3 social studies required, 4 social studies recommended.

## The Inside Word
With rising national interest in the South, it won't be long before the academic strength found at Oglethorpe attracts wider attention and more applicants. At present, it's much easier to gain admission here than at many universities of similar quality. Go to Atlanta for a campus interview—you'll leave impressed.

## FINANCIAL AID
*Students should submit:* FAFSA, institution's own financial aid form, state aid form. No deadline for regular filing. The Princeton Review suggests that all financial aid forms be submitted as soon as possible after January 1. *Need-based scholarships/grants offered:* Pell, SEOG, state scholarships/grants, private scholarships, the school's own gift aid. *Loan aid offered:* Direct Subsidized Stafford, Direct Unsubsidized Stafford, Direct PLUS, FFEL Subsidized Stafford, FFEL Unsubsidized Stafford, FFEL PLUS, Federal Perkins. Federal Work-Study Program available. Institutional employment available. Applicants will be notified of awards on a rolling basis beginning on or about January 1. Off-campus job opportunities are excellent.

## FROM THE ADMISSIONS OFFICE
"Promising students and outstanding teachers come together at Oglethorpe University in an acclaimed program of liberal arts and sciences. Here you'll find an active intellectual community on a beautiful English Gothic campus just 10 miles from the center of Atlanta, capital of the Southeast, site of the 1996 Summer Olympics, and home to 4 million people. If you want challenging academics, the opportunity to work closely with your professors, and the stimulation of a great metropolitan area, consider Oglethorpe, a national liberal arts college in a world-class city."

### SELECTIVITY

| | |
|---|---|
| Admissions Rating | 85 |
| # of applicants | 602 |
| % of applicants accepted | 90 |
| % of acceptees attending | 35 |

#### FRESHMAN PROFILE
| | |
|---|---|
| Range SAT Verbal | 560-680 |
| Average SAT Verbal | 617 |
| Range SAT Math | 540-650 |
| Average SAT Math | 603 |
| Range ACT Composite | 23-29 |
| Average ACT Composite | 26 |
| Minimum TOEFL | 550 |
| Average HS GPA | 3.7 |
| % graduated top 10% of class | 43 |
| % graduated top 25% of class | 73 |
| % graduated top 50% of class | 99 |

#### DEADLINES
| | |
|---|---|
| Priority admission | 12/30 |
| Nonfall registration? | yes |

#### APPLICANTS ALSO LOOK AT
**AND OFTEN PREFER**
Emory
Florida State

**AND SOMETIMES PREFER**
U. Georgia
U. of the South
Furman
Georgia Tech.
Vanderbilt

**AND RARELY PREFER**
Mercer
Berry

### FINANCIAL FACTS

| | |
|---|---|
| Financial Aid Rating | 91 |
| Tuition | $18,990 |
| Room and board | $6,360 |
| Books and supplies | $600 |
| Required fees | $450 |
| % frosh receiving aid | 66 |
| % undergrads receiving aid | 61 |
| Avg frosh grant | $11,018 |
| Avg frosh loan | $2,934 |

# Ohio Northern University

525 South Main Street, Ada, OH 45810 • Admissions: 419-772-2260 • Fax: 419-772-2313

## CAMPUS LIFE

| | |
|---|---|
| Quality of Life Rating | 80 |
| Type of school | private |
| Affiliation | Methodist |
| Environment | rural |

### STUDENTS

| | |
|---|---|
| Total undergrad enrollment | 2,281 |
| % male/female | 53/47 |
| % from out of state | 12 |
| % live on campus | 60 |
| % in (# of) fraternities | 25 (8) |
| % in (# of) sororities | 22 (4) |
| % African American | 2 |
| % Asian | 1 |
| % Caucasian | 96 |
| % Hispanic | 1 |
| % international | 1 |
| # of countries represented | 15 |

### SURVEY SAYS . . .
Frats and sororities dominate social scene
Athletic facilities are great
Classes are small
Great computer facilities
Student publications are ignored
Lousy off-campus food
Students don't like Ada, OH
Students are very religious
Low cost of living
Lousy food on campus

## ACADEMICS

| | |
|---|---|
| Academic Rating | 80 |
| Calendar | quarter |
| Student/faculty ratio | 13:1 |
| Profs interesting rating | 92 |
| Profs accessible rating | 93 |
| % profs teaching UG courses | 100 |
| Avg reg class size | 10-19 students |

### MOST POPULAR MAJORS
Biology/biological sciences
Pharmacy (PharmD, BS/BPharm)
Industrial production technologies/technicians

## STUDENTS SPEAK OUT

### Academics
" 'Large enough to challenge, small enough to care' applies 100 percent at ONU!" With an average class size of under 25, students benefit from "small classes" in which professors "make [an] effort to get to know each student." Because professors take such an interest, one junior says, they "make me want to do well!" Despite being a small university, ONU offers over 60 majors and "lots of variety in classes." And the curriculum is challenging. "I didn't have to work hard in high school," a freshman reports, "but I do here!" This combination of rigor, attention, and academic variety means that "Ohio Northern has a lot to offer" the dedicated student. And after the student days are over, ONU invites its students into a web of professional and alumni networks. This prompts one senior to write that a student who decides to attend ONU "can have the opportunities to become a leader in today's world."

### Life
Before you sign on at ONU, you should be aware that "Ada is not a booming metropolis." With just more than 5,000 residents in town, the undergrad and law-school population (which totals almost 3,300) bears the burden of finding its own fun. And "there is fun to be had," one sophomore says, "it just depends on how creative you are." Many Polar Bears find their entertainment through activities sponsored by the "SPC (Student Planning Committee), sororities, fraternities, or service organizations." Other times, students will venture into the town for "bowling, movies," or, when they're feeling especially adventurous, to the Lima Mall, in nearby Lima, a town of over 40,000. Parties are also part of the university portrait here—particularly "on Tuesday nights and weekends." But don't count on having a few too many drinks and inviting a member of the opposite sex back to your room for a little late-night, um, bonding. "Visitation hours are ridiculous and outdated," gripes a freshman student, referring to the university policy that says that guys can only go into girls' rooms, and vice versa, from 10 A.M. to 11 P.M., Sunday through Thursday, and 10 A.M. to 1 A.M. on Friday and Saturday. If this bothers you, here's some good news: the university is now reconsidering this policy. At the moment, there's even one "experimental" residential hall with 24-hour access for all.

### Student Body
Ohio Northern University is a private institution with liberal arts and professional programs that's affiliated with the United Methodist Church. Not everyone who goes here is Methodist, though, and some students notice that the so-called " 'religious' students and 'nonreligious' students don't mix very much." But when you look at the big picture, "all students are friendly and seem to get along well with one another." ONU has a "pretty conservative, uniform" student body, though you're still bound to run into "diverse personalities" all over campus. Personalities, many students admit, are perhaps the only signs of diversity on campus. "I wish we had more diversity," one student complains. "Everyone is upper-middle class, white, and a science or engineering major!" says another. But they're also a "friendly" group, which is important when you're at a "small school" in a small Ohio town. In an undergraduate pool of about 3,000, "the majority of students know each other," and, with the dual spirits of competition and cooperation at work, there's a vibrant "atmosphere created by its students." One freshman admits, "I was so worried coming here because I didn't know anyone, but it's been great!"

# OHIO NORTHERN UNIVERSITY

FINANCIAL AID: 419-772-2272 • E-MAIL: ADMISSIONS-UG@ONU.EDU • WEBSITE: WWW.ONU.EDU

## ADMISSIONS
*Very important factors considered include:* secondary school record, standardized test scores. *Important factors considered include:* class rank, extracurricular activities, interview. *Other factors considered include:* alumni/ae relation, character/personal qualities, essays, minority status, recommendations, talent/ability, volunteer work, work experience. SAT I or ACT required. TOEFL required of all international applicants. High school diploma or GED is required. *High school units required/recommended:* 16 total required; 22 total recommended; 4 English required, 2 math required, 4 math recommended, 2 science required, 3 science recommended, 2 science lab required, 2 foreign language recommended, 2 social studies required, 3 social studies recommended, 2 history required, 4 elective required.

## The Inside Word
Solid grades from high school are a pretty sure ticket for admission to Ohio Northern. Students who are above average academically are in good positions to take advantage of a very large number of no-need scholarships.

## FINANCIAL AID
*Students should submit:* FAFSA, institution's own financial aid form. Regular filing deadline is June 1. The Princeton Review suggests that all financial aid forms be submitted as soon as possible after January 1. *Need-based scholarships/grants offered:* Pell, SEOG, state scholarships/grants, private scholarships, the school's own gift aid. *Loan aid offered:* FFEL Subsidized Stafford, FFEL Unsubsidized Stafford, FFEL PLUS, Federal Perkins, college/university loans from institutional funds, alternative loans, Federal Health Professions Loan. Federal Work-Study Program available. Institutional employment available. Applicants will be notified of awards on a rolling basis beginning on or about February 15. Off-campus job opportunities are good.

## FROM THE ADMISSIONS OFFICE
"Ohio Northern's purpose is to help students develop into self-reliant, mature men and women capable of clear and logical thinking and sensitive to the higher values of truth, beauty, and goodness. ONU selects its student body from among those students possessing characteristics congruent with the institution's objectives. Generally, a student must be prepared to use the resources of the institution to achieve personal and educational goals."

### SELECTIVITY

| | |
|---|---|
| Admissions Rating | 78 |
| # of applicants | 2,469 |
| % of applicants accepted | 89 |
| % of acceptees attending | 34 |

### FRESHMAN PROFILE
| | |
|---|---|
| Range SAT Verbal | 510-610 |
| Average SAT Verbal | 560 |
| Range SAT Math | 530-650 |
| Average SAT Math | 590 |
| Range ACT Composite | 23-28 |
| Average ACT Composite | 25 |
| Minimum TOEFL | 550 |
| Average HS GPA | 3.6 |
| % graduated top 10% of class | 40 |
| % graduated top 25% of class | 69 |
| % graduated top 50% of class | 90 |

### DEADLINES
| | |
|---|---|
| Priority admission | 12/1 |
| Regular admission | 8/15 |
| Nonfall registration? | yes |

### APPLICANTS ALSO LOOK AT AND SOMETIMES PREFER
Miami University
Ohio State University–Columbus
Wittenberg University
Bowling Green State
University of Toledo

### FINANCIAL FACTS

| | |
|---|---|
| Financial Aid Rating | 89 |
| Tuition | $24,935 |
| Room and board | $6,030 |
| Books and supplies | $900 |
| Required fees | $210 |
| % frosh receiving aid | 86 |
| % undergrads receiving aid | 83 |

# OHIO STATE UNIVERSITY—COLUMBUS

ENARSON HALL, 154 W. 12TH AVENUE, COLUMBUS, OH 43210 • ADMISSIONS: 614-292-3980 • FAX: 614-292-4818

## CAMPUS LIFE

| | |
|---|---|
| Quality of Life Rating | 78 |
| Type of school | public |
| Environment | urban |

### STUDENTS
| | |
|---|---|
| Total undergrad enrollment | 36,855 |
| % male/female | 52/48 |
| % from out of state | 11 |
| % from public high school | 88 |
| % live on campus | 24 |
| % in (# of) fraternities | 5 (33) |
| % in (# of) sororities | 6 (22) |
| % African American | 9 |
| % Asian | 6 |
| % Caucasian | 81 |
| % Hispanic | 2 |
| % international | 4 |
| # of countries represented | 89 |

### SURVEY SAYS . . .
Students are cliquish
Lots of beer drinking
Everyone loves the Buckeyes
(Almost) everyone smokes
Lots of classroom discussion
(Almost) everyone plays intramural sports
Ethnic diversity on campus
Student publications are popular
Lab facilities are great

## ACADEMICS

| | |
|---|---|
| Academic Rating | 67 |
| Calendar | quarter |
| Student/faculty ratio | 13:1 |
| Avg lab size | 20-29 students |
| Avg reg class size | 10-19 students |

### MOST POPULAR MAJORS
English language and literature
Biology/biological sciences
Psychology

## STUDENTS SPEAK OUT

### Academics
At a school "probably best known for football," many students agree that Ohio State "is growing in academic strength." Courses "emphasize critical thinking," and "the school offers every imaginable class." It can, however, be "difficult to get into the classes that you want and need. I'm even an honors student with priority scheduling, and I have problems." Another student writes, "More classes should be available so the freshman class is not shut out." Some undergraduates describe professors as "devoted to teaching" and "very intelligent and helpful," while others point out that "it is difficult to be in contact with some professors due to the amount of research that goes on here." But when professors are unavailable, "TAs are very easy to get in touch with." Advising seems to be a case-by-case matter at OSU. One student reports, "My advisor has assisted me in deciding on my major, and she set me up with a mentor." But others comment, "Students are forced to find out much more for themselves," prompting the widespread sentiment, "No wonder everyone takes five years to graduate." Widely considered the "best value for your dollar," Ohio State all in all offers "a real-world experience and worldwide access to the best of the best."

### Life
Ohio State social life flourishes in an atmosphere where "there are parties all the time, everywhere." The Greek community can be exclusive, with several students noting that at fraternity parties "people risk being rejected at the door because they are not cool enough or not female." Luckily, the campus offers an abundance of alternatives: "There's so much to do on any given night, it's hard to remember you're not on vacation." The size of the school provides for options galore, meaning, "If you can't find it through Ohio State, it may not exist." During warm weather, students hang out in The Oval, "the best place on Earth to socialize and relax." And of course in the fall, Buckeye football is a campuswide obsession. One student proudly points out, "There aren't too many schools that can fill a 110,000-person stadium for football games." If on-campus events ever fail to entertain, the surrounding capital city of Columbus "caters to both partiers and those who enjoy the arts." Overall, life at OSU "will surely give you the total college experience you're looking for."

### Student Body
"With more than 48,000 students [undergraduate and graduate], you have just about every type of person: Rastafarians, hippies, ROTC participants, party goers, Greeks, athletes. You cannot label OSU students because there are just so many with so much diversity." Despite this variety, "the sense of community and oneness is very strong," and a common opinion is that "Ohio State is probably one of the biggest schools with such a sense of camaraderie." Racial and ethnic diversity prevails at the university, with one student commenting, "People who decide to come to Ohio State do so knowing they will be immersed in ethnicity. The community is really comfortable because of this." Other students remark, however, that it is "difficult to interact with other ethnicities." The school's residence life department "works really hard to incorporate diversity and insure that students are getting a well-rounded education." Regarding geographical variety, one student states, "As an out-of-state freshman, it can be a little difficult to make connections with people because everyone seems to be from the same small towns in Ohio." But reportedly the strongly conservative population is "friendly and accepting of anyone who is a Buckeye."

# OHIO STATE UNIVERSITY—COLUMBUS

FINANCIAL AID: 614-292-0300 • E-MAIL: ASKABUCKEYE@OSU.EDU • WEBSITE: WWW.OSU.EDU

## ADMISSIONS
*Very important factors considered include:* class rank, secondary school record, standardized test scores. *Important factors considered include:* extracurricular activities, minority status, talent/ability, volunteer work, work experience. *Other factors considered include:* essays, geographical residence, recommendations, state residency. SAT I or ACT required. TOEFL required of all international applicants. High school diploma or GED is required. *High school units required/recommended:* 4 English required, 3 math required, 4 math recommended, 2 science required, 3 science recommended, 2 science lab required, 2 foreign language required, 3 foreign language recommended, 2 social studies required, 3 social studies recommended, 1 elective required.

## The Inside Word
Although admissions officers consider extracurriculars and other personal characteristics of candidates, there is a heavy emphasis on numbers—grades, rank, and test scores. Although admissions standards have become increasingly competitive in recent years, OSU is still worth a shot for the average student. The university's great reputation and affordable cost make it a good choice for anyone looking at large schools.

## FINANCIAL AID
*Students should submit:* FAFSA. The Princeton Review suggests that all financial aid forms be submitted as soon as possible after January 1. *Need-based scholarships/grants offered:* Pell, SEOG, state scholarships/grants, private scholarships, the school's own gift aid. *Loan aid offered:* Direct Subsidized Stafford, Direct Unsubsidized Stafford, Direct PLUS, Federal Perkins, Federal Nursing, college/university loans from institutional funds. Federal Work-Study Program available. Institutional employment available. Applicants will be notified of awards on or about April 1. Off-campus job opportunities are good.

## FROM THE ADMISSIONS OFFICE
"The Ohio State University is Ohio's leading center for teaching, research, and public service. Our exceptional faculty, innovative programs, supportive services, and extremely competitive tuition costs make Ohio State one of higher education's best values. Our central campus is in Columbus, Ohio, the state's largest city. About 48,000 students from every county in Ohio, every state in the nation, and over 87 foreign nations are enrolled at Ohio state. Our faculty include Nobel Prize winners, Rhodes Scholars, members of the National Academy of Sciences, widely published writers, and noted artists and musicians. Our campus boasts world-class facilities like the Wexner Center for the Arts, the nation's largest medical teaching facility, and the new, multibuilding Fisher College of Business. From classes and residence halls to concerts and seminars to clubs and sports and honoraries to Frisbee games on the Oval, Ohio State offers opportunities to develop talents and skills while meeting a variety of people. At Ohio State, you're sure to find a place to call your own."

### SELECTIVITY
★ ★ ☆ ☆

| | |
|---|---|
| Admissions Rating | 73 |
| % of acceptees attending | 41 |
| # accepting a place on wait list | 120 |
| % admitted from wait list | 27 |

### FRESHMAN PROFILE
| | |
|---|---|
| Range SAT Verbal | 520-630 |
| Average SAT Verbal | 575 |
| Range SAT Math | 540-660 |
| Average SAT Math | 594 |
| Range ACT Composite | 23-28 |
| Average ACT Composite | 25 |
| Minimum TOEFL | 527 |
| Average HS GPA | 4.0 |
| % graduated top 10% of class | 33 |
| % graduated top 25% of class | 66 |
| % graduated top 50% of class | 91 |

### DEADLINES
| | |
|---|---|
| Regular admission | 2/15 |
| Nonfall registration? | yes |

### APPLICANTS ALSO LOOK AT AND OFTEN PREFER
Miami U.
Ohio U.
Case Western
Bowling Green State
Purdue Univ.
U. Cincinnati

**AND RARELY PREFER**
Bellarmine

### FINANCIAL FACTS
★ ★ ★ ☆

| | |
|---|---|
| Financial Aid Rating | 84 |
| In-state tuition | $4,788 |
| Out-of-state tuition | $13,554 |
| Room and board | $6,031 |
| Books and supplies | $936 |
| % frosh receiving aid | 48 |
| % undergrads receiving aid | 45 |
| Avg frosh grant | $3,410 |
| Avg frosh loan | $2,702 |

# OHIO UNIVERSITY—ATHENS

120 CHUBB HALL, ATHENS, OH 45701 • ADMISSIONS: 740-593-4100 • FAX: 740-593-0560

## CAMPUS LIFE

| | |
|---|---|
| Quality of Life Rating | 82 |
| Type of school | public |
| Environment | rural |

### STUDENTS
| | |
|---|---|
| Total undergrad enrollment | 17,343 |
| % male/female | 45/55 |
| % from out of state | 9 |
| % from public high school | 82 |
| % live on campus | 44 |
| % in (# of) fraternities | 12 (21) |
| % in (# of) sororities | 14 (12) |
| % African American | 3 |
| % Asian | 1 |
| % Caucasian | 95 |
| % Hispanic | 1 |
| % international | 2 |
| # of countries represented | 100 |

### SURVEY SAYS . . .
Beautiful campus
Athletic facilities are great
Campus easy to get around
Great library
Great computer facilities
Lousy food on campus
Registration is a pain
Student publications are popular

## ACADEMICS

| | |
|---|---|
| Academic Rating | 72 |
| Calendar | quarter |
| Student/faculty ratio | 20:1 |
| Profs interesting rating | 71 |
| Profs accessible rating | 92 |
| % profs teaching UG courses | 100 |
| % classes taught by TAs | 19 |
| Avg lab size | 10-19 students |
| Avg reg class size | 10-19 students |

## STUDENTS SPEAK OUT

### Academics
Students believe that the academic level at Ohio University is underrated ("Classes are definitely not as easy as some believe") and uniformly praise their education. "It's a wonderful school with great professors who are genuinely interested in the concepts they are teaching us." The journalism program earns especially high praise, though some journalism students complain that they have a difficult time getting into classes within the major. Most professors are held in high regard and "are very nice and accessible outside of class." Ohio operates on a quarterly calendar, and many students laud the system. Though there are few teaching assistants, some students complain that in certain subjects the TAs are difficult to understand because their command of the English language is weak. First-year students speak of an excellent academic support system: "I was scared that I would get lost in classes, but the teachers were right there to help me find my way." The administration is also appreciated. The advisors are "great," and the dean of students is "personable." The university has attempted to improve the class registration system by implementing online registration which students see as "a step in the right direction."

### Life
Ohio University students describe themselves as "low maintenance" when it comes to having fun. Those who are of age go to the downtown bars for dancing and partying. The annual Halloween celebration is legendary; students "party for an entire weekend," with mounted police overseeing the festivities. Students appreciate the "beautiful" campus and because "there really are not a lot of things to do in Athens," students take advantage of the 300-plus on-campus clubs and organizations. Many are associated with the Greek system, and they believe that fraternities and sororities improve campus life. Students support the athletic programs and laud the "new and huge" rec center. Movies are also a popular diversion. Many say that they spend most of their weeknights studying because it is easy to fall behind in a quarterly system if one is not diligent. The campus food needs improvement. "I gave up meat at the first glimpse of what they served me," mutters one journalism major. Students also want the parking situation upgraded.

### Student Body
Nearly 91 percent of Ohio's "laid-back" students are Caucasian, and a majority of the students are "middle class, so . . . everyone seems to be on an even financial level and out to actually get an education, while at the same time enjoying the freedom and experience of college." Students say that their peers are friendly, and only a few are bothered by the lack of on-campus diversity. "There aren't enough minorities," although the University is seeking to improve diversity through recruitment. Students feel safe on campus.

392 ■ THE BEST 351 COLLEGES

# OHIO UNIVERSITY—ATHENS

FINANCIAL AID: 740-593-4141 • E-MAIL: ADMISSIONS@OHIOU.EDU • WEBSITE: WWW.OHIOU.EDU

## ADMISSIONS

*Very important factors considered include:* class rank, secondary school record, standardized test scores. *Other factors considered include:* alumni/ae relation, essays, extracurricular activities, geographical residence, minority status, recommendations, state residency, talent/ability, work experience. SAT I or ACT required; ACT preferred. High school diploma or GED is required. *High school units required/recommended:* 16 total recommended; 4 English recommended, 3 math recommended, 3 science recommended, 2 foreign language recommended, 3 social studies recommended, 1 visual or performing arts recommended.

### The Inside Word

There's little mystery in applying to Ohio U. The admissions process follows the formula approach very closely, and those whose numbers plug in well will get good news.

## FINANCIAL AID

*Students should submit:* FAFSA. The Princeton Review suggests that all financial aid forms be submitted as soon as possible after January 1. *Need-based scholarships/grants offered:* Pell, SEOG, state scholarships/grants, private scholarships, the school's own gift aid. *Loan aid offered:* Direct Subsidized Stafford, Direct Unsubsidized Stafford, Direct PLUS, Federal Perkins, college/university loans from institutional funds. Federal Work-Study Program available. Institutional employment available. Applicants will be notified of awards on or about April 1. Off-campus job opportunities are good.

## FROM THE ADMISSIONS OFFICE

"Chartered in 1804, Ohio University symbolizes America's early commitment to higher education. Its historic campus provides a setting matched by only a handful of other universities in the country. Students choose Ohio University mainly because of its academic strength, but the beautiful setting and college-town atmosphere are also factors in their decision. Ohio University is the central focus of Athens, Ohio, located approximately 75 miles southeast of Columbus. We encourage prospective students to come for a visit and experience the beauty and academic excellence of Ohio University."

## SELECTIVITY
★ ★ ☆ ☆

| | |
|---|---|
| Admissions Rating | 79 |
| # of applicants | 13,195 |
| % of applicants accepted | 75 |
| % of acceptees attending | 37 |

### FRESHMAN PROFILE

| | |
|---|---|
| Range SAT Verbal | 500-600 |
| Average SAT Verbal | 540 |
| Range SAT Math | 500-610 |
| Average SAT Math | 550 |
| Range ACT Composite | 21-26 |
| Average ACT Composite | 23 |
| Minimum TOEFL | 550 |
| Average HS GPA | 3.3 |
| % graduated top 10% of class | 18 |
| % graduated top 25% of class | 50 |
| % graduated top 50% of class | 90 |

### DEADLINES

| | |
|---|---|
| Regular admission | 2/1 |
| Nonfall registration? | yes |

### APPLICANTS ALSO LOOK AT AND OFTEN PREFER
Ohio State U
Miami of Ohio

**AND SOMETIMES PREFER**
Oberlin
Kent State
Penn State at University Park
Wittenberg
U of Cincinnati
U of Dayton

**AND RARELY PREFER**
Bowling Green State
Purdue U at West Lafayette
Indiana U at Bloomington

## FINANCIAL FACTS
★ ★ ★ ☆

| | |
|---|---|
| Financial Aid Rating | 82 |
| In-state tuition | $6,336 |
| Out-of-state tuition | $13,818 |
| Room and board | $6,777 |
| Books and supplies | $810 |
| % frosh receiving aid | 46 |
| % undergrads receiving aid | 45 |
| Avg frosh grant | $3,853 |

# OHIO WESLEYAN UNIVERSITY

61 SOUTH SANDUSKY STREET, DELAWARE, OH 43015 • ADMISSIONS: 740-368-3020 • FAX: 740-368-3314

## CAMPUS LIFE

| | |
|---|---|
| Quality of Life Rating | 83 |
| Type of school | private |
| Affiliation | Methodist |
| Environment | suburban |

### STUDENTS

| | |
|---|---|
| Total undergrad enrollment | 1,935 |
| % male/female | 46/54 |
| % from out of state | 40 |
| % from public high school | 75 |
| % live on campus | 81 |
| % in (# of) fraternities | 44 (13) |
| % in (# of) sororities | 34 (8) |
| % African American | 5 |
| % Asian | 2 |
| % Caucasian | 79 |
| % Hispanic | 2 |
| % international | 11 |
| # of countries represented | 52 |

### SURVEY SAYS . . .
Lots of beer drinking
Frats and sororities dominate social scene
Hard liquor is popular
(Almost) everyone smokes
Registration is a breeze
Students are happy
Ethnic diversity on campus
No one cheats
Students don't get along with local community
Students don't like Delaware, OH

## ACADEMICS

| | |
|---|---|
| Academic Rating | 88 |
| Calendar | semester |
| Student/faculty ratio | 13:1 |
| % profs teaching UG courses | 100 |
| Avg lab size | 10-19 students |
| Avg reg class size | 10-19 students |

### MOST POPULAR MAJORS
Business/managerial economics
Zoology/animal biology
Psychology

## STUDENTS SPEAK OUT

### Academics

Students love the academic approach at Ohio Wesleyan University, where their curriculum leads them to discover "how various disciplines can be integrated to form a greater whole, how to question what we know, and how to critically analyze the world around us." As one student put it, "The overall experience at OWU is one of practicum," a constant focus on practical application of advanced theory. Students also brag of the "countless opportunities and experiences in a variety of fields waiting for students" at OWU. "If there's something you want," explained one student, "all you have to do is ask and someone will help you get it." Undergrads warn that "while classes can be tough, professors really want you to succeed and truly learn the material." Instructors are truly mentors. "Their real reason for being here is to teach," students agree. "They may also do research, but that is secondary and they always use us (undergrad students) to assist with any research (which looks great on our resumes)." Noted one student, "It's incredible to walk around campus and have both faculty and administrators call you by your first name. I've been able to develop great relationships with professors, which has allowed me to learn so much more on a personal level." Students also praise the "great new science center" and note that "by next semester, we are supposed to be optically connected, which should [make] our Internet run much [more smoothly]."

### Life

OWU students "want to have a good time, but are very studious when it comes to class work. Students have their priorities straight at OWU." Once they've fulfilled their academic obligations, though, undergrads feel free to cut loose. Most agree that "Ohio Wesleyan always has a variety of things going on. If you really like the party scene, you can find that, but if you are not looking for that, there are many things that you can do instead." While "Greek life is popular, the Student Activities Board provides an enormous amount of fun options" away from Frat Row, as the board is "very in tune with students' wishes. They provide free movies once a month at the local movie theater and get bands to play at our Springfest concert." Undergrads also have "tons of clubs to choose from." Reports one, "There are clubs that are religious in nature: Tauheed (Islamic), Hillel (Jewish), Methodist Student Movement . . . and many others. I think these groups enrich life on campus far beyond any other aspect." Students here are "very community service–oriented. There are many opportunities for students to be engaged in serving the community in Delaware, Columbus, and pretty much anywhere in the world (every Spring Break Mission Week allows that)." Hometown Delaware gets poor marks, but OWU's proximity to OSU and Columbus eases the pain.

### Student Body

OWU is home to a "diverse group of students, especially for a school with" less than 2,000 undergraduates. "The student body prides itself on its diversity. Because of this, we enjoy a gamut of ethnic clubs and social events. It creates an atmosphere in which you can learn, not only about the richness of other cultures, but more about yourself as well." The student body includes "a large international student population, which fits in wonderfully on our campus: a lot of brilliantly smart Pakistani and Indian kids," as well as "Ohio kids and a surprisingly large population from Connecticut." One thing students here share in common: they are "involved, involved, involved in many student clubs, community service organizations, and other groups."

# OHIO WESLEYAN UNIVERSITY

FINANCIAL AID: 740-368-3050 • E-MAIL: OWUADMIT@OWU.EDU • WEBSITE: WEB.OWU.EDU

## ADMISSIONS

*Very important factors considered include:* character/personal qualities, interview, recommendations, secondary school record. *Important factors considered include:* alumni/ae relation, class rank, essays, extracurricular activities, geographical residence, minority status, standardized test scores, talent/ability, volunteer work. *Other factors considered include:* work experience. SAT I or ACT required; SAT II recommended. TOEFL required of all international applicants. High school diploma or GED is required. *High school units required/recommended:* 16 total recommended; 4 English recommended, 3 math recommended, 3 science recommended, 3 foreign language recommended, 3 social studies recommended.

### The Inside Word

OWU's high admit rate garners it both a competetive admit pool, as well as a high yield of those students. Students won't encounter super-selective academic standards for admission, but they will have to put some thought into the completion of their applications. The university's thorough admissions process definitely emphasizes the personal side of candidate evaluation.

## FINANCIAL AID

*Students should submit:* FAFSA, institution's own financial aid form. Regular filing deadline is March 15. The Princeton Review suggests that all financial aid forms be submitted as soon as possible after January 1. *Need-based scholarships/grants offered:* Pell, SEOG, state scholarships/grants, private scholarships, the school's own gift aid. *Loan aid offered:* FFEL Subsidized Stafford, FFEL Unsubsidized Stafford, FFEL PLUS, Federal Perkins, state loans, college/university loans from institutional funds. Federal Work-Study Program available. Institutional employment available. Applicants will be notified of awards on a rolling basis beginning on or about January 15. Off-campus job opportunities are excellent.

## FROM THE ADMISSIONS OFFICE

"Balance is the key word that describes Ohio Wesleyan. For example: 46 percent male, 54 percent female; 40 percent members of Greek life, 60 percent not; National Colloquium Program; Top Division III sports program; small-town setting of 25,000, near the 16th largest city in U.S. (Columbus, Ohio); excellent faculty/student ratio; outstanding fine and performing arts programs."

### SELECTIVITY

| | |
|---|---|
| Admissions Rating | 80 |
| # of applicants | 2,212 |
| % of applicants accepted | 80 |
| % of acceptees attending | 31 |
| # accepting a place on wait list | 6 |
| % admitted from wait list | 100 |
| # of early decision applicants | 29 |
| % accepted early decision | 86 |

### FRESHMAN PROFILE

| | |
|---|---|
| Range SAT Verbal | 540-650 |
| Average SAT Verbal | 602 |
| Range SAT Math | 540-650 |
| Average SAT Math | 608 |
| Range ACT Composite | 23-28 |
| Average ACT Composite | 27 |
| Minimum TOEFL | 550 |
| Average HS GPA | 3.3 |
| % graduated top 10% of class | 26 |
| % graduated top 25% of class | 50 |
| % graduated top 50% of class | 76 |

### DEADLINES

| | |
|---|---|
| Early decision | 12/1 |
| Early decision notification | 12/30 |
| Priority admission | 3/1 |
| Nonfall registration? | yes |

### APPLICANTS ALSO LOOK AT
**AND OFTEN PREFER**
Cornell University
Harvard College
American University
**AND SOMETIMES PREFER**
Wheaton College (MA)
Gettysburg College
**AND RARELY PREFER**
Kenyon College
Miami University
Denison University
College of Wooster
Ohio State University—Columbus

### FINANCIAL FACTS

| | |
|---|---|
| Financial Aid Rating | 86 |
| Tuition | $25,080 |
| Room and board | $7,110 |
| Books and supplies | $800 |
| Required fees | $360 |
| % frosh receiving aid | 60 |
| % undergrads receiving aid | 55 |
| Avg frosh grant | $12,861 |
| Avg frosh loan | $3,586 |

# PENNSYLVANIA STATE UNIVERSITY—UNIVERSITY PARK

201 SHIELDS BUILDING, UNIVERSITY PARK, PA 16802-3000 • ADMISSIONS: 814-865-5471 • FAX: 814-863-7590

## CAMPUS LIFE

| | |
|---|---|
| Quality of Life Rating | 78 |
| Type of school | public |
| Environment | suburban |

### STUDENTS

| | |
|---|---|
| Total undergrad enrollment | 34,829 |
| % male/female | 54/46 |
| % from out of state | 24 |
| % live on campus | 36 |
| % in (# of) fraternities | 13 (55) |
| % in (# of) sororities | 10 (25) |
| % African American | 4 |
| % Asian | 5 |
| % Caucasian | 87 |
| % Hispanic | 3 |
| % international | 2 |

### SURVEY SAYS . . .
Everyone loves the Nittany Lions
Lots of beer drinking
Athletic facilities are great
Great library
Frats and sororities dominate social scene
Student newspaper is popular
Hard liquor is popular
Campus is beautiful

## ACADEMICS

| | |
|---|---|
| Academic Rating | 87 |
| Calendar | semester |
| Student/faculty ratio | 17:1 |

## STUDENTS SPEAK OUT

### Academics
At a helluva big school like Pennsylvania State University, "you can find anything to do academically. If you want a school that will hold your hand, go to Swarthmore. If you're an independent, self-motivated person, come here." The school's main branch offers its students a mind-boggling array of majors, from turfgrass science to ancient Mediterranean studies to aerospace engineering. Engineering at PSU "is a fantastic bargain, provided that you are willing to put in the work." Programs in business, education, and computer science are also excellent. Students warn that "in order to thrive within this gigantic university, you must be able to create your own little world in which to exist. Otherwise, you are not only liable but guaranteed to get lost in the crowd." Several survey respondents offer strategies for coping with PSU's vastness. Writes one, "The longer you are at PSU, the more tricks you learn, and the better and easier it becomes. Here's one: Schedule 24 credits at the beginning of the semester, then pick the five or six classes with the best professors and drop the rest." Offers another, "If you sit in front of classes, you can't tell that there are 150 people behind you." Professors "are very smart and know their stuff, but they are poor communicators." Notes one student, "How good professors are basically depends on two things: your interest in the subject and, more importantly, [whether] they can teach. You can tell some professors are here just to do research, while others can actually teach." While some feel that "TAs are depended on too much" here, others argue that "everyone has negative comments about TAs, but some are actually better, more down-to-earth, and easier to get in touch with than the professors." Administration of the school is unsurprisingly sluggish; recounts one student, "I'm in my fourth semester and I've had two classes cancelled for the semester and one class had a day/time shift. "

### Life
With a student population the size of many American towns, Penn State can offer a wide variety of social options. "Anything you want to do on a weekend," explains one student, "you can find a group of people to do it with. It's not just about drinking. There are concerts, arts, club activities, everything." While it may not be just about drinking, most agree that "Penn State is a party school no matter what anyone says. We throw a party for any reason." Adds another student, "People drink a lot because all there [are] in this town are bars." When students tire of drinking in bars, they . . . drum roll please . . . drink at fraternities! The biggest thing on campus, however, is Nittany Lion football. Reports one student, "Kids go two or three hours early for front-row seats." Students approve of the "beautiful" campus but warn that "it is a pain in the ass to get around campus. Buses are always packed and the campus is huge." They appreciate the school's rural setting, however, which "allows easy access to lots of outdoors activities, like biking, hiking, skiing, canoeing, and boating." As an added bonus, University Park is a "good location for access to major cities (D.C., Baltimore, Philadelphia, Pittsburgh), all three to four hours away." The town itself, however, "is overpriced and pretentious."

### Student Body
The 35,000-plus "very sociable, kind, and easy to talk to" undergraduates of Penn State represent a wide array of attitudes and backgrounds. Writes one student, "A wonderful thing about a large school is that you can find people and opinions from across the board." Geographically, though, "diversity is in short supply, with a large majority of students coming from Pennsylvania." Even though the minority population is proportionally small, they are still 3,000. Unfortunately, "races at PSU segregate themselves. There is no built-in racism; it's all by personal choice." The pragmatic, nonintellectual approach of the majority here doesn't appeal to everyone. To detractors, "the students are all right, but they're like high school students, just a little older."

# PENNSYLVANIA STATE UNIVERSITY—UNIVERSITY PARK

FINANCIAL AID: 814-865-6301 • WEBSITE: WWW.PSU.EDU/ADMISSIONS

## ADMISSIONS

*Very important factors considered include:* secondary school record, standardized test scores. *Other factors considered include:* alumni/ae relation, character/personal qualities, class rank, essays, extracurricular activities, recommendations, talent/ability, volunteer work, work experience. SAT I or ACT required. TOEFL required of all international applicants. High school diploma or GED is required. *High school units required/recommended:* 4 English required, 3 math required, 3 science required, 2 foreign language required, 3 social studies required.

### The Inside Word

Penn State is deluged with applicants (they claim to receive more SAT score reports than any other college in the country), which makes it especially important for candidates to have better than average grades and test scores. Although a personal essay and information on extracurricular activities are requested, the university's formula focuses on the numbers. At schools this large it's hard for the admissions process to be more individualized.

## FINANCIAL AID

*Students should submit:* FAFSA. No deadline for regular filing. The Princeton Review suggests that all financial aid forms be submitted as soon as possible after January 1. *Need-based scholarships/grants offered:* Pell, SEOG, state scholarships/grants, private scholarships, the school's own gift aid. *Loan aid offered:* FFEL Subsidized Stafford, FFEL Unsubsidized Stafford, FFEL PLUS, Federal Perkins, college/university loans from institutional funds, private loans. Federal Work-Study Program available. Applicants will be notified of awards on a rolling basis beginning on or about February 15. Off-campus job opportunities are good.

## FROM THE ADMISSIONS OFFICE

"Unique among large public universities, Penn State combines the nearly 35,000-student setting of its University Park campus with 20 academically and administratively integrated undergraduate locations—small-college settings ranging in size from 600 to 3,400 students. Each year, more than 60 percent of incoming freshmen begin their studies at these residential and commuter campuses, while nearly 40 percent begin at the University Park Campus. The smaller locations focus on the needs of new students by offering the first two years of most Penn State baccalaureate degrees in settings that stress close interaction with faculty. Depending on the major selected, students may choose to complete their degree at University Park or one of the smaller locations. Your application to Penn State qualifies you for review for any of our campuses. Your two choices of location are reviewed in the order given. Entrance difficulty is based, in part, on the demand. Due to its popularity, the University Park campus is the most competitive for admission."

## SELECTIVITY

| | |
|---|---|
| Admissions Rating | 86 |
| # of applicants | 27,604 |
| % of applicants accepted | 57 |
| % of acceptees attending | 38 |

### FRESHMAN PROFILE

| | |
|---|---|
| Range SAT Verbal | 530-630 |
| Average SAT Verbal | 593 |
| Range SAT Math | 560-670 |
| Average SAT Math | 617 |
| Minimum TOEFL | 550 |
| Average HS GPA | 3.5 |
| % graduated top 10% of class | 41 |
| % graduated top 25% of class | 78 |
| % graduated top 50% of class | 96 |

### DEADLINES

| | |
|---|---|
| Priority admission | 11/30 |
| Nonfall registration? | yes |

### APPLICANTS ALSO LOOK AT AND OFTEN PREFER

Carnegie Mellon
Cornell
Lehigh
U of Maryland at College Park
U of Michigan

### AND SOMETIMES PREFER

U of Virginia
Johns Hopkins
Georgetown
Harvard
Emory

## FINANCIAL FACTS

| | |
|---|---|
| Financial Aid Rating | 89 |
| In-state tuition | $9,431 |
| Out-of-state tuition | $18,922 |
| Room and board | $6,000 |
| Books and supplies | $864 |
| Required fees | $374 |
| % frosh receiving aid | 44 |
| % undergrads receiving aid | 49 |
| Avg frosh grant | $2,800 |
| Avg frosh loan | $3,193 |

# PEPPERDINE UNIVERSITY

24255 PACIFIC COAST HIGHWAY, MALIBU, CA 90263 • ADMISSIONS: 310-456-4392 • FAX: 310-456-4861

## CAMPUS LIFE

| Quality of Life Rating | 88 |
|---|---|
| Type of school | private |
| Affiliation | Church of Christ |
| Environment | suburban |

### STUDENTS

| Total undergrad enrollment | 3,153 |
|---|---|
| % male/female | 44/56 |
| % from out of state | 48 |
| % live on campus | 50 |
| % in (# of) fraternities | 15 (6) |
| % in (# of) sororities | 15 (8) |
| % African American | 7 |
| % Asian | 9 |
| % Caucasian | 55 |
| % Hispanic | 11 |
| % international | 7 |
| % Native American | 2 |
| # of countries represented | 70 |

### SURVEY SAYS . . .
Very little drug use
Frats and sororities dominate social scene
Students love Malibu, CA
Great food on campus
Dorms are like palaces
Students are very religious
Very little beer drinking
Library needs improving
Very little hard liquor
Computer facilities need improving

## ACADEMICS

| Academic Rating | 82 |
|---|---|
| Calendar | semester |
| Student/faculty ratio | 12:1 |
| Profs interesting rating | 94 |
| Profs accessible rating | 92 |
| % profs teaching UG courses | 100 |
| Avg lab size | 10-19 students |
| Avg reg class size | 10-19 students |

### MOST POPULAR MAJORS
Business administration/management
Organizational communication
Psychology

## STUDENTS SPEAK OUT

### Academics

The academic experience at Pepperdine is no day at the beach. While most professors "are very dedicated to teaching and helping their students learn," they hold high standards and expect the students to live up to them. "Yeah, it's hard," writes a student, "and you have to put a lot of time into your studies." But it's not just the intellect that professors nurture at Pepperdine. "All aspects are cultivated here: intellectual, spiritual, emotional, social." The spiritual aspect is notably strong. "Sixty percent of the faculty has to be Church of Christ." While religion doesn't make its way into every classroom, students do hear about it "at the weekly convocation series. This is a mandatory meeting, often with religious undertones. Many of the students enjoy this highly religious atmosphere, but to the nondevout, it can be a little overwhelming." Overall, students find little reason to complain about the academic life at Pepperdine. It's "challenging." It's "personal." And it all takes place in an unbeatable location. "To be honest," admits one student, "attending Pepperdine equates to attending classes at an oceanside resort."

### Life

"When it's warm out, everyone's at the beach." Go figure. For many students, "the beach is visible" from their dorm rooms and when they finally pull themselves from their "breathtaking" bedside views, they "walk to class with the Pacific Ocean right there." So it's not at all surprising that catching some rays or studying under a beach umbrella or surfing the waves are favorite pastimes for Pepperdine students. In fact, "on days when homework is put aside, living at Pepperdine can seem . . . like an extended vacation." Still, it's a fairly tame vacation. Aside from beach bumming and superstar gazing, "there isn't much to do in Malibu." "The town shuts down at 10," moans one student. "It sucks because you always think to rent a movie at 10:05, and Blockbuster closed five minutes ago." Life on campus is kept under control by strict drug and alcohol policies and rules dictating that "from 2 A.M. to 10 A.M., guys aren't allowed in girls' residence halls, and vice versa." Though it is a "dry campus," "the majority of the students do drink," which means you're likely to find a crowd at the nearby "Malibu Inn" or "just chillin' " with their alcoholic contraband in the dorms. "For fun, Pepperdine tries to put on a lot of on-campus activities." But students will tell you that "those aren't very fun." The real fun, according to undergraduates, is found away from campus. Students often head "to UCLA or USC for parties," or "party down on Sunset Boulevard, or somewhere in L.A."

### Student Body

"Not too far from L.A.," you'll find the oceanside community of Malibu where there is a high incidence of celebrity sightings, great surf, and unfailing sunshine. And right there in the heart of Malibu's Santa Monica Mountains sits Pepperdine University. Fittingly, a good deal of students on "Pepperdine Island" "look good, drive super nice cars, and wear all the expensive brand names." According to the university, "Pepperdine is a Christian university committed to the highest standards of academic excellence and Christian values, where students are strengthened for lives of purpose, service, and leadership." And while students here will admit that the "religious" and "wealthy" "stereotypes" aren't completely off the mark, they'll warn you not to have too narrow a perception of the student body. If you look closely, you'll find "the surfer and valley girl," as well as the "jock, the brain, the princess, and the basketcase." "Pepp," as some students affectionately call it, is composed of people "from diverse backgrounds"—at least ethnically. Socially, however, this group of students tends to fall into "cliques"—and these groups are especially evident around dinnertime. "Ask anyone on campus, and they'll tell you which group sits where in the cafeteria."

398 ■ THE BEST 351 COLLEGES

# PEPPERDINE UNIVERSITY

FINANCIAL AID: 310-456-4301 • E-MAIL: ADMISSION-SEAVER@PEPPERDINE.EDU • WEBSITE: WWW.PEPPERDINE.EDU

## ADMISSIONS
*Very important factors considered include:* character/personal qualities, essays, extracurricular activities, recommendations, religious affiliation/commitment, secondary school record, standardized test scores. *Important factors considered include:* talent/ability, volunteer work. *Other factors considered include:* alumni/ae relation, interview, minority status, work experience. SAT I or ACT required. TOEFL required of all international applicants. High school diploma or GED is required. *High school units required/recommended:* 25 total recommended; 4 English recommended, 4 math recommended, 4 science recommended, 3 foreign language recommended, 3 social studies recommended, 3 history recommended, 2 elective recommended.

## The Inside Word
A stunning physical location enables the admissions office to produce beautiful catalogs and viewbooks, which, when combined with the university's reputation for academic quality, help to attract a large applicant pool. In addition to solid grades and test scores, successful applicants typically have well-rounded extracurricular backgrounds. Involvement in school, church, and community is an overused cliché in the world of college admissions, but at Pepperdine it's definitely one of the ingredients in successful applications.

## FINANCIAL AID
*Students should submit:* FAFSA, institution's own financial aid form. Regular filing deadline is February 15. The Princeton Review suggests that all financial aid forms be submitted as soon as possible after January 1. *Need-based scholarships/grants offered:* Pell, SEOG, state scholarships/grants, private scholarships, the school's own gift aid. *Loan aid offered:* FFEL Subsidized Stafford, FFEL Unsubsidized Stafford, FFEL PLUS, Federal Perkins, state loans, college/university loans from institutional funds. Federal Work-Study Program available. Institutional employment available. Applicants will be notified of awards on or about April 15. Off-campus job opportunities are excellent.

## FROM THE ADMISSIONS OFFICE
"As a selective university, Pepperdine seeks students who show promise of academic achievement at the collegiate level. However, we also seek students who are committed to serving the university community, as well as others with whom they come into contact. We look for community service activities, volunteer efforts, and strong leadership qualities, as well as a demonstrated commitment to academic studies and an interest in the liberal arts."

### SELECTIVITY

| | |
|---|---|
| Admissions Rating | 86 |
| # of applicants | 5,613 |
| % of applicants accepted | 36 |
| % of acceptees attending | 41 |
| # accepting a place on wait list | 416 |

### FRESHMAN PROFILE
| | |
|---|---|
| Range SAT Verbal | 550-660 |
| Average SAT Verbal | 612 |
| Range SAT Math | 580-680 |
| Average SAT Math | 628 |
| Range ACT Composite | 24-29 |
| Average ACT Composite | 26 |
| Minimum TOEFL | 550 |
| Average HS GPA | 3.7 |
| % graduated top 10% of class | 72 |
| % graduated top 25% of class | 95 |
| % graduated top 50% of class | 99 |

### DEADLINES
| | |
|---|---|
| Regular notification | 4/1 |
| Nonfall registration? | yes |
| Regular admission | 1/15 |

### APPLICANTS ALSO LOOK AT AND OFTEN PREFER
USC
Stanford
UCLA
U of San Diego
U of Pennsylvania
UC Santa Barbara

### AND SOMETIMES PREFER
UC San Diego
Santa Clara
UC Irvine, UC Berkeley
Vanderbilt, NYU

### AND RARELY PREFER
Loyola Marymount U
Occidental, Biola U
Chapman, Gonzaga

### FINANCIAL FACTS

| | |
|---|---|
| Financial Aid Rating | 87 |
| Tuition | $26,280 |
| Room and board | $7,930 |
| Books and supplies | $500 |
| Required fees | $90 |
| % frosh receiving aid | 77 |
| % undergrads receiving aid | 75 |
| Avg frosh grant | $30,548 |
| Avg frosh loan | $5,554 |

THE BEST 351 COLLEGES ■ 399

# PITZER COLLEGE

1050 NORTH MILLS AVENUE, CLAREMONT, CA 91711-6101 • ADMISSIONS: 909-621-8129 • FAX: 909-621-8770

## CAMPUS LIFE

| Quality of Life Rating | 85 |
|---|---|
| Type of school | private |
| Environment | suburban |

### STUDENTS

| Total undergrad enrollment | 954 |
|---|---|
| % male/female | 38/62 |
| % from out of state | 49 |
| % live on campus | 75 |
| % African American | 6 |
| % Asian | 12 |
| % Caucasian | 46 |
| % Hispanic | 15 |
| % international | 2 |
| # of countries represented | 12 |

### SURVEY SAYS . . .
No one plays intramural sports
Registration is a breeze
Great computer facilities
Diverse students interact
Intercollegiate sports unpopular or nonexistent
Students aren't religious
Political activism is hot
Great library

## ACADEMICS

| Academic Rating | 87 |
|---|---|
| Calendar | semester |
| Student/faculty ratio | 12:1 |
| Profs interesting rating | 96 |
| Profs accessible rating | 97 |
| % profs teaching UG courses | 100 |
| Avg reg class size | 10-19 students |

### MOST POPULAR MAJORS
English language and literature
Psychology
Sociology

## STUDENTS SPEAK OUT

### Academics

Pitzer students wear their activist label proudly; it doesn't stop there though, profs and administrators intimately understand the school's common theme of social responsibility and embrace it. The professors, reports one senior, "are a very diverse and proactive bunch who are genuinely interested in their own subjects as well as stimulating thought" in general. Because professors at this "small, liberal, socially aware" college "are actively interested in their students," a student at Pitzer can garner an education that is "a fun, creative, and enriching experience." In fact, at a place where professors often "act like peers" and "validate Pitzer's [socially conscious] reputation more than the students do," you're even likely to see professors "protest alongside" their activist students. Many students enjoy the "fluid" Pitzer curriculum that gives them "the power to design their own coursework and their majors." What they enjoy much less is the administration. But students aren't unanimously critical of management; a freshman notes that the administration is getting better at "involving students in decisions that affect our future."

### Life

Life at Pitzer is lively. Students know how to "work hard and party hard," and when it comes to partying, they're creative. Of course, there are the usual college parties at Pitzer and at the other four Claremont Colleges. And there are frequent trips to nearby Los Angeles. But what truly earmarks the caliber of student life at Pitzer is the string of creative social events it boasts. There are activities like "playing guitars/drums/singing, wherever and whenever," and taking trips to "the mountains . . . desert, ocean"—all within driving distance, if you have a car. "It is hard to be here without a car, though," warns a senior from Massachusetts. One of the reasons students want to get away from campus is because Claremont itself "is not a very active city." Also, the "dorms are a little shabby and depressing." But all in all, students enjoy Pitzer, which, along with its nearby sister schools, allows students to get "a small college experience with a university feel."

### Student Body

Clustered into a 12-block area with the four other Claremont Colleges, Pitzer is a liberal arts and sciences institution full of "creative, open-minded, and insane people." Though "it was once said that Pitzer was a school of aging hippies," today you're just as likely to see a student who looks like he just "walked out of a J.Crew catalog" as you are to see a student with a tie-dyed shirt and Birkenstocks. People tend to be politically aware and active, though beware if your views lean even a little toward the conservative: "They tend not to tolerate political views to the right of Lenin," one freshman observes of his classmates. Because you'll find "hard workers" as well as students "with a more laid-back work ethic" at Pitzer, there's a comfortable spot in the student body for both the bookworm and social bug. In fact, the "diversity" of personalities is one of the prime forms of entertainment at Pitzer. Students here are, on the whole, "ridiculously friendly."

400 ■ THE BEST 351 COLLEGES

# PITZER COLLEGE

FINANCIAL AID: 909-621-8208 • E-MAIL: ADMISSION@PITZER.EDU • WEBSITE: WWW.PITZER.EDU

## ADMISSIONS

*Very important factors considered include:* character/personal qualities, class rank, essays, extracurricular activities, minority status, recommendations, secondary school record, talent/ability, community service. *Important factors considered include:* geographical residence, interview, work experience. *Other factors considered include:* alumni/ae relation. TOEFL required of all international applicants. *High school units required/recommended:* 4 English recommended plus related writing courses, 3 math recommended, 3 laboratory science recommended, 3 social and behavioral science recommended (including history), 3 foreign language recommended. Pitzer has adopted a new admission policy for first-year students applying for admission for fall 2004 in order to provide applicants with greater flexibility in presenting application materials that accurately reflect their diverse academic abilities and potentials. All students must submit the Common Application, Pitzer's Supplement to the Common Application, a $50 application fee, high school transcript(s), and transcripts of any college attended. In addition, students that fall below a cumulative GPA of 3.50 or the top 10 percent of their graduating class must submit standardized test scores or AP test scores or International Baccalaureate tests or a graded paper and graded advanced math exam (details available from the Admissions Office).

### The Inside Word

This is a place where applicants can feel confident in letting their thoughts flow freely on admissions essays. Not only does the committee read them (a circumstance more rare in college admissions than one is led to believe), but they've set up the process to emphasize them! Thus, what you have to say for yourself will go much further than numbers in determining your suitability for Pitzer. Paying greater attention to essays also helps Pitzer create a dynamic and engaging freshman class each year.

## FINANCIAL AID

*Students should submit:* FAFSA, CSS/Financial Aid PROFILE, state aid form, noncustodial (divorced/separated) parent's statement, business/farm supplement. Regular filing deadline is February 1. The Princeton Review suggests that all financial aid forms be submitted as soon as possible after January 1. *Need-based scholarships/grants offered:* Pell, SEOG, state scholarships/grants, private scholarships, the school's own gift aid. *Loan aid offered:* FFEL Subsidized Stafford, FFEL Unsubsidized Stafford, FFEL PLUS, Federal Perkins, college/university loans from institutional funds. Federal Work-Study Program available. Institutional employment available. Applicants will be notified of awards on or about April 1. Off-campus job opportunities are good.

## FROM THE ADMISSIONS OFFICE

"Pitzer is about opportunities. It's about possibilities. The students who come here are looking for something different from the usual 'take two courses from column A, two courses from column B, and two courses from column C.' That kind of arbitrary selection doesn't make a satisfying education at Pitzer. So we look for students who want to have an impact on their own education, who want the chief responsibility—with help from their faculty advisors—in designing their own futures."

## SELECTIVITY

| | |
|---|---|
| Admissions Rating | 83 |
| # of applicants | 2,323 |
| % of applicants accepted | 56 |
| % of acceptees attending | 18 |

### FRESHMAN PROFILE

| | |
|---|---|
| Range SAT Verbal | 570-670 |
| Average SAT Verbal | 624 |
| Range SAT Math | 550-670 |
| Average SAT Math | 610 |
| Range ACT Composite | 23-27 |
| Average ACT Composite | 25 |
| Minimum TOEFL | 590 |
| Average HS GPA | 3.5 |
| % graduated top 10% of class | 23 |
| % graduated top 50% of class | 93 |

### DEADLINES

| | |
|---|---|
| Early action | 12/1 |
| Regular admission | 1/15 |
| Regular notification | 4/1 |

### APPLICANTS ALSO LOOK AT AND OFTEN PREFER
Claremont McKenna
Occidental
Pomona
UCLA
UC Berkeley
USC
Scripps

### AND SOMETIMES PREFER
Boston U
Colorado College
Lewis & Clark
NYU
Whitman

### AND RARELY PREFER
George Washington U
Pepperdine, Reed
U of Puget Sound

## FINANCIAL FACTS

| | |
|---|---|
| Financial Aid Rating | 89 |
| Tuition | $25,264 |
| Room and board | $7,370 |
| Books and supplies | $850 |
| Required fees | $2,992 |
| % frosh receiving aid | 34 |
| % undergrads receiving aid | 45 |
| Avg frosh grant | $23,864 |
| Avg frosh loan | $2,626 |

# POMONA COLLEGE

333 NORTH COLLEGE WAY, CLAREMONT, CA 91711-6312 • ADMISSIONS: 909-621-8134 • FAX: 909-621-8952

## CAMPUS LIFE

| | |
|---|---|
| Quality of Life Rating | 91 |
| Type of school | private |
| Environment | suburban |

### STUDENTS
| | |
|---|---|
| Total undergrad enrollment | 1,551 |
| % male/female | 50/50 |
| % from out of state | 66 |
| % from public high school | 61 |
| % live on campus | 97 |
| % in (# of) fraternities | 5 (4) |
| % African American | 6 |
| % Asian | 13 |
| % Caucasian | 60 |
| % Hispanic | 8 |
| % international | 2 |

### SURVEY SAYS . . .
Great library
School is well run
Registration is a breeze
Dorms are like palaces
(Almost) no one smokes
Very small frat/sorority scene
No one plays intramural sports
Lousy food on campus

## ACADEMICS

| | |
|---|---|
| Academic Rating | 96 |
| Calendar | semester |
| Student/faculty ratio | 9:1 |
| Profs interesting rating | 96 |
| Profs accessible rating | 98 |
| % profs teaching UG courses | 100 |
| Avg lab size | 10-19 students |
| Avg reg class size | 10-19 students |

### MOST POPULAR MAJORS
English language and literature
Biology/biological sciences
Economics

## STUDENTS SPEAK OUT

### Academics
When students at Pomona say their "professors are really interesting, interested, and accessible," they really mean it. "Ever been skinny dipping with a professor?" one senior asks. Though there's no guarantee that you'll get to see your professors in the buff, you're sure to meet a healthy number of professors whom you "can cultivate a close relationship with." Remarks one student, "I had dinner with the dean last night, I received a personal e-mail from two profs in the last 24 hours, and my history prof wrote more about my paper than I did." Students at Pomona choose classes from "a wide range of topics" offered by the college's 26 departments. Although "academics are highly valued by students," they're "never a source of extreme stress." Campus administrators get mixed reviews ranging from "disconnected" to "plugged-in." However, Pomona students are quick to point out that they are always accessible. One students sums up the experience at Pomona with this commment: "It's kind of like going to summer camp with a lot of work." Another goes even further: "Our college is the happiest place on earth. It's like living in Disneyland 24 hours a day."

### Life
"People at Pomona amaze me," waxes one sophomore. "They can drink more than humanly possible Monday, Tuesday, Wednesday, Thursday, and then ace their organic chem final that Friday." There are few opportunities for Pomona students to party off campus, because "unfortunately the City of Claremont is in denial of its being a college town." However, Pomona students have no trouble finding a party *on* campus. Many students said they found it difficult to balance work and play at Pomona—the classes, the social scene, and the ever-present Southern California sunshine. However, strike a balance they do: "We work hard and play hard . . . more often than not it's on the same day." Anyone would have difficulty in labeling Pomona, as "the activities are as diverse as the people." The college offers a slew of diversions for students, who go to "movies, speakers, and concerts," "to the pool, the beach, and the mountains," and take advantage of "the fun, [and] free classes" like "piano lessons" and "ju-jitsu." Most students enjoy being "so close to L.A.," which is about 35 miles west. Not surprisingly, Pomona's geography is one of the school's draws. A freshman loves "being half an hour away from pro basketball, pro baseball, skiing, the beach, museums, nightclubs, and especially Disneyland!" And let's not forget the weather. "Where else can you spend a winter afternoon studying by the pool after a morning of intense classes?"

### Student Body
Pomona students boast they're "some of the easiest people to get along with." This is a West Coast school at its best, without any of "the East Coast high-strung mentality." While students are "smart," they're also "laid back." And they're a political bunch, too. "Just like the administration, they are very focused on being 'PC' and promoting 'free speech.' " Speaking freely isn't as accepted, however, when "your opinion doesn't agree with the left-wingers who dominate the campus." One student who describes himself as "right wing" complains that his fellow students "just reiterate what their liberal parents and educators have ingrained in 'em." Of course, there are also the students who can be "kind of lazy" and spend their time pondering the less-than-important questions of life, like how can they "get really drunk"? But don't let a slight disposition for sleeping and partying fool you; as one sophomore remarks, "I'm constantly surprised by the talent I'm surrounded by."

# POMONA COLLEGE

FINANCIAL AID: 909-621-8205 • E-MAIL: ADMISSIONS@POMONA.EDU • WEBSITE: WWW.POMONA.EDU

## ADMISSIONS

*Very important factors considered include:* character/personal qualities, class rank, essays, extracurricular activities, interview, recommendations, secondary school record, standardized test scores, talent/ability. *Other factors considered include:* alumni/ae relation, geographical residence, minority status, volunteer work, work experience. TOEFL required of all international applicants. *High school units required/recommended:* 4 English required, 3 math required, 4 math recommended, 3 science required, 2 science lab required, 3 foreign language required, 4 foreign language recommended, 2 social studies required.

### The Inside Word

Even though it is tough to get admitted to Pomona, students will find the admissions staff to be accessible and engaging. An applicant pool full of such well-qualified students as those who typically apply, in combination with the college's small size, necessitates that candidates undergo as personal an admissions evaluation as possible. This is how solid matches are made and how Pomona does a commendable job of keeping an edge on the competition.

## FINANCIAL AID

*Students should submit:* FAFSA, CSS/Financial Aid PROFILE, state aid form, noncustodial (divorced/separated) parent's statement, business/farm supplement, tax returns for both the student and parents. Regular filing deadline is February 1. The Princeton Review suggests that all financial aid forms be submitted as soon as possible after January 1. *Need-based scholarships/grants offered:* Pell, SEOG, state scholarships/grants, private scholarships, the school's own gift aid. *Loan aid offered:* FFEL Subsidized Stafford, FFEL Unsubsidized Stafford, FFEL PLUS, Federal Perkins, college/university loans from institutional funds. Federal Work-Study Program available. Institutional employment available. Applicants will be notified of awards on or about April 10. Off-campus job opportunities are excellent.

## FROM THE ADMISSIONS OFFICE

"Perhaps the most important thing to know about Pomona College is that we are what we say we are. There is enormous integrity between the statements of mission and philosophy governing the college and the reality that students, faculty, and administrators experience. The balance in the curriculum is unusual. Sciences, social sciences, humanities, and the arts receive equal attention, support, and emphasis. Most importantly, the commitment to undergraduate education is absolute. Teaching awards remain the highest honor the trustees can bestow upon faculty. The typical method of instruction is the seminar and the average class size of 14 offers students the opportunity to become full partners in the learning process. Our location in the Los Angeles basin and in Claremont, with five other colleges, provides a remarkable community."

---

### SELECTIVITY

| | |
|---|---:|
| **Admissions Rating** | 97 |
| # of applicants | 4,230 |
| % of applicants accepted | 23 |
| % of acceptees attending | 39 |
| # of early decision applicants | 345 |
| % accepted early decision | 33 |

#### FRESHMAN PROFILE

| | |
|---|---:|
| Range SAT Verbal | 690-760 |
| Average SAT Verbal | 730 |
| Range SAT Math | 680-750 |
| Average SAT Math | 720 |
| Range ACT Composite | 30-33 |
| Average ACT Composite | 32 |
| Minimum TOEFL | 600 |
| Average HS GPA | 3.9 |
| % graduated top 10% of class | 84 |
| % graduated top 25% of class | 89 |
| % graduated top 50% of class | 100 |

#### DEADLINES

| | |
|---|---:|
| Early decision | 11/15 |
| Early decision notification | 12/15 |
| Regular admission | 1/2 |
| Regular notification | 4/10 |

#### APPLICANTS ALSO LOOK AT AND OFTEN PREFER
Harvard
UC—Berkeley
Stanford
Yale, Princeton

#### AND SOMETIMES PREFER
UCLA
Dartmouth
Williams
Wesleyan U.
Claremont McKenna

#### AND RARELY PREFER
UC—Davis
Pitzer

### FINANCIAL FACTS

| | |
|---|---:|
| **Financial Aid Rating** | 91 |
| Tuition | $25,730 |
| Room and board | $9,600 |
| % frosh receiving aid | 51 |
| % undergrads receiving aid | 52 |
| Avg frosh grant | $20,300 |
| Avg frosh loan | $2,000 |

# PRINCETON UNIVERSITY

PO Box 430, Admission Office, Princeton, NJ 08544-0430 • Admissions: 609-258-3060 • Fax: 609-258-6743

## CAMPUS LIFE

| | |
|---|---|
| Quality of Life Rating | 86 |
| Type of school | private |
| Environment | suburban |

### STUDENTS

| | |
|---|---|
| Total undergrad enrollment | 4,779 |
| % male/female | 52/48 |
| % from out of state | 86 |
| % from public high school | 55 |
| % live on campus | 97 |
| % African American | 9 |
| % Asian | 13 |
| % Caucasian | 70 |
| % Hispanic | 7 |
| % international | 7 |

### SURVEY SAYS . . .
Lots of classroom discussion
Registration is a breeze
Diverse students interact
No one cheats
(Almost) everyone smokes
Computer lab facilities need improving
Intercollegiate sports unpopular or nonexistent
Lousy food on campus
No one plays intramural sports

## ACADEMICS

| | |
|---|---|
| Academic Rating | 99 |
| Calendar | semester |
| Student/faculty ratio | 6:1 |
| Profs interesting rating | 94 |
| Profs accessible rating | 91 |

### MOST POPULAR MAJORS
History
English language and literature
Political science and government

## STUDENTS SPEAK OUT

### Academics

Princeton University is arguably the most undergraduate-friendly member of the Ivy League. "The lack of a large graduate school at Princeton allows professors to focus more on the undergraduate population, which is a significant contrast to other top schools in the nation." Students rate professors from "stars of academia" to "unknowns who are there because they are great at teaching." With more than 4,500 undergrads, Princeton is no stranger to lecture courses. But "all the bigger lectures are broken down into precepts"—small, once-a-week discussion groups where students are given a greater degree of personal attention. While many of the precepts are run by TAs "who don't always have wonderful teaching skills," others are led by faculty members. One exuberant student says, "I walked into my first precept of the semester and saw that my preceptor was none other than James McPherson, the greatest living Civil War historian." History, politics, English, and economics are the most popular majors. But, argues a student, "there are basically no weak departments at Princeton. Whatever subject you choose to major in, you will have the world's foremost experts in the field instructing you." All students must complete "independent work" in their junior year and "a thesis" as seniors. The university calls these requirements "the hallmark of a Princeton education," and students rave that it "is fantastic because of the close relationships it fosters between students and their professor-advisors who supervise all independent work."

### Life

"Two words: THE STREET." "The Street," as students call it, is Prospect Avenue, where one finds Princeton's famous eating clubs. "It's impossible to explain Princeton's social life without describing the Eating Clubs." These are "Princeton's version of coed fraternities," and at the end of sophomore year the majority of students join one—either through lottery or a selection process called "bicker." Members get "free" food and "free" beer, not to mention access to an array of social events. Students' descriptions of the clubs range from "quite good" to "pompous and ridiculous." New students quickly realize that the town of Princeton "offers little diversion for a college student." That's why "most of an undergraduate's social life occurs" on campus. The university provides "various performances, dances, fashion shows, cultural shows, plays, and theatre," not to mention a plentitude of extracurricular clubs and athletics. The new student center "has movies, TVs, a chic coffee shop with live jazz, a smoothie and milkshake bar, plenty of room to chill, computers, and, of course, great food." And, yes, Princeton students study. A lot. "I think most Princeton students find time to keep up with their work, do extracurriculars, and party," surmises a student. "The only thing that gets sacrificed is sleep."

### Student Body

"At first, most (students) seem like your typical college kids. It's only after you live with them that you begin to see how incredible they are." While Princeton's administration is still working hard to outrun the university's "preppy white image," it's having no problem drawing in brilliant students. "I learn more talking to my friends at 3 A.M. than I'll ever learn from a Nobel Prize winner," writes one satisfied student. The undergrads here range from championship athletes to award-winning musicians—and everyone in between. And they come from a range of backgrounds. As one student puts it, "Princeton is one of the few schools in the country where the son or daughter of a wealthy senator can befriend a math Olympiad winner whose parents didn't finish high school." Others do complain about the lack of racial diversity on campus: "Princeton is numerically diverse (i.e., they have a healthy percentage of minority students), but it seems somewhat homogenous." This aside, one student assures, "As a minority, I don't feel any discrimination." Sure, students here "can be somewhat pretentious." But hey, every once in a while "it can be difficult being bunched together with a group of overachievers."

# PRINCETON UNIVERSITY

FINANCIAL AID: 609-258-3330 • WEBSITE: WWW.PRINCETON.EDU

## ADMISSIONS

*Very important factors considered include:* character/personal qualities, essays, extracurricular activities, recommendations, secondary school record, standardized test scores, talent/ability, volunteer work, work experience. *Important factors considered include:* alumni/ae relation, minority status. *Other factors considered include:* class rank, interview. SAT I or ACT required; SAT I preferred; SAT II also required. TOEFL required of all international applicants. High school diploma is required and GED is not accepted. *High school units required/recommended:* 18 total recommended; 4 English recommended, 4 math recommended, 2 science recommended, 2 science lab recommended, 4 foreign language recommended, 2 history recommended.

### The Inside Word

Princeton is much more open about the admissions process than the rest of their Ivy compatriots. The admissions staff evaluates candidates' credentials using a 1–5 rating scale, common among highly selective colleges. In the initial screening of applicants, admissions staff members assigned to particular regions of the country eliminate weaker students before the admissions committee makes its evaluation. Princeton's recommendation to interview should be considered a requirement, given the ultra-competitive nature of the applicant pool. In addition, three SAT IIs are required; no joke, indeed.

## FINANCIAL AID

*Students should submit:* Princeton accepts, but does not require, the CSS/PROFILE application. The primary application is the Princeton Financial Aid Application, on the Web at www.princeton.edu. This online form has no fee. The FAFSA is also required. Regular filing deadline is February 1. *Need-based scholarships/grants offered:* Pell, SEOG, state scholarships/grants, private scholarships, the school's own gift aid. Princeton eliminated student loans in 2001–2002 and replaced them with additional grants. Since then, no student has been required to borrow as part of their aid award. Federal Work-Study Program available. Institutional employment available. Applicants will be notified of awards on or about April 1. Off-campus job opportunities are good.

## FROM THE ADMISSIONS OFFICE

"Methods of instruction [at Princeton] vary widely, but common to all areas . . . is a strong emphasis on individual responsibility and the free interchange of ideas. This is displayed most notably in the wide use of preceptorials and seminars, in the provision of independent study for all upperclass students and qualified underclass students, and in the availability of a series of special programs to meet a range of individual interests. The undergraduate college encourages the student to be an independent seeker of information . . . and to assume responsibility for gaining both knowledge and judgment that will strengthen later contributions to society."

### SELECTIVITY
★★★★

| | |
|---|---|
| Admissions Rating | 99 |
| # of applicants | 14,521 |
| % of applicants accepted | 11 |
| % of acceptees attending | 73 |

### FRESHMAN PROFILE

| | |
|---|---|
| Minimum TOEFL | 630 |
| % graduated top 10% of class | 95 |
| % graduated top 25% of class | 99 |
| % graduated top 50% of class | 100 |

### DEADLINES

| | |
|---|---|
| Early decision | 11/1 |
| Early decision notification | 12/15 |
| Regular admission | 1/1 |
| Regular notification | 4/3 |

### APPLICANTS ALSO LOOK AT AND SOMETIMES PREFER
Harvard
Yale
Stanford
MIT

### AND RARELY PREFER
Dartmouth
Brown
Duke
Columbia
Williams

### FINANCIAL FACTS

| | |
|---|---|
| Financial Aid Rating | 83 |
| Tuition | $28,540 |
| Room and board | $8,109 |
| Books and supplies | $790 |
| % frosh receiving aid | 46 |
| % undergrads receiving aid | 43 |
| Avg frosh grant | $23,000 |

# PROVIDENCE COLLEGE

RIVER AVENUE AND EATON STREET, PROVIDENCE, RI 02918 • ADMISSIONS: 401-865-2535 • FAX: 401-865-2826

## CAMPUS LIFE

| Quality of Life Rating | 79 |
|---|---|
| Type of school | private |
| Affiliation | Roman Catholic |
| Environment | suburban |

### STUDENTS

| Total undergrad enrollment | 4,371 |
|---|---|
| % male/female | 42/58 |
| % from out of state | 87 |
| % from public high school | 63 |
| % live on campus | 76 |
| % African American | 2 |
| % Asian | 2 |
| % Caucasian | 85 |
| % Hispanic | 2 |
| % international | 1 |

### SURVEY SAYS . . .

Diversity lacking on campus
Everyone loves the Friars
Hard liquor is popular
Students are cliquish
(Almost) everyone plays intramural sports
Very small frat/sorority scene
Students are very religious
Registration is a pain
Library needs improving
Lousy food on campus

## ACADEMICS

| Academic Rating | 78 |
|---|---|
| Calendar | semester |
| Student/faculty ratio | 14:1 |
| Profs interesting rating | 92 |
| Profs accessible rating | 89 |
| % profs teaching UG courses | 100 |
| Avg lab size | 10-19 students |
| Avg reg class size | 10-19 students |

### MOST POPULAR MAJORS
Marketing/marketing management
Special education
Biology/biological sciences

## STUDENTS SPEAK OUT

### Academics

Providence College: Welcome to an enjoyable but "demanding" academic experience. Students attend Providence because it is a small Catholic school with a reputation for its strong liberal arts program. The required two-year humanities course, "The Development of Western Civilization," is highly regarded and "comes in handy when watching Jeopardy." Some students complain that it also "lacks perspective outside" of that which is provided by the "white Catholic male" professors. Students appreciate that there are no TAs and that professors are, as one senior political science major puts it, "friendly and easily accessible." Professors "go out of their way to help students—even those not in their classes," a junior communications major brags. Though introductory classes tend to be easy, upper-level classes are "interesting and challenging." The Honors Program is "excellent," and the education program also garners high praise. The administration is "very rigid, keeping in close accordance with traditional Catholic policy," one junior reports, though students admit that the administration is also "very easy to communicate with." Class registration is "frustrating" because some students complain that athletes are provided preferential treatment.

### Life

"Life at Providence College involves working hard during the week and partying on the weekends." Speaking of other entertainment options, one senior management major notes, "there are also many theaters, shows, and intellectually stimulating events in and around the Providence College campus." Downtown Providence is a popular destination. The city's numerous quality restaurants are standard haunts. Students also spend a good deal of time working for various community service organizations. The college's basketball team plays in the powerful Big East conference and often fights its way into the NCAA Tournament. The hockey team is also a popular draw. A political science major speculates that "Friar hockey games [have] become the biggest social event on campus." Students are unhappy with the on-campus food, which one sophomore calls "just plain bad," and the dorms. They also complain that the exercise facilities are insufficient and that the school needs an indoor track. Students say that the nearby Indian casinos are a great place to blow off some steam.

### Student Body

A great sense of community pervades Providence College, thanks largely to the fact that students are "very involved on campus, especially through volunteer work." Some students sadly note that their peers "are very likely to conform to the latest styles and social norms." One sophomore admits that her fellow students are "mostly white, Irish-Catholic Republicans, and if you don't fit that mold, you're looked upon as different." Some students tend to be "cliquey" and "overly materialistic" as well as "shallow" and "snobbish," and diversity is sorely lacking. "We need more people from different backgrounds, and not just minorities, to open people up to seeing things another way." One biology major affirms, "The lack of diversity is frustrating." Nevertheless, students overwhelmingly admit that their peers are extremely friendly. "There is a familial atmosphere" at Providence College.

# PROVIDENCE COLLEGE

FINANCIAL AID: 401-865-2286 • E-MAIL: PCADMISS@PROVIDENCE.EDU • WEBSITE: WWW.PROVIDENCE.EDU

## ADMISSIONS
*Very important factors considered include:* secondary school record. *Important factors considered include:* character/personal qualities, class rank, essays, extracurricular activities, recommendations, standardized test scores, talent/ability, volunteer work. *Other factors considered include:* alumni/ae relation, geographical residence, minority status, state residency, work experience. SAT I or ACT required; SAT II recommended. TOEFL required of all international applicants. High school diploma is required and GED is not accepted. *High school units required/recommended:* 16 total required; 18 total recommended; 4 English required, 3 math required, 4 math recommended, 3 science required, 4 science recommended, 2 science lab required, 3 science lab recommended, 3 foreign language required, 1 social studies required, 2 history required.

### The Inside Word
Providence's reputation for quality is solidly in place among above-average graduates of northeastern Catholic high schools, who account for almost a quarter of the applicant pool. The strength of these candidates is one of the primary factors that allow the college to be choosy about who gets in. Successful candidates usually project a well-rounded, conservative image.

## FINANCIAL AID
*Students should submit:* FAFSA, CSS/Financial Aid PROFILE. Regular filing deadline is February 1. The Princeton Review suggests that all financial aid forms be submitted as soon as possible after January 1. *Need-based scholarships/grants offered:* Pell, SEOG, state scholarships/grants, private scholarships, the school's own gift aid. *Loan aid offered:* Direct Subsidized Stafford, Direct Unsubsidized Stafford, Direct PLUS, FFEL Subsidized Stafford, FFEL Unsubsidized Stafford, FFEL PLUS, Federal Perkins. Federal Work-Study Program available. Institutional employment available. Applicants will be notified of awards on or about April 1. Off-campus job opportunities are excellent.

## FROM THE ADMISSIONS OFFICE
"Infused with the history, tradition, and learning of a 700-year-old Catholic teaching order, the Dominican Friars, Providence College offers a value-affirming environment where students are enriched through spiritual, social, physical, and cultural growth as well as through intellectual development. Providence College offers over 35 programs of study leading to baccalaureate degrees in business, education, the sciences, arts, and humanities. Our faculty is noted for a strong commitment to teaching. A close student/faculty relationship allows for in-depth classwork, independent research projects, and detailed career exploration. While noted for the physical facilities and academic opportunities associated with larger universities, Providence also fosters personal growth through a small, spirited, family-like atmosphere that encourages involvement in student activities and athletics."

### SELECTIVITY

| | |
|---|---|
| **Admissions Rating** | 83 |
| # of applicants | 7,347 |
| % of applicants accepted | 49 |
| % of acceptees attending | 24 |
| # accepting a place on wait list | 399 |
| % admitted from wait list | 88 |

### FRESHMAN PROFILE
| | |
|---|---|
| Range SAT Verbal | 540-630 |
| Average SAT Verbal | 587 |
| Range SAT Math | 550-640 |
| Average SAT Math | 596 |
| Range ACT Composite | 23-28 |
| Average ACT Composite | 25 |
| Minimum TOEFL | 550 |
| Average HS GPA | 3.4 |
| % graduated top 10% of class | 42 |
| % graduated top 25% of class | 81 |
| % graduated top 50% of class | 99 |

### DEADLINES
| | |
|---|---|
| Regular admission | 1/15 |
| Regular notification | 4/1 |
| Nonfall registration? | yes |

### APPLICANTS ALSO LOOK AT AND OFTEN PREFER
Boston College
Holy Cross
Notre Dame
Tufts
Georgetown

**AND SOMETIMES PREFER**
Villanova
Fairfield
Stonehill
Fordham, Boston U

**AND RARELY PREFER**
U of New Hampshire
U of Connecticut, St. John's
Scranton, St. Anselm

### FINANCIAL FACTS

| | |
|---|---|
| **Financial Aid Rating** | 81 |
| Tuition | $21,665 |
| Room and board | $8,500 |
| Books and supplies | $650 |
| Required fees | $320 |
| % frosh receiving aid | 67 |
| % undergrads receiving aid | 64 |
| Avg frosh grant | $9,570 |
| Avg frosh loan | $4,125 |

# PURDUE UNIVERSITY—WEST LAFAYETTE

1080 SCHLEMAN HALL, WEST LAFAYETTE, IN 47907 • ADMISSIONS: 765-494-1776 • FAX: 765-494-0544

## CAMPUS LIFE

| | |
|---|---|
| Quality of Life Rating | 79 |
| Type of school | public |
| Environment | suburban |

### STUDENTS

| | |
|---|---|
| Total undergrad enrollment | 30,908 |
| % male/female | 58/42 |
| % from out of state | 24 |
| % in (# of) fraternities | 18 (46) |
| % in (# of) sororities | 17 (25) |
| % African American | 3 |
| % Asian | 4 |
| % Caucasian | 82 |
| % Hispanic | 2 |
| % international | 6 |
| # of countries represented | 120 |

### SURVEY SAYS . . .
Everyone loves the Boilermakers
Lots of beer drinking
Hard liquor is popular
Students are cliquish
Frats and sororities dominate social scene
Musical organizations are hot
Campus difficult to get around
Great computer facilities
Lab facilities are great
Lousy food on campus

## ACADEMICS

| | |
|---|---|
| Academic Rating | 68 |
| Calendar | semester |
| Student/faculty ratio | 16:1 |
| Profs interesting rating | 91 |
| Profs accessible rating | 92 |
| Avg lab size | 20-29 students |
| Avg reg class size | 20-29 students |

## STUDENTS SPEAK OUT

### Academics
Purdue is a big school, and while it can boast a stock of "great professors," it still has the expected pitfalls of most institutions of its girth. "Classes should be easier to get into," grumbles one freshman. Class sizes range from the intimate to the gargantuan, and students who get stuck in the latter wish they had "more time to associate with students one on one." Many students report that the majority of their intro classes are taught by teaching assistants, and TAs even run several upper-level courses. This can be a particular problem when "teaching assistants suck," as one sophomore puts it. The less-than-attractive aspects of Purdue's academics cause some students to think that Purdue "is not what they make it out to be." But on the flipside, some students say that you can get a terrific education if you simply go after it, like this junior, who wrote, "Even though it is a large size school, I get the help I need." And a seldom-mentioned perk of Purdue's academic plan as structured on its physical plant is that "all your classes are within walking distance of each other."

### Life
It shouldn't be a shock to hear that "football games are a big thing that everyone attends" at Purdue. And it shouldn't be surprising to be told that Purdue students "like to party!" In fact, you probably won't be caught off guard by anything that you learn about Purdue's social life—except, maybe, that some students like to spend their free hours on the campus's "mud volleyball courts." Otherwise, many students adhere to a routine that goes something like this: "Go to class, eat some food, play some video games, drink some beer, & sleep." With a good number of hungry livers on campus, Purdue's social scene offers plenty of opportunities to go to "fraternities and apartment parties" and drink the night away. But it's not all fun from a keg; "there are many things to get involved with, like intramural sports, clubs, and exercising." In regard to life away from campus, students seem to think West Lafayette is an "average" town, with individual opinions ranging from calling it "excellent" to whining that "the town smells." The campus itself is "beautiful," and the students who live on it manage to find a "good mixture of school and social life." There are some, however, who would rather spend their days in bedrooms instead of classrooms. Explains a freshman, "Quite a few people are nymphos!"

### Student Body
There are about 30,000 undergraduates at the main West Lafayette campus of Purdue. With a number like this, it's not surprising that people seem to "just keep to themselves." But don't let big numbers scare you—"there are so many students that it's easy to make friends and find people with common interests." Students will admit that their population is not "as diverse as we let on to be." One black student from Indianapolis writes that she "never felt what it is like to be a minority until I came to Purdue." But the Purdue stock assures that it's a "friendly" one. As one new member of campus says, "the students at Purdue are very helpful, and I know if I ever need anything, they will be there."

# PURDUE UNIVERSITY—WEST LAFAYETTE

FINANCIAL AID: 765-494-5050 • E-MAIL: ADMISSIONS@ADMS.PURDUE.EDU • WEBSITE: WWW.PURDUE.EDU

## ADMISSIONS
*Very important factors considered include:* class rank, secondary school record, standardized test scores. *Other factors considered include:* alumni/ae relation, recommendations, state residency. SAT I or ACT required. TOEFL required of all international applicants. High school diploma or GED is required. *High school units required/recommended:* 4 English required, 3 math required, 2 science required, 3 science recommended, 2 science lab required, 3 science lab recommended, 2 foreign language recommended.

### The Inside Word
The fact that Purdue holds class rank as one of its most important considerations in the admission of candidates is troublesome. There are far too many inconsistencies in ranking policies and class size among the 25,000-plus high schools in the U.S. to place so much weight on an essentially incomparable number. The university's high admit rate thankfully renders the issue relatively moot, even though applications have increased.

## FINANCIAL AID
*Students should submit:* FAFSA. The Princeton Review suggests that all financial aid forms be submitted as soon as possible after January 1. *Need-based scholarships/grants offered:* Pell, SEOG, state scholarships/grants, private scholarships, the school's own gift aid. *Loan aid offered:* FFEL Subsidized Stafford, FFEL Unsubsidized Stafford, FFEL PLUS, Federal Perkins, college/university loans from institutional funds. Federal Work-Study Program available. Institutional employment available. Applicants will be notified of awards on or about April 15. Off-campus job opportunities are good.

## FROM THE ADMISSIONS OFFICE
"Although it is one of America's largest universities, Purdue does not 'feel' big to its students. The main campus in West Lafayette was built around a master plan that keeps walking time between classes to a maximum of 12 minutes. Purdue is a comprehensive university with an international reputation in a wide range of academic fields. A strong work ethic prevails at Purdue. As a member of the Big 10, Purdue has a strong and diverse athletic program. Purdue offers nearly 600 clubs and organizations. The residence halls and Greek community offer many participatory activities for students. Numerous convocations and lectures are presented each year. Purdue is all about people, and allowing students to grow academically as well as socially, preparing them for the real world."

## SELECTIVITY

| | |
|---|---|
| Admissions Rating | 76 |
| # of applicants | 22,872 |
| % of applicants accepted | 76 |
| % of acceptees attending | 36 |

### FRESHMAN PROFILE
| | |
|---|---|
| Range SAT Verbal | 500-610 |
| Average SAT Verbal | 555 |
| Range SAT Math | 530-660 |
| Average SAT Math | 595 |
| Range ACT Composite | 23-28 |
| Average ACT Composite | 26 |
| Minimum TOEFL | 550 |
| % graduated top 10% of class | 28 |
| % graduated top 25% of class | 62 |
| % graduated top 50% of class | 93 |

### DEADLINES
| | |
|---|---|
| Priority admission | 3/1 |
| Nonfall registration? | yes |

### APPLICANTS ALSO LOOK AT AND SOMETIMES PREFER
Indiana U at Bloomington
Valparaiso
U of Illinois
Rose-Hulman

## FINANCIAL FACTS

| | |
|---|---|
| Financial Aid Rating | 83 |
| In-state tuition | $5,580 |
| Out-of-state tuition | $16,260 |
| Room and board | $6,340 |
| Books and supplies | $830 |
| % frosh receiving aid | 38 |
| % undergrads receiving aid | 36 |

# RANDOLPH-MACON COLLEGE

Box 5005-5505, Ashland, VA 23005 • Admissions: 804-752-7305 • Fax: 804-752-4707

## CAMPUS LIFE

| Quality of Life Rating | 87 |
|---|---|
| Type of school | private |
| Affiliation | Methodist |
| Environment | suburban |

### STUDENTS

| | |
|---|---|
| Total undergrad enrollment | 1,154 |
| % male/female | 50/50 |
| % from out of state | 35 |
| % from public high school | 65 |
| % live on campus | 85 |
| % in (# of) fraternities | 45 (6) |
| % in (# of) sororities | 45 (5) |
| % African American | 5 |
| % Asian | 1 |
| % Caucasian | 92 |
| % Hispanic | 2 |
| % international | 1 |
| # of countries represented | 16 |

### SURVEY SAYS . . .
Frats and sororities dominate social scene
Lots of beer drinking
Campus easy to get around
Hard liquor is popular
(Almost) everyone smokes
Campus is beautiful
Athletic facilities are great
Great computer facilities

## ACADEMICS

| Academic Rating | 79 |
|---|---|
| Calendar | 4-1-4 |
| Student/faculty ratio | 11:1 |
| % profs teaching UG courses | 100 |
| Avg reg class size | 10-19 students |

### MOST POPULAR MAJORS
Business/managerial economics
English language and literature
Psychology

## STUDENTS SPEAK OUT

### Academics

If what you seek is a "great education to prepare you for the real world while still having a great, fun social life," then Randolph-Macon College just might be the undergraduate institution for you. The curriculum provides a solid liberal arts education to the pragmatic student body. Undergrads here are accomplished—one in four proceeds immediately to grad school upon graduation. As one student tells it, "Word is that R-MC is easy to get into but hard to stay [in], and I believe that's completely true; you really have to work to get what you want out of your experience." Support comes primarily from a dedicated faculty; explained one student, "Our slogan says it best: 'Believe in the Moment of Connection.' Our professors are very close to us. The administration tries to be." More than one undergraduate thinks "the greatest strength of my school has to be its size and the many benefits that come with that. We are only a little over 1,000 students, so classes are never over 25 students." On the downside, "the problem with such a small school is that only so many classes can be offered because there is not an excess of students to take them and not a lot of professors to teach them." Membership in the Seven College Consortium of Virginia mitigates this problem somewhat.

### Life

"Greek life is a major part of campus life at our school," observes one R-MC student. Surprisingly few students here complain about the divisive effect Greek organizations often present, however, probably because "they provide so many student activities, even for those students who are not members." Notes one student approvingly, "Everyone gets along no matter what the differences may be (e.g., Greeks and non-Greeks are all friends). People look out for each other here. There is a real sense of community." This unity is obvious at every Yellow Jackets' home game; "sporting events such as men's basketball and football are popular, and they have a pretty big turnout for their games," writes one student. Outdoor enthusiasts speak highly of Macon Outdoors, a campus organization "dedicated to exploring the outdoors" through "rafting, skiing, hiking, kayaking, mountain biking, canoeing, and rock climbing" trips. Complains one student, "I have trouble finding things to do on the weekends because I don't drink." Some students commit to clubs, organizations, and public service. Those who don't usually frequent the Greek houses or "entertain themselves in downtown Richmond," just a half-hour to the south.

### Student Body

Randolph Macon is "slowly becoming more diverse"; even so, the vast majority of undergraduates "come from a mid- to upper-socioeconomic-level background and tend to be Republican." The typical student is "from Virginia, Maryland, or Pennsylvania" and mostly "concerns him- or herself with the ongoing social aspects of campus, with little to no regard for what is going on in the outside world," writes one undergrad. Students here are sociable and easygoing about their academic commitments: "People . . . go out and party and still get their work done." Undergraduates are often "involved in many different aspects of college life . . . . [They are] active in sports (either competitive or intramural) and most likely also have a job somewhere on campus or in the nearby community."

410 ■ THE BEST 351 COLLEGES

# RANDOLPH-MACON COLLEGE

FINANCIAL AID: 804-752-7259 • E-MAIL: ADMISSIONS@RMC.EDU • WEBSITE: WWW.RMC.EDU

## ADMISSIONS

*Very important factors considered include:* secondary school record. *Important factors considered include:* class rank, recommendations, standardized test scores. *Other factors considered include:* alumni/ae relation, character/personal qualities, essays, extracurricular activities, interview, minority status, talent/ability, volunteer work. SAT I or ACT required; SAT I preferred; SAT II also recommended. TOEFL required of all international applicants. High school diploma or GED is required. *High school units required/recommended:* 16 total required; 22 total recommended; 4 English required, 3 math required, 4 math recommended, 3 science required, 4 science recommended, 2 science lab required, 4 science lab recommended, 2 foreign language required, 4 foreign language recommended, 1 social studies required, 4 social studies recommended, 2 history required, 1 elective required.

## The Inside Word

Candidates who are above-average students and testers are very likely to receive scholarships at Randolph-Macon. The college has a low yield of admits who enroll, and every strong student who signs on gives the freshman academic profile a boost. If the competition among Virginia colleges weren't so strong, admission to Randolph-Macon would be much tougher.

## FINANCIAL AID

*Students should submit:* FAFSA, state aid form. The Princeton Review suggests that all financial aid forms be submitted as soon as possible after January 1. *Need-based scholarships/grants offered:* Pell, SEOG, state scholarships/grants, private scholarships, the school's own gift aid. *Loan aid offered:* FFEL Subsidized Stafford, FFEL Unsubsidized Stafford, FFEL PLUS, Federal Perkins, college/university loans from institutional funds. Federal Work-Study Program available. Institutional employment available. Applicants will be notified of awards on or about April 1. Off-campus job opportunities are good.

## FROM THE ADMISSIONS OFFICE

"Randolph-Macon College, located in historic Ashland, just north of Richmond, is a co-educational, liberal arts and sciences college with a mission fulfilled through a combination of personal interaction and academic rigor. The student/faculty ratio is 11:1 and the average class size is 16 students. Enrollment is kept at approximately 1,150 to maintain this intimate atmosphere. Randolph-Macon College has an outstanding national reputation for its internships, study abroad, and undergraduate research. Founded in 1830, Randolph-Macon College is the oldest United Methodist Church–affiliated college in the nation, is a Phi Beta Kappa college, and is ranked as a Baccalaureate I college by the Carnegie Foundation. It offers the broadest liberal arts core curriculum of any college in Virginia.

"The College prepares students for any future, including success in securing a job or in gaining acceptance to graduate or professional school. The College offers a wide variety of social and recreational opportunities through more than 100 campus organizations. Forty percent of the students participate in one or more community service activities; 70 percent play intramural sports; 45 percent join a fraternity or sorority; and everyone has a voice in student government. A new $9.5 million sports and recreation center is very popular with students, and a new performing arts center opened this year. In addition, freshmen residence halls are now under extensive renovation and a new 'Peaks of Excellence' center is being constructed."

## SELECTIVITY

| Admissions Rating | 77 |
|---|---|
| # of applicants | 1,689 |
| % of applicants accepted | 78 |
| % of acceptees attending | 29 |
| # accepting a place on wait list | 14 |
| # of early decision applicants | 55 |
| % accepted early decision | 73 |

### FRESHMAN PROFILE

| Range SAT Verbal | 500-610 |
|---|---|
| Average SAT Verbal | 560 |
| Range SAT Math | 500-600 |
| Average SAT Math | 552 |
| Minimum TOEFL | 550 |
| Average HS GPA | 3.2 |
| % graduated top 10% of class | 20 |
| % graduated top 25% of class | 50 |
| % graduated top 50% of class | 81 |

### DEADLINES

| Early decision | 12/1 |
|---|---|
| Early decision notification | 12/20 |
| Priority admission | 2/1 |
| Regular admission | 3/1 |
| Regular notification | 4/1 |
| Nonfall registration? | yes |

### APPLICANTS ALSO LOOK AT AND OFTEN PREFER
U of Virginia
### AND SOMETIMES PREFER
James Madison
Virginia Tech
Washington and Lee
Hampden-Sydney
### AND RARELY PREFER
Mary Washington
Roanoke
Sweet Briar
U of Richmond

## FINANCIAL FACTS

| Financial Aid Rating | 91 |
|---|---|
| Tuition | $19,480 |
| Room and board | $5,715 |
| Books and supplies | $600 |
| Required fees | $565 |
| % frosh receiving aid | 52 |
| % undergrads receiving aid | 50 |
| Avg frosh grant | $11,491 |
| Avg frosh loan | $3,600 |

# RANDOLPH-MACON WOMAN'S COLLEGE

2500 RIVERMONT AVENUE, LYNCHBURG, VA 24503-1526 • ADMISSIONS: 800-745-7692 • FAX: 434-947-8996

## CAMPUS LIFE

| | |
|---|---|
| Quality of Life Rating | 88 |
| Type of school | private |
| Affiliation | Methodist |
| Environment | suburban |

### STUDENTS
| | |
|---|---|
| Total undergrad enrollment | 764 |
| % from out of state | 55 |
| % from public high school | 82 |
| % live on campus | 90 |
| % African American | 8 |
| % Asian | 3 |
| % Caucasian | 85 |
| % Hispanic | 3 |
| % international | 11 |
| # of countries represented | 48 |

### SURVEY SAYS . . .
Students are religious
Political activism is hot
Theater is hot
(Almost) everyone plays intramural sports
Unattractive campus
Campus difficult to get around

## ACADEMICS

| | |
|---|---|
| Academic Rating | 93 |
| Calendar | semester |
| Student/faculty ratio | 9:1 |
| Profs interesting rating | 75 |
| Profs accessible rating | 73 |
| % profs teaching UG courses | 100 |
| Avg lab size | 10-19 students |
| Avg reg class size | 10-19 students |

### MOST POPULAR MAJORS
English language and literature
Biology/biological sciences
Psychology

## STUDENTS SPEAK OUT

### Academics
Students at Randolph-Macon Woman's College love the small-school charm that imbues their academic experience. "This is NOT a finishing school," undergrads here say time and again. It's the kind of place where "many professors seem to take it upon themselves as a personal mission to not award high grades" and course work is "difficult. It is not too bad to get along if you took a few AP courses in high school, but if you just skated through easier classes, you may have trouble." Professors, the women here agree, are "without a doubt the best thing about R-MWC . . . . They care about the students, and actually interact with them." Students also love R-MWC's honor code, which they describe as "amazing. Self-scheduled exams, freedom in leaving belongings in public areas, and a general feeling of cooperation are wonderful things to have in a college environment." These assets help make up for Macon's shortcomings, which include "a student body so small that it leaves only a few options in terms of classes" and a registration system that "flows like a clogged toilet."

### Life
Tradition is central to R-MWC extracurricular life. These traditions include the Even-Odd rivalry ("women that graduate in even years are even and women that graduate in odd years are odd; it helps create a bond based on graduation year"); Ring Week ("where juniors and [freshmen] are paired up to exchange little gifts and the first year decorates the junior's door and gives the junior her ring"); and Pumpkin Parade ("similar to Ring Week, but with sophomores and seniors, pumpkin carving, and a candlelight parade"). Students love these distinguishing touches, but wish the school could supplement them with a more active social calendar. Explained one student, "We are completely restricted by the school's visitation and alcohol policies. The school seems to still be stuck in an era when most schools in the area were single-sex and there was more incentive for men to come here." As a result, "many students feel they must go off-campus for fun," and so they do, road-tripping to "Charlottesville, home of UVA, which attracts a lot of live music," and Roanoke, which "has a decent nightlife, with three nightclubs and an all-night coffee shop." They rarely hang around hometown Lynchburg, which "is not a college town, despite having over 12,000 college students (combining our school, Liberty University, Lynchburg College, and Sweet Briar College)." As they do every time we survey them, the women of R-MWC brag that "we have the best dining service! They cook us real food (and I'm talking real chicken parmesan, steak, fried cod, shrimp) and if you can't find anything to eat (which is next to impossible), just go find Jeff, our head chef. He'll make you whatever you want!"

### Student Body
"There is definitely a range" of women at R-MWC, "from the super-traditional girly girls who spend many a weekend at Hampden-Sydney or VMI looking for their future husbands to very liberal feminists who never look for guys; from girls who party and drink nearly every weekend to girls [who] think that a good time is a hot cup of tea and a Jane Austen novel." Students tell us that "everyone gets along pretty well. . . . Of course, on an all-female campus, there's always someone PMS-ing, but that's life." Many speak of a sense of sisterhood; as one student explained, "With so few students, all of them women, and nearly all living on campus, it is understandable that we would be a bit closer than many other colleges." Another benefit of attending an all-women's college: "It really decreases the emphasis on fashion, makeup, and the like."

# RANDOLPH-MACON WOMAN'S COLLEGE

FINANCIAL AID: 434-947-8128 • E-MAIL: ADMISSIONS@RMWC.EDU • WEBSITE: WWW.RMWC.EDU

## ADMISSIONS

*Very important factors considered include:* character/personal qualities, essays, recommendations, secondary school record. *Important factors considered include:* class rank, extracurricular activities, standardized test scores, talent/ability. *Other factors considered include:* alumni/ae relation, interview, minority status, volunteer work, work experience. SAT I or ACT required. TOEFL required of all international applicants. High school diploma or GED is required. *High school units required/recommended:* 16 total required; 4 English recommended, 3 math recommended, 2 science recommended, 2 science lab recommended, 4 foreign language recommended, 2 history recommended, 2 elective recommended.

### The Inside Word

The admissions process at Randolph-Macon Woman's College works pretty much as it does at most small liberal arts colleges, with one worthwhile exception: Each candidate is assigned to an admissions staff member who functions as an advocate for the student throughout the process. It's nice to have somewhat regular contact with someone in the admissions office over the course of the cycle. This saves time restating problems, questions, and circumstances every time you call or write. It also helps the college make a strong positive impression on applicants.

## FINANCIAL AID

*Students should submit:* FAFSA, state aid form. No deadline for regular filing. The Princeton Review suggests that all financial aid forms be submitted as soon as possible after January 1. *Need-based scholarships/grants offered:* Pell, SEOG, state scholarships/grants, private scholarships, the school's own gift aid. *Loan aid offered:* FFEL Subsidized Stafford, FFEL Unsubsidized Stafford, FFEL PLUS, Federal Perkins. Federal Work-Study Program available. Institutional employment available. Applicants will be notified of awards on a rolling basis beginning on or about March 1. Off-campus job opportunities are good.

## FROM THE ADMISSIONS OFFICE

"Randolph-Macon Woman's College students appreciate the College's personalized approach to their educational program. Their individualized Macon Plan, which includes study abroad, internships, career guidance, leadership development, and one-on-one faculty advising, allows the student superior opportunities and direction in achieving their goals and dreams. The Honor System is a vital part of life at R-MWC, providing students with a living and learning environment based on integrity, trust, and mutual respect. A diverse student population from 43 states and 47 countries offers exceptional opportunities to learn about different cultures and perspectives. The College's solid academic reputation coupled with an impressive array of alumnae who are leaders in nearly every career field imaginable positions R-MWC as one of the finest liberal arts colleges in the nation.

"If you are bright, ambitious, and motivated, Randolph-Macon Woman's College is the place for you!"

## ADMISSIONS

| | |
|---|---|
| **Admissions Rating** | **80** |
| # of applicants | 723 |
| % of applicants accepted | 85 |
| % of acceptees attending | 33 |
| # of early decision applicants | 32 |
| % accepted early decision | 81 |

### FRESHMAN PROFILE

| | |
|---|---|
| Range SAT Verbal | 540-640 |
| Average SAT Verbal | 592 |
| Range SAT Math | 510-620 |
| Average SAT Math | 564 |
| Range ACT Composite | 23-28 |
| Average ACT Composite | 25 |
| Minimum TOEFL | 550 |
| Average HS GPA | 3.4 |
| % graduated top 10% of class | 39 |
| % graduated top 25% of class | 65 |
| % graduated top 50% of class | 93 |

### DEADLINES

| | |
|---|---|
| Early decision | 11/15 |
| Early decision notification | 12/15 |
| Regular admission | 3/1 |
| Nonfall registration? | yes |

### APPLICANTS ALSO LOOK AT AND OFTEN PREFER
Duke
Wellesley
Smith

### AND SOMETIMES PREFER
U of Virginia
William and Mary
Mount Holyoke
Sweet Briar

### AND RARELY PREFER
Virginia Tech
Hollins
James Madison

## FINANCIAL FACTS

| | |
|---|---|
| **Financial Aid Rating** | **92** |
| Tuition | $18,900 |
| Room and board | $7,560 |
| Required fees | $380 |
| % frosh receiving aid | 65 |
| % undergrads receiving aid | 62 |
| Avg frosh grant | $14,400 |
| Avg frosh loan | $2,461 |

# REED COLLEGE

3203 SE WOODSTOCK BOULEVARD, PORTLAND, OR 97202-8199 • ADMISSION: 503-777-7511 • FAX: 503-777-7553

## CAMPUS LIFE

| | |
|---|---|
| Quality of Life Rating | 84 |
| Type of school | private |
| Environment | suburban |

### STUDENTS
| | |
|---|---|
| Total undergrad enrollment | 1,363 |
| % male/female | 46/54 |
| % from out of state | 79 |
| % from public high school | 66 |
| % live on campus | 57 |
| % African American | 1 |
| % Asian | 5 |
| % Caucasian | 68 |
| % Hispanic | 4 |
| % international | 3 |
| # of countries represented | 38 |

### SURVEY SAYS . . .
Diversity lacking on campus
No one cheats
Students love Portland, OR
(Almost) everyone smokes
Registration is a breeze
Class discussions encouraged

## ACADEMICS

| | |
|---|---|
| Academic Rating | 98 |
| Calendar | semester |
| Student/faculty ratio | 10:1 |
| Profs interesting rating | 95 |
| Profs accessible rating | 99 |
| % profs teaching UG courses | 100 |
| Avg lab size | 10-19 students |
| Avg reg class size | 10-19 students |

### MOST POPULAR MAJORS
Biology/biological sciences
Psychology
English language and literature

## STUDENTS SPEAK OUT

### Academics
Tucked away in the Pacific Northwest, Reed College is a hidden acorn in the forest of academia. A Reed education combines a traditional classical curriculum with a progressive atmosphere that de-emphasizes grades and encourages intellectual discussion both in and out of class. Classes are intense and the workload is extremely challenging. A junior math major concurs, "Sometimes I do homework for one class as a break from work for another class. But it's a lot of fun and intellectually exciting." Students driven by comparing their grades to those of their peers need not apply. "This school is not for everyone. It is for people who consider themselves intellectuals and are driven to work not out of competition but for the intellectual endeavor," one student counsels. Reed's professors are generally well respected for both their intelligence and accessibility. Professors teach classes; TA's are nonexistent. "Most professors are incredibly accessible and almost all put their students ahead of their research," one junior economics student comments. Still, one senior English major opines that "while lauded for its academic standards, I find many parts of Reed's curriculum to be outdated and Eurocentric." Students agree that the student/administration relationship is much stronger than it is at most universities. To prospective applicants, one junior forewarns, "No matter how smart you are, kiddo, Reed will kick your butt. It's up to you to decide whether that's a good thing or not."

### Life
Students cite Reed's location in rainy Portland, Oregon, as one of the major reasons that they stay inside and study. Recently, Reed's administration has given other good reasons to stay inside, with recent renovations to the library, sports center, biology building, and studio art building and a new educational technology center. Reed's demanding academic schedule ensures that "one learns a great deal here, but that means lots of studying and lots of stress." According to a freshman, "People like to sit inside and 'expand their minds.' Sometimes this means reading. Often this means other substances." When they do venture off campus, students take advantage of what Portland has to offer: scenes for "foodies" and "film buffs" and "excellent music venues, bookstores, shops, and an excellent public transportation system." Of course nearby national parks, the Pacific Ocean, and Mount Hood offer plenty to those interested in the outdoors, including "snow camping, climbing, hiking, trips to the beach," "rafting, kayaking" and "year-round snowboarding."

### Student Body
Most students note the lack of on-campus diversity. Reed offers "a diversity of white American subcultures that is really quite amazing." While students regard their classmates as "smart" and "inspiring," they are, at the same time, "weird, creative, and radical in theory. I find them to be self-centered, cynical, homogeneously rich, [and] white." Still, Reed students are inspired by their classmates' creativity. "I never know when someone might ride by on a flaming bicycle or paint the bathrooms green," notes one biochemistry major. Reed students challenge each other academically but focus on intellectual stimulation instead of on grades. An English major reflects, "Sometimes Reedies derive too much of our identities from our academic abilities, which can feed a dismissive and overly interrogative atmosphere." A first-year theater major sums up the student attitude at Reed: "If academia is a religion, we're pretty damned pious."

# REED COLLEGE

FINANCIAL AID: 800-547-4750 • E-MAIL: ADMISSION@REED.EDU • WEBSITE: WWW.REED.EDU

## ADMISSIONS
*Very important factors considered include:* essays, secondary school record. *Important factors considered include:* class rank, interview, recommendations, standardized test scores. *Other factors considered include:* alumni/ae relation, character/personal qualities, extracurricular activities, talent/ability, volunteer work, work experience. SAT I or ACT required; SAT I preferred; SAT II also recommended. TOEFL required of all international applicants. High school diploma or GED is required. *High school units required/recommended:* 23 total recommended; 4 English recommended, 3 math recommended, 3 science recommended, 3 science lab recommended, 3 foreign language recommended, 4 history/social studies recommended.

## The Inside Word
Despite the progressive nature of the educational attitudes and student body at Reed, the college zealously avoids such labeling in admissions literature, preferring to portray itself in a much more traditional fashion. While a social conscience is definitely an asset, applicants should devote particular attention to discussing their intellectual curiosity and academic interests in essays and/or interviews.

## FINANCIAL AID
*Students should submit:* FAFSA, institution's own financial aid form, CSS/Financial Aid PROFILE, noncustodial (divorced/separated) parent's statement. Regular filing deadline is January 1. The Princeton Review suggests that all financial aid forms be submitted as soon as possible after January 1. *Need-based scholarships/grants offered:* Pell, SEOG, state scholarships/grants, private scholarships, the school's own gift aid. *Loan aid offered:* FFEL Subsidized Stafford, FFEL Unsubsidized Stafford, FFEL PLUS, Federal Perkins, state loans. Federal Work-Study Program available. Institutional employment available. Applicants will be notified of awards on or about April 1. Off-campus job opportunities are good.

## FROM THE ADMISSIONS OFFICE
"Dedication to the highest standards of academic scholarship is central to a Reed education. A well-structured curriculum and small classes with motivated students and dedicated faculty provide the environment in which a student's quest for learning can be given broad rein. Students most likely to derive maximum benefit from a Reed education are individuals who possess a high degree of self-discipline and a genuine enthusiasm for academic work."

## SELECTIVITY

| | |
|---|---|
| Admissions Rating | 89 |
| # of applicants | 2,276 |
| % of applicants accepted | 44 |
| % of acceptees attending | 31 |
| # accepting a place on wait list | 358 |
| % admitted from wait list | 4 |
| # of early decision applicants | 161 |
| % accepted early decision | 67 |

### FRESHMAN PROFILE
| | |
|---|---|
| Range SAT Verbal | 660-760 |
| Average SAT Verbal | 667 |
| Range SAT Math | 620-710 |
| Average SAT Math | 704 |
| Range ACT Composite | 29-32 |
| Average ACT Composite | 30 |
| Minimum TOEFL | 600 |
| Average HS GPA | 3.8 |
| % graduated top 10% of class | 51 |
| % graduated top 25% of class | 85 |
| % graduated top 50% of class | 100 |

### DEADLINES
| | |
|---|---|
| Early decision | 11/15 |
| Early decision notification | 12/15 |
| Regular admission | 1/15 |
| Regular notification | 4/1 |

### APPLICANTS ALSO LOOK AT AND OFTEN PREFER
Stanford
### AND SOMETIMES PREFER
Oberlin
U of Chicago
### AND RARELY PREFER
St. John's (MD)

## FINANCIAL FACTS

| | |
|---|---|
| Financial Aid Rating | 79 |
| Tuition | $29,000 |
| Room and board | $7,750 |
| Books and supplies | $950 |
| Required fees | $200 |
| % frosh receiving aid | 55 |
| % undergrads receiving aid | 55 |
| Avg frosh grant | $20,162 |
| Avg frosh loan | $2,258 |

# RENSSELAER POLYTECHNIC INSTITUTE

110 EIGHTH STREET, TROY, NY 12180-3590 • ADMISSIONS: 518-276-6216 • FAX: 518-276-4072

## CAMPUS LIFE

| Quality of Life Rating | 82 |
|---|---|
| Type of school | private |
| Environment | suburban |

### STUDENTS

| Total undergrad enrollment | 5,139 |
|---|---|
| % male/female | 75/25 |
| % from out of state | 47 |
| % from public high school | 79 |
| % live on campus | 55 |
| % in (# of) fraternities | 35 (29) |
| % in (# of) sororities | 20 (6) |
| % African American | 4 |
| % Asian | 13 |
| % Caucasian | 71 |
| % Hispanic | 5 |
| % international | 4 |

### SURVEY SAYS . . .
Great computer facilities
Lots of beer drinking
Frats and sororities dominate social scene
Registration is a breeze
Lab facilities are great
Hard liquor is popular
Ethnic diversity on campus
Athletic facilities are great

## ACADEMICS

| Academic Rating | 87 |
|---|---|
| Calendar | semester |
| Student/faculty ratio | 16:1 |
| Avg lab size | 10-19 students |
| Avg reg class size | 20-29 students |

## STUDENTS SPEAK OUT

### Academics

Prestigious profs and a boot camp–style curriculum distinguish Rensselaer Polytechnic Institute, an engineering and management powerhouse in upstate New York. "One of my professors is the CIO here, and another worked at Amazon.com and chiefly developed the one-click shopping; yet another is a security expert for the network," brags one of many students who tout their instructors' credentials. Their teaching ability, of course, is another matter: "While some professors engage students and take an active role, many others mumble and seem to just regurgitate a lecture that they have given hundreds of times before." Undergraduates also want you to know that "some of the professors do not speak English well enough to fully convey their teachings and opinions on certain subjects." Most departments here, however, offer more chances for hands-on research than you'll find at comparable institutions: "The school has a great undergraduate research program for students to get involved in actual research programs that you might have to wait until grad school for otherwise," reports one engineer. Outside the school's areas of specialty, the quality of courses drops off. "Humanities and social sciences are hell," warns one student. "Any hope that reading the course catalog inspires within you will be crushed when you realize that if [a course is] offered (almost never happens), it's filled entirely by seniors." Students also complain of "a continual struggle between students and administration. The administration has an extreme tendency to skip student input before implementing decisions that directly affect the student body."

### Life

"Everyone at RPI is pretty focused on academics," students here say, "and if you aren't, you don't last particularly long. I've lost two roommates so far." A heavy academic load isn't the only check on RPI social life. There's also hometown Troy, which one student describes as "every run-down town you've ever seen in a movie." Nearby Albany isn't much better; cautioned one undergrad, "The tour guides hype to prospectives the opportunities to visit Albany for entertainment, but having lived most of my life in Albany, I can honestly say that there isn't much more to do there than there is in Troy." Thus, the job of providing entertainment at RPI falls largely to the Greek system. "The social life at RPI is mostly made up of Greeks," explains one student. "Even non-Greeks go to frat parties because there isn't much else to do." Those uninterested in the Greeks have few options; as one put it, "A large majority of non-Greek students evacuate the campus on every available weekend to go to Montreal, NYC, Boston, and points west." Or they plant themselves in front of their computers, working problem sets and playing video games. Some venture outdoors: "The school has great proximity to the Adirondack Mountains and to southern Vermont for day hikes and skiing all winter." During hockey season—"our only Division I sport"—they follow the Red Hawks.

### Student Body

The student body at RPI is divided between "geeky engineer types who never actually interact with the social scene" and "manager types who are more socially adept [and] who shun what they call 'the engineers' to the point of being excessively rude about them behind their backs." The geeks are pretty much all male, which "works out well because the ratio of females to males is quite low, so this alarming trend actually benefits the regular student who likes to socialize and basically have a good time." Not that the women here can't be a bit geeky, too; as one student recounts, "True story: My first week here, I saw a fight in the dining hall between two girls over which was the best Final Fantasy game. Not a discussion or an argument, a fight. They were in each others' faces yelling. So yeah, there are some strange people here." The large international population includes "lots of Chinese and Indians. You learn a lot about different cultures from the people here."

# RENSSELAER POLYTECHNIC INSTITUTE

FINANCIAL AID: 518-276-6813 • E-MAIL: ADMISSIONS@RPI.EDU • WEBSITE: WWW.RPI.EDU

## ADMISSIONS

*Very important factors considered include:* secondary school record. *Important factors considered include:* standardized test scores. *Other factors considered include:* alumni/ae relation, character/personal qualities, class rank, essays, extracurricular activities, geographical residence, minority status, recommendations, talent/ability, volunteer work, work experience. SAT I or ACT required. TOEFL required of all international applicants. High school diploma or GED is required. *High school units required/recommended:* 15 total required; 4 English required, 4 math required, 4 science required, 3 social studies required.

### The Inside Word

Although scores and numbers may not be the only consideration of the admissions committee at RPI, it is important to remember that you have to have high ones in order to stay in the running for admission. Here in Troy and at many other highly selective colleges and universities, the first review weeds out those who are academically weak and without any special considerations. Underrepresented minorities and women are high on the list of desirables in the applicant pool here, and go through the admissions process without any hitches if reasonably well qualified.

## FINANCIAL AID

*Students should submit:* FAFSA. No deadline for regular filing. The Princeton Review suggests that all financial aid forms be submitted as soon as possible after January 1. *Need-based scholarships/grants offered:* Pell, SEOG, state scholarships/grants, private scholarships, the school's own gift aid. *Loan aid offered:* Direct Subsidized Stafford, Direct Unsubsidized Stafford, Direct PLUS, FFEL Subsidized Stafford, FFEL Unsubsidized Stafford, FFEL PLUS, Federal Perkins, college/university loans from institutional funds. Federal Work-Study Program available. Institutional employment available. Applicants will be notified of awards on or about March 20. Off-campus job opportunities are good.

## FROM THE ADMISSIONS OFFICE

"Rensselaer emphasizes the study of technology and science, preparing students for today's high-tech world. The university is devoted to the discovery and dissemination of knowledge and its application to the service of humanity. Rensselaer has been in the forefront of scientific and professional education since its founding in 1824, and today its reputation for educational excellence draws students from every state and more than 81 countries. Recently constructed Barton Hall is state-of-the-art housing with Web and Ethernet access in all rooms and conference rooms, plus a fully wired lounge. Rensselaer has recently completed construction of a $6 million fitness center and a $9.5 million renovation to the student union. The Institute will break ground on two major facilities: a center for biotechnology and interdisciplinary studies that will advance the work of expanding research portfolio, and an experimental media and performing arts center that will significantly enrich the campus experience and build programs in the electronic arts."

## SELECTIVITY

| | |
|---|---|
| Admissions Rating | 83 |
| # of applicants | 5,480 |
| % of applicants accepted | 70 |
| % of acceptees attending | 27 |
| # of early decision applicants | 200 |
| % accepted early decision | 83 |

### FRESHMAN PROFILE

| | |
|---|---|
| Range SAT Verbal | 580-680 |
| Average SAT Verbal | 611 |
| Range SAT Math | 640-720 |
| Average SAT Math | 671 |
| Range ACT Composite | 24-28 |
| Average ACT Composite | 27 |
| Minimum TOEFL | 550 |
| % graduated top 10% of class | 65 |
| % graduated top 25% of class | 91 |
| % graduated top 50% of class | 99 |

### DEADLINES

| | |
|---|---|
| Early decision | 11/15 |
| Early decision notification | 12/31 |
| Regular admission | 1/1 |
| Regular notification | 3/31 |
| Nonfall registration? | yes |

### APPLICANTS ALSO LOOK AT AND OFTEN PREFER
Princeton
MIT, Cornell U.

### AND SOMETIMES PREFER
Carnegie Mellon
Boston U.
Lehigh
Worcester Poly.
U. Rochester

### AND RARELY PREFER
Binghamton U.
Clarkson, SUNY—Buffalo
Syracuse, RIT

## FINANCIAL FACTS

| | |
|---|---|
| Financial Aid Rating | 85 |
| Tuition | $26,400 |
| Room and board | $8,902 |
| Books and supplies | $1,528 |
| Required fees | $770 |
| % frosh receiving aid | 70 |
| % undergrads receiving aid | 70 |
| Avg frosh grant | $16,992 |
| Avg frosh loan | $4,800 |

# RHODES COLLEGE

OFFICE OF ADMISSIONS, 2000 NORTH PARKWAY, MEMPHIS, TN 38112 • ADMISSIONS: 901-843-3700 • FAX: 901-843-3631

## CAMPUS LIFE

| | |
|---|---|
| Quality of Life Rating | 92 |
| Type of school | private |
| Affiliation | Presbyterian |
| Environment | urban |

### STUDENTS

| | |
|---|---|
| Total undergrad enrollment | 1,541 |
| % male/female | 44/56 |
| % from out of state | 71 |
| % live on campus | 75 |
| % in (# of) fraternities | 51 (7) |
| % in (# of) sororities | 58 (5) |
| % African American | 4 |
| % Asian | 3 |
| % Caucasian | 86 |
| % Hispanic | 1 |
| % international | 1 |
| # of countries represented | 13 |

### SURVEY SAYS...
Theater is hot
Frats and sororities dominate social scene
Athletic facilities are great
No one cheats
Beautiful campus
Lousy food on campus
Students get along with local community
Class discussions encouraged
Students are very religious
Diverse students interact

## ACADEMICS

| | |
|---|---|
| Academic Rating | 89 |
| Calendar | semester |
| Student/faculty ratio | 11:1 |
| Profs interesting rating | 97 |
| Profs accessible rating | 99 |
| % profs teaching UG courses | 100 |
| Avg lab size | 10-19 students |
| Avg reg class size | 10-19 students |

### MOST POPULAR MAJORS
Business administration
English language and literature
Biology/biological sciences

## STUDENTS SPEAK OUT

### Academics

Regarding this private college in the heart of Memphis, a sophomore writes, "Rhodes is the perfect school for those looking for a small, liberal arts school in the urban South." With a solid reputation, a "fortified learning environment," and a "small student-teacher ratio," Rhodes's students are by and large quite pleased with their choice of school. Writes a senior, "If you enroll in college for the right reasons, those being academic reasons, the Rhodes academic standard is second to none. If you plan on going to college with your 'MTV These Are the Best Years of My Life, I'm Here to Find Myself' attitude, stay home." In addition to the well-respected honor code, as well as excellent study abroad and experiential education opportunities (e.g., studying urban planning by working in downtown Memphis), it's a caring, accessible faculty that makes the difference to Rhodes undergrads. A junior art major provides an example: "I am very close to my professors. I have borrowed their clothes, slept in their beds (without them there—I house-sit), shared dinner, brought cookies, swam in their Jacuzzi. We are like family." A benefit of this close personal attention is the fact that students can "write their own majors" and "approach any professor about getting a class started, like Arabic or playwriting." Of course, there's always a down side: "They will hunt you down, however, if you miss a class." Listening to students extends to the administration as well. "You know student input is important when the president of the college knows your name," writes a senior. The result of all this attention? A happy, satisfied student body.

### Life

With its "beautiful" and "serene" neo-Gothic campus (ivied walls and all) and its high incidence of Beautiful People, Rhodes "is like a posh country club," notes a senior. "Everyone is polite, intelligent, wealthy, and good looking—professors and students included." Socially, people do things in large groups, and one sophomore writes of the pack mentality: "The community calls us Rhodents, and the rumor mill here is worse than at a private, boarding, 100-student, all-girl high school in the country." Greek affiliation at the school is over 50 percent, and while the current administration is trying to minimize its influence, many students resist their efforts. There are those who would like Rhodes to widen its horizon a bit—"get more f/n liberal," as one student puts it. Others practice what they preach: "I particularly enjoy writing for the newspaper and [playing] intramural sports," states one senior. "People are very interested in community service and activity in Memphis." Not surprisingly, it's in the city where most non-Rhodents seem to find solace. With a "growing art scene" and "all sorts of entertainment and culture," Memphis provides a nearby haven for independent spirits. "I've left campus and found a niche for myself in Memphis," writes a senior. "There's too much to do off campus to waste time here."

### Student Body

"Not a helluva lot of diversity," quips a sophomore. A senior explains, "Students tend to be southern and rich, and many have a hard time getting past their own background, but [they're] extremely friendly." The friendliness seems genuine, however, and built on a solid foundation of time spent together. Notes a senior, "In a classroom situation there is so much interaction between the students that you build solid friendships. This is the sort of campus where you know everyone and never feel like you're alone. You always can go to someone... student, faculty, or staff." As for the lack of diversity, the administration is trying to turn the situation around. What's more, some like the chance to define themselves against the crowd. A heavy metal–loving senior sings the praises of being a fish out of water (or a rat without a pack?): "Abercrombie & Fitch, Birkenstocks, Phish, Widespread, Dave Matthews. This is what to expect. Then again, it's kind of fun to stand out like a sore thumb."

418 ■ THE BEST 351 COLLEGES

# RHODES COLLEGE

FINANCIAL AID: 901-843-3810 • E-MAIL: ADMINFO@RHODES.EDU • WEBSITE: WWW.RHODES.EDU

## ADMISSIONS

*Very important factors considered include:* class rank, secondary school record, standardized test scores. *Important factors considered include:* alumni/ae relation, character/personal qualities, essays, extracurricular activities, interview, minority status, recommendations, talent/ability. *Other factors considered include:* geographical residence, state residency, volunteer work, work experience. SAT I or ACT required. TOEFL required of all international applicants. High school diploma or GED is required. *High school units required/recommended:* 16 total required; 4 English required, 3 math required, 4 math recommended, 2 science required, 2 science lab required, 2 foreign language required, 2 social studies required, 2 history required, 3 elective required.

### The Inside Word

Rhodes is one of the best kept secrets in higher education, familiar mainly to those in the Southeast but beginning to develop more national recognition. Its student body is very impressive academically. Only the college's upper-echelon competition—the best universities in the South—prevents the admissions committee from being even more selective. Even so, candidates should be prepared for a thorough review of their academic qualifications and the match they make with Rhodes.

## FINANCIAL AID

*Students should submit:* FAFSA, CSS/Financial Aid PROFILE, business/farm supplement. The Princeton Review suggests that all financial aid forms be submitted as soon as possible after January 1. *Need-based scholarships/grants offered:* Pell, SEOG, state scholarships/grants, private scholarships, the school's own gift aid. *Loan aid offered:* FFEL Subsidized Stafford, FFEL Unsubsidized Stafford, FFEL PLUS, Federal Perkins. Federal Work-Study Program available. Institutional employment available. Applicants will be notified of awards on or about April 10. Off-campus job opportunities are good.

## FROM THE ADMISSIONS OFFICE

"It's not just one characteristic that makes Rhodes different from other colleges, it's a special blend of features that sets us apart. We are a selective liberal arts college, yet without a cutthroat atmosphere; we are a small community, yet located in a major city; we are in a metropolitan area, yet offer one of the most beautiful and serene campuses in the nation. Our students are serious about learning and yet know how to have fun . . . in an atmosphere of trust and respect brought about by adherence to the honor code. And they know that learning at Rhodes doesn't mean sitting in a lecture hall and memorizing the professor's lecture. It means interaction, discussion, and a process of teacher and student discovering knowledge together. Community service is an integral part of the culture at Rhodes. Our students are keenly aware of their social responsibility and over 80 percent are involved as volunteers throughout their college years. Rhodes is a place that welcomes new people and new ideas. It's a place of energy and light, not of apathy and complacency. Everyone who is a part of the Rhodes community is striving to be the best at what she/he does."

## SELECTIVITY

| | |
|---|---|
| Admissions Rating | 85 |
| # of applicants | 2,345 |
| % of applicants accepted | 70 |
| % of acceptees attending | 27 |
| # accepting a place on wait list | 287 |
| % admitted from wait list | 18 |
| # of early decision applicants | 102 |
| % accepted early decision | 83 |

### FRESHMAN PROFILE

| | |
|---|---|
| Range SAT Verbal | 590-700 |
| Average SAT Verbal | 644 |
| Range SAT Math | 600-690 |
| Average SAT Math | 640 |
| Range ACT Composite | 26-30 |
| Average ACT Composite | 28 |
| Minimum TOEFL | 550 |
| Average HS GPA | 3.6 |
| % graduated top 10% of class | 50 |
| % graduated top 25% of class | 78 |
| % graduated top 50% of class | 95 |

### DEADLINES

| | |
|---|---|
| Early decision | 11/1 |
| Early decision notification | 12/1 |
| Priority admission | 2/1 |
| Regular admission | 2/1 |
| Regular notification | 4/1 |
| Nonfall registration? | yes |

### APPLICANTS ALSO LOOK AT AND OFTEN PREFER
Duke, Davidson, U. of the South

### AND SOMETIMES PREFER
Wake Forest, Emory
U. Tennessee—Knoxville
Wesleyan Coll., Vanderbilt

### AND RARELY PREFER
Centre
Randolph-Macon Woman's

## FINANCIAL FACTS

| | |
|---|---|
| Financial Aid Rating | 90 |
| Tuition | $22,628 |
| Room and board | $6,382 |
| Books and supplies | $760 |
| Required fees | $310 |
| % frosh receiving aid | 43 |
| % undergrads receiving aid | 37 |
| Avg frosh grant | $10,256 |
| Avg frosh loan | $3,423 |

THE BEST 351 COLLEGES ■ 419

# RICE UNIVERSITY

PO Box 1892, Houston, TX 77251-1892 • Admissions: 713-348-7423 • Fax: 713-348-5952

## CAMPUS LIFE

| | |
|---|---|
| Quality of Life Rating | 86 |
| Type of school | private |
| Environment | urban |

### STUDENTS

| | |
|---|---|
| Total undergrad enrollment | 2,787 |
| % male/female | 53/47 |
| % from out of state | 46 |
| % live on campus | 73 |
| % African American | 7 |
| % Asian | 14 |
| % Caucasian | 54 |
| % Hispanic | 11 |
| % international | 3 |

### SURVEY SAYS . . .
No one cheats
(Almost) everyone plays intramural sports
Great off-campus food
Class discussions are rare
(Almost) no one smokes
Ethnic diversity on campus

## ACADEMICS

| | |
|---|---|
| Academic Rating | 96 |
| Calendar | semester |
| Student/faculty ratio | 5:1 |
| Profs interesting rating | 92 |
| Profs accessible rating | 90 |
| % profs teaching UG courses | 96 |
| Avg reg class size under 10 students |  |

### MOST POPULAR MAJORS
Economics
Biology/biological sciences
Electrical and computer engineering

## STUDENTS SPEAK OUT

### Academics

At a university renowned for engineering and the sciences, professors across the board give "lectures so good I want to cry." Undergraduates enjoy access to top faculty—"The Physics 101 teacher is also the dean of the physics department"—as well as a "wide array of resources for internships and research projects" and plenty of financial aid. Rice is described as free of "East-Coast competitiveness" and boasts a solid honor code that governs academic life, allowing for group work and take-home exams. Students like being treated like real grownups: "The trust is great." This "utopian undergraduate environment," takes some shots for its registration system, but hey, what's one complaint! One blissful transfer student chirps, "Everyone at Rice wants to see you reach your goals" . . . guess she found her El Dorado. In addition, the personable vice president of student affairs gets high marks for staying connected to the student body by "memorizing each new student's name and a few interesting things about them."

### Life

Rice social life is defined by the college system wherein dorms serve as "coed fraternities/sororities" and provide an "instant social net," which soon turns into "cults" or "tribe-like identities." Rivalries between colleges at this "nerdy party school" are heated but friendly, especially in powder puff football. Campus parties, often replete with themes and costumes, "are safe and well attended," partly due to the school's notably lenient alcohol policies. As the administration gets more conservative, many traditional Rice pranks and rituals are dying a politically correct death; many students share the sentiment, "I hope tradition wins." Some antagonism exists between the "vocal" Christian community and the nonreligious population, which exhibits significant "anti-Christian sentiment." The secure and usually picturesque campus is marred by construction—"Everywhere I turn stands another crane"—which aims to solve the housing shortage but remains an eyesore until fruition. Venturing "beyond the hedges," as students refer to the off-campus world, Houston offers "anything you want to do" including "nearby dance and jazz clubs."

### Student Body

At a "school notoriously composed of geeks, dorks, and nerds," Rice is home to students who are generally "very future-oriented, looking for internships, summer jobs, and study abroad programs," to the extent that, "if it won't look good on a resume, most students aren't interested." Students discuss diversity in terms of personality rather than race: "Everyone is an individual, with an interesting story and different background, so you don't have as many large cliques of people who all think alike." The more moneyed students are called "pretentious" and "self-important," and reportedly "students that are not rich, white, or straight are tolerated only superficially." On the other hand, a student comments, "We are here to learn and become friends, not show off our cars." Many female students agree that "the environment for women leaves a bit to be desired at times," partially due to the "politically apathetic" environment that tolerates some ongoing male-centric practices.

# RICE UNIVERSITY

FINANCIAL AID: 713-348-4958 • E-MAIL: ADMISSION@RICE.EDU • WEBSITE: WWW.RICE.EDU

## ADMISSIONS
*Very important factors considered include:* character/personal qualities, class rank, essays, extracurricular activities, recommendations, secondary school record, standardized test scores, talent/ability. *Other factors considered include:* alumni/ae relation, geographical residence, interview, state residency, volunteer work, work experience. SAT I or ACT required; SAT II also required. TOEFL required of all international applicants. *High school units required:* 16 total required; 4 English, 3 math, 2 science, 2 science lab, 2 foreign language, 2 social studies, 3 elective. However, competitive candidates go far beyond the minimum requirements.

### The Inside Word
Rice has gotten loads of positive publicity over the past few years. As a result, what was already an extremely selective university is even more so. Candidates with less than the most impressive applications are not likely to last long in the admissions process.

## FINANCIAL AID
*Students should submit:* FAFSA, CSS/Financial Aid PROFILE, noncustodial (divorced/separated) parent's statement, business/farm supplement. Regular filing deadline is March 1. The Princeton Review suggests that all financial aid forms be submitted as soon as possible after January 1. *Need-based scholarships/grants offered:* Pell, SEOG, state scholarships/grants, private scholarships, the school's own gift aid. *Loan aid offered:* FFEL Subsidized Stafford, FFEL Unsubsidized Stafford, FFEL PLUS, Federal Perkins, college/university loans from institutional funds. Federal Work-Study Program available. Institutional employment available. Applicants will be notified of awards on a rolling basis. Off-campus job opportunities are excellent. Merit aid offered.

## FROM THE ADMISSIONS OFFICE
"Student applications are reviewed within the context of the division to which they apply. Admission committee decisions are based not only on high school grades and test scores but also on such qualities as leadership, participation in extracurricular activities, and personal creativity. Admission is extremely competitive; Rice attempts to seek out and identify those students who have demonstrated exceptional ability and the potential for personal and intellectual growth."

## SELECTIVITY

| | |
|---|---|
| Admissions Rating | 98 |
| # of applicants | 7,079 |
| % of applicants accepted | 24 |
| % of acceptees attending | 42 |
| # of early decision applicants | 488 |
| % accepted early decision | 32 |

### FRESHMAN PROFILE
| | |
|---|---|
| Range SAT Verbal | 650-750 |
| Range SAT Math | 670-770 |
| Range ACT Composite | 28-33 |
| Minimum TOEFL | 550 |
| % graduated top 10% of class | 83 |
| % graduated top 25% of class | 92 |
| % graduated top 50% of class | 99 |

### DEADLINES
| | |
|---|---|
| Early decision | 11/1 |
| Early decision notification | 12/15 |
| Regular admission | 1/10 |
| Regular notification | 4/1 |

### APPLICANTS ALSO LOOK AT AND OFTEN PREFER
Stanford
Harvard
MIT

### AND SOMETIMES PREFER
Duke
Northwestern U

### AND RARELY PREFER
Chicago
UT Austin

## FINANCIAL FACTS

| | |
|---|---|
| Financial Aid Rating | 86 |
| Tuition | $18,850 |
| Room and board | $7,880 |
| Books and supplies | $800 |
| Required fees | $820 |
| % frosh receiving aid | 32 |
| % undergrads receiving aid | 30 |

# RIDER UNIVERSITY

2083 LAWRENCEVILLE ROAD, LAWRENCEVILLE, NJ 08648-3099 • FAX: 609-896-5042

## CAMPUS LIFE

| Quality of Life Rating | 78 |
|---|---|
| Type of school | private |
| Environment | suburban |

### STUDENTS

| Total undergrad enrollment | 4,284 |
|---|---|
| % male/female | 41/59 |
| % from out of state | 21 |
| % from public high school | 80 |
| % live on campus | 64 |
| % in (# of) fraternities | 15 (8) |
| % in (# of) sororities | 16 (7) |
| % African American | 8 |
| % Asian | 4 |
| % Caucasian | 78 |
| % Hispanic | 5 |
| % international | 2 |

### SURVEY SAYS . . .
Hard liquor is popular
Lab facilities need improving
Registration is a breeze
Student publications are ignored
Students aren't very religious
Students don't like
Lawrenceville, NJ

## ACADEMICS

| Academic Rating | 77 |
|---|---|
| Calendar | semester |
| Student/faculty ratio | 13:1 |
| Profs interesting rating | 74 |
| Profs accessible rating | 81 |
| % profs teaching UG courses | 95 |
| Avg lab size | 10-19 students |
| Avg reg class size | 10-19 students |

### MOST POPULAR MAJORS
Business
Communications studies/speech
communication and rhetoric
Elementary education and teaching

## STUDENTS SPEAK OUT

### Academics
Business-related studies and elementary education are the biggest drawing cards at Rider University, an institution that combines the intimacy and mentorship of a teaching college with the broad academic offerings of a university. Students brag that "you can tell an overwhelming majority of the professors really care about their students and enjoy their job. They are very easy to find and always willing to help." The College of Business Administration (CBA) receives near-universal accolades; writes one enthusiastic undergraduate, "The CBA offers excellent courses that help you not only learn the materials but also understand them." Students are especially bullish about the accounting program and DAARSTOC, an experiential "executive skill-building program" meant to develop in students "interview skills, stand-up speaking abilities, conflict resolution skills, [and] group dynamics." Smaller but equally prestigious is Rider's Westminster Choir College, a choral school with its campus in beautiful Princeton. Students report that "the performance opportunities, the talent of the teachers (in performance and pedagogy), and the music education program" are top-notch, but complain that "classrooms consist of mostly temporary cottage-like rooms, which is a bad thing. And our budget is tight, as it is with a lot of art schools. . . . [But] if someone wanted to make a few million dollars worth of donations, we'd be set."

### Life
Rider undergrads report that "life at Rider is quite laid-back. Most of the week is spent going to class, with work in the evening, but weekends are when the fun starts. Being close to a huge movie theater and having free movies at our student center always gives students something to watch." Rider is also home to an active Greek scene, and students tell us that "during Rush there is always plenty to do because the fraternities are the best hangout spots." Otherwise, life here is subdued but satisfying; according to undergrads, "The campus usually goes to local bars during the week." Such a pace leaves some yearning for more, provoking glass-half-full types to point out that "some students complain that there is nothing to do, when in reality they are lazy. Almost every day a different event is happening, and campus entertainment is also a big part of life here. Famous bands, comedians, lectures, and magicians always are coming to campus." Students at the Choir College tell us that "Westminster is a very quiet campus. . . . It is definitely a conservatory atmosphere. For fun, we walk around Princeton or go see a movie, go out to dinner. Nothing extremely unique." Students on both campuses happily point out that Philadelphia, Trenton, and New York are all easily accessible by train.

### Student Body
Rider students want you to know that they are typical college students, no more and no less; writes one, "Some think, some drink, some even stink, but we will all learn our own ways of doing things and what we want from life during our time here at school." African-Americans make up the largest minority group at this predominantly Caucasian campus where "people of different races interact but most stick to their own." Students are quick to point out that "there are many diverse student groups on campus. Each person belongs [to] at least one organization, which caters to his/her interest. These student groups/organizations foster unity, commitment, and social interaction with other students, faculty members, and staff." Some students at the Lawrenceville campus complain of cliquishness, especially among the Greek community. Music students report that Westminster, on the contrary, "is one of the least cliquish environments I have ever experienced. The majority of the students are voice majors, and along with that comes drama queens but also an intense passion for life and music. Since everyone in the school is in a choir, you meet with your whole class for an hour, four days of the week. This creates a bond that I don't think anything else could create."

# RIDER UNIVERSITY

E-MAIL: ADMISSIONS@RIDER.EDU • WEBSITE: WWW.RIDER.EDU

## ADMISSIONS

*Very important factors considered include:* essays, secondary school record, standardized test scores. *Important factors considered include:* class rank. *Other factors considered include:* recommendations, character/personal qualities, extracurricular activities, talent/ability. SAT I or ACT required. TOEFL required of all international applicants. High school diploma or GED is required. *High school units required/recommended:* 16 total required; 4 English required, 3 math required, 3 science recommended, 2 foreign language recommended, 2 social studies recommended, 2 history recommended.

## The Inside Word

In the admissions world there are two all-important mandates: recruit the college's home state, and recruit JERSEY! As a school in the Garden State, Rider deserves some special attention for the diverse group of students it brings in each year. Students who wish to attend need to have a solid academic record and good test scores. A few bumps in your academic past, however, shouldn't pose too much of a threat.

## FINANCIAL AID

*Students should submit:* FAFSA. Priority filing deadline is March 1. The Princeton Review suggests that all financial aid forms be submitted as soon as possible after January 1. *Need-based scholarships/grants offered:* Pell, SEOG, state scholarships/grants, private scholarships, the school's own gift aid. *Loan aid offered:* FFEL Subsidized Stafford, FFEL Unsubsidized Stafford, FFEL PLUS, Federal Perkins, state loans, college/university loans from institutional funds, alternative loans. Federal Work-Study Program available. Institutional employment available. Applicants will be notified of awards on a rolling basis beginning on or about April 1. Off-campus job opportunities are excellent.

### SELECTIVITY

| | |
|---|---:|
| Admissions Rating | 75 |
| # of applicants | 4,091 |
| % of applicants accepted | 82 |
| % of acceptees attending | 29 |

#### FRESHMAN PROFILE

| | |
|---|---:|
| Range SAT Verbal | 470-560 |
| Average SAT Verbal | 510 |
| Range SAT Math | 470-580 |
| Average SAT Math | 520 |
| Minimum TOEFL | 550 |
| Average HS GPA | 3.1 |
| % graduated top 10% of class | 11 |
| % graduated top 25% of class | 37 |
| % graduated top 50% of class | 71 |

#### DEADLINES

| | |
|---|---:|
| Nonfall registration? | yes |

### FINANCIAL FACTS

| | |
|---|---:|
| Financial Aid Rating | 84 |
| Tuition | $20,590 |
| Room and board | $8,060 |
| Books and supplies | $1,000 |
| Required fees | $460 |
| % frosh receiving aid | 69 |
| % undergrads receiving aid | 65 |
| Avg frosh grant | $17,171 |
| Avg frosh loan | $3,613 |

# RIPON COLLEGE

300 SEWARD STREET, PO BOX 248, RIPON, WI 54971 • ADMISSIONS: 800-947-4766 • FAX: 920-748-8335

## CAMPUS LIFE

★ ★ ☆ ☆

| | |
|---|---|
| Quality of Life Rating | 79 |
| Type of school | private |
| Environment | rural |

### STUDENTS

| | |
|---|---|
| Total undergrad enrollment | 987 |
| % male/female | 47/53 |
| % from out of state | 32 |
| % from public high school | 75 |
| % live on campus | 90 |
| % in (# of) fraternities | 49 (5) |
| % in (# of) sororities | 27 (3) |
| % African American | 2 |
| % Asian | 1 |
| % Caucasian | 89 |
| % Hispanic | 4 |
| % international | 2 |

### SURVEY SAYS . . .
Lots of beer drinking
Registration is a breeze
(Almost) everyone plays intramural sports
Hard liquor is popular
Campus is beautiful
Students are happy
Very little drug use
Ethnic diversity lacking on campus

## ACADEMICS

| | |
|---|---|
| Academic Rating | 83 |
| Calendar | semester |
| Student/faculty ratio | 14:1 |
| % profs teaching UG courses | 100 |
| Avg lab size | 10-19 students |
| Avg reg class size | 10-19 students |

### MOST POPULAR MAJORS
Business administration/management
Education
Biology/biological sciences

## STUDENTS SPEAK OUT

### Academics
Most students here are glad they chose Ripon. As one undergrad told us, "I'm glad I went to a small school where I gets lots of personalized help and everyone—professors, administrators, town people—is so friendly because it's so small." Student satisfaction with their experiences here is especially impressive since some complained of recent staff reductions, shortened library hours, and delayed improvements and additions to the school. The profs, undergrads agree, "love to teach" and offer an educational experience that is "very personalized. The faculty and staff do their best at providing a wealth of knowledge through individual interaction. Classes tend to have many discussions, and the student's opinion is the basis for learning." Agrees another student, "From the president to professors, everyone goes out of their way to cater to the students' needs. It's an open-door policy at all levels." Several students singled out the mathematics and economics departments, deeming them "superb." If you're seeking "a nice, little hometown college in the middle of Farmland, Wisconsin, with a friendly laid-back atmosphere that doesn't require too much from its students," Ripon College might just be the place for you.

### Life
Because the town of Ripon "doesn't have a lot more to offer socially than bars, and the larger towns are all a half-hour to [an] hour away," life at Ripon College revolves around "the big social scene in the dorms (nearly all students live on-campus)" as well as the school's robust Greek community. Students describe an active campus, complete with an arts scene ("Virtually every play is sold out each season . . . and there are several art and photo shows"), sporting events ("We try to support our sports teams as much as possible, especially football and basketball. It's easy because you are friends with the people playing. A lot of people are involved in intercollegiate and intramural sports. We are a sports-oriented campus"), student organizations ("There are about 30 clubs on campus, and the student senate and campus political groups are very active"), and, of course, partying ("For about half of the weekends, there is usually a lounge party sponsored by a fraternity. When these occur, independents, Greeks, and freshmen all seem to come together for a night of fun"). Comedians and speakers visit this remote campus with surprising frequency; reported one student, "Groups like College Republicans bring in high-profile speakers like Ben Stein and Alan Keyes during weeknights." And while the town of Ripon itself is dead, larger towns are not too far afield. Oshkosh and Fond du Lac are about a half-hour's drive off; Milwaukee and Madison offer a wider variety of options for those up for a 90-minute trek.

### Student Body
"I think there are two types of typical students" at Ripon, reported one student. "One is friendly, outgoing, majoring in at least two subjects, and involved in lots of activities. The other does nothing except varsity sports and is majoring in exercise science, but is moderately good-looking." Diversity is minimal here, since "we are a small campus in the middle of nowhere Wisconsin. The typical student is white and middle-class, usually from the Midwest." However, "there is quite a sizable minority from other places," especially from overseas. Notes one freshman, "I am from Nevada, and there are two Russians and three natives of Hong Kong on my floor alone." The majority fit the Abercrombie & Fitch mold, while "atypical students look like the remnants of a bad Nickelodeon show, all trying their hardest to be the most different."

# RIPON COLLEGE

FINANCIAL AID: 920-748-8101 • E-MAIL: ADMINFO@RIPON.EDU • WEBSITE: WWW.RIPON.EDU

## ADMISSIONS
*Very important factors considered include:* interview, secondary school record. *Important factors considered include:* character/personal qualities, class rank, extracurricular activities, recommendations, standardized test scores. *Other factors considered include:* alumni/ae relation, essays, talent/ability, volunteer work. SAT I or ACT required. TOEFL required of all international applicants. High school diploma or GED is required. *High school units required/recommended:* 17 total required; 4 English required, 2 math required, 4 math recommended, 2 science required, 4 science recommended, 2 foreign language recommended, 2 social studies required, 4 social studies recommended.

### The Inside Word
Candidates for admission to Ripon should prepare their applications with the knowledge that they will be subjected to a very thorough and demanding review. Even though the college faces formidable competition from other top midwestern liberal arts colleges and highly selective universities, the admissions staff succeeds at enrolling a very impressive freshman class each year. That doesn't happen without careful matchmaking and a lot of personal attention.

## FINANCIAL AID
*Students should submit:* FAFSA. No deadline for regular filing. The Princeton Review suggests that all financial aid forms be submitted as soon as possible after January 1. *Need-based scholarships/grants offered:* Pell, SEOG, state scholarships/grants, private scholarships, the school's own gift aid. *Loan aid offered:* FFEL Subsidized Stafford, FFEL Unsubsidized Stafford, FFEL PLUS, Federal Perkins. Federal Work-Study Program available. Institutional employment available. Applicants will be notified of awards on a rolling basis beginning on or about March 1. Off-campus job opportunities are good.

## FROM THE ADMISSIONS OFFICE
"Since its founding in 1851, Ripon College has adhered to the philosophy that the liberal arts offer the richest foundation for intellectual, cultural, social, and spiritual growth. Academic strength is a 150-year tradition at Ripon. We attract excellent professors who are dedicated to their disciplines; they in turn attract bright, committed students from 36 states and 19 countries. Ripon has a national reputation for academic excellence—evidenced by a 2002 Rhodes Scholar, the College's third, and a 2003 Fulbright Scholar—as well as a friendly, relaxed atmosphere, small class size, and the availability of outstanding facilities. Ripon is also a community. Not only do you see your professor in the classroom, but you can relate to them in a variety of other social situations. Ripon offers a rigorous curriculum in 30 major areas, including unique pre-professional programs. There is also ample opportunity for co-curricular involvement."

## SELECTIVITY

| | |
|---|---|
| Admissions Rating | 80 |
| # of applicants | 934 |
| % of applicants accepted | 84 |
| % of acceptees attending | 32 |

### FRESHMAN PROFILE
| | |
|---|---|
| Range SAT Verbal | 570-640 |
| Average SAT Verbal | 599 |
| Range SAT Math | 540-670 |
| Average SAT Math | 602 |
| Range ACT Composite | 22-26 |
| Average ACT Composite | 24 |
| Minimum TOEFL | 550 |
| Average HS GPA | 3.3 |
| % graduated top 10% of class | 26 |
| % graduated top 25% of class | 53 |
| % graduated top 50% of class | 85 |

### DEADLINES
| | |
|---|---|
| Priority admission | 3/15 |
| Nonfall registration? | yes |

### APPLICANTS ALSO LOOK AT AND OFTEN PREFER
Lawrence U
U of Wisconsin at Madison
Marquette U

### AND SOMETIMES PREFER
Illinois Wesleyan
Grinnell College

### AND RARELY PREFER
Beloit College
Lake Forest College
Cornell College
St. Olaf College

## FINANCIAL FACTS

| | |
|---|---|
| Financial Aid Rating | 89 |
| Tuition | $19,700 |
| Room and board | $5,055 |
| Books and supplies | $500 |
| Required fees | $240 |
| % frosh receiving aid | 77 |
| % undergrads receiving aid | 76 |
| Avg frosh grant | $11,125 |
| Avg frosh loan | $2,751 |

# ROCHESTER INSTITUTE OF TECHNOLOGY

60 LOMB MEMORIAL DRIVE, ROCHESTER, NY 14623 • ADMISSIONS: 716-475-6631 • FAX: 716-475-7424

## CAMPUS LIFE

| Quality of Life Rating | 74 |
|---|---|
| Type of school | private |
| Environment | suburban |

### STUDENTS
| | |
|---|---|
| Total undergrad enrollment | 12,279 |
| % male/female | 69/31 |
| % from out of state | 40 |
| % from public high school | 85 |
| % live on campus | 60 |
| % in (# of) fraternities | 7 (19) |
| % in (# of) sororities | 5 (10) |
| % African American | 5 |
| % Asian | 7 |
| % Caucasian | 75 |
| % Hispanic | 3 |
| % international | 5 |
| # of countries represented | 90 |

### SURVEY SAYS . . .
Very little drug use
Musical organizations aren't popular
Great computer facilities
Student publications are ignored
Popular college radio
Unattractive campus
Campus difficult to get around
Student government is unpopular
Intercollegiate sports unpopular or nonexistent
Political activism is (almost) nonexistent

## ACADEMICS

| Academic Rating | 80 |
|---|---|
| Calendar | quarter |
| Student/faculty ratio | 13:1 |
| Profs interesting rating | 91 |
| Profs accessible rating | 94 |
| % profs teaching UG courses | 95 |
| Avg lab size | 10-19 students |
| Avg reg class size | 10-19 students |

### MOST POPULAR MAJORS
Information technology
Mechanical engineering
Photography

## STUDENTS SPEAK OUT

### Academics
The "very prestigious" Rochester Institute of Technology is a demanding arts and technology school with a humanist approach to academics: the school requires every student, regardless of major, to complete a core curriculum of liberal arts courses. Students love or endure the requirements in order to benefit from RIT's modern classrooms, "exceptional" laboratories, and "state-of-the-art" equipment. Classes, students report, are "difficult and require a lot of work," a situation made more intense by a quarterly academic schedule that causes courses to fly by. "It's impossible to get ahead of your work," writes one student. "The trick is to not fall too far behind." Most professors are "accessible" and are "genuinely concerned with their students' success." Students enjoy "classes [that] are small so you can get more individual attention along with the fast pace." All told, students concede that an RIT education is a stressful one, but feel "the stress is worth it" because "graduates are in demand." One reason why grads are able to land prime jobs is RIT's co-op program, which allows students to gain hands-on experience in paid internships. Participating companies include biggies like Xerox, Kodak, and Bausch & Lomb. Each year, over 2,600 RIT co-op students work in more than 1,300 firms around the country.

### Life
"Since RIT is such an intense learning environment, there isn't a lot of time left for extracurricular activities," says one student. When students do find some time to put their books and laptops away, they "go to movies, work out at the gym, or hang out in somebody's room" playing video games. For more lively entertainment, students often "travel to other schools for parties." Greek life provides a social outlet for some students, though at least as many despise fraternities and sororities. The result is a deeply divided campus, with Greeks complaining of an "anti-frat sentiment" and independents griping that fraternities and sororities act like they own the campus. Others complain that "the general setup of the school makes it difficult to meet and interact with those outside your major." However, most agree it is "extremely easy to make friends at RIT."

### Student Body
The "hard-working" and "goal-orientated" students of RIT hail from all 50 states and 90 countries. And they say that their peers "are very friendly and mix well together no matter what race." The glue that binds them, according to many, is stress. "Camaraderie is often essential to survive the hellish upper-level courses. Having friends in your major really helps to relieve stress and work better." With heavy workloads burdening them, RIT undergrads have little time for and less interest in the outside world. "If I only had one word with which to describe RIT students," notes one student, "it would be 'focused.'"

# ROCHESTER INSTITUTE OF TECHNOLOGY

FINANCIAL AID: 716-475-2186 • E-MAIL: ADMISSIONS@RIT.EDU • WEBSITE: WWW.RIT.EDU

## ADMISSIONS

*Very important factors considered include:* secondary school record. *Important factors considered include:* class rank, minority status, standardized test scores. *Other factors considered include:* alumni/ae relation, character/personal qualities, essays, extracurricular activities, geographical residence, interview, recommendations, talent/ability, volunteer work, work experience. SAT I or ACT required. TOEFL required of all international applicants. High school diploma or GED is required. *High school units required/recommended:* 22 total required; 4 English required, 2 math required, 3 math recommended, 2 science required, 3 science recommended, 1 science lab required, 2 science lab recommended, 3 foreign language recommended, 4 social studies required, 4 social studies recommended, 10 elective required.

### The Inside Word

RIT is not as competitive as the top tier of technical schools, but its location and contacts with major research corporations make it a top choice for many students. The acceptance rate is deceptively high when considered in conjunction with the student academic profile and the high yield of admitted students who enroll. There is a strong element of self-selection at work in the applicant pool; the successful candidate is one who is solid academically and ready to hit the ground running.

## FINANCIAL AID

*Students should submit:* FAFSA, state aid form. The Princeton Review suggests that all financial aid forms be submitted as soon as possible after January 1. *Need-based scholarships/grants offered:* Pell, SEOG, state scholarships/grants, private scholarships, the school's own gift aid. *Loan aid offered:* Direct Subsidized Stafford, Direct Unsubsidized Stafford, Direct PLUS, Federal Perkins, private bank loans. Federal Work-Study Program available. Institutional employment available. Applicants will be notified of awards on a rolling basis beginning on or about March 15. Off-campus job opportunities are excellent.

## FROM THE ADMISSIONS OFFICE

"A nationally respected leader in professional and career-oriented education, RIT has been described as one of America's most imitated institutions and has been recognized as one of the nation's leading universities. RIT has also been rated the number one comprehensive university in the East for its scientific and technology programs. RIT's strength lies in its dedication to providing superior career preparation for today's students. This has attracted excellent faculty to RIT and has led to the development of academic programs that combine small classes and an emphasis on undergraduate teaching, modern classroom facilities, and work experience gained through the university's cooperative education program. Few universities provide RIT's variety of career-oriented programs. Our eight colleges offer outstanding programs in business, engineering, art and design, science and mathematics, liberal arts, photography, hotel management, computer science, and other areas. RIT's National Technical Institute for the Deaf (NTID) is the world's largest mainstreamed college program for the deaf and hearing impaired."

## SELECTIVITY

| | |
|---|---|
| Admissions Rating | 85 |
| # of applicants | 8,697 |
| % of applicants accepted | 69 |
| % of acceptees attending | 39 |
| # accepting a place on wait list | 125 |
| % admitted from wait list | 20 |
| # of early decision applicants | 830 |
| % accepted early decision | 81 |

### FRESHMAN PROFILE

| | |
|---|---|
| Range SAT Verbal | 540-640 |
| Range SAT Math | 570-670 |
| Range ACT Composite | 25-28 |
| Minimum TOEFL | 525 |
| Average HS GPA | 3.7 |
| % graduated top 10% of class | 31 |
| % graduated top 25% of class | 65 |
| % graduated top 50% of class | 92 |

### DEADLINES

| | |
|---|---|
| Early decision | 12/15 |
| Early decision notification | 1/15 |
| Priority admission | 2/15 |
| Regular admission | 3/15 |
| Nonfall registration? | yes |

### APPLICANTS ALSO LOOK AT AND OFTEN PREFER
Cornell University
### AND SOMETIMES PREFER
Rensselaer Polytechnic Institute
University of Rochester
Carnegie Mellon
### AND RARELY PREFER
SUNY Buffalo
Clarkson University
Syracuse

## FINANCIAL FACTS

| | |
|---|---|
| Financial Aid Rating | 81 |
| Tuition | $19,470 |
| Room and board | $7,527 |
| Books and supplies | $600 |
| Required fees | $510 |
| % frosh receiving aid | 70 |
| % undergrads receiving aid | 67 |
| Avg frosh grant | $9,800 |
| Avg frosh loan | $3,900 |

# ROLLINS COLLEGE

CAMPUS BOX 2720, WINTER PARK, FL 32789-4499 • ADMISSIONS: 407-646-2161 • FAX: 407-646-1502

## CAMPUS LIFE

| Quality of Life Rating | 84 |
|---|---|
| Type of school | private |
| Environment | suburban |

### STUDENTS

| Total undergrad enrollment | 1,723 |
|---|---|
| % from out of state | 48 |
| % from public high school | 55 |
| % live on campus | 63 |
| % in (# of) fraternities | 38 (5) |
| % in (# of) sororities | 40 (6) |
| % African American | 4 |
| % Asian | 3 |
| % Caucasian | 78 |
| % Hispanic | 8 |
| % international | 4 |
| # of countries represented | 31 |

### SURVEY SAYS . . .
Ethnic diversity on campus
Students are religious
Student publications are popular
Popular college radio
No one cheats
Great on-campus food
Lousy off-campus food

## ACADEMICS

| Academic Rating | 85 |
|---|---|
| Calendar | semester |
| Student/faculty ratio | 11:1 |
| Profs interesting rating | 75 |
| Profs accessible rating | 75 |
| % profs teaching UG courses | 100 |
| Avg reg class size | 10-19 students |

### MOST POPULAR MAJORS
International business
English language and literature
Psychology

## STUDENTS SPEAK OUT

### Academics

Students at small, exclusive Rollins College in Winter Park, Florida (just six miles north of Orlando), praise their school for its devoted faculty, attentive administration, and "solid reputation for academics, which has job recruiters impressed." Professors here earn high marks because they "genuinely care about their students and are always willing to help in or outside of class about any issue. Every teacher I have had has proved to be excellent at keeping lectures interesting and getting students involved." Also, "due to small class sizes, it is very easy to find a time to meet, and you aren't jockeying with 100 other students for five minutes of the professor's time." In such an environment, "you get a lot of personal attention," leading to a student body extremely satisfied with its academic experience. The school gets bonus points for "numerous study abroad programs that are easy to become involved in" and "an appeals committee that meets every week and actually pays attention to students' problems. . . . The small school atmosphere minimizes the bureaucratic bull."

### Life

"Don't be surprised to see a group of frat guys lying by the pool in their plaid and checkered bathing suits, drinking martinis and discussing the hot spots of the Caribbean," as one student describes a typical day on the Rollins campus, adding, "Let's put it this way: we have shirts that say 'Rollins College Country Club.'" In keeping with the country club vibe, the Rollins campus has a "laid-back atmosphere. If you are someone who wants to spend a few extra years just relaxing, Rollins is definitely the place." The campus is "beautiful, in the Spanish style." Undergrads also appreciate how "the small campus means no walk to class is more than five minutes, and everything is very accessible." Academics are demanding here, but even so, "partying is not just reserved for the weekends!" During the week, students try to finish their studies early enough to "go clubbing in downtown Orlando." Notes one student, "The local music scene in Orlando is pretty strong, and it's always worthwhile to check out the bands." On weekends, "everyone heads to their condos at the nearby beaches." The allure of the beach means that "the campus really empties out on the weekends." Students also pack up and head for the shore on Fox Day, "when the school president puts a big fox statue on the school lawn. It means that all classes are canceled. Everyone goes to the beach." Students agree that Orlando is great for shopping, restaurants, and fun.

### Student Body

The students of Rollins College are rich. How rich are they? As one undergrad put it, "It's wall-to-wall trust funds. Lots of Prada and Gucci. It's not uncommon to see students driving BMWs, Mercedes, and other fancy and expensive cars. The girls never wear the same clothes twice and they brush their hair during class." As one African American student told us, "It's like *90210* revisited. Most minority students feel very much out of place and, to some degree, lost." But the rich kids generally don't mind the company, naturally, and some of the less well-to-do find their niche as well. Writes one plebeian, "I think there are definitely some snobs here, but they are still nice people. A lot of kids here went to boarding schools, so sometimes you'll find kids that think the world should revolve around them because they have money. I'm from a public school, though, and I have no trouble getting along with them." Many also warn that "Rollins is small. . . . It's high school all over again. 'So and so is dating so and so and oh-my-gosh, did you hear about her?' A lot of the cattiness and snobbishness that people talk about is not just rumor."

# ROLLINS COLLEGE

FINANCIAL AID: 407-646-2395 • E-MAIL: ADMISSION@ROLLINS.EDU • WEBSITE: WWW.ROLLINS.EDU

## ADMISSIONS

*Very important factors considered include:* secondary school record. *Important factors considered include:* essays, extracurricular activities, recommendations, standardized test scores, talent/ability. *Other factors considered include:* alumni/ae relation, character/personal qualities, class rank, geographical residence, campus visit, minority status, religious affiliation/commitment, state residency, volunteer work, work experience. SAT I or ACT required. TOEFL required of all international applicants whose primary language is not English. High school diploma or GED is required. *High school units required/recommended:* 17 total required; 24 total recommended; 4 English required, 3 math required, 4 math recommended, 2 science required, 4 science recommended, 2 foreign language required, 3 foreign language recommended, 2 social studies required, 3 social studies recommended, 2 history required, 3 history recommended, 2 elective required, 3 elective recommended.

### The Inside Word

It's fairly important to put together a well-rounded candidacy when applying to Rollins. Academic standards are moderate, but the admissions committee puts a great deal of emphasis on the whole package when evaluating candidates. Despite this thorough personal approach, solid numbers will still be enough on their own to get you admitted, provided you don't take the process too lightly.

## FINANCIAL AID

*Students should submit:* FAFSA, institution's own financial aid form. Regular filing deadline is March 1. The Princeton Review suggests that all financial aid forms be submitted as soon as possible after January 1. *Need-based scholarships/grants offered:* Pell, SEOG, state scholarships/grants, private scholarships, the school's own gift aid. *Loan aid offered:* Direct Subsidized Stafford, Direct Unsubsidized Stafford, Direct PLUS, Federal Perkins, college/university loans from institutional funds. Federal Work-Study Program available. Institutional employment available. Applicants will be notified of awards on a rolling basis beginning on or about March 1. Off-campus job opportunities are excellent.

## FROM THE ADMISSIONS OFFICE

"As you begin the college selection process, you should remember that you're in control of your destiny. While the grades you've earned and the scores you've achieved are very important in the college's review of your credentials, places like Rollins pay serious attention to your personal side—your interests, talents, strengths, values, and potential to contribute to college life. Don't sell yourself short in the process. Be proud of what you've accomplished and who you are, and be ready to describe yourself honestly. If you can visit the campus, make sure you meet with an admission representative and take a student-led campus tour. During your visit, you'll find that we encourage you to talk about yourself and what you do well. If you have a portfolio of your artwork or a scrapbook of your accomplishments, bring it with you. Your essay is equally important in describing yourself. Write it in your own voice, and read it aloud when you're finished. It shouldn't sound like an essay, but like a conversation. And most of all, it should be about you! Many colleges appreciate your personal side and look for ways to know you better. Take advantage of that in the college selection process."

## SELECTIVITY

| | |
|---|---|
| Admissions Rating | 84 |
| # of applicants | 2,307 |
| % of applicants accepted | 63 |
| % of acceptees attending | 32 |
| # accepting a place on wait list | 175 |
| % admitted from wait list | 22 |
| # of early decision applicants | 280 |
| % accepted early decision | 69 |

### FRESHMAN PROFILE

| | |
|---|---|
| Range SAT Verbal | 530-620 |
| Average SAT Verbal | 576 |
| Range SAT Math | 530-630 |
| Average SAT Math | 580 |
| Range ACT Composite | 22-26 |
| Average ACT Composite | 24 |
| Minimum TOEFL | 550 |
| Average HS GPA | 3.4 |
| % graduated top 10% of class | 40 |
| % graduated top 25% of class | 71 |
| % graduated top 50% of class | 90 |

### DEADLINES

| | |
|---|---|
| Early decision I | 11/15 |
| Early decision I notification | 12/15 |
| Early decision II | 1/15 |
| Early decision II notification | 2/1 |
| Regular admission | 2/15 |
| Regular notification | 4/1 |
| Nonfall registration? | yes |

### APPLICANTS ALSO LOOK AT

**AND OFTEN PREFER**
U. Richmond

**AND SOMETIMES PREFER**
Emory, Furman
U. Florida, U. Miami

**AND RARELY PREFER**
U. of Central Florida
Stetson, Eckerd

## FINANCIAL FACTS

| | |
|---|---|
| Financial Aid Rating | 82 |
| Tuition | $23,205 |
| Room and board | $7,341 |
| Books and supplies | $520 |
| Required fees | $677 |
| % frosh receiving aid | 39 |
| % undergrads receiving aid | 42 |
| Avg frosh grant | $12,654 |
| Avg frosh loan | $3,536 |

THE BEST 351 COLLEGES ■ 429

# ROSE-HULMAN INSTITUTE OF TECHNOLOGY

5500 WABASH AVENUE, CM 1, TERRE HAUTE, IN 47803-3999 • ADMISSIONS: 812-877-8213 • FAX: 812-877-8941

## CAMPUS LIFE

| | |
|---|---|
| **Quality of Life Rating** | **79** |
| Type of school | private |
| Environment | suburban |

### STUDENTS

| | |
|---|---|
| Total undergrad enrollment | 1,800 |
| % male/female | 82/18 |
| % from out of state | 51 |
| % from public high school | 87 |
| % live on campus | 54 |
| % in (# of) fraternities | 47 (8) |
| % in (# of) sororities | 46 (2) |
| % African American | 2 |
| % Asian | 3 |
| % Caucasian | 94 |
| % Hispanic | 1 |
| % international | 1 |
| # of countries represented | 12 |

### SURVEY SAYS . . .
High cost of living
Political activism is hot
(Almost) everyone smokes
Popular college radio
School is well run
Great on-campus food
Students are cliquish

## ACADEMICS

| | |
|---|---|
| **Academic Rating** | **89** |
| Calendar | quarter |
| Student/faculty ratio | 13:1 |
| Profs interesting rating | 80 |
| Profs accessible rating | 74 |
| % profs teaching UG courses | 100 |
| Avg lab size | 20-29 students |
| Avg reg class size | 20-29 students |

### MOST POPULAR MAJORS
Electrical, electronics, and communications engineering
Mechanical engineering
Chemical engineering

## STUDENTS SPEAK OUT

### Academics

The engineering school with a heart: that could be the slogan for the Rose-Hulman Institute of Technology, according to students here. "Everyone here is very personable and accessible," writes one undergrad. "There aren't too many schools where the president will routinely sit down and eat lunch with the students." Agrees another, "The relationships are very personal. I've had teachers invite us to their house and even come in late at night to hold a study session. When I see a professor around town, it's so cool to talk to them. They know who you are." The "small class size and individual attention to students' needs" at Rose "ensure that a rigorous engineering curriculum is understood by all students." Rigorous indeed—as one engineer put it, "Rose is a great school if you have no problem with devoting your life to studying for four years." The workload requires "110 percent effort" and the material can be downright soporific; explains one student, "The Rose-Hulman professors' ability to send their students into a zombie-like state from the amount of homework and studying is matched only by the excitement they show during classes while teaching stuff they love." As you might expect, profs here "all have quirks ranging from being an anglophile to being a hippie to climbing Mt. Kilimanjaro." In this way, they match the students; explains one, "The professors are all really unique; you know you have the right major when they remind you of you." One such idiosyncratic student thinks—and writes—like a pirate. Quoth the scholar-brigand of his instructors: "Argh, the profs, they be good, matey. I be gettin' a good book-learnin'."

### Life

As at most engineering schools, "Life at Rose is spent mostly studying and always worrying if we haven't. Everyone is excited about the good salaries they will earn after college, or the stuff they'll be equipped to do." Reports one student, "Everything revolves around homework. Last year after two guys in the sophomore engineering curriculum disagreed about an equation, one hogtied the other and scribbled his version all over his body. This is our idea of a joke." When books are closed and computers shut down, Rose is a "very Greek-oriented" school; "For the most part, if you're an upperclassman and aren't Greek, you've got nothing to do," complains one sophomore engineer. Some here make their own entertainment ("We have hall sports. This includes shooting frozen oranges at cardboard boxes with slingshots. And lubricating the floor and sliding in your socks," reports one resourceful undergrad), while many others simply "spend a lot of time in their rooms on their computers. We like to tool it up . . . play LAN games on our kick-ass network. Yeah!" Intramural sports are also popular. Terre Haute, unfortunately, doesn't offer much in the way of off-campus diversion. Now, you are no doubt wondering: "What do the pirates at Rose-Hulman do for fun?" Answer: "Thar she blows! We enjoy math and cars and sports and women."

### Student Body

Rose's "religious, conservative" students "have glasses [and] pasty white skin," and are mostly "hard working, small-town kids that learn well hands-on. There are a lot of incredibly technically gifted students here. It is a techie's paradise!" The majority "are male and have problems communicating with members of the opposite sex (welcome to an engineering school!)." These self-described "tools" like to "play video games constantly or computer games," although a sizable subpopulation is into athletics. "We're very diverse socially," notes one wry student. "We have everyone from computer nerds to computer jocks." The few women here note, kind of optimistically, that "the odds are good, but the goods are odd." Pirates here are apparently homophobes; wrote one, "Shiver me timbers, they hate gay people and love naked wenches."

430 ■ THE BEST 351 COLLEGES

# ROSE-HULMAN INSTITUTE OF TECHNOLOGY

FINANCIAL AID: 812-877-8259 • E-MAIL: ADMIS.OFC@ROSE-HULMAN.EDU • WEBSITE: WWW.ROSE-HULMAN.EDU

## ADMISSIONS

*Very important factors considered include:* class rank, secondary school record, standardized test scores. *Important factors considered include:* character/personal qualities, minority status, recommendations. *Other factors considered include:* alumni/ae relation, extracurricular activities, interview, talent/ability, volunteer work, work experience. SAT I or ACT required. TOEFL required of all international applicants. High school diploma is required and GED is not accepted. *High school units required/recommended:* 16 total required; 4 English required, 4 math required, 5 math recommended, 2 science required, 3 science recommended, 2 science lab required, 2 social studies required, 4 elective required.

### The Inside Word

Seven years ago, after 100 years as an all-male institution, Rose-Hulman opened its doors to women. The results have been largely successful—each of the last two freshman classes were 20 percent women. The Institute expects to continue at this pace as it builds up the female presence on its campus; thus, for adventurous, ambitious, and technologically-minded women, Rose-Hulman will be a relatively easy admit for the foreseeable future. "Relatively" is the key word here; academic standards are high and so are the expectations of the admissions committee.

## FINANCIAL AID

*Students should submit:* FAFSA. No deadline for regular filing. The Princeton Review suggests that all financial aid forms be submitted as soon as possible after January 1. *Need-based scholarships/grants offered:* Pell, SEOG, state scholarships/grants, the school's own gift aid. *Loan aid offered:* Direct Subsidized Stafford, Direct Unsubsidized Stafford, Direct PLUS, Federal Perkins. Federal Work-Study Program available. Institutional employment available. Applicants will be notified of awards on or about March 10. Off-campus job opportunities are good.

## FROM THE ADMISSIONS OFFICE

"Rose-Hulman is generally considered one of the premier undergraduate colleges of engineering and science. We are nationally known as an institution that puts teaching above research and graduate programs. At Rose-Hulman, professors (not graduate students) teach the courses and conduct their own labs. Department chairmen teach freshmen. To enhance the teaching at Rose-Hulman, computers have become a prominent addition to not only our labs but also in our classrooms and residence halls. Additionally, all students are now required to purchase laptop computers. Ninety million dollars in new facilities have been added in the last six years."

---

### SELECTIVITY

| | |
|---|---|
| Admissions Rating | 92 |
| # of applicants | 3,207 |
| % of applicants accepted | 65 |
| % of acceptees attending | 22 |

#### FRESHMAN PROFILE

| | |
|---|---|
| Range SAT Verbal | 570-670 |
| Average SAT Verbal | 620 |
| Range SAT Math | 640-720 |
| Average SAT Math | 680 |
| Range ACT Composite | 27-31 |
| Average ACT Composite | 29 |
| Minimum TOEFL | 550 |
| % graduated top 10% of class | 73 |
| % graduated top 25% of class | 96 |
| % graduated top 50% of class | 100 |

#### DEADLINES

| | |
|---|---|
| Priority admission | 12/1 |
| Regular admission | 3/1 |

#### APPLICANTS ALSO LOOK AT AND OFTEN PREFER

Carnegie Mellon University
Case Western Reserve University
University of Illinois—Urbana-Champaign
Purdue University—West Lafayette

#### AND SOMETIMES PREFER

Massachusetts Institute of Technology
Georgia Institute of Technology
Washington University in St. Louis
Northwestern University

#### AND RARELY PREFER

University of Michigan—Ann Arbor
Ohio State University—Columbus

### FINANCIAL FACTS

| | |
|---|---|
| Financial Aid Rating | 84 |
| Tuition | $24,255 |
| Room and board | $6,720 |
| Books and supplies | $900 |
| Required fees | $435 |
| % frosh receiving aid | 77 |
| % undergrads receiving aid | 73 |
| Avg frosh grant | $5,649 |
| Avg frosh loan | $5,000 |

# RUTGERS UNIVERSITY—NEW BRUNSWICK

65 DAVIDSON ROAD, PISCATAWAY, NJ 08854-8097 • ADMISSIONS: 732-932-4636 • FAX: 732-445-0237

## CAMPUS LIFE

| | |
|---|---|
| **Quality of Life Rating** | 72 |
| Type of school | public |
| Environment | suburban |

### STUDENTS

| | |
|---|---|
| Total undergrad enrollment | 28,070 |
| % male/female | 47/53 |
| % from out of state | 11 |
| % African American | 8 |
| % Asian | 22 |
| % Caucasian | 56 |
| % Hispanic | 8 |
| % international | 3 |
| # of countries represented | 99 |

### SURVEY SAYS . . .
Great library
Athletic facilities are great
Political activism is hot
Students don't get along with local community
Large classes
Campus difficult to get around
Ethnic diversity on campus
Unattractive campus
Lots of long lines and red tape

## ACADEMICS

| | |
|---|---|
| **Academic Rating** | 82 |
| Calendar | semester |
| Student/faculty ratio | 14:1 |
| Profs interesting rating | 89 |
| Profs accessible rating | 90 |
| % profs teaching UG courses | 80 |
| % classes taught by TAs | 20 |

## STUDENTS SPEAK OUT

### Academics

For most undergrads, the choice to come to Rutgers is primarily an economic one; even for out-of-state students, this public university provides a name-brand education at a discount rate. Once they arrive, though, most students are surprised to discover not just a cheap school but also a top-notch university, one that can offer the 28,000 undergraduates on its New Brunswick campus academic opportunities in practically every field under the sun. Students report finding RU's size daunting at first ("It is very easy to get lost in the crowd here," warns one sophomore), but eventually they learn to work the system and get the most of their myriad opportunities. Writes one, "As I grew up at this school I learned to like it more, especially as I got into research. Based on my experiences I would rate Rutgers as great for doing research—that is, if you know how to use the school." Agrees another, "Rutgers University promotes education that helps individuals to explore learning in an independent manner. Students are challenged by professors to solve problems and expand their critical thinking skills. When entering the working world, I felt totally prepared. Learning is continuous at this school." Professors are "great but the higher up the ladder you go, the bigger the egos," explains a junior. Teaching assistants, unfortunately, are often "unqualified, unprepared, or just unable to effectively teach classes." Consequently, "Rutgers is basically a do-it-yourself school where you have to occasionally look for help." Don't look to the administration, though, unless you're prepared for the "RU Screw," or, as one student put it—less colorfully and more diplomatically—"some bureaucratic difficulty."

### Life

At Rutgers "there is no lack of activities for the interested, motivated student," says a sophomore. "It's just a matter of keeping your eyes and ears open to take advantage of everything" Rutgers has to offer. Writes another student, "Rutgers has provided a multitude of opportunities for me to grow through community service," as well as clubs and other organizations. Activities "range from the Rutgers Ambulance Service to Model United Nations to one of the best college newspapers in the country." Intercollegiate sports are popular, and students report a decent variety of movies and plays presented on campus. The Greek system is thriving but not overwhelming, and parties of all kinds are "going on practically every night." Even so, some feel that life in New Brunswick leaves something to be desired. "Thank God we are near New York City," writes one. "Otherwise, I hope you like drinking beer in a basement because that is what everyone does until they turn 21." Philadelphia is also an easy train ride away.

### Student Body

As a public university that draws lots of nontraditional students (i.e., part-timers, continuing education students), "RU students are very representative of people in the real world. It takes all kinds." Attests one student, "Few campuses offer the same diversity of lifestyles" or "so many diverse social groups." Students are "friendly, active, and involved. I have made many friendships here that will last an entire lifetime." And while they may not have the time to hang out and grab a beer (since many have families, jobs, and the like), "most are easy to get along with and quite friendly. I do a lot of group work with them and they're just great. . . . Everyone is willing to offer their advice or knowledge."

# RUTGERS UNIVERSITY—NEW BRUNSWICK

FINANCIAL AID: 732-932-7057 • E-MAIL: ADMISSIONS@ASB-UGADM.RUTGERS.EDU • WEBSITE: WWW.RUTGERS.EDU

## ADMISSIONS

*Very important factors considered include:* class rank, secondary school record, standardized test scores. *Other factors considered include:* extracurricular activities, geographical residence, minority status, state residency, talent/ability, volunteer work, work experience. SAT I or ACT required. TOEFL required of all international applicants. High school diploma or GED is required. *High school units required/recommended:* 16 total required; 4 English required, 3 math required, 4 math recommended, 2 science required, 2 foreign language required, 5 elective required.

### The Inside Word

New Jersey residents are finally acknowledging that the flagship of their state university system is among the finest public universities in the nation. As a result, getting in keeps getting tougher every year as more and more New Jersey residents elect to stay home for college.

## FINANCIAL AID

*Students should submit:* FAFSA. No deadline for regular filing. The Princeton Review suggests that all financial aid forms be submitted as soon as possible after January 1. *Need-based scholarships/grants offered:* Pell, SEOG, state scholarships/grants, the school's own gift aid. *Loan aid offered:* Direct Subsidized Stafford, Direct Unsubsidized Stafford, Direct PLUS, Federal Perkins, state loans, college/university loans from institutional funds, other educational loans. Federal Work-Study Program available. Institutional employment available. Applicants will be notified of awards on a rolling basis beginning on or about February 15. Off-campus job opportunities are good.

## FROM THE ADMISSIONS OFFICE

"Rutgers, The State Universtiy of New Jersey, one of only 61 members of the Association of American Universities, is a research university, which attracts students from across the nation and around the world. What does it take to be accepted for admission to Rutgers University? There's no single answer to that question. Our primary emphasis is on your past academic performance as indicated by your high school grades (particularly in required academic subjects), your class rank, the strength of your academic program, your standardized test scores on the SAT or ACT, any special talents you may have, and your participation in school and community activities. We seek students with a broad diversity of talents, interests, and backgrounds. Above all else, we're looking for students who will get the most out of a Rutgers education—students with the intellect, initiative, and motivation to make full use of the opportunities we have to offer."

## SELECTIVITY

| | |
|---|---|
| Admissions Rating | 88 |
| # of applicants | 26,678 |
| % of applicants accepted | 55 |
| % of acceptees attending | 35 |

### FRESHMAN PROFILE

| | |
|---|---|
| Range SAT Verbal | 530-630 |
| Average SAT Verbal | 582 |
| Range SAT Math | 560-670 |
| Average SAT Math | 613 |
| Minimum TOEFL | 550 |
| % graduated top 10% of class | 36 |
| % graduated top 25% of class | 75 |
| % graduated top 50% of class | 98 |

### DEADLINES

| | |
|---|---|
| Priority admission | 12/01 |
| Regular notification | 2/28 |

### APPLICANTS ALSO LOOK AT AND OFTEN PREFER
U. Penn
Cornell U.
Virginia

### AND SOMETIMES PREFER
Penn State—U. Park
Boston Coll.
New Jersey Tech
Montclair State

### AND RARELY PREFER
Trenton State
Seton Hall
George Washington

## FINANCIAL FACTS

| | |
|---|---|
| Financial Aid Rating | 82 |
| In-state tuition | $5,770 |
| Out-of-state tuition | $11,746 |
| Room and board | $7,200 |
| Books and supplies | $750 |
| Required fees | $1,538 |
| % frosh receiving aid | 49 |
| % undergrads receiving aid | 47 |
| Avg frosh grant | $6,598 |
| Avg frosh loan | $3,816 |

THE BEST 351 COLLEGES ■ 433

# St. Anselm College

100 Saint Anselm Drive, Manchester, NH 03102-1310 • Admissions: 888-4ANSELM • Fax: 603-641-7550

## CAMPUS LIFE

| | |
|---|---|
| Quality of Life Rating | 80 |
| Type of school | private |
| Affiliation | Roman Catholic |
| Environment | suburban |

### STUDENTS

| | |
|---|---|
| Total undergrad enrollment | 1,956 |
| % male/female | 43/57 |
| % from out of state | 77 |
| % from public high school | 65 |
| % live on campus | 85 |
| % Asian | 1 |
| % Caucasian | 96 |
| % Hispanic | 1 |
| % international | 1 |
| # of countries represented | 15 |

### SURVEY SAYS . . .
Great on-campus food
Students are religious
Lab facilities are great
No one cheats
Registration is a breeze
Student government is popular

## ACADEMICS

| | |
|---|---|
| Academic Rating | 79 |
| Calendar | semester |
| Student/faculty ratio | 14:1 |
| Profs interesting rating | 81 |
| Profs accessible rating | 82 |
| % profs teaching UG courses | 100 |
| Avg lab size | 10-19 students |
| Avg reg class size | 10-19 students |

### MOST POPULAR MAJORS
Nursing
Business administration/management
Psychology

## STUDENTS SPEAK OUT

### Academics

Just about every St. Anselm student will agree that the greatest strength of this school is the faculty. "My professors are all awesome," crows one undergrad. "They're also very accessible and urge us to come to them." With just under 2,000 students, St. Anselm adheres to an "anti-inflation grading policy," which one student claims "makes it impossible to get over a C!" Hence, the nickname of the school, "St. A," is sometimes changed to "St. C." The stringent grading policy, however, is "very challenging and encourages the students to work harder." One common complaint is that there should be "a larger selection of majors to choose from," and many students specifically cite a need for more attention to fine arts, eastern theologies, and music. And while some students claim it's "difficult to create change on campus because St. Anselm is deeply rooted in tradition," the majority agree that "the administrators are always open to student input," and, as one students states, "I have been pushed to excel by professors who quickly assessed my abilities and truly wanted me to achieve what I was capable of."

### Life

Formed in 1889 in southern New Hampshire by Benedictine Monks, Saint Anselm sometimes has earned a reputation as "a large bunch of Catholic do-gooders, but at the same time . . . a large bunch of fallen Catholic partiers!" Located near Manchester, the students "usually only party on Thursdays, Fridays, and Saturdays. . . . the weekends always revolve around drinking since there's not much else to do." Campus "can be boring because there are not a lot of places to go and have a fun time, but we do have a few clubs near by." No official Greek system adds to the rush off campus when class ends. One student is a big fan of "taking road trips to Boston or Portsmouth" and another is a huge proponent of the many campus events "like outdoor movies on the quad, laser tag, concerts, and our own game shows." For outdoorsmen, one student suggests taking "advantage of the excellent rock climbing, snow-shoeing, hiking, camping, and skiing that the area has to offer." For the indoors type, on the other hand, there are a few complaints. While "new, beautiful townhouses were built for upper classmen," one student feels that "dorm availability for freshmen" is a problem.

### Student Body

Budgeting one's time is important to a St. Anselm student. "It takes me so long to get to class because every five steps there is someone new to stop and say 'Hi' to and to talk to. Everyone is so friendly." With only 2,000 students, "everyone knows what is going on in everyone's life." And while some think this breeds "high-school-like cliques," another student likes how "the college tries to foster a 'Community of Respect,' and I do believe they succeed in that attempt." Many students hail from New England and are predominantly Catholic and Caucasian. Others, more inclined to fashion metaphors, label their peers "stereotypical Abercrombie-Finch cookie cutter," "snobby J.Crew," and "Gap poster children." In fact, a majority of students feel that "the lack of diversity of races, lifestyles, and backgrounds is St. Anselm's biggest weakness." But most agree "the school has a lot to offer people. There are sports, groups, SGA, etc. . . . There is plenty for a student to be involved in." Warning to first-time visitors: the school is run primarily by Benedictine monks and although most students feel "the life of the monks who run the school is inspiring to anyone who meets them," another warns that it takes some time to "get used to men walking around in long, black robes."

# ST. ANSELM COLLEGE

FINANCIAL AID: FINANCIAL_AID@ANSELM.EDU • WEBSITE: WWW.ANSELM.EDU

## ADMISSIONS

*Very important factors considered include:* character/personal qualities, secondary school record. *Important factors considered include:* class rank, essays, recommendations, standardized test scores, talent/ability. *Other factors considered include:* alumni/ae relation, extracurricular activities, geographical residence, interview, minority status, volunteer work, work experience. SAT I or ACT required. TOEFL required of all international applicants. High school diploma or GED is required. *High school units required/recommended:* 18 total required; 20 total recommended; 4 English required, 3 math required, 4 math recommended, 3 science required, 4 science recommended, 3 science lab required, 2 foreign language required, 4 foreign language recommended, 2 social studies required, 1 history required, 2 history recommended, 3 elective required.

### The Inside Word

St. Anselm gets a predominately regional applicant pool, and Massachusetts is one of its biggest suppliers of students. An above average-academic record should be more than adequate to gain admission.

## FINANCIAL AID

*Students should submit:* FAFSA, CSS/Financial Aid PROFILE, federal tax returns for parent(s) and student. The Princeton Review suggests that all financial aid forms be submitted as soon as possible after January 1. *Need-based scholarships/grants offered:* Pell, SEOG, state scholarships/grants, private scholarships, the school's own gift aid. *Loan aid offered:* FFEL Subsidized Stafford, FFEL Unsubsidized Stafford, FFEL PLUS, Federal Perkins, GATE Loans. Federal Work-Study Program available. Institutional employment available. Applicants will be notified of awards on a rolling basis beginning on or about March 10. Off-campus job opportunities are excellent.

## FROM THE ADMISSIONS OFFICE

"Why St. Anselm? The answer lies with our graduates. Not only do our alumni go on to successful careers in medicine, law, human services, and other areas, but they also make connections on campus that last a lifetime. With small classes, professors are accessible and approachable. The Benedictine monks serve not only as founders of the college, but as teachers, mentors, and spiritual leaders.

"St. Anselm is rich in history, but certainly not stuck in a bygone era. In fact, the college has launched a $50 million fundraising campaign, which will significantly increase funding for financial aid, academic programs, and technology. New initiatives include the New Hampshire Institute of Politics, where the guest list includes every major candidate from the 2000 presidential race, as well as other political movers and shakers. Not a political junkie? No problem. The NHIOP is a diverse undertaking that also involves elements of psychology, history, theology, ethics, and statistics.

"St. Anselm encourages students to challenge themselves academically and to lead lives that are both creative and generous. On that note, more than 40 percent of our students participate in community service locally and globally. Each year, about 150 students take part in Spring Break Alternative to help those less fortunate across the United States and Latin America. High expectations and lofty goals are hallmarks of a St. Anselm College education, and each student is encouraged to achieve his/her full potential here. Why St. Anselm? Accept the challenge and soon you will discover your own answers."

### ADMISSIONS

| | |
|---|---:|
| Admissions Rating | 86 |
| # of applicants | 3,018 |
| % of applicants accepted | 73 |
| % of acceptees attending | 29 |
| # accepting a place on wait list | 213 |
| # of early decision applicants | 81 |
| % accepted early decision | 83 |

#### FRESHMAN PROFILE

| | |
|---|---:|
| Range SAT Verbal | 510-600 |
| Average SAT Verbal | 551 |
| Range SAT Math | 510-600 |
| Average SAT Math | 556 |
| Range ACT Composite | 21-25 |
| Average ACT Composite | 23 |
| Minimum TOEFL | 550 |
| Average HS GPA | 3.1 |
| % graduated top 10% of class | 14 |
| % graduated top 25% of class | 47 |
| % graduated top 50% of class | 87 |

#### DEADLINES

| | |
|---|---:|
| Early decision | 12/1 |
| Early decision notification | 12/15 |
| Nonfall registration? | yes |

#### APPLICANTS ALSO LOOK AT AND OFTEN PREFER
Boston College
Fairfield University
College of the Holy Cross
Providence College
Stonehill College

#### AND SOMETIMES PREFER
Saint Michael's College
U. Massachusetts—Amherst
U. New Hampshire

#### AND RARELY PREFER
Assumption College
Merrimack College

### FINANCIAL FACTS

| | |
|---|---:|
| Financial Aid Rating | 82 |
| Tuition | $21,410 |
| Room and board | $8,090 |
| Books and supplies | $750 |
| Required fees | $520 |
| % frosh receiving aid | 91 |
| % undergrads receiving aid | 82 |
| Avg frosh grant | $7,696 |
| Avg frosh loan | $2,427 |

THE BEST 351 COLLEGES ■ 435

# Saint Bonaventure University

PO Box D, Saint Bonaventure, NY 14778 • Admissions: 716-375-2400 • Fax: 716-375-4005

## CAMPUS LIFE

| | |
|---|---|
| Quality of Life Rating | 85 |
| Type of school | private |
| Affiliation | Roman Catholic |
| Environment | rural |

### STUDENTS

| | |
|---|---|
| Total undergrad enrollment | 2,229 |
| % male/female | 46/54 |
| % from out of state | 21 |
| % from public high school | 71 |
| % live on campus | 76 |

### SURVEY SAYS . . .
Great library
Lousy food on campus
Great computer facilities
Beautiful campus
Campus easy to get around
Athletic facilities are great
Low cost of living
Lots of beer drinking

## ACADEMICS

| | |
|---|---|
| Academic Rating | 77 |
| Calendar | semester |
| Student/faculty ratio | 15:1 |
| Profs interesting rating | 78 |
| Profs accessible rating | 94 |
| % profs teaching UG courses | 98 |
| Avg lab size | 10-19 students |
| Avg reg class size | 10-19 students |

### MOST POPULAR MAJORS
Journalism
Elementary education and teaching
Psychology

## STUDENTS SPEAK OUT

### Academics

In the mid-1990s, the faculty at St. Bonaventure created a division of the university called Clare College. The college now serves as the headquarters for all core-curriculum courses. To graduate, each student has to complete 12 of the Clare College courses, in addition to taking care of a major. In essence, it's not much different from most universities. But from the student perspective (and this is one of the nicer students), the "Clare College program needs work." Clare College aside, students at Bona's (as they affectionately call it) appreciate their academic experience—especially the professors. Not only are profs "funny," but they're also always endearing themselves to their students by doing things like giving out "their home phone numbers in case you need help" after close of business. "One of my professors lives in his office, I think," surmises a journalism major. "Profs are very nice," chirps a sophomore business major, adding, "Even if I get bad grades, I still can't hate them." Small class sizes ensure that students are able to work closely with their professors. "This school has provided me with more than $80,000 worth of knowledge," writes a senior.

### Life

St. Bonaventure was a thirteenth-century bishop. Translated, his name means, "Oh, good fortune!" If you ask students at St. Bonaventure University, they'll tell you that, when it comes to socializing, it's an apt name indeed. On the whole, people who come to Bona's feel fortunate that they did. Students here basically "live it up," according to one junior. Well, "Bonaventure is a party school," and while the university is not without its list of organizations and activities, most students prefer to find their own fun at the bars or parties. An "estimated 80 percent of students drink four times a week," guesses a junior, adding that those numbers are "not bad if you can moderate it with studies." Of course, not all students find their entertainment in a bottle. And "if a student complains all there is to do is drink, it's their fault!" A sophomore elementary education major says she easily has "fun with . . . friends doing non-alcoholic activities." While the "very small town" of St. Bonaventure doesn't have much to offer the students culture-wise—except for bars—campus activities like intercollegiate sports (participating and spectating), the campus radio station, and "CAB [Campus Activities Board] activities" add to the after-class options. What students don't do for fun is eat. In the apropos words of a freshman, "The food is icky."

### Student Body

A profile of the average St. Bonaventure student would look something like this: "Middle-upper class," a strong penchant for drink, a love of sports, and "very friendly." This is just a profile, of course. Some students are "a little stuck up," or "cliquey," though on the whole "no matter where you go on campus, you always say 'hi' and smile to everyone." Actually, the general friendliness of the campus is so pervasive that students feel like "Bona" (as they call it) is just "one big family." While "the strong Catholic tradition leaves" students "very friendly," they're also "very close-minded to alternative lifestyles and ways of viewing" the world. Although many of the students are eager to get out and support the Bona's sports teams, they'll also tell you that "Division I athletes think they are God's gift to the school." But you shouldn't let a few inflated heads stop you from finding your place at St. Bonaventure. As one senior declares, "I make a new friend everyday, seriously."

# SAINT BONAVENTURE UNIVERSITY

FINANCIAL AID: 716-375-2528 • E-MAIL: ADMISSIONS@SBU.EDU • WEBSITE: WWW.SBU.EDU

## ADMISSIONS
*Very important factors considered include:* character/personal qualities, interview, recommendations, secondary school record. *Important factors considered include:* essays, extracurricular activities, standardized test scores, talent/ability, volunteer work. *Other factors considered include:* alumni/ae relation, class rank, work experience. SAT I or ACT required; SAT I recommended. TOEFL required of all international applicants. High school diploma or GED is required. *High school units required/recommended:* 19 total recommended; 4 English required, 3 math required, 3 science required, 3 science lab recommended, 2 foreign language required, 4 social studies required.

## The Inside Word
Saint Bonaventure is a safety for many students applying to more selective Catholic universities, but it does a good job of enrolling a sizable percentage of its admits. Most solid students needn't worry about admission; even so, candidates who rank St. Bonnie as a top choice should still submit essays and interview.

## FINANCIAL AID
*Students should submit:* FAFSA, institution's own financial aid form, state aid form. The Princeton Review suggests that all financial aid forms be submitted as soon as possible after January 1. *Need-based scholarships/grants offered:* Pell, SEOG, state scholarships/grants, private scholarships, the school's own gift aid. *Loan aid offered:* FFEL Subsidized Stafford, FFEL Unsubsidized Stafford, FFEL PLUS, Federal Perkins, college/university loans from institutional funds. Federal Work-Study Program available. Institutional employment available. Applicants will be notified of awards on a rolling basis beginning on or about April 1. Off-campus job opportunities are excellent.

## FROM THE ADMISSIONS OFFICE
"The Saint Bonaventure University family has been imparting the Franciscan tradition to men and women of a rich diversity of backgrounds for more than 130 years. This tradition encourages all who become a part of it to face the world confidently, respect the earthly environment, and work for productive change in the world. The charm of our campus and the inspirational beauty of the surrounding hills provide a special place where growth in learning and living is abundantly realized. The Richter Student Fitness Center, scheduled to be completed in 2004, will provide all students with state-of-the-art facilities for athletics and wellness. Academics at Saint Bonaventure are challenging. Small classes and personalized attention encourage individual growth and development for students. Saint Bonaventure's nationally known Schools of Arts and Sciences, Business Administration, Journalism/Mass Communication, and Education offer majors in 31 disciplines. The School of Graduate Studies also offers several programs leading to the master's degree."

### SELECTIVITY

| | |
|---|---|
| Admissions Rating | 77 |
| # of applicants | 1,704 |
| % of applicants accepted | 88 |
| % of acceptees attending | 39 |

### FRESHMAN PROFILE
| | |
|---|---|
| Range SAT Verbal | 480-570 |
| Average SAT Verbal | 523 |
| Range SAT Math | 480-580 |
| Average SAT Math | 531 |
| Range ACT Composite | 20-25 |
| Average ACT Composite | 22 |
| Minimum TOEFL | 550 |
| Average HS GPA | 3.1 |
| % graduated top 10% of class | 12 |
| % graduated top 25% of class | 35 |
| % graduated top 50% of class | 70 |

### DEADLINES
| | |
|---|---|
| Priority admission | 2/1 |
| Regular admission | 4/15 |
| Nonfall registration? | yes |

### APPLICANTS ALSO LOOK AT
**AND OFTEN PREFER**
Villanova
Geneseo State
Providence

**AND SOMETIMES PREFER**
LeMoyne
Siena
Ithaca
SUNY—Buffalo
Niagara

**AND RARELY PREFER**
Syracuse

### FINANCIAL FACTS

| | |
|---|---|
| Financial Aid Rating | 88 |
| Tuition | $17,190 |
| Room and board | $6,594 |
| Books and supplies | $735 |
| Required fees | $635 |
| % frosh receiving aid | 74 |
| % undergrads receiving aid | 71 |
| Avg frosh grant | $8,641 |
| Avg frosh loan | $3,050 |

THE BEST 351 COLLEGES ■ 437

# ST. JOHN'S COLLEGE (MD)

PO BOX 2800, ANNAPOLIS, MD 21404 • ADMISSIONS: 410-626-2522 • FAX: 410-269-7916

## CAMPUS LIFE

| | |
|---|---|
| **Quality of Life Rating** | 87 |
| Type of school | private |
| Environment | urban |

### STUDENTS
| | |
|---|---|
| Total undergrad enrollment | 465 |
| % male/female | 55/45 |
| % from out of state | 85 |
| % from public high school | 67 |
| % live on campus | 66 |
| % Asian | 2 |
| % Caucasian | 92 |
| % Hispanic | 3 |
| % international | 3 |
| # of countries represented | 15 |

### SURVEY SAYS . . .
Theater is hot
No one cheats
Registration is a breeze
Diversity lacking on campus
(Almost) everyone plays intramural sports
Class discussions encouraged
Intercollegiate sports unpopular or nonexistent
Political activism is (almost) nonexistent
Diverse students interact

## ACADEMICS

| | |
|---|---|
| **Academic Rating** | 92 |
| Calendar | semester |
| Student/faculty ratio | 8:1 |
| Profs interesting rating | 98 |
| Profs accessible rating | 98 |
| % profs teaching UG courses | 100 |
| Avg reg class size | 10-19 students |

## STUDENTS SPEAK OUT

### Academics
St. John's gets back to basics with a classical education focused exclusively on 100 seminal texts of western civilization, concentrating on philosophy but also covering math, science, literature, and music. Rather than professors, "tutors" with a "passion for teaching" serve to "guide the discussion and keep it on track, but they are there to learn as much as we are." Considering that tutors are required to eventually teach every course, they are experts in cross-subject integration, a goal of the St. John's education. Students form close relationships with their tutors: "Without a doubt, there will be one who changes you forever." Seeing as the dean is simply a "tutor with a title," students say, "The administration? Well, I know all seven of them." Some undergrads find the set academic program "very limiting," but others point out, "I often have the freedom to concentrate on my interests because many essays have quite broad subject assignments." Students are "challenged to dive into our civilization's deepest texts, look into their soul, and really learn." They share the uncommon belief that "philosophy is self-evidently relevant and terribly important." A student tells us, "It felt like I had been asleep before I read these books." In summary, one student writes, "If you want to discover how math, language, and literature can be heartbreakingly beautiful, come to St. John's."

### Life
Life and academics are virtually one and the same at St. John's. For example, one student says that he "sits in a diner and reads Dante" for fun. Others claim, "This is the place to sit up late at night with a bottle of wine talking about philosophy and the cosmos," and often, "students will still be debating metaphysics as they slip into drunken oblivion." All of this boozing is seen as an "escape from the gravity of the subject matter we face daily in class." The weekends begin early among Johnnies; Wednesday nights are known as "New Year's Eve" since the partying begins at midnight. Other than that, the "famous St. John's waltz parties" attract crowds, and for another break from mental acrobatics, "the intramural program here is extremely well-run and lots of fun. It's sports the way that they were meant to be played." Continuing the old-school flavor of the place, the only intercollegiate sports are fencing, crew, and croquet. Generally, students enjoy their "process of shared inquiry," adding "think hard" to the "work hard, play hard" equation.

### Student Body
Amid the student body of 500 "Johnnies," the average student is described as "extremely pretentious, but highly intellectual." This "bright, self-confident, and neurotic" group sometimes displays an "almost complete lack of social graces," unless one counts being "both debauched and brilliant." Bringing the classroom into the interpersonal realm, often the "jokes and conversations center too much on philosophy and the program." The population shows evidence of the "general maturing effects of reading what we read" as they "learn to care for oneself in the transcendental sense." St. John's undergraduates may be regarded as "pretty strange" for their drive to "learn for the sake of learning." But at long last these high school misfits agree that they have "finally met other people like me." If the Annapolis crew gets too familiar, students have the option of transferring to the school's Santa Fe campus for a new crop of cohorts.

# ST. JOHN'S COLLEGE (MD)

FINANCIAL AID: 410-626-2502 • E-MAIL: ADMISSIONS@SJCA.EDU • WEBSITE: WWW.SJCA.EDU

## ADMISSIONS

*Very important factors considered include:* essays. *Important factors considered include:* alumni/ae relation, character/personal qualities, interview, recommendations, secondary school record. *Other factors considered include:* class rank, extracurricular activities, minority status, standardized test scores, talent/ability, volunteer work, work experience. TOEFL required of all international applicants. High school diploma or GED is required. *High school units required/recommended:* 4 English recommended, 3 math required, 4 math recommended, 3 science recommended, 3 science lab recommended, 2 foreign language required, 4 foreign language recommended, 2 social studies recommended, 2 history recommended.

### *The Inside Word*

St. John's has one of the most personal admissions processes in the country. The applicant pool is highly self-selected and extremely bright, so don't be fooled by the high acceptance rate—every student who is offered admission deserves to be here. Candidates who don't give serious thought to the kind of match they make with the college and devote serious energy to their essays are not likely to be successful.

## FINANCIAL AID

*Students should submit:* FAFSA, CSS/Financial Aid PROFILE, noncustodial (divorced/separated) parent's statement, business/farm supplement. No deadline for regular filing. The Princeton Review suggests that all financial aid forms be submitted as soon as possible after January 1. *Need-based scholarships/grants offered:* Pell, SEOG, state scholarships/grants, the school's own gift aid. *Loan aid offered:* FFEL Subsidized Stafford, FFEL Unsubsidized Stafford, FFEL PLUS, Federal Perkins, college/university loans from institutional funds. Federal Work-Study Program available. Institutional employment available. Applicants will be notified of awards on a rolling basis beginning on or about November 1. Off-campus job opportunities are excellent.

## FROM THE ADMISSIONS OFFICE

"The purpose of the admission process is to determine whether an applicant has the necessary preparation and ability to complete the St. John's program satisfactorily. The essays are designed to enable applicants to give a full account of themselves. They can tell the committee much more than statistical records reveal. Previous academic records show whether an applicant has the habits of study necessary at St. John's. Letters of reference, particularly those of teachers, are carefully read for indications that the applicant has the maturity, self-discipline, ability, energy, and initiative to succeed in the St. John's program. St. John's attaches little importance to 'objective' test scores, and no applicant is accepted or rejected because of such scores."

### SELECTIVITY

| | |
|---|---|
| Admissions Rating | 85 |
| # of applicants | 450 |
| % of applicants accepted | 71 |
| % of acceptees attending | 39 |

### FRESHMAN PROFILE

| | |
|---|---|
| Range SAT Verbal | 660-750 |
| Range SAT Math | 590-690 |
| Minimum TOEFL | 600 |
| % graduated top 10% of class | 46 |
| % graduated top 25% of class | 74 |
| % graduated top 50% of class | 99 |

### DEADLINES

| | |
|---|---|
| Priority admission | 3/1 |
| Nonfall registration? | yes |

### APPLICANTS ALSO LOOK AT

**AND OFTEN PREFER**
Swarthmore College
University of Chicago
University of Virginia

**AND SOMETIMES PREFER**
Smith College
Reed College
Kenyon College
Oberlin College

**AND RARELY PREFER**
Bard College
Hampshire College

### FINANCIAL FACTS

| | |
|---|---|
| Financial Aid Rating | 91 |
| Tuition | $25,790 |
| Room and board | $6,770 |
| Books and supplies | $275 |
| Required fees | $200 |
| % frosh receiving aid | 53 |
| % undergrads receiving aid | 56 |
| Avg frosh grant | $14,207 |
| Avg frosh loan | $3,125 |

# ST. JOHN'S COLLEGE (NM)

1160 CAMINO CRUZ BLANCA, SANTA FE, NM 87505 • ADMISSIONS: 505-984-6060 • FAX: 505-984-6162

## CAMPUS LIFE

| | |
|---|---|
| Quality of Life Rating | 90 |
| Type of school | private |
| Environment | urban |

### STUDENTS

| | |
|---|---|
| Total undergrad enrollment | 454 |
| % male/female | 55/45 |
| % from out of state | 90 |
| % from public high school | 75 |
| % live on campus | 75 |
| % African American | 1 |
| % Asian | 3 |
| % Caucasian | 89 |
| % Hispanic | 6 |
| % international | 2 |
| # of countries represented | 8 |

### SURVEY SAYS . . .
Students love Santa Fe, NM
Great off-campus food
Student government is popular
Students are happy
Student publications are popular
(Almost) everyone smokes
Lots of long lines and red tape
Library needs improving
Lousy food on campus

## ACADEMICS

| | |
|---|---|
| Academic Rating | 92 |
| Calendar | semester |
| Student/faculty ratio | 8:1 |
| Profs interesting rating | 97 |
| Profs accessible rating | 98 |
| % profs teaching UG courses | 100 |
| Avg reg class size | 10-19 students |

## STUDENTS SPEAK OUT

### Academics

Imagine a college with no tests, no lectures, no majors, no professors. Well, what you're imagining is St. John's College. Now when they say no professors, they don't really mean no professors. They mean that the well-trained members of the faculty are "tutors." Because there are "no lecture classes," "St. John's College is kind of like a congress—it's run by discussions." Students meet in tutorials of only a small group of classmates and in labs and seminars that consist of no more than 22 students; in each setting, the groups discuss their responses to readings of primary works. Once a week, the entire student body congregates for a collective lecture. "The academic experience is what you make of it," writes a senior. "Since there is little 'formal' evaluation, it is possible to get by doing almost nothing." But that's not usually the case because the expectations of preparation and participation often force "everyone to think critically." There's no question that the St. John's style isn't for everyone. As one student puts it, "The Johnny is the student who is miserable everywhere else."

### Life

At a college like St. John's, where students all major in liberal arts and take largely the same courses and where the student body is small enough to cram onto a small ship, one of two things happens: either students embrace each other, like a family, or they scatter. Both of these scenarios play out at St. John's. One freshman notes that "people around here find their social lives and thoughts intertwined with the academic." This often means that even spare hours are crowded with "philosophy, philosophy, philosophy, books, books, books." But it's not all exercise of the cerebral cortex. "People think of everything—from Plato to Play-Doh." Many students prefer to get away from campus—away from where it feels that everyone is always pondering "the meaning of life, the universe, and everything . . . it's very tiring." Fortunately, "the beautiful surrounding land" and the city of Santa Fe provide plenty of distractions for the students who need it. "People go hiking, rafting, biking," and "there are several excellent hot springs near here." The college provides a fair share of outlets, too—ranging from groups like the Film Society to pottery and fencing classes. But athletes beware: the college does not participate in formal competition with other schools, nor does it dish out scholarships. But hulking linebackers aren't what St. John's needs. It needs students who have the guts and grit to "wake up hung over, go to classes, write papers and do Greek homework, get drunk and start fistfights over what Plato really said til 4:00 in the morning, sleep, repeat."

### Student Body

In some of their fellow classmates' eyes, St. John's students are "the most intelligent, well-traveled, interesting people"—people who can be "very witty," though "sometimes manic." When other students look around them, they see "the weirdest bunch of insomniac, alcoholic, philosophy nerds you've ever seen." While you're sure to find some geeks and freaks and pranksters wandering around this Santa Fe campus, you'll also find a balance of "quite grounded and humble" students. Because of St. John's' nontraditional curriculum (no tests, no majors, and, well, you get the picture), it tends to attract students who rarely fit any late-teenage stereotypes. In general, this means that students are accepting of each other and "there's no pressure to act in certain ways." Although St. John's' undergrads represent an array "of contrasting backgrounds," many are white and share the self-perception of "an aspiring writer or lawyer." "Johnnies are a bunch of nuts," writes an undergrad, "but we really come together as some sort of close dysfunctional family. The question is whether our dysfunction is the sort you're after."

# ST. JOHN'S COLLEGE (NM)

FINANCIAL AID: 505-984-6058 • E-MAIL: ADMISSIONS@MAIL.SJCSF.EDU • WEBSITE: WWW.SJCSF.EDU

## ADMISSIONS
*Very important factors considered include:* character/personal qualities, essays, interview, talent/ability. *Important factors considered include:* extracurricular activities, recommendations, secondary school record. *Other factors considered include:* class rank, standardized test scores, volunteer work, work experience. TOEFL and SAT I required of all international applicants. *High school units required/recommended:* 18 total recommended; 3 math required, 4 math recommended, 3 science recommended, 3 science lab recommended, 2 foreign language required, 4 foreign language recommended, 2 social studies recommended, 2 history recommended.

### The Inside Word
Self-selection drives this admissions process—over one-half of the entire applicant pool each year indicates that St. John's is their first choice, and half of those admitted send in tuition deposits. Even so, no one in admissions takes things for granted, and neither should any student considering an application. The admissions process is highly personal on both sides of the coin. Only the intellectually curious and highly motivated need apply.

## FINANCIAL AID
*Students should submit:* FAFSA, CSS/Financial Aid PROFILE, noncustodial (divorced/separated) parent's statement, business/farm supplement. The Princeton Review suggests that all financial aid forms be submitted as soon as possible after January 1. *Need-based scholarships/grants offered:* Pell, SEOG, state scholarships/grants, private scholarships, the school's own gift aid. *Loan aid offered:* Direct Subsidized Stafford, Direct Unsubsidized Stafford, Direct PLUS, Federal Perkins, college/university loans from institutional funds. Federal Work-Study Program available. Institutional employment available. Applicants will be notified of awards on a rolling basis beginning on or about December 1. Off-campus job opportunities are good.

## FROM THE ADMISSIONS OFFICE
"St. John's appeals to students who value good books, love to read, and are passionate about discourse and debate. There are no lectures and virtually no tests or electives. Instead, classes of 16–20 students occur around conference tables where professors are as likely to be asked to defend their points of view as are students. Great books provide the direction, context, and stimulus for conversation. The entire student body adheres to the same, all-required arts and science curriculum. Someone once said 'A classic is a house we still live in,' and at St. John's, students and professors alike approach each reading on the list as if the ideas it holds were being expressed for the first time—questioning the logic behind a geometrical proof, challenging the premise of a scientific development, or dissecting the progression of modern political theory as it unfolds."

## SELECTIVITY

| | |
|---|---|
| Admissions Rating | 82 |
| # of applicants | 358 |
| % of applicants accepted | 80 |
| % of acceptees attending | 48 |
| # accepting a place on wait list | 10 |
| % admitted from wait list | 60 |

### FRESHMAN PROFILE
| | |
|---|---|
| Range SAT Verbal | 630-720 |
| Average SAT Verbal | 700 |
| Range SAT Math | 560-650 |
| Average SAT Math | 600 |
| Range ACT Composite | 26-30 |
| Average ACT Composite | 27 |
| Minimum TOEFL | 550 |
| % graduated top 10% of class | 23 |
| % graduated top 25% of class | 46 |
| % graduated top 50% of class | 77 |

### DEADLINES
| | |
|---|---|
| Priority admission | 3/1 |
| Regular notification | rolling |
| Nonfall registration? | yes |

### APPLICANTS ALSO LOOK AT AND OFTEN PREFER
U of Chicago
Stanford

**AND SOMETIMES PREFER**
Rice
Colorado College
Claremont McKenna

**AND RARELY PREFER**
Grinnell
Whitman
Oberlin

## FINANCIAL FACTS

| | |
|---|---|
| Financial Aid Rating | 85 |
| Tuition | $28,840 |
| Room and board | $7,320 |
| Books and supplies | $275 |
| Required fees | $200 |
| % frosh receiving aid | 71 |
| % undergrads receiving aid | 71 |
| Avg frosh grant | $15,788 |
| Avg frosh loan | $3,405 |

# ST. LAWRENCE UNIVERSITY

PAYSON HALL, CANTON, NY 13617 • ADMISSIONS: 315-229-5261 • FAX: 315-229-5818

## CAMPUS LIFE

★ ★ ★ ☆

| | |
|---|---|
| Quality of Life Rating | 83 |
| Type of school | private |
| Environment | rural |

### STUDENTS

| | |
|---|---|
| Total undergrad enrollment | 2,150 |
| % male/female | 47/53 |
| % from out of state | 46 |
| % from public high school | 72 |
| % live on campus | 95 |
| % in (# of) fraternities | 15 (4) |
| % in (# of) sororities | 23 (4) |
| % African American | 2 |
| % Asian | 1 |
| % Caucasian | 74 |
| % Hispanic | 2 |
| % international | 4 |

### SURVEY SAYS . . .
Beautiful campus
Students are religious
Everyone loves the saints
Students get along with local community
Frats and sororities dominate social scene
Political activism is hot
Campus difficult to get around
Students are happy

## ACADEMICS

★ ★ ★ ★

| | |
|---|---|
| Academic Rating | 91 |
| Calendar | semester |
| Student/faculty ratio | 12:1 |
| Profs interesting rating | 75 |
| Profs accessible rating | 75 |
| % profs teaching UG courses | 99 |
| Avg lab size | 10-19 students |
| Avg reg class size | 10-19 students |

### MOST POPULAR MAJORS
Psychology
Economics
English language and literature

## STUDENTS SPEAK OUT

### Academics

St. Lawrence students love the "really comfortable, home-like atmosphere" engendered by "the size of the student body and the relative isolation of our campus from any real cities." Small class sizes are the norm at this small liberal arts college in the "north country" of New York State, meaning that "classes are discussion seminars rather than lectures. This allows students to make a more personal connection—not only with their fellow students, but also with their fellow professors." Professors "are all passionate about their subjects, easy to talk to, have good senses of humor, and available outside of class. If you can't make it to their office hours, they are willing to schedule a meeting time." Add "great research, independent projects, internships, and study abroad opportunities in 14 countries" as well as "a great diversity of classes offered here that makes it is almost impossible to not become enriched," and you'll understand why students here feel so favorably about SLU academics. But wait; there's more! Students also tell us that "the alumni connections are amazing and a great thing to have later on after college, especially for internships or actual jobs."

### Life

"At St. Lawrence, there isn't much to do for fun except make your own fun." Some students here immerse themselves in campus life; writes one, "It's most important to be extremely active and try to enjoy what the campus has to offer to the fullest. From intramurals to the student government, there is always something to interest everyone." Students enthusiastically support their Division I hockey teams, which "add interest on an otherwise dull campus in the dead of winter," and enjoy special events like Peak Weekend ("It's for those who hike, I mean really hike, and those who just like to own hiking stuff. The Outing Club, the nation's oldest collegiate outdoors club, attempts to get college students on all 36 high peaks in the Adirondacks") and Snowbowl ("lots of sledding and beer"). Most students eventually find their way to SLU's lively party scene. "We do drink a lot," confesses one student. "The school tries to hide it, but St. Lawrence students can handle their booze almost any night of the week and still keep pace with the demanding academic program." For many, "the social scene at St. Lawrence gets a little monotonous. The area doesn't have much to offer, and the main weekend activities revolve around drinking with friends." Many warn that winters are long and exceedingly cold. Road trips to Canada, especially to Ottawa or Montreal, are popular diversions.

### Student Body

St. Lawrence has long had a reputation as a preppy haven. Students here tell us that about half the student body fits that stereotype; writes one, the typical "Larry" likes "wearing his polo shirt with the collar turned up, [wearing] a North Face fleece, and carrying a Nalgene bottle. A Muffy, the female Larry, can be spotted with her Vera Bradley bags, Tiffany's heart bracelet, and an inordinate number of shoes." Admits one majority student, "St. Lawrence plays into the hands of the classic prep, so many of us seem to come from New England boarding schools, while the remainder are from upscale areas. We look and act like we stepped right out of the pages of The Official Preppy Handbook, and most of us seem proud of it." However, "there are also environmentalists, hippies, the outdoors people, and everyone else" at SLU, although "there aren't many punks and skaters, and people of these types tend to find themselves the token 'oddball' of the dorm." Everyone seems to agree that "we are quite a 'white' school and are lacking a bit in diversity." Many here are "involved in everything. I can't think of anyone who doesn't have extracurriculars. There is an organization for anything you can imagine." Many are active in community service.

# ST. LAWRENCE UNIVERSITY

FINANCIAL AID: 315-229-5265 • E-MAIL: ADMISSIONS@STLAWU.EDU • WEBSITE: WWW.STLAWU.EDU

## ADMISSIONS

*Very important factors considered include:* character/personal qualities, recommendations, secondary school record. *Important factors considered include:* class rank, essays, extracurricular activities, interview, minority status, standardized test scores. *Other factors considered include:* alumni/ae relation, geographical residence, talent/ability, volunteer work, work experience. SAT I or ACT required. TOEFL required of all international applicants. High school diploma or GED is required. *High school units required/recommended:* 20 total recommended; 4 English recommended, 4 math recommended, 4 science recommended, 4 foreign language recommended, 2 social studies recommended, 2 history recommended.

## The Inside Word

St. Lawrence has a rough time convincing students to commit to spending four years in relative isolation. Serious competition from many fine northeastern colleges also causes admissions standards to be less selective than the university would like. This makes St. Lawrence an especially good choice for academically sound but average students who are seeking an excellent small college experience and/or an outdoorsy setting.

## FINANCIAL AID

*Students should submit:* FAFSA, institution's own financial aid form, noncustodial (divorced/separated) parent's statement, income tax returns/W-2s. Regular filing deadline is February 15. The Princeton Review suggests that all financial aid forms be submitted as soon as possible after January 1. *Need-based scholarships/grants offered:* Pell, SEOG, state scholarships/grants, the school's own gift aid. *Loan aid offered:* Direct Subsidized Stafford, Direct Unsubsidized Stafford, FFEL Subsidized Stafford, FFEL Unsubsidized Stafford, FFEL PLUS, Federal Perkins, college/university loans from institutional funds, GATE Loans. Federal Work-Study Program available. Institutional employment available. Applicants will be notified of awards on or about March 30. Off-campus job opportunities are poor.

## FROM THE ADMISSIONS OFFICE

"St. Lawrence is an independent, nondenominational, liberal arts and sciences university located in northern New York. The student body of 2,000 men and women choose from among more than 30 majors and minors; classes are small, with an emphasis on experiential learning, interdisciplinary study, and independent research. St. Lawrence is a residential college where living and learning are combined through the First-Year Program, theme cottages, and international study. St. Lawrence students are well rounded and involved, with many drawn to the 1,000-acre campus for the opportunity it provides for outdoor recreation. The campus, located in the town of Canton, is halfway between the Adirondack Park and the city of Ottawa. Students are active in various organizations centered on the arts, politics, community service, and athletics, with 32 intercollegiate teams offered. St. Lawrence alumni are loyal and active, providing internships for undergraduates and demonstrating their commitment through giving generously of their time and resources."

## SELECTIVITY

| | |
|---|---|
| Admissions Rating | 86 |
| # of applicants | 2,867 |
| % of applicants accepted | 65 |
| % of acceptees attending | 33 |
| # accepting a place on wait list | 123 |
| % admitted from wait list | 2 |
| # of early decision applicants | 166 |
| % accepted early decision | 80 |

### FRESHMAN PROFILE

| | |
|---|---|
| Range SAT Verbal | 520-620 |
| Average SAT Verbal | 570 |
| Range SAT Math | 520-620 |
| Average SAT Math | 570 |
| Range ACT Composite | 21-27 |
| Average ACT Composite | 24 |
| Minimum TOEFL | 600 |
| Average HS GPA | 3.3 |
| % graduated top 10% of class | 31 |
| % graduated top 25% of class | 62 |
| % graduated top 50% of class | 92 |

### DEADLINES

| | |
|---|---|
| Early decision | 11/15 |
| Early decision notification | 12/15 |
| Regular admission | 2/15 |
| Nonfall registration? | yes |

### APPLICANTS ALSO LOOK AT
**AND OFTEN PREFER**
Middlebury
Colby, Colgate
U. Vermont
**AND SOMETIMES PREFER**
Hamilton
Syracuse, Bates
Skidmore
U. New Hampshire
**AND RARELY PREFER**
Union (NY)
Denison

## FINANCIAL FACTS

| | |
|---|---|
| Financial Aid Rating | 83 |
| Tuition | $27,985 |
| Room and board | $7,755 |
| Books and supplies | $650 |
| Required fees | $205 |
| % frosh receiving aid | 85 |
| % undergrads receiving aid | 85 |
| Avg frosh grant | $18,341 |
| Avg frosh loan | $5,009 |

THE BEST 351 COLLEGES ■ 443

# SAINT LOUIS UNIVERSITY

221 NORTH GRAND BOULEVARD, SAINT LOUIS, MO 63103 • ADMISSIONS: 314-977-2500 • FAX: 314-977-3079

## CAMPUS LIFE

| Quality of Life Rating | 80 |
|---|---|
| Type of school | private |
| Affiliation | Roman Catholic |
| Environment | urban |

### STUDENTS
| | |
|---|---|
| Total undergrad enrollment | 7,178 |
| % male/female | 46/54 |
| % from out of state | 47 |
| % live on campus | 51 |
| % in (# of) fraternities | 16 (11) |
| % in (# of) sororities | 17 (4) |
| % African American | 7 |
| % Asian | 4 |
| % Caucasian | 71 |
| % Hispanic | 3 |
| % international | 3 |
| # of countries represented | 80 |

### SURVEY SAYS . . .
Theater is hot
Political activism is hot
Lots of classroom discussion
Classes are small
Campus difficult to get around

## ACADEMICS

| Academic Rating | 79 |
|---|---|
| Calendar | semester |
| Student/faculty ratio | 12:1 |
| Profs interesting rating | 73 |
| Profs accessible rating | 72 |
| Avg lab size | 20-29 students |
| Avg reg class size | 10-19 students |

### MOST POPULAR MAJORS
Business
Biology/biological sciences
Psychology

## STUDENTS SPEAK OUT

### Academics
Students praise Saint Louis University, a big-city Jesuit school, as "a small, private institution that really cares for its students. Due to its small size, you aren't just a 'face in the crowd' here." A renowned physical therapy/occupational therapy program, the "nationally ranked aviation school," the pre-med program, and the "recently expanded Cook School of Business" receive the highest praise here, but students report that, in all areas, "the classes are really small and teachers are really accessible, once you get past your introductory classes." Students in the most prestigious programs report that "there is a heavy workload, and everybody is pretty serious about studying during the week and even on the weekends." Others tell us that "academics are what you want them to be here. If you want a challenge, you can find those classes easily. If you want the easy way out, ask around for names of those professors" that offer them. Profs at SLU "really make an effort to reach out to the students and make us think. Also, they are available outside class and genuinely help out anyone in need." Undergrads also appreciate the way that "SLU tries to give every student the opportunity to grow and learn by offering many ways to get involved. The academic [curriculum] works together with the residence hall system, and all support the experience gained from participating in student organizations and extracurricular activities."

### Life
Like most students in big cities, undergrads at Saint Louis University report that their extracurricular fun usually takes place beyond the campus gates. "The great thing about SLU is that it is located in a very urban environment with tons of cultural and entertaining things to do," explains one student. "There's never a dull moment. We have easy access . . . to museums, zoos, the Fox Theatre, and downtown sporting events." Adds another, "There's Forest Park to visit on nice days, the Arch, the Science Center, a fabulous zoo, ice skating, movie theaters, and lots of great malls." The campus is connected to most city hot spots by MetroLink, St. Louis' light rail system; some here wish the school would offer shuttle bus service, but most seem to handle the public transportation experience without much trouble. Those who choose not to venture out can enjoy "a beautiful campus, with tons of fountains, statues, and flowers." The Greeks exert a major influence on campus social life, and "there is a strong separation between Greeks and non-Greeks. Since there aren't houses—just a Greek dorm—there aren't any open parties. Greek functions tend to be exclusive."

### Student Body
Drawing heavily from private Catholic schools in the Midwest, Saint Louis University is home to "many students who are preppy, snobby, rich kids." However, "since SLU gives out good scholarships, the economic classes here vary a little bit." Diversity is enhanced by the fact that "there [are] a great deal of international students, since we have our own campus in Madrid." Minority representation is considerable, too, although most here agree that "all the different races and ethnic groups are segregated." Some feel the school could do better in this area; as one put it, "I also wish there was more diversity; not only ethnically, but different kinds of personalities. It seems that while most people here are down-to-earth, everyone is preppy. I wish we had more hippie types, and musicians, and the like: something different." Many here consider themselves "smart, caring, and into volunteering/helping out the community."

# SAINT LOUIS UNIVERSITY

FINANCIAL AID: 314-977-2350 • E-MAIL: ADMITME@SLU.EDU • WEBSITE: WWW.SLU.EDU

## ADMISSIONS

*Important factors considered include:* secondary school record, standardized test scores. *Other factors considered include:* character/personal qualities, essays, extracurricular activities, recommendations, volunteer work. SAT I or ACT required. TOEFL required of all international applicants. High school diploma or GED is required. *High school units required/recommended:* 20 total recommended; 4 English recommended, 4 math recommended, 3 science recommended, 3 foreign language recommended, 3 social studies recommended, 3 elective recommended.

### The Inside Word

Students who are ranked in the top half of their graduating class will have a fairly easy path to admission at Saint Louis. Those who are not can find success in the admissions process by being a minority, having a top Catholic school diploma, or possessing a major talent in soccer.

## FINANCIAL AID

*Students should submit:* FAFSA. Regular filing deadline is March 1. The Princeton Review suggests that all financial aid forms be submitted as soon as possible after January 1. *Need-based scholarships/grants offered:* Pell, SEOG, state scholarships/grants, private scholarships, the school's own gift aid. *Loan aid offered:* FFEL Subsidized Stafford, FFEL Unsubsidized Stafford, FFEL PLUS, Federal Perkins, Federal Nursing, short-term loans. Federal Work-Study Program available. Applicants will be notified of merit awards on a rolling basis beginning on or about October 15. Need-based awards notification begins February 1. Off-campus job opportunities are excellent.

## FROM THE ADMISSIONS OFFICE

"A hot midwestern university with a growing national and international reputation, Saint Louis University gives students the knowledge, skills, and values to build a successful career and make a difference in the lives of those around them.

"Students live and learn in a safe and attractive campus environment. The beautiful urban, residential campus offers loads of internship, outreach, and recreational opportunities. Ranked as one of the best educational values in the country, the University welcomes students from all 50 states and 80 foreign countries who pursue rigorous majors that invite individualization. Accessible faculty, study abroad opportunities, and many small, interactive classes make SLU a great place to learn.

"A leading Jesuit, Catholic university, SLU's goal is to graduate men and women of competence and conscience—individuals who are not only capable of making wise decisions, but who also understand why they made them. Since 1818, Saint Louis University has been dedicated to academic excellence, service to others, and preparing students to be leaders in society. Saint Louis University truly is the place . . . *where knowledge touches lives.*"

### SELECTIVITY

| | |
|---|---|
| Admissions Rating | 77 |
| # of applicants | 5,992 |
| % of applicants accepted | 72 |
| % of acceptees attending | 33 |

#### FRESHMAN PROFILE
| | |
|---|---|
| Range SAT Verbal | 530-640 |
| Average SAT Verbal | 585 |
| Range SAT Math | 530-655 |
| Average SAT Math | 595 |
| Range ACT Composite | 23-28 |
| Average ACT Composite | 26 |
| Minimum TOEFL | 525 |
| Average HS GPA | 3.5 |
| % graduated top 10% of class | 32 |
| % graduated top 25% of class | 61 |
| % graduated top 50% of class | 88 |

#### DEADLINES
| | |
|---|---|
| Priority admission | 12/1 |
| Regular admission | 8/1 |
| Nonfall registration? | yes |

#### APPLICANTS ALSO LOOK AT AND OFTEN PREFER
U Notre Dame

#### AND SOMETIMES PREFER
Marquette
Purdue U
Washington U
U of Illinois at Urbana-Champaign
U of Missouri at Columbia

#### AND RARELY PREFER
Bradley
Rockhurst
Southwest Missouri State
Tulane
U of Missouri at St Louis

### FINANCIAL FACTS

| | |
|---|---|
| Financial Aid Rating | 92 |
| Tuition | $20,840 |
| Room and board | $7,310 |
| Books and supplies | $1,040 |
| Required fees | $168 |
| % frosh receiving aid | 73 |
| % undergrads receiving aid | 67 |
| Avg frosh grant | $13,575 |
| Avg frosh loan | $6,797 |

# SAINT MARY'S COLLEGE OF CALIFORNIA

PO Box 4800, Moraga, CA 94575-4800 • Admissions: 925-631-4224 • Fax: 925-376-7193

## CAMPUS LIFE

| | |
|---|---|
| Quality of Life Rating | 89 |
| Type of school | private |
| Affiliation | Roman Catholic |
| Environment | suburban |

### STUDENTS

| | |
|---|---|
| Total undergrad enrollment | 3,401 |
| % male/female | 40/60 |
| % from out of state | 11 |
| % from public high school | 57 |
| % live on campus | 62 |
| % African American | 6 |
| % Asian | 10 |
| % Caucasian | 60 |
| % Hispanic | 18 |
| % international | 2 |
| # of countries represented | 21 |

### SURVEY SAYS . . .
Classes are small
Beautiful campus
Campus easy to get around
Campus feels safe
Musical organizations aren't popular
Very small frat/sorority scene
Class discussions encouraged
Theater is unpopular
Lousy food on campus
Political activism is (almost) nonexistent

## ACADEMICS

| | |
|---|---|
| Academic Rating | 91 |
| Calendar | 4-1-4 |
| Student/faculty ratio | 13:1 |
| Profs interesting rating | 96 |
| Profs accessible rating | 98 |
| % profs teaching UG courses | 100 |
| Avg reg class size | 20-29 students |

### MOST POPULAR MAJORS
Business administration/management
Communications studies/speech communication and rhetoric
Political science and government

## STUDENTS SPEAK OUT

### Academics

With a core curriculum centered on the "one-of-a-kind" Great Books Seminar Program, and a strong affiliation with the Roman Catholic church, this small private college manages to keep one foot firmly planted in tradition, while the other is pointed straight towards the future. The school's "beautiful" campus—located in the heart of the Bay Area close to San Francisco—"is booming with new buildings, technologies, and media," yet the school's classic approach encourages undergrads to gain a solid liberal arts foundation before they head into one of the school's many pre-professional majors, such as business administration. "I can't think of any other school that allows students to soak up some sun while discussing the dominant 'Amazonian' women and their roles in Lysistrata," writes a sophomore. With a little less than 2,500 undergrads, small "seminar-style discussions" and lots of "personal attention" are guaranteed; and while "no one has a cow if you don't come to class," notes another sophomore, "students here know that missing a class is as bad as not calling Mom back after she's left yet another message." And like Mom, professors are student-focused and very available. Says a junior, "I have been very pleased with my academic experience. My professors have all been extremely accessible and interested in seeing me succeed." Faculty and administration are described as "friendly" and "willing to help." Writes another junior, "They work hard to get to know you as a person." A first-year provides an unusual example of faculty devotion: "Last week, my professor in 'Culture and Community' bought my whole class Round Table Pizza and before that, Starbucks, and before that, Ben & Jerry's. I love my professors here!" And while with all this fussing over the student body may make it hard to leave, SMC encourages students to widen their educational horizons by offering a January term every year during which students pursue nontraditional themes, internships, and travel, as well as study abroad programs at affiliated Catholic institutions in Rome, France, and England.

### Life

Only a short BART ride away from San Francisco, yet far enough away to offer hiking, biking, skating, and climbing just minutes from campus, "gorgeous" Saint Mary's is ideally situated to provide a little something for every type of student. It's also a "community-oriented" school, improved since the inception of a new student union building last year. In terms of campus life, crew and other sports are reasonably popular, as is the Campus Ministry—"a great way to get involved." And while many students mention the lack of a weekend scene at SMC due to the fact that many of its students live in nearby towns, "a new sprouting of on-campus activities makes life here much more exciting." Still, writes one junior, "Moraga is a very upper-class white town, and the students here are those usually with money, so they go home on weekends a lot as there isn't much to do. It sucks for out-of-state students, socially, unless they find friends with cars and generosity." Of course there's always the good old college standby: "meet at students' rooms, listen to music, dance, and drink."

### Student Body

Though SMC students have the reputation of being fairly conservative, Roman Catholic, and career-oriented (and a bit "behind in diversity," notes a first-year), a sophomore notes that "many aren't as serious about academics as I'd expected." She continues, "They're not too spiritual and they like to have fun." One thing is certain: Most students point out that "everyone is very friendly" at SMC, and a senior takes it a step further, saying, "The best thing about this school is the people you meet."

# SAINT MARY'S COLLEGE OF CALIFORNIA

FINANCIAL AID: 925-631-4370 • E-MAIL: SMCADMIT@STMARYS-CA.EDU • WEBSITE: WWW.STMARYS-CA.EDU

## ADMISSIONS

*Very important factors considered include:* secondary school record, standardized test scores. *Important factors considered include:* essays, recommendations. *Other factors considered include:* alumni/ae relation, character/personal qualities, class rank, extracurricular activities, geographical residence, interview, minority status, religious affiliation/commitment, talent/ability, volunteer work, work experience. SAT I or ACT required. TOEFL required of all international applicants. High school diploma or GED is required. *High school units required/recommended:* 16 total required; 17 total recommended; 4 English required, 3 math required, 4 math recommended, 2 science required, 3 science recommended, 1 science lab required, 2 foreign language required, 3 foreign language recommended, 1 social studies required, 1 history required, 3 elective required.

### The Inside Word

The typical St. Mary's admit is a better-than-average student who has attending a Catholic college very high on his or her list of preferences. The applicant pool is full of such candidates. Candidates should give serious attention to the application process, as they are guaranteed close scrutiny despite the college's high admit rate.

## FINANCIAL AID

*Students should submit:* FAFSA, state aid form. Regular filing deadline is March 2. The Princeton Review suggests that all financial aid forms be submitted as soon as possible after January 1. *Need-based scholarships/grants offered:* Pell, SEOG, state scholarships/grants, private scholarships, the school's own gift aid. *Loan aid offered:* FFEL Subsidized Stafford, FFEL Unsubsidized Stafford, FFEL PLUS, Federal Perkins. Federal Work-Study Program available. Institutional employment available. Applicants will be notified of awards on a rolling basis beginning on or about April 15. Off-campus job opportunities are excellent.

## FROM THE ADMISSIONS OFFICE

"Today St. Mary's College continues to offer a value-oriented education by providing a classical liberal arts background second to none. The emphasis here is on teaching an individual how to think independently and responsibly, how to analyze information in all situations, and how to make choices based on logical thinking and rational examination. Such a program develops students' ability to ask the right questions and to formulate meaningful answers, not only within their professional careers but also for the rest of their lives. St. Mary's College is committed to preparing young men and women for the challenge of an ever-changing world, while remaining faithful to an enduring academic and spiritual heritage. We believe the purpose of a college experience is to prepare men and women for an unlimited number of opportunities. We believe this is best accomplished by educating the whole person, both intellectually and ethically. We strive to recruit, admit, enroll and graduate students who are generous, faith-filled, and human, and we believe this is reaffirmed in our community of Brothers, in our faculty, and in our personal concern for each student."

### SELECTIVITY

| | |
|---|---|
| Admissions Rating | 79 |
| # of applicants | 3,021 |
| % of applicants accepted | 85 |
| % of acceptees attending | 25 |
| # accepting a place on wait list | 74 |
| % admitted from wait list | 43 |

#### FRESHMAN PROFILE

| | |
|---|---|
| Range SAT Verbal | 500-600 |
| Average SAT Verbal | 551 |
| Range SAT Math | 500-600 |
| Average SAT Math | 552 |
| Minimum TOEFL | 525 |
| Average HS GPA | 3.4 |

#### DEADLINES

| | |
|---|---|
| Priority admission | 11/30 |
| Regular admission | 2/1 |
| Nonfall registration? | yes |

#### APPLICANTS ALSO LOOK AT AND OFTEN PREFER
Notre Dame
UC Berkeley
Stanford

#### AND SOMETIMES PREFER
UC Davis
Loyola Marymount
UC San Diego
Santa Clara

#### AND RARELY PREFER
Gonzaga
UC Santa Barbara
U of the Pacific
UC Santa Cruz

### FINANCIAL FACTS

| | |
|---|---|
| Financial Aid Rating | 82 |
| Tuition | $23,640 |
| Room and board | $9,075 |
| Books and supplies | $846 |
| Required fees | $135 |
| % frosh receiving aid | 66 |
| % undergrads receiving aid | 60 |
| Avg frosh loan | $3,818 |

# ST. MARY'S COLLEGE OF MARYLAND

ADMISSIONS OFFICE, 18952 EAST FISHER ROAD, ST. MARY'S CITY, MD 20686-3001 • ADMISSIONS: 800-492-7181 • FAX: 240-895-5001

## CAMPUS LIFE
★ ★ ★ ☆

| | |
|---|---|
| Quality of Life Rating | 81 |
| Type of school | public |
| Environment | rural |

### STUDENTS
| | |
|---|---|
| Total undergrad enrollment | 1,823 |
| % male/female | 40/60 |
| % from out of state | 15 |
| % from public high school | 80 |
| % live on campus | 76 |
| % African American | 7 |
| % Asian | 4 |
| % Caucasian | 82 |
| % Hispanic | 3 |
| # of countries represented | 25 |

### SURVEY SAYS . . .
Classes are small
No one cheats
Beautiful campus
Campus easy to get around
Lab facilities need improving
Great computer facilities
Library needs improving
Lousy off-campus food
Lousy food on campus

## ACADEMICS
★ ★ ★ ☆

| | |
|---|---|
| Academic Rating | 83 |
| Calendar | semester |
| Student/faculty ratio | 12:1 |
| Profs interesting rating | 94 |
| Profs accessible rating | 95 |
| % profs teaching UG courses | 100 |
| Avg lab size | 10-19 students |
| Avg reg class size | 10-19 students |

### MOST POPULAR MAJORS
Biology/biological sciences
Economics
Psychology

## STUDENTS SPEAK OUT

### Academics
A small, private liberal arts school experience at state school prices: that's what regularly puts St. Mary's College in Maryland at or near the top of everyone's "Best Buys in Education" lists. Students here appreciate what the school offers, bragging about the "accessible and friendly" faculty, the availability of "lots of interdisciplinary courses and programs, basically lots of academic flexibility," and an administration that is "very open to student input and always willing to hold discussions and Q & A sessions." Students agree that "St. Mary's is well deserving of its 'Honors College' label. It makes you work for your degree with challenging classes that require a lot of work outside of class." Every student here may complete an extensive senior project, a "student-initiated, culminating experience" that is "the centerpiece of the honors college curriculum." Students are assisted in their endeavors by professors whom they "call by their first names and never hesitate to ask for private meetings when we have concerns or even just want to chat." Also, "another plus is that most of the profs are willing to take on freshmen to help with research if they want to do it. There are incredible opportunities here."

### Life
The secluded campus of St. Mary's College, students agree, "is absolutely breathtaking. It is right on the St. Mary's River, and the sunsets are magnificent! It is so calm and peaceful. There are these beautiful benches all over the campus, but the best ones are right on the water in a little garden. If you go and sit on those benches, all your troubles melt away. Also, the buildings are gorgeous." Not surprisingly, students "spend a lot of time on the river, either sailing, kayaking, or swimming." Many complain that there is little else to do. "It is rather isolated here," students tell us. "Town is 20 minutes away, even the closest McDonald's." ("Town," by the way, is historic St. Mary's City, the first capital of Maryland and host to many historical reenactments.) More than a few students, however, report having little trouble finding diversions: "There [are] always activities sponsored by the school, and there's always spontaneous fun" like "grabbing cafeteria trays, inflatable chairs, and garbage bags and sledding on this hill near my dorm. The whole school shows up, and everyone is laughing and having a great time." Some "chase the peacocks while drunk, watch movies, shop at Wal-Mart, drive an hour to get to a mall, go to lectures." Students also tell us that "community service is big here . . . . A majority of the college volunteers on a regular basis, and not only the students, but professors as well. I think that's pretty damn cool." Sports are popular; writes one undergrad, "My school is Division III, so the athletes aren't playing to be noticed, they're playing because they enjoy it. Our guys and girls lacrosse, sailing, and crew teams are very popular and ranked well."

### Student Body
"The initial impression I got of SMCM was on my campus tour when random people walking by, said 'hello,' and told me to come here," explains one student. Sure, there are different cliques, like the athletes, the hippies, the administration-involved, etc., but everyone mixes and gets along." Most are hardworking and driven to succeed; notes one undergrad, "The students here are so motivated, both inside and outside the classroom. Students work hard at school, and they work hard in their extracurricular activities." The small student body means that "everyone here knows everyone else. Don't expect to come here and be anonymous." Racial diversity isn't as pronounced as most students would like it; reports one student, "Most people are white. There is a visible black population though. Most students are liberal (especially environmentally). There are many different groups here: the jocks, the 'nerds,' the preps, the hippies, etc. But everyone seems to get along pretty well. Everyone is nice."

448 ■ THE BEST 351 COLLEGES

# ST. MARY'S COLLEGE OF MARYLAND

FINANCIAL AID: 240-895-3000 • E-MAIL: ADMISSIONS@SMCM.EDU • WEBSITE: WWW.SMCM.EDU

## ADMISSIONS
*Very important factors considered include:* essays, secondary school record, standardized test scores. *Important factors considered include:* extracurricular activities, recommendations, talent/ability. *Other factors considered include:* alumni/ae relation, character/personal qualities, geographical residence, interview, minority status, state residency, volunteer work, work experience. SAT I or ACT required; SAT I preferred. TOEFL required of all international applicants. High school diploma or GED is required. *High school units required/recommended:* 20 total required; 22 total recommended; 4 English required, 3 math required, 3 science required, 2 science lab recommended, 2 foreign language recommended, 3 social studies required, 7 elective required.

### The Inside Word
There are few better choices than St. Mary's for better-than-average students who are not likely to get admitted to one of the top 50 or so colleges in the country. It is likely that if funding for public colleges is able to stabilize, or even grow, that this place will soon be joining the ranks of the best. Now is the time to take advantage, before the academic expectations of the admissions committee start to soar.

## FINANCIAL AID
*Students should submit:* FAFSA. Regular filing deadline is March 1. The Princeton Review suggests that all financial aid forms be submitted as soon as possible after January 1. *Need-based scholarships/grants offered:* Pell, SEOG, state scholarships/grants, private scholarships, the school's own gift aid. *Loan aid offered:* FFEL Subsidized Stafford, FFEL Unsubsidized Stafford, FFEL PLUS, Federal Perkins. Federal Work-Study Program available. Institutional employment available. Applicants will be notified of awards on or about April 1. Off-campus job opportunities are good.

## FROM THE ADMISSIONS OFFICE
"St. Mary's College of Maryland . . . occupies a distinctive niche and represents a real value in American higher education. It is a public college, dedicated to the ideal of affordable, accessible education but committed to quality teaching and excellent programs for undergraduate students. The result is that St. Mary's offers the small college experience of the same high caliber usually found at prestigious private colleges, but at public college prices. Designated by the state of Maryland as 'Its Public Honors College,' one of only two public colleges in the nation to hold that distinction, St. Mary's has become increasingly attractive to high school students. Admission is very selective."

## SELECTIVITY

| | |
|---|---:|
| **Admissions Rating** | 90 |
| # of applicants | 1,884 |
| % of applicants accepted | 59 |
| % of acceptees attending | 38 |
| # accepting a place on wait list | 115 |
| % admitted from wait list | 37 |
| # of early decision applicants | 314 |
| % accepted early decision | 61 |

### FRESHMAN PROFILE
| | |
|---|---:|
| Range SAT Verbal | 570-670 |
| Average SAT Verbal | 624 |
| Range SAT Math | 560-650 |
| Average SAT Math | 608 |
| Minimum TOEFL | 550 |
| Average HS GPA | 3.5 |
| % graduated top 10% of class | 44 |
| % graduated top 25% of class | 79 |
| % graduated top 50% of class | 97 |

### DEADLINES
| | |
|---|---:|
| Early decision | 12/1 |
| Early decision notification | 1/1 |
| Priority admission | 12/1 |
| Regular admission | 1/15 |
| Regular notification | 4/1 |
| Nonfall registration? | yes |

### APPLICANTS ALSO LOOK AT AND OFTEN PREFER
William and Mary
U. Delaware
Lehigh
Bucknell

### AND SOMETIMES PREFER
Dickinson
James Madison
Loyola Coll. (MD)
U. Maryland—Coll. Park
Towson State

## FINANCIAL FACTS

| | |
|---|---:|
| **Financial Aid Rating** | 86 |
| In-state tuition | $6,925 |
| Out-of-state tuition | $12,260 |
| Room and board | $6,613 |
| Books and supplies | $870 |
| Required fees | $1,157 |
| % frosh receiving aid | 42 |
| % undergrads receiving aid | 45 |
| Avg frosh grant | $4,000 |
| Avg frosh loan | $2,625 |

# ST. OLAF COLLEGE

1520 ST. OLAF AVENUE, NORTHFIELD, MN 55057-1098 • ADMISSIONS: 507-646-3025 • FAX: 507-646-3832

## CAMPUS LIFE

| | |
|---|---|
| Quality of Life Rating | 88 |
| Type of school | private |
| Affiliation | Lutheran |
| Environment | rural |

### STUDENTS

| | |
|---|---|
| Total undergrad enrollment | 3,041 |
| % male/female | 41/59 |
| % from out of state | 46 |
| % from public high school | 85 |
| % live on campus | 96 |
| % African American | 1 |
| % Asian | 4 |
| % Caucasian | 89 |
| % Hispanic | 1 |
| % international | 1 |
| # of countries represented | 28 |

### SURVEY SAYS . . .
Great library
No one cheats
Campus feels safe
Campus is beautiful
Dorms are like palaces
Very little drug use
Lousy food on campus
Students are cliquish
Student publications are ignored

## ACADEMICS

| | |
|---|---|
| Academic Rating | 92 |
| Calendar | 4-1-4 |
| Student/faculty ratio | 13:1 |
| Profs interesting rating | 97 |
| Profs accessible rating | 98 |
| % profs teaching UG courses | 100 |
| Avg lab size | 10-19 students |
| Avg reg class size | 20-29 students |

### MOST POPULAR MAJORS
Economics
Biology/biological sciences
English language and literature

## STUDENTS SPEAK OUT

### Academics

St. Olaf, a small Lutheran college in Minnesota, utilizes a 4-1-4 academic calendar, allowing students a winter term to travel or pursue individual projects. Study abroad is encouraged, and an adventurous group of students take advantage of the around-the-world program, which hits five countries in as many months. The school prides itself on its music department, especially its renowned choir. Students appreciate that "even nonmusic majors have the opportunity to participate in bands and choirs." Professors are caring, as is shown in their willingness to "approach you if you're struggling and express concern." Luckily, the "professors really want to be here. They want to be teaching college kids." Equally personable, the new president is "regularly spotted chatting with students outside of the commons." Students are upset, however, that certain "important programs," including the communications department, "were cut without faculty and student input." They also express a get-a-clue attitude towards the administration, claiming they are "in denial" about topics such as drinking on this dry campus. One student admonishes the Board of Regents to "open your eyes; it's the twenty-first century."

### Life

Various opinions crop up regarding St. Olaf's dry-campus policy. One student writes, "I think it [helps us] avoid a lot of potential hazards in college and generally leads to a healthier lifestyle among the student body." On the other hand, a peer counters, "Just about everyone seems to agree this is a ridiculous policy since we are all adults." Virtually everyone lives on campus for all four years, attending "student government-sponsored activities such as DJs, speakers, dances, bands, comedians." Considering the strong music department, performances draw big crowds. "A male a cappella ensemble that sings mostly Gregorian chant is actually more popular here than the football games." To get away from campus (a.k.a. "Little Suburbia"), students can take free buses to Carleton College, Timberwolves games, or other Twin Cities' happenings, all under an hour away. Those looking for politics will probably be happy here at "one of the most activist campuses in Minnesota" and one "fairly liberal in the Christian religious sphere." The environment allows for "serious contemplation of one's religious beliefs without forcing Christianity or Lutheranism on anyone."

### Student Body

One student aptly explains the "cookie-cutter" quotient at St. Olaf: "Even though I'm white and upper-middle class, I sometimes feel out of place because I'm not a blond, Lutheran, Norwegian-American." A senior adds, however, that "diversity on campus and appreciation of this diversity has increased significantly since I was a freshman." St. Olaf has an active GLOW (Gay, Lesbian, Or Whatever) club, and even amid the religious environment, sexuality issues are openly discussed. A straight, Christian student who thinks homosexuality is a sin says of a friend, "He is homosexual, and yet we have loved each other and found ways to communicate through the hard issues rather than just avoiding them or each other." Full of future Peace Corps participants, St. Olaf is home to 3,000 "good citizens" who "volunteer time both on and off campus." The resilience of the campus community was recently demonstrated when three students were tragically killed by a drunk driver. One student writes, "I know it sounds morbid, but our campus was at its best when these kids died because you could really see what a family we are here at Olaf."

# ST. OLAF COLLEGE

FINANCIAL AID: 507-646-3019 • E-MAIL: ADMISSIONS@STOLAF.EDU • WEBSITE: WWW.STOLAF.EDU

## ADMISSIONS
*Very important factors considered include:* secondary school record. *Important factors considered include:* essays, recommendations, standardized test scores. *Other factors considered include:* alumni/ae relation, character/personal qualities, class rank, extracurricular activities, geographical residence, interview, minority status, religious affiliation/commitment, state residency, talent/ability, volunteer work, work experience. SAT I or ACT required. TOEFL required of all international applicants. High school diploma or GED is required. *High school units required/recommended:* 15 total recommended; 3 English recommended, 3 math recommended, 2 science recommended, 1 science lab recommended, 2 foreign language recommended, 2 history or social science recommended.

### The Inside Word
St. Olaf truly deserves a more national reputation; the place is a bastion of excellence and has always crossed applications with the best schools in the Midwest. Despite its lack of widespread recognition, it is a great choice. Candidates benefit from the relative anonymity of the college through an admissions process, which, while demanding, isn't as tough as other colleges of St. Olaf's caliber.

## FINANCIAL AID
*Students should submit:* FAFSA, CSS/Financial Aid PROFILE, noncustodial (divorced/separated) parent's statement. No deadline for regular filing. The Princeton Review suggests that all financial aid forms be submitted as soon as possible after January 1. *Need-based scholarships/grants offered:* Pell, SEOG, state scholarships/grants, private scholarships, the school's own gift aid. *Loan aid offered:* FFEL Subsidized Stafford, FFEL Unsubsidized Stafford, FFEL PLUS, Federal Perkins, Federal Nursing, state loans, college/university loans from institutional funds. Federal Work-Study Program available. Institutional employment available. Applicants will be notified of awards on a rolling basis beginning on or about March 1. Off-campus job opportunities are fair.

## FROM THE ADMISSIONS OFFICE
"St. Olaf College provides an education in the liberal arts that is rooted in the Christian gospel and offered with a global perspective. Sixty-seven percent of each graduating class will have studied overseas during the four years at St. Olaf. The Center for Integrative Studies and Great Conversation programs offer alternatives to the traditional curriculum."

## SELECTIVITY

| | |
|---|---|
| Admissions Rating | 86 |
| # of applicants | 2,624 |
| % of applicants accepted | 73 |
| % of acceptees attending | 41 |
| # accepting a place on wait list | 56 |
| % admitted from wait list | 18 |
| # of early decision applicants | 125 |
| % accepted early decision | 88 |

### FRESHMAN PROFILE
| | |
|---|---|
| Range SAT Verbal | 590-690 |
| Average SAT Verbal | 639 |
| Range SAT Math | 580-690 |
| Average SAT Math | 635 |
| Range ACT Composite | 25-30 |
| Average ACT Composite | 27 |
| Minimum TOEFL | 550 |
| Average HS GPA | 3.6 |
| % graduated top 10% of class | 50 |
| % graduated top 25% of class | 79 |
| % graduated top 50% of class | 97 |

### DEADLINES
| | |
|---|---|
| Early decision | 11/15 |
| Early decision notification | 12/15 |
| Priority admission | 2/1 |
| Nonfall registration? | yes |

### APPLICANTS ALSO LOOK AT AND OFTEN PREFER
Carleton
**AND SOMETIMES PREFER**
Grinnell
Macalester
**AND RARELY PREFER**
Luther
Gustavus Adolphus

## FINANCIAL FACTS

| | |
|---|---|
| Financial Aid Rating | 89 |
| Tuition | $23,650 |
| Room and board | $4,850 |
| Books and supplies | $850 |
| Required fees | $0 |
| % frosh receiving aid | 60 |
| % undergrads receiving aid | 58 |
| Avg frosh grant | $12,210 |
| Avg frosh loan | $3,680 |

# SALISBURY UNIVERSITY

ADMISSIONS OFFICE, 1101 CAMDEN AVENUE, SALISBURY, MD 21801 • ADMISSIONS: 410-543-6161 • FAX: 410-546-6016

## CAMPUS LIFE

| | |
|---|---|
| Quality of Life Rating | 77 |
| Type of school | public |
| Environment | rural |

### STUDENTS

| | |
|---|---|
| Total undergrad enrollment | 6,206 |
| % male/female | 43/57 |
| % from out of state | 18 |
| % from public high school | 80 |
| % live on campus | 32 |
| % in (# of) fraternities | 5 (4) |
| % in (# of) sororities | 7 (4) |
| % African American | 8 |
| % Asian | 2 |
| % Caucasian | 83 |
| % Hispanic | 2 |
| % international | 1 |

### SURVEY SAYS . . .
Classes are small
(Almost) everyone smokes
Musical organizations aren't popular
Lots of conservatives on campus
Computer facilities need improving
Library needs improving
Lab facilities are great
Student government is unpopular

## ACADEMICS

| | |
|---|---|
| Academic Rating | 77 |
| Calendar | 4-1-4 |
| Student/faculty ratio | 17:1 |
| Profs interesting rating | 72 |
| Profs accessible rating | 73 |
| % profs teaching UG courses | 100 |
| % classes taught by TAs | 2 |
| Avg lab size | 20-29 students |
| Avg reg class size | 20-29 students |

### MOST POPULAR MAJORS
Business administration/management
Communications studies/speech communication and rhetoric
Elementary education and teaching

## STUDENTS SPEAK OUT

### Academics

Career-minded students on and around the Delmarva Peninsula would be hard pressed to find a better bargain than Salisbury University. The school's super-low tuition is further discounted by an unusually large endowment, funded by such business magnates as Frank Perdue (for whom the business school is named). Salisbury's greatest strengths are in education, business administration, accounting, engineering, communications, and, of course, its proximity to beachfront property. Writes one student, "We're close to the beach and have great weather, challenging courses, great people: what more could a person ask for?" Students appreciate the fact that they receive an exceptional amount of attention in return for their low tuition; reports one undergrad, "What I like most about this school is how much the professor's are willing to help students both inside and outside of class. There are also study groups and tutors available for many different subjects." Adds another, "Many of the professors try to actually teach the material instead of just lecturing about it and make time available outside of class for any problems. The class sizes are usually about the same size as most high school classes, except for lecture hall classes." Although nearly all students are satisfied at Salisbury, a few echo this sentiment: "This school is decent without being excellent in any one area. It's like driving a Ford Escort. It will get you from A to B, but not particularly fast or in good style."

### Life

Students describe a sedate life on Salisbury's "absolutely gorgeous and very well-kept" campus; explains one, "For fun a bunch of us will rent a movie during the weeknights, then on weekends go out to several different parties, usually ending up at one of the apartments nearby to play drinking games and hang out. The only real place to go and hang out on weekends is the mall. Salisbury is not a college town at all." Nearby resort town Ocean City, on the other hand, is lots of fun, especially during warmer months. "Ocean City (the beach) is only about a half hour away, so when you can get a free afternoon, it is wonderful!" notes one student; adds another, "The beach being so close is a definite plus." Still, many say that "[Ocean City] is nice, but certainly not a New York; or a Washington, D.C.; or even a Cleveland. There are things to do that are entertaining, but most of the time you've got to find stuff to do on your own." Students report a large contingent of beer drinkers among their midst but warn that "the town has begin to cut down on underage drinking, which has resulted in lots of citations. If you party smart, you can keep out of trouble." Athletic activities "are very important here. There is always some physical activity going on. Whether it's playing an intercollegiate, club, or intramural sport, or watching someone else play, there's always something."

### Student Body

Salisbury undergrads "are some of the nicest and most wholesome X'ers you will ever meet. There are several types of students on campus: the idealistic activists, the apathetic me-firster business majors, the evangelical Christians, the Christian lefties, the Euro-Buddhists, the ethnic minorities, and the moderates." Another student fond of dividing classmates up by type adds that "there are those who are here to learn academically, those who are here to party and skate through classes, and those who are here to develop academically, socially and individually. Within each group the students get along." Notes one student, "The only problem is that there is not a great deal of [racial] diversity. The university tries to bring in more diversity, but it is very difficult." Quality academic programs combined with the low out-of-state tuition attract an unusually large number of students from Delaware, New Jersey, Pennsylvania, and Virginia.

# SALISBURY UNIVERSITY

FINANCIAL AID: 410-543-6165 • E-MAIL: ADMISSIONS@SALISBURY.EDU • WEBSITE: WWW.SALISBURY.EDU

## ADMISSIONS

*Very important factors considered include:* secondary school record. *Important factors considered include:* class rank, standardized test scores. *Other factors considered include:* alumni/ae relation, character/personal qualities, essays, extracurricular activities, geographical residence, minority status, recommendations, state residency, talent/ability, volunteer work, work experience. SAT I or ACT required; SAT I preferred. TOEFL required of all international applicants. High school diploma or GED is required. *High school units required/recommended:* 14 total required; 18 total recommended; 4 English required, 3 math required, 4 math recommended, 3 science required, 4 science recommended, 2 science lab required, 3 science lab recommended, 2 foreign language required, 3 foreign language recommended, 3 social studies required.

### The Inside Word

As a part of the new wave of public institutions of higher learning focusing their energies on undergraduate research, Salisbury State has seen its admissions standards and the quality of its freshman class steadily improve over the past few years. As a result, candidate review is also more personalized than the formula-driven approaches of most public colleges. The admissions committee will pay close attention to the match you make with the University, evaluating your entire background instead of simply your numbers—though most students are strong academically to begin with.

## FINANCIAL AID

*Students should submit:* FAFSA. Regular filing deadline is December 31. The Princeton Review suggests that all financial aid forms be submitted as soon as possible after January 1. *Need-based scholarships/grants offered:* Pell, SEOG, state scholarships/grants, the school's own gift aid. *Loan aid offered:* Direct Subsidized Stafford, Direct Unsubsidized Stafford, Direct PLUS, Federal Perkins. Federal Work-Study Program available. Institutional employment available. Applicants will be notified of awards on a rolling basis beginning on or about April 1. Off-campus job opportunities are good.

## FROM THE ADMISSIONS OFFICE

"Friendly, convenient, safe, and beautiful are just a few of the words used to describe the campus of Salisbury University. The campus is a compact, self-contained community that offers the full range of student services. Beautiful, traditional-style architecture and impeccably landscaped grounds combine to create an atmosphere that inspires learning and fosters student pride. Located just 30 minutes from the beaches of Ocean City, Maryland, SU students enjoy a year-round resort social life as well as an inside track on summer jobs. Situated less than two hours from the urban excitement of Baltimore and Washington, D.C., greater Salisbury makes up for its lack of size—its population is about 80,000—by being strategically located. Within easy driving distance of a number of other major cities, including New York City, Philadelphia, and Norfolk, Salisbury is the hub of the Delmarva Peninsula, a mostly rural region flavored by the salty air of the Chesapeake Bay and Atlantic Ocean."

---

### SELECTIVITY

| | |
|---|---|
| Admissions Rating | 84 |
| # of applicants | 5,298 |
| % of applicants accepted | 50 |
| # accepting a place on wait list | 762 |
| % admitted from wait list | 14 |
| # of early decision applicants | 575 |
| % accepted early decision | 53 |

### FRESHMAN PROFILE

| | |
|---|---|
| Range SAT Verbal | 520-600 |
| Average SAT Verbal | 555 |
| Range SAT Math | 530-610 |
| Average SAT Math | 571 |
| Minimum TOEFL | 595 |
| Average HS GPA | 3.4 |
| % graduated top 10% of class | 22 |
| % graduated top 25% of class | 55 |
| % graduated top 50% of class | 87 |

### DEADLINES

| | |
|---|---|
| Early decision | 12/15 |
| Early decision notification | 1/15 |
| Regular admission | 1/15 |
| Regular notification | 3/15 |
| Nonfall registration? | yes |

### APPLICANTS ALSO LOOK AT AND SOMETIMES PREFER
U of Maryland at Baltimore County
Towson
St. Mary's or Maryland
**AND RARELY PREFER**
U of Maryland at College Park

### FINANCIAL FACTS

| | |
|---|---|
| Financial Aid Rating | 84 |
| In-state tuition | $4,804 |
| Out-of-state tuition | $10,568 |
| Room and board | $6,530 |
| Books and supplies | $675 |
| Required fees | $1,430 |
| % frosh receiving aid | 43 |
| % undergrads receiving aid | 39 |

# SAMFORD UNIVERSITY

800 LAKESHORE DRIVE, BIRMINGHAM, AL 35229 • ADMISSIONS: 205-726-3673 • FAX: 205-726-2171

## CAMPUS LIFE

| Quality of Life Rating | 89 |
|---|---|
| Type of school | private |
| Affiliation | Baptist |
| Environment | suburban |

### STUDENTS

| Total undergrad enrollment | 2,853 |
|---|---|
| % male/female | 37/63 |
| % from out of state | 52 |
| % from public high school | 64 |
| % live on campus | 63 |
| % in (# of) fraternities | 30 (7) |
| % in (# of) sororities | 31 (8) |
| % African American | 6 |
| % Asian | 1 |
| % Caucasian | 90 |
| % Hispanic | 1 |

### SURVEY SAYS . . .
Lab facilities are great
Low cost of living
Students are religious
Ethnic diversity lacking on campus
Lots of conservatives
Very little drug use
Very little hard liquor

## ACADEMICS

| Academic Rating | 81 |
|---|---|
| Calendar | 4-1-4 |
| Student/faculty ratio | 13:1 |
| Profs interesting rating | 93 |
| Profs accessible rating | 90 |
| % profs teaching UG courses | 72 |
| Avg lab size | under 10 students |
| Avg reg class size | 10-19 students |

### MOST POPULAR MAJORS
Nursing/registered nurse training (RN, ASN, BSN, MSN)
Business administration/management
Human development and family studies

## STUDENTS SPEAK OUT

### Academics
Located in a cultural center of the American South, Samford's campus "is the orgasmic pinnacle of landscaping and architecture." And on this "beautiful campus," you'll find academic halls where professors foster "both spiritual and mental growth." While many students feel the professors are great, it sometimes appears that "the administration chooses teachers for their personalities rather than their teaching abilities." Other criticism stems from the institution's pervasive Christian fervor, like one sophomore who feels as if she's "bombarded with Christianity" in her classes. Some dissent with this view, as does a senior who counters that while "Christ is centered in many places," she still believes that she and her peers "have the freedom to make choices." If one makes an effort, getting to know the professors is a cinch. And here's some good news: "If your professors know you, they can't flunk you." At least that's what most students hope.

### Life
"Good clean fun" is what a lot of Samford students are looking for, and they find it in the form of things such as "Frisbee, croquet, going to the dog tracks," going "out to eat, to coffee houses, to the movies, to the theatre," or attending church. But the largest single source of social diversion here is "Greek, Greek, Greek." The 15 Greek organizations are, for the most part, highly esteemed and upstanding groups of students. While "many people drink at Samford," the ones who are involved in fraternities and sororities are reluctant to "admit it in front of their Greek organization" because Greek life here is supposed to be more about social service than social life. Of course, pledging fraternities and cracking open cans of beer aren't the only things to do within the Samford walls. "We have a wide variety of activities that provide on-campus" entertainment, claims an undergrad. But the most important activity is keeping up with schoolwork: "I run cross-country and track," writes a sophomore, but "it is second priority to school work." You'll find some students who think that "people don't let loose and have enough fun here," but others enjoy the quiet campus life. What students collectively complain about is campus policy. "Parking," for instance, "is terrible," and "the visitation hours" in dorms make students feel as though they "are stuck in the fifties!" When students need a taste of life outside of Samford, they have plenty of options at their doorstep. "Birmingham is close to Nashville, Atlanta, New Orleans, and Florida [i.e., the beach]." And, of course, Birmingham itself is a city of more than 250,000 people. For the student with a little eye for adventure, boredom is nowhere in sight.

### Student Body
Southern Baptists of Alabama founded Samford a century and a half ago. It's not surprising, then, that students report sharing classes and dorms with a bunch of "holy rollers." Nonetheless, Samford is open to people of all faiths and denominations, and its students are, for the most part, "really friendly." "One of the main reasons I came to this school is because of the friendliness of the students," recalls one junior. Samford students say that incoming freshman should expect to find "that most of the students are from the same backgrounds" ("white, upper/middle class, Christian") and that these similarities have bred narrow-mindedness in more than a few undergraduates. Samford students would welcome "more diversity" of the ethnic and racial variety as well as "personality wise." So a prospect's best bet is to find the portion of the student body that "is incredibly friendly and involved." If one can do this, she may end up feeling like the senior who on our survey exclaimed: "AWESOME—a great environment [in which] to be a student!"

# SAMFORD UNIVERSITY

FINANCIAL AID: 800-888-7245 • E-MAIL: ADMISSION@SAMFORD.EDU • WEBSITE: WWW.SAMFORD.EDU

## ADMISSIONS
*Very important factors considered include:* character/personal qualities, recommendations, secondary school record, standardized test scores. *Important factors considered include:* class rank, essays, extracurricular activities, religious affiliation/commitment, talent/ability. *Other factors considered include:* alumni/ae relation, geographical residence, interview, minority status, state residency, volunteer work, work experience. SAT I or ACT required. TOEFL required of all international applicants. High school diploma or GED is required. *High school units required/recommended:* 4 English required, 3 math required, 2 science recommended, 2 science lab recommended, 2 foreign language recommended, 3 social studies recommended, 3 history recommended, 3 elective recommended.

### The Inside Word
Samford's use of admission credentials in scholarship considerations is something that is quite common at colleges across the country. Students should always complete their applications as if such is the case. Even for universities where you are clearly admissible academically, giving some additional attention to essays and visiting for an interview can make the difference between being a scholarship winner and taking on an additional summer job.

## FINANCIAL AID
*Students should submit:* FAFSA. No deadline for regular filing. The Princeton Review suggests that all financial aid forms be submitted as soon as possible after January 1. *Need-based scholarships/grants offered:* Pell, SEOG, state scholarships/grants, private scholarships, the school's own gift aid, United Negro College Fund. *Loan aid offered:* FFEL Subsidized Stafford, FFEL Unsubsidized Stafford, FFEL PLUS, Federal Perkins, college/university loans from institutional funds. Federal Work-Study Program available. Institutional employment available. Applicants will be notified of awards on a rolling basis beginning on or about March 1. Off-campus job opportunities are excellent.

## FROM THE ADMISSION OFFICE
"Students who are drawn to Samford are well-rounded individuals who not only expect to be challenged, but are excited by the prospect. It is the critical and creative way you think, it is the articulate way you write and speak, it is the joy of learning that stays with you throughout your life, and it is the clarity of decision-making guided by Christian principles."

### SELECTIVITY

| | |
|---|---|
| **Admissions Rating** | 78 |
| # of applicants | 1,954 |
| % of applicants accepted | 89 |
| % of acceptees attending | 38 |

### FRESHMAN PROFILE
| | |
|---|---|
| Range SAT Verbal | 520-620 |
| Average SAT Verbal | 572 |
| Range SAT Math | 530-640 |
| Average SAT Math | 581 |
| Range ACT Composite | 22-28 |
| Average ACT Composite | 25 |
| Minimum TOEFL | 550 |
| Average HS GPA | 3.7 |
| % graduated top 10% of class | 42 |
| % graduated top 25% of class | 66 |
| % graduated top 50% of class | 90 |

### DEADLINES
| | |
|---|---|
| Priority admission | 6/1 |
| Regular admission | 8/15 |
| Nonfall registration? | yes |

### APPLICANTS ALSO LOOK AT AND OFTEN PREFER
Vanderbilt
Furman

### AND SOMETIMES PREFER
Baylor
Florida State
U. Georgia
Auburn

### FINANCIAL FACTS

| | |
|---|---|
| **Financial Aid Rating** | 90 |
| Tuition | $12,294 |
| Room and board | $4,994 |
| % frosh receiving aid | 40 |
| % undergrads receiving aid | 41 |
| Avg frosh grant | $2,446 |
| Avg frosh loan | $8,693 |

# SANTA CLARA UNIVERSITY

500 EL CAMINO REAL, SANTA CLARA, CA 95053 • ADMISSIONS: 408-554-4700 • FAX: 408-554-5255

## CAMPUS LIFE

| Quality of Life Rating | 88 |
|---|---|
| Type of school | private |
| Affiliation | Roman Catholic |
| Environment | suburban |

### STUDENTS

| | |
|---|---|
| Total undergrad enrollment | 4,643 |
| % male/female | 44/56 |
| % from out of state | 35 |
| % from public high school | 52 |
| % live on campus | 47 |
| % African American | 2 |
| % Asian | 21 |
| % Caucasian | 56 |
| % Hispanic | 13 |
| % international | 3 |

### SURVEY SAYS . . .
Political activism is hot
Student publications are popular
Everyone loves the Broncos
Registration is a breeze
Students are not very happy
Students are cliquish
Very little drug use
(Almost) no one listens to college radio
Theater is unpopular
Lousy food on campus

## ACADEMICS

| Academic Rating | 84 |
|---|---|
| Calendar | quarter |
| Student/faculty ratio | 12:1 |
| Profs interesting rating | 94 |
| Profs accessible rating | 91 |
| % profs teaching UG courses | 74 |
| Avg lab size | 10-19 students |
| Avg reg class size | 20-29 students |

## STUDENTS SPEAK OUT

### Academics
Santa Clara University is a bustling microcosm within the bustling Silicon Valley. And like all communities, it has its ripened spots and its rotten spots. The administration, for instance, is one of the things SCU students say they could do without because it's often "dominating" and "not willing to sit down with students" to discuss issues. But you're not likely to hear similar complaints about the faculty because they are "really accessible," and "very talented and educated in their areas." With a 12:1 student/teacher ratio, SCU students spend three quarters a year working closely with their profs. A freshman proclaims, "The professors have made all the difference for me here." At the end of each student's academic path lies one of three degrees: BA, BS, or BS in commerce. As students pursue their diplomas, they quickly discover that even with the careful guidance of professors, school can be tedious around these parts. It's like "Stanford with the workload," sighs a junior. Maybe that's true, but don't forget that it's also like Stanford with the palm trees.

### Life
With a bronco as the school mascot, you might expect that the SCU Broncos are a little rough and wild. Actually, they're relatively tame. "The most common pastime" at Santa Clara is "simply hanging out with a group of friends." For a lot of students, the off-campus Greek system [unaffiliated with the university] serves as a social vehicle. "It's introduced me to so many people," states a junior sorority member. Even if the Broncos aren't the most indulgent students in America, they know how to enjoy a good party, though. "There are always parties of some sort on the weekend." And because the school is small—contained in 104 acres—students are likely to succeed if they try to sniff out a party. The smallness of the school also has its ill effects. "Since school is so small, you have to watch what you do and say because rumors fly." But overall, "life in the 'bubble' is pretty nice," summarizes a student. And when it's not so nice, there's always the expanse of the Bay Area just outside your door, which is, of course, "a great place to go out." Oh, and the beaches of nearby Santa Cruz are only half an hour away.

### Student Body
Down near the tip of the San Francisco Bay, wedged between Sunnyvale and San Jose, you'll find the city of Santa Clara. And in this city, a cluster of about 4,600 undergrads and 3,400 grads makes up the student body of Santa Clara University. As is the case at many religiously affiliated institutions, the students of Santa Clara are about 54 percent Roman Catholic and are not particularly religious. But that's not to say that they see themselves as especially diverse group, either. "NO diversity," moans one despairing student. For the most part, they're "friendly and open," which is good since the school is small enough that students tend "to see the same people every day." Some students will tell you that their classmates are a cliquey crew who "are very segregated" when social hours roll around. But others will scoff at such a notion, countering that "the students at SCU have made SCU the great place it is."

# SANTA CLARA UNIVERSITY

FINANCIAL AID: 408-554-4505 • E-MAIL: UGADMISSIONS@SCU.EDU • WEBSITE: WWW.SCU.EDU

## ADMISSIONS

*Very important factors considered include:* essays, recommendations, secondary school record, standardized test scores. *Important factors considered include:* character/personal qualities, extracurricular activities, talent/ability, volunteer work. *Other factors considered include:* alumni/ae relation, class rank, geographical residence, minority status, work experience. SAT I or ACT required. TOEFL required of all international applicants. High school diploma is required and GED is not accepted. *High school units required/recommended:* 18 total required; 19 total recommended; 4 English required, 4 math required, 3 science required, 4 science recommended, 1 science lab required, 2 science lab recommended, 3 foreign language required, 4 foreign language recommended, 1 social studies required, 2 social studies recommended, 1 history required, 2 history recommended, 2 social studies required.

### The Inside Word

Santa Clara deserves recognition as a rising star that still manages to be highly personal and accessible. It's always better when an admissions staff regards you as a person, not an enrollment target. Unfortunately, such is not always the case. It would be hard to find a place that is more receptive to minority students. There is a very significant minority presence here because Santa Clara works hard and earnestly to make everyone feel at home. The university's popularity is increasing across the board, which proves that nice guys sometimes finish first.

## FINANCIAL AID

*Students should submit:* FAFSA, CSS/Financial Aid PROFILE. No deadline for regular filing. The Princeton Review suggests that all financial aid forms be submitted as soon as possible after January 1. *Need-based scholarships/grants offered:* Pell, SEOG, state scholarships/grants, private scholarships, the school's own gift aid. *Loan aid offered:* Direct Subsidized Stafford, Direct Unsubsidized Stafford, Direct PLUS, Federal Perkins, private alternative loans. Federal Work-Study Program available. Institutional employment available. Applicants will be notified of awards on a rolling basis beginning on or about April 1. Off-campus job opportunities are excellent.

## FROM THE ADMISSIONS OFFICE

"Santa Clara University, located one hour south of San Francisco, offers its undergraduates an opportunity to be educated within a challenging, dynamic, and caring community. The university blends a sense of tradition and history (as the oldest college in California) with a vision that values innovation and a deep commitment to social justice. Santa Clara's faculty members are talented scholars who are demanding, supportive, and accessible. The students are serious about academics, are ethnically diverse, and enjoy a full range of athletic, social, community service, religious, and cultural activities—both on campus and through the many options presented by our northern California location. The undergraduate program includes three divisions: the College of Arts and Sciences, the School of Business, and the School of Engineering."

## SELECTIVITY

★ ★ ★ ☆

| | |
|---|---|
| Admissions Rating | 80 |
| # of applicants | 5,842 |
| % of applicants accepted | 70 |
| % of acceptees attending | 28 |
| # accepting a place on wait list | 164 |
| % admitted from wait list | 54 |

### FRESHMAN PROFILE

| | |
|---|---|
| Range SAT Verbal | 550-650 |
| Average SAT Verbal | 601 |
| Range SAT Math | 560-660 |
| Average SAT Math | 618 |
| Range ACT Composite | 23-28 |
| Average ACT Composite | 27 |
| Minimum TOEFL | 550 |
| Average HS GPA | 3.6 |
| % graduated top 10% of class | 41 |
| % graduated top 25% of class | 75 |
| % graduated top 50% of class | 96 |

### DEADLINES

| | |
|---|---|
| Regular admission | 1/15 |
| Regular notification | 4/1 |
| Nonfall registration? | yes |

### APPLICANTS ALSO LOOK AT AND OFTEN PREFER

UC Berkeley
UC Davis
Stanford
Notre Dame
UCLA

### AND SOMETIMES PREFER

Pomona, UC Irvine
UC Santa Barbara
UC San Diego
Loyola Marymount

### AND RARELY PREFER

U of Oregon
UC Santa Cruz
U of San Francisco
San Jose State

## FINANCIAL FACTS

★ ★ ★ ☆

| | |
|---|---|
| Financial Aid Rating | 83 |
| Tuition | $25,365 |
| Room and board | $9,336 |
| Books and supplies | $1,224 |
| % frosh receiving aid | 48 |
| % undergrads receiving aid | 48 |
| Avg frosh grant | $7,728 |
| Avg frosh loan | $2,512 |

# SARAH LAWRENCE COLLEGE

ONE MEAD WAY, BRONXVILLE, NY 10708-5999 • ADMISSIONS: 914-395-2510 • FAX: 914-395-2676

## CAMPUS LIFE

| | |
|---|---|
| Quality of Life Rating | 76 |
| Type of school | private |
| Environment | suburban |

### STUDENTS

| | |
|---|---|
| Total undergrad enrollment | 1,226 |
| % male/female | 26/74 |
| % from out of state | 79 |
| % from public high school | 65 |
| % live on campus | 87 |
| % African American | 6 |
| % Asian | 5 |
| % Caucasian | 77 |
| % Hispanic | 4 |
| % international | 4 |

### SURVEY SAYS . . .
No one cheats
(Almost) everyone smokes
Class discussions encouraged
Classes are small
Political activism is hot
Intercollegiate sports unpopular or nonexistent
No one plays intramural sports
Campus easy to get around
Students don't get along with local community

## ACADEMICS

| | |
|---|---|
| Academic Rating | 93 |
| Calendar | semester |
| Student/faculty ratio | 6:1 |
| Profs interesting rating | 95 |
| Profs accessible rating | 98 |
| % profs teaching UG courses | 100 |
| Avg reg class size | 10-19 students |

## STUDENTS SPEAK OUT

### Academics

At Sarah Lawrence, there's no such thing as a test, core requirement, or major. The SLC equivalent of a test, explains one sophomore, involves "sitting in a room with 10 classmates and a brilliant teacher and working hard enough to participate in a discussion without looking like an idiot." However, don't be fooled, for what SLC doesn't give in tests, it does make up for in papers; many, many papers! The downside of this unrestrictive approach is that students who aren't organized, disciplined, and self-motivated can find themselves fumbling through an "unfocused education." If students find that they're losing their way—or just need to chat about classes, or personal life, or the future—they can always talk to their "don." The system of donning at Sarah Lawrence links each student with a personal advisor (professor) who helps guide the student's education. As you might expect, "good professors are extremely enthusiastic and intelligent," while "bad profs are average and boring." Sometimes it's tough to get into classes—especially popular ones like "photography, writing, and some lit classes." Regardless of what courses students end up in, they know that they'll be busy. "Work flows steadily" from every academic font on this campus. Students don't mind the rigor, though. In fact, one freshman only wishes "we could take more classes."

### Life

Imagine that all the "brilliant weirdos," "introverted poetic types," "artistic geniuses," and "social martyrs" from high school came together in one place—that place is Sarah Lawrence. SLC's extracurricular activities are what you make them. One freshman puts it nicely: "There are tons of activities going on all the time. I don't think a day goes by when there isn't some sort of guest performer or speaker or student performance going on." Other students flee campus every chance they get for everyone's favorite enchanted isle—Manhattan, 15 miles away. Whether they choose to stay or go, Sarah Lawrence offers a pretty unique experience for everyone. On the whole, Sarah Lawrence's hometown gets bad ratings, as "Bronxville is a sleepy little hamlet with an average income of around $350,000, so the neighbors aren't exactly into all-night raging parties." This can be a sore spot if you're a student who likes to "play hard and work hard," but party life does exist, in all its incantations. A sophomore says it's the drugs that serve as the social grease on the rusty hinges of the student body, but another says, "There are people who only want to party and get wasted, but there are also quite a few people who would much rather go to a movie or watch one in their room with some friends." Whatever your bag, Sarah Lawrence can please on many levels. Larger events on campus tend to be big crowd pleasers, like the Cross Dress Cabaret (Drag Queen and King crowned, of course), the Dive-in-Movie (only 65 at this one . . . the pool can't fit anymore!) and more than a handful of poetry slams. And if this all gets to be too much, students can wander over to the library and into The Pillow Room—a space cluttered with big cushions where students can read a book, take a nap, or try to figure out how they're going to come up with the train fare into the city next weekend.

### Student Body

On any given day at Sarah Lawrence, you're likely to see a mix of "hipsters, artists, intellectuals, and slackers." And most of these people are intent on fostering and exhibiting their individualism. This translates to a healthy population of creative minds, though it also leads to some problems. "It's hard to create a community from a lot of individuals," says one student. Another calls Sarah Lawrence the "un-community," and says that the college "focuses so much on individualism" that "no one remembers to stop and say 'hello.'" With about three-quarters of the student population being white as well as "extremely liberal," it sometimes seems that "the student body is much more homogenous than they like to believe." But as you'll find at any campus, generalities don't tell the whole story. "Students at times can be cold, pretentious, and alienating," concedes one sophomore. "But at other times [they] can be warm, generous, and accepting. It's a bit of a bipolar campus."

# SARAH LAWRENCE COLLEGE

FINANCIAL AID: 914-395-2570 • E-MAIL: SLCADMIT@MAIL.SLC.EDU • WEBSITE: WWW.SLC.EDU

## ADMISSIONS
*Very important factors considered include:* character/personal qualities, essays, recommendations, secondary school record. *Important factors considered include:* extracurricular activities, talent/ability, volunteer work, work experience. *Other factors considered include:* alumni/ae relation, class rank, geographical residence, interview, minority status, standardized test scores. SAT I or ACT required. TOEFL required of all international applicants. *High school units required/recommended:* 4 English required, 2 math required, 4 math recommended, 2 science required, 4 science recommended, 2 foreign language required, 4 foreign language recommended, 4 social studies recommended, 2 history required, 4 history recommended.

### The Inside Word
The public generally views Sarah Lawrence as an artsy "alternative" college. The college itself avoids this image, preferring instead to evoke an impression that aligns them with more traditional and prestigious northeastern colleges such as the Ivies, Little Ivies, and former Seven Sisters. Both the total number of applicants and the selectivity of the admissions process have increased over the past few years.

## FINANCIAL AID
*Students should submit:* FAFSA, CSS/Financial Aid PROFILE, noncustodial (divorced/separated) parent's statement. Regular filing deadline is February 1. The Princeton Review suggests that all financial aid forms be submitted as soon as possible after January 1. *Need-based scholarships/grants offered:* Pell, SEOG, state scholarships/grants, private scholarships, the school's own gift aid. *Loan aid offered:* FFEL Subsidized Stafford, FFEL Unsubsidized Stafford, FFEL PLUS, Federal Perkins. Federal Work-Study Program available. Institutional employment available. Applicants will be notified of awards on or about April 1. Off-campus job opportunities are good.

## FROM THE ADMISSIONS OFFICE
"Students who come to Sarah Lawrence are curious about the world, and they have an ardent desire to satisfy that curiosity. Sarah Lawrence offers such students two innovative academic structures: the seminar/conference system and the arts components. Courses in the humanities, social sciences, natural sciences, and mathematics are taught in the seminar/conference style. The seminars enroll an average of 11 students and consist of lecture, discussion, readings, and assigned papers. For each seminar, students also have private tutorials, called conferences, where they conceive of individualized projects and shape them under the direction of professors. Arts components let students combine history and theory with practice. Painters, printmakers, photographers, sculptors and filmmakers, composers, musicians, choreographers, dancers, actors, and directors work in readily available studios, editing facilities, and darkrooms, guided by accomplished professionals. The secure, wooded campus is 30 minutes from New York City, and the diversity of people and ideas at Sarah Lawrence make it an extraordinary educational environment."

## SELECTIVITY

| | |
|---|---:|
| Admissions Rating | 90 |
| # of applicants | 2,667 |
| % of applicants accepted | 40 |
| % of acceptees attending | 30 |
| # accepting a place on wait list | 264 |
| # of early decision applicants | 192 |
| % accepted early decision | 46 |

### FRESHMAN PROFILE
| | |
|---|---:|
| Range SAT Verbal | 610-710 |
| Average SAT Verbal | 660 |
| Range SAT Math | 530-650 |
| Average SAT Math | 590 |
| Range ACT Composite | 24-29 |
| Average ACT Composite | 27 |
| Minimum TOEFL | 600 |
| Average HS GPA | 3.6 |
| % graduated top 10% of class | 34 |
| % graduated top 25% of class | 77 |
| % graduated top 50% of class | 97 |

### DEADLINES
| | |
|---|---:|
| Early decision | 11/15 |
| Early decision notification | 12/15 |
| Regular admission | 1/1 |
| Regular notification | 4/1 |

### APPLICANTS ALSO LOOK AT AND OFTEN PREFER
NYU
Vassar
Barnard

### AND SOMETIMES PREFER
Smith
Oberlin
Bard

### AND RARELY PREFER
Mount Holyoke
Hampshire
Goucher

## FINANCIAL FACTS

| | |
|---|---:|
| Financial Aid Rating | 80 |
| Tuition | $28,680 |
| Room and board | $10,494 |
| Books and supplies | $600 |
| Required fees | $680 |
| % frosh receiving aid | 46 |
| % undergrads receiving aid | 51 |
| Avg frosh grant | $18,268 |
| Avg frosh loan | $2,370 |

# SCRIPPS COLLEGE

1030 COLUMBIA AVENUE, CLAREMONT, CA 91711 • ADMISSIONS: 909-621-8149 • FAX: 909-607-7508

## CAMPUS LIFE

| | |
|---|---|
| Quality of Life Rating | 82 |
| Type of school | private |
| Environment | suburban |

### STUDENTS

| | |
|---|---|
| Total undergrad enrollment | 798 |
| % from out of state | 52 |
| % from public high school | 63 |
| % live on campus | 93 |
| % African American | 4 |
| % Asian | 14 |
| % Caucasian | 60 |
| % Hispanic | 6 |
| % international | 2 |
| # of countries represented | 16 |

### SURVEY SAYS . . .
Campus is beautiful
Campus easy to get around
Dorms are like palaces
Great library
Campus feels safe
Lab facilities are great
No one cheats
Great computer facilities
Political activism is hot

## ACADEMICS

| | |
|---|---|
| Academic Rating | 92 |
| Calendar | semester |
| Student/faculty ratio | 11:1 |
| % profs teaching UG courses | 100 |
| Avg class size | 10-19 students |

### MOST POPULAR MAJORS
English language and literature
Biology/biological sciences
Psychology

## STUDENTS SPEAK OUT

### Academics

The young women at Scripps College encounter "very involved and politically aware" professors who are "excited to hear what you think about." Students enjoy plenty of out-of-class contact with instructors: "A lot of teachers eat in the dining hall, and on any given day there are probably eight faculty members eating lunch in Malot Commons." The core curriculum is "hell to get through, but it's kind of a bonding experience for all the first-years to complain about, and it sticks with you forever." Discussion plays a large part in Scripps's small classes; as one state-school transfer puts it, "I feel like I've died [and] gone to heaven." Most students agree, "Although the workload is very high and demanding, it is worth [it]," but several survey respondents lament, "students here are very competitive when it comes to grades." As one of the Claremont Colleges, Scripps encourages students to take classes at any of the four other schools, which, according to one undergrad, "allows me so many options for courses." Some people encounter difficulty in registering for classes, "but professors are flexible about letting you into a class if there is room." Complaints are logged regarding the "rather stuffy" administration, which has a reputation for being "unresponsive to our needs and desires." Others believe that those in charge "treat the school as a corporation for profit rather than an institution of learning." Personal interaction with higher-ups is available, whether it's "petting President Bekavac's dogs" or chatting with the load advisor "for a half-hour about how I am adjusting to life here." In any case, by the time students graduate, they have been "taught to think differently, to think for myself."

### Life

The Scripps campus itself "doesn't really have parties. The dorms are like hotels, which is nice, but not exactly conducive to socializing and fun." But the other Claremont campuses, such as Harvey Mudd, where "the blended drinks flow like water," are "more party and drinking friendly." The result is that "between the five colleges, there are parties six nights a week." As much as students appreciate the options and "estrogen-balancing effect" provided by the other campuses, they also like "coming back to Scripps to sleep and relax in peace." Aside from campus parties, students strike out for Los Angeles, which is an hour away, or drive to local movie theaters and shopping centers. The campus café, the Motley, draws a loyal crowd for blackberry mochas, musical events, and art exhibits. When students aren't "organizing around social justice issues," they might be found "painting pet rocks for each other" or "creating elaborate sock puppet plays." The fitness facility is called "a pretty busy place," though "not a lot of Scripps students participate in sports," besides ever-popular Frisbee.

### Student Body

"Scrippsies" could be described as "pretty liberal, artsy, and philisophical" women who "know their own opinions and aren't ashamed of them." Hailing mostly from the West Coast, the population includes "wealthy, pretty party girls; lesbians; heterosexual feminists; political activists; and quiet, studious types." Though there is an "outspoken queer population," some students feel the outside world gets the "mistaken impression that we are all lesbians." Several respondents note that the campus displays "some ethnic diversity, but it's still overwhelmingly white." One student tells us the population includes "some Asian students, fewer Hispanic students, and even fewer black students." Certain people attest to a "marginalization of women of color," but a 52-year-old Latina reports that she feels "well received in all my classes," despite being married and living off campus. Overall, this lively, contentious, and intelligent community "somehow strangely mixes together and makes one really interesting group."

460 ■ THE BEST 351 COLLEGES

# SCRIPPS COLLEGE

FINANCIAL AID: 909-621-8275 • E-MAIL: ADMOFC@AD.SCRIPPSCOL.EDU • WEBSITE: WWW.SCRIPPSCOL.EDU

## ADMISSIONS
*Very important factors considered include:* alumni/ae relation, character/personal qualities, extracurricular activities, interview, recommendations, secondary school record. *Important factors considered include:* class rank, essays, geographical residence, minority status, standardized test scores, state residency, talent/ability, volunteer work, work experience. SAT I or ACT required. TOEFL required of all international applicants. High school diploma or GED is required. *High school units required/recommended:* 4 English recommended, 4 math recommended, 4 science recommended, 4 foreign language recommended.

## The Inside Word
With a graded paper required in addition to application essays, it is safe to say that Scripps is going to take a long, hard look at the writing ability of its candidates. Colleges that require such papers often use them to temper the unnatural aura that sometimes envelops the application essay-writing process; a school paper will usually reflect a student's work under more normal circumstances. Here's a classic case where you should pay little heed to the high admit rate; academic standards are formidable and admissions committee expectations high.

## FINANCIAL AID
*Students should submit:* FAFSA, CSS/Financial Aid PROFILE, noncustodial (divorced/separated) parent's statement, business/farm supplement, verification worksheet, parent's and student's federal tax returns. February 1 deadline for regular filing. The Princeton Review suggests that all financial aid forms be submitted as soon as possible after January 1. *Need-based scholarships/grants offered:* Pell, SEOG, state scholarships/grants, private scholarships, the school's own gift aid. *Loan aid offered:* FFEL Subsidized Stafford, FFEL Unsubsidized Stafford, FFEL PLUS, Federal Perkins, college/university loans from institutional funds. Federal Work-Study Program available. Institutional employment available. Applicants will be notified of awards on or about April 1. Off-campus job opportunities are fair.

## FROM THE ADMISSIONS OFFICE
"At Scripps we believe that learning involves much more than amassing information. The truly educated person is one who can think analytically, communicate effectively, and make confident, responsible choices. Scripps classes are small (the average class size is 12) so that they foster an atmosphere where students feel comfortable participating, testing old assumptions, and exploring new ideas. Our curriculum is based on the traditional components of a liberal arts education: a set of general requirements in a wide variety of disciplines including foreign language, natural science, and writing; a multicultural requirement; a major that asks you to study one particular field in depth; and a variety of electives that allows considerable flexibility. What distinguishes Scripps from other liberal arts colleges is an emphasis on interdisciplinary courses."

## SELECTIVITY
★ ★ ★ ☆

| | |
|---|---|
| Admissions Rating | 84 |
| # of applicants | 1,371 |
| % of applicants accepted | 58 |
| % of acceptees attending | 28 |
| # accepting a place on wait list | 151 |
| % admitted from wait list | 1 |
| # of early decision applicants | 88 |
| % accepted early decision | 30 |

### FRESHMAN PROFILE
| | |
|---|---|
| Range SAT Verbal | 620-720 |
| Average SAT Verbal | 666 |
| Range SAT Math | 600-690 |
| Average SAT Math | 641 |
| Range ACT Composite | 26-30 |
| Average ACT Composite | 28 |
| Minimum TOEFL | 600 |
| Average HS GPA | 3.8 |
| % graduated top 10% of class | 62 |
| % graduated top 25% of class | 86 |
| % graduated top 50% of class | 100 |

### DEADLINES
| | |
|---|---|
| Early decision I | 11/1 |
| Early decision I notification | 12/15 |
| Early decision II | 1/1 |
| Early decision II notification | 2/1 |
| Regular admission | 2/1 |
| Regular notification | 4/1 |
| Nonfall registration? | yes |

### APPLICANTS ALSO LOOK AT
**AND OFTEN PREFER**
Smith, Wellesley
UC—Berkeley
Occidental
UC—San Diego
**AND SOMETIMES PREFER**
Mount Holyoke
UCLA, Pomona, Bryn Mawr
Claremont McKenna

## FINANCIAL FACTS
★ ★ ★ ★

| | |
|---|---|
| Financial Aid Rating | 90 |
| Tuition | $25,568 |
| Room and board | $8,300 |
| Books and supplies | $800 |
| Required fees | $132 |
| % frosh receiving aid | 60 |
| % undergrads receiving aid | 46 |
| Avg frosh grant | $20,140 |
| Avg frosh loan | $2,998 |

# SEATTLE UNIVERSITY

ADMISSIONS OFFICE, 900 BROADWAY, SEATTLE, WA 98122-4340 • ADMISSIONS: 206-296-2000

## CAMPUS LIFE

| Quality of Life Rating | 80 |
|---|---|
| Type of school | private |
| Affiliation | Roman Catholic-Jesuit |
| Environment | urban |

### STUDENTS
| | |
|---|---|
| Total undergrad enrollment | 3,561 |
| % male/female | 39/61 |
| % from out of state | 36 |
| % live on campus | 41 |
| % African American | 5 |
| % Asian | 24 |
| % Caucasian | 54 |
| % Hispanic | 7 |
| % Native American | 1 |
| % international | 9 |

### SURVEY SAYS . . .
Students get along with local community
Students love Seattle, WA
Student publications are popular
Diverse students interact
Classes are small
High cost of living
School is well run
Theater is hot

## ACADEMICS

| Academic Rating | 84 |
|---|---|
| Calendar | quarter |
| Student/faculty ratio | 14:1 |
| Profs interesting rating | 75 |
| Profs accessible rating | 73 |
| % profs teaching UG courses | 73 |
| % classes taught by TAs | 0 |
| Avg lab size | 10-19 students |
| Avg reg class size | 20-29 students |

### MOST POPULAR MAJORS
marketing/marketing management
finance
nursing/registered nurse training (RN, ASN, BSN, MSN)

## STUDENTS SPEAK OUT

### Academics
When students say that their "professors tend to rival gods" and think they're "like manna from heaven—smart, sweet, sharp, challenging," one might suspect exaggeration. But students here will tell you that their high opinions of the professors are right on the money. Sure, there are "a few nutty professors, and a few horrible ones," but most students appreciate the "very interactive" educations they receive in the small, personal classrooms and under accessible profs. Many undergrads will tell you that the pervasive Jesuit focus on social service is one the university's crowning attributes. "SU does a good job teaching about the importance of serving others . . . and being a part of the world we live in. I think I am a far more open-minded person now than when I was a freshman." To promote diversity of thought, the university requires that students "take two religion classes and three philosophy classes."

### Student Life
The campus is only one part of Seattle University. "The city is the other part of the school." And students generally agree that "life off campus and in the city is awesome." SU is "within walking distance" of "a plethora of quirky and inexpensive coffee shops, vintage stores, movie theatres, performance theatres, dance clubs, open markets, and parks." "Have you ever heard of Broadway in Seattle? Or Capitol Hill?" asks one student. Broadway and Capitol Hill comprise this lively area immediately surrounding campus, and "it is a crazy place to venture." "From drag queens to homeless people, it epitomizes urban life." If students want to escape city living, this too is quite easy. "You can drive for an hour and hit the slopes," says an outdoor enthusiast. "We've got excellent winter and summer outdoor fun." Even with all of this activity swirling outside the campus walls, students and administration try to provide plenty of on-campus social options. Although "the school has no Greek system," it's certainly not an atmosphere starved of parties. "There are drugs and alcohol here," and some of the big bashes are even school sponsored. After these fêtes students sober up and realize that the day is full of other options, such as "speakers and roundtable discussions and luncheons and conferences." At night, students settle into their dorm rooms, which some claim are inadequate. Others say that the dorms are safe and nurturing environments, with "priests living on every floor, plus two RAs, and tons of support groups." With the many perks at SU, there remains one challenge for students who haven't grown up in the Pacific Northwest: "You need to get used to the rain."

### Students
"The only way to describe students" at Seattle University "is with the word community." "Yeah, people have their groups of friends, but it's not like you can't hang out with anyone and everyone" here. SU undergraduates "are very diverse in preferences, from ravers to religious to athletic." It's true that "many are [from the] upper class," but even these students "don't have a classist mentality." One undergrad reports, "As for diversity, there have been times when I've looked around while in a crowd of students and realized I was the only straight white person there." "The ethnic mix is healthy" at this university in the Pacific Northwest, and "even though most students are Christian, they lean to the left politically." The biggest lesson you can learn about Seattle University is that its student body is a conglomerate of many individuals. "Everyone does his or her own thing," sums up one student.

# SEATTLE UNIVERSITY

Fax: 206-296-5656 • E-mail: admissions@seattleu.edu • Website: www.seattleu.edu

## ADMISSIONS

*Very important factors considered by the admissions committee include:* recommendations, secondary school record, standardized test scores, and volunteer work. *Important factors considered include:* class rank, essays, extracurricular activities, geographical residence, and talent/ability. *Other factors considered include:* alumni/ae relation, character/personal qualities, interview, minority status, state residency, and work experience. SAT I or ACT required. TOEFL required of all international applicants. High school diploma or GED is required. *High school units required/recommended:* 18 total required; 4 English required, 3 math required, 2 science required, 3 science recommended, 2 science lab required, 3 science lab recommended, 2 foreign language required, 3 social studies required, 2 elective required.

### The Inside Word

Like most Catholic universities, Seattle places a heavy premium on community service. Candidates with a record demonstrating commitment to helping others have a definite leg up at this competitive school.

## FINANCIAL AID

*Students should submit:* FAFSA. The Princeton Review suggests that all financial aid forms be submitted as soon as possible after January 1. *Need-based scholarships/grants offered:* Pell, SEOG, state scholarships/grants, private scholarships, and the school's own gift aid. *Loan aid offered:* Direct Subsidized Stafford, Direct Unsubsidized Stafford, Direct PLUS, Federal Perkins, and Federal Nursing. Federal Work-Study Program available. Institutional employment available. Applicants will be notified of awards on a rolling basis beginning on or about April 1. Off-campus job opportunities are excellent.

## FROM THE ADMISSIONS OFFICE

"Seattle University provides an ideal environment for motivated students interested in self-reliance, awareness of different cultures, social justice, and the fulfillment that comes from making a difference. Our location in the center of one of the nation's most diverse and progressive cities enables us to attract a student body, faculty, and staff rich in diversity. Our urban setting promotes the development of leadership skills and independence as well as providing a variety of opportunities for students to apply what they learn through internships, clinical experiences, and volunteer work. It is an environment that allows us to 'connect the mind to what matters.'

"Our academic offerings are designed to provide leadership opportunities as well as to develop global awareness and enable graduates to serve society through a demanding liberal arts and sciences foundation. In the Jesuit tradition we teach our students how to think, not what to think. Professional undergraduate offerings include highly respected schools of business, nursing, and science and engineering, as well as career-oriented liberal arts programs such as creative writing, journalism, communications, and criminal justice.

"While located in the center of the city, Seattle University is a true residential campus, including students from 49 states and territories and 71 different nations. Washington State has designated the campus as an 'official backyard sanctuary' for its striking landscaping and environmentally conscious practices—several buildings enjoy official 'green' designations, and the student-run recycling program continually receives national recognition. Additionally, Seattle University is proud of its distinction as the most ethnically diverse institution in the Northwest—all students are valued and respected for their individual strengths, experiences, and worth."

## SELECTIVITY

| | |
|---|---|
| Admissions Rating | 79 |
| # of applicants | 2,951 |
| % of applicants accepted | 82 |
| % of acceptees attending | 28 |
| # accepting a place on wait list | 179 |
| % admitted from wait list | 1 |

### FRESHMAN PROFILE

| | |
|---|---|
| Range SAT Verbal | 500-610 |
| Average SAT Verbal | 562 |
| Range SAT Math | 500-620 |
| Average SAT Math | 561 |
| Range ACT Composite | 23-29 |
| Average ACT Composite | 26 |
| Minimum TOEFL | 520 |
| Average HS GPA | 3.5 |
| % graduated top 10% of class | 28 |
| % graduated top 25% of class | 58 |
| % graduated top 50% of class | 86 |

### DEADLINES

| | |
|---|---|
| Regular admission | 2/1 |
| Nonfall registration? | yes |

### APPLICANTS ALSO LOOK AT AND OFTEN PREFER
Santa Clara University
U of Puget Sound
### AND SOMETIMES PREFER
Gonzaga U
U of Portland
U of Washington
### AND RARELY PREFER
Western Washington
Pacific Lutheran

## FINANCIAL FACTS

| | |
|---|---|
| Financial Aid Rating | 79 |
| Tuition | $20,070 |
| Room and board | $6,858 |
| Books and supplies | $1,125 |

THE BEST 351 COLLEGES ■ 463

# SETON HALL UNIVERSITY

400 South Orange Avenue, South Orange, NJ 07079-2697 • Admissions: 973-761-9332 • Fax: 973-275-2040

## CAMPUS LIFE

| | |
|---|---|
| **Quality of Life Rating** | **80** |
| Type of school | private |
| Affiliation | Roman Catholic |
| Environment | suburban |

### STUDENTS

| | |
|---|---|
| Total undergrad enrollment | 5,080 |
| % male/female | 48/52 |
| % from out of state | 21 |
| % from public high school | 70 |
| % live on campus | 42 |
| % in (# of) fraternities | 6 (11) |
| % in (# of) sororities | 5 (12) |
| % African American | 11 |
| % Asian | 9 |
| % Caucasian | 54 |
| % Hispanic | 9 |
| % international | 2 |

### SURVEY SAYS . . .
(Almost) everyone smokes
Lots of beer drinking
Great computer facilities
Everyone loves the Pirates
Frats and sororities dominate social scene
Hard liquor is popular
Popular college radio
Campus easy to get around
Ethnic diversity on campus
Students don't get along with local community

## ACADEMICS

| | |
|---|---|
| **Academic Rating** | **83** |
| Calendar | semester |
| Student/faculty ratio | 14:1 |
| % profs teaching UG courses | 65 |
| % classes taught by TAs | 1 |
| Avg lab size | 10-19 students |
| Avg reg class size | 10-19 students |

### MOST POPULAR MAJORS
Finance
Communications studies/speech communication and rhetoric
Nursing/registered nurse training (RN, ASN, BSN, MSN)

## STUDENTS SPEAK OUT

### Academics

Students at Seton Hall praise their school's pre-professional and career-specific programs. The education department, for example, "has a wonderful staff who are readily available and very resourceful," writes one future teacher. A nursing student reported having "an overall good experience with my professors." And a business student bragged that everyone in the b-school is "helpful, nice, and accessible." Students generally praise the deans as "very personable," and report that priests "are very nice too." There's general approbation of the full-time professors, who "work hard to help the students" and who, "because of our wireless campus and email system, are very accessible day or night!" Despite all these assets, Seton Hall also receives some very loud complaints from its undergraduates. "Registration and the money aspect are horrible," most here agree. They also warn that "advisors are the worst part of the entire process. They either don't know what they're doing or they just don't care." Others grouse that "the instructors for the core classes haven't been the best quality" and that "a lot of adjunct professors arrive here after a long day's work at their other job and don't teach us anything." Summing up both the good and bad here, one student writes, "At Seton Hall you can find small class sizes, professors who care, students who are willing to help each other and a feeling like you belong to a really big family. Seton Hall . . . has its problems with parking for commuters, living spaces for residents, long lines at the financial aid office, and even longer lines at the bookstore to buy high-priced books."

### Life

"A lot of parties go on at Seton Hall" even though the university "has worked really hard to prevent students from doing the typical party scene." Notes one student, "At the beginning of last year, Seton Hall started putting pressure on the South Orange Police. The parties are at Greek houses, which are off campus, and now most parties get broken up by the cops." The university crackdown is the result of frequent complaints from the school's neighbors; notes one student bluntly, "The town of South Orange hates college students." As a result, students either hit the frat parties or "travel away from campus, and usually away from South Orange if they plan to do most things." The net result is that many students feel that "Seton Hall University has absolutely no social life for a student who cares naught for alcohol." A good portion of the student body goes home after classes; as one student put it, "On the weekends the place is so deserted." Many who stick around "just take the train to New York City, which isn't that expensive or hard to get to. It's only a 20-minute ride, so it's what most of us do for fun here. We head for a bar or club in the city." About the only time the campus truly comes together is to watch the Pirates shoot hoops.

### Student Body

Seton Hall is "a very ethnically and culturally diverse school," but by nearly all accounts, students separate themselves into ethnic and racial enclaves. Students typically "are from New York or New Jersey. They are Catholic and either white or Hispanic. On the weekends, everyone goes home, so the campus is deserted except for out-of-state and international students." Mr. Blackwell would probably side with those who complained that their classmates "wear way too much makeup and try to be J.Lo or Ja Rule. It's sick." Added another critic, "Black pants, tight shirts, and the 'Jersey' look, which is trendy, set the tone. There's Coach, Fendi, Gucci, and Tiffany's everywhere. These people think they're upper class." Undergrads tend to be "uninterested in politics at the local, state, and national levels." Most are "involved in at least one extracurricular activity, have a part-time job, and know when to have fun and when to buckle down to do their work."

# SETON HALL UNIVERSITY

FINANCIAL AID: 973-761-9332 • E-MAIL: THEHALL@SHU.EDU • WEBSITE: WWW.ADMISSIONS.SHU.EDU

## ADMISSIONS

*Very important factors considered include:* essays, recommendations, secondary school record, standardized test scores. *Important factors considered include:* extracurricular activities, volunteer work, work experience. *Other factors considered include:* character/personal qualities, class rank, interview, talent/ability. SAT I or ACT required. TOEFL required of all international applicants. High school diploma or GED is required. *High school units required/recommended:* 16 total required; 4 English required, 3 math required, 1 science required, 1 science lab required, 2 foreign language required, 2 social studies required, 4 elective required.

### The Inside Word

Getting into Seton Hall shouldn't be too stressful for most average students who have taken a full college-prep curriculum in high school. In the New York metropolitan area there are a lot of schools with similar characteristics, and collectively they take away the large proportion of Seton Hall's admits. Above average students who are serious about the university should be able to parlay their interest into some scholarship dollars, over 300 full scholarships this year.

## FINANCIAL AID

*Students should submit:* FAFSA. No deadline for regular filing. The Princeton Review suggests that all financial aid forms be submitted as soon as possible after January 1. *Need-based scholarships/grants offered:* Pell, SEOG, state scholarships/grants, private scholarships, the school's own gift aid. *Loan aid offered:* Direct Subsidized Stafford, Direct Unsubsidized Stafford, Direct PLUS, Federal Perkins, state loans, college/university loans from institutional funds. Federal Work-Study Program available. Institutional employment available. Applicants will be notified of awards on a rolling basis beginning on or about March 15. Off-campus job opportunities are excellent.

## FROM THE ADMISSIONS OFFICE

"As the oldest and largest diocesan university in the United States, Seton Hall University is committed to providing its students with a diverse environment focusing on academic excellence and ethical development. Outstanding faculty, a technologically advanced campus, and a values-centered curriculum challenge Seton Hall students. Through these things and the personal attention students receive, they are prepared to be leaders in their professional and community lives in a global society. Seton Hall's campus offers students up-to-date facilities, including an award-winning library facility opened in 1994 and the state-of-the art Kozlowski Hall, which opened in 1997. The university has invested more than $25 million in the past five years to provide its students and faculty with leading edge information technology. The Mobile Computing Program is widely recognized as one of the nation's best. In 1999 and 2000, Seton Hall was ranked as one of the nation's Most Wired universities by *Yahoo! Internet Life* magazine. Recent additions to Seton Hall's academic offerings include the School of Diplomacy and International Relations and a number of dual-degree health sciences programs, including physical therapy, physician assistant, and occupational therapy."

## SELECTIVITY

| | |
|---|---|
| Admissions Rating | 77 |
| # of applicants | 5,575 |
| % of applicants accepted | 85 |
| % of acceptees attending | 25 |
| # accepting a place on wait list | 1,239 |
| % admitted from wait list | 87 |

### FRESHMAN PROFILE

| | |
|---|---|
| Range SAT Verbal | 480-590 |
| Average SAT Verbal | 539 |
| Range SAT Math | 490-600 |
| Average SAT Math | 548 |
| Range ACT Composite | 22-27 |
| Average ACT Composite | 25 |
| Minimum TOEFL | 550 |
| Average HS GPA | 3.2 |
| % graduated top 10% of class | 24 |
| % graduated top 25% of class | 50 |
| % graduated top 50% of class | 80 |

### DEADLINES

| | |
|---|---|
| Priority admission | 3/1 |
| Nonfall registration? | yes |

### APPLICANTS ALSO LOOK AT AND OFTEN PREFER
Rutgers U.
NYU
Villanova

### AND SOMETIMES PREFER
Fairfield
Fordham
U. Conn

### AND RARELY PREFER
St. Bonaventure
Hofstra

## FINANCIAL FACTS

| | |
|---|---|
| Financial Aid Rating | 81 |
| Tuition | $18,780 |
| Room and board | $8,302 |
| Books and supplies | $1,100 |
| Required fees | $2,050 |

# SIENA COLLEGE

515 LOUDON ROAD, LOUDONVILLE, NY 12211 • ADMISSIONS: 518-783-2423 • FAX: 518-783-2436

## CAMPUS LIFE

| Quality of Life Rating | 75 |
| --- | --- |
| Type of school | private |
| Affiliation | Roman Catholic |
| Environment | suburban |

### STUDENTS

| Total undergrad enrollment | 3,405 |
| --- | --- |
| % male/female | 43/57 |
| % from out of state | 20 |
| % live on campus | 70 |
| % African American | 2 |
| % Asian | 2 |
| % Caucasian | 90 |
| % Hispanic | 3 |
| # of countries represented | 6 |

### SURVEY SAYS . . .
Musical organizations aren't popular
Diversity lacking on campus
Students love Loudonville, NY
Classes are small
(Almost) everyone plays intramural sports
Very small frat/sorority scene
Theater is unpopular
Computer facilities need improving
Registration is a pain

## ACADEMICS

| Academic Rating | 74 |
| --- | --- |
| Calendar | semester |
| Student/faculty ratio | 14:1 |
| Profs interesting rating | 91 |
| Profs accessible rating | 92 |
| % profs teaching UG courses | 100 |
| Avg lab size | 10-19 students |
| Avg reg class size | 20-29 students |

### MOST POPULAR MAJORS
Biology
Accounting
Psychology

## STUDENTS SPEAK OUT

### Academics

Students at Siena College have very mixed feelings about their education. They praise their favorite professors because they are "always available and willing to help with anything." And they're "creative and open-minded" to boot. The history program gets especially high marks. Professors "not only know what they are talking about, [but] they [also] know how to relay the information to students in a user-friendly way," writes a senior psychology major. Despite the small classes, "some professors tend to lecture too much and don't get the students involved." Students also complain that they have a difficult time registering for the most desired classes, which therefore makes "the good teachers impossible to get." The administration also gets mixed reviews. While a sophomore English major believes, "Those who don't look at the administration as the enemy from day one get listened to with relative seriousness," most students say that the lack of communication between the administration and themselves is a major problem. One senior history major describes the administration as "a bunch of bureaucrats on valium who are underpaid and consequently don't care." She adds that the various administrative offices "treat students like juvenile delinquents."

### Life

Although Loudonville is not far from the bars of Albany, the lack of transportation is a problem—one that encourages many students to stay in town, where entertainment options are seriously limited. Some students "get all dolled up in their party best and pile 12 to a taxi"; however, because taxis are expensive, which makes it difficult to get off campus, many students go to the upperclassmen's townhouses to pour a few down the hatch. However, there are other things to do on campus: students attend movies, and a number enjoy their association with a medieval history club—the Society for Creative Anachronism. The gym is well used, the dorms are overcrowded, and students go out to dinner as often as they can because the on-campus food leaves much to be desired.

### Student Body

Siena's students are primarily Catholic and conservative. Some believe that the "upper-middle-class Catholic students are unacquainted with reality." An English major describes his fellows as "good people who do very stupid things." Students complain about the evident lack of diversity on campus; this is not surprising considering that over 90 percent of the students are Caucasian. "There is some diversity," a chemistry major says, "but it's primarily Abercrombie-wearing Dave Matthews fans." A senior history major decries the "closed-mindedness" that she observes among her schoolmates. Students describe their peers as "friendly" but "cliquey." Overall, "students here . . . are nice and usually show respect for you," a business major writes. "They are able to get along together pretty well."

# SIENA COLLEGE

FINANCIAL AID: 518-783-2427 • E-MAIL: ADMIT@SIENA.EDU • WEBSITE: WWW.SIENA.EDU

## ADMISSIONS

*Very important factors considered include:* secondary school record. *Important factors considered include:* essays, recommendations, standardized test scores. *Other factors considered include:* alumni/ae relation, character/personal qualities, class rank, extracurricular activities, talent/ability, volunteer work, work experience. SAT I or ACT required. TOEFL required of all international applicants. High school diploma or GED is required. *High school units required/recommended:* 14 total required; 19 total recommended; 4 English required, 3 math required, 4 math recommended, 3 science required, 4 science recommended, 3 science lab required, 4 science lab recommended, 3 foreign language recommended, 1 social studies required, 3 history required.

### The Inside Word

Students who have consistently solid grades should have no trouble getting admitted. There is hot competition for students between colleges in New York State; Siena has to admit the large majority of its applicants in order to meet freshman class enrollment targets.

## FINANCIAL AID

*Students should submit:* FAFSA, state aid form. The Princeton Review suggests that all financial aid forms be submitted as soon as possible after January 1. *Need-based scholarships/grants offered:* Pell, SEOG, state scholarships/grants, private scholarships, the school's own gift aid, Siena Grants, Franciscan Community Grants. *Loan aid offered:* FFEL Subsidized Stafford, FFEL Unsubsidized Stafford, FFEL PLUS, Federal Perkins. Federal Work-Study Program available. Institutional employment available. Applicants will be notified of awards on or about April 1. Off-campus job opportunities are good.

## FROM THE ADMISSIONS OFFICE

"Siena is a coeducational, independent liberal arts college with a Franciscan tradition. It is a community where the intellectual, personal, and social growth of all students is paramount. Siena's faculty calls forth the best Siena students have to give—and the students do the same for them. Students are competitive, but not at each other's expense. Siena's curriculum includes 23 majors in three schools—liberal arts, science, and business. In addition, there are over a dozen pre-professional and special academic programs. With a student-faculty ratio of 14:1, class size ranges between 15 and 35 students. Siena's 152-acre campus is located in Loudonville, a suburban community within two miles of the New York State seat of government in Albany. With 15 colleges in the area, there is a wide variety of activities on weekends. Regional theater, performances by major concert artists, and professional sports events compete with the activities on the campus. Within 50 miles are the Adirondacks, the Berkshires, and the Catskills, providing outdoor recreation throughout the year. Because the capital region's easy, friendly lifestyle is so appealing, many Siena graduates try to find their first jobs in upstate New York."

### SELECTIVITY

| | |
|---|---:|
| **Admissions Rating** | 74 |
| # of applicants | 3,945 |
| % of applicants accepted | 58 |
| % of acceptees attending | 30 |
| # of early decision applicants | 117 |
| % accepted early decision | 9 |

### FRESHMAN PROFILE

| | |
|---|---:|
| Range SAT Verbal | 510-590 |
| Average SAT Verbal | 550 |
| Range SAT Math | 520-610 |
| Average SAT Math | 567 |
| Range ACT Composite | 24-27 |
| Average ACT Composite | 26 |
| Minimum TOEFL | 550 |
| % graduated top 10% of class | 24 |
| % graduated top 25% of class | 63 |
| % graduated top 50% of class | 94 |

### DEADLINES

| | |
|---|---:|
| Early decision | 12/1 |
| Early decision notification | 12/15 |
| Priority admission | 3/1 |
| Regular admission | 3/1 |
| Regular notification | 3/15 |
| Nonfall registration? | yes |

### APPLICANTS ALSO LOOK AT AND OFTEN PREFER
Villanova
Providence

### AND SOMETIMES PREFER
Fairfield
Marist
SUNY Albany
U of Scranton
Loyola College of Maryland

### AND RARELY PREFER
Oswego State
Fredonia State
LeMoyne
Syracuse
UConn

### FINANCIAL FACTS

| | |
|---|---:|
| **Financial Aid Rating** | 80 |
| Tuition | $17,555 |
| Room and board | $7,215 |
| Books and supplies | $745 |
| Required fees | $540 |
| % frosh receiving aid | 92 |
| % undergrads receiving aid | 89 |

# SIMMONS COLLEGE

300 THE FENWAY, BOSTON, MA 02115 • ADMISSIONS: 617-521-2051 • FAX: 617-521-3190

## CAMPUS LIFE

★ ★ ★ ☆

| Quality of Life Rating | 86 |
| --- | --- |
| Type of school | private |
| Environment | urban |

### STUDENTS

| Total undergrad enrollment | 1,373 |
| --- | --- |
| % from out of state | 43 |
| % from public high school | 81 |
| % live on campus | 75 |
| % African American | 7 |
| % Asian | 7 |
| % Caucasian | 76 |
| % Hispanic | 4 |
| % international | 4 |
| # of countries represented | 26 |

### SURVEY SAYS . . .
Students love Boston, MA
Profs teach upper levels
Students are cliquish
Great off-campus food
Students are happy
High cost of living

## ACADEMICS

| Academic Rating | 88 |
| --- | --- |
| Calendar | semester |
| Student/faculty ratio | 12:1 |
| Profs interesting rating | 94 |
| Profs accessible rating | 94 |
| % profs teaching UG courses | 100 |
| Avg reg class size | 10-19 students |

### MOST POPULAR MAJORS
Nursing/registered nurse training (RN, ASN, BSN, MSN)
Biology
Communications

## STUDENTS SPEAK OUT

### Academics

Have you ever heard of "Dan—The Man—Cheever"? Most Simmons students have. "The president is down to earth. He lets the students call him 'Dan—The Man,'" after all. In fact, most students find the administration and the faculty to be "very accessible." Overall, students believe Simmons provides an "academic experience" that is "excellent" and "truly interactive." "Professors here go the extra mile"—though it should be said that "some of them are windbags and like hearing themselves talk." No matter what they think of their professors, students can definitely lodge a complaint or two against the curriculum. For instance, a "performing arts department is needed," and there's "only one music prof—icky." They also could do without Culture Matters, an "extremely disappointing, ineffective, and not challenging" course that all first-year students have to take. But if your cards fall right, you'll find that "every class ends up being your favorite class." Because the "work load is heavy" across the board, Simmons students get the sense that they're "all in this together." A sophomore adds, "Especially when we all have to cross Brookline Avenue, the four-lane road with no crosswalk."

### Life

There are more than 50 clubs and organizations at Simmons, though you wouldn't know it by talking to the students. "Campus life is nonexistent," remarks a freshman. "Clubs and sports are often ignored." So what exactly do Simmons students do for fun? For those who choose to stick around campus, not much. "Girls have knitting parties, eat a lot of take out, and do laundry on Saturday nights." Others "just hang out, drink, smoke, and make out." But for those who are looking for a little more excitement, they've got Boston—and 15 nearby colleges—at their fingertips. The city of Boston can provide not only "a great opportunity to go to see movies, plays, musicals, [and] go to museums and shopping," but also the chance to meet other college-agers at "bars and clubs." And when they feel up for a good old-fashioned keg party, the Simmons women "go to frats at the larger schools" that are nearby, especially Boston University and MIT. And for sports fans, "Red Sox and Bruins games" are good ways to spend an evening. But at the end of any good evening, Simmons students return to "quiet" dorms on campus, dorms that according to some, "are like dungeons." So you're not likely to find boys or a party or an Ethernet hookup in your dorm room. But you just have to keep in mind that "Simmons is a great learning environment while Boston is a great social environment."

### Student Body

Take 1,200 female undergraduates, drop them in the heart of Boston, and what do you get? Simmons College, of course. "It's all women, white, majority middle class," which makes one Latina student exclaim, "More diversity, PLEASE, GOD!" According to one junior, Simmons "students come in two types: conservative, rich, and closed-minded, and then liberal, middle or lower class, and working for progress and diversity at Simmons." While "there are a lot of activists at Simmons," there is also an apathetic contingent in the student body. One student complains that her classmates are "snobby and stick within their own cliques." "A lot of people say Simmons women are snobby, but I find the complete opposite," dissents a freshman. One thing's for sure: when they're not listening to Britney or waging a political crusade, they're lost in their coursework. The fact that they're "very dedicated" to their studies is the common bond among Simmons students.

468 ■ THE BEST 351 COLLEGES

# SIMMONS COLLEGE

FINANCIAL AID: 617-521-2001 • E-MAIL: UGADM@SIMMONS.EDU • WEBSITE: WWW.SIMMONS.EDU

## ADMISSIONS

*Very important factors considered include:* secondary school record. *Important factors considered include:* character/personal qualities, class rank, essays, recommendations, standardized test scores. *Other factors considered include:* alumni/ae relation, extracurricular activities, interview, talent/ability, volunteer work, work experience. SAT I or ACT required. TOEFL required of all international applicants. High school diploma or GED is required. *High school units required/recommended:* 15 total required; 4 English required, 3 math required, 4 math recommended, 3 science required, 3 foreign language required, 4 foreign language recommended, 3 social studies required, 4 social studies recommended.

### The Inside Word

Most of the best women's colleges in the country are in the Northeast, including those Seven Sister schools (roughly the female equivalent of the formerly all-male Ivies) that remain women's colleges. The competition for students is intense, and although Simmons is a strong attraction for many women, there are at least a half-dozen competitors who draw the better students away. For the majority of applicants there is little need for anxiety while awaiting a decision. Its solid academics, Boston location, and bountiful scholarship program make Simmons well worth considering for any student opting for a women's college.

## FINANCIAL AID

*Students should submit:* FAFSA. The Princeton Review suggests that all financial aid forms be submitted as soon as possible after January 1. *Need-based scholarships/grants offered:* Pell, SEOG, state scholarships/grants, private scholarships, the school's own gift aid. *Loan aid offered:* FFEL Subsidized Stafford, FFEL Unsubsidized Stafford, FFEL PLUS, Federal Perkins, state loans, college/university loans from institutional funds. Federal Work-Study Program available. Institutional employment available. Applicants will be notified of awards on a rolling basis. Off-campus job opportunities are good.

## FROM THE ADMISSIONS OFFICE

"Simmons believes passionately in an 'educational contract' that places students first and helps them build successful careers, lead meaningful lives, and realize a powerful return on their investment.

"Simmons is truly a 100-year-old university in Boston, with a tradition of providing women with a collaborative environment that stimulates dialogue, enhances listening, catalyzes action, and spurs personal and professional growth.

"Simmons honors this contract by delivering a quality education and measurable success through our singular approach to professional preparation, intellectual exploration, and community orientation."

---

### SELECTIVITY

| | |
|---|---|
| Admissions Rating | 77 |
| # of applicants | 1,753 |
| % of applicants accepted | 68 |
| % of acceptees attending | 27 |
| # accepting a place on wait list | 18 |
| % admitted from wait list | 0 |

### FRESHMAN PROFILE

| | |
|---|---|
| Range SAT Verbal | 500-600 |
| Average SAT Verbal | 554 |
| Range SAT Math | 490-590 |
| Average SAT Math | 542 |
| Range ACT Composite | 19-25 |
| Average ACT Composite | 23 |
| Minimum TOEFL | 560 |
| % graduated top 10% of class | 24 |
| % graduated top 25% of class | 47 |
| % graduated top 50% of class | 80 |
| Average HS GPA | 3.1 |

### DEADLINES

| | |
|---|---|
| Regular admission | 2/1 |
| Regular notification | 4/15 |
| Nonfall registration? | yes |

### APPLICANTS ALSO LOOK AT
**AND OFTEN PREFER**
Boston Coll.
Boston U.
Mount Holyoke
Wellesley
Bryn Mawr

**AND SOMETIMES PREFER**
Wheaton (MA)
Northeastern U.
Smith

**AND RARELY PREFER**
U. Mass—Amherst
U. New Hampshire

### FINANCIAL FACTS

| | |
|---|---|
| Financial Aid Rating | 80 |
| Tuition | $22,860 |
| Room and board | $9,458 |
| Books and supplies | $640 |
| Required fees | $690 |
| % frosh receiving aid | 88 |
| % undergrads receiving aid | 65 |

# SIMON'S ROCK COLLEGE OF BARD

84 ALFORD ROAD, GREAT BARRINGTON, MA 01230 • ADMISSIONS: 413-528-7312 • FAX: 413-528-7334

## CAMPUS LIFE

★ ★ ★ ☆

| | |
|---|---|
| Quality of Life Rating | 84 |
| Type of school | private |
| Environment | rural |

### STUDENTS

| | |
|---|---|
| Total undergrad enrollment | 409 |
| % male/female | 41/59 |
| % from out of state | 80 |
| % from public high school | 70 |
| % live on campus | 86 |
| % African American | 3 |
| % Asian | 5 |
| % Caucasian | 74 |
| % Hispanic | 3 |
| % international | 1 |

### SURVEY SAYS . . .
Ethnic diversity on campus
Lots of classroom discussion
Political activism is hot
Theater is hot
Very small frat/sorority scene
Athletic facilities need improving
Intercollegiate sports unpopular or nonexistent

## ACADEMICS

| | |
|---|---|
| Academic Rating | 93 |
| Calendar | semester |
| Student/faculty ratio | 8:1 |
| Profs interesting rating | 80 |
| Profs accessible rating | 76 |
| % profs teaching UG courses | 100 |
| Avg lab size | 10-19 students |
| Avg reg class size | 10-19 students |

### MOST POPULAR MAJORS
Dramatic/theatre arts and stagecraft
Mathematics
Ethnic, cultural minority, and gender studies

## STUDENTS SPEAK OUT

### Academics

Tiny Simon's Rock College of Bard, which admits exceptional high school sophomores and juniors to its college-level program, "is a fantastic opportunity for students who were either bored in high school (the overachievers) or the really smart kids who never did a damn thing, but want to now. Hating high school isn't enough, though; you really have to work hard here." With barely 400 enrollees, "there are usually only about 8 people in a class. You can take the class wherever you want it to go. And if you can't, you can stay after and talk it over with the teacher one-on-one." The school offers students the freedom "to do independent study or take a 300-level course as a freshman or do practically anything else. All you have to do is ask." Notes one student, "This school is really one giant test of one's own motivation and determination." Although "there isn't a huge variety of majors and classes available," students tell us that "every semester when the course catalog comes out, it's never a question of finding interesting courses to take; it's always a matter of working them into a workable schedule." They also explain that "because of the interdisciplinary nature of academics here, the limited number of majors isn't a huge problem." Furthermore, "if something you want to study isn't being covered, it's remarkably easy to set up a tutorial dedicated to that subject because professors are extraordinarily available and receptive."

### Life

"Life at Simon's Rock can be very boring since it's located in a small town," undergrads at this tiny college concede, "but you can find happiness with your friends and student life staff." Diversion comes primarily in the form of "a peculiar form of 'hanging out'—Simon's Rock should really be a verb rather than a noun. This sort of hanging out involves either being outside smoking or inside watching the *Fight Club* DVD a lot, and having conversations that range from the emotionally charged to goofy to intellectual." Go-getters note that "the schools is always really helpful to students. Since many of the students are younger, some too young to drive, they offer town trips every day, and on weekends they often take groups to go ice-skating, bowling, roller skating, miniature golfing, or just to the movies. They also have mall trips, and student groups often go to other colleges to meet other students and to get ideas as to how to incorporate Simon's Rock into the larger college community." Many, however, don't take advantage of these opportunities, instead resorting to immersion in computer games, pot-smoking, or pure tedium. Location and the size of the school are major roadblocks to a more active social scene. "It would be nice if there were stronger campus organizations, but it's difficult for that to happen given the small size of the school and the demanding nature of the classes," explains one student. Notes another, "The location of the school doesn't help one bit." It's so secluded that "there's no television reception, and cell phones are useless, too."

### Student Body

Traditionally regarded as a lefty-weirdo haven, Simon's Rock "seems to be getting more conservative and preppy with each entering class." The transition is a slow one, however. According to one student "the average Simon's Rock student probably smokes both cigarettes and marijuana, is interested in arts and humanities, considers him- or herself to be politically active, and is probably vegetarian or vegan." And oddballs still predominate; as one student put it, "We all come from something abnormal, due to the fact that we are entering college a year or two early. And these abnormalities, although strikingly different, form a common bond." Adds another, "The townies call us 'the freaks on the hill.' My mom calls us 'the patients.'" Because it's a school of 400 students, "everyone knows everybody."

470 ■ THE BEST 351 COLLEGES

# SIMON'S ROCK COLLEGE OF BARD

FINANCIAL AID: 413-528-7297 • E-MAIL: ADMIT@SIMONS-ROCK.EDU • WEBSITE: WWW.SIMONS-ROCK.EDU

## ADMISSIONS
*Very important factors considered include:* character/personal qualities, essays, interview, recommendations, talent/ability. *Important factors considered include:* extracurricular activities, secondary school record, standardized test scores, volunteer work. *Other factors considered include:* alumni/ae relation, minority status, work experience. SAT I or ACT required. TOEFL required of all international applicants. *High school units required/recommended:* 15 total recommended; 2 English recommended, 2 math recommended, 2 science recommended, 1 science lab recommended, 2 foreign language recommended, 2 social studies recommended, 2 history recommended, 2 elective recommended.

### The Inside Word
There is no other college like Simon's Rock in the country, and no other similar admissions process. Applying to college doesn't get any more personal, and thus any more demanding, than it does here. If you're not ready to tap your potential as a thinker in college beginning with completion of the application, avoid Simon's Rock. Simply hating high school isn't going to get you in. Self-awareness, intellectual curiosity, and a desire for more formidable academic challenges than those typically found in high school will.

## FINANCIAL AID
*Students should submit:* FAFSA, CSS/Financial Aid PROFILE, noncustodial (divorced/separated) parent's statement. Regular filing deadline is June 15. The Princeton Review suggests that all financial aid forms be submitted as soon as possible after January 1. *Need-based scholarships/grants offered:* Pell, SEOG, state scholarships/grants, private scholarships, the school's own gift aid. *Loan aid offered:* Direct Subsidized Stafford, Direct Unsubsidized Stafford, Direct PLUS, FFEL Subsidized Stafford, FFEL Unsubsidized Stafford, FFEL PLUS, Federal Perkins, state loans. Federal Work-Study Program available. Institutional employment available. Applicants will be notified of awards on a rolling basis beginning on or about April 15. Off-campus job opportunities are good.

## FROM THE ADMISSIONS OFFICE
"Simon's Rock is dedicated to one thing: to allow bright highly motivated students the opportunity to pursue college work leading to the AA and BA degrees at an age earlier than our national norm."

### SELECTIVITY
★ ★ ★ ★

| | |
|---|---|
| Admissions Rating | 91 |
| # of applicants | 480 |
| % of applicants accepted | 50 |
| % of acceptees attending | 64 |

### FRESHMAN PROFILE
| | |
|---|---|
| Range SAT Verbal | 580-660 |
| Average SAT Verbal | 640 |
| Range SAT Math | 490-640 |
| Average SAT Math | 600 |
| Range ACT Composite | 22-28 |
| Average ACT Composite | 26 |
| Minimum TOEFL | 550 |

### DEADLINES
| | |
|---|---|
| Regular admission | 7/1 |
| Regular notification | rolling |

### FINANCIAL FACTS
★ ★ ★ ☆

| | |
|---|---|
| Financial Aid Rating | 88 |
| Tuition | $27,180 |
| Room and board | $7,160 |
| Books and supplies | $1,000 |
| Required fees | $235 |
| % frosh receiving aid | 68 |
| % undergrads receiving aid | 63 |

# Skidmore College

815 North Broadway, Saratoga Springs, NY 12866-1632 • Admissions: 518-580-5570 • Fax: 518-580-5584

## CAMPUS LIFE

| | |
|---|---|
| **Quality of Life Rating** | **94** |
| Type of school | private |
| Environment | suburban |

### STUDENTS

| | |
|---|---|
| Total undergrad enrollment | 2,506 |
| % male/female | 40/60 |
| % from out of state | 71 |
| % from public high school | 60 |
| % live on campus | 77 |
| % African American | 3 |
| % Asian | 5 |
| % Caucasian | 75 |
| % Hispanic | 4 |
| % international | 1 |

### SURVEY SAYS . . .
Great library
Students love Saratoga Springs, NY
Great computer facilities
Dorms are like palaces
Diversity lacking on campus
No one plays intramural sports
Class discussions encouraged

## ACADEMICS

| | |
|---|---|
| **Academic Rating** | **84** |
| Calendar | semester |
| Student/faculty ratio | 11:1 |
| Profs interesting rating | 94 |
| Profs accessible rating | 94 |
| % profs teaching UG courses | 100 |
| Avg lab size | 10-19 students |
| Avg reg class size | 10-19 students |

## STUDENTS SPEAK OUT

### Academics

Skidmore College, a small liberal arts school in upstate New York, boasts strengths in the "liberal arts, fine arts, and performing arts." In addition, Skidmore offers excellent pre-professional programs and programs in education and social work. A core curriculum—the Liberal Studies sequence—exposes students to the "greatest hits" of western arts and sciences and provides "a valuable supplement to a solid liberal arts education." Says one student of the curriculum, "Skidmore embraces versatility. It's the training ground for modern Leonardo da Vincis, Aristotles, and tap-dancing brain surgeons." Students at Skidmore enjoy a relaxed but rigorous academic atmosphere in which "academics are challenging yet manageable" and the workload is "just right. I think I was well prepared for the academic atmosphere here. Just when things seem too easy, something challenging comes along, and vice versa." Professors are "fun and interesting. They seem to love what they do." Writes an undergrad, "Professors are always available to talk to. They are so helpful and friendly. Not only can you talk to them about academics but you can get advice on life in general." About the only beef students have with the faculty is that "we need more professors in order to expand the number of courses offered." Undergrads are more circumspect about the administration, complaining that "students have very little input in what happens on this campus. Decisions are made behind closed doors." For a select group of "highly motivated and talented students," Skidmore offers the Honors Forum, "an enriched combination of academic and co-curricular opportunities."

### Life

For those who enjoy crisp autumns, beautiful campuses, and lovely small cities, Skidmore offers an excellent quality of life. "The campus is beautiful, dorms are awesome, and Saratoga Springs is great!" gushes one student. "It's a 30,000-person town with the facilities and entertainment of a town three times its size. Wonderful coffee shops [and a] great night life" are among the most popular amenities. Students are quick to point out that "for the outdoorsy types, the Adirondacks are an hour drive away" and that "Lake George is beautiful and less than 30 minutes away." One student remarks that there's "lots of stuff to do here with nature. Mad nice parks. We usually do outdoor activities for fun (hiking, biking, Frisbee, etc.) until the sun goes down, then we usually consume a lot of alcohol and do a variety of drugs." Students also note that "big cities [New York, Boston] are four hours away . . . a little too far, but there are buses and trains." Albany is close by for students needing an instant fix of urban style. On campus, "students are highly involved in clubs and other extracurriculars," but "sports and school spirit are lacking." Offers one undergrad, "There is always something going on: lectures, bands, plays, free movies on weekends, bowling, laser tag. . . . I think this may account for the low support of sports." Skidmore has no Greek scene, which many here see as "a plus. Off-campus parties are fun, relaxed environments."

### Student Body

"Skidmore students," explains one undergrad, "are generally considered wealthy, spoiled, privileged people. To a certain extent, it's true. But at the same time, you can surround yourself with people who do not fit the stereotype. There are many hard-working, down-to-earth people here." Comments another, "Skidmore is, unfortunately, a pretty homogeneous place. The administration works hard to give financial aid. Without it, the cost of tuition would make this place completely exclusive. All issues of diversity directly relate to money." Some report that "all the different types of people—jocks, thespians, artists, hippies, and preps—all interact well together. It isn't uncommon to have friends in all circles." Others complain that students are very cliquey. One woman warns prospective female applicants that "the students at Skidmore are mostly women. The ratio of men to women is about 2:3, which is really good if you're a straight guy because a lot of the men here are gay."

# SKIDMORE COLLEGE

FINANCIAL AID: 518-580-5750 • E-MAIL: ADMISSIONS@SKIDMORE.EDU • WEBSITE: WWW.SKIDMORE.EDU

## ADMISSIONS

*Very important factors considered include:* recommendations, secondary school record. *Important factors considered include:* character/personal qualities, class rank, essays, extracurricular activities, standardized test scores, talent/ability, volunteer work, work experience. *Other factors considered include:* alumni/ae relation, geographical residence, interview, minority status. SAT I or ACT required. TOEFL required of all international applicants. High school diploma or GED is required. *High school units required/recommended:* 4 English recommended, 4 math recommended, 4 science recommended, 3 science lab recommended, 4 foreign language recommended, 4 social studies recommended.

## The Inside Word

Although Skidmore overlaps applicants with some of the best colleges and universities in the Northeast, it's mainly viewed as a safety. Still, this makes for a strong applicant pool, and those students who do enroll give the college a better-than-average freshman academic profile. The entire admissions operation at Skidmore is impressive and efficient, proof that number two does indeed try harder.

## FINANCIAL AID

*Students should submit:* FAFSA, CSS/Financial Aid PROFILE, state aid form. Regular filing deadline is January 15. The Princeton Review suggests that all financial aid forms be submitted as soon as possible after January 1. *Need-based scholarships/grants offered:* Pell, SEOG, state scholarships/grants, the school's own gift aid. *Loan aid offered:* FFEL Subsidized Stafford, FFEL Unsubsidized Stafford, FFEL PLUS, Federal Perkins. Federal Work-Study Program available. Institutional employment available. Applicants will be notified of awards on or about April 1. Off-campus job opportunities are good.

## FROM THE ADMISSIONS OFFICE

"Skidmore's Liberal Studies Curriculum is a highly interdisciplinary core curriculum that enriches a student's first two years of study. Students take one course in each of four liberal studies areas, beginning that Liberal Studies I: The Human Experience. This is a cornerstone course that is team-taught to all freshmen by 28 professors from virtually every department in the college. It involves lectures, performances, films, and regular small group discussions. Students then take one more liberal studies course in one of the three succeeding semesters. The purpose of these two courses is to show the important academic interrelationships across disciplines, across cultures, and across time. The result is that our students learn to look for connections among the disciplines rather than see them in isolation. With this interdisciplinary foundation under their belts by the end of the sophomore year, students are better prepared to then select a major (or combination of majors) that matches their interests."

### SELECTIVITY

| | |
|---|---|
| Admissions Rating | 83 |
| # of applicants | 5,606 |
| % of applicants accepted | 46 |
| % of acceptees attending | 25 |
| # accepting a place on wait list | 347 |
| % admitted from wait list | 1 |
| # of early decision applicants | 406 |
| % accepted early decision | 57 |

### FRESHMAN PROFILE

| | |
|---|---|
| Range SAT Verbal | 580-670 |
| Average SAT Verbal | 630 |
| Range SAT Math | 580-660 |
| Average SAT Math | 620 |
| Range ACT Composite | 25-28 |
| Average ACT Composite | 27 |
| Minimum TOEFL | 580 |
| Average HS GPA | 3.4 |
| % graduated top 10% of class | 41 |
| % graduated top 25% of class | 74 |
| % graduated top 50% of class | 97 |

### DEADLINES

| | |
|---|---|
| Early decision | 12/1 |
| Early decision notification | 1/1 |
| Regular admission | 1/15 |
| Regular notification | 4/1 |
| Nonfall registration? | yes |

### APPLICANTS ALSO LOOK AT
**AND OFTEN PREFER**
Trinity (CT)
Middlebury
Vassar
**AND SOMETIMES PREFER**
American
Syracuse
Boston U.
**AND RARELY PREFER**
Clark

### FINANCIAL FACTS

| | |
|---|---|
| Financial Aid Rating | 81 |
| Tuition | $27,700 |
| Room and board | $7,835 |
| Books and supplies | $650 |
| Required fees | $280 |
| % frosh receiving aid | 40 |
| % undergrads receiving aid | 42 |
| Avg frosh grant | $17,342 |
| Avg frosh loan | $2,336 |

# SMITH COLLEGE

7 COLLEGE LANE, NORTHAMPTON, MA 01063 • ADMISSIONS: 413-585-2500 • FAX: 413-585-2527

## CAMPUS LIFE

| | |
|---|---|
| **Quality of Life Rating** | **92** |
| Type of school | private |
| Environment | suburban |

### STUDENTS

| | |
|---|---|
| Total undergrad enrollment | 2,647 |
| % from out of state | 76 |
| % from public high school | 74 |
| % live on campus | 87 |
| % African American | 5 |
| % Asian | 10 |
| % Caucasian | 62 |
| % Hispanic | 6 |
| % international | 6 |
| # of countries represented | 55 |

### SURVEY SAYS . . .
Lots of liberals
Profs teach upper-level courses
Lab facilities are great
No one watches intercollegiate sports
Political activism is hot
Student publications are popular
Class discussions encouraged

## ACADEMICS

| | |
|---|---|
| **Academic Rating** | **94** |
| Calendar | semester |
| Student/faculty ratio | 9:1 |
| Profs interesting rating | 97 |
| Profs accessible rating | 98 |
| % profs teaching UG courses | 100 |
| Avg lab size | 10-19 students |
| Avg reg class size | 10-19 students |

### MOST POPULAR MAJORS
Psychology
Economics
Political science and government

## STUDENTS SPEAK OUT

### Academics

Ask any student why she decided to come to Smith, and you're bound to hear about its "academic reputation." While students tend to think the classes at Smith are "interesting but not thrilling," they also believe that the school does live up to its reputation. With "small classes" and "no distribution requirements," students are given the academic freedom and attention that they need to succeed. "The support systems" provided by professors and other students are crucial aids as "Smithies," as Smith students refer to themselves, dive headlong into the hard work that they find in almost every class. "There's great tutoring and writing help available," reports one junior. "And professors and other students always want to help everyone." In fact, professors are looked upon as "minor deities" in these parts, not only because they "are always accessible and open to questions," but also because they are "extremely intelligent" and dedicated to their fields of study. Students, in turn, become dedicated to their own fields of study. As a result, academics can be very consuming at Smith. "I study my ass off—everyone does," writes one sophomore. "If you don't, you will not last here."

### Life

Smithies are known far and wide for their acceptance of alternative lifestyles and a liberal-minded academic and extracurricular dedication to social issues. Notwithstanding these activist principles, Smithies are the kind of students that "study for fun." Because of the campus "house system," which provides "country-club comfort" of living for students, many Smithies reveal that they form their closest friendships with other women in their respective houses. Soon after arriving at Smith, students realize that "this is not a party school," which means it's a "good deal quieter than coed institutions." But that's not to suggest that it's boring. Activities run the gamut from "playing Scrabble on a Friday night" to "organizing a rally" to singing with the campus a cappella group, The Smithereens, to attending "lectures, theatre, dance shows, improv comedy," to just hanging out with friends and talking "a lot about emotions, equality, justice, the government, and larger religious and existential questions." Smith is also part of the Five College Consortium (along with Amherst, Mount Holyoke, and Hampshire Colleges, and the University of Massachusetts—Amherst). When Smithies go looking for parties, they appreciate the "easy access to the other four colleges in the area." And "the good thing is the bus (to these colleges) is free and runs til 3 A.M. on the weekends!" Smithies also take advantage of their location in the heart of Northhampton, which many students believe to be "the greatest town ever!" "Northhampton is a wonderful place—funky and diverse, with tons of activities—movies, shopping, parks, bars and pubs," and "fun stores and restaurants." In other words, if you just look a little, you'll "never have a problem finding something to do here."

### Student Body

Smithies are a "rather homogenous" bunch of about 2,600 students almost universally "intent on their studies." A large majority of them are "of a lefty bent" as far as politics go, and they're vocal about their opinions. "If you're not open-minded, you'll be miserable at Smith," one freshman warns. This outspoken liberalism isn't appreciated by all of the students, though. "I feel like I'm going to be lynched if I'm not PC enough," a student says. Some students—who hadn't anticipated the strong presence of liberal and lesbian cultures at Smith—complain that "the college does not present an accurate description of students" in its admissions literature. This means that "Smith can be a hard place to adjust to" when you actually join its ranks as a freshman. For the most part, once students realize that they're a part of a "smart, assertive, wacky" student body, they tend to settle quite cozily into the "beautiful campus" and the challenging college life at Smith.

# SMITH COLLEGE

FINANCIAL AID: 413-585-2530 • E-MAIL: ADMISSIONS@SMITH.EDU • WEBSITE: WWW.SMITH.EDU

## ADMISSIONS

*Very important factors considered include:* character/personal qualities, recommendations, secondary school record. *Important factors considered include:* class rank, essays, extracurricular activities, interview, standardized test scores, talent/ability. *Other factors considered include:* alumni/ae relation, minority status, volunteer work, work experience. SAT I or ACT required; SAT II recommended. TOEFL required of all international applicants. *High school units required/recommended:* 15 total recommended; 4 English recommended, 3 math recommended, 3 science recommended, 3 science lab recommended, 3 foreign language recommended, 2 history recommended.

### The Inside Word

Don't be fooled by the relatively high acceptance rate at Smith (or at other top women's colleges). The applicant pool here is small and highly self-selected, and it's fairly tough to get admitted. Only women who have taken the most challenging course loads in high school and achieved at a superior level will be competitive.

## FINANCIAL AID

*Students should submit:* FAFSA, institution's own financial aid form, CSS/Financial Aid PROFILE, noncustodial (divorced/separated) parent's statement, business/farm supplement. Regular filing deadline is February 1. The Princeton Review suggests that all financial aid forms be submitted as soon as possible after January 1. *Need-based scholarships/grants offered:* Pell, SEOG, state scholarships/grants, the school's own gift aid. *Loan aid offered:* Direct Subsidized Stafford, Direct Unsubsidized Stafford, FFEL PLUS, Federal Perkins, state loans, college/university loans from institutional funds. Federal Work-Study Program available. Institutional employment available. Applicants will be notified of awards on or about April 1. Off-campus job opportunities are excellent.

## FROM THE ADMISSIONS OFFICE

"Smith students choose from 1,000 courses in more than 50 areas of study. There are no specific course requirements outside the major; students meet individually with faculty advisers to plan a balanced curriculum. Smith programs offer unique opportunities, including the chance to study abroad, or at another college in the United States, and to learn firsthand about the federal government. The Ada Comstock Scholars Program encourages women beyond the traditional age to return to college and complete their undergraduate studies. Smith is located in the scenic Connecticut River valley of western Massachusetts near a number of other outstanding educational institutions. Through the Five College Consortium, Smith, Amherst, Hampshire, and Mount Holyoke colleges and the University of Massachusetts enrich their academic, social, and cultural offerings by means of joint faculty appointments, joint courses, student and faculty exchanges, shared facilities, and other cooperative arrangements."

### SELECTIVITY

| | |
|---|---|
| Admissions Rating | 97 |
| # of applicants | 3,047 |
| % of applicants accepted | 53 |
| % of acceptees attending | 42 |
| # accepting a place on wait list | 174 |
| # of early decision applicants | 224 |
| % accepted early decision | 70 |

#### FRESHMAN PROFILE

| | |
|---|---|
| Range SAT Verbal | 590-700 |
| Average SAT Verbal | 660 |
| Range SAT Math | 580-670 |
| Average SAT Math | 640 |
| Range ACT Composite | 24-30 |
| Average ACT Composite | 27 |
| Minimum TOEFL | 600 |
| Average HS GPA | 3.8 |
| % graduated top 10% of class | 58 |
| % graduated top 25% of class | 90 |
| % graduated top 50% of class | 99 |

#### DEADLINES

| | |
|---|---|
| Early decision | 11/15 |
| Early decision notification | 12/15 |
| Regular admission | 1/15 |
| Regular notification | 4/1 |

**APPLICANTS ALSO LOOK AT AND SOMETIMES PREFER**
Brown University
Wellesley College
**AND RARELY PREFER**
Mount Holyoke College

### FINANCIAL FACTS

| | |
|---|---|
| Financial Aid Rating | 79 |
| Tuition | $27,330 |
| Room and board | $9,490 |
| Books and supplies | $1,500 |
| Required fees | $214 |
| % frosh receiving aid | 61 |
| % undergrads receiving aid | 64 |
| Avg frosh grant | $21,874 |
| Avg frosh loan | $2,674 |

# SONOMA STATE UNIVERSITY

1801 East Cotati Avenue, Rohnert Park, CA 94928 • Admissions: 707-664-2778 • Fax: 707-664-2060

## CAMPUS LIFE

| | |
|---|---|
| Quality of Life Rating | 82 |
| Type of school | public |
| Environment | suburban |

### STUDENTS

| | |
|---|---|
| Total undergrad enrollment | 6,278 |
| % male/female | 36/64 |
| % from out of state | 1 |
| % from public high school | 87 |
| % live on campus | 29 |
| % in (# of) fraternities | 6 (4) |
| % in (# of) sororities | 5 (4) |
| % African American | 2 |
| % Asian | 5 |
| % Caucasian | 65 |
| % Hispanic | 10 |
| % international | 2 |

### SURVEY SAYS...
Campus is beautiful
Great library
Lots of beer drinking
Great computer facilities
Hard liquor is popular
Students are happy
Dorms are like palaces
Students don't get along with local community

## ACADEMICS

| | |
|---|---|
| Academic Rating | 70 |
| Calendar | semester |
| Student/faculty ratio | 21:1 |
| % profs teaching UG courses | 98 |
| % classes taught by TAs | 1 |
| Avg lab size | 10-19 students |
| Avg reg class size | 10-19 students |

### MOST POPULAR MAJORS
Business administration/management
Liberal arts and sciences/liberal studies
Psychology

## STUDENTS SPEAK OUT

### Academics
Like most state schools, lately Sonoma State University is struggling to cope with reduced government funding. While students here still brag about "personalized classroom experiences" and "good, easily available advising," an increasing number express concerns over cutbacks. "Not enough teachers are hired full-time," writes one student, "and because of this, many teachers teach at more than one campus. These teachers are not as accessible and less familiar with how the subject is taught across the campus." Still, many students praise Sonoma's full-time faculty ("Professors have been very thorough and helpful in teaching subjects, and they seem genuinely pleased to be sharing their knowledge with each class") and its marquee programs in music, business, environmental studies, and liberal studies. They warn that introductory general education (GE) classes are really "very easy." "The GE professors seem to only be going through the motions, like because it was a GE class, it didn't really matter. Upper-division teaching, however, is excellent, with superior professors directly connected to current job fields."

### Life
"The atmosphere is laid-back" at Sonoma State University. A little too laid-back for many; students tell us that "everyone complains about there being nothing to do" here. One problem lies with Sonoma's hometown of Rohnert Park, which has "no college-town atmosphere." Students describe it as "a family kind of place. It's a very small town with only a few bars." The other is the proximity of more enticing destinations: Chico ("On the weekends the school is fairly quiet, as most students make the trek to Chico State for some fun," writes one student), Santa Rosa ("lots of bars and malls"), and, of course, San Francisco, which is less than an hour's drive from campus. With so many students heading elsewhere for fun, "the campus pretty much closes down on weekends, so there's not much to do at school then." Students report that "the university is really good about attaining entertainment like movie nights, comedians, local bands playing in the quad, and field trips off campus," but also tell us that such events are not always well attended. "Collegiate and intramural sports are popular among a wide variety of students," but not enough to keep the majority of students on campus once classes end. On a positive note, students brag that "the coast and redwoods are nearby and are a great place for a drive or a walk," that the "residential communities are amazing. We live in phat-ass apartments. It's way nicer than any other schools' dorms I have ever seen," and that "great local wine is consumed in copious amounts here."

### Student Body
Many SSU undergrads concede that "there is little diversity" on this "mostly white, mostly female, middle- to upper-class campus." Students feel that SSU has a good diversity of personality types, however. "Since SSU is strong in liberal arts, media, sciences, and business, there are all types here, and good students represent all shapes, colors, and political opinions across the spectrum." Notes one undergrad, "Some of us study very hard, others hardly at all; some spend years messing around, some get in and out very quickly; some are courteous and helpful, others are deterrents to learning." Another observes that "there is a big gay population, but they're not ostentatious. There are large Jewish and Christian populations. Everyone is pretty much accepted at face value, whether you play lacrosse or major in computer science."

# SONOMA STATE UNIVERSITY

FINANCIAL AID: 707-664-2389 • E-MAIL: ADMITME@SONOMA.EDU • WEBSITE: WWW.SONOMA.EDU

## ADMISSIONS

*Very important factors considered include:* secondary school record, standardized test scores. *Important factors considered include:* geographical residence, minority status, state residency. SAT I or ACT required. TOEFL required of all international applicants. High school diploma or GED is required. *High school units required/recommended:* 16 total required; 4 English required, 3 math required, 2 science required, 1 science lab required, 2 foreign language required, 1 history required, 3 elective required.

### The Inside Word

Admission by formula is the rule at Sonoma State, consistent with its role in the Cal State system. Plug in to the formula and sign up for class—there's no mystery to candidate selection here. Solid courses, grades, and test scores lead the way into the freshman class.

## FINANCIAL AID

*Students should submit:* FAFSA. The Princeton Review suggests that all financial aid forms be submitted as soon as possible after January 1. *Need-based scholarships/grants offered:* Pell, SEOG, state scholarships/grants, private scholarships, the school's own gift aid. *Loan aid offered:* Direct Subsidized Stafford, Direct Unsubsidized Stafford, Direct PLUS, Federal Perkins. Federal Work-Study Program available. Institutional employment available. Applicants will be notified of awards on a rolling basis beginning on or about March 15. Off-campus job opportunities are good.

## FROM THE ADMISSIONS OFFICE

"Sonoma State University occupies 275 acres in the beautiful wine country of Sonoma County, in northern California. Located at the foot of the Sonoma hills, the campus is an hour's drive north of San Francisco and centrally located between the Pacific Ocean to the west and the wine country to the north and east. SSU is deeply committed to the teaching of the liberal arts and sciences. The campus has earned a national reputation as a leader in integrating the use of technology into its curriculum. Within its 32 academic departments, SSU awards bachelor's degrees in 41 areas of specialization and master's degrees in 14 areas. In addition, the university offers a joint master's degree in mathematics with San Francisco State University. The campus ushered in the 21st century with the opening of a new library and technology center, the Jean and Charles Schulz Information Center."

## SELECTIVITY

| | |
|---|---:|
| Admissions Rating | 71 |
| # of applicants | 5,006 |
| % of applicants accepted | 92 |
| % of acceptees attending | 23 |

### FRESHMAN PROFILE

| | |
|---|---:|
| Range SAT Verbal | 460-570 |
| Average SAT Verbal | 514 |
| Range SAT Math | 470-570 |
| Average SAT Math | 516 |
| Minimum TOEFL | 500 |
| Average HS GPA | 3.1 |
| % graduated top 10% of class | 11 |
| % graduated top 25% of class | 38 |
| % graduated top 50% of class | 77 |

### DEADLINES

| | |
|---|---:|
| Priority admission | 11/30 |
| Regular admission | 1/31 |
| Nonfall registration? | yes |

## FINANCIAL FACTS

| | |
|---|---:|
| Financial Aid Rating | 84 |
| Out-of-state tuition | $7,380 |
| Room and board | $6,921 |
| Books and supplies | $846 |
| Required fees | $2,032 |
| % frosh receiving aid | 34 |
| % undergrads receiving aid | 37 |
| Avg frosh grant | $1,200 |
| Avg frosh loan | $2,454 |

# SOUTHERN METHODIST UNIVERSITY

PO Box 750296, Dallas, TX 75275-0296 • Admissions: 214-768-2058 • Fax: 214-768-2507

## CAMPUS LIFE

| | |
|---|---|
| Quality of Life Rating | 91 |
| Type of school | private |
| Affiliation | Methodist |
| Environment | suburban |

### STUDENTS

| | |
|---|---|
| Total undergrad enrollment | 6,210 |
| % male/female | 46/54 |
| % from out of state | 36 |
| % from public high school | 61 |
| % live on campus | 48 |
| % in (# of) fraternities | 37 (15) |
| % in (# of) sororities | 38 (12) |
| % African American | 6 |
| % Asian | 7 |
| % Caucasian | 78 |
| % Hispanic | 9 |
| % international | 5 |
| # of countries represented | 92 |

### SURVEY SAYS . . .
Beautiful campus
Students love Dallas, TX
Great off-campus food
Campus easy to get around
Great computer facilities
Student publications are ignored
Students aren't religious
Lousy food on campus

## ACADEMICS

| | |
|---|---|
| Academic Rating | 82 |
| Calendar | semester |
| Student/faculty ratio | 12:1 |
| Profs interesting rating | 88 |
| Profs accessible rating | 95 |
| Avg lab size | 10-19 students |
| Avg reg class size | 10-19 students |

### MOST POPULAR MAJORS
Finance
Marketing/marketing management
Psychology

## STUDENTS SPEAK OUT

### Academics
Many students tell us they chose Southern Methodist because of its "academic experience." SMU has bragging rights in many areas; some of the highlights include their business and management programs housed within the nationally recognized Cox School of Business, as well as other pre-professional programs. Critiques of SMU's faculty ran the gamut; however, there was a common theme of "close interaction between students and faculty." Professors as well as administrators are "genuinely devoted" and "easily accessible." For students interested in fine arts, the Meadows School "is incredible and isolated from the rest of the school." Another strength at SMU is the "very proactive" career center with its "strong ties to local industry." One journalism student tells us, "We take tons of trips to Dallas media companies and meet lots of professionals, finding many opportunities for internships." Additionally, the "international office is excellent," managing to send close to one-third of students to foreign lands. The administration "actively seeks the voice of the students," prompting comments like, "It is the students who run the university, not as much the administration." The administration could be accused of being helpful to the point of "babying" students: "If there is a problem, SMU will throw money at it until it goes away."

### Life
Social life equals Greek life at SMU, so much so that one student advises prospective freshmen to "be Greek, or don't go at all." In the sea of fraternity and sorority jerseys, many students point out the positive aspects of the robust Greek system, including "a strong sense of campus community." This community is also known as a "socialite breeding ground" where "you've never seen so many BMWs in [your] life," and "'Your father is a CEO of what?' " is a well-worn pickup line. Though "football isn't popular, tailgating is," and other teams, including men's soccer, have attracted a healthy following as of late. Dallas "is the perfect environment for a university," with "the campus only 5 to 10 minutes away from the downtown district of museums, jazz, clubs, and bars." Though students write that "plenty of alternatives to drinking" exist, community service organizations seem to be one of the few options.

### Student Body
Students tell us at SMU "you see as many Prada backpacks as Jansport." One student claims, "Generally, it's like living amongst Barbie dolls." Many tend to put "social life ahead of academic career," meaning they "spend more time making sure they look good for class than preparing for it." Generalizations aside, another student points out, "If you can get past the stereotypes, you can meet so many great people who are very different from yourself." Among the "generally conservative" population, some "artsy" and "very eclectic students" can be found, but only a "tiny number of politically active people and intellectuals" manage to survive. Though "minority students are definitely marginalized," the university is "working to create a more open and diverse environment, and making good progress." One undergraduate enjoys hanging out with her "diverse group of friends from all over the U.S. and the world."

# SOUTHERN METHODIST UNIVERSITY

FINANCIAL AID: 214-768-3417 • E-MAIL: UGADMISSION@SMU.EDU • WEBSITE: WWW.SMU.EDU

## ADMISSIONS

*Very important factors considered include:* essays, recommendations, secondary school record, standardized test scores. *Important factors considered include:* character/personal qualities, class rank, extracurricular activities, talent/ability, volunteer work, work experience. *Other factors considered include:* alumni/ae relation, interview. SAT I or ACT required. TOEFL required of all international applicants. High school diploma is required and GED is not accepted. *High school units required/recommended:* 15 total required; 4 English required, 3 math required, 4 math recommended, 3 science required, 4 science recommended, 2 science lab required, 3 science lab recommended, 2 foreign language required, 3 foreign language recommended, 1 social studies required, 2 social studies recommended, 2 history required, 3 history recommended.

### The Inside Word

SMU's School of the Arts is one of the best in the country, and applicants face a very competitive admissions process. The university in general is not quite as selective, but the expectations are high enough so that average students with academic inconsistencies or weak test scores can expect to encounter a rocky road to admission.

## FINANCIAL AID

*Students should submit:* FAFSA. The Princeton Review suggests that all financial aid forms be submitted as soon as possible after January 1. *Need-based scholarships/grants offered:* Pell, SEOG, state scholarships/grants, private scholarships, the school's own gift aid. *Loan aid offered:* FFEL Subsidized Stafford, FFEL Unsubsidized Stafford, FFEL PLUS, Federal Perkins, state loans, college/university loans from institutional funds. Federal Work-Study Program available. Institutional employment available. Applicants will be notified of awards on a rolling basis beginning on or about March 15. Off-campus job opportunities are excellent.

## FROM THE ADMISSIONS OFFICE

"At SMU, you'll enjoy The Education of Your Life and the Life of Your Education. More than 80 challenging academic majors are offered in small classes taught by professors recognized for their teaching and research. Top students in the sciences can participate in joint programs with UT—Southwestern Medical Center at Dallas. Opportunities abound for study abroad, internships, and undergraduate research, along with participation in the new Honors Program. SMU underscores its commitment to outstanding instruction through the Center for Teaching Excellence and the new Academy of Distinguished Teachers. Outside of class, SMU sponsors more than 175 student organizations, 450 artistic performances, and lecture programs enabling students to interact with world leaders. Recently SMU has added 14 new or renovated facilities, 171 new scholarships, and 16 new academic positions. SMU welcomes a diverse student body from all 50 states, the District of Columbia, and 86 foreign countries, and fosters cross-cultural understanding through campus programs. In addition, SMU's tuition ranks among the lowest compared with private institutions nationwide. Find out more at www.smu.edu/admission."

## SELECTIVITY

| | |
|---|---|
| Admissions Rating | 82 |
| # of applicants | 6,152 |
| % of applicants accepted | 66 |
| % of acceptees attending | 34 |
| # accepting a place on wait list | 353 |
| % admitted from wait list | 16 |

### FRESHMAN PROFILE

| | |
|---|---|
| Range SAT Verbal | 540-630 |
| Range SAT Math | 550-650 |
| Range ACT Composite | 23-28 |
| Minimum TOEFL | 550 |
| Average HS GPA | 3.5 |
| % graduated top 10% of class | 35 |
| % graduated top 25% of class | 65 |
| % graduated top 50% of class | 91 |

### DEADLINES

| | |
|---|---|
| Priority admission | 1/15 |
| Regular notification | 3/15 |
| Nonfall registration? | yes |

### APPLICANTS ALSO LOOK AT AND OFTEN PREFER
Vanderbilt
U of Southern California
### AND SOMETIMES PREFER
UT Austin
Trinity U
U of Miami
Tulane
### AND RARELY PREFER
TCU
Baylor
U of Colorado at Boulder
U of Arizona

## FINANCIAL FACTS

| | |
|---|---|
| Financial Aid Rating | 90 |
| Tuition | $19,466 |
| Room and board | $7,954 |
| Books and supplies | $600 |
| Required fees | $2,476 |
| % frosh receiving aid | 37 |
| % undergrads receiving aid | 37 |

# SOUTHWESTERN UNIVERSITY

ADMISSIONS OFFICE, PO BOX 770, GEORGETOWN, TX 78627-0770 • ADMISSIONS: 512-863-1200 • FAX: 512-863-9601

## CAMPUS LIFE

| Quality of Life Rating | 81 |
|---|---|
| Type of school | private |
| Affiliation | Methodist |
| Environment | suburban |

### STUDENTS

| Total undergrad enrollment | 1,266 |
|---|---|
| % male/female | 41/59 |
| % from out of state | 9 |
| % from public high school | 84 |
| % live on campus | 80 |
| % in (# of) fraternities | 34 (3) |
| % in (# of) sororities | 33 (4) |
| % African American | 3 |
| % Asian | 3 |
| % Caucasian | 78 |
| % Hispanic | 13 |
| # of countries represented | 10 |

### SURVEY SAYS . . .
Theater is hot
Frats and sororities dominate social scene
No one cheats
Athletic facilities are great
Registration is a pain
Intercollegiate sports unpopular or nonexistent
Class discussions encouraged
Lousy off-campus food

## ACADEMICS

| Academic Rating | 84 |
|---|---|
| Calendar | semester |
| Student/faculty ratio | 10:1 |
| Profs interesting rating | 91 |
| Profs accessible rating | 92 |
| % profs teaching UG courses | 100 |
| Avg lab size | under 10 students |
| Avg reg class size | 10-19 students |

### MOST POPULAR MAJORS
Business/commerce
Communications studies/speech communication and rhetoric
Biology/biological sciences

## STUDENTS SPEAK OUT

### Academics

Students laud the personal touches that distinguish the Southwestern University academic experience. "For anyone who doesn't want to get lost in the crowd," writes one student, "this is the school for you. The environment may seem like you're in a 'bubble,' but the small population allows students to really get to know their professors, and vice versa." Agrees another, "Southwestern is definitely a school that prides itself in the concept of personal interaction. I have professors that call me when I am absent from class! I wouldn't get that if I had attended a larger, less personal school." Students also appreciate the sense that they have a hand in shaping the university's future; notes one, "Southwestern University is continually developing and redefining its core values and goals. There are so many ways for students to get involved in planning the future of this school." Another adds, "The administration, professors, and other staff members are very open to comments and help outside the classroom." Students approve of the "writing intensive" core curriculum, an "excellent" study abroad program (nearly 50 percent of the students here spend time overseas), and the Brown Symposium, a two-day series of seminars during spring semester for which classes are suspended and scholars from around the world deliver lectures and lead discussions.

### Life

Students at Southwestern report a heavy workload. Writes one, "The classes here are hard but not impossible. A fellow student wrote in the campus newspaper, the Megaphone, that after a four-year stint here, you'd be well prepared for the rigors of hell. Maybe. Come here and be prepared to study." Undergrads do find time to unwind, however, most often at one of the Greek houses. "Greek life is the outlet many people [resort] to in order to have fun," report many students here. The town of Georgetown offers little help, as "it is not a college town at all—to find food after 9 P.M. we drive to Round Rock, which is about 20 minutes away." For a really big time, students head to Austin, about 30 minutes off by automobile, where they go clubbing. "Austin is full of many music venues where promising new artists as well as well-known bands can be seen performing for relatively low prices," writes one student. Others point out that a trip to the capital offers the opportunity to hang out with UT undergrads. Opportunities for sports and other outdoor activities exist, with students telling us they enjoy camping, canoeing, and caving on weekends. Many volunteer for community service, often through one of the campus' religious organizations.

### Student Body

The students of Southwestern "get along very well for the most part. But why wouldn't they? It's a fairly homogenous group. Mostly white, upper-middle-class, Daddy's-little-girl Texans. Everyone likes to think they're a liberal, but when confronted with diversity of any kind, they find it weird." Students have a distinctly Texan attitude, believing that "Texas is the entire world and they need never leave it. On move-in day, one parent told me that I was 'practically a foreign exchange student'—I'm from New Mexico! It can be an okay experience, but it will be different for non-Texans." There are "a few PCU types" mixed into the crowd, "but generally the students are willing to get involved without becoming cause-heads. Most students here are extremely friendly and accepting of who you are." Sums up one undergrad: "SU is a very small liberal arts college—1,200 students, if that. [Actually, the official undergraduate enrollment is a little more than 1,250.] About a thousand of us live on campus. Sure, there are assholes, and overly wealthy snobs, and drunks, and stoners, and Jesus freaks, and lesbians, etc., but you're gonna find that on any campus, except perhaps Bob Jones U. The point is, all that doesn't matter. Everyone, with very few exceptions, gets along fine with everyone else."

# SOUTHWESTERN UNIVERSITY

FINANCIAL AID: 512-863-1259 • E-MAIL: ADMISSION@SOUTHWESTERN.EDU • WEBSITE: WWW.SOUTHWESTERN.EDU

## ADMISSIONS
*Very important factors considered include:* secondary school record. *Important factors considered include:* class rank, essays, extracurricular activities, interview, recommendations, standardized test scores. *Other factors considered include:* alumni/ae relation, character/personal qualities, geographical residence, religious affiliation/commitment, talent/ability. SAT I or ACT required. TOEFL required of all international applicants. High school diploma or GED is required. *High school units required/recommended:* 17 total recommended; 4 English recommended, 4 math recommended, 3 science recommended, 2 science lab recommended, 2 foreign language recommended, 3 social studies recommended, 3 history recommended, 1 elective recommended.

## The Inside Word
Southwestern is one of the best "sleepers" in the nation. Admissions standards are high, but they would be even more so if more people knew of this place. Academic excellence abounds, the administration is earnest and helpful, and the school has attracted national recognition. If you could thrive in a small-town, close-knit environment, Southwestern definitely deserves a look.

## FINANCIAL AID
*Students should submit:* FAFSA, institution's own financial aid form. The Princeton Review suggests that all financial aid forms be submitted as soon as possible after January 1. *Need-based scholarships/grants offered:* Pell, SEOG, state scholarships/grants, private scholarships, the school's own gift aid. *Loan aid offered:* FFEL Subsidized Stafford, FFEL Unsubsidized Stafford, FFEL PLUS, Federal Perkins, state loans, college/university loans from institutional funds, Gold and Silver Star private educational loan program. Federal Work-Study Program available. Institutional employment available. Applicants will be notified of awards on a rolling basis beginning on or about February 15. Off-campus job opportunities are good.

## FROM THE ADMISSIONS OFFICE
"On the outskirts of Texas's vibrant capital city of Austin is Southwestern University, the state's first institution of higher learning. Southwestern is committed to helping students achieve personal and professional success as well as a passion for life-long learning. The Paideia Program, funded in 2002 by an $8.5 million grant, is a distinctive new option for select students beginning the sophomore year that provides opportunities to compare, contrast, and integrate knowledge and skills gained in various areas of study. In addition to their regular studies, students work with the same Paideia Professor over a three-year period in seminar groups of ten. They work to discover the powerful connections between Southwestern's rigorous academic experience and the dynamic programs available outside the classroom—through leadership, service, intercultural learning, and collaborative research or creative works. All Southwestern students discover that a premiere liberal arts education leads to high acceptance rates into prestigious graduate and professional programs and careers right out of college. Southwestern is today what it has always been: a highly personal liberal arts experience that equips students with the strengths they need to develop fulfilling lives."

### SELECTIVITY

| | |
|---|---|
| Admissions Rating | 84 |
| # of applicants | 1,572 |
| % of applicants accepted | 61 |
| % of acceptees attending | 36 |
| # accepting a place on wait list | 43 |
| % admitted from wait list | 26 |
| # of early decision applicants | 177 |
| % accepted early decision | 75 |

### FRESHMAN PROFILE
| | |
|---|---|
| Range SAT Verbal | 570-660 |
| Average SAT Verbal | 621 |
| Range SAT Math | 570-670 |
| Average SAT Math | 615 |
| Range ACT Composite | 24-29 |
| Average ACT Composite | 26 |
| Minimum TOEFL | 570 |
| Average HS GPA | 3.5 |
| % graduated top 10% of class | 60 |
| % graduated top 25% of class | 91 |
| % graduated top 50% of class | 99 |

### DEADLINES
| | |
|---|---|
| Early decision | 11/1 |
| Early decision notification | 12/1 |
| Priority admission | 1/15 |
| Regular admission | 2/15 |
| Regular notification | 4/15 |

### APPLICANTS ALSO LOOK AT AND OFTEN PREFER
Rice
Vanderbilt

### AND SOMETIMES PREFER
Rhodes
Texas A&M
Trinity U
Tulane, UT Austin

### AND RARELY PREFER
Austin College, Baylor
Southern Methodist
TCU

### FINANCIAL FACTS

| | |
|---|---|
| Financial Aid Rating | 88 |
| Tuition | $18,870 |
| Room and board | $6,540 |
| Books and supplies | $700 |
| % frosh receiving aid | 56 |
| % undergrads receiving aid | 51 |
| Avg frosh grant | $12,116 |
| Avg frosh loan | $3,008 |

# SPELMAN COLLEGE

350 SPELMAN LANE SOUTH WEST, ATLANTA, GA 30314 • ADMISSIONS: 800-982-2411 • FAX: 404-215-7788

## CAMPUS LIFE

| Quality of Life Rating | 82 |
|---|---|
| Type of school | private |
| Environment | urban |

### STUDENTS
| | |
|---|---|
| Total undergrad enrollment | 1,899 |
| % from out of state | 75 |
| % from public high school | 84 |
| % live on campus | 62 |
| % in (# of) sororities | 1 (4) |
| % African American | 100 |
| % international | 3 |

### SURVEY SAYS . . .
Theater is hot
Student publications are ignored
Students don't get along with local community
Class discussions are rare
High cost of living
Very little beer drinking
Lab facilities are great
Library needs improving
Very little hard liquor
Athletic facilities need improving

## ACADEMICS

| Academic Rating | 83 |
|---|---|
| Calendar | semester |
| Profs interesting rating | 94 |
| Profs accessible rating | 88 |
| % profs teaching UG courses | 100 |

## STUDENTS SPEAK OUT

### Academics
Students at historically black all-women's Spelman College feel that the experience here is not simply academic in nature. "Attending Spelman College," explains an undergraduate, "is not just an excellent undergraduate experience, but also a lifetime of memories built in four years. It is true that upon entering Spelman you are a girl; through your duration at Spelman you become a Spelman woman; and at graduation you become a successful, black Spelman graduate. All of which are impressive titles that Spelmanites carry through their life." Students are aware of Spelman's stellar reputation; indeed, most chose the school because it is known for producing successful graduates. As one undergrad told us, "If you graduate a Spelmanite, 9 times out of 10, you will be successful. The staff is dedicated to getting you into medical school, law school, graduate school, or a job. You will not have to do it all by yourself. Many prestigious medical schools, graduate schools, law schools, and companies recruit at Spelman." Although small, Spelman provides access to a wide variety of studies through the Atlanta University Center (AUC), a five-college consortium that creates "a big school's library, activities, etc., all because of shared resources. We are also able to take classes at any of the undergraduate schools within the AUC." A new science facility "is equipped to bring science majors into the new millennium in full force," thereby eliminating one of the school's Achilles heels. The quantifiable results here are undeniable; one-third of Spelman grads hold degrees in the sciences. Students gush that their "professors are extremely dedicated to their students; they know their field and teach it to their students well. They are very open and pretty easy to reach."

### Life
Undergraduates report that "campus life at Spelman is somewhat dead on the weekends; however, that's because there are five other schools in the AUC (Spelman, Morehouse College, Clark, Atlanta University, Morris Brown College, and the Interdenominational Theological Center), and since we're all within a 3- to 15-minute walk, it's not hard to find something to do." Undergrads want you to know that going to an all-women's college does not mean you must lead a cloistered existence; explains one student, "Since Spelman is located in the Atlanta University Center, we have the opportunity to interact with about 10,000 students each day. Ladies, a large number of those students are men. Contrary to popular belief, we are not surrounded by women all day. As a matter of fact, I see more minority men living in Atlanta and going to Spelman than all of my friends who attended schools at home in New York or in that area." Greek parties at Spelman and Morehouse are generally big events; also popular are extracurricular clubs, particularly those involved with community service and leadership organizations. Students love greater Atlanta, where "there is always something to do"; Spelman women love the nightclub scene as well as movies, the theater, restaurants, and museums.

### Student Body
The women of Spelman agree that "the concept of 'Spelman Sisterhood' cannot be easily explained. However, once you step on our campus, it is very apparent. We are taught to treat each other like a family; we may not always get along, we may have our differences, and we may not always like each other, but we do love each other." Undergraduates are typically "high achievers, and we all have a somewhat high level of competition amongst ourselves. It is not a cutthroat type of competition, but one that encourages our fellow sisters to do and be our best at all times." The typical Spelman student is religious (church services are a regular part of most students' lives), socially conservative, and politically liberal.

# SPELMAN COLLEGE

FINANCIAL AID: 404-681-3643 • E-MAIL: ADMISS@SPELMAN.EDU • WEBSITE: WWW.SPELMAN.EDU

## ADMISSIONS

SAT I or ACT required. High school diploma or GED is required. *High school units required/recommended:* 15 total required; 4 English required, 2 math required, 3 math recommended, 2 science required, 3 science recommended, 2 foreign language required, 3 foreign language recommended, 2 social studies required, 2 elective required.

### The Inside Word

No historically black college in the country has a more competitive admissions process than Spelman, and on top of this, application totals were up 25 percent last season. Successful candidates show strong academic records with challenging course loads and solid grades. Applicant evaluation here is very personal; it is quite important to show depth of character and social consciousness.

## FINANCIAL AID

*Students should submit:* FAFSA, institution's own financial aid form. The Princeton Review suggests that all financial aid forms be submitted as soon as possible after January 1. *Loan aid offered:* FFEL Subsidized Stafford, FFEL PLUS. Federal Work-Study Program available. Institutional employment available. Applicants will be notified of awards on or about April 2. Off-campus job opportunities are fair.

## FROM THE ADMISSIONS OFFICE

"As an outstanding historically black college for women, Spelman strives for academic excellence in liberal arts education. This predominantly residential private college provides students with an academic climate conducive to the full development of their intellectual and leadership potential. The college is a member of the Atlanta University Center consortium, and Spelman students enjoy the benefits of a small college while having access to the resources of the other four participating institutions. The purpose extends beyond intellectual development and professional career preparation of students. It seeks to develop the total person. The college provides an academic and social environment that strengthens those qualities that enable women to be self-confident as well as culturally and spiritually enriched. This environment attempts to instill in students both an appreciation for the multicultural communities of the world and a sense of responsibility for bringing about positive change in those communities."

### SELECTIVITY

| | |
|---|---|
| Admissions Rating | 89 |

#### FRESHMAN PROFILE
| | |
|---|---|
| Range SAT Verbal | 500-600 |
| Average SAT Verbal | 549 |
| Range SAT Math | 500-599 |
| Average SAT Math | 524 |
| Range ACT Composite | 21-24 |
| Average ACT Composite | 22 |
| Average HS GPA | 3.1 |

#### DEADLINES
| | |
|---|---|
| Early decision | 11/15 |
| Early decision notification | 12/31 |
| Regular admission | 2/1 |
| Regular notification | 4/1 |
| Nonfall registration? | yes |

#### APPLICANTS ALSO LOOK AT
**AND OFTEN PREFER**
Georgia Tech.
**AND SOMETIMES PREFER**
Howard
Hampton
Clark Atlanta
Tuskegee
Florida A&M
**AND RARELY PREFER**
U. Maryland—College Park
Emory
U. Georgia

### FINANCIAL FACTS

| | |
|---|---|
| Financial Aid Rating | 87 |
| Tuition | $9,250 |
| Room and board | $6,560 |
| Books and supplies | $750 |
| Required fees | $1,600 |

# STANFORD UNIVERSITY

520 LASUEN MALL, OLD UNION 232, STANFORD, CA 94305-3005 • ADMISSIONS: 650-723-2091 • FAX: 650-723-6050

## CAMPUS LIFE

| | |
|---|---|
| Quality of Life Rating | 89 |
| Type of school | private |
| Environment | suburban |

### STUDENTS
| | |
|---|---|
| Total undergrad enrollment | 6,731 |
| % male/female | 52/48 |
| % from out of state | 47 |
| % from public high school | 69 |
| % live on campus | 99 |
| % African American | 10 |
| % Asian | 24 |
| % Caucasian | 48 |
| % Hispanic | 11 |
| % Native American | 2 |
| % international | 5 |

### SURVEY SAYS . . .
Registration is a breeze
Political activism is hot
Everyone loves the Cardinal
Student publications are popular
Ethnic diversity on campus
Students don't like Stanford, CA
(Almost) no one listens to college radio
Very little drug use
Students are cliquish

## ACADEMICS

| | |
|---|---|
| Academic Rating | 92 |
| Calendar | quarter |
| Student/faculty ratio | 7:1 |
| Profs interesting rating | 93 |
| Profs accessible rating | 86 |
| Avg lab size | 10-19 students |
| Avg reg class size | 10-19 students |

### MOST POPULAR MAJORS
Biology/biological sciences
Economics
Computer science

## STUDENTS SPEAK OUT

### Academics
Students choose Stanford University for its unique blend of "world class" academics, "zesty spirit," "laid-back lifestyle," and "beautiful weather." Undergrads agree that Stanford lives up to its reputation as "an amazingly hard academic institution with a laid-back atmosphere" teeming with "brilliant and down-to-earth" professors. Stanford will particularly appeal to those looking for a serious school that "doesn't take itself too seriously," as illustrated by a freshman who recounts, "My intro to psych prof spent the last day of class lip synching to The Wiz and dancing around in cowboy boots, and giving everyone in the class hugs as they left from the final. He may be a little over the top, but he loves teaching, just as all Stanford profs do." On that note, students say the faculty is "approachable" and "often have opportunities for you to get involved in research." Those looking for a supportive, small-college atmosphere, however, should consider other private universities. "There is very little hand holding" at Stanford. Many complain that the required first-year humanities program is "excruciating." Underclassmen tell us that newer programs like freshmen and sophomore seminars and "free summer Sophomore College" provide new students with "small classes and generous interaction with celebrated faculty members."

### Life
"Life is generally laid-back" at Stanford, but it's not exactly an afternoon at the beach. "Over-commitment is a huge issue in that students are academically oriented and then use up the rest of their energy reserves on volunteer work, musical and theater productions, [or] athletics," explains one student. "Everybody is involved in everything," sighs another. While some praise the active lifestyle, others feel "too many of the students are so focused on their work that they don't even care to meet new people or to socialize." When not packing their schedules with extracurricular activities, Stanford undergrads like to "study while sunbathing," "go to Stanford basketball games, fountain hop, play Doom and Snood, listen to MP3s," "hang out at the Coffee House," "go to San Francisco, go out to eat, go to the Pez Museum, go for hikes in the foothills, go to the beach," and "engage in [other] outdoor activities." In addition, since 96 percent of Stanford undergrads live on campus and the administration "is very lenient about the drinking policy," it's not a surprise that undergrads attend "a lot of parties on campus."

### Student Body
"I get the feeling that everyone here is really intelligent and driven, but for some reason, pretending not to be," writes one astute undergrad. Indeed, Stanford students like to retain the image that "kids at Stanford are running around with surfboards saying 'dude' all the time," though they're in actuality "bright people with goals and drive," "pre-professionals," "current and future Olympians," and "academic Gods." The result is a campus of "closet studiers" who act like ducks on a pond: "serene on top, pedaling like crazy below." Though Stanford "does a good job of keeping its student body diverse" and "ethnic centers are very active," most say that there are "class, racial, and ethnic divisions." "I feel as though ethnic groups are highly segregated," opines one student, while another explains, "Though it is easy to meet people from different backgrounds, there is a certain tendency to form cliques. One must actively set out to interact in order to make the most of this diversity."

484 ■ THE BEST 351 COLLEGES

# STANFORD UNIVERSITY

FINANCIAL AID: 650-723-3058 • E-MAIL: ADMISSION@STANFORD.EDU • WEBSITE: HTTP://ADMISSION.STANFORD.EDU

## ADMISSIONS

*Very important factors considered include:* character/personal qualities, class rank, essays, recommendations, secondary school record, standardized test scores. *Important factors considered include:* extracurricular activities, talent/ability. *Other factors considered include:* alumni/ae relation, geographical residence, minority status, volunteer work, work experience. SAT I or ACT required; SAT I preferred; SAT II also recommended. High school diploma or GED is required. *High school units required/recommended:* 20 total recommended; 4 English recommended, 4 math recommended, 3 science recommended, 3 science lab recommended, 3 foreign language recommended, 2 social studies recommended, 1 history recommended.

### The Inside Word

Not only is Stanford a pinnacle of academic excellence, but among the nation's ultra-selective universities it is one of the most compassionate toward students, both those who attend and those who aspire to attend. It isn't easy for an admissions staff to be warm and caring when your reputation is based in part on how many candidates you say "no" to. In our opinion, Stanford is the best of the best in this regard. Students who haven't devoted themselves to excellence in the same fashion that Stanford itself has are not likely to meet with success in gaining admission.

## FINANCIAL AID

*Students should submit:* FAFSA, CSS/Financial Aid PROFILE. The Princeton Review suggests that all financial aid forms be submitted as soon as possible after January 1. *Need-based scholarships/grants offered:* Pell, SEOG, state scholarships/grants, private scholarships, the school's own gift aid. *Loan aid offered:* FFEL Subsidized Stafford, FFEL Unsubsidized Stafford, FFEL PLUS, Federal Perkins, GATE Loans. Federal Work-Study Program available. Institutional employment available. Applicants will be notified of awards on a rolling basis beginning on or about April 2. Off-campus job opportunities are excellent.

## FROM THE ADMISSIONS OFFICE

"Stanford students are risk-takers who set high standards, show initiative, and have the courage to push themselves. We offer such students renowned yet approachable faculty members, extraordinary academic resources, and a living and learning environment that rewards those who seek excellence in everything they do. From their first days on campus, Stanford students can explore virtually unlimited opportunities that will fuel their intellectual passions and help them fulfill their academic and personal promise."

## SELECTIVITY

| | |
|---|---|
| Admissions Rating | 99 |
| # of applicants | 18,599 |
| % of applicants accepted | 13 |
| % of acceptees attending | 69 |
| # accepting a place on wait list | 592 |
| % admitted from wait list | 9 |
| # of early decision applicants | 2,384 |
| % accepted early decision | 23 |

### FRESHMAN PROFILE

| | |
|---|---|
| Range SAT Verbal | 660-760 |
| Range SAT Math | 690-780 |
| Range ACT Composite | 28-33 |
| Average HS GPA | 3.9 |
| % graduated top 10% of class | 88 |
| % graduated top 25% of class | 97 |
| % graduated top 50% of class | 99 |

### DEADLINES

| | |
|---|---|
| Single-choice early action | 11/1 |
| Early action notification | 12/15 |
| Regular admission | 12/15 |
| Regular notification | 4/1 |

## FINANCIAL FACTS

| | |
|---|---|
| Financial Aid Rating | 85 |
| Tuition | $27,204 |
| Room and board | $8,680 |
| Books and supplies | $1,155 |
| % frosh receiving aid | 47 |
| % undergrads receiving aid | 44 |
| Avg frosh grant | $25,334 |

# STATE UNIVERSITY OF NEW YORK AT ALBANY

1400 WASHINGTON AVENUE, ALBANY, NY 12222 • ADMISSIONS: 518-442-5435 • FAX: 518-442-5383

## CAMPUS LIFE

| | |
|---|---|
| Quality of Life Rating | 68 |
| Type of school | public |
| Environment | suburban |

### STUDENTS

| | |
|---|---|
| Total undergrad enrollment | 11,953 |
| % male/female | 50/50 |
| % from out of state | 5 |
| % live on campus | 58 |
| % in (# of) fraternities | 4 (19) |
| % in (# of) sororities | 5 (15) |
| % African American | 9 |
| % Asian | 6 |
| % Caucasian | 65 |
| % Hispanic | 7 |
| % international | 2 |
| # of countries represented | 87 |

### SURVEY SAYS . . .
Class discussions are rare
Students don't get along with local community
Students are cliquish
Ethnic diversity on campus
Large classes
Unattractive campus

## ACADEMICS

| | |
|---|---|
| Academic Rating | 70 |
| Calendar | semester |
| Student/faculty ratio | 21:1 |
| Profs interesting rating | 89 |
| Profs accessible rating | 88 |
| % profs teaching UG courses | 91 |
| % classes taught by TAs | 13 |
| Avg lab size | 10-19 students |
| Avg reg class size | 20-29 students |

### MOST POPULAR MAJORS
Business administration/management
English language and literature
Psychology

## STUDENTS SPEAK OUT

### Academics

SUNY—Albany lures students with an affordable, quality education—an uncommon combination these days. The psychology, business, and English programs are popular. Unfortunately, these departments are often very large, which causes a number of problems. A senior business administration major voices, "Many of the professors are disinterested and lack substance. It just seems as though a substantial portion of the faculty doesn't care about the student body." SUNY—Albany is a research university. Accordingly, professors "don't want to teach and quite a few don't even know how to teach." Students also complain that classes are impersonal. "My name is my social security number," one junior writes, and in popular majors, class sizes do not decrease in upper-level courses. One senior theater major points out that "the [classes] tend to be different from department to department. Some are huge, cold, and impersonal, while others are small and extremely good about giving attention to the individual." Science students love the new research library, and many students rave about the design of the campus. "Everything is in a rectangular area so it's easy to get from class to class," writes one. The administration takes some serious lumps. "Class registration is preposterous. There are too many students and not enough classes or room in classes," one junior psychology major writes. Advisors do not fare well either. A disappointed psychology major comments, "It is nearly impossible to get an appointment with my advisor. He's always too busy." Another adds, "I don't know my advisor's name. I have never met [him] because I've always seen grad students or associates." Despite those disillusioned by little student-faculty interaction, for many students Albany "is a good school if you like big schools."

### Life

Students at SUNY—Albany know that studying is only one ingredient in the smorgasbord that is a rewarding college experience. "We're not a party school. We just have lots of parties, drinking, and drugs. Okay, I guess we are a party school," one senior psychology major admits. "Students care more about partying than studying. If they have to choose between studying or going out and getting drunk, the latter usually prevails." Another senior adds that students only make an effort "when it comes to getting drunk. They spend all night trying to accomplish that." On the upside, downtown Albany, though "always cold and gray," provides "many entertainment opportunities." The area contains numerous inexpensive bars and clubs, and "anyone with a library card could get into [them]." Thursday, Friday, and Saturday are popular party nights, though students agree, "there are parties almost every night." Students complain about the cafeteria food and the lack of parking. "If you have a class after 9 A.M., it's difficult to find a spot." The school also needs to improve a few facilities. One senior math major writes, "Many of the classrooms are disgusting. Walls are dirty, desks are small, and the blackboards don't erase."

### Student Body

SUNY—Albany is a diverse campus where students "all get along like pigs in a blanket." The university is popular among students who reside in the Northeast because of its central location. A junior criminal justice major writes that "SUNY—Albany is one of the few schools where you can walk around campus and feel like you're in Beverly Hills, then in a minute feel like you're in Flatbush." GDIs do not hold the Greek system in high regard. While students are generally friendly, many of them form cliques "like in high school," leading to some campus tension. Nevertheless, one junior psychology major writes, "Everyone has a generally friendly attitude."

# STATE UNIVERSITY OF NEW YORK AT ALBANY

FINANCIAL AID: 518-442-5757 • E-MAIL: UGADMISSIONS@ALBANY.EDU • WEBSITE: WWW.ALBANY.EDU

## ADMISSIONS
*Very important factors considered include:* character/personal qualities, class rank, secondary school record, standardized test scores. *Important factors considered include:* essays, recommendations. *Other factors considered include:* extracurricular activities, geographical residence, minority status, talent/ability, volunteer work. SAT I or ACT required; SAT I preferred. TOEFL required of all international applicants. High school diploma or GED is required. *High school units required/recommended:* 18 total required; 4 English required, 2 math required, 4 math recommended, 2 science required, 3 science recommended, 2 science lab required, 3 science lab recommended, 3 foreign language recommended, 3 social studies required, 2 history required, 5 elective required.

## The Inside Word
While the SUNY system's budgetary woes have abated to a degree, funding uncertainties continue to be a problem. Applications and standards are on the rise. Albany is the third most selective SUNY campus. Perhaps the university's status as the training camp site for the New York Giants will bring both revenue and facilities to aid a turnaround. Without increased private funding, Albany is likely to remain a relatively easy path into a SUNY university center.

## FINANCIAL AID
*Students should submit:* FAFSA. New York State residents will receive an Express TAP Application one month after filing FAFSA. The Princeton Review suggests that all financial aid forms be submitted as soon as possible after January 1. *Need-based scholarships/grants offered:* Pell, SEOG, state scholarships/grants, private scholarships, the school's own gift aid. *Loan aid offered:* FFEL Subsidized Stafford, FFEL Unsubsidized Stafford, FFEL PLUS, Federal Perkins, college/university loans from institutional funds. Federal Work-Study Program available. Institutional employment available. Applicants will be notified of awards on a rolling basis beginning on or about April 1. Off-campus job opportunities are good.

## FROM THE ADMISSIONS OFFICE
"Albany continues to see a growth in the quality of its applicants and has become increasingly selective, with an admission rate of just above 50 percent. Out-of-state and international enrollments are also increasing as metro Albany receives greater national visibility for its educational opportunities. (It's ranked third in the *Places Rated Almanac*.) UAlbany will be the new home of the research and development center of International Sematech North, a consortium of the world leaders in computer chip manufacturing. The Presidential Scholars Program continues to attract top-achieving students, and Project Renaissance, the unique freshman-year experience, also remains a very popular option for students interested in UAlbany's high-quality, affordable college experience."

## SELECTIVITY

| | |
|---|---|
| Admissions Rating | 79 |
| # of applicants | 17,667 |
| % of applicants accepted | 56 |
| % of acceptees attending | 23 |

### FRESHMAN PROFILE
| | |
|---|---|
| Range SAT Verbal | 500-600 |
| Average SAT Verbal | 567 |
| Range SAT Math | 520-610 |
| Average SAT Math | 583 |
| Minimum TOEFL | 550 |
| Average HS GPA | 3.6 |
| % graduated top 10% of class | 16 |
| % graduated top 25% of class | 54 |
| % graduated top 50% of class | 92 |

### DEADLINES
| | |
|---|---|
| Priority admission | 12/1 |
| Regular admission | 3/1 |
| Nonfall registration? | yes |

### APPLICANTS ALSO LOOK AT AND OFTEN PREFER
Cornell U
Binghamton U
**AND SOMETIMES PREFER**
U of Rochester
Fordham
Syracuse
Siena
UMass at Amherst
**AND RARELY PREFER**
Hofstra

## FINANCIAL FACTS

| | |
|---|---|
| Financial Aid Rating | 74 |
| In-state tuition | $3,400 |
| Out-of-state tuition | $8,300 |
| Room and board | $7,052 |
| Books and supplies | $800 |
| Required fees | $1,420 |
| % frosh receiving aid | 54 |
| % undergrads receiving aid | 53 |
| Avg frosh grant | $4,310 |
| Avg frosh loan | $4,113 |

# STATE UNIVERSITY OF NY AT BINGHAMTON

PO Box 6000, Binghamton, NY 13902-6001 • Admissions: 607-777-2171 • Fax: 607-777-4445

## CAMPUS LIFE

| Quality of Life Rating | 75 |
|---|---|
| Type of school | public |
| Affiliation | none |
| Environment | suburban |

### STUDENTS

| Total undergrad enrollment | 10,328 |
|---|---|
| % male/female | 48/52 |
| % from out of state | 4 |
| % from public high school | 87 |
| % live on campus | 57 |
| % in (# of) fraternities | 10 (10) |
| % in (# of) sororities | 10 (10) |
| % African American | 5 |
| % Asian | 17 |
| % Caucasian | 52 |
| % Hispanic | 6 |
| % international | 3 |
| # of countries represented | 85 |

### SURVEY SAYS . . .
Class discussions are rare
Students don't get along with local community
Students are cliquish
Ethnic diversity on campus
Large classes

## ACADEMICS

| Academic Rating | 84 |
|---|---|
| Calendar | semester |
| Student/faculty ratio | 21:1 |
| Profs interesting rating | 91 |
| Profs accessible rating | 88 |
| % profs teaching UG courses | 90 |
| % classes taught by TAs | 10 |
| Avg lab size | 20-29 students |
| Avg reg class size | 10-19 students |

### MOST POPULAR MAJORS
Business administration/management
English language and literature
Psychology

## STUDENTS SPEAK OUT

### Academics
A highly regarded state school, SUNY—Binghamton is said to be "perfect for those looking to get in and out with a good and inexpensive education." Reportedly, students "can experiment with ideas, think freely, and get the tools to expand their view of the world." Professors are respected for their intelligence and prominence in their fields, but in terms of teaching skills, students dream, "Maybe I'll eventually get into a class where I don't have to teach myself." According to some, just enrolling in "the courses you want or need can be nearly impossible." While some characterize the administration as "efficient and friendly," most remain decidedly "dissatisfied" with the top brass. One student tells us, "Getting the answers to questions about your major or any other thing is very difficult."

### Life
The Binghamton experience includes a "politically active campus" amid a "lack of school spirit." One student notes, "There are really no traditions on campus," though the popular pastime of "smoking in nonsmoking buildings" may soon count as one. Free time is filled with "a huge variety of stuff to do, ranging from cultural, religious, and political events, to lots of artsy stuff, to lots of good old-fashioned getting drunk." Since Binghamton is "by no means a party school," social activities centered on something other than alcohol are common. Reports one student, "They have recently begun showing movies in the Union on weekends, along with late-night billiards and bowling." The surrounding city of "Binghamton is not the best of cities. It is, however, cheap and accessible" with "movie theaters, bowling alleys, skating rinks, restaurants, and shopping galore." Though "the 'townies' don't like us very much," the two-dollar cab fare into town keeps student influx high. The campus is "not too country and only a few hours from N.Y.C.," but upperclassmen can hunker down in their widely praised on-campus apartment housing. In summary, a student explains, "Even though it wasn't anyone's first choice, everyone likes it."

### Student Body
SUNY—Binghamton is reportedly home to "a million closet geniuses." A conspicuous segment of the population—who want to achieve good grades and are always pleased with the low price they pay for tuition—is said to be "preoccupied with the latest Gucci and Versace product lines." Regarding students' personal transport, "The cars in the parking lot are worth more than my house." Attracting many students from New York City and Long Island, a rift between down- and up-staters is sometimes apparent, though the majority shares a "typical white middle-class" background. Students believe there is "not much mingling" between racial and ethnic groups; some even report "large racial and ethnic cleavages." One comments, "The many forms of diversity on campus come at the expense of true campus cohesiveness." One gay undergraduate male writes, "I have found the school to be relatively tolerant of my orientation." Tolerance comes with the territory in another's opinion: "New York is a melting pot; therefore, many, if not all, of the students are well aware of the diverse cultures of the world, and this awareness makes them respectful."

# STATE UNIVERSITY OF NEW YORK AT BINGHAMTON

FINANCIAL AID: 607-777-2428 • E-MAIL: ADMIT@BINGHAMTON.EDU • WEBSITE: WWW.BINGHAMTON.EDU

## ADMISSIONS

*Very important factors considered include:* secondary school record, standardized test scores. *Important factors considered include:* class rank, essays, extracurricular activities, minority status, talent/ability. *Other factors considered include:* alumni/ae relation, character/personal qualities, geographical residence, recommendations, state residency, volunteer work, work experience. SAT I or ACT required. TOEFL required of all international applicants. High school diploma or GED is required. *High school units required/recommended:* 16 total required; 4 English required, 3 math required, 4 math recommended, 2 science required, 3 science recommended, 3 foreign language required, 2 social studies required, 3 history recommended.

### The Inside Word

Binghamton's admissions process is highly selective, but fairly simple. Candidates go through a process that first considers academic qualifications, primarily through numbers, and then takes a relatively brief look at other components of the application. Out-of-state enrollment is miniscule for a public university of Binghamton's reputation, but the University's enrollment management strategy includes enhancing efforts to recruit students from further afield.

## FINANCIAL AID

*Students should submit:* FAFSA. The Princeton Review suggests that all financial aid forms be submitted as soon as possible after January 1. *Need-based scholarships/grants offered:* Pell, SEOG, state scholarships/grants, private scholarships, the school's own gift aid. *Loan aid offered:* Direct Subsidized Stafford, Direct Unsubsidized Stafford, Direct PLUS, Federal Perkins, Federal Nursing, college/university loans from institutional funds. Federal Work-Study Program available. Institutional employment available. Applicants will be notified of awards on a rolling basis beginning on or about March 15. Off-campus job opportunities are excellent.

## FROM THE ADMISSIONS OFFICE

"Binghamton University prides itself on excellent teaching and solid research from a faculty remarkably accessible to students. Students have the opportunity to engage in research with faculty and, together, they have designed projects and coauthored papers. Teaching and mentoring by faculty builds students' confidence and competence, encouraging them to become independent learners. Binghamton University welcomes serious students interested in working toward a productive future in our dynamic academic community."

## SELECTIVITY

| | |
|---|---|
| Admissions Rating | 92 |
| # of applicants | 18,315 |
| % of applicants accepted | 42 |
| % of acceptees attending | 27 |
| # accepting a place on wait list | 219 |
| % admitted from wait list | 100 |

### FRESHMAN PROFILE

| | |
|---|---|
| Range SAT Verbal | 550-640 |
| Average SAT Verbal | 599 |
| Range SAT Math | 590-690 |
| Average SAT Math | 637 |
| Range ACT Composite | 24-29 |
| Average ACT Composite | 26 |
| Minimum TOEFL | 550 |
| Average HS GPA | 3.6 |
| % graduated top 25% of class | 86 |
| % graduated top 50% of class | 99 |

### DEADLINES

| | |
|---|---|
| Priority admission | 1/15 |
| Nonfall registration? | yes |

### APPLICANTS ALSO LOOK AT AND OFTEN PREFER
Cornell U
NYU
U Penn
Columbia

### AND SOMETIMES PREFER
U of Michigan
Clarkson U
Penn State

### AND RARELY PREFER
SUNY Geneseo
SUNY Buffalo
SUNY Albany
Syracuse

## FINANCIAL FACTS

| | |
|---|---|
| Financial Aid Rating | 75 |
| In-state tuition | $3,400 |
| Out-of-state tuition | $8,300 |
| Room and board | $6,412 |
| Books and supplies | $800 |
| Required fees | $1,317 |
| % frosh receiving aid | 43 |
| % undergrads receiving aid | 49 |
| Avg frosh grant | $3,806 |
| Avg frosh loan | $3,116 |

# STATE UNIVERSITY OF NEW YORK AT BUFFALO

15 Capen Hall, Buffalo, NY 14260 • Admissions: 888-UB-ADMIT • Fax: 716-645-6411

## CAMPUS LIFE

| Quality of Life Rating | 69 |
|---|---|
| Type of school | public |
| Environment | suburban |

### STUDENTS

| Total undergrad enrollment | 16,536 |
|---|---|
| % male/female | 55/45 |
| % from out of state | 2 |
| % live on campus | 21 |
| % in (# of) fraternities | 1 (10) |
| % in (# of) sororities | 1 (12) |
| % African American | 8 |
| % Asian | 10 |
| % Caucasian | 71 |
| % Hispanic | 4 |
| % international | 5 |
| # of countries represented | 106 |

### SURVEY SAYS . . .
Ethnic diversity on campus
(almost) everyone smokes
Lots of beer drinking
Great computer facilities
Great library
Student newspaper is popular
Athletic facilities are great
Hard liquor is popular

## ACADEMICS

| Academic Rating | 76 |
|---|---|
| Calendar | semester |
| Student/faculty ratio | 14:1 |
| % profs teaching UG courses | 64 |
| % classes taught by TAs | 20 |
| Avg lab size | 20-29 students |
| Avg reg class size | 20-29 students |

### MOST POPULAR MAJORS
Business administration/management
Communications studies/speech
communication and rhetoric
Psychology

## STUDENTS SPEAK OUT

### Academics
A "wonderful variety of majors" and an "inexpensive" education await those willing to brave the frosty winters of New York State's northwestern academic outpost, SUNY—Buffalo. Engineering, business, and pre-med are the major draws here, but other disciplines (especially communications and the liberal arts and sciences) also offer competitive programs. Students report that "classes are big, which kind of sucks." Instruction in large lectures, many feel, is "not very easy. They expect you to understand right away what they understand. Also, they need to get more experienced instructors instead of using TAs to teach courses." Classes improve, though, at the upper levels, where "professors relate well to students, are accessible, and overall, keep learning interesting." Buffalo's administration "communicates very poorly with students," not a very unusual situation at a large state university. Even so, students cheerfully acknowledge Buffalo's many assets, which include "great computer facilities," as well as "wonderful" research opportunities, a great library, and "an [excellent] Honors Program."

### Life
SUNY—Buffalo is situated on two distinct campuses, a "south urban" campus within the city limits of the city and a "north rural (or suburban)" campus just outside of town. South Campus is home to the medical sciences, while most other departments are headquartered to the north. Other departments and the School of Architecture and Planning are split between the two campuses. Students feel that the university is relatively easy to get around. From South Campus "it's very easy to go out and do stuff. We're close to the theater district." Downtown is also home to "the bars of Main Street or Chippewa Street," music venues, and a bevy of great pizzerias. At the northern campus, however, "either you go to frats and dance clubs and get wasted or you don't. If you don't, there's really nothing else for you to do here. If you want a life, you need a car." Adds one student, "Greeks make up only 2 percent of the population but are so evident around North Campus. They don't have a good reputation at all! " For those desirous of more constructive pursuits, "there's something for everyone"; the student newspaper, minority student organizations, student government, and sports are all popular. A sophomore tells us that "getting involved is easy, and it makes a big school like UB feel smaller." Students give parking and campus food an adamant thumbs down and warn all upstate neophytes that "UB lives up to the isolated tundra stereotype of Buffalo."

### Student Body
The student body at UB "is broad and diverse, enabling students to gain valuable cultural insight." And therefore, "we treat each other with respect," notes one white student, a sentiment apparently confirmed by an African American student who feels "Buffalo has a great deal to offer minority students." Leaning to the left-of-center politically, most UB students we surveyed don't consider themselves particularly politically active. As a whole, they're a "generally friendly" lot who rate themselves as pretty happy, if lacking a little "school spirit" and a strong sense of community. Writes one, "It's hard to make a lot of friends with such a large commuter population."

# STATE UNIVERSITY OF NEW YORK AT BUFFALO

FINANCIAL AID: 866-838-7257 • E-MAIL: UB-ADMISSIONS@BUFFALO.EDU • WEBSITE: WWW.BUFFALO.EDU

## ADMISSIONS

*Very important factors considered include:* class rank, secondary school record, standardized test scores. *Other factors considered include:* essays, extracurricular activities, minority status, recommendations, talent/ability, volunteer work. SAT I or ACT required. TOEFL required of all international applicants. High school diploma or GED is required. *High school units required/recommended:* 17 total recommended; 4 English recommended, 3 math recommended, 3 science recommended, 3 foreign language recommended, 4 social studies recommended.

## The Inside Word

Buffalo was formerly a private university and was absorbed into the SUNY system. Its admissions process reflects this private heritage to the extent possible (applications are centrally processed for the entire system in Albany). It's one of the few SUNY schools with a freshman academic profile higher than its published admissions standards. Although Binghamton is academically the most selective of the SUNY University Centers, Buffalo is in many ways closer to what other states refer to as the flagship of the state system.

## FINANCIAL AID

*Students should submit:* FAFSA. The Princeton Review suggests that all financial aid forms be submitted as soon as possible after January 1. *Need-based scholarships/grants offered:* Pell, SEOG, state scholarships/grants, private scholarships, the school's own gift aid, Federal Nursing. *Loan aid offered:* Direct Subsidized Stafford, Direct Unsubsidized Stafford, Direct PLUS, Federal Perkins, Federal Nursing, college/university loans from institutional funds. Federal Work-Study Program available. Applicants will be notified of awards on a rolling basis beginning on or about February 1. Off-campus job opportunities are good.

## FROM THE ADMISSIONS OFFICE

"The University at Buffalo (UB) is among the nation's finest public research universities—a learning community where you'll work side by side with world-renowned faculty, including Nobel, Pulitzer, National Medal of Science, and other award winners. As the largest, most comprehensive university center in the State University of New York (SUNY) system, UB offers more undergraduate majors than any public university in New York or New England. With opportunities for joint degrees and combined five-year bachelor's and master's degrees, you'll be free to chart an academic course that meets your individual goals—you can even design your own major. Our unique University Honors and University at Buffalo Scholars scholarship programs offer an enhanced academic experience, including advanced research opportunities, faculty mentors, and special seminars. The university is committed to providing the latest information technology—UB was ranked as the nation's 10th most-wired university by *Yahoo! Internet Life* magazine. UB also places a high priority on offering an exciting campus environment. With nonstop festivals, Division I sporting events, concerts, and visiting lecturers, you'll have plenty to do outside of the classroom. We encourage you and your family to visit campus to see UB up close and in person. Our Visit UB campus tours and presentations are offered year-round."

## SELECTIVITY

| | |
|---|---|
| Admissions Rating | 82 |
| # of applicants | 16,057 |
| % of applicants accepted | 61 |
| % of acceptees attending | 31 |
| # of early decision applicants | 417 |
| % accepted early decision | 63 |

### FRESHMAN PROFILE

| | |
|---|---|
| Range SAT Verbal | 500-600 |
| Average SAT Verbal | 566 |
| Range SAT Math | 520-630 |
| Average SAT Math | 589 |
| Average ACT Composite | 29 |
| Minimum TOEFL | 550 |
| Average HS GPA | 3.1 |
| % graduated top 10% of class | 21 |
| % graduated top 25% of class | 57 |
| % graduated top 50% of class | 92 |

### DEADLINES

| | |
|---|---|
| Early decision | 11/1 |
| Early decision notification | 12/1 |
| Priority admission | 11/1 |
| Nonfall registration? | yes |

### APPLICANTS ALSO LOOK AT AND OFTEN PREFER
SUNY—Albany
Binghamton U.
Cornell U., NYU

### AND SOMETIMES PREFER
Syracuse, Alfred
U. Rochester
SUNY—Stony Brook
Boston U.

### AND RARELY PREFER
U. Mass—Amherst
Penn State—Univ. Park
U. Conn.

## FINANCIAL FACTS

| | |
|---|---|
| Financial Aid Rating | 80 |
| In-state tuition | $3,400 |
| Out-of-state tuition | $8,300 |
| Room and board | $6,512 |
| Books and supplies | $750 |
| Required fees | $1,450 |
| % frosh receiving aid | 65 |
| % undergrads receiving aid | 52 |
| Avg frosh grant | $5,225 |
| Avg frosh loan | $4,050 |

# STATE UNIVERSITY OF NEW YORK COLLEGE AT GENESEO

1 COLLEGE CIRCLE, GENESEO, NY 14454-1401 • ADMISSIONS: 716-245-5571 • FAX: 716-245-5550

## CAMPUS LIFE

| | |
|---|---|
| Quality of Life Rating | 71 |
| Type of school | public |
| Environment | rural |

### STUDENTS
| | |
|---|---|
| Total undergrad enrollment | 5,387 |
| % male/female | 36/64 |
| % from out of state | 1 |
| % from public high school | 94 |
| % live on campus | 58 |
| % in (# of) fraternities | 10 (10) |
| % in (# of) sororities | 12 (10) |
| % African American | 2 |
| % Asian | 5 |
| % Caucasian | 90 |
| % Hispanic | 3 |
| % international | 1 |

### SURVEY SAYS . . .
Lots of beer drinking
Lots of classroom discussion
Athletic facilities need improving
Registration is a pain
Low cost of living
Ethnic diversity lacking on campus

## ACADEMICS

| | |
|---|---|
| Academic Rating | 77 |
| Calendar | semester |
| Student/faculty ratio | 19:1 |
| Profs interesting rating | 71 |
| Profs accessible rating | 76 |
| % profs teaching UG courses | 100 |
| Avg reg class size | 20-29 students |

### MOST POPULAR MAJORS
Special education
Psychology
Business administration/management

## STUDENTS SPEAK OUT

### Academics

Future undergrads seeking a small-school experience at state-school prices would do well to consider SUNY—Geneseo, the competitive liberal arts campus located in one of the system's northern outposts. Gushes one student, "Geneseo's greatest strength is in academics. I was warned that it would be hard to access professors at a state school, but at Geneseo, nothing could be further from the truth. My class sizes are small, my professors all know me personally, and they are always available to discuss anything with their students. The academic work is incredibly challenging—it requires a lot of time and effort to succeed here. I'm proud of the rigorous academic standards at Geneseo." Other students warn, however, that "professors vary by department, and it's very clear that there is a bias toward specific departments that the school is known for." The school's most prominent programs include "excellent" dance and theatre programs, a "great" school of business, and popular psychology and biology departments. The best professors here "take time to get to know you on a personal level and are extremely accessible inside and outside of the classroom. Because our university is geared more toward the undergraduate as opposed to the graduate, the professors will bend over backwards to help you." The administration, "particularly when it comes to financial aid and bills, is somewhat lacking, but I guess compared to other schools is average."

### Life

The studious undergrads of Geneseo report that their campus "is a quiet place, for the most part. [But] if you are looking for parties, you will be able to find them. At the same time, we have so many organizations that put on performances (several choirs, an orchestra, several bands, two drama clubs, etc.) that no one can ever be bored." A sizeable Greek contingent hosts the majority of weekend bashes; explains one frat member, "Many complain about the Greek population, but it offers a great number of opportunities and experiences, and especially friendships. There is a large number of Greeks in Geneseo, and it does create a boundary with some individuals, but for every one of those there are two others who do not feel that way." Outside the Greek scene, students note that "there are also always plays or musical events on campus to attend. Movies are played for reduced prices as well. Most people are content with the activities." Students also praise their "beautiful campus," although they wish there weren't so many hills to climb, especially during the snowy winter months. They also gripe that "because we are a state school, there is not a lot of money, and construction projects seem to take forever, and there always seems to be something that is falling apart." The town of Geneseo gets poor grades; writes one student, "Geneseo can be a bit boring . . . . Sometimes the most fun we can have is riding the bus to and from Wal-Mart." Students roadtrip to Rochester, which is only 30 minutes away by car or school-sponsored bus.

### Student Body

Students on the "mostly female" (about two-thirds, to be exact) Geneseo campus agree that "Geneseo is a great place, but it isn't exactly an accurate representation of the real world. The student body is very homogenous, mostly white middle- to upper-middle class. More diversity would be nice." Others do note some diversity, pointing out that "the campus is rather divided socioeconomically. You can go to the overcrowded parking lots to see that. A lot of parents pay for their kids to come here because it is so reasonably priced and will buy them expensive cars and give them spending money and everything. Then there are the students who are holding down several part-time jobs, have loans, and are paying for college themselves." Undergrads here "are extremely friendly." Writes one student, "I would have no problem going to a dining hall alone, and if I saw another student alone, joining them and having a conversation."

492 ■ THE BEST 351 COLLEGES

# STATE UNIVERSITY OF NEW YORK COLLEGE AT GENESEO

FINANCIAL AID: 716-245-5321 • E-MAIL: ADMISSIONS@GENESEO.EDU • WEBSITE: WWW.GENESEO.EDU

## ADMISSIONS

*Very important factors considered include:* class rank, secondary school record, standardized test scores. *Important factors considered include:* essays, extracurricular activities, minority status, recommendations, talent/ability. *Other factors considered include:* character/personal qualities, volunteer work. SAT I or ACT required. TOEFL required of all international applicants. High school diploma or GED is required. *High school units required/recommended:* 20 total recommended; 4 English recommended, 4 math recommended, 4 science recommended, 4 foreign language recommended, 4 social studies recommended.

### The Inside Word

Geneseo is the most selective of SUNY's 13 undergraduate colleges and more selective than three of SUNY's university centers. No formula approach is used here. Expect a thorough review of both your academic accomplishments (virtually everyone here graduated in the top half of their high school classes) and your extracurricular/personal side. Admissions standards are tempered only by a somewhat low yield of admits who enroll; this keeps the admit rate higher than it might otherwise be.

## FINANCIAL AID

*Students should submit:* FAFSA, state aid form. The Princeton Review suggests that all financial aid forms be submitted as soon as possible after January 1. *Need-based scholarships/grants offered:* Pell, SEOG, state scholarships/grants, private scholarships, the school's own gift aid. *Loan aid offered:* FFEL Subsidized Stafford, FFEL Unsubsidized Stafford, FFEL PLUS, Federal Perkins, state loans, alternative loans. Federal Work-Study Program available. Institutional employment available. Applicants will be notified of awards on a rolling basis beginning on or about March 15. Off-campus job opportunities are fair.

## FROM THE ADMISSIONS OFFICE

"Geneseo has carved a distinctive niche among the nation's premier public liberal arts colleges. Founded in 1871, the college occupies a 220-acre hillside campus in the historic Village of Geneseo, overlooking the scenic Genesee Valley. As a residential campus—with nearly two-thirds of the students living in college residence halls—it provides a rich and varied program of social, cultural, recreational, and scholarly activities. Geneseo is noted for its distinctive core curriculum and the extraordinary opportunities it offers undergraduates to pursue independent study and research with faculty who value close working relationships with talented students. Equally impressive is the remarkable success of its graduates, nearly one-third of whom study at leading graduate and professional schools immediately following graduation."

### SELECTIVITY

| | |
|---|---|
| Admissions Rating | 92 |
| # accepting a place on wait list | 2,735 |
| % admitted from wait list | 7 |
| # of early decision applicants | 265 |
| % accepted early decision | 50 |

#### FRESHMAN PROFILE
| | |
|---|---|
| Range SAT Verbal | 580-650 |
| Average SAT Verbal | 619 |
| Range SAT Math | 590-660 |
| Average SAT Math | 626 |
| Range ACT Composite | 25-28 |
| Average ACT Composite | 27 |
| Minimum TOEFL | 525 |
| Average HS GPA | 3.6 |
| % graduated top 10% of class | 49 |
| % graduated top 25% of class | 81 |
| % graduated top 50% of class | 99 |

#### DEADLINES
| | |
|---|---|
| Early decision | 11/15 |
| Early decision notification | 12/15 |
| Regular admission | 1/15 |
| Nonfall registration? | yes |

#### APPLICANTS ALSO LOOK AT
**AND OFTEN PREFER**
Binghamton U.
Cornell U.

**AND SOMETIMES PREFER**
U. Rochester
SUNY—Buffalo
Boston College
SUNY—Albany
Colgate

**AND RARELY PREFER**
Hamilton
Ithaca
St. Bonaventure

### FINANCIAL FACTS

| | |
|---|---|
| Financial Aid Rating | 79 |
| In-state tuition | $3,400 |
| Out-of-state tuition | $8,300 |
| Room and board | $5,660 |
| Books and supplies | $700 |
| Required fees | $910 |
| % frosh receiving aid | 45 |
| % undergrads receiving aid | 47 |
| Avg frosh grant | $1,585 |
| Avg frosh loan | $2,975 |

# STEPHENS COLLEGE

1200 EAST BROADWAY, BOX 2121, COLUMBIA, MO 65215 • ADMISSIONS: 573-876-7207 • FAX: 573-876-7237

## CAMPUS LIFE

| | |
|---|---|
| Quality of Life Rating | 79 |
| Type of school | private |
| Environment | suburban |

### STUDENTS

| | |
|---|---|
| Total undergrad enrollment | 596 |
| % male/female | 5/95 |
| % from out of state | 57 |
| % from public high school | 75 |
| % live on campus | 70 |
| % in (# of) sororities | 8 (2) |
| % African American | 9 |
| % Asian | 1 |
| % Caucasian | 84 |
| % Hispanic | 4 |
| # of countries represented | 5 |

### SURVEY SAYS . . .
*Athletic facilities need improving
No one watches intercollegiate sports
No one plays intramural sports
Campus easy to get around
Registration is a breeze
Students are happy*

## ACADEMICS

| | |
|---|---|
| Academic Rating | 70 |
| Calendar | semester |
| Student/faculty ratio | 10:1 |
| % profs teaching UG courses | 100 |
| Avg lab size | under 10 students |
| Avg reg class size | under 10 students |

### MOST POPULAR MAJORS
Fashion/apparel design
Drama and dramatics/theatre arts
Education

## STUDENTS SPEAK OUT

### Academics

"It's all about theater, dance, fashion design, and marketing" at Stephens College, a small all-women's school (almost, that is; the school admits a few men to its theater department) "with an emphasis in almost every class on women's history and women's issues." Stephens is "a strict school academically, which really prepares you for the real world. Small classes and teachers who really care can be a great blessing for your education." The school's very existence and success, students say, empower them. "Stephens is about providing confidence and the ability to back that confidence up, for women, in a predominantly male world," explains one undergrad. Profs receive high marks for their "amazing real-world experience in their fields. The theatre professors have actually acted and directed in the business, the dance professors are from New York, and the Broadcasting teacher spent many years on TV." Better still, they know how to share their expertise with undergrads; as one student told us, "You really have an opportunity to bond with [profs] and make them your friend once you're done with their class. They're always willing to listen to what you have to say and how you feel about what they're teaching." On the downside, students feel that the "non-arts departments need more attention" and that "the facilities here are outdated, and the library is weak and in need of updates."

### Life

Stephens students love Columbia, "a three-college town where there's always something to do." The city has a lot to offer these aesthetically inclined undergrads; explains one student, "The largest majors on campus are theater, fashion, and dance, so most of our student body is very creative. Even those not in one of these majors have an appreciation for art, and there are a lot of opportunities in downtown Columbia for us to see independent film, a poetry reading, a local musician, or the work of a local artist." Because "Mizzou is two blocks away, girls have all the chances in the world to meet guys" and "go hang out at frat parties." Students here tell us that "the majority of our student body aren't hard partiers, and those who are tend to live off-campus where they can drink and party to their own satisfaction." Most here are too busy and too deeply involved in their studies to devote much time to partying. Wrote one theater major, "As far as theater is concerned, most of us are completely consumed by the department, which is a good thing. Like Annie Potts said of her experience here, you really do 'eat, breathe, live theater.' Most of us seem to love being so busy, but others don't like the idea of rehearsing or working on a crew a good deal of the afternoon and evening and then having to do homework way into the wee hours of the morning." Just about everyone here agrees that "the food is really bad and greasy."

### Student Body

"There is no 'typical Stephens woman,'" many Stephens women insist. "We are all unique: short, tall, fat, thin, black, white, Asian, Hispanic, brainiac, or sorority lover . . .we all find our niche here." Others tell us that "Stephens is mostly white students, but everyone here observes diversity and at least respects it" and report that "most students are middle class and from Missouri, or from a surrounding state. Most are in the arts (theater, dance, fashion)." Students outside the most popular majors "are respected by professors, but don't always get treated the same by students." Notes one undergrad, "While there are definite social cliques—the fashion majors, dancers, theatre people, etc.—we all get along." As at many unaffiliated women's schools, "Sexual orientation isn't an issue here. There is a good mixture of heterosexual and gay/bisexual people. It may seem like there are quite a few lesbians and bisexuals, but in reality it's just that they feel more open here."

# STEPHENS COLLEGE

FINANCIAL AID: 573-876-7106 • E-MAIL: APPLY@SC.STEPHENS.EDU • WEBSITE: WWW.STEPHENS.EDU

## ADMISSIONS

*Very important factors considered include:* character/personal qualities, essays, recommendations, secondary school record, standardized test scores. *Important factors considered include:* extracurricular activities, interview, talent/ability, volunteer work. *Other factors considered include:* work experience. SAT I or ACT required. TOEFL required of all international applicants. High school diploma or GED is required. *High school units required/recommended:* 12 total recommended; 4 English recommended, 2 math recommended, 2 science recommended, 2 foreign language recommended, 2 social studies recommended.

### The Inside Word

Each candidate's application is read by three members of the admissions committee, and essays carry much more significance than test scores. You'll get a lot of personal attention from the admissions staff here; with the kind of competition Stephens faces for students, they have to work pretty hard here to bring in the freshman class. Their success is a testament to the quality of the college.

## FINANCIAL AID

*Students should submit:* FAFSA. No deadline for regular filing. The Princeton Review suggests that all financial aid forms be submitted as soon as possible after January 1. *Need-based scholarships/grants offered:* Pell, SEOG, state scholarships/grants, private scholarships, the school's own gift aid. *Loan aid offered:* Direct Subsidized Stafford, Direct Unsubsidized Stafford, Direct PLUS, Federal Perkins. Federal Work-Study Program available. Institutional employment available. Applicants will be notified of awards on a rolling basis beginning on or about February 1. Off-campus job opportunities are excellent.

## FROM THE ADMISSIONS OFFICE

"A national private liberal arts college for women in the Midwest, Stephens College was established in 1833 as Columbia's first institution of higher education. Students are encouraged to arrange a campus visit.

"The women's college setting offers stimulating classroom discussion and close interaction with professors and peers. Bridging theory and application, students engage in hands-on learning opportunities (education majors in our on-campus children's laboratory school and theatre in Iowa, for example) as well as internship experiences in their first year of study. The Stephens campus is within walking distance of a thriving downtown, shared by more than 26,000 students at area colleges and universities. An extensive network of Stephens alumnae are always willing to assist students with employment searches upon graduation."

## SELECTIVITY

| | |
|---|---|
| Admissions Rating | 73 |
| # of applicants | 335 |
| % of applicants accepted | 83 |
| % of acceptees attending | 44 |

### FRESHMAN PROFILE

| | |
|---|---|
| Range SAT Verbal | 510-630 |
| Average SAT Verbal | 566 |
| Range SAT Math | 480-580 |
| Average SAT Math | 513 |
| Range ACT Composite | 21-26 |
| Average ACT Composite | 24 |
| Minimum TOEFL | 550 |
| Average HS GPA | 3.5 |
| % graduated top 10% of class | 43 |
| % graduated top 25% of class | 67 |
| % graduated top 50% of class | 88 |

### DEADLINES

| | |
|---|---|
| Regular notification | rolling |
| Nonfall registration? | yes |

### APPLICANTS ALSO LOOK AT AND SOMETIMES PREFER
U. Missouri—Columbia
William Woods

### AND RARELY PREFER
Butler

## FINANCIAL FACTS

| | |
|---|---|
| Financial Aid Rating | 91 |
| Tuition | $17,360 |
| Room and board | $6,900 |
| Books and supplies | $750 |
| % frosh receiving aid | 73 |
| % undergrads receiving aid | 65 |
| Avg frosh grant | $10,600 |
| Avg frosh loan | $2,000 |

# STETSON UNIVERSITY

421 N. WOODLAND BOULEVARD, UNIT 8378, DELAND, FL 32723 • ADMISSIONS: 800-688-0101 • FAX: 386-822-7112

## CAMPUS LIFE

| | |
|---|---|
| **Quality of Life Rating** | **75** |
| Type of school | private |
| Environment | suburban |

### STUDENTS

| | |
|---|---|
| Total undergrad enrollment | 2,142 |
| % male/female | 42/58 |
| % from out of state | 23 |
| % from public high school | 75 |
| % live on campus | 69 |
| % in (# of) fraternities | 33 (8) |
| % in (# of) sororities | 29 (6) |
| % African American | 4 |
| % Asian | 2 |
| % Caucasian | 85 |
| % Hispanic | 5 |
| % international | 3 |
| # of countries represented | 43 |

### SURVEY SAYS . . .
Athletic facilities are great
Campus is beautiful
No one cheats
Campus easy to get around
Classes are small
Ethnic diversity lacking on campus
Students don't like DeLand, FL

## ACADEMICS

| | |
|---|---|
| **Academic Rating** | **79** |
| Calendar | semester |
| Student/faculty ratio | 11:1 |
| Profs interesting rating | 72 |
| Profs accessible rating | 74 |
| % profs teaching UG courses | 98 |
| Avg lab size | 10-19 students |
| Avg reg class size | 10-19 students |

## STUDENTS SPEAK OUT

### Academics

"My dean threw a picnic for the School of Music. What does that say?" asks a freshman music theory and composition major. One thing it says is that Stetson, with a 11:1 student/faculty ratio, allows its students "to have one-on-one discussions with faculty and staff whenever you need it. You're not just a number." It also says that Stetson has a strong music department, and it should, since it pays particular attention to this corner of campus. "If you really have an interest in art, music, or spirituality, this is a great center of culture and learning." Nonetheless, some students complain that the university plays favorites, giving too many "scholarships to music school students and athletes, not to smart kids." This is all part of a general dissatisfaction with an administration that, students say, is mired in "a large amount of bureaucracy." In many students' eyes, the professors make up for this shortfall. "Stetson's strongest point is its professors," writes one student. Another is a little more even-handed, reporting that when professors "enjoy what they do, they're amazing. When they don't, they stink." So the key is this: Research the professor before signing up for a class.

### Life

If you ask students at Stetson about their impressions of hometown DeLand, you're likely to hear something to the effect of, "This is not DeLand, it's 'Deadland.'" Fortunately, when they get stir crazy, students can hop in the car and "drive over to Daytona or Orlando," each of them about a half hour away. As the "area is bursting with beauty," taking a day trip isn't a bad way to while away free hours. (But having a car on campus comes at a cost because "parking is a nightmare.") Back on campus, students can enjoy "orchestra concerts, lectures, art shows, and the like." Students also "play games, play intramurals, play Frisbee, play ping-pong, look at the weather," which "is absolutely beautiful." And, of course, there are the parties. "This is a party school," and while "fraternities are extremely popular" and play a central role in the university's campus life, students manage to find parties wherever there's room for a bottle and a few bodies. "Thursday night is the most popular night to go out" at Stetson, and "most students try to cram into two local bars" in town. When they're not drinking—or studying, or driving to the beach—they are eating. Unfortunately, students think their school could stand to improve the quality of on-campus cuisine. One idealistic junior admits that she longs "to have a student union building with Starbucks, Burger King, Pizza Hut, and a Subway." Most students, though, would probably settle for a tastier vegetarian option.

### Student Body

One thing's for sure about Stetson students: They feel no need to flatter each other. "The student body consists of BMW- and Mercedes-driving spoiled kids who don't know the meaning of work," a sophomore from Pennsylvania complains. "A bunch of shallow nincompoops," another adds. A junior, coming to the defense of his peers, admits that while there are "many upper-class rich snobs," there is also "a good amount of down-to-earth people to balance it out." Whether their noses are in the air or to the books, Stetson's students tend to "stick within their own groups" of friends. And "there is a fairly strong separation between those students involved in Greek life and those that are not"—an important thing to note because the school recognizes 14 very active Greek organizations. But it's not as if anyone "openly hates anyone" here, which means that all in all "everything seems to run pretty smoothly." Because students come to Stetson from 44 states and 43 foreign countries, the easy smiles and Southern drawl are welcomed novelties. But even the students who can't seem to get enough of Stetson and its surroundings admit that there's "not enough diversity" among their classmates.

# STETSON UNIVERSITY

FINANCIAL AID: 386-822-7120 • E-MAIL: ADMISSIONS@STETSON.EDU • WEBSITE: WWW.STETSON.EDU

## ADMISSIONS
*Very important factors considered include:* secondary school record. *Important factors considered include:* character/personal qualities, class rank, essays, extracurricular activities, interview, recommendations, standardized test scores, talent/ability, volunteer work, work experience. *Other factors considered include:* alumni/ae relation, geographical residence, minority status, state residency. SAT I or ACT required; SAT I preferred. TOEFL required of all international applicants. High school diploma or GED is required. *High school units required/recommended:* 16 total required; 4 English required, 3 math required, 3 science required, 2 foreign language required, 2 social studies required, 2 elective required.

### The Inside Word
Stetson is a university with strong academic offerings, yet moderate admissions standards. Solid B students with slightly-above-average test scores should encounter few obstacles to admission. What sort of fit a candidate makes with the university is in many ways more important than numbers, and the admissions committee closely evaluates applicants' personal sides.

## FINANCIAL AID
*Students should submit:* FAFSA, institution's own financial aid form. Regular filing deadline is February 15. The Princeton Review suggests that all financial aid forms be submitted as soon as possible after January 1. *Need-based scholarships/grants offered:* Pell, SEOG, state scholarships/grants, private scholarships, the school's own gift aid. *Loan aid offered:* FFEL Subsidized Stafford, FFEL Unsubsidized Stafford, FFEL PLUS, Federal Perkins, state loans, college/university loans from institutional funds. Federal Work-Study Program available. Institutional employment available. Applicants will be notified of awards on a rolling basis. Off-campus job opportunities are good.

## FROM THE ADMISSIONS OFFICE
"What does it mean to be academically adventuresome? For students with bright, active minds, Stetson University is the place to find out. Stetson is a place to energetically engage the world around you. To think. To imagine. To question. To discover. To be wide open to all the intellectual adventures you will discover on this unique and beautiful campus in central Florida. Stetson has a special commitment to make values an important part of the learning process and everyday life on campus. Whether your interest is business, music, or more than 40 majors in our College of Arts and Sciences, Stetson has a challenging program for you. It all adds up to the academic prestige that Stetson has enjoyed since 1883. Excite your mind at Stetson University."

### SELECTIVITY

| | |
|---|---|
| Admissions Rating | 81 |

#### FRESHMAN PROFILE
| | |
|---|---|
| Range SAT Verbal | 510-620 |
| Average SAT Verbal | 566 |
| Range SAT Math | 500-610 |
| Average SAT Math | 557 |
| Range ACT Composite | 21-27 |
| Average ACT Composite | 24 |
| Minimum TOEFL | 550 |
| Average HS GPA | 3.6 |
| % graduated top 10% of class | 32 |
| % graduated top 25% of class | 61 |
| % graduated top 50% of class | 90 |

#### DEADLINES
| | |
|---|---|
| Early decision | 11/1 |
| Early decision notification | 11/15 |
| Priority admission | 1/1 |
| Regular admission | 3/1 |
| Nonfall registration? | yes |

#### APPLICANTS ALSO LOOK AT
**AND OFTEN PREFER**
University of Florida
**AND SOMETIMES PREFER**
Florida State University
Rollins College
University of Miami
University of Central Florida
University of Richmond
**AND RARELY PREFER**
Mercer University—Macon
Samford University
Eckerd College

### FINANCIAL FACTS

| | |
|---|---|
| Financial Aid Rating | 83 |
| Tuition | $20,425 |
| Room and board | $6,855 |
| Books and supplies | $800 |
| Required fees | $1,080 |
| % frosh receiving aid | 59 |
| % undergrads receiving aid | 58 |
| Avg frosh grant | $14,325 |
| Avg frosh loan | $5,217 |

THE BEST 351 COLLEGES ■ 497

# STEVENS INSTITUTE OF TECHNOLOGY

CASTLE POINT ON HUDSON, HOBOKEN, NJ 07030 • ADMISSIONS: 800-458-5323 • FAX: 201-216-8348

## CAMPUS LIFE

| Quality of Life Rating | 74 |
|---|---|
| Type of school | private |
| Environment | suburban |

### STUDENTS

| Total undergrad enrollment | 1,729 |
|---|---|
| % male/female | 75/25 |
| % from out of state | 35 |
| % live on campus | 75 |
| % in (# of) fraternities | 30 (9) |
| % in (# of) sororities | 33 (3) |
| % African American | 5 |
| % Asian | 25 |
| % Caucasian | 51 |
| % Hispanic | 10 |
| % international | 7 |
| # of countries represented | 68 |

### SURVEY SAYS . . .
Students love Hoboken, NJ
Musical organizations aren't popular
Class discussions are rare
Popular college radio
Library needs improving
Lousy food on campus
Lab facilities are great
Political activism is (almost) nonexistent
Computer facilities need improving

## ACADEMICS

| Academic Rating | 82 |
|---|---|
| Calendar | semester |
| Student/faculty ratio | 9:1 |
| Profs interesting rating | 86 |
| Profs accessible rating | 91 |
| % profs teaching UG courses | 100 |
| Avg lab size | 10-19 students |
| Avg reg class size | 20-29 students |

### MOST POPULAR MAJORS
Computer science
Computer engineering
Mechanical engineering

## STUDENTS SPEAK OUT

### Academics
Students looking for a highly regarded engineering school near a major city need look no further than Stevens Institute of Technology in Hoboken, New Jersey. Of course, some students point out that Stevens is one of those techie schools that "tries to be broad-based, but isn't." Students don't come to Stevens for the humanities. Professors are "brilliant" but also "often too smart for their own good." They sometimes forget that students are not yet experts in their field and accordingly, "their expectations are quite high." They "need to stop reading the text to us." Many believe that their professors "are basically just here to do research and write books." Also, many of the TAs for labs and recitations are not native speakers of English. "Half the time, you have to guess what the professor is saying," a junior electrical engineering major says. First- and second-year students find the school's mandatory course load a relief—one less thing for them to worry about. Of course, the workload is significant, and many students worry as much about the grading curve as they do about passing classes that they consider superfluous. Nevertheless, the "engineering department and comp-sci programs are great." Students also tell us that the co-op programs are very strong, and the school's career services center is very helpful. The school also reportedly does an excellent job supporting students with any extra tutoring they might need.

### Life
Stevens students love the campus because it is located in Hoboken, a town with numerous bars and restaurants across the Hudson from New York City. "It is the best view of New York you could ever get," one student writes. New York offers numerous opportunities for diversion, and students often go to the movies in Greenwich Village. The campus itself is small and "park-like," which makes it "easy to get to classes from the dorms." Students, especially those who are underage, go to parties at the fraternities and sororities. While Stevens is not a commuter school, a large number of students go home on the weekend. However, athletics is a big draw, with over 70 percent of undergraduates participating. Studying is a must on week nights if one is to keep up with the workload. Students also report a dislike for on-campus fare, and all agree that parking is difficult in Hoboken. Also, students wish clubs and student organizations had better support from the school's administration.

### Student Body
It's not surprising on a campus whose male population is greater than 75 percent that the primary complaint is that there aren't enough female students. While most students are friendly and noncompetitive, there is a good percentage of "anti-social types who just sit at their computers all day." Those not involved with the Greek community tend to form cliques based on their ethnicity. Students feel like they know everyone because the campus and the student body are so small. While there are many students "who'd rather stay in on a Saturday night and play network games rather than go out and enjoy Manhattan or Hoboken," there are very bright people at Stevens, "so you're bound to come across some interesting characters." In general, Stevens's students get along because they are united by a common goal: "To get a great education that will put us out in the world with a very good salary."

# STEVENS INSTITUTE OF TECHNOLOGY

FINANCIAL AID: 201-216-5194 • E-MAIL: ADMISSIONS@STEVENS-TECH.EDU • WEBSITE: WWW.STEVENS-TECH.EDU

## ADMISSIONS

*Very important factors considered include:* interview, secondary school record, standardized test scores. *Important factors considered include:* character/personal qualities, class rank, extracurricular activities, talent/ability. *Other factors considered include:* alumni/ae relation, essays, recommendations, volunteer work, work experience. SAT I or ACT required; SAT I preferred. TOEFL required of all international applicants. High school diploma is required and GED is not accepted. *High school units required/recommended:* 4 English required, 4 math required, 3 science required, 4 science recommended, 3 science lab required, 4 science lab recommended, 2 foreign language recommended, 2 social studies recommended, 2 history recommended, 4 elective recommended.

### The Inside Word

Stevens is indeed impressive and legitimately near the top of the "second tier" of technical schools. Above-average students who would run into difficulty trying to gain admission to the MITs and Caltechs of the world will find a much more receptive admissions process here. Given its solid reputation and metropolitan New York location, it's an excellent choice for techies who want to establish their careers in the area.

## FINANCIAL AID

*Students should submit:* FAFSA. No deadline for regular filing. The Princeton Review suggests that all financial aid forms be submitted as soon as possible after January 1. *Need-based scholarships/grants offered:* Pell, SEOG, state scholarships/grants, private scholarships, the school's own gift aid. *Loan aid offered:* Direct Subsidized Stafford, Direct Unsubsidized Stafford, Direct PLUS, Federal Perkins, state loans, Signature Loans, TERI Loans. Federal Work-Study Program available. Institutional employment available. Applicants will be notified of awards on a rolling basis beginning on or about March 30. Off-campus job opportunities are excellent.

## FROM THE ADMISSIONS OFFICE

"The quality and achievements of our graduates are the greatest hallmarks of the Stevens education. Approximately 100 percent have had technical, pre-professional experience outside the classroom during their undergraduate years. Among other benefits, this enables them to be the finest candidates for prestigious graduate schools or positions of employment in industry. Striking indications of this are that all students seeking a full-time position receive a job offer prior to graduation from the institute, and Stevens ranks 11th among the Top 550 institutions that produce presidents, vice presidents, and directors of U.S. companies. However, outstanding academic excellence needs to be balanced with an outstanding campus life, and at Stevens students will find 70 student organizations and NCAA Division III athletics. Plus, the Hoboken location overlooking the Hudson River and New York City skyline offers a campus environment like no other."

## SELECTIVITY

| | |
|---|---|
| Admissions Rating | 85 |
| # of applicants | 2,049 |
| % of applicants accepted | 50 |
| % of acceptees attending | 38 |
| # accepting a place on wait list | 166 |
| % admitted from wait list | 17 |
| # of early decision applicants | 76 |
| % accepted early decision | 47 |

### FRESHMAN PROFILE

| | |
|---|---|
| Range SAT Verbal | 540-660 |
| Range SAT Math | 610-730 |
| Minimum TOEFL | 550 |
| Average HS GPA | 3.8 |

### DEADLINES

| | |
|---|---|
| Early decision | 11/1 |
| Early decision notification | 12/15 |
| Priority admission | 11/15 |
| Regular admission | 2/15 |

### APPLICANTS ALSO LOOK AT AND OFTEN PREFER
RPI
Carnegie Mellon
Lehigh
Cornell U.

### AND SOMETIMES PREFER
New Jersey Tech
Rutgers U.

## FINANCIAL FACTS

| | |
|---|---|
| Financial Aid Rating | 89 |
| Tuition | $24,500 |
| Room and board | $8,100 |
| Books and supplies | $900 |
| Required fees | $250 |
| % frosh receiving aid | 74 |
| % undergrads receiving aid | 70 |
| Avg frosh grant | $19,140 |
| Avg frosh loan | $2,500 |

THE BEST 351 COLLEGES ■ 499

# STONY BROOK UNIVERSITY (SUNY)

OFFICE OF ADMISSIONS, STONY BROOK, NY 11794-1901 • ADMISSIONS: 631-632-9898 • FAX: 631-632-9898

## CAMPUS LIFE

| | |
|---|---|
| Quality of Life Rating | 68 |
| Type of school | public |
| Environment | suburban |

### STUDENTS

| | |
|---|---|
| Total undergrad enrollment | 14,224 |
| % male/female | 52/48 |
| % from out of state | 3 |
| % from public high school | 90 |
| % live on campus | 50 |
| % African American | 10 |
| % Asian | 25 |
| % Caucasian | 37 |
| % Hispanic | 8 |
| % international | 4 |

### SURVEY SAYS . . .
Musical organizations aren't popular
High cost of living
Popular college radio
(Almost) everyone smokes
Students don't get along with local community
Large classes
Unattractive campus
Campus difficult to get around
Students are not very happy

## ACADEMICS

| | |
|---|---|
| Academic Rating | 75 |
| Calendar | semester |
| Student/faculty ratio | 18:1 |
| Profs interesting rating | 87 |
| Profs accessible rating | 88 |
| Avg lab size | 20-29 students |
| Avg reg class size | 10-19 students |

### MOST POPULAR MAJORS
Psychology
Business management
Biology

## STUDENTS SPEAK OUT
### Academics
The State University of New York at Stony Brook "is what you make it. You can take a rigorous, challenging curriculum or you can take Basketweaving 101." Most choose the former route, attending Stony Brook in hopes of earning a valuable degree in the sciences and engineering at public-school prices. A nationally renowned graduate research center ("Our research facilities are awesome!!"), Stony Brook comes complete with all of the advantages and drawbacks one would expect to find in a large university. Students "are very much on their own here." Professors "are usually too into lecturing as opposed to making sure students understand what they are being taught. There are few excellent professors, a large sum of nonchalant professors, and a few no-care professors." Notes one student, "Studying electrical engineering at Stony Brook is one of the most brutal and crushing experiences a person can have. The required work is voluminous and extremely challenging and there is almost no support whatsoever: TAs don't speak English and the professors are, for the most part, unhelpful. On the plus side, the professors are extremely knowledgeable." Upperclassmen have access to better teachers and smaller classes and are accordingly more positive about the school. Writes one, "My upper-division professors are fabulous. They do all their own research and have developed their own views on their subjects. The lack of real professors during freshman and sophomore year was awful, but these past two years have made up for it." Students in the Honors College also laud the "priority registration, close-knit group of students," and the fact that the program "encourages students to question everything and to think freely." As for the administration, a typical student asks, "Administration? It's a state school, the people who bring you the DMV. Sadly, the civil-service taint is felt here at the school big time."

### Life
Several factors conspire to make Stony Brook's campus one of the nation's least active socially. First, many students are deeply immersed in science and engineering and thus have little time for socializing. "Most people here," explains one student, "think about chemistry. Once they're done with that, they think about chemistry some more. Then they go home for the weekend." Second, many undergrads commute to Stony Brook for classes only. The parking situation, it should be noted, does little to encourage commuters to stick around: it is "a major crisis for most commuter students" because so few spaces are available. Of those who reside on campus, many go home nearly every weekend. Third, "Port Jefferson and Stony Brook aren't great college towns, although they're getting better" as they add "shopping, entertainment, and many local bars and clubs with a young crowd." As a result, many feel that "there is nothing to do for fun. On weekends this place is dead, a ghost campus until Monday morning." A small but vocal minority protest that "some people feel that there is nothing to do on this campus because our campus is portrayed as a suitcase college . . . but by being part of a group or team, your life on campus is a lot more fun, with parties, mixers, etc." With "Campus Recreation making small improvements every year," perhaps Stony Brook is growing closer to a more typical undergraduate social environment.

### Student Body
The diversity of SUNY SB's student body "is a great asset to the campus because it allows students to get to know other cultures, races, etc., and to become more tolerant and understanding of human beings as a whole." Students "generally keep to their own ethnic groups but also get along with other students." While "some students seem exceptionally smart, interesting, etc., others fall into the basic Long Island 'big hair and muscle car' category. And many, of course, are science geeks." Because the many commuters here usually come only for classes and study sessions, "it's hard to meet people."

# STONY BROOK UNIVERSITY (SUNY)

FINANCIAL AID: 631-632-6840 • E-MAIL: UGADMISSIONS@NOTES.CC.SUNYSB.EDU • WEBSITE: WWW.STONYBROOK.EDU

## ADMISSIONS

*Very important factors considered include:* secondary school record, standardized test scores. *Important factors considered include:* class rank, essays, extracurricular activities, interview, talent/ability. *Other factors considered include:* alumni/ae relation, recommendations. SAT I or ACT required; SAT II recommended. TOEFL required of all international applicants. High school diploma or GED is required. *High school units required/recommended:* 14 total required; 19 total recommended; 4 English required, 3 math required, 4 math recommended, 3 science required, 4 science recommended, 2 foreign language required, 3 foreign language recommended, 4 social studies required.

### The Inside Word

Graduate programs continue to receive national accolades, and the New York State legislature has been somewhat kinder to SUNY of late. Stony Brook's athletic programs have moved to NCAA Division I, America East Conference, in hopes of generating greater visibility and increases in applications. For the near future, admission will remain relatively easy for solid students.

## FINANCIAL AID

*Students should submit:* FAFSA. The Princeton Review suggests that all financial aid forms be submitted as soon as possible after January 1. *Need-based scholarships/grants offered:* Pell, SEOG, state scholarships/grants. *Loan aid offered:* FFEL Subsidized Stafford, FFEL Unsubsidized Stafford, FFEL PLUS, Federal Perkins. Federal Work-Study Program available. Institutional employment available. Applicants will be notified of awards on a rolling basis beginning on or about March 1. On- and off-campus job opportunities are excellent.

## FROM THE ADMISSIONS OFFICE

"Stony Brook University has a philosophy of encouraging excellence. This commitment to excellence shows in the many different merit scholarship programs we offer high-achieving students, including special scholarships offered to Intel Science Talent Research and National Merit Scholarship Competition finalists and semifinalists as well as valedictorians and salutatorians.

"At Stony Brook we offer our undergraduates one of the finest educations available. Stony Brook's faculty rank among the best in the country and pride themselves on creating a discovery-rich environment on campus. Just this past year, the American Association of Colleges & Universities recognized Stony Brook as one of only 16 'Leadership Institutions' for innovation and commitment to undergraduates. We invite students who possess both intellectual curiosity and academic ability to explore countless exciting opportunities available at Stony Brook to learn, discover, and create."

## SELECTIVITY

| | |
|---|---|
| Admissions Rating | 80 |
| # of applicants | 16,849 |
| % of applicants accepted | 54 |
| % of acceptees attending | 27 |

### FRESHMAN PROFILE

| | |
|---|---|
| Range SAT Verbal | 500-590 |
| Average SAT Verbal | 545 |
| Range SAT Math | 550-650 |
| Average SAT Math | 599 |
| Minimum TOEFL | 550 |
| Average HS GPA | 3.5 |
| % graduated top 10% of class | 26 |
| % graduated top 25% of class | 63 |
| % graduated top 50% of class | 93 |

### DEADLINES

| | |
|---|---|
| Priority admission | 12/1 |
| Regular admission | rolling |
| Regular notification | rolling |
| Nonfall registration? | yes |

### APPLICANTS ALSO LOOK AT AND OFTEN PREFER
NYU
SUNY Binghamton
Cornell U

### AND SOMETIMES PREFER
SUNY Buffalo
Penn State
Boston U
SUNY Albany

### AND RARELY PREFER
Syracuse
Rochester Institute of Technology

## FINANCIAL FACTS

| | |
|---|---|
| Financial Aid Rating | 73 |
| In-state tuition | $3,400 |
| Out-of-state tuition | $8,300 |
| Room and board | $7,174 |
| Books and supplies | $900 |
| Required fees | $958 |
| % frosh receiving aid | 50 |
| % undergrads receiving aid | 60 |
| Avg frosh grant | $4,043 |
| Avg frosh loan | $2,153 |

THE BEST 351 COLLEGES ■ 501

# SUSQUEHANNA UNIVERSITY

514 UNIVERSITY AVENUE, SELINSGROVE, PA 17870 • ADMISSIONS: 570-372-4260 • FAX: 570-372-2722

## CAMPUS LIFE
★★★★

| | |
|---|---|
| Quality of Life Rating | 94 |
| Type of school | private |
| Affiliation | Lutheran |
| Environment | rural |

### STUDENTS
| | |
|---|---|
| Total undergrad enrollment | 1,995 |
| % male/female | 42/58 |
| % from out of state | 38 |
| % from public high school | 86 |
| % live on campus | 80 |
| % in (# of) fraternities | 25 (4) |
| % in (# of) sororities | 28 (4) |
| % African American | 2 |
| % Asian | 2 |
| % Caucasian | 93 |
| % Hispanic | 2 |
| % international | 1 |

### SURVEY SAYS . . .
Lots of beer drinking
Athletic facilities are great
Students don't get along with local community
Ethnic diversity lacking on campus
Campus easy to get around
Classes are small
Low cost of living

## ACADEMICS

| | |
|---|---|
| Academic Rating | 91 |
| Calendar | semester |
| Student/faculty ratio | 14:1 |
| Profs interesting rating | 93 |
| Profs accessible rating | 93 |
| % profs teaching UG courses | 100 |
| Avg lab size | 10-19 students |
| Avg reg class size | 10-19 students |

### MOST POPULAR MAJORS
Business administration/management
Communications studies/speech communication and rhetoric
Biology/biological sciences

## STUDENTS SPEAK OUT

### Academics
Professors and the administration at Susquehanna University get "two thumbs up" from students, considering that they "over-exert themselves and work above and beyond the expected." According to a psychology student, "The academic and administrative departments are very well run," and the faculty is described as "kind and knowledgeable" as well as "pretty cool and very interesting." Small-school personal attention is readily available: "Everyone so far has taken an interest in me," writes an English major. Others tell us they visit "professors at home and have very close relationships with them." About ten percent of the student body are members of the Honors program, and over half of Susquehanna undergraduates receive some form of financial aid, often merit-based. The university prides itself on its writing program, part of the English major, which features small workshop classes and frequent student readings of fiction, creative non-fiction, poetry, screenplays, and plays.

### Life
Stranded in rural Pennsylvania, surrounded by "too many Amish," Susquehanna students report that there's "not much to do except go to the one bar in town" or "paint your toenails" for fun. A junior qualifies these opinions, reporting that "Selinsgrove is a small town, but a nice small town." The Pocono ski area is nearby for those itching to hit the slopes, but the closest urban life rafts lie at least three hours away in Philadelphia or Pittsburgh. The on-campus social scene "is decent the first year, but after that, if you aren't Greek, it gets old fast," reports a sophomore, and it can be tough to find "somewhere to go to do something besides drink." School-sponsored activities exist, but a senior music major wishes there were "more activities that students would actually go to." A more optimistic student writes, "We go to the campus coffee house, rent movies, and take trips to Wal-Mart. There are so many things to get involved in or do." Many undergraduates praise "the look" of the "beautiful campus," which is home to 80 percent of the student population.

### Student Body
One undergrad writes, "SU definitely lacks diversity. It's mostly rich, over-achieving white kids, and the few minorities here tend to only socialize with each other. However, everyone is friendly and gets along." Other students agree that there's "not much discrimination" but that "it's hard to differentiate" between individual members of the "well-dressed," "peaceful," and "really white" student body. A freshman also notes a need to increase "diversity, not just culturally, but in every aspect of the word," seeing as only about 8 percent are international or students of color. Seemingly, "Everyone is from a hick town. They are (many times) small-minded geeks plastered with Greek letters which now make them cool." The advantages of a small school include a public relations major's view that it's possible to "get to know so many people on a personal level." Everyone "smiles all the time," making it "quite easy to make friends," in the experience of one freshman. "I am surprised how people can fool around so much and still do so well," comments an RA.

502 ■ THE BEST 351 COLLEGES

# SUSQUEHANNA UNIVERSITY

FINANCIAL AID: 570-372-4450 • E-MAIL: SUADMISS@SUSQU.EDU • WEBSITE: WWW.SUSQU.EDU

## ADMISSIONS

*Very important factors considered include:* class rank, secondary school record, standardized test scores. *Important factors considered include:* character/personal qualities, essays, interview, minority status, recommendations, talent/ability. *Other factors considered include:* alumni/ae relation, extracurricular activities, geographical residence, religious affiliation/commitment, state residency, volunteer work, work experience. SAT II recommended. TOEFL required of all international applicants. High school diploma or GED is required. *High school units required/recommended:* 18 total required; 22 total recommended; 4 English required, 3 math required, 4 math recommended, 3 science required, 4 science recommended, 2 science lab required, 3 science lab recommended, 2 foreign language required, 3 foreign language recommended, 1 social studies required, 2 social studies recommended, 1 history required, 2 elective required.

### The Inside Word

Susquehanna is about as low profile as universities come in the age of MTV. Getting in is made easier by the serious competition the university faces from numerous like institutions in the region, some with significantly better reputations.

## FINANCIAL AID

*Students should submit:* FAFSA, CSS/Financial Aid PROFILE, state aid form, business/farm supplement. Regular filing deadline is May 1. The Princeton Review suggests that all financial aid forms be submitted as soon as possible after January 1. *Need-based scholarships/grants offered:* Pell, SEOG, state scholarships/grants, private scholarships, the school's own gift aid. *Loan aid offered:* FFEL Subsidized Stafford, FFEL Unsubsidized Stafford, FFEL PLUS, Federal Perkins, college/university loans from institutional funds. Federal Work-Study Program available. Institutional employment available. Applicants will be notified of awards on a rolling basis beginning on or about January 15. Off-campus job opportunities are good.

## FROM THE ADMISSIONS OFFICE

"Students tell us they are getting both a first-rate education and practical experience to help them be competitive upon graduation. Faculty, especially in psychology, marketing, and the sciences, regularly encourage students in their research. Students also do internships at such sites as the White House, Continental Insurance, Estee Lauder, State Street Global Advisors, and Cable News Network. About 90 percent of our graduates go on for advanced degrees or get jobs in their chosen field within six months of graduation. Keeping up with the latest in information technology is easy for our students now that all residence hall rooms have connections to the computer network. Even though the university has six micro-computing laboratories, including one open 24 hours a day, many students find it convenient to use their own PCs to 'surf the 'Net' from their rooms. . . . Small classes, the opportunity to work closely with professors, and the sense of campus community all contribute to the educational experience here. . . . More than 100 student organizations provide lots of opportunity for leadership and involvement in campus life."

## SELECTIVITY

★ ★ ★ ☆

| | |
|---|---|
| Admissions Rating | 81 |
| # of applicants | 2,411 |
| % of applicants accepted | 63 |
| % of acceptees attending | 33 |
| # accepting a place on wait list | 114 |
| % admitted from wait list | 11 |
| # of early decision applicants | 184 |
| % accepted early decision | 76 |
| % admitted from wait list | 12 |

### FRESHMAN PROFILE

| | |
|---|---|
| Range SAT Verbal | 530-620 |
| Range SAT Math | 540-630 |
| Minimum TOEFL | 550 |
| % graduated top 10% of class | 38 |
| % graduated top 25% of class | 72 |
| % graduated top 50% of class | 97 |

### DEADLINES

| | |
|---|---|
| Early decision | 1/1 |
| Early decision notification | 1/15 |
| Regular admission | 3/1 |
| Nonfall registration? | yes |

### APPLICANTS ALSO LOOK AT AND OFTEN PREFER
Bucknell University
Villanova University
Lafayette College
Ithaca College

### AND SOMETIMES PREFER
Muhlenberg College
Gettysburg College
Dickinson State University

### AND RARELY PREFER
Pennsylvania State University—University Park
Elizabethtown College
Lebanon Valley College

## FINANCIAL FACTS

★ ★ ★ ★

| | |
|---|---|
| Financial Aid Rating | 94 |
| Tuition | $21,930 |
| Room and board | $6,260 |
| Books and supplies | $600 |
| Required fees | $320 |
| % frosh receiving aid | 65 |
| % undergrads receiving aid | 68 |
| Avg frosh grant | $10,515 |
| Avg frosh loan | $3,300 |

# SWARTHMORE COLLEGE

500 COLLEGE AVENUE, SWARTHMORE, PA 19081 • ADMISSIONS: 610-328-8300 • FAX: 610-328-8580

## CAMPUS LIFE

| Quality of Life Rating | 85 |
|---|---|
| Type of school | private |
| Environment | suburban |

### STUDENTS

| Total undergrad enrollment | 1,479 |
|---|---|
| % from out of state | 83 |
| % from public high school | 55 |
| % live on campus | 93 |
| % in (# of) fraternities | 6 (2) |
| % African American | 7 |
| % Asian | 16 |
| % Caucasian | 54 |
| % Hispanic | 9 |
| % international | 6 |

#### SURVEY SAYS . . .
Campus is beautiful
Campus easy to get around
Political activism is hot
Ethnic diversity on campus
Great library
No one cheats
Musical organizations are hot
Great computer facilities

## ACADEMICS

| Academic Rating | 98 |
|---|---|
| Calendar | semester |
| Student/faculty ratio | 8:1 |
| % profs teaching UG courses | 100 |
| Avg lab size | 10-19 students |
| Avg reg class size | 10-19 students |

#### MOST POPULAR MAJORS
Biology/biological sciences
Economics
Political science and government

## STUDENTS SPEAK OUT

### Academics

"A Swarthmore day is a 28-hour day," notes one student, reflecting on the notoriously heavy workload at this elite liberal arts school. Don't let the reputation scare you off, though; as one student explained, "Academics at Swat are hard; everyone knows that coming in. But that doesn't mean they aren't enjoyable." Furthermore, "Swarthmore has a tremendous support network anchored by the professors and administration (as well as other students). When help is needed, there is always someone to turn to." The support is essential, since "the overall stress level here is high from balancing classes, activities, and social life." What do students get in return for their fretting and sweating? Academic freedom, for one; "students at Swarthmore manage to study anything and everything that interests them and may do so [to] whatever depth they choose." They also get "campus resources, including many public computers, electronics in the classroom, and free transportation to nearby campuses and Philadelphia to name a few." And let's not forget professors who "love to really get to know their students. They email you back within an hour, invite you to their homes for dinner, ask you to baby-sit for their kids, and always schedule appointments out of their office hours." Finally, students here enjoy an environment in which "learning is the goal, not the means." One thing they don't get, though, is great grades; as one student told us, "As one of our T-shirts says: 'Anywhere else it would have been an A.'"

### Life

Life at Swarthmore, most here agree, is "intense. Between the challenging classes, extracurricular commitments, and small community, people here tend to stress a lot and complain frequently. However, just about everybody who makes it through to graduation looks back on their four (or five or six) years as the most incredible time in their life." On top of their mountain of schoolwork, students "tend to be very involved in campus life and in a wide range of activities. People can be in student government and active in a minority organization and in a play, all at the same time." Accordingly, students have to get their fun on the run and learn to enjoy little pleasures. "Swatties love to have discussions," writes one student. "They will talk about a subject, everything from the gender politics of *Wuthering Heights* to the imagery of *Lord of the Rings*, for hours on end." They also "love walking around the gorgeous campus and taking walks in the acres of [the] well-kept arboretum around us." When it's time to party, Swatties do it for free: all on-campus activities are paid for out of the student activity fund. Notes one student, "It's quite possible to go months without spending money on things to do." Others, however, warn that "campus events are enjoyable for the first two years, but after that get a little old." That's when students head off campus, not to surrounding Swarthmore, which is "a pretty small suburb," but to Philadelphia. There's a train stop "at the foot of campus" that runs kids straight downtown.

### Student Body

The "brilliant, creative, engaging, and always ready for a discussion on anything and everything" students of Swarthmore maintain "a very high level of intellectual and social idealism." This social idealism manifests itself in a pervasive political leftism; "almost everyone is so far left politically/ideologically that the Democratic party seems right-wing," explains one undergrad. Many here are "over-involved. A typical Swattie is involved in a ludicrous number of extracurriculars: clubs, sports, volunteering, committees (besides all the work for class!)." Also, "whether a jock or a partygoer, a published writer or world traveler, everyone at Swarthmore has a little bit of dork deep down inside of them, and it's the common bond between us all." As one student put it, "People are unconcerned with matters of fashion, pop culture, and sometimes hygiene." Most Swatties "come from an upper-middle-class background."

# SWARTHMORE COLLEGE

FINANCIAL AID: 610-328-8358 • E-MAIL: ADMISSIONS@SWARTHMORE.EDU • WEBSITE: WWW.SWARTHMORE.EDU

## ADMISSIONS
*Very important factors considered include:* character/personal qualities, class rank, essays, recommendations, secondary school record, standardized test scores. *Important factors considered include:* extracurricular activities. *Other factors considered include:* alumni/ae relation, geographical residence, interview, minority status, talent/ability, volunteer work, work experience. SAT I or ACT required; SAT II also required.

### The Inside Word
Swarthmore is as good as they come; among liberal arts colleges there is none better. Candidates face an admissions process that is appropriately demanding and thorough. Even the best qualified of students need to complete their applications with a meticulous approach—during candidate evaluation, serious competition is just another file away. Those who are fortunate enough to be offered admission usually have shown the committee that they have a high level of intellectual curiosity, self-confidence, and motivation.

## FINANCIAL AID
*Students should submit:* FAFSA, institution's own financial aid form, CSS/Financial Aid PROFILE, state aid form, noncustodial (divorced/separated) parent's statement, business/farm supplement, federal tax return, W-2 statements, year-end paycheck stub. Regular filing deadline is mid-February. The Princeton Review suggests that all financial aid forms be submitted as soon as possible after January 1. *Need-based scholarships/grants offered:* Pell, SEOG, state scholarships/grants, private scholarships, the school's own gift aid. *Loan aid offered:* FFEL Subsidized Stafford, FFEL Unsubsidized Stafford, FFEL PLUS, Federal Perkins, state loans, college/university loans from institutional funds. Federal Work-Study Program available. Institutional employment available. Applicants will be notified of awards on or about April 1. Off-campus job opportunities are poor.

## FROM THE ADMISSIONS OFFICE
"Swarthmore is a highly selective college of liberal arts and engineering, located 11 miles southwest of Philadelphia. Founded as a coeducational institution in 1864, it is nonsectarian but reflects many traditions and values of its Quaker founders and attracts students who are engaged in the community as well as the classroom. Swarthmore's Honors Program provides an option to study in small seminars during the junior and senior years. A small school by deliberate policy, Swarthmore has an enrollment of about 1,450, with a student/faculty ratio of 8:1. It attracts students from 50 states and 42 countries."

### SELECTIVITY

| | |
|---|---:|
| Admissions Rating | 98 |
| # of applicants | 3,886 |
| % of applicants accepted | 24 |
| % of acceptees attending | 40 |
| # of early decision applicants | 360 |
| % accepted early decision | 43 |

### FRESHMAN PROFILE
| | |
|---|---:|
| Range SAT Verbal | 670-770 |
| Average SAT Verbal | 718 |
| Range SAT Math | 680-760 |
| Average SAT Math | 715 |
| % graduated top 10% of class | 90 |
| % graduated top 25% of class | 99 |
| % graduated top 50% of class | 100 |

### DEADLINES
| | |
|---|---:|
| Early decision I | 11/15 |
| Early decision I notification | 12/15 |
| Early decision II | 1/1 |
| Early decision II notification | 2/1 |
| Regular admission | 1/1 |
| Regular notification | 4/1 |

### APPLICANTS ALSO LOOK AT
**AND OFTEN PREFER**
Harvard
Princeton
Yale

**AND SOMETIMES PREFER**
Amherst
Columbia
Brown
Williams

**AND RARELY PREFER**
Cornell
Georgetown
Haverford
Wesleyan

### FINANCIAL FACTS

| | |
|---|---:|
| Financial Aid Rating | 83 |
| Tuition | $27,272 |
| Room and board | $8,530 |
| Books and supplies | $944 |
| Required fees | $290 |
| % frosh receiving aid | 48 |
| % undergrads receiving aid | 49 |
| Avg frosh grant | $21,656 |
| Avg frosh loan | $1,989 |

# SWEET BRIAR COLLEGE

PO Box B, Sweet Briar, VA 24595 • Admissions: 434-381-6142 • Fax: 434-381-6152

## CAMPUS LIFE

★ ★ ★ ★

| | |
|---|---|
| Quality of Life Rating | 94 |
| Type of school | private |
| Environment | rural |

### STUDENTS

| | |
|---|---|
| Total undergrad enrollment | 688 |
| % male/female | 3/97 |
| % from out of state | 57 |
| % from public high school | 77 |
| % live on campus | 89 |
| % African American | 4 |
| % American Indian | 1 |
| % Asian | 3 |
| % Caucasian | 86 |
| % Hispanic | 3 |
| % international | 3 |
| # of countries represented | 15 |

### SURVEY SAYS . . .
Great food on campus
No one cheats
Student government is popular
Campus feels safe
Dorms are like palaces
Class discussions encouraged
Students get along with local community

## ACADEMICS

| | |
|---|---|
| Academic Rating | 91 |
| Calendar | semester |
| Student/faculty ratio | 8:1 |
| Profs interesting rating | 97 |
| Profs accessible rating | 99 |
| % profs teaching UG courses | 100 |
| Avg reg class size | under 10 students |

### MOST POPULAR MAJORS
Psychology
English and creative writing
Biology

## STUDENTS SPEAK OUT

### Academics
Nestled in the foothills of Virginia's Blue Ridge Mountains, Sweet Briar's romantic name and distinctly southern location might lead the uninitiated to think its ladies are receiving instruction in the fine arts of swooning, eyelash batting, and fork placement. Not so. SBC has "cutting-edge" programs like Law & Society, the Center for Civic Renewal, and an environmental science program that includes, as one junior puts it, "3,250 acres of outdoor campus—woods, lakes, mountains—like having your own personal ecology laboratory." Sweet Briar's strengths also include highly focused instruction, a well-designed advisor program, and excellent professor-student dynamics: "Sweet Briar prides itself on small classes, individual attention, and a supportive environment," writes one student. "In a class of seven people, the professors won't let you fail." One sophomore remarks, "It's not just easy to find your professors here, it's hard to avoid them." Plus, everyone could use a little protection once they get out into the big bad world. Notes a sophomore: "The alumnae network is incredible."

### Life
While there's certainly no shortage of enthusiasm for life at Sweet Briar (one student warns, "if I loved it any more than I already do, I would buy it up and keep it")—there are varying opinions about the ups and downs of socializing on and off campus. Writes a senior, "Life at Sweet Briar can get pretty dull with no men around, and the college has been characterized as a 'suitcase school' as many leave during the weekend to visit neighboring colleges"—which include Hampden-Sydney College, University of Virginia, and Washington and Lee. Fairly strict alcohol policies also "force people to go off campus to have fun," though there have been concerted efforts by the administration in the last few years to improve SBC's social programming, which now includes "feature films, musicians, lectures, theater, 'Dell Parties,' casino nights, and formals throughout the year." Though there are the occasional trips to movies, the Wal-Mart, and a local country-and-western bar, a junior complains that "the town is much like Deliverance, and I just want to escape." Despite the negatives, SBC women manage to make the best of the situation, citing the school's stunning location on "a really beautiful campus with lots of great trails for running, hiking, mountain biking, and horseback riding."

### Student Body
Sweet Briar women are, in general, happy, active, involved, and mutually supportive. As one sophomore puts it, "The goals they have set for themselves are high and challenging." Adds another, "Living with 600 women changes the way you interact with women overall. Women respect women here." Of course, there are always your slightly irritating overachievers (e.g., "I sing in choir, am a class officer, am the chair of the Saturday Enrichment Program, ride on the fall team, have two campus jobs and a boyfriend!"), but on the whole SBC seems to offer students a noncompetitive, friendly atmosphere in which to pursue their studies. One student lauds "the encouragement of the women here to be all they can and to do whatever [they] want [with their] futures." And though a few students remarked on the ethnic and economic homogeneity of the student body, others disagreed. "Some people think we're a lily-white country club," writes a junior. "They've never been here. I have made friends from a wide variety of countries, cultures, races, and lifestyles. We're friends not because of some phony diversity movement, but because we're united by our academic pursuits." You go girl!

# SWEET BRIAR COLLEGE

FINANCIAL AID: 434-381-6156 • E-MAIL: ADMISSIONS@SBC.EDU • WEBSITE: WWW.SBC.EDU

## ADMISSIONS

*Very important factors considered include:* secondary school record. *Important factors considered include:* class rank, essays, extracurricular activities, recommendations, standardized test scores. *Other factors considered include:* alumni/ae relation, character/personal qualities, interview, minority status, talent/ability, volunteer work, work experience. SAT I or ACT required. TOEFL required of all international applicants. High school diploma or GED is required. *High school units required/recommended:* 16 total required; 20 total recommended; 4 English required, 3 math required, 4 math recommended, 3 science required, 4 science recommended, 2 science lab required, 3 foreign language required, 4 foreign language recommended, 1 social studies required, 2 social studies recommended, 2 history required.

## The Inside Word

A small applicant pool tempers selectivity greatly but also allows the admissions committee to take a longer look at most candidates than is typical in college admission. Despite the small applicant pool, candidates are usually well-qualified academically.

## FINANCIAL AID

*Students should submit:* FAFSA, noncustodial (divorced/separated) parent's statement, business/farm supplement. The Princeton Review suggests that all financial aid forms be submitted as soon as possible after January 1. *Need-based scholarships/grants offered:* Pell, SEOG, state scholarships/grants, private scholarships, the school's own gift aid. *Loan aid offered:* Direct Subsidized Stafford, Direct Unsubsidized Stafford, Direct PLUS, Federal Perkins, college/university loans from institutional funds. Federal Work-Study Program available. Institutional employment available. Applicants will be notified of awards on a rolling basis beginning on or about March 1. Off-campus job opportunities are good.

## FROM THE ADMISSIONS OFFICE

"The woman who applies to Sweet Briar is mature and far-sighted enough to know what she wants from her college experience. She is intellectually adventuresome, more willing to explore new fields, and more open to challenging her boundaries. Sweet Briar attracts the ambitious, confident woman who enjoys being immersed not only in a first-rate academic program, but in a variety of meaningful activities outside the classroom. Our students take charge and revel in their accomplishments. This attitude follows graduates, enabling them to compete confidently in the corporate world and in graduate school."

## SELECTIVITY

★ ★ ★ ☆

| | |
|---|---|
| Admissions Rating | 81 |
| # of applicants | 420 |
| % of applicants accepted | 86 |
| % of acceptees attending | 42 |
| # of early decision applicants | 43 |
| % accepted early decision | 93 |

### FRESHMAN PROFILE

| | |
|---|---|
| Range SAT Verbal | 530-660 |
| Average SAT Verbal | 590 |
| Range SAT Math | 490-610 |
| Average SAT Math | 550 |
| Range ACT Composite | 22-27 |
| Average ACT Composite | 24 |
| Minimum TOEFL | 580 |
| Average HS GPA | 3.5 |
| % graduated top 10% of class | 30 |
| % graduated top 25% of class | 59 |
| % graduated top 50% of class | 90 |

### DEADLINES

| | |
|---|---|
| Early decision | 12/1 |
| Early decision notification | 12/15 |
| Regular admission | 2/1 |
| Nonfall registration? | yes |

### APPLICANTS ALSO LOOK AT AND OFTEN PREFER

William & Mary
Mount Holyoke
Randolph-Macon Women's

### AND SOMETIMES PREFER

Hollins
Vanderbilt
U of Richmond

## FINANCIAL FACTS

★ ★ ★ ★

| | |
|---|---|
| Financial Aid Rating | 94 |
| Tuition | $19,700 |
| Room and board | $8,040 |
| Books and supplies | $600 |
| Required fees | $200 |
| Avg frosh grant | $9,093 |
| Avg frosh loan | $3,002 |

# SYRACUSE UNIVERSITY

201 TOLLEY, ADMINISTRATION BUILDING, SYRACUSE, NY 13244 • ADMISSIONS: 315-443-3611

## CAMPUS LIFE

| | |
|---|---|
| Quality of Life Rating | 84 |
| Type of school | private |
| Environment | urban |

### STUDENTS
| | |
|---|---|
| Total undergrad enrollment | 10,936 |
| % male/female | 44/56 |
| % from out of state | 56 |
| % from public high school | 78 |
| % live on campus | 73 |
| % in (# of) fraternities | 8 (22) |
| % in (# of) sororities | 13 (20) |
| % African American | 6 |
| % Asian | 5 |
| % Caucasian | 73 |
| % Hispanic | 4 |
| % international | 3 |
| # of countries represented | 61 |

### SURVEY SAYS . . .
Student publications are popular
Diverse students interact
Everyone loves the Orangemen
Frats and sororities dominate social scene
Students are cliquish
Athletic facilities are great
Lousy off-campus food
Lab facilities need improving
Students aren't religious

## ACADEMICS

| | |
|---|---|
| Academic Rating | 87 |
| Calendar | semester |
| Student/faculty ratio | 12:1 |
| Profs interesting rating | 73 |
| Profs accessible rating | 73 |
| % profs teaching UG courses | 98 |
| % classes taught by TAs | 6 |
| Avg lab size | 10-19 students |
| Avg reg class size | 20-29 students |

### MOST POPULAR MAJORS
Information science/studies
Psychology
Political science and government

## STUDENTS SPEAK OUT

### Academics
Students choose Syracuse University for the tremendous scope of its offerings, its excellent resources (including "a fantastic library!") and of course, its national reputation. Among its nine academic divisions, SU boasts notable programs in business, engineering, visual and performing arts, and natural sciences. It is probably best known, however, for the "amazing" Newhouse School of Communications, which is universally thought to be "one of the best in the country" and includes one of the nation's top broadcast journalism programs. Like most universities, "this school is very research oriented." Warns one student, "Syracuse University is supposedly a student-centered research campus; however, if the students don't know and act upon that, they'll get lost in the crowd." Instruction varies markedly from one division to the next, with journalism profs earning the highest marks. Notes one sophomore, "Some professors are captivating and others are awful. The TAs, in my experience, are uninformed, dull, and disinterested. The class sizes usually prevent individual interaction between students and teachers." Complains one math education major, "There is no doubt in my mind that the professors know their stuff, but a large portion of them don't know how to present the material in a beneficial manner." The administration generally receives favorable reviews; writes one student, "The school's administration is very accessible . . . many of them go to great lengths to accommodate your needs as a student. This helps reduce the stress of the whole academic experience." Many students, however, complain that the administration nickels-and-dimes them with "lots of extra charges on top of the very expensive tuition."

### Life
Students are split in their assessment of the social scene at Syracuse. Detractors badmouth the town ("dull and depressing . . . the local establishments—stores, shops, etc.—could use some restoration"), the weather ("This is the third most overcast city in the U.S.—lots of rain"), and the variety of available entertainment ("A car is needed to go anywhere that has culture," writes one student; says another, "No one leaves campus except to go to the mall. Culture in Syracuse is nonexistent"). Others disagree, pointing out that "there's more to do in Syracuse than people give it credit for. Many people go to the campus bars for entertainment. By far they are the most popular, but there are other things to do, like bowling, dancing, coffee houses, etc." They also point to a moderately active Greek system that "provides more stuff to do, especially since there isn't much to do in local areas. Bars are big here, as are casual drugs like marijuana. This could be a very depressing place or the best time ever." All students agree that drinking is a popular pastime, explaining that "SU is a drinking school, not a party school." They also agree that intercollegiate sports, especially football, basketball, and lacrosse, are huge. Sums up one student, "If you like sports, snow, and beer, this is a great school for you."

### Student Body
"People think that the only type of people that come here are rich spoiled kids from Long Island," writes one SU student. "In reality, those are the ones that stick out the most, but there are many different types of people here." Indeed, undergrads at SU represent "a diverse student population with diverse interests." However, according to most students, different populations rarely intermingle. "I would love to believe that we all get along," writes one African American junior, "but we segregate from each other based on Greek life, race, religion, class, etc. It's rather sad: some just live in a bubble and think SU is A-OK. We have some work to do."

# SYRACUSE UNIVERSITY

FINANCIAL AID: 315-443-1513 • E-MAIL: ORANGE@SYR.EDU • WEBSITE: WWW.SYRACUSE.EDU

## ADMISSIONS
*Very important factors considered include:* character/personal qualities, class rank, essays, interview, recommendations, secondary school record, standardized test scores. *Important factors considered include:* talent/ability. *Other factors considered include:* alumni/ae relation, extracurricular activities, minority status, volunteer work, work experience. SAT I or ACT required; SAT I preferred. TOEFL required of all international applicants. High school diploma or GED is required. *High school units required/recommended:* 20 total required; 21 total recommended; 4 English required, 3 math required, 3 science required, 3 science lab required, 2 foreign language required, 3 foreign language recommended, 3 social studies required, 5 elective required.

### The Inside Word
Thanks to nationally competitive athletic teams and the Newhouse School of Communications, Syracuse draws a large applicant pool. At the same time, it has reduced the size of the freshman class, so the university has gotten more selective over the past few years. Most above-average students should still be strong candidates; though many weaker students are also able to benefit from Syracuse's individualized admissions process, they must show true promise in order to have a shot. Candidates for the Newhouse School will encounter even greater competition for admission.

## FINANCIAL AID
*Students should submit:* FAFSA, CSS/Financial Aid PROFILE. Regular filing deadline is February 1. The Princeton Review suggests that all financial aid forms be submitted as soon as possible after January 1. *Need-based scholarships/grants offered:* Pell, SEOG, state scholarships/grants, the school's own gift aid. *Loan aid offered:* FFEL Subsidized Stafford, FFEL Unsubsidized Stafford, FFEL PLUS, Federal Perkins, Federal Nursing. Federal Work-Study Program available. Institutional employment available. Applicants will be notified of awards on or about April 1. Off-campus job opportunities are good.

## FROM THE ADMISSIONS OFFICE
"Syracuse University is set on a beautiful residential campus that encompasses more than 200 acres and 170 buildings. Situated on a hill, overlooking downtown Syracuse, the school gives students the opportunity to enjoy the traditional college environment while realizing the social and recreational opportunities of a medium-size city.

"Syracuse University is committed to priorities that place its students first and foremost in importance. Small classes, intensive advising, emphasis on transition to college in the first year, and active learning characterize a systematic approach to assuring a productive teaching and learning environment. Improved classroom opportunities through smaller classes provide students with close attention from faculty.

"In virtually every aspect of students' lives at Syracuse, choices abound. The range of courses available, opportunities for study abroad and internships, the scope of residential living possibilities, the array of co-curricular and extracurricular clubs and organizations (there are nearly 300), and the opportunity to participate in the Honors Program makes SU an exciting place to attend. Students at Syracuse University have the choice of more than 200 undergraduate majors and nearly 70 undergraduate minors. Syracuse combines the best characteristics of a research institution with a traditional focus on the highest quality teaching, advising, and mentoring. It is a student-centered research university, and is committed to giving students the very best educational experiences available."

### SELECTIVITY

| | |
|---|---:|
| Admissions Rating | 88 |
| # of applicants | 13,644 |
| % of applicants accepted | 69 |
| % of acceptees attending | 31 |
| # of early decision applicants | 715 |
| % accepted early decision | 65 |

### FRESHMAN PROFILE
| | |
|---|---:|
| Range SAT Verbal | 550-640 |
| Range SAT Math | 570-660 |
| Minimum TOEFL | 550 |
| Average HS GPA | 3.5 |
| % graduated top 10% of class | 41 |
| % graduated top 25% of class | 79 |
| % graduated top 50% of class | 98 |

### DEADLINES
| | |
|---|---:|
| Early decision | 11/15 |
| Early decision notification | 12/31 |
| Regular admission | 1/1 |
| Nonfall registration? | yes |

### APPLICANTS ALSO LOOK AT AND SOMETIMES PREFER
NYU
Cornell
Boston U
Penn State
U of Maryland

### FINANCIAL FACTS

| | |
|---|---:|
| Financial Aid Rating | 83 |
| Tuition | $24,170 |
| Room and board | $9,590 |
| Books and supplies | $1,162 |
| Required fees | $960 |
| % frosh receiving aid | 55 |
| % undergrads receiving aid | 56 |
| Avg frosh grant | $13,400 |
| Avg frosh loan | $3,300 |

# TCU

Office of Admissions, TCU Box 297013, Fort Worth, TX 76129 • Admissions: 817-257-7490 • Fax: 817-257-7268

## CAMPUS LIFE

| | |
|---|---|
| Quality of Life Rating | 88 |
| Type of school | private |
| Affiliation | Disciples of Christ |
| Environment | suburban |

### STUDENTS

| | |
|---|---|
| Total undergrad enrollment | 6,851 |
| % male/female | 42/58 |
| % from out of state | 23 |
| % from public high school | 94 |
| % live on campus | 46 |
| % in (# of) fraternities | 34 (13) |
| % in (# of) sororities | 38 (16) |
| % African American | 5 |
| % Asian | 2 |
| % Caucasian | 78 |
| % Hispanic | 6 |
| % international | 5 |
| # of countries represented | 75 |

### SURVEY SAYS . . .

Frats and sororities dominate social scene
Campus easy to get around
Students love Fort Worth, TX
Campus is beautiful
Great off-campus food
Students are happy
Lots of beer drinking, Great library
Campus feels safe
Registration is a breeze
Everyone loves the Horned Frogs
Great computer facilities
Student newspaper is popular
School is well run
Dorms are like palaces

## ACADEMICS

| | |
|---|---|
| Academic Rating | 78 |
| Calendar | semester |
| Student/faculty ratio | 15:1 |
| % profs teaching UG courses | 97 |
| % classes taught by TAs | 2 |
| Avg lab size | 10-19 students |
| Avg reg class size | 10-19 students |

## STUDENTS SPEAK OUT

### Academics

TCU, students tell us, "is a medium-size school that lets everyone feel like they're in a community college environment." It's a university large enough to provide students with excellent research opportunities, yet small enough that most professors and administrators have open-door policies. Reports one student, "Most of the professors here treat us more like equals than students; it's nice to have professors who don't look down on you because you're young." Similarly, administrators "almost always have open doors so students can go in and chat with them." TCU is not without its big-school problems, however; several students here complain that "the advisors are not totally sure what they are doing, and I hear a lot of students are not sure what classes to take, and are misinformed about some curriculum courses." For serious students, however, TCU's only major drawback is the student body; writes one disappointed undergrad, "Most people are not thinking much at all except for the next test. There is not a strong forum for exchanging ideas and it's not cultivated outside the classroom." Adds another ambitious scholar, "TCU is a party school. The majority of the students could care less about learning . . . . [They] are mostly concerned about what party they are going to on Friday night." Opportunities for the highly motivated exist in the honors program ("pushed me to new levels of studying and learning") and the study abroad program ("Studying abroad was perhaps one of the most eye-opening and amazing experiences I [had] in my years at TCU. I went to Australia, and learned so much about myself just from taking myself out of the 'TCU Bubble'").

### Life

"TCU is all about Greek Life," students here agree; the school "has an overwhelming Greek population that permeates, and sadly sometimes overshadows, the actual education aspect of the school." As one student put it, "If you are interested in Greek life, then TCU is definitely the place for you. Even though statistics show that only 35 to 40 percent of students are Greek, the reality is that it feels as if 90 to 95 percent are. They always have mixers, fund-raisers, and many other functions that make them very visible on campus." Be forewarned that "there is a huge pressure to be a part of Greek recruitment as a freshman. . . . [Those] who don't join any organizations often feel really isolated. It's all about social connections here." Because "Greek housing is located in a completely separate area of campus and is far away from the other residence halls," the Greeks socialize only with each other, leaving the few independents to fend for themselves. Fortunately, there's Fort Worth, which is "great for going out and exploring. There are great places to eat and shop and even some great places to go and enjoy the culture. We love the stockyards and Billy Bob's." There's also an active bar scene right across the street from campus; also nearby "you can find the zoo, botanical gardens, or a nearby strip of shops where students can go and hang out." A little further down the road is Dallas. Of course, there's always TCU sports and the home team Horned Frogs; notes one student, "Being in Texas, everyone rallies around the football team. Games are a big deal, and lots of people go."

### Student Body

"Everyone here is good-looking and never seems to go to class." The typical student is "rich, white, and Greek," "conservative, but friendly," and "very marriage-oriented; we joke about obtaining a 'Mrs.' degree." Alternative students, "the ones who wear dreads, or skater clothes, or have funky-dyed hair, all band together. All ten of them." Diversity at TCU arrives primarily in the form of international students, who "mostly associate among themselves." Most students are devout Christians who manage to reconcile their beliefs with the school's vigorous party scene.

510 ■ THE BEST 351 COLLEGES

# TCU

FINANCIAL AID: 817-257-7858 • E-MAIL: FROGMAIL@TCU.EDU • WEBSITE: WWW.TCU.EDU

## ADMISSIONS

*Very important factors considered include:* character/personal qualities, class rank, essays, recommendations, secondary school record, standardized test scores. *Important factors considered include:* extracurricular activities, geographical residence, minority status, religious affiliation/commitment, talent/ability, volunteer work, work experience. *Other factors considered include:* alumni/ae relation, interview. SAT I or ACT required. TOEFL required of all international applicants. High school diploma is required and GED is not accepted. *High school units required/recommended:* 17 total required; 24 total recommended; 4 English required, 3 math required, 4 math recommended, 3 science required, 4 science recommended, 2 foreign language required, 4 foreign language recommended, 3 social studies required, 4 social studies recommended, 2 elective required, 4 elective recommended.

### The Inside Word

The most important element of the admissions process at TCU is finding the right student to fill their classes. Most applicants are admitted, notwithstanding TCU's challenging academic standards.

## FINANCIAL AID

*Students should submit:* FAFSA, institution's own financial aid form. Regular filing deadline is May 1. The Princeton Review suggests that all financial aid forms be submitted as soon as possible after January 1. *Need-based scholarships/grants offered:* Pell, SEOG, state scholarships/grants, private scholarships, the school's own gift aid, United Negro College Fund. *Loan aid offered:* FFEL Subsidized Stafford, FFEL Unsubsidized Stafford, FFEL PLUS, Federal Perkins, Federal Nursing, state loans, college/university loans from institutional funds. Federal Work-Study Program available. Institutional employment available. Applicants will be notified of awards on a rolling basis beginning on or about March 1. Off-campus job opportunities are excellent.

## FROM THE ADMISSIONS OFFICE

"TCU is a major teaching and research university with the feel of a small college. The friendly campus community welcomes new students before classes begin, at Frog Camp, where students find three days of fun meeting new friends, learning campus traditions, and serving the community. The TCU experience continues with opportunities like freshman seminars that are small classes with top faculty; cutting-edge technology and equipment such as Internet access in every residence hall room and major classroom and lab upgrades; a liberal arts and sciences core curriculum; and real-life application through faculty-directed research, group projects, and internships. While TCU faculty members are recognized for research, their main focus is on teaching and mentoring students. The historic relationship to the Christian Church (Disciples of Christ) means that instead of imposing a particular viewpoint, TCU encourages students to consider and follow their own beliefs. The university's mission—to educate individuals to think and act as ethical leaders and responsible citizens in the global community—influences everything from course work to study abroad to the way Horned Frogs act and interact. From National Merit Scholars to those just now realizing their academic potential, TCU attracts and serves students who are learning to change the world."

---

### SELECTIVITY

★★★☆

| | |
|---|---|
| Admissions Rating | 80 |
| # of applicants | 6,137 |
| % of applicants accepted | 71 |
| % of acceptees attending | 33 |
| # accepting a place on wait list | 273 |
| % admitted from wait list | 96 |

### FRESHMAN PROFILE

| | |
|---|---|
| Range SAT Verbal | 510-620 |
| Range SAT Math | 520-630 |
| Range ACT Composite | 21-27 |
| Minimum TOEFL | 550 |
| % graduated top 10% of class | 28 |
| % graduated top 25% of class | 64 |
| % graduated top 50% of class | 94 |

### DEADLINES

| | |
|---|---|
| Regular admission | 2/15 |
| Regular notification | 4/1 |
| Nonfall registration? | yes |

### APPLICANTS ALSO LOOK AT AND SOMETIMES PREFER

UT Austin
Trinity U
Texas A&M
Rice
Baylor

### AND RARELY PREFER

SMU
Austin College
Southwestern U

### FINANCIAL FACTS

| | |
|---|---|
| Financial Aid Rating | 83 |
| Tuition & fees | $17,590 |
| Room and board | $5,780 |
| Books and supplies | $750 |
| % frosh receiving aid | 42 |
| % undergrads receiving aid | 40 |

# TEMPLE UNIVERSITY

1801 NORTH BROAD STREET, PHILADELPHIA, PA 19122-6096 • ADMISSIONS: 215-204-7200 • FAX: 215-204-5694

## CAMPUS LIFE

| | |
|---|---|
| Quality of Life Rating | 81 |
| Type of school | public |
| Environment | urban |

### STUDENTS
| | |
|---|---|
| Total undergrad enrollment | 21,429 |
| % male/female | 42/58 |
| % from out of state | 25 |
| % from public high school | 78 |
| % live on campus | 27 |
| % in (# of) fraternities | 1 (13) |
| % in (# of) sororities | 1 (12) |
| % African American | 23 |
| % Asian | 8 |
| % Caucasian | 57 |
| % Hispanic | 4 |
| % international | 4 |
| # of countries represented | 130 |

### SURVEY SAYS . . .
Ethnic diversity on campus
(Almost) everyone smokes
Athletic facilities are great
Everyone loves the Owls
Lots of beer drinking
Great computer facilities
Great library
Great off-campus food
Hard liquor is popular

## ACADEMICS

| | |
|---|---|
| Academic Rating | 72 |
| Calendar | semester |
| Student/faculty ratio | 14:1 |
| Avg lab size | 20-29 students |
| Avg reg class size | 20-29 students |

### MOST POPULAR MAJORS
Elementary education and teaching
Journalism
Psychology

## STUDENTS SPEAK OUT

### Academics

Temple students love their school for its ability to integrate "a good education with significant life experiences." The school has earned a "great scholastic reputation" while prioritizing "real-life, hands-on experience with internships, co-ops, and experiential learning that prepare you for life beyond college." Many students agree that Temple helps students "develop thinking skills, ask questions, and wake up to see what the reality is." Professors are praised for "incorporating things from outside of the classroom into the lectures and discussions." Instructors both "know their material" and find "effective ways to relate it to the students." The University's heterogeneous student body is reflected in the faculty, "a diverse, intelligent group" that "finds delight in sharing their knowledge with us." In particular, students gush about the professors and classes in the honors program. Honors classes "tend to be smaller, more interesting, and contain people who seem to actually enjoy learning." These courses provide "an atmosphere where discussions create more learning than a lecture would." The "extremely supportive" professors involved in the program "go out of their way to keep in contact with the students." For those not enrolled in the honors program, "course selection and advising can be difficult." One student values that Temple "can also be very interesting and experimental with its class offerings." As far as logistics go, one respondent writes, " I have had no problem contacting [the] administration when I need help with a problem." Though a few students say, "The bureaucracy sucks," most agree that "the education can be magic." Not to mention affordable.

### Life

Temple's urban location largely defines the campus' feel. Though the school organizes "free good food, movies, guest speakers, parties, festivals, and cultural bus trips," most students choose to make their own fun in surrounding Philadelphia, "which is easy because we are directly connected to public transportation." Undergraduates agree, "From theatre and museums to shops, clubs, and cafés, Philly has a lot to do." Students just have to "be able to take care of themselves in the city" since the surrounding area is described as "dodgy." One respondent articulates both sides of the issue: "Temple's main strength is the fact that it is in Philadelphia, but this takes away much of the close-knit campus feel." Certain issues do bring people together: "Political activism has become more popular recently, especially concerns over the government and foreign affairs." Fraternities pitch in on the weekend social scene, throwing parties attended mainly by underclassmen and those who live on campus. Commuters claim to have a "completely different life" than their resident counterparts, marked mainly by parking headaches.

### Student Body

One student sums it up when she writes, "We call it Diversity University." Repeatedly, surveys emphasize that the undergraduate population comprises students from every imaginable racial, ethnic, religious, and class background. A few unifying factors do emerge: "A typical student is a fairly hardworking, goal-oriented, middle-class American looking to carve out a future for his or herself." But as soon as you think you have a beat on it, someone says, "It is impossible to define a typical student because Temple is full of every different type of person." Students appreciate the diversity, claiming that the mix of "various backgrounds challenges opinions and feeds into active class discussions." In this "huge melting pot," respondents claim, "everyone's differences become their connection to other people." Certain students shatter the utopian image by telling us, "Most people seem to stick to their own groups, dictated by either major, race, [or] economic status." Other people call the campus "annoyingly anonymous" because it is "very much a commuter school." Despite these minor grumbles, Temple students predominantly "look past the stereotypes" and accept their peers "for whom they are and what they are trying to achieve."

# TEMPLE UNIVERSITY

FINANCIAL AID: 215-204-8760 • E-MAIL: TUADM@MAIL.TEMPLE.EDU • WEBSITE: WWW.TEMPLE.EDU

## ADMISSIONS

*Very important factors considered include:* class rank, secondary school record. *Important factors considered include:* standardized test scores. *Other factors considered include:* alumni/ae relation, character/personal qualities, essays, extracurricular activities, recommendations, talent/ability, volunteer work, work experience. SAT I or ACT required. TOEFL required of all international applicants. High school diploma or GED is required. *High school units required/recommended:* 16 total required; 22 total recommended; 4 English required, 3 math required, 4 math recommended, 2 science required, 3 science recommended, 1 science lab required, 2 science lab recommended, 2 foreign language required, 2 social studies required, 1 history required, 2 history recommended, 1 elective required, 3 elective recommended.

### The Inside Word

Nearly 50 percent of Temple's applicants are from outside Pennsylvania; 25 percent are from the Philadelphia area, and 25 percent from elsewhere in Pennsylvania. Admissions standards are moderately selective in general (61 percent acceptance rate), but candidates for the College of Music, in particular, face a rigorous review.

## FINANCIAL AID

*Students should submit:* FAFSA. The Princeton Review suggests that all financial aid forms be submitted as soon as possible after January 1. *Need-based scholarships/grants offered:* Pell, SEOG, state scholarships/grants, private scholarships, the school's own gift aid, Federal Nursing. *Loan aid offered:* FFEL Subsidized Stafford, FFEL Unsubsidized Stafford, FFEL PLUS, Federal Perkins, Federal Nursing, college/university loans from institutional funds. Federal Work-Study Program available. Institutional employment available. Applicants will be notified of awards on a rolling basis beginning on or about February 15. Off-campus job opportunities are excellent.

## FROM THE ADMISSIONS OFFICE

"Temple combines the academic resources and intellectual stimulation of a large research university with the intimacy of a small college. The university experienced record growth in attracting new students from all 50 states and over 125 countries: up 60 percent in three years. Students choose from 119 undergraduate majors. Special academic programs include honors, learning communities for first-year undergraduates, co-op education, and study abroad. Temple has seven regional campuses, including Main Campus and the Health Sciences Center in historic Philadelphia, suburban Temple University, Ambler, and overseas campuses in Tokyo and Rome. Main Campus is home to the Tuttleman Learning Center, with 1,000 computer stations linked to Paley Library. The Center is a hub for emerging learning technologies, and is designed for the high-tech students of today and tomorrow. The Liacouras Center is a state-of-the-art entertainment, recreation, and sports complex that hosts concerts, plays, trade shows, and college and professional athletics. It also includes the Independence Blue Cross Student Recreation Center, a major fitness facility for students now and in the future. Students can also take advantage of the new Student Fieldhouse. The university has constructed two new dorms, built to meet an unprecedented demand for main campus housing."

### SELECTIVITY

| | |
|---|---|
| Admissions Rating | 79 |
| # of applicants | 15,288 |
| % of applicants accepted | 61 |
| % of acceptees attending | 39 |

#### FRESHMAN PROFILE

| | |
|---|---|
| Range SAT Verbal | 490-590 |
| Average SAT Verbal | 536 |
| Range SAT Math | 490-590 |
| Average SAT Math | 532 |
| Range ACT Composite | 19-24 |
| Minimum TOEFL | 525 |
| Average HS GPA | 3.2 |
| % graduated top 10% of class | 20 |
| % graduated top 25% of class | 50 |
| % graduated top 50% of class | 88 |

#### DEADLINES

| | |
|---|---|
| Regular admission | 4/1 |
| Nonfall registration? | yes |

#### APPLICANTS ALSO LOOK AT AND OFTEN PREFER

U Pennsylvania
U Pittsburgh
Penn State at University Park
Lehigh

#### AND SOMETIMES PREFER

Villanova
Rutgers
St. Joseph's U
Drexel
NYU

#### AND RARELY PREFER

Westchester U
Widener U
Gettysburg College
LaSalle U

### FINANCIAL FACTS

| | |
|---|---|
| Financial Aid Rating | 75 |
| In-state tuition | $7,602 |
| Out-of-state tuition | $13,856 |
| Room and board | $7,112 |
| Books and supplies | $800 |
| Required fees | $460 |
| % frosh receiving aid | 70 |
| % undergrads receiving aid | 67 |

THE BEST 351 COLLEGES ■ 513

# Texas A&M University—College Station

ADMISSIONS COUNSELING, COLLEGE STATION, TX 77843-1265 • ADMISSIONS: 979-845-3741 • FAX: 979-847-8737

## CAMPUS LIFE

| | |
|---|---|
| **Quality of Life Rating** | **89** |
| Type of school | public |
| Environment | suburban |

### STUDENTS
| | |
|---|---|
| Total undergrad enrollment | 45,083 |
| % male/female | 51/49 |
| % from out of state | 3 |
| % live on campus | 27 |
| % in (# of) fraternities | 4 (26) |
| % in (# of) sororities | 6 (20) |
| % African American | 2 |
| % Asian | 3 |
| % Caucasian | 84 |
| % Hispanic | 9 |
| % international | 1 |
| # of countries represented | 115 |

### SURVEY SAYS . . .
Everyone loves the Aggies
Athletic facilities are great
(Almost) everyone plays intramural sports
Class discussions are rare
Political activism is hot
Large classes
Students are very religious
Students get along with local community
Campus difficult to get around
(Almost) no one smokes

## ACADEMICS

| | |
|---|---|
| **Academic Rating** | **81** |
| Calendar | semester |
| Student/faculty ratio | 21:1 |
| Profs interesting rating | 89 |
| Profs accessible rating | 90 |
| % profs teaching UG courses | 75 |
| % classes taught by TAs | 25 |
| Avg lab size | 10-19 students |
| Avg reg class size | 20-29 students |

### MOST POPULAR MAJORS
Operations management and supervision
Biological and physical sciences
Psychology

## STUDENTS SPEAK OUT

### Academics
Tradition-laden Texas A&M neatly divides its student body in two: those who live, breathe, and die A&M maroon, and those who can't figure out what all the fuss is about. Explains one student, "A&M has tradition, tradition, and some more tradition. If you get involved, it will sweep you along (sometimes to the detriment of your studies), but if you aren't the type to buy into it, it can take longer to find friends with similar interests." Not surprisingly, those who get swept up love the place; those who don't usually exit before their four years are up. To its champions, "Texas A&M is a great place. It's very big and has lots of students, so it can be very overwhelming for a first-semester freshman, but once you learn the ropes and how to do things" things get a lot better. Detractors warn that "at times, I feel like I am only a number to a lot of my professors. My advisor is not always available either." They also complain that "Texas A&M is so concerned about research and money and the prestige that accompanies both that they feel a great researcher equals [a] great instructor." Aggie boosters disagree, saying that "A&M's obvious focus is on research, but not to the overall detriment of undergraduates." All agree that A&M has superior schools of engineering, veterinary science, and business, and also that the vast alumni network is an invaluable resource to graduates.

### Life
Attending A&M is not just an academic decision; for most, it is a lifestyle choice. "Aggies are fanatical about being Aggies" and "share a fabulous heritage." If you love school spirit and want to be a part of some of the greatest college traditions offered by humankind, this is the place for you. Leading the way is A&M's military training program, the Corps of Cadets. A member boasts, "It is the best leadership training in the nation. We are known as 'keepers of the spirit' and 'founders of tradition.' " Another tradition is "saying 'Howdy' to everyone that you pass. That is just one of the many things I like about the Aggies. We get along very well." With more than 700 student organizations, a first-class student union, and a thriving Greek community, A&M offers just about anything for the student who feels at home in College Station. For those few who don't, life can get pretty monotonous. Writes one such student, "Nightlife consists of either going to a country bar, some smoked-filled bar teeming with other guys, going to a party (more beer and guys), or just hauling ass to Austin, Houston, or even [Dallas/Fort Worth]. For fun I like to dream about this upcoming August when I shall graduate and never set foot here again." P.S.: Football is HUGE here.

### Student Body
Because of A&M's many cherished traditions, students here "are strongly bonded by the fact that we are all Aggies. There is a deep camaraderie that extends long after you graduate. No matter where you are later in life, if you see an Aggie ring, you have an instant bond with that person. Many students are here because of that camaraderie, and that's what makes A&M such an amazing place." Those who don't fit in, however, have a difficult time. Explains one Aggie, "The first thing I will admit about A&M is that it is very conservative. While most of the students are open-minded about the differences between us, there is a small yet visible group of students who are very close-minded. The one flaw I can point out about A&M is that people of minorities—whether a religious minority, a racial minority, or a minority based on sexual orientation—are not necessarily encouraged to come here by what they see. . . . Honestly, we are a school of white, heterosexual, Christian students."

# TEXAS A&M UNIVERSITY—COLLEGE STATION

FINANCIAL AID: 979-845-3236 • E-MAIL: ADMISSIONS@TAMU.EDU • WEBSITE: WWW.TAMU.EDU

## ADMISSIONS

*Very important factors considered include:* class rank, extracurricular activities, secondary school record, standardized test scores, state residency, talent/ability. *Important factors considered include:* essays, volunteer work, work experience. *Other factors considered include:* alumni/ae relation, character/personal qualities, geographical residence, recommendations. SAT I or ACT required. TOEFL required of all international applicants. High school diploma or GED is required. *High school units required/recommended:* 16 total required; 19 total recommended; 4 English required, 3 math required, 2 science required, 3 science recommended, 2 science lab required, 2 foreign language required, 3 foreign language recommended, 2 social studies required, 1 history required.

## The Inside Word

Texas A&M has a very impressive record of enrolling strong students. A super-high percentage of these admits enroll, which, when combined with the university's impressive graduation rate, is probably the best testament to A&M's reputation. Don't be deceived by the fairly high admit rate, however—for it to be significantly lower, there would have to be a huge increase in the size of the already enormous applicant pool. African American and Hispanic applicants may find it somewhat easier going, as applications from those groups declined last season. Affirmative action issues in Texas ultimately cloud the picture for out-of-state minority applicants, at least until it becomes more clear what steps will or will not be taken in the admissions processes at Texas schools. The current approach guarantees admission for those Texas students graduating in the top 10 percent of their high school class.

## FINANCIAL AID

*Students should submit:* FAFSA, institution's own financial aid form, financial aid transcripts (for transfer students). The Princeton Review suggests that all financial aid forms be submitted as soon as possible after January 1. *Need-based scholarships/grants offered:* Pell, SEOG, state scholarships/grants, private scholarships, the school's own gift aid. *Loan aid offered:* FFEL Subsidized Stafford, FFEL Unsubsidized Stafford, FFEL PLUS, Federal Perkins, state loans, college/university loans from institutional funds. Federal Work-Study Program available. Institutional employment available. Applicants will be notified of awards on a rolling basis beginning on or about April 15. Off-campus job opportunities are good.

## FROM THE ADMISSIONS OFFICE

"Established in 1876 as the first public college in the state, Texas A&M University today has become a world leader in teaching, research, and public service. Located in College Station in the heart of Texas, it is centrally situated among three of the country's 10 largest cities—Dallas, Houston, and San Antonio. Texas A&M is the only university to be ranked nationally among the top 10 in these four areas: enrollment (fall 1997 enrollment was 41,461), enrollment of top students (7th in number of new National Merit Scholars for fall 1997), value of research (7th with $367 million in 1997), and endowment (10th in endowment with $2.4 billion as of 1997)."

### SELECTIVITY

| | |
|---|---|
| Admissions Rating | 83 |
| # of applicants | 17,284 |
| % of applicants accepted | 68 |
| % of acceptees attending | 59 |
| # accepting a place on wait list | 1,518 |
| % admitted from wait list | 45 |

### FRESHMAN PROFILE

| | |
|---|---|
| Range SAT Verbal | 520-630 |
| Average SAT Verbal | 576 |
| Range SAT Math | 550-660 |
| Average SAT Math | 602 |
| Range ACT Composite | 22-27 |
| Average ACT Composite | 25 |
| Minimum TOEFL | 550 |
| % graduated top 10% of class | 55 |
| % graduated top 25% of class | 89 |
| % graduated top 50% of class | 99 |

### DEADLINES

| | |
|---|---|
| Regular admission | 2/15 |
| Nonfall registration? | yes |

### APPLICANTS ALSO LOOK AT

**AND OFTEN PREFER**
Rice
**AND SOMETIMES PREFER**
UT Austin
Texas Tech
LSU at Baton Rouge
Baylor
**AND RARELY PREFER**
Southern Methodist
Stephen F. Austin State
Southwest Texas

### FINANCIAL FACTS

| | |
|---|---|
| Financial Aid Rating | 86 |
| In-state tuition | $2,640 |
| Out-of-state tuition | $9,180 |
| Room and board | $6,030 |
| Books and supplies | $818 |
| Required fees | $4,748 |
| % frosh receiving aid | 29 |
| % undergrads receiving aid | 28 |
| Avg frosh grant | $3,280 |
| Avg frosh loan | $4,350 |

# TRINITY COLLEGE

300 SUMMIT STREET, HARTFORD, CT 06016 • ADMISSIONS: 860-297-2180 • FAX: 860-297-2287

## CAMPUS LIFE

| Quality of Life Rating | 80 |
|---|---|
| Type of school | private |
| Environment | urban |

### STUDENTS

| Total undergrad enrollment | 2,098 |
|---|---|
| % male/female | 48/52 |
| % from out of state | 78 |
| % from public high school | 54 |
| % live on campus | 95 |
| % in (# of) fraternities | 27 (7) |
| % in (# of) sororities | 22 (7) |
| % African American | 6 |
| % Asian | 6 |
| % Caucasian | 69 |
| % Hispanic | 5 |
| % international | 2 |
| # of countries represented | 35 |

### SURVEY SAYS...
Diversity lacking on campus
Everyone loves the Bantams
Great computer facilities
Great food on campus
Class discussions encouraged

## ACADEMICS

| Academic Rating | 84 |
|---|---|
| Calendar | semester |
| Student/faculty ratio | 9:1 |
| Profs interesting rating | 95 |
| Profs accessible rating | 98 |
| % profs teaching UG courses | 100 |
| Avg lab size | 20-29 students |
| Avg reg class size | 10-19 students |

### MOST POPULAR MAJORS
History
Economics
Political science and government

## STUDENTS SPEAK OUT

### Academics

Students at Trinity College enjoy an uncommon degree of academic intimacy and comfort. Notes one, "Trinity is a small school where it is easy to form strong relationships with professors, administration, and even the buildings and grounds staff." Agrees another, "There is no line between faculty, administration, and students. We work hard together; we play hard together. We are a proud campus!" While students appreciate the bond they form with faculty, they also enjoy the degree of autonomy Trinity's academic approach grants them. Even the curricular requirements here provide opportunities for independence, as students are allowed to choose from a number of courses to fulfill each requirement and to design their own "integration of knowledge" sequence. One engineering major boasts, "Trinity has given me educational opportunities not normally available to undergraduates. I've been involved in graduate-level research since freshman year, have the ability to take graduate courses through the consortium, have an internship through Hartford Hospital, and have presented research at a conference." Profs here earn high marks both for teaching ability ("professors allow the make-up of the class to direct what type of class it is: discussion, group work, field trips, visual aids, lecture, etc.") and accessibility ("I have had some absolutely amazing professors who are accessible outside the classroom and go out of their way to know students"). Students save their highest praise, though, for the school president, who "is really involved. He's even called our room before regarding a question."

### Life

"Trinity is a party school!" proudly exclaim students, who hasten to add that it's not all play here. "People at this school like to have fun," offers one student, "but they know when it's time to buckle down and do some work." A senior qualifies that assessment, opining that "the 'work hard, play hard' ethic still applies here, although profs are sometimes too lenient and students can get away with doing little work or getting extensions." During extracurricular hours, students enjoy theme parties such as the 1980s Dance and the Nastee Greek parties, productions by the school's "strong" theater department, lectures ("We had Cornell West and two descendents of Thomas Jefferson—one black, one white—here recently"), Greek life ("beneficial to all"), and athletic events ("Intercollegiate sports are big here. I can always count on my roommates and friends to show up [at] my games"). They also appreciate the location ("between Boston and New York") of Hartford and report that "Trinity is in a bad neighborhood, but downtown Hartford offers restaurants, theater, and a world-class museum." The lovely campus boasts "the most beautiful chapel on the East Coast."

### Student Body

The students of Trinity are "so friendly, so interesting, everyone gets along." Their harshest critics say they are "rich, shallow, in a bubble. I get along with them, but I wish people cared less about how Daddy didn't put enough money in their checking account." Those looking at the bright side see that "all are passionate about something: a sport, theater, the newspaper, Saturday nights." Minority students are few and far between here. Writes one African American undergrad, "This school needs more support for minority students." Notes a white student, "Black and Hispanic kids are quite noticeably segregated."

# TRINITY COLLEGE

FINANCIAL AID: 860-297-2046 • E-MAIL: ADMISSIONS.OFFICE@TRINCOLL.EDU • WEBSITE: WWW.TRINCOLL.EDU

## ADMISSIONS
*Very important factors considered include:* secondary school record. *Important factors considered include:* character/personal qualities, class rank, essays, extracurricular activities, interview, minority status, recommendations, standardized test scores, talent/ability. *Other factors considered include:* alumni/ae relation, geographical residence, volunteer work, work experience. TOEFL required of all international applicants. High school diploma or GED is required. *High school units required/recommended:* 16 total required; 4 English required, 3 math required, 2 science required, 2 science lab required, 2 foreign language required, 2 history required.

### The Inside Word
Trinity's Ivy safety status and well-deserved reputation for academic quality enables it to enroll a fairly impressive student body, but many of its best applicants go elsewhere. The price tag is high, and the college's competitors include a large portion of the best schools in the country. Minority candidates with sound academic backgrounds will encounter a most accommodating admissions committee.

## FINANCIAL AID
*Students should submit:* FAFSA, CSS/Financial Aid PROFILE, noncustodial (divorced/separated) parent's statement, federal income tax returns. Regular filing deadline is February 1. The Princeton Review suggests that all financial aid forms be submitted as soon as possible after January 1. *Need-based scholarships/grants offered:* Pell, SEOG, state scholarships/grants, private scholarships, the school's own gift aid. *Loan aid offered:* Direct Subsidized Stafford, Direct Unsubsidized Stafford, Direct PLUS, FFEL Subsidized Stafford, FFEL Unsubsidized Stafford, FFEL PLUS, Federal Perkins, college/university loans from institutional funds. Federal Work-Study Program available. Institutional employment available. Applicants will be notified of awards on or about April 1. Off-campus job opportunities are good.

## FROM THE ADMISSIONS OFFICE
"An array of distinctive curricular options—including an interdisciplinary neuroscience major and a professionally accredited engineering degree program, a unique Human Rights Program, a tutorial college for selected sophomores, a Health Fellows Program, and interdisciplinary programs such as the Cities Program, Interdisciplinary Science Program, and InterArts—is one reason record numbers of students are applying to Trinity. In fact, applications are up 80 percent over the past five years. In addition, the college has been recognized for its commitment to diversity; students of color have represented approximately 20 percent of the freshman class for the past four years, setting Trinity apart from many of its peers. Trinity's capital city location offers students unparalleled 'real-world' learning experiences to complement classroom learning. Students take advantage of extensive opportunities for internships for academic credit and community service, and these opportunities extend to Trinity's global learning sites in cities around the world. Trinity's faculty is a devoted and accomplished group of exceptional teacher-scholars; our 100-acre campus is beautiful; Hartford is an educational asset that differentiates Trinity from other liberal arts colleges; our global connections and foreign study opportunities prepare students to be good citizens of the world; and our graduates go on to excel in virtually every field. We invite you to learn more about why Trinity might be the best choice for you."

---

### SELECTIVITY
★ ★ ★ ★

| | |
|---|---:|
| Admissions Rating | 94 |
| # of applicants | 5,417 |
| % of applicants accepted | 36 |
| % of acceptees attending | 28 |
| # accepting a place on wait list | 433 |
| # of early decision applicants | 522 |
| % accepted early decision | 50 |

### FRESHMAN PROFILE
| | |
|---|---:|
| Range SAT Verbal | 590-690 |
| Average SAT Verbal | 630 |
| Range SAT Math | 600-690 |
| Average SAT Math | 642 |
| Range ACT Composite | 24-29 |
| Average ACT Composite | 27 |
| Minimum TOEFL | 550 |
| % graduated top 10% of class | 56 |
| % graduated top 25% of class | 83 |
| % graduated top 50% of class | 98 |

### DEADLINES
| | |
|---|---:|
| Early decision | 11/15 |
| Early decision notification | 12/15 |
| Regular admission | 1/15 |
| Regular notification | 4/1 |

### APPLICANTS ALSO LOOK AT
**AND OFTEN PREFER**
Amherst
Yale, Harvard
U. Penn
Tufts
**AND SOMETIMES PREFER**
Middlebury
Wesleyan U.
**AND RARELY PREFER**
Boston U
Colgate
Connecticut Coll.
Fairfield

### FINANCIAL FACTS

| | |
|---|---:|
| Financial Aid Rating | 82 |
| Tuition | $27,170 |
| Room and board | $7,380 |
| Books and supplies | $850 |
| Required fees | $1,432 |
| % frosh receiving aid | 44 |
| % undergrads receiving aid | 47 |
| Avg frosh grant | $25,000 |
| Avg frosh loan | $3,521 |

# TRINITY UNIVERSITY

1 Trinity Place, San Antonio, TX 78212 • Admissions: 210-999-7207 • Fax: 210-999-8164

## CAMPUS LIFE

| | |
|---|---|
| Quality of Life Rating | 92 |
| Type of school | private |
| Affiliation | Presbyterian |
| Environment | urban |

### STUDENTS

| | |
|---|---|
| Total undergrad enrollment | 2,357 |
| % male/female | 47/53 |
| % from out of state | 31 |
| % from public high school | 67 |
| % live on campus | 78 |
| % African American | 2 |
| % Asian | 5 |
| % Caucasian | 70 |
| % Hispanic | 11 |
| % international | 1 |

### SURVEY SAYS . . .
No one cheats
Registration is a breeze
Dorms are like palaces
Great off-campus food
Great on-campus food
Students love San Antonio, TX

## ACADEMICS

| | |
|---|---|
| Academic Rating | 91 |
| Calendar | semester |
| Student/faculty ratio | 11:1 |
| Profs interesting rating | 96 |
| Profs accessible rating | 98 |
| % profs teaching UG courses | 100 |
| Avg lab size | 20-29 students |
| Avg reg class size | 10-19 students |

### MOST POPULAR MAJORS
Business administration/management
Mass communications/media studies
Foreign languages/modern languages

## STUDENTS SPEAK OUT

### Academics

"It's cool to be smart and studious" at Trinity. "You have to be to survive," a sophomore tells us. A common refrain is that the university "doesn't have the reputation it deserves" considering the rigorous academic line-up. Professors garner high praise from their protégés: "They care about students and are gifted teachers," comments a poli-sci major, while a senior adds, "They don't hesitate to act as mentors." Students also speak well of the university's head honchos, noting, "Our president and VP of student affairs sit down with students in the dining hall at lunch; they are in view and accessible." The rest of the administration is less popular, accused of being money-grubbing "conservative cronies" who "treat us like we're in middle school." The biggest gripe concerns class availability. "You can walk in to registration with an ideal schedule and walk out with five pink slips—no classes. Then you have to beg the professors to let you in," reports a junior.

### Life

Though fraternities and sororities dominate the social scene at Trinity, they're counterbalanced, according to one sophomore, by a "prevalent volunteer and social organization community." "If you love to party, this is the place; if you don't like to party, this is also the place," adds a freshman. A divide, however, persists: "For those who choose not to participate in the Greek system, good luck making friends with those who do because the mentality is usually, 'You are either in or you're not.'" Either way, off-campus options abound. "Since Austin and Mexico are just an hour in either direction, road trips are always good to go," enthuses a senior, and downtown San Antonio offers "the river, jazz, cigar shops, and concerts" to those with acceptable IDs. Many students decry the mandatory three years of on-campus living, but the "huge dorm rooms and maid service" ease the pain. Overall, sums up one senior, "Everything is taken care of, everything is handed to you" at Trinity.

### Student Body

Many students note the Trinity population's general affluence ("our parking lots look like luxury car dealerships") and religious leanings ("Don't say you're an atheist unless you want 2,500 Christians trying to convert you!"). Others characterize their peers as a bit on the geeky side, with one senior pointing specifically to the fact that "we talk about oligarchies and plate tectonics a bit more often than normal." A strong "sense of camaraderie" exists among undergraduates, possibly because "students are different enough to keep it interesting, but similar enough to be comfortable." A sophomore comments, "While I will admit that racial diversity isn't that high, the diversity of personalities is extensive. Most people are very different in their attitudes and opinions." But her perception is questioned by a political science major who wishes "more non-Texas students" were attracted to the school and a sophomore drama major who begs, "Please let interesting people come!" A homebody senior concludes, "We don't go to many sporting events, we don't really go out, but damn it, we're good alumni."

# TRINITY UNIVERSITY

FINANCIAL AID: 210-999-8315 • E-MAIL: ADMISSIONS@TRINITY.EDU • WEBSITE: WWW.TRINITY.EDU

## ADMISSIONS

*Very important factors considered include:* character/personal qualities, class rank, secondary school record, standardized test scores. *Important factors considered include:* essays, extracurricular activities, recommendations, talent/ability. *Other factors considered include:* alumni/ae relation, geographical residence, interview, state residency, volunteer work, work experience. SAT I recommended. TOEFL required of all international applicants. High school diploma or GED is required. *High school units required/recommended:* 19 total required; 20 total recommended; 4 English required, 3 math required, 4 math recommended, 3 science required, 2 science lab required, 3 science lab recommended, 2 foreign language required, 3 foreign language recommended, 3 social studies required, 1 elective required.

## The Inside Word

There is no disputing that Trinity has bought academic excellence in its student body. For this reason alone, above-average students who need significant financial assistance in order to attend college should definitely consider applying. While Trinity's actions may be less than noble, there is no question that it's an extremely capable student body and that there are significant benefits to be derived from attending.

## FINANCIAL AID

*Students should submit:* FAFSA. Regular filing deadline is April 1. The Princeton Review suggests that all financial aid forms be submitted as soon as possible after January 1. *Need-based scholarships/grants offered:* Pell, SEOG, state scholarships/grants, private scholarships, the school's own gift aid. *Loan aid offered:* FFEL Subsidized Stafford, FFEL Unsubsidized Stafford, FFEL PLUS, Federal Perkins, state loans, college/university loans from institutional funds. Federal Work-Study Program available. Institutional employment available. Applicants will be notified of awards on or about April 1. Off-campus job opportunities are good.

## FROM THE ADMISSIONS OFFICE

"Three qualities separate Trinity University from other selective, academically challenging institutions around the country. First, Trinity is unusual in the quality and quantity of resources devoted almost exclusively to its undergraduate students. Those resources give rise to a second distinctive aspect of Trinity—its emphasis on undergraduate research. Our students prefer being involved over observing. With superior laboratory facilities and strong, dedicated faculty, our undergraduates fill many of the roles formerly reserved for graduate students. With no graduate assistants, our professors often go to their undergraduates for help with their research. Finally, Trinity stands apart for the attitude of its students. In an atmosphere of academic camaraderie and fellowship, our students work together to stretch their minds and broaden their horizons. For quality of resources, for dedication to undergraduate research, and for the disposition of its student body, Trinity University holds a unique position in American higher education."

## SELECTIVITY

| | |
|---|---|
| Admissions Rating | 84 |
| # of applicants | 3,108 |
| % of applicants accepted | 69 |
| % of acceptees attending | 31 |
| # accepting a place on wait list | 58 |
| % admitted from wait list | 47 |
| # of early decision applicants | 55 |
| % accepted early decision | 82 |

### FRESHMAN PROFILE

| | |
|---|---|
| Range SAT Verbal | 580-690 |
| Average SAT Verbal | 630 |
| Range SAT Math | 610-690 |
| Average SAT Math | 650 |
| Range ACT Composite | 27-31 |
| Average ACT Composite | 29 |
| Minimum TOEFL | 570 |
| Average HS GPA | 3.5 |
| % graduated top 10% of class | 49 |
| % graduated top 25% of class | 88 |
| % graduated top 50% of class | 97 |

### DEADLINES

| | |
|---|---|
| Early decision | 11/1 |
| Early decision notification | 12/15 |
| Priority admission | 2/1 |
| Regular notification | 4/1 |
| Nonfall registration? | yes |

### APPLICANTS ALSO LOOK AT
**AND OFTEN PREFER**
Rice
Duke
U. Texas—Austin
**AND SOMETIMES PREFER**
TCU, Tulane
Vanderbilt, SMU
Texas A&M
**AND RARELY PREFER**
Rhodes

## FINANCIAL FACTS

| | |
|---|---|
| Financial Aid Rating | 87 |
| Tuition | $18,402 |
| Room and board | $7,290 |
| Books and supplies | $620 |
| Required fees | $775 |
| % frosh receiving aid | 43 |
| % undergrads receiving aid | 40 |
| Avg frosh grant | $11,066 |
| Avg frosh loan | $2,739 |

THE BEST 351 COLLEGES ■ 519

# TRUMAN STATE UNIVERSITY

McClain Hall 205, 100 East Normal, Kirksville, MO 63501 • Admissions: 660-785-4114 • Fax: 660-785-7456

## CAMPUS LIFE

| | |
|---|---|
| Quality of Life Rating | 87 |
| Type of school | public |
| Environment | rural |

### STUDENTS

| | |
|---|---|
| Total undergrad enrollment | 5,636 |
| % male/female | 41/59 |
| % from out of state | 24 |
| % from public high school | 78 |
| % live on campus | 48 |
| % in (# of) fraternities | 30 (19) |
| % in (# of) sororities | 21 (11) |
| % African American | 4 |
| % Asian | 2 |
| % Caucasian | 90 |
| % Hispanic | 2 |
| % international | 4 |
| # of countries represented | 49 |

### SURVEY SAYS . . .
Campus easy to get around
Campus is beautiful
Lots of beer drinking
Campus feels safe
Athletic facilities are great
Great library
Great computer facilities
Frats and sororities dominate social scene
Ethnic diversity lacking on campus

## ACADEMICS

| | |
|---|---|
| Academic Rating | 86 |
| Calendar | semester |
| Student/faculty ratio | 15:1 |
| % profs teaching UG courses | 97 |
| % classes taught by TAs | 4 |
| Avg lab size | 20-29 students |
| Avg reg class size | 20-29 students |

### MOST POPULAR MAJORS
Business administration/management
English language and literature
Biology/biological sciences

## STUDENTS SPEAK OUT

### Academics
Truman State University, a "highly selective school that strives to provide a quality education at an affordable price," offers "students willing to be pushed academically" a demanding but worthwhile undergraduate experience. "Truman is known for its rigorous classes and is not for the faint at heart," cautions one undergrad. Others temper their warnings, reporting that "the academics can be challenging, but not overwhelming. There are some tough classes, but those only serve to teach me more." Students agree that a Truman degree is worth the hard work because "the school has a great reputation. Job recruiters know that Truman graduates are high quality." Excellent professors soften the impact of the heavy workload; "the teachers are incredibly student-oriented and they are always available for assistance," explains one undergrad. Observes another, "I think people who are willing to move to Kirksville to teach are here . . . because they like what they do." The administration makes every effort to keep class sizes small, a fact students appreciate. "The size of Truman is really one of its greatest strengths. Truman provides a very 'at home' kind of feeling," notes one student. "The classes are small and you get to know the people in your major throughout your years, so there is always great networking after college," adds another.

### Life
The workload is heavy at Truman State, so "people at this school tend to study hard during the week and leave the weekends for partying." The weekend party scene is fairly active: "Weekend nights are usually spent at house parties or the bars, which tend to be popular hangouts for local students," one student reports, even though "alcohol rules are extremely strict. There is a bit of tension between the community and campus in the area of parties and enforcement of alcohol laws." Many here remain happily outside the party scene, telling us that they remain busy by "hiking or boating at Thousand Hills State Park; seeing a play, movie, musical, or performance on campus; participating in discussion groups; watching movies with friends; and enjoying any number of other activities." Others note that "many students join organizations to meet others with like interests." The Student Activities Board "is always bringing movies, comedians, and music acts to campus for free or a small fee." The Greek community is also active here: "Greeks lead almost every major organization on campus," writes one undergrad. All of these options help make up for the fact that hometown Kirksville "is the smallest town ever. There is not a lot to do in town on a Friday or Saturday night." Some see an upside to Kirksville's size and remote location: "Even though Kirksville is small, it is very quaint and the people are very friendly. It really grows on you," writes one student.

### Student Body
If you want to envision the Truman State student body, you should "think midwestern. Think conservative living. Think very smart. Truman is not a place to come if any of these things freak you out." Truman "does not have a lot of diversity." In fact, most here agree that "Truman needs to work on recruiting a more diverse student body. There's a big need to avoid just enrolling white, straight midwesterners." Students brag, "Being a highly selective university, Truman draws some of the best and brightest in the area," but also see a downside: "Unfortunately, the typical student is pretty dorky. Many of our students care so much about academics that they care very little about their appearance." A substantial number of Truman undergrads are "religious; we have a large Catholic population from the St. Louis area." Most "have pretty conservative views; however, they are also incredibly down-to-earth and friendly." The school has a "high female-to-male ratio."

# TRUMAN STATE UNIVERSITY

FINANCIAL AID: 660-785-4130 • E-MAIL: ADMISSIONS@TRUMAN.EDU • WEBSITE: WWW.TRUMAN.EDU

## ADMISSIONS
*Very important factors considered include:* class rank, secondary school record, standardized test scores. *Important factors considered include:* essays, extracurricular activities. *Other factors considered include:* alumni/ae relation, character/personal qualities, geographical residence, interview, minority status, recommendations, state residency, talent/ability, volunteer work, work experience. SAT I or ACT required; ACT preferred. TOEFL required of all international applicants. High school diploma or GED is required. *High school units required/recommended:* 16 total required; 17 total recommended; 4 English required, 3 math required, 4 math recommended, 3 science required, 2 foreign language required, 3 social studies required.

### The Inside Word
Truman is among the next-in-line among public universities joining the ranks of the highly selective. It's tough to get admitted here, even though application totals declined somewhat last year. Serious students with conservative attitudes make the best match.

## FINANCIAL AID
*Students should submit:* FAFSA, institution's own financial aid form. The Princeton Review suggests that all financial aid forms be submitted as soon as possible after January 1. *Need-based scholarships/grants offered:* Pell, SEOG, state scholarships/grants, private scholarships, the school's own gift aid. *Loan aid offered:* FFEL Subsidized Stafford, FFEL Unsubsidized Stafford, FFEL PLUS, Federal Perkins, Federal Nursing, state loans, college/university loans from institutional funds. Federal Work-Study Program available. Institutional employment available. Applicants will be notified of awards on a rolling basis beginning on or about April 15. Off-campus job opportunities are good.

## FROM THE ADMISSIONS OFFICE
"Truman's talented student body enjoys small classes where undergraduate research and personal interaction with professors are the norm. Truman's commitment to providing an exemplary liberal arts and sciences education with nearly 200 student organizations and outstanding internship and study abroad opportunities allows students to compete in top graduate schools and the job market."

### SELECTIVITY

| | |
|---|---|
| Admissions Rating | 82 |
| # of applicants | 5,132 |
| % of applicants accepted | 79 |
| % of acceptees attending | 36 |

#### FRESHMAN PROFILE
| | |
|---|---|
| Range SAT Verbal | 560-680 |
| Average SAT Verbal | 614 |
| Range SAT Math | 550-660 |
| Average SAT Math | 606 |
| Range ACT Composite | 25-30 |
| Average ACT Composite | 27 |
| Minimum TOEFL | 550 |
| Average HS GPA | 3.8 |
| % graduated top 10% of class | 47 |
| % graduated top 25% of class | 82 |
| % graduated top 50% of class | 98 |

#### DEADLINES
| | |
|---|---|
| Priority admission | 11/15 |
| Regular admission | 3/1 |
| Nonfall registration? | yes |

#### APPLICANTS ALSO LOOK AT AND OFTEN PREFER
Washington U
U of Missouri at Columbia
St. Louis U

#### AND SOMETIMES PREFER
Southwest Missouri State
U of Illinois at Urbana-Champaign

#### AND RARELY PREFER
U of Iowa
Illinois State
Illinois Wesleyan

### FINANCIAL FACTS

| | |
|---|---|
| Financial Aid Rating | 86 |
| In-state tuition | $4,600 |
| Out-of-state tuition | $8,400 |
| Room and board | $5,072 |
| Books and supplies | $600 |
| Required fees | $56 |
| % frosh receiving aid | 26 |
| % undergrads receiving aid | 36 |
| Avg frosh grant | $4,103 |
| Avg frosh loan | $3,462 |

# TUFTS UNIVERSITY

BENDETSON HALL, MEDFORD, MA 02155 • ADMISSIONS: 617-627-3170 • FAX: 617-627-3860

## CAMPUS LIFE

| | |
|---|---|
| **Quality of Life Rating** | **89** |
| Type of school | private |
| Environment | suburban |

### STUDENTS

| | |
|---|---|
| Total undergrad enrollment | 4,910 |
| % male/female | 45/55 |
| % from out of state | 76 |
| % from public high school | 61 |
| % live on campus | 75 |
| % in (# of) fraternities | 15 (10) |
| % in (# of) sororities | 4 (3) |
| % African American | 8 |
| % Asian | 14 |
| % Caucasian | 58 |
| % Hispanic | 9 |
| % international | 7 |

### SURVEY SAYS...
Great library
Student newspaper is popular
Campus easy to get around
Campus feels safe
Great off-campus food
Campus is beautiful
Great on-campus food
Lots of beer drinking

## ACADEMICS

| | |
|---|---|
| **Academic Rating** | **91** |
| Calendar | semester |
| Student/faculty ratio | 9:1 |
| % profs teaching UG courses | 100 |
| % classes taught by TAs | 1 |
| Avg lab size | 10-19 students |
| Avg reg class size | 10-19 students |

## STUDENTS SPEAK OUT

### Academics

Students at Tufts University, "a friendly school with great opportunities both at the school and in the Boston area," think it's the perfect size, "small enough to feel like a small New England liberal arts college, but big enough to offer great variety." A big plus is that "Tufts' small size gives undergrads opportunities to do individual research with excellent professors. It's fairly common for undergraduates to get published, too." Unlike many research-oriented universities, Tufts allows TAs to "only teach labs and study groups. Professors teach the actual classes, so you get a much more detailed, informed education." Professors here are "amazing, caring, intelligent individuals who take time to work with students." The school offers such a variety of courses that "the trouble is not finding enough classes to take, but rather choosing from the amazing selection." Although strong in many areas, Tufts earns especially good marks from students for its programs in engineering, international relations, pre-med studies, and the sciences. Luckily, "academics are serious without being cutthroat," which students appreciate. They also love the "awesome study abroad opportunities" the school offers. Student complaints center primarily on financial issues: "The endowment is small, so things like classroom and dorm renovation lag behind. The school tends to nickel and dime students a lot, which is also directly tied to the endowment issues," notes a typical respondent.

### Life

Students at Tufts really do, as the old cliché goes, have the best of both worlds: a campus abuzz with activity and a world-class city just a few stops away on the T. On campus, "most kids here are pretty active in something . . . community service, writing, sports, whatever interests them." Writes one student, "I almost feel like there is too much going on at Tufts. You sometimes have to make a conscious effort to avoid the activities on campus just so you can get your work done." Adds another, "Tufts has so many performing groups, there is something to go see almost every night, and definitely every weekend. Lots of performances and exhibits are free, as are lectures. We have lots of speakers come to campus (almost every group brings people to talk), and lectures are well publicized and generally interesting." A cappella competitions are surprisingly popular; sports are less so. "The only well-attended football game is homecoming and everyone there is too drunk to even watch." As for the surrounding city, the campus is located "just down the road [from] Davis Square, home of sweet bars, nice restaurants, and a solid concert/movie/play venue. The subway is right there; Harvard Square is two stops away; Lansdowne Street is about 25 to 30 minutes away." Students here love the specialty residences (e.g., language houses, arts houses) that allow students with common interests to live together; they warn, however, that "housing for juniors and seniors is a big problem . . . because Tufts does not guarantee housing to upperclassmen."

### Student Body

There are lots of stereotypes of the Tufts student body, and according to our survey, they're mostly true. "It's true what they say about Tufts; the school is filled with bitter Ivy League rejects," writes one student. Adds another, "There are a ton of well-off Jewish kids from the Northeast who wear Abercrombie and listen to Guster all the time. But there are just as many kids who don't fit that cookie-cutter view." In fact, "there is a lot of diversity for such an expensive campus. One-quarter of the student body is a racial or ethnic minority. Plus, there's an active gay community." Although diverse, the student body is not well integrated; explains one student, "The best analogy I've heard to describe Tufts students is the TV dinner. You see, we have all kinds of different flavors, but each [is] segregated into different compartments."

522 ■ THE BEST 351 COLLEGES

# TUFTS UNIVERSITY

FINANCIAL AID: 617-627-3528 • E-MAIL: ADMISSIONS.INQUIRY@ASE.TUFTS.EDU • WEBSITE: WWW.TUFTS.EDU

## ADMISSIONS
*Very important factors considered include:* secondary school record. *Important factors considered include:* character/personal qualities, class rank, essays, extracurricular activities, minority status, recommendations, standardized test scores, talent/ability, volunteer work, work experience. *Other factors considered include:* alumni/ae relation, geographical residence, interview. TOEFL required of all international applicants. High school diploma or GED is required. *High school units required/recommended:* 4 English recommended, 3 math recommended, 2 science recommended, 3 foreign language recommended, 2 history recommended.

## The Inside Word
Tufts has little visibility outside the Northeast and little personality either. Still it manages to attract and keep an excellent student body, mostly from right inside its own backyard. In order to be successful, candidates must have significant academic accomplishments and submit a thoroughly well-prepared application—the review is rigorous and the standards are high.

## FINANCIAL AID
*Students should submit:* FAFSA, CSS/Financial Aid PROFILE, noncustodial (divorced/separated) parent's statement, business/farm supplement, parent's and student's federal income tax returns. Regular filing deadline is February 15. The Princeton Review suggests that all financial aid forms be submitted as soon as possible after January 1. *Need-based scholarships/grants offered:* Pell, SEOG, state scholarships/grants, private scholarships, the school's own gift aid. *Loan aid offered:* FFEL Subsidized Stafford, FFEL Unsubsidized Stafford, FFEL PLUS, Federal Perkins, state loans, college/university loans from institutional funds. Federal Work-Study Program available. Institutional employment available. Applicants will be notified of awards on or about April 5. Off-campus job opportunities are good.

## FROM THE ADMISSIONS OFFICE
"Tufts University, on the boundary between Medford and Somerville, sits on a hill overlooking Boston, five miles northwest of the city. The campus is a tranquil New England setting within easy access by subway and bus to the cultural, social, and entertainment resources of Boston and Cambridge. "Since its founding in 1852 by members of the Universalist church, Tufts has grown from a small liberal arts college into a nonsectarian university of over 7,000 students. By 1900 the college had added a medical school, a dental school, and graduate studies. The University now also includes the Fletcher School of Law and Diplomacy, the Graduate School of Arts and Sciences, the School of Veterinary Medicine, the School of Nutrition, the Sackler School of Graduate Biomedical Sciences, and the Gordon Institute of Engineering Management."

## SELECTIVITY

| | |
|---|---|
| Admissions Rating | 97 |
| # of applicants | 14,308 |
| % of applicants accepted | 27 |
| % of acceptees attending | 34 |
| # of early decision applicants | 1,230 |
| % accepted early decision | 43 |

### FRESHMAN PROFILE
| | |
|---|---|
| Range SAT Verbal | 610-710 |
| Range SAT Math | 640-720 |
| Range ACT Composite | 26-31 |
| Minimum TOEFL | 100 (CBT) |
| % graduated top 10% of class | 72 |
| % graduated top 25% of class | 94 |
| % graduated top 50% of class | 100 |

### DEADLINES
| | |
|---|---|
| Early decision | 11/15 |
| Early decision notification | 12/15 |
| Regular admission | 1/1 |
| Regular notification | 4/1 |

### APPLICANTS ALSO LOOK AT AND OFTEN PREFER
Harvard
Duke
Brown
Dartmouth
U. Penn

### AND SOMETIMES PREFER
Northwestern U.
U. Mass—Amherst

### AND RARELY PREFER
Boston Coll.
Brandeis

## FINANCIAL FACTS

| | |
|---|---|
| Financial Aid Rating | 84 |
| Tuition | $26,213 |
| Room and board | $7,987 |
| Books and supplies | $700 |
| Required fees | $679 |
| % frosh receiving aid | 36 |
| % undergrads receiving aid | 41 |
| Avg frosh grant | $19,183 |
| Avg frosh loan | $3,356 |

# TULANE UNIVERSITY

6823 ST. CHARLES AVENUE, NEW ORLEANS, LA 70118-5680 • ADMISSIONS: 504-865-5731 • FAX: 504-862-8715

## CAMPUS LIFE

| Quality of Life Rating | 88 |
|---|---|
| Type of school | private |
| Environment | urban |

### STUDENTS

| Total undergrad enrollment | 7,701 |
|---|---|
| % male/female | 47/53 |
| % from out of state | 66 |
| % from public high school | 55 |
| % live on campus | 55 |
| % in (# of) fraternities | 12 (15) |
| % in (# of) sororities | 15 (9) |
| % African American | 9 |
| % Asian | 5 |
| % Caucasian | 73 |
| % Hispanic | 4 |
| % international | 3 |
| # of countries represented | 100 |

### SURVEY SAYS . . .
Hard liquor is popular
Great off-campus food
Lots of beer drinking
Students love New Orleans, LA
Athletic facilities are great
(Almost) everyone smokes
Campus easy to get around
Students are happy

## ACADEMICS

| Academic Rating | 85 |
|---|---|
| Calendar | semester |
| Student/faculty ratio | 10:1 |
| % profs teaching UG courses | 89 |
| % classes taught by TAs | 9 |
| Avg lab size | 10-19 students |
| Avg reg class size | 10-19 students |

### MOST POPULAR MAJORS
Engineering
Social sciences
Business/commerce

## STUDENTS SPEAK OUT

### Academics
"Every state should have a Tulane," writes a soon-to-be-graduated senior. With "small classes, great financial aid, and a fabulous city" to offer students, private, mid-size Tulane University consistently attracts top-notch students from all around the country and world who are drawn to the school because of its "excellent academic reputation." A second-year is impressed by the "creativity of professors" and their "willingness to teach dynamic and nontraditional material," while a freshman notes that "Tulane is really trying to reach out to the undergraduates, which means you could end up with the president of the university as your professor—I did!" Still, for many Tulane prospectives, it was "location, location, location" that proved to be a deciding factor for attending. The Big Easy's legendary culture, history, and nightlife far outweigh some of Tulane's weaker spots—which, according to those we surveyed, include a few old-guard profs who could "put an entire room of Starbucks customers to sleep" and an administration that's well intentioned but "full of red tape." A junior describes the situation this way: "The administration is more than willing to ask students for input, but they have a little earwax buildup or something, because they aren't the best at *hearing* that input." What's more, with Bourbon Street around the corner, "focusing in a city like New Orleans is not always easy." Thank goodness for 8:00 A.M. calculus; notes a sophomore, "if one actually attends class, there is quite a bit to learn here."

### Life
"During the week we think about classes and homework," writes a freshman. "During the weekends? Yeah, we try to think as little as possible." So goes life at this "mad fun" campus in a "great city" and a "beautiful part of town." Of course, the city that celebrates Mardi Gras with so much, well, alcohol could be a bit tough on the GPA (and the liver), and many an undergrad might ask themselves (as this existentially minded sophomore did), "Do I drink because of poor grades, or do I have poor grades because I drink?" Deep. Fortunately, a first-year offers advice: "After the first few months of school, hanging out with smelly drunk tourists on Bourbon Street gets kind of old. That's when you finally begin to appreciate the rest of New Orleans for what it is—a city with museums and restaurants and history. That's why I love Tulane." Indeed, with N'awlins' "excellent selection of music clubs," parks, industry, nightlife and culture—not to mention "bikini weather in February"—undergrads who don't venture beyond the "Mardi Gras debauchery" are missing much of what the city has to offer. A junior points out, "there are a lot of great groups/programs on campus," and many students consider its facilities unmatched, including a rec center that one sophomore calls "the best I've ever seen."

### Student Body
Summarizes one sanguine student we surveyed, "There is a place for just about every person—and we all fit into the puzzle. I love being here!" Of course, there are those who'd disagree. One senior finds his fellow students "apathetic and drunk," while a junior notes that "most of them are really shallow." Our junior concludes, "There's a saying that you're either a smart kid here on scholarship, or a rich kid looking for the ultimate party school." Is it all scholarship kids and the filthy rich? Not so, argues one undergraduate, "Tulane represents a very diverse montage of students . . . . Students exude the spirit of New Orleans and Tulane, making the social experience encouraging and charming."

524 ■ THE BEST 351 COLLEGES

# TULANE UNIVERSITY

FINANCIAL AID: 504-865-5723 • E-MAIL: UNDERGRAD.ADMISSION@TULANE.EDU • WEBSITE: WWW.TULANE.EDU

## ADMISSIONS
*Very important factors considered include:* class rank, secondary school record, standardized test scores. *Important factors considered include:* essays, recommendations. *Other factors considered include:* alumni/ae relation, character/personal qualities, extracurricular activities, geographical residence, talent/ability, volunteer work, work experience. SAT I or ACT required. TOEFL required of all international applicants. High school diploma or GED is required. *High school units required/recommended:* 4 English required, 3 math required, 4 math recommended, 3 science required, 4 science recommended, 3 science lab required, 2 foreign language required, 3 foreign language recommended, 3 social studies required, 3 history required.

### The Inside Word
Tulane's applicant pool is highly national in origin and very sound academically. The university's competitors include many of the best universities in the country, which tempers its selectivity significantly due to the loss of admitted students. Nonetheless, Tulane is an excellent choice for just about anyone looking for a quality institution that is on the move. Prestige and the value of a Tulane degree stand to increase as the South continues to grow in population and political influence.

## FINANCIAL AID
*Students should submit:* FAFSA, CSS/Financial Aid PROFILE, noncustodial (divorced/separated) parent's statement, business/farm supplement. Regular filing deadline is February 1. The Princeton Review suggests that all financial aid forms be submitted as soon as possible after January 1. *Need-based scholarships/grants offered:* Pell, SEOG, state scholarships/grants, private scholarships. *Loan aid offered:* FFEL Subsidized Stafford, FFEL Unsubsidized Stafford, FFEL PLUS, Federal Perkins. Federal Work-Study Program available. Institutional employment available. Applicants will be notified of awards on a rolling basis beginning on or about February 1. Off-campus job opportunities are good.

## FROM THE ADMISSIONS OFFICE
"With 5,000 full-time undergraduate students in five divisions, Tulane University offers the personal attention and teaching excellence traditionally associated with liberal arts colleges together with the facilities and interdisciplinary resources found only at major research universities—with both complemented by the exciting, historic setting of New Orleans, America's most interesting city. Senior faculty regularly teach introductory and lower-level courses, and 74 percent of the classes have 25 or fewer students. The close student-teacher relationship pays off. Tulane graduates are among the country's most likely to be selected for several prestigious fellowships that support graduate study abroad. Founded in 1834 and reorganized as Tulane University in 1884, Tulane is one of the major private research universities in the South. The Tulane campus offers a traditional collegiate setting in an attractive residential neighborhood."

### SELECTIVITY

| | |
|---|---|
| Admissions Rating | 84 |
| # of applicants | 13,006 |
| % of applicants accepted | 56 |
| # accepting a place on wait list | 81 |
| % admitted from wait list | 129 |
| # of early decision applicants | 127 |
| % accepted early decision | 63 |

### FRESHMAN PROFILE
| | |
|---|---|
| Range SAT Verbal | 610-700 |
| Average SAT Verbal | 655 |
| Range SAT Math | 610-700 |
| Average SAT Math | 648 |
| Range ACT Composite | 28-32 |
| Minimum TOEFL | 550 |
| % graduated top 10% of class | 58 |
| % graduated top 25% of class | 85 |
| % graduated top 50% of class | 98 |

### DEADLINES
| | |
|---|---|
| Early decision | 11/1 |
| Early decision notification | 12/15 |
| Regular admission | 1/15 |
| Regular notification | 4/1 |

### APPLICANTS ALSO LOOK AT AND OFTEN PREFER
Duke
Vanderbilt
Emory

### AND SOMETIMES PREFER
UT Austin
Northwestern U
Florida State
Washington U

### AND RARELY PREFER
Skidmore
SMU
U of Richmond
Rollins

### FINANCIAL FACTS

| | |
|---|---|
| Financial Aid Rating | 92 |
| Tuition | $26,100 |
| Room and board | $7,392 |
| Books and supplies | $1,000 |
| Required fees | $2,210 |
| % frosh receiving aid | 46 |
| % undergrads receiving aid | 43 |
| Avg frosh grant | $15,700 |
| Avg frosh loan | $3,460 |

# TUSKEGEE UNIVERSITY

KRESGE CENTER, 3RD FLOOR, TUSKEGEE, AL 36088 • ADMISSIONS: 334-727-8500 • FAX: 334-727-5750

## CAMPUS LIFE

| | |
|---|---|
| **Quality of Life Rating** | **65** |
| Type of school | private |
| Environment | rural |

### STUDENTS
| | |
|---|---|
| Total undergrad enrollment | 2,608 |
| % male/female | 43/57 |
| % from out of state | 58 |
| % live on campus | 55 |
| % in (# of) fraternities | 6 (5) |
| % in (# of) sororities | 5 (6) |
| % African American | 81 |
| % international | 1 |

### SURVEY SAYS . . .
Popular college radio
Student publications are ignored
Frats and sororities dominate social scene
Theater is hot
Students don't get along with local community
Registration is a pain
Students don't like Tuskegee, AL
Athletic facilities need improving

## ACADEMICS

| | |
|---|---|
| **Academic Rating** | **74** |
| Calendar | semester |
| Student/faculty ratio | 13:1 |
| Profs interesting rating | 89 |
| Profs accessible rating | 89 |
| Avg reg class size | 10-19 students |

### MOST POPULAR MAJORS
Electrical engineering
Biology
Business

## STUDENTS SPEAK OUT

### Academics

Booker T. Washington founded this "prestigious historically black university" over a century ago. In the intervening years, Tuskegee University has built a "proud" tradition to accompany its "great historical background." Despite several quality liberal arts departments and a great veterinary program (over 70 percent of the African American veterinarians in the world trained here), Tuskegee is proudest of its strong engineering program, which enrolls nearly a quarter of the students. Tuskegee graduates more African American aerospace science engineers than any other school. For the record, it also produces the most African American military officers—including West Point and the Naval Academy. "Extremely caring" professors teach nearly all of the "small," discussion-oriented classes here, a fact not lost on the appreciative students. "I love my professors," beams an English major. They are "great, helpful, nurturing, and always there to help." Also, some professors are "good with one-on-one help." The administration, on the other hand, is universally unpopular for its unhelpful, "negative attitude." Registration is perhaps the biggest problem. Students also complain that "a few buildings could use some work," especially a handful of dilapidated dorms, and the roads on campus are in need of repair. Despite these complaints, students say they would "choose Tuskegee every time." "The Tuskegee experience shapes you as an individual," explains a political science major. "As far as establishing a sound African American foundation for students, it's the best there is."

### Life

For some students here, especially those from metropolitan centers, campus life "takes some getting used to," as one junior reports. Tuskegee, Alabama, is a sleepy southern town "out in the country" where, according to some students, there is "nothing to do" except "visiting friends and renting videos." Other students say their campus is "a lot of fun." Tuskegee has a "great" marching band that is "a way of life" for its members. There is also Greek life. On campus, Greek life is tremendously popular; fraternity and sorority parties are well attended and the festivities of Greek Week are a huge draw. Students also look forward to homecoming ("the best time of the year" because "the campus is overrun by many visitors, alumni, and thrill seekers") and an annual spring festival. When campus is not hopping, nearby Auburn (home to Auburn University) is a popular destination, as is the urban metropolis of Atlanta. "If you don't have a car," though, "you are out of luck." If you do have a car, events that bring Tuskegee students together with students from other historically African American colleges, such as Freaknic in Atlanta and Black College Week in Daytona Beach, are popular road trip destinations.

### Student Body

The "wonderful, cooperative, and encouraging" students at Tuskegee are a "very congenial," generally studious bunch: schoolwork takes up a great deal of the average student's day. When students finally put their books away, though, "it's like one big, beautiful family." Without a doubt, "student unity" prevails on this campus in a way that is truly "unique." It's all part of the Tuskegee experience, to which so many students allude. "Everyone seems to get along with each other," says a senior. "We have our differences, but when it comes down to it, we stick together." The majority of the students come from the South, and they are "extremely socially diverse (geographically, financially, religiously)," but students from all different social strata manage to "interact well, providing a stimulating environment."

526 ■ THE BEST 351 COLLEGES

# TUSKEGEE UNIVERSITY

FINANCIAL AID: 334-727-8201 • E-MAIL: ADMISSIONS@TUSKEGEE.EDU • WEBSITE: WWW.TUSKEGEE.EDU

## ADMISSIONS

*Very important factors considered include:* recommendations, secondary school record, standardized test scores, talent/ability. *Important factors considered include:* alumni/ae relation, class rank. *Other factors considered include:* character/personal qualities, geographical residence, state residency, volunteer work, work experience. SAT I or ACT required. TOEFL required of all international applicants. High school diploma or GED is required. *High school units required/recommended:* 16 total required; 4 English required, 3 math required, 2 science required, 3 social studies required, 4 elective required.

### The Inside Word

Tuskegee University has a solid reputation and draws a large pool of above-average candidates. Academic accomplishments in high school are first and foremost ingredients of a successful application for admission, but there is no doubt that the committee takes a close look at all aspects of candidate files. Don't downplay the importance of recommendations and a well-rounded extracurricular background.

## FINANCIAL AID

*Students should submit:* FAFSA, institution's own financial aid form, CSS/Financial Aid PROFILE. The Princeton Review suggests that all financial aid forms be submitted as soon as possible after January 1. *Need-based scholarships/grants offered:* Pell, SEOG, state scholarships/grants, private scholarships, the school's own gift aid, United Negro College Fund. *Loan aid offered:* Direct Subsidized Stafford, Direct Unsubsidized Stafford, Direct PLUS, FFEL Subsidized Stafford, FFEL Unsubsidized Stafford, FFEL PLUS, Federal Perkins, state loans, college/university loans from institutional funds. Federal Work-Study Program available. Institutional employment available. Off-campus job opportunities are good.

## FROM THE ADMISSIONS OFFICE

"With distinctive strengths in the sciences, engineering and other professions, the university's basic mission is to provide educational programs of exceptional quality that promote the development of liberally prepared and professionally-oriented people. The university is rooted in a history of successfully educating black Americans to understand themselves against the background of their total heritage and the promise of their individual and collective future. A primary mission has been to prepare them to play effective professional and leadership roles in society and to become productive citizens in the national and world community. Tuskegee University continues to be dedicated to these broad aims."

## SELECTIVITY

| | |
|---|---|
| Admissions Rating | 73 |
| # of applicants | 1,902 |
| % of applicants accepted | 81 |
| % of acceptees attending | 49 |

### FRESHMAN PROFILE

| | |
|---|---|
| Range SAT Verbal | 340-540 |
| Average SAT Verbal | 441 |
| Range SAT Math | 370-550 |
| Average SAT Math | 438 |
| Range ACT Composite | 17-20 |
| Average ACT Composite | 19 |
| Minimum TOEFL | 500 |
| Average HS GPA | 3.2 |
| % graduated top 10% of class | 20 |
| % graduated top 25% of class | 59 |
| % graduated top 50% of class | 100 |

### DEADLINES

| | |
|---|---|
| Regular notification | rolling |
| Nonfall registration? | yes |

### APPLICANTS ALSO LOOK AT AND SOMETIMES PREFER
Florida A&M
Spelman
Howard
Hampton
Alabama A&M

### AND RARELY PREFER
U of Alabama
Auburn
Alabama State

## FINANCIAL FACTS

| | |
|---|---|
| Financial Aid Rating | 86 |
| Tuition | $11,060 |
| Room and board | $5,940 |
| Books and supplies | $848 |
| Required fees | $300 |
| % frosh receiving aid | 66 |
| % undergrads receiving aid | 66 |
| Avg frosh grant | $2,500 |
| Avg frosh loan | $2,625 |

# UNION COLLEGE

GRANT HALL, SCHENECTADY, NY 12308 • ADMISSIONS: 518-388-6112 • FAX: 518-388-6986

## CAMPUS LIFE

| Quality of Life Rating | 77 |
|---|---|
| Type of school | private |
| Environment | suburban |

### STUDENTS

| Total undergrad enrollment | 2,147 |
|---|---|
| % male/female | 53/47 |
| % from out of state | 54 |
| % from public high school | 70 |
| % live on campus | 80 |
| % in (# of) fraternities | 21 (14) |
| % in (# of) sororities | 25 (4) |
| % African American | 3 |
| % Asian | 5 |
| % Caucasian | 84 |
| % Hispanic | 4 |
| % international | 3 |
| # of countries represented | 21 |

### SURVEY SAYS . . .
Lots of beer drinking
Frats and sororities dominate social scene
Popular college radio
Profs teach upper-levels
Hard liquor is popular
Students don't like Schenectady, NY
Students are cliquish

## ACADEMICS

| Academic Rating | 87 |
|---|---|
| Calendar | trimester |
| Student/faculty ratio | 11:1 |
| Profs interesting rating | 95 |
| Profs accessible rating | 98 |
| % profs teaching UG courses | 100 |
| Avg lab size | 10-19 students |
| Avg reg class size | 10-19 students |

### MOST POPULAR MAJORS
Psychology
Political science and government
Economics

## STUDENTS SPEAK OUT

### Academics
Students are attracted to Union College by the great variety of courses available at a school that has fewer than 2,500 undergrads. The enrollment ensures that class sizes are small and that professors have the time to get to know their students. "Academically, Union is great," a senior political science major avers. "Classes are interesting," and professors are, "caring," accessible, and approachable. Professors "go out of their way to . . . get involved on campus," a junior political science major writes, and "many even give you their home numbers." TAs are nowhere to be found. There are a few professors on campus who aren't as highly regarded, and a math major grumbles, "The school puts too much emphasis on selecting professors with good reputations, [instead of] selecting professors who actually can teach and speak English." Students rave about the trimester calendar, according to which they only take three classes at a time. "You never feel too bogged down," one first-year student writes. Students do, however, want to be able to register online. The "conservative" administration is, for the most part, disliked. "The bureaucracy at this school makes the IRS look like a well-oiled machine," a senior history major gripes.

### Life
"Union's a blast," a sophomore beams. "We go to the same two hole-in-the-wall places where we see the same people as always," writes a less enthusiastic classmate. Campus student organizations "work hard to schedule events," but students often forsake those events for frat parties. Still, "the number of clubs we have is great," a senior Spanish major gushes. "There is a club for everything from sign language to ballroom dancing." Theme houses provide an alternative to those not interested in Greek life. Campus sports are popular, as are on-campus movies and concerts. Though students complain that there is little to do in "less-than-desirable" Schenectady, they admit that the area offers much in the way of volunteer opportunities. Many students are involved in the Big Brothers/Big Sisters program. Students are also "within a few hours of New York and Boston, and below the Adirondack Mountains, where prime skiing and hiking" opportunities abound. Students feel that campus security is too strict and that athletic facilities could stand some improvement.

### Student Body
Union's students describe themselves as "apathetic" and "conservative" and "rich snobs." Most come from the East Coast. "If Daddy bought you an SUV and you're from Jersey, you'll fit right in here," a computer engineering major quips. One female student comments that most of her female peers "live by Cosmo," and a junior adds, "There's a division: the Kate Spade, Jeep Grand Cherokee, sorority and frat boy types, versus the rest of the world." Students are "cliquey," and a first-year student marvels, "I have never seen so many North Face Jackets and Kate Spade bags in one place." A sociology major observes, "Many students, especially those involved in the Greek system, view college as one continuous party with the disadvantage of having to take finals at the end of each term to be able to come back." Many students describe their peers as "polite" and "friendly," and people "smile and say 'hi' as they pass between classes." One English major believes, however, that most of her peers view college "as a means to an end—money—[and] not an intellectual adventure."

528 ■ THE BEST 351 COLLEGES

# UNION COLLEGE

FINANCIAL AID: 518-388-6123 • E-MAIL: ADMISSIONS@UNION.EDU • WEBSITE: WWW.UNION.EDU

## ADMISSIONS

*Very important factors considered include:* class rank, secondary school record. *Important factors considered include:* alumni/ae relation, character/personal qualities, essays, extracurricular activities, interview, minority status, recommendations, talent/ability, volunteer work. *Other factors considered include:* geographical residence, standardized test scores, state residency, work experience. SAT I or ACT required. TOEFL required of all international applicants. High school diploma or GED is required. *High school units required/recommended:* 16 total required; 24 total recommended; 4 English required, 3 math required, 4 math recommended, 2 science required, 4 science recommended, 2 science lab required, 4 science lab recommended, 2 foreign language required, 4 foreign language recommended, 1 social studies required, 2 social studies recommended, 1 history required, 2 history recommended.

### The Inside Word

In this age of MTV-type admissions videos and ultra-glossy promotional literature, Union is decidedly more low-key than most colleges. The college is a bastion of tradition and conservatism and sticks to what it knows best when it comes to recruitment and admission. Students who are thinking about Union need to be prepared with as challenging a high school curriculum as possible and solid grades across the board.

## FINANCIAL AID

*Students should submit:* FAFSA, CSS/Financial Aid PROFILE, state aid form, noncustodial (divorced/separated) parent's statement, business/farm supplement. Regular filing deadline is February 1. The Princeton Review suggests that all financial aid forms be submitted as soon as possible after January 1. *Need-based scholarships/grants offered:* Pell, SEOG, state scholarships/grants, private scholarships, the school's own gift aid. *Loan aid offered:* FFEL Subsidized Stafford, FFEL Unsubsidized Stafford, FFEL PLUS, Federal Perkins, college/university loans from institutional funds. Federal Work-Study Program available. Institutional employment available. Applicants will be notified of awards on or about April 1. Off-campus job opportunities are good.

## FROM THE ADMISSIONS OFFICE

"'Breadth' and 'flexibility' characterize the Union academic program. Whether the subject is the poetry of ancient Greece or the possibilities of developing fields such as nanotechnology, Union students can choose among nearly 1,000 courses—a range that is unusual among America's highly selective colleges. Students can major in a single field, combine work in two or more departments, or even create their own organizing theme major. Undergraduate research is strongly encouraged, and nearly 70 percent of Union's students take advantage of the College's extensive international study program."

## ADMISSIONS

| | |
|---|---:|
| Admissions Rating | 91 |
| # of applicants | 3,828 |
| % of applicants accepted | 45 |
| % of acceptees attending | 33 |
| # accepting a place on wait list | 405 |
| % admitted from wait list | 18 |
| # of early decision applicants | 249 |
| % accepted early decision | 74 |

### FRESHMAN PROFILE

| | |
|---|---:|
| Range SAT Verbal | 550-650 |
| Average SAT Verbal | 610 |
| Range SAT Math | 590-680 |
| Average SAT Math | 630 |
| Minimum TOEFL | 600 |
| Average HS GPA | 3.5 |
| % graduated top 10% of class | 58 |
| % graduated top 25% of class | 81 |
| % graduated top 50% of class | 96 |

### DEADLINES

| | |
|---|---:|
| Early decision | 11/15 |
| Early decision notification | 12/15 |
| Regular admission | 1/15 |
| Regular notification | 4/1 |

### APPLICANTS ALSO LOOK AT AND OFTEN PREFER
Colgate
Colby
Tufts

### AND SOMETIMES PREFER
Hamilton
Lehigh
Lafayette
Skidmore
Connecticut College
Trinity College

### AND RARELY PREFER
U of Rochester
Rensselaer Polytechnic

## FINANCIAL FACTS

| | |
|---|---:|
| Financial Aid Rating | 81 |
| Tuition | $27,246 |
| Room and board | $6,738 |
| Books and supplies | $450 |
| Required fees | $268 |
| % frosh receiving aid | 48 |
| % undergrads receiving aid | 51 |
| Avg frosh grant | $19,846 |
| Avg frosh loan | $2,745 |

# UNITED STATES AIR FORCE ACADEMY

HQ USAFA/RRS, 2304 CADET DRIVE, SUITE 200, USAF ACADEMY, CO 80840-5025 • ADMISSIONS: 719-333-2520 • FAX: 719-333-3012

## CAMPUS LIFE

| | |
|---|---|
| Quality of Life Rating | 88 |
| Type of school | public |
| Environment | suburban |

### STUDENTS

| | |
|---|---|
| Total undergrad enrollment | 4,219 |
| % from out of state | 95 |
| % live on campus | 100 |
| % African American | 6 |
| % Asian | 5 |
| % Caucasian | 82 |
| % Hispanic | 6 |
| % international | 1 |
| # of countries represented | 22 |

### SURVEY SAYS . . .
Very little drug use
Musical organizations aren't popular
Everyone loves the Falcons
Student publications are ignored
Classes are small
Athletic facilities need improving
Lab facilities are great

## ACADEMICS

| | |
|---|---|
| Academic Rating | 99 |
| Calendar | semester |
| Student/faculty ratio | 8:1 |
| Profs interesting rating | 96 |
| Profs accessible rating | 100 |
| % profs teaching UG courses | 100 |
| Avg lab size | 10-19 students |
| Avg reg class size | 10-19 students |

### MOST POPULAR MAJORS
Business administration/management
Engineering
Social sciences

## STUDENTS SPEAK OUT

### Academics

Cadets speak glowingly of the United States Air Force Academy, training ground for tomorrow's elite Air Force officers. Writes a typical student, "I am convinced that USAFA is the best education available . . . . [It's] one giant fraternity, where all cadets endure the challenge of academics, athletics, and military instruction. This place produces the best leaders and prepares its cadets for anything they will encounter." The workload here, by all accounts, is tremendous; as one student put it, "They purposely place 25 hours of tasks in every 24-hour day. It's tough, but if you work as a team and put forth all your effort every day, this place won't be too bad." Fortunately, professors "do not go home after they leave class. They stay for a full day, giving extra instruction whenever needed." Students appreciate the fact that "the funding for all aspects of education (not just academics, [but also] athletics, leadership, and character) is essentially unlimited, so the absolute best is not an exception: it is a rule." The "large core here" ensures cadets "some unique undergrad experiences like working with electron microscopes, nuclear magnetic resonance, and real cadavers." The curriculum also includes "classes in honor, character development, human relations and leadership. During the summer we have other programs . . . [like] Jump (skydiving) and Soaring (flying gliders)." Even those overwhelmed by the school's demands admit that though "it's about the last place on Earth you would want to attend, it's the first place on Earth you would want to be from."

### Life

Life at USAFA is rigorous, to put it mildly. "It's hard; there's so much to do with 23 credit hours, athletics, military stuff, religion, and community service," writes one cadet. "Overall it's a good experience; we learn time management very quickly." Freshman year—fourth class cadet status, technically speaking—is "quite harsh," filled with a back-breaking academic schedule, training evaluations conducted by upperclassmen (sentimentally referred to as "beatdowns"), mandatory athletics, and frequent training sessions. Weekends "are a welcome relief," writes one fourth class cadet, "except for one weekend a month when inspections, parades, and training sessions happen all Friday evening and into Saturday afternoon." Things improve somewhat in subsequent years, although "you can't go out during the school week until your senior year, and even then it's very limited, so our occasional free weekends are the times when we all let loose." In fact, until senior year, students' lives "are very structured, time allotted to do everything." During their rare sojourns off campus, students find that "the location is great because it affords students the opportunity to ski, hike, fish, shop, and just about anything else you could want to do." Notes one student, "There are two big cities (Denver and Colorado Springs) within driving distance and they both have active night scenes."

### Student Body

The "straightforward, open-minded, goal-oriented individuals" who populate the USAFA "are teammates. We'd help each other out of trouble in a second. We're that close." Explains one student, "Due to the military stresses placed on them in the first year, they make great friends much quicker then I would imagine civilian students would in their freshman year." This closeness continues throughout their educations; explains one, "Without my fellow classmates there would be no way for me to make it through USAFA. Everyone here is extremely competitive, but we all help each other out as much as possible because we are in this institution together. You will NEVER understand the awesome level of friendship here." Cadets "get along really well, for the most part. We also have our share of geeks, athletes, and power-hungry tightwads who make the place less than amiable, but for the most part they even out and we all get along." Many cadets reported that "attitudes here have become more serious since September 11. There is a sense of purpose and drive, and a clear goal" shared by all.

# UNITED STATES AIR FORCE ACADEMY

E-MAIL: RR_WEBMAIL@USAFA.AF.MIL • WEBSITE: WWW.ACADEMYADMISSIONS.COM

## ADMISSIONS

*Very important factors considered include:* character/personal qualities, interview, secondary school record, standardized test scores. *Important factors considered include:* class rank, extracurricular activities, volunteer work, work experience. *Other factors considered include:* essays, recommendations, talent/ability. SAT I or ACT required. *High school units required/recommended:* 4 English recommended, 4 math recommended, 4 science recommended, 2 foreign language recommended, 3 social studies recommended, 1 computer recommended, 1 elective recommended.

### The Inside Word

Candidates to the service academies face some of America's most challenging admissions standards. Air Force is no exception in this regard. In addition to a very rigorous academic review, students must first win a nomination from their congressman and pass a demanding physical fitness exam. If you make it through, it's worth the hard work and effort—few students turn down an offer of admission and the chance to join the fold of an elite student body. Admit rates are among the nation's lowest annually.

## FINANCIAL AID

The Princeton Review suggests that all financial aid forms be submitted as soon as possible after January 1. Off-campus job opportunities are poor.

### SELECTIVITY

| | |
|---|---:|
| **Admissions Rating** | 99 |
| # of applicants | 9,041 |
| % of applicants accepted | 17 |
| % of acceptees attending | 79 |

### FRESHMAN PROFILE

| | |
|---|---:|
| Range SAT Verbal | 590-680 |
| Average SAT Verbal | 633 |
| Range SAT Math | 620-700 |
| Average SAT Math | 658 |
| Average HS GPA | 3.8 |
| % graduated top 10% of class | 57 |
| % graduated top 25% of class | 85 |
| % graduated top 50% of class | 98 |

### DEADLINES

| | |
|---|---:|
| Regular admission | 1/31 |
| Regular notification | 4/1 |

### APPLICANTS ALSO LOOK AT AND SOMETIMES PREFER

U.S. Coast Guard Academy
U.S. Military Academy
U.S. Naval Academy
U.S. Merchant Marine Academy

### FINANCIAL FACTS

| | |
|---|---:|
| **Financial Aid Rating** | 99 |

# UNITED STATES COAST GUARD ACADEMY

31 Mohegan Avenue, New London, CT 06320-8103 • Admissions: 800-883-8724 • Fax: 860-701-6700

## CAMPUS LIFE

| | |
|---|---|
| Quality of Life Rating | 85 |
| Type of school | public |
| Environment | suburban |

### STUDENTS

| | |
|---|---|
| Total undergrad enrollment | 985 |
| % from out of state | 93 |
| % live on campus | 100 |
| % African American | 5 |
| % Asian | 5 |
| % Caucasian | 82 |
| % Hispanic | 6 |
| % international | 2 |

### SURVEY SAYS . . .
Classes are small
Great library
Lots of classroom discussion
Lab facilities are great
Diverse students interact
No one cheats

## ACADEMICS

| | |
|---|---|
| Academic Rating | 99 |
| Calendar | semester |
| Student/faculty ratio | 10:1 |
| % profs teaching UG courses | 100 |
| Avg lab size | 10-19 students |
| Avg reg class size | 20-29 students |

### MOST POPULAR MAJORS
Civil engineering
Electrical, electronics, and communications engineering
Environmental/environmental health engineering

## STUDENTS SPEAK OUT

### Academics

"It's free, you get paid, and you have a job promised to you when you graduate." For most at the United States Coast Guard Academy, that's a parlay too enticing to refuse. That's right; students at CGA not only get a completely free ride, but also a small stipend and a Coast Guard gig waiting at the end of the line. Others choose CGA because they want an extremely challenging, extremely disciplined college experience; those cadets don't leave disappointed. "The Coast Guard Academy is one of the best overall learning opportunities that the United States has to offer. Cadets here are challenged in many aspects, including physically, mentally, and academically" by a curriculum that includes mandatory sports and drilling as well as an average of 20 credit hours per semester. "Classes are small, which allows for superb instruction." And "profs really care and will spend a lot of time out of the classroom for us." All this helps take some of the sting off the fact that "cadets get an average of 5 hours of sleep a night because the academic load is tremendous." Agrees one student, "The hardest aspect of going to school here is the lack of time to complete the assignments, or deciding which ones you are going to complete given your time." The hard work pays off, most agree: "The experience, although extremely demanding, leaves one feeling quite proud of what he has accomplished."

### Life

There is "little to no downtime" for cadets at CGA, since academic and athletic requirements cram students' weekdays full. "We can basically only have fun on the weekends, when we get liberty. During the week, there is no time for anything but school" is how one cadet puts it. Many here resent the school's strict, occasionally "illogical" regulations. "Micromanaging every aspect of our lives gets old after a few days . . . let alone four years," writes one cadet. Students particularly dislike the strict drug and alcohol policy ("No drugs, ever. Caught twice drinking [underage] and you're expelled") and the rule requiring all barracks doors to remain open from 0600 to 2200. Once weekends come around, "we leave, if we can get liberty. That's the way it is in a barracks." Because "New London is a horrendously barren town," cadets try to go elsewhere; Boston, Providence, and New York are all favorite destinations. Those stuck in town "head for Connecticut College across the street," where there are "many opportunities to take part in the more artistic/scholarly activities" as well as keg parties. Life at CGA is not without its pleasures, however; the school has "an amazing sports program for a Division III school," and "the summer programs either on Coast Guard boats or spent at the Academy instructing the incoming 'Swabs'" can be "the best summers of your life. I have been able to fly Coast Guard helicopters and aircraft and participate in the exchange cadet program to the United States Military Academy at West Point during my junior year."

### Student Body

"There are few other institutions on this planet that bring groups of people together the way service academies do," explains one Coast Guard cadet. "At times the closeness of the Academy can drive you crazy, but overall it enriches the institution and the experience." Puns one student, "We are all in the same boat." Coast Guard cadets "are very competitive by nature, and the corps of cadets is full of Type A personalities." They "tend to come from small communities" and be "very conservative and outgoing." Regardless of their differences, "the system requires a basic professional respect for others that one must practice most of the time." Of course, "there are a few bad apples, like anywhere." "Sometimes the Academy atmosphere, rules, etc. have a way of bringing out the worst in people," explains one cadet. "The Academy system has a way of creating conflict between people. Luckily, most of these people get weeded out eventually."

# UNITED STATES COAST GUARD ACADEMY

E-MAIL: ADMISSIONS@CGA.USCG.MIL • WEBSITE: WWW.CGA.EDU

## ADMISSIONS

*Very important factors considered include:* character/personal qualities, class rank, extracurricular activities, secondary school record, standardized test scores. *Important factors considered include:* essays, recommendations, talent/ability. *Other factors considered include:* alumni/ae relation, interview, volunteer work, work experience. SAT I or ACT required. TOEFL required of all international applicants. High school diploma or GED is required. *High school units required/recommended:* 4 English required, 4 math required.

### The Inside Word

The Coast Guard is the smallest service academy, regarded by many as a well-kept secret. Just like the other military service academies, admission is highly selective. Candidates must go through a rigorous admissions process that includes a medical exam and physical fitness evaluation. Those who pass muster join a very proud service. If you're a woman and thinking about a service academy, be aware that the Corps of Cadets at the Coast Guard Academy is 30 percent women!

## FINANCIAL AID

The Coast Guard Academy is tuition-free.

## FROM THE ADMISSIONS OFFICE

"Founded in 1876, the United State Coast Guard Academy has a proud tradition as one of the finest colleges in the country. When you've earned your four-year Bachelor of Science degree and a commission as an Ensign, you're prepared professionally, physically, and mentally as a leader and lifelong learner. You'll build friendships to last a lifetime, study with inspiring teachers in small classes, and train during the summer aboard America's Tall Ship EAGLE and the service's newest, most sophisticated ships and aircraft. Top performers spend their senior summer traveling on exciting internships. No Congressional nominations, appointments are awarded competitively on a nationwide basis. Graduates must serve for five years and have unmatched opportunities to attend flight training and graduate school, all funded by the Coast Guard. Your leadership potential and desire to serve your fellow Americans are what counts. Our student body reflects the best America has to offer—with all its potential and diversity!"

---

### SELECTIVITY

| | |
|---|---|
| Admissions Rating | 98 |
| # accepting a place on wait list | 161 |

#### FRESHMAN PROFILE

| | |
|---|---|
| Range SAT Verbal | 580-670 |
| Average SAT Verbal | 620 |
| Range SAT Math | 610-680 |
| Average SAT Math | 640 |
| Range ACT Composite | 25-30 |
| Average ACT Composite | 27 |
| Minimum TOEFL | 500 |
| % graduated top 10% of class | 48 |
| % graduated top 25% of class | 88 |
| % graduated top 50% of class | 100 |

#### DEADLINES

| | |
|---|---|
| Regular admission | 12/15 |

#### APPLICANTS ALSO LOOK AT AND SOMETIMES PREFER

U.S. Air Force Academy
U.S. Military Academy
U.S. Naval Academy
U.S. Merchant Marine Academy

### FINANCIAL FACTS

| | |
|---|---|
| Financial Aid Rating | 99 |
| Required fees | $3,000 |

# United States Merchant Marine Academy

Office of Admissions, Kings Point, NY 11024-1699 • Admissions: 516-773-5391 • Fax: 516-773-5390

## CAMPUS LIFE

★ ★ ★ ☆

| | |
|---|---|
| **Quality of Life Rating** | **84** |
| Type of school | public |
| Affiliation | none |
| Environment | suburban |

### STUDENTS

| | |
|---|---|
| Total undergrad enrollment | 943 |
| % from out of state | 86 |
| % from public high school | 50 |
| % live on campus | 100 |
| % international | 2 |
| # of countries represented | 4 |

### SURVEY SAYS . . .
Instructors are good teachers
No one cheats
School is well run
Campus easy to get around
Great computer facilities
Diverse students interact
Class discussions encouraged
Very little drug use

## ACADEMICS

★ ★ ★ ☆

| | |
|---|---|
| **Academic Rating** | **84** |
| Calendar | trimester |
| Student/faculty ratio | 11:1 |
| Profs interesting rating | 84 |
| Profs accessible rating | 83 |

## STUDENTS SPEAK OUT

### Academics

Mention sailors and most people think of swearing, drinking, and port-of-call carousing, and while this image applies on rare occasions to students at the United States Merchant Marine Academy, the focus here is decidedly on academics. At the beginning of the second semester of freshman year, midshipmen select a major—one of six available: "deck or engine, [meaning Marine Transportation or Marine Engineering] with a few subcategories in each." From that point forward, they have their course schedule laid out by the Academy. "I get one elective in four years," one midshipman notes. The academic program receives high praise, specifically because classroom learning is complemented by "one of four years of actual working experience." That experience comes during Sea Year, and students say, "Sea Year Courses, which are done while training on various merchant ships throughout the world, are the most difficult of the academy's courses." Professors are characterized as "dedicated," some to the point of being "slave drivers." The small classes, lack of TAs, and mandatory class attendance policy ensure that students get the attention they need to manage the "very heavy course load" and regimental requirements. Even deans pitch in and "tutor students when they can." Students submit mixed opinions when it comes to the administration, though the superintendent is widely respected. Some midshipmen perceive an "open door" attitude from administrators, but others claim that the "administration thinks we are whiny brats." Most students look forward to the high-paying careers available to them after graduation and appreciate the "excellent leadership training" they receive at the Academy.

### Life

"This school is a country club if you disregard the marching," one USMMA student observes. Marching and other regimental activities constitute much of life in Kings Point, prompting some students to feel at times like "inmates" on campus. Some report "sleeping two to four hours a night" to accommodate the intense academic and regimental schedule. Basically, "freshmen don't have lives," but even first-years point out, "We are here to train." As they progress, midshipmen begin to enjoy more "individual freedoms [and] privileges, which are granted based upon seniority and individual performance." To blow off steam, "most people work out nearly every day or play sports." When the weekend rolls around, "it's all about New York City," which is only 20 to 30 minutes away by train. One student writes, "I typically utilize some of our perks, such as free admission to Mets games, the U.S. Open, Yankees games, and David Letterman." Though rumors suggest "a few people have actually gone into museums," during these outings to the Big Apple, students mainly hit the bars, "on the prowl due to the lack of women at school." Other people choose to "sail all over Long Island on the weekends." A common sentiment goes something like, "Life at school is very busy and there are not many times to just 'chill,' as my regular college friends call it."

### Students

The typical USMMA student is reported to be a "white male between the ages of 18 and 22"; only about 100 women attend the Academy. Also, the population includes "very few students that are of a different ethnicity," but one minority student writes frankly, "I have not found this to be a problem." This might be partly due to the pervasive notion that "having people from many different areas of the country and world makes for an increased awareness of life in general and how people act." Respondents agree that "most students have similar political views," which translates to "no hippies." "Everyone becomes 'typical' by necessity because of the regimentation of the school." Strong bonds form during an "indoctrination period" that each incoming class undergoes, the "evident esprit de corps" solidified by the "cramped quarters" and "repressive regime" in which they exist. These solid connections endure after graduates set sail: "The merchant marine community is so small that there is also the advantage of an excellent network of contacts."

# UNITED STATES MERCHANT MARINE ACADEMY

EMAIL: ADMISSIONS@USMMA.EDU • WEBSITE: WWW.USMMA.EDU

## ADMISSIONS

*Very important factors considered by the admissions committee include:* character/personal qualities, secondary school record, and standardized test scores. *Important factors considered include:* class rank, essays, extracurricular activities, recommendations, and talent/ability. *Other factors considered include:* interview, minority status, state residency, volunteer work, and work experience. SAT I or ACT required. TOEFL required of all international applicants. High school diploma is required and GED is not accepted. *High school units required/recommended:* 18 total are required; 4 English required, 4 English recommended, 3 math required, 4 math recommended, 3 science required, 4 science recommended, 1 science lab required, 2 science lab recommended, 2 foreign language recommended, 4 social studies recommended, 8 elective required.

## The Inside Word

Academic criteria are only part of the admissions game here; you must also meet the Academy's physical requirements. The school catalog has three pages on requirements concerning vision, hearing, weight and body fat percent, skin condition, and respiratory health. You also need to know how to swim.

## FINANCIAL AID

*Students should submit:* FAFSA and institution's own financial aid form. Regular filing deadline is May 1. The Princeton Review suggests that all financial aid forms be submitted as soon as possible after January 1. *Need-based scholarships/grants offered:* Pell. Loan aid offered: FFEL subsidized Stafford, and FFEL PLUS. Applicants will be notified of awards on a rolling basis beginning on or about January 31. Off-campus job opportunities are poor.

## FROM THE ADMISSIONS OFFICE

"What makes the U.S. Merchant Marine Academy different from the other federal service academies? The difference can be summarized in two phrases that appear in our publications. The first: 'The World Is Your Campus.' You will spend a year at sea—a third of your sophomore year and two-thirds of your junior year—teamed with a classmate aboard a U.S. merchant ship. You will visit an average of 18 foreign nations while you work and learn in a mariner's true environment. You will graduate with seafaring experience and as a citizen of the world. The second phrase is 'Options and Opportunities.' Unlike students at the other federal academies, who are required to enter the service connected to their academy, you have the option of working in the seagoing merchant marine and transportation industry, or applying for active duty in the Navy, Coast Guard, Marine Corps, Air Force, or Army. Nearly 29 percent of our most recent graduating class entered various branches of the Armed Forces with an officer rank. As a graduate of the U.S. Merchant Marine Academy, you will receive a Bachelor of Science degree, a government-issued merchant marine officer's license, and a Naval Reserve commission (unless you have been accepted for active military duty). No other service academy offers so attractive a package."

## SELECTIVITY

| | |
|---|---|
| Admissions Rating | 98 |
| # of applicants | 1,586 |
| % of applicants accepted | 24 |
| % of acceptees attending | 74 |
| # accepting a place on wait list | 113 |
| % admitted from wait list | 15 |

### FRESHMAN PROFILE

| | |
|---|---|
| Range SAT Verbal | 620-670 |
| Average SAT Verbal | 600 |
| Range SAT Math | 600-650 |
| Average SAT Math | 610 |
| Average ACT Composite | 27 |
| Minimum TOEFL | 550 |
| % graduated top 10% of class | 16 |
| % graduated top 25% of class | 75 |
| % graduated top 50% of class | 100 |

### DEADLINES

| | |
|---|---|
| Early decision | 11/1 |
| Regular admission | 3/1 |

### APPLICANTS ALSO LOOK AT AND OFTEN PREFER
US Naval Academy
### AND SOMETIMES PREFER
US Coast Guard Academy
US Air Force Academy
US Military Academy
### AND RARELY PREFER
SUNY Maritime College
Massachusetts Maritime Academy
Maine Maritime Academy

## FINANCIAL FACTS

| | |
|---|---|
| Financial Aid Rating | 99 |
| Avg frosh loan | $2,625 |

# UNITED STATES MILITARY ACADEMY

600 Thayer Road, West Point, NY 10996-1797 • Admissions: 914-938-4041 • Fax: 914-938-3021

## CAMPUS LIFE

| Quality of Life Rating | 78 |
| --- | --- |
| Type of school | public |
| Environment | suburban |

### STUDENTS

| Total undergrad enrollment | 4,154 |
| --- | --- |
| % from out of state | 92 |
| % from public high school | 86 |
| % live on campus | 100 |
| % African American | 8 |
| % Asian | 5 |
| % Caucasian | 79 |
| % Hispanic | 6 |
| % international | 1 |

### SURVEY SAYS . . .
School is run well
Campus feels safe
No one cheats
Registration is a breeze
Different students interact
Students don't like West Point, NY
Very little drug use
Very little hard liquor
Lousy off-campus food
Student publications are ignored

## ACADEMICS

| Academic Rating | 99 |
| --- | --- |
| Calendar | semester |
| Student/faculty ratio | 7:1 |
| Profs interesting rating | 96 |
| Profs accessible rating | 99 |
| % profs teaching UG courses | 100 |

## STUDENTS SPEAK OUT

### Academics

"West Point is unique in many ways: a military institution, a first-class university, and a national landmark all rolled into one," explains one cadet. "Our motto is 'duty, honor, country,' and sometimes duty looms much larger than the rest. Life is hard here, but its difficulty makes it fulfilling." The West Point approach—to cram as much activity into one day as humanly possible—is "very tough. Learn to prioritize. If you procrastinate, you die. Be ready not to sleep." Notes one student, "Academics are tough, but it's the fact that you have no time to study that makes it hard." Life is strictly regimented here, as one would expect. Writes one student, "West Point is similar to high school, at times almost too similar. We start at 7, stop for lunch at 12, and then continue until 3. Classes are small, which means every professor knows your name." For nearly all freshmen and sophomores, "There is no class choice. All classes are required." And even upperclassmen warn that "it's the military: You pick the major, they choose the classes." Fortunately for students, "the professors here, for the most part, are amazing. They understand how rigorous our life is and will tutor you personally every day for hours if you need it." Cadets are the first to admit that this school is not for everyone. "The school is focused toward military development and officership, so if you don't want to be in the Army, don't come!" warns one. Concludes another, "West Point is a machine that takes you in, chews you up, and spits you out—but somehow you are tremendously better person for it." Upon graduation, cadets are commissioned as Second Lieutenants in the U.S. Army and must serve a minimum of five years of active duty.

### Life

As far as extracurricular life is concerned, a student's tenure at West Point is neatly divided in half. Simply put, for their first two years, students have no extracurricular life. Writes one student, "Because I am a sophomore, otherwise known as a 'Yuk,' I have no privileges (like going to the movies or to the mall). I am stuck in the cadet area studying." During their final two years, students are given greater freedom. Explains one upperclassman, "There is not much to do here in the first two years, but once you receive off-post privileges there is more available." The town surrounding the beautiful campus, Highland Falls, is small, so even when cadets do leave campus, they find very little to do unless they have wheels. Writes one student, "If you're not a cow (junior) or a first (senior) with a car, you are hard-pressed to have fun. If you do have a car, New York City and New Jersey aren't so far off. It also helps to be on a sports team." Intercollegiate athletic events are well attended here, even though Army's teams generally lose more often than they win. Army's popular football team, for one, competes in Conference USA, where it is usually overmatched by Tulane, Houston, Louisville, and Southern Mississippi, among others. The lacrosse team is much better, ranking 20th in the nation at the end of the 2000 season. Intramural sports are unusually popular for the simple reason that "all students not on varsity teams must play intramurals here. It's not an option." Mostly, though, life at West Point is defined by study, exercise, and plenty of drilling. "If you don't want to work hard, run, or be in the Army, do not come here," advises a senior.

### Student Body

West Point's undergraduates represent a "great diversity of students and different backgrounds." However, as one cadet pointed out, "Relationships with other students are always filtered through the lens of leadership." As a result, "some get along, and some don't. But one thing about West Point is that I would trust any of [my classmates] with my life—and someday I may have to." Adds another student, "Students here all get along. They are forced to because of our mission in life: to become officers. Teamwork is essential. There are no individuals here." Minority discrimination "does not occur because it is simply not allowed here."

# UNITED STATES MILITARY ACADEMY

FINANCIAL AID: 914-938-3516 • E-MAIL: 8DAD@EXMAIL.USMA.ARMY.MIL • WEBSITE: WWW.USMA.EDU

## ADMISSIONS

*Very important factors considered include:* essays, extracurricular activities, recommendations, secondary school record, standardized test scores. *Important factors considered include:* character/personal qualities, interview, minority status, talent/ability. *Other factors considered include:* geographical residence, volunteer work, work experience. SAT I or ACT required. High school diploma or GED is required. *High school units required/recommended:* 19 total recommended; 4 English recommended, 4 math recommended, 2 science recommended, 2 science lab recommended, 2 foreign language recommended, 3 social studies recommended, 1 history recommended, 3 elective recommended.

## The Inside Word

Students considering a candidacy at West Point need to hit the ground running in the second half of their junior year. Don't delay initiating the application and nomination processes; together they constitute a long, hard road that includes not one but several highly competitive elements. Successful candidates must demonstrate strength both academically and physically, be solid citizens and contributors to society, and show true fortitude and potential for leadership. Admissions processes at other top schools can seem like a cakewalk compared to this, but those who get a nomination and pass muster through the physical part of the process have made it through the hardest part.

## FINANCIAL AID

The Princeton Review suggests that all financial aid forms be submitted as soon as possible after January 1.

### SELECTIVITY

| | |
|---|---:|
| Admissions Rating | 99 |
| # of applicants | 11,473 |
| % of applicants accepted | 13 |
| % of acceptees attending | 74 |

### FRESHMAN PROFILE
| | |
|---|---:|
| Range SAT Verbal | 570-670 |
| Average SAT Verbal | 627 |
| Range SAT Math | 590-680 |
| Average SAT Math | 641 |
| Range ACT Composite | 26-30 |
| Average ACT Composite | 28 |
| Average HS GPA | 3.7 |
| % graduated top 10% of class | 50 |
| % graduated top 25% of class | 81 |
| % graduated top 50% of class | 97 |

### DEADLINES
| | |
|---|---:|
| Priority admission | 12/1 |
| Regular admission | 3/21 |

### APPLICANTS ALSO LOOK AT
**AND OFTEN PREFER**
U. Rochester
**AND SOMETIMES PREFER**
U.S. Naval Acad.
Notre Dame
Villanova
Tulane U.
U. Oklahoma
**AND RARELY PREFER**
U. Florida
Carnegie Mellon

### FINANCIAL FACTS

| | |
|---|---:|
| Financial Aid Rating | 99 |
| Books and supplies | $664 |

# UNITED STATES NAVAL ACADEMY

117 DECATUR ROAD, ANNAPOLIS, MD 21402 • ADMISSIONS: 410-293-4361 • FAX: 410-295-1815

## CAMPUS LIFE

| | |
|---|---|
| Quality of Life Rating | 84 |
| Type of school | public |
| Environment | suburban |

### STUDENTS

| | |
|---|---|
| Total undergrad enrollment | 4,309 |
| % from out of state | 94 |
| % from public high school | 60 |
| % live on campus | 100 |
| % African American | 6 |
| % Asian | 4 |
| % Caucasian | 80 |
| % Hispanic | 8 |
| % international | 1 |
| # of countries represented | 24 |

### SURVEY SAYS . . .
Very little drug use
Everyone loves the Midshipmen
(Almost) everyone plays intramural sports
Classes are small
Popular college radio
Unattractive campus
Campus difficult to get around
Library needs improving
Lab facilities are great
Computer facilities need improving

## ACADEMICS

| | |
|---|---|
| Academic Rating | 99 |
| Calendar | semester |
| Student/faculty ratio | 7:1 |
| Profs interesting rating | 94 |
| Profs accessible rating | 100 |
| % profs teaching UG courses | 100 |
| Avg reg class size | 10-19 students |

### MOST POPULAR MAJORS
Systems engineering
Economics
Political science and government

## STUDENTS SPEAK OUT

### Academics

Future Naval and Marine officers at the USNA—known as "midshipmen" or just "mids"—enter an academic world distinct from that their civilian counterparts do. First of all, the academy dictates all freshman-year classes and virtually all courses outside of a student's major in subsequent years. Professors differ in that "the only research [they] run is as a secondary researcher to an undergraduate project." Focussed on teaching, the mix of civilian and military professors couldn't be more accessible: "On several occasions my chemistry professor has come up to my company area and gone room to room helping people in first-year chemistry." The administration is less popular, characterized as "ridiculously overbearing and intrusive" and accused of "micromanaging every aspect of our life." Some students praise the efficiency born of the military chain of command, but others whine, "The administration runs things so well because we have little choice and no way to disagree." The "outrageous punishments" are said to "only make people cynical and unhappy." Deep-seated traditions and mounds of paperwork ensure that "you cannot change a thing, no matter how ridiculous it is." The free tuition, room, and board, along with a guaranteed job at graduation, make the hassles easier to swallow.

### Life

A common refrain is that the academy is "a good place to be from but not to be at." One midshipman admits, "People don't pick this place for the lifestyle." But others state that the atmosphere can be "wonderful and challenging." However, incarceration analogies are alarmingly common: one student writes, "You are in jail for four years." Plebes (freshmen) are given only 12 hours of freedom per week, from 10 A.M. to 10 P.M. on Saturdays; the rest of the time they are on campus and in uniform, prohibited from driving or wearing civilian clothes until they are juniors. Though life is "very restricted," one student claims, "It is for a purpose and has worth." Drinking laws are strictly enforced, and no alcohol is allowed on campus. Thus, "for fun, we get the hell away from the academy," which generally means getting plowed in Annapolis, visiting nearby colleges such as UVA and Georgetown, or seeing a movie at the mall. Local sponsor families provide relief for students, mostly in the form of home-cooked meals.

### Student Body

Not many colleges have students who say, "We must be prepared to die for one another." As part of "the biggest fraternity in the world," mids take camaraderie to a new level while fiercely "competing against each other to be the best." There is a fair share of ruthless climbers, "who don't mind who they have to step on to get one rung higher up the ladder." It's still tough to be female at this historically male institution; "strained male-female relationships" are commonly noted. But though "girls aren't treated too well, minorities are treated great" because "we share a common thread which lowers the traditional racial boundaries." Being in uniform also means that "you can't tell who comes from money and who doesn't." Amid this "type A," "moral, intelligent," "goal-oriented," and "aloof" student body, "liberal opinions are hard to find." One student observes a split between "those who buy into the indoctrination system and those who rebel." A student from the latter group warns against "group-think syndrome," concluding that "being an individual can be a good thing."

# UNITED STATES NAVAL ACADEMY

E-MAIL: WEBMAIL@GWMAIL.USNA.COM • WEBSITE: WWW.USNA.EDU

## ADMISSIONS

*Very important factors considered include:* character/personal qualities, class rank, essays, extracurricular activities, interview, recommendations, secondary school record, standardized test scores. *Important factors considered include:* talent/ability. *Other factors considered include:* alumni/ae relation, geographical residence, volunteer work, work experience. SAT I or ACT required. TOEFL required of all international applicants. *High school units required/recommended:* 4 English recommended, 4 math recommended, 2 science recommended, 1 science lab recommended, 2 foreign language recommended, 2 history recommended.

### The Inside Word

It doesn't take a genius to recognize that getting admitted to Annapolis requires true strength of character; simply completing the arduous admissions process is an accomplishment worthy of remembrance. Those who have successful candidacies are strong, motivated students, and leaders in both school and community. Perseverance is an important character trait for anyone considering the life of a midshipman—the application process is only the beginning of a truly challenging and demanding experience.

## FINANCIAL AID

The Princeton Review suggests that all financial aid forms be submitted as soon as possible after January 1.

## FROM THE ADMISSIONS OFFICE

"The Naval Academy offers you a unique opportunity to associate with a broad cross-section of the country's finest young men and women. You will have the opportunity to pursue a four-year program that develops you mentally, morally, and physically as no civilian college can. As you might expect, this program is demanding, but the opportunities are limitless and more than worth the effort. To receive an appointment to the academy, you need four years of high school preparation to develop the strong academic, athletic, and extracurricular background required to compete successfully for admission. You should begin preparing in your freshman year and apply for admission at the end of your junior year. Selection for appointment to the academy comes as a result of a complete evaluation of your admissions package and completion of the nomination process. Complete admissions guidance may be found at www.usna.edu."

---

### SELECTIVITY
★ ★ ★ ★

| | |
|---|---|
| Admissions Rating | 99 |
| # of applicants | 12,331 |
| % of applicants accepted | 12 |
| % of acceptees attending | 83 |

### FRESHMAN PROFILE

| | |
|---|---|
| Range SAT Verbal | 530-640 |
| Average SAT Verbal | 637 |
| Range SAT Math | 560-670 |
| Average SAT Math | 663 |
| Minimum TOEFL | 500 |
| % graduated top 10% of class | 57 |
| % graduated top 25% of class | 84 |
| % graduated top 50% of class | 96 |

### DEADLINES
Regular admission     2/15

### APPLICANTS ALSO LOOK AT AND OFTEN PREFER
Harvard
Duke
Stanford
U. Virginia
U.S. Air Force Acad.

### AND SOMETIMES PREFER
U.S. Military Acad.
Georgia Tech.
MIT
Penn State—Univ. Park
U. Michigan—Ann Arbor

### AND RARELY PREFER
Purdue U.
Boston U.

### FINANCIAL FACTS
★ ★ ★ ★

Financial Aid Rating     99

# UNIVERSITY OF ALABAMA—TUSCALOOSA

Box 870132, Tuscaloosa, AL 35487 • Admissions: 205-348-5666 • Fax: 205-348-9046

## CAMPUS LIFE

| Quality of Life Rating | 75 |
| --- | --- |
| Type of school | public |
| Environment | suburban |

### STUDENTS

| Total undergrad enrollment | 15,441 |
| --- | --- |
| % male/female | 47/53 |
| % from out of state | 20 |
| % from public high school | 89 |
| % live on campus | 23 |
| % in (# of) fraternities | 16 (27) |
| % in (# of) sororities | 24 (19) |
| % African American | 15 |
| % Asian | 1 |
| % Caucasian | 83 |
| % Hispanic | 1 |
| % international | 1 |

### SURVEY SAYS . . .
Everyone loves the Crimson Tide
Lots of beer drinking
Campus is beautiful
(Almost) everyone smokes
Athletic facilities are great
Frats and sororities dominate social scene
Hard liquor is popular
Great library
Students are happy
Great off-campus food

## ACADEMICS

| Academic Rating | 76 |
| --- | --- |
| Calendar | semester |
| Student/faculty ratio | 18:1 |
| % profs teaching UG courses | 76 |
| % classes taught by TAs | 14 |
| Avg lab size | 10-19 students |
| Avg reg class size | 10-19 students |

### MOST POPULAR MAJORS
Finance
Marketing/marketing management
Public administration

## STUDENTS SPEAK OUT

### Academics

Students at University of Alabama, a gargantuan southern state university, believe that several factors help to mitigate the impersonality typical of other mega-universities. "Because Alabama is in the South, there is an overall friendliness between professors and students, as long as you show up for class not hung-over, as many students do," explains one student. "As a freshman, I have already developed strong bonds with two of my professors. Out of all my introductory classes, only one is a large lecture class. I love it here!" This big school is also made to feel a little smaller by "great student advisors. You can walk in anytime and get one to talk to you about your grades, progress, or problems. If you slip up and have a bad semester, they're there for you." As at most big schools, "it is the luck of the draw in getting a good teacher or professor," and "the administration is OK at best. They are fairly helpful during registration, and the records office usually runs pretty smoothly. However, the financial aid office and Student Receivables (bursar's office) are ridiculous." Undergrads choose from nine educational divisions: commerce and business administration, education, communication, engineering, arts and sciences, nursing, social work, human environmental sciences, and New College—a unique, independent study program. They observe that "while the bigger colleges have nicer facilities and equipment, the smaller colleges have more faculty and support for each student."

### Life

Students report that "Alabama is a great place if you are looking for a good time, from going to the bars, to sitting on the porch with friends, to a huge victory party (after football games). We have anything you would want to do on any night of the week." More than a few students, it should be noted, mentioned with pride that 'Bama received a "#2 Party School" ranking in a previous edition of this book. Those not into partying often agree that "life at Alabama is fairly monotonous. There is 'The Strip,' the main street through the campus with bars and restaurants and other little shops, and that's about it. There are no clubs here, just several bars, and that's pretty much the only entertainment on weekends." There's also a large, powerful, and, by many accounts, elitist Greek scene here; writes one student, "The thing at Alabama is to be Greek. If you aren't, there are a lot of things unavailable to you." Students adore their Crimson Tide teams; reports one student, "People really love sports here, especially football. It's a really athletic school with great recreational facilities."

### Student Body

The "overwhelmingly conservative" students of 'Bama admit to a wide, well-defined divide running between the Greek and independent communities. Writes one GDI, "The Greeks can be nice individually, but as a group they can be somewhat snobbish." Independents especially resent the sense that "the Greek system here at the university, referred to by many simply as 'The Machine,' basically runs the school. They control the SGA and nearly every campus group. For non-Greek students, it's hard to escape from under their umbrella." Students report that "there's a lot of ethnic diversity here at UA; however, the groups almost never mix. I wouldn't say there's any animosity. The groups just don't have anything in common with each other." Some go further; groused one Jewish student, "Make no mistake about it, there is more racism here than I have ever experienced in my life . . . . Even in the campus dining area, there is a clear line of the 'white side' and the 'black side.'"

# UNIVERSITY OF ALABAMA—TUSCALOOSA

FINANCIAL AID: 205-348-6756 • E-MAIL: UAADMIT@UA.EDU • WEBSITE: WWW.UA.EDU

## ADMISSIONS

*Very important factors considered include:* secondary school record. *Important factors considered include:* class rank, standardized test scores. *Other factors considered include:* alumni/ae relation, character/personal qualities, essays, extracurricular activities, interview, recommendations, talent/ability, volunteer work, work experience. SAT I or ACT required. TOEFL required of all international applicants. High school diploma or GED is required. *High school units required/recommended:* 15 total required; 19 total recommended; 4 English required, 3 math required, 4 math recommended, 3 science required, 4 science recommended, 2 science lab required, 1 foreign language required, 2 foreign language recommended, 3 social studies required, 4 social studies recommended, 1 history required, 5 elective required.

### The Inside Word

There's no mystery in Alabama's formula-driven approach to admission; any solid "B" student is likely to meet with success. What selectivity there is in the process exists mainly because of the volume of applications. Recommendations are not likely to play a significant role in the admission of applicants unless they are borderline candidates.

## FINANCIAL AID

*Students should submit:* FAFSA. No deadline for regular filing. The Princeton Review suggests that all financial aid forms be submitted as soon as possible after January 1. *Need-based scholarships/grants offered:* Pell, SEOG, state scholarships/grants, private scholarships, the school's own gift aid, Federal Nursing. *Loan aid offered:* Direct Subsidized Stafford, Direct Unsubsidized Stafford, Direct PLUS, Federal Perkins, college/university loans from institutional funds. Federal Work-Study Program available. Institutional employment available. Applicants will be notified of awards on or about April 1. Off-campus job opportunities are good.

## FROM THE ADMISSIONS OFFICE

"Since its founding in 1831 as the first public university in the state, the University of Alabama has been committed to providing the best, most complete education possible for its students. Our commitment to that goal means that as times change, we sharpen our focus and methods to keep our graduates competitive in their fields. By offering outstanding teaching in a solid core curriculum enhanced by multimedia classrooms and campus-wide computer labs, the University of Alabama keeps its focus on the future while maintaining a traditional college atmosphere. Extensive international study opportunities, internship programs, and co-operative education placements help our students prepare for successful futures. Consisting of 14 colleges and schools offering 275 degrees in over 150 fields of study, the university gives its students a wide range of choices and offers courses of study at the bachelor's, master's, specialist, and doctoral levels. The university emphasizes quality and breadth of academic opportunities, and challenging programs for the well-prepared students through the university Honors Program, International Honors Program, and Computer-Based Honors Programs. One-third of undergraduates are from out-of-state providing an enriching social and cultural environment."

## SELECTIVITY

| | |
|---|---:|
| Admissions Rating | 80 |
| # of applicants | 7,322 |
| % of applicants accepted | 85 |
| % of acceptees attending | 43 |

### FRESHMAN PROFILE

| | |
|---|---:|
| Range SAT Verbal | 490-620 |
| Average SAT Verbal | 547 |
| Range SAT Math | 490-620 |
| Average SAT Math | 546 |
| Range ACT Composite | 21-26 |
| Average ACT Composite | 23 |
| Minimum TOEFL | 500 |
| Average HS GPA | 3.4 |
| % graduated top 10% of class | 27 |
| % graduated top 25% of class | 54 |
| % graduated top 50% of class | 82 |

### DEADLINES

| | |
|---|---:|
| Priority admission | 3/1 |
| Regular admission | 7/1 |
| Nonfall registration? | yes |

### APPLICANTS ALSO LOOK AT AND OFTEN PREFER

U. Georgia
Florida State
U. Tennessee
Vanderbilt U.
Birmingham-Southern Coll.

### AND SOMETIMES PREFER

Auburn U.
Oglethorpe U.
Loyola U. New Orleans
Samford U.
Mississippi State U.

## FINANCIAL FACTS

| | |
|---|---:|
| Financial Aid Rating | 83 |
| In-state tuition | $3,556 |
| Out-of-state tuition | $9,624 |
| Room and board | $4,232 |
| Books and supplies | $700 |
| % frosh receiving aid | 30 |
| % undergrads receiving aid | 46 |
| Avg frosh grant | $5,174 |
| Avg frosh loan | $4,667 |

# UNIVERSITY OF ARIZONA

PO Box 210040, Tucson, AZ 85721-0040 • Admissions: 520-621-3237 • Fax: 520-621-9799

## CAMPUS LIFE

| | |
|---|---|
| Quality of Life Rating | 71 |
| Type of school | public |
| Environment | urban |

### STUDENTS

| | |
|---|---|
| Total undergrad enrollment | 28,278 |
| % male/female | 47/53 |
| % from out of state | 30 |
| % from public high school | 90 |
| % live on campus | 18 |
| % in (# of) fraternities | 11 (25) |
| % in (# of) sororities | 13 (20) |
| % African American | 3 |
| % Asian | 6 |
| % Caucasian | 70 |
| % Hispanic | 15 |
| % international | 4 |

### SURVEY SAYS . . .
Everyone loves the Wildcats
Frats and sororities dominate social scene
Athletic facilities are great
(Almost) everyone plays intramural sports
Student government is popular
Ethnic diversity on campus
Student publications are popular
Large classes
Students get along with local community
Diverse students interact

## ACADEMICS

| | |
|---|---|
| Academic Rating | 72 |
| Calendar | semester |
| Student/faculty ratio | 19:1 |
| Profs interesting rating | 91 |
| Profs accessible rating | 95 |
| % profs teaching UG courses | 77 |
| % classes taught by TAs | 21 |
| Avg lab size | 20-29 students |
| Avg reg class size | 20-29 students |

### MOST POPULAR MAJORS
Psychology
Political science and government
Communications studies/speech communication and rhetoric

## STUDENTS SPEAK OUT

### Academics
Maybe it's all the sunshine in Tucson that makes students so wildly enthusiastic about the University of Arizona, or maybe it's just that this school does a great job making its students a number-one priority. Whatever the cause, students at U of A are nothing short of impassioned about their school, academically and otherwise: "I couldn't imagine attending any other school. Every experience I have had at U of A has been excellent." Says another student, "My experience at U of A has been wonderful! I've had professors and classes I'll never forget." And another reports, "My professors have always been willing to help me outside of class (and always respond to my questioning e-mails!)." The University of Arizona has much to offer students by way of academics, including a demanding engineering program and strong departments in molecular and cellular biology and chemistry, as well as in English and the social sciences. The emphasis on research at this institution offers students the opportunity to work with professors outside of class as well, which "gives students a great opportunity to be part of a published work." The administration receives decent marks from U of A students. One writes, "I have been overly impressed with the administration and professors' availability throughout my experience here." Several students point directly to the new president, Peter Likins, as the source of their smooth relations: "We are really excited. . . . [He] has amply shown that he cares about students."

### Life
It's a virtual love-fest as far as student relations go at U of A. But maybe it's just the sunny weather that puts everyone in such a good mood: "We're all just coolio at U of A!" boasts one enthusiast. "I LOVE the students here. Everyone is very outgoing, active, and friendly and always willing to make new friends." And how could they not? The opportunities to socialize are ever present with all the great outdoor activities available to students in the general area. "Life is a blast! There are always interesting activities, concerts, clubs and such to get involved with. I am always busy . . . never a dull moment," writes one student. Says another active U of Aer, "My friends and I go to the movies, dinner, miniature golfing, go-carting, hiking, back-packing, mountain biking, rollerblading, or just go for coffee for a late night of talking." Sports are extremely popular: "Intramural sports teams are big and very good. People get very involved with teams, especially the NCAA basketball champs." The city of Tucson itself is campus-friendly, and town-gown relations are good: "The town of Tucson is built up around the U of A, so there is a tremendous amount of community spirit and support." Although most agree that a car is necessary, parking can be a problem.

### Student Body
Students at U of A describe each other as "friendly, spirited, and involved in campus life." Greek life is popular, though as one student comments, "Sometimes it's harder to get to know someone who is in the Greek system if you are not in it." Another agrees, "The Greek system tends to be a bit exclusive." Diversity, however, doesn't seem to be a problem. As this student observes, "I'd never met so many people from other cultures until I came to U of A." Says another, "There is a large, diverse population full of interesting people."

# UNIVERSITY OF ARIZONA

FINANCIAL AID: 520-621-1858 • E-MAIL: APPINFO@ARIZONA.EDU • WEBSITE: WWW.ARIZONA.EDU

## ADMISSIONS

*Very important factors considered include:* secondary school record. *Important factors considered include:* class rank, standardized test scores. *Other factors considered include:* character/personal qualities, essays, extracurricular activities, geographical residence, interview, minority status, recommendations, state residency, talent/ability, volunteer work, work experience. SAT I or ACT required. High school diploma or GED is required. *High school units required/recommended:* 16 total required; 4 English required, 4 math required, 3 science required, 3 science lab required, 2 foreign language required, 1 social studies required, 1 history required.

### The Inside Word

The University of Arizona uses formulas and cutoffs in the admissions process; however, the admissions office prides itself on reading every application. Volume processing means that very little time is spent on individual applicants: you either have what is required, or you don't.

## FINANCIAL AID

*Students should submit:* FAFSA. The Princeton Review suggests that all financial aid forms be submitted as soon as possible after January 1. *Need-based scholarships/grants offered:* Pell, SEOG, state scholarships/grants, private scholarships, the school's own gift aid, Federal Nursing. *Loan aid offered:* FFEL Subsidized Stafford, FFEL Unsubsidized Stafford, FFEL PLUS, Federal Perkins, Federal Nursing, college/university loans from institutional funds. Federal Work-Study Program available. Institutional employment available. Applicants will be notified of awards on a rolling basis beginning on or about April 1. Off-campus job opportunities are good.

## FROM THE ADMISSIONS OFFICE

"Surrounded by mountains and the dramatic beauty of the Sonoran Desert, the University of Arizona offers a top-drawer education in a resort-like setting. Some of the nation's highest ranked departments make their homes at this oasis of learning in the desert. In addition to producing cloudless sunshine 350 days per year, the clear Arizona skies provide an ideal setting for one of the country's best astronomy programs. Other nationally rated programs include nursing, sociology, management information systems, anthropology, creative writing, and computer and aerospace engineering. The university balances a strong research component with an emphasis on teaching—faculty rolls include Nobel and Pulitzer Prize winners. Famous Chinese astrophysicist and political dissident Fang Lizhi continues his landmark studies here; he now teaches physics to undergraduates. The wealth of academic choices—the university offers 118 majors—is supplemented by an active, progressive campus atmosphere; conference-winning basketball, softball, and football teams; and myriad recreational opportunities."

### SELECTIVITY

| | |
|---|---|
| Admissions Rating | 75 |
| # of applicants | 19,832 |
| % of applicants accepted | 86 |
| % of acceptees attending | 34 |

#### FRESHMAN PROFILE

| | |
|---|---|
| Range SAT Verbal | 490-600 |
| Average SAT Verbal | 543 |
| Range SAT Math | 500-620 |
| Average SAT Math | 556 |
| Range ACT Composite | 21-26 |
| Average ACT Composite | 23 |
| % graduated top 10% of class | 32 |
| % graduated top 25% of class | 59 |
| % graduated top 50% of class | 87 |

#### DEADLINES

| | |
|---|---|
| Priority admission | 10/1 |
| Regular admission | 4/1 |
| Nonfall registration? | yes |

#### APPLICANTS ALSO LOOK AT AND OFTEN PREFER
UC Irvine
U of Washington

**AND SOMETIMES PREFER**
U of Colorado at Boulder
UCLA
UC Santa Barbara
U of Wisconsin at Madison
Ohio U

**AND RARELY PREFER**
Baylor
Arizona State
Northern Arizona

### FINANCIAL FACTS

| | |
|---|---|
| Financial Aid Rating | 86 |
| In-state tuition | $3,604 |
| Out-of-state tuition | $12,374 |
| Room and board | $6,568 |
| Books and supplies | $735 |
| Required fees | $85 |
| % frosh receiving aid | 36 |
| % undergrads receiving aid | 47 |

# UNIVERSITY OF ARKANSAS—FAYETTEVILLE

200 SILAS HUNT HALL, FAYETTEVILLE, AR 72701 • ADMISSIONS: 479-575-5346 • FAX: 479-575-7515

## CAMPUS LIFE

| | |
|---|---|
| Quality of Life Rating | 82 |
| Type of school | public |
| Environment | urban |

### STUDENTS

| | |
|---|---|
| Total undergrad enrollment | 12,889 |
| % male/female | 51/49 |
| % from out of state | 11 |
| % from public high school | 95 |
| % live on campus | 41 |
| % in (# of) fraternities | 14 (15) |
| % in (# of) sororities | 18 (12) |
| % African American | 6 |
| % Asian | 3 |
| % Caucasian | 86 |
| % Hispanic | 2 |
| % international | 3 |

### SURVEY SAYS . . .
*Everyone loves the Razorbacks
Lots of beer drinking
(Almost) everyone smokes
Athletic facilities are great
Frats and sororities dominate social scene
Great off-campus food
Hard liquor is popular
Students love Fayetteville, AR*

## ACADEMICS

| | |
|---|---|
| Academic Rating | 80 |
| Calendar | semester |
| Student/faculty ratio | 16:1 |
| Profs interesting rating | 82 |
| Profs accessible rating | 78 |
| % profs teaching UG courses | 100 |
| % classes taught by TAs | 26 |
| Avg lab size | 20-29 students |
| Avg reg class size | 20-29 students |

### MOST POPULAR MAJORS
Marketing/marketing management
Computer science
Curriculum and instruction

## STUDENTS SPEAK OUT

### Academics
Like the Wal-Mart chain headquartered in its home city, the University of Arkansas offers just about anything anyone could want at a reasonable cost. And many students bring a Wal-Mart shopper's attitude to their academic duties; they want to get in, get what they need with as little hassle as possible, and get out as quickly and easily as possible. That's not to say there aren't hard workers and serious students here. Rather, it's that the vast majority simply want career-advancing degrees and good football tickets, and not necessarily in that order. As one bookworm glumly noted, "Most classes that are offered as discussion-based evolve into lectures, but this is as much the fault of poor student preparation as anything else." As at many large state universities, "With professors, you win some, and you lose some. Too many of the professors and grad students are here for their research and not . . . to share their knowledge." The administration, students tell us, "is just like any other bureaucracy." Reported one undergrad, "I have no idea who my academic dean is, and anytime there is a problem with my transcript, it seems as if I have to run in circles to take care of it." Despite these drawbacks, UA still has plenty to offer: a "good learning opportunity, if you know how to take advantage of it" at a fraction of the cost charged by smaller, upscale/boutique schools.

### Life
At UA, "people seem to really focus on their studies when they have to, but when the weekend comes around, everyone does something besides study." During football season, that "something" is cheering on the Razorbacks, who "are a huge part of this school." Reports one student, "On game days, off-campus students have virtually no access to campus, and I think even on campus students have to find another place to park their cars." Students also flock to Dickson Street, "the major street in town, located just down the hill from the school. Within the past ten years it's turned into a solid three blocks of bars, liquor stores, and restaurants." Consequently, "there's a lot of partying. . . . There are quite a few clubs in town for people who like to dance and some nice bars and restaurants for the quieter ones. The Greek scene here, most agree, is pretty big. There's more to UA than just football and keggers, however; the Walton Arts Center and Dickson Street Theater help nurture a "strong arts scene. . . . Many of the local coffee shops display local work. There is also a very strong indie music scene." Also, "Fayetteville is surrounded by great natural beauty, so things like fishing, hiking, camping, climbing, spelunking, and other outdoor stuff is easily accessible."

### Student Body
Most UA undergrads concede that "the largest group on campus consists of white kids from all over the state who arrive at the university more excited about the social aspects . . . than the academic aspects." Even though this seems the norm, one can find "many students who are quite intense about their education; the honors students especially" tend to be "scholarly." As at many southern schools, students have a propensity for religion and conservatism. "We are in the Bible Belt, so Christianity is a big deal, and white, southern look-alikes are [the norm]," explains one student, "but there are many foreign students, and people still come from all over the country." One international notes that "the university does a wonderful job at bringing [foreign students] into the community through the International Students' Office. For instance, I was part of a Conversation Group during my freshman year that met once a week to help us become comfortable with speaking English."

# UNIVERSITY OF ARKANSAS—FAYETTEVILLE

FINANCIAL AID: 479-575-5346 • E-MAIL: UOFA@UARK.EDU • WEBSITE: WWW.UARK.EDU/ADMISSIONS

## ADMISSIONS

*Very important factors considered include:* secondary school record, standardized test scores. *Important factors considered include:* class rank. *Other factors considered include:* alumni/ae relation, character/personal qualities, essays, extracurricular activities, geographical residence, state residency, talent/ability, volunteer work, work experience. SAT I or ACT required. TOEFL required of all international applicants. High school diploma or GED is required. *High school units required/recommended:* 16 total required; 4 English required, 3 math required, 3 science required, 2 science lab required, 2 foreign language recommended, 3 social studies required, 3 elective required.

### The Inside Word

Admission is very straightforward here at Arkansas' flagship university campus. Average college prep students (with a 2.75 or better GPA) will encounter a clear path into the freshman class. The university will also consider those with lower grades for possible conditional admission.

## FINANCIAL AID

*Students should submit:* FAFSA. No deadline for regular filing. The Princeton Review suggests that all financial aid forms be submitted as soon as possible after January 1. *Need-based scholarships/grants offered:* Pell, SEOG, state scholarships/grants, private scholarships, the school's own gift aid. *Loan aid offered:* FFEL Subsidized Stafford, FFEL Unsubsidized Stafford, FFEL PLUS, Federal Perkins, state loans, college/university loans from institutional funds. Federal Work-Study Program available. Institutional employment available. Applicants will be notified of awards on a rolling basis beginning on or about April 1. Off-campus job opportunities are excellent.

## FROM THE ADMISSIONS OFFICE

"The University of Arkansas's drive to emerge as one of the top 50 public research universities in America got a tremendous boost in April 2002 when the University received a $300 million gift from the Walton Family Charitable Support Foundation. The gift—the largest ever made to a public university—will be used to establish and endow an undergraduate honors college providing full financial support to nearly 2,000 high achieving students. The university's growing academic stature is reflected in the accomplishments of its students' winning the nation's most prestigious academic honors. Since 1990, University of Arkansas undergraduates have had 10 students named to the USA Today All-USA College Academic Team and won 24 Barry Goldwater Scholarships in Science and Mathematics, 12 National Science Foundation Graduate Fellowships, 10 Fulbright Scholarships in International Studies, 6 British Marshall Scholarships, 6 Harry S. Truman Scholarships, 4 Morris K. Udall Scholarships, 3 James Madison Scholarships, 3 Tylenol Scholarships, and 1 Rhodes Scholarship (although the University has produced 10 Rhodes Scholars over its history). As The Chronicle of Higher Education pointed out in its September 14, 2001, issue, 'Last year, when Harvard was shut out of the Rhodes and Yale was passed over for the Marshall, Arkansas won one of each.' Students get much more than a school with a door-opening academic reputation, however. The University offers 208 academic programs—which is more than many universities twice our size offer—which means you can find the major that's right for you. Yet as research universities go, we're on the small, intimate side. That means smaller classes and more individual attention from faculty. The University is located in Fayetteville, a small city situated on the beautiful Ozark Plateau, with friendly people, safe streets, a moderate climate, racial and ethnic diversity, awesome recreational opportunities, a robust economy, a vibrant cultural life, and all the excitement you would expect from a great college town."

## SELECTIVITY

| | |
|---|---:|
| Admissions Rating | 81 |
| # of applicants | 5,025 |
| % of applicants accepted | 86 |
| % of acceptees attending | 52 |

### FRESHMAN PROFILE

| | |
|---|---:|
| Range SAT Verbal | 510-640 |
| Average SAT Verbal | 576 |
| Range SAT Math | 520-650 |
| Average SAT Math | 587 |
| Range ACT Composite | 22-28 |
| Average ACT Composite | 25 |
| Minimum TOEFL | 550 |
| Average HS GPA | 3.6 |
| % graduated top 10% of class | 36 |
| % graduated top 25% of class | 65 |
| % graduated top 50% of class | 91 |

### DEADLINES

| | |
|---|---:|
| Priority admission | 11/15 |
| Regular admission | 8/15 |
| Nonfall registration? | yes |

### APPLICANTS ALSO LOOK AT
**AND OFTEN PREFER**
U of Central Arkansas
**AND SOMETIMES PREFER**
Arkansas State
**AND RARELY PREFER**
Oklahoma State

## FINANCIAL FACTS

| | |
|---|---:|
| Financial Aid Rating | 91 |
| In-state tuition | $3,573 |
| Out-of-state tuition | $9,945 |
| Room and board | $4,744 |
| Books and supplies | $840 |
| Required fees | $883 |
| % frosh receiving aid | 43 |
| % undergrads receiving aid | 43 |
| Avg frosh grant | $5,854 |
| Avg frosh loan | $4,169 |

# UNIVERSITY OF CALIFORNIA—BERKELEY
Office of Undergraduate Admission, 110 Sproul Hall #5800, Berkeley, CA 94720-5800 • Admissions: 510-642-3175

## CAMPUS LIFE

| Quality of Life Rating | 75 |
| --- | --- |
| Type of school | public |
| Environment | urban |

### STUDENTS

| Total undergrad enrollment | 23,835 |
| --- | --- |
| % male/female | 46/54 |
| % from out of state | 11 |
| % from public high school | 85 |
| % live on campus | 35 |
| % in (# of) fraternities | 11 (38) |
| % in (# of) sororities | 10 (19) |
| % African American | 4 |
| % Asian | 42 |
| % Caucasian | 30 |
| % Hispanic | 10 |
| % international | 3 |

### SURVEY SAYS . . .
Ethnic diversity on campus
Political activism is hot
Everyone loves the Bears
Different students interact
Campus difficult to get around
Lousy food on campus
(Almost) no one listens to college radio

## ACADEMICS

| Academic Rating | 90 |
| --- | --- |
| Calendar | semester |
| Student/faculty ratio | 16:1 |
| Profs interesting rating | 91 |
| Profs accessible rating | 88 |
| % profs teaching UG courses | 100 |
| Avg reg class size | 10-19 students |

### MOST POPULAR MAJORS
Computer engineering
English language and literature
Political science and government

## STUDENTS SPEAK OUT

### Academics
"Only the best come to Berkeley," observes one current undergraduate. Because of Berkeley's size and the absence of hand-holding professors, "Berkeley is a place for the more independent-minded students who are used to doing things on their own." "Shy people need not apply." While professors are willing to help students outside of the classroom, it's up to the students to initiate contact, and this can be intimidating when you're talking about "supremely intelligent" professors who're teaching classes of 500. Across the board, Berkeley profs are "extremely demanding, which in turn makes the academic experience one of the toughest in the nation." Sighs one student, "You can study your pants off and end up with a C." Online lectures are popular ways for students here to recap the topic of any given day's lecture. Many lectures are also supplemented by "smaller discussion groups" that "are led by" TAs that "range from wonderful to terrible." As a good number of students gripe, "The primary drawback to attending school at Berkeley is the bureaucracy." In the words of one undergrad, "Berkeley is #1 for red tape."

### Life
According to one student, "Berkeley is the center of the universe." "There is SO much going on on campus that it's hard to summarize." Spend a day at Berkeley, and you're likely to find everything "from themed frat parties to barbecues to football games to theater performances to watching jazz at Yoshi's to sneaking into the Greek Theater at midnight on the last day of classes to listen to the UC Berkeley Men's Octet perform to watching friends' dance and choral performances to attending protests, and everything in between." One student describes a typical walk to class this way: "I'll see Christian conservatives debating with students over abortion, with Hare Krishnas dancing around them, next to the Legalize Porn table." Sproul Plaza is the soapbox center of campus—the equivalent of London's legendary Speaker's Corner—"where different groups set up information tables to gain members and support." Regardless of where your interests lie, you'll find some cause to cleave to with "over 300 different student organizations" looking to swell their ranks. Parties? Never tough to find. Students also report that "drugs are very popular" here. Many students find their thrills just wandering around the surrounding town. "The city of Berkeley is ORGASMIC," raves one. And "the huge resources" of the entire Bay Area are in easy reach. San Francisco, for instance, is "just a 15 minute BART [Bay Area Rapid Transit] ride away." "As Clark Kerr, a former Chancellor of our university once said, 'If you are bored with Berkeley, you are bored with life.'" But proceed with caution, writes one student. "Don't be like me and fail your classes because you get caught up in all the lovely things to do."

### Student Body
"There are hippies and stoners and gutter punks and preppy, Abercrombie-and-Fitch-donning, cell-phone-carrying socialites. There are frat boys and odd-ball co-opers, the politically zealous and the religious fanatics, the atheists and the trannies" at Berkeley. "The students are crazy, hailing from all geographical, philosophical, socioeconomic, political, and psychological points of view," reports one student. And they're "united by one thing: their hatred for Stanford—er, I mean thirst for learning." Sure, students here take their studies seriously, but when the competitive academic life is set aside, they're a laid-back crowd. "My fellow students and I all share the prevalent California attitude that everything is great and that things will work out." The most prevalent trait among the Berkeley student body, however, is independence. In some students' minds, this means that their classmates are "people that will really change the world, discover the cure for something, save a country, build the better mousetrap." In other students' minds, this means their classmates are "soulless GPA mongers" whose only concern is a good grade.

# UNIVERSITY OF CALIFORNIA—BERKELEY

Fax: 510-642-7333 • Financial Aid: 510-642-6442 • Website: www.berkeley.edu

## ADMISSIONS

*Very important factors considered include:* essays, secondary school record, state residency. *Important factors considered include:* character/personal qualities, extracurricular activities, standardized test scores, talent/ability, volunteer work, work experience. *Other factors considered include:* geographical residence. SAT I or ACT required; SAT II also required. TOEFL required of all international applicants. High school diploma or GED is required. *High school units required/recommended:* 15 total required; 4 English required, 3 math required, 4 math recommended, 2 science required, 3 science recommended, 2 science lab required, 3 science lab recommended, 2 foreign language required, 3 foreign language recommended, 2 social studies required, 2 history required, 2 elective required.

### The Inside Word

The state of California's discontinuation of affirmative action in the UC admission process has created much uncertainty regarding the future of candidate selection in the system. There is little room for deviation in any applicant's statistical profile, but out-of-state students will find the going even tougher, with available spaces few and far between. Still, minority acceptances remain lower than before the ban. Berkeley is the most selective campus of the university system.

## FINANCIAL AID

*Students should submit:* FAFSA, state aid form. No deadline for regular filing. The Princeton Review suggests that all financial aid forms be submitted as soon as possible after January 1. *Need-based scholarships/grants offered:* Pell, SEOG, state scholarships/grants, private scholarships, the school's own gift aid. *Loan aid offered:* Direct Subsidized Stafford, Direct Unsubsidized Stafford, Direct PLUS, Federal Perkins. Federal Work-Study Program available. Institutional employment available. Applicants will be notified of awards on a rolling basis. Off-campus job opportunities are excellent.

## FROM THE ADMISSIONS OFFICE

"One of the top public universities in the nation and the world, the University of California, Berkeley offers a vast range of courses and a full menu of extracurricular activities. Berkeley's academic programs are internationally recognized for their excellence. Undergraduates can choose one of 100 majors. Thirty-five departments are top-ranked, more than any other college or university in the country. Access to one of the foremost university libraries enriches studies. There are 23 specialized libraries on campus and distinguished museums of anthropology, paleontology, and science."

### SELECTIVITY

| | |
|---|---|
| Admissions Rating | 96 |

#### FRESHMAN PROFILE

| | |
|---|---|
| Range SAT Verbal | 570-700 |
| Average SAT Verbal | 629 |
| Range SAT Math | 620-740 |
| Average SAT Math | 671 |
| Minimum TOEFL | 550 |
| Average HS GPA | 4.2 |
| % graduated top 10% of class | 98 |
| % graduated top 25% of class | 100 |

#### DEADLINES

| | |
|---|---|
| Regular admission | 11/30 |
| Regular notification | 3/31 |
| Nonfall registration? | yes |

#### APPLICANTS ALSO LOOK AT AND OFTEN PREFER
Stanford
#### AND SOMETIMES PREFER
UC Los Angeles
#### AND RARELY PREFER
UC Davis
UC San Diego
UC Santa Barbara
UC Santa Cruz

### FINANCIAL FACTS

| | |
|---|---|
| Financial Aid Rating | 85 |
| Out-of-state tuition | $12,009 |
| Room and board | $10,608 |
| Books and supplies | $1,108 |
| Required fees | $4,200 |
| % frosh receiving aid | 48 |
| % undergrads receiving aid | 45 |

# UNIVERSITY OF CALIFORNIA—DAVIS

178 Mark Hall, UC Davis, Davis, CA 95616 • Admissions: 530-752-2971 • Fax: 530-752-1280

## CAMPUS LIFE

| Quality of Life Rating | 82 |
|---|---|
| Type of school | public |
| Environment | suburban |

### STUDENTS

| Total undergrad enrollment | 22,750 |
|---|---|
| % male/female | 44/56 |
| % from out of state | 4 |
| % from public high school | 85 |
| % live on campus | 25 |
| % in (# of) fraternities | 9 (28) |
| % in (# of) sororities | 9 (21) |
| % African American | 3 |
| % Asian | 35 |
| % Caucasian | 43 |
| % Hispanic | 10 |
| % international | 1 |

### SURVEY SAYS . . .
Great library
Popular college radio
High cost of living
Large classes
(Almost) no one smokes
Student publications are popular

## ACADEMICS

| Academic Rating | 78 |
|---|---|
| Calendar | quarter |
| Student/faculty ratio | 19:1 |
| Profs interesting rating | 91 |
| Profs accessible rating | 91 |
| Avg lab size | 20-29 students |
| Avg reg class size | 20-29 students |

## STUDENTS SPEAK OUT

### Academics

Opportunities abound at UC—Davis for the self-starter willing to grab them. The key to distinguishing yourself among the 20,000-plus undergrads here, students say, is to take the initiative. Points out one student, "Access to your professors is there; it's how you choose to use it that makes a difference. This is college; they don't hold your hand through the process, but they are always delighted to help you out." Others note that "at UC—Davis, there are numerous opportunities to get involved with the school and local community, to participate in athletic events, or to pursue other interests" and that "the opportunities for undergraduate research are quite extensive." Students report that "as with every school there are good professors and bad professors. You just have to hope that you get the good ones." Mandatory intro courses are large, and "at the lower division/introductory class levels, much of your grade is determined by your discussion leader/TA. Fortunately, in my experience the grad students in these positions are some of the most brilliant people on the planet." Students prefer upper division courses, which provide "an excellent opportunity to discuss issues in detail with other students and the professor." Students see an academic benefit to their location: "Being in the middle of agriculture and not near any real hot spots drives you to the books a little faster," explains one.

### Life

Don't come to Davis looking for a huge party scene; you won't find it here. Notes one student, "Davis is a very small town, and sometimes it is hard to find things to do. If you aren't 21, it sucks! If you are, it is better, but there are only about four bars in the whole town, so you really don't have much variety in your life." Options are indeed limited; as one student reports, "Thursday night is frat party night. Friday night is frat party night with option of clubbing at a very few local clubs. Saturday is frat party night, too. And for those who don't do the frat parties, there are two movie theatres." For some, the situation is idyllic; writes one undergrad, "Davis is the perfect town to go to college in: not too big, still has a small, college-town feel." Some "find the availability of outdoor activities" here "very pleasing." Many, however, find the slow pace suffocating, complaining that "there is absolutely nothing to do here." When they need to accelerate things a bit, "a lot of people go to Tahoe, Sacramento, or San Francisco to find fun." Students agree that "the campus is gorgeous, and getting to, from, and around campus on a bicycle is very easy." "Bike paths abound" in this cycle-friendly town, "as do bike-specific traffic lights. Every building has a bike 'parking lot' so you can hop off and walk into class."

### Student Body

The "nice and helpful" undergraduates of Davis are mostly "hardworking, lower- to middle-class people. They take their education seriously and respect everyone equally." A student body so large is bound to run the gamut; as one student puts it, "There's a regular bunch of students here ranging from punkster to raver, from suburbia to urban and witty to wicked." Mostly, though, "everyone looks normal, which was a big surprise to me. At high school I was used to seeing people dressed everywhere from Goth to drag. Here even someone who dyes their hair sticks out." Many students report that "there is a lot of interracial tension. The school is very pro-minority, which is a positive thing, and the majority of the student body is made up of minority students. But minority groups tend to stick with members of their same ethnicity, and there is little cross-cultural interaction." Some hopefully report that "despite racial tension, there is unity among students. Well, figures. Why wouldn't there be unity among 26,000 students stuffed into a town that takes a whole 15 minutes to drive through?"

# UNIVERSITY OF CALIFORNIA—DAVIS

FINANCIAL AID: 530-752-2390 • E-MAIL: WHY@UCDAVIS.EDU • WEBSITE: WWW.UCDAVIS.EDU

## ADMISSIONS
*Very important factors considered include:* essays, secondary school record, standardized test scores. *Important factors considered include:* extracurricular activities, leadership, talent/ability. *Other factors considered include:* geographical residence. SAT I or ACT required, SAT II also required. TOEFL required of all international applicants. High school diploma or GED is required. *High school units required/recommended* (all units in years): 4 English required, 2 history/social science required, 3 math required, 3 math recommended, 2 lab science required, 3 lab science recommended, 2 foreign language required, 3 foreign language recommended, 1 visual/performing arts required, 1 college prep elective required.

### The Inside Word
California's discontinuation of affirmative action in the UC admission process has created much uncertainty regarding the future of candidate selection in the system. A higher percentage of students are admitted to Davis than to Berkeley or UCLA, but don't forget that the UC system in general is geared toward the best and brightest of California's high school students.

## FINANCIAL AID
*Students should submit:* FAFSA. The Princeton Review suggests that all financial aid forms be submitted as soon as possible after January 1. Federal Work-Study Program available. Institutional employment available. Off-campus job opportunities are good.

## FROM THE ADMISSIONS OFFICE
"UC Davis prides itself on its academic rigor and its vibrant college-town atmosphere. In a recent survey that included undergraduate students from eight of the UC campuses, UC Davis students were second most likely to recommend their school to prospective applicants. UC Davis has programs that are ranked among the best in the nation as well as more than 100 majors. The most satisfied students at UC Davis are those who take advantage of the myriad opportunities, including social and recreational events, research and internship positions, and programs such as UC Davis Washington Center or Bodega Marine Laboratory."

---

### SELECTIVITY
★ ★ ★ ☆

| | |
|---|---|
| Admissions Rating | 84 |

#### FRESHMAN PROFILE
| | |
|---|---|
| Average SAT Verbal | 598 |
| Average SAT Math | 637 |
| Average ACT Composite | 28 |
| Minimum TOEFL | 550 |
| Average HS GPA | 3.8 |
| % graduated top 10% of class | 95 |
| % graduated top 25% of class | 100 |
| % graduated top 50% of class | 100 |

#### DEADLINES
| | |
|---|---|
| Regular admission | 11/30 |
| Regular notification | 3/31 |
| Nonfall registration? | yes |

#### APPLICANTS ALSO LOOK AT
**AND OFTEN PREFER**
UC Berkeley
UCLA
**AND SOMETIMES PREFER**
UC Santa Barbara
UC Santa Cruz
Cal Poly
**AND RARELY PREFER**
UC San Diego
UC Irvine
UC Riverside

### FINANCIAL FACTS

| | |
|---|---|
| Financial Aid Rating | 86 |
| Out-of-state tuition | $16,131 |
| Room and board | $8,764 |
| Books and supplies | $1,162 |
| Required fees | $4,645 |
| % frosh receiving aid | 49 |
| % undergrads receiving aid | 62 |
| Avg frosh grant | $6,500 |
| Avg frosh loan | $3,300 |

# UNIVERSITY OF CALIFORNIA—IRVINE

Office of Admissions, 204 Administration Building, Irvine, CA 92697-1075 • Admissions: 949-824-6703 • Fax: 949-824-2711

## CAMPUS LIFE

| | |
|---|---|
| Quality of Life Rating | 78 |
| Type of school | public |
| Environment | suburban |

### STUDENTS
| | |
|---|---|
| Total undergrad enrollment | 19,179 |
| % male/female | 48/52 |
| % from out of state | 3 |
| % from public high school | 66 |
| % live on campus | 26 |
| % African American | 2 |
| % Asian | 51 |
| % Caucasian | 24 |
| % Hispanic | 11 |
| % international | 3 |

### SURVEY SAYS . . .
High cost of living
Class discussions are rare
Popular college radio
Student publications are ignored
Large classes
Intercollegiate sports unpopular or nonexistent
Lots of TAs teach upper-level courses
Athletic facilities need improving

## ACADEMICS

| | |
|---|---|
| Academic Rating | 71 |
| Calendar | quarter |
| Student/faculty ratio | 18:1 |
| Profs interesting rating | 90 |
| Profs accessible rating | 87 |
| Avg lab size | 20-29 students |
| Avg reg class size | 20-29 students |

### MOST POPULAR MAJORS
Biology/biological sciences
Economics
Sociology

## STUDENTS SPEAK OUT

### Academics
This "research-oriented institution" offers students a wealth of opportunity to try their hands at the work of actual professionals. This plays out especially well in majors like biology, the discipline for which "UCI is best known." Irvine "is a school that adamantly believes in 'hands-on' learning," notes one student. As you'll find at most big universities, students' biggest gripe is that they have little access to their professors. One student thinks this is for the better: "The professors are monotone and mundane! I have found it's easier to sleep in class than in the dorms." Another disagrees: "We do have great teachers, and when you finally do have them as teachers it is great." TAs abound here, but since "teaching assistants are great" and are "sometimes . . . way better than the professors," few students find them cause for whining. The key at UC Irvine is to do your homework before you sign up for a class—find out who's teaching a certain course and whether that professor or TA has received positive reviews. Most students find the efforts of the administration "adequate," though a few feel it can be "bull-headed at times."

### Life
A quick shot south of Los Angeles, Irvine is so close to the ocean that one student suggests they change the name to "UC—Newport Beach. How much better does that sound?" When freshmen first set foot on campus, they're invited into the UC Irvine community through the nationally recognized SPOP program, which one student calls "the greatest orientation program on the planet." Students quickly find, however, that the campus social scene could stand improvement. This sentiment stems partly from the fact that "UCI is a big commuter school," with many students returning home when classes end. "They should stay at school and have some fun," suggests one student. Those who do stick around "love to party." "Greek life is a highlight of UC Irvine," but diversion also "involves local clubs and bars on the weekend, or else trips to L.A. or local mountains or the beach." And for the thirsty, "there is also a bar on campus, which is cool." As far as the town itself goes, "Irvine is a beautiful, yet boring" town. "Most things within walking distance of the campus are closed around 9 P.M." and the campus' wealthy, crotchety neighbors "have very sensitive hearing and are extremely light sleepers." One student explains that "life in Irvine is very posh due to the commercial culture that overruns Orange County." But while "life behind the Orange Curtain is certainly slow . . . there is a certain charm in that."

### Student Body
Irvine is one of the few colleges in America where Caucasians are part of the minority. In fact, more than half of the students here are of Asian descent. While students of different backgrounds tend to form cliques, overall, a "harmonious atmosphere" pervades the campus. You'll find all sorts here, from "computer geeks and jocks" to "party animals and stoners." Most students are natives of Southern California, and also, it seems, from privileged backgrounds. According to one undergraduate, "Many students here are trendy, driving fancy cars, riding scooters on campus, carrying cell phones, and well dressed." "Overall, students at UCI get along well," though some students complain that their peers creepily "walk around like they're cold and empty and can't see anyone," which means a lot of people run into each other. And at Irvine, you'll likely bump into students who range from "exceedingly intelligent to obscenely stupid." But it's up to you to decide on the people with whom you want to associate. With more than 17,000 students, most undergraduates here find a place to fit in.

# UNIVERSITY OF CALIFORNIA—IRVINE

FINANCIAL AID: 949-824-6261 • WEBSITE: WWW.UCI.EDU

## ADMISSIONS
*Very important factors considered include:* essays, secondary school record, standardized test scores. *Important factors considered include:* character/personal qualities, extracurricular activities, talent/ability, volunteer work. *Other factors considered include:* work experience. SAT I or ACT required; SAT II also required. TOEFL required of all international applicants. High school diploma or GED is required. *High school units required/recommended:* 15 total required; 18 total recommended; 4 English required, 3 math required, 4 math recommended, 2 science required, 3 science recommended, 2 science lab required, 3 science lab recommended, 2 foreign language required, 3 foreign language recommended, 2 history and social science required, 1 visual/performing arts required.

### The Inside Word
The state of California's voter referendum that banned affirmative action in the UC admission process has created much uncertainty regarding the future of candidate selection in the system, and African American and Hispanic admissions have fallen as a result. Few out-of-state students consider Irvine, which lessens the competition among those applicants who are well qualified.

## FINANCIAL AID
*Students should submit:* FAFSA. The Princeton Review suggests that all financial aid forms be submitted as soon as possible after January 1. *Need-based scholarships/grants offered:* Pell, SEOG, the school's own gift aid. *Loan aid offered:* Direct Subsidized Stafford, Direct Unsubsidized Stafford, Direct PLUS, FFEL Subsidized Stafford, Federal Perkins. Federal Work-Study Program available. Institutional employment available. Applicants will be notified of awards on or about May 1. Off-campus job opportunities are excellent.

## FROM THE ADMISSIONS OFFICE
"UCI offers programs designed to provide students with a foundation on which to continue developing their intellectual, aesthetic, and moral capacity. The programs and curricula are based on the belief that a student's collective university experience should provide understanding and insight, which are the bases for an intellectual identity and lifelong learning. An important aspect of the educational approach at UCI is the emphasis placed on student involvement in independent study, research, and the creative process as a complement to classroom study. Independent research in laboratories, field study, involvement in writing workshops, and participation in fine arts productions are normal elements of the UCI experience."

### SELECTIVITY

| | |
|---|---|
| Admissions Rating | 79 |
| # of applicants | 30,598 |
| % of applicants accepted | 56 |
| % of acceptees attending | 23 |

#### FRESHMAN PROFILE
| | |
|---|---|
| Range SAT Verbal | 510-620 |
| Range SAT Math | 560-650 |
| Minimum TOEFL | 550 |
| Average HS GPA | 3.7 |
| % graduated top 10% of class | 95 |
| % graduated top 25% of class | 100 |

#### DEADLINES
| | |
|---|---|
| Priority admission | 11/30 |
| Regular notification | 3/30 |

#### APPLICANTS ALSO LOOK AT AND OFTEN PREFER
UC Berkeley
UCLA
Stanford
UC San Diego

#### AND SOMETIMES PREFER
U of Southern California
UC Santa Cruz
UC Davis
UC Santa Barbara
UC Riverside

### FINANCIAL FACTS

| | |
|---|---|
| Financial Aid Rating | 84 |
| In-state tuition | $4,739 |
| Out-of-state tuition | $19,284 |
| Room and board | $7,380 |
| Books and supplies | $1,355 |
| Required fees | $4,739 |
| % frosh receiving aid | 47 |
| % undergrads receiving aid | 47 |
| Avg frosh grant | $7,263 |

# UNIVERSITY OF CALIFORNIA—LOS ANGELES

405 HILGARD AVENUE, LOS ANGELES, CA 90095 • ADMISSIONS: 310-825-3101 • FAX: 310-206-1206

## CAMPUS LIFE

| | |
|---|---|
| **Quality of Life Rating** | **79** |
| Type of school | public |
| Environment | urban |

### STUDENTS

| | |
|---|---|
| Total undergrad enrollment | 24,899 |
| % male/female | 44/56 |
| % from out of state | 3 |
| % from public high school | 80 |
| % live on campus | 30 |
| % in (# of) fraternities | 12 (27) |
| % in (# of) sororities | 9 (18) |
| % African American | 4 |
| % Asian | 36 |
| % Caucasian | 33 |
| % Hispanic | 15 |
| % international | 3 |
| # of countries represented | 100 |

### SURVEY SAYS . . .
Everyone loves the Bruins
Students love Los Angeles, CA
Frats and sororities dominate social scene
Great food on campus
Great library
Large classes
Student publications are popular
Lots of TAs teach upper-level courses
Dorms are like dungeons
Campus difficult to get around
Computer facilities are great

## ACADEMICS

| | |
|---|---|
| **Academic Rating** | **85** |
| Calendar | quarter |
| Student/faculty ratio | 17:1 |
| Profs interesting rating | 89 |
| Profs accessible rating | 86 |
| Avg lab size | 20-29 students |
| Avg reg class size | 10-19 students |

## STUDENTS SPEAK OUT

### Academics

UCLA is a place for students who know how to work on their own. "Realistically, this is a very big school," one student tells us, and "you have to be out for yourself, searching for answers, or else you will fall behind." Unlike students at smaller universities and colleges, UCLA students say that their professors aren't there to serve as mentors. "Professors are there to deliver the information," explains one undergrad. "It's up to you to bang your head against the wall to try to understand it." Few students will deny that professors are good researchers, but many students wish the profs were as good at communicating as they are at researching. For this reason, teaching assistants (who often lead small, mandatory discussion groups that are based on professors' lectures, as well as do most of the grading) are often the "most useful" tools "in helping you know your strengths and weaknesses." As far as the professors themselves go, students have a range of opinions. Some call the profs "arrogant"; others say they're all "wonderful." If you get a "bad apple," don't worry: UCLA runs on the quarter system, so you'll be onto a new class soon enough. By the time senior year rolls around, competition can get fierce as students vie for a respectable spot along the grade curve. One student groans about "the heavy competition," saying, "I had never been so stressed in my entire life before I came to UCLA." A classmate retorts, "Competition? Any good school is competitive."

### Life

Two words on the social opportunities at UCLA: wide open. The village of Westwood is a little city within an enormous one, and while students will be the first to admit that it's not the most exciting part of town, it has a wealth of "food and movie" options. And while we're on the subject, movie stars live in the neighborhoods close to campus (Beverly Hills is about two miles away), which makes for celebrity sightings galore. When nighttime rolls round, "the [active] Greek system" has a lock on freshman and sophomore minds. For students over 21, the plentitude of bars and clubs are popular destinations. There's a lot to L.A. beyond Westwood, though. "If you have a car or aren't afraid of the bus, you can always go to Santa Monica, Hollywood, and many other popular places." Another student adds, "The campus is 10 minutes from the beach and the promenade, less than half an hour to Sunset Boulevard and the Hollywood clubs, and only a couple hours to the snow in winter." But many students are just as happy to stay around Westwood in their free time. Especially because of the top-notch food they find in the dorm cafeterias and at the nearby restaurants. "Forget the freshman 15," advises one student. "Try the freshman 115."

### Student Body

With upwards of 25,000 undergrads on campus (and almost 12,000 grad students on top of that), most students "don't think there's one single characterization that could define the typical Bruin." Just look around, and you're likely to see "the serious scholar, the researcher, the activist, the religious individual, the partier, the artist, the service-oriented student," etc. But while "there is definitely diversity as far as race and culture," students report that Bruin undergrads tend to form cliques, often along racial and ethnic lines. Regardless, most students are pleased with UCLA's diversity. A few years into the UCLA experience, however, the gloss of diversity and friendliness wears away, and students become aware "of a strong sense of competition." According to one student, the competitiveness among upperclassmen is bred by a "grading system based on curves." In other words, don't be too nice to that guy you bump into on Bruin Walk, the main campus thoroughfare; he may just be the one who knocks you out of A range in that dreadful biochemistry class.

552 ■ THE BEST 351 COLLEGES

# UNIVERSITY OF CALIFORNIA—LOS ANGELES

FINANCIAL AID: 310-206-0400 • E-MAIL: UGADM@SAONET.UCLA.EDU • WEBSITE: WWW.UCLA.EDU

## ADMISSIONS

*Important factors considered include:* secondary school record, standardized test scores, state residency, talent/ability, volunteer work, extracurricular activities, work experience. SAT I or ACT required; SAT II also required. TOEFL required of all international applicants. High school diploma or GED is required. *High school units required/recommended:* 4 English required, 3 math required, 4 math recommended, 2 science required, 3 science recommended, 2 science lab required, 3 science lab recommended, 2 foreign language required, 3 foreign language recommended, 2 history required, 1 visual and performing arts required, 1 elective required.

### The Inside Word

Since California's voters acted to discontinue affirmative action in the UC admission process, there was much uncertainty regarding the future of candidate selection in the system. Through innovative policies UCLA still attracts and admits respectable numbers of African American and Hispanic students. UCLA is the second most selective university in the UC system.

## FINANCIAL AID

*Students should submit:* FAFSA. No deadline for regular filing. The Princeton Review suggests that all financial aid forms be submitted as soon as possible after January 1. *Need-based scholarships/grants offered:* Pell, SEOG, state scholarships/grants, private scholarships, the school's own gift aid, United Negro College Fund, Federal Nursing, National Merit Scholarship. *Loan aid offered:* FFEL Subsidized Stafford, FFEL Unsubsidized Stafford, FFEL PLUS, Federal Perkins, Federal Nursing, state loans, college/university loans from institutional funds. Federal Work-Study Program available. Institutional employment available. Applicants will be notified of awards on a rolling basis beginning on or about March 15. Off-campus job opportunities are good.

## FROM THE ADMISSIONS OFFICE

"Undergraduates arrive at UCLA from throughout California and around the world with exceptional levels of academic preparation. They are attracted by our acclaimed degree programs, distinguished faculty, and the beauty of a park-like campus set amid the dynamism of the nation's second largest city. UCLA's highly ranked undergraduate programs incorporate cutting-edge technology and teaching techniques that hone the critical-thinking skills and the global perspectives necessary for success in our rapidly changing world. The diversity of these programs draws strength from a student body that mirrors the cultural and ethnic vibrancy of Los Angeles. Generally ranked among the nation's top half-dozen universities, UCLA is at once distinguished and dynamic, academically rigorous and responsive."

### SELECTIVITY
★ ★ ★ ★

| | |
|---|---|
| Admissions Rating | 94 |
| # of applicants | 43,443 |
| % of applicants accepted | 24 |
| % of acceptees attending | 41 |

### FRESHMAN PROFILE

| | |
|---|---|
| Range SAT Verbal | 550-670 |
| Average SAT Verbal | 611 |
| Range SAT Math | 590-720 |
| Average SAT Math | 653 |
| Range ACT Composite | 22-29 |
| Average ACT Composite | 26 |
| Minimum TOEFL | 550 |
| Average HS GPA | 4.1 |
| % graduated top 10% of class | 97 |

### DEADLINES

| | |
|---|---|
| Regular admission | 11/30 |
| Regular notification | 3/30 |

### FINANCIAL FACTS
★ ★ ★ ☆

| | |
|---|---|
| Financial Aid Rating | 89 |
| Out-of-state tuition | $12,379 |
| Room and board | $10,452 |
| Books and supplies | $1,344 |
| Required fees | $4,878 |
| % frosh receiving aid | 49 |
| % undergrads receiving aid | 50 |
| Avg frosh grant | $8,534 |
| Avg frosh loan | $3,996 |

# UNIVERSITY OF CALIFORNIA—RIVERSIDE

1120 HINDERAKER HALL, RIVERSIDE, CA 92521 • ADMISSIONS: 909-787-4531 • FAX: 909-787-6344

## CAMPUS LIFE

| Quality of Life Rating | 81 |
|---|---|
| Type of school | public |
| Environment | suburban |

### STUDENTS

| Total undergrad enrollment | 14,124 |
|---|---|
| % male/female | 46/54 |
| % from out of state | 1 |
| % from public high school | 90 |
| % live on campus | 28 |
| % in (# of) fraternities | 3 (16) |
| % in (# of) sororities | 3 (14) |
| % African American | 6 |
| % Asian | 41 |
| % Caucasian | 23 |
| % Hispanic | 23 |
| % international | 2 |
| # of countries represented | 22 |

### SURVEY SAYS...
No one cheats
Political activism is hot
Theater is hot
Dorms are like palaces
Athletic facilities need improving
(Almost) no one smokes
Registration is a pain

## ACADEMICS

| Academic Rating | 74 |
|---|---|
| Calendar | quarter |
| Student/faculty ratio | 19:1 |
| % profs teaching UG courses | 100 |
| Avg lab size | 20-29 students |
| Avg reg class size | 20-29 students |

### MOST POPULAR MAJORS
Business administration/management
Biology/biological sciences
Social sciences

## STUDENTS SPEAK OUT

### Academics

Students at the University of California—Riverside call their school an "excellent learning environment" with "instructors who actually care about the students and teach for the love of teaching." One student writes, "People used to think that UC Riverside was the bastard child of the UC system. It's not." In fact, a junior business major proclaims that he actually chose Riverside over heavy hitters UC Berkeley and UCLA, crowing that "the academic element [at Riverside] is unbeatable." Many undergraduates are drawn by the "great computer science program," others by the "generous financial aid." Students praise professors for being "very understanding and easily accessible." One respondent tells us, "Upper-division classes are very personal and a great chance to get to know professors." Certain students complain, however, that "high-level courses should not be taught by graduate students," which a few seem to be. A senior psychology major whines that, as at many large state universities, "some professors are more interested in their research than talking to undergraduates." Another student feels that "some of my classes are watered down," while others ask for "more lab sections." Riverside is experiencing some "growing pains" as the enrollment increases somewhat dramatically, and this may be the cause of some of the glitches students perceive in the administrative processes. One senior reports, "Administrators hide in their offices and pray you don't come to see them," and several surveys claim that the administration spends too much time interfering with the Greek system. Another undergrad counters these assertions, though, declaring that he chose Riverside because it "caters to each student's needs." Overall, the school is set up so that students have "a great opportunity to interact with staff, faculty, and administrators."

### Life

Day-to-day existence at Riverside is defined by the "great campus and community environment." A high percentage of respondents commented on the school's physical beauty ("I like the fact that it is so green"), with only minor complaints regarding the ongoing construction. Students agree that the campus "could always use more programming," but many undergraduates stay involved with extracurricular activities. A savvy business major notes, for instance, that "our clubs and organizations have many professional ties." Most people think a football team is in order to improve school spirit. In the meantime, it's the fraternities and sororities that bring the campus together. "Without the Greek system, UCR would be boring." People also perceive a need for more "events where the different cliques come together." Since the surrounding area is "not very exciting," most people "leave Riverside to have fun," which requires wheels. Still, some civic-minded students think locally: "We need to help out the surrounding community, especially East Riverside, right down the street."

### Student Body

The Riverside population is "small but not too small" (at least by UC standards), just the right size so that students "start to recognize a lot of faces," making the whole place feel "very comfortable and homey." One student comments, "You get to know a lot of people from the dorms in your first year." Most students count the campus' marked diversity as one of the school's greatest strengths: "I never thought I would meet so many people who are so different from me with whom I have so much in common." Amid this heterogeneous group, everyone seems "easy to get along with" and "pretty chill." Certain people report that their peers are "generally quiet and not voluntarily social," while others feel the student body is largely "friendly and sociable." Either way, students appreciate the environment where "everyone is always willing to help anyone."

# UNIVERSITY OF CALIFORNIA—RIVERSIDE

FINANCIAL AID: 909-787-3878 OR 3879 • E-MAIL: DISCOVER@POP.UCR.EDU • WEBSITE: WWW.UCR.EDU

## ADMISSIONS
*Very important factors considered include:* secondary school record, standardized test scores. *Important factors considered include:* essays. *Other factors considered include:* extracurricular activities, talent/ability, volunteer work, work experience. SAT I or ACT required; SAT II also required. TOEFL required of all international applicants. High school graduation, GED, or California HS Proficiency Exam is required. *High school units required/recommended:* 15 total required; 4 English required, 3 math required, 2 science lab required, 2 language other than English required, 2 history required, 1 visual and performing arts required, 1 elective required.

## The Inside Word
The state of California's ban on affirmative action in the UC admission process has created much uncertainty regarding the future of candidate selection in the system. Though African American and Hispanic admissions have dropped system-wide, UC Riverside stands out in its ability to fight this decline—it's one of only two UC schools where minority admissions have grown. Riverside's admit rate is sufficiently high to mean smooth sailing for those who fit into the formulas well.

## FINANCIAL AID
*Students should submit:* FAFSA, state aid form. The Princeton Review suggests that all financial aid forms be submitted as soon as possible after January 1. *Need-based scholarships/grants offered:* Pell, SEOG, state scholarships/grants, private scholarships, the school's own gift aid. *Loan aid offered:* Direct Subsidized Stafford, Direct Unsubsidized Stafford, Direct PLUS, Federal Perkins, college/university loans from institutional funds. Federal Work-Study Program available. Institutional employment available. Applicants will be notified of awards on a rolling basis beginning on or about March 1. Off-campus job opportunities are excellent.

## FROM THE ADMISSIONS OFFICE
"The University of California—Riverside offers the quality, rigor, and facilities of a major research institution, while assuring its undergraduates personal attention and a sense of community. Academic programs, teaching, advising, and student services all reflect the supportive attitude that characterizes the campus. Among the exceptional opportunities are the UCR/UCLA Thomas Haider Program in Biomedical Sciences, which provides an exclusive path to UCLA's Geffen School of Medicine; the University Honors Program; an extensive undergraduate research program; UC's largest undergraduate degree program in business administration; and UC's only bachelor's degree in creative writing. More than 200 student clubs and organizations and a variety of athletic and arts events give students a myriad of ways to get involved and have fun."

## SELECTIVITY

| | |
|---|---:|
| Admissions Rating | 80 |
| # of applicants | 22,975 |
| % of applicants accepted | 86 |
| % of acceptees attending | 18 |

### FRESHMAN PROFILE
| | |
|---|---:|
| Range SAT Verbal | 440-560 |
| Average SAT Verbal | 504 |
| Range SAT Math | 490-620 |
| Average SAT Math | 553 |
| Range ACT Composite | 18-23 |
| Average ACT Composite | 21 |
| Minimum TOEFL | 550 |
| Average HS GPA | 3.5 |
| % graduated top 10% of class | 94 |
| % graduated top 25% of class | 100 |

### DEADLINES
| | |
|---|---:|
| Priority admission | 11/1 |
| Regular admission | 11/30 |
| Nonfall registration? | yes |

### APPLICANTS ALSO LOOK AT AND OFTEN PREFER
UC Berkeley
UCLA
UC Irvine

### AND SOMETIMES PREFER
UC Davis
Cal Poly
Claremont McKenna
UC Santa Barbara
UC Santa Cruz

### AND RARELY PREFER
U of San Diego
U of Southern California

## FINANCIAL FACTS

| | |
|---|---:|
| Financial Aid Rating | 85 |
| Out-of-state tuition | $11,775 |
| Room and board | $8,200 |
| Books and supplies | $1,300 |
| Required fees | $4,421 |
| % frosh receiving aid | 60 |
| % undergrads receiving aid | 61 |
| Avg frosh grant | $7,648 |
| Avg frosh loan | $9,672 |

# UNIVERSITY OF CALIFORNIA—SAN DIEGO

9500 GILMAN DRIVE, 0021, LA JOLLA, CA 92093-0021 • ADMISSIONS: 858-534-4831

## CAMPUS LIFE

| | |
|---|---|
| Quality of Life Rating | 83 |
| Type of school | public |
| Environment | suburban |

### STUDENTS

| | |
|---|---|
| Total undergrad enrollment | 19,088 |
| % male/female | 48/52 |
| % from out of state | 2 |
| % live on campus | 33 |
| % in (# of) fraternities | 10 (19) |
| % in (# of) sororities | 10 (14) |
| % African American | 1 |
| % Asian | 34 |
| % Caucasian | 37 |
| % Hispanic | 10 |
| % international | 1 |
| # of countries represented | 70 |

### SURVEY SAYS . . .
Athletic facilities are great
Great library
Campus is beautiful
Campus feels safe
Great computer facilities
Registration is a breeze
Lab facilities are great

## ACADEMICS

| | |
|---|---|
| Academic Rating | 83 |
| Calendar | quarter |
| Student/faculty ratio | 19:1 |
| Avg lab size | 20-29 students |
| Avg reg class size | 10-19 students |

## STUDENTS SPEAK OUT

### Academics

UCSD, most students agree, "is dedicated to math and the sciences," the departments in which it has built its reputation as a statewide powerhouse. Pre-meds and engineers agree that it's Valhalla (that is, if your idea of Valhalla involves dawn-to-midnight studying); others temper their enthusiasm, telling us that "academically, it varies. I always hear how fabulous this place is for science majors, but nonscience majors get the shaft." Which is too bad, since there are other solid departments here; they simply take a back seat to the star attractions. Like most prestigious math and science schools, "UCSD does not focus its energy on the undergraduate experience. It works to maintain the happiness of its faculty and the administration, often at the cost of student happiness." Because many classes involve lectures by profs and discussion sections led by TAs, "how much you get out of a class is really determined by how good your TA is, not the professor." While some TAs are excellent, others "do not know the class material thoroughly, and tend to confuse us." No wonder one engineer told us that "when you get into college, you have to learn to be proactive. You literally teach yourself in a lot of the classes." Students are much more bullish on UCSD's administration, thanks largely to the six-college system, which divides the large university into smaller schools. "What is great about UCSD is its college system. It is really like six small liberal arts colleges all located next to each other," writes one student. Many here warn that the quarterly academic calendar really ratchets up the pressure; "once third week hits, you have papers/midterms every week until finals."

### Life

Students at UCSD agree that theirs is not the typical college experience. "The university definitely suffers from a lack of social life," most here agree, the combined result of a hardworking student body and inhospitable surroundings. It's the kind of place where "for fun, a lot of people are glued to their computers playing computer games or talking on AIM." Hometown La Jolla offers no help; explains one student, "La Jolla . . . is extremely snobby. They won't let fast food restaurants or new movie theaters be built. . . . In general, without a car at UCSD, you aren't going to get to do anything." There is a Greek system here, but "La Jolla banned a Greek Row and won't allow for them to own houses." Adds one student, "The major problem is that rent is so high in this area that . . . there is no concentrated student population other than on campus." Because of the lack of any sense of community at UCSD, "there is no school spirit." On the bright side, "we live in paradise, because the beaches are so close. Surfing is very popular. So are intramural sports." Those fortunate enough to have cars report "a great indie movie, art, theatre, and music scene in San Diego," but add that "the best concerts are mostly 21+, so too bad for 18-year-olds." But frosh still manage to get their kicks. As one freshman put it, "The border is half an hour away, and clubs in Tijuana offer drinking and dancing for the 18- to 20-year-olds. What do you think we do?"

### Student Body

Because of UCSD's prominent pre-med and engineering programs, "most students here are goal-oriented nerds who like to study all the time." Notes one undergrad, "The typical student is an Asian or Caucasian biology or engineering student that spends 60 hours a week studying, .0002 hours a week socializing with other people, .003 hours a week bathing, and the rest of the time is spent playing Counter-Strike." The school is also home to "lots of stoners, and most of them are chill," as well as "a strong religious . . . community." The school is large enough for each subpopulation to create its own cozy community.

556 ■ THE BEST 351 COLLEGES

# UNIVERSITY OF CALIFORNIA—SAN DIEGO

FINANCIAL AID: 858-534-4480 • E-MAIL: ADMISSIONSINFO@UCSD.EDU • WEBSITE: WWW.UCSD.EDU

## ADMISSIONS
*Very important factors considered include:* essays, secondary school record, standardized test scores, talent/ability, volunteer work, work experience. SAT I or ACT required; SAT II also required. TOEFL required of all international applicants. High school diploma or GED is required. *High school units required/recommended:* 15 total required; 4 English required, 3 math required, 4 math recommended, 2 science required, 3 science recommended, 2 science lab required, 3 science lab recommended, 2 foreign language required, 3 foreign language recommended, 2 history required, 1 elective required, 1 visual and performing arts required.

## The Inside Word
The state of California's discontinuance of affirmative action in the UC admission process created much uncertainty regarding the future of candidate selection in the system, and admissions of African American and Hispanic students have fallen significantly system-wide. Increased national awareness and its reputation for excellence in the sciences is making UCSD more and more popular with high school seniors. Even greater selectivity cannot be far behind.

## FINANCIAL AID
*Students should submit:* FAFSA, state aid form. Regular filing deadline is June 1. The Princeton Review suggests that all financial aid forms be submitted as soon as possible after January 1. *Need-based scholarships/grants offered:* Pell, SEOG, state scholarships/grants, private scholarships, the school's own gift aid. *Loan aid offered:* FFEL Subsidized Stafford, FFEL Unsubsidized Stafford, FFEL PLUS, Federal Perkins, college/university loans from institutional funds, alternative loans. Federal Work-Study Program available. Institutional employment available. Applicants will be notified of awards on a rolling basis beginning on or about March 15. Off-campus job opportunities are excellent.

## FROM THE ADMISSIONS OFFICE
"UCSD is recognized for the exceptional quality of its academic programs: a recent Johns Hopkins study rated UCSD faculty 1st nationally among public institutions in science; *U.S. News & World Report* rates UCSD 7th in the nation among state-supported colleges and universities; Kiplinger's "100 Best Values in Public Colleges" ranks UCSD 10th in the nation. UCSD ranks 5th in the nation and 1st in the University of California system for the amount of federal research dollars spent on research and development; and the university ranks 10th in the nation in the excellence of its graduate programs and the quality of its faculty, according to the most recent National Research Council college rankings."

## SELECTIVITY

| | |
|---|---|
| Admissions Rating | 84 |
| # of applicants | 38,187 |
| % of applicants accepted | 43 |
| % of acceptees attending | 24 |

### FRESHMAN PROFILE
| | |
|---|---|
| Average SAT Verbal | 593 |
| Average SAT Math | 646 |
| Average ACT Composite | 25 |
| Minimum TOEFL | 550 |
| Average HS GPA | 3.95 |
| % graduated top 10% of class | 99 |
| % graduated top 25% of class | 100 |

### DEADLINES
| | |
|---|---|
| Regular admission | 11/30 |
| Regular notification | 3/15 |

### APPLICANTS ALSO LOOK AT AND OFTEN PREFER
UC Los Angeles
UC Berkeley

### AND SOMETIMES PREFER
UC Davis
Stanford
Cal Poly

### AND RARELY PREFER
San Diego State

## FINANCIAL FACTS

| | |
|---|---|
| Financial Aid Rating | 84 |
| In-state tuition | $3,950 |
| Out-of-state tuition | $12,480 |
| Room and board | $8,066 |
| Books and supplies | $1,221 |
| Required fees | $3,950 |
| % frosh receiving aid | 58 |
| % undergrads receiving aid | 61 |
| Avg frosh grant | $5,014 |
| Avg frosh loan | $4,668 |

# UNIVERSITY OF CALIFORNIA—SANTA BARBARA

OFFICE OF ADMISSIONS, 1210 CHEADLE HALL, SANTA BARBARA, CA 93106 • ADMISSIONS: 805-893-2881 • FAX: 805-893-2676

## CAMPUS LIFE

| Quality of Life Rating | 89 |
|---|---|
| Type of school | public |
| Environment | suburban |

### STUDENTS

| Total undergrad enrollment | 17,714 |
|---|---|
| % male/female | 48/52 |
| % from out of state | 5 |
| % from public high school | 83 |
| % live on campus | 22 |
| % in (# of) fraternities | 8 (19) |
| % in (# of) sororities | 10 (18) |
| % African American | 3 |
| % Asian | 16 |
| % Caucasian | 61 |
| % Hispanic | 17 |
| % international | 1 |

### SURVEY SAYS . . .
Beautiful campus
Campus easy to get around
Students love Santa Barbara, CA
Great off-campus food
Athletic facilities are great
Student publications are ignored
Students are cliquish
(Almost) no one smokes
Students get along with local community

## ACADEMICS

| Academic Rating | 74 |
|---|---|
| Calendar | quarter |
| Student/faculty ratio | 17:1 |
| Profs interesting rating | 72 |
| Profs accessible rating | 96 |
| Avg lab size | 20-29 students |
| Avg reg class size | 10-19 students |

## STUDENTS SPEAK OUT

### Academics

"I came to this school expecting beer, beaches, and babes," writes a sophomore. "I was thrilled to find exceptional teachers; eager, intellectual students—and beer, beaches, and babes!" While many of its undergrads did choose this "beautiful," "laid-back" state school for reasons not quite academic ("sun," "beach," "girls/guys," and "location" seem to be the decisive factors), the University of California at Santa Barbara, with its "friendly people," "strong liberal faculty" and excellent programs in the sciences and math—as well as in foreign languages, English, theater, and writing—make the school a good choice for the sociable student looking for a solid liberal arts education. Faculty gets high marks all around, and though there's no avoiding a couple of duds once in a while, UCSB students seem to take all things in stride. A first-year explains: "Most of my professors have been interesting, informative, and inspiring. Of course, there have been a few who have lulled me to sleep better than any soft bed I have ever encountered. In general, though, they get an A+—even if I wasn't reciprocated with the same grade." Administrators, too, are well liked—one senior claims that they seem "even stonier than the students"—and work hard to provide resources and services for UCSB's traditional and nontraditional students. (However, the school could stand to improve its academic counseling and computer facilities, say undergrads.) Basically, academic success at UCSB "all depends on your approach," concludes a wise freshman. "If you are motivated and determined, you will get the classes you want and the information and resources you need. If you sit around at the beach and just expect to get into all your classes, you will be 'watching the waves' for a while."

### Life

"UCSB is the greatest place on earth. Nowhere else in the country can you get a college experience like here. Isla Vista is like Disneyland for 20-year-olds." High praise coming from southern California, the land of fun and sun. UCSB has something of a reputation for taking the good life seriously—it's the "University of Casual Sex and Beer," joke undergrads—and the bustling, upscale communities of Isla Vista and Santa Barbara only serve to heighten the experience. "It's a very big party school," writes a second-year, "similar to a Bourbon Street atmosphere." Many students claim that they spend the first few years "trying to find a balance between academics and social life," not an easy task when you've got the beach, surfing, hiking, barbecues, football, Frisbee golf, parties, and downtown S.B. (not to mention L.A. in an hour and a half) luring you away. Of course, not everyone is so enamored of the outdoorsy, party-hearty culture; some students make it their business to get away, to "Vegas, L.A., San Diego," all within a day's drive of campus. Still, it's hard to complain when the only campus improvement one freshman could think of is "moving sidewalks with back massage specialists everywhere."

### Student Body

Students' bodies might be a more apt description of what's on a UCSBer's mind a good portion of the time. "Hot chicks"? Got 'em. "Good looking guys?" That too. This isn't to say students at Santa Barbara don't appreciate their peers' "open-mindedness" and "easy-going, laid-back" personalities, but at UCSB a premium seems to be placed on being nice looking, too. Some students complain about the amount of navel gazing (prettily pierced, of course) that goes on at the U.: "They are largely selfish and unmotivated, except to get what they want," writes a senior; while a junior notes that "many don't want to go outside of their own bubble." Despite some complaints about diversity ("white is over-represented," notes a senior) and substance use ("lots of pot smokers/alcoholics"), many UCSB students remark that their fellow students are "the most open-minded anywhere."

# UNIVERSITY OF CALIFORNIA—SANTA BARBARA

FINANCIAL AID: 805-893-2432 • E-MAIL: APPINFO@SA.UCSB.EDU • WEBSITE: WWW.UCSB.EDU

## ADMISSIONS

*Very important factors include:* grades in required course work, standardized test scores, essays, extracurricular activities, talent/ability, volunteer work, work experience. SAT I or ACT required; 3 SAT II exams also required. TOEFL is required of international applicants. High school diploma or GED is required. *High school units required/recommended:* 15 total required; 2 history/social science required, 3 math required, 4 math recommended, 2 laboratory science required, 3 laboratory science recommended, 2 language other than English required, 3 language other than English recommended, 1 visual and performing arts required, 1 college preparatory elective required.

### The Inside Word

Although applications from members of underrepresented minority groups dipped following the 1997 state ban on the use of affirmative action in admissions, the picture has changed dramatically in the past few years. As a result of UC—Santa Barbara's vigorous outreach and recruiting efforts, applications from members of underrepresented minority groups have climbed steadily, as have acceptances. For the fall 2001 entering freshman class, the number of applicants accepted who are members of underrepresented minority groups has returned to pre-1997 levels.

## FINANCIAL AID

*Students should submit:* FAFSA. Regular filing deadline is May 31. The Princeton Review suggests that all financial aid forms be submitted as soon as possible after January 1. *Need-based scholarships/grants offered:* Pell, SEOG, state scholarships/grants, the school's own gift aid. *Loan aid offered:* Direct PLUS, Federal Perkins. Federal Work-Study Program available. Institutional employment available. Applicants will be notified of awards on a rolling basis beginning on or about March 15. Off-campus job opportunities are fair.

## FROM THE ADMISSIONS OFFICE

"The University of California Santa Barbara is a major research institution offering undergraduate and graduate education in the arts, humanities, sciences and technology, and social sciences. Large enough to have excellent facilities for study, research, and other creative activities, the campus is also small enough to foster close relationships among faculty and students. The faculty numbers more than 900. A member of the most distinguished system of public higher education in the nation, UC Santa Barbara is committed equally to excellence in scholarship and instruction. Through the general education program, students acquire good grounding in the skills, perceptions, and methods of a variety of disciplines. In addition, because they study with a research faculty, they not only acquire basic skills and broad knowledge but also are exposed to the imagination, inventiveness, and intense concentration that scholars bring to their work. UCSB is one of 62 members of the prestigous Association of American Universities."

## SELECTIVITY

| | |
|---|---:|
| Admissions Rating | 82 |
| # of applicants | 34,703 |
| % of applicants accepted | 51 |
| % of acceptees attending | 22 |

### FRESHMAN PROFILE

| | |
|---|---:|
| Range SAT Verbal | 510-620 |
| Average SAT Verbal | 570 |
| Range SAT Math | 550-660 |
| Average SAT Math | 602 |
| Range ACT Composite | 23-28 |
| Average ACT Composite | 25 |
| Minimum TOEFL | 500 |
| Average HS GPA | 3.7 |

### DEADLINES

| | |
|---|---:|
| Regular admission | 11/30 |
| Regular notification | 3/15 |
| Nonfall registration? | yes |

### APPLICANTS ALSO LOOK AT AND OFTEN PREFER
UC—Berkeley
UC—San Diego
UC—Irvine
UCLA

### AND SOMETIMES PREFER
UC—Davis
Pomona
Loyola Marymount

### AND RARELY PREFER
U. Pacific
UC—Riverside
UC—Santa Cruz

## FINANCIAL FACTS

| | |
|---|---:|
| Financial Aid Rating | 81 |
| In-state tuition | $4,600 |
| Out-of-state tuition | $12,379 |
| Room and board | $8,642 |
| Books and supplies | $1,225 |
| Required fees | $2,600 |
| % frosh receiving aid | 94 |
| % undergrads receiving aid | 42 |
| Avg frosh grant | $3,703 |
| Avg frosh loan | $4,477 |

# UNIVERSITY OF CALIFORNIA—SANTA CRUZ

OFFICE OF ADMISSIONS, COOK HOUSE, 1156 HIGH STREET, SANTA CRUZ, CA 95064 • ADMISSIONS: 831-459-4008 • FAX: 831-459-4452

## CAMPUS LIFE

★ ★ ★ ★

| | |
|---|---|
| Quality of Life Rating | 93 |
| Type of school | public |
| Environment | suburban |

### STUDENTS

| | |
|---|---|
| Total undergrad enrollment | 12,881 |
| % male/female | 44/56 |
| % from out of state | 5 |
| % from public high school | 96 |
| % live on campus | 42 |
| % in (# of) fraternities | 1 (9) |
| % in (# of) sororities | 1 (7) |
| % African American | 2 |
| % Asian | 17 |
| % Caucasian | 54 |
| % Hispanic | 14 |
| % international | 1 |

### SURVEY SAYS . . .
Campus is beautiful
Great library
Students are happy
Great computer facilities
Political activism is hot
Campus feels safe
Athletic facilities are great
Great off-campus food

## ACADEMICS

| | |
|---|---|
| Academic Rating | 81 |
| Calendar | Quarter |
| Student/faculty ratio | 19:1 |
| Avg lab size | 10-19 students |
| Avg reg class size | 20-29 students |

### MOST POPULAR MAJORS
Psychology
Biology/biological sciences
English language and literature

## STUDENTS SPEAK OUT

### Academics

UC Santa Cruz continues to be one of the best deals in California higher education—especially for students looking for a gentler, kinder, more community-oriented college experience. What makes UCSC special? "Natural beauty, small classes, and accessible professors," say students, who seem to appreciate the school's unique blend of big-school resources and small-school liberal arts atmosphere, set along some of the most beautiful coastline in northern California. "It's an excellent college for undergrads," writes a first-year. "All courses are taught by professors, who are generally good teachers." Students say that the school's "fabulous" academics—especially in the natural and computer sciences, language studies, linguistics, film, and digital media studies—are largely a result of the "easygoing," "helpful," and "approachable" faculty. Even UCSC's grading system reflects a concern for the individual student. For the most part, students receive "performance evaluations"—short summations of performance and progress—as well as traditional letter grades. With such an individually oriented environment, how could UCSC not have the perfect recipe for bliss! Some students, however, complain about a certain amount of administrative inefficiency. Santa Cruz is sometimes "not terribly well organized," writes a sophomore, "though I don't think that it's significantly worse than any other large institution." Class scheduling and overcrowding can sometimes be a problem, and there's some concern that the school's current expansion will only worsen the situation. There's something about Santa Cruz that defies the kind of bureaucratic-machine vibe that infuses other large state schools, though. Take it from a wee freshman: "UCSC has done a great job in helping me feel right at home as a Banana Slug!"

### Life

While most students give high marks to Santa Cruz's "secluded" and "gorgeous" location and "laid-back" atmosphere, one sophomore concedes that with so much to do out of doors, the life of the mind can sometimes take a backseat to the life of the mountains and ocean (with a slightly bizarre carney-style boardwalk called "The Strip" in between). With opportunities for mountain biking, surfing, hiking, hot-tubbing, or just hanging out at the beach literally at students' back doors, Santa Cruz is sometimes criticized for being a little too idyllic; yet it's clear that the Banana Slugs wouldn't have it any other way. "Life here at Santa Cruz is so relaxed," says a junior. Of course certain things can get a rise out of this normally mellow crowd. Many UCSCers are politically and environmentally active, and as housing in the area is far beyond most students' budgets, some have joined in a call for better and cheaper residential options. As for social life, Santa Cruz has your standard supply of "bars, restaurants, [and] movie theatres." Frats don't seem particularly overbearing at the school, though they are an option. Basically, kids like to do what they do everywhere (albeit in a hot tub overlooking the Pacific): "Party, party, and party some more."

### Student Body

It probably wouldn't surprise anyone that Santa Cruz students tend to like each other—a lot. "The majority of the students here are open-minded and friendly" is a typical characterization, as are "liberal," "open," "fun," and "unique." Again, the Banana Slug emphasis on community: "You have a voice here and a place to be someone," notes a junior. And while there are bound to be some "stuck up jerks" in any crowd of several thousand, students at UCSC seem to experience a genuine camaraderie with their peers. Still, there's room for improvement: cultural and economic diversity is sorely lacking. With the university's imminent expansion, however, even some of the school's reputed insularity and homogeneity is bound to change for the better.

# UNIVERSITY OF CALIFORNIA—SANTA CRUZ

FINANCIAL AID: 831-459-2963 • E-MAIL: ADMISSIONS@CATS.UCSC.EDU • WEBSITE: WWW.ADMISSIONS.UCSC.EDU

## ADMISSIONS

*Very important factors considered include:* class rank, secondary school record, standardized test scores, state residency. *Important factors considered include:* essays. *Other factors considered include:* character/personal qualities, extracurricular activities, geographical residence, recommendations, talent/ability, volunteer work, work experience. SAT I or ACT required, SAT II also required. TOEFL required of all international applicants. High school diploma or GED is required. *High school units required/recommended:* 15 total required; 18 total recommended; 4 English required, 3 math required, 4 math recommended, 2 science required, 3 science recommended, 2 foreign language required, 3 foreign language recommended, 1 history required, 2 social studies required.

### The Inside Word

Don't be deceived by the high acceptance rate at Santa Cruz; there are lots of engaging, intellectually motivated students here, and only active learners need apply. The state of California's ban on affirmative action in the UC admission process has created much uncertainty regarding the future of candidate selection in the system, but Santa Cruz is one of only two UC units that have been able to keep minority admission rates from declining precipitously.

## FINANCIAL AID

*Students should submit:* FAFSA, state aid form. Regular filing deadline is May 1. The Princeton Review suggests that all financial aid forms be submitted as soon as possible after January 1. *Need-based scholarships/grants offered:* Pell, SEOG, state scholarships/grants, private scholarships, the school's own gift aid. *Loan aid offered:* Direct Subsidized Stafford, Direct Unsubsidized Stafford, Direct PLUS, Federal Perkins, college/university loans from institutional funds. Federal Work-Study Program available. Institutional employment available. Applicants will be notified of awards on a rolling basis beginning on or about April 1. Off-campus job opportunities are good.

## FROM THE ADMISSIONS OFFICE

"Since its founding in 1965, UC Santa Cruz has earned a national reputation as a campus devoted to excellence in undergraduate teaching, graduate study and research, and professional education. Its academic plan and physical design combine the advantages of a small-college setting with the intensive research and academic strengths traditional to the University of California. At UC Santa Cruz, undergraduate courses are taught by the same faculty who conduct cutting-edge research. In a national survey of more than 60 elite research universities by the Association of American Universities, UC Santa Cruz ranked 15th for students in all disciplines whose bachelor's degrees led to doctorates. The campus is growing selectively and is investing half a billion dollars in new and improved infrastructure."

## SELECTIVITY

| | |
|---|---|
| Admissions Rating | 80 |
| # of applicants | 20,616 |
| % of applicants accepted | 80 |
| % of acceptees attending | 19 |

### FRESHMAN PROFILE

| | |
|---|---|
| Range SAT Verbal | 500-620 |
| Average SAT Verbal | 564 |
| Range SAT Math | 520-630 |
| Average SAT Math | 573 |
| Range ACT Composite | 21-26 |
| Average ACT Composite | 23 |
| Minimum TOEFL | 550 |
| Average HS GPA | 3.5 |

### DEADLINES

| | |
|---|---|
| Regular admission | 11/30 |
| Regular notification | 3/31 |
| Nonfall registration? | yes |

### APPLICANTS ALSO LOOK AT AND OFTEN PREFER
Stanford
UCLA
UC Berkeley

### AND SOMETIMES PREFER
UC Davis
UC Santa Barbara
UC San Diego

### AND RARELY PREFER
UC Riverside
San Jose State
San Francisco State

## FINANCIAL FACTS

| | |
|---|---|
| Financial Aid Rating | 87 |
| Out-of-state tuition | $12,379 |
| Room and board | $9,355 |
| Books and supplies | $1,170 |
| Required fees | $4,300 |
| % frosh receiving aid | 41 |
| % undergrads receiving aid | 47 |

# UNIVERSITY OF CHICAGO

1116 EAST 59TH STREET, CHICAGO, IL 60637 • ADMISSIONS: 773-702-8650 • FAX: 773-702-4199

## CAMPUS LIFE

| | |
|---|---|
| Quality of Life Rating | 73 |
| Type of school | private |
| Environment | urban |

### STUDENTS

| | |
|---|---|
| Total undergrad enrollment | 4,236 |
| % male/female | 50/50 |
| % from out of state | 78 |
| % from public high school | 70 |
| % live on campus | 66 |
| % in (# of) fraternities | 12 (9) |
| % in (# of) sororities | 5 (2) |
| % African American | 4 |
| % Asian | 16 |
| % Caucasian | 71 |
| % Hispanic | 8 |
| % international | 8 |
| # of countries represented | 34 |

### SURVEY SAYS . . .
Great library
Students love Chicago, IL
Lab facilities need improving
Students don't get along with local community
Students aren't religious
Athletic facilities need improving
Student government is unpopular
Campus difficult to get around

## ACADEMICS

| | |
|---|---|
| Academic Rating | 94 |
| Calendar | quarter |
| Student/faculty ratio | 4:1 |
| Profs interesting rating | 91 |
| Profs accessible rating | 92 |
| % profs teaching UG courses | 90 |

## STUDENTS SPEAK OUT

### Academics

Rigor, reputation, and a world-renowned faculty. The "Three Rs (and a lower case w)"—as well as a common core curriculum—are the reasons why many students choose the University of Chicago, despite Hyde Park's bone-chilling winters, strangely aggressive squirrel population, and what some might see as the school's "elitist, pretentious" attitude. Chances are, you've already heard that at U of C, "academic life is central and very rigorous." Rumor has it that the faculty has racked up more Nobel Prizes than any other university in the world. One junior agrees: "The professors are world-class and know how to teach. Where else can you see a nationally known physicist launch himself out of class to demonstrate nonrelativistic mechanics?" Nor is it just in the sciences that U of C excels. Notes a sophomore, "We have a writing program that actually tries to teach us to write well." Of course, such brilliance requires a sacrifice. "When you come here," warns a first-year, "you become a nerd and the library is your second home." Of course, the school's quarter system and its notable lack of grade inflation can make for a rather pressurized environment at times—"like an axe is ready to drop any minute," writes one student. Still, most wouldn't have it any other way: "Most people, although they wouldn't admit it, like the work that they do." Concludes a second-year, "The University of Chicago is the greatest academic experience of my life. It has introduced me to a world of knowledge I never before knew existed. And the Chicago weather has made me strong."

### Life

On the University of Chicago's reputation as being "the place where fun comes to die," many students choose to look at the bright side: "Learning happens here," quips a glass-is-half-full type. "People go to movies, to coffee, to restaurants, to Math Club." Others aren't so zen: "With all the other core requirements we have to fulfill there should be social skills in there, too. The computer science majors need remedial bathing." A more balanced look at the school is offered by the following senior: "The academic life is the be-all and end-all of U. Chicago. If you're not into your studies and don't enjoy the intellectual life, chances are that you will think U of C is boring. "Of course, the proximity to Chicago makes even the dullest Math Club meeting an opportunity to get out and explore the Windy City, which has "one of the most beautiful skylines in the world" and where "the theatre and restaurant scenes are particularly good." Although campus itself could stand a few more social options, the administration has been trying to upgrade its image in this area over the last few years, making a more concerted effort to address quality-of-life issues such extracurricular activities, student transportation, and safety. Pluses? "Housing is exceptional," according to one student. "Where else can you have a kitchen, living room, and dining room with an excellent view of Lake Michigan?" Then there's the "legendary" Scav Hunt, quintessentially U of C: "Each spring the school nearly shuts down as students rush to answer obscure trivia, party on rooftops on other campuses, and try—successfully—to cobble together nuclear reactors."

### Student Body

"Prospectives be warned," writes a junior. "We are not the stereotypical, boring, academic, nonfun students we are rumored to be!" One student argues, "People here are smart, quick-witted, and aware of the world around them." Sure, "everyone is smart, which means some very interesting people and some who are annoying and egotistical," but look at what's inside, urges a sophomore. "Their sarcasm may make them seem cynical, but it merely masks idealism struggling to exist in a nonideal world. Students here are not friendly, they're honest. You may not feel as 'welcome' or as warm and fuzzy as at other schools, but here at least you know where you stand." But if you're still concerned about the nerd factor, take heart. Writes a junior, "I'm a nerd, and I like it a lot here. So I'm guessing that, if you're a nerd, you'll like it a lot here too."

# UNIVERSITY OF CHICAGO

FINANCIAL AID: 773-702-8666 • WEBSITE: WWW.UCHICAGO.EDU

## ADMISSIONS

*Very important factors considered include:* essays, recommendations, secondary school record. *Important factors considered include:* character/personal qualities, class rank, standardized test scores, talent/ability. *Other factors considered include:* alumni/ae relation, extracurricular activities, interview, minority status, volunteer work, work experience. SAT I or ACT required. TOEFL required of all international applicants. *High school units required/recommended:* 4 English recommended, 4 math recommended, 4 science recommended, 3 foreign language recommended, 2 social studies recommended, 2 history recommended.

## The Inside Word

While excellent grades in tough courses and high test scores are the norm for applicants to the university, what really counts is what's on your mind. This is a cerebral institution, and thinkers stand out in the admissions process. Think about yourself, think about what you'd like to know more about, think about why you want to attend the university. Once you have some answers, begin writing your essays. And remember that universities that are this selective and recommend interviews should always be taken up on their recommendation.

## FINANCIAL AID

The Princeton Review suggests that all financial aid forms be submitted as soon as possible after January 1. Federal Work-Study Program available. Institutional employment available. Off-campus job opportunities are excellent.

## FROM THE ADMISSIONS OFFICE

"Chicago is a place where talented young intellectuals, writers, mathematicians, and scientists come to learn in a setting that rewards hard work and prizes initiative and creativity. It is also a place where collegiate life is urban, yet friendly and open, and free of empty traditionalism and snobbishness. Chicago is the right choice for students who know that they would thrive in an intimate classroom setting. Classes at Chicago are small, emphasizing discussion with faculty members whose research is always testing the limits of their chosen fields. Our students: They take chances; they delight us when they pursue a topic on their own for the fun of it; they display an articulate voice in papers and in discussion; they do not accept our word for everything but respect good argument; they are fanciful or solid at the right time. Most often they are students who choose the best courses available, who take a heavier load than necessary because they are curious and not worried about the consequences, who let curiosity and energy spill over into activities and sports, who are befriended by the best and toughest teachers, and who finish what they set out to do."

---

### SELECTIVITY

| | |
|---|---|
| Admissions Rating | 96 |
| # of applicants | 8,139 |
| % of applicants accepted | 42 |
| % of acceptees attending | 33 |
| # accepting a place on wait list | 754 |
| % admitted from wait list | 10 |

### FRESHMAN PROFILE

| | |
|---|---|
| Range SAT Verbal | 660-750 |
| Range SAT Math | 650-750 |
| Range ACT Composite | 28-32 |
| Minimum TOEFL | 600 |
| % graduated top 10% of class | 79 |
| % graduated top 25% of class | 94 |
| % graduated top 50% of class | 100 |

### DEADLINES

| | |
|---|---|
| Regular admission | 1/1 |
| Regular notification | 4/1 |

### APPLICANTS ALSO LOOK AT AND OFTEN PREFER

University of Pennsylvania
Yale University
Columbia University
Columbia College
Harvard College

### AND SOMETIMES PREFER

Cornell University
University of California—Berkeley
Northwestern University

### AND RARELY PREFER

Georgetown University
University of Michigan—Ann Arbor
New York University
Washington University in St. Louis

### FINANCIAL FACTS

| | |
|---|---|
| Financial Aid Rating | 85 |
| Tuition | $27,324 |
| Room and board | $8,728 |
| Books and supplies | $1,061 |
| Required fees | $501 |
| % frosh receiving aid | 58 |
| % undergrads receiving aid | 56 |
| Avg frosh grant | $20,616 |
| Avg frosh loan | $4,000 |

# UNIVERSITY OF COLORADO—BOULDER

Campus Box 30, Boulder, CO 80309-0030 • Admissions: 303-492-6301 • Fax: 303-492-7115

## CAMPUS LIFE

| | |
|---|---|
| Quality of Life Rating | 84 |
| Type of school | public |
| Environment | suburban |

### STUDENTS

| | |
|---|---|
| Total undergrad enrollment | 25,158 |
| % male/female | 53/47 |
| % from out of state | 33 |
| % live on campus | 24 |
| % in (# of) fraternities | 8 (17) |
| % in (# of) sororities | 12 (15) |
| % African American | 2 |
| % Asian | 6 |
| % Caucasian | 81 |
| % Hispanic | 6 |
| % international | 1 |
| # of countries represented | 100 |

### SURVEY SAYS . . .
Campus is beautiful
Lots of beer drinking
Hard liquor is popular
Students love Boulder, CO
Campus easy to get around
Great off-campus food
Athletic facilities are great
Students are happy
Great computer facilities
Lab facilities are great

## ACADEMICS

| | |
|---|---|
| Academic Rating | 82 |
| Calendar | semester |
| Student/faculty ratio | 16:1 |
| % profs teaching UG courses | 75 |
| % classes taught by TAs | 19 |
| Avg lab size | 20-29 students |
| Avg reg class size | 10-19 students |

### MOST POPULAR MAJORS
Psychology
Communications
Cell/cellular and molecular biology

## STUDENTS SPEAK OUT

### Academics
Whether you're looking for a backbreaking foray into the world of science, a four-year ski vacation, or something in between, you're likely to find it at the University of Colorado's flagship campus in Boulder. "CU is all about opportunity," explains one undergrad, "from the opportunity to 'Ski and Get D's to Get Degrees' to the opportunity to live your life doing research in a lab." CU boasts strong programs in engineering, the sciences, business, and journalism, all bolstered by "excellent computer resources" and "exceptional laboratory facilities, which can be used by underclassmen (even freshmen)." Like most large state schools, CU is "geared toward research, which results in some teachers who do not have the best teaching skills." Given that, a surprising number of respondents told us that "professors and teaching assistants are usually willing to spend time with you as long as you make the effort to seek them out" and that "teachers are constantly telling us about ways to further our education outside of school, and most make some sort of effort to get to know students personally." Another plus is that "many profs are from industry, so they really know what they are talking about, which makes it easier to pay attention." The Honors Program, students agree, is "exceptional for a large university; the classes are challenging, the discussions are interesting, and the professors are the best on campus." As one undergrad sums it up, "The school gives those students who really want an education a great one, and for those who don't, it's a great place to ski!"

### Life
Students come to CU for the peerless quality of life, and by nearly all accounts, that's exactly what they get. The key to it all is "location, location, location." The city of Boulder offers "an endless amount of things to do. From concerts to coffee shops, movies to lecturers, or shopping to parties, as well as just about every sport or outdoor activity, you'll never have an excuse to be bored." And "if that is not enough, Denver is only 30 minutes away." Those willing to travel a little farther harvest what most consider the area's pearl: some of the best skiing and snowboarding to be found anywhere. But students don't have to go anywhere to achieve bliss: "It is hard not to be happy when you live on such a beautiful campus. It's absolutely amazing: open courtyards shaded by beautiful trees, old brick buildings filled with warmth, and the towering Flatirons peering down from the west." The campus is "100 percent pedestrian and bicycle. We have over 15,000 bikes on campus," a testament to the crunchy granola vibe that permeates the university and surrounding town. Add an "awesome rec center," "a multitude of clubs and organizations to belong to," and popular Division I varsity, club, and intramural sports programs, and you begin to understand why so many here agree that "CU is all about having a great time in a beautiful place while learning new and interesting things."

### Student Body
The CU student body consists of "a combination of rich kids and hippies, kids who don't care about classwork, and kids who are super-competitive, studying hard during the week and letting loose on the weekends." The typical CU student "is fairly well-off, white, and genuinely nice." The engineering program is more diverse than most here, since "about one-quarter of all the students are foreign." CU has a relatively high out-of-state population; it's "exciting to know so many people from so many different areas." "Many out-of-state students come from California or Texas," and "there is a large visual disparity from the in-state students just lucky to have a chance to get to school here, to your Ms. Beverly Hills decked out in the latest designer wear [and] Tiffany & Co. jewelry and driving her Mercedes that her daddy gave her." Students skew left politically; there are lots of "diversity thugs and enviro-hippies."

564 ■ THE BEST 351 COLLEGES

# UNIVERSITY OF COLORADO—BOULDER

FINANCIAL AID: 303-492-5091 • E-MAIL: APPLY@COLORADO.EDU • WEBSITE: WWW.COLORADO.EDU

## ADMISSIONS
*Very important factors considered include:* GPA, secondary school record, standardized test scores. *Important factors considered include:* essays, geographical residence, contribution to diversity status, recommendations, state residency. *Other factors considered include:* alumni/ae relation, character/personal qualities, extracurricular activities, talent/ability, volunteer work, work experience. SAT I or ACT required. TOEFL required of all international applicants. High school diploma or GED is required. *High school units required/recommended:* 16 total required; 4 English required, 3 math required, 3 science required, 2 science lab required, 3 foreign language required, 3 social studies required, 1 history required.

## The Inside Word
In response to past concerns in Colorado about overly high percentages of out-of-staters being admitted to CU, the out-of-state population has been monitored more carefully than once was the case. Non-Coloradans will definitely find the going a bit tougher than will Colorado residents.

## FINANCIAL AID
*Students should submit:* FAFSA, tax return required. No deadline for regular filing; April 1 priority deadline. The Princeton Review suggests that all financial aid forms be submitted as soon as possible after January 1. *Need-based scholarships/grants offered:* Pell, SEOG, state scholarships/grants, private scholarships, the school's own gift aid. *Loan aid offered:* Direct Subsidized Stafford, Direct Unsubsidized Stafford, Direct PLUS, Federal Perkins, college/university loans from institutional funds, loans from private lenders. Federal Work-Study Program available. Institutional employment available. Applicants will be notified of awards on a rolling basis beginning on or about February 1. Off-campus job opportunities are excellent.

## FROM THE ADMISSIONS OFFICE
"The University of Colorado at Boulder, founded in 1876, is a major teaching and research university. Four undergraduate colleges and three schools offer over 3,400 courses in more than 150 fields of study. CU—Boulder offers more than 85 programs that lead to a bachelor's degree. Forty-six percent of all undergraduate course sections enroll no more than 19 students and 86 percent enroll fewer than 50. CU has over 70 research centers and institutes, and has numerous partnerships with businesses. CU—Boulder emphasizes a total learning environment, and many 'academic neighborhoods' tap community resources. Some academic programs allow students to take small classes in their residence halls. In addition, nonresidential programs like FallFEST group new students in courses and small discussion sections of no more than 25 students throughout the fall semester. CU—Boulder has been ranked 17th among all public colleges and universities in Yahoo's list of the 100 most 'wired' colleges and 9th among all public universities in federally funded research. CU—Boulder has traditionally been a leader in the space sciences. Most recently, CU faculty and students designed and built instruments for NASA's Galileo spacecraft now orbiting Jupiter, and a $12 million instrument for the Cassini Mission to Saturn. Faculty members include a Nobel Prize winner in chemistry, 17 members of the National Academy of Sciences, 14 members of the American Academy of Arts and Sciences, and 10 members of the National Academy of Engineering."

## SELECTIVITY

| | |
|---|---|
| Admissions Rating | 84 |
| # of applicants | 19,152 |
| % of applicants accepted | 80 |
| % of acceptees attending | 36 |
| # accepting a place on wait list | 412 |
| % admitted from wait list | 3 |

### FRESHMAN PROFILE
| | |
|---|---|
| Range SAT Verbal | 520-620 |
| Average SAT Verbal | 569 |
| Range SAT Math | 540-640 |
| Average SAT Math | 590 |
| Range ACT Composite | 22-27 |
| Average ACT Composite | 25 |
| Minimum TOEFL | 500 |
| Average HS GPA | 3.5 |
| % graduated top 10% of class | 23 |
| % graduated top 25% of class | 56 |
| % graduated top 50% of class | 91 |

### DEADLINES
| | |
|---|---|
| Regular admission | 1/15 |
| Nonfall registration? | yes |

### APPLICANTS ALSO LOOK AT AND OFTEN PREFER
UC—Berkeley
Stanford
UC—Santa Cruz

### AND SOMETIMES PREFER
Northwestern U.
Colorado State
Arizona State
U. Arizona
Oregon State

### AND RARELY PREFER
U. Oregon
U. Vermont

## FINANCIAL FACTS

| | |
|---|---|
| Financial Aid Rating | 82 |
| In-state tuition | $3,361 |
| Out-of-state tuition | $19,607 |
| Room and board | $7,323 |
| Books and supplies | $1,163 |
| Required fees | $790 |
| % frosh receiving aid | 24 |
| % undergrads receiving aid | 25 |
| Avg frosh grant | $2,875 |
| Avg frosh loan | $2,842 |

THE BEST 351 COLLEGES ■ 565

# UNIVERSITY OF CONNECTICUT

2131 HILLSIDE ROAD, U-3088, STORRS, CT 06268-3088 • ADMISSIONS: 860-486-3137 • FAX: 860-486-1476

## CAMPUS LIFE

★ ★ ☆ ☆

| Quality of Life Rating | 70 |
| --- | --- |
| Type of school | public |
| Environment | rural |

### STUDENTS

| Total undergrad enrollment | 14,716 |
| --- | --- |
| % male/female | 48/52 |
| % from out of state | 23 |
| % live on campus | 72 |
| % in (# of) fraternities | 7 (18) |
| % in (# of) sororities | 7 (9) |
| % African American | 5 |
| % Asian | 6 |
| % Caucasian | 75 |
| % Hispanic | 5 |
| % international | 1 |
| # of countries represented | 107 |

### SURVEY SAYS . . .
Everyone loves the Huskies
Popular college radio
Campus difficult to get around
Large classes
Lots of long lines and red tape

## ACADEMICS

| Academic Rating | 71 |
| --- | --- |
| Calendar | semester |
| Student/faculty ratio | 17:1 |
| Profs interesting rating | 89 |
| Profs accessible rating | 89 |
| Avg lab size | 10-19 students |
| Avg reg class size | 10-19 students |

### MOST POPULAR MAJORS
Business
Political science
Engineering

## STUDENTS SPEAK OUT

### Academics

Students at the University of Connecticut's flagship campus in Storrs tell us that they chose their school for "the wide variety of opportunities it provides its students to get involved and get ahead." Undergrads here also cite as big pluses "undergraduate research, study abroad, career services/internships, cooperative education programs," "more than 90 majors, including an individualized major which allows students to design their own plan of study, and over 200 clubs and activities. There is literally something for everyone." Business administration, music, theater, education, computer science, and engineering are among the disciplines garnering students' specific praise here. As at many large state schools, many warn that "introductory courses are not that great. It gets better as you progress as a student." Profs are "surprisingly helpful when students go to their office hours and tend to return emails the same day," although "with [UConn] being a research university, you sometimes get stuck with professors that are just too intelligent to be teaching." Of course, for the right student, the presence of so many researchers "provides a great experience. You can find numerous opportunities to get involved in professors' research projects." Many here appreciate the fact that "larger lectures are almost always broken into discussion sections of 20–25 students that meet once a week." Being the flagship university for the state of Connecticut doesn't hurt either. Connecticut profited, not once, but twice from state grants of $1 billion each, first in 1996 and then again in 2002. Students directly benefit from this windfall of dough in that every residence hall, academic building, sports facility, program office, etc. is being completely refurbished, torn down and rebuilt, or simply added anew to campus.

### Life

As a large university, UConn has the resources to support a wide variety of campus activities. Big-name acts "come to the university's Jorgensen Auditorium; they're amazing and with student ticket prices are a wonderfully cheap way to see great shows." On a smaller scale, "there are many students who enjoy the concerts of UConn Underground, numerous films, lectures, plays, and other activities going on in the dorms on a nightly basis." Furthermore, "there are so many clubs and organizations to be involved with that if you're bored on campus, it's because of your own laziness." Even so, a surprising number of students here claim that "there is nothing to do here except party." One reason is that many of the nonparty activities end early; explains one student, "UConn has a great campus life, which ends at 10 P.M. every day. Unfortunately because of that, alcohol is a popular late-night substitute. Activities are available . . . if you look hard enough and are open to different cultural and artistic experiences." Don't look in hometown Storrs, though, which "is not a college town. There is nothing to do off campus without driving at least 20 minutes." Do, however, look in the stadiums, arenas, and gymnasiums, as "the University of Connecticut offers strong Division I athletic programs in addition to a vast selection of club and intramural sports." Most here agree that "Spring Weekend is the highlight of the year. Three straight days (starting on a Thursday) of parties with crowds up to and over 10,000 people: just an overall amazing experience."

### Student Body

While "the large size of UConn means that there's not one typical student," we're told that most students here "have a good balance of school and social life. They work hard during the week and enjoy the weekend." Many are serious about success but not necessarily about book learning for its own sake; they "know that it's OK to skip at least one or two classes a week and to show up late because no one will say anything." Students are split regarding diversity. While some describe the typical UConn student as "white, middle/upper class, and from Connecticut," others point to "our five cultural centers, [where] it's easy for students to fit in and feel a part of a community."

# UNIVERSITY OF CONNECTICUT

FINANCIAL AID: 860-486-2819 • E-MAIL: BEAHUSKY@UCONN.EDU • WEBSITE: WWW.UCONN.EDU

## ADMISSIONS
*Very important factors considered include:* class rank, secondary school record, standardized test scores, talent/ability. *Important factors considered include:* character/personal qualities, essays, extracurricular activities, minority status, recommendations, volunteer work. *Other factors considered include:* alumni/ae relation, geographical residence, state residency, work experience. SAT I or ACT required. TOEFL required of all international applicants. High school diploma or GED is required. *High school units required/recommended:* 16 total required; 4 English required, 3 math required, 2 science required, 2 science lab required, 2 foreign language required, 3 foreign language recommended, 2 social studies required, 3 elective required.

### The Inside Word
While no formulas or cutoffs may be used at UConn in the admissions process, getting in is still simply a matter of decent courses, grades, and tests. The $2 billion building program coupled with the recent high national profiles of the UConn men's and women's basketball teams has resulted in an increase in applications and in turn an increase in selectivity. With an incoming freshman class of more than 3,000, UConn is now holding enrollment steady for eager Huskies-to-be.

## FINANCIAL AID
*Students should submit:* FAFSA. No deadline for regular filing. The Princeton Review suggests that all financial aid forms be submitted as soon as possible after January 1. *Need-based scholarships/grants offered:* Pell, SEOG, state scholarships/grants, private scholarships, the school's own gift aid. *Loan aid offered:* FFEL Subsidized Stafford, FFEL Unsubsidized Stafford, FFEL PLUS, Federal Perkins. Federal Work-Study Program available. Institutional employment available. Applicants will be notified of awards on a rolling basis beginning on or about March 1. Off-campus job opportunities are good.

## FROM THE ADMISSIONS OFFICE
"The University of Connecticut provides students with high quality education, personalized attention, and a wide range of social and cultural opportunities. There are 29 students in the average undergraduate class. From award-winning actors to the federal reserve board chair, fascinating speakers and world leaders have lectured on campus within the past year, while students have taken in shows by premier dance, jazz, and rock performers. Transportation to campus events is convenient and safe; most students walk to class or ride university shuttlebuses. Through UCONN 2000 and 21st-Century UConn, landmark building programs totaling $2.3 billion, the university is erecting state-of-the-art academic and residential facilities. Among the projects: A new Center for Undergraduate Education, unifying student support services in one central location and providing speedy answers to student concerns. Because of a variety of innovations like this one, UConn is transforming the undergraduate experience and fast becoming a school of choice for a new generation of achievement-oriented students."

## SELECTIVITY

| | |
|---|---|
| Admissions Rating | 79 |
| # of applicants | 13,760 |
| % of applicants accepted | 62 |
| % of acceptees attending | 37 |
| # accepting a place on wait list | 628 |
| % admitted from wait list | 9 |

### FRESHMAN PROFILE
| | |
|---|---|
| Range SAT Verbal | 520-610 |
| Average SAT Verbal | 565 |
| Range SAT Math | 530-630 |
| Average SAT Math | 584 |
| Minimum TOEFL | 550 |
| % graduated top 10% of class | 26 |
| % graduated top 25% of class | 65 |
| % graduated top 50% of class | 96 |

### DEADLINES
| | |
|---|---|
| Regular admission | 3/1 |
| Nonfall registration? | yes |

### APPLICANTS ALSO LOOK AT
**AND OFTEN PREFER**
Syracuse University
Boston College
Boston University
University of Maryland—College Park
University of Delaware
**AND SOMETIMES PREFER**
Pennsylvania State University—University Park
Providence College
Villanova University
Northeastern University
Rutgers University—New Brunswick
**AND RARELY PREFER**
University of Rhode Island
Marist College
University of Massachusetts—Amherst
Hofstra University
University of New Hampshire

## FINANCIAL FACTS

| | |
|---|---|
| Financial Aid Rating | 83 |
| In-state tuition | $5,260 |
| Out-of-state tuition | $16,044 |
| Room and board | $6,888 |
| Books and supplies | $725 |
| Required fees | $1,540 |
| % frosh receiving aid | 48 |
| % undergrads receiving aid | 47 |
| Avg frosh grant | $5,124 |
| Avg frosh loan | $3,108 |

THE BEST 351 COLLEGES ■ 567

# UNIVERSITY OF DALLAS

1845 EAST NORTHGATE DRIVE, IRVING, TX 75062 • ADMISSIONS: 972-721-5266 • FAX: 972-721-5017

## CAMPUS LIFE

| | |
|---|---|
| Quality of Life Rating | 91 |
| Type of school | private |
| Affiliation | Roman Catholic |
| Environment | suburban |

### STUDENTS

| | |
|---|---|
| Total undergrad enrollment | 1,218 |
| % male/female | 44/56 |
| % from out of state | 46 |
| % from public high school | 49 |
| % live on campus | 60 |
| % African American | 2 |
| % Asian | 7 |
| % Caucasian | 67 |
| % Hispanic | 15 |
| % international | 2 |

### SURVEY SAYS . . .
Students are religious
Campus easy to get around
(Almost) everyone smokes
No one cheats
Lots of beer drinking
Students are happy
Theater is hot

## ACADEMICS

| | |
|---|---|
| Academic Rating | 84 |
| Calendar | semester |
| Student/faculty ratio | 12:1 |
| % profs teaching UG courses | 10 |
| Avg lab size | 10-19 students |
| Avg reg class size | 10-19 students |

### MOST POPULAR MAJORS
English language and literature
Biology/biological sciences
Political science and government

## STUDENTS SPEAK OUT

### Academics

In their "distinctly Catholic academic and social setting," University of Dallas students immerse themselves in a core curriculum featuring the poster boys of western thought: "Homer, Virgil, Dante, Milton, Plato, Aristotle, Locke, Aquinas, Shakespeare—you get the idea." The academic experience is intense; "You become the core, and the core becomes you." This course of study "helps me understand my culture, including the political, economic, scientific, and philosophical arenas, by showing me its origins." Even amid these lofty texts, students claim, "the subject matter is never purely theoretical or divorced from morality. I am encouraged to think about how I can use what I've learned to be a better person." Class sizes are kept very small, and the resulting education "surpasses Ivy League schools," according to one fired-up respondent. The "surpassingly excellent" faculty is "the main attraction of the school." These "world-renowned thinkers" reportedly "care deeply about the intellectual growth of their students." An astronomical number of students study abroad, mainly at the University's Rome campus. "The Rome program definitely helps everybody on campus to develop their individuality while creating life-long friends." Some students express concern about the direction the administration has laid out for the future of the school, claiming that the focus has shifted from "learning for learning's sake" to "sporting events and business." Nonetheless, students can engage in dialogue with the administrators, who are "very helpful, even [during] the most stressful times of the year."

### Life

Though University of Dallas students know how to hit the books, traditional drunken revelry does occur, in the form of parties at upperclassmen apartments or the weekly "Thank God It's Thursday" events. The campus, however, "offers options other than drinking and partying." These include "sword fighting in the courtyard at three in the morning," "reenacting Trojan wars," "crocheting afghans," and "lauding Tolkien." And as we all know, "there is nothing like discussing Dante at two in the morning at the local IHOP with fellow stressed students." Slightly less geeked-out, "the student activities organization always has something planned on campus, be it concerts, comedians, hypnotists, or dances." Students look forward to annual Groundhog Day festivities, which include hayrides and a school-wide party that lasts until the early-morning hours. People with cars can take full advantage of the plentiful Dallas attractions, but those without wheels find themselves mostly campus-bound. As one student sums up the social scene, "UD is about discovering truth through studying the classics and living a complete life, which includes spiritual, emotional, and physical aspects, as well as the intellectual."

### Student Body

Most strikingly, UD students are "strongly, almost eccentrically, grounded in Orthodox Catholic principles." More than one respondent to our survey offers "sheltered, conservative, middle-class, and white" as appropriate adjectives to describe the undergraduate population. "Unfortunately, there's not much diversity in ethnicity," most here agree. Those who do differ from the norm report some friction: "I'm a pretty liberal Democrat and would support issues like abortion and gay rights, for example, and most people here are appalled by that." Another "minority" student writes, "As one of the few Protestants on campus, I feel like I fit in, and no one forces Catholicism on me." Certain respondents attest that "atypical students are uncommon, but don't have trouble fitting in." Perhaps that owes itself to the fact that "the school tries, with great success, to unify the students in each graduating class." Basically, anyone with "a beer in one hand and the complete works of Plato in the other" can hang. Bottom line, the school stands as a "utopia for the odd," reflected in the rally cry, "We are definitely all geeks here, but we like it that way!"

568 ■ THE BEST 351 COLLEGES

# UNIVERSITY OF DALLAS

FINANCIAL AID: 972-721-5266 • E-MAIL: UNDADMIS@ACAD.UDALLAS.EDU • WEBSITE: WWW.UDALLAS.EDU

## ADMISSIONS

*Very important factors considered include:* class rank, essays, secondary school record, standardized test scores. *Important factors considered include:* recommendations. *Other factors considered include:* alumni/ae relation, character/personal qualities, extracurricular activities, talent/ability, volunteer work, work experience. SAT I or ACT required. TOEFL required of all international applicants. High school diploma or GED is required. *High school units required/recommended:* 23 total required; 27 total recommended; 4 English required, 3 math required, 3 science required, 4 science recommended, 2 foreign language required, 4 foreign language recommended, 2 social studies required, 3 social studies recommended, 1 history required, 4 elective required.

### The Inside Word

The university's conservative nature places significant emphasis on "fit" in the admissions process. Having a solid academic background counts, but what kind of match a candidate makes with Dallas can be even more important.

## FINANCIAL AID

*Students should submit:* FAFSA, institution's own financial aid form. Regular filing deadline is March 1. The Princeton Review suggests that all financial aid forms be submitted as soon as possible after January 1. *Need-based scholarships/grants offered:* Pell, SEOG, state scholarships/grants, private scholarships, the school's own gift aid. *Loan aid offered:* FFEL Subsidized Stafford, FFEL Unsubsidized Stafford, FFEL PLUS, Federal Perkins, state loans. Federal Work-Study Program available. Institutional employment available. Applicants will be notified of awards on a rolling basis beginning on or about March 15. Off-campus job opportunities are good.

## FROM THE ADMISSIONS OFFICE

"Quite unabashedly, the curriculum at the University of Dallas is based on the supposition that truth and virtue exist and are the proper objects of search in an education. The curriculum further supposes that this search is best pursued through an acquisition of philosophical and theological principles on the part of a student and has for its analogical field a vast body of great literature—perhaps more extensive than is likely to be encountered elsewhere—supplemented by a survey of the sweep of history and an introduction to the political and economic principles of society. An understanding of these subjects, along with an introduction to the quantitative and scientific worldview and a mastery of a language, is expected to form a comprehensive and coherent experience, which, in effect, governs the intellect of a student in a manner that develops independence of thought in its most effective mode."

## SELECTIVITY

| | |
|---|---|
| Admissions Rating | 80 |
| # of applicants | 1,688 |
| % of applicants accepted | 69 |
| % of acceptees attending | 34 |

### FRESHMAN PROFILE

| | |
|---|---|
| Range SAT Verbal | 560-670 |
| Average SAT Verbal | 620 |
| Range SAT Math | 540-650 |
| Average SAT Math | 600 |
| Range ACT Composite | 25-28 |
| Average ACT Composite | 27 |
| Minimum TOEFL | 550 |
| % graduated top 10% of class | 38 |
| % graduated top 25% of class | 66 |
| % graduated top 50% of class | 89 |

### DEADLINES

| | |
|---|---|
| Priority admission | 12/1 |
| Regular admission | 1/15 |
| Regular notification | 1/15 |
| Nonfall registration? | yes |

### APPLICANTS ALSO LOOK AT AND OFTEN PREFER
U. Texas—Austin
U. Texas—Dallas
Trinity U.

### AND SOMETIMES PREFER
Baylor
St. Louis
U. Denver
U. Texas—Arlington
SMU

## FINANCIAL FACTS

| | |
|---|---|
| Financial Aid Rating | 87 |
| Tuition | $17,612 |
| Room and board | $6,494 |
| Books and supplies | $850 |
| Required fees | $450 |
| % frosh receiving aid | 85 |
| % undergrads receiving aid | 81 |
| Avg frosh grant | $6,800 |
| Avg frosh loan | $4,750 |

# UNIVERSITY OF DAYTON

300 COLLEGE PARK DRIVE, DAYTON, OH 45469-1300 • ADMISSIONS: 937-229-4411 • FAX: 937-229-4729

## CAMPUS LIFE

| | |
|---|---|
| Quality of Life Rating | 87 |
| Type of school | private |
| Affiliation | Roman Catholic |
| Environment | suburban |

### STUDENTS

| | |
|---|---|
| Total undergrad enrollment | 7,085 |
| % male/female | 50/50 |
| % from out of state | 33 |
| % from public high school | 51 |
| % live on campus | 95 |
| % in (# of) fraternities | 15 (14) |
| % in (# of) sororities | 18 (10) |
| % African American | 4 |
| % Asian | 1 |
| % Caucasian | 88 |
| % Hispanic | 2 |
| % international | 1 |
| # of countries represented | 46 |

### SURVEY SAYS . . .
Lots of beer drinking
Campus easy to get around
(Almost) everyone smokes
Great computer facilities
Students are happy
Campus is beautiful
Hard liquor is popular
Registration is a breeze
(Almost) everyone plays intramural sports
Great off-campus food

## ACADEMICS

| | |
|---|---|
| Academic Rating | 80 |
| Calendar | semester |
| Student/faculty ratio | 15:1 |
| % profs teaching UG courses | 97 |
| Avg lab size | 10-19 students |
| Avg reg class size | 20-29 students |

### MOST POPULAR MAJORS
Business/marketing
Engineering
Education

## STUDENTS SPEAK OUT

### Academics
University of Dayton, a midsize university "rooted in the Marianist tradition and Catholic faith," provides its largely career-oriented students with an ethics-based liberal arts education. "My school is all about our 'Learn, Lead, Serve' motto that comes from our Marianist influence," brags one of the many undergraduates who praise a wide array of departments, including engineering, drama, education, and marketing. Students appreciate that their school is large enough to maintain a broad selection of courses, yet small enough to provide mentoring and one-on-one teaching. "Since the undergraduate population is only 7,000, it is easy to have access to professors," reports one student, "while also having plenty of opportunities, such as those that are found at bigger schools." Better still, "professors are some of the best around. Many do research at Wright Patterson Air Force Base, which is nearby." Students give the new administration mixed reviews. Some tell us that administrators "seem to be very upbeat about the future, and very interested in the students, what they have to offer seems very promising." Others, however, worry that "the school's administration is out to shed itself of the party school image, and they think that throwing money and technology at the school will solve their problems, instead of getting at the root problems." One of those root problems, writes one undergrad, is that "some teachers and classes are brought down by mediocre students." Even so, most here speak highly of the overall UD experience, satisfied with the sense that "the focus at Dayton is not only grades and learning, but also taking care of us as young adults in need of mentors."

### Life
Some kids go to college to escape the ghetto; at UD, the opposite occurs. "The Ghetto, an infamous neighborhood composed of old houses, most of which the University owns, [is] filled with undergrad students, mostly juniors and seniors," explains one undergrad. While "drinking in the Ghetto is the main activity" of many Dayton students, "the experience of the Ghetto is about much more than wild parties . . . . You learn to live in a community built on respect for one another." Dayton has long had a reputation as a party school, and an especially democratic one at that; "there is no such thing as 'list' parties at Dayton; rather, everyone is accepted everywhere," reports one student. "I know this is hard to believe, but it's the truth, and one of the main reasons I love this place so much." However, "while UD is known as a party school, it really isn't that bad. There are plays, movies, and special activities that Student Government sets up for those who don't want to drink. For fun we go to the movies, out to eat, or to the mall. I think the University of Dayton provides plenty of interesting things to do on the weekend." UD also has "all kinds of intramural sports that students love to play; I think we had 5,000 students play softball last spring."

### Student Body
The "J.Crew and Abercrombie" crowd at UD is "dominated by white Catholic kids from private schools," primarily from Ohio, Pennsylvania, and Indiana. Writes one student, "Most students are what my friends and I call the three C's: Caucasian, Catholic (nonpracticing, of course!), and conservative. I am atypical in that I am a liberal Democrat. For students like me, there are student organizations such as Students Allies (gay, lesbian, transgender, etc.), College Democrats, Amnesty International, and Pax Christi (pacifist group)." Many here noted "the university's commitment toward making UD more diverse, reflected in its scholarship and grant-giving this year." Several students told us that "diversity is improving but could still go a long way." Many undergrads are involved in "serving the community of Dayton and reaching out to those less fortunate."

# UNIVERSITY OF DAYTON

FINANCIAL AID: 937-229-4311 • E-MAIL: ADMISSION@UDAYTON.EDU • WEBSITE: WWW.UDAYTON.EDU

## ADMISSIONS

*Very important factors considered include:* secondary school record. *Important factors considered include:* class rank, standardized test scores, talent/ability. *Other factors considered include:* alumni/ae relation, character/personal qualities, essays, extracurricular activities, interview, minority status, recommendations, volunteer work, work experience. SAT I or ACT required. TOEFL required of all international applicants. High school diploma or GED is required. *High school units required/recommended:* 16 total recommended; 4 English recommended, 3 math recommended, 2 science recommended, 3 social studies recommended, 4 elective recommended.

### The Inside Word

While Dayton reviews all applicants individually in regard to their potential for success at the university, its high admit rate means that there's little for all but the weakest applicants to worry about concerning admission.

## FINANCIAL AID

*Students should submit:* FAFSA. The Princeton Review suggests that all financial aid forms be submitted as soon as possible after January 1. *Need-based scholarships/grants offered:* Pell, SEOG, state scholarships/grants, private scholarships. *Loan aid offered:* FFEL Subsidized Stafford, FFEL Unsubsidized Stafford, FFEL PLUS, Federal Perkins, state loans, college/university loans from institutional funds, GATE Loans. Federal Work-Study Program available. Institutional employment available. Applicants will be notified of awards on a rolling basis beginning on or about February 20. Off-campus job opportunities are good.

## FROM THE ADMISSIONS OFFICE

"The University of Dayton is respected as one of the nation's leading Catholic universities. We offer the resources and diversity of a comprehensive university and the attention and accessibility of a small college. All university-owned housing is fully wired for direct high-speed connection to the Internet as well as our 78-channel cable system. The technology-enhanced learning and student computer initiative ensures students use of the tools that will prepare them for a technology-dependent workplace. Our programs of study, impressive 110-acre campus, advanced research facilities, NCAA Division I intercollegiate athletics, and international alumni network are big-school advantages. Small class sizes, undergraduate emphasis, student-centered faculty and staff, residential campus life, and friendliness are all attractive small-school qualities. The University of Dayton is committed to student success. Our educational mission is to recognize the talents you bring as an individual and help you reach your potential."

## SELECTIVITY

| | |
|---|---|
| Admissions Rating | 78 |
| # of applicants | 7,496 |
| % of applicants accepted | 84 |
| % of acceptees attending | 26 |
| # accepting a place on wait list | 37 |
| % admitted from wait list | 100 |

### FRESHMAN PROFILE

| | |
|---|---|
| Range SAT Verbal | 500-610 |
| Average SAT Verbal | 557 |
| Range SAT Math | 510-630 |
| Average SAT Math | 575 |
| Range ACT Composite | 22-27 |
| Average ACT Composite | 24 |
| Minimum TOEFL | 550 |
| % graduated top 10% of class | 18 |
| % graduated top 25% of class | 41 |
| % graduated top 50% of class | 75 |

### DEADLINES

| | |
|---|---|
| Priority admission | 1/1 |
| Nonfall registration? | yes |

### APPLICANTS ALSO LOOK AT
### AND OFTEN PREFER
Miami U
Notre Dame
### AND SOMETIMES PREFER
Ohio U
Ohio State
Xavier
Marquette
John Carrol
### AND RARELY PREFER
Purdue
U of Cincinnati
Toledo

## FINANCIAL FACTS

| | |
|---|---|
| Financial Aid Rating | 82 |
| Tuition | $18,390 |
| Room and board | $5,890 |
| Required fees | $570 |
| % frosh receiving aid | 63 |
| % undergrads receiving aid | 56 |
| Avg frosh grant | $6,406 |
| Avg frosh loan | $4,263 |

# UNIVERSITY OF DELAWARE

116 HULLIHEN HALL, NEWARK, DE 19716 • ADMISSIONS: 302-831-8123 • FAX: 302-831-6905

## CAMPUS LIFE

| | |
|---|---|
| Quality of Life Rating | 84 |
| Type of school | public |
| Environment | suburban |

### STUDENTS

| | |
|---|---|
| Total undergrad enrollment | 17,486 |
| % male/female | 42/58 |
| % from out of state | 59 |
| % from public high school | 80 |
| % live on campus | 48 |
| % in (# of) fraternities | 15 (15) |
| % in (# of) sororities | 15 (15) |
| % African American | 5 |
| % Asian | 3 |
| % Caucasian | 88 |
| % Hispanic | 3 |
| % international | 1 |
| # of countries represented | 100 |

### SURVEY SAYS . . .
Frats and sororities dominate social scene
Class discussions are rare
Hard liquor is popular
(Almost) everyone smokes
Great library
Large classes
Campus difficult to get around
Student government is unpopular
Dorms are like dungeons
Lots of TAs teach upper-level courses

## ACADEMICS

| | |
|---|---|
| Academic Rating | 79 |
| Calendar | 4-1-4 |
| Student/faculty ratio | 12:1 |
| Profs interesting rating | 90 |
| Profs accessible rating | 96 |
| % profs teaching UG courses | 95 |
| % classes taught by TAs | 5 |
| Avg lab size | 20-29 students |
| Avg reg class size | 20-29 students |

## STUDENTS SPEAK OUT

### Academics
Located at the very center of an urban corridor that stretches from New York City to Washington, D.C., the University of Delaware manages to provide its undergrads with a traditional university education and the opportunity to engage in a meaningful way in today's global society. Besides the old-school virtues of "a beautiful campus, strong academic reputation, and wonderful people," UD was one of the first universities to offer study abroad programs on every continent (as one senior points out, "Who could pass up learning French in Martinique—or economics in Australia—during the winter?"). Additionally, besides being the recipient of a huge influx of funds during the last few years to upgrade their technological capabilities and connectivity, it's also one of the only schools in the country designated a land-grant, sea-grant, urban-grant, and space-grant institution. All that and professors who are "excellent, accessible" and remember students' names too? Yes, writes a junior, "especially when they sense you have a question or concern, or haven't completed an assignment." A top-notch, selective Honors Program and opportunities for undergraduate research "allow for a rigorous academic career," notes one upperclassman—so do the "demanding but fun" classes. And though there are some complaints about "poor teaching style" and an administration that cares more about prospective, rather than currently enrolled, students ("All the construction makes it hard to drive around!" gripes a junior), undergrads realize that the school's many excellent resources, a fairly good financial aid program, and an administration and faculty that are "genuinely interested in students" generally make for a "positive" university experience.

### Life
A UD sophomore waxes philosophical: "Life at the University of Delaware is just that, life! There are tough times and easy times, and all along the way you have so many avenues of help available." In keeping with their take on academics, UD students seem to favor a positive approach to life on this large, "fun," and always interesting college campus. "There is always something to do," claims a junior. Whether it be partying at the residence halls of one of the many different schools that make up the university, going to see an a capella concert, a student play, or an athletic event, or just hanging out at one of the local watering holes, undergrads seem to agree that at UD "there's too much to do and not enough time to do it." (Even "seasonal events like hayrides" get a mention.) As for partying, though one senior makes the case that "instead of using the school to broaden their horizons and think, students use it to get drunk every weekend," another points out that at UD, "you have plenty of options if drinking is not your thing." Newark is a "nice, small" town, after all, and if that's not enough, well, there's always a hayride.

### Student Body
"Extremely friendly" peeps who "say 'hi' just because they're crossing the street towards each other" are just one reason why students love UD. Its "warm environment" and "easygoing atmosphere" are a couple more. "The overall student body is a very accepting group of individuals," adds a sophomore. "It makes such a large school more welcoming and inviting." Some would argue that these "individuals" are really one big "white, Abercrombie, upper-middle-class yuppie." There is also the sense that many students are apolitical, self-segregated, and a tad "stuck up." Notes a self-identified "left-wing" senior, "I like my friends, but it took me a while to find progressive activist students on a conservative, apathetic campus like this one."

# UNIVERSITY OF DELAWARE

FINANCIAL AID: 302-831-8761 • E-MAIL: ADMISSIONS@UDEL.EDU • WEBSITE: WWW.UDEL.EDU/VIEWBOOK

## ADMISSIONS

*Very important factors considered include:* essays, secondary school record. *Important factors considered include:* character/personal qualities, class rank, extracurricular activities, geographical residence, recommendations, standardized test scores, state residency, talent/ability. *Other factors considered include:* alumni/ae relation, minority status, volunteer work, work experience. SAT I or ACT required; SAT II recommended. TOEFL required of all international applicants. High school diploma or GED is required. *High school units required/recommended:* 16 total required; 4 English required, 2 math required, 4 math recommended, 2 science required, 3 science recommended, 1 science lab required, 2 foreign language required, 4 foreign language recommended, 1 social studies required, 2 social studies recommended, 2 history required, 3 history required.

### *Inside Word*

Most students applying to Delaware face a moderately selective admissions process focused mainly on grades and tests with some focus on nonacademic characteristics. Those who seek to enter the university's honors program need to be far more thorough in completing their applications and much better prepared academically in order to gain admission. The honors program has high expectations; from what we know, it appears to be well worth it.

## FINANCIAL AID

*Students should submit:* FAFSA. Regular filing deadline is March 15. The Princeton Review suggests that all financial aid forms be submitted as soon as possible after January 1. *Need-based scholarships/grants offered:* Pell, SEOG, state scholarships/grants, private scholarships, the school's own gift aid. *Loan aid offered:* Direct Subsidized Stafford, Direct Unsubsidized Stafford, Direct PLUS, Federal Perkins, Federal Nursing. Federal Work-Study Program available. Institutional employment available. Applicants will be notified of awards on a rolling basis beginning on or about March 15. Off-campus job opportunities are good.

## FROM THE ADMISSIONS OFFICE

"The University of Delaware is a major national research university with a long-standing commitment to teaching and serving undergraduates. It is one of only a few universities in the country designated as a land-grant, sea-grant, urban-grant, and space-grant institution. The academic strength of this university is found in its highly selective Honors Program, nationally recognized Undergraduate Research Program, and its successful alumni, including three Rhodes Scholars since 1998. The University of Delaware offers the wide range of majors and course offerings expected of a university, but in spirit remains a small place where you can interact with your professors and feel at home. The beautiful green campus is ideally located at the very center of the East Coast 'megacity' that stretches from New York City to Washington, D.C. All of these elements, combined with an endowment approaching $1 billion and a spirited Division I athletics program make the University of Delaware a tremendous value."

## SELECTIVITY

| | |
|---|---|
| Admissions Rating | 83 |
| # of applicants | 20,365 |
| % of applicants accepted | 48 |
| % of acceptees attending | 35 |
| # accepting a place on wait list | 1,578 |
| % admitted from wait list | 3 |
| # of early decision applicants | 1,256 |
| % accepted early decision | 49 |

### FRESHMAN PROFILE

| | |
|---|---|
| Range SAT Verbal | 530-620 |
| Range SAT Math | 550-650 |
| Range ACT Composite | 22-27 |
| Minimum TOEFL | 550 |
| Average HS GPA | 3.5 |
| % graduated top 10% of class | 34 |
| % graduated top 25% of class | 75 |
| % graduated top 50% of class | 97 |

### DEADLINES

| | |
|---|---|
| Early decision | 11/15 |
| Early decision notification | 12/15 |
| Priority admission | 1/15 |
| Regular admission | 2/15 |
| Regular notification | 3/15 |
| Nonfall registration? | yes |

### APPLICANTS ALSO LOOK AT

**AND OFTEN PREFER**
U. Virginia

**AND SOMETIMES PREFER**
U. Conn.
U. Richmond
Virginia Tech
U. Vermont

**AND RARELY PREFER**
Penn State—Univ. Park
U. Maryland—Coll. Park
Rutgers U.

## FINANCIAL FACTS

| | |
|---|---|
| Financial Aid Rating | 83 |
| In-state tuition | $5,190 |
| Out-of-state tuition | $14,720 |
| Room and board | $5,822 |
| Books and supplies | $800 |
| Required fees | $570 |
| % frosh receiving aid | 43 |
| % undergrads receiving aid | 37 |
| Avg frosh grant | $4,200 |
| Avg frosh loan | $3,500 |

# UNIVERSITY OF DENVER

UNIVERSITY HALL, ROOM 110, 2197 S. UNIVERSITY BLVD., DENVER, CO 80208 • ADMISSIONS: 303-871-2036 • FAX: 303-871-3301

## CAMPUS LIFE

| | |
|---|---|
| Quality of Life Rating | 83 |
| Type of school | private |
| Environment | suburban |

### STUDENTS

| | |
|---|---|
| Total undergrad enrollment | 4,257 |
| % male/female | 42/58 |
| % from out of state | 50 |
| % live on campus | 43 |
| % in (# of) fraternities | 23 (8) |
| % in (# of) sororities | 22 (5) |
| % African American | 4 |
| % Asian | 5 |
| % Caucasian | 79 |
| % Hispanic | 7 |
| % international | 5 |

### SURVEY SAYS . . .
Theater is hot
Frats and sororities dominate social scene
Students love Denver, CO
Student publications are ignored
Political activism is (almost) nonexistent

## ACADEMICS

| | |
|---|---|
| Academic Rating | 81 |
| Calendar | quarter |
| Student/faculty ratio | 9:1 |
| Profs interesting rating | 94 |
| Profs accessible rating | 92 |
| Avg lab size | 10-19 students |
| Avg reg class size | 10-19 students |

## STUDENTS SPEAK OUT

### Academics

Known for its business, mass communications, public relations, and digital media programs ("The Daniels College of Business is an excellent new academic facility"), DU is no slouch academically, though at least one student complains that sometimes "it seems that Denver University is more of a business than a school." This sentiment is echoed in a sophomore's claim that DU "needs more majors," and another's that "arts and humanities need to be treated equally with business." With an administration that's "always available" and "seems to care about students and their success," however, it looks like DU is "definitely becoming more focused on academics"—a welcome sign for those who are interested in seeing the school deepen its traditional liberal arts curriculum. Still, many DU students like its "professionalism," and there are few complaints about classes like "Communication & Popular Culture" and "Human Sexuality." One junior remarks, "I love DU because I always have fun stories about classes to tell my friends back home." Professors are the real gem at the University of Denver; almost across the board, students praise the school's small class sizes, personal attention, and devoted faculty. Writes one sophomore, "My honors courses have all been great, offering me material I never could get anywhere else. How was I to know that during the Black Plague all they thought about was sex?" Of course, there's always a cynic. Comments one senior, "There are enough unmotivated students that don't care about school that the teachers have plenty of time and enthusiasm for those who care." But, hey, when the reigning feeling about the school is that it is "a great academic experience which also guarantees a great time," who's complaining?

### Life

Writes one junior: "DU is the perfect size. It is big enough to offer diversity yet small enough to foster connectedness." A sense of community is clearly important for most DU undergrads, many of whom join the school's flourishing Greek system. "People who are in Greek houses are the most involved," states a sophomore, and there does seem to be a sense amongst the student body that the school could "offer more to non-Greeks." One rather blunt junior describes campus life this way: "Most people don't think much and go to frat parties and get wasted for fun," while another says pretty much the same thing in just three words: "Greek is awesome!" Alternatives? "The best skiing in the country right out the back door" and the obvious draw of Denver, Colorado's biggest city, "which provides a variety of recreational activities," writes a sophomore. Another sings the town's praises by saying, "Being in Denver is great—downtown for clubs, bars, shopping, food. And being in an industrial city is wonderful: internships, jobs, opportunities." Overall, concludes a junior, "There is always something to do and usually people to do it with."

### Student Body

Denver prides itself on a certain brand of individuality; notes a first year: "The students at DU all appear the same on the outside but are anything but the same when you get to know them." One student might be a mom raising a two-year-old while taking classes full time, while another might be one of the school's many international students at DU to study business or management. Writes a junior, "Students at DU are pretty accepting and open-minded. I get along and we get along with each other." And while the school has been accused of being "cliquey" and "comprised of mostly overprivileged rich kids," the majority of the student body are "great friends," writes a sophomore. With a beautiful campus and the mountains an hour-and-a-half away, it shouldn't come as a surprise that "most of the people at DU are pretty laid back and easygoing." And, writes a senior, they're "all smiles." With all that snow and those pearly whites gleaming, just be sure to pack your shades.

574 ■ THE BEST 351 COLLEGES

# UNIVERSITY OF DENVER

Financial Aid: 303-871-4026 • E-mail: admission@du.edu • Website: www.du.edu

## ADMISSIONS

*Very important factors considered include:* secondary school record. *Important factors considered include:* character/personal qualities, class rank, extracurricular activities, standardized test scores, talent/ability, volunteer work, work experience. *Other factors considered include:* alumni/ae relation, essays, geographical residence, recommendations. Interview and SAT I or ACT required of all students. TOEFL required of all international applicants. High school diploma or GED is required. *High school units required/recommended:* 4 English required, 4 math required, 3 science required, 2 science lab required, 2 foreign language required.

### The Inside Word

Any good student will find getting admitted to Denver to be a fairly straightforward process.

## FINANCIAL AID

*Students should submit:* FAFSA. The Princeton Review suggests that all financial aid forms be submitted as soon as possible after January 1. *Need-based scholarships/grants offered:* Pell, SEOG, state scholarships/grants, private scholarships, the school's own gift aid. *Loan aid offered:* Direct Subsidized Stafford, Direct Unsubsidized Stafford, Direct PLUS, FFEL Subsidized Stafford, FFEL Unsubsidized Stafford, FFEL PLUS, Federal Perkins, college/university loans from institutional funds. Federal Work-Study Program available. Institutional employment available. Applicants will be notified of awards on or about April 1. Off-campus job opportunities are excellent.

## FROM THE ADMISSIONS OFFICE

"Founded in 1864, the University of Denver offers an educational experience characterized by adventurous learning and innovative mentoring from a caring faculty. Our undergraduate students come from all across the United States and from more than 90 countries to study in an environment that nurtures potential and passion. The new Hyde Interview requirement provides all applicants the opportunity to give a voice to their application while assisting DU with admission decisions.

"DU is continually developing educational initiatives that help students prepare for an ever-changing world. Among our offerings: living and learning communities that provide residential space and extracurricular programming for students interested in particular areas; a grant program for students that funds everything from research to creative endeavors; and hundreds of internship opportunities that put students in laboratories, corporate offices, government agencies, and cultural settings. In addition, an experimental leadership program emphasizes ethics, community service, and citizenship.

"DU's 25-acre University Park campus, located in a quiet residential neighborhood, is eight miles from downtown Denver and a half-hour's drive from the Rocky Mountain foothills. DU students enjoy an active lifestyle with plenty of opportunities to recreate in the Rockies, cheer on one of the city's many professional sports teams, or enjoy downtown's lively arts and entertainment scene."

## SELECTIVITY

| | |
|---|---:|
| Admissions Rating | 78 |
| # of applicants | 4,305 |
| % of applicants accepted | 86 |
| % of acceptees attending | 23 |

### FRESHMAN PROFILE

| | |
|---|---:|
| Range SAT Verbal | 510-610 |
| Average SAT Verbal | 555 |
| Range SAT Math | 500-610 |
| Average SAT Math | 567 |
| Range ACT Composite | 21-27 |
| Average ACT Composite | 24 |
| Minimum TOEFL | 500 |
| Average HS GPA | 3.4 |
| % graduated top 10% of class | 38 |
| % graduated top 25% of class | 62 |
| % graduated top 50% of class | 85 |

### DEADLINES

| | |
|---|---:|
| Nonfall registration? | yes |

### APPLICANTS ALSO LOOK AT AND OFTEN PREFER
U. Colorado—Boulder
### AND SOMETIMES PREFER
U. Puget Sound
U. Vermont

## FINANCIAL FACTS

| | |
|---|---:|
| Financial Aid Rating | 85 |
| Tuition | $22,680 |
| Room and board | $6,987 |
| Required fees | $574 |
| % frosh receiving aid | 40 |
| % undergrads receiving aid | 40 |
| Avg frosh grant | $9,800 |
| Avg frosh loan | $6,500 |

# UNIVERSITY OF FLORIDA

PO Box 114000, 201 Criser Hall, Gainesville, FL 32611-4000 • Admissions: 352-392-1365 • Fax: 352-392-3987

## CAMPUS LIFE

| | |
|---|---|
| Quality of Life Rating | 83 |
| Type of school | public |
| Environment | suburban |

### STUDENTS

| | |
|---|---|
| Total undergrad enrollment | 34,031 |
| % male/female | 47/53 |
| % from out of state | 5 |
| % live on campus | 21 |
| % in (# of) fraternities | 15 (29) |
| % in (# of) sororities | 15 (18) |
| % African American | 8 |
| % Asian | 7 |
| % Caucasian | 72 |
| % Hispanic | 11 |
| % international | 1 |

### SURVEY SAYS . . .
Lots of beer drinking
Everyone loves the Gators
Athletic facilities are great
Hard liquor is popular
Frats and sororities dominate social scene
Student newspaper is popular
Great library
Campus is beautiful
(Almost) everyone plays intramural sports
Ethnic diversity on campus

## ACADEMICS

| | |
|---|---|
| Academic Rating | 84 |
| Calendar | semester |
| Student/faculty ratio | 21:1 |
| Avg lab size | 10-19 students |
| Avg reg class size | 20-29 students |

## STUDENTS SPEAK OUT

### Academics

Students describe the University of Florida as a school that can be as difficult or easy as they want to make it. Some cruise through by adhering to the principle that "the key to taking classes here is to understand the system and find the scattered easy classes. There are at least two easy teachers in every department. Find them and take every class they offer." Others take a more arduous route; writes one, "UF is very academically challenging, especially when you get into your upper-division courses, and especially in the hard sciences. People who say otherwise are taking doofus electives like 'Insects, Molds, and Mildews' to boost their GPA." Intro level courses are mostly "huge lectures where students sit—silently—and professors lecture indifferently." "The academic experience becomes rewarding," however, "once upper-level classes are reached. Classes are much smaller, and I have been able to know my professors better because I have them for more that one course." Many students love the "TV and WEB classes, which are very convenient. . . . The one good thing about the administration is they put everything online on this thing called ISIS and send a weekly e-mail." Sums up one student, "Because UF is such a large university, it is easy to feel overwhelmed and lost. But if you try to get involved and get to know the facilities you have at hand, UF has soooo many opportunities it's ridiculous."

### Life

"What, UF is a school? I thought they were just a football team." So writes one student who pithily sums up many students' reverent attitude toward the Gators' gridiron powerhouse. "Life revolves around Gator football," explains one student, "and on game days the campus is crowded with visitors, alumni, and students, making parking impossible." Students love the men's basketball team, too; in fact, students here just love sports, plain and fancy. "Intramural sports here kick arse," and undergrads participate in "a lot of outdoor activities. The school provides students with a lake of our own where we can use sailboats, canoes, jet skis, etc., all for free." When nighttime rolls around, "People go to clubs for fun. There are a lot of raves and keg parties." Also, "the Greek system is extremely popular on campus and they always have stuff going on. It is a good way to meet a ton of people." Much of hometown Gainesville commerce is tailored to serving the large student body, leading students to observe that "Gainesville has pretty much everything, including a ton of bars with something for anyone Greek, non-Greek, gay, Hispanic, Afro-American. If you don't like going out, the Gulf of Mexico is 45 minutes to the west, and the Atlantic is 1.5 hours east. Orlando is 1 hour away. The list goes on. Because of its size, student life at UF is limited only by your imagination, time, and/or course load."

### Student Body

At UF "there are so many students that everyone should be able to find a niche." Once students find their niche, most lock in; reports one student, "Different groups don't really mix. Each has its own thing going and doesn't seem to involve others." Among these groups are "large outspoken Christian groups" and a "large Greek population." Notes one student, "The only downfall is that Greek life is pretty dominant, but hey, if you like that kind of thing, you'll be in heaven." Concludes one student, "It's a mixed bag between really amazing people who work hard and have good direction . . . and the spoiled yuppie brats who don't know how lucky they are to be here and what life is all about beyond MTV."

576 ■ THE BEST 351 COLLEGES

# UNIVERSITY OF FLORIDA

FINANCIAL AID: 352-392-1275 • E-MAIL: FRESHMAN@UFL.EDU • WEBSITE: WWW.UFL.EDU

## ADMISSIONS

SAT I or ACT required. High school diploma or GED is required. *High school units required/recommended:* 15 total required; 4 English required, 3 math required, 3 science required, 2 science lab required, 2 foreign language required, 3 social studies required. A personal written statement is required.

## The Inside Word

Practically every other high school graduate in the state applies to UF, which gives the admissions staff a huge pool of candidates to choose from. The selection process is driven by numbers, with little personal attention afforded anyone but athletes, legacies, minorities, and National Merit Scholars. Out-of-state students will find that getting into this "party school" isn't at all easy. With budget cuts further restricting enrollment, it won't be long before admission to Florida is as difficult for out-of-staters as it is at such top public universities as North Carolina and Virginia.

## FINANCIAL AID

*Students should submit:* FAFSA. The Princeton Review suggests that all financial aid forms be submitted as soon as possible after January 1. *Need-based scholarships/grants offered:* Pell, SEOG, state scholarships/grants, private scholarships, the school's own gift aid. *Loan aid offered:* Direct Subsidized Stafford, Direct Unsubsidized Stafford, Direct PLUS, Federal Perkins, college/university loans from institutional funds. Federal Work-Study Program available. Institutional employment available. Applicants will be notified of awards on a rolling basis beginning on or about April 1. Off-campus job opportunities are fair.

## FROM THE ADMISSIONS OFFICE

"University of Florida students come from more than 100 countries, all 50 states, and every one of the 67 counties in Florida. Nineteen percent of the student body is comprised of graduate students. Approximately 2,300 African American students, 3,300 Hispanic students, and 2,200 Asian American students attend UF. Ninety percent of the entering freshmen rank above the national mean of scores on standard entrance exams. UF consistently ranks near the top among public universities in the number of new National Merit and Achievement scholars in attendance."

### SELECTIVITY

| | |
|---|---|
| Admissions Rating | 88 |
| # of applicants | 20,119 |
| % of applicants accepted | 58 |
| % of acceptees attending | 56 |
| # of early decision applicants | 2,952 |
| % accepted early decision | 60 |

### FRESHMAN PROFILE

| | |
|---|---|
| Range SAT Verbal | 550-660 |
| Range SAT Math | 580-680 |
| Range ACT Composite | 24-29 |
| Average HS GPA | 3.8 |
| % graduated top 10% of class | 71 |
| % graduated top 25% of class | 89 |
| % graduated top 50% of class | 97 |

### DEADLINES

| | |
|---|---|
| Early decision | 10/1 |
| Early decision notification | 12/1 |
| Regular admission | 1/13 |
| Nonfall registration? | yes |

### FINANCIAL FACTS

| | |
|---|---|
| Financial Aid Rating | 82 |
| In-state tuition | $2,581 |
| Out-of-state tuition | $12,046 |
| Room and board | $5,640 |
| Books and supplies | $780 |
| % frosh receiving aid | 34 |
| % undergrads receiving aid | 34 |
| Avg frosh grant | $3,994 |
| Avg frosh loan | $2,341 |

THE BEST 351 COLLEGES ■ 577

# UNIVERSITY OF GEORGIA

TERRELL HALL, ATHENS, GA 30602 • ADMISSIONS: 706-542-8776 • FAX: 706-542-1466

## CAMPUS LIFE

| | |
|---|---|
| Quality of Life Rating | 88 |
| Type of school | public |
| Environment | suburban |

### STUDENTS

| | |
|---|---|
| Total undergrad enrollment | 24,983 |
| % male/female | 44/56 |
| % from out of state | 11 |
| % from public high school | 87 |
| % live on campus | 23 |
| % in (# of) fraternities | 12 (23) |
| % in (# of) sororities | 18 (22) |
| % African American | 5 |
| % Asian | 4 |
| % Caucasian | 85 |
| % Hispanic | 2 |
| % international | 1 |

### SURVEY SAYS . . .
Everyone loves the Bulldogs
Students love Athens, GA
Athletic facilities are great
Frats and sororities dominate social scene
Great food on campus
Large classes
Student publications are popular
Theater is unpopular
Student government is unpopular
Dorms are like dungeons

## ACADEMICS

| | |
|---|---|
| Academic Rating | 80 |
| Calendar | semester |
| Student/faculty ratio | 13:1 |
| Profs interesting rating | 91 |
| Profs accessible rating | 94 |
| % profs teaching UG courses | 80 |
| % classes taught by TAs | 18 |
| Avg reg class size | 20-29 students |

## STUDENTS SPEAK OUT
### Academics
Students seeking a "very good" education at a low cost should consider the University of Georgia. Though a large state school, the 2,000-member honors program is highly regarded. Some honors students believe that it is not as challenging as honors programs at other universities, but they still praise the professors and the small class sizes. They also note that registration is a breeze. The registration process for non-Honors students, however, needs improvement. "There are some fabulous professors in the English department," asserts on student. "I'll go to class even when there isn't an attendance policy." Professors get mixed reviews. One student says, "The professors are very smart, yet their teaching is average." Another notes that upper-level professors "rock," while lower-level professors are nowhere near as good. The major problem is that students often get "discouraged from the start" because the quality of professors in the lower-level classes is significantly lower than the quality of those professors who teach upper-level courses. Students praise the administration and say that the university runs smoothly, though they decry the lack of parking spaces and class availability.

### Life
Look up "college town" in a dictionary and you'll likely find Athens included somewhere in the definition. Its legendary music scene spawned the B-52s and REM, and the town's primary purpose is to cater to the 24,000 students who attend UGA. The town is chock full of terrific clubs, excellent restaurants, and fantastic coffeehouses. There are plenty of bars and pubs as well, and students call the college experience "great." The UGA football team is usually nationally ranked, and the recreational sports facility "is without equal." The other unifying force is the Greek system. Students admit that they party "a lot," but they also study a great deal. There are over 400 student groups, so most students have no problem finding something interesting and fun to do. Obviously, school spirit runs unchecked at UGA.

### Student Body
UGA students are very courteous and friendly once you get to know them. Though this is a bit of a daunting task at first, students find that they assimilate and make friends relatively quickly. "Most people don't socialize in class," points out one first-year. "You get to know people through clubs, Greek life, and stuff like that." Overall, most students get along, though some are not fond of the Greek system and complain, "the emphasis on Greek life and football are out of control." Still, "I have almost never had any problem of any kind with fellow students," a senior history major admits. Diversity is lacking—not surprising on a campus where 85 percent of the students are Caucasian. One student sums up her peers at UGA: "The students here are mostly future-oriented. We like to have fun, but at the same time, we know when it's time to work."

# UNIVERSITY OF GEORGIA

FINANCIAL AID: 706-542-6147 • E-MAIL: under2@admissions.uga.edu • WEBSITE: www.uga.edu

## ADMISSIONS

*Very important factors considered include:* secondary school record, standardized test scores. *Other factors considered include:* essays, extracurricular activities, recommendations, talent/ability, volunteer work, work experience. SAT I or ACT required. TOEFL required of all international applicants. High school diploma or GED is required. *High school units required/recommended:* 16 total required; 20 total recommended; 4 English required, 4 math required, 3 science required, 2 science lab required, 2 foreign language required, 3 social studies required.

### The Inside Word

UGA is one of the more popular choices among southern college-bound students. The admissions process is very straightforward, but few large universities have as much success as Georgia in converting admits to enrollees, which makes candidate evaluation fairly selective. So does the fantastically successful Hope Scholarship Program for Georgia residents, now being emulated throughout the United States. Since student satisfaction and interest in the university show no sign of a decline any time soon, look for circumstances to remain the same for the foreseeable future.

## FINANCIAL AID

*Students should submit:* FAFSA. Priority filing deadline is March 1. *Need-based scholarships/grants offered:* Pell, SEOG, state scholarships/grants, private scholarships, the school's own gift aid. *Loan aid offered:* Direct Subsidized Stafford, Direct Unsubsidized Stafford, Direct PLUS, Federal Perkins, college/university loans from institutional funds. Federal Work-Study Program available. Institutional employment available. Applicants will be notified of awards on a rolling basis. Off-campus job opportunities are good.

## FROM THE ADMISSIONS OFFICE

"The University of Georgia's academic reputation continues to rise, largely on the accomplishments of its best undergraduates. This year, only Harvard, Yale, Brown, and UGA had students selected for the four highly prestigious Rhodes, Marshall, Truman, and Goldwater scholarships. UGA offers a large but friendly campus community in a vibrant yet easygoing college town. To experience the excitement of UGA, most prospective students visit Athens, a 90-minute drive northeast of the Atlanta airport. Contact our Visitors Center for tour information and reservations. Visit our website to request admissions materials and view the weekday schedule of admissions information sessions. The first-year application for admission also serves as the initial application for Honors Program membership, merit scholarships, and Regents Waivers of out-of-state tuition, all highly competitive processes."

### SELECTIVITY
★★★☆

| | |
|---|---|
| Admissions Rating | 85 |
| # of applicants | 12,786 |
| % of applicants accepted | 65 |
| % of acceptees attending | 51 |

### FRESHMAN PROFILE

| | |
|---|---|
| Range SAT Verbal | 550-640 |
| Average SAT Verbal | 604 |
| Range SAT Math | 560-650 |
| Average SAT Math | 611 |
| Range ACT Composite | 24-29 |
| Minimum TOEFL | 213 (CBT) |
| Average HS GPA | 3.7 |

### DEADLINES

| | |
|---|---|
| Early action | 11/1 |
| Regular admission | 2/1 |
| Regular notification | 4/1 |
| Nonfall registration? | yes |

### APPLICANTS ALSO LOOK AT AND OFTEN PREFER
UNC Chapel Hill
U of Virginia
Duke
Wake Forest
Spelman

### AND SOMETIMES PREFER
Georgia Tech
Emory
Vanderbilt
Furman
U of Florida

### AND RARELY PREFER
Georgia Southern
Georgia State
Auburn
Mercer
Clemson
Florida State
U of Tennessee at Knoxville

### FINANCIAL FACTS
★★★★

| | |
|---|---|
| Financial Aid Rating | 90 |
| In-state tuition | $3,208 |
| Ou-of-state tuition | $13,984 |
| Room and board | $5,756 |
| Books and supplies | $700 |
| Required fees | $870 |
| % frosh receiving aid | 27 |
| % undergrads receiving aid | 26 |

# UNIVERSITY OF HAWAII—MANOA

2600 CAMPUS ROAD, SSC ROOM 001, HONOLULU, HI 96822 • ADMISSIONS: 808-956-8975 • FAX: 808-956-4148

## CAMPUS LIFE

| | |
|---|---|
| Quality of Life Rating | 81 |
| Type of school | public |
| Environment | urban |

### STUDENTS
| | |
|---|---|
| Total undergrad enrollment | 12,054 |
| % male/female | 44/56 |
| % from out of state | 17 |
| % from public high school | 67 |
| % live on campus | 18 |
| % African American | 1 |
| % Asian | 77 |
| % Caucasian | 20 |
| % Hispanic | 2 |
| % international | 6 |
| # of countries represented | 77 |

### SURVEY SAYS . . .
Students love Honolulu, HI
Popular college radio
Musical organizations aren't popular
Class discussions are rare
Great off-campus food
Large classes
Ethnic diversity on campus
Unattractive campus
Political activism is (almost) nonexistent
TAs teach lower-level classes

## ACADEMICS

| | |
|---|---|
| Academic Rating | 74 |
| Calendar | semester |
| Student/faculty ratio | 12:1 |
| Profs interesting rating | 73 |
| Profs accessible rating | 76 |
| Avg lab size | 10-19 students |
| Avg reg class size | 10-19 students |

### MOST POPULAR MAJORS
Biology/biological sciences
Psychology
Art/art studies

## STUDENTS SPEAK OUT

### Academics

The University of Hawaii at Manoa, the flagship campus of the University of Hawaii system, is undoubtedly an affordable institution. But don't let this trick you into thinking that its academic offerings are second-rate. UHM offers particularly strong programs in disciplines like tropical agriculture, oceanography, volcanology, and Hawaiian, Asian, and Pacific cultural studies. Still, students on the humanities side of things sometimes feel shortchanged. According to one such student, "Here the sciences get all the money and places like the business/art/economics buildings are a disgrace." The professors here are generally seen as "wonderful" and "knowledgeable"—though it doesn't hurt to "ask around" to find out which professors are particularly outstanding. UHM students also boast that many of their professors have gained "real-life experience" in their fields, which allows them to provide practical insights in the classroom. Professors are criticized, however, because of a two-and-a-half week strike last year that kept profs out of the classrooms—and largely out of touch with students—as they waged a war for more competitive salaries. But with a new president now in charge of things, students are beginning to build renewed confidence in the administration and faculty. "Changes are coming," writes one optimistic student, and these changes "will make the university even better than what it is now."

### Life

Life in general is pretty good at UHM. With terrific tropical weather year-round and easy access to the beach, students have no problem spending their days in the sun. "Seeing as we are in Hawaii, I surf for fun," offers one student. Students also enjoy their parties, though UHM is by no means a party school. *Why not?* you ask. *After all, this is Hawaii.* The answer might be that Manoa is "a commuter school," where you'll meet many older students who don't live on campus, who hold one or two or three steady jobs, or "who are going back to school after raising kids." The school's largely nontraditional student body produces a campus social scene typical of many commuter schools: reasonably active during the week but relatively dead on weekends. So whether it's taking a blanket to the beach for a Monday-morning study session or taking a bottle of booze to the campus apartments for a Friday-night party, students who live on campus here are basically left to their own devices as far as finding fun goes. Aside from parties, the on-campus residents enjoy activities such as volleyball, clubbing, watching movies, and, of course, watching the Pacific sunsets.

### Student Body

When students say that "Aloha spirit" is alive and well at UHM, they mean that the people here are "super friendly" and "laid back" and "easy to get along with." Despite the "easygoing" atmosphere at Manoa, the campus community is not particularly tight. For one thing, UHM "is a commuter-based school," which means that many students leave campus by nightfall. Also, "many of the kids that go to UHM have grown up in Honolulu and all went to high school together and maintain that tightness of high school"—something that students from afar sometimes find problematic. One thing that's admirably noteworthy about this student body is its diversity. While people from different ethnic backgrounds tend to cluster together, the overall exposure to different cultures provides UHM students of all strains "with a great learning experience." One white student tells us that "going to UHM is the first time I have been in the minority. I will walk into a classroom and be the only white girl." Overall, "everyone seems to get along, regardless of race or gender."

580 ■ THE BEST 351 COLLEGES

# UNIVERSITY OF HAWAII—MANOA

FINANCIAL AID: 808-956-7251 • E-MAIL: AR-INFO@HAWAII.EDU • WEBSITE: WWW.UHM.HAWAII.EDU

## ADMISSIONS

*Very important factors considered include:* secondary school record, standardized test scores. *Important factors considered include:* class rank, state residency. *Other factors considered include:* character/personal qualities, essays, extracurricular activities, geographical residence, interview, recommendations, talent/ability. SAT I or ACT required. TOEFL required of all international applicants. High school diploma or GED is required. *High school units required/recommended:* 4 English required, 3 math required, 3 science required, 2 foreign language recommended, 3 social studies required, 4 elective required.

## The Inside Word

A 2.8 high school GPA meets the University's minimum standards for admission. Though preference is given to state residents for admission, in practice there's room for just about any better-than-average student in the freshman class here.

## FINANCIAL AID

*Students should submit:* FAFSA, institution's own financial aid form. The Princeton Review suggests that all financial aid forms be submitted as soon as possible after January 1. *Need-based scholarships/grants offered:* Pell, SEOG, state scholarships/grants, private scholarships, the school's own gift aid, Federal Nursing. *Loan aid offered:* FFEL Subsidized Stafford, FFEL Unsubsidized Stafford, FFEL PLUS, Federal Perkins, Federal Nursing, state loans, college/university loans from institutional funds. Federal Work-Study Program available. Institutional employment available. Applicants will be notified of awards on a rolling basis beginning on or about March 26. Off-campus job opportunities are fair.

### SELECTIVITY
★ ★ ★ ☆

| | |
|---|---:|
| Admissions Rating | 81 |
| # of applicants | 4,565 |
| % of applicants accepted | 71 |
| % of acceptees attending | 51 |

### FRESHMAN PROFILE

| | |
|---|---:|
| Range SAT Verbal | 470-570 |
| Average SAT Verbal | 525 |
| Range SAT Math | 510-610 |
| Average SAT Math | 563 |
| Minimum TOEFL | 500 |
| Average HS GPA | 3.3 |
| % graduated top 10% of class | 23 |
| % graduated top 25% of class | 58 |
| % graduated top 50% of class | 90 |

### DEADLINES

| | |
|---|---:|
| Priority admission | 11/1 |
| Regular admission | 6/1 |
| Nonfall registration? | yes |

### FINANCIAL FACTS
★ ★ ★ ☆

| | |
|---|---:|
| Financial Aid Rating | 84 |
| In-state tuition | $3,312 |
| Out-of-state tuition | $9,792 |
| Room and board | $6,101 |
| Books and supplies | $1,049 |
| Required fees | $152 |
| % frosh receiving aid | 28 |
| % undergrads receiving aid | 30 |
| Avg frosh grant | $3,015 |
| Avg frosh loan | $1,420 |

# UNIVERSITY OF IDAHO

ADMISSIONS OFFICE, MOSCOW, ID 83844-4264 • ADMISSIONS: 208-885-6326 • FAX: 208-885-9119

## CAMPUS LIFE

★ ★ ★ ☆

| | |
|---|---|
| Quality of Life Rating | 84 |
| Type of school | public |
| Environment | rural |

### STUDENTS

| | |
|---|---|
| Total undergrad enrollment | 9,368 |
| % male/female | 54/46 |
| % from out of state | 19 |
| % African American | 1 |
| % Asian | 2 |
| % Caucasian | 88 |
| % Hispanic | 3 |
| % international | 2 |

### SURVEY SAYS . . .
Ethnic diversity on campus
Great on-campus food
Students are religious
Classes are small
No one cheats
Very little beer drinking

## ACADEMICS

| | |
|---|---|
| Academic Rating | 75 |
| Calendar | semester |
| Student/faculty ratio | 19:1 |
| Profs interesting rating | 82 |
| Profs accessible rating | 80 |
| % profs teaching UG courses | 70 |
| % classes taught by TAs | 20 |
| Avg lab size | 10-19 students |
| Avg reg class size | 10-19 students |

## STUDENTS SPEAK OUT

### Academics

With an academic setting that allows students to "grow in all aspects of life," the University of Idaho has earned a reputation as a "great school for a great price." Some students point out that fees are on the rise—as it is at most state universities—but they acknowledge that the administration "can't improve anything when they don't have the money." While the budget is being slashed, students feel that the school "runs smoothly" thanks to the "very organized" administration. The "friendly and helpful staff" helps students access the right people, who are "great once you find what building they've moved to." On the academic front, the electrical engineering program garners praise, though students across departments complain about "not being able to understand foreign teachers and TAs." On the whole, students find professors to be "very personable outside of class and very knowledgeable." Instructors "want to be here" and "really do want us to succeed and understand the material." Students also report that they "really get to know their instructors." One undergraduate tells us, "Learning is fun and comes more easily due to the fact that professors don't act superior. They treat you as an equal." The only hitch seems to be problems registering for courses: "I could only get into one class toward my major [during a certain semester]," writes a junior in visual communications.

### Life

In the small town of Moscow, Idaho, students report, "there's not much to do but hang out with friends." One undergraduate notes a lusting among his cohorts for a more urban setting: "People are generally happy but want to live in a larger city." Many people seem perfectly content, however, in an "atmosphere that allows the students to be active within the community." Other mellowed-out students concur, with the sentiment "I like to have a laid-back lifestyle, and I am able to do it here." Certain students wish for "more activities to do off campus," but others gladly forgo cheesy techno clubs for the abundant outdoor opportunities: hiking, camping, fishing, and hunting in the area are favorite pastimes. Students use multiple exclamation points when expressing their joy derived from the campus' cushy student recreation center, replete with a new climbing wall. Idaho students can often be found "working out or playing sports for fun," and devoted fans flock to football and basketball games. Students also get out to see "local bands and shows at the Red Hawk," or they "go out to movies or find a party." Fraternities manage to facilitate a steady flow of your standard ragers, and one member diplomatically points out, "Greek life is fun, but I don't know what non-Greeks think about it." Overall, the campus and surrounding environs amount to "a unique college experience" with a "a very homey feel."

### Student Body

The most common descriptors of the student population at Idaho would have to be "laid-back" and "easygoing." Among these "down-to-earth" kids, people "don't have to try to fit in." Some students do perceive, however, "a wall between the Greek system and other students," largely based on the sentiment that "some Greeks have a big ego problem on this campus. So do a lot of athletes." This kind of tension makes some students feel that UI is "just like high school all over again." Luckily, undergraduates report more harmony between other groups. "I believe that most students, regardless of race, religion, or year, get along splendidly." Though some students say, "There are students from everywhere, and there is a lot of diversity around our campus," others wish for "more minority and cultural group recognition." Because the university "isn't too big or too small," students report, "everyone gets to know each other pretty well." Overall, undergraduates find their peers "easy to get along with and work with" as well as "very cheerful and friendly."

582 ■ THE BEST 351 COLLEGES

# UNIVERSITY OF IDAHO

FINANCIAL AID: 208-885-6312 • E-MAIL: NSS@UIDAHO.EDU • WEBSITE: WWW.UIDAHO.EDU

## ADMISSIONS
*Very important factors considered include:* secondary school record, standardized test scores. SAT I or ACT required; SAT I preferred. High school diploma or GED is required. *High school units required/recommended:* 15 total required; 4 English required, 3 math required, 3 science required, 1 science lab required, 1 foreign language required, 2 social studies required, 1 elective required.

### The Inside Word
Idaho's admissions process is typical of large universities and easy to deal with—it doesn't get any more straightforward than this. A small number of college-age students in Idaho means out-of-staters face little in the way of any constraints above and beyond in-state standards.

## FINANCIAL AID
The Princeton Review suggests that all financial aid forms be submitted as soon as possible after January 1. Federal Work-Study Program available. Institutional employment available. Applicants will be notified of awards on a rolling basis. Off-campus job opportunities are good.

## FROM THE ADMISSIONS OFFICE
"The University of Idaho combines the best of both worlds. We are the major research university in the state of Idaho, the state's land grant university, and a safe, residential environment. Moscow's small size and the supportive surrounding community provide the ideal atmosphere for a total learning experience."

---

### SELECTIVITY

| | |
|---|---:|
| Admissions Rating | 74 |
| # of applicants | 3,936 |
| % of applicants accepted | 82 |
| % of acceptees attending | 53 |

#### FRESHMAN PROFILE
| | |
|---|---:|
| Average SAT Verbal | 549 |
| Average SAT Math | 559 |
| Average ACT Composite | 23 |
| Average HS GPA | 3.4 |
| % graduated top 10% of class | 18 |
| % graduated top 25% of class | 45 |
| % graduated top 50% of class | 76 |

#### DEADLINES
| | |
|---|---:|
| Regular admission | 8/1 |
| Nonfall registration? | yes |

#### APPLICANTS ALSO LOOK AT AND SOMETIMES PREFER
Boise State
Washington State

### FINANCIAL FACTS

| | |
|---|---:|
| Financial Aid Rating | 80 |
| Out-of-state tuition | $6,720 |
| Room and board | $6,550 |
| Books and supplies | $1,188 |
| Required fees | $3,044 |

---

THE BEST 351 COLLEGES ■ 583

# UNIVERSITY OF ILLINOIS—URBANA-CHAMPAIGN

901 WEST ILLINOIS STREET, URBANA, IL 61801 • ADMISSIONS: 217-333-0302 • FAX: 217-333-9758

## CAMPUS LIFE

| | |
|---|---|
| Quality of Life Rating | 75 |
| Type of school | public |
| Environment | urban |

### STUDENTS

| | |
|---|---|
| Total undergrad enrollment | 28,750 |
| % male/female | 52/48 |
| % from out of state | 7 |
| % live on campus | 30 |
| % in (# of) fraternities | 17 (55) |
| % in (# of) sororities | 22 (30) |
| % African American | 7 |
| % Asian | 14 |
| % Caucasian | 72 |
| % Hispanic | 6 |
| % international | 2 |
| # of countries represented | 51 |

### SURVEY SAYS . . .
Frats and sororities dominate social scene
Everyone loves the Fighting Illini
Lots of beer drinking
Ethnic diversity on campus
Student publications are popular
Students are cliquish
Students don't like Urbana, IL
Students are not very happy
Lousy food on campus
Very little drug use

## ACADEMICS

| | |
|---|---|
| Academic Rating | 82 |
| Calendar | semester |
| Student/faculty ratio | 15:1 |
| Profs interesting rating | 90 |
| Profs accessible rating | 90 |
| % profs teaching UG courses | 89 |
| Avg lab size | 20-29 students |
| Avg reg class size | 20-29 students |

### MOST POPULAR MAJORS
Biology/biological sciences
Psychology

## STUDENTS SPEAK OUT

### Academics
Renowned research center University of Illinois—Urbana-Champaign offers students a multitude of options and opportunities, especially in its nationally acclaimed engineering and business programs. "The size is a huge benefit because of all of the resources available," students agree. Yet as at most big schools, quality of instruction varies widely. "Like everywhere, you have to take the bad with the good," explains one student. "I think that the good outweighs the bad for the most part here." Undergrads point out that "many TAs do the 'real' teaching while the professor just makes the exams," and while some feel that "most of TAs are not experienced and do not teach adequately," others feel just as strongly that "teaching assistants have a very unfair reputation. I have found that the best teachers are TAs. They are only a few years older than you and are still students, and therefore empathetic. They also understand the material very well." Many report that "the high number of TAs and even profs who don't have the best grasp of English, however brilliant they may be, can make things unnecessarily difficult." Nearly all would warn that "the school is large. If you don't have the presence of mind to get the stuff you [need to] get done taken care of, no one else will. I would never expect extra attention from the faculty here." In terms of administrative duties, expect "huge spools of red tape. I put in a petition in October, and I still haven't heard back. It's now the end of February."

### Life
Many Illini tell us that they "did not know it before coming here, but the U of I is a huge party school." The campus is "very Greek; it seems like everyone is in a fraternity or sorority." Students mostly like to party at the school's numerous bars, each of which allows students 19 and over to enter (although theoretically the drinking age is 21). Writes one student, "There's not much to do in the cornfields of Champaign-Urbana [sic], but the 20-plus bars on campus really take care of that problem. Most people go out on weekends, to the bars, house/apartment parties, and after-hours parties at fraternities. During the week, many people go out as well. The weekend definitely starts on Thursday, though." Agrees another undergrad, "Nightlife for most consists of attending the campus bars. Period." Nonpartiers, including many in the school's sizeable religious contingent, "often congregate in their dorm rooms with a movie, a bunch of people from their floor, and pizza from Papa John's, a traditional campus establishment. There are a million organizations to be involved in," but according to one student, "At least a third of them are religiously affiliated, though, so unless you plan on joining every church on campus, that narrows it down a bit." Sports "seem to play a bigger role of importance than even academics, unfortunately. I guess it's pretty typical of a Big 10 university."

### Student Body
"It seems like every kind of group you can imagine is represented" at U of I. "There are the Greeks, there are the athletes—either club, intramural, or Division I athletes who hang out with each other 24/7—there are the conservatives, the nerds, the ethnic groups—Hispanic, Black, Indian, Asian, European, etc.—the goths, the hippies, and on and on the list goes." Many agree that "there is not much meshing of the different ethnic and social groups" on campus. Students are united on game day, though; writes one undergrad, "For a campus of over 30,000 students, it's a pretty tight bunch. Everyone is friendly. Plus, there's a lot of school spirit. During the football season everyone is wearing orange and blue. There's definitely a sense of pride in being part of the University of Illinois."

584 ■ THE BEST 351 COLLEGES

# UNIVERSITY OF ILLINOIS—URBANA-CHAMPAIGN

FINANCIAL AID: 217-333-0100 • E-MAIL: ADMISSIONS@OAR.UIUC.EDU • WEBSITE: WWW.UIUC.EDU

## ADMISSIONS

*Very important factors considered include:* class rank, secondary school record, standardized test scores. *Important factors considered include:* essays, minority status, talent/ability. *Other factors considered include:* character/personal qualities, extracurricular activities, geographical residence, recommendations, state residency, volunteer work, work experience. SAT I or ACT required. TOEFL required of all international applicants. High school diploma or GED is required. *High school units required/recommended:* 4 English required, 3 math required, 2 science required, 2 science lab required, 2 foreign language required, 2 social studies required, 2 elective required.

## The Inside Word

Few candidates are deceived by Illinois' relatively high acceptance rate; the university has a well-deserved reputation for expecting applicants to be strong students, and those who aren't usually don't bother to apply. Despite a jumbo applicant pool, the admissions office reports that every candidate is individually reviewed, which deserves mention as rare in universities of this size.

## FINANCIAL AID

*Students should submit:* FAFSA. Regular filing deadline is March 15. The Princeton Review suggests that all financial aid forms be submitted as soon as possible after January 1. *Need-based scholarships/grants offered:* Pell, SEOG, state scholarships/grants, private scholarships, the school's own gift aid. *Loan aid offered:* Direct Subsidized Stafford, Direct Unsubsidized Stafford, Direct PLUS, Federal Perkins, college/university loans from institutional funds. Federal Work-Study Program available. Institutional employment available. Applicants will be notified of awards on or about April 1. Off-campus job opportunities are excellent.

## FROM THE ADMISSIONS OFFICE

"The campus has been aptly described as a collection of neighborhoods constituting a diverse and vibrant city. The neighborhoods are of many types: students and faculty within a department; people sharing a room or house; the members of a professional organization, a service club, or an intramural team; or simply people who, starting out as strangers sharing a class or a study lounge or a fondness for a weekly film series, have become friends. And the city of this description is the university itself—a rich cosmopolitan environment constructed by students and faculty to meet their educational and personal goals. The quality of intellectual life parallels that of other great universities, and many faculty and students who have their choice of top institutions select Illinois over its peers. While such choices are based often on the quality of individual programs of study, another crucial factor is the 'tone' of the campus life that is linked with the virtues of midwestern culture. There is an informality and a near-absence of pretension which, coupled with a tradition of commitment to excellence, creates an atmosphere that is unique among the finest institutions."

## SELECTIVITY

| | |
|---|---|
| Admissions Rating | 85 |
| # of applicants | 19,930 |
| % of applicants accepted | 62 |
| % of acceptees attending | 51 |

### FRESHMAN PROFILE

| | |
|---|---|
| Range SAT Verbal | 550-670 |
| Average SAT Verbal | 613 |
| Range SAT Math | 600-720 |
| Average SAT Math | 660 |
| Range ACT Composite | 25-30 |
| Average ACT Composite | 27 |
| Minimum TOEFL | 550 |
| % graduated top 10% of class | 55 |
| % graduated top 25% of class | 86 |
| % graduated top 50% of class | 99 |

### DEADLINES

| | |
|---|---|
| Regular admission | 1/1 |
| Nonfall registration? | yes |

### APPLICANTS ALSO LOOK AT
**AND OFTEN PREFER**
Northwestern U.
U. Michigan—Ann Arbor
U. Wisconsin—Madison
Purdue
Washington U.
**AND SOMETIMES PREFER**
U. Michigan—Ann Arbor
Northern Illinois
Miami U.
**AND RARELY PREFER**
U. Kentucky
Loyola U. Chicago
Illinois State
Southern Illinois—Edwardsville

## FINANCIAL FACTS

| | |
|---|---|
| Financial Aid Rating | 80 |
| In-state tuition | $5,226 |
| Out-of-state tuition | $13,046 |
| Room and board | $6,090 |
| Books and supplies | $740 |
| Required fees | $1,304 |
| % frosh receiving aid | 40 |
| % undergrads receiving aid | 38 |

THE BEST 351 COLLEGES ■ 585

# UNIVERSITY OF IOWA

107 CALVIN HALL, IOWA CITY, IA 52242 • ADMISSIONS: 319-335-3847 • FAX: 319-333-1535

## CAMPUS LIFE

| | |
|---|---|
| Quality of Life Rating | 85 |
| Type of school | public |
| Environment | suburban |

### STUDENTS

| | |
|---|---|
| Total undergrad enrollment | 20,487 |
| % male/female | 45/55 |
| % from out of state | 33 |
| % from public high school | 89 |
| % live on campus | 28 |
| % in (# of) fraternities | 12 (23) |
| % in (# of) sororities | 13 (17) |
| % African American | 2 |
| % Asian | 3 |
| % Caucasian | 88 |
| % Hispanic | 2 |
| % international | 1 |
| # of countries represented | 122 |

### SURVEY SAYS...
Lots of beer drinking
Hard liquor is popular
(Almost) everyone smokes
Everyone loves the Hawkeyes
Great computer facilities
Students love Iowa City, IA
Great off-campus food
Student newspaper is popular
Campus is beautiful
Students are happy

## ACADEMICS

| | |
|---|---|
| Academic Rating | 77 |
| Calendar | semester |
| Student/faculty ratio | 15:1 |
| % profs teaching UG courses | 100 |
| Avg lab size | 20-29 students |
| Avg reg class size | 10-19 students |

### MOST POPULAR MAJORS
Business administration/management
Communications studies/speech
communication and rhetoric
Psychology

## STUDENTS SPEAK OUT

### Academics

Applicants to a big state school like Iowa sometimes fear "drowning in general education classes," but many current Hawkeyes point out, "You can make it personal" with some effort, since "not very many professors have a line of students waiting to hang out at office hours, even though they'd like [them] to." Professors "have a passion for the material," and most complement that with "the passion to teach the material." As at most large state universities, certain undergraduates feel their instructors stay "so buried in their research that they probably wouldn't come to class if a waiting student hadn't called them on their cell." Other students point out that "professors have a presence, but the school does rely on teaching assistants." On the whole, however, "most professors... attempt to present lectures in an interesting forum." Respondents single out the writing department as "highly regarded," and tout the honors program as "the ticket to ride for anyone with academic concern." Administrators receive high marks from students, who say they are "readily accessible and extremely supportive—so much so that it borders on mentoring and parental advocacy." Some students, however, see the "very parental" administration as their mortal foe, claiming that they "work with the city council on anti-student policies." Complaints also pop up surrounding the ongoing tuition hikes. In general, however, the campus "seems to run very smoothly," and the people in charge appear "attuned to students' opinions." Overall, the university offers students "a diverse and liberal learning environment" where everyone can "prepare [a] future in an atmosphere of fun and opportunity."

### Life

Social life revolves around three things at Iowa: the downtown bars, Hawkeye football, and Christian groups. The "beautiful town" of Iowa City "has a lot to offer," mainly in the form of bars, "packed to capacity every night of the week." The resulting scene is "quite crazy, and most everyone seems to enjoy it." The campus' location right in the thick of things allows the "weekend to start on Tuesday and end on Sunday" even though the on-campus sororities and fraternities are dry. Some people resist the pull and take advantage of the "good restaurants and coffee shops on or near campus." Other alcohol-free options include "improv theater and musical events"; it seems "there's always some sort of live performance going on here." Hawkeye pride abounds—"It's all about sports"—and students congregate for rowdy tailgating sessions on game days during football season. Aside from drinking and cheering, many in the student body keep "involved in campus Christian groups, like, 24-7." Put it all together, and you've got a school that "offers a true big-time college experience in a very unique and exciting town."

### Student Body

In the large, somewhat diverse milieu of the University of Iowa, students say, "You can be whoever you want to be and still have a big group of friends." Though many call it "your average white-dominated midwestern university," numerous students claim their school is "surprisingly open-minded, considering the location." One student expands, "The school's reputation of diversity is helped tremendously by the graduate student population." Also, the diversity lies in "social backgrounds rather than racial backgrounds." People may come from the Iowa sticks or the urban spread of Chicago, but the school still "lacks a good social atmosphere for minorities." Several surveys point out the university's intent to attract more students of color. On-campus groups do provide a framework for discussing "various ethnicities, sexual orientations, religious backgrounds, etc." Even if most people are "Christian, middle-class Dave Matthews fans who love the bars," they also share the common traits of "friendliness, enthusiasm, and openness."

# UNIVERSITY OF IOWA

FINANCIAL AID: 319-335-1450 • E-MAIL: ADMISSIONS@UIOWA.EDU • WEBSITE: WWW.UIOWA.EDU

## ADMISSIONS

*Very important factors considered include:* class rank, secondary school record, standardized test scores. *Other factors considered include:* alumni/ae relation, minority status, state residency, talent/ability. SAT I or ACT required. TOEFL required of all international applicants. High school diploma or GED is required. *High school units required/recommended:* 15 total required; 4 English required, 3 math required, 3 science required, 2 foreign language required, 4 foreign language recommended, 3 social studies required.

### The Inside Word

Iowa's admissions process is none too personal, but on the other hand, candidates know exactly what is necessary to get admitted. The majority of applicants are fairly good students, most get in, and a lot choose to attend. That helps make Iowa the solid academic community it is.

## FINANCIAL AID

*Students should submit:* FAFSA, institution's own financial aid form. No deadline for regular filing. The Princeton Review suggests that all financial aid forms be submitted as soon as possible after January 1. *Need-based scholarships/grants offered:* Pell, SEOG, state scholarships/grants, private scholarships, the school's own gift aid, Federal Nursing. *Loan aid offered:* Direct Subsidized Stafford, Direct Unsubsidized Stafford, Direct PLUS, Federal Perkins, Federal Nursing, college/university loans from institutional funds. Federal Work-Study Program available. Institutional employment available. Applicants will be notified of awards on a rolling basis beginning on or about March 1. Off-campus job opportunities are excellent.

## FROM THE ADMISSIONS OFFICE

"The University of Iowa has strong programs in the creative arts, being the home of the first Writers Workshop and now housing the world-renowned International Writing Program. It also has strong programs in communication studies, journalism, political science, English, and psychology, and was the birthplace of the discipline of speech pathology and audiology. It offers excellent programs in the basic health sciences and health care programs, led by the top-ranked College of Medicine and the closely associated University Hospitals and Clinics."

## SELECTIVITY

| | |
|---|---|
| Admissions Rating | 80 |
| # of applicants | 13,079 |
| % of applicants accepted | 84 |
| % of acceptees attending | 38 |

### FRESHMAN PROFILE

| | |
|---|---|
| Range SAT Verbal | 520-650 |
| Range SAT Math | 540-670 |
| Range ACT Composite | 22-27 |
| Minimum TOEFL | 530 |
| Average HS GPA | 3.5 |
| % graduated top 10% of class | 21 |
| % graduated top 25% of class | 50 |
| % graduated top 50% of class | 89 |

### DEADLINES

| | |
|---|---|
| Regular admission | 4/1 |
| Nonfall registration? | yes |
| Priority Application | 2/1 |

### APPLICANTS ALSO LOOK AT
**AND OFTEN PREFER**
Northwestern U.
U. Illinois—Urbana-Champaign
**AND SOMETIMES PREFER**
Iowa State
U. Northern Iowa
Indiana U.—Bloomington
Drake
Grinnell
**AND RARELY PREFER**
Illinois State
U. Wisconsin—Madison
Cornell Coll.
U. Missouri—Rolla

## FINANCIAL FACTS

| | |
|---|---|
| Financial Aid Rating | 82 |
| In-state tuition | $4,342 |
| Out-of-state tuition | $14,634 |
| Room and board | $5,930 |
| Books and supplies | $840 |
| Required fees | $651 |
| % frosh receiving aid | 38 |
| % undergrads receiving aid | 42 |
| Avg frosh grant | $1,650 |
| Avg frosh loan | $2,250 |

# UNIVERSITY OF KANSAS

OFFICE OF ADMISSIONS AND SCHOLARSHIPS, 1502 IOWA STREET, LAWRENCE, KS 66045 • ADMISSIONS: 785-864-3911

## CAMPUS LIFE

| Quality of Life Rating | 83 |
|---|---|
| Type of school | public |
| Environment | urban |

### STUDENTS
| | |
|---|---|
| Total undergrad enrollment | 20,605 |
| % male/female | 48/52 |
| % from out of state | 33 |
| % live on campus | 18 |
| % in (# of) fraternities | 15 (25) |
| % in (# of) sororities | 18 (18) |
| % African American | 3 |
| % Asian | 4 |
| % Caucasian | 83 |
| % Hispanic | 3 |
| % international | 7 |
| # of countries represented | 118 |

### SURVEY SAYS . . .
Everyone loves the Jayhawks
Students love Lawrence, KS
Frats and sororities dominate social scene
Great off-campus food
Large classes
Registration is a pain
Student publications are popular
Theater is unpopular
Lab facilities are great

## ACADEMICS

| Academic Rating | 75 |
|---|---|
| Calendar | semester |
| Student/faculty ratio | 15:1 |
| Profs interesting rating | 92 |
| Profs accessible rating | 95 |
| % profs teaching UG courses | 100 |
| % classes taught by TAs | 24 |
| Avg lab size | 10-19 students |
| Avg reg class size | 20-29 students |

### MOST POPULAR MAJORS
Biology/biological sciences
Psychology
Business administration/management

## STUDENTS SPEAK OUT

### Academics
The University of Kansas produces students satisfied with their education. Professors are always accessible. According to a biology major, "All professors have office hours and most offer workshops making them accessible to KU students." Professors are "usually at the top of their field," writes one music major. The key to being successful at KU, advises a sophomore, is to "take advantage of the resources available (i.e. TAs, libraries, instructors)." The professors make an excellent impression on first-year students; as one first-year architecture student gushes, "Every teacher I have had or met I want to chill with on the weekends, but sometimes it just doesn't work out." Dangit. While students like their professors, they are less enamored of the administration. Reports are mixed concerning the undergrad academic experience, as one student will gush, "Academically, the University of Kansas exceeded my expectations," while another will declare, "The University of Kansas will always be a good school for average kids from large midwestern cities."

### Life
"Lawrence is a rather alternative, obscure community, typical of a college town. The college students are the number one priority here." Students note that both the campus and the town are beautiful. A senior journalism major happily comments that "the town and university [are] very liberal and open-minded. Anyone is willing to hear you speak your mind as long as you can back it up." Students appreciate the different opportunities that life in Lawrence provides. "If you're going to stay in and do work, that's cool. If you're going to go to the bars, that's cool. If you're going to stay in and party, or go to a house party, everything is cool and fun to do." A sophomore sociology major adds that it isn't difficult to find a party in certain off-campus neighborhoods, as "you can walk down the party streets and smell the alcohol." Some believe that the city can be "a little boring" if one doesn't party. The university's basketball team is a perennial national powerhouse, and students wish that the football team would be as successful.

### Student Body
As would be expected of a large, state university in middle America, students at the University of Kansas are "typical Midwest: middle-class, friendly, laid-back, and white." Most students agree that the university needs more diversity, "both ethnically and from rural areas." There is little mixing between social groups. As one junior history major puts it, "Frat boys hang out with frat boys. Nader lovers hang out with earth-friendly types. Goths chill with goths. It's segregated but united by alcohol." Still, students agree that most of their classmates are "friendly and supportive." One first-year student testifies that his life has been altered by his classmates. "The people here are incredible. I was an edgy person when I came here, but everyone's so courteous that it changes you." A sophomore sums up life at the University of Kansas: "Everyone here is friendly. You can literally just say hi to someone on campus and they will be more than delighted to respond [in a] friendly [manner]."

# UNIVERSITY OF KANSAS

Fax: 785-864-5017 • Financial Aid: 785-864-4700 • E-mail: adm@ku.edu • Website: www.ku.edu

## ADMISSIONS

*Very important factors considered include:* class rank, secondary school record, standardized test scores. *Important factors considered include:* geographical residence, state residency. SAT I or ACT required. High school diploma or GED is required. *High school units required/recommended:* 14 total required; 17 total recommended; 4 English required, 3 math required, 4 math recommended, 3 science required (1 year of science must be chemistry or physics), 2 foreign language recommended, 3 social studies required, 1 computer technology required.

### The Inside Word

A no-sweat approach to admissions. So who gets denied? Weak out-of-state candidates, who are apparently in large supply in the Kansas applicant pool. But in-state students will have to face the music with new admissions standards starting in 2001.

## FINANCIAL AID

*Students should submit:* FAFSA. Regular filing deadline is March 1. The Princeton Review suggests that all financial aid forms be submitted as soon as possible after January 1. *Need-based scholarships/grants offered:* Pell, SEOG, state scholarships/grants, private scholarships, the school's own gift aid. *Loan aid offered:* Direct Subsidized Stafford, Direct Unsubsidized Stafford, Direct PLUS, Federal Perkins, college/university loans from institutional funds. Federal Work-Study Program available. Institutional employment available. Applicants will be notified of awards on a rolling basis beginning on or about April 1. Off-campus job opportunities are excellent.

## FROM THE ADMISSIONS OFFICE

"The University of Kansas has a long and distinguished tradition for academic excellence. Outstanding students from Kansas and across the nation are attracted to KU because of its strong academic reputation, beautiful campus, affordable cost of education, and contagious school spirit. KU provides students extraordinary opportunities in honors programs, research, internships, and study abroad. The university is located in Lawrence (40 minutes from Kansas City), a community of 80,000 regarded as one of the nation's best small cities for its arts scene, live music, and historic downtown."

---

### SELECTIVITY

| | |
|---|---|
| Admissions Rating | 81 |
| # of applicants | 9,573 |
| % of applicants accepted | 67 |
| % of acceptees attending | 63 |
| # accepting a place on wait list | 175 |
| % admitted from wait list | 71 |

### FRESHMAN PROFILE

| | |
|---|---|
| Range ACT Composite | 21-27 |
| Average ACT Composite | 24 |
| Average HS GPA | 3.4 |
| % graduated top 10% of class | 28 |
| % graduated top 25% of class | 56 |
| % graduated top 50% of class | 87 |

### DEADLINES

| | |
|---|---|
| Priority admission | 1/15 |
| Regular admission | 4/1 |
| Regular notification | rolling |
| Nonfall registration? | yes |

### APPLICANTS ALSO LOOK AT AND OFTEN PREFER
U of Notre Dame
Duke U

### AND SOMETIMES PREFER
U of Nebraska
U of Missouri at Columbia
U of Missouri at Kansas City
Kansas State
Wichita State
U of Colorado at Boulder

### AND RARELY PREFER
U of Illinois at Urbana-Champaign
Colorado State

### FINANCIAL FACTS

| | |
|---|---|
| Financial Aid Rating | 81 |
| In-state tuition | $2,921 |
| Out-of-state tuition | $10,124 |
| Room and board | $4,822 |
| Books and supplies | $750 |
| Required fees | $563 |
| % frosh receiving aid | 44 |
| % undergrads receiving aid | 46 |
| Avg frosh grant | $3,777 |
| Avg frosh loan | $2,502 |

# UNIVERSITY OF KENTUCKY

100 FUNKHOUSER BUILDING, LEXINGTON, KY 40506 • ADMISSIONS: 859-257-2000 • FAX: 859-257-3823

## CAMPUS LIFE

| | |
|---|---|
| Quality of Life Rating | 83 |
| Type of school | public |
| Environment | urban |

### STUDENTS
| | |
|---|---|
| Total undergrad enrollment | 17,830 |
| % male/female | 48/52 |
| % from out of state | 17 |
| % live on campus | 25 |
| % in (# of) fraternities | 15 (19) |
| % in (# of) sororities | 18 (16) |
| % African American | 5 |
| % Asian | 2 |
| % Caucasian | 91 |
| % Hispanic | 1 |
| % international | 1 |
| # of countries represented | 113 |

### SURVEY SAYS . . .
Everyone loves the Wildcats
Great library
(Almost) everyone smokes
Student newspaper is popular
Lots of beer drinking
Great computer facilities
Great off-campus food
Hard liquor is popular
Frats and sororities dominate social scene

## ACADEMICS

| | |
|---|---|
| Academic Rating | 77 |
| Calendar | semester |
| Student/faculty ratio | 16:1 |
| % profs teaching UG courses | 76 |
| % classes taught by TAs | 24 |
| Avg reg class size | 20-29 students |

## STUDENTS SPEAK OUT

### Academics

Most students choose UK for its "fun, laid-back lifestyle, blended nicely with an educational experience." For the most part, they get what they came for. Some concede that "the academic experience is very impersonal. You are not given the attention sometimes needed due to class size." "As in every large state university, it is easy to get lost with 30,000 other students in the mix. If you are not a proactive student, the likelihood of you succeeding to get out of here in four years is slim to none." They also report that as in "any big school, you have teachers that care and want to help you learn, and you also have professors that don't give a [expletive] about you, or if you learn, as long as they get paid." And since math and science figure so prominently here, it should come as no surprise that "many of the teachers and the TAs that teach labs and classes are foreign, and that's fine. But when their English is not good enough for a class composed primarily of English-speaking students, this is a serious problem." Despite these drawbacks, students are generally happy here: the academic experience meets their expectations. Plus, many here feel that "the current administration (and especially the current president) have done much to improve the campus for students." Undergraduates are thus hopeful about the university's future.

### Life

"Life at UK is very dominated by sports," students here agree. Men's varsity football and hockey (a club team) are both well supported, but "basketball reigns supreme. Basketball games in the state of Kentucky are a way of life. If this is news to you, maybe UK isn't the school you want to think about." Undergrads "spend long nights at the ticket lottery just to get tickets to [basketball] games, which are always sold out." On game day, the night's match-ups are just about all anyone on campus discusses. As game time approaches, students gather for pregame parties, then head to Rupp Arena to shout their heads off. While sports are central to UK life, they aren't the alpha and omega. Undergrads tell us that "there is a very popular Greek life"; that "student organizations are popular, with about 300 official clubs"; and that "student government is trying to bring more campus activities than there used to be." "A large number of students also like to do outdoor activities like rock climbing and camping." Hometown Lexington has "lots of excellent restaurants . . . many theaters, several bowling alleys, a roller-skating rink, ice skating, mini golf—pretty much any activity you can think of, you can probably find it nearby." Students report that drinking is a popular pastime despite the enforced dry-campus policy. This policy, students inform us, encourages them "to party off campus." Few here report any difficulty accessing alcohol, but most agree that the university and town do their best to make drinking a hassle: "Cops around here are not so nice; they bust parties all the time," gripes one student.

### Student Body

"Most UK students are friendly natives who share the same southern values and get along very well," undergrads here report. Adds one student, "There are a lot of standard-issue fraternity guys and sorority girls. I can't go ten feet without seeing a girl who completely dresses up for class like it's a fashion show." Still, because of the school's immensity, many feel that "there is no 'typical student' at UK. There are many different types of students here; however, the different types don't usually mix together. Everyone has a niche on campus and they are all separate." Although there are pockets of hard workers scattered throughout the university, the average student here "studies lightly Sunday through Wednesday and parties hard Thursday through Saturday."

# UNIVERSITY OF KENTUCKY

FINANCIAL AID: 859-257-3172 • E-MAIL: ADMISSIO@UKY.EDU • WEBSITE: WWW.UKY.EDU

## ADMISSIONS

*Very important factors considered include:* secondary school record, standardized test scores. *Important factors considered include:* extracurricular activities, volunteer work, community involvement. *Other factors considered include:* character/personal qualities and optional essay. SAT I or ACT required. TOEFL required of all international applicants. High school diploma or GED is required.

### The Inside Word

High volume of applications has more to do with Kentucky's selectivity than any other factor. Given the recent successes of the Wildcats in NCAA basketball, more apps are likely to be on the way.

## FINANCIAL AID

*Students should submit:* FAFSA. The Princeton Review suggests that all financial aid forms be submitted as soon as possible after January 1. *Need-based scholarships/grants offered:* Pell, SEOG, state scholarships/grants, private scholarships, the school's own gift aid. *Loan aid offered:* Federal Perkins, Federal Nursing. Federal Work-Study Program available. Institutional employment available. Applicants will be notified of awards on a rolling basis beginning on or about May 1. Off-campus job opportunities are excellent.

## FROM THE ADMISSIONS OFFICE

"The University of Kentucky offers you an outstanding learning environment and quality instruction through its excellent faculty. Of the 1,892 full-time faculty, 98 percent hold the doctorate degree or the highest degree in their field of study. Many are nationally and internationally known for their research, distinguished teaching, and scholarly service to Kentucky, the nation, and the world. UK's scholars (students, faculty, and alumni) have been honored by Nobel, Pulitzer, Rhodes, Fulbright, Guggenheim, and Grammy Awards, and most recently the Metropolitan Opera and the Marshall Foundation. Yet, with a student/teacher ratio of only 16:1, UK faculty are accessible and willing to answer your questions and discuss your interests."

### SELECTIVITY

| | |
|---|---:|
| Admissions Rating | 79 |
| # of applicants | 8,879 |
| % of applicants accepted | 82 |
| % of acceptees attending | 51 |

### FRESHMAN PROFILE

| | |
|---|---:|
| Range ACT Composite | 22-27 |
| Average ACT Composite | 25 |
| Minimum TOEFL | 527 |

### DEADLINES

| | |
|---|---:|
| Priority admission | 2/15 |
| Regular admission | 2/15 |
| Nonfall registration? | yes |

### APPLICANTS ALSO LOOK AT AND OFTEN PREFER
Centre Coll.
Transylvania
Miami University
Indiana University

### AND SOMETIMES PREFER
U. Tennessee—Knoxville
Eastern Kentucky
U. Louisville
Western Kentucky
Bellarmine

### AND RARELY PREFER
U. Illinois—Urbana-Champaign
Purdue U.—West Lafayette
Ohio State—Columbus
Florida State
U. Florida

### FINANCIAL FACTS

| | |
|---|---:|
| Financial Aid Rating | 90 |
| In-state tuition | $3,480 |
| Out-of-state tuition | $10,032 |
| Room and board | $4,050 |
| Books and supplies | $600 |
| Required fees | $495 |
| % frosh receiving aid | 32 |
| % undergrads receiving aid | 34 |
| Avg frosh grant | $3,525 |
| Avg frosh loan | $3,769 |

# THE UNIVERSITY OF MAINE

5713 CHADBOURNE HALL, ORONO, ME 04469-5713 • ADMISSIONS: 207-581-1561 • FAX: 207-581-1213

## CAMPUS LIFE

★ ★ ☆ ☆

| Quality of Life Rating | 73 |
|---|---|
| Type of school | public |
| Environment | rural |

### STUDENTS
| Total undergrad enrollment | 8,817 |
|---|---|
| % male/female | 48/52 |
| % from out of state | 14 |
| % live on campus | 43 |
| % African American | 1 |
| % Asian | 1 |
| % Caucasian | 95 |
| % Hispanic | 1 |
| % international | 2 |
| # of countries represented | 73 |

### SURVEY SAYS . . .
Everyone loves the Black Bears
Students aren't religious
Lots of beer drinking
High cost of living
Class discussions are rare
Large classes
Great computer facilities
Campus difficult to get around
Campus is beautiful
Lousy food on campus

## ACADEMICS

| Academic Rating | 71 |
|---|---|
| Calendar | semester |
| Student/faculty ratio | 15:1 |
| Profs interesting rating | 91 |
| Profs accessible rating | 94 |
| % profs teaching UG courses | 76 |
| % classes taught by TAs | 6 |
| Avg lab size | 10-19 students |
| Avg reg class size | 20-29 students |

### MOST POPULAR MAJORS
Business administration/management
Education
Engineering

## STUDENTS SPEAK OUT

### Academics
The University of Maine is academic nirvana for any student looking to turn a love of the outdoors into a career. Top-ranked programs in wildlife ecology and forestry, as well as a major called Parks, Recreation, and Tourism, turn out the future park rangers and conservation scientists of America. "It is a nurturing and comfortable atmosphere for learning with intelligent, caring professors," writes a sophomore about the English department. Disagreeing, another student warns, "Don't come to U. Maine if you want one-on-one attention," referring to "huge classes" typical to freshman year students. A call for "higher academic standards" is a common sentiment; a first-year complains, "They shouldn't have graduate students teaching classes," and a senior recalls, "My advisor did nothing to help advise me." In a fair summary, one student writes that his course work has been, "challenging, tiring, inspiring, and boring all rolled into one semester." On the administrative side, there's concern that students are treated "like second-class citizens." Plus, "relations between the president and the student body are strained," a women's studies major reports. But for most attendees, the bottom line is that "you get your money's worth in terms of tuition and living costs."

### Life
Smack in the middle of the "Vacation Land" state, University of Maine students hit both the hiking trails and the bottle for diversion. A native New Yorker says going to school with outdoorsy types has exposed her to a "much healthier lifestyle, socially, mentally, physically, and environmentally." But a freshman observes, "Since we live in Maine, the only thing to do is party. Every night." Cheering on Black Bear teams, especially in hockey, is a rabid obsession, to the point that many students feel the school should "focus on students, not athletics." For nonvarsity athletes, "intramural sports are the best. They give me opportunities to meet people, have fun, and stay in shape between study sessions," quips a sophomore. A typical senior tells us, "My life is made up of active involvement in campus organizations along with participation in recreational sports and outdoor activities." Other undergrads participate in "the progressive groups on campus, which are awesome and very active."

### Student Body
Considering that state universities recruit mainly from their home state, a sociology major is compelled to write, "I think for our area we are pretty diverse." Since that area is Maine, that means a predominantly snow-white group, made up of "your typical Maine-iacs" and "great people with good attitudes." Describing the aesthetic of her northeastern cohorts, a senior writes, "General fashion on campus is somewhere between a Grateful Dead concert and an L.L. Bean catalog." It follows that they're concerned with things like making their campus "more green-friendly." A sophomore calls his peers "naïve about the world outside of Maine," but apparently, "you would have to try not to like them." According to another student, "There is a strong sense of community among students at this school, and that is something to be proud of." "Everyone is welcomed with open arms," concludes one of his classmates.

# THE UNIVERSITY OF MAINE

FINANCIAL AID: 207-581-1324 • E-MAIL: UM-ADMIT@MAINE.EDU • WEBSITE: WWW.UMAINE.EDU

## ADMISSIONS

*Very important factors considered include:* secondary school record, standardized test scores. *Important factors considered include:* class rank, essays. *Other factors considered include:* alumni/ae relation, recommendations, state residency. SAT I or ACT required; SAT I preferred. TOEFL required of all international applicants. High school diploma or GED is required. *High school units required/recommended:* 17 total required; 24 total recommended; 4 English required, 3 math required, 4 math recommended, 2 science required, 3 science recommended, 2 science lab required, 3 science lab recommended, 2 foreign language required, 2 social studies required, 3 social studies recommended, 1 history recommended, 2 elective required, 4 elective recommended.

### The Inside Word

The University of Maine is much smaller than most public flagship universities, and its admissions process reflects this; it is a much more personal approach than most others use. Candidates are reviewed carefully for fit with their choice of college and major, and the committee will contact students regarding a second choice if the first doesn't seem to be a good match. Prepare your application as if you are applying to a private university.

## FINANCIAL AID

*Students should submit:* FAFSA. The Princeton Review suggests that all financial aid forms be submitted as soon as possible after January 1. *Need-based scholarships/grants offered:* Pell, SEOG, state scholarships/grants, private scholarships, the school's own gift aid. *Loan aid offered:* FFEL Subsidized Stafford, FFEL Unsubsidized Stafford, FFEL PLUS, Federal Perkins, state loans. Federal Work-Study Program available. Institutional employment available. Applicants will be notified of awards on a rolling basis beginning on or about March 15. Off-campus job opportunities are good.

## FROM THE ADMISSIONS OFFICE

"The University of Maine offers students a wide array of academic and social programs, including clubs, organizations, professional societies, and religious groups. We strive to help students feel welcome and to provide opportunities for them to become an integral part of the campus community. Visit our beautiful campus and become better acquainted with this community. Take a guided campus tour and learn about campus facilities, services and technologies, and living and dining. Our student tour guides give a first-hand view of the Black Bear experience. During your visit, meet with faculty and admission staff to learn more about your program of interest and our academic climate. The University of Maine's commitment to educational excellence and community building will be reinforced when you visit our campus!"

## SELECTIVITY

| | |
|---|---|
| Admissions Rating | 76 |
| # of applicants | 5,249 |
| % of applicants accepted | 79 |
| % of acceptees attending | 43 |

### FRESHMAN PROFILE

| | |
|---|---|
| Range SAT Verbal | 480-590 |
| Average SAT Verbal | 539 |
| Range SAT Math | 490-610 |
| Average SAT Math | 547 |
| Range ACT Composite | 20-26 |
| Average ACT Composite | 23 |
| Minimum TOEFL | 530 |
| Average HS GPA | 3.2 |
| % graduated top 10% of class | 23 |
| % graduated top 25% of class | 50 |
| % graduated top 50% of class | 89 |

### DEADLINES

| | |
|---|---|
| Nonfall registration? | yes |

### APPLICANTS ALSO LOOK AT AND OFTEN PREFER
U of Vermont
### AND SOMETIMES PREFER
U of New Hampshire
UConn
Colby
### AND RARELY PREFER
U of Rhode Island
UMass at Amherst

## FINANCIAL FACTS

| | |
|---|---|
| Financial Aid Rating | 81 |
| In-state tuition | $4,380 |
| Out-of-state tuition | $12,450 |
| Room and board | $5,922 |
| Books and supplies | $700 |
| Required fees | $1,170 |
| % frosh receiving aid | 73 |
| % undergrads receiving aid | 57 |
| Avg frosh grant | $5,329 |
| Avg frosh loan | $2,974 |

THE BEST 351 COLLEGES ■ 593

# UNIV. OF MARYLAND, BALTIMORE COUNTY

1000 HILLTOP CIRCLE, BALTIMORE, MD 21250 • ADMISSIONS: 410-455-2291 • FAX: 410-455-1094

## CAMPUS LIFE

| | |
|---|---|
| Quality of Life Rating | 76 |
| Type of school | public |
| Environment | suburban |

### STUDENTS

| | |
|---|---|
| Total undergrad enrollment | 9,549 |
| % male/female | 52/48 |
| % from out of state | 8 |
| % from public high school | 84 |
| % live on campus | 33 |
| % in (# of) fraternities | 3 (11) |
| % in (# of) sororities | 3 (10) |
| % African American | 15 |
| % Asian | 16 |
| % Caucasian | 56 |
| % Hispanic | 3 |
| % international | 5 |

### SURVEY SAYS . . .
Very little drug use
(Almost) everyone smokes
Class discussions are rare
Popular college radio
High cost of living
Large classes
Unattractive campus
Ethnic diversity on campus
Campus difficult to get around

## ACADEMICS

| | |
|---|---|
| Academic Rating | 74 |
| Calendar | 4-1-4 |
| Student/faculty ratio | 17:1 |
| Profs interesting rating | 73 |
| Profs accessible rating | 77 |
| % profs teaching UG courses | 100 |
| % classes taught by TAs | 2 |
| Avg lab size | 10-19 students |
| Avg reg class size | 10-19 students |

### MOST POPULAR MAJORS
Information technology
Psychology
Visual and performing arts

## STUDENTS SPEAK OUT

### Academics

The University of Maryland, Baltimore County has prospered over the last few years, and its bragging rights echoed in the comments of their students. In the not-so-distant past, UMBC primarily served a student body of bright Marylanders who had underachieved in high school. UMBC offered them a chance to prove their academic worth, and so they'd come, bust their humps for good grades, and then transfer out to "better" schools. In the process, UMBC developed a reputation as a solid, no-nonsense school that pushed students to their limits. A UMBC degree began to carry greater cachet, and, consequently, more and more kids started to stick around for the full four years. Out-of-state students started arriving, and today Baltimore's commuter campus is well on the way to transforming itself into a residential school with a strong regional reputation. Students here report that "the focus of UMBC's academia lies in scientific research," and while professors "are very accessible and willing to make time for students outside of office hours and class," undergrads also warn that "the quality of professors varies quite widely, especially at the intro level. In the upper-level courses, however, I have taken, the professors are generally very knowledgeable and courteous." UMBC is a "very competitive, very academic school" that is "not for slackers," but students note that "there are many programs here to help those who have trouble academically." Students warn that UMBC's administration requires "far too many procedures . . . complications, and hassles."

### Life

Although more and more a residential campus, UMBC is still growing into the shoes of a full-to-capacity residential college. Significant growth is especially true for this year's freshman class with nearly 80 percent living on campus. "The on-campus community isn't as large as most schools," explains one student, "but the school is building, and building, and keeping on building new dorms, so the on-campus community is growing. There are a lot more things to do on campus now then there was when I was a freshman." Most sponsored activities take place in The Commons, UMBC's new center for campus life. During the week there are "tons of school-sponsored social events (which can be lame sometimes but are usually pretty cool). The only times there aren't many people around are weekends. They [weekends, not students] can be absolutely dead." Campus life is further dampened by school drinking policies: "The campus is very strict about drinking and noise. People having fun in the dorms or apartment areas quickly arouses attention from the authorities because it is so unusual." Accordingly, "most people leave campus for fun. The average UMBC student spends his Friday night in Baltimore at a club. Otherwise he's sitting in his dorm room playing Counter-Strike." Adds one student, "Fun is going to Baltimore's Inner Harbor (you better have money because it's expensive). There is also Fells Point for the drinkers among us (very dirty). If not that, D.C. isn't that far away, and it's cleaner anyway."

### Student Body

"There is a lot of diversity at UMBC, which is good," students tell us, although many feel that "there are some serious problems with ethnic cliques." "Most of my friends here are white," explains one white student, "for the simple reason that the different races just don't seem to interact as much." Most communication among different groups occurs in the classroom, allowing students to "learn so much about other cultures and ethnicities. It's an experience and understanding I could not have gotten elsewhere."

# UNIVERSITY OF MARYLAND, BALTIMORE COUNTY

FINANCIAL AID: 410-455-2387 • E-MAIL: ADMISSIONS@UMBC.EDU • WEBSITE: WWW.UMBC.EDU

## ADMISSIONS

*Very important factors considered include:* secondary school record, standardized test scores. *Important factors considered include:* class rank, essays, recommendations. *Other factors considered include:* character/personal qualities, extracurricular activities, interview, talent/ability, volunteer work, work experience. SAT I or ACT required. TOEFL required of all international applicants. High school diploma or GED is required. *High school units required/recommended:* 22 total required; 23 total recommended; 4 English required, 3 math required, 4 math recommended, 3 science required, 2 science lab required, 2 foreign language required, 2 social studies required, 2 history required, 4 elective required.

## The Inside Word

The State of Maryland seems blessed with several strong, small, public universities in addition to its flagship campus at College Park. UMBC is one of those to watch; its national visibility and admissions standards are on the rise. Strong students are attracted by UMBC's emphasis on academic achievement. As a result, the admissions committee has grown to expect evidence of challenging academic course work throughout high school from its candidates, preferably at the honors or AP level. This competitive path will give you the best shot for admission if you're an eager learner looking for a campus where the academic experience is engaging.

## FINANCIAL AID

*Students should submit:* FAFSA. No deadline for regular filing. The Princeton Review suggests that all financial aid forms be submitted as soon as possible after January 1. *Need-based scholarships/grants offered:* Pell, SEOG, state scholarships/grants, private scholarships, the school's own gift aid. *Loan aid offered:* FFEL Subsidized Stafford, FFEL Unsubsidized Stafford, FFEL PLUS, Federal Perkins. Federal Work-Study Program available. Institutional employment available. Applicants will be notified of awards on a rolling basis beginning on or about March 15. Off-campus job opportunities are excellent.

## FROM THE ADMISSIONS OFFICE

"UMBC students find out quickly that learning at an honors university takes place in many different ways and in a variety of settings. Students discover an environment with a strong undergraduate liberal arts and sciences focus. A midsize public research university, UMBC provides students with opportunities to work with nationally recognized faculty on research ranging from AIDS prevention and environmental issues affecting Chesapeake Bay to computer graphics and animation. The 2003 Kaplan/Newsweek 'How to Get Into College' guide names UMBC as one of 'America's Hot Schools.' UMBC's academic reputation and industry partnerships help to place students in promising careers and leading graduate programs. In fact, one-third of UMBC students immediately go on to many of the nation's finest graduate or professional schools including Harvard, Johns Hopkins, Yale, and Stanford."

### SELECTIVITY

| | |
|---|---|
| Admissions Rating | 80 |
| # of applicants | 5,211 |
| % of applicants accepted | 63 |
| % of acceptees attending | 41 |
| # accepting a place on wait list | 300 |
| % admitted from wait list | 13 |

### FRESHMAN PROFILE

| | |
|---|---|
| Range SAT Verbal | 540-640 |
| Average SAT Verbal | 592 |
| Range SAT Math | 570-670 |
| Average SAT Math | 621 |
| Range ACT Composite | 23-28 |
| Average ACT Composite | 25 |
| Minimum TOEFL | 220 |
| Average HS GPA | 3.5 |
| % graduated top 10% of class | 30 |
| % graduated top 25% of class | 60 |
| % graduated top 50% of class | 90 |

### DEADLINES

| | |
|---|---|
| Priority admission | 11/1 |
| Regular admission | 2/1 |
| Nonfall registration? | yes |

### APPLICANTS ALSO LOOK AT
**AND OFTEN PREFER**
Johns Hopkins
Virginia Tech
**AND SOMETIMES PREFER**
Penn State
U. Virginia
U. Maryland College Park
U. Delaware
**AND RARELY PREFER**
St. Mary's (MD)
Towson

### FINANCIAL FACTS

| | |
|---|---|
| Financial Aid Rating | 83 |
| In-state tuition | $4,614 |
| Out-of-state tuition | $10,798 |
| Room and board | $6,780 |
| Books and supplies | $800 |
| Required fees | $1,748 |
| % frosh receiving aid | 53 |
| % undergrads receiving aid | 54 |
| Avg frosh grant | $6,212 |
| Avg frosh loan | $2,566 |

# UNIVERSITY OF MARYLAND, COLLEGE PARK

MITCHELL BUILDING, COLLEGE PARK, MD 20742-5235 • ADMISSIONS: 301-314-8385 • FAX: 301-314-9693

## CAMPUS LIFE

| Quality of Life Rating | 69 |
|---|---|
| Type of school | public |
| Environment | suburban |

### STUDENTS

| Total undergrad enrollment | 25,179 |
|---|---|
| % male/female | 51/49 |
| % from out of state | 25 |
| % live on campus | 39 |
| % in (# of) fraternities | 9 (27) |
| % in (# of) sororities | 10 (20) |
| % African American | 13 |
| % Asian | 14 |
| % Caucasian | 59 |
| % Hispanic | 5 |
| % international | 3 |

### SURVEY SAYS . . .
Student publications are popular
Ethnic diversity on campus
Everyone loves the Terrapins
Frats and sororities dominate social scene
Great on-campus food
Campus difficult to get around
Students are not very happy
Students are cliquish
Students don't like College Park, MD
(Almost) no one listens to college radio

## ACADEMICS

| Academic Rating | 75 |
|---|---|
| Calendar | semester |
| Student/faculty ratio | 13:1 |
| Profs interesting rating | 89 |
| Profs accessible rating | 90 |
| Avg lab size | 20-29 students |
| Avg reg class size | 20-29 students |

### MOST POPULAR MAJORS
Political science and government
Criminology
Computer science

## STUDENTS SPEAK OUT

### Academics
The very affordable University of Maryland is a major research university that offers a "professional atmosphere" and, for those who qualify, an exemplary Honors Program with small classes and lots of personal attention. As at many of the behemoth state universities, though, large lecture classes are the norm for the typical student. Excellent engineering, physics, economics, and business departments provide just a few of the near-limitless choices awaiting the self-starter here. Writes one student, "To the self-directed, enterprising student, Maryland affords immense opportunity. To those with no talent for getting through endless bureaucracy, go somewhere else!" Maryland's core curriculum, usually completed during the first two years, requires students to fulfill a wide range of distribution requirements. During their senior year, undergrads must complete two seminars designed to help integrate these disparate core courses into their major fields of study. Students write that their final two years here are better and more enjoyable than the first two. As one junior explains, "At first you feel like a number, but as you get into your upper-level classes and classes for your major, teachers become more available and there is more individual attention." Professors vary from those who are "interesting, provide humor, and keep me relatively awake" to those who "teach just so they can do research." Of the latter type, one biology major reports that "if you learn to be assertive, professors and staff are more than willing to give you some of their precious time." Students complain that "advising is horrible. There should be someone to advise you not to be advised by an advisor." As for administration, "for a big campus, it runs pretty smoothly."

### Life
Maryland's "huge, largely diverse," and "great campus" has "something for everyone." To some, it's "Party Park," with "lotsa parties and cool bars. You can walk down the street and always find a good party." Others focus on the immensely popular intercollegiate sports teams. Gushes one student, "Men's basketball is huge. Games are so much fun!" Football and lacrosse also pull in big crowds. Intramural sports are big, as are the literally hundreds of clubs and extracurricular activities housed on campus. Fraternities and sororities also exert a "pretty strong" influence on campus life and provide numerous social activities. Writes one undergrad, "There is always something going on on campus and off campus, and if it doesn't suit you, D.C. is only a Metro ride away." The nation's capital has "plenty to do . . . lots of concerts," clubs, and restaurants, while Baltimore, "only 30 minutes away by car," boasts an ever-expanding downtown nightlife. College Park's choice location also provides abundant opportunities for work and "great internships," not only in the two major cities but also in nearby Annapolis, Maryland's capital. Students complain that their hometown, College Park, does not live "up to its potential" and caution that having your own wheels makes city jaunts much easier. Beware though: "We really need more parking spaces. And we need to build more dorms. No one should have to live in a double room with two other roommates. That is torture."

### Student Body
Maryland students are, by and large, a pleasant group. Writes one undergrad, "If you smile at someone, they'll be sure to smile back. Even with a campus of 30,000, you're bound to run into someone you know." Most consider themselves "easy-going" and "apathetic" but "decent people who wish to hold on to their beliefs without criticism." By Maryland state law, "70 percent come from Maryland. Some are nice, some aren't." The majority are "suburban white kids from public schools," but a substantial student-of-color population means that "the diversity at UMCP is great; however, there is little interaction between groups of different cultures."

# UNIVERSITY OF MARYLAND, COLLEGE PARK

FINANCIAL AID: 301-314-9000 • E-MAIL: UM-ADMIT@UGA.UMD.EDU • WEBSITE: WWW.MARYLAND.EDU

## ADMISSIONS

*Very important factors considered include:* secondary school record, standardized test scores. *Important factors considered include:* class rank, essays, recommendations, state residency, talent/ability. *Other factors considered include:* alumni/ae relation, character/personal qualities, extracurricular activities, geographical residence, minority status, volunteer work, work experience. SAT I or ACT required; SAT I preferred. TOEFL required of all international applicants. High school diploma or GED is required. *High school units required/recommended:* 16 total required; 17 total recommended; 4 English required, 3 math required, 4 math recommended, 2 science required, 2 science lab required, 2 foreign language required, 3 social studies required.

### The Inside Word

Maryland's initial candidate review process emphasizes academic credentials and preparedness. Through this first review, roughly 20 percent of the applicant pool is either admitted or denied. The remaining 80 percent are then evaluated in depth by admissions officers and reviewed by an admissions committee of seven, who collectively decide upon each candidate. Don't take essays and the compilation of other personal material that is required of applicants lightly. It's uncommon for a large university to devote this kind of attention to candidate selection. Perhaps this explains why so many of the students here made Maryland their first choice.

## FINANCIAL AID

*Students should submit:* FAFSA. Regular filing deadline is June 30. The Princeton Review suggests that all financial aid forms be submitted as soon as possible after January 1. *Need-based scholarships/grants offered:* Pell, SEOG, state scholarships/grants, private scholarships, the school's own gift aid. *Loan aid offered:* FFEL Subsidized Stafford, FFEL Unsubsidized Stafford, FFEL PLUS, Federal Perkins. Federal Work-Study Program available. Institutional employment available. Applicants will be notified of awards on or about April 1. Off-campus job opportunities are excellent.

## FROM THE ADMISSIONS OFFICE

"Commitment to excellence, to diversity, to learning—these are the hallmarks of a Maryland education. As the state's flagship campus and one of the nation's leading public universities, Maryland offers students and faculty the opportunity to come together to explore and create knowledge, to debate and discover our similarities and our differences, and to serve as a model of intellectual and cultural excellence for the state and the nation's capital. With leading programs in engineering, business, journalism, architecture, and the sciences, the university offers an outstanding educational value."

### SELECTIVITY

| | |
|---|---:|
| Admissions Rating | 81 |
| # of applicants | 23,117 |
| % of applicants accepted | 43 |
| % of acceptees attending | 39 |
| # accepting a place on wait list | 1,816 |
| % admitted from wait list | 28 |

### FRESHMAN PROFILE

| | |
|---|---:|
| Range SAT Verbal | 570-670 |
| Range SAT Math | 600-700 |
| Minimum TOEFL | 575 |
| Average HS GPA | 3.9 |
| % graduated top 10% of class | 58 |
| % graduated top 25% of class | 90 |
| % graduated top 50% of class | 100 |

### DEADLINES

| | |
|---|---:|
| Priority admission | 12/1 |
| Regular admission | 1/20 |
| Nonfall registration? | yes |

### APPLICANTS ALSO LOOK AT AND OFTEN PREFER
U Delaware
### AND SOMETIMES PREFER
Penn State
### AND RARELY PREFER
U Virginia

### FINANCIAL FACTS

| | |
|---|---:|
| Financial Aid Rating | 82 |
| In-state tuition | $4,572 |
| Out-of-state tuition | $13,336 |
| Room and board | $7,241 |
| Books and supplies | $808 |
| Required fees | $1,098 |
| % frosh receiving aid | 40 |
| % undergrads receiving aid | 40 |
| Avg frosh grant | $4,858 |
| Avg frosh loan | $3,301 |

# UNIVERSITY OF MASSACHUSETTS—AMHERST

UNIVERSITY ADMISSIONS CENTER, AMHERST, MA 01003 • ADMISSIONS: 413-545-0222 • FAX: 413-545-4312

## CAMPUS LIFE

| Quality of Life Rating | 74 |
|---|---|
| Type of school | public |
| Environment | suburban |

### STUDENTS
| | |
|---|---|
| Total undergrad enrollment | 18,606 |
| % male/female | 49/51 |
| % from out of state | 18 |
| % from public high school | 90 |
| % live on campus | 60 |
| % in (# of) fraternities | 3 (21) |
| % in (# of) sororities | 7 (12) |
| % African American | 5 |
| % Asian | 7 |
| % Caucasian | 76 |
| % Hispanic | 4 |
| % international | 2 |
| # of countries represented | 114 |

### SURVEY SAYS . . .
Everyone loves the Minutemen
Students love Amherst, MA
Hard liquor is popular
Great off-campus food
Class discussions are rare
Large classes
Lousy food on campus
Unattractive campus
Lab facilities are great
Student publications are popular

## ACADEMICS

| Academic Rating | 72 |
|---|---|
| Calendar | semester |
| Student/faculty ratio | 19:1 |
| Profs interesting rating | 92 |
| Profs accessible rating | 95 |
| % profs teaching UG courses | 88 |
| % classes taught by TAs | 12 |
| Avg lab size | 20-29 students |
| Avg reg class size | 20-29 students |

### MOST POPULAR MAJORS
Communications studies/speech
communication and rhetoric
English language and literature
Biology/biological sciences

## STUDENTS SPEAK OUT

### Academics
State-run University of Massachusetts at Amherst offers "a great education in a liberal but structured environment," according to its students. Like many large schools, it's "a wonderful university providing countless opportunities to get involved with other students. UMass is fun and active; there is always something going on at UMass every day of the week." The university also suffers from several typical large-school maladies, including a lumbering, inefficient administration and a wide range in the quality of instruction. Of profs, opinions range from the positively positive ("All the professors love their work and it shows") to the qualifiedly positive ("The professors are an amalgamation. I've had great teachers I'll never forget and ones I already have forgotten because they were so useless. Overall, this is a good experience, but that's overall"). There are even those who caustically fume that "there are several hundred professors at UMass. By simple law of averages, some of them should be reasonably interesting. Apparently UMass does not know its math." Others complain that "the teachers are OK, but the conditions—in the auditorium-style classrooms—inhibit learning because of external irritations like stuffiness, overheating, small chairs and desks so you can't write comfortably, etc. It's not a good atmosphere for intense concentration." Membership in the Five College Consortium helps to soften some of the griping, as it allows students to use the resources available at the nearby warmer-and-fuzzier campuses of Amherst, Hampshire, Smith, and Mount Holyoke.

### Life
Smack in the middle of the Pioneer Valley, UMass—Amherst is an idyllic setting for collegiate New England-philes. Amherst "is a great little town" with "plenty of things to do," and "good skiing and hiking are nearby." So too are the towns of Northampton, Springfield, and a little further down the line, Albany, New York. Writes one student, "We're close enough to large cities to access them but far enough away to have a small-town feel." The large university, as well as several smaller schools close by, creates an environment in which "there's always something to do no matter what you like." Fraternities and sororities "exist . . . but do not dominate the social scene." University-sponsored clubs are very popular; as one student notes, "There are many groups available to join—hang-gliding club, dance team, animal rights coalition, bridge club, etc." As far as the night scene goes, there's always a good time to be had nearby: "When it comes to having fun, there's everything from parties to dancing to restaurants, movies, or a band playing anywhere at almost any given time." Are there downsides to this little slice o' heaven? The campus itself, for one. "Be prepared to eat, breathe, and live concrete. Bland, uninteresting concrete. UMass is a large slab of gray concrete dropped in the middle of farmland," warns one student. Students also grouse loudly and frequently about the food. Says one, "They really need to improve the food. It's like a poison that kills you a little each time."

### Student Body
UMass undergrads agree that theirs is a diverse population. As one student muses, "UMass is like a big bag of potpourri, made up of a thousand different scents, which, when brought together, create the strongest and sweetest of aromas." Even so, "the students, while pretty cool, are definitely segregated." Undergrads say their fellow students are "friendly, fun, and some are even concerned about real life beyond the UMass community," but they feel they're not as pointy-headed as their neighbors at Amherst College. As one student puts it, "I'd like to think this is a fairly intellectual environment and a good place to learn, but there are still quite a few dumbasses lolling about."

# UNIVERSITY OF MASSACHUSETTS—AMHERST

FINANCIAL AID: 413-545-0801 • E-MAIL: MAIL@ADMISSIONS.UMASS.EDU • WEBSITE: WWW.UMASS.EDU

## ADMISSIONS

*Very important factors considered include:* essays, secondary school record. *Important factors considered include:* character/personal qualities, extracurricular activities, standardized test scores, state residency, talent/ability. *Other factors considered include:* alumni/ae relation, class rank, minority status, recommendations, volunteer work, work experience. SAT I or ACT required. TOEFL required of all international applicants. High school diploma or GED is required. *High school units required/recommended:* 16 total required; 4 English required, 3 math required, 3 science required, 2 science lab required, 2 foreign language required, 2 social studies required, 2 elective required.

### The Inside Word

Gaining admission to UMass is generally not particularly difficult, but an increase in applications last year resulted in the University increasing its selectivity. Still, most applicants with solid grades in high school should be successful. UMass is a great choice for students who might have a tougher time getting in at the other Five College Consortium members.

## FINANCIAL AID

*Students should submit:* FAFSA. The Princeton Review suggests that all financial aid forms be submitted as soon as possible after January 1. *Need-based scholarships/grants offered:* Pell, SEOG, state scholarships/grants, private scholarships, the school's own gift aid. *Loan aid offered:* Direct Subsidized Stafford, Direct Unsubsidized Stafford, Direct PLUS, Federal Perkins, state loans, William D. Ford Federal Direct (subsidized and unsubsidized) Loans. Federal Work-Study Program available. Institutional employment available. Applicants will be notified of awards on a rolling basis beginning on or about April 1. Off-campus job opportunities are good.

## FROM THE ADMISSIONS OFFICE

"The University of Massachusetts—Amherst is the largest public university in New England, offering its students an almost limitless variety of academic programs and activities. Nearly 100 majors are offered, including a unique program called Bachelor's Degree with Individual Concentration (BDIC) in which students create their own program of study. The outstanding faculty of 1,100 includes novelist John Wideman, Pulitzer Prize winners Madeleine Blais and James Tate, National Medal of Science winner Lynn Margulis, and five members of the prestigious National Academy of Sciences. Students can take courses through the honors program and sample classes at nearby Amherst, Hampshire, Mount Holyoke, and Smith Colleges at no extra charge. Students can take classes in the residence halls with other dorm residents through Residential Academic Programs (RAP), and first-year students may be asked to participate in the Talent Advancement Programs (TAP) in which students with the same majors live and take classes together. And the university's extensive library system is the largest at any public institution in the Northeast. Extracurricular activities include more than 200 clubs and organizations, fraternities and sororities, multicultural and religious centers, and NCAA Division I sports for men and women. Award-winning student-operated businesses, the largest college daily newspaper in the region, and an active student government provide hands-on experiences. About 5,000 students a year participate in the intramural sports program. The picturesque New England town of Amherst offers shopping and dining, and the ski slopes of western Massachusetts and southern Vermont are close by."

## SELECTIVITY

| | |
|---|---|
| Admissions Rating | 75 |
| # of applicants | 20,449 |
| % of applicants accepted | 58 |
| % of acceptees attending | 28 |

### FRESHMAN PROFILE

| | |
|---|---|
| Range SAT Verbal | 500-620 |
| Average SAT Verbal | 554 |
| Range SAT Math | 510-630 |
| Average SAT Math | 571 |
| Minimum TOEFL | 550 |
| Average HS GPA | 3.4 |
| % graduated top 10% of class | 21 |
| % graduated top 25% of class | 56 |
| % graduated top 50% of class | 92 |

### DEADLINES

| | |
|---|---|
| Regular admission | 1/15 |
| Nonfall registration? | yes |

### APPLICANTS ALSO LOOK AT

**AND OFTEN PREFER**
Dartmouth
Boston Coll.

**AND SOMETIMES PREFER**
U. Vermont
U. New Hampshire
U. Conn
Boston U.
Syracuse

**AND RARELY PREFER**
Northeastern U.
U. Rhode Island
SUNY—Albany
U. Maine—Orono
Worcester Poly.

## FINANCIAL FACTS

| | |
|---|---|
| Financial Aid Rating | 79 |
| In-state tuition | $1,714 |
| Out-of-state tuition | $9,937 |
| Room and board | $5,472 |
| Books and supplies | $500 |
| % frosh receiving aid | 46 |
| % undergrads receiving aid | 44 |

THE BEST 351 COLLEGES ■ 599

# UNIVERSITY OF MIAMI

Office of Admission, PO Box 248025, Coral Gables, FL 33124-4616 • Admissions: 305-284-4323 • Fax: 305-284-2507

## CAMPUS LIFE

| | |
|---|---|
| **Quality of Life Rating** | **89** |
| Type of school | private |
| Environment | suburban |

### STUDENTS

| | |
|---|---|
| Total undergrad enrollment | 9,794 |
| % male/female | 43/57 |
| % from out of state | 44 |
| % live on campus | 41 |
| % in (# of) fraternities | 13 (14) |
| % in (# of) sororities | 13 (9) |
| % African American | 10 |
| % Asian | 6 |
| % Caucasian | 54 |
| % Hispanic | 27 |
| % international | 7 |

### SURVEY SAYS . . .
Campus is beautiful
Athletic facilities are great
Everyone loves the Hurricanes
Ethnic diversity on campus
Students love Coral Gables, FL
Great off-campus food
Campus easy to get around
Great computer facilities
Lots of beer drinking

## ACADEMICS

| | |
|---|---|
| **Academic Rating** | **82** |
| Calendar | semester |
| Student/faculty ratio | 13:1 |
| Avg lab size | 10-19 students |
| Avg reg class size | 10-19 students |

## STUDENTS SPEAK OUT

### Academics

Fine academics, coupled with an unbeatable quality of life, are what draw students to the University of Miami. "Studying doesn't seem like such a chore when you're studying in the sun, under palm trees, with an ocean breeze blowing," explains one student. Agrees another, "Attending University of Miami is like being on vacation all year long while at the same time having to put in a fair amount of work time." Pre-medical studies are a key drawing card here, as are the "good music and film programs." Students tell us that "for a large research university, UM is run efficiently," although they warn that "in the larger departments, where professors have more classes to teach, some simply have no time to meet students outside the classroom." Professors are generally good; "sure, you get a dud somewhere in between the outstanding ones, but overall the faculty is very impressive," writes one undergrad. Students also appreciate how "classes are taught in an interesting fashion with extra learning methods, such as trips to courts, films, the school's museum visits, etc., to keep it fun."

### Life

University of Miami, students tell us, "is like a resort. You walk to class and you pass the lake and all the palm trees and it's just gorgeous." In fact, the idyllic tropical setting is the primary reason many choose UM over, say, Big East rival Syracuse. Students love the "amazing weather, as long as you don't mind buttloads of rain every once in a while"; the easy access to the beach; the "state-of-the-art fitness center that offers free exercise classes, an indoor pool, and a Jacuzzi"; and the hopping club scene in South Beach. "On Friday and Saturday nights there's a shuttle to both South Beach and Coconut Grove, so a lot of people will go hang out there," students tell us; even so, most agree that a car is pretty close to a necessity here. "If you don't have a car to get out of Coral Gables, you have to lock yourself in your room and do some mind-altering substance," warns one student. Alcohol and drugs, students tell us, are easy to come by. Even so, many insist that "while there are lots of fun parties, this is not as big a party school as the rest of the world thinks." It is, however, a huge football school. Writes one student, "Football is life at UM. We have the best football team in the country. Every Saturday, the entire student body converges at the Orange Bowl to watch our Hurricanes romp their opponents."

### Student Body

At "Club UM," the typical student "wears designer clothes to class and heels (if female), drives a BMW, has a cell phone attached to her ear (probably speaking another language, such as Spanish or Portuguese), works out every day of the week, parties at least three times a week, and (if female) has her books tucked away in her Coach backpack." This student "tends to be more concerned with their appearance than average, and tends to be self-absorbed." Many "come from New York or New Jersey. There is a strong Hispanic population and a strong Jewish population." However, "there are a good number of atypical students as well, and they fit in simply by wearing normal clothes to class, less makeup, and not conforming to the superficial tendencies of the rest of the students." Many agree that the student body's most compelling asset is its sizable international population. "You learn a lot from classes, but you end up learning more from the people that you associate yourself with, so in the case of UM with its huge international population and range of students, you end up with a first-class education about the world," writes one student.

# UNIVERSITY OF MIAMI

FINANCIAL AID: 305-284-5212 • E-MAIL: ADMISSION@MIAMI.EDU • WEBSITE: WWW.MIAMI.EDU/ADMISSIONS

## ADMISSIONS
*Very important factors considered include:* class rank, essays, recommendations, secondary school record, standardized test scores. *Other factors considered include:* alumni/ae relation, character/personal qualities, extracurricular activities, geographical residence, minority status, state residency, talent/ability, volunteer work, work experience. SAT I or ACT required. TOEFL required of all international applicants. High school diploma or GED is required. *High school units required/recommended:* 16 total recommended; 4 English recommended, 4 math recommended, 3 science recommended, 2 science lab recommended, 2 foreign language recommended, 3 social studies recommended.

### The Inside Word
Over the years Miami has gotten far more national attention for the escapades of the 'Canes on and off the football field than it has for academic excellence. But anyone who takes a closer look will find national-caliber programs in several areas. Candidates who apply for the schools of music and marine sciences will face lots of competition and rigorous screening from the admissions committee.

## FINANCIAL AID
*Students should submit:* FAFSA. The Princeton Review suggests that all financial aid forms be submitted as soon as possible after January 1. *Need-based scholarships/grants offered:* Pell, SEOG, state scholarships/grants, private scholarships, the school's own gift aid, Federal Nursing. *Loan aid offered:* FFEL Subsidized Stafford, FFEL Unsubsidized Stafford, FFEL PLUS, Federal Perkins, Federal Nursing, Signature Student Loan (alternative loan program). Federal Work-Study Program available. Institutional employment available. Applicants will be notified of awards on a rolling basis beginning on or about March 1. Off-campus job opportunities are excellent.

## FROM THE ADMISSIONS OFFICE
"The University of Miami in Coral Gables, Florida, is an innovative private research university in a location unlike any other in the country. Located 10 miles from the vibrant international city of Miami, UM's 9,000 undergraduates come from every state and 114 nations, allowing people of many cultures to challenge and champion each other. Faculty work closely with students, and internships and research experiences are integral to academic life. Students work hard as community volunteers and exert leadership in a range of lively clubs and organizations, including the student-managed TV station, radio station, and newspaper."

---

### SELECTIVITY
★★★☆

| | |
|---|---|
| **Admissions Rating** | 86 |
| # of applicants | 15,909 |
| % of applicants accepted | 44 |
| % of acceptees attending | 30 |
| # of early decision applicants | 779 |
| % accepted early decision | 37 |

### FRESHMAN PROFILE
| | |
|---|---|
| Range SAT Verbal | 550-650 |
| Range SAT Math | 570-670 |
| Range ACT Composite | 25-30 |
| Minimum TOEFL | 550 |
| Average HS GPA | 4.0 |
| % graduated top 10% of class | 55 |
| % graduated top 25% of class | 87 |
| % graduated top 50% of class | 98 |

### DEADLINES
| | |
|---|---|
| Early decision | 11/15 |
| Early decision notification | 12/15 |
| Regular admission | 2/1 |
| Regular notification | 4/15 |
| Nonfall registration? | yes |

### APPLICANTS ALSO LOOK AT
**AND OFTEN PREFER**
Duke
**AND SOMETIMES PREFER**
NYU
Vanderbilt
Boston U
USC
**AND RARELY PREFER**
Florida State

### FINANCIAL FACTS
★★★☆

| | |
|---|---|
| **Financial Aid Rating** | 86 |
| Tuition | $24,378 |
| Room and board | $8,062 |
| Books and supplies | $775 |
| Required fees | $432 |
| % frosh receiving aid | 57 |
| % undergrads receiving aid | 54 |

# UNIVERSITY OF MICHIGAN—ANN ARBOR

1220 STUDENT ACTIVITIES BUILDING, ANN ARBOR, MI 48109-1316 • ADMISSIONS: 734-764-7433 • FAX: 734-936-0740

## CAMPUS LIFE

| | |
|---|---|
| **Quality of Life Rating** | **80** |
| Type of school | public |
| Environment | urban |

### STUDENTS

| | |
|---|---|
| Total undergrad enrollment | 24,547 |
| % male/female | 49/51 |
| % from out of state | 34 |
| % from public high school | 80 |
| % live on campus | 37 |
| % in (# of) fraternities | 38 (16) |
| % in (# of) sororities | 22 (15) |
| % African American | 8 |
| % Asian | 12 |
| % Caucasian | 64 |
| % Hispanic | 4 |
| % international | 4 |
| # of countries represented | 129 |

### SURVEY SAYS . . .
Everyone loves the Wolverines
Lots of beer drinking
Great library
Great computer facilities
Students love Ann Arbor, MI
Hard liquor is popular
Student newspaper is popular
Great off-campus food
Lab facilities are great
(Almost) everyone plays intramural sports

## ACADEMICS

| | |
|---|---|
| **Academic Rating** | **89** |
| Calendar | trimester |
| Student/faculty ratio | 15:1 |
| Avg lab size | 20-29 students |
| Avg reg class size | 10-19 students |

### MOST POPULAR MAJORS
Mechanical engineering
Economics
English language and literature

## STUDENTS SPEAK OUT

### Academics
For many enrolled at the University of Michigan, attending the school has been a lifelong dream: "I've always wanted to come here—since I was a kid," writes one junior. With majors ranging from violin performance and art to aerospace engineering and molecular biology (and everything in between)—in addition to one of the best faculties in the world—it's no wonder most University of Michigan undergrads are confident in their school's solid reputation of "quality and prestige." The school's a national powerhouse in nearly every aspect: academics (both undergrad and graduate), research, athletics, and student activism, not to mention its thriving social scene and excellent location in Ann Arbor, a town that's "not too big, but has a lot going on." On top of all this, it's a relative bargain for in-state students and still cheaper than comparable private institutions for out-of-staters. Notes another senior, "The academics at U of M are second to none—including the Ivy League." Research opportunities, location near central Michigan industry, "well-qualified" yet "friendly and approachable" professors, as well as the fact that "every department is in the Top 10 list" make Michigan an excellent choice for students looking for a top-quality, large university with unparalleled facilities and staff at a relatively low price. But make sure you like 'em big, because Michigan is simply that. With about 25,000 undergrads packing the lecture halls, you'll probably share this senior's desire for "more personal attention and less GSIs [graduate student instructors]." While you're first starting out you might find, like this first year did, that at Michigan it's "everyone for themselves. . . . you must seek to find your own place."

### Life
Diversity, student activism, and a college town with "piles to do"—one has the sense that things are all good in Ann Arbor. A junior describes the situation this way: "The amount and quality of extracurricular activities here are phenomenal. It almost makes me want to take one class per term so I can use all my time for these activities." And that's just at the university! A classic, just-big-enough "college town," Ann Arbor, too, is known for its "great downtown restaurants and bars, and very diverse culture." U of M is also a "sports heaven" and athletics can play a big part in undergraduate life if students are so inclined. "House parties on the weekends" are also an outlet, though one senior complains that "a lot of people drink and use alcohol as a means of escapism. They think it's fun." Her social outlet? "Dancing, working out, reading"—and though finding a "social atmosphere that is moral and healthy" can be tough for chem-free students, at such a big school a kindred soul's bound to turn up sooner rather than later.

### Student Body
"Students here are great," writes a junior. "There's never a shortage of new people to meet." A sophomore elaborates: "As can be expected, social groups form along distinct boundaries, but friendships abound." Sure there are your "elitists" and "spoiled rich kids," but as a senior points out, academics are the ties that bind: "People are pretty friendly," he writes, "very school-oriented." As a result, there's some division according to discipline—English majors hang out with English majors and the like. Jokes a senior, "They are generally friendly in my program. Outside of engineering they aren't friendly." U of M can be "ethnically separated," too, but for the most part, the student vibe seems to be summed up in this junior's statement: "I really like the student atmosphere here. Lots of diversity, and I've learned a lot."

602 ■ THE BEST 351 COLLEGES

# UNIVERSITY OF MICHIGAN—ANN ARBOR

FINANCIAL AID: 734-763-6600 • ADMISS. WEBSITE: WWW.ADMISSIONS.UMICH.EDU • FINANCIAL AID WEBSITE: WWW.FINAID.UMICH.EDU

## ADMISSIONS

*Very important factors considered include:* secondary school record. *Important factors considered include:* curriculum, minority status, standardized test scores, state residency, talent/ability. *Other factors considered include:* alumni/ae relation, character/personal qualities, essays, extracurricular activities, geographical residence, recommendations, volunteer work. SAT I or ACT required. TOEFL required of all non-native speakers of English. High school diploma or GED is required. *High school units required/recommended:* Advised to take 20 total units, specific subject pattern tied to school, college, or division requirements. 1–2 science lab and 3 social studies required, 2 history recommended.

### The Inside Word

Michigan's admissions process combines both formulaic and personal components in its evaluation of candidates. Making the cut is tough—and is getting even tougher for out-of-state applicants, though the university definitely wants them in large numbers. There are simply loads of applicants from outside the state. If being a Wolverine is high on your list of choices, make sure you're well prepared, and since Michigan admits on a rolling basis—apply early! Michigan establishes an enormous waitlist each year. Controversies surrounding Michigan's approach to affirmative action have resulted in significant changes in the manner in which candidates are evaluated, with greater emphasis now given to aspects of candidates' backgrounds that are not quantified by grades and scores.

## FINANCIAL AID

*Students should submit:* FAFSA plus parent's and student's 1040s by February 15. There is no separate institutional financial aid or scholarship application. Merit scholarships are awarded based on the application for admission, therefore early application for admission (prior to November 15) is strongly advised. *Need-based scholarships/grants offered:* Pell, SEOG, state scholarships/grants, private scholarships, the school's own gift aid. *Loan aid offered:* Direct Subsidized Stafford, Direct Unsubsidized Stafford, Direct PLUS, Federal Perkins, Federal Nursing, state loans, college/university loans from institutional funds, Michigan Loan Program, Health Professional Student Loans. Federal Work-Study Program available. Institutional employment available. Applicants will be notified of awards on a rolling basis beginning on or about March 15. Off-campus job opportunities are excellent.

## FROM THE ADMISSIONS OFFICE

"Michigan is a place of incredible possibility. Students shape that possibility according to their diverse interests, goals, energy, and initiative. Undergraduate education is in the academic spotlight at Michigan, offering more than 200 fields of study in 11 schools and colleges; more than 150 first-year seminars with 18 or fewer students taught by senior faculty; composition classes of 20 or fewer students; more than 1,200 first- and second-year students in undergraduate research partnerships with faculty; and numerous service learning programs linking academics with volunteerism. Some introductory courses have large lectures, but these are combined with labs or small group discussions where students get plenty of individualized attention. A Michigan degree is one of distinction and promise; graduates are successful in medical, law, and graduate schools all over the nation and world and 75 percent who enter the work force after graduation secure positions within nine months."

## SELECTIVITY

| | |
|---|---|
| Admissions Rating | 91 |
| # of applicants | 25,081 |
| % of applicants accepted | 49 |
| % of acceptees attending | 42 |
| # accepting a place on wait list | 1,150 |

### FRESHMAN PROFILE

| | |
|---|---|
| Range SAT Verbal | 570-670 |
| Average SAT Verbal | 622 |
| Range SAT Math | 610-720 |
| Average SAT Math | 661 |
| Range ACT Composite | 26-30 |
| Average ACT Composite | 28 |
| Minimum TOEFL | 570 |
| Average HS GPA | 3.8 |

### DEADLINES

| | |
|---|---|
| Regular admission | 2/1 |
| Nonfall registration? | yes |

### APPLICANTS ALSO LOOK AT AND OFTEN PREFER

Harvard
Duke
Stanford
Princeton
Brown
U of Pennsylvania

### AND SOMETIMES PREFER

Northwestern
NYU
Washington U
Cornell
Notre Dame

### AND RARELY PREFER

Michigan State
Boston U
Penn State

## FINANCIAL FACTS

| | |
|---|---|
| Financial Aid Rating | 87 |
| In-state tuition | $7,765 |
| Out-of-state tuition | $24,489 |
| Room and board | $6,620 |
| Books and supplies | $938 |
| Required fees | $187 |
| % frosh receiving aid | 77 |
| % undergrads receiving aid | 63 |
| Avg frosh grant | $8,309 |
| Avg frosh loan | $5,937 |

THE BEST 351 COLLEGES ■ 603

# UNIVERSITY OF MINNESOTA—TWIN CITIES

231 PILLSBURY DRIVE, SE, 240 WILLIAMSON HALL, MINNEAPOLIS, MN 55455-0213 • ADMISSIONS: 612-625-2008 • FAX: 612-626-1693

## CAMPUS LIFE

★ ★ ☆ ☆

| | |
|---|---|
| Quality of Life Rating | 74 |
| Type of school | public |
| Environment | urban |

### STUDENTS

| | |
|---|---|
| Total undergrad enrollment | 28,103 |
| % male/female | 48/52 |
| % from out of state | 18 |
| % live on campus | 22 |
| % African American | 4 |
| % Asian | 8 |
| % Caucasian | 82 |
| % Hispanic | 2 |
| % international | 2 |

### SURVEY SAYS...
Students love Minneapolis, MN
Athletic facilities are great
Class discussions are rare
Political activism is hot
Students aren't religious
Campus difficult to get around
Large classes
Lots of TAs teach upper-level courses
Student publications are popular
Unattractive campus

## ACADEMICS

| | |
|---|---|
| Academic Rating | 71 |
| Calendar | semester |
| Student/faculty ratio | 15:1 |
| Profs interesting rating | 90 |
| Profs accessible rating | 89 |
| Avg lab size | 10-19 students |
| Avg reg class size | 10-19 students |

## STUDENTS SPEAK OUT

### Academics

Students at the University of Minnesota—Twin Cities take a pragmatic approach to their academic experiences. "I think for what I am paying I am getting a very good deal," writes one. "I have great and extremely well-qualified professors.... Also, at a school this large the opportunities seem nearly endless." Students identify a definite hierarchy among departments, with "star" programs like business and technology receiving the most attention from the administration; other areas, such as the arts, "lack funding" and often offer too few courses. At the Carlson School of Management, the U's business program, "teachers are well experienced and offer excellent information in class. The school also has several computer labs kept in fantastic condition." The prestigious Institute of Technology receives similarly high marks, although many students complain that "professors can't speak English very well and this makes it difficult to learn." Throughout the university, "professors mostly try to get involved with us. It's hard because it's such a huge university. The lecture halls are so large that unless you make the effort, the professor probably won't be able to tell you apart from someone else." The university's administration "is pretty good except for services like the bursar or financial aid/scholarships office. They do quite poorly in this area."

### Life

"There is something for everyone" at the large, urban U of M campus. Explains one student, "There are hundreds of groups, from activist groups to club sports. You can go to Dinkytown, Uptown, the Mall of America, Downtown Minneapolis, St. Paul, etc." For some, the city is the chief attraction; as one undergrad told us, "Living in Minneapolis is great! It's a friendly town, yet has all the perks of a big city: theaters, major league sports, museums, concerts! The Dalai Lama is even coming to speak here this semester." For others, it's the myriad opportunities to get involved in campus activities; wrote one student, "Sports are big.... This community is strong in the arts as well. It's very diverse, so if you want it, we probably have it. Unless you want year-round surfing." Many agree that "going out and having fun is what goes on on the weekends. Frat and house parties are very popular weekend activities. People also enjoy clubs and bars. Weekdays, hanging out at coffee shops to chat and do homework is popular." The weather here, undergrads warn, is not for everyone. Writes one, "For about a week after the first snow, we all careen around like horny antelopes, sliding to class in half the time it takes to walk there. After that it turns into drudgery and everybody pretty much stays inside.... The worst part isn't the snow or the dark, though; it's the lack of color for six months that really gets to you after a while."

### Student Body

Undergrads report that "the University of Minnesota attracts a wide range of people—there are traditionally aged students and some older people as well. I've had classes with a range of 17 (still in high school) to 60." More than a few arrive from the northern countryside; reports one caustic urbanite, "I've noticed that the city is really a foreign atmosphere to some people. They are here as tourists and are merely waiting for the day when they can return to their cornfields in relief and brag about their experiences in the big city." By Minnesotan standards, the U draws an ethnically diverse population; explains one student, "Minnesota tends to be pretty Caucasian, but the U draws people of every ethnic background, which is cool." Many warn that "[because] this university is huge... you have to make serious effort to keep in contact with people, because you won't see them unless you have a class with them."

# UNIVERSITY OF MINNESOTA—TWIN CITIES

FINANCIAL AID: 612-624-1665 • E-MAIL: ADMISSIONS@TC.UMN.EDU • WEBSITE: ADMISSIONS.TC.UMN.EDU

## ADMISSIONS

*Very important factors considered include:* class rank, secondary school record, standardized test scores, competitiveness of curriculum. *Other factors considered include:* character/personal qualities, extracurricular activities, geographical residence, state residency, talent/ability, volunteer work, work experience. SAT I or ACT required. High school diploma or GED is required. *High school units required/recommended:* 16 total required; 4 English required, 3 math required, 3 science required, 2 foreign language required, 3 social studies required, 1 visual and/or performing arts required.

### The Inside Word

Despite what looks to be a fairly choosy admissions rate, it's the sheer volume of applicants that creates a selective situation at Minnesota. Admission is by formula; only those with weak course selections and inconsistent academic records need to work up a sweat over getting admitted.

## FINANCIAL AID

*Students should submit:* FAFSA. Priority deadline for filing is February 15. The Princeton Review suggests that all financial aid forms be submitted as soon as possible after January 1. *Need-based scholarships/grants offered:* Pell, SEOG, state scholarships/grants, private scholarships, the school's own gift aid, NSS, ROTC scholarships, academic merit scholarships, athletic scholarships. *Loan aid offered:* Direct Subsidized Stafford, Direct Unsubsidized Stafford, Direct PLUS, Federal Perkins, Federal Nursing, state loans, college/university loans from institutional funds, NSL, private loans. Federal Work-Study Program available. Institutional employment available. Applicants will be notified of awards on a rolling basis. Off-campus job opportunities are excellent.

## FROM THE ADMISSIONS OFFICE

"Known globally as a leader in teaching, research, and public service, the University of Minnesota ranks among the top 25 public universities in the nation. The classic Big 10 campus, located in the heart of the Minneapolis–St. Paul metropolitan area, provides a world-class setting for lifelong learning. In addition to the top-notch academic programs (and more than 145 undergraduate degrees), the university offers an Undergraduate Research Opportunities Program that is a national model; one of the largest study abroad programs in the country; 20,000 computers available for use in labs across campus; and extraordinary opportunities for internships, employment, and personal enrichment. Students can pursue interests in more than 400 official student organizations. Committed to offering its students an education that is not only outstanding but competitively priced, the university has been recognized as a 'best value' and 'best buy.' Students from other states may qualify for discounted tuition through one of the university's reciprocity agreements. Plus, the university awards a number of academic scholarships to qualified freshmen. The university community is a broad mix of ethnic backgrounds, interests, and cultures from all 50 states and 110 foreign countries, creating a welcoming feeling on campus. Beyond campus, the dynamic communities of Minneapolis and St. Paul offer something for everyone—a nationally recognized arts and theater community, a thriving entertainment industry, a host of Fortune 500 companies, four glorious seasons of outdoor recreation, exciting professional sports, shopping, and restaurants for every taste."

## SELECTIVITY

| | |
|---|---|
| Admissions Rating | 80 |
| # of applicants | 14,724 |
| % of applicants accepted | 74 |
| % of acceptees attending | 47 |

### FRESHMAN PROFILE

| | |
|---|---|
| Range SAT Verbal | 540-660 |
| Average SAT Verbal | 593 |
| Range SAT Math | 550-670 |
| Average SAT Math | 612 |
| Range ACT Composite | 22-28 |
| Average ACT Composite | 25 |
| Minimum TOEFL | 550 |
| % graduated top 10% of class | 30 |
| % graduated top 25% of class | 65 |
| % graduated top 50% of class | 92 |

### DEADLINES

| | |
|---|---|
| Regular admission | 12/15 |
| Nonfall registration? | yes |

### APPLICANTS ALSO LOOK AT AND OFTEN PREFER
Northwestern
U of Michigan at Ann Arbor
### AND SOMETIMES PREFER
U of Wisconsin at Madison
Iowa Sate

## FINANCIAL FACTS

| | |
|---|---|
| Financial Aid Rating | 79 |
| In-state tuition | $5,420 |
| Out-of-state tuition | $15,994 |
| Room and board | $5,696 |
| Books and supplies | $730 |
| Required fees | $860 |
| % frosh receiving aid | 48 |
| % undergrads receiving aid | 46 |
| Avg frosh grant | $6,346 |
| Avg frosh loan | $3,874 |

# UNIVERSITY OF MISSISSIPPI

145 MARTINDALE, UNIVERSITY, MS 38677 • ADMISSIONS: 662-915-7226 • FAX: 662-915-5869

## CAMPUS LIFE

| Quality of Life Rating | 87 |
| --- | --- |
| Type of school | public |
| Environment | rural |

### STUDENTS
| | |
| --- | --- |
| Total undergrad enrollment | 10,661 |
| % male/female | 47/53 |
| % from out of state | 32 |
| % from public high school | 70 |
| % live on campus | 28 |
| % in (# of) fraternities | 32 (19) |
| % in (# of) sororities | 34 (13) |
| % African American | 13 |
| % Asian | 1 |
| % Caucasian | 85 |
| % international | 1 |
| # of countries represented | 68 |

### SURVEY SAYS . . .
Frats and sororities dominate social scene
Hard liquor is popular
Instructors are good teachers
Everyone loves the Rebels
Students get along with local community
Low cost of living
Library needs improving
Theater is unpopular

## ACADEMICS

| Academic Rating | 76 |
| --- | --- |
| Calendar | semester |
| Student/faculty ratio | 21:1 |
| Profs interesting rating | 79 |
| Profs accessible rating | 77 |
| Avg lab size | 20-29 students |
| Avg reg class size | 10-19 students |

### MOST POPULAR MAJORS
Business administration/management
Marketing/marketing management
Elementary education and teaching

## STUDENTS SPEAK OUT

### Academics
For many, University of Mississippi—"Ole Miss" to friends—is as much a lifestyle choice as an academic one. "The best aspect of Ole Miss is the southern pride and the beauty that you experience," explains one undergrad. Students here single out the business school and programs in pharmacology and accounting for special praise; education is also a popular major. Professors, many agree, "are highly accessible and are willing to work with you and meet with you whenever you need to speak with them. They are also extraordinarily friendly, making an effort to talk to you if there seems to be something wrong." Administrators also receive remarkably high grades for a large state school: "The administration is incredibly supportive as well. I am so comfortable with the administration that I can walk up to the chancellor and start a conversation without a second thought," writes a typical undergrad. Students also love the strong alumni network and the McDonnell-Barksdale Honors College ("small, discussion-oriented classes"). Although the subject of some debate, the school's efforts to update its image wins many students' support; writes one, "The school is getting rid of the old symbols like the Confederate battle flag and things like that. They really are trying to make things better for all people," notes one student approvingly.

### Life
You should know that "people either really like Ole Miss or really hate Ole Miss. It is a Greek-oriented school, and if you aren't that type of person, or an athlete, you probably won't like the school." Football is the alpha and omega of fall semester; on game day "the Grove, a 15-acre park in the center of campus, is packed with tents. Under each tent, friends and family gather to eat and drink. Some people bring candelabras, white linen, and fine china. This is without doubt the greatest tradition in college football; it's Mississippi Mardi Gras." The Greeks, who claim one-third of the student body, are integral to the action. "On game nights fraternities have big parties at their houses with kegs and hooch." Students tell us that Ole Miss is "a huge party school." Students also note the "unbelievably beautiful campus. The trees [and] green grass in the Grove, the old historic buildings on the circle . . . there is nothing else quite like the atmosphere here at Ole Miss."

### Student Body
"Ole Miss is the central meeting place of well-to-do southerners," a place where "everybody's father is somebody and every girl is beautiful and expects to get her way." "There are a lot of rich kids here," explains one student. "It seems like every other car in the parking lot is an Infiniti or a Jaguar or a Range Rover." Students extend the courtesies of southern hospitality, however, as "everyone is always greeting one another with a common 'Hello' or 'Hey, how are you doing?'" Under this veneer of cordiality, however, the student body is divided by "a very strong Greek system." Writes one independent, "You are an oddball if you are not in a sorority or a fraternity. We call them 'packs,' the groups of Greek guys and girls that roam around the town square and campus." While a demanding education can certainly be had at Ole Miss, it's also possible to glide through. "A lot of students don't come here to get an education. That's a major problem, but probably not the university's fault," writes one undergrad.

606 ■ THE BEST 351 COLLEGES

# UNIVERSITY OF MISSISSIPPI

FINANCIAL AID: 662-915-7175 • E-MAIL: ADMISSIONS@OLEMISS.EDU • WEBSITE: WWW.OLEMISS.EDU

## ADMISSIONS

*Very important factors considered include:* secondary school record. *Important factors considered include:* class rank, standardized test scores. *Other factors considered include:* alumni/ae relation, state residency, talent/ability. SAT I or ACT required. TOEFL required of all international applicants. High school diploma or GED is required. *High school units required/recommended:* 15 total required; 4 English required, 3 math required, 4 math recommended, 3 science required, 4 science recommended, 3 science lab required, 1 foreign language required, 2 foreign language recommended, 1 social studies required, 2 social studies recommended, 2 history required, 1 elective required.

### The Inside Word

The admissions process at Ole Miss is relatively stress-free. Solid high school achievement in college-prep courses will open the doors for most applicants.

## FINANCIAL AID

*Students should submit:* FAFSA. No deadline for regular filing, recommended filing by February 15. *Need-based scholarships/grants offered:* Pell, SEOG, state scholarships/grants, private scholarships, the school's own gift aid. *Loan aid offered:* FFEL Subsidized Stafford, FFEL Unsubsidized Stafford, FFEL PLUS, Federal Perkins, college/university loans from institutional funds. Federal Work-Study Program available. Institutional employment available. Applicants will be notified of awards on a rolling basis beginning on or about April 1. Off-campus job opportunities are good.

## FROM THE ADMISSIONS OFFICE

"The flagship university of the state, the University of Mississippi, widely known as Ole Miss, offers extraordinary opportunities through more than 100 areas of study, including programs such as the McDonnell-Barksdale Honors College and the Croft Institute for International Studies. UM students are the only public university students in the state who have the opportunity to be tapped by the nation's oldest and most prestigious honor society, Phi Beta Kappa. Strong academic programs and a rich and varied campus life have helped Ole Miss graduate 24 Rhodes Scholars.

"The campus is diverse; 35 percent come from other states and countries and 13 percent are African American. Significant campus improvements in 2003 included the $25 million Gertrude Ford Performing Arts Center and a new privately funded campus memorial honoring the integration of higher education. UM ranks 27th in the nation among public universities for endowment per student. Ole Miss hosts 20 research centers, including the National Center for Justice and the Rule of Law, which provides training on investigating and prosecuting cybercrime; the William Winter Institute for Racial Reconciliation; and the National Center for Natural Products Research.

"The University is located in Oxford, consistently recognized as a great college town and as a center for writers and other artists. Like Ole Miss, Oxford is modest in size and large in the opportunities it provides residents, offering many of the advantages of a larger place in a friendly and open environment."

### SELECTIVITY

| | |
|---|---|
| Admissions Rating | 77 |
| # of applicants | 7,603 |
| % of applicants accepted | 67 |
| % of acceptees attending | 44 |

#### FRESHMAN PROFILE

| | |
|---|---|
| Range ACT Composite | 20-26 |
| Average ACT Composite | 23 |
| Minimum TOEFL | 550 |
| Average HS GPA | 3.4 |
| % graduated top 10% of class | 35 |
| % graduated top 25% of class | 52 |
| % graduated top 50% of class | 85 |

#### DEADLINES

| | |
|---|---|
| Priority admission | 6/15 |
| Regular admission | 7/20 |
| Nonfall registration? | yes |

### FINANCIAL FACTS

| | |
|---|---|
| Financial Aid Rating | 90 |
| In-state tuition | $3,916 |
| Out-of-state tuition | $8,826 |
| Room and board | $5,300 |
| Books and supplies | $800 |
| % frosh receiving aid | 34 |
| % undergrads receiving aid | 38 |

# UNIVERSITY OF MISSOURI—ROLLA

106 PARKER HALL, ROLLA, MO 65409 • ADMISSIONS: 573-341-4165 • FAX: 573-341-4082

## CAMPUS LIFE

★ ★ ★ ☆

| | |
|---|---|
| Quality of Life Rating | 81 |
| Type of school | public |
| Environment | rural |

### STUDENTS

| | |
|---|---|
| Total undergrad enrollment | 3,849 |
| % male/female | 75/25 |
| % from out of state | 22 |
| % from public high school | 85 |
| % in (# of) fraternities | 27 (20) |
| % in (# of) sororities | 24 (6) |
| % African American | 5 |
| % Asian | 3 |
| % Caucasian | 86 |
| % Hispanic | 2 |
| % international | 3 |
| # of countries represented | 38 |

### SURVEY SAYS . . .
Political activism is hot
High cost of living
No one cheats
Student publications are popular
Very little beer drinking

## ACADEMICS

| | |
|---|---|
| Academic Rating | 80 |
| Calendar | semester |
| Student/faculty ratio | 14:1 |
| Profs interesting rating | 80 |
| Profs accessible rating | 74 |
| % profs teaching UG courses | 88 |
| % classes taught by TAs | 14 |
| Avg lab size | 10-19 students |
| Avg reg class size | 20-29 students |

### MOST POPULAR MAJORS
Computer science
Electrical, electronics, and communications engineering
Mechanical engineering

## STUDENTS SPEAK OUT

### Academics
Students looking for "serious, no-frills engineering studies" flock to Rolla, where "research programs and post-graduation job placement" are often listed among the school's strengths. The course work is "not designed for the lazy," and a senior tells us, "Most people here are highly dedicated, reflected by our average graduating GPA." Students relish this academic community, relieved "finally to be among my mental peers." Most students find their professors "very knowledgeable and easy to talk to" as well as "interesting and experienced." Certain respondents see the faculty as "research oriented," but others say they are "very involved with undergraduates." Instructors are known to "act tough," but a junior writes that those who are "aloof in class" can be "laid-back and human in the office." Students find themselves slaving for those top grades: "Nobody cares if you spend 30 hours a week in a two-credit-hour lab." Some students wish for more discussion in classes, complain about under-staffing, and lament certain outdated facilities. But the "programs offered that assist students with their academic program and overall well-being" more than compensate for any shortcomings. However, they succeed in creating an atmosphere that "teaches great leadership qualities" and produces "graduates who know what they're doing," according to a junior in the computer engineering department.

### Life
Life at UMR revolves around academics, which is reflected in the buildings themselves, "built for utility, not art." One student writes, "The reason people come to school here is not to have fun," but many people appreciate that "the environment provides very few distractions from the education that I am paying for." Those looking for a respite from the "strictly business" vibe are "forced to be creative." That translates to "climbing the abandoned nine-story building or building flame throwers" with surprising frequency. Typical geek pastimes, such as Magic tournaments, computer games, and something called the "SAE formula car group," occupy students when they aren't studying, and one respondent reports, "Role playing happens around the clock." (Meaning avatars, not French maids, we assume.) Rolla "ain't no place to party," and "people who like to drink a lot are unsatisfied because there aren't many bars," aside from the campus pub, The Grotto. The Student Union Board attempts to lure people away from the monitor's glow, but "a lot of people don't support campus activities." Though the surrounding city offers "no malls or clubs," the Ozarks provide an outdoor playground, with plenty of places for caving, fishing, hunting, and hiking. In a typically practical Rolla statement, one student concludes, "We came for the engineering degree, not the city."

### Student Body
At a school full of engineers and computer scientists, it's not surprising to find high representation of "somewhat introverted white males who rarely tear themselves away from the computer." Though these "antisocial weirdos" may "not get out much," certain students assure us that they can be "very nice and social when necessary." "Frat boys" add some diversity of personality to the student body, but some respondents feel that "too much of the campus population is Greek." Many of Rolla's young men complain about the paucity of women, but one Don Juan quips, "If you eliminate all the guys who are attached or just plain pathetic, the odds are pretty even." The ladies themselves mostly enjoy the advantageous ratio, but a female student writes, "Sometimes a female will run into a person who doesn't believe that girls can be engineers." Students perceive "factions of each minority," noting that "foreign students flock together and rarely interact with the rest of us." Overall, Rolla enjoys the harmony that comes from common purpose: "Despite the diverse campus, everybody seems to get along."

608 ■ THE BEST 351 COLLEGES

# UNIVERSITY OF MISSOURI—ROLLA

FINANCIAL AID: 800-522-0938 • E-MAIL: UMROLLA@UMR.EDU • WEBSITE: WWW.UMR.EDU

## ADMISSIONS
*Very important factors considered include:* class rank, secondary school record, standardized test scores. *Important factors considered include:* recommendations. *Other factors considered include:* character/personal qualities, essays, extracurricular activities, interview, talent/ability, volunteer work, work experience. SAT I or ACT required. TOEFL required of all international applicants. High school diploma or GED is required. *High school units required/recommended:* 17 total required; 4 English required, 4 math required, 3 science required, 1 science lab required, 2 foreign language required, 3 social studies required, 1 fine arts required.

### *The Inside Word*
This public university admissions committee functions pretty much the same as most others; admission is based on numbers and course distribution requirements. The applicant pool is small, well-qualified, and self-selected; despite the extremely high admit rate, only strong students are likely to meet with success.

## FINANCIAL AID
*Students should submit:* FAFSA. No deadline for regular filing. The Princeton Review suggests that all financial aid forms be submitted as soon as possible after January 1. *Need-based scholarships/grants offered:* Pell, SEOG, state scholarships/grants, private scholarships, the school's own gift aid, United Negro College Fund. *Loan aid offered:* Direct Subsidized Stafford, Direct Unsubsidized Stafford, Federal Perkins, state loans, college/university loans from institutional funds. Federal Work-Study Program available. Institutional employment available. Applicants will be notified of awards on a rolling basis beginning on or about April 1. Off-campus job opportunities are excellent.

## FROM THE ADMISSIONS OFFICE
"Widely recognized as one of our nation's best universities for engineering, sciences, computer science, and technology, the University of Missouri—Rolla also offers programs in information science, business, and liberal arts. Personal attention, access to leadership opportunities, research projects, and co-ops and internships mean students are well prepared for the future. A 98 percent career placement rate across all majors and a 90-plus percent placement rate to medical, law, and other professional schools tells the tale; UMR offers a terrific undergraduate experience and value for your money."

## SELECTIVITY
★ ★ ★ ☆

| | |
|---|---|
| Admissions Rating | 83 |
| # of applicants | 1,976 |
| % of applicants accepted | 90 |

### FRESHMAN PROFILE
| | |
|---|---|
| Range ACT Composite | 25-30 |
| Average ACT Composite | 27 |
| Minimum TOEFL | 550 |
| Average HS GPA | 3.5 |
| % graduated top 10% of class | 40 |
| % graduated top 25% of class | 70 |
| % graduated top 50% of class | 94 |

### DEADLINES
| | |
|---|---|
| Priority admission | 12/1 |
| Regular admission | 7/1 |
| Nonfall registration? | yes |

### APPLICANTS ALSO LOOK AT AND OFTEN PREFER
U. Illinois—Urbana-Champaign
MIT
U. Missouri—Columbia
Truman State
U. Wisconsin—Madison

### AND SOMETIMES PREFER
U. Iowa
Georgia Tech.
Purdue U.—West Lafayette

## FINANCIAL FACTS
★ ★ ★ ☆

| | |
|---|---|
| Financial Aid Rating | 85 |
| In-state tuition | $4,602 |
| Out-of-state tuition | $13,755 |
| Room and board | $5,230 |
| Books and supplies | $850 |
| Required fees | $778 |
| % frosh receiving aid | 49 |
| % undergrads receiving aid | 50 |
| Avg frosh grant | $5,900 |
| Avg frosh loan | $3,400 |

# UNIVERSITY OF MONTANA—MISSOULA

103 LODGE BUILDING, MISSOULA, MT 59812 • ADMISSIONS: 406-243-6266 • FAX: 406-243-5711

## CAMPUS LIFE

| | |
|---|---|
| Quality of Life Rating | 79 |
| Type of school | public |
| Environment | urban |

### STUDENTS

| | |
|---|---|
| Total undergrad enrollment | 10,828 |
| % male/female | 47/53 |
| % from out of state | 26 |
| % from public high school | 56 |
| % live on campus | 20 |
| % in (# of) fraternities | 6 (8) |
| % in (# of) sororities | 5 (4) |
| % Asian | 1 |
| % Caucasian | 90 |
| % Hispanic | 1 |
| % international | 2 |

### SURVEY SAYS . . .
Students are religious
Dorms are like palaces
Great on-campus food
Lousy off-campus food

## ACADEMICS

| | |
|---|---|
| Academic Rating | 79 |
| Calendar | semester |
| Student/faculty ratio | 22:1 |
| Profs interesting rating | 70 |
| Profs accessible rating | 72 |
| % profs teaching UG courses | 100 |
| % classes taught by TAs | 7 |
| Avg lab size | 20-29 students |
| Avg reg class size | 10-19 students |

### MOST POPULAR MAJORS
Business, management, marketing, and related support services
Education
English language and literature

## STUDENTS SPEAK OUT

### Academics

Students at University of Montana—Missoula love the gestalt of their school, telling us that "Missoula is one of the best places to be: friendly people, supportive faculty, a great sense of community, fantastic educational opportunities, and beautiful, beautiful scenery!" Montana receives praise for its offerings in a broad range of subjects—English literature, wildlife biology, business, and communications are just a few our respondents named—although students worry that recent state financial problems will cause some departments to shrink or even disappear. In the wake of budget cuts, many here resent the school's focus on intercollegiate athletics; "the contrast of the buildings on campus is ridiculous," complained a typical undergrad. "We have [a] fancy stadium and sport center, but we have [a] crappy and dilapidated math building, for example." Others gripe that UM sets the academic bar too low; "if you want to learn a lot, you must pay attention and study a lot out of desire. The course load is not very demanding," writes one student. For students seeking a greater challenge, "The honors college is a lifesaver. Honors classes are small and taught by many of the university's best professors. All the resources for an unmatched education are here, as long as you are willing to take responsibility for finding them." UM professors "are easy to relate to, because they are in Montana for the same reason we are . . . outdoor recreation!" They are also "very accessible and grade reasonably."

### Life

"Missoula is definitely a granola town," students at UM agree. "Everyone is very earthy, into the environment and the outdoors." Campus life mirrors the life of the town; UM students tend to be hippie-ish, outdoorsy types who, atypically, love football. When not immersed in their studies, undergrads here "are usually enjoying the amazing outdoor possibilities. Missoula is known for its beautiful mountains and streams, which lend themselves to almost any outdoor activity." Despite "three ski mountains within an hour," during the cold winters "activities are harder to come by." The social scene kicks up after the "Montana winter retreats in time for the summer fire season." Students of drinking age enjoy a lively bar scene; "the nightlife for those over 21 is great. There are bars and places for you to hang out no matter what kind of person you are," explains one student. Life is less active for the under-21 set; as one student told us, "UM needs to improve on entertainment for students on and off campus who are under 21. There is nowhere to really go to dance if you are not of age. Besides going to the movies, bowling, and maybe ice skating, you are limited." Underclassmen can't simply fall back on the frat-party scene since "Greek life is not a huge thing here." In the fall, it's all about football; "Griz football is huge here. People live and die for their football around here."

### Student Body

Students at UM are "very open and friendly. It is easy to meet people in any class or just out in the open oval." The student body includes "lots of people from the East Coast. Kids come out here, get into the laid-back vibe, turn into hippies (trustafarians, they're called), and 30 years down the road they still live in Missoula. No one ever wants to leave!" Like hometown Missoula (but unlike the rest of Montana), "there is a very liberal sense of politics at UM. The town reinforces that, making it easy for a person to hold and stick to their personal values." Fortunately, "while people out here tend to be pretty opinionated, everyone still gets along royally. Students are very respectful of others." Most here agree that "the school community could use a little more diversity."

# UNIVERSITY OF MONTANA—MISSOULA

FINANCIAL AID: 406-243-5373 • E-MAIL: ADMISS@SELWAY.UMT.EDU • WEBSITE: WWW.UMT.EDU

## ADMISSIONS
*Very important factors considered include:* class rank, standardized test scores. *Important factors considered include:* extracurricular activities, secondary school record, talent/ability. *Other factors considered include:* interview, minority status, recommendations, volunteer work, work experience. SAT I or ACT required. TOEFL required of all international applicants. High school diploma or GED is required. *High school units required/recommended:* 4 English required, 3 math required, 2 science required, 2 science lab required, 3 social studies required.

### The Inside Word
Montana's rolling admissions process places few demands on its applicants. Most students with a college-prep curriculum in high school and average grades should encounter no trouble gaining admission.

## FINANCIAL AID
*Students should submit:* FAFSA, institution's own financial aid form. No deadline for regular filing. The Princeton Review suggests that all financial aid forms be submitted as soon as possible after January 1. *Need-based scholarships/grants offered:* Pell, SEOG, state scholarships/grants, private scholarships, the school's own gift aid. *Loan aid offered:* FFEL Subsidized Stafford, FFEL Unsubsidized Stafford, FFEL PLUS, Federal Perkins. Federal Work-Study Program available. Institutional employment available. Applicants will be notified of awards on a rolling basis beginning on or about April 1. Off-campus job opportunities are excellent.

## FROM THE ADMISSIONS OFFICE
"There's something special about this place. It's something different for each person. For some, it's the blend of academic quality and outdoor recreation. For others, it's size. Not too big. Not too little. Just right. Thirteen thousand students. A community that could pass for a cozy college town or a bustling big city, depending on your point of view. There's a lot happening, but you won't get lost. There are the people. Friendly. Diverse. They come from all over the world to study and learn and to live a good life. Mostly to live a good life. They come to a place to be inspired. A place where they feel comfortable yet challenged. Some never leave. Most never want to."

### SELECTIVITY

| | |
|---|---|
| Admissions Rating | 76 |
| # of applicants | 3,560 |
| % of applicants accepted | 88 |
| % of acceptees attending | 61 |

### FRESHMAN PROFILE
| | |
|---|---|
| Range SAT Verbal | 450-600 |
| Average SAT Verbal | 550 |
| Range SAT Math | 470-590 |
| Average SAT Math | 540 |
| Range ACT Composite | 20-25 |
| Average ACT Composite | 22 |
| Minimum TOEFL | 500 |
| Average HS GPA | 3.2 |
| % graduated top 10% of class | 14 |
| % graduated top 25% of class | 33 |
| % graduated top 50% of class | 66 |

### DEADLINES
| | |
|---|---|
| Regular notification | rolling |
| Nonfall registration? | yes |

### APPLICANTS ALSO LOOK AT AND SOMETIMES PREFER
Montana State
U Colorado
Colorado State
U Oregon
Washington State
U Idaho
U Washington

### FINANCIAL FACTS

| | |
|---|---|
| Financial Aid Rating | 89 |
| In-state tuition | $2,873 |
| Out-of-state tuition | $9,868 |
| Room and board | $5,090 |
| Books and supplies | $700 |
| Required fees | $1,115 |
| % frosh receiving aid | 48 |
| % undergrads receiving aid | 50 |
| Avg frosh grant | $2,500 |
| Avg frosh loan | $2,849 |

THE BEST 351 COLLEGES ■ 611

# UNIVERSITY OF NEBRASKA—LINCOLN

1410 Q STREET, LINCOLN, NE 68588-0417 • ADMISSIONS: 402-472-2023 • FAX: 402-472-0670

## CAMPUS LIFE

| | |
|---|---|
| Quality of Life Rating | 88 |
| Type of school | public |
| Environment | urban |

### STUDENTS

| | |
|---|---|
| Total undergrad enrollment | 18,118 |
| % male/female | 52/48 |
| % from out of state | 14 |
| % live on campus | 25 |
| % in (# of) fraternities | 15 (26) |
| % in (# of) sororities | 17 (16) |
| % African American | 2 |
| % Asian | 2 |
| % Caucasian | 89 |
| % Hispanic | 2 |
| % international | 3 |
| # of countries represented | 124 |

### SURVEY SAYS . . .
Everyone loves the Cornhuskers
(Almost) everyone plays intramural sports
Frats and sororities dominate social scene
Students are happy
Student publications are popular
Great off-campus food
Class discussions are rare
Large classes
Library needs improving

## ACADEMICS

| | |
|---|---|
| Academic Rating | 75 |
| Calendar | semester |
| Student/faculty ratio | 19:1 |
| Profs interesting rating | 80 |
| Profs accessible rating | 75 |
| % classes taught by TAs | 17 |
| Avg lab size | 20-29 students |
| Avg reg class size | 20-29 students |

## STUDENTS SPEAK OUT

### Academics

Students at University of Nebraska—Lincoln tell us that their school offers "the opportunities of a large school, but with a small school feel." Nebraska achieves its "small school feel" by dividing its 18,000 undergraduates into it's undergraduate colleges: Agricultural Sciences and Natural Resources, Architecture, Arts & Sciences, Business Administration, Engineering and Technology, Fine & Performing Arts, Human Resources and Family Sciences, Journalism and Mass Communication, and Teachers. Further personal touches are supplied by "a very strong and prominent Greek system as well as one of the best residence hall systems in the area." Students brag that UNL offers "great access to research opportunities combined with good access to professors and community" and that "the full professors are quite good, although the TAs and graduate assistants often leave something to be desired." Even with all the intimate touches, UNL's scope can be a little intimidating; the resultant fears, however, are relatively easy to overcome. As one student put it, "My freshman year, I was scared to death of the large lecture halls. I took my parents' advice, though, and got to know my professors. I have discovered that they are there to help you if you just make a little effort to show that you need or want it." Surprisingly (considering this is a state school), undergrads here report "very little red tape to deal with. Bills are easy to pay in person or online, class registration is a breeze, and any concerns I have had have been answered promptly by administration."

### Life

Lincoln's nation of 18,000 Cornhuskers agrees that "athletics, both intramural and intercollegiate, are a big part of the culture at Nebraska. It has a unifying effect among students and impacts the social life of most. The best part of the school year is definitely the football season." There's more to life in Lincoln than game day, however. Students here enjoy an active social life that centers on the Greek houses (especially for those under 21) and O Street and its "30+ bars that are packed with college kids on weekends." Our respondents report that alcohol is popular "even though UNL is a dry campus . . . . The rule is strictly enforced." Student opinions vary on hometown Lincoln. Some brag that "Lincoln is definitely a 'college town'" because "less than two blocks away [from campus] are the historic HayMarket, movie theaters, the Lied Center for Performing Arts, and the bar and club district." Others, noting that much of the entertainment near campus is limited to the 21-and-over crowd, complain that "there's not a lot to do in this town, so it helps to have good friends to spend time with." Summing up campus life, one student writes the following: "Sports and beer—that's Nebraska nightlife. People try to change and do different things, but it always comes back to sports and beer." Adds another, "Either you drink or you go to Bible study. That's it. And some people do both!"

### Student Body

While most students at UNL "are from Nebraska or surrounding areas," "there are students from every state and many, many countries" at the university. "There are more minority and international students now than when I first started college in 1999," notes one senior, although most here agree that "there is not a lot of diversity on campus." A sizable number of students are "very religious," and "many of them try and force this on others, who do not wish it." On the upside, "most students are involved with at least one organization on campus," and "because football is so big and many of our other athletic teams are excellent (volleyball, wrestling, gymnastics, bowling), there's a real emphasis among the student body on exercise and athletics."

# UNIVERSITY OF NEBRASKA—LINCOLN

FINANCIAL AID: 402-472-2030 • E-MAIL: NUHUSKER@UNL.EDU • WEBSITE: WWW.UNL.EDU

## ADMISSIONS

*Very important factors considered include:* class rank, secondary school record, standardized test scores. *Important factors considered include:* talent/ability. *Other factors considered include:* alumni/ae relation, geographical residence, minority status, recommendations. SAT I or ACT required. TOEFL required of all international applicants. High school diploma or GED is required. *High school units required/recommended:* 16 total required; 4 English required, 4 math required, 3 science required, 1 science lab required, 2 foreign language required, 3 social studies required, 1 history recommended.

### The Inside Word

Like most large-scale universities, Nebraska—Lincoln admits a huge freshman class each year. The need for numbers is reflected in an admissions process that concentrates on them—your course selection, GPA, and test scores will be all they need to see. Unless you've had troubles academically, they're likely to welcome you aboard, though some programs have higher expectations than others.

## FINANCIAL AID

*Students should submit:* FAFSA. No deadline for regular filing. The Princeton Review suggests that all financial aid forms be submitted as soon as possible after January 1. *Need-based scholarships/grants offered:* Pell, SEOG, state scholarships/grants, private scholarships, the school's own gift aid. *Loan aid offered:* Direct Subsidized Stafford, Direct Unsubsidized Stafford, Direct PLUS, Federal Perkins, college/university loans from institutional funds. Federal Work-Study Program available. Institutional employment available. Applicants will be notified of awards on a rolling basis beginning on or about April 15. Off-campus job opportunities are excellent.

## FROM THE ADMISSIONS OFFICE

"Chartered in 1869, the University of Nebraska—Lincoln has since grown to become a major international research university, offering 149 undergraduate majors and 118 graduate programs. While 90 percent of the 23,000 students come from Nebraska, students from every state and 110 countries choose the university for its comprehensive programs and reputation for quality. Nebraska is classified as a Carnegie I Research Institution, recognizing the university's commitment to research funding and quality scholarship, and has been a member of the Association of American Universities since 1909—one of only 62 universities to claim this prestigious membership. These affiliations ensure Nebraska students are taught by nationally and internationally recognized faculty who are experts in their fields, bringing the latest discoveries into their classrooms. Lincoln—Nebraska's capital with a population of more than 213,000—offers the comfort and security of a college town with the cultural and entertainment opportunities of a larger city."

### SELECTIVITY

| | |
|---|---|
| Admissions Rating | 91 |
| # of applicants | 7,631 |
| % of applicants accepted | 90 |
| % of acceptees attending | 53 |

### FRESHMAN PROFILE

| | |
|---|---|
| Range SAT Verbal | 500-640 |
| Average SAT Verbal | 570 |
| Range SAT Math | 520-660 |
| Average SAT Math | 589 |
| Range ACT Composite | 21-27 |
| Average ACT Composite | 24 |
| Minimum TOEFL | 525 |
| % graduated top 10% of class | 26 |
| % graduated top 25% of class | 53 |
| % graduated top 50% of class | 85 |

### DEADLINES

| | |
|---|---|
| Priority admission | 1/15 |
| Regular admission | 6/30 |
| Nonfall registration? | yes |

### FINANCIAL FACTS

| | |
|---|---|
| Financial Aid Rating | 84 |
| In-state tuition | $3,345 |
| Out-of-state tuition | $9,938 |
| Room and board | $4,875 |
| Books and supplies | $756 |
| Required fees | $780 |
| % frosh receiving aid | 41 |
| % undergrads receiving aid | 40 |
| Avg frosh grant | $3,934 |
| Avg frosh loan | $2,588 |

# UNIVERSITY OF NEVADA—LAS VEGAS

4505 MARYLAND PARKWAY, BOX 451021, LAS VEGAS, NV 89154-1021 • ADMISSIONS: 702-895-3443 • FAX: 702-895-1118

## CAMPUS LIFE

| | |
|---|---|
| Quality of Life Rating | 90 |
| Type of school | public |
| Environment | urban |

### STUDENTS

| | |
|---|---|
| Total undergrad enrollment | 19,761 |
| % male/female | 44/56 |
| % from out of state | 21 |
| % live on campus | 8 |
| % in (# of) fraternities | 7 (8) |
| % in (# of) sororities | 5 (6) |
| % African American | 8 |
| % Asian | 14 |
| % Caucasian | 57 |
| % Hispanic | 10 |
| % international | 4 |
| # of countries represented | 84 |

### SURVEY SAYS . . .

(Almost) everyone plays intramural sports
Everyone loves the Runnin' Rebels
Athletic facilities are great
Dorms are like palaces
Great off-campus food
(Almost) no one listens to college radio
Student publications are ignored

## ACADEMICS

| | |
|---|---|
| Academic Rating | 74 |
| Calendar | semester |
| Student/faculty ratio | 19:1 |
| Profs interesting rating | 86 |
| Profs accessible rating | 97 |
| % profs teaching UG courses | 88 |
| % classes taught by TAs | 11 |
| Avg lab size | 10-19 students |
| Avg reg class size | 20-29 students |

### MOST POPULAR MAJORS

Hotel/motel administration/management
Communications studies/speech communication and rhetoric
Elementary education and teaching

## STUDENTS SPEAK OUT

### Academics

Established in the late 1950s, UNLV is young, and there's no doubt that it's experienced some growing pains along the way. But "the notion that UNLV is an oasis for party-goers, strippers, and gambling is changing," declaims a junior business management major. "Each year we get better teachers, better classes, etc." Indeed, UNLV students almost uniformly dig their professors. "Our professors are real people," writes a sophomore. "Most of them really seem to care about students," adds a classmate. A more even-handed student believes that "instructors are either extremely talented or extremely incompetent." Incompetence seems to be endemic amongst teaching assistants. One biology major groans, "I am appalled at the TAs' ability to teach well-educated students like vapid kindergartners." But since UNLV is a state school with a wide range of professors and TAs, students who do a little homework before signing up for a course should be able to avoid instructors of the "very boring" or "incompetent" types. UNLV offers around 65 courses of study, including its highly acclaimed hotel management program. And students with the right credentials can take advantage of the Honors College, an academic track that provides the advantages of small classes, close interaction with faculty members, early registration, and scholarship opportunities. And all UNLV Rebels can take advantage of the new—and much esteemed—library on campus. As one student tells us, "Now you can actually get a good education and still have fun in Sin City."

### Life

"It's Vegas baby!"—the self-described Entertainment Capital of the World. As you can probably imagine, there's plenty here to distract even the most diligent student from chemistry homework. "There are so many concerts here it boggles my mind," raves a sophomore, while others point to "clubbing" and "cruising the strip" as opportunities to strut and pick up. There is an age factor, though. "If you are 21, you have fun," reports one student. Then he reconsiders, adding, "If you have a fake, you have fun." Students under 21 often turn to campus activities, which receive mixed reviews. "Our school is a commuter school," writes a junior, "so not much happens as far as campus life." Yet others tell us that there's "always something going on." A good example of this is the annual music fest, Rebelpalooza. Also, "fraternities and sororities are very active." Translation: Parties aren't too hard to find. For the athletically inclined, there are 16 Division I sports teams and 20 intramural teams. And for the intellectually or artistically inclined, events like the Charles Vanda Master Series and the Barrick Lecture Series have summoned to campus guest speakers and performers such as Mark Russell, David Broder, James Carville, Mary Matalin, and Cokie Roberts. The Barbara Greenspan Lecture Series presented former president Bill Clinton in April 2002. Campus and community theatres, galleries, and museums are also a draw. And let's not forget the great outdoors. With an average yearly temperature of 79 degrees, students "often go hiking and camping on Mount Charleton," "skiing at Lee Canyon," and when they're up for a five-hour road trip, they hit the beaches of southern California.

### Student Body

Nontraditional is perhaps the best way to describe the student body at UNLV. The average undergrad here is around 25, and many students commute to campus. Some students praise the diversity of the undergrad population while others would like to see "more ethnicity." One of the reasons that students may not appreciate the campus's multicultural makeup is that "students never get together at this university." "Small cliques" plaster the landscape here, often separated according to race, Greek letters/GDIs, or friends from the area who knew each other before coming to UNLV. As a result, one hotel management major describes the university as "more of a tossed salad than a melting pot." Still, the general feeling is that this is an "awesome," "laid-back" group that, as a whole, can be "friendly, popular, smart, witty, funny."

# UNIVERSITY OF NEVADA—LAS VEGAS

FINANCIAL AID: 702-895-3424 • E-MAIL: UNDRGRADADMISION@CCMAIL.NEVADA.EDU • WEBSITE: WWW.UNLV.EDU

## ADMISSIONS

*Very important factors considered include:* secondary school record. *Other factors considered include:* standardized test scores. TOEFL required of all international applicants. High school diploma or GED is required. *High school units required/recommended:* 13 total required; 4 English required, 3 math required, 3 science required, 2 science lab required, 3 social studies required.

### The Inside Word

The admissions process at UNLV is pretty direct. The focus is on academic achievement as gauged by your course selection, grades, and test scores. A minimum of a 2.5 cumulative, unweighted GPA is required, which is atypical of more selective universities that factor in weighting for AP and honors courses. Student who fall short of course unit requirements can sometimes get admitted anyway due to a higher GPA or test scores

## FINANCIAL AID

*Students should submit:* FAFSA, institution's own financial aid form. No deadline for regular filing. The Princeton Review suggests that all financial aid forms be submitted as soon as possible after January 1. *Need-based scholarships/grants offered:* Pell, SEOG, state scholarships/grants, private scholarships, the school's own gift aid. *Loan aid offered:* Direct Subsidized Stafford, Direct Unsubsidized Stafford, Direct PLUS, Federal Perkins, state loans, college/university loans from institutional funds. Federal Work-Study Program available. Institutional employment available. Applicants will be notified of awards on a rolling basis beginning on or about April 1. Off-campus job opportunities are excellent.

## FROM THE ADMISSIONS OFFICE

"The University of Nevada—Las Vegas is located in one of the fastest-growing, most exciting areas of the country, in the beautiful desert Southwest. Its distinctive programs include a world-class College of Hotel Administration, with the Las Vegas Strip as its lab; the new William S. Boyd School of Law; a nationally recognized honors college; a community-involved environmental studies program; innovative desert environment programs; international education opportunities; accredited architecture, social work, and business schools; a new physical therapy program; and numerous research centers and interdisciplinary programs. A $50 million library, with a state-of-the-art book retrieval system, opened in 2000. UNLV is also known for its nationally competitive intercollegiate athletics programs."

## SELECTIVITY

| | |
|---|---|
| Admissions Rating | 73 |
| # of applicants | 5,538 |
| % of applicants accepted | 82 |
| % of acceptees attending | 55 |

### FRESHMAN PROFILE

| | |
|---|---|
| Range SAT Verbal | 430-560 |
| Average SAT Verbal | 501 |
| Range SAT Math | 450-570 |
| Average SAT Math | 514 |
| Range ACT Composite | 19-24 |
| Average ACT Composite | 21 |
| Minimum TOEFL | 500 |
| Average HS GPA | 3.2 |
| % graduated top 10% of class | 19 |
| % graduated top 25% of class | 49 |
| % graduated top 50% of class | 84 |

### DEADLINES

| | |
|---|---|
| Priority admission | 5/15 |
| Regular admission | 7/15 |
| Nonfall registration? | yes |

## FINANCIAL FACTS

| | |
|---|---|
| Financial Aid Rating | 84 |
| In-state tuition | $2,670 |
| Out-of-state tuition | $11,157 |
| Room and board | $6,140 |
| Books and supplies | $850 |
| Required fees | $126 |
| % frosh receiving aid | 44 |
| % undergrads receiving aid | 42 |
| Avg frosh grant | $5,660 |
| Avg frosh loan | $2,505 |

THE BEST 351 COLLEGES ■ 615

# UNIVERSITY OF NEW HAMPSHIRE

4 GARRISON AVENUE, DURHAM, NH 03824 • ADMISSIONS: 603-862-1360 • FAX: 603-862-0077

## CAMPUS LIFE

| | |
|---|---|
| Quality of Life Rating | 87 |
| Type of school | public |
| Environment | rural |

### STUDENTS

| | |
|---|---|
| Total undergrad enrollment | 11,496 |
| % male/female | 43/57 |
| % from out of state | 43 |
| % from public high school | 78 |
| % live on campus | 51 |
| % in (# of) fraternities | 5 (10) |
| % in (# of) sororities | 5 (5) |
| % African American | 1 |
| % Asian | 2 |
| % Caucasian | 90 |
| % Hispanic | 1 |
| % international | 1 |
| # of countries represented | 28 |

### SURVEY SAYS . . .
Lots of beer drinking
Campus is beautiful
Great library
Athletic facilities are great
Everyone loves the Wildcats
Hard liquor is popular
Students are happy
(Almost) everyone smokes
Great off-campus food
(Almost) everyone plays intramural sports

## ACADEMICS

| | |
|---|---|
| Academic Rating | 75 |
| Calendar | semester |
| Student/faculty ratio | 14:1 |
| % profs teaching UG courses | 77 |
| % classes taught by TAs | 4 |
| Avg lab size | 10-19 students |
| Avg reg class size | 10-19 students |

### MOST POPULAR MAJORS
Business administration/management
English language and literature
Psychology

## STUDENTS SPEAK OUT

### Academics

As is the case at most large, public universities, professors at UNH don't coddle students. It's up to the latter to take the initiative to get to know the former or to locate the resources they need to develop academically. Enterprising students will find, however, that "the professors are very open" when approached. Notwithstanding a few bad-apple instructors, most students report that their "professors are excellent." Some of the highlights of UNH academics include the Undergraduate Research Opportunities Program (UROP), which matches students interested in doing independent research with an appropriate faculty advisor and hooks them up with the necessary funds to accomplish said research. The engineering department gets rave reviews as well. Some students complain that they have trouble finding quiet space to work on their studies, though: "The library closes promptly at midnight Sunday-Thursday, and 8 P.M. on Friday and Saturday." But most of the student dissatisfaction at UNH stems from the administrative problems, such as class registration. A sophomore grumbles, "I have not been able to enroll in any of my first-choice courses. This is due to overbooking and the classes not being offered."

### Life

Hockey is basically an institution at UNH, drawing a consistent stream of participants and spectators, since "UNH [intercollegiate] hockey tickets are free to students." In general, athleticism runs deep at this "beautiful" campus in the "kind of isolated" town of Durham, New Hampshire. "Skiing, biking, hiking"—all of these outdoor activities are easy to access. For the indoors-inclined, student-run activities, including "laser tag, bingo, bowling, poetry and story readings," as well as "local band performances," are popular. For chem-free students "there is an organization here called Weekend Warriors that sponsors nonalcoholic events like carnivals and movie nights." For drinkers, "Frat Row"—center of the "huge Greek life" on campus—is a popular party destination. Recreational drug use also has its place at UNH. According to an undergrad, "The University of New Hampshire is drenched with a sweet perfume—the tireless scent of a blunt and an open bottle." Still, some students say that the university's "party school" label is not entirely deserved because most people "only drink on occasion or choose not to drink at all." Students don't find much to do in tiny hometown Durham. Instead, when they need time away from school, students take advantage of the "shuttle service" to nearby "cities like Dover, Newmarket, and Portsmouth."

### Student Body

About 60 percent of UNH students hail from New Hampshire, with many others coming from nearby Massachusetts, Maine, and Connecticut. "Ethnic diversity is strongly lacking" on campus, which leads some students to cry, "HOMOGENEOUS." But just in skin color. One student offers this colorful breakdown: "It works like this—there are two extremes, the Super Preps and the Hippies. The Super Preps wear Abercrombie and Fitch and drink imported beer. They are generally stodgy and stuck up, upper-class suburban kids who couldn't get into Ivy League schools. On the other side of the spectrum you have the hippies. They wear anything earthy, secondhand, or hand-made. They don't drink beer, they drink chai and smoke pot. In between these two extremes lies most of the UNH population. You have your jocks who drink Natty Ice and keg beer and generally associate with other jocks. You have your Trendoids who carry cell phones and constantly change their wardrobe. You have your Greeks who are loyal to each other despite the fact that they aren't a respectable bunch. You've got your usual conglomeration of sluts and drawer-droppers who go out on weekends in search of anything that is remotely human and willing to have sex with it. You've got your free spirits who run the Student Cable Access Network (SCAN) and will do anything anywhere as long as it's fun. You've got your druggies who smoke anything you can roll into a cigarette paper." Despite all of these cliques, "these groups will interact with each other" and "have fun together."

# UNIVERSITY OF NEW HAMPSHIRE

FINANCIAL AID: 603-862-3600 • E-MAIL: ADMISSIONS@UNH.EDU • WEBSITE: WWW.UNH.EDU

## ADMISSIONS
*Very important factors considered include:* secondary school record. *Important factors considered include:* class rank, essays, recommendations, standardized test scores, state residency. *Other factors considered include:* alumni/ae relation, character/personal qualities, extracurricular activities, geographical residence, minority status, talent/ability, volunteer work, work experience. SAT I or ACT required, SAT I preferred. TOEFL required of all international applicants. High school diploma or GED is required. *High school units required/recommended:* 18 total recommended; 4 English recommended, 4 math recommended, 4 science recommended, 4 science lab recommended, 3 foreign language recommended, 3 social studies recommended.

### The Inside Word
New Hampshire's emphasis on academic accomplishment in the admissions process makes it clear that the admissions committee is looking for students who have taken high school seriously. Standardized tests take as much of a backseat here as is possible at a large public university.

## FINANCIAL AID
*Students should submit:* FAFSA. The Princeton Review suggests that all financial aid forms be submitted as soon as possible after January 1. *Need-based scholarships/grants offered:* Pell, SEOG, state scholarships/grants, private scholarships, the school's own gift aid. *Loan aid offered:* FFEL Subsidized Stafford, FFEL Unsubsidized Stafford, FFEL PLUS, Federal Perkins, state loans, college/university loans from institutional funds. Federal Work-Study Program available. Institutional employment available. Applicants will be notified of awards on a rolling basis beginning on or about March 1. Off-campus job opportunities are excellent.

## FROM THE ADMISSIONS OFFICE
"The University of New Hampshire is a public university founded in 1866 with an undergraduate population of 11,000 students. UNH offers an excellent education at a reasonable cost to students with a broad range of interests. Over 100 majors, 2,000 courses, and 130 student clubs and organizations are offered. Programs that provide valuable experience include the honors program, undergraduate research, internships, study abroad, and national exchange. UNH's location also caters to a wide range of interests. The campus itself is in a small town setting, surrounded by woods and farms; within 20 minutes is the Atlantic coastline, and just over an hour away are the White Mountains, Boston, and Portland."

### SELECTIVITY

| | |
|---|---|
| Admissions Rating | 78 |
| # of applicants | 10,376 |
| % of applicants accepted | 77 |
| % of acceptees attending | 34 |

#### FRESHMAN PROFILE
| | |
|---|---|
| Range SAT Verbal | 500-590 |
| Average SAT Verbal | 546 |
| Range SAT Math | 510-610 |
| Average SAT Math | 558 |
| Minimum TOEFL | 550 |
| % graduated top 10% of class | 18 |
| % graduated top 25% of class | 53 |
| % graduated top 50% of class | 94 |

#### DEADLINES
| | |
|---|---|
| Regular admission | 2/1 |
| Regular notification | 4/15 |
| Nonfall registration? | yes |

#### APPLICANTS ALSO LOOK AT AND OFTEN PREFER
Boston College
University of Vermont

**AND SOMETIMES PREFER**
Syracuse University
Boston University
University of Massachusetts—Amherst
University of Connecticut
Northeastern University

**AND RARELY PREFER**
University of Rhode Island
University of Maine
Keene State College

### FINANCIAL FACTS

| | |
|---|---|
| Financial Aid Rating | 86 |
| Books and supplies | $1,300 |
| % frosh receiving aid | 54 |
| % undergrads receiving aid | 53 |
| Avg frosh grant | $6,630 |
| Avg frosh loan | $3,538 |

# UNIVERSITY OF NEW MEXICO

OFFICE OF ADMISSIONS, STUDENT SERVICES CENTER 150, ALBUQUERQUE, NM 87131-2046 • ADMISSIONS: 800-225-5866

## CAMPUS LIFE

★ ★ ☆ ☆

| | |
|---|---|
| Quality of Life Rating | 78 |
| Type of school | public |
| Environment | urban |

### STUDENTS

| | |
|---|---|
| Total undergrad enrollment | 16,806 |
| % male/female | 43/57 |
| % from out of state | 12 |
| % live on campus | 11 |
| % African American | 3 |
| % Asian | 4 |
| % Caucasian | 50 |
| % Hispanic | 33 |
| % international | 1 |

### SURVEY SAYS . . .
Everyone loves the Lobos
Very little drug use
Popular college radio
Great library
Class discussions are rare
Ethnic diversity on campus
Large classes
Lots of long lines and red tape
Lots of TAs teach upper-level courses
Lab facilities are great

## ACADEMICS

| | |
|---|---|
| Academic Rating | 71 |
| Calendar | semester |
| Student/faculty ratio | 17:1 |
| Profs interesting rating | 74 |
| Profs accessible rating | 73 |
| Avg lab size | 20-29 students |
| Avg reg class size | 20-29 students |

### MOST POPULAR MAJORS
Elementary education and teaching
General studies
Psychology

## STUDENTS SPEAK OUT

### Academics

At a terrific bargain, especially for state residents, students overwhelmingly describe their academic experience at UNM as "worth the money." When students here rave about their academics, they tend to mention things like the "good student/professor communication," the challenging "University Honors Program," or the terrific resources of the business school. Education, engineering, pre-medical sciences, and business are the popular majors here. But these only represent the tip of the scholastic iceberg in sunny Albuquerque; undergrads choose from nearly 150 majors and concentrations. The biggest problem with undergrad courses is that many are led "by TAs who really don't know how to teach well." But when students do get the chance to work closely with actual professors, they find them "extremely helpful" and "extraordinarily knowledgeable in their fields." As you'll find at many large, state institutions, people here are more likely to complain about the administration—and its bureaucratic nature—than to praise it. "It is very hard to access the administration when specific funding is needed or specific issues need [addressing]," writes an upperclassman. One Hispanic student believes the administration is out-of-touch and hypocritical, billing itself as a "Hispanic serving institution" and then allowing the "Chicano studies program" to fall into "a sad state of affairs due to virtually NO funding." If the cards fall right, however, one finds "a great academic experience at the University of New Mexico."

### Life

The UNM campus is replete with Spanish Pueblo revival architecture, a visual display that reflects the fusion of cultures present here. Fittingly, "there are many cultural activities" during any given week to help students "appreciate the differences" among people in the world around them. And speaking of the world around them, students take advantage of the nearby nature by "biking and hiking" and participating in "just about any outdoor activity" one can conceive. Though located in the heart of Albuquerque, UNM is only "about a 30-minute drive to a hike in the mountains, two hours from a lake, one hour from the art and culture of Santa Fe, and in just about any direction there is a Native American reservation." Albuquerque itself, however, "is admittedly lackluster." While UNM is officially a "dry campus," students have no problem finding places to throw a party. Aside from the staple frat parties, "there are the infamous 'Rugby House' parties" and regular bashes thrown by the large off-campus population, leading some students to complain that "getting drunk and getting high is the number-one priority here." Others point to outings to the "huge movie theatre" and "sports-plex" nearby, or to leisure hours of "bowling" and "golf." "It's just about people doing what they like and enjoying themselves," offers one non-drinking sophomore. "There's nothing wrong with that."

### Student Body

The student body at UNM is decidedly nontraditional. Numerous students commute, though there's definitely also an on-campus contingent. And most students here "have full or part-time jobs," though they also make time to hit the books. The average age of UNM undergrads is somewhere in the mid-20s. Almost 30 percent of the population is Hispanic and 11 percent is Native American, providing a racial ratio that is laudably unusual on the American higher-ed landscape. "At the University of New Mexico we pride ourselves on diversity," comments one undergraduate. In fact, the only diversity that's notably absent is geographic diversity; about 90 percent of UNM students hail from the Land of Enchantment. This statistic reportedly "makes it hard on those of us who are from out of state" because many people seem to have formed their cliques before coming to college.

# UNIVERSITY OF NEW MEXICO

Fax: 505-277-6686 • Financial Aid: 505-277-2041 • E-mail: apply@unm.edu • Website: www.unm.edu

## ADMISSIONS

*Very important factors considered include:* secondary school record. *Important factors considered include:* class rank, standardized test scores. *Other factors considered include:* essays, recommendations. SAT I or ACT required; ACT preferred. TOEFL required of all international applicants. High school diploma or GED is required. *High school units required/recommended:* 13 total required; 4 English required, 3 math required, 2 science required, 1 science lab required, 2 foreign language required, 2 social studies required, 1 history required.

## The Inside Word

UNM's rolling admissions process is quite typical of large public universities. Consideration is based nearly entirely on courses, grades, and test scores, though recommendations can sometimes help a candidate. Solid average students should encounter no difficulty in gaining an offer of admission.

## FINANCIAL AID

*Students should submit:* FAFSA. No deadline for regular filing. The Princeton Review suggests that all financial aid forms be submitted as soon as possible after January 1. *Need-based scholarships/grants offered:* Pell, SEOG, state scholarships/grants, private scholarships, the school's own gift aid, Federal Nursing. *Loan aid offered:* Direct Subsidized Stafford, Direct Unsubsidized Stafford, Federal Perkins, Federal Nursing, state loans, college/university loans from institutional funds. Federal Work-Study Program available. Institutional employment available. Applicants will be notified of awards on a rolling basis beginning on or about April 15. Off-campus job opportunities are excellent.

## FROM THE ADMISSIONS OFFICE

"The University of New Mexico is a major research institution nestled in the heart of multi-cultural Albuquerque on one of the nation's most beautiful and unique campuses. Students learn in an environment graced by distinctive southwestern architecture, beautiful plazas and fountains, spectacular art and a national arboretum . . . all within view of the 10,000-foot Sandia Mountains. At UNM, diversity is a way of learning with education enriched by a lively mix of students being taught by a world-class research faculty that includes a Nobel laureate, a MacArthur Fellow, and members of several national academies. UNM offers more than 225 degree programs and majors and has earned national recognition in dozens of disciplines, ranging from primary care medicine and clinical law to engineering, photography, Latin American history, and intercultural communications. Research and the quest for new knowledge fuels the university's commitment to an undergraduate education where students work side by side with many of the finest scholars in their fields."

## SELECTIVITY

| | |
|---|---|
| Admissions Rating | 75 |
| # of applicants | 6,232 |
| % of applicants accepted | 77 |
| % of acceptees attending | 59 |

### FRESHMAN PROFILE

| | |
|---|---|
| Range SAT Verbal | 510-610 |
| Average SAT Verbal | 572 |
| Range SAT Math | 480-590 |
| Average SAT Math | 525 |
| Range ACT Composite | 19-24 |
| Average ACT Composite | 22 |
| Minimum TOEFL | 550 |
| Average HS GPA | 3.3 |
| % graduated top 10% of class | 18 |
| % graduated top 25% of class | 46 |
| % graduated top 50% of class | 80 |

### DEADLINES

| | |
|---|---|
| Regular admission | 6/15 |
| Nonfall registration? | yes |

## FINANCIAL FACTS

| | |
|---|---|
| Financial Aid Rating | 83 |
| In-state tuition | $3,313 |
| Out-of-state tuition | $11,954 |
| Room and board | $5,910 |
| Books and supplies | $744 |
| % frosh receiving aid | 47 |
| % undergrads receiving aid | 50 |

# UNIVERSITY OF NEW ORLEANS

Office of Admissions—AD 103, Lakefront, New Orleans, LA 70148 • Admissions: 504-280-6000 • Fax: 504-280-5522

## CAMPUS LIFE

★★★☆

| | |
|---|---|
| Quality of Life Rating | 83 |
| Type of school | public |
| Environment | urban |

### STUDENTS

| | |
|---|---|
| Total undergrad enrollment | 13,189 |
| % male/female | 43/57 |
| % from out of state | 6 |
| % from public high school | 62 |
| % live on campus | 9 |
| % in (# of) fraternities | 2 (8) |
| % in (# of) sororities | 2 (6) |
| % African American | 24 |
| % Asian | 6 |
| % Caucasian | 55 |
| % Hispanic | 6 |
| % international | 3 |

### SURVEY SAYS . . .
High cost of living
Students love New Orleans, LA
Great food on campus
Class discussions are rare
Popular college radio
Very little hard liquor
Ethnic diversity on campus
Unattractive campus
Very little beer drinking
Dorms are like dungeons

## ACADEMICS

| | |
|---|---|
| Academic Rating | 71 |
| Calendar | semester |
| Student/faculty ratio | 25:1 |
| Profs interesting rating | 69 |
| Profs accessible rating | 82 |
| Avg reg class size | 20-29 students |

### MOST POPULAR MAJORS
Business administration/management
Liberal arts and sciences/liberal studies
Engineering science

## STUDENTS SPEAK OUT

### Academics

Though the name may conjure up images of masquerades and Mardi Gras, students at the University of New Orleans declare that they are "serious to learn" and came to UNO for its "record of high academic standards for its graduates." A large, public university, UNO boasts a "great engineering program" and a renowned naval architecture curriculum, as well as strong biology, business, and English departments, in which students say you get a lot of "bang for your buck." Courses can be tough, as reported by one student: "Academically, my experience at University of New Orleans has been rewarding. My professors challenge me, and I like the fact that here at UNO, grades aren't a given." Despite the overall size, students agree that UNO offers "generally small classes," but are also sure to point out that it suffers a few instructional drawbacks that most universities of its girth do. In particular, many complain that the "student teachers are terrible." One embittered undergrad recounts, "Only the higher-level course instructors seem to be able to speak fluent English, so that the people who need the most actual instruction are forced to attempt to ferret out their lesson from garbled attempts at explaining." As with most large schools, the administration receives its share of complaints, including the popular refrain, "Too much paperwork." Most importantly, students report, "the financial aid department needs a total overhaul." Jokes one, "Trying to get your financial aid is like trying to swallow a pool cue sideways."

### Life

Students say life at UNO "is as close to real life as college can get." As "the student body at UNO consists mainly of working students," the majority of whom commute, many "just come to school and go to class, then go home." As a result, "campus life isn't as involved as other schools," and "a lot of extracurricular effort is put into academics." Students are also quick to remind you, however, that "the school is in New Orleans, party capital of the world, so most students go to school here and party at surrounding places." Perhaps one student best summed up life at UNO thusly: "UNO is a great school for people who want to learn, and the city is great for people who want to party." As for those looking for more typically collegiate distractions, students report that on campus "fraternities and sororities plan activities, as well as the student housing counsel," and that "organizations on campus are very diverse and there is an organization for everybody on campus." Writes one undergrad, "We have a number of student organizations, and every organization has its own activities. The clubs/organizations are very social, so we usually support one another by attending and participating in each others' activities."

### Student Body

Students consider UNO as likely "one of the most diverse campuses in the state of Louisiana." Overall, students report that they "see little prejudice or unfairness," in the classroom and have found their "classmates to be tolerant of others and their beliefs." Some benefit from the school's diversity, as with one student who claims, "I have had the opportunity to meet friends from other parts of the world and backgrounds." Others point out, however, that "most of the African American students do not intermingle with the other students." On the whole, UNO's student body is both "friendly and capable," "willing to help each other out," and "social."

620 ■ THE BEST 351 COLLEGES

# UNIVERSITY OF NEW ORLEANS

FINANCIAL AID: 504-280-6603 • E-MAIL: ADMISSIONS@UNO.EDU • WEBSITE: WWW.UNO.EDU

## ADMISSIONS

*Very important factors considered include:* secondary school record, standardized test scores. *Other factors considered include:* alumni/ae relation, character/personal qualities, class rank, essays, extracurricular activities, interview, recommendations, state residency, talent/ability, volunteer work, work experience. SAT I or ACT required. TOEFL required of all international applicants. High school diploma or GED is required. *High school units required/recommended:* 4 English required, 3 math required, 3 science required, 2 foreign language required, 3 social studies required, 2 elective required.

### The Inside Word

It doesn't really get any more direct than the admissions process at UNO. The primary emphasis in candidate evaluation at this public university on the shores of Lake Ponchartrain is on test scores. If you've got a 950 combined SAT or a 20 composite on the ACT, you'll get in with minimal hassle. Course selection and GPA get the rest of the admissions committee's attention.

## FINANCIAL AID

*Students should submit:* FAFSA, institution's own financial aid form. The Princeton Review suggests that all financial aid forms be submitted as soon as possible after January 1. *Need-based scholarships/grants offered:* Pell, SEOG, state scholarships/grants, private scholarships, the school's own gift aid. *Loan aid offered:* FFEL Subsidized Stafford, FFEL Unsubsidized Stafford, FFEL PLUS, Federal Perkins, college/university loans from institutional funds. Federal Work-Study Program available. Institutional employment available. Applicants will be notified of awards on a rolling basis beginning on or about April 20. Off-campus job opportunities are excellent.

## FROM THE ADMISSIONS OFFICE

"Knowledge is perishable and careers inconstant. Corporate and government leaders are looking to higher education for solutions to their immediate needs. The University of New Orleans provides these leaders with graduates who can contribute to the economic, social, and academic growth of their industries now and into the future. UNO embraces its mission by providing the best educational opportunities for undergraduate and graduate students, conducting world-class research, and serving a diverse community in critical areas. The university's general level of excellence is reflected in its students and faculty. Its Centers of Excellence, which address important community needs, are recognized as among the best in the world. UNO's most outstanding offerings include a doctoral program in conservation biology providing training in the most advanced molecular biological techniques; the largest U.S. undergraduate program in naval architecture and marine engineering; one of the top 25 film programs in the country; and the only graduate arts administration program in the Gulf South."

### SELECTIVITY
★ ★ ☆ ☆

| | |
|---|---|
| Admissions Rating | 74 |
| # of applicants | 5,011 |
| % of applicants accepted | 66 |
| % of acceptees attending | 59 |

### FRESHMAN PROFILE

| | |
|---|---|
| Range SAT Verbal | 480-610 |
| Average SAT Verbal | 553 |
| Range SAT Math | 450-590 |
| Average SAT Math | 535 |
| Range ACT Composite | 18-23 |
| Average ACT Composite | 21 |
| Minimum TOEFL | 550 |

### DEADLINES

| | |
|---|---|
| Priority admission | 7/1 |
| Regular admission | 8/31 |
| Regular notification | 8/31 |
| Nonfall registration? | yes |

### FINANCIAL FACTS
★ ★ ★ ☆

| | |
|---|---|
| Financial Aid Rating | 92 |
| In-state tuition | $2,876 |
| Out-of-state tuition | $9,920 |
| Room and board | $3,888 |
| Books and supplies | $1,150 |
| Required fees | $150 |
| % frosh receiving aid | 27 |
| % undergrads receiving aid | 30 |
| Avg frosh grant | $3,500 |
| Avg frosh loan | $2,600 |

# UNIV. OF NORTH CAROLINA—ASHEVILLE

CPO #2210, 117 LIPINSKY HALL, ASHEVILLE, NC 28804-8510 • ADMISSIONS: 828-251-6481 • FAX: 828-251-6482

## CAMPUS LIFE

| | |
|---|---|
| Quality of Life Rating | 89 |
| Type of school | public |
| Environment | suburban |

### STUDENTS

| | |
|---|---|
| Total undergrad enrollment | 3,351 |
| % male/female | 42/58 |
| % from out of state | 11 |
| % live on campus | 33 |
| % in (# of) fraternities | 5 (4) |
| % in (# of) sororities | 4 (2) |
| % African American | 2 |
| % Asian | 2 |
| % Caucasian | 92 |
| % Hispanic | 1 |
| % international | 1 |

### SURVEY SAYS . . .
Campus feels safe
Campus is beautiful
Students love Asheville, NC
Dorms are like palaces
Great off-campus food
(Almost) everyone smokes
Lots of beer drinking
Great computer facilities

## ACADEMICS

| | |
|---|---|
| Academic Rating | 83 |
| Calendar | semester |
| Student/faculty ratio | 14:1 |
| % profs teaching UG courses | 100 |
| Avg lab size | 10-19 students |
| Avg reg class size | 10-19 students |

### MOST POPULAR MAJORS
Psychology
Management
Environmental science

## STUDENTS SPEAK OUT

### Academics

At the University of North Carolina—Asheville, the emphasis lies on the "freedom of the individual mind." The "challenging liberal arts curriculum," with a "major emphasis on the humanities and social sciences," provides an environment that "encourages you to think." The professors "know who you are and care about how you do," displaying not only impressive academic credentials but "a desire to actually teach and help their students in and out of class." Many faculty members "keep in active contact with their students through e-mail" and take time to address personal concerns as well as classroom issues. When the material gets overwhelming, "help is always available, and professors do not mind putting in overtime to help you understand a concept." One student reports easy interpersonal relations, assuring readers, "I could ask a prof to have coffee and this would not be weird." The administration functions transparently according to students: "They're there, but you would hardly know it unless you need to find them." The chancellor garners popularity by showing up "not only at events, but sometimes just in the dining hall. He is very warm and keeps a good relationship with the student body." Generally, the higher-ups "do not interfere in the lives of students," and the only complaint we hear is that "the state school penny-pinching is extremely evident." Finances aside, the staff, administration, and faculty combine to facilitate a "liberating education based on what life really means."

### Life

Students flock to this UNC campus "for the liberal atmosphere that Asheville provides." Known as a progressive and "completely college-friendly" town, Asheville "caters to the granola heads" and ensures that "there is a new cause on campus every week, from Amnesty International to trout ponds. Capitalism is a dirty word, and the views are socialistic." The picturesque mountain setting only adds to this bohemian lifestyle. Some students gripe, "The weekends are generally kind of dead around here" because people go home or hang out off campus. Other respondents qualify that judgment: "Those who complain of having nothing to do are only looking on campus, so if that is what a potential student is looking for, they may get bored here." On the fiesta front, "getting drunk is, like, a pastime, and frat parties are widely known," but many students agree that "drinking and partying are not really a priority because of all the other things offered either on campus or in town." Options include "plenty of pizza places and movie theatres," "lots of art galleries," "hanging out and watching TV," and "studying the Bible." Student organizations occupy free time, and many undergraduates join them "not only to become involved, but to rise to leadership positions."

### Student Body

Students at UNC—Asheville manage to strike the typically elusive balance of being "very mellow and down to earth, but surprisingly driven." These "children of Deadheads" and "mountain people" tend to be "environmentally friendly types," but "plenty of nonhippies, some rednecks, and a small but growing population of ethnic minorities" round out the student body. To put it bluntly, "this school is extremely white and unaware of the lack of race relations," according to one student, and many people would encourage the school to "make itself available to more students of varying ethnic backgrounds." Others contend, "We don't have many minorities, but we have a broad diversity in the types of people we do have." Reportedly, atypical students "are accepted here without question," but though they "fit in fine," they "tend not to mingle." Thanks to an open-minded atmosphere and common interests among the population, "most of the time one sees smiles on the faces of the students here."

# UNIVERSITY OF NORTH CAROLINA—ASHEVILLE

FINANCIAL AID: 828-251-6535 • E-MAIL: ADMISSIONS@UNCA.EDU • WEBSITE: WWW.UNCA.EDU

## ADMISSIONS
*Very important factors considered include:* class rank, secondary school record. *Important factors considered include:* standardized test scores. *Other factors considered include:* alumni/ae relation, character/personal qualities, essays, extracurricular activities, geographical residence, interview, recommendations, state residency, talent/ability, volunteer work, work experience. SAT I or ACT required. TOEFL required of all international applicants. High school diploma is required and GED is not accepted. *High school units required/recommended:* 12 total required; 18 total recommended; 4 English required, 3 math required, 4 math recommended, 3 science required, 4 science recommended, 2 science lab required, 3 science lab recommended, 2 foreign language required, 1 social studies required, 1 history required, 4 elective recommended.

### The Inside Word
UNC—Asheville is one of those relatively unknown gems in higher education. Recent publicity has fueled increases in applications and in turn boosted selectivity. The university is dynamic and eager to take advantage of this newfound recognition. No doubt admissions will become more and more competitive as the cycle repeats itself. For students who seek a public education in a smaller campus environment than places like Chapel Hill, this is a great choice.

## FINANCIAL AID
*Students should submit:* FAFSA. No deadline for regular filing. The Princeton Review suggests that all financial aid forms be submitted as soon as possible after January 1. *Need-based scholarships/grants offered:* Pell, SEOG, state scholarships/grants, private scholarships, the school's own gift aid. *Loan aid offered:* Direct Subsidized Stafford, Direct Unsubsidized Stafford, Direct PLUS, Federal Perkins, state loans, college/university loans from institutional funds. Federal Work-Study Program available. Institutional employment available. Applicants will be notified of awards on a rolling basis beginning on or about March 15. Off-campus job opportunities are good.

## FROM THE ADMISSIONS OFFICE
"If you want to learn how to think, how to analyze and solve problems on your own, and how to become your own best teacher, a broad-based liberal arts education is the key. UNC—Asheville focuses on undergraduates, with a core curriculum covering humanities, language and culture, arts and ideas, and health and fitness. Students thrive in small classes, with a faculty dedicated first of all to teaching. The liberal arts emphasis develops discriminating thinkers, expert and creative communicators with a passion for learning. These are qualities you need for today's challenges and the changes of tomorrow."

### SELECTIVITY

| | |
|---|---|
| Admissions Rating | 82 |
| # of applicants | 1,937 |
| % of applicants accepted | 67 |
| % of acceptees attending | 33 |

#### FRESHMAN PROFILE
| | |
|---|---|
| Range SAT Verbal | 530-640 |
| Average SAT Verbal | 586 |
| Range SAT Math | 520-630 |
| Average SAT Math | 574 |
| Range ACT Composite | 21-27 |
| Average ACT Composite | 24 |
| Minimum TOEFL | 550 |
| Average HS GPA | 3.7 |
| % graduated top 10% of class | 24 |
| % graduated top 25% of class | 61 |
| % graduated top 50% of class | 97 |

#### DEADLINES
| | |
|---|---|
| Priority admission | 10/15 |
| Regular admission | 3/15 |
| Nonfall registration? | yes |

#### APPLICANTS ALSO LOOK AT AND OFTEN PREFER
Warren Wilson

#### AND SOMETIMES PREFER
UNC—Chapel Hill
North Carolina State
Appalachian State

#### AND RARELY PREFER
UNC—Wilmington
UNC—Greensboro
Western Carolina
UNC—Charlotte

### FINANCIAL FACTS

| | |
|---|---|
| Financial Aid Rating | 88 |
| In-state tuition | $1,592 |
| Out-of-state tuition | $9,997 |
| Room and board | $4,650 |
| Books and supplies | $800 |
| Required fees | $1,365 |
| % frosh receiving aid | 38 |
| % undergrads receiving aid | 39 |
| Avg frosh grant | $3,660 |
| Avg frosh loan | $4,102 |

# UNIV. OF NORTH CAROLINA—CHAPEL HILL

JACKSON HALL 153A—CAMPUS BOX 2200, CHAPEL HILL, NC 27599 • ADMISSIONS: 919-966-3621 • FAX: 919-962-3045

## CAMPUS LIFE

| | |
|---|---|
| Quality of Life Rating | 90 |
| Type of school | public |
| Environment | suburban |

### STUDENTS
| | |
|---|---|
| Total undergrad enrollment | 15,961 |
| % male/female | 40/60 |
| % from out of state | 18 |
| % from public high school | 83 |
| % live on campus | 43 |
| % African American | 11 |
| % Asian | 6 |
| % Caucasian | 79 |
| % Hispanic | 2 |
| % international | 1 |
| # of countries represented | 100 |

### SURVEY SAYS . . .
Students love the Tar Heels
Students love Chapel Hill, NC
Political activism is hot
Great library
Registration is a pain
Large classes
Student publications are popular
Ethnic diversity on campus
Lots of TAs teach upper-level courses

## ACADEMICS

| | |
|---|---|
| Academic Rating | 88 |
| Calendar | semester |
| Student/faculty ratio | 14:1 |
| Profs interesting rating | 92 |
| Profs accessible rating | 94 |
| % profs teaching UG courses | 68 |
| % classes taught by TAs | 31 |
| Avg lab size | 10-19 students |
| Avg reg class size | 20-29 students |

### MOST POPULAR MAJORS
Business administration/management
Communications studies/speech communication and rhetoric
Psychology

## STUDENTS SPEAK OUT

### Academics
Those lucky enough to live in North Carolina have a low-tuition, high-reputation option right in Chapel Hill. In a rare instance for a state school, the administration is described as "very organized" and "eager to help manage your schedule." Apparently, the level of faculty-staff cooperation is high: "Administration and professors work together to facilitate an environment that is conducive to the educational goals of all students," opines one satisfied senior. Professors get high marks, often portrayed as "focused on the individual" and "happy to meet outside of class." In the words of one junior, there is an academic feeling of "curiosity, desire to learn, and excitement" where teachers "inspire me to work harder." A senior biochemistry major remarks, "I have been challenged in all facets of academics at Carolina," and a junior adds, "I have never been surrounded by such educated minds." It seems that the only complaint amid this "excellent intellectual atmosphere" is a slightly rough registration process for freshmen.

### Life
A full life is the name of the game at Carolina. Students enjoy the best of both worlds, a "small-school atmosphere with large-school resources," and they have all the "opportunities to excel in what they enjoy." One senior English major chose UNC—Chapel Hill because of its "good balance of academic and social life," while another senior was attracted because "both working and playing hard are encouraged." A schoolmate echoes, "We are well rounded with academics, athletics, and activities." More specifically, "from student government to Web servers to Friday parties, life is good." Tar Heel sports are popular, especially men's basketball, and pick-up games are always looking for fresh challengers. Chapel Hill, essentially a quaint extension of the campus, is a "fun college town," and "people go out every weekend to clubs, bars, and parties." In terms of the grounds, a senior states, "The school is beautiful except that everywhere you turn there's construction."

### Student Body
A diverse student body is drawn to UNC. "Students at Carolina are from different backgrounds socially as well as economically. The diversity here encourages each and every student to learn more about themselves and others," comments one senior. Another observes, "People often group themselves by race. Not everyone does, and it is probably better than many places, but it still occurs." A nursing student says the school is "far more diverse than I expected." A sophomore poli-sci major notes, "There is more motivation for progress among students than I can imagine existing elsewhere." Academically, students are "motivated," and outside the classroom, "they like to party; they're fun." The school's friendly character is illustrated by the declaration that "it is impossible not to meet people on the campus bus." The "60:40 girl-guy ratio" is cited by a guy as one of the school's greatest strengths, but male or female, "each student can find his or her social, academic, and athletic niche." A junior says his peers are "the best part of UNC. There are so many friendly, outgoing, and interesting people to meet. I've never felt like I didn't belong here."

624 ■ THE BEST 351 COLLEGES

# UNIVERSITY OF NORTH CAROLINA—CHAPEL HILL

FINANCIAL AID: 919-962-8396 • E-MAIL: UADM@EMAIL.UNC.EDU • WEBSITE: WWW.UNC.EDU

## ADMISSIONS
*Very important factors considered include:* character/personal qualities, class rank, essays, extracurricular activities, recommendations, secondary school record, standardized test scores, state residency, talent/ability. *Important factors considered include:* alumni/ae relation, minority status, volunteer work, work experience. SAT I or ACT required. TOEFL required of all international applicants. High school diploma is required and GED is not accepted. *High school units required/recommended:* 4 English required, 3 math required, 4 math recommended, 3 science required, 4 science recommended, 1 science lab required, 2 foreign language required, 4 foreign language recommended, 1 social studies required, 3 social studies recommended, 1 history required, 2 elective required.

### The Inside Word
UNC's admissions process is highly selective. North Carolina students compete against other students from across the state for 82 percent of all spaces available in the freshman class; out-of-state students compete for the remaining 18 percent of the spaces. State residents will find the admissions standards high, and out-of-state applicants will find that it's one of the hardest offers of admission to come by in the country.

## FINANCIAL AID
*Students should submit:* FAFSA, CSS/Financial Aid PROFILE. The Princeton Review suggests that all financial aid forms be submitted as soon as possible after January 1. *Need-based scholarships/grants offered:* Pell, SEOG, state scholarships/grants, private scholarships, the school's own gift aid, state grants. *Loan aid offered:* FFEL Subsidized Stafford, FFEL Unsubsidized Stafford, FFEL PLUS, Federal Perkins, state loans, college/university loans from institutional funds, alternative loans. Federal Work-Study Program available. Institutional employment available. Applicants will be notified of awards on a rolling basis beginning on or about March 15. Off-campus job opportunities are good.

## FROM THE ADMISSIONS OFFICE
"One of the leading research and teaching institutions in the world, UNC—Chapel Hill offers first-rate faculty, innovative academic programs, and students who are smart, friendly, and committed to public service. Students take full advantage of extensive undergraduate research opportunities, a study abroad program with programs on every continent except Antarctica, and 400-plus clubs and organizations. And we offer all this in Chapel Hill, one of the greatest and most welcoming college towns anywhere. We invite you to visit. Talk with our professors. Attend a class. Spend time with some students. Walk across the campus on which public education was born."

### SELECTIVITY

| | |
|---|---|
| Admissions Rating | 91 |
| # of applicants | 17,141 |
| % of applicants accepted | 35 |
| % of acceptees attending | 57 |

#### FRESHMAN PROFILE
| | |
|---|---|
| Range SAT Verbal | 580-680 |
| Average SAT Verbal | 625 |
| Range SAT Math | 600-690 |
| Average SAT Math | 642 |
| Range ACT Composite | 24-30 |
| Average ACT Composite | 27 |
| Minimum TOEFL | 600 |
| Average HS GPA | 4.1 |
| % graduated top 10% of class | 71 |
| % graduated top 25% of class | 94 |
| % graduated top 50% of class | 99 |

#### DEADLINES
| | |
|---|---|
| Regular admission | 1/15 |

#### APPLICANTS ALSO LOOK AT AND OFTEN PREFER
Princeton
Harvard
**AND SOMETIMES PREFER**
Duke
Brown
U of Virginia
**AND RARELY PREFER**
North Carolina State
U of Maryland at College Park
Tulane
Rutgers

### FINANCIAL FACTS

| | |
|---|---|
| Financial Aid Rating | 88 |
| In-state tuition | $2,814 |
| Out-of-state tuition | $14,098 |
| Room and board | $5,805 |
| Books and supplies | $800 |
| Required fees | $1,042 |
| % frosh receiving aid | 29 |
| % undergrads receiving aid | 29 |
| Avg frosh grant | $5,845 |
| Avg frosh loan | $2,684 |

# UNIV. OF NORTH CAROLINA—GREENSBORO

123 MOSSMAN BUILDING, GREENSBORO, NC 27402-6170 • ADMISSIONS: 336-334-5243 • FAX: 336-334-4180

## CAMPUS LIFE

| | |
|---|---|
| **Quality of Life Rating** | 78 |
| Type of school | public |
| Environment | urban |

### STUDENTS

| | |
|---|---|
| Total undergrad enrollment | 10,751 |
| % male/female | 33/67 |
| % from out of state | 9 |
| % from public high school | 95 |
| % live on campus | 36 |
| % in (# of) fraternities | 8 (10) |
| % in (# of) sororities | 6 (9) |
| % African American | 20 |
| % Asian | 3 |
| % Caucasian | 73 |
| % Hispanic | 2 |
| % international | 1 |

### SURVEY SAYS . . .
Frats and sororities dominate social scene
Athletic facilities are great
Great computer facilities
Student publications are ignored
Political activism is (almost) nonexistent
Ethnic diversity on campus
Diverse students interact

## ACADEMICS

| | |
|---|---|
| **Academic Rating** | 67 |
| Calendar | semester |
| Student/faculty ratio | 15:1 |
| Profs interesting rating | 69 |
| Profs accessible rating | 67 |
| Avg lab size | 20-29 students |
| Avg reg class size | 20-29 students |

### MOST POPULAR MAJORS
Nursing/registered nurse training (RN, ASN, BSN, MSN)
Business administration/management
Elementary education and teaching

## STUDENTS SPEAK OUT

### Academics
For a biggish state university, UNC—Greensboro provides a pleasing amount of student-faculty interaction. According to one student, "If you take an interest in their subject[s], professors at UNCG will go out of their way to talk with you after class, set up appointments for times outside of their office hours, or maybe even meet for coffee." Opinions on the professors vary from "very knowledgeable and skilled" to "didn't know what they were doing and had no idea how boring they were" a difference in opinion not uncommon at a large university. The good news is that "if you are highly motivated, you can run away with the show." Motivated or not, students seem irritated about their graduation requirements. But stick it out and you'll realize, as many other students have, that "you can [have] a good academic experience here."

### Life
Some students describe UNC—Greensboro as a "suitcase school." Because many undergrads tend to head home on the weekends, the university faces a particular brand of social challenge: how to get students to stay on campus? Undergrads report that the university is acknowledging this problem and taking strides in the right direction. Writes one upperclassman, "Last year . . . you could either go to a frat party that was full of drunken idiots or you could stay in your room and do nothing. However, this year there seems to be things like movies on the quad, more interesting speakers, comedians, step shows, talent shows, and many more interesting activities." While "there aren't that many parties" here, Greensboro students have no problem getting down: "The fraternities are very strong" and are responsible for many of the livelier parties. Off campus, students can be found at the city's "three large clubs," as well as a handful of "smaller clubs/bars that provide an outlet for local musicians." One sports fan grumbles that "intercollegiate sports are NONEXISTENT" at Greensboro, while an athlete optimistically points out that Greensboro has "a great recreation center with racquetball courts and a pool and Cybex gym equipment." As students progress through their education, they move further away from campus life. After freshman and sophomore years, "off-campus housing is very popular," and students become more involved in the Greensboro community. This is when they really take advantage of the "several interesting shops and restaurants" nearby, as well as "a pretty good assortment of . . . semi-professional sports, concerts, mall, and parks."

### Student Body
With a little over a myriad of undergrads, UNC Greensboro "is a small university in comparison to other public universities, but it is big enough for a variety of people—poor and rich, rural and urban, in state and out of state, and international." Students lament, however, that many of their classmates are commuters. One undergrad points out that "a vast majority" of the students "are from the Greensboro/Winston-Salem/High Point area," and about 90 percent are North Carolina residents. In general, though, the combination of non-Carolinians and minorities on campus supply students with enough diversity to make their college experience interesting. And while Greensboro, like most schools, has its share of slackers, it's also home to a healthy number of "very goal-oriented" students who constantly breathe life into the intellect of the campus.

# UNIVERSITY OF NORTH CAROLINA—GREENSBORO

FINANCIAL AID: 336-334-5702 • E-MAIL: UNDERGRAD_ADMISSIONS@UNCG.EDU • WEBSITE: WWW.UNCG.EDU

## ADMISSIONS

*Important factors considered include:* secondary school record, standardized test scores. *Other factors considered include:* class rank. SAT I or ACT required; SAT I preferred. TOEFL required of all international applicants. High school diploma or GED is required. *High school units required/recommended:* 15 total required; 4 English required, 3 math required, 3 science required, 1 science lab required, 2 foreign language required, 1 social studies required, 1 history required, 1 elective required.

### The Inside Word

UNC—Greensboro has yet to gain much attention outside of regional circles so, at least for the moment, gaining admission is not particularly difficult. The usual public university considerations apply; expect the admissions office to focus on grades and test scores, and not much else. Out-of-staters will find a much smoother path to admission here than at Chapel Hill and will still be within reasonable reach of internship and career possibilities in the Research Triangle.

## FINANCIAL AID

*Students should submit:* FAFSA. No deadline for regular filing. The Princeton Review suggests that all financial aid forms be submitted as soon as possible after January 1. *Need-based scholarships/grants offered:* Pell, SEOG, state scholarships/grants, private scholarships, the school's own gift aid. *Loan aid offered:* FFEL Subsidized Stafford, FFEL Unsubsidized Stafford, FFEL PLUS, Federal Perkins, state loans. Federal Work-Study Program available. Institutional employment available. Applicants will be notified of awards on a rolling basis beginning on or about April 1. Off-campus job opportunities are good.

## FROM THE ADMISSIONS OFFICE

"For the student who wants more than a small college offers but who would feel lost at a large university, UNC Greensboro is the perfect size. It is a diverse yet close-knit community where its 10,000 undergraduates can flourish as individuals. Students find a healthy balance of academic seriousness and collegiate fun, programs from the BA to the PhD, and charming traditions and cutting-edge scholarship. The UNCG faculty has long been known for exceptional teaching and research, combined with a genuinely caring attitude toward undergraduates. Students choose UNCG for the reputation of its academic programs and faculty, low costs, size, the convenient location in a friendly southern city, and the warm, inviting feeling of its beautiful campus. Students enjoy experiences such as residential colleges, internships, study abroad, small discussion classes, 14 NCAA Division I sports, and more than 150 student organizations."

### SELECTIVITY

| | |
|---|---|
| Admissions Rating | 69 |
| # of applicants | 7,065 |
| % of applicants accepted | 76 |
| % of acceptees attending | 39 |

#### FRESHMAN PROFILE

| | |
|---|---|
| Range SAT Verbal | 460-570 |
| Average SAT Verbal | 519 |
| Range SAT Math | 470-570 |
| Average SAT Math | 514 |
| Minimum TOEFL | 550 |
| Average HS GPA | 3.4 |
| % graduated top 10% of class | 12 |
| % graduated top 25% of class | 42 |
| % graduated top 50% of class | 85 |

#### DEADLINES

| | |
|---|---|
| Priority admission | 3/1 |
| Regular admission | 8/1 |
| Regular notification | rolling |
| Nonfall registration? | yes |

### FINANCIAL FACTS

| | |
|---|---|
| Financial Aid Rating | 86 |
| In-state tuition | $1,717 |
| Out-of-state tuition | $12,091 |
| Room and board | $4,460 |
| Books and supplies | $1,156 |
| Required fees | $1,288 |
| % frosh receiving aid | 48 |
| % undergrads receiving aid | 60 |

THE BEST 351 COLLEGES ■ 627

# UNIVERSITY OF NORTH DAKOTA

Box 8357, Grand Forks, ND 58202 • Admissions: 701-777-4463 • Fax: 701-777-2696

## CAMPUS LIFE

| | |
|---|---|
| Quality of Life Rating | 78 |
| Type of school | public |
| Environment | urban |

### STUDENTS

| | |
|---|---|
| Total undergrad enrollment | 10,277 |
| % male/female | 53/47 |
| % from out of state | 42 |
| % from public high school | 85 |
| % live on campus | 26 |
| % in (# of) fraternities | 9 (13) |
| % in (# of) sororities | 9 (7) |
| % African American | 1 |
| % Asian | 1 |
| % Caucasian | 95 |
| % Hispanic | 1 |
| % international | 2 |
| # of countries represented | 61 |

### SURVEY SAYS . . .
Lots of beer drinking
Hard liquor is popular
(Almost) everyone smokes
Everyone loves the Fighting Sioux
Frats and sororities dominate social scene
Great computer facilities
Ethnic diversity lacking on campus

## ACADEMICS

| | |
|---|---|
| Academic Rating | 73 |
| Calendar | semester |
| Student/faculty ratio | 18:1 |
| % profs teaching UG courses | 85 |
| Avg lab size | 20-29 students |
| Avg reg class size | 20-29 students |

### MOST POPULAR MAJORS
Nursing/registered nurse training (RN, ASN, BSN, MSN)
Elementary education and teaching
Aeronautics/aviation/aerospace science and technology

## STUDENTS SPEAK OUT

### Academics
"A history of producing hardworking professionals and a strong alumni association" are just two of the many reasons students choose to come to the University of North Dakota. Affordability and the chance to "receive a great education while still having tons of fun" are two more. Students here brag about a variety of programs, the nationally renowned aviation program ("one of the best anywhere"), the "super business and engineering schools, and a great social work program" among them. Like most large state universities, UND offers a wide range of options, making it "great for students who definitely know what their career path is, and great for those students who are still searching for their direction." Atypically for a big school, "classes are small, which makes learning easier," and "there are a large number of professors and other faculty members dedicated to making sure every student receives the best possible education. If there is a problem or a student needs assistance, people are willing to listen and help out." To many, though, UND's large and active alumni network is the school's chief asset. Explains one student, "Alumni are amazing. They really look out for one another. It establishes an immediate connection. You say to someone in Florida, 'I graduated from UND,' and they will give you a job or find you one."

### Life
North Dakota, its students brag, is home to "the best hockey team on earth," and most here would agree that intercollegiate sports—not just hockey, but also football, women's basketball, and swimming—are central to campus life. Some think sports are a little too central; complains one, "Don't get me wrong; I love hockey and football as much as the next guy. But when some faculty on campus literally have their offices in closets, and UND is buying the hockey players engraved suitcases and matching jackets, it's a little pathetic." When there's no game to attend, students enjoy a lively party scene. "Life at UND is study during the week and party on the weekend," explains one student. "Frats have many parties and the college has events going most weekends." Undergrads also report that "the university programming is usually really good. In the dorms, there is Residence Life Cinema, which has great movies . . . . They have concerts at the new arena." Hometown Grand Forks "isn't a huge city, so there's not a whole lot of places for students under 21 to go to." However, "once a student turns 21, there are a lot of bars, and most of them are pretty fun." Students appreciate how "the campus and the town are pretty safe," but wish the school would build some underground walkways: "It's subzero most of the year and we must often walk 10 to 15 minutes around campus!" writes one student. Road trips to Canada are popular among students with access to vehicles.

### Student Body
According to some students here, geography is destiny; as one put it, "In North Dakota, the land is flat and unchanging. At UND, most of the students are the same way: everyone looks and basically acts the same. This is good and bad, and stems from the fact that most of the students here are from the tri-state region. Not many kids from other parts of the country want to go to school so far north." The exceptions to the rule "are athletes and aviation students, who add diversity. Everyone else is a Caucasian with blonde hair. We live in a Scandinavian area. It's bound to happen!" Students also note that many of their classmates "are from farms or the city of Grand Forks." Most agree that a friendly midwestern vibe pervades the campus. Writes one undergrad, "Students here are extremely nice and never put anyone down."

# UNIVERSITY OF NORTH DAKOTA

FINANCIAL AID: 701-777-3121 • E-MAIL: ENROLSER@SAGE.UND.NODAK.EDU • WEBSITE: WWW.UND.EDU

## ADMISSIONS
*Very important factors considered include:* secondary school record, standardized test scores. *Other factors considered include:* class rank, essays, recommendations. SAT I or ACT required; ACT preferred. TOEFL required of all international applicants. High school diploma or GED is required. *High school units required/recommended:* 4 English required, 3 math required, 3 science required, 3 science lab required, 1 foreign language recommended, 3 social studies required.

## The Inside Word
North Dakota shapes up as a low-stress choice with little pressure on applicants. Its sound reputation serves as a reminder that a highly selective admissions profile isn't an indicator of the quality of a university. Who graduates is much more important than who gets admitted or denied.

## FINANCIAL AID
*Students should submit:* FAFSA. The Princeton Review suggests that all financial aid forms be submitted as soon as possible after January 1. *Need-based scholarships/grants offered:* Pell, SEOG, state scholarships/grants, private scholarships, the school's own gift aid. *Loan aid offered:* FFEL Subsidized Stafford, FFEL Unsubsidized Stafford, FFEL PLUS, Federal Perkins, Federal Nursing, college/university loans from institutional funds. Federal Work-Study Program available. Institutional employment available. Applicants will be notified of awards on or about May 15. Off-campus job opportunities are excellent.

## FROM THE ADMISSIONS OFFICE
"More than 12,000 students come to the University of North Dakota each year, from every state in the nation and more than 60 countries. They're impressed by our academic excellence, about 170 major fields of study, our dedication to the liberal arts mission, and alumni success record. Nearly all of the university's new students rank in the top half of their high school classes, with about half in the top quarter. As the oldest and most diversified institution of higher education in the Dakotas, Montana, Wyoming, and western Minnesota, UND is a comprehensive teaching and research university. Yet the university provides individual attention that may be missing at very large universities. UND graduates are highly regarded among prospective employers. Representatives from more than 200 regional and national companies recruit UND students every year. Our campus is approximately 98 percent accessible."

## SELECTIVITY

| | |
|---|---|
| Admissions Rating | 77 |
| # of applicants | 3,628 |
| % of applicants accepted | 72 |
| % of acceptees attending | 77 |

### FRESHMAN PROFILE
| | |
|---|---|
| Range ACT Composite | 20-26 |
| Average ACT Composite | 23 |
| Minimum TOEFL | 525 |
| Average HS GPA | 3.4 |
| % graduated top 10% of class | 16 |
| % graduated top 25% of class | 40 |
| % graduated top 50% of class | 74 |

### DEADLINES
| | |
|---|---|
| Regular admission | 7/1 |
| Nonfall registration? | yes |

### APPLICANTS ALSO LOOK AT AND OFTEN PREFER
U. Nebraska—Lincoln
U. Colorado—Boulder
Notre Dame

### AND SOMETIMES PREFER
Moorhead State
U. Minnesota
Bismarck State
Concordia Coll. (Moorhead, MN)
U. Wisconsin—Madison

### AND RARELY PREFER
Marquette

## FINANCIAL FACTS

| | |
|---|---|
| Financial Aid Rating | 80 |
| Out-of-state tuition | $8,594 |
| Room and board | $3,987 |
| Books and supplies | $700 |
| Required fees | $708 |
| % frosh receiving aid | 47 |
| % undergrads receiving aid | 53 |
| Avg frosh grant | $2,512 |
| Avg frosh loan | $5,102 |

THE BEST 351 COLLEGES ■ 629

# UNIVERSITY OF NOTRE DAME

220 Main Building, Notre Dame, IN 46556 • Admissions: 574-631-7505 • Fax: 574-631-8865

## CAMPUS LIFE

| | |
|---|---|
| Quality of Life Rating | 80 |
| Type of school | private |
| Affiliation | Roman Catholic |
| Environment | suburban |

### STUDENTS
| | |
|---|---|
| Total undergrad enrollment | 8,261 |
| % male/female | 53/47 |
| % from out of state | 88 |
| % from public high school | 50 |
| % live on campus | 75 |
| % African American | 3 |
| % Asian | 4 |
| % Caucasian | 84 |
| % Hispanic | 8 |
| % international | 3 |
| # of countries represented | 80 |

### SURVEY SAYS . . .
Everyone loves the Fighting Irish
(Almost) everyone plays intramural sports
Diversity lacking on campus
Great library
Great computer facilities
Students are very religious
Students don't like Notre Dame, IN
(Almost) no one smokes
Student publications are popular

## ACADEMICS

| | |
|---|---|
| Academic Rating | 92 |
| Calendar | semester |
| Student/faculty ratio | 12:1 |
| Profs interesting rating | 92 |
| Profs accessible rating | 92 |
| % profs teaching UG courses | 94 |
| % classes taught by TAs | 7 |
| Avg lab size | 10-19 students |
| Avg reg class size | 10-19 students |

### MOST POPULAR MAJORS
Pre-medicine/pre-medical studies
Business administration/management
Engineering

## STUDENTS SPEAK OUT

### Academics
Students at Notre Dame don't mince words when it comes to boasting about the education and experiences they've received at their beloved alma mater. Call it Irish Pride. A senior provides a perfect example: "Notre Dame, besides simply BEING college football, is great academically. You are practically guaranteed a job when you leave as long as you kept your grades at decent levels through school. What's more, ND is able to attract not only some of the best students, but also the best teachers." What is it about Notre Dame that engenders such love and devotion? It's the holy trinity of "tradition, faith, and academics" that sets Notre Dame apart, argue undergrads, who also find comfort in ND's "strong sense of community" and "unparalleled school spirit." These last two—and an alumni network that's been called "the biggest fraternity in the world"—are what "make all this studying bearable," notes a sophomore. For the most part, undergrads praise Notre Dame's faculty, curriculum, and resources, noting that the school's strong emphasis on classical liberal arts courses such as theology and philosophy, its top-notch science program, as well as its honor code, exemplify ND's "commitment to instilling quality and character" in its students. Being a big research school, there are the usual complaints about TA's teaching classes (though an honors student points out that she's gotten "the cream of the crop"—"three heads of departments as teachers already, and I'm a freshman!"). This is balanced, however, by the sense that "people really care about you at Notre Dame. You're not another number, but rather, you're respected as an intelligent human. You're expected to treat others in the same way, which creates a wonderful atmosphere."

### Life
A sophomore provides a window onto life at ND: "It's a Catholic university and football is so big that my friends from other schools often ask what we do: pray all the time? Or does everything shut down if the football team loses . . . ." So goes life in Notre Dame-dominated South Bend, Indiana, a few hours drive from anywhere (mostly kids go to Chicago, which is 90 minutes away, for big-city fun). Still, Domers love it: "Life is wonderful!," waxes a junior. "Football games are a little slice of heaven out here—and I am not kidding. Tailgating under a golden dome—what could be better?" Of course not everyone is so smitten with Notre Dame's "tradition of tradition," especially on matters of personal autonomy, choice, and day-to-day life at this conservative religious school. A first-year—living the "painful life of a pagan liberal at Notre Dame"—charges that "it is a sexist campus where women are rarely promoted and sometimes professors are just outright crude to women." Ouch! Yet, despite some distinctly un-twenty-first-century rules and regulations (such as single sex dorms and "parietals"—essentially curfews designed to keep men out of women's rooms and vice versa), most students are okay with Notre Dame's social set up.

### Student Body
A little bit more Irish Pride—this time from a senior: "Notre Dame has the best student body in the country. The students are what make the school." Coming from a Domer, it's probably a bit of an exaggeration; still, students are, for the most part, agreed upon the fact that "the sense of community and the 'Notre Dame Family' are the most valuable part of the university." And while there's a bit of a problem with homogeneity (the typical ND student is "a rich white kid that's Abercrombie and Fitched out wearing a North Face because we do face arctic temperatures out here in Indiana . . ."), a sophomore points out that "the school is trying to become more modern/activist/chic." The problem? "We're dealing with a Catholic institution," notes our wise sophomore, "and the Catholic Church changes about as fast as molasses."

630 ■ THE BEST 351 COLLEGES

# UNIVERSITY OF NOTRE DAME

FINANCIAL AID: 574-631-6436 • E-MAIL: ADMISSIO.1@ND.EDU • WEBSITE: WWW.ND.EDU

## ADMISSIONS
*Very important factors considered include:* character/personal qualities, class rank, essays, extracurricular activities, recommendations, secondary school record, standardized test scores, talent/ability. *Other factors considered include:* alumni/ae relation, minority status, religious affiliation/commitment, volunteer work, work experience. SAT I or ACT required. TOEFL required of all international applicants. High school diploma is required and GED is not accepted. *High school units required/recommended:* 16 total required; 23 total recommended; 4 English required, 3 math required, 4 math recommended, 2 science required, 4 science recommended, 2 foreign language required, 4 foreign language recommended, 2 history required, 4 history recommended, 3 elective required.

### The Inside Word
For most candidates, getting admitted to Notre Dame is pretty tough. Legacies, however, face some of the most favorable admissions conditions to be found at any highly selective university. Unofficially, athletic talents seem to have some influence on the committee as well: An enormous percentage of the total student body holds at least one varsity letter from high school, and many were team captains. Perhaps it's merely coincidence, but even so, candidates who tap well into the Notre Dame persona are likeliest to succeed.

## FINANCIAL AID
*Students should submit:* FAFSA, CSS/Financial Aid PROFILE, noncustodial (divorced/separated) parent's statement, business/farm supplement. Signed federal income tax return, and W-2 forms may be requested on an individual basis. Regular filing deadline is February 15. The Princeton Review suggests that all financial aid forms be submitted as soon as possible after January 1. *Need-based scholarships/grants offered:* Pell, SEOG, state scholarships/grants, private scholarships, the school's own gift aid, Alumni Club Scholarships. *Loan aid offered:* FFEL Subsidized Stafford, FFEL Unsubsidized Stafford, FFEL PLUS, Federal Perkins, privately funded student loans. Federal Work-Study Program available. Institutional employment available. Applicants will be notified of awards on or about April 1. Off-campus job opportunities are good.

## FROM THE ADMISSIONS OFFICE
"Notre Dame is a Catholic university, which means it offers unique opportunities for academic, ethical, spiritual, and social service development. The First Year of Studies program provides special assistance to our students as they make the adjustment from high school to college. The first-year curriculum includes many core requirements, while allowing students to explore several areas of possible future study. Each residence hall is home to students from all classes; most will live in the same hall for all their years on campus. An average of 93 percent of entering students will graduate within five years."

## SELECTIVITY

| | |
|---|---|
| Admissions Rating | 99 |
| # of applicants | 9,744 |
| % of applicants accepted | 34 |
| % of acceptees attending | 58 |
| # accepting a place on wait list | 477 |
| % admitted from wait list | 48 |

### FRESHMAN PROFILE
| | |
|---|---|
| Range SAT Verbal | 620-720 |
| Average SAT Verbal | 665 |
| Range SAT Math | 650-730 |
| Average SAT Math | 685 |
| Range ACT Composite | 30-33 |
| Average ACT Composite | 31 |
| Minimum TOEFL | 550 |
| % graduated top 10% of class | 82 |
| % graduated top 25% of class | 95 |
| % graduated top 50% of class | 100 |

### DEADLINES
| | |
|---|---|
| Regular admission | 1/9 |
| Regular notification | 4/1 |

### APPLICANTS ALSO LOOK AT AND OFTEN PREFER
Princeton
Stanford

### AND SOMETIMES PREFER
Cornell
Duke
Northwestern
Georgetown

### AND RARELY PREFER
U of Michigan
U of Illinois
Boston College

## FINANCIAL FACTS

| | |
|---|---|
| Financial Aid Rating | 84 |
| Tuition | $25,510 |
| Room and board | $6,510 |
| Books and supplies | $850 |
| Required fees | $342 |
| % frosh receiving aid | 46 |
| % undergrads receiving aid | 40 |

# UNIVERSITY OF OKLAHOMA

1000 ASP AVENUE, NORMAN, OK 73019-4076 • ADMISSIONS: 405-325-2251 • FAX: 405-325-7124

## CAMPUS LIFE

| | |
|---|---|
| Quality of Life Rating | 75 |
| Type of school | public |
| Environment | suburban |

### STUDENTS
| | |
|---|---|
| Total undergrad enrollment | 20,193 |
| % male/female | 50/50 |
| % from out of state | 21 |
| % live on campus | 21 |
| % in (# of) fraternities | 17 (19) |
| % in (# of) sororities | 25 (12) |
| % African American | 6 |
| % Asian | 5 |
| % Caucasian | 74 |
| % Hispanic | 4 |
| % international | 4 |
| # of countries represented | 100 |

### SURVEY SAYS . . .
Frats and sororities dominate social scene
Everyone loves the Sooners
Great food on campus
Theater is hot
Large classes
Students get along with local community
Student publications are popular
Students are very religious

## ACADEMICS

| | |
|---|---|
| Academic Rating | 73 |
| Calendar | semester |
| Student/faculty ratio | 21:1 |
| Profs interesting rating | 91 |
| Profs accessible rating | 86 |
| % classes taught by TAs | 19 |
| Avg lab size | 20-29 students |
| Avg reg class size | 20-29 students |

### MOST POPULAR MAJORS
Management information systems
Psychology
Sociology

## STUDENTS SPEAK OUT

### Academics
Weather is not small talk at Oklahoma University, considering that "OU has the best severe weather meteorological school in the world (really)." Aside from this distinction, the school prides itself on attracting high numbers of National Merit Scholars. In general, students comment, "Even though many of the introductory lecture classes are very large (100 to 400 students), professors find ways to give us attention on a more personal level." Though instructors sometimes "teach like the students already know the material," they are highly devoted. One student writes, "My professor stopped by my place of work to answer questions I had in class because I couldn't come to office hours." The administration can be more distant: "It is really hard to get in touch with a dean if you need to." President Boren is a favorite topic of discussion, with some students claiming, "He is loved and respected by all here at OU, and he even teaches a government class each semester. What a guy!" Others criticize, "To him, the school is a monetarily motivated political publicity stunt." The financial focus is further reflected in the comment, "They need to go ahead and just incorporate. It's run like a business."

### Life
Football is life at Oklahoma, with one student commenting, "Having a national championship football team is the school's biggest strength." Since "everyone loves the Sooners," some contend that "it doesn't matter if [we're] national champions or big fat losers, nothing is more fun than a Saturday afternoon in Owens Field." Greek life attracts about a quarter of OU students, and a divide between Greeks and independents is noticeable. One undergrad writes, "I am in a sorority, so sometimes I feel like I only socialize with people of the Greek system. I wish it were not like that, though." Many students share the sentiment; comments another Sooner, "Sometimes you have to look very hard to find something to do besides party." Optimists point out, however, that "there is always something planned through the campus activities council." Dubbed a "suitcase school," the university sees many of its 20,000 students head back home on the weekends. Those remaining don't find much to do in the town of Norman besides "bowling or pool." Luckily, Oklahoma City, with its Bricktown district "providing cool clubs and bars," is only 20 minutes away.

### Student Body
Drawing students mainly from Oklahoma, "very white bread, top-40 listening, trend-following, yuppies to be" dominate the OU student population. Most think about "how much fun they're having, the football team, and finding a significant other and getting married." The overriding "provincialism" can translate into a pleasant "courteousness" where "the guys always open doors." It's widely agreed that "student diversity is low" and there is "very little mixing between ethnicities." One student tells us, "Sometimes it seems as if minority students are only here to make the school look good." Matters were only made worse when the school "just recently stopped awarding minority scholarships." One student tells us, "As a Black female, I feel overlooked and underexposed" at a school generally "dominated by men." (The male/female ratio is actually 50/50.) Other students report that "homophobia still exists in a big way at OU." Religiously, "being in the Bible Belt, it is hard at times if you fall far from Christianity."

632 ■ THE BEST 351 COLLEGES

# UNIVERSITY OF OKLAHOMA

FINANCIAL AID: 405-325-4521 • E-MAIL: ADMREC@OU.OU.EDU • WEBSITE: WWW.OU.EDU

## ADMISSIONS

*Important factors considered include:* class rank, secondary school record, standardized test scores. *Other factors considered include:* essays, recommendations, state residency. SAT I or ACT required. TOEFL required of all international applicants. High school diploma or GED is required. *High school units required/recommended:* 15 total required; 4 English required, 3 math required, 2 science required, 2 science lab required, 3 foreign language recommended, 1 social studies required, 2 history required, 3 elective required.

### The Inside Word

It's plain from the approach of Oklahoma's evaluation process that candidates needn't put much energy into preparing supporting materials for their applications. This is one place that is going to get you a decision pronto—your numbers will call the shots.

## FINANCIAL AID

*Students should submit:* FAFSA, institution's own financial aid form. No deadline for regular filing. The Princeton Review suggests that all financial aid forms be submitted as soon as possible after January 1. *Need-based scholarships/grants offered:* Pell, SEOG, state scholarships/grants, private scholarships, the school's own gift aid, United Negro College Fund. *Loan aid offered:* FFEL Subsidized Stafford, FFEL Unsubsidized Stafford, FFEL PLUS, Federal Perkins, Federal Nursing, college/university loans from institutional funds. Federal Work-Study Program available. Institutional employment available. Applicants will be notified of awards on a rolling basis beginning on or about March 15. Off-campus job opportunities are excellent.

## FROM THE ADMISSIONS OFFICE

"Ask yourself some significant questions. What are your ambitions, goals, and dreams? Do you desire opportunity, and are you ready to accept challenge? What do you hope to gain from your educational experience? Are you looking for a university that will provide you with the tools, resources, and motivation to convert ambitions, opportunities, and challenges into meaningful achievement? To effectively answer these questions you must carefully seek out your options, look for direction, and make the right choice. The University of Oklahoma combines a unique mixture of academic excellence, varied social cultures, and a variety of campus activities to make your educational experience complete. At OU, comprehensive learning is our goal for your life. Not only do you receive a valuable classroom learning experience, but OU is also one of the finest research institutions in the United States. This allows OU students the opportunity to be a part of technology in progress. It's not just learning, it's discovery, invention, and dynamic creativity, a hands-on experience that allows you to be on the cutting edge of knowledge. Make the right choice and consider the University of Oklahoma!"

## SELECTIVITY

| | |
|---|---|
| Admissions Rating | 77 |
| # of applicants | 7,248 |
| % of applicants accepted | 89 |
| % of acceptees attending | 60 |
| # accepting a place on wait list | 53 |
| % admitted from wait list | 52 |

### FRESHMAN PROFILE

| | |
|---|---|
| Average SAT Verbal | 582 |
| Average SAT Math | 591 |
| Range ACT Composite | 23-28 |
| Average ACT Composite | 25 |
| Minimum TOEFL | 550 |
| Average HS GPA | 3.6 |
| % graduated top 10% of class | 32 |
| % graduated top 25% of class | 67 |
| % graduated top 50% of class | 91 |

### DEADLINES

| | |
|---|---|
| Regular admission | 6/1 |
| Nonfall registration? | yes |

### APPLICANTS ALSO LOOK AT AND OFTEN PREFER
Washington U.
Rice

### AND SOMETIMES PREFER
Baylor
U. Texas—Austin
U. Kansas

## FINANCIAL FACTS

| | |
|---|---|
| Financial Aid Rating | 84 |
| In-state tuition | $2,163 |
| Out-of-state tuition | $7,311 |
| Room and board | $5,030 |
| Books and supplies | $913 |
| Required fees | $766 |
| % frosh receiving aid | 48 |
| % undergrads receiving aid | 49 |
| Avg frosh grant | $3,711 |
| Avg frosh loan | $4,996 |

# UNIVERSITY OF OREGON

1217 UNIVERSITY OF OREGON, EUGENE, OR 97403-1217 • ADMISSIONS: 541-346-3201 • FAX: 541-346-5815

## CAMPUS LIFE

| | |
|---|---|
| Quality of Life Rating | 79 |
| Type of school | public |
| Environment | urban |

### STUDENTS

| | |
|---|---|
| Total undergrad enrollment | 16,047 |
| % male/female | 46/54 |
| % from out of state | 25 |
| % from public high school | 90 |
| % live on campus | 21 |
| % in (# of) fraternities | 10 (14) |
| % in (# of) sororities | 10 (9) |
| % African American | 2 |
| % Asian | 7 |
| % Caucasian | 79 |
| % Hispanic | 3 |
| % international | 6 |

### SURVEY SAYS . . .
Everyone loves the Ducks
Political activism is hot
Great library
Students aren't religious
Registration is a breeze
Dorms are like dungeons
Large classes
Student publications are popular

## ACADEMICS

| | |
|---|---|
| Academic Rating | 73 |
| Calendar | quarter |
| Student/faculty ratio | 19:1 |
| Profs interesting rating | 90 |
| Profs accessible rating | 89 |
| % profs teaching UG courses | 100 |
| % classes taught by TAs | 22 |
| Avg reg class size | 20-29 students |

### MOST POPULAR MAJORS
Business administration
Journalism
Psychology

## STUDENTS SPEAK OUT

### Academics

If you're looking for a tough and rewarding academic challenge, many students suggest that the Honors College at UO is the way to go. Explains one, "The Honors College has provided me with an experience that I did not expect would be available in a large, public institution such as this." Another Honors College student relates that the profs in the program are "funny, honest, and fairly easy going." Honors College aside, bright spots abound in the academic halls of this campus. Among the highly esteemed programs at UO are psychology, journalism, music, business, and the hard sciences. Reputation doesn't always tell the whole story, though, according to one jaded undergrad who calls the journalism program "overrated," adding that "most of the journalism professors are egomaniacs who just want you to know how important they were 10 years ago." In other corners of campus, academics tend to be "way too easy" or professors fail "to create any sort of challenge." So the ticket is to do a little research on a major before you sign on the dotted line. If you land in one of UO's many stellar programs, you'll find professors who are excited to teach and eager to get to know their students: "Professors are always talking about visiting them in their offices, and when you go they are happy to see you and help you." Professors are particularly accessible in the upper-level courses as opposed to the larger intro classes, which are often led by TAs, whose ability to teach is sometimes questionable. But if problems ever mount, the administration is open to hearing so from the students. "The president of our university has an open-door policy, as do all the administrators," writes one student.

### Life

At UO, "social life is varied depending on your own desires. You could spend every weekend going to frat parties or the bars or spend every weekend at a poetry reading, play, or concert." Though the campus offers a wealth of extracurricular opportunities, the uncontested champion of school-related activities is sports, watching them in particular. "The best thing about this place is Duck football and basketball," raves a student. Only about 10 percent of undergraduates join Greek organizations, but frats and sororities still manage to provide a few social options a week. Off-campus bashes are popular on the weekends, but "the newly established Eugene Police 'Party Patrol' has severely limited the scope of such house parties." Regarding the city of Eugene itself, students agree "there isn't much to do" here. But the city's offerings have not gone unmentioned; seasonal music festivals and the thriving Saturday Market are big draws. And let's not forget the people of Eugene. The city is known for a regular cast of eccentrics, like "Frog the 'Funniest Joke Book in the World' man, Free God News man, and Bible Jim, who comes to preach and piss everyone off a few times a year." Eugene is only "an hour from the coast, an hour from the mountains, and we have forests right in our back yard." And for the urban crawlers, "day or night trips to Portland are always an option" since Portland is only an hour up the road.

### Student Body

"Laid back" is the best way to describe the University of Oregon student body. Some students tell us that Oregon attracts "a bunch of damn hippies," while others remind us that it's a big school where you'll also find students who are "yuppie, preppy, snobby, left-wing, hyper-activist, or altogether too apathetic." Some of the common traits among these northwestern Ducks are their liberal tendencies ("People who come to UO as liberal democrats leave feeling like conservatives," a student says) and their geographical origins (nearly 75 percent come from in state). "I think the student body is more politically aware and active than most," opines a student. Overall, assures one undergrad, "campus relations are relatively good."

634 ■ THE BEST 351 COLLEGES

# UNIVERSITY OF OREGON

FINANCIAL AID: 541-346-3211 • E-MAIL: UOADMIT@OREGON.UOREGON.EDU • WEBSITE: WWW.UOREGON.EDU

## ADMISSIONS

*Very important factors considered include:* secondary school record, standardized test scores. SAT I or ACT required. TOEFL required of all international applicants. High school diploma or GED is required. *High school units required/recommended:* 14 total required; 4 English required, 3 math required, 2 science required, 1 science lab recommended, 2 foreign language required, 3 social studies required.

### The Inside Word

Oregon's admissions process is essentially a formula; it's not likely that anything beyond your grades, rank, and tests will play much of a part in getting you admitted.

## FINANCIAL AID

*Students should submit:* FAFSA. The Princeton Review suggests that all financial aid forms be submitted as soon as possible after January 1. *Need-based scholarships/grants offered:* Pell, SEOG, state scholarships/grants, private scholarships, the school's own gift aid. *Loan aid offered:* Direct Subsidized Stafford, Direct Unsubsidized Stafford, Direct PLUS, Federal Perkins, college/university loans from institutional funds. Federal Work-Study Program available. Institutional employment available. Applicants will be notified of awards on a rolling basis beginning on or about April 1. Off-campus job opportunities are good.

## FROM THE ADMISSIONS OFFICE

"The University of Oregon is internationally recognized for academic excellence, research opportunities for undergraduates, and commitment to the liberal arts and sciences. The UO's emphasis of 'learning communities'—small, personalized teaching environments—is a national model for undergraduate education. Programs in architecture, literature, journalism, biology, creative writing, physics, and music are nationally competitive. The university's inspiring Northwest location, situated an hour west of the Cascade Mountains and an hour east of the Pacific coast, offers incredible recreation and education options, including field studies in geology and marine biology. The university is currently listed as one of 21 best buys in the country."

## SELECTIVITY

| | |
|---|---|
| Admissions Rating | 80 |
| # of applicants | 9,889 |
| % of applicants accepted | 86 |
| % of acceptees attending | 38 |

### FRESHMAN PROFILE

| | |
|---|---|
| Range SAT Verbal | 492-610 |
| Average SAT Verbal | 551 |
| Range SAT Math | 494-608 |
| Average SAT Math | 551 |
| Minimum TOEFL | 500 |
| Average HS GPA | 3.5 |
| % graduated top 10% of class | 21 |
| % graduated top 25% of class | 52 |
| % graduated top 50% of class | 85 |

### DEADLINES

| | |
|---|---|
| Regular admission | 1/15 |
| Nonfall registration? | yes |

### APPLICANTS ALSO LOOK AT AND OFTEN PREFER
UC Berkeley
UC Davis

### AND SOMETIMES PREFER
U of Washington
U of Colorado at Boulder
U of Portland
U of Arizona
UC Santa Cruz

### AND RARELY PREFER
Willamette

## FINANCIAL FACTS

| | |
|---|---|
| Financial Aid Rating | 87 |
| In-state tuition | $2,907 |
| Out-of-state tuition | $13,896 |
| Room and board | $6,252 |
| Books and supplies | $876 |
| Required fees | $1,323 |
| % frosh receiving aid | 39 |
| % undergrads receiving aid | 45 |

# UNIVERSITY OF PENNSYLVANIA

1 COLLEGE HALL, PHILADELPHIA, PA 19104 • ADMISSIONS: 215-898-7507 • FAX: 215-898-9670

## CAMPUS LIFE

★ ★ ★ ☆

| Quality of Life Rating | 85 |
| --- | --- |
| Type of school | private |
| Environment | urban |

### STUDENTS

| Total undergrad enrollment | 9,742 |
| --- | --- |
| % male/female | 51/49 |
| % from out of state | 81 |
| % from public high school | 56 |
| % live on campus | 96 |
| % in (# of) fraternities | 11 (34) |
| % in (# of) sororities | 8 (10) |
| % African American | 6 |
| % Asian | 18 |
| % Caucasian | 50 |
| % Hispanic | 6 |
| % international | 9 |

### SURVEY SAYS . . .
Registration is a breeze
Great library
Theater is hot
Student publications are popular
(Almost) no one listens to college radio
Musical organizations are hot
Large classes

## ACADEMICS

| Academic Rating | 97 |
| --- | --- |
| Calendar | semester |
| Student/faculty ratio | 6:1 |
| Profs interesting rating | 91 |
| Profs accessible rating | 96 |
| Avg reg class size | 10-19 students |

### MOST POPULAR MAJORS
Finance
Psychology
Economics

## STUDENTS SPEAK OUT

### Academics

Penn is one of the hottest names in American higher education, and students here tell us that its reputation is well deserved. First of all, there's the top-notch faculty. Writes one giddy freshman, "I mean, I've already had profs who are world famous." And while "professors expect students to think for themselves," they're usually open to "one-on-one instruction during office hours if lectures are not sufficient." In addition to office hours, undergraduates can access professors through freshman seminar classes, and many profs live right on campus. Many students agree, however, that some of their professors are most interested in their research and "only teach because they have to." With so many professors involved in academic inquiry, "research opportunities [for undergraduates] abound." Regardless of professorial focus, Penn students across the board tell us they're challenged and satisfied. A few complain, however, that a pervasive business-like mentality among students, faculty, and administrators sometimes makes Penn seem "more practical than intellectual." Other complaints involve the large "intro and lecture courses" and the hit-or-miss quality of TAs. All things considered, complaints are few and far between. "My one regret is that I won't have time to take all the classes I'm intrigued by," sighs a student.

### Life

"This is the only Ivy where you can have a normal college experience in terms of social life," declares one Penn student. "People study during the week, and then know how to party on the weekends." Whether the partying occurs in the main hall of a frat house, in the living room of an off-campus apartment, or on the dance floor of an Old City club, you can be sure that parties here are "frequent, loud, and a lot of fun." In many cases, the amount of fun that students can have depends on their course of study. "There are four main schools: engineering, business (Wharton), nursing, and the college," explains a student, "and each have different amounts of work. History majors go out every night of the week, Wharton people have their weekends start on Thursday, and engineering students are always doing work." The university offers "a wealth of various cultural shows every weekend—comedy, musical, dramatic, and ethnic. And people also find time to go to movies and, of course, to athletic events." While not all sports are widely supported by the student body, "football and basketball games are huge events, especially the Princeton rivalry games." Penn students also take advantage of the city surrounding them. From "downtown Philly," campus is only "a 5-minute bus or cab ride, or a 15-minute walk." As one of the largest cities in the United States, Philadelphia is an urban sprawl of history, shopping, restaurants, bars, clubs, theatres, parks, and museums. The part-bohemian/part-commercial South Street is favorite spot for students and native Philadelphians alike. "West Philadelphia, where the university is located, is not the greatest place in the world," admits one student. "But there are wonderful places to eat and the campus is very safe." One senior notes that the neighborhood has changed dramatically—for the better—over the last four years.

### Student Body

Penn is often referred to as "The Social Ivy" because its students are rumored to be the hardest partiers in the Ivy League. Many students wear this badge proudly. One student notes that because many students come from families at "the higher end" of the financial ladder, it can sometimes seem that Penn students "were all born with silver spoons in" an unprintable part of their anatomies. For a significant portion of the Penn population, fashion savvy and "designer labels" seem to be social denominators. But Penn is too large a university to let generalities tell the whole story, and despite the stereotypes, the university boasts an admirably diverse student body. And while students admit that racial "self-segregation" often occurs, they also say that on the whole everyone is "very friendly" with each other.

636 ■ THE BEST 351 COLLEGES

# UNIVERSITY OF PENNSYLVANIA

FINANCIAL AID: 215-898-1988 • E-MAIL: INFO@ADMISSIONS.UGAO.UPENN.EDU • WEBSITE: WWW.UPENN.EDU

## ADMISSIONS

*Very important factors considered include:* character/personal qualities, essays, recommendations, secondary school record. *Important factors considered include:* alumni/ae relation, extracurricular activities, standardized test scores. *Other factors considered include:* class rank, geographical residence, interview, minority status, talent/ability, volunteer work, work experience. TOEFL required of all international applicants. High school diploma or GED is required. *High school units required/recommended:* 17 total required; 4 English required, 4 math required, 3 science required, 3 foreign language required, 3 social studies required, 2 history required.

### The Inside Word

After a small decline three cycles ago, applications are once again climbing at Penn—the fourth increase in five years. The competition in the applicant pool is formidable. Applicants can safely assume that they need to be one of the strongest students in their graduating class in order to be successful.

## FINANCIAL AID

*Students should submit:* FAFSA, institution's own financial aid form, CSS/Financial Aid PROFILE, parent's and student's federal income tax returns (for verification). The Princeton Review suggests that all financial aid forms be submitted as soon as possible after January 1. *Need-based scholarships/grants offered:* Pell, SEOG, state scholarships/grants, private scholarships, the school's own gift aid. *Loan aid offered:* FFEL Subsidized Stafford, FFEL Unsubsidized Stafford, FFEL PLUS, Federal Perkins, Federal Nursing, college/university loans from institutional funds, Penn Guaranteed Loan. Federal Work-Study Program available. Institutional employment available. Applicants will be notified of awards on or about April 1. Off-campus job opportunities are excellent.

## FROM THE ADMISSIONS OFFICE

"The nation's first university, the University of Pennsylvania had its beginnings in 1740, some 36 years before Thomas Jefferson, Benjamin Franklin (Penn's founder), and their fellow revolutionaries went public in Philadelphia with incendiary notions about life, liberty and the pursuit of happiness. Today, Penn continues in the spirit of the Founding Fathers, developing the intellectual, discussion-oriented seminars that comprise the majority of our course offerings, shaping innovative new courses of study, and allowing a remarkable degree of academic flexibility to its undergraduate students.

"Penn is situated on a green, tree-lined, 260-acre, urban campus, four blocks west of the Schuylkill River in Philadelphia. The broad lawns that connect Penn's stately halls embody a philosophy of academic freedom within our undergraduate schools. Newly developed interdisciplinary programs fusing classical disciplines with practical, professional options enable Penn to define cutting-edge academia in and out of the classroom. Students are encouraged to partake in study and research that may extend into many of the graduate and professional schools. As part of our College House system, Penn's Faculty Masters engage students in academic and civic experience while leading residential programs that promote an environment where living and learning intersect around the clock.

"Penn students are part of a dynamic community that includes a traditional campus, a lively neighborhood, and a city rich in culture and diversity. Whether your interests include artistic performance, community involvement, student government, athletics, fraternities and sororities, or cultural and religious organizations, you'll find many different options. Most importantly, students at Penn find that their lives in and out of the classroom compliment each other and are full, interesting and busy. We invite you to visit Penn in Philadelphia. You'll enjoy the revolutionary spirit of the campus and city."

## SELECTIVITY

| | |
|---|---|
| Admissions Rating | 99 |
| # of applicants | 18,784 |
| % of applicants accepted | 21 |
| % of acceptees attending | 62 |
| # accepting a place on wait list | 152 |
| % admitted from wait list | 14 |
| # of early decision applicants | 3,037 |
| % accepted early decision | 39 |

### FRESHMAN PROFILE

| | |
|---|---|
| Range SAT Verbal | 650-740 |
| Average SAT Verbal | 688 |
| Range SAT Math | 680-760 |
| Average SAT Math | 716 |
| Range ACT Composite | 28-32 |
| Average ACT Composite | 30 |
| Minimum TOEFL | 600 |
| Average HS GPA | 3.8 |
| % graduated top 10% of class | 91 |
| % graduated top 25% of class | 98 |
| % graduated top 50% of class | 100 |

### DEADLINES

| | |
|---|---|
| Early decision | 11/1 |
| Early decision notification | 12/15 |
| Regular admission | 1/1 |
| Regular notification | 4/1 |

### APPLICANTS ALSO LOOK AT AND OFTEN PREFER
Princeton University
Yale University
Stanford University
Harvard College

### AND SOMETIMES PREFER
Brown University
Duke University
Columbia University

### AND RARELY PREFER
Cornell University
Georgetown University
Northwestern University

## FINANCIAL FACTS

| | |
|---|---|
| Financial Aid Rating | 83 |
| Tuition | $25,078 |
| Room and board | $8,224 |
| Books and supplies | $760 |
| Required fees | $2,910 |
| % frosh receiving aid | 41 |
| % undergrads receiving aid | 42 |
| Avg frosh grant | $24,285 |

THE BEST 351 COLLEGES ■ 637

# UNIVERSITY OF PITTSBURGH—PITTSBURGH

ALUMNI HALL 4227 FIFTH AVENUE, FIRST FLOOR, PITTSBURGH, PA 15260 • ADMISSIONS: 412-624-7488 • FAX: 412-648-8815

## CAMPUS LIFE

★ ★ ★ ☆

| | |
|---|---|
| Quality of Life Rating | 88 |
| Type of school | public |
| Environment | urban |

### STUDENTS

| | |
|---|---|
| Total undergrad enrollment | 17,910 |
| % male/female | 48/52 |
| % from out of state | 15 |
| % live on campus | 42 |
| % in (# of) fraternities | 10 (21) |
| % in (# of) sororities | 7 (15) |
| % African American | 9 |
| % Asian | 4 |
| % Caucasian | 82 |
| % Hispanic | 1 |
| % international | 1 |

### SURVEY SAYS . . .
Lots of beer drinking
(Almost) everyone smokes
Great library
Student newspaper is popular
Everyone loves the Panthers
Great off-campus food
Great computer facilities
Hard liquor is popular
Students love Pittsburgh, PA
Students are happy

## ACADEMICS

| | |
|---|---|
| Academic Rating | 78 |
| Calendar | semester |
| Student/faculty ratio | 17:1 |
| Avg lab size | 20-29 students |
| Avg reg class size | 10-19 students |

## STUDENTS SPEAK OUT

### Academics

Many University of Pittsburgh students feel "happy that we discovered this amazing yet quite underrated school." They cite the English and science programs as two of the strongest, and one student tells us, "The nursing program is excellent and prepares you for the real world." The university offers "tons of diverse courses in any one semester," and students are encouraged to take a term abroad, "which is the best thing you can do." Some people see Pitt as "primarily a research school," but "it's stated university policy that professors are easy to see." The faculty "urges us to question things and provides an environment where we feel comfortable doing that." These "instructors and mentors" are known for being "passionate about what they teach" and "helpful both during lecture and during their office hours." Students appreciate that they "draw from real-world experience as a complement to their academic knowledge." Advisors provide additional academic support: "We meet one-on-one with our advisors at least twice a semester, and mine has always gotten me the classes I needed at the times I needed with the professors I want." The administration receives high marks "for advancing the university, raising money, recruiting strong applicants, and managing public affairs." Though they may "look out for our best interests," administrators are seen as "a bit detached," "extremely inaccessible," and "nearly impossible to reach." Recent tuition hikes only exacerbate this unfavorable assessment. Nonetheless, Pitt provides a scholastic climate where undergraduates "learn so much and grow as people." A senior writes, "It has been quite challenging, but I am thankful for my time here. It just goes to prove that I have a strong degree behind me."

### Life

The Pitt existence can be "extremely busy with academics, extracurricular activities, internships, part-time jobs, work-study positions, and social life." With more than 300 student organizations, there's room for everyone to "do their own thing." Aside from some safety issues, students love their location in the Oakland section of Pittsburgh, "home to many restaurants and bars, making for a very social atmosphere." Students looking to enrich themselves take advantage of the "Carnegie Museums across the street" and the popular Pitt Arts program, which "provides discounted or free tickets to various cultural events around Pittsburgh." Couple that with free public transit for students, and one student writes, "What can beat free transportation, dinner, a symphony ticket, and dessert afterward?" The only better plan could be cheering on the top-notch football and basketball squads—season tickets set students back only 20 bucks. On campus, "the weekends are full of fun with activities planned through different student organizations and great parties." Though some students claim "the majority of students drink on the weekends," many people think the "novelty of fraternity parties tends to wear off pretty fast."

### Student Body

The 18,000 undergarduate students attending Pitt form "a diverse group of students that, from what I have seen, interact easily and on a regular basis." One student observes, "We are amazingly diverse, and everyone is not only respectful, but also curious and excited to learn about and meet new people." Other respondents report that "people of the same ethnic group or background usually hang together." Even with approximately 14 percent of the student body members of minorities, one student points out, "Unfortunately, that is low for a city school." The minority populations organize effectively, in groups including the Black Action Society, Rainbow Alliance, and Asian Students Alliance. Amid this "wide spectrum of students" with a "broad range of interests," most are "friendly, outgoing, involved, motivated, and responsible." Most people seem to find their niche among "academically focused and open-minded" peers.

# UNIVERSITY OF PITTSBURGH—PITTSBURGH

FINANCIAL AID: 412-624-7488 • E-MAIL: OAFA@PITT.EDU • WEBSITE: WWW.PITT.EDU

## ADMISSIONS

*Very important factors considered include:* secondary school record, standardized test scores. *Important factors considered include:* class rank. *Other factors considered include:* essays, extracurricular activities, interview, recommendations, talent/ability, volunteer work, work experience. SAT I or ACT required; SAT I preferred. TOEFL required of all international applicants. High school diploma or GED is required. *High school units required/recommended:* 15 total required; 4 English required, 3 math required, 3 science (with lab) required, 1 social science required (3 recommended), 4 elective required (of which 3 in one foreign language are recommended).

### The Inside Word

Applicants to Pitt, as at most large public universities, are admitted primarily on the strength of basic qualifiers like grades and test scores. If you are serious about Pitt, rolling admissions allows you to get a decision earlier than most colleges notify their applicants.

## FINANCIAL AID

*Students should submit:* FAFSA, institution's own financial aid form. No deadline for regular filing. The Princeton Review suggests that all financial aid forms be submitted as soon as possible after January 1. *Need-based scholarships/grants offered:* Pell, SEOG, the school's own gift aid, College Work Study Program (CWS). *Loan aid offered:* FFEL Subsidized Stafford, FFEL Unsubsidized Stafford, FFEL PLUS, Federal Perkins, Federal Nursing, VA, HEAL. Federal Work-Study Program available. Institutional employment available. Applicants will be notified of awards on a rolling basis beginning on or about March 15. Off-campus job opportunities are excellent.

## FROM THE ADMISSIONS OFFICE

"The University of Pittsburgh is one of 62 members of the Association of American Universities, a prestigious group whose members include the major research universities of North America. There are nearly 400 degree programs available at the 16 Pittsburgh campus schools (two offering only undergraduate degree programs, four offering graduate degree programs, and ten offering both) and four regional campuses, allowing students a wide latitude of choices, both academically and in setting and style, size and pace of campus. Programs ranked nationally include philosophy, history and philosophy of science, chemistry, economics, English, history, physics, political science, and psychology. The University Center for International Studies is ranked one of the exemplary international programs in the country by the Council on Learning; and the Semester at Sea Program takes students to different ports of call around the world on an ocean liner."

### SELECTIVITY

| | |
|---|---|
| **Admissions Rating** | 84 |
| # of applicants | 15,888 |
| % of applicants accepted | 55 |
| % of acceptees attending | 36 |

### FRESHMAN PROFILE

| | |
|---|---|
| Range SAT Verbal | 540-640 |
| Average SAT Verbal | 595 |
| Range SAT Math | 560-650 |
| Average SAT Math | 607 |
| Range ACT Composite | 24-29 |
| Average ACT Composite | 26 |
| Minimum TOEFL | 500 |
| % graduated top 10% of class | 39 |
| % graduated top 25% of class | 74 |
| % graduated top 50% of class | 97 |

### DEADLINES

| | |
|---|---|
| Priority admission | 3/1 |
| Nonfall registration? | yes |

### APPLICANTS ALSO LOOK AT AND OFTEN PREFER
Virginia Tech
Boston U
NYU
U of Penn
Carnegie Mellon

### AND SOMETIMES PREFER
U of Delaware
Penn State
U of Maryland

### AND RARELY PREFER
Indiana U of Pennsylvania
Temple
Slippery Rock
Duquesne

### FINANCIAL FACTS

| | |
|---|---|
| **Financial Aid Rating** | 80 |
| In-state tuition | $7,868 |
| Out-of-state tuition | $16,676 |
| Room and board | $6,470 |
| Books and supplies | $700 |
| Required fees | $660 |
| % frosh receiving aid | 56 |
| % undergrads receiving aid | 55 |

# UNIVERSITY OF PUGET SOUND

1500 NORTH WARNER, TACOMA, WA 98416 • ADMISSION: 800-396-7191 • FAX: 253-879-3993

## CAMPUS LIFE

| | |
|---|---|
| Quality of Life Rating | 86 |
| Type of school | private |
| Environment | suburban |

### STUDENTS

| | |
|---|---|
| Total undergrad enrollment | 2,604 |
| % male/female | 40/60 |
| % from out of state | 69 |
| % from public high school | 77 |
| % live on campus | 64 |
| % in (# of) fraternities | 20 (4) |
| % in (# of) sororities | 29 (5) |
| % African American | 2 |
| % Asian | 10 |
| % Caucasian | 78 |
| % Hispanic | 3 |
| % international | 1 |
| # of countries represented | 20 |

### SURVEY SAYS . . .
Classes are small
Campus easy to get around
Intercollegiate sports unpopular or nonexistent
Dorms are like palaces
Great off-campus food
Great on-campus food

## ACADEMICS

| | |
|---|---|
| Academic Rating | 91 |
| Calendar | semester |
| Student/faculty ratio | 11:1 |
| Profs interesting rating | 95 |
| Profs accessible rating | 98 |
| % profs teaching UG courses | 97 |
| Avg lab size | 10-19 students |
| Avg reg class size | 10-19 students |

### MOST POPULAR MAJORS
Business administration/management
English language and literature
Psychology

## STUDENTS SPEAK OUT

### Academics
Students tell us that "the small community at UPS makes it easy to get to know the administrators and teachers at a personal level." Of course, among a left-leaning student body there are bound to be criticisms. A music major states that administrators "are more concerned with students who are going to come here and those who have already graduated than they [are with] those of us currently enrolled." Another student adds, "The administration has its flaws but overall it runs very smoothly." In contrast, professors are generally commended. They "become involved in our lives because they care about us and our education," writes a junior. A sophomore in the psychology department gushes, "Professors give you incentive to rise to their challenges because they are so wonderful!" Financial aid is often cited as one of the school's strong points, along with study abroad programs and academic counseling services.

### Life
UPS's location offers students access to the natural wonders of the Pacific Northwest—the Olympic rain forest, the Cascades, and Mt. Rainier—as well as the urban perks of nearby Seattle. A senior psychology student comments, "A car is a must to have any fun aside from crashing parties," because in Tacoma itself, "Target is the place to be." An English major clarifies, "After a couple of years, [Tacoma] either grows on you or you can't wait to leave." On campus, "it's a small community. For some, that makes it comfortable and safe, but others find it constrictive or too dull." Fraternities and sororities propel social life, but in return, "there is some animosity toward Greeks. Aside from wanting "less rain, more school spirit" ("You often see people wearing sweatshirts with the names of other schools"), most students report "a high quality of life," where "the food is good and the dorm rooms are huge."

### Student Body
Our sources report that location is everything in Tacoma. "All the freshmen live in the beautiful dorms, and all the upperclassmen live in the hideous off-campus housing, where they can drink without hassles." Describing the make-up of the UPS population, a political science student muses, "This place couldn't get much whiter or upper middle class or suburbanite," which closely conforms to a classmate's quip, "We're like vanilla ice cream." Another student counters, "the student population is not very diverse, but it is getting better. The campus tends to be cliquey, but if you make an effort, it really isn't too difficult to meet new people." In the home-state of "alternative" culture, rebellion just doesn't fly anymore, in the eyes of one senior: "In an effort to be 'independent,' 'different,' or 'emo,' kids end up being just as alike and conformist as the Greeks they turn their noses up at."

# UNIVERSITY OF PUGET SOUND

FINANCIAL AID: 800-396-7192 • E-MAIL: ADMISSION@UPS.EDU • WEBSITE: WWW.UPS.EDU

## ADMISSIONS

*Very important factors considered include:* secondary school record, standardized test scores. *Important factors considered include:* alumni/ae relation, character/personal qualities, essays, extracurricular activities, minority status, recommendations, talent/ability. *Other factors considered include:* class rank, interview, volunteer work, work experience. SAT I or ACT required; SAT I preferred. TOEFL required of all international applicants. High school diploma or GED is required. *High school units required/recommended:* 19 total recommended; 4 English recommended, 4 math recommended, 4 science recommended, 4 science lab recommended, 3 foreign language recommended, 3 social studies recommended, 3 history recommended.

## The Inside Word

The University of Puget Sound is on the right track with its willingness to supply students with detailed information about how the selection process works. If universities in general were more forthcoming about candidate evaluation, college admission wouldn't be the angst-ridden exercise that it is for so many students. All students are aware that their academic background is the primary consideration of every admissions committee. How they are considered as individuals remains mysterious. At Puget Sound, it is clear that people mean more to the university than its freshman profile and that candidates can count on a considerate and caring attitude before, during, and after the review process.

## FINANCIAL AID

*Students should submit:* FAFSA. Regular filing deadline is February 1. The Princeton Review suggests that all financial aid forms be submitted as soon as possible after January 1. *Need-based scholarships/grants offered:* Pell, SEOG, state scholarships/grants, private scholarships, the school's own gift aid. *Loan aid offered:* FFEL Subsidized Stafford, FFEL Unsubsidized Stafford, FFEL PLUS, Federal Perkins, state loans, private education loans. Federal Work-Study Program available. Institutional employment available. Applicants will be notified of awards on a rolling basis beginning on or about March 15. Off-campus job opportunities are excellent.

## FROM THE ADMISSIONS OFFICE

"For over 100 years, students from many locations and backgrounds have chosen to join our community. It is a community committed to excellence—excellence in the classroom and excellence in student organizations and activities. Puget students are serious about rowing and writing, management and music, skiing and sciences, leadership and languages. At Puget Sound you'll be challenged—and helped—to perform at the peak of your ability."

### SELECTIVITY

| | |
|---|---|
| Admissions Rating | 86 |
| # of applicants | 4,154 |
| % of applicants accepted | 72 |
| % of acceptees attending | 22 |
| # accepting a place on wait list | 119 |
| % admitted from wait list | 17 |
| # of early decision applicants | 175 |
| % accepted early decision | 95 |

### FRESHMAN PROFILE

| | |
|---|---|
| Range SAT Verbal | 580-685 |
| Average SAT Verbal | 631 |
| Range SAT Math | 580-670 |
| Average SAT Math | 622 |
| Range ACT Composite | 25-29 |
| Average ACT Composite | 27 |
| Minimum TOEFL | 550 |
| Average HS GPA | 3.6 |
| % graduated top 10% of class | 43 |
| % graduated top 25% of class | 75 |
| % graduated top 50% of class | 94 |

### DEADLINES

| | |
|---|---|
| Early decision | 11/15 |
| Early decision notification | 12/15 |
| Priority admission | 2/1 |
| Regular admission | 5/1 |
| Nonfall registration? | yes |

### APPLICANTS ALSO LOOK AT AND OFTEN PREFER
Stanford
Northwestern, Pomona
**AND SOMETIMES PREFER**
U of Washington
Whitman, Lewis & Clark
Willamette, Colorado College
**AND RARELY PREFER**
U of Oregon
Gonzaga, Linfield College
Albertson College

### FINANCIAL FACTS

| | |
|---|---|
| Financial Aid Rating | 88 |
| Tuition | $23,780 |
| Room and board | $6,140 |
| Books and supplies | $1,000 |
| Required fees | $165 |
| % frosh receiving aid | 59 |
| % undergrads receiving aid | 57 |
| Avg frosh grant | $10,448 |
| Avg frosh loan | $5,981 |

# UNIVERSITY OF REDLANDS

PO Box 3080, Redlands, CA 92373-0999 • Admissions: 909-335-4074 • Fax: 909-335-4089

## CAMPUS LIFE

| | |
|---|---|
| Quality of Life Rating | 88 |
| Type of school | private |
| Environment | suburban |

### STUDENTS

| | |
|---|---|
| Total undergrad enrollment | 2,088 |
| % male/female | 40/60 |
| % from out of state | 26 |
| % live on campus | 76 |
| % in (# of) fraternities | 22 (7) |
| % in (# of) sororities | 51 (5) |
| % African American | 3 |
| % Asian | 5 |
| % Caucasian | 61 |
| % Hispanic | 12 |
| % international | 2 |
| # of countries represented | 10 |

### SURVEY SAYS . . .
Frats and sororities dominate social scene
Classes are small
Theater is hot
Everyone loves the Bulldogs
Student publications are ignored
Library needs improving
Musical organizations are hot
Lab facilities are great
Students don't like Redlands, CA
Class discussions encouraged

## ACADEMICS

| | |
|---|---|
| Academic Rating | 89 |
| Calendar | other |
| Student/faculty ratio | 13:1 |
| Profs interesting rating | 95 |
| Profs accessible rating | 98 |
| % profs teaching UG courses | 100 |
| Avg reg class size | 10-19 students |

### MOST POPULAR MAJORS
Business administration/management
Liberal arts and sciences studies and humanities
Sociology

## STUDENTS SPEAK OUT

### Academics
Undergraduates at University of Redlands love the independence their education affords them; explains one, "Classes give you a lot of flexibility to pursue what interests you. Students often determine the path a class takes." The hallmark of the Redlands approach is the Johnston Center for Integrated Studies, where students may "follow any path one chooses without compromising anything" by designing their own courses of study and even creating their own disciplines. Notes one student, "The Johnston Center has been particularly key to my academic success, providing the motivation to take control of my own education." Students laud the UOR faculty, reporting that "the professors for the most part are great . . . . They're almost always available outside of class, and my advisor bends over backwards to make things happen for me." Adds one student, "The professors are mostly excellent, as they are there to teach, and to teach undergraduates. This has made for a highly enjoyable undergraduate experience!" Class sizes are extremely small, which enables students "to be looked at as individual people instead of just numbers." The administration is "supportive," but many complain about the "useless bureaucracy" that seems unnecessary at such a small institution. A junior liberal studies major summarizes the educational experience at UOR: "First year, they hold your hand long enough to allow students to [get] what they want out of the University of Redlands. From there on, what you put in is what you walk away with."

### Life
Students agree that "Redlands is a quiet town where everything except Del Taco and Wal-Mart close at 6 P.M." Reports one student, "The center of all culture and life in the city of Redlands is the Krikorian movie theater. For those who want to do other things, you either have to go home or off campus to the [nearby] beaches, the mountains, or Los Angeles, about an hour's drive from here. A car or a good friend with a car is invaluable." Students appreciate the fact that "all of Southern California's beauty, the beaches and mountains, are nearby. Redlands is essentially on the outskirts of everything." On campus, "frats and sororities are very big," and "there are over 90 clubs and organizations for you to get involved in [to] enhance your college experience." Students love to party; writes one, "For fun we have theme parties, no matter what day of the week." Drinking is popular with students, although many in the school's sizeable religious population find their classmates' bibulousness offensive. "I try to be tolerant of other people's lifestyles regardless of my own, but this school really pushes me to my limits," complains one. Students of all types enjoy the sense that "life is very relaxed around here. It's sunny and you wear shorts and sandals all the time."

### Student Body
"There isn't much diversity among the student population," at the University of Redlands, undergrads here admit, "but the atmosphere is friendly and open." Explains one student, "It is very possible to meet diverse students, but as a whole, the student body does not seem very diverse. Even so, I've made a number of really good friends from quite different backgrounds. You have to make an effort, though." Some here find their classmates "a little too conservative and religious." Others complain of a pervading superficiality; "The student body is friendly, but more often than not, more interested in frat parties and alcohol than anything else," writes one undergrad. Adds another, "There is a general acceptance of being ordinary at UOR. Students don't always seem to strive for academic, artistic, or musical excellence where they could."

# UNIVERSITY OF REDLANDS

FINANCIAL AID: 909-335-4047 • E-MAIL: ADMISSIONS@UOR.EDU • WEBSITE: WWW.REDLANDS.EDU

## ADMISSIONS

*Very important factors considered include:* essays, recommendations, secondary school record. *Important factors considered include:* character/personal qualities, standardized test scores. *Other factors considered include:* alumni/ae relation, extracurricular activities, geographical residence, interview, minority status, talent/ability, volunteer work, work experience. SAT I or ACT required. TOEFL required of all international applicants. High school diploma or GED is required. *High school units required/recommended:* 13 total required; 16 total recommended; 4 English required, 3 math required, 2 science required, 3 science recommended, 2 science lab required, 3 science lab recommended, 2 foreign language required, 3 foreign language recommended, 2 social studies required, 3 social studies recommended, 2 history recommended.

### The Inside Word

The University of Redlands is a solid admit for any student with an above average high school record. Candidates who are interested in pursuing self-designed programs through the University's Johnston Center will find the admissions process to be distinctly more personal than it generally is; the center is interested in intellectually curious, self-motivated students and puts a lot of energy into identifying and recruiting them.

## FINANCIAL AID

*Students should submit:* FAFSA, GPA verification form for California residents. The Princeton Review suggests that all financial aid forms be submitted as soon as possible after January 1. *Need-based scholarships/grants offered:* Pell, SEOG, state scholarships/grants, private scholarships, the school's own gift aid. *Loan aid offered:* FFEL Subsidized Stafford, FFEL Unsubsidized Stafford, FFEL PLUS, Federal Perkins, college/university loans from institutional funds, alternative loans. Federal Work-Study Program available. Institutional employment available. Applicants will be notified of awards on a rolling basis beginning on or about February 28. Off-campus job opportunities are good.

## FROM THE ADMISSIONS OFFICE

"We've created an unusually blended curriculum of the liberal arts and pre-professional study because we think education is about learning how to think and learning how to do. For example, our environmental studies students have synthesized their study of computer science, sociology, biology, and economics to develop an actual resource management plan for the local mountain communities. Our creative writing program encourages internships with publishing or television production companies so that when our graduates send off their first novel, they can pay the rent as magazine writers. We educate managers, poets, environmental scientists, teachers, musicians, and speech therapists to be reflective about culture and society so that they can better understand and improve the world they'll enter upon graduation."

### SELECTIVITY

| | |
|---|---|
| Admissions Rating | 74 |
| # of applicants | 2,499 |
| % of applicants accepted | 76 |
| % of acceptees attending | 32 |

#### FRESHMAN PROFILE

| | |
|---|---|
| Range SAT Verbal | 520-610 |
| Average SAT Verbal | 565 |
| Range SAT Math | 520-630 |
| Average SAT Math | 574 |
| Range ACT Composite | 21-26 |
| Average ACT Composite | 24 |
| Minimum TOEFL | 550 |
| Average HS GPA | 3.5 |
| % graduated top 10% of class | 33 |
| % graduated top 25% of class | 69 |
| % graduated top 50% of class | 93 |

#### DEADLINES

| | |
|---|---|
| Priority admission | 2/1 |
| Regular admission | 12/15 |
| Nonfall registration? | yes |

#### APPLICANTS ALSO LOOK AT AND OFTEN PREFER
Occidental
U. Penn

#### AND SOMETIMES PREFER
Pitzer
UC—Irvine
UC—Santa Barbara
U. of the Pacific
U. San Diego

#### AND RARELY PREFER
Whittier
Pepperdine
U. Southern Cal

### FINANCIAL FACTS

| | |
|---|---|
| Financial Aid Rating | 88 |
| Tuition | $22,450 |
| Room and board | $8,114 |
| Books and supplies | $850 |
| Required fees | $300 |
| % frosh receiving aid | 68 |
| % undergrads receiving aid | 71 |
| Avg frosh grant | $11,887 |
| Avg frosh loan | $3,860 |

# UNIVERSITY OF RHODE ISLAND

14 UPPER COLLEGE ROAD, KINGSTON, RI 02881-1391 • ADMISSIONS: 401-874-7000 • FAX: 401-874-5523

## CAMPUS LIFE

| | |
|---|---|
| Quality of Life Rating | 81 |
| Type of school | public |
| Environment | rural |

### STUDENTS
| | |
|---|---|
| Total undergrad enrollment | 10,784 |
| % male/female | 44/56 |
| % from out of state | 38 |
| % from public high school | 92 |
| % live on campus | 33 |
| % in (# of) fraternities | 7 (9) |
| % in (# of) sororities | 11 (11) |
| % African American | 4 |
| % Asian | 3 |
| % Caucasian | 77 |
| % Hispanic | 4 |

### SURVEY SAYS . . .
Frats and sororities dominate social scene
Everyone loves the Rams
(Almost) everyone smokes
Great computer facilities
Lab facilities are great
Hard liquor is popular
Large classes
Lousy food on campus
Campus difficult to get around
High cost of living
Musical organizations aren't popular

## ACADEMICS

| | |
|---|---|
| Academic Rating | 73 |
| Calendar | semester |
| Student/faculty ratio | 18:1 |
| Profs interesting rating | 91 |
| Profs accessible rating | 93 |
| % profs teaching UG courses | 83 |
| % classes taught by TAs | 8 |
| Avg lab size | 10-19 students |
| Avg reg class size | 20-29 students |

### MOST POPULAR MAJORS
Pharmacy (PharmD, BS/BPharm)
Communications studies/speech communication and rhetoric
Psychology

## STUDENTS SPEAK OUT

### Academics
The mostly pre-professional students at the University of Rhode Island tell us their school has "respectable academics." Although some classes are huge, the smaller sections and seminars students deem "extremely helpful." Regarding the quality of the professors and teaching assistants who instruct these courses, student opinion is decidedly mixed. There are professors who "don't care about you at all" and whose "teaching skills leave much to be desired," but "there are also some good, challenging ones." Indeed, a great many profs at URI are "engaged and interested in what they're trying to teach" and "well-informed and knowledgeable in their subjects." Several electrical engineers single out the faculty in their department as "exceptional." Also, "though there are a lot of graduate assistants and new professors teaching lower-level classes, they do a great job," pledges a junior. Students give a thumbs-up to the "good computer labs" here and say the administration is "accommodating." In addition to a nationally celebrated oceanography program, popular majors at URI include education, business, engineering, psychology, communications, nursing, and pharmacy.

### Life
The alcohol policies on this "quintessential New England" campus are strict—"too strict," according to some students. To drink, "we have to drive to the bars—there's not much on campus," laments a junior. Still, the parties seem to be making a comeback. Between the happening "off-campus party scene" and "strong Greek system," many students manage to "get blasted" on a regular basis. For students who do pledge, "Greek Week and Homecoming are the best times of the year." Beyond partying, students enjoy "sports, ice skating, shopping, bowling," or one of the more than 80 organizations offered by the Student Entertainment Committee and the Office of Student Life. But be aware that "this is a big school," declares a junior. "If you feel the need to be pampered, you're in the wrong place. If you are an easily adjustable person, you can find your niche and really fit in." The newly powerful men's basketball team is very popular; "I love cheering for the school," beams a freshman. URI students also focus locally, "always helping the community." On campus, "classrooms are old and buildings are run down," and security is an issue, but the "atrocious" parking situation is "the biggest problem" at the school. When they need a big-city fix, students head off to Providence, about 40 minutes away by car, or Boston, a little farther at two hours.

### Student Body
Lots of students choose URI because it is "close to home" and "cheap," especially for in-state residents, who make up a majority here. Approximately 62 percent of the students at URI hail from Rhode Island; the next most represented states—New Jersey and Massachusetts—show up a distant second with about 11 percent each. While some students are "snobby," most describe themselves as "easygoing," "polite," "helpful," and "very friendly." One first-year says she gets along with other students "like friends from home." The overall population is reasonably diverse, and "for the most part, everyone gets along," although different ethnic groups "do not mesh well." Students report "quite a bit of racial tension" on campus.

# UNIVERSITY OF RHODE ISLAND

Financial Aid: 401-874-9500 • E-mail: uriadmit@eta1.uri.edu • Website: www.uri.edu/admissions

## ADMISSIONS

*Very important factors considered include:* secondary school record. *Important factors considered include:* character/personal qualities, class rank, geographical residence, minority status, standardized test scores, state residency, talent/ability. *Other factors considered include:* alumni/ae relation, essays, extracurricular activities, interview, recommendations, volunteer work, work experience. SAT I or ACT required. TOEFL required of all international applicants. High school diploma or GED is required. *High school units required/recommended:* 18 total required; 4 English required, 3 math required, 4 math recommended, 2 science required, 3 science recommended, 2 science lab required, 2 foreign language required, 3 foreign language recommended, 2 social studies required, 3 social studies recommended, 5 elective required.

## The Inside Word

Any candidate with solid grades is likely to find the university's admissions committee to be welcoming. The yield of admits who enroll is low and the state's population small. Out-of-state students are attractive to URI because they are sorely needed to fill out the student body. Students who graduate in the top 10 percent of their class are good scholarship bets.

## FINANCIAL AID

*Students should submit:* FAFSA. No deadline for regular filing. The Princeton Review suggests that all financial aid forms be submitted as soon as possible after January 1. *Need-based scholarships/grants offered:* Pell, SEOG, state scholarships/grants, private scholarships, the school's own gift aid. *Loan aid offered:* Direct Subsidized Stafford, Direct Unsubsidized Stafford, Direct PLUS, Federal Perkins, Federal Nursing, college/university loans from institutional funds, health professions loan. Federal Work-Study Program available. Institutional employment available. Applicants will be notified of awards on a rolling basis beginning on or about March 15. Off-campus job opportunities are excellent.

## FROM THE ADMISSIONS OFFICE

"Outstanding freshman candidates with minimum SAT scores of 1150 who rank in the top third of their class are eligible for consideration for a Centennial Scholarship ranging up to full tuition. The scholarships are renewable each semester if the student maintains continuous full-time enrollment and a 3.0 average or better. Eligibility requires a completed admissions application received by our December 15 Early Action deadline. Applications and information received after December 15 cannot be considered. (High school students who present more than 23 college credits are considered transfer applicants and are not eligible for Centennial Scholarships). Like the permanent granite cornerstones that grace its stately buildings, the University of Rhode Island was founded in the lasting tradition of the land-grant colleges and later became one of the original crop of national sea-grant colleges. Observing its centennial in 1992, the state's largest university prepares its students to meet the challenges of the twenty-first century."

## SELECTIVITY

| | |
|---|---|
| Admissions Rating | 72 |
| # of applicants | 11,072 |
| % of applicants accepted | 69 |
| % of acceptees attending | 31 |

### FRESHMAN PROFILE

| | |
|---|---|
| Range SAT Verbal | 490-590 |
| Average SAT Verbal | 549 |
| Range SAT Math | 500-610 |
| Average SAT Math | 562 |
| Minimum TOEFL | 550 |
| Average HS GPA | 3.4 |
| % graduated top 10% of class | 16 |
| % graduated top 25% of class | 59 |
| % graduated top 50% of class | 89 |

### DEADLINES

| | |
|---|---|
| Priority admission | 12/15 |
| Regular admission | 2/1 |
| Nonfall registration? | yes |

## FINANCIAL FACTS

| | |
|---|---|
| Financial Aid Rating | 79 |
| In-state tuition | $3,864 |
| Out-of-state tuition | $13,334 |
| Room and board | $7,402 |
| Books and supplies | $800 |
| Required fees | $1,990 |
| % frosh receiving aid | 74 |
| % undergrads receiving aid | 72 |

# UNIVERSITY OF RICHMOND

28 WESTHAMPTON WAY, RICHMOND, VA 23173 • ADMISSIONS: 804-289-8640 • FAX: 804-287-6003

## CAMPUS LIFE

| | |
|---|---|
| Quality of Life Rating | 96 |
| Type of school | private |
| Environment | suburban |

### STUDENTS

| | |
|---|---|
| Total undergrad enrollment | 2,998 |
| % male/female | 47/53 |
| % from out of state | 84 |
| % from public high school | 70 |
| % live on campus | 92 |
| % in (# of) fraternities | 32 (8) |
| % in (# of) sororities | 49 (8) |
| % African American | 5 |
| % Asian | 4 |
| % Caucasian | 89 |
| % Hispanic | 2 |
| % international | 6 |
| # of countries represented | 70 |

### SURVEY SAYS . . .
*Frats and sororities dominate social scene*
*Students love Richmond, VA*
*Diversity lacking on campus*
*Great food on campus*
*Athletic facilities are great*
*Students get along with local community*
*Class discussions encouraged*

## ACADEMICS

| | |
|---|---|
| Academic Rating | 90 |
| Calendar | semester |
| Student/faculty ratio | 10:1 |
| Profs interesting rating | 95 |
| Profs accessible rating | 99 |
| % profs teaching UG courses | 100 |
| Avg reg class size | 20-29 students |

### MOST POPULAR MAJORS
Business administration/management
Biology/biological sciences
Political science and government

## STUDENTS SPEAK OUT

### Academics
Students at University of Richmond love the benefits of attending a small, undergraduate-oriented school. "One of the greatest positives about the University of Richmond is its small size," explains one student. "My teachers almost always know my name, even years after I had them as instructors." Adds another, "I have some friends who have attended large state schools and they are perpetually astonished by how small my classes are, while I can't imagine a classroom with 200 to 300 people in it." A caring and committed faculty enhances the educational experience here; students sense that "professors are here to teach first and foremost," "really want you to do well, and they actually appreciate your getting to know them." They "are extremely accessible, and even offer to come to campus on weekends if you need extra help." Students also enjoy "an excellent advising system" and an administration that makes sure "everything on campus runs very smoothly." Complaints center on some restrictive administrative policies, the required first-year course ("It is like an AP English literature course: we read 10 or so books, analyze them, have discussions, and write papers. Many of us do not see the point"), and the insular nature of life on campus ("Welcome to the bubble!!! College is supposed to be the next step toward the 'real world' but Richmond is not quite close enough").

### Life
For most students at UR, "social life tends to revolve around the Greek system. The place to be on Friday night is Fraternity Row." Other orbits exist, however; explains one student, "Weekend culture revolves around Fraternity Row, but I have never been to the Row and still manage to amuse myself. I attend arts performances in our arts building, which is beautiful and accommodates many different groups. There is a prominent D-Hall (dining hall) culture among more intellectual students; they sit and talk for hours after dinner or even after lunch on Fridays. Much non-Greek weekend activity revolves around religious organizations and sports teams. We take trips to Virginia Beach or Washington, D.C., or even just into Richmond. If you have a car, this is a great place to be. It's only when I can't find a friend with a car that I sometimes get bored on weekends." Students agree that "Richmond is a terrific city, with great restaurants, museums, bars, theaters, etc." and love the fact that "We're also two hours away from the ocean, two hours away from the mountains, an hour and a half from D.C., so road trips are frequent." They also appreciate that UR is "small enough that when you walk to classes you will always run into people you know, but it's big enough that you can't know everybody. There are definite groups of people; you have to find your niche, but basically, everyone is just nice."

### Student Body
The students at University of Richmond are "extremely ambitious: it feels like everyone was class president in high school. But for the most part they are also very down-to-earth, friendly, and helpful." Most agree there is a sameness to the student body, and "sometimes it's easy to see where the nickname 'the University of Rich Men' came from." Observes one undergrad, "Students here are generally white and upper-middle-class to upper-class. There is not much diversity, aside from a large percentage of international students, many from Latin America and Eastern Europe." Students' commitment to religion is divided into "two different extremes: there are religious people, and there are students who have set religion aside for a while."

646 ■ THE BEST 351 COLLEGES

# UNIVERSITY OF RICHMOND

FINANCIAL AID: 804-289-8438 • E-MAIL: ADMISSIONS@RICHMOND.EDU • WEBSITE: WWW.RICHMOND.EDU

## ADMISSIONS
*Very important factors considered include:* secondary school record. *Important factors considered include:* character/personal qualities, class rank, essays, standardized test scores, talent/ability. *Other factors considered include:* alumni/ae relation, extracurricular activities, geographical residence, minority status, recommendations, state residency, volunteer work, work experience. TOEFL required of all international applicants. High school diploma or GED is required. *High school units required/recommended:* 16 total required; 20 total recommended; 4 English required, 3 math required, 4 math recommended, 2 science required, 4 science recommended, 2 science lab required, 4 science lab recommended, 2 foreign language required, 4 foreign language recommended, 2 history required, 4 history recommended.

### The Inside Word
There may not be an admissions formula, but two SAT II: Subject Tests are an important application requirement; we'd advise candidates to prepare for them thoroughly, since they outweigh the SAT I. When used with a measure of flexibility and a willingness to consider other factors, as Richmond does, there is nothing inherently wrong with such an approach. There does appear to be an effort to look at the candidate's record carefully and thoroughly. Make no mistake: Course of study, high school performance, and test scores are the most important parts of your application, but Richmond also makes sure that all files are read at least three times before a final decision has been rendered.

## FINANCIAL AID
*Students should submit:* FAFSA, institution's own financial aid form. Regular filing deadline is February 25. The Princeton Review suggests that all financial aid forms be submitted as soon as possible after January 1. *Need-based scholarships/grants offered:* Pell, SEOG, state scholarships/grants, private scholarships, the school's own gift aid. *Loan aid offered:* Direct Subsidized Stafford, Direct Unsubsidized Stafford, Direct PLUS, Federal Perkins. Federal Work-Study Program available. Institutional employment available. Applicants will be notified of awards on or about April 1. Off-campus job opportunities are good.

## FROM THE ADMISSIONS OFFICE
"The University of Richmond combines the characteristics of a small college with the dynamics of a large university. The unique size, beautiful suburban campus, and world-class facilities offer students an extraordinary mix of opportunities for personal growth and intellectual achievement. At Richmond, students are encouraged to engage themselves in their environment. Discussion and dialogue are the forefront of the academic experience, while research, internships, and international experiences are important components of students' co-curricular lives. The university is committed to providing undergraduate students with a rigorous academic experience, while integrating these studies with opportunities for experiential learning and promoting total individual development."

### SELECTIVITY
★★★★

| | |
|---|---|
| Admissions Rating | 91 |
| # of applicants | 5,895 |
| % of applicants accepted | 41 |
| % of acceptees attending | 33 |
| # accepting a place on wait list | 961 |
| # of early decision applicants | 366 |
| % accepted early decision | 54 |

### FRESHMAN PROFILE
| | |
|---|---|
| Range SAT Verbal | 600-690 |
| Range SAT Math | 620-700 |
| Range ACT Composite | 27-30 |
| Minimum TOEFL | 550 |
| % graduated top 10% of class | 55 |
| % graduated top 25% of class | 95 |
| % graduated top 50% of class | 99 |

### DEADLINES
| | |
|---|---|
| Early decision | 11/15 |
| Early decision notification | 12/15 |
| Regular admission | 1/15 |
| Regular notification | 4/1 |

### APPLICANTS ALSO LOOK AT AND OFTEN PREFER
William and Mary
U.Virginia
UNC—Chapel Hill
Duke

### AND SOMETIMES PREFER
Wake Forest
James Madison
Tulane
Vanderbilt
Washington and Lee

### AND RARELY PREFER
Lafayette
Lehigh

### FINANCIAL FACTS

| | |
|---|---|
| Financial Aid Rating | 83 |
| Tuition | $23,730 |
| Room and board | $5,160 |
| Books and supplies | $1,000 |
| % frosh receiving aid | 34 |
| % undergrads receiving aid | 30 |

# UNIVERSITY OF ROCHESTER

BOX 270251, ROCHESTER, NY 14627-0251 • ADMISSIONS: 716-275-3221 • FAX: 716-461-4595

## CAMPUS LIFE

| | |
|---|---|
| **Quality of Life Rating** | **82** |
| Type of school | private |
| Environment | suburban |

### STUDENTS

| | |
|---|---|
| Total undergrad enrollment | 4,665 |
| % male/female | 54/46 |
| % from out of state | 50 |
| % live on campus | 80 |
| % in (# of) fraternities | 26 (17) |
| % in (# of) sororities | 19 (11) |
| % African American | 5 |
| % Asian | 13 |
| % Caucasian | 66 |
| % Hispanic | 4 |
| % international | 4 |

### SURVEY SAYS . . .
Popular college radio
Great library
Theater is hot
Dorms are like palaces
(Almost) everyone plays intramural sports
Intercollegiate sports unpopular or nonexistent
Athletic facilities need improving
Large classes
Musical organizations are hot

## ACADEMICS

| | |
|---|---|
| **Academic Rating** | **88** |
| Calendar | semester |
| Student/faculty ratio | 8:1 |
| Profs interesting rating | 94 |
| Profs accessible rating | 90 |
| Avg reg class size | 10-19 students |

## STUDENTS SPEAK OUT

### Academics

The University of Rochester has traditionally been known best for its math and science departments. However, the "home of the Bausch & Lomb scholars and Xerox" has enough diversity in its academic offerings to "dispel the myth that the U of R is solely an engineering/pre-med breeding ground." Although numerous students consider the workload "heavy and tough—they don't mess around!" most also believe their rigorous courses are "extremely rewarding." Rochester has several unique opportunities to offer its students; one is the world-renowned Eastman School of Music (the administration encourages qualified students to take courses there). Distinct to the U of R is a program called "Take Five," an attractive option for students who find themselves unable to fit enough courses of interest into a four-year schedule. One student writes, "As a chemical engineer, I have very little time to take courses outside my major. The U of R has given me the opportunity to stay here for an additional year—tuition-free—to pursue my interest in Japanese history and culture." While some students claim that certain professors "are more interested in their research than they are in undergrads," in general students here are positive and enthusiastic about their academic life; some consider the U of R "better than the Ivies but without the reputation—it's the jewel of upper New York State."

### Life

Cold weather is a given in Rochester: "Siberia for eight months of the year" is a popular description among students we surveyed. It is actually possible to avoid a great deal of winter misery by using the convenient indoor tunnels beneath the campus. Nevertheless, the consensus seems to be that of one student who notes, "I just wish we could take the whole school and place it in California or somewhere where there is no snow." Despite the academic pressures at the U of R (or perhaps because of them), weekends are full of partying opportunities. Fraternities and sororities figure prominently in the social scene, and Greek activities dominate. One student observes, "Many people claim to be anti-Greek, but they tend to show up at frat parties anyway." There are varying degrees of social contentment here; some students have "too many parties to choose from," some contend that "freshman males lead lives of quiet desperation," and some prefer to socialize electronically in the generally comfy and spacious dorms.

### Student Body

The typical student at the University of Rochester is politically moderate, not politically active. A small private school, despite its public-sounding name, the U of R has made an effort to increase student diversity, and minorities account for more than a fifth of the student body. However, some students still feel "the minority population is lacking . . . especially in the black and Hispanic sectors."

# UNIVERSITY OF ROCHESTER

FINANCIAL AID: 716-275-3226 • E-MAIL: ADMIT@ADMISSIONS.ROCHESTER.EDU • WEBSITE: WWW.ROCHESTER.EDU

## ADMISSIONS

*Very important factors considered include:* secondary school record, standardized test scores. *Important factors considered include:* character/personal qualities, class rank, essays, recommendations, talent/ability. *Other factors considered include:* alumni/ae relation, extracurricular activities, minority status, volunteer work, work experience. SAT I or ACT required. TOEFL required of all international applicants. High school diploma or GED is required. *High school units required/recommended:* 4 total recommended; 4 English recommended, 4 math recommended, 3 science recommended, 4 science lab recommended, 2 foreign language recommended, 2 social studies recommended.

### The Inside Word

The University of Rochester is definitely a good school, but the competition takes away three-fourths of the university's admits. Many students use Rochester as a safety; this hinders the university's ability to move up among top national institutions in selectivity. It also makes U of R a very solid choice for above-average students who aren't Ivy material.

## FINANCIAL AID

*Students should submit:* FAFSA, CSS/Financial Aid PROFILE, state aid form, noncustodial (divorced/separated) parent's statement. Regular filing deadline is February 1. The Princeton Review suggests that all financial aid forms be submitted as soon as possible after January 1. *Need-based scholarships/grants offered:* Pell, SEOG, state scholarships/grants, private scholarships, the school's own gift aid. Federal Work-Study Program available. Institutional employment available. Applicants will be notified of awards on or about April 1. Off-campus job opportunities are excellent.

## FROM THE ADMISSIONS OFFICE

"A campus visit can be one of the most important (and most enjoyable) components of a college search. Visiting Rochester can provide you with the opportunity to experience for yourself the traditions and innovations of our university. Whether you visit a class, tour the campus, or meet with a professor or coach, you'll learn a great deal about the power of a Rochester education—with advantages that begin during your undergraduate years and continue after graduation. No other school combines the wealth of academic programs on the personal scale that the University of Rochester offers. Our students achieve academic excellence in a university setting that encourages frequent, informal contact with distinguished faculty. Our faculty-designed 'Rochester Renaissance Curriculum' allows students to spend as much of their time as possible studying subjects they enjoy so much that they stop watching the clock,' says William Scott Green, dean of the undergraduate college. At the heart of the Renaissance Curriculum is the Quest Program. Quest courses are seminar-sized offerings that encourage you to solve problems through investigations and exploration . . . much the same way our faculty do. Working alongside your professor, you will test theories and explore education frontiers on a campus with some of the best resources in the world, driven by a curriculum that is truly unprecedented."

### SELECTIVITY

| | |
|---|---:|
| Admissions Rating | 88 |
| # of applicants | 10,930 |
| % of applicants accepted | 49 |
| % of acceptees attending | 21 |
| # accepting a place on wait list | 336 |
| # of early decision applicants | 375 |
| % accepted early decision | 52 |

### FRESHMAN PROFILE

| | |
|---|---:|
| Range SAT Verbal | 600-700 |
| Average SAT Verbal | 665 |
| Range SAT Math | 620-710 |
| Average SAT Math | 687 |
| Range ACT Composite | 27-32 |
| Average ACT Composite | 30 |
| Minimum TOEFL | 550 |
| % graduated top 10% of class | 60 |
| % graduated top 25% of class | 88 |
| % graduated top 50% of class | 99 |

### DEADLINES

| | |
|---|---:|
| Early decision | 11/15 |
| Early decision notification | 12/15 |
| Regular admission | 1/20 |
| Regular notification | 4/1 |
| Nonfall registration? | yes |

### APPLICANTS ALSO LOOK AT AND OFTEN PREFER
Cornell U.
Washington U.
Binghamton U.
SUNY—Buffalo

### AND SOMETIMES PREFER
Boston U.
SUNY—Albany
U. Vermont
Syracuse
NYU

### AND RARELY PREFER
Franklin & Marshall

### FINANCIAL FACTS

| | |
|---|---:|
| Financial Aid Rating | 83 |
| Tuition | $24,150 |
| Room and board | $8,185 |
| Books and supplies | $575 |
| Required fees | $644 |
| % frosh receiving aid | 55 |
| % undergrads receiving aid | 59 |

THE BEST 351 COLLEGES ■ 649

# UNIVERSITY OF SAN DIEGO

5998 ALCALÁ PARK, SAN DIEGO, CA 92110-2492 • FAX: 619-260-6836

## CAMPUS LIFE

| Quality of Life Rating | 88 |
|---|---|
| Type of school | private |
| Affiliation | Roman Catholic |
| Environment | urban |

### STUDENTS

| Total undergrad enrollment | 4,837 |
|---|---|
| % male/female | 39/61 |
| % from out of state | 39 |
| % from public high school | 65 |
| % live on campus | 48 |
| % in (# of) fraternities | 15 (5) |
| % in (# of) sororities | 25 (5) |
| % African American | 2 |
| % Asian | 7 |
| % Caucasian | 70 |
| % Hispanic | 16 |
| % international | 3 |
| # of countries represented | 63 |

### SURVEY SAYS . . .
Campus is beautiful
Campus feels safe
Great off-campus food
Lab facilities need improving
Musical organizations aren't popular
Lots of beer drinking
Students love San Diego, CA
Lousy food on campus

## ACADEMICS

| Academic Rating | 82 |
|---|---|
| Calendar | 4-1-4 |
| Student/faculty ratio | 15:1 |
| Profs interesting rating | 80 |
| Profs accessible rating | 85 |
| % profs teaching UG courses | 100 |
| Avg lab size | 10-19 students |
| Avg reg class size | 10-19 students |

### MOST POPULAR MAJORS
Business administration/management
Communications studies/speech communication and rhetoric
Psychology

## STUDENTS SPEAK OUT

### Academics

"Class sizes are small," discussion is encouraged, and the professors "take a lot of pride in (giving) personal attention to the student" at this Southern Californian Catholic institution. One undergrad gushes, "Professors are all very accessible and love it when you come by to office hours." Some students complain about the workload that results from professors who think "that their class is the only class you are taking." And, yes, professors are the ones handing out assignments at USD: "I have never had a teacher's assistant instructing a class," remarks a student. While USD undergraduates are generally pleased with their professors, they'd like to see profs teaching a wider variety of subjects; writes one student, "The biggest complaint I have (and I know I speak for 90 percent of the campus) is that there are too few majors offered here and too few classes available." This, of course, is more of an administrative issue than an academic one. In fact, students here register most of their complaints against the administration. "Being a Catholic university," explains one undergrad, "they fail to see students' lifestyles in the 21st century. For example, they ignore the fact that most students are sexually active, and their policy is to not provide students with information about birth control." Another student adds, "It wouldn't hurt for USD to recognize the issues plaguing students and address them."

### Life

One of the founders of USD, Mother Rosalie Hill, felt that education was best carried out in a beautiful and harmonious atmosphere. Today, students continue to reap the benefits of Mother Hill's vision. "The campus is one of the most beautiful campuses there is," brags one student, referring to the 180-acre spread adorned with lavish white buildings, palm trees, year-round flora, an ever-present grounds crew, and a breathtaking view of Mission Bay's Pacific waters. Many upperclassmen take advantage of their location by renting beach houses, which double as the sites of most USD parties. Great off-campus housing means that "there aren't many parties on campus," which in turn means students often venture away from USD to find entertainment. That's just dandy with most, as "San Diego is the best college town in the U.S. We have Mexico right down the street, beautiful beaches, a rocking city, beautiful canyons, and L.A. two hours north of us." And since ID is definitely required in San Diego bars, "Students under 21 go to Tijuana, which is 20 to 30 minutes away." On campus, many students involve themselves in Greek life, and "sports, intercollegiate and intramurals, are very popular here, especially soccer and basketball." Somehow, students manage to whittle out some time to study. They'll be the first to admit, however, that sometimes USD seems more like "an expensive resort" than a university.

### Student Body

"One of the reasons I chose USD is because the students are so friendly," declares one student. And since she came to USD, she says she's been able to "interact with different minorities and people of different sexual orientation." While most USD students agree that their classmates are "generally cordial," many would dispute the notion that USD is a "diverse" campus. "We need more minorities here to add some color and flavor to this campus," suggests one psychology major. USD students would also like to see classmates from a broader range of socioeconomic backgrounds. "A lot of kids are really well off and as a result are extremely spoiled and self-centered," writes a student. But look hard enough, and you'll find that "there are down-to-earth, hard workers as well." You won't have to look as hard for women. "If you're a guy, it's paradise," raves a male student. "The ratio of girls to guys is like 65:35." Another male elucidates, "The women at USD are absolutely gorgeous." Perhaps tellingly, none of the women completing our survey mentioned the handsomeness of the male population.

# UNIVERSITY OF SAN DIEGO

EMAIL: USDOFAS@SANDIEGO.EDU • WEBSITE: WWW.SANDIEGO.EDU/UGADMISS

## ADMISSIONS

*Very important factors considered include:* secondary school record, standardized test scores. *Important factors considered include:* character/personal qualities, essays, extracurricular activities, recommendations, talent/ability. *Other factors considered include:* alumni/ae relation, class rank, minority status, religious affiliation/commitment, volunteer work, work experience. SAT I or ACT required; SAT I preferred; SAT II also recommended. TOEFL required of all international applicants. High school diploma or GED is required. *High school units required/recommended:* 20 total recommended; 4 English recommended, 4 math recommended, 4 science recommended, 4 science lab recommended, 4 foreign language recommended, 4 social studies recommended.

### The Inside Word

Applicants to the University of San Diego will find a unique place with a remarkable amount of diversity in its 4,000-student population. Academically, the school offers a solid liberal arts core with close interaction between professors—all in one of the most livable cities anywhere. Solid test scores and high schools grades should be a given for applicants.

## FINANCIAL AID

*Students should submit:* FAFSA, institution's own financial aid form. Regular filing deadline is February 20. The Princeton Review suggests that all financial aid forms be submitted as soon as possible after January 1. *Need-based scholarships/grants offered:* Pell, SEOG, state scholarships/grants, private scholarships, the school's own gift aid. *Loan aid offered:* FFEL Subsidized Stafford, FFEL Unsubsidized Stafford, FFEL PLUS, Federal Perkins, state loans, college/university loans from institutional funds, nonfederal loan programs. Federal Work-Study Program available. Institutional employment available. Applicants will be notified of awards on a rolling basis beginning on or about March 1. Off-campus job opportunities are excellent.

## FROM THE ADMISSIONS OFFICE

"Looking at the University of San Diego is easy on the eyes. But really seeing our true character demands a little work.

"It is easy to focus on the obvious: the incredible beauty of the campus, the region's unparalleled climate and livability, long lists of recreational and co-curricular opportunities, the vitality of students walking through the central plaza, or even the obvious expressions of USD's Catholic character. But to focus on the superficial would be misleading.

"While the beach is nearby, USD is a serious academic institution. And while the campus is stunning, the people make the difference. More than 7,000 candidates vie for 1,000 freshman openings. But to see the 'average' freshman as a 3.8 GPA or a 1210 SAT score would miss the person. Each is unique—selected on expressions of diversity, leadership, service, talent, and essential human character. Faculty, too, are rigorously screened. USD draws over 100 candidates for every faculty opening, and this screening goes well beyond their lists of publications or the names on their diplomas. To challenge and inspire, they bring innovative approaches to undergraduate research, experiential learning, and faculty mentoring.

"While often compared to much larger institutions, USD seeks to be recognized for undergraduate teaching and residential learning. In comparison to schools of similar character, USD's academic offerings are truly impressive; a small sample includes marine biology, environmental studies, Latino studies, communication studies, e-commerce, and professional programs in engineering, business, nursing, and education, each of which complements a rigorous liberal arts base. New facilities demonstrate this diversity, including a state-of-the-art science center, the Kroc Institute for Peace and Justice, and the Jenny Craig Sports Pavilion."

## ADMISSIONS

| | |
|---|---:|
| Admissions Rating | 80 |
| # of applicants | 6,815 |
| % of applicants accepted | 53 |
| % of acceptees attending | 29 |
| # accepting a place on wait list | 104 |
| % admitted from wait list | 25 |

### FRESHMAN PROFILE

| | |
|---|---:|
| Range SAT Verbal | 520-620 |
| Average SAT Verbal | 570 |
| Range SAT Math | 540-640 |
| Average SAT Math | 590 |
| Range ACT Composite | 23-27 |
| Average ACT Composite | 26 |
| Minimum TOEFL | 550 |
| Average HS GPA | 3.7 |
| % graduated top 10% of class | 46 |
| % graduated top 25% of class | 82 |
| % graduated top 50% of class | 97 |

### DEADLINES

| | |
|---|---:|
| Priority admission | 1/5 |
| Regular admission | 1/5 |
| Regular notification | 4/15 |
| Nonfall registration? | yes |

### APPLICANTS ALSO LOOK AT
### AND OFTEN PREFER
UC Los Angeles
### AND SOMETIMES PREFER
UC San Diego
### AND RARELY PREFER
San Diego State U

## FINANCIAL FACTS

| | |
|---|---:|
| Financial Aid Rating | 87 |
| Tuition | $21,880 |
| Room and board | $9,130 |
| Books and supplies | $1,206 |
| Required fees | $108 |
| % frosh receiving aid | 51 |
| % undergrads receiving aid | 47 |
| Avg frosh grant | $19,729 |
| Avg frosh loan | $4,605 |

THE BEST 351 COLLEGES ■ 651

# UNIVERSITY OF SAN FRANCISCO

2130 FULTON STREET, SAN FRANCISCO, CA 94117 • ADMISSIONS: 415-422-6563 • FAX: 415-422-2217

## CAMPUS LIFE

| | |
|---|---|
| Quality of Life Rating | 89 |
| Type of school | private |
| Affiliation | Roman Catholic |
| Environment | urban |

### STUDENTS

| | |
|---|---|
| Total undergrad enrollment | 4,695 |
| % male/female | 37/63 |
| % from out of state | 38 |
| % from public high school | 51 |
| % live on campus | 54 |
| % in (# of) fraternities | 2 (4) |
| % in (# of) sororities | 2 (4) |
| % African American | 6 |
| % Asian | 27 |
| % Caucasian | 42 |
| % Hispanic | 14 |
| % international | 7 |
| # of countries represented | 78 |

### SURVEY SAYS . . .
Students love San Francisco, CA
Great off-campus food
Student government is popular
Students are happy
Student publicatications are popular
Very small frat/sorority scene
(Almost) everyone smokes

## ACADEMICS

| | |
|---|---|
| Academic Rating | 79 |
| Calendar | 4-1-4 |
| Student/faculty ratio | 16:1 |
| Profs interesting rating | 91 |
| Profs accessible rating | 86 |
| % profs teaching UG courses | 75 |
| Avg lab size | 10-19 students |
| Avg reg class size | 10-19 students |

### MOST POPULAR MAJORS
Business administration/management
Psychology
Nursing/registered nurse training (RN, ASN, BSN, MSN)

## STUDENTS SPEAK OUT

### Academics

Despite what the name may lead you to believe, the University of San Francisco is not a state school, but a relatively small, private, Jesuit university. And the Jesuit tradition of educating the entire individual is in full effect at USF. Many students here find their professors to be "easily accessible, brilliant, and caring," and classes tend to be fairly small. Students here don't just slide straight into major-specific courses, though. They instead spend two years working through a 50-unit General Education Curriculum (GEC). Some students are grateful for the exposure the core classes offer them, while plenty of others find them to be "way too many," and roadblocks to taking the courses they really want to take. For the most part the students are enthusiastic about the academics here. Classes tend to be tough, but very few students find them overly demanding, and there are definitely those who find them just plain easy. The professors at USF may be accessible and receptive, but the administration catches a lot more flak from the students, especially when it comes to issues of supporting student organizations and the dreaded complaints about bureaucracy.

### Life

Located a little north of dead center of the peninsula on which San Francisco lies, USF has on all sides a city perpetually pulling students off campus. "Haight/Ashbury is just six blocks" in one direction, with its "restaurants, window-shopping, and thrift/vintage stores" while "Golden Gate Park is just around the corner." If the urge moves them, it's easy for students to play the part of the "tourist for the weekend and check out the Golden Gate Bridge or Alcatraz." The lackluster campus life is most apparent on the weekends, when students pour out to the bars on nearby Geary and Clement Street. And despite the dearth of school spirit, traditional house parties abound. Some optimistic types argue that there is fun to be had on campus, like the ironically named "dead hour" on Thursdays when there are "live bands that perform in the school plaza, and . . . vendors that come outside to sell their products to students." And one night a week USF sponsors a "club night" during which it turns "the entire first floor of the University Center into a dance club with themed rooms." The more laid-back "people just have fun in their rooms . . . get booze and such."

### Student Body

Talk about a diverse campus: USF is one of a handful of national-caliber universities in which white students aren't a majority. The University has made an exceptional use of its prized location in San Francisco and its Jesuit heritage to bring in students from a wide array of backgrounds and cultures. "There are all sorts of students here: from all different states, countries, and backgrounds. The students are very diverse, as diversity is something this school emphasizes a lot." USF's multicultural atmosphere has made it a great place for a large number of active cultural clubs on campus. With so much exposure to so many different types of people both on and off campus, it's not surprising that many students here regard themselves and their peers as being "very open-minded" and accepting of students from different backgrounds. In the end, odds are whatever type of person you're looking to find, you're likely to meet them at USF.

# UNIVERSITY OF SAN FRANCISCO

FINANCIAL AID: 415-422-6303 • E-MAIL: ADMISSION@USFCA.EDU • WEBSITE: WWW.USFCA.EDU

## ADMISSIONS

*Very important factors considered include:* recommendations, secondary school record, standardized test scores. *Important factors considered include:* class rank, essays. *Other factors considered include:* alumni/ae relation, character/personal qualities, extracurricular activities, interview, minority status, talent/ability, volunteer work. SAT I or ACT required; SAT I preferred. TOEFL required of all international applicants. High school diploma or GED is required. *High school units required/recommended:* 20 total recommended; 4 English recommended, 3 math recommended, 2 science recommended, 2 science lab recommended, 2 foreign language recommended, 3 social studies recommended, 6 elective recommended.

### The Inside Word

The admissions committee at USF is not purely numbers-focused. They'll evaluate your full picture here, using your academic strengths and weaknesses along with your personal character strengths, essays, and recommendations to assess your suitability for admission. It's matchmaking. If you fit well in the USF community, you'll be welcome

## FINANCIAL AID

*Students should submit:* FAFSA. The Princeton Review suggests that all financial aid forms be submitted as soon as possible after January 1. *Need-based scholarships/grants offered:* Pell, SEOG, state scholarships/grants, private scholarships, the school's own gift aid, Federal Nursing. *Loan aid offered:* Direct PLUS, FFEL PLUS, Federal Perkins, Federal Nursing. Federal Work-Study Program available. Institutional employment available. Off-campus job opportunities are excellent.

### SELECTIVITY

| | |
|---|---|
| Admissions Rating | 80 |
| # of applicants | 3,590 |
| % of applicants accepted | 82 |
| % of acceptees attending | 28 |

### FRESHMAN PROFILE
| | |
|---|---|
| Range SAT Verbal | 510-610 |
| Range SAT Math | 510-610 |
| Range ACT Composite | 21-26 |
| Minimum TOEFL | 550 |
| Average HS GPA | 3.4 |
| % graduated top 10% of class | 27 |
| % graduated top 25% of class | 60 |
| % graduated top 50% of class | 88 |

### DEADLINES
| | |
|---|---|
| Priority admission | 2/1 |
| Nonfall registration? | yes |

### APPLICANTS ALSO LOOK AT AND OFTEN PREFER
UC Berkeley
UC Davis
U of Southern California
Santa Clara U

### AND SOMETIMES PREFER
Loyola Marymount
St. Mary's College
UC Santa Cruz

### AND RARELY PREFER
Fordham
Boston College

### FINANCIAL FACTS

| | |
|---|---|
| Financial Aid Rating | 84 |
| Tuition | $23,220 |
| Room and board | $9,350 |
| Books and supplies | $800 |
| Required fees | $120 |
| % frosh receiving aid | 59 |
| % undergrads receiving aid | 56 |
| Avg frosh grant | $17,497 |
| Avg frosh loan | $5,366 |

# UNIVERSITY OF SCRANTON

800 LINDEN STREET, SCRANTON, PA 18510 • ADMISSIONS: 570-941-7540 • FAX: 570-941-5928

## CAMPUS LIFE

| | |
|---|---|
| **Quality of Life Rating** | **77** |
| Type of school | private |
| Affiliation | Roman Catholic |
| Environment | urban |

### STUDENTS

| | |
|---|---|
| Total undergrad enrollment | 4,060 |
| % male/female | 42/58 |
| % from out of state | 48 |
| % from public high school | 52 |
| % live on campus | 47 |
| % African American | 1 |
| % Asian | 2 |
| % Caucasian | 87 |
| % Hispanic | 3 |
| % international | 1 |

### SURVEY SAYS . . .
Lots of beer drinking
Low cost of living
Lots of classroom discussion
Students don't like Scranton, PA
Students are cliquish

## ACADEMICS

| | |
|---|---|
| **Academic Rating** | **77** |
| Calendar | semester |
| Student/faculty ratio | 13:1 |
| Profs interesting rating | 80 |
| Profs accessible rating | 84 |
| % profs teaching UG courses | 98 |
| Avg lab size | 10-19 students |
| Avg reg class size | 10-19 students |

## STUDENTS SPEAK OUT

### Academics

The "intimacy between faculty and students" at the University of Scranton is illustrated by one freshman's comment, "My professors are more like my friends." This buddy-buddy relationship, combined with small class sizes, allows for individual attention and depth of study. "My teachers don't base grades on robotic regurgitation of their lectures. They evaluate my performance on original and creative thought," states a senior English major. One purist undergrad is pleased that Scranton maintains a "rigorous insistence on competency in certain 'old-school' disciplines: logic, rhetoric, and effective writing." Scranton's physical therapy, occupational therapy, and education programs are also routinely praised. A sophomore, does, however, sing the familiar small-private-school blues, characterizing Scranton academics as "average" and "not worth what we pay." Word has it that the administration "works hard to produce a socially active and learning-conducive environment." Some general complaints center around limited course availability and meager career services, though registration is reported to be "a breeze."

### Life

The Jesuit environment defines much of Scranton life, from the thriving campus ministry program to a plethora of school-sponsored sober activities, including dances, bands, and a popular coffee house. "Even as a no-alcohol person, I find so much to do," claims a content freshman. Of course, booze finds its way even into this den of Catholicism. A junior theology major notes the unusual triad of activities, "Drink Coronas, pray, study," and a sophomore corroborates with, "We have a good time, mostly at the bar." As far as the city of Scranton goes, a junior tells us "it ain't Canaan" but "it's cheap to live" and the lack of Studio 54–type nightlife "keeps you focused on school work." An industrious sophomore points out, "Though hard to fathom, I've seen Carmen performed by the London City Opera, the band Moe, and David Sedaris all within minutes of the campus." So though there's not much in terms of athletics or school spirit, a sophomore philosophy major exclaims, "Scranton should be called ScranFUN!"

### Student Body

The Scranton student population can generally be divided into "partiers and religious people, with no middle ground," according to a female senior. But in class on a Tuesday, it could be tough to tell the two groups apart. A freshman observes, "There is no variety when it comes to the student body," which is described as "white, Catholic, and upper-middle class" as well as "very conservative and closed-minded at times." Scranton is an insular and close-knit place: "The school is very concerned with creating a community. It worked—being at school is like forgetting about everything else," comments a senior. One student points out the benefits of living with the God squad, that the student body "exemplifies the Christian attribute of loving one's neighbor." A sophomore agrees and writes, "This was easily the friendliest, warmest, most welcoming campus I visited. My experience here has strengthened this view."

# UNIVERSITY OF SCRANTON

FINANCIAL AID: 570-941-7700 • E-MAIL: ADMISSIONS@SCRANTON.EDU • WEBSITE: WWW.SCRANTON.EDU

## ADMISSIONS

*Very important factors considered include:* secondary school record. *Important factors considered include:* class rank, standardized test scores. *Other factors considered include:* alumni/ae relation, character/personal qualities, essays, extracurricular activities, interview, minority status, recommendations, talent/ability, volunteer work, work experience. SAT I or ACT required. TOEFL required of all international applicants. High school diploma or GED is required. *High school units required/recommended:* 16 total required; 4 English required, 3 math required, 4 math recommended, 1 science required, 2 science recommended, 2 foreign language required, 2 social studies required, 3 social studies recommended.

### The Inside Word

Admission to Scranton gets harder each year. A steady stream of smart kids from the tri-state area keeps classes full and the admit rate low. Successful applicants will need solid grades and test scores. As with many religiously affiliated schools, students should be a good match philosophically as well.

## FINANCIAL AID

*Students should submit:* FAFSA. No deadline for regular filing. The Princeton Review suggests that all financial aid forms be submitted as soon as possible after January 1. *Need-based scholarships/grants offered:* Pell, SEOG, state scholarships/grants, private scholarships, the school's own gift aid. *Loan aid offered:* FFEL Subsidized Stafford, FFEL Unsubsidized Stafford, FFEL PLUS, Federal Perkins. Federal Work-Study Program available. Institutional employment available. Applicants will be notified of awards on a rolling basis beginning on or about March 1. Off-campus job opportunities are good.

## FROM THE ADMISSIONS OFFICE

"A Jesuit institution in Pennsylvania's Pocono northeast region, The University of Scranton is known for many things, especially its outstanding academics, state-of-the art campus and technology, and exceptional sense of community. Founded in 1888, the University offers more than 80 undergraduate and graduate academic programs of study in five colleges and schools.

"For nine consecutive years, *U.S. News & World Report*'s America's Best Colleges edition has ranked the University among the ten finest master's universities in the North—fourth in the 2003 edition. The University also joined the elite colleges profiled in The Princeton Review's *The 345 Best Colleges*. The University was profiled in the 2003 edition of Kaplan Publishing's *The Unofficial, Unbiased Insider's Guide to the 320 Most Interesting Colleges*. As well, the University was rated 39th among the nation's 100 most-wired colleges in *Yahoo! Internet Life* magazine's 2001 edition and is one of only 100 schools in the nation on Templeton's Honor Roll of Character-Building Colleges.

"Scranton has a history of success in preparing students for medical school, law school, and the nation's most prestigious scholarships and fellowships. In 2002, the acceptance rate for graduating seniors from the University into medical and related schools reached an all-time high of 100 percent. Law schools accepted 72 percent of the graduating seniors who applied in 2002. In the past three years, Scranton students have earned a remarkable 12 Fulbright Fellowships, a Goldwater Scholarship, two Truman Scholarships, four Freeman Awards, a Jack Kent Cooke Scholarship, two NCAA Post-Graduate Scholarships, two Rotary Ambassadorial Scholarships, a DeRance Scholarship, and two State Farm Fellowships for Exceptional Students. In the spring of 2003, applications for admission reached an all-time high. Students are encouraged to apply early for admission and can do so online with no application fee at www.scranton.edu/apply."

## ADMISSIONS

| Admissions Rating | 85 |
|---|---|
| # of applicants | 5,121 |
| % of applicants accepted | 70 |
| % of acceptees attending | 27 |
| # accepting a place on wait list | 430 |
| % admitted from wait list | 17 |

### FRESHMAN PROFILE

| Range SAT Verbal | 510-610 |
|---|---|
| Average SAT Verbal | 565 |
| Range SAT Math | 520-620 |
| Average SAT Math | 562 |
| Minimum TOEFL | 500 |
| Average HS GPA | 3.4 |
| % graduated top 10% of class | 30 |
| % graduated top 25% of class | 64 |
| % graduated top 50% of class | 91 |

### DEADLINES

| Regular admission | 3/1 |
|---|---|
| Nonfall registration? | yes |

### APPLICANTS ALSO LOOK AT AND OFTEN PREFER
Villanova
Saint Joseph's U
Fairfield
U of Delaware

### AND SOMETIMES PREFER
Penn State at University Park
Fordham
Loyola Maryland

## FINANCIAL FACTS

| Financial Aid Rating | 79 |
|---|---|
| Tuition | $20,248 |
| Room and board | $8,770 |
| Books and supplies | $900 |
| Required fees | $200 |
| % frosh receiving aid | 68 |
| % undergrads receiving aid | 63 |
| Avg frosh grant | $10,217 |
| Avg frosh loan | $3,300 |

# UNIVERSITY OF SOUTH CAROLINA—COLUMBIA

OFFICE OF ADMISSIONS, COLUMBIA, SC 29208 • ADMISSIONS: 803-777-7700 • FAX: 803-777-0101

## CAMPUS LIFE

| | |
|---|---|
| Quality of Life Rating | 75 |
| Type of school | public |
| Environment | urban |

### STUDENTS

| | |
|---|---|
| Total undergrad enrollment | 16,567 |
| % male/female | 46/54 |
| % from out of state | 21 |
| % live on campus | 47 |
| % in (# of) fraternities | 17 (18) |
| % in (# of) sororities | 17 (12) |
| % African American | 17 |
| % Asian | 3 |
| % Caucasian | 73 |
| % Hispanic | 2 |
| % international | 2 |

### SURVEY SAYS . . .
Frats and sororities dominate social scene
(Almost) everyone smokes
Hard liquor is popular
Lots of beer drinking
Students are cliquish
Campus difficult to get around
Large classes
Ethnic diversity on campus
Students get along with local community

## ACADEMICS

| | |
|---|---|
| Academic Rating | 65 |
| Calendar | semester |
| Student/faculty ratio | 17:1 |
| Profs interesting rating | 91 |
| Profs accessible rating | 88 |
| % profs teaching UG courses | 61 |
| % classes taught by TAs | 23 |
| Avg lab size | 20-29 students |
| Avg reg class size | 20-29 students |

## STUDENTS SPEAK OUT

### Academics

Home of the mighty "Gamecocks" (favored lid of the white-hat crowd), University of South Carolina undergrads don't mince words when it comes to why they chose their school: "Had what I needed at the best price," writes a junior media arts major. "It's in the South, it's in a city, and it has a good journalism school," adds a senior. Offering all the strengths of a traditional liberal arts university—in addition to several pre-professional tracks (popular majors include journalism, business, advertising, and public relations)—this state school is usually the first choice for South Carolina residents who want a solid education, a fun college experience in a big city and the option to go home for mom's grits and sweet potato pie on the weekends. For a big university, USC's "professor accessibility" is second to none—"I was very impressed with the quality and availability of the faculty," declares a sophomore. And though some complain that "a few of the teachers are so old they seem to have no passion for what they're doing," most students are of the opinion that USC's profs are "interesting and intelligent—some even seem like real people sometimes!" On the money front, students are a bit less forgiving. A junior explains the situation like this: "A lack of funding forced USC to make severe budget cuts this year, yet the powers that be still find money to dramatically raise the football coach's salary. It is evident the school's top priority is not academic in nature." While undergrads praise the school's job opportunities and commitment to diversity, as well as its willingness to "keep up with new technology," shoddy maintenance of campus facilities and lax security are considered deficits, as is the aforementioned privileging of athletics over academics. Still, students at South Carolina seem generally happy. Says a sophomore, "It's not bad. There's room for improvement, but I'd say that it's pretty good to be at USC."

### Life

"In general," writes a junior, USC students "go to bars, play sports, and go to frat parties." Columbia's Five Points and The Vista are where most students go to socialize, though for the under-21 crowd, going Greek seems to be the path of least resistance. A strong fraternity/sorority presence on campus isn't to everyone's liking, however. Notes another junior, "There seems to be a lack of individuality among students here. For fun, I get away from campus." A senior agrees: "There's a lot of animosity between Greeks and non-Greeks," she writes. At the same time, students praise the school's "many student organizations" and "awareness of social issues." Writes a sophomore, "I love USC. There is so much to do on and off campus. People are involved in a variety of religious, musical, political, [and] sports-related clubs." And though some USC students might agree with this first-year's words—"College is a lot more boring that I thought it would be"—we like this junior's more positive summation of life at the University of South Carolina: "It's lovely walking through campus. The grass is almost always green."

### Student Body

Perhaps it's a southern stereotype—slow as molasses and all that—but despite their pointed remarks about academics, University of South Carolina students seem to see themselves as a fairly laid-back bunch. "Everyone is friendly and easy to get along with," chirps a junior, while a typically mellow sophomore adds, "Most are easygoing, some are jerks . . . that's life." Diversity seems to be a particular strength of USC's; notes another sophomore, "Most people here are accepting and understanding. I have seen very few, if any, cases of discrimination or bias on campus." Perhaps there is something to the legendary southern hospitality, after all. A junior is only half-joking when she writes, "It's amazing to think that someone opening a door for you is a mentionable event, but so many people do that here. It's a nice addition to my day."

# UNIVERSITY OF SOUTH CAROLINA—COLUMBIA

FINANCIAL AID: 803-777-8134 • E-MAIL: ADMISSIONS-UGRAD@SC.EDU • WEBSITE: WWW.SC.EDU

## ADMISSIONS

*Very important factors considered include:* secondary school record, standardized test scores. *Other factors considered include:* recommendations, talent/ability. SAT I or ACT required. TOEFL required of all international applicants. High school diploma or GED is required. *High school units required/recommended:* 19 total required; 4 English required, 3 math required, 3 science required, 3 science lab required, 2 foreign language required, 2 social studies required, 1 history required, 4 elective required.

## *The Inside Word*

The admissions process at South Carolina is formula-driven and not particularly demanding. A solid academic performance in high school should do the trick. For the past three years, USC has had to close its admissions to the freshman class early, as the number of applicants has risen. So it is important to meet the application deadline.

## FINANCIAL AID

*Students should submit:* FAFSA. The Princeton Review suggests that all financial aid forms be submitted as soon as possible after January 1. *Need-based scholarships/grants offered:* Pell, SEOG, state scholarships/grants, private scholarships, the school's own gift aid, United Negro College Fund. *Loan aid offered:* FFEL Subsidized Stafford, FFEL Unsubsidized Stafford, FFEL PLUS, Federal Perkins, Federal Nursing. Federal Work-Study Program available. Institutional employment available. Applicants will be notified of awards on a rolling basis beginning on or about April 15. Off-campus job opportunities are excellent.

## FROM THE ADMISSIONS OFFICE

"Nestled among ancient oaks and beautiful green spaces, University of South Carolina sits in the center of Columbia, South Carolina, the state's capital city. A major research university, USC awards baccalaureate, master's, and doctoral degrees, and is known for its top-ranked academic programs. For example, USC is currently ranked number one in the nation for undergraduate international business by U.S. News & World Report. Other programs are regularly listed in the top 25, including advertising, public relations, and marine science. Additionally, the magazine recognizes USC's pioneering efforts in freshman outreach as number one for Programs That Really Work. USC's Honors College is one of the nation's best, offering Ivy League quality at state college costs. Academic major choices are plentiful, with more than 80 options available. USC also has a graduate school, school of law, school of medicine, and professional degree programs. The University offers quality student support in such areas as career development, disability services, and computer lab access. The campus and surrounding community also have great entertainment, cultural, and recreational outlets. A new 18,000-seat arena brings national concerts to town and serves as home to USC basketball. And students enjoy USC's newly opened, $40 million fitness center featuring state-of-the-art equipment and amenities. Beyond city borders, South Carolina's world-famous beaches and the Blue Ridge Mountains are each less than a three-hour drive away. Growing numbers of students are discovering that the University of South Carolina is the right choice for them."

## SELECTIVITY

| | |
|---|---|
| Admissions Rating | 74 |
| # of applicants | 12,016 |
| % of applicants accepted | 70 |
| % of acceptees attending | 42 |

### FRESHMAN PROFILE

| | |
|---|---|
| Range SAT Verbal | 500-610 |
| Average SAT Verbal | 558 |
| Range SAT Math | 510-620 |
| Average SAT Math | 569 |
| Range ACT Composite | 21-26 |
| Average ACT Composite | 24 |
| Minimum TOEFL | 550 |
| Average HS GPA | 3.7 |
| % graduated top 10% of class | 24 |
| % graduated top 25% of class | 56 |
| % graduated top 50% of class | 88 |

### DEADLINES

| | |
|---|---|
| Priority admission | 12/1 |
| Regular admission | 12/1 |
| Nonfall registration? | yes |

### APPLICANTS ALSO LOOK AT
**AND OFTEN PREFER**
UNC Chapel Hill
**AND SOMETIMES PREFER**
Clemson
**AND RARELY PREFER**
Wake Forest

## FINANCIAL FACTS

| | |
|---|---|
| Financial Aid Rating | 80 |
| In-state tuition | $5,548 |
| Out-of-state tuition | $14,886 |
| Room and board | $5,327 |
| Books and supplies | $720 |
| Required fees | $200 |
| % frosh receiving aid | 80 |
| % undergrads receiving aid | 70 |
| Avg frosh grant | $3,400 |
| Avg frosh loan | $3,000 |

# UNIVERSITY OF SOUTH DAKOTA

414 EAST CLARK, VERMILLION, SD 57069 • ADMISSIONS: 605-677-5434 • FAX: 605-677-6753

## CAMPUS LIFE

| Quality of Life Rating | 81 |
|---|---|
| Type of school | public |
| Environment | rural |

### STUDENTS

| Total undergrad enrollment | 5,769 |
|---|---|
| % male/female | 39/61 |
| % from out of state | 23 |
| % from public high school | 93 |
| % live on campus | 19 |
| % in (# of) fraternities | 20 (8) |
| % in (# of) sororities | 12 (4) |
| % African American | 1 |
| % Asian | 1 |
| % Caucasian | 86 |
| % Hispanic | 1 |
| % Native American | 2 |
| % international | 1 |
| # of countries represented | 38 |

### SURVEY SAYS . . .
Student government is popular
Student newspaper is popular
Frats and sororities dominate social scene
Students are happy
Lab facilities need improving
Computer facilities need improving
Athletic facilities need improving

## ACADEMICS

| Academic Rating | 71 |
|---|---|
| Calendar | semester |
| Student/faculty ratio | 14:1 |
| Profs interesting rating | 77 |
| Profs accessible rating | 81 |
| % profs teaching UG courses | 94 |
| % classes taught by TAs | 6 |
| Avg reg class size under 10 students | |

### MOST POPULAR MAJORS
Psychology
Biology
Business administration/management

## STUDENTS SPEAK OUT

### Academics

USD is made up of 100 programs in eight schools, including the state's only medical school, law school, and college of fine arts. While not every program is open to them, undergraduates here are generally pleased with the academic exposure and opportunity that surrounds them. Perhaps just as enticing as the spectrum of selection at USD is the price. South Dakota's flagship university offers notably low tuition rates, as well as "nice scholarships." Students find themselves studying under a faculty that is "very kind, understanding, and determined to make us learn." For the most part, professors here "have a good sense of humor" and give the 5,000 or so undergrads "ample time to meet with them before and after class." Some students say that niceness doesn't always make a good teacher, though. The few professors here who "babble on even when half the class is asleep" get low marks. When students need a break from the lecture hall, they find relief—and stimulation—in the range of "research and internship opportunities" available here. Overall, summarizes one student, "academics are challenging, but not enough to give you a mental breakdown."

### Life

USD is located in Vermillion, a city of 10,000 that lies on bluffs overlooking the Missouri River in South Dakota's southeast corner. While students can't deny that Vermillion is a quaint, safe, comfortable town, they find little to spark their excitement here. When they need a dose of something resembling urban life, they head 25 miles southeast to Sioux City, Iowa, or, when they're feeling particularly ambitious, 65 miles north to the even larger Sioux Falls. One student tells us that many classmates "make time for extracurricular activities," which include "academic clubs (biology club, math club, etc.), intramural sports, and the school newspaper," as well as "tae kwon do, fencing, and church activities." This being the case, one student opines, "Very rarely should anyone be bored on our campus." Sports are especially good at bringing the campus to life—particularly when one of the USD Coyote teams hosts a game at their impressive arena, the DakotaDome. But athletic match-ups and after-hours speakers don't satiate everybody's social urges. "Life is pretty boring," moans one student, and therefore "most people party." As you'll find at almost every university, drinking and drugs have a prominent role in some students' lives, but many say they don't have much time for partying. "Most students here work in addition to going to school full-time," explains an English major. "The younger ones only think about the parties. The older ones are finally at the point where they know this is going to affect the rest of their lives." In other words, as the years press on, students learn to drop some of the partying and "focus on their academics."

### Student Body

Undergraduates at the University of South Dakota "have the midwestern courtesy and kindness thing going on." And there's good reason for this. More than 85 percent of this student body comes from South Dakota and its neighboring states. Because of the aura of friendliness at the university, one student writes, "I always feel comfortable walking up to a fellow student and asking a question or just talking." Another agrees: "I'd feel comfortable approaching anyone. They are all very laid-back and fun-loving." The biggest complaint by USD students is the noticeable absence of "diverse peoples." At times, this lack of diversity translates to a lack of student interest in the world beyond USD. One tuned-in student mutters, "Students are very apathetic towards politics and society in general." But some of the university's alums stand as proof that this stereotype doesn't always fit. Ten South Dakotan governors have attended USD, as well as many state supreme court justices. And let's not forget news anchor Tom Brokaw, sports commentator Pat O'Brien, and *USA Today* founder Al Neuharth—all three earned their degrees at USD.

# UNIVERSITY OF SOUTH DAKOTA

FINANCIAL AID: 605-677-5446 • E-MAIL: ADMISS@USD.EDU • WEBSITE: WWW.USD.EDU

## ADMISSIONS

*Very important factors considered include:* class rank, secondary school record, standardized test scores. *Other factors considered include:* essays, extracurricular activities, minority status, recommendations, talent/ability. SAT I or ACT required; ACT preferred. TOEFL required of all international applicants. High school diploma or GED is required. *High school units required/recommended:* 16 total required; 17 total recommended; 4 English required, 3 math required, 3 science required, 3 science lab required, 3 social studies required.

### The Inside Word

Given the relatively small numbers of college-bound students coming from South Dakota's high schools each year, the university's rolling admission policy is nearly open admission. Solid college-prep students should encounter no trouble in gaining admission.

## FINANCIAL AID

*Students should submit:* FAFSA. No deadline for regular filing. The Princeton Review suggests that all financial aid forms be submitted as soon as possible after January 1. *Need-based scholarships/grants offered:* Pell, SEOG, private scholarships, the school's own gift aid, Federal Nursing. *Loan aid offered:* FFEL Subsidized Stafford, FFEL Unsubsidized Stafford, FFEL PLUS, Federal Perkins, Federal Nursing, college/university loans from institutional funds. Federal Work-Study Program available. Institutional employment available. Applicants will be notified of awards on a rolling basis beginning on or about May 3. Off-campus job opportunities are good.

## FROM THE ADMISSIONS OFFICE

"USD, a doctorate-granting university with liberal arts emphasis, has a strong academic reputation. Old Main, the campus focal point, houses the Honors Program, high-tech classrooms, and more. Among the many programs on campus are three Centers of Excellence including the center on Ambulatory Medical Student Education. Innovative, this program has a physician-patient approach, which provides learning opportunities in primary care medicine. The Disaster Mental Health Institute, internationally recognized, provides unique programs in disaster mental health response. The W.O. Farber Center for Civic Leadership, which prepares students in leadership, offers academic, enrichment, and community-outreach programs. The center sponsors internationally prominent speakers such as retired U.S. Army General Colin Powell, former President Gerald Ford, NBC News anchor Tom Brokaw, and others. USD's alumni include: NBC's Tom Brokaw, *USA Today* founder Allen Neuharth, motivational speaker Joan Brock, writers Peter Dexter, *Penny Whistle* book author Meredith Auld Brokaw, Pat O'Brien, USD President James W. Abbott, and World War II ace Joe Foss, among others."

---

### SELECTIVITY

★★☆☆

| | |
|---|---|
| Admissions Rating | 73 |
| # of applicants | 2,539 |
| % of applicants accepted | 86 |
| % of acceptees attending | 51 |

#### FRESHMAN PROFILE

| | |
|---|---|
| Range ACT Composite | 19-25 |
| Average ACT Composite | 22 |
| Minimum TOEFL | 560 |
| Average HS GPA | 3.1 |
| % graduated top 10% of class | 10 |
| % graduated top 25% of class | 31 |
| % graduated top 50% of class | 63 |

#### DEADLINES

| | |
|---|---|
| Nonfall registration? | yes |

#### APPLICANTS ALSO LOOK AT AND OFTEN PREFER
U of Nebraska at Lincoln
Mankato State

#### AND SOMETIMES PREFER
South Dakota State
Augustana

#### AND RARELY PREFER
Mount Marty College
Northern State
Dakota State

### FINANCIAL FACTS

★★★☆

| | |
|---|---|
| Financial Aid Rating | 84 |
| In-state tuition | $2,163 |
| Out-of-state tuition | $6,875 |
| Room and board | $3,505 |
| Books and supplies | $700 |
| Required fees | $2,042 |
| % frosh receiving aid | 58 |
| % undergrads receiving aid | 59 |
| Avg frosh grant | $2,127 |
| Avg frosh loan | $2,065 |

# UNIVERSITY OF SOUTHERN CALIFORNIA

UNIVERSITY PARK, LOS ANGELES, CA 90089 • ADMISSIONS: 213-740-1111 • FAX: 213-740-6364

## CAMPUS LIFE

★★★☆

| | |
|---|---|
| Quality of Life Rating | 80 |
| Type of school | private |
| Environment | urban |

### STUDENTS
| | |
|---|---|
| Total undergrad enrollment | 16,145 |
| % male/female | 50/50 |
| % from out of state | 33 |
| % from public high school | 62 |
| % live on campus | 37 |
| % in (# of) fraternities | 16 (25) |
| % in (# of) sororities | 17 (18) |
| % African American | 7 |
| % Asian | 21 |
| % Caucasian | 48 |
| % Hispanic | 13 |
| % international | 8 |

### SURVEY SAYS . . .
Frats and sororities dominate social scene
Everyone loves the Trojans
High cost of living
Great computer facilities
Great library
Ethnic diversity on campus
Student publications are popular

## ACADEMICS

| | |
|---|---|
| Academic Rating | 80 |
| Calendar | semester |
| Student/faculty ratio | 10:1 |
| Profs interesting rating | 92 |
| Profs accessible rating | 90 |
| Avg lab size | 20-29 students |
| Avg reg class size | 10-19 students |

### MOST POPULAR MAJORS
Communications studies/speech communication and rhetoric
Psychology
Business administration/management

## STUDENTS SPEAK OUT

### Academics
Students looking for a "cutting-edge" university located in such a heavenly place as the City of Angels ought to turn an eye to the University of Southern California, named School of the Year by *Time/Princeton Review College Guide* in 2000. USC students gush about their "dedicated" faculty, unlike most other large research universities, all general education courses are taught by senior, tenured faculty, not part-timers or graduate assistants. The theater and film departments are (can you believe it?) extremely popular, and journalism students appreciate the fact that many of their classes are taught by real-life journalists. "Where else can . . . you see your teacher in class and then on the 11 o'clock news?" a broadcast journalism major asks. The mathematics and art departments also receive high marks. A little initiative goes a long way here because "everyone wants to help you, but you have to ask first." The administration is "too bureaucratic" but students believe that, like Big Government with a conscience, it's "committed to ensuring that we receive a top-rate education." A junior business major declares, "I would never want to go to any other school but USC." Graduating students find that being a Trojan has its advantages in the working world, because USC alumni (approximately 250,000 living) are everywhere and are known to help new alumni find employment.

### Life
USC's location allows u-grads to sample all that Los Angeles has to offer. Specifically, students love the beach (which is only a 10-minute drive away), the clubs, and all aspects of the entertainment industry. Students frequently attend movies (Hello? Hollywood?). Having a car on campus is a major advantage because the public transit system isn't as reliable. Students say that "there's always a party to go to," especially on "The Row"—a legendary group of fraternity houses located near campus. The Greek system is big here, and "Trojan pride" is infectious. Students support the university's football team regardless of its record, and games against cross-town rival UCLA raise school spirit to a fever pitch. The weather in Southern California is usually pretty close to paradisal. With all that the university and the surrounding areas have to offer, a senior theater major editorializes, "You've got to be pretty tough on yourself to go to classes with all the distractions." A sophomore adds, "Coming to USC is like getting a giant dinner plate and having all-access to a world-class buffet. There are so many opportunities, it's almost overwhelming."

### Student Body
USC is one of the more diverse campuses profiled in Best 345. Contrary to what that diversity might imply, however, students of the same ethnic group tend to form "socially segregated" ethnic cliques. Still, students say that their peers are "the school's best asset." Many credit the warm climate (which decreases the necessity for restrictive clothing) for helping them to meet people, and students constantly mention how attractive their peers are, calling them "beautiful" and "awesome" as well as "sexy" and "cute." Of course, some complain that the "'California—beauty-is-everything-mindset' can get tiring sometimes." A senior biology major points out that students are "very competitive" and that "nobody wants to help you or study with you." Despite the cutthroat academics, the "Trojan family" bonds people, no matter what. One enthusiastic sophomore writes, "Whenever you see someone wearing USC clothing around town, you say 'Fight On!'"

# UNIVERSITY OF SOUTHERN CALIFORNIA

FINANCIAL AID: 213-740-1111 • E-MAIL: UGRD@USC.EDU • WEBSITE: WWW.USC.EDU

## ADMISSIONS
*Very important factors considered include:* secondary school record, standardized test scores, talent/ability. *Important factors considered include:* character/personal qualities, essays, extracurricular activities, interview, recommendations. *Other factors considered include:* alumni/ae relation, minority status, volunteer work, work experience. SAT I or ACT required. High school diploma is required and GED is not accepted. *High school units required/recommended:* 16 total required; 4 English required, 3 math required, 4 math recommended, 2 science required, 4 science recommended, 2 science lab required, 3 science lab recommended, 2 foreign language required, 3 foreign language recommended, 2 social studies required, 3 social studies recommended, 3 elective required.

### The Inside Word
The high national visibility of its athletic teams and glamorous images has long enabled USC to maintain a large applicant pool. Recently, though, this athletic powerhouse has become an academic powerhouse. Admissions is solidly competitive. USC is looking for top students who are motivated and ready to take advantage of all the resources of a large, urban research university.

## FINANCIAL AID
*Students should submit:* FAFSA, CSS/Financial Aid PROFILE, business/farm supplement, parent's and student's federal income tax forms with all schedules and W-2s, income documentation for nonfilers. Regular filing deadline is February 28. The Princeton Review suggests that all financial aid forms be submitted as soon as possible after January 1. *Need-based scholarships/grants offered:* Pell, SEOG, state scholarships/grants, private scholarships, the school's own gift aid. *Loan aid offered:* FFEL Subsidized Stafford, FFEL Unsubsidized Stafford, FFEL PLUS, Federal Perkins, credit-ready and credit-based loans from private sources. Federal Work-Study Program available. Institutional employment available. Applicants will be notified of awards on a rolling basis beginning on or about March 15. Off-campus job opportunities are excellent.

## FROM THE ADMISSIONS OFFICE
"One of the best ways to discover if USC is right for you is to walk around campus, talk to students, and get a feel for the area both as a place to study and a place to live. If you can't visit, we hold admission information programs around the country. Watch your mailbox for an invitation or send us an e-mail if you're interested."

### SELECTIVITY

| | |
|---|---|
| Admissions Rating | 83 |
| # of applicants | 28,362 |
| % of applicants accepted | 30 |
| % of acceptees attending | 32 |

#### FRESHMAN PROFILE
| | |
|---|---|
| Range SAT Verbal | 600-700 |
| Average SAT Verbal | 652 |
| Range SAT Math | 640-720 |
| Average SAT Math | 683 |
| Range ACT Composite | 27-31 |
| Average ACT Composite | 30 |
| Average HS GPA | 4.0 |
| % graduated top 10% of class | 80 |
| % graduated top 25% of class | 90 |
| % graduated top 50% of class | 99 |

#### DEADLINES
| | |
|---|---|
| Priority admission | 12/10 |
| Regular admission | 1/10 |
| Regular notification | 4/1 |
| Nonfall registration? | yes |

#### APPLICANTS ALSO LOOK AT
**AND OFTEN PREFER**
UC Berkeley
Stanford
**AND SOMETIMES PREFER**
NYU
Northwestern
UCLA
**AND RARELY PREFER**
UC Irvine
UC Santa Barbara

### FINANCIAL FACTS

| | |
|---|---|
| Financial Aid Rating | 85 |
| Tuition | $26,464 |
| Room and board | $8,512 |
| Books and supplies | $644 |
| Required fees | $490 |
| % frosh receiving aid | 43 |
| % undergrads receiving aid | 50 |
| Avg frosh grant | $24,917 |
| Avg frosh loan | $3,016 |

# UNIVERSITY OF TENNESSEE—KNOXVILLE

320 STUDENT SERVICE BUILDING, CIRCLE PARK DRIVE, KNOXVILLE, TN 37996 • ADMISSIONS: 865-974-2184 • FAX: 865-974-6341

## CAMPUS LIFE

★ ★ ☆ ☆

| Quality of Life Rating | 79 |
| --- | --- |
| Type of school | public |
| Environment | urban |

### STUDENTS

| Total undergrad enrollment | 19,956 |
| --- | --- |
| % male/female | 49/51 |
| % from out of state | 14 |
| % live on campus | 32 |
| % in (# of) fraternities | 15 (26) |
| % in (# of) sororities | 20 (17) |
| % African American | 7 |
| % Asian | 3 |
| % Caucasian | 87 |
| % Hispanic | 1 |
| % international | 2 |
| # of countries represented | 90 |

### SURVEY SAYS . . .
Everyone loves the Volunteers
Lots of beer drinking
(Almost) everyone smokes
Athletic facilities are great
Hard liquor is popular
Great library
Frats and sororities dominate social scene
Great off-campus food

## ACADEMICS

| Academic Rating | 73 |
| --- | --- |
| Calendar | semester |
| Student/faculty ratio | 18:1 |
| % profs teaching UG courses | 88 |
| % classes taught by TAs | 18 |
| Avg lab size | 10-19 students |
| Avg reg class size | 20-29 students |

## STUDENTS SPEAK OUT

### Academics
As at many large state schools, "the academic experience can be a good one" at University of Tennessee—Knoxville for the student who "puts in quite a bit more effort to have a well-rounded education rather than the 'party school' education that my university tends to promote." Agrees one undergrad, "You can get an incredible education here if you work at it a little bit. The instructors are great. Many of the departments here have national recognition, like anthropology (due to Dr. William Bass, the famous forensics anthropologist), child and family studies (due to Cheryl Buehler), philosophy medical ethics courses (due to Glenn Graber), and a fantastic psychology undergraduate program." The business and engineering programs also receive students' plaudits. Tennessee undergrads warn, however, that getting that great education requires a ton of initiative; "the only way to get things done at this school is simply be aggressive," explains one senior. Big-school bureaucratic nightmares, combined with professors who "only care about getting published," leave many here feeling slighted; they refer to this feeling as "the Big Orange Screw."

### Life
"Life at this school is centered on sports," UT undergrads agree. "You can't beat a UT fan!" In the fall, football dominates campus life; students tell us that "football games really bring the school, community, and entire state together to support a wonderful team." Adds one undergrad, "Next to Baptists, football fans are the largest religious group on campus." In the spring, it's all about the "outstanding" men's and women's basketball teams. As one student put it, "I hate to admit it, but academics aren't as important here as football and basketball." Before games, after games, and when there are no games, UT students party up. "A lot of people seem to come to UT to party," students report. "Some freshmen come here, get dressed up and go out every night, get trashed and never make it to class." Much of the activity centers on "The Strip" ("the main road that runs through campus") and surrounds, which students here have dubbed "constant party zones." Teetotalers should note that "there's so many people up here that if partying really isn't your thing, you can always find something else to do." For example, "there is a club for everything, from swing dancing to Frisbee throwing." Also, "UT is pretty good about having some really awesome guest speakers. The two I found most intriguing recently were Sonja Sanchez and Kurt Vonnegut." Many here love to escape to the Smoky Mountains, which are just a 20-minute drive from campus.

### Student Body
"Clique is the word" at UT, where many students, it seems, arrive with a network of friends already in tow. "There are a lot of social cliques here, and most of them stem from high school," writes one student. "There is a definite feeling that no one wants to make new friends." Adds another undergrad, "It seems like UT is a big Memphis and Nashville reunion, just moved a little east. The student body is "mostly white, middle-to-upper-class, somewhat religious . . . and loves to party!" Students warn that "the Greek life is very dominant here, and some of them are not so friendly with those that are not in a sorority or a fraternity." Even so, the surface pleasures of southern gentility are evident, at least to outsiders; as one Yankee reports, "I came from Washington, D.C., so everyone is much friendlier here. You get on the elevator and people say 'Hi.' If you did that at home, people would give you looks."

662 ■ THE BEST 351 COLLEGES

# UNIVERSITY OF TENNESSEE—KNOXVILLE

FINANCIAL AID: 865-974-3131 • E-MAIL: ADMISSIONS@UTK.EDU • WEBSITE: WWW.UTK.EDU

## ADMISSIONS

*Very important factors considered include:* secondary school record, standardized test scores. *Other factors considered include:* alumni/ae relation, character/personal qualities, class rank, extracurricular activities, minority status, recommendations. SAT I or ACT required. TOEFL required of all international applicants. High school diploma or GED is required. *High school units required/recommended:* 14 total required; 4 English required, 3 math required, 2 science required, 1 science lab required, 2 foreign language required, 1 social studies required, 1 history required.

### *The Inside Word*

Don't expect any attention to be given to your essays or extracurriculars at Tennessee unless you are not "automatically admissible." The university takes in a jumbo freshman class and has to use a fairly straightforward approach to getting these kids admitted. Standards are the same for out-of-state applicants as for in-state, but the school's mix of in-state/out-of-state students is firm, since it is set by policy of the Board of Trustees.

## FINANCIAL AID

*Students should submit:* FAFSA, institution's own financial aid form. November 1 priority deadline for scholarship application. March 1 priority deadline for FAFSA. *Need-based scholarships/grants offered:* Pell, SEOG, state scholarships/grants, private scholarships, the school's own gift aid. *Loan aid offered:* FFEL Subsidized Stafford, FFEL Unsubsidized Stafford, FFEL PLUS, Federal Perkins, college/university loans from institutional funds. Federal Work-Study Program available. Applicants will be notified of awards on a rolling basis beginning on or about April 1. Off-campus job opportunities are good.

## FROM THE ADMISSIONS OFFICE

"The University of Tennessee—Knoxville is the place where you belong if you're interested in outstanding resources and unlimited opportunities to foster your personal and academic growth. Nine colleges offer more than 120 majors to students from all 50 states and 95 foreign countries. More than 300 clubs and organizations on campus offer opportunities for fun, challenge, and service. UTK is a place where students take pride in belonging to a 200-year-old tradition and celebrate the excitement of 'the Volunteer spirit.' We invite you to explore the many advantages UTK has to offer."

---

### SELECTIVITY

| | |
|---|---|
| Admissions Rating | 77 |
| # of applicants | 9,724 |
| % of applicants accepted | 58 |
| % of acceptees attending | 65 |

#### FRESHMAN PROFILE

| | |
|---|---|
| Range SAT Verbal | 500-600 |
| Average SAT Verbal | 551 |
| Range SAT Math | 500-610 |
| Average SAT Math | 549 |
| Range ACT Composite | 21-27 |
| Average ACT Composite | 24 |
| Minimum TOEFL | 523 |
| Average HS GPA | 3.4 |
| % graduated top 10% of class | 27 |
| % graduated top 25% of class | 54 |
| % graduated top 50% of class | 83 |

#### DEADLINES

| | |
|---|---|
| Early action | 11/1 |
| Regular admission | 2/1 |
| Regular notification | rolling |
| Nonfall registration? | yes |

#### APPLICANTS ALSO LOOK AT
##### AND OFTEN PREFER
Middle Tennessee State
Auburn
Emory
##### AND SOMETIMES PREFER
U. Florida
Vanderbilt
U. Georgia
##### AND RARELY PREFER
U. Kentucky
East Tennessee State
Clemson
U. of the South

### FINANCIAL FACTS

| | |
|---|---|
| Financial Aid Rating | 83 |
| In-state tuition | $3,476 |
| Out-of-state tuition | $11,578 |
| Room and board | $4,912 |
| Books and supplies | $1,090 |
| Required fees | $580 |
| % frosh receiving aid | 34 |
| % undergrads receiving aid | 35 |

THE BEST 351 COLLEGES ■ 663

# UNIVERSITY OF TEXAS—AUSTIN

JOHN W. HARGIS HALL, AUSTIN, TX 78712-1111 • ADMISSIONS: 512-475-7440 • FAX: 512-475-7475

## CAMPUS LIFE

★ ★ ★ ☆

| | |
|---|---|
| Quality of Life Rating | 86 |
| Type of school | public |
| Environment | urban |

### STUDENTS

| | |
|---|---|
| Total undergrad enrollment | 39,661 |
| % male/female | 50/50 |
| % from out of state | 9 |
| % live on campus | 17 |
| % in (# of) fraternities | 10 (26) |
| % in (# of) sororities | 14 (22) |
| % African American | 4 |
| % Asian | 17 |
| % Caucasian | 62 |
| % Hispanic | 14 |
| % international | 4 |
| # of countries represented | 126 |

### SURVEY SAYS . . .
Everyone loves the Longhorns
Students love Austin, TX
Athletic facilities are great
Great library
Great off-campus food
Great computer facilities
Ethnic diversity on campus
Students get along with local community

## ACADEMICS

| | |
|---|---|
| Academic Rating | 83 |
| Calendar | semester |
| Student/faculty ratio | 19:1 |
| Avg reg class size | 40-49 students |

### MOST POPULAR MAJORS
Liberal arts
Biology/biological sciences
Computer sciences

## STUDENTS SPEAK OUT

### Academics

Attending the largest school in the country, UT Austin students, numbering more than 50,000 (undergraduate and graduate) at last count, "can be swallowed by the behemoth without leaving a ripple." Notwithstanding its girth, the administration "does an admirable job of coping with the numbers in a way that is as personal as possible." Technology alleviates some of the problems; "most services, from paying bills directly from your checking account to renewing library books, are available online." The Web also helps undergrads hone in on the best professors, providing detailed "ratings from a student-completed survey." Generally, instructors "are very willing to talk outside of class, but in class it is hard to get individual attention." The widespread issue of non-English-speaking TAs was taken to a new level at UT Austin when "someone had to come in to translate our questions and write on the blackboard." A common sentiment calls for an "emphasis on helping students improve instead of weeding them out," which could lower the "huge drop-out rate" and help more students graduate in four years. Even though "registering for classes can be a nightmare for freshmen, especially if you miss orientation," certain programs ease the transition for first-year students. Many students recommend "that freshmen participate in a freshman seminar or freshman interest group," which "allow you to take three classes with the same group of people."

### Life

The throngs of people make for plenty of activity at UT Austin. Clubs run rampant: "We have over 800 student organizations, including the Phallic Artisans Society." But perhaps the biggest group of all is the one comprising football fanatics. "Mighty Longhorn football has a cult following," even "for students who aren't really interested in sports." The fall season finds the "stadium packed with 83,000 fans wearing our burnt orange with pride." Greek life also thrives at the university, where "foam parties seem to be particularly popular." These kids know how to drink, with one student telling us, "I think I've consumed more alcohol than water" since arriving. When the parties pause, political life kicks in. Reportedly, "if there is a controversy, you can count on students from both sides creating interest groups." Students call the surrounding city of Austin—which claims to be the "live music capital of the world"—a "huge selling point" for the school. This "very liberal city in a very conservative state" offers "something for everyone, be it theater, live music, dance clubs, parties, or public parks." Famous Sixth Street comprises "a mile-long strip with nothing but bars." For nature lovers, there are "ample outdoor activities such as hike and bike trails, natural springs, lakes, and rivers." Many undergraduates share this sentiment: "I hope to live here after I graduate."

### Student Body

Though nearly 90 percent of Longhorns hail from Texas, diversity is high and acceptance permeates the student body. One student credits the administration for the smooth relations: "The university puts a lot of effort into tolerance and nondiscrimination, and I think it pays off." Apparently, "Gentiles or Jews, Taiwanese or Africans, Abilene rednecks or Dallas jetsetters, Democrats or Republicans, we love 'em all." Many students cite the "overall quality of race relations" among the school's greatest strengths, though they observe that there are "relatively few Hispanics and Blacks in comparison to [their corresponding percentages of the] state's population." Aside from race, students observe that "there are more sexually open people here when compared to many schools." No matter what package they come in—"Fanatic holy rollers or pierced and tattooed sadists," "top-of-class mega-stars to people who just don't get it"—students tend to be "smart people with genuine ambition."

664 ■ THE BEST 351 COLLEGES

# UNIVERSITY OF TEXAS—AUSTIN

FINANCIAL AID: 512-475-6282 • E-MAIL: ASKADMIT@UTS.CC.UTEXAS.EDU • WEBSITE: WWW.UTEXAS.EDU

## ADMISSIONS
*Very important factors considered include:* class rank, secondary school record. *Important factors considered include:* essays, extracurricular activities, standardized test scores, talent/ability, volunteer work, work experience. *Other factors considered include:* character/personal qualities, geographical residence, recommendations, state residency. SAT I or ACT required. TOEFL required of all international applicants. High school diploma or GED is required. *High school units required/recommended:* 15.5 total required; 4 English required, 3 math required, 4 math recommended, 2 science required, 3 science recommended, 2 foreign language required, 3 foreign language recommended, 3 social studies required, 1.5 elective required.

### The Inside Word
Top faculty and super facilities draw a mega-sized applicant pool to UT, as does Longhorn football. Texas wants top athletes in each entering class, to be sure. But it also seeks students who are well qualified academically, and it gets loads of them. Both the university and Austin are thriving intellectual communities; Austin has the highest per capita book sales of any city in the United States. Many students continue on to grad school without ever leaving, which is understandable—it's hard to spend any time here without developing an affinity for the school and the city. Legal judgments against affirmative action in the state of Texas (covering the entire fifth circuit of the federal court) have resulted in higher minority applications this year.

## FINANCIAL AID
*Students should submit:* FAFSA. No deadline for regular filing. The Princeton Review suggests that all financial aid forms be submitted as soon as possible after January 1. *Need-based scholarships/grants offered:* Pell, SEOG, state scholarships/grants, private scholarships, the school's own gift aid, Federal Nursing. *Loan aid offered:* FFEL Subsidized Stafford, FFEL Unsubsidized Stafford, FFEL PLUS, Federal Perkins, state loans, college/university loans from institutional funds. Federal Work-Study Program available. Institutional employment available. Applicants will be notified of awards on a rolling basis beginning on or about March 15. Off-campus job opportunities are good.

## FROM THE ADMISSIONS OFFICE
"UT Austin is a large, research-oriented university located in the capital of Texas, at the edge of the beautiful hill country of Texas. More than 50,000 students representing 50 states and 126 foreign countries live and learn in a competitive academic environment. A strong intercollegiate athletic program for both men and women is supplemented by an intramural athletic program that is available to all students as well as faculty and staff. An undergraduate advising center for undeclared majors, a career choice information center, and college placement centers provide advising, career counseling, and placement. Other student services include an honors center, counseling and student health centers, and a study abroad office. The university serves as a cultural center to the community at large as well as to students, faculty, and staff. A performing arts center is host to Broadway plays, the Austin Civic Opera, the Austin Symphony, and visiting musical and dance groups throughout the year. A strong faculty, fine facilities and student services, and a commitment to undergraduate education make UT Austin one of the truly great universities in America and in the world."

### SELECTIVITY
★ ★ ★ ☆

| | |
|---|---|
| Admissions Rating | 88 |
| # of applicants | 22,179 |
| % of applicants accepted | 61 |
| % of acceptees attending | 59 |

### FRESHMAN PROFILE
| | |
|---|---|
| Range SAT Verbal | 540-650 |
| Average SAT Verbal | 596 |
| Range SAT Math | 570-680 |
| Average SAT Math | 626 |
| Range ACT Composite | 22-28 |
| Average ACT Composite | 26 |
| Minimum TOEFL | 550 |
| % graduated top 10% of class | 53 |
| % graduated top 25% of class | 87 |
| % graduated top 50% of class | 99 |

### DEADLINES
| | |
|---|---|
| Regular admission | 2/1 |
| Nonfall registration? | yes |

### FINANCIAL FACTS
★ ★ ★ ☆

| | |
|---|---|
| Financial Aid Rating | 87 |
| In-state tuition | $2,640 |
| Out-of-state tuition | $9,180 |
| Room and board | $5,975 |
| Books and supplies | $736 |
| Required fees | $1,310 |
| % frosh receiving aid | 55 |
| % undergrads receiving aid | 52 |
| Avg frosh grant | $5,630 |
| Avg frosh loan | $3,100 |

# UNIVERSITY OF THE PACIFIC

3601 Pacific Avenue, Stockton, CA 95211 • Admissions: 800-959-2867 • Fax: 209-946-2413

## CAMPUS LIFE

| | |
|---|---|
| Quality of Life Rating | 85 |
| Type of school | private |
| Environment | suburban |

### STUDENTS

| | |
|---|---|
| Total undergrad enrollment | 3,233 |
| % male/female | 42/58 |
| % from out of state | 11 |
| % from public high school | 82 |
| % live on campus | 62 |
| % in (# of) fraternities | 20 (8) |
| % in (# of) sororities | 21 (7) |
| % African American | 3 |
| % Asian | 26 |
| % Caucasian | 50 |
| % Hispanic | 10 |
| % international | 3 |
| # of countries represented | 59 |

### SURVEY SAYS . . .
Popular college radio
Students are religious
Political activism is hot
Theater is hot
Great on-campus food
Campus difficult to get around

## ACADEMICS

| | |
|---|---|
| Academic Rating | 80 |
| Calendar | differs by program |
| Student/faculty ratio | 13:1 |
| Profs interesting rating | 78 |
| Profs accessible rating | 74 |
| Avg lab size | 10-19 students |
| Avg reg class size | 10-19 students |

### MOST POPULAR MAJORS
Business administration
Biology
Pre-pharmacy

## STUDENTS SPEAK OUT

### Academics

Students love the "big-school experience with a small-school feel" provided by University of the Pacific, a midsize private university with one of the nation's loveliest campuses (West Coast filmmakers frequently use it as a stand-in for East Coast schools). The university is "very diversified. Though many of the students are in the sciences, there are still many in math, sports, music, theatre, [and] psychology." Students praise an accelerated degree program in pharmacy as well as those in pre-law and pre-business. "This school is all about accelerated programs," opines one undergrad. Pacific is also home to the "first accredited conservatory of music in the western states" and boasts a renowned international relations program. Despite a breadth of offerings that often portends impersonal education and bureaucratic nightmares, U of Pacific manages to give its students "a personal experience. There are no automated phone-answering services; we talk to real people after the first or second ring." Professors "are always there for you, whether you have questions, need help, or just want some career advice." Notes one undergrad, "I never knew college would be like this. I never expected to get e-mails from professors wondering if I was okay because I had missed a class."

### Life

Because hometown Stockton "is not a great college town"—"there isn't much else to do besides go to bars"—a "social life at U of Pacific must be found on campus." As a result, "Greek life is extremely popular (pretty much the sum extent of the social scene post–freshman year for the majority of students here)." As one student puts it, "The Greek system rules the social aspect of the school. Each weekend at least one of the fraternities or sororities has something planned. Sometimes the parties are exclusive, but for the most part anyone can go." Unfortunately, "sororities and parties are not to everyone's taste," which is why "too many people leave for home on the weekends." Others just "hang out with friends, watch movies, or go out to dinner." Opportunities do exist for those interested in extracurricular clubs and organizations; notes one undergrad, "The greatest thing about UPacific is the chance to get involved. With hundreds of clubs and a low campus population, anyone can get elected and make a difference at Pacific." Intercollegiate sports teams in baseball, volleyball, and basketball draw the occasional crowd; many here long for the return of intercollegiate football. Most here agree, though, that a car is essential to fun-seekers. "The beach, the mountains, the desert, and Reno are only a few hours by car, making it easy to take a last-minute road trip," notes one student. Adds another, "San Francisco is an hour away, and you could club or spend the day out there doing anything and everything."

### Student Body

The U of P student body divides itself into several well-defined subcommunities, students here agree. "There's an obvious difference between Greeks and non-Greeks," for example. Science students, who make up a significant proportion of the population, often keep to themselves. A large Asian population also is largely self-segregated from the white majority. As one student put it, "There are very different cliques around campus, and by the end of your first year you find yourself immersed in one . . . either a Greek clique, an Asian clique, a science one, a Christian, conservatory, etc." Students hasten to add that all groups get along well enough, and many here are proud of the fact that "the campus is very diverse, more than just ethnically, but also financially." As one student reported, "While the university is very expensive at face value, most students easily receive enough financial aid to make it conceivable for any income-level student to attend." Lotharios, take note: It seems like "there's one boy to every two girls" at U of Pacific. Happy hunting!

# UNIVERSITY OF THE PACIFIC

FINANCIAL AID: 209-946-2421 • E-MAIL: ADMISSIONS@UOP.EDU • WEBSITE: WWW.UOP.EDU

## ADMISSIONS

*Very important factors considered include:* secondary school record. *Important factors considered include:* essays, extracurricular activities, recommendations, standardized test scores. *Other factors considered include:* alumni/ae relation, character/personal qualities, class rank, geographical residence, minority status, talent/ability, volunteer work, work experience. SAT I or ACT required. TOEFL required of all international applicants. High school diploma or GED is required. *High school units required/recommended:* 16 total required; 4 English recommended, 3 math recommended, 2 science recommended, 2 science lab recommended, 2 foreign language recommended, 1 history recommended, 3 elective recommended.

### *The Inside Word*

Pacific's small applicant pool and average yield of admits who enroll results in an admissions profile that is less competitive than the academic quality of the freshmen might predict. Test scores count less than a consistently solid academic performance in high school toward getting admitted. The out-of-state population is small; candidates from far afield can expect this to benefit them to a minor degree.

## FINANCIAL AID

*Students should submit:* FAFSA. No deadline for regular filing. The Princeton Review suggests that all financial aid forms be submitted as soon as possible after January 1. *Need-based scholarships/grants offered:* Pell, SEOG, state scholarships/grants, private scholarships, the school's own gift aid. *Loan aid offered:* Direct Subsidized Stafford, Direct Unsubsidized Stafford, Direct PLUS, FFEL Subsidized Stafford, FFEL Unsubsidized Stafford, FFEL PLUS, Federal Perkins, state loans. Federal Work-Study Program available. Institutional employment available. Applicants will be notified of awards on a rolling basis beginning on or about March 15. Off-campus job opportunities are good.

## FROM THE ADMISSIONS OFFICE

"One of the most concise ways of describing the University of the Pacific is that it is 'a major university in a small college package.' Our 3,100 undergraduates get the personal attention that you would expect at a small, residential college. But they also have the kinds of opportunities offered at much larger institutions, including more than 80 majors and programs; 90 student organizations; drama, dance, and musical productions; 16 NCAA Division I athletic teams; and two dozen club and intramural sports. We offer undergraduate major programs in the arts, sciences and humanities, business, education, engineering, international studies, music, pharmacy, and health sciences. Some of the more unique aspects of our academic programs include the following: we have the only independent, coed, nonsectarian liberal arts and sciences college located between Los Angeles and central Oregon; we have the only undergraduate professional school of international studies in California—and it's the only one in the nation that actually requires you to study abroad; we have the only engineering program in the West that requires students to complete a year's worth of paid work experience as part of their degree; our Conservatory of Music focuses on performance but also offers majors in music management, music therapy, and music education; and we offer several accelerated programs in business, dentistry, education, law, and pharmacy. Our beautiful New England–style main campus is located in Stockton (population 250,000) and is within two hours or less of San Francisco, Santa Cruz, Yosemite National Park, and Lake Tahoe."

## SELECTIVITY

★ ★ ☆ ☆

| | |
|---|---|
| Admissions Rating | 75 |
| # of applicants | 3,736 |
| % of applicants accepted | 71 |
| % of acceptees attending | 26 |
| # accepting a place on wait list | 107 |

### FRESHMAN PROFILE

| | |
|---|---|
| Range SAT Verbal | 510-610 |
| Average SAT Verbal | 559 |
| Range SAT Math | 540-650 |
| Average SAT Math | 595 |
| Range ACT Composite | 22-26 |
| Average ACT Composite | 24 |
| Minimum TOEFL | 475 |
| Average HS GPA | 3.5 |
| % graduated top 10% of class | 46 |
| % graduated top 25% of class | 74 |
| % graduated top 50% of class | 95 |

### DEADLINES

| | |
|---|---|
| Priority admission | 1/15 |
| Nonfall registration? | yes |

### APPLICANTS ALSO LOOK AT AND OFTEN PREFER
UC—Berkeley
UC—Davis

### AND SOMETIMES PREFER
U. Southern Cal
CalPoly—San Luis Obispo
UCLA
U. Redlands
U. Arizona

### AND RARELY PREFER
Santa Clara

## FINANCIAL FACTS

★ ★ ★ ★

| | |
|---|---|
| Financial Aid Rating | 91 |
| Tuition | $22,180 |
| Room and board | $7,198 |
| Books and supplies | $1,206 |
| Required fees | $375 |
| % frosh receiving aid | 80 |
| % undergrads receiving aid | 82 |

THE BEST 351 COLLEGES

# UNIVERSITY OF THE SOUTH

735 UNIVERSITY AVENUE, SEWANEE, TN 37383-1000 • ADMISSIONS: 931-598-1238 • FAX: 931-598-3248

## CAMPUS LIFE

| Quality of Life Rating | 89 |
|---|---|
| Type of school | private |
| Affiliation | Episcopal |
| Environment | rural |

### STUDENTS

| Total undergrad enrollment | 1,340 |
|---|---|
| % male/female | 47/53 |
| % from out of state | 76 |
| % from public high school | 52 |
| % live on campus | 92 |
| % in (# of) fraternities | 45 (11) |
| % in (# of) sororities | 43 (6) |
| % African American | 5 |
| % Asian | 1 |
| % Caucasian | 93 |
| % Hispanic | 1 |
| % international | 2 |
| # of countries represented | 25 |

### SURVEY SAYS . . .
Major frat and sorority scene
Lots of beer drinking
Hard liquor is popular
Campus is beautiful
Students are happy
Campus feels safe
Students are cliquish
Lousy food on campus
Students don't like Sewanee, TN
Student publications are ignored
Very little drug use

## ACADEMICS

| Academic Rating | 89 |
|---|---|
| Calendar | semester |
| Student/faculty ratio | 10:1 |
| Profs interesting rating | 98 |
| Profs accessible rating | 99 |
| % profs teaching UG courses | 100 |
| Avg lab size | 10-19 students |
| Avg reg class size | 10-19 students |

## STUDENTS SPEAK OUT

### Academics
The University of the South, a.k.a. Sewanee, boasts "eloquent" professors who are "enthusiastic about teaching." One student gushes that she has had "almost exclusively amazing professors" who help her "learn about life." It's a close academic community where teachers "really motivate their students," and even the dean "always stops to say hello and get feedback." A common complaint among students is that there is "zero grade inflation" at Sewanee, which they see as a disadvantage considering the bloated GPAs at other schools. One student feels "very frustrated" by the university's diligent application of the bell curve because it "puts Sewanee grads in a worse position when it comes to grad schools and the job search." Students report the presence of a "strong honor code," stating, "no one cheats, steals, or lies at this school," but they also appeal to the administration to show more "consistency with rules." Certain students complain of too much "mothering," including enforcement of "no-cut days," while others accuse the administration of letting their "political agendas dictate policy."

### Life
Greek life is alive and kicking in Sewanee, with close to 90 percent of students involved in sororities and fraternities. One junior qualifies this number, however, commenting, "60 percent of them aren't typical Greeks." Tell that to a freshman who writes, "Fun apparently means getting wasted and regurgitating your daddy's tuition money in the basement of a fraternity house. Sign me up!" Those who remain unaffiliated still attend the open parties—"pretty much the entire school goes to them every weekend"—but most agree that "independents are in limbo." A senior woman observes, "If you aren't a drinker, your social life will suffer" because there is virtually "no social alternative to frats." Off-campus options are far flung: "You have to travel at least 45 minutes for clubs, bars, or concerts," comments a senior. The campus' isolation has a definite upside, though. When students aren't partying, they enjoy the great outdoors, with nature "literally in your backyard." The 10,000-acre campus and surrounding area provides opportunities for kayaking, rock climbing, caving, hiking, and swimming, and the Sewanee Outing Program routinely organizes trips.

### Student Body
One senior chooses the following four adjectives to describe his cohorts: "white, upper-middle-class, southern, Episcopalian." The student body is characterized as "sheltered" and "homogeneous," to the extent of all having the same "Sewanee haircut." Students definitely see opportunities for increasing diversity, "not just in ethnicity but also in religion, geography, and interests." Cliques are endemic, with one student explaining, "There are groups for everyone, including people who would never join a stereotypical group." Factions form to the extent that "once you find your clique, there is little social interaction with other students." Cynics say that University of the South students "get along because they're all the same," but Sewanee devotees claim that "when we come together, it becomes an almost mystical experience." Several students point out that "male-female relationships" could be improved and note that "socially diverse groups sometimes butt heads." Considering the school's location, there are logically plenty of "outdoorsy types" and "Eagle Scouts." Overall, Sewanee prides itself on being a "tightly woven community" of "athletic, intelligent party animals."

# UNIVERSITY OF THE SOUTH

FINANCIAL AID: 931-598-1312 • E-MAIL: COLLEGEADMISSION@SEWANEE.EDU • WEBSITE: WWW.SEWANEE.EDU

## ADMISSIONS

*Very important factors considered include:* recommendations, secondary school record. *Important factors considered include:* character/personal qualities, essays, extracurricular activities, standardized test scores, volunteer work, work experience. *Other factors considered include:* alumni/ae relation, class rank, geographical residence, interview, minority status, talent/ability. SAT I or ACT required. TOEFL required of all international applicants. High school diploma is required and GED is not accepted. *High school units required/recommended:* 13 total required; 20 total recommended; 4 English required, 3 math required, 4 math recommended, 2 science required, 4 science recommended, 2 science lab required, 3 science lab recommended, 2 foreign language required, 4 foreign language recommended, 1 social studies required, 2 social studies recommended, 1 history required, 2 history recommended.

## The Inside Word

The admissions office at Sewanee is very personable and accessible to students. Its staff includes some of the most well-respected admissions professionals in the South, and it shows in the way they work with students. Despite a fairly high acceptance rate, candidates who take the admissions process here lightly may find themselves disappointed. Applicant evaluation is too personal for a lackadaisical approach to succeed.

## FINANCIAL AID

*Students should submit:* FAFSA, institution's own financial aid form. The Princeton Review suggests that all financial aid forms be submitted as soon as possible after January 1. *Need-based scholarships/grants offered:* Pell, SEOG, state scholarships/grants, private scholarships, the school's own gift aid. *Loan aid offered:* FFEL Subsidized Stafford, FFEL Unsubsidized Stafford, FFEL PLUS, Federal Perkins, state loans, college/university loans from institutional funds. Federal Work-Study Program available. Institutional employment available. Applicants will be notified of awards on or about April 1. Off-campus job opportunities are fair.

## FROM THE ADMISSIONS OFFICE

"The University of the South, popularly known as Sewanee, is consistently ranked among the top tier of national liberal arts universities. Sewanee is committed to an academic curriculum that focuses on the liberal arts as the most enlightening and valuable form of undergraduate education. Founded by leaders of the Episcopal church in 1857, Sewanee continues to be owned by 28 Episcopal dioceses in 12 states. The university is located on a 10,000-acre campus atop Tennessee's Cumberland Plateau between Chattanooga and Nashville. The university has an impressive record of academic achievement—23 Rhodes Scholars and 23 NCAA Postgraduate Scholarship recipients have graduated from Sewanee."

## SELECTIVITY

| | |
|---|---:|
| Admissions Rating | 87 |
| # of applicants | 1,669 |
| % of applicants accepted | 71 |
| % of acceptees attending | 31 |
| # accepting a place on wait list | 59 |
| % admitted from wait list | 47 |
| # of early decision applicants | 95 |
| % accepted early decision | 76 |

### FRESHMAN PROFILE

| | |
|---|---:|
| Range SAT Verbal | 560-660 |
| Range SAT Math | 550-650 |
| Range ACT Composite | 24-28 |
| Minimum TOEFL | 550 |
| Average HS GPA | 3.4 |
| % graduated top 10% of class | 35 |
| % graduated top 25% of class | 69 |
| % graduated top 50% of class | 94 |

### DEADLINES

| | |
|---|---:|
| Early decision | 11/15 |
| Early decision notification | 12/15 |
| Regular admission | 2/1 |
| Regular notification | 4/1 |

### APPLICANTS ALSO LOOK AT
**AND OFTEN PREFER**
UNC Chapel Hill
Washington and Lee
Virginia
**AND SOMETIMES PREFER**
Davidson
Vanderbilt
Wake Forest
**AND RARELY PREFER**
Rhodes
U of Georgia
U of Tennessee at Knoxville

## FINANCIAL FACTS

| | |
|---|---:|
| Financial Aid Rating | 87 |
| Tuition | $21,140 |
| Room and board | $5,950 |
| Books and supplies | $600 |
| Required fees | $200 |
| % frosh receiving aid | 38 |
| % undergrads receiving aid | 40 |

# UNIVERSITY OF TORONTO

315 BLOOR STREET WEST, TORONTO, ON M5S 1A3 • ADMISSIONS: 416-978-2190 • FAX: 416-978-7022

## CAMPUS LIFE

| | |
|---|---|
| Quality of Life Rating | 80 |
| Type of school | public |
| Environment | urban |

### STUDENTS

| | |
|---|---|
| Total undergrad enrollment | 40,341 |
| % male/female | 44/56 |
| % from out of state | 4 |
| % live on campus | 20 |
| % international | 4 |

### SURVEY SAYS . . .
Students love Toronto
Classes are small
Popular college radio
High cost of living
Musical organizations aren't popular
Lots of classroom discussion
Very little hard liquor
Very little beer drinking

## ACADEMICS

| | |
|---|---|
| Academic Rating | 76 |
| Calendar | differs by program |
| Student/faculty ratio | 15:1 |
| Profs interesting rating | 83 |
| Profs accessible rating | 77 |
| Avg reg class size | 10-19 students |

### MOST POPULAR MAJORS
Environmental studies
Computer science
English language and literature

## STUDENTS SPEAK OUT

### Academics

University of Toronto is the quintessential large public university, offering its students "excellent research opportunities," "a wide variety of co-op programs," "multiculturalism and a huge selection of courses," and, unfortunately, the impersonality of "a huge student body that makes one feel like just one more in a crowd." Students warn that there's "not much outreach to us students" and "not enough staff to run the school smoothly." In other words, self-sufficiency is a requirement to succeed here. Making the U of T experience even more stressful is its notoriously demanding academics. Students warn that "professors are extremely difficult graders. They require immense commitment to studying. You can't ever slack off or fall behind." As a result, "students are extremely competitive. Grades are all-important to many." Upping the ante is the fact that "everyone wants to get a good GPA to get into the 'specialist' programs, which I think should be open to everyone who is interested, not only to those who have a specific GPA." Toronto profs are a mixed bag; writes one student, "Professors are either extremely helpful or . . . they don't give a hoot about you." Many note that "professors seem more personable and approachable in higher-level courses." Summing up the U of T experience, one student writes, "The strength of this school is also its biggest weakness: it is really, really big. That means we get the best academics, researchers, city, etc. However, if you like the small-town experience, don't come here."

### Life

Toronto students generally agree that their school is not conducive to an active social scene. Many factors, they report, contribute to the dearth of extracurricular life here. As one student puts it, "Since U of T is extremely large, it has a huge student population and it is hard to feel like you actually belong and are wanted here." The large commuter population means that "many here are already in their own cliques formed previously, and it is very hard to find a good group of people to spend time with on campus." Finally, there's the intensity of the academic pressure and the competitiveness among students, which means that a student's schedule typically consists of nothing more than "going to class, studying, procrastinating, cramming before a test, drinking to celebrate afterward, and sleeping a lot." On a positive note, some tell us that "if you make an effort to participate, you'll probably find an organization that is suitable for you because the school is so large. There are revolver clubs and Kendo clubs, for example, to name just two." Fortunately, hometown Toronto is a major metropolis offering a near-endless stream of options. As one student put it, "The best thing about U of T is that it is right in the middle of Toronto." Students here also like the fact that "all the buildings are connected. Therefore there is no need to go outside in the roaring winds to run from class to class."

### Student Body

"There is no typical student" at U of T because "Toronto is a multicultural city, and the university is in the middle of that." The school is home to "a high concentration of Indian and East Asian students. Most stay within their own ethnic groups." Because the majority of students live off campus, "the typical student is a commuter who spends most of her time on the bus or subway going from the university to where [she lives]. I think students feel very isolated, and it is hard for them to get involved with school activities." That sense of isolation is further intensified by the sense that "many of the students are very competitive and do not help each other out." Competition is most pronounced, students agree, in the sciences and engineering; humanities students, conversely, report a more friendly, cooperative atmosphere. Because of the relatively small population of campus residents, "there is a lack of participation in anything nonacademic, and there is very little (if any) school spirit."

# UNIVERSITY OF TORONTO

FINANCIAL AID: 416-978-2190 • E-MAIL: ASK@ADM.UTORONTO.CA • WEBSITE: WWW.UTORONTO.CA

## ADMISSIONS
*Very important factors considered include:* class rank, secondary school record, standardized test scores. SAT I required. High school diploma or GED is required.

### The Inside Word
The University of Toronto is one of Canada's best, and its admissions process is appropriately selective. American candidates: Give yourself extra time to research and prepare for filing an application You're an international student here, and some additional paperwork is required in order to attend—though the hassles are ultimately minimal, and the financial bargain substantial.

## FINANCIAL AID
The Princeton Review suggests that all financial aid forms be submitted as soon as possible after January 1. Federal Work-Study Program available. Off-campus job opportunities are excellent.

## FROM THE ADMISSIONS OFFICE
"The University of Toronto is committed to being an internationally significant research university with undergraduate, graduate, and professional programs of study."

### SELECTIVITY
★ ★ ★ ☆

| | |
|---|---|
| Admissions Rating | 82 |
| # of applicants | 54,474 |
| % of applicants accepted | 60 |
| % of acceptees attending | 38 |

### FRESHMAN PROFILE
| | |
|---|---|
| Average HS GPA | 3.0 |

### DEADLINES
| | |
|---|---|
| Regular admission | 3/1 |

### FINANCIAL FACTS
★ ★ ★ ☆

| | |
|---|---|
| Financial Aid Rating | 83 |
| In-state tuition | $3,951 |
| Out-of-state tuition | $8,755 |
| Room and board | $4,930 |
| Books and supplies | $1,050 |
| Required fees | $527 |

Note: All figures in Canadian dollars

# UNIVERSITY OF TULSA

600 SOUTH COLLEGE AVENUE, TULSA, OK 74104 • ADMISSIONS: 800-331-3050 • FAX: 918-631-5003

## CAMPUS LIFE

| | |
|---|---|
| Quality of Life Rating | 76 |
| Type of school | private |
| Affiliation | Presbyterian |
| Environment | urban |

### STUDENTS

| | |
|---|---|
| Total undergrad enrollment | 2,691 |
| % male/female | 48/52 |
| % from out of state | 24 |
| % from public high school | 78 |
| % live on campus | 52 |
| % in (# of) fraternities | 21 (7) |
| % in (# of) sororities | 23 (9) |
| % African American | 9 |
| % Asian | 3 |
| % Caucasian | 72 |
| % Hispanic | 3 |
| % international | 11 |
| # of countries represented | 71 |

### SURVEY SAYS . . .
Great off-campus food
Classes are small
Students love Tulsa, OK
Great library
Students aren't very religious
Registration is a pain
Theater is unpopular

## ACADEMICS

| | |
|---|---|
| Academic Rating | 81 |
| Calendar | semester |
| Student/faculty ratio | 11:1 |
| Profs interesting rating | 75 |
| Profs accessible rating | 81 |
| % profs teaching UG courses | 100 |
| Avg lab size | 10-19 students |
| Avg reg class size | 10-19 students |

### MOST POPULAR MAJORS
Business administration/management
Psychology
Biology/biological sciences

## STUDENTS SPEAK OUT

### Academics
"My school is the secret of the South," boasts one student about her experience at the University of Tulsa. With a student population of just under 3,000 undergraduates, TU is one of the smaller schools in the region. For Tulsa students, the smaller, more intimate feel of their university lies at the crux of their academic experience here. "At Tulsa you are treated as a person by the profs, not just a number because our class sizes are so small." And as one student notes, "many professors encourage you to call them at home and will always make time for a student." The general enthusiasm the students share over their professors extends to the university's administration, which has a reputation with undergraduates ranging from "very helpful" to "wonderful." Classes here can be very challenging (especially for engineering students), but not overly burdensome. Students caution, however, not to expect too much from the school's general education requirements.

### Life
Intramural sports, a little Frisbee golf, dances, and a large host of student organizations do a good job of filling in the social details on campus. That's not to say that things are perfect here in Tulsa. As nice and as friendly as everybody may be, there's a bit of problem with the old school spirit. According to one student, "Our student government could stand to improve, especially in the area of promoting a more active campus." The University of Tulsa is a wet campus; thanks to the strong, yet intimate, Greek system that's at the heart of most students' social life. The Greeks are everywhere, and you can bet that most students are happy to have them around to throw parties on the weekend. Here you don't need to be in a fraternity or sorority to enjoy the weekend revelry, though. All you need, in fact, is a valid university ID. If the Greek system isn't really your scene, though, be prepared to be a little more creative in the city of Tulsa, where you can visit a "world-renowned art museum," "go to horse races," "watch minor league sporting events," or hit the "local bars, which are always fun to go hang out at." Homebodies aren't marginalized, either; several students told us that other favorite pastimes include hanging out in dorms and apartments, talking "about just about everything, from the latest in computer technology to who broke up with who last weekend."

### Student Body
This is Tulsa, Oklahoma, where as one student put it, it's practically "a rule that you must be nice to everyone." And although many students hail from midwestern states, diversity prevails. This is partly due to TU's strong engineering program, which goes a long way in attracting international students from all over the world. "My fellow students come from varying backgrounds and are thus very diverse in interests and personalities," writes one student. As at many colleges, though, people of different backgrounds "tend to socialize within their own ethnicities." Most students also seem to think that Greeks and GDIs get along well. All the right social factors—small population, a student body unusually diverse for the region, and a vibrant hometown—conspire to create a place where "everyone finds a niche while being able to remain friends with diverse individuals."

672 ■ THE BEST 351 COLLEGES

# UNIVERSITY OF TULSA

E-MAIL: ZIHW@UTULSA.EDU • WEBSITE: WWW.UTULSA.EDU

## ADMISSIONS
*Very important factors considered include:* class rank, interview, secondary school record. *Important factors considered include:* extracurricular activities, recommendations, standardized test scores, talent/ability. *Other factors considered include:* alumni/ae relation, character/personal qualities, essays, minority status, volunteer work, work experience. SAT I or ACT required. TOEFL required of all international applicants. High school diploma or GED is required. *High school units required/recommended:* 16 total recommended; 4 English recommended, 3 math recommended, 3 science recommended, 2 science lab recommended, 2 foreign language recommended, 1 social studies recommended, 2 history recommended, 1 elective recommended.

## The Inside Word
TU is a university with solid academic offerings, a strong sense of community, lots of student-faculty interaction, and attainable admission standards. The school's commitment to undergrads is clear. One of TU's most impressive programs, The Tulsa Undergraduate Research Challenge (TURC), allows undergrads to complete research along with faculty.

## FINANCIAL AID
*Students should submit:* FAFSA, institution's own financial aid form. The Princeton Review suggests that all financial aid forms be submitted as soon as possible after January 1. *Need-based scholarships/grants offered:* Pell, SEOG, state scholarships/grants, private scholarships, the school's own gift aid. *Loan aid offered:* FFEL Subsidized Stafford, FFEL Unsubsidized Stafford, FFEL PLUS, Federal Perkins. Federal Work-Study Program available. Institutional employment available. Applicants will be notified of awards on a rolling basis beginning on or about March 1. Off-campus job opportunities are excellent.

## FROM THE ADMISSIONS OFFICE
"The University of Tulsa is a private university with a comprehensive scope. Students choose from more than 80 majors offered through three undergraduate colleges—Arts and Sciences, Business Administration, and Engineering and Natural Sciences. Their curriculum can be customized with collaborative research, joint BA/MBA and BA/Law degree programs, and an Honors Program, among other options. Professors are equally committed to teaching undergraduates and to scholarly research. This results in extraordinary individual achievement, as demonstrated by the nationally competitive scholarships TU students have won since 1995: 30 Goldwater Scholars, 6 Truman Scholars, 2 Udall Scholars, and 3 Marshall Scholars. Since 1994 campus life has benefited from more than $35 million in new student apartments and residence hall renovations. The 8,300-seat Reynolds Arena, completed in 1998, is home to the standout Golden Hurricane NCAA Division I men's basketball team, campus events, and concerts. A 40-acre sports complex includes a student fitness center and indoor tennis center (both opened in 2001) that will host the 2004 NCAA Division I men's tennis finals. An outdoor adventure freshman orientation program launches an entire first-year experience dedicated to developing students' full potential."

## SELECTIVITY

| | |
|---|---|
| Admissions Rating | 82 |
| # of applicants | 2,077 |
| % of applicants accepted | 73 |
| % of acceptees attending | 36 |

### FRESHMAN PROFILE
| | |
|---|---|
| Range SAT Verbal | 540-700 |
| Average SAT Verbal | 610 |
| Range SAT Math | 540-700 |
| Average SAT Math | 620 |
| Range ACT Composite | 22-30 |
| Average ACT Composite | 26 |
| Minimum TOEFL | 500 |
| Average HS GPA | 3.7 |
| % graduated top 10% of class | 57 |
| % graduated top 25% of class | 75 |
| % graduated top 50% of class | 100 |

### DEADLINES
| | |
|---|---|
| Priority admission | 2/1 |
| Regular notification | rolling |
| Nonfall registration? | yes |

### APPLICANTS ALSO LOOK AT AND OFTEN PREFER
Southern Methodist
TCU
Oklahoma State
U of Oklahoma

### AND SOMETIMES PREFER
Washington U
Tulane
Baylor
Trinity U

### AND RARELY PREFER
Texas A&M at College Station
U of Kansas
U of Missouri at Columbia

## FINANCIAL FACTS

| | |
|---|---|
| Financial Aid Rating | 81 |
| Tuition | $15,656 |
| Room and board | $5,610 |
| Books and supplies | $1,200 |
| Required fees | $80 |
| % frosh receiving aid | 48 |
| % undergrads receiving aid | 50 |
| Avg frosh grant | $10,574 |
| Avg frosh loan | $4,686 |

# UNIVERSITY OF UTAH

201 SOUTH 1460 EAST, ROOM 250S, SALT LAKE CITY, UT 84112-9057 • ADMISSIONS: 801-581-7281 • FAX: 801-585-7864

## CAMPUS LIFE

| | |
|---|---|
| Quality of Life Rating | 86 |
| Type of school | public |
| Environment | urban |

### STUDENTS

| | |
|---|---|
| Total undergrad enrollment | 22,648 |
| % male/female | 55/45 |
| % from out of state | 10 |
| % from public high school | 95 |
| % live on campus | 10 |
| % in (# of) fraternities | 5 (7) |
| % in (# of) sororities | 5 (6) |
| % African American | 1 |
| % Asian | 4 |
| % Caucasian | 83 |
| % Hispanic | 4 |
| % international | 3 |

### SURVEY SAYS . . .

(Almost) everyone plays intramural sports
Everyone loves the Utes
Dorms are like palaces
Great food on campus
Computer facilities need improving
Library needs improving
Lab facilities need improving

## ACADEMICS

| | |
|---|---|
| Academic Rating | 71 |
| Calendar | semester |
| Student/faculty ratio | 16:1 |
| Profs interesting rating | 81 |
| Profs accessible rating | 84 |
| % profs teaching UG courses | 87 |
| % classes taught by TAs | 16 |
| Avg lab size | 20-29 students |
| Avg reg class size | 10-19 students |

### MOST POPULAR MAJORS
Business administration/management
Pre-medicine/pre-medical studies
Special education

## STUDENTS SPEAK OUT

### Academics

For most University of Utah undergrads, about 90 percent of whom come from in state, this large and well-respected public research university offers the best of both worlds—it's "close to home" and less than an hour away from "the best snowboarding in the world." Academics aren't bad either; jokes a junior, "This institution has a highly understated abundance of well-respected tenured professors. They are well-known, serious scholars who could get a Valley Girl interested in any major you can think of." Utah is widely known for its excellent, practically immeasurable resources and facilities, as well as its plethora of programs and majors. In courses that range from pre-med and bioengineering to film studies and modern dance, "top-rate" and "research-focused" professors "really seem like they want to teach the class something beyond general information." And though "classes are big," as a first year points out, "professors are willing to work with students on a personal level." Of course, this isn't always the case; argues a senior, "The faculty are great, but sometimes they become distracted by research and writing and quit focusing heavily on teaching." That's when "students need to be able to take initiative," notes another senior. As for the school's leviathan administration, the vote seems split. A senior waxes about "people willing to help whenever needed with anything from counseling to advising to student involvement or advocacy." But a sophomore disagrees: "It is impossible to get a lot of things done here. They give students the runaround."

### Life

With such a bucolic campus (Utah perches on a long and steep hill that overlooks beautiful downtown Salt Lake City), it's no surprise that most students consider Utah "pretty tame." A senior explains the situation at the fairly quiet, "spread-out" campus: "We are a commuter campus, and so mostly students come here, go to work, and go home. But," she adds, "Salt Lake City has amazing mountains, so people spend a lot of time snowboarding, skiing, hiking, and biking." While some call Utah's "clean, wholesome community" boring and uneventful, others will note "only boring people get bored." Writes a particularly involved first-year, "I'm extremely busy, and the school is full of all kinds of activities—from working and volunteering to studying and playing." Another gets involved in a different way (and we thought Salt Lake was a dry city!): "People in college get drunk and have sex. College is a time for growth and exploration—and yes, this takes place in the classroom but also outside of it." Dorm life seems to provoke a similar split. A junior paints a rosy picture: "The friends you make in the residence halls will be the friends you have all your life." A classmate sees it differently: "The dorms are built and maintained to look nice. They are designed, however, to inhibit any kind of student community."

### Student Body

Though University of Utah students come from all over the world, the school has a hard time shaking its reputation of being mostly a "religious" school, where "if you're non-Mormon, it seems as if you don't fit." This situation isn't helped by the fairly homogenous student body (about three-quarters of which self-identifies as white). Writes a first-year, "This campus has no diversity, ethnically or religiously. There is a narrow-mindedness here that I did not grow up with." Still, there's hope: "People off campus are way different from those who live on," notes a senior. And though the school's different groups can be "cliquish," a junior points out that "everyone is really friendly and willing to talk to you if you make a little effort to talk to them." A first-year provides a helpful summing up for prospectives: "There are no real in-betweens," he writes. "It's usually a love-hate thing."

674 ■ THE BEST 351 COLLEGES

# UNIVERSITY OF UTAH

FINANCIAL AID: 801-581-6211 • WEBSITE: WWW.UTAH.EDU

## ADMISSIONS

*Very important factors considered include:* secondary school record, standardized test scores. *Important factors considered include:* talent/ability. *Other factors considered include:* class rank, extracurricular activities, interview, minority status, recommendations. SAT I or ACT required; ACT preferred. TOEFL required of all international applicants. High school diploma or GED is required. *High school units required/recommended:* 15 total required; 4 English required, 2 math required, 2 science required, 1 science lab required, 2 foreign language required, 1 history required, 4 elective required.

### The Inside Word

Utah is another state in which low numbers of high school grads keep selectivity down at its public flagship university. Admission is based primarily on the big three: course selection, grades, and test scores; if you've got a 3.0 GPA or better and average test scores, you're close to a sure bet for admission.

## FINANCIAL AID

*Students should submit:* FAFSA. No deadline for regular filing. The Princeton Review suggests that all financial aid forms be submitted as soon as possible after January 1. *Need-based scholarships/grants offered:* Pell, SEOG, state scholarships/grants, private scholarships, the school's own gift aid. *Loan aid offered:* FFEL Subsidized Stafford, FFEL Unsubsidized Stafford, FFEL PLUS, Federal Perkins, Federal Nursing, college/university loans from institutional funds. Federal Work-Study Program available. Institutional employment available. Applicants will be notified of awards on a rolling basis beginning on or about April 24. Off-campus job opportunities are good.

## FROM THE ADMISSIONS OFFICE

"The University of Utah is a distinctive community of learning in the American West. Today's 25,000 students are from every state and 109 foreign countries. The U has research ties worldwide, with national standing among the top comprehensive research institutions. The U offers majors in 73 undergraduate and 94 graduate subjects. Nationally recognized honors and undergraduate research programs stimulate intellectual inquiry. Undergraduates collaborate with faculty on important investigations. The U's intercollegiate athletes compete in the NCAA Division I Mountain West Conference. The men's basketball team has been nationally ranked for several years, as have our women's gymnastics and skiing teams. The U's location in Salt Lake City provides easy access to the arts, theater, Utah Jazz basketball, and hockey. Utah's Great Outdoors—skiing, hiking, and five national parks—are nearby. The university will be the site for the opening and closing ceremonies and the Athletes Village for the 2002 Winter Olympic Games.

"Residential Living has greatly expanded the opportunity for students to live on campus with a new and wide variety of housing. Heritage Commons, located in historic Fort Douglas on campus, consists of 21 newly constructed buildings, including 3 residence hall–style facilities, which accommodate more than 2,500 students."

### SELECTIVITY
★★☆☆

| | |
|---|---|
| Admissions Rating | 71 |
| # of applicants | 5,802 |
| % of applicants accepted | 85 |
| % of acceptees attending | 71 |

### FRESHMAN PROFILE

| | |
|---|---|
| Range ACT Composite | 20-26 |
| Average ACT Composite | 24 |
| Minimum TOEFL | 500 |
| Average HS GPA | 3.5 |
| % graduated top 10% of class | 26 |
| % graduated top 25% of class | 49 |
| % graduated top 50% of class | 79 |

### DEADLINES

| | |
|---|---|
| Priority admission | 2/15 |
| Regular admission | 5/15 |
| Nonfall registration? | yes |

### FINANCIAL FACTS
★★★☆

| | |
|---|---|
| Financial Aid Rating | 82 |
| In-state tuition | $1,823 |
| Out-of-state tuition | $5,646 |
| Room and board | $5,036 |
| Books and supplies | $1,086 |
| % frosh receiving aid | 66 |
| % undergrads receiving aid | 69 |

# UNIVERSITY OF VERMONT

OFFICE OF ADMISSIONS, 194 S. PROSPECT STREET, BURLINGTON, VT 05401-3596 • ADMISSIONS: 802-656-3370 • FAX: 802-656-8611

## CAMPUS LIFE

| Quality of Life Rating | 88 |
|---|---|
| Type of school | public |
| Environment | suburban |

### STUDENTS

| Total undergrad enrollment | 8,792 |
|---|---|
| % male/female | 44/56 |
| % from out of state | 61 |
| % from public high school | 70 |
| % live on campus | 52 |
| % in (# of) fraternities | 9 (10) |
| % in (# of) sororities | 6 (5) |
| % African American | 1 |
| % Asian | 2 |
| % Caucasian | 94 |
| % Hispanic | 2 |
| % international | 1 |
| # of countries represented | 40 |

### SURVEY SAYS . . .
Students love Burlington, VT
Diversity lacking on campus
Great off-campus food
Musical organizations aren't popular
Students aren't religious
Large classes
Student government is unpopular
Dorms are like dungeons

## ACADEMICS

| Academic Rating | 76 |
|---|---|
| Calendar | semester |
| Student/faculty ratio | 13:1 |
| Profs interesting rating | 92 |
| Profs accessible rating | 94 |
| % profs teaching UG courses | 85 |
| % classes taught by TAs | 2 |
| Avg lab size | 10-19 students |
| Avg reg class size | 10-19 students |

### MOST POPULAR MAJORS
Business administration/management
English language and literature
Psychology

## STUDENTS SPEAK OUT

### Academics
There's no denying that many choose University of Vermont for its lovely ski-resort location and party-school reputation, but that doesn't mean students can't get a first-rate education here as well. Explains one student, "There may be some kids who are here for a good time and a good time only, but many of us are here for a strong education." Others point out that "if you take an active role in your education—if you really believe that no one is going to hand it to you—it is easy to get a great education here." UVM's overall academic reputation is quite solid, and deservedly so. The university is particularly strong in animal science and health- and environment-related areas; students report that psychology, political science, and business and management are also popular majors. Undergrads note that "despite large class sizes, the professors are very dynamic and really get the class involved" and that "the larger classes are intimidating, but most offer helpful discussion groups that are small and more personal." Advises one student, "To get the most out of your tuition, use as many study aids as you can, including study groups, tutors, professors, and supplemental instruction. They will all improve your grades, and they are usually free to students." Professors receive unusually high praise for state-university instructors. Students commend them as "down-to-earth and easy to relate to" and report that they're "open [to] discussions, ideas, and suggestions. A lot of my professors encourage creativity and care about their students and their performance." The administration, on the other hand, "is a nightmare. Getting things done in the UVM bureaucracy is like pulling teeth."

### Life
Just how intense the party scene is at UVM is a matter of some debate. According to many, "Our school is a shameless party school. People here think about where their next beer is coming from." Others take a more nuanced view, explaining that "it's true that UVM is a big party school, but only for those who choose it. There are many students here who study hard, have fun with their friends, participate in athletic activities, and still make the grade." For those who do choose partying, "people smoke a lot of pot, and there are some good hallucinogens floating around, but not quite as much drinking as other colleges. This is good, though—it makes the atmosphere chill instead of drunk and rowdy." That is, until "The Man" shows up. "Police are always in the dorms, and they have little respect for students and our rights," complain several undergrads. Whatever their differences on the topic of partying, nearly all students agree that UVM is ideally located for those who love outdoor winter activities. "What other school has ski mountains 20 minutes away, a lake 5 minutes away, and a beach 10 minutes away?" asks one student. Students also love Burlington, saying it's "an amazing town for its size. There are a ton of things to do, and its location on the lake is beautiful." Town features include "concerts, shows, movies, tons of stores, the waterfront: there's always life downtown." Students work hard during the week, but "on the weekends," notes one student, "most of us go downtown shopping or to the lake during the day. At night, we go to the dance clubs or off-campus parties," though, of course, "always pre-gamed (i.e. drunk or stoned before we arrive)."

### Student Body
Many UVM undergrads feel that their student body provides "a wide variety of social groups. From hippies to jocks, UVM has it all." To these happy undergrads, "the atmosphere up here is real laid-back and relaxed. I noticed when I first came up here that if you smile at someone or say 'hi' to a stranger, they almost always say 'hi' back. People up here are cool." They also note that "the school does an excellent job of making its many out-of-state students feel comfortable, accepted, and appreciated. For us, this truly is a home away from home." Even so, there are more than a few who complain that "sometimes I feel as if I'm surrounded by hippies, extreme environmentalists, and communists. [Though] they aren't that widespread on campus, they're just very vocal."

# UNIVERSITY OF VERMONT

FINANCIAL AID: 802-656-3156 • E-MAIL: ADMISSIONS@UVM.EDU • WEBSITE: WWW.UVM.EDU

## ADMISSIONS
*Very important factors considered include:* secondary school record. *Important factors considered include:* alumni/ae relation, character/personal qualities, class rank, essays, minority status, standardized test scores, state residency. *Other factors considered include:* extracurricular activities, geographical residence, interview, recommendations, talent/ability, volunteer work, work experience. SAT I or ACT required. TOEFL required of all international applicants. High school diploma or GED is required. *High school units required/recommended:* 16 total required; 4 English required, 3 math required, 2 science required, 1 science lab required, 2 foreign language required, 3 social studies required.

## The Inside Word
UVM is one of the most popular public universities in the country, and its admissions standards are significantly more competitive for out-of-state students. Nonresidents shouldn't get too anxiety-ridden about getting in; more than half of the student body comes from elsewhere. Candidates with above-average academic profiles should be in good shape.

## FINANCIAL AID
*Students should submit:* FAFSA. Regular filing deadline is March 15. The Princeton Review suggests that all financial aid forms be submitted as soon as possible after January 1. *Need-based scholarships/grants offered:* Pell, SEOG, state scholarships/grants, private scholarships, the school's own gift aid, Federal Nursing. *Loan aid offered:* FFEL Subsidized Stafford, FFEL Unsubsidized Stafford, FFEL PLUS, Federal Perkins, Federal Nursing, college/university loans from institutional funds. Federal Work-Study Program available. Institutional employment available. Applicants will be notified of awards on a rolling basis beginning on or about March 15. Off-campus job opportunities are excellent.

## FROM THE ADMISSIONS OFFICE
"The University of Vermont blends the close faculty-student relationships most commonly found in a small liberal arts college with the dynamic exchange of knowledge associated with a research university. This is not surprising because UVM is both. A comprehensive research university offering nearly 100 undergraduate majors and extensive offerings through its Graduate College and College of Medicine, UVM has chosen to keep its enrollment relatively small. UVM prides itself on the richness of its undergraduate experience. Distinguished senior faculty teach introductory courses in their fields. They also advise not only juniors and seniors, but also first- and second-year students, and work collaboratively with undergraduates on research initiatives. Students find extensive opportunities to test classroom knowledge in field through practicums, academic internships, and community service. More than 90 student organizations (involving 80 percent of the student body), 26 Division I varsity teams, 18 intercollegiate club and 24 intramural sports programs, and a packed schedule of cultural events fill in where the classroom leaves off."

## SELECTIVITY

| | |
|---|---|
| Admissions Rating | 77 |
| # of applicants | 9,776 |
| % of applicants accepted | 71 |
| % of acceptees attending | 26 |
| # accepting a place on wait list | 380 |
| % admitted from wait list | 24 |
| # of early decision applicants | 245 |
| % accepted early decision | 70 |

### FRESHMAN PROFILE
| | |
|---|---|
| Range SAT Verbal | 520-620 |
| Average SAT Verbal | 568 |
| Range SAT Math | 520-620 |
| Average SAT Math | 574 |
| Range ACT Composite | 22-27 |
| Average ACT Composite | 24 |
| Minimum TOEFL | 550 |
| % graduated top 10% of class | 19 |
| % graduated top 25% of class | 55 |
| % graduated top 50% of class | 91 |

### DEADLINES
| | |
|---|---|
| Early decision | 11/1 |
| Early decision notification | 12/15 |
| Regular admission | 1/15 |
| Regular notification | 3/31 |
| Nonfall registration? | yes |

### APPLICANTS ALSO LOOK AT AND OFTEN PREFER
Skidmore College
Syracuse University
University of Colorado—Boulder

### AND RARELY PREFER
University of Rhode Island
University of Massachusetts—Amherst
Ithaca College

## FINANCIAL FACTS

| | |
|---|---|
| Financial Aid Rating | 83 |
| In-state tuition | $8,696 |
| Out-of-state tuition | $21,748 |
| Room and board | $6,680 |
| Books and supplies | $800 |
| Required fees | $940 |
| % frosh receiving aid | 54 |
| % undergrads receiving aid | 50 |
| Avg frosh grant | $8,208 |
| Avg frosh loan | $4,239 |

THE BEST 351 COLLEGES ■ 677

# UNIVERSITY OF VIRGINIA

Office of Admission, PO Box 400160, Charlottesville, VA 22906 • Admissions: 434-982-3200 • Fax: 434-924-3587

## CAMPUS LIFE

| | |
|---|---|
| Quality of Life Rating | 90 |
| Type of school | public |
| Environment | suburban |

### STUDENTS

| | |
|---|---|
| Total undergrad enrollment | 13,805 |
| % male/female | 46/54 |
| % from out of state | 28 |
| % from public high school | 75 |
| % live on campus | 46 |
| % in (# of) fraternities | 30 (32) |
| % in (# of) sororities | 30 (22) |
| % African American | 10 |
| % Asian | 11 |
| % Caucasian | 73 |
| % Hispanic | 3 |
| % international | 4 |
| # of countries represented | 97 |

### SURVEY SAYS . . .
Great on-campus food
Students are religious
Popular college radio
Students get along with local community
Theater is hot
Computer facilities need improving
Athletic facilities need improving

## ACADEMICS

| | |
|---|---|
| Academic Rating | 93 |
| Calendar | semester |
| Student/faculty ratio | 16:1 |
| Profs interesting rating | 77 |
| Profs accessible rating | 79 |
| % classes taught by TAs | 18 |
| Avg lab size | 10-19 students |
| Avg reg class size | 10-19 students |

### MOST POPULAR MAJORS
Business/commerce
Psychology
Economics

## STUDENTS SPEAK OUT

### Academics

Regarded as one of the country's premier state universities, University of Virginia offers an "excellent all-around college experience: great, intelligent students; wonderful intercollegiate sports; phenomenal faculty; and, of course, excellent academics." Students appreciate that "unlike other publics, there is not a tendency for students at UVA to be lost in paperwork and bureaucracy. The people who work in the administrative offices are very nice and understanding; perhaps this is a product of 'southern hospitality.' Also, professors at UVA are not only accessible but hospitable." Indeed, "most professors at UVA are eager to get to know the students. Many bend over backward to help students and understand what is important to the students." Additionally, "UVA has an extraordinary number of professors who are both dedicated teachers and [at the] top of their fields." Students also tell us that "your education does not end at the classroom. There are numerous opportunities related to service in which you can learn to become part of your community and give back to people who need help. In addition, there are numerous cultural, social, and athletic organizations, all of which allow you to pursue a well-rounded education."

### Life

"For all the hard-core nature of academics at UVA, it is still a really fun place to be," students here agree, especially if you love frat parties ("Greek life is very prominent at the university"). For students who "do not enjoy alcohol . . . there are many other things to do. The University of Virginia is located about 20 miles from the Blue Ridge Mountains, where you can go for a nice hike. Winter Green is about an hour away from Charlottesville (for those who enjoy skiing or playing golf). The James River is about 40 minutes away for those who enjoy tubing or rafting." Nor is travel off campus necessary, as the school itself offers a "diversity of activities! If you play sports, dance, act, like intellectual activities, [or] participate in the strong student self-governance, you can do it at UVA." The school also attracts "awesome speakers, including Isabel Allende, Ralph Nader, the Dalai Lama, and Archbishop Desmond Tutu, to name a few that have come while I've been here." Students may just choose to sit back and enjoy the beautiful campus itself; writes one student, "When I finished my last final first year, I walked out of my classroom elated. But as I passed the historical Lawn and the beautiful amphitheater, my heart dropped at the thought of having to leave such gorgeous surroundings." Virginia is a school rich in tradition, a fact appreciated by most students. Traditions include streaking across the Lawn ("The tradition is to start from the Rotunda, sprint down to Homer—located in front of Old Cabell hall—and kiss his butt, and sprint back. Then you look through the keyhole at the top of the steps of the rotunda to see if you can see Thomas Jefferson"), "dressing up to go to athletic events," and the Honor Code.

### Student Body

Virginia has long had a reputation as a preppy haven, a reputation students tell us is well deserved. "UVA is quite a preppy, well-to-do school," writes one undergrad. "It's the perfect school for frat boys who like to wear Gucci shoes and sorority girls who dig Versace." Not everyone fits the mold; explains one student, "Upon closer inspection, you'll realize that the student population includes people of all walks of life." The student body has its share of "gun-toting, abortion-hating, Confederacy-loving students; insane-worker, dedicated-to-a-fault, anal-about-cleanliness students; and 'eccentric to a point that begs the question not of whether, but of when they'll be committed' students." Although fairly diverse, "UVA is very segregated. Different ethnic groups do not mix very much, and the Greek population is an entity unto [itself]." Political activism "is not big at the university at all. The student body is largely more conservative-leaning, and the flaming liberals don't have too much of an impact of student life."

678 ■ THE BEST 351 COLLEGES

# UNIVERSITY OF VIRGINIA

FINANCIAL AID: 804-982-6000 • E-MAIL: UNDERGRAD-ADMISSION@VIRGINIA.EDU • WEBSITE: WWW.VIRGINIA.EDU

## ADMISSIONS

*Very important factors considered include:* alumni/ae relation, minority status, secondary school record, state residency. *Important factors considered include:* character/personal qualities, class rank, essays, extracurricular activities, recommendations, standardized test scores, talent/ability. *Other factors considered include:* geographical residence, volunteer work, work experience. SAT I or ACT required; SAT I preferred; SAT II also required. TOEFL required of all international applicants. High school diploma or GED is required. *High school units required/recommended:* 16 total required; 4 English required, 4 math required, 2 science required, 4 science recommended, 2 foreign language required, 1 social studies required, 3 social studies recommended.

## The Inside Word

Even many Virginia residents regard trying to get into UVA as a feeble attempt. The competition doesn't get much more severe, and only the most capable and impressive candidates stand to be offered admission. The volume of out-of-state applications borders on enormous when considered in conjunction with available spots in the entering class.

## FINANCIAL AID

*Students should submit:* FAFSA, institution's own financial aid form. The Princeton Review suggests that all financial aid forms be submitted as soon as possible after January 1. *Need-based scholarships/grants offered:* Pell, SEOG, state scholarships/grants, private scholarships, the school's own gift aid. *Loan aid offered:* Direct Subsidized Stafford, Direct Unsubsidized Stafford, Direct PLUS, Federal Perkins, Federal Nursing, college/university loans from institutional funds. Federal Work-Study Program available. Institutional employment available. Applicants will be notified of awards on or about April 5. Off-campus job opportunities are fair.

## FROM THE ADMISSIONS OFFICE

"Admission to competitive schools requires strong academic credentials. Students who stretch themselves and take rigorous courses (honors level and Advanced Placement courses, when offered) are significantly more competitive than those who do not. Experienced admission officers know that most students are capable of presenting superb academic credentials, and the reality is that a very high percentage of those applying do so. Other considerations, then, come into play in important ways for academically strong candidates, as they must be seen as 'selective' as well as academically competitive."

### SELECTIVITY

| | |
|---|---|
| Admissions Rating | 94 |
| # of applicants | 14,320 |
| % of applicants accepted | 39 |
| % of acceptees attending | 54 |
| # accepting a place on wait list | 1,157 |
| % admitted from wait list | 13 |
| # of early decision applicants | 2,384 |
| % accepted early decision | 40 |

### FRESHMAN PROFILE

| | |
|---|---|
| Range SAT Verbal | 600-700 |
| Average SAT Verbal | 647 |
| Range SAT Math | 620-720 |
| Average SAT Math | 668 |
| Range ACT Composite | 25-31 |
| Average ACT Composite | 28 |
| Minimum TOEFL | 600 |
| Average HS GPA | 4.0 |
| % graduated top 10% of class | 84 |
| % graduated top 25% of class | 97 |
| % graduated top 50% of class | 99 |

### DEADLINES

| | |
|---|---|
| Early decision | 11/1 |
| Early decision notification | 12/1 |
| Regular admission | 1/2 |
| Regular notification | 4/1 |

### APPLICANTS ALSO LOOK AT AND OFTEN PREFER
Duke
Georgetown U.

### AND SOMETIMES PREFER
William and Mary
UNC—Chapel Hill
Virginia Tech

### AND RARELY PREFER
George Washington
Bucknell
Boston U.

### FINANCIAL FACTS

| | |
|---|---|
| Financial Aid Rating | 88 |
| In-state tuition | $4,584 |
| Out-of-state tuition | $20,604 |
| Room and board | $5,591 |
| Books and supplies | $900 |
| Required fees | $1,565 |
| % frosh receiving aid | 22 |
| % undergrads receiving aid | 22 |

# UNIVERSITY OF WASHINGTON

1410 NE CAMPUS PARKWAY, 320 SCHMITZ BOX 355840, SEATTLE, WA 98195-5840 • ADMISSIONS: 206-543-9686 • FAX: 206-685-3655

## CAMPUS LIFE

★ ★ ★ ☆

| | |
|---|---|
| Quality of Life Rating | 86 |
| Type of school | public |
| Environment | urban |

### STUDENTS

| | |
|---|---|
| Total undergrad enrollment | 28,362 |
| % male/female | 48/52 |
| % from out of state | 15 |
| % live on campus | 17 |
| % in (# of) fraternities | 12 (30) |
| % in (# of) sororities | 11 (18) |
| % African American | 3 |
| % Asian | 25 |
| % Caucasian | 56 |
| % Hispanic | 4 |
| % international | 3 |

### SURVEY SAYS . . .
Students love Seattle, WA
Everyone loves the Huskies
Theater is hot
Great off-campus food
Large classes
Dorms are like dungeons
Ethnic diversity on campus
Lots of TAs teach upper-level
courses
Campus difficult to get around

## ACADEMICS

| | |
|---|---|
| Academic Rating | 77 |
| Calendar | quarter |
| Student/faculty ratio | 11:1 |
| Profs interesting rating | 91 |
| Profs accessible rating | 92 |
| Avg lab size | 20-29 students |
| Avg reg class size | 20-29 students |

## STUDENTS SPEAK OUT

### Academics

With 17 colleges and over 3,000 professors, the University of Washington offers a mind-boggling array of opportunities to the right type of student. Writes one such undergrad, "The school is wonderful because you can take a class in practically anything you want and your teachers always make themselves available to you." Students warn that "it is very easy to get lost in a big school like this. So you gotta watch out for yourself!" They also appreciate, however, the safeguards built into the system to help them find their way. Explains one student, "For approximately half of the class time the lectures are broken into small class-sized discussion groups. It's a wonderful system." Many undergrads find themselves "pleasantly surprised, even as a freshman, as to the amount of individual attention that is available even at such a huge school as UW. [They] just had to learn to seek it out." As at many large, research-oriented schools, "most professors are not very effective teachers. Students tend to learn more in quiz sections with TAs." Writes one student, "The abilities of TAs should never be underestimated. They have played a significant role in my learning, and I feel completely comfortable and confident in their knowledge." A quarterly academic calendar "goes by fast, but you feel like you learn a great deal."

### Life

Students at UW enjoy the best of both worlds: a vibrant, busy campus surrounded by a great neighborhood and a world-class city. Most students find time to take advantage of all that UW's environs have to offer. Writes one student, "Seattle is a great city with a wide variety of things to do and many if not all of the students have taken advantage of that fact." The city offers "so much to do for fun. On weekends in the fall there's always football games and Mariners games. And of course, you can always explore downtown Seattle, visit Pike's Market, Space Needle, Seattle Center, and GameWorks." A university-distributed 'U-Pass' "provides free and discounted bus service throughout the area." Closer to home is the U-District, an "eclectic and interesting" neighborhood surrounding the school. Students call the main drag "the Ave" and report it offers "anything you could ever want: wonderful food and lots of stuff to do at night and on the weekends." Students enjoy sports ("we have excellent workout facilities and trails to go running or biking as well"), "very crazy frat parties," and "numerous campus activities to suit every taste." As if all this weren't enough, students also happily report that "because we are fairly close to the mountains, skiing and snowboarding are very popular in the winter. From December to April every Saturday morning there is always a group to go up to the ski pass with." Is there anything about life here students don't love? "It rains more then any place I've ever been," grouse many students.

### Student Body

"You can find someone of every race, religion, nationality" at U of W, students tell us. "No matter what kind of person you are, you'll find someone that you can get along with. The atmosphere is incredibly accepting and friendly." Writes one student, "My fellow peers are generally open-minded, fun-loving people. The college kids in Seattle are a diverse group that comes from all over as well as from Washington, so it creates a nice atmosphere." Politically, "the student population is an interesting blend. The editor of the major campus newspaper is an ultra-radical leftist and there is a large leftist campus, but also a very vocal College Republican crowd. In general, there is much heated debate, but it tends to confine itself to appropriate forums." Students warn that "because the school is so large, it is hard to interact with a lot of people."

680 ■ THE BEST 351 COLLEGES

# UNIVERSITY OF WASHINGTON

FINANCIAL AID: 206-543-6101 • E-MAIL: ASKUWADM@U.WASHINGTON.EDU • WEBSITE: WWW.WASHINGTON.EDU

## ADMISSIONS

*Very important factors considered include:* secondary school record. *Important factors considered include:* standardized test scores, state residency. *Other factors considered include:* alumni/ae relation, class rank, essays, extracurricular activities, talent/ability, volunteer work, work experience. SAT I or ACT required. *High school units required/recommended:* 4 English required, 3 math required, 4 math recommended, 2 science required, 3 science recommended, 1 science lab required, 2 science lab recommended, 2 foreign language required, 3 foreign language recommended, 3 social studies required, 4 social studies recommended.

### *The Inside Word*

Like the other five public colleges in Washington, UW uses an admissions index (AI) as part of its initial review of applications, taking into account the student's GPA, as well as combined SAT I or composite ACT scores, course selection, personal statements, and essays. A student whose qualifications exceed expectations in all of these areas may be a "turbo admit"; all other applications receive an intensive review, which evaluates evidence of academic rigor in the student's curriculum, a challenging senior year, academic awards, personal statement, school and community activities, educational and economic disadvantage, personal adversity, grade trends, special talents in the arts, and cultural awareness. UW notes the importance of these qualitative factors as it moves away from AI-driven decisions.

## FINANCIAL AID

*Students should submit:* FAFSA. The Princeton Review suggests that all financial aid forms be submitted as soon as possible after January 1. *Need-based scholarships/grants offered:* Pell, SEOG, state scholarships/grants, private scholarships, the school's own gift aid. *Loan aid offered:* Direct Subsidized Stafford, Direct Unsubsidized Stafford, Direct PLUS, Federal Perkins, Federal Nursing, college/university loans from institutional funds. Federal Work-Study Program available. Institutional employment available. Applicants will be notified of awards on a rolling basis beginning on or about April 1. Off-campus job opportunities are good.

## FROM THE ADMISSIONS OFFICE

"Undergraduates benefit from the exciting opportunities for research and service, while learning from professors who are at the forefront of generating new knowledge."

### SELECTIVITY

| | |
|---|---|
| Admissions Rating | 82 |
| # of applicants | 15,950 |
| % of applicants accepted | 68 |
| % of acceptees attending | 44 |

### FRESHMAN PROFILE
| | |
|---|---|
| Range SAT Verbal | 510-630 |
| Range SAT Math | 550-660 |
| Range ACT Composite | 22-28 |
| Average HS GPA | 3.7 |
| % graduated top 10% of class | 44 |
| % graduated top 25% of class | 80 |
| % graduated top 50% of class | 97 |

### DEADLINES
| | |
|---|---|
| Regular admission | 1/15 |
| Regular notification | 4/15 |
| Nonfall registration? | yes |

### APPLICANTS ALSO LOOK AT
**AND OFTEN PREFER**
USC
UC—San Diego
Seattle U.
**AND SOMETIMES PREFER**
Wetern Wash. U.
U. of Oregon
U. Colorado—Boulder
**AND RARELY PREFER**
Washington St. U.
U. of Puget Sound

### FINANCIAL FACTS

| | |
|---|---|
| Financial Aid Rating | 86 |
| In-state tuition | $4,636 |
| Out-of-state tuition | $15,337 |
| Room and board | $6,570 |
| Books and supplies | $822 |
| Required fees | $469 |
| % frosh receiving aid | 33 |
| % undergrads receiving aid | 40 |
| Avg frosh loan | $3,376 |

# UNIVERSITY OF WISCONSIN—MADISON

161 BEACON HALL, 500 LINCOLN DRIVE, MADISON, WI 53706 • ADMISSIONS: 608-262-3961 • FAX: 608-262-7708

## CAMPUS LIFE

| | |
|---|---|
| Quality of Life Rating | 84 |
| Type of school | public |
| Environment | urban |

### STUDENTS
| | |
|---|---|
| Total undergrad enrollment | 29,708 |
| % male/female | 47/53 |
| % from out of state | 30 |
| % from public high school | 70 |
| % live on campus | 26 |
| % in (# of) fraternities | 9 (25) |
| % in (# of) sororities | 8 (9) |
| % African American | 2 |
| % Asian | 5 |
| % Caucasian | 90 |
| % Hispanic | 2 |
| % international | 3 |
| # of countries represented | 100 |

### SURVEY SAYS . . .
Lots of beer drinking
Hard liquor is popular
Everyone loves the Badgers
Students love Madison, WI
Great library
Great off-campus food
Campus is beautiful
Great computer facilities
Student newspaper is popular
Students are happy

## ACADEMICS

| | |
|---|---|
| Academic Rating | 88 |
| Calendar | semester |
| Student/faculty ratio | 13:1 |
| % profs teaching UG courses | 90 |
| Avg lab size | 20-29 students |
| Avg reg class size | 10-19 students |

### MOST POPULAR MAJORS
Psychology
Communications studies/speech
communication and rhetoric
Political science and government

## STUDENTS SPEAK OUT

### Academics
One of the most prestigious state universities in the country, the University of Wisconsin—Madison employs professors who "are all extremely talented, and most are great teachers as well." It's said that "everyone from administration to TAs challenges students to think deeply and insightfully. They want the best all the time. They enjoy teaching, and we enjoy learning." The problem with attending an undoubtedly "great research institution," however, is that the faculty sometimes "cares less about the students than their research," comments a psychology major. Another student agrees, claiming that it's "tough for students to get in touch with professors and administration." A competitive spirit reigns at Wisconsin, and one sophomore wishes courses were geared for "success rather than hoping [other] people will fail." Difficulties lie in "finishing in four years," "getting classes of choice as a freshman," and "transferring credits" from other schools. Students also complain about a lack of career placement services and remark that "advising is a bitch. I still don't know who my advisor is."

### Life
Political activism is a cornerstone of Madison life, to a degree that one junior comments, "It can get irritating. How many rallies can you have?" When students aren't protesting, there's "lots of partying, but also lots of studying," writes a freshman. Wisconsin's reputation as a party school ("Beer goes well with all activities") has diminished in the past few years, and one senior says, "The alcohol scene is over-hyped—there's other stuff to do." That "stuff" includes "plays, concerts, an overwhelming number of organizations on campus," and Badger sporting events. The city of Madison is widely considered the ultimate college town, with a senior bragging that "State Street compares to Bourbon Street on weekend nights." The city is also a big kids' playground "for biking, running, sports, and water activities." A content math major summarizes, "No better college atmosphere can be found anywhere than in Madison with so many things to do. People come just to see how much students care for and love the opportunities the campus offers."

### Student Body
The University of Wisconsin—Madison is home to "nice Midwest people" who are characterized as a "fun and crazy bunch." Amid a sea of undergraduates, one student comments, "people are friendly and willing to chat in class, which makes the large college seem smaller and more welcoming." A senior questions her classmates' priorities, opining that many are "least interested in school and the community." Some students are well-versed in studying "just enough for an A or B," but others are perpetually "way too driven and stressed out," according to a senior. The politically aware student body bends over backwards to defend the Wisconsin brand of diversity, emphasizing that the campus population is "very socio-economically diverse" even if it is "very segregated" and in sore need of "minority recruitment and retention." Interaction between students and locals is limited; one Madison native states that "most students do not know the city or its people."

# UNIVERSITY OF WISCONSIN—MADISON

FINANCIAL AID: 608-262-3060 • E-MAIL: ONWISCONSIN@ADMISSIONS.WISC.EDU • WEBSITE: WWW.WISC.EDU

## ADMISSIONS

*Very important factors considered include:* class rank, secondary school record. *Important factors considered include:* recommendations, standardized test scores, state residency, talent/ability. *Other factors considered include:* alumni/ae relation, character/personal qualities, essays, extracurricular activities, interview, minority status, volunteer work, work experience. SAT I or ACT required. TOEFL required of all international applicants. High school diploma or GED is required. *High school units required/recommended:* 17 total required; 20 total recommended; 4 English required, 3 math required, 4 math recommended, 3 science required, 4 science recommended, 2 foreign language required, 3 social studies required, 4 social studies recommended.

### The Inside Word

Wisconsin has high expectations of its candidates and virtually all of them relate to numbers. Though not at the top tier of selectivity, this is admissions-by-formula at its most refined state. Nonresidents will encounter a very selective process.

## FINANCIAL AID

*Students should submit:* FAFSA, institution's own financial aid form. No deadline for regular filing. The Princeton Review suggests that all financial aid forms be submitted as soon as possible after January 1. *Need-based scholarships/grants offered:* Pell, SEOG, state scholarships/grants, private scholarships, the school's own gift aid. *Loan aid offered:* FFEL Subsidized Stafford, FFEL Unsubsidized Stafford, FFEL PLUS, Federal Perkins, Federal Nursing, state loans, college/university loans from institutional funds. Federal Work-Study Program available. Institutional employment available. Applicants will be notified of awards on a rolling basis beginning on or about April 1. Off-campus job opportunities are excellent.

## FROM THE ADMISSIONS OFFICE

"Admission decisions of quality and fairness take time. We don't promise to be the fastest out of the box, but we do guarantee a complete, fair, and thorough decision. We want applicants to provide us with as much information about themselves as they think is necessary for a group of people who don't know them to reach a favorable decision."

## SELECTIVITY

| | |
|---|---|
| **Admissions Rating** | 91 |
| # of applicants | 21,211 |
| % of applicants accepted | 60 |
| % of acceptees attending | 43 |

### FRESHMAN PROFILE

| | |
|---|---|
| Range SAT Verbal | 560-670 |
| Average SAT Verbal | 613 |
| Range SAT Math | 610-710 |
| Average SAT Math | 652 |
| Range ACT Composite | 25-30 |
| Average ACT Composite | 27 |
| Minimum TOEFL | 550 |
| Average HS GPA | 3.6 |
| % graduated top 10% of class | 55 |
| % graduated top 25% of class | 93 |
| % graduated top 50% of class | 99 |

### DEADLINES

| | |
|---|---|
| Priority admission | 2/1 |
| Regular admission | 2/1 |
| Nonfall registration? | yes |

### APPLICANTS ALSO LOOK AT AND OFTEN PREFER

U of Illinois at Urbana
U of Michigan at Ann Arbor
U of Minnesota at Twin Cities
Northwestern

### AND SOMETIMES PREFER

Marquette
U of Wisconsin at La Crosse
U of Iowa
U of Colorado at Boulder
U of Wisconsin at Milwaukee

## FINANCIAL FACTS

| | |
|---|---|
| **Financial Aid Rating** | 82 |
| In-state tuition | $4,426 |
| Out-of-state tuition | $18,426 |
| Room and board | $4,005 |
| Books and supplies | $680 |
| % frosh receiving aid | 30 |
| % undergrads receiving aid | 31 |

# UNIVERSITY OF WYOMING

ADMISSIONS OFFICE, PO BOX 3435, LARAMIE, WY 82071 • ADMISSIONS: 307-766-5160 • FAX: 307-766-4042

## CAMPUS LIFE

| | |
|---|---|
| **Quality of Life Rating** | 76 |
| Type of school | public |
| Environment | rural |

### STUDENTS

| | |
|---|---|
| Total undergrad enrollment | 9,250 |
| % male/female | 47/53 |
| % from out of state | 26 |
| % live on campus | 24 |
| % in (# of) fraternities | 8 (9) |
| % in (# of) sororities | 5 (4) |
| % African American | 1 |
| % Asian | 1 |
| % Caucasian | 87 |
| % Hispanic | 4 |
| % international | 1 |

### SURVEY SAYS . . .
*Theater is hot*
*Everyone loves the Cowboys*
*Diversity lacking on campus*
*(Almost) everyone plays intramural sports*
*Students get along with local community*
*Lab facilities are great*

## ACADEMICS

| | |
|---|---|
| **Academic Rating** | 71 |
| Calendar | semester |
| Student/faculty ratio | 15:1 |
| Profs interesting rating | 76 |
| Profs accessible rating | 73 |
| % profs teaching UG courses | 97 |
| % classes taught by TAs | 9 |
| Avg lab size | 10-19 students |
| Avg reg class size | 20-29 students |

## STUDENTS SPEAK OUT

### Academics

Students choose the University of Wyoming for its excellence in the natural sciences and engineering as well as for its relatively intimate size. "The University of Wyoming is not too big or too small," brags one Colorado native who chose UW over his larger home state university. Students note that "all teachers and administrators are accessible to students, and they are very approachable" and brag that "professors here are really dedicated to undergraduates, though we do have a lot of graduates here too. They are very approachable and I would consider myself friends with several of them. They are widely respected in their fields, too." The "non-threatening" administration "has made an outstanding effort in recent years to provide better access to student services" and to improve registration and records. This is not to say, however, that UW does not have its share of "red tape and paperwork." Students' other complaints center on the libraries, which "need more modern books and should have a wider variety of selection." Besides science and engineering, elementary education, psychology, and social work are popular majors here. "The Honors Program here is excellent," many report, and as an added plus, "the tuition is cheap both for in- and out-of-state students."

### Life

UW attracts a large number of outdoor enthusiasts, students tell us. "People are generally connected to the outdoors and love to go hiking, biking, and rock climbing as often as possible. Wyoming is beautiful and has lots of recreational opportunities, without the crowds of other states," explains one undergrad. Adds another, "Most people at the University of Wyoming ski, snowboard, backpack, fish, mountain bike, and party." Hometown Laramie is full of "cute coffee shops and restaurants," the town is "very welcoming," and conveniently, "Laramie isn't too far from the wilderness, so outdoorsy things are not only the best route to go, but also the easiest." Students also report that "intramural sports are also quite common, as is the attendance of intercollegiate sports, in particular men's basketball." Some complain that "sometimes, especially in the winter, it's hard to find stuff to do here." Luckily, "Cheyenne and Fort Collins, Colorado, aren't far away." When students get the itch for serious civilization, it's "about two hours to Denver." Students gripe about the physical plant ("The buildings here are . . . historical, shall we say? The need for renovation is apparent but it should be noted that the campus is undergoing a renovation piece by piece").

### Student Body

Students insist that "Wyoming is a friendly place. Where else can you walk in the middle of the night without too much concern?" Students agree that "the majority of our students get along well, regardless of their differences." Students are "just a laid-back, easygoing group of individuals who don't care where you came from or how much your parents make" and who "tend to stay with their own groups (white with whites, blacks with blacks, Chinese with Chinese, etc.)." There is a "good mix of city and rural kids" as well as a large religious population. UW has a "fair share of Libertarians and Republicans. Democrats and liberals are the minority in Wyoming."

# UNIVERSITY OF WYOMING

FINANCIAL AID: 307-766-2116 • E-MAIL: UNDERGRADUATEADMISSION@UWYO.EDU • WEBSITE: WWW.UWYO.EDU

## ADMISSIONS
*Very important factors considered include:* secondary school record, standardized test scores. *Important factors considered include:* essays, recommendations. *Other factors considered include:* character/personal qualities, extracurricular activities, geographical residence, interview, state residency, talent/ability. TOEFL required of all international applicants. High school diploma or GED is required. *High school units required/recommended:* 13 total required; 19 total recommended; 4 English required, 3 math required, 3 science and 3 science lab required, 3 cultural context recommended.

### The Inside Word
The admissions process at Wyoming is fairly formula-driven. State residents need a minimum 2.75 high school GPA in order to gain admission. Nonresidents have to have a 3.0 GPA. That and some solid test scores will open the door to Laramie.

## FINANCIAL AID
*Students should submit:* FAFSA. No deadline for regular filing. The Princeton Review suggests that all financial aid forms be submitted as soon as possible after January 1. *Need-based scholarships/grants offered:* Pell, SEOG, state scholarships/grants, private scholarships, the school's own gift aid. *Loan aid offered:* FFEL Subsidized Stafford, FFEL Unsubsidized Stafford, FFEL PLUS, Federal Perkins, private loans. Federal Work-Study Program available. Institutional employment available. Applicants will be notified of awards on a rolling basis. Off-campus job opportunities are good.

## FROM THE ADMISSIONS OFFICE
"The entire admission staff have analyzed why we love UW and Laramie. We think it primarily boils down to size and location. The University of Wyoming and Laramie are relatively small, affording students the opportunity to get personal attention and develop a close rapport with their professors. They can easily make friends and find peers with similar interests and values. Over 200 student organizations offer students a great way to get involved and encourage growth and learning. Couple the small size with a great location and you have a winning combination. Laramie sits between the Laramie and the Snowy Range Mountains. There are numerous outdoor activities in which one can participate. Furthermore, the university works hard to attract other great cultural events. Major label recording artists come to UW as well as some of today's great minds. In all, the University of Wyoming is a great place to be because of its wonderful blend of a small town atmosphere with 'big city' activities."

## ADMISSIONS

| | |
|---|---|
| Admissions Rating | 75 |
| # of applicants | 2,954 |
| % of applicants accepted | 95 |
| % of acceptees attending | 52 |

### FRESHMAN PROFILE
| | |
|---|---|
| Range SAT Verbal | 460-580 |
| Range SAT Math | 480-600 |
| Range ACT Composite | 20-26 |
| Average ACT Composite | 23 |
| Minimum TOEFL | 525 |
| Average HS GPA | 3.4 |
| % graduated top 10% of class | 20 |
| % graduated top 25% of class | 45 |
| % graduated top 50% of class | 76 |

### DEADLINES
| | |
|---|---|
| Priority admission | 3/1 |
| Regular admission | 8/10 |
| Nonfall registration? | yes |

## FINANCIAL FACTS

| | |
|---|---|
| Financial Aid Rating | 85 |
| In-state tuition | $2,400 |
| Out-of-state tuition | $8,064 |
| Room and board | $5,120 |
| Books and supplies | $800 |
| Required fees | $597 |
| % frosh receiving aid | 85 |
| % undergrads receiving aid | 94 |
| Avg frosh grant | $3,321 |
| Avg frosh loan | $1,188 |

# URSINUS COLLEGE

URSINUS COLLEGE, ADMISSIONS OFFICE, COLLEGEVILLE, PA 19426 • ADMISSIONS: 610-409-3200 • FAX: 610-409-3662

## CAMPUS LIFE

| | |
|---|---|
| Quality of Life Rating | 79 |
| Type of school | private |
| Environment | suburban |

### STUDENTS

| | |
|---|---|
| Total undergrad enrollment | 1,324 |
| % male/female | 43/57 |
| % from out of state | 36 |
| % from public high school | 68 |
| % live on campus | 91 |
| % in (# of) fraternities | 15 (9) |
| % in (# of) sororities | 25 (5) |
| % African American | 8 |
| % Asian | 4 |
| % Caucasian | 86 |
| % Hispanic | 2 |
| % international | 3 |

### SURVEY SAYS . . .
Frats and sororities dominate social scene
Popular college radio
Lots of beer drinking
Library needs improving
Lousy off-campus food
Low cost of living

## ACADEMICS

| | |
|---|---|
| Academic Rating | 81 |
| Calendar | semester |
| Student/faculty ratio | 11:1 |
| Profs interesting rating | 92 |
| Profs accessible rating | 91 |
| % profs teaching UG courses | 100 |
| Avg lab size | 10-19 students |
| Avg reg class size | under 10 students |

### MOST POPULAR MAJORS
Biology/biological sciences
Psychology
Economics

## STUDENTS SPEAK OUT

### Academics

"An amazing biology department" and an equally excellent chemistry department that churn out viable candidates for the nation's top medical schools are the star attractions at Ursinus College. Students here also speak highly of the political science department and the education program, but most would quickly concede that the medical sciences are king here. Pre-meds "get a lot in the way of academic advantages. Our chemistry building was recently updated, so there is a lot of availability of technology," including a fully networked campus. All freshmen receive a laptop "with the programs already on it" so that everyone can log on and tap into the information stream. At the threat of becoming too technology- and science-driven, Ursinus several years ago instituted a liberal studies curriculum encompassing English, math, science, and foreign language. Students approve, believing the core "is the reason that graduate schools enjoy leeching students away from the college." Professors "really know us due to the small size of classes, and are really there for us when we need them." They teach "courses that force you to think 'outside the box' and connect all areas of your life to help you become a fully integrated person." Students also appreciate how Ursinus provides "the opportunity to push beyond our requirements to work closely with professors and administrators in independent and honors research." The administration "is fairly accessible and willing to listen to our concerns," while the career services office "is constantly informing students of internship or job opportunities." Some students complain that it is not easy enough for upperclassmen to get into the electives of their choice.

### Life

"Greek organizations are very popular" with the students of Ursinus, most of whom agree that "there's not a whole lot to do in this area," which is why "people spend most of the weekend drinking" at parties. Reports one, "The Greek system is the foundation of all of the partying that goes on here." One type of party unique to the school is a 'dated,' a semi-formal dance sponsored by a Greek organization. "Dateds are amazing fun in the fall," writes one student, "with at least two per weekend, as buses take students to a banquet hall full of alcohol and great music for four hours, only to return to campus [so students can] party some more!" Other than frat parties, activity is sparse, though "campus activities are held about once every two weeks or so, and they're usually pretty entertaining." Hometown Collegeville is "boring. Almost everything in Collegeville closes at 9 P.M. and there's very little excitement within walking distance. Having a car on campus (which many do) is an important asset [for] reaching a nearby Lazer Tag facility or the mammoth King of Prussia Mall." Philadelphia is two and a half inconvenient hours away by public transportation; grouses one student, "The college promo literature made it seem that a student could go to Philly any time they wanted without having to have a car on campus. No one really does this and I'm not even sure if it is a possibility." Many students also complain about dining hall food: "The food was really good, but this year it got really bad. If the food could go back to normal, it'd be great again."

### Student Body

Undergrads at Ursinus "are friendly, but can get very cliquey." Students divide into cliques according to area of study, graduating class, and of course, Greek affiliation. "Many people play sports" here, while "others are really into politics and still others are very art- and music-inclined." The small student body lends an air of informality to the campus: "People here aren't worried about how you look all the time. You can go to class in sweatpants or you can go to class in a skirt—no one cares." Students are proud to report that "a key word at Ursinus is tolerance. We have a very active Gay-Straight Alliance, which sponsors many events."

# URSINUS COLLEGE

FINANCIAL AID: 610-409-3600 • E-MAIL: ADMISSIONS@URSINUS.EDU • WEBSITE: WWW.URSINUS.EDU

## ADMISSIONS

*Very important factors considered include:* class rank, extracurricular activities, secondary school record. *Important factors considered include:* alumni/ae relation, essays, minority status, recommendations, standardized test scores, talent/ability, volunteer work, work experience. *Other factors considered include:* character/personal qualities, geographical residence, interview. SAT I or ACT required; SAT II recommended. TOEFL required of all international applicants. High school diploma or GED is required. *High school units required/recommended:* 16 total required; 20 total recommended; 4 English required, 3 math required, 4 math recommended, 1 science required, 3 science recommended, 1 science lab required, 2 foreign language required, 4 foreign language recommended, 1 social studies required, 3 social studies recommended, 5 elective required.

### The Inside Word

The admission process at Ursinus is very straightforward; about 70 percent of those who apply get in. Grades, test scores, and class rank count for more than anything else, and unless you are academically inconsistent, you'll likely get good news.

## FINANCIAL AID

*Students should submit:* FAFSA, institution's own financial aid form, CSS/Financial Aid PROFILE. Regular filing deadline is February 15. The Princeton Review suggests that all financial aid forms be submitted as soon as possible after January 1. *Need-based scholarships/grants offered:* Pell, SEOG, state scholarships/grants, private scholarships, the school's own gift aid. *Loan aid offered:* FFEL Subsidized Stafford, FFEL Unsubsidized Stafford, FFEL PLUS, Federal Perkins, college/university loans from institutional funds. Federal Work-Study Program available. Institutional employment available. Applicants will be notified of awards on or about April 1. Off-campus job opportunities are excellent.

## FROM THE ADMISSIONS OFFICE

"Located one-half hour from center-city Philadelphia, the college boasts a beautiful 140-acre campus that includes the Residential Village (renovated Victorian-style homes that decorate the Main Street and house our students) and the nationally recognized Berman Museum of Art. Ursinus is a member of the Centennial Conference, competing both in academics and in intercollegiate athletics with institutions such as Dickinson, Franklin and Marshall, Gettysburg, and Muhlenberg. The academic environment is enhanced with such fine programs as a chapter of Phi Beta Kappa, an Early Assurance Program to medical school with the Medical College of Pennsylvania, and myriad student exchanges both at home and abroad. A heavy emphasis is placed on student research—an emphasis that can only be carried out with the one-on-one attention Ursinus students receive from their professors."

## SELECTIVITY

| | |
|---|---|
| Admissions Rating | 80 |
| # of applicants | 1,547 |
| % of applicants accepted | 78 |
| % of acceptees attending | 36 |
| # accepting a place on wait list | 12 |
| # of early decision applicants | 199 |
| % accepted early decision | 80 |

### FRESHMAN PROFILE

| | |
|---|---|
| Range SAT Verbal | 540-640 |
| Average SAT Verbal | 595 |
| Range SAT Math | 550-650 |
| Average SAT Math | 598 |
| Minimum TOEFL | 550 |
| Average HS GPA | 3.5 |
| % graduated top 10% of class | 40 |
| % graduated top 25% of class | 80 |
| % graduated top 50% of class | 94 |

### DEADLINES

| | |
|---|---|
| Early decision | 1/15 |
| Early decision notification | 1/31 |
| Priority admission | 2/15 |
| Regular admission | 2/15 |
| Regular notification | 4/1 |
| Nonfall registration? | yes |

### APPLICANTS ALSO LOOK AT AND OFTEN PREFER

Swarthmore
Princeton
Brown
Haverford
Johns Hopkins

### AND SOMETIMES PREFER

Villanova
Gettysburg
Dickinson
St. Joseph's U.
Franklin & Marshall

## FINANCIAL FACTS

| | |
|---|---|
| Financial Aid Rating | 89 |
| Tuition | $26,200 |
| Room and board | $6,600 |
| Books and supplies | $600 |
| % frosh receiving aid | 78 |
| % undergrads receiving aid | 75 |

# VALPARAISO UNIVERSITY

Office of Admission, Kretzmann Hall, Valparaiso, IN 46383-9978 • Admissions: 219-464-5011 • Fax: 219-464-6898

## CAMPUS LIFE

| | |
|---|---|
| Quality of Life Rating | 73 |
| Type of school | private |
| Affiliation | Lutheran |
| Environment | rural |

### STUDENTS

| | |
|---|---|
| Total undergrad enrollment | 2,910 |
| % male/female | 47/53 |
| % from out of state | 66 |
| % from public high school | 81 |
| % live on campus | 65 |
| % in (# of) fraternities | 24 (8) |
| % in (# of) sororities | 20 (7) |
| % African American | 3 |
| % Asian | 2 |
| % Caucasian | 88 |
| % Hispanic | 3 |
| % international | 3 |
| # of countries represented | 37 |

### SURVEY SAYS . . .
Frats and sororities dominate social scene
No one cheats
Musical organizations are hot
Student government is popular
Lots of beer drinking
Library needs improving
Students are cliquish
Students don't like Valparaiso, IN
Very little drug use

## ACADEMICS

| | |
|---|---|
| Academic Rating | 76 |
| Calendar | semester |
| Student/faculty ratio | 13:1 |
| Profs interesting rating | 93 |
| Profs accessible rating | 91 |
| % profs teaching UG courses | 100 |
| Avg lab size | 10-19 students |
| Avg reg class size | 10-19 students |

### MOST POPULAR MAJORS
Elementary education and teaching
Biology/biological sciences
Nursing/registered nurse training (RN, ASN, BSN, MSN)

## STUDENTS SPEAK OUT

### Academics

The students at Valparaiso University—affectionately called "Valpo" by all affiliated with the school—consider it a successful hybrid of large university and small liberal arts college. With 60 fields of study in four colleges (arts and sciences, nursing, business, and engineering), Valpo undergrads can select from a broad academic slate of majors the likes of which are found at large universities, and many of which train them for specific careers. Most undergrads also have to complete a battery of core requirements in order to graduate. But what the students—almost every student we surveyed—seem to appreciate the most is the easy access to professors that is often an earmark of small institutions. "Every school now seems to say that the professors are very personable, but how many schools can say that their professors have dinner with students, let them borrow their cars to take into Chicago for interviews, travel to Istanbul with them, or let them house-sit while they are away for a semester?" Aside from the strong profs, Valparaiso has built some other enticing features in its offerings, like the "neat program for freshmen called Valpo Core, which combines first-year English, history, theology, and a number of other humanities classes into one five-credit class, taken each of the first two semesters." Something that they're less enthusiastic about is the library. But one student is pleased to report that "Valpo will have a much-needed new library by fall 2004." Overall, a freshman tells us, there's no doubt that the "Valpo atmosphere is conducive to learning."

### Life

Just because Valpo students tend to be religious and just because "theoretically Valpo is a dry campus" doesn't mean that these students don't know how to cut loose: "It's undeniable that alcohol is big here," and "if people don't drink in the dorms they go to the frat houses." About a quarter of all students join fraternities and sororities, and these Greeks bear the collective onus of maintaining a healthy party scene on campus. Students report, though, that "people get in trouble for alcohol on a normal basis" because of the strict campus policies and the relentless local police. Beyond the keggers, students get "involved with intramurals, student government, and the many (other) organizations that are found here." And there's always a strong turnout at the Valparaiso Crusaders men's basketball games. When students take a few steps off of campus, they find themselves in the town of Valparaiso, "the greatest hick town the world has ever seen." Still, it's "close enough to Chicago to escape the small-town atmosphere" if the students need to. And the Indiana Dunes National Lakeshore on Lake Michigan is just a quick car ride away. "It's a very relaxing and laid-back atmosphere," sums up a freshman.

### Student Body

Affiliated with the Lutheran Church, the most distinctive feature of the undergraduate body is its "religious" flavor. "If you don't believe in God don't come here because it can become a very cold" place if you don't, according to one student. She estimates that "80 percent of students are ultra-conservative and are adamant about evangelizing their faith." The traditional stance taken by most students sometimes leads to problems. For instance, "sexual orientation is a sore point at Valparaiso." But overall, squabbles are rare, and this student population of 3,000 prides itself on its "friendliness." "No matter where you go you see smiling faces," raves a sophomore, a phenomenon referred to as "the Valpo Smile." Crusaders are the first to admit, however, that they're not the most diverse bunch around. "We are all upper-middle-class white kids with stable homes and not too much drama in our lives," one student tells us. Students believe, however, that their commonalities are the bedrock of many friendships.

# VALPARAISO UNIVERSITY

FINANCIAL AID: 219-464-5015 • E-MAIL: UNDERGRAD.ADMISSIONS@VALPO.EDU • WEBSITE: WWW.VALPO.EDU

## ADMISSIONS

*Very important factors considered include:* secondary school record. *Important factors considered include:* class rank, extracurricular activities, standardized test scores, talent/ability. *Other factors considered include:* alumni/ae relation, character/personal qualities, essays, interview, minority status, recommendations, religious affiliation/commitment, volunteer work. SAT I or ACT required. TOEFL required of all international applicants. High school diploma or GED is required. *High school units required/recommended:* 4 English required, 3 math required, 4 math recommended, 2 science required, 3 science recommended, 2 science lab required, 3 science lab recommended, 2 foreign language required, 3 social studies required, 3 elective required.

### The Inside Word

Valparaiso admits the vast majority of those who apply, but candidates should not be overconfident. Places like this fill a special niche in higher education and spend a good deal of time assessing the match a candidate makes with the university, even if the expected better-than-average high school record is present. Essays and extracurriculars can help you get admitted if your transcript is weak.

## FINANCIAL AID

*Students should submit:* FAFSA. The Princeton Review suggests that all financial aid forms be submitted as soon as possible after January 1. *Need-based scholarships/grants offered:* Pell, SEOG, state scholarships/grants, private scholarships, the school's own gift aid. *Loan aid offered:* Direct Subsidized Stafford, Direct Unsubsidized Stafford, Direct PLUS, Federal Perkins, college/university loans from institutional funds. Federal Work-Study Program available. Institutional employment available. Applicants will be notified of awards on a rolling basis beginning on or about March 1. Off-campus job opportunities are good.

## FROM THE ADMISSIONS OFFICE

"Valpo provides students a blend of academic excellence, social experience, and spiritual exploration. The concern demonstrated by faculty and administration for the total well-being of students reflects a long history as a Lutheran-affiliated university."

### SELECTIVITY

| | |
|---|---|
| Admissions Rating | 79 |
| # of applicants | 3,117 |
| % of applicants accepted | 84 |
| % of acceptees attending | 27 |

### FRESHMAN PROFILE

| | |
|---|---|
| Range SAT Verbal | 530-630 |
| Average SAT Verbal | 583 |
| Range SAT Math | 530-650 |
| Average SAT Math | 596 |
| Range ACT Composite | 23-29 |
| Average ACT Composite | 26 |
| Minimum TOEFL | 550 |
| % graduated top 10% of class | 34 |
| % graduated top 25% of class | 68 |
| % graduated top 50% of class | 93 |

### DEADLINES

| | |
|---|---|
| Priority admission | 1/15 |
| Regular admission | 8/15 |
| Nonfall registration? | yes |

### APPLICANTS ALSO LOOK AT AND OFTEN PREFER
Indiana U at Bloomington
Purdue U at West Lafayette
U of Illinois at Urbana-Champaign

### AND SOMETIMES PREFER
Marquette
Bradley
Augustana (IL)
Illinois Wesleyan
Butler

### FINANCIAL FACTS

| | |
|---|---|
| Financial Aid Rating | 82 |
| Tuition | $20,000 |
| Room and board | $5,480 |
| Books and supplies | $700 |
| Required fees | $638 |
| % frosh receiving aid | 69 |
| % undergrads receiving aid | 64 |
| Avg frosh grant | $12,533 |
| Avg frosh loan | $5,661 |

# VANDERBILT UNIVERSITY

2305 WEST END AVENUE, NASHVILLE, TN 37203 • ADMISSIONS: 615-322-2561 • FAX: 615-343-7765

## CAMPUS LIFE

★★★☆

| | |
|---|---|
| Quality of Life Rating | 89 |
| Type of school | private |
| Environment | urban |

### STUDENTS

| | |
|---|---|
| Total undergrad enrollment | 6,146 |
| % male/female | 48/52 |
| % from out of state | 80 |
| % from public high school | 60 |
| % live on campus | 84 |
| % in (# of) fraternities | 34 (19) |
| % in (# of) sororities | 50 (12) |
| % African American | 6 |
| % Asian | 6 |
| % Caucasian | 77 |
| % Hispanic | 4 |
| % international | 2 |
| # of countries represented | 52 |

### SURVEY SAYS . . .
Frats and sororities dominate social scene
Diversity lacking on campus
Athletic facilities are great
Students are cliquish
Registration is a breeze
Political activism is (almost) nonexistent

## ACADEMICS

| | |
|---|---|
| Academic Rating | 94 |
| Calendar | semester |
| Student/faculty ratio | 9:1 |
| Profs interesting rating | 92 |
| Profs accessible rating | 90 |
| Avg lab size | 10-19 students |
| Avg reg class size | under 10 students |

### MOST POPULAR MAJORS
Engineering science
Psychology
Sociology

## STUDENTS SPEAK OUT

### Academics
Smack in the middle of one of the nation's fastest growing regions, venerable Vanderbilt University gives students a taste of both the New and Old South. The school offers "academics on a par with any Ivy League school," which provide a major toehold in the area's high-tech economy. And all in a genteel setting. "There is a sense of academic excellence here," writes one undergraduate, "but without the cutthroat competition." A broad and comprehensive core curriculum covers writing, humanities, mathematics, and natural and social sciences. The "grading standards are stringent," and there is definitely an "adherence to traditional values" at Vandy. There is also an honor code, which students say it is best not to trifle with. Many of the professors here are "outstanding" and "excited about teaching," especially in the liberal arts and sciences. These professors are "so helpful and interested in the students that it's almost overwhelming." Others don't quite rise to their peers' level; reports one student, "The teaching abilities vary widely, from mumbling lecturers to educational gods." The "capable" administration "does a really good job running the university." Student opinion of the administration has improved with the arrival of a new chancellor, who "has made an incredible effort to make the administration open to discussion with students."

### Life
Most undergrads agree that the Greeks dominate the Vandy campus, reporting that "Vanderbilt students' social lives revolve around the Greek system, from football games to week and weekend nights." The Greeks are also active in extracurriculars, "providing ways to get involved in campus and in the Nashville community at large." A few students feel that "although Greek life is a big part of the social scene, it isn't the only thing to do" and point out that "there are a lot of organizations for people interested in every aspect of extracurricular life." Undergrads refer to their environment as "the Vanderbubble," a "sheltered and comfortable" place where students "work hard" during the week and "play hard" during the "almost entirely party-oriented" weekends. Besides frat parties, the bars and clubs and "great nightlife" of Nashville are "just five minutes away." A lot "of variety as far as dining and entertainment" awaits students off campus, and, of course, "great concerts" abound. Nashville is "Music City, after all." However, "cabs are expensive," and "you have to have a car to do any of these cool things." On campus, "the Rites of Spring is a big outdoor party on Alumni Lawn with great music" and "tons of fun." In the fall, "dressing up and taking dates to football games is a great tradition at Vandy." Students rave about the recreation center, which is "120,000 square feet of perfection." The most often cited negative: the weather in Nashville. Don't forget to "bring your umbrella."

### Student Body
As some students describe it, the Vanderbilt student body comes straight out of a southern debutante ball. "Prestige matters" to these "conservative" adherents to "a cult of southern gentility and graciousness." Some of these ladies and gentlemen "tend to be somewhat snobbish and cliquish" while others are "very friendly." Students add that "you learn pretty quickly that, even though superficially a lot of people look the same, everyone has had very different experiences and come[s] from a different background." Agrees one student, "There are groups of very different students here: sorority girls, jocks, brains, and people who are a mix." The campus is not as racially diverse as many students would like it to be, though the school has come a long way in the past few years.

# VANDERBILT UNIVERSITY

FINANCIAL AID: 615-322-3591 • E-MAIL: ADMISSIONS@VANDERBILT.EDU • WEBSITE: WWW.VANDERBILT.EDU

## ADMISSIONS
*Very important factors considered include:* character/personal qualities, class rank, essays, extracurricular activities, recommendations, secondary school record, standardized test scores, talent/ability. *Other factors considered include:* alumni/ae relation, geographical residence, minority status, volunteer work, work experience. SAT I or ACT required; SAT II recommended. TOEFL required of all international applicants. *High school units required/recommended:* 17 total required; 24 total recommended; 4 English required, 3 math required, 4 math recommended, 2 science required, 3 science recommended, 2 science lab required, 3 science lab recommended, 2 foreign language required, 3 foreign language recommended, 2 social studies required, 3 social studies recommended, 2 history required, 2 elective recommended.

### The Inside Word
Vanderbilt's strong academic reputation has positioned the university among the most selective in the South. Make no mistake, the applicant pool is competitive and all apps are read by at least three admissions counselors; students should not downplay the importance of submitting strong essays and recommendations—they make the difference for some candidates.

## FINANCIAL AID
*Students should submit:* FAFSA, CSS/Financial Aid PROFILE, noncustodial (divorced/separated) parent's statement. The Princeton Review suggests that all financial aid forms be submitted as soon as possible after January 1. *Need-based scholarships/grants offered:* Pell, SEOG, state scholarships/grants, private scholarships, the school's own gift aid. *Loan aid offered:* FFEL Subsidized Stafford, FFEL Unsubsidized Stafford, FFEL PLUS, Federal Perkins, Federal Nursing, college/university loans from institutional funds. Federal Work-Study Program available. Institutional employment available. Applicants will be notified of awards on or about April 1. Off-campus job opportunities are excellent.

## FROM THE ADMISSIONS OFFICE
"Exceptional accomplishment and high promise in some field of intellectual endeavor are essential. The student's total academic and nonacademic record is reviewed in conjunction with recommendations and personal essays. For students at Blair School of Music, the audition is a prime consideration."

## SELECTIVITY

| | |
|---|---:|
| **Admissions Rating** | 94 |
| # of applicants | 9,836 |
| % of applicants accepted | 46 |
| % of acceptees attending | 35 |
| # accepting a place on wait list | 529 |
| % admitted from wait list | 1 |
| # of early decision applicants | 891 |
| % accepted early decision | 50 |

### FRESHMAN PROFILE
| | |
|---|---:|
| Range SAT Verbal | 610-700 |
| Range SAT Math | 640-720 |
| Range ACT Composite | 27-31 |
| Minimum TOEFL | 570 |
| % graduated top 10% of class | 74 |
| % graduated top 25% of class | 93 |
| % graduated top 50% of class | 99 |

### DEADLINES
| | |
|---|---:|
| Early decision | 11/1 |
| Early decision notification | 12/15 |
| Priority admission | 1/2 |
| Regular admission | 2/15 |
| Regular notification | 4/1 |
| Nonfall registration? | yes |

### APPLICANTS ALSO LOOK AT AND OFTEN PREFER
U of Virginia
Princeton
Notre Dame
Cornell U
Georgetown U

**AND SOMETIMES PREFER**
Duke, Emory
Wake Forest
Northwestern U
Dartmouth

**AND RARELY PREFER**
Tulane
Washington U
Boston College
Southern Methodist, Rhodes

## FINANCIAL FACTS

| | |
|---|---:|
| **Financial Aid Rating** | 85 |
| Tuition | $26,400 |
| Room and board | $9,060 |
| Books and supplies | $950 |
| Required fees | $687 |
| % frosh receiving aid | 40 |
| % undergrads receiving aid | 42 |

# Vassar College

124 Raymond Avenue, Poughkeepsie, NY 12604 • Admissions: 845-437-7300 • Fax: 845-437-7063

## CAMPUS LIFE

| | |
|---|---|
| Quality of Life Rating | 82 |
| Type of school | private |
| Environment | suburban |

### STUDENTS

| | |
|---|---|
| Total undergrad enrollment | 2,472 |
| % male/female | 40/60 |
| % from out of state | 72 |
| % from public high school | 60 |
| % live on campus | 95 |
| % African American | 5 |
| % Asian | 10 |
| % Caucasian | 78 |
| % Hispanic | 6 |
| % international | 5 |
| # of countries represented | 41 |

### SURVEY SAYS . . .

(Almost) everyone plays intramural sports
Students get along with local community
Diverse students interact
Library needs improving

## ACADEMICS

| | |
|---|---|
| Academic Rating | 94 |
| Calendar | semester |
| Student/faculty ratio | 9:1 |
| Profs interesting rating | 70 |
| Profs accessible rating | 70 |
| % profs teaching UG courses | 100 |
| Avg lab size | 10-19 students |
| Avg reg class size | 10-19 students |

### MOST POPULAR MAJORS

English language and literature
Psychology
Political science and government

## STUDENTS SPEAK OUT

### Academics

Students say that Vassar's goal is "teaching students to think," and that the college achieves this end by affording undergraduates a high degree of academic freedom. "Vassar trusts that I can achieve my academic goals without strict guidance" is one common sentiment among students. Most here "love that we have no core curriculum," leaving them time to pursue their "genuine interests." Though the "workload is very challenging," students feel supported by their "impressive, friendly, empathetic," and "very encouraging" professors. "If you had a question for one of my professors after class, she would talk to you for half an hour and not realize how much time had gone by," writes a sophomore. Instructors "love what they do and want you to do well," and the small class sizes "force us to contribute to discussions." Students perceive "significant academic competitiveness" among undergraduates; writes one, "Sometimes Vassar students are a bit too intense about academics." A few complaints arise regarding the "limited number of classes and sections." Certain students groan that the administration "likes to maintain absurd amounts of authority." Still others call for "increased communication between administration and students." But a sophomore offer the following challenge: "Tell me any other college where the president would take the time to e-mail me personally to tell me that she's a fan of my newspaper column." In the end, a student in the American culture department avers that a Vassar education is "about self-development and intellectual glory."

### Life

In their fairly isolated location in the Hudson Valley, most students feel "restricted to on-campus activities." Luckily, "on any given Friday, there's usually a concert, lecture, play, and comedy performance." Other students frequent The Mug, the college's dance club and bar, or hit the live music performances at the campus café every Thursday. One student writes, "For fun, most people are drinking," and another adds that students have "no social life if you don't drink or take drugs recreationally." The administration, however, has been "cracking down lately with new party rules," putting a damper on the scene. As an alternative, students happily resort to sledding on cafeteria trays, also known as traying. When this grows tiresome—or when the snow melts—students take advantage of their "great location close to New York City." Several respondents note the abundant "opportunities for leadership positions and internships" at Vassar, emphasizing that "the activist groups here are great." Surveys repeatedly praise the beautiful campus, the perfect surroundings in which to pursue Vassar students' favorite pastime of all: "finding yourself."

### Student Body

The most common opinion regarding the undergraduate population of Vassar goes something like, "An atypical student here is the sort who would be a typical student elsewhere." In a place where students "conform by not conforming," the climate remains "very accepting of individuality," prompting one student to describe her peers as "tolerant, almost to the point of apathy." If forced to pin down a stereotype, one might try one or all of: "hippie, style conscious, smart, left wing, idealist, East-Village-y." Less generous characterizations call students "white rich kids with holes in their clothes" or "liberal people feeling good about it." Though some people see "no ideological diversity," others are quick to point out that the campus is "getting more conservative" and that "there are spiritual and religious people here." The student body is "very accepting in terms of sexuality," which can be a boon, considering that 60 percent of the population is female. Basically, these "pretty people with lots of talent" will continue to "pride themselves on being unique and involved" and "overthinking virtually everything."

# VASSAR COLLEGE

FINANCIAL AID: 845-437-5320 • E-MAIL: ADMISSIONS@VASSAR.EDU • WEBSITE: WWW.VASSAR.EDU

## ADMISSIONS
*Very important factors considered include:* secondary school record. *Important factors considered include:* character/personal qualities, class rank, essays, recommendations, standardized test scores. *Other factors considered include:* alumni/ae relation, extracurricular activities, geographical residence, interview, minority status, talent/ability, volunteer work, work experience. TOEFL required of all international applicants. High school diploma or GED is required. *High school units required/recommended:* 16 total recommended; 4 English recommended, 4 math recommended, 3 science recommended, 2 science lab recommended, 4 foreign language recommended, 3 social studies recommended, 2 history recommended.

## The Inside Word
Vassar is relatively frank about its standards; you won't get much more direct advice from colleges about how to get admitted. The admissions process here follows very closely the practices of most prestigious northeastern schools. Your personal side—essays, extracurriculars, interview, etc.—is not going to do a lot for you if you don't demonstrate significant academic accomplishments. Multiple applicants from the same high school will be compared against each other as well as the entire applicant pool. Males and minorities are actively courted by the admissions staff, and the college is sincere in its commitment.

## FINANCIAL AID
*Students should submit:* FAFSA, institution's own financial aid form, CSS/Financial Aid PROFILE, state aid form, noncustodial (divorced/separated) parent's statement, business/farm supplement. Regular filing deadline is February 1. The Princeton Review suggests that all financial aid forms be submitted as soon as possible after January 1. *Need-based scholarships/grants offered:* Pell, SEOG, state scholarships/grants, private scholarships, the school's own gift aid. *Loan aid offered:* FFEL Subsidized Stafford, FFEL Unsubsidized Stafford, FFEL PLUS, Federal Perkins, college/university loans from institutional funds. Federal Work-Study Program available. Institutional employment available. Applicants will be notified of awards on or about April 3. Off-campus job opportunities are fair.

## FROM THE ADMISSIONS OFFICE
"Vassar presents a rich variety of social and cultural activities, clubs, sports, living arrangements, and regional attractions. Vassar is a vital, residential college community recognized for its respect for the rights and individuality of others."

### SELECTIVITY
★★★★

| | |
|---|---|
| **Admissions Rating** | 95 |
| # of applicants | 5,733 |
| % of applicants accepted | 26 |
| % of acceptees attending | 43 |
| # accepting a place on wait list | 400 |
| # of early decision applicants | 508 |
| % accepted early decision | 50 |

### FRESHMAN PROFILE
| | |
|---|---|
| Range SAT Verbal | 640-730 |
| Average SAT Verbal | 686 |
| Range SAT Math | 630-700 |
| Average SAT Math | 664 |
| Range ACT Composite | 28-32 |
| Minimum TOEFL | 600 |
| % graduated top 10% of class | 65 |
| % graduated top 25% of class | 95 |
| % graduated top 50% of class | 99 |

### DEADLINES
| | |
|---|---|
| Early decision | 11/15 |
| Early decision notification | 12/15 |
| Regular admission | 1/1 |
| Regular notification | 4/1 |

### APPLICANTS ALSO LOOK AT AND OFTEN PREFER
Brown
Yale
**AND SOMETIMES PREFER**
Wesleyan
Columbia
NYU
**AND RARELY PREFER**
Skidmore
Union (NY)

### FINANCIAL FACTS

| | |
|---|---|
| **Financial Aid Rating** | 86 |
| Tuition | $27,550 |
| Room and board | $7,340 |
| Books and supplies | $800 |
| Required fees | $410 |
| % frosh receiving aid | 54 |
| % undergrads receiving aid | 53 |
| Avg frosh grant | $19,917 |
| Avg frosh loan | $2,797 |

THE BEST 351 COLLEGES ■ 693

# VILLANOVA UNIVERSITY

800 LANCASTER AVENUE, VILLANOVA, PA 19085-1672 • ADMISSIONS: 610-519-4000 • FAX: 610-519-6450

## CAMPUS LIFE

| Quality of Life Rating | 87 |
|---|---|
| Type of school | private |
| Affiliation | Roman Catholic |
| Environment | suburban |

### STUDENTS
| | |
|---|---|
| Total undergrad enrollment | 7,375 |
| % male/female | 49/51 |
| % from out of state | 66 |
| % from public high school | 55 |
| % live on campus | 67 |
| % in (# of) fraternities | 6 (7) |
| % in (# of) sororities | 25 (8) |
| % African American | 3 |
| % Asian | 5 |
| % Caucasian | 85 |
| % Hispanic | 6 |
| % international | 2 |

### SURVEY SAYS . . .
Musical organizations are hot
School is well run
Lousy off-campus food
Unattractive campus

## ACADEMICS

| Academic Rating | 82 |
|---|---|
| Calendar | semester |
| Student/faculty ratio | 13:1 |
| % profs teaching UG courses | 100 |
| Avg lab size | 10-19 students |
| Avg reg class size | 10-19 students |

### MOST POPULAR MAJORS
Biology/biological sciences
Psychology
Finance

## STUDENTS SPEAK OUT

### Academics
Students at Villanova feel that their university "helps everyone to be their best on a personal and academic level." The challenging course work and Catholic environment draw young scholars eager to jump in on "great class discussions" and work with professors who are "easy to approach." Instructors are known to "go out of their way to accommodate students," whether that means "inviting everyone who was going to be on campus over for Thanksgiving" or "giving out their cell phone numbers in case we are screwed on an assignment." This "great rapport" allows professors to "help you learn about the material and about yourself." Undergraduates see that the faculty "reaches out and wants to meet their students," which is part of what helps them all to be "good at their job and enjoy what they're doing." We get mixed reviews regarding the administration, with some students calling them "extremely helpful" and others "a big hassle." Overall, however, the campus seems to "run pretty smoothly," and students feel they are "a face with a name, not a number."

### Life
The Villanova lifestyle combines academics with top-notch athletics and plenty of opportunities for fun. The typical schedule runs: "learn four days a week, get hammered two days a week, and save the world on the other day." The get-hammered portion is brought to you by your friendly neighborhood frat house. "Greeks provide a great social life, but you don't have to be a brother or a sister to have a good time." Students say, "I always manage to drink in some dorm room," but it can be "hard to have a lot of fun because of strict [alcohol] policies." Some think that "the rules are too strict," but they can still head to "the Brick Bar, which is pretty popular when the beer is cheap." For those not interested in bending the hooch regulations, "there are a lot of nonalcohol activities, too," including "late-night movies," theater performances, supporting the perennially successful basketball team, and listening to the ever-popular radio station. Some undergrads complain that "the campus is secluded," meaning they "must go to Philly for fun," but creative fun seekers claim "the town around campus has some good surprises." Student life is rounded out by "so many volunteer opportunities [that] it's overwhelming." Many people participate in the campus ministry, and many agree that "the religious presence here is completely optional but really adds to the sense of community and charity."

### Student Body
A field guide to Villanova students might describe them as "white kids from different suburbs across the country," the progeny of "upper-middle-class, Catholic" families. Sometimes known as "Vanilla-nova," the university is "hurting for diversity," but also seems to be "making good progress to diversify the school." For now, the majority of students either are "pretty preppy or they're guidos." Certain plebeians call their peers "snobbish" and snipe that "being academic comes second to looking good." The "motivated, bright, and outgoing" population includes "very few atypical students." Those who deviate from the "fun-loving, studious, career-oriented" norm may be few in number, but they "find their own niche." Others argue that within this "family environment" of "involved, intelligent, and witty" students, they do count a "decent number of interesting/quirky people."

# VILLANOVA UNIVERSITY

FINANCIAL AID: 610-519-4010 • E-MAIL: GOTOVU@EMAIL.VILLANOVA.EDU • WEBSITE: WWW.VILLANOVA.EDU

## ADMISSIONS

*Factors considered include:* alumni/ae relation, character/personal qualities, class rank, essays, extracurricular activities, geographical residence, minority status, recommendations, secondary school record, standardized test scores, volunteer work, work experience. SAT I or ACT required. TOEFL required of all international applicants. High school diploma or GED is required. *High school units required/recommended:* 18 total required; 20 total recommended; 4 English required, 4 math required, 4 science required, 2 science lab required, 3 science lab recommended, 2 foreign language required, 4 foreign language recommended.

### *The Inside Word*

Villanova has a very solid and growing reputation among Catholic universities nationally, yet is less competitive for admissions than the top tier of schools like Georgetown and Notre Dame. If Villanova is your first choice, be careful. As is the case at many universities, Early Action applicants face higher academic standards than those for the regular pool. This university is a very sound option, whether high on your list of choices or as a safety school.

## FINANCIAL AID

*Students should submit:* FAFSA, institution's own financial aid form. Regular filing deadline is February 15. The Princeton Review suggests that all financial aid forms be submitted as soon as possible after January 1. *Need-based scholarships/grants offered:* Pell, SEOG, state scholarships/grants, private scholarships, the school's own gift aid. *Loan aid offered:* Direct Subsidized Stafford, Direct Unsubsidized Stafford, Direct PLUS, FFEL Subsidized Stafford, FFEL Unsubsidized Stafford, FFEL PLUS, Federal Perkins, state loans. Federal Work-Study Program available. Institutional employment available. Applicants will be notified of awards on or about April 1. Off-campus job opportunities are excellent.

## FROM THE ADMISSIONS OFFICE

"The University is a community of persons of diverse professional, academic, and personal interests who in a spirit of collegiality cooperate to achieve their common goals and objectives in the transmission, the pursuit, and the discovery of knowledge.... Villanova attempts to enroll students with diverse social, geographic, economic, and educational backgrounds.... Villanova welcomes students who consider it desirable to study within the philosophical framework of Christian Humanism.... Finally, this community seeks to reflect the spirit of St. Augustine by the cultivation of knowledge, by respect for individual differences, and by adherence to the principle that mutual love and respect should animate every aspect of University life."

—*Villanova University Mission Statement*

### SELECTIVITY

| | |
|---|---:|
| Admissions Rating | 83 |
| # of applicants | 10,897 |
| % of applicants accepted | 47 |
| % of acceptees attending | 31 |
| # accepting a place on wait list | 2,212 |
| % admitted from wait list | 20 |

### FRESHMAN PROFILE

| | |
|---|---:|
| Range SAT Verbal | 580-650 |
| Average SAT Verbal | 605 |
| Range SAT Math | 610-680 |
| Average SAT Math | 633 |
| Average ACT Composite | 27 |
| Minimum TOEFL | 550 |
| Average HS GPA | 3.6 |
| % graduated top 10% of class | 41 |
| % graduated top 25% of class | 57 |
| % graduated top 50% of class | 96 |

### DEADLINES

| | |
|---|---:|
| Regular admission | 1/7 |
| Regular notification | 4/1 |

### APPLICANTS ALSO LOOK AT AND OFTEN PREFER
Notre Dame
Georgetown

### AND SOMETIMES PREFER
Boston College
Holy Cross

### AND RARELY PREFER
Loyola
Providence
Fairfield

### FINANCIAL FACTS

| | |
|---|---:|
| Financial Aid Rating | 79 |
| Tuition | $23,540 |
| Room and board | $8,330 |
| Books and supplies | $800 |
| Required fees | $550 |
| % frosh receiving aid | 47 |
| % undergrads receiving aid | 47 |

# VIRGINIA TECH
UNDERGRADUATE ADMISSIONS, 201 BURRUSS HALL, BLACKSBURG, VA 24061 • ADMISSIONS: 540-231-6267 • FAX: 540-231-3242

## CAMPUS LIFE

| | |
|---|---|
| Quality of Life Rating | 86 |
| Type of school | public |
| Environment | rural |

### STUDENTS
| | |
|---|---|
| Total undergrad enrollment | 21,468 |
| % male/female | 59/41 |
| % from out of state | 27 |
| % from public high school | 95 |
| % live on campus | 39 |
| % in (# of) fraternities | 13 (34) |
| % in (# of) sororities | 15 (16) |
| % African American | 6 |
| % Asian | 7 |
| % Caucasian | 82 |
| % Hispanic | 2 |
| % international | 3 |

### SURVEY SAYS . . .
Everyone loves the Hokies
Students are happy
Class discussions are rare
Political activism is hot
Students are religious
High cost of living
(Almost) everyone smokes
Hard liquor is popular
Large classes

## ACADEMICS

| | |
|---|---|
| Academic Rating | 81 |
| Calendar | semester |
| Student/faculty ratio | 17:1 |
| % profs teaching UG courses | 75 |

### MOST POPULAR MAJORS
Communications studies/speech communication and rhetoric
Engineering
Biology/biological sciences

## STUDENTS SPEAK OUT

### Academics
For 20,000-plus bright, goal-oriented Virginia undergraduates, Virginia Polytechnic and State University offers the perfect mixture of academic theory and practical application (and, of course, football). As one student explains, "I feel that many schools, like University of Virginia, have excellent academics, but do not offer a real-world mentality attached to that education. Virginia Tech has the best of both worlds. I feel that upon graduation I will have a successful professional life that will be easily transitioned into." Tech students also appreciate how their school "is a place where people really care about learning and are proud of their studies, but they also know how to enjoy life and not just spend all their time in the books." Undergrads here speak highly of the "excellent engineering department," "the state's only veterinary school," and "solid business and computer science departments." Profs here, as at most tech schools, are a mixed bag; "some professors are great, while others are dreadful," reports one engineer. "Fortunately, there's this really useful website where you can evaluate teachers that you have had, and check up on what teachers that you may have are like." Most here agree that the quality of instruction—as well as the interest level of the material—improves as they progress through school. "All professors are helpful, but the more high-level classes you take, the even-more-helpful the professors are. I have had a very good academic experience here." Students note that VT has not been immune to the nationwide epidemic of state budget-cutting; reports one undergrad, "With the recent huge budget cuts in Virginia, students will be paying more and getting less."

### Life
Students tell us that "life at VT is pretty laid-back, for the most part. Students are expected to work hard for good grades, and they generally do. Monday through Thursday is pretty academically geared. But come Thursday night, it's all about the party." Notes one student, "Most people start partying on Thursday night. They go downtown to one of the many local bars, go to a frat party, or go to an apartment party. There are so many apartments off campus that there are at least ten parties at anyone's fingertips at one time. We party hard and we love our sports." Hokie football reigns supreme on the Blacksburg campus; volleyball and women's basketball both have also fielded competitive squads in recent seasons. If you're not into partying or sports, students warn, "There's not much more available aside from the restaurants and local theatre. Since most of the things to do, like bowling or the big movie theatre, are located in the next town (about 15 minutes by car), they are somewhat uncompelling." Agrees one student, "Wal-Mart is about as much fun as it gets for the nonpartiers, as there are pretty slim pickings if you don't party." Hometown Blacksburg, most admit, "doesn't offer much." The closest city, Roanoke, is about an hour's drive from campus.

### Student Body
Students at VT are bright but not necessarily intellectually curious: "We're very concerned about doing well, though not necessarily learning" is how one student puts it. While "the typical student is white, dresses in clothes from Abercrombie, Structure, Gap, American Eagle, etc. . . . and obviously comes from a white-collar family," there are "many atypical students, probably just under 50 percent of the student body. The school is big enough so that cliques are impossible." As one student put it, "The campus is really diverse, and everyone can find a place not just with people like them, but with almost anyone." As a rule, "people here are generally pretty laid-back and friendly," eschewing the cutthroat competitiveness that characterizes many engineering and tech schools.

# VIRGINIA TECH

FINANCIAL AID: 540-231-5179 • E-MAIL: VTADMISS@VT.EDU • WEBSITE: WWW.VT.EDU

## ADMISSIONS
*Very important factors considered include:* secondary school record, standardized test scores. *Important factors considered include:* extracurricular and after-school activities. *Other factors considered include:* alumni/ae relation, essays, extracurricular activities, geographical residence, minority status, recommendations, state residency, talent/ability, volunteer work, work experience. SAT I or ACT required; SAT I preferred; SAT II also recommended. TOEFL required of all international applicants. High school diploma or GED is required. *High school units required/recommended:* 18 total required; 4 English required, 3 math required, 2 science required, 3 science recommended, 2 science lab required, 3 foreign language recommended, 1 social studies required, 1 history required, 3 elective required.

### The Inside Word
When compared to applying to UVA or William and Mary, getting into Virginia Tech is a cakewalk. Tech has a great reputation, which from a careerist point of view makes it well worth considering.

## FINANCIAL AID
*Students should submit:* FAFSA, General Scholarship Application. Regular filing deadline is March 11. The Princeton Review suggests that all financial aid forms be submitted as soon as possible after January 1. *Need-based scholarships/grants offered:* Pell, SEOG, state scholarships/grants, private scholarships, the school's own gift aid, cadet scholarships/grants. *Loan aid offered:* Direct Subsidized Stafford, Direct Unsubsidized Stafford, Direct PLUS, FFEL PLUS, Federal Perkins, college/university loans from institutional funds. Federal Work-Study Program available. Institutional employment available. Applicants will be notified of awards on or about April 15. Off-campus job opportunities are good.

## FROM THE ADMISSIONS OFFICE
"Virginia Tech offers the opportunities of a large research university in a small-town setting. Undergraduates choose from more than 75 majors in 7 colleges, including nationally ranked business, forestry, and engineering schools, as well as excellent computer science, biology, communication studies, and architecture programs. Technology is a key focus, both in classes and in general. All first-year students are required to own a personal computer, each residence hall room has Ethernet connections, and every student is provided e-mail and Internet access. Faculty incorporate a wide variety of technology into class, utilizing chat rooms, online lecture notes, and multimedia presentations. The university offers cutting-edge facilities for classes and research, abundant opportunities for advanced study in the Honors Program, undergraduate research opportunities, study abroad, internships, and cooperative education. Students enjoy more than 500 organizations, which offer something for everyone. Tech offers the best of both worlds—everything a large university can provide and a small-town atmosphere."

### SELECTIVITY

| | |
|---|---:|
| Admissions Rating | 84 |
| # of applicants | 18,321 |
| % of applicants accepted | 65 |
| % of acceptees attending | 41 |
| # accepting a place on wait list | 500 |
| % admitted from wait list | 0 |
| # of early decision applicants | 2,250 |
| % accepted early decision | 20 |

### FRESHMAN PROFILE
| | |
|---|---:|
| Range SAT Verbal | 540-630 |
| Average SAT Verbal | 600 |
| Range SAT Math | 570-650 |
| Average SAT Math | 650 |
| Minimum TOEFL | 550 |
| Average HS GPA | 3.6 |
| % graduated top 10% of class | 40 |
| % graduated top 25% of class | 80 |
| % graduated top 50% of class | 99 |

### DEADLINES
| | |
|---|---:|
| Early decision | 11/1 |
| Early decision notification | 12/15 |
| Regular admission | 1/15 |
| Regular notification | 4/1 |
| Nonfall registration? | yes |

### APPLICANTS ALSO LOOK AT AND OFTEN PREFER
James Madison U
U of Virginia
**AND SOMETIMES PREFER**
Virginia Commonwealth
**AND RARELY PREFER**
U Maryland
UNC Chapel Hill
William and Mary

### FINANCIAL FACTS

| | |
|---|---:|
| Financial Aid Rating | 82 |
| In-state tuition | $5,095 |
| Out-of-state tuition | $15,029 |
| Room and board | $4,084 |
| Books and supplies | $900 |
| Required fees | $905 |
| % frosh receiving aid | 43 |
| % undergrads receiving aid | 45 |
| Avg frosh grant | $9,030 |
| Avg frosh loan | $11,625 |

THE BEST 351 COLLEGES ■ 697

# WABASH COLLEGE

PO Box 352, 301 W. Wabash Avenue, Crawfordsville, IN 47933 • Admissions: 765-361-6225 • Fax: 765-361-6437

## CAMPUS LIFE

| | |
|---|---|
| Quality of Life Rating | 82 |
| Type of school | private |
| Environment | suburban |

### STUDENTS

| | |
|---|---|
| Total undergrad enrollment | 912 |
| % from out of state | 26 |
| % from public high school | 92 |
| % live on campus | 99 |
| % in (# of) fraternities | 65 (10) |
| % African American | 7 |
| % Asian | 3 |
| % Caucasian | 84 |
| % Hispanic | 6 |
| % international | 3 |
| # of countries represented | 13 |

### SURVEY SAYS . . .
Frats dominate social scene
Everyone loves the Giants
(Almost) everyone plays intramural sports
No one cheats
Campus feels safe
Students don't like Crawfordsville, IN
Class discussions encouraged
Student publications are popular

## ACADEMICS

| | |
|---|---|
| Academic Rating | 93 |
| Calendar | semester |
| Student/faculty ratio | 11:1 |
| Profs interesting rating | 98 |
| Profs accessible rating | 99 |
| % profs teaching UG courses | 100 |
| Avg lab size | 10-19 students |
| Avg reg class size | 10-19 students |

### MOST POPULAR MAJORS
History
English language and literature
Political science and government

## STUDENTS SPEAK OUT

### Academics

All-male Wabash College produces graduates who exemplify "the Gentleman's Rule," Wabash's brief but all-inclusive code of conduct: "Every student should behave as a gentleman and responsible citizen on and off campus." Students report that every interaction at Wabash is colored by students', faculty members', and administrators' commitment to the rule. Writes one student, "I think the Gentleman's Rule, which is our only code of conduct, not only is applicable for the students, but also for the faculty and administrators as well. They really do a good job listening to the concerns of the students and work on improving the learning environment on the campus." Professors here constitute "a knowledgeable and wonderful group of people. They push us to the furthest extent possible so that we can do the most with our given ability. I've never worked so hard in my life, and I've never gotten so much out of anything, academically, socially, and personally, as I have from Wabash." Students must complete a required core of liberal arts courses, fulfill a major concentration, and pass comprehensive written and oral examinations in order to graduate. Their efforts are abetted by access to exceptional facilities; as one student reports, "In a college as small as Wabash, it is sometimes amazing to consider all the facilities we have at our fingertips. The computer labs are all over campus and available to anyone very easily. I think our library is the best I have yet to see, and I know our recreational/athletic facilities are the envy of Division III schools."

### Life

You probably wouldn't expect much in the way of wild partying from an all-male campus with demanding academics, and during weekdays, you'd be right. Weekends, however, are a whole other matter at Wabash. Reports one student, "From the start of Sunday night to Friday night students are busy studying . . . . On weekends, however, the party life here is awesome. The school is known throughout the state for having the best parties anywhere and is definitely worth the drive for girls and guys." Students brag that Wabash is a "very wet campus" where drunken misconduct is restrained not by campus police but rather by the Gentleman's Rule; writes one undergrad, "Basically, if we conduct ourselves like gentlemen, both on and off campus, no one gets in trouble. This is a very risky way of disciplining a college campus, but it works. We do a lot of drinking and partying on the weekends and a little during the week, but as long as we are mature about it, no one gets in trouble and everyone has a good time." Sports are very big with students, as is the Greek system, which reportedly snags nearly three-quarters of all undergraduates. Hometown Crawfordsville has "all of the essentials but lacks the versatility of a bigger city"; fortunately, "there are two larger cities close by that can provide the extra entertainment needed." Students occasionally "venture to other schools for parties and things because they aren't that far: Purdue, Ball State, Butler, and Indiana University are all really close."

### Student Body

The "studious, disciplined, naturally intelligent, and for the most part well-spoken" undergraduates of Wabash regard each other as brothers. "Unity on campus is prevalent," students agree, "mostly because of tradition. Traditions like Chapel Sing and the Monon Bell game bring all students on campus together." These brothers do squabble on occasion. "The only problem I find is being an independent on a campus that is almost three-quarters Greek," complains one student. "Members of some of the fraternities seem to really look down on independent students." Responds a frat brother, "There are rivalries, but when it comes time for Wabash to compete or show her collective power, everyone is there sporting the scarlet and white." Students are "ridiculously conservative," and while "not everyone is religious, those who are are very religious." In recent years "the student body has gotten much more diverse, and that has helped the atmosphere rather than caused problems."

698 ■ THE BEST 351 COLLEGES

# WABASH COLLEGE

FINANCIAL AID: 765-361-6370 • E-MAIL: ADMISSIONS@WABASH.EDU • WEBSITE: WWW.WABASH.EDU

## ADMISSIONS

*Very important factors considered include:* class rank, secondary school record. *Important factors considered include:* recommendations, standardized test scores. *Other factors considered include:* alumni/ae relation, character/personal qualities, essays, extracurricular activities, geographical residence, interview, minority status, state residency, talent/ability, volunteer work, work experience. SAT I or ACT required. TOEFL required of all international applicants. High school diploma or GED is required. *High school units required/recommended:* 17 total recommended; 4 English recommended, 4 math recommended, 3 science recommended, 2 science lab recommended, 2 foreign language recommended, 2 social studies recommended, 2 history recommended.

### The Inside Word

Wabash is one of the few remaining all-male colleges in the country, and like the rest it has a small applicant pool. The pool is highly self-selected, and the academic standards for admission, while selective, are not particularly demanding. However, Wabash is tough to graduate from—don't consider it if you aren't prepared to work.

## FINANCIAL AID

*Students should submit:* FAFSA, CSS/Financial Aid PROFILE, federal tax returns and W-2 statements. Regular filing deadline is March 1. The Princeton Review suggests that all financial aid forms be submitted as soon as possible after January 1. *Need-based scholarships/grants offered:* Pell, state scholarships/grants, private scholarships, the school's own gift aid. *Loan aid offered:* FFEL Subsidized Stafford, FFEL Unsubsidized Stafford, FFEL PLUS, college/university loans from institutional funds. Institutional employment available. Applicants will be notified of awards on or about April 1. Off-campus job opportunities are excellent.

## FROM THE ADMISSIONS OFFICE

"Wabash College is different—and distinctive—from other liberal arts colleges. Different in that Wabash is an outstanding college for men only. Distinctive in the quality and character of the faculty, in the demanding nature of the academic program, in the farsightedness and maturity of the men who enroll, and in the richness of the traditions that have evolved throughout its 168-year history. Wabash is, preeminently, a teaching institution, and fundamental to the learning experience is the way faculty and students talk to each other: with mutual respect for the expression of informed opinion. For example, students who collaborate with faculty on research projects are considered their peers in the research—an esteem not usually extended to undergraduates. The college takes pride in the sense of community that such a learning environment fosters. But perhaps the single most striking aspect of student life at Wabash is personal freedom. The college has only one rule: 'The student is expected to conduct himself at all times, both on and off the campus, as a gentleman and a responsible citizen.' Wabash College treats students as adults, and such treatment attracts responsible freshmen and fosters their independence and maturity."

### SELECTIVITY

| | |
|---|---|
| Admissions Rating | 87 |
| # of applicants | 1,287 |
| % of applicants accepted | 50 |
| % of acceptees attending | 42 |
| # accepting a place on wait list | 86 |
| % admitted from wait list | 7 |
| # of early decision applicants | 58 |
| % accepted early decision | 81 |

### FRESHMAN PROFILE

| | |
|---|---|
| Range SAT Verbal | 530-620 |
| Average SAT Verbal | 576 |
| Range SAT Math | 560-655 |
| Average SAT Math | 609 |
| Range ACT Composite | 23-28 |
| Average ACT Composite | 26 |
| Minimum TOEFL | 550 |
| Average HS GPA | 3.6 |
| % graduated top 10% of class | 32 |
| % graduated top 25% of class | 68 |
| % graduated top 50% of class | 95 |

### DEADLINES

| | |
|---|---|
| Early decision | 11/15 |
| Early decision notification | 12/15 |
| Priority admission | 12/15 |
| Nonfall registration? | yes |

### APPLICANTS ALSO LOOK AT AND OFTEN PREFER
Indiana U
Purdue U

### AND SOMETIMES PREFER
DePauw
Hanover
Butler

### AND RARELY PREFER
Franklin College
Miami of Ohio

### FINANCIAL FACTS

| | |
|---|---|
| Financial Aid Rating | 89 |
| Tuition | $20,829 |
| Room and board | $6,717 |
| Books and supplies | $600 |
| Required fees | $386 |
| % frosh receiving aid | 77 |
| % undergrads receiving aid | 68 |
| Avg frosh grant | $18,668 |
| Avg frosh loan | $3,301 |

THE BEST 351 COLLEGES ■ 699

# WAGNER COLLEGE

ONE CAMPUS ROAD, STATEN ISLAND, NY 10301 • ADMISSIONS: 718-390-3411 • FAX: 718-390-3105

## CAMPUS LIFE

| | |
|---|---|
| **Quality of Life Rating** | 76 |
| Type of school | private |
| Affiliation | Lutheran |
| Environment | urban |

### STUDENTS

| | |
|---|---|
| Total undergrad enrollment | 1,739 |
| % male/female | 41/59 |
| % from out of state | 55 |
| % from public high school | 57 |
| % live on campus | 77 |
| % African American | 6 |
| % Asian | 4 |
| % Caucasian | 77 |
| % Hispanic | 6 |
| % international | 2 |
| # of countries represented | 16 |

### SURVEY SAYS . . .
*Lots of beer drinking
Students aren't very religious
Hard liquor is popular
Students don't like Staten Island, NY
Great off-campus food*

## ACADEMICS

| | |
|---|---|
| **Academic Rating** | 76 |
| Calendar | semester |
| Student/faculty ratio | 15:1 |
| Profs interesting rating | 73 |
| Profs accessible rating | 80 |
| % profs teaching UG courses | 100 |

## STUDENTS SPEAK OUT

### Academics
Wagner has some flagship majors that earn it a national reputation, and many students apply to the college specifically for these disciplines. However, the college's recently revamped liberal arts curriculum gives it up-to-date bragging rights. Ah, and did we mention that the campus overlooks La Isla MANHATTAN? Wagner students are no strangers to using the city as a classroom and for internships. As one senior puts its, "New York is our classroom." Student opinion at Wagner runs the spectrum from thrilled to disgruntled. Across the board, the small class sizes and "resourceful, witty, and inspiring" professors "create a really positive atmosphere" for study. "I feel challenged, yet professors are helpful," writes a junior, agreeing with others who note that the faculty is "always willing to give of out-of-class time to help with accelerated research projects." On the administrative side, reviews remain mixed. "The upper administration seems to distance themselves from everyone else, but if you request their attention they will give it to you." Referring to the disconnect between the administration and the student body, one student notes, "Students have a loud voice," but many wish they had more say regarding the administrative choices made for the school—both for students and the campus itself.

### Life
Proximity to the unlimited opportunities of the Big Apple is one of Wagner's strongest selling points; the school provides free transportation to the Staten Island ferry, making access easy. "It's a great life here because you can go into the city, but actually get out of it and sleep when you go back to your dorm," explains a sophomore. A senior majoring in theater notes the "Location, location, location. No college is more beautiful or more beautifully located than Wagner." Oddly enough, the second most commonly mentioned aspect of Wagner life is the architectural material of choice: brick. A sociology major notes sarcastically, "I think we could use a few more bricks," and a fellow student adds, "Bricks, bricks everywhere!" Meticulous "leaf-blowing and lawn-maintenance" practices also contribute to the campus' pristine look. When they are not lured away by the city's attractions, students enjoy "on-campus activities, such as comedy nights, films, and plays." Fraternity and sorority members agree that "Greek life rocks!" though other students note that "People don't do anything unless there's alcohol." All factors considered, a sophomore declares, "[I'm] having the time of my life."

### Student Body
Wagner students' general opinion of each other is pretty typical. "People here are your everyday college students: they chain smoke, bitch about the food, get drunk, go to class, [and] sleep long hours," remarks a junior majoring in technical theater. Others believe that Wagner-ites are "very open-minded" and "supportive of each other in activities," but "rumors tend to spread like wildfire." A clear division exists between students who live on campus and those who live off, with residents griping that commuters "don't realize anything outside of Staten Island exists." In spite of these opposing camps, many students laud the "sense of community" at Wagner and comment, "The people here are great. While we all have our own groups, everyone is friendly to each other." A common refrain goes, "I have made many friends here." One sophomore writes, "We are an extremely diverse social group coming from all aspects of society and different family backgrounds and different viewpoints."

# WAGNER COLLEGE

FINANCIAL AID: 718-390-3183 • E-MAIL: ADMISSIONS@WAGNER.EDU • WEBSITE: WWW.WAGNER.EDU

## ADMISSIONS
*Very important factors considered include:* secondary school record, standardized test scores. *Important factors considered include:* class rank, essays, interview, recommendations, talent/ability. *Other factors considered include:* alumni/ae relation, character/personal qualities, extracurricular activities, geographical residence, minority status, volunteer work. SAT I or ACT required; SAT I preferred; SAT II also recommended. TOEFL required of all international applicants. High school diploma is required and GED is not accepted. *High school units required/recommended:* 18 total required; 21 total recommended; 4 English required, 3 math required, 4 math recommended, 2 science required, 3 science recommended, 2 foreign language required, 3 social studies required, 4 social studies recommended, 4 elective required.

### The Inside Word
Wagner has profited in recent years from a renewed interest in urban colleges. In other words, don't take the application process too lightly. Applicants are met with a college admissions staff dedicated to finding the right students for their school. Wagner's pioneering efforts in experiential learning for all students make its recent resurgence well earned.

## FINANCIAL AID
*Students should submit:* FAFSA. Regular filing deadline is April 15. The Princeton Review suggests that all financial aid forms be submitted as soon as possible after January 1. *Need-based scholarships/grants offered:* Pell, SEOG, state scholarships/grants, private scholarships, the school's own gift aid, Lutheran Scholarships. *Loan aid offered:* FFEL Subsidized Stafford, FFEL Unsubsidized Stafford, FFEL PLUS, Federal Perkins, Federal Nursing. Federal Work-Study Program available. Institutional employment available. Off-campus job opportunities are good.

## FROM THE ADMISSIONS OFFICE
"At Wagner College, we attract and develop active learners and future leaders. Wagner College has received national acclaim (Time magazine, American Association of Colleges and Universities) for its innovative curriculum, 'The Wagner Plan for the Practical Liberal Arts.' At Wagner, we capitalize on our unique geography; we are a traditional, scenic, residential campus, which happens to sit atop a hill on an island overlooking lower Manhattan. Our location allows us to offer a program that couples required off-campus experiences (internships), with 'learning community' clusters of courses. This program begins in the first semester and continues through the senior capstone experience in the major. Fieldwork and internships, writing-intensive reflective tutorials, connected learning, 'reading, writing, and doing' . . . at Wagner College our students truly discover 'the practical liberal arts in New York City.'"

## ADMISSIONS

| | |
|---|---|
| Admissions Rating | 78 |
| # of applicants | 2,413 |
| % of applicants accepted | 66 |
| % of acceptees attending | 33 |
| # of early decision applicants | 74 |
| % accepted early decision | 29 |

### FRESHMAN PROFILE
| | |
|---|---|
| Range SAT Verbal | 510-620 |
| Average SAT Verbal | 560 |
| Range SAT Math | 520-610 |
| Average SAT Math | 560 |
| Average ACT Composite | 25 |
| Minimum TOEFL | 550 |
| Average HS GPA | 3.5 |
| % graduated top 10% of class | 17 |
| % graduated top 25% of class | 50 |
| % graduated top 50% of class | 91 |

### DEADLINES
| | |
|---|---|
| Early decision | 11/15 |
| Early decision notification | 1/1 |
| Priority admission | 2/15 |
| Regular admission | 3/15 |
| Nonfall registration? | yes |

### APPLICANTS ALSO LOOK AT AND OFTEN PREFER
Muhlenberg
NYU
Fairfield

### AND SOMETIMES PREFER
Drew
Fordham
Hobart & William Smith

### AND RARELY PREFER
Marist
Manhattan
Quinnipiac

## FINANCIAL FACTS

| | |
|---|---|
| Financial Aid Rating | 80 |
| Tuition | $18,000 |
| Room and board | $6,500 |
| Books and supplies | $625 |
| % frosh receiving aid | 75 |
| % undergrads receiving aid | 68 |
| Avg frosh grant | $6,965 |
| Avg frosh loan | $5,660 |

# WAKE FOREST UNIVERSITY

Box 7305, Reynolda Station, Winston-Salem, NC 27109 • Admissions: 336-758-5201 • Fax: 336-758-4324

## CAMPUS LIFE

| Quality of Life Rating | 87 |
| --- | --- |
| Type of school | private |
| Environment | suburban |

### STUDENTS

| Total undergrad enrollment | 4,045 |
| --- | --- |
| % male/female | 49/51 |
| % from out of state | 71 |
| % from public high school | 67 |
| % live on campus | 75 |
| % in (# of) fraternities | 37 (14) |
| % in (# of) sororities | 50 (9) |
| % African American | 7 |
| % Asian | 3 |
| % Caucasian | 88 |
| % Hispanic | 2 |
| % international | 1 |

### SURVEY SAYS . . .

Everyone loves the Demon Deacons
Beautiful campus
Political activism is hot
Athletic facilities are great
Great library
Student publications are ignored
Students aren't religious
(Almost) no one listens to college radio

## ACADEMICS

| Academic Rating | 93 |
| --- | --- |
| Calendar | semester |
| Student/faculty ratio | 10:1 |
| Profs interesting rating | 80 |
| Profs accessible rating | 85 |
| % profs teaching UG courses | 100 |
| Avg lab size | 10-19 students |
| Avg reg class size | 10-19 students |

### MOST POPULAR MAJORS
Communications
Psychology
Business/commerce

## STUDENTS SPEAK OUT

### Academics

Students at Wake Forest agree that "lots of opportunities and resources that are typically available only at larger schools," "great technology (everyone gets a laptop upon entering)," a "small student population, and small classes" are what distinguish their school from the pack. That, and a wicked-hard grading system; many here warn that "grading is extremely rigid, with no curves, extra credit, or other benefits to the students. . . . Overall, I have found that a C can be achieved with little to no effort, B's are possible with a significant amount of work, and A's are virtually impossible." They love their professors, whom they describe as "down to earth and easy to talk to," "at the top of their fields, and very knowledgeable in their respective areas of expertise." The administration earns similar plaudits ("Friendly through-and-through. Must be that southern hospitality" is how one student puts it). Many here wish the school would reduce the number of core requirements, telling us that "the amount of core courses leaves little room to explore interests outside a major/minor. Forget about electives if you're double majoring or have a minor."

### Life

As one student puts it, "I can sum up fun at Wake pretty easily: Monday through Wednesday everyone works, Wednesday night everyone drinks, Thursday people study for Friday tests, Friday through Sunday everyone drinks like rock stars, and Sunday everyone goes to the library." The lively party scene here revolves around the Greeks and area bars and clubs. Frat parties "are completely open and welcoming to all students and provide dancing and free beer," but upperclassmen eventually "tire of the frat scene. Even so, we are comfortable with the social options at Wake." Many complain about the university's restrictive regulations, especially those concerning alcohol. Beyond the party scene, "opportunities to get involved on campus abound: there are a ton of clubs, teams, and organizations to join." Students brag that "we're in the ACC, so we have some of the best athletics in the nation" and also note that "there is always so much going on on-campus, whether that is a local/school band in the coffeehouse, a play in the theater, or just a movie playing in your suite." Most here agree that "student life is very campus-centered . . . in spite of the fact that there are good things to do in the surrounding area. For example, the NC School of the Arts is in town and puts on fantastic works, but most students are unaware of it." They also agree that the campus is "gorgeous." Opinion is split on hometown Winston-Salem; the town has its boosters, but most here feel that it "isn't exactly a college town."

### Student Body

"Most students are conservative, clean-cut, studious, easygoing, and involved in many activities on campus and in the community." The majority are also "white, upper-middle-class, very Christian, Republican, and Greek." Adds one student, "'Diversified' is the last word that could ever be used to describe Wake, but honestly, most like it that way. The few that do stand out are pointed out and would hardly be said to fit in." Some disagree, telling us that "more and more students here are choosing to pull away from the stereotype, and so atypical students fit in fairly well." Nearly all concede, however, that "The school is hugely lacking in a minority presence. What minorities there are tend to self-segregate, and the social separation perpetuates itself." Athletics form a common bond for most here; "anyone overweight really stands out as an oddity," writes one undergrad.

# WAKE FOREST UNIVERSITY

FINANCIAL AID: 336-758-5154 • E-MAIL: ADMISSIONS@WFU.EDU • WEBSITE: WWW.WFU.EDU

## ADMISSIONS

*Very important factors considered include:* character/personal qualities, class rank, secondary school record, standardized test scores. *Important factors considered include:* alumni/ae relation, essays, extracurricular activities, minority status, recommendations, religious affiliation/commitment, talent/ability, volunteer work. *Other factors considered include:* geographical residence, state residency. SAT I required; SAT II recommended. TOEFL required of all international applicants. High school diploma or GED is required. *High school units required/recommended:* 16 total required; 20 total recommended; 4 English required, 3 math required, 4 math recommended, 1 science required, 4 science recommended, 2 foreign language required, 4 foreign language recommended, 2 social studies required, 4 social studies recommended.

## The Inside Word

An applicant to Wake Forest undergoes very close scrutiny from the admissions committee; many very solid candidates wind up on the wait list. Fortunately, the admissions staff is as friendly and accessible as the university's students rate the whole place. Successful candidates typically show impressive extracurricular accomplishments as well as academic excellence, and are good matches with the university's personality.

## FINANCIAL AID

*Students should submit:* FAFSA, CSS/Financial Aid PROFILE, state aid form, noncustodial (divorced/separated) parent's statement. No deadline for regular filing. The Princeton Review suggests that all financial aid forms be submitted as soon as possible after January 1. *Need-based scholarships/grants offered:* Pell, SEOG, state scholarships/grants, private scholarships, the school's own gift aid. *Loan aid offered:* FFEL Subsidized Stafford, FFEL Unsubsidized Stafford, FFEL PLUS, Federal Perkins, state loans, college/university loans from institutional funds, alternative loans. Federal Work-Study Program available. Institutional employment available. Applicants will be notified of awards on or about April 1. Off-campus job opportunities are excellent.

## FROM THE ADMISSIONS OFFICE

"Wake Forest University has been dedicated to the liberal arts for over a century and a half; this means education in the fundamental fields of human knowledge and achievement. It seeks to encourage habits of mind that ask why, that evaluate evidence, that are open to new ideas, that attempt to understand and appreciate the perspective of others, that accept complexity and grapple with it, that admit error, and that pursue truth. Wake Forest is among a small, elite group of American colleges and universities recognized for their outstanding academic quality. It offers small classes taught by full-time faculty—not graduate assistants—and a commitment to student interaction with those professors. Students are all provided IBM ThinkPads and color printers. Classrooms and residence halls are fully networked. Wake Forest maintains a need-blind admissions policy by which qualified students are admitted regardless of their financial circumstances."

## SELECTIVITY

| | |
|---|---|
| Admissions Rating | 95 |
| # of applicants | 5,995 |
| % of applicants accepted | 41 |
| % of acceptees attending | 41 |
| # of early decision applicants | 618 |
| % accepted early decision | 58 |

### FRESHMAN PROFILE

| | |
|---|---|
| Range SAT Verbal | 600-680 |
| Range SAT Math | 620-710 |
| Minimum TOEFL | 550 |
| % graduated top 10% of class | 62 |
| % graduated top 25% of class | 91 |
| % graduated top 50% of class | 98 |

### DEADLINES

| | |
|---|---|
| Early decision | 11/15 |
| Early decision notification | 12/15 |
| Regular admission | 1/15 |
| Regular notification | 4/1 |
| Nonfall registration? | yes |

### APPLICANTS ALSO LOOK AT
**AND OFTEN PREFER**
UNC Chapel Hill
Duke
North Carolina State
**AND SOMETIMES PREFER**
U of Virginia
Vanderbilt

## FINANCIAL FACTS

| | |
|---|---|
| Financial Aid Rating | 86 |
| Tuition | $24,750 |
| Books and supplies | $700 |
| Avg frosh grant | $17,343 |
| Avg frosh loan | $4,674 |

# WARREN WILSON COLLEGE

PO Box 9000, Asheville, NC 28815 • Admissions: 800-934-3536 • Fax: 828-298-1440

## CAMPUS LIFE

| Quality of Life Rating | 83 |
|---|---|
| Type of school | private |
| Affiliation | Presbyterian |
| Environment | suburban |

### STUDENTS

| Total undergrad enrollment | 781 |
|---|---|
| % male/female | 39/61 |
| % from out of state | 79 |
| % from public high school | 77 |
| % live on campus | 88 |
| % African American | 2 |
| % Asian | 1 |
| % Caucasian | 95 |
| % Hispanic | 1 |
| % international | 5 |

### SURVEY SAYS . . .
Diverse students interact
High cost of living
Students are cliquish
Very little drug use

## ACADEMICS

| Academic Rating | 85 |
|---|---|
| Calendar | other |
| Student/faculty ratio | 12:1 |
| Profs interesting rating | 90 |
| Profs accessible rating | 80 |
| % profs teaching UG courses | 100 |
| Avg lab size | 10-19 students |
| Avg reg class size | 10-19 students |

### MOST POPULAR MAJORS
Environmental science
English language and literature
Fine/studio arts

## STUDENTS SPEAK OUT

### Academics

"It's all about the Triad" at Warren Wilson College. No, our respondents aren't talking about the Greensboro/High Point/Winston-Salem metropolitan area, but rather Wilson's "unique requirements to work 15 hours a week and perform community service" as integral parts of the curriculum. The goal of the Triad, according to the school, is to foster "community, creativity, learning, and a sense of harmony with the environment." Most here feel it achieves that goal handily. "Work and service are very important," explains one undergrad. "People here are realistic, yet willing to work hard toward making positive change in the world." Students also appreciate the strong community ties that the Wilson program creates: "Our professors are our peers. We teach and learn together" is how one student puts it. Writes another, "Professors are understanding and treat you like an actual person; they notice your bad days, are genuinely concerned if you are not working up to your potential, and are always available for help outside of class." Similarly, "the administration is exceptionally interested in the students and student wellness." Some here feel, however, that "the focus on academics could be stronger." Warns one student, "Some profs can make you laugh for hours and never actually teach you anything." Adds another, "The real excitement is in seminar/discussion classes, where you actually get to interact with the people around you. If it weren't for the average academics at this school, it'd be Valhalla." Even so, most feel that Wilson offers an enriching, empowering academic experience. As one student puts it, "It's all about the kids. We are this place; we own it."

### Life

Life under the Triad program takes some getting used to. Explains one freshman, "When I first got here, it felt like summer camp, too much fun. Now I've settled into academics, and it's excellent. Life of the Mind and Life of the Bawdy Politic blended into a great experience." Fun, maybe, but definitely time- and labor-intensive. As one student tells us, "Since we're a work school, there isn't a lot of time to hang out. We kind of hang out and walk around campus." Students also "watch movies, drink, go to town, cook, etc. for fun. Life's pretty fun and laid-back here." Others enjoy "school-sponsored and community-sponsored activities. They're very popular." Some even "go for hikes in the woods, swim in the pond, and be children of Mother Earth." Mother Earth, hmm? No wonder "some call it a 'hippie' school. But that doesn't mean it's a bunch of kids getting stoned all the time. It's very progressive. People here are very conscious about current issues, locally and worldwide. Many students here are activist types." Wilson's hometown, Asheville, is a quaint mountain city long regarded as a North Carolina hippie haven.

### Student Body

"Wilson is known as a hippie college," students tell us, "but there is a startling diversity of other kinds of alterna-creatures here. We have our punk rockers; we have our socialists; we have girls who shave. Everybody here smiles and says 'hello.'" Politically, the school is not quite so diverse: "This college consists of various facets of the left wing: the Democrats, the Greens, and the anarchists. No Republican has ever set foot on this campus. Ever. If they did, they'd probably be pelted to death with hand-rolled cigarette butts," writes one undergrad. Students share another common characteristic: "We all come to class all covered in dirt from being working young lads and lasses. We don't usually brush our hair." Notes another student, "We're a stinky bunch of kids, that's for damned sure, but we're all united by this idealism that would get us accosted at any other school. Just the fact that the person goes to Wilson, a school with such a unique vision of education, is enough to automatically classify them as cool."

# WARREN WILSON COLLEGE

FINANCIAL AID: 828-298-3325 • E-MAIL: ADMIT@WARREN-WILSON.EDU • WEBSITE: WWW.WARREN-WILSON.EDU

## ADMISSIONS

*Very important factors considered include:* character/personal qualities, essays, interview, secondary school record, standardized test scores, volunteer work, work experience. *Important factors considered include:* class rank, recommendations. *Other factors considered include:* alumni/ae relation, extracurricular activities, state residency, talent/ability. SAT I or ACT required. TOEFL required of all international applicants. High school diploma or GED is required. *High school units required/recommended:* 12 total required; 4 English required, 3 math required, 2 science required, 2 science lab required, 2 foreign language recommended, 3 social science required.

### The Inside Word

Warren Wilson is a college for thinkers with a deep sense of social commitment. The admissions process clearly reflects the committee's desire for solid academic achievement in successful candidates, but they also take a close and careful look at the person being considered. It isn't supercompetitive to get in here, but only candidates who make good matches with the college are offered admission.

## FINANCIAL AID

*Students should submit:* FAFSA, institution's own financial aid form. The Princeton Review suggests that all financial aid forms be submitted as soon as possible after January 1. *Need-based scholarships/grants offered:* Pell, SEOG, state scholarships/grants, private scholarships, the school's own gift aid. *Loan aid offered:* FFEL Subsidized Stafford, FFEL Unsubsidized Stafford, FFEL PLUS, Federal Perkins, college/university loans from institutional funds. Federal Work-Study Program available. Institutional employment available. Applicants will be notified of awards on a rolling basis beginning on or about March 2. Off-campus job opportunities are good.

## FROM THE ADMISSIONS OFFICE

"This book is a 'Guide to the Best 345 Colleges,' but Warren Wilson College may not be the best college for many students. There are 3,500 colleges in the U.S., and there is a best place for everyone. The 'best college' is one that has the right size, location, programs, and above all, the right feel for you, even if it is not listed here. Warren Wilson College may be the best choice if you think and act independently, actively participate in your education, and want a college that provides a sense of community. Your hands will get dirty here, your mind will be stretched, and you'll not be anonymous. If you are looking for the traditional college experience with football and frats, and a campus-on-a-quad, this probably is not the right place. However, if you want to be a part of an academic community that works and serves together, this might be exactly what you are looking for."

### SELECTIVITY

| | |
|---|---|
| Admissions Rating | 79 |
| # of early decision applicants | 58 |
| % accepted early decision | 83 |

#### FRESHMAN PROFILE

| | |
|---|---|
| Range SAT Verbal | 520-670 |
| Average SAT Verbal | 579 |
| Range SAT Math | 490-620 |
| Average SAT Math | 544 |
| Range ACT Composite | 22-28 |
| Average ACT Composite | 24 |
| Minimum TOEFL | 550 |
| Average HS GPA | 3.3 |
| % graduated top 10% of class | 18 |
| % graduated top 25% of class | 42 |
| % graduated top 50% of class | 77 |

#### DEADLINES

| | |
|---|---|
| Early decision | 11/15 |
| Regular admission | 3/15 |
| Nonfall registration? | yes |

#### APPLICANTS ALSO LOOK AT AND OFTEN PREFER
Earlham
**AND SOMETIMES PREFER**
Northland
Evergreen
**AND RARELY PREFER**
ASU
Antioch

### FINANCIAL FACTS

| | |
|---|---|
| Financial Aid Rating | 91 |
| Tuition | $16,674 |
| Room and board | $5,120 |
| Books and supplies | $724 |
| Required fees | $200 |
| % frosh receiving aid | 48 |
| % undergrads receiving aid | 50 |
| Avg frosh loan | $2,325 |

THE BEST 351 COLLEGES ■ 705

# WASHINGTON AND LEE UNIVERSITY

LETCHER AVENUE, LEXINGTON, VA 24450-0303 • ADMISSIONS: 540-463-8710 • FAX: 540-463-8062

## CAMPUS LIFE

| Quality of Life Rating | 92 |
|---|---|
| Type of school | private |
| Environment | suburban |

### STUDENTS

| Total undergrad enrollment | 1,750 |
|---|---|
| % male/female | 53/47 |
| % from out of state | 82 |
| % live on campus | 64 |
| % in (# of) fraternities | 80 (15) |
| % in (# of) sororities | 72 (5) |
| % African American | 4 |
| % Asian | 2 |
| % Caucasian | 92 |
| % Hispanic | 1 |
| % international | 4 |
| # of countries represented | 47 |

### SURVEY SAYS . . .
Frats and sororities dominate social scene
No one cheats
Diversity lacking on campus
Hard liquor is popular
Student publications are popular
Class discussions encouraged

## ACADEMICS

| Academic Rating | 96 |
|---|---|
| Calendar | differs by program |
| Student/faculty ratio | 11:1 |
| Profs interesting rating | 98 |
| Profs accessible rating | 99 |
| % profs teaching UG courses | 100 |
| Avg lab size | under 10 students |
| Avg reg class size | 10-19 students |

### MOST POPULAR MAJORS
Business administration/management
Journalism
Economics

## STUDENTS SPEAK OUT

### Academics

While not the best-known small, traditional, liberal arts school on the East Coast, Washington and Lee may well be the best loved by its students. The school is not for everyone—see *Student Body*, below—but for those who fit the mold, W&L is a "little utopian society" that offers "really small classes" and a "strong sense of community among the students, faculty, and administration." These factors help mitigate the heavy workload here. Writes one student, "Academically, W&L is very challenging, but the small classes and group discussions make it very easy to participate and learn." Students say the faculty is "extremely helpful and always accessible" and appreciate professors who "epitomize southern hospitality. They're amazing!" All classes are taught by full professors; W&L has "no TAs, which is excellent." Undergrads are equally sanguine about the administration, reporting that the "administration and departments bend over backwards to help you out. If you are serious about learning and not just willing but want to work for your education, W&L will present excellent opportunities." The school runs on an unusual academic schedule, featuring two full-length terms (fall and winter) and a mandatory six-week term in the spring, during which students participate in seminars and internships or travel abroad. W&L also has a very popular Honor System that allows students to schedule their own nonproctored exams and leave their dorm rooms unlocked. Take-home, closed-book examinations are not uncommon, and "the buildings are open 24/7" as well. Brags one student, "The Honor System dominates life on campus and is a large part of what makes this university so special."

### Life

Students at W&L really, really want you to know how much they drink. More than a few, in fact, are deeply offended that they dropped in this publication's "Drinking School" ranking last year. We'll let the students set the record straight. Writes one, "W&L allows students to pursue a wide range of academics while maintaining a strong sense of drunkenness." Adds another, "W&L is Utopia, with frat parties and kegs added." Indeed, the W&L social universe revolves around the Greek scene. Comments one student, "We have the greatest fraternity scene in the country. Period. If you like bourbon and Coke or beer flowing like water, there is no place to go but here." Agrees another, "We like to get our drink on." Because "fraternity parties are open to everyone, except for special functions," W&L suffers less from Greek/independent antagonism than do many other Greek-dominated campuses. During nondrinking hours, "club and intramural sports are popular. The opportunities for satisfying extracurricular activities are excellent." Students also love to "go tubing in the river, play Frisbee in the quad, dance all night long," hang out in their "palatial dorms," or walk across their postcard-perfect, ivy-covered campus. But when it comes right down to it, "basically, students study their asses off during the week, then party their asses off on the weekend. 'Work hard, drink hard' is our motto."

### Student Body

"W&L is often described as having a student body like a country club: white, well-off, Republican," explains one student. "Many students here come from families of wealth. My little Neon is parked next to a Lexus, a Saab, and a brand-new SUV—in the freshman lot!" Students concur that the "conservative, clean-cut, red-blooded American boys and girls" who attend W&L are "fun-loving, ambitious, and elitist." Writes one African American undergrad, "You can tell some of them have never even been around minority students before." Those who fit in agree that "never before have I met friendlier people. A lot of our students [approximately 10 percent] are from Texas, so friendliness is an inherent trait." Those who don't fit in either transfer out or endure a long four years.

# WASHINGTON AND LEE UNIVERSITY

FINANCIAL AID: 540-463-8715 • E-MAIL: ADMISSIONS@WLU.EDU • WEBSITE: WWW.WLU.EDU

## ADMISSIONS

*Very important factors considered include:* character/personal qualities, extracurricular activities, secondary school record, standardized test scores. *Important factors considered include:* class rank, recommendations. *Other factors considered include:* alumni/ae relation, essays, geographical residence, minority status, state residency, talent/ability, volunteer work, work experience. SAT I or ACT required; SAT II also required. High school diploma is required and GED is not accepted. *High school units required/recommended:* 16 total required; 4 English required, 3 math required, 4 math recommended, 1 science required, 3 science recommended, 1 science lab required, 2 foreign language required, 3 foreign language recommended, 1 social studies required, 1 history required, 2 history recommended, 4 elective required.

### *The Inside Word*

If you're looking for a bastion of southern tradition, Washington and Lee is one of the foremost. Its admissions process is appropriately traditional, and highly selective. Under these circumstances, it is always best to take a cautious and conservative approach to preparing your candidacy. Smart applicants have taken the toughest courses available to them in high school—the minimum requirements aren't likely to help you gain admission. Neither will a glib approach to the personal side of the application; a well-written essay is what they're after.

## FINANCIAL AID

*Students should submit:* FAFSA, CSS/Financial Aid PROFILE, noncustodial (divorced/separated) parent's statement, business/farm supplement. The Princeton Review suggests that all financial aid forms be submitted as soon as possible after January 1. *Need-based scholarships/grants offered:* Pell, SEOG, state scholarships/grants, private scholarships, the school's own gift aid. *Loan aid offered:* FFEL Subsidized Stafford, FFEL Unsubsidized Stafford, FFEL PLUS, Federal Perkins, college/university loans from institutional funds. Federal Work-Study Program available. Institutional employment available. Applicants will be notified of awards on or about April 3. Off-campus job opportunities are fair.

## FROM THE ADMISSIONS OFFICE

"W&L, the nation's ninth oldest college, is a small, private, liberal arts school located in the heart of the beautiful Shenandoah Valley. As one might expect, W&L possesses an inordinate amount of history. Quality teaching both in and out of the classroom, and the development of students into well-rounded leaders, summarize the school's primary goals. An average W&L class contains 15 students, and courses are taught by the school's full-time faculty members; no graduate students or teacher assistants are on the faculty. W&L possesses a uniquely broad and deep curriculum, as well as a time-honored, student-run Honor System that allows students a wide range of freedoms. W&L is a highly competitive school, where students will receive a first-rate, personalized education, develop leadership skills, enjoy life outside of the classroom, and reap the innumerable postgraduation benefits of a W&L education."

## SELECTIVITY
★ ★ ★ ★

| | |
|---|---|
| Admissions Rating | 99 |
| # of applicants | 3,188 |
| % of applicants accepted | 31 |
| % of acceptees attending | 46 |
| # accepting a place on wait list | 268 |
| % admitted from wait list | 13 |
| # of early decision applicants | 402 |
| % accepted early decision | 55 |

### FRESHMAN PROFILE
| | |
|---|---|
| Range SAT Verbal | 640-720 |
| Range SAT Math | 640-720 |
| Range ACT Composite | 28-30 |
| Average HS GPA | 4.0 |
| % graduated top 10% of class | 80 |
| % graduated top 25% of class | 96 |
| % graduated top 50% of class | 100 |

### DEADLINES
| | |
|---|---|
| Early decision | 12/1 |
| Early decision notification | 12/22 |
| Regular admission | 1/15 |
| Regular notification | 4/1 |

### APPLICANTS ALSO LOOK AT
**AND OFTEN PREFER**
U of Virginia
Duke
**AND SOMETIMES PREFER**
Davidson
William and Mary
UNC Chapel Hill
Georgetown
**AND RARELY PREFER**
Rhodes
Vanderbilt
Wake Forest
U of Richmond
U of Georgia

## FINANCIAL FACTS

| | |
|---|---|
| Financial Aid Rating | 86 |
| Tuition | $22,900 |
| Room and board | $6,205 |
| Books and supplies | $1,480 |
| Required fees | $195 |
| % frosh receiving aid | 26 |
| % undergrads receiving aid | 27 |

# WASHINGTON STATE UNIVERSITY

370 LIGHTY STUDENT SERVICES BUILDING, PULLMAN, WA 99164 • ADMISSIONS: 509-335-5586 • FAX: 509-335-4902

## CAMPUS LIFE

★ ★ ☆ ☆

| | |
|---|---|
| Quality of Life Rating | 76 |
| Type of school | public |
| Environment | rural |

### STUDENTS

| | |
|---|---|
| Total undergrad enrollment | 18,024 |
| % male/female | 47/53 |
| % from out of state | 13 |
| % from public high school | 96 |
| % live on campus | 34 |
| % in (# of) fraternities | 13 (24) |
| % in (# of) sororities | 13 (15) |
| % African American | 3 |
| % Asian | 5 |
| % Caucasian | 76 |
| % Hispanic | 3 |
| % international | 4 |
| # of countries represented | 102 |

### SURVEY SAYS . . .
Frats and sororities dominate social scene
Everyone loves the Cougars
(Almost) everyone plays intramural sports
Hard liquor is popular
Registration is a breeze
Large intro classes
Theater is unpopular
Dorms are like dungeons
Student publications are popular

## ACADEMICS

★ ☆ ☆ ☆

| | |
|---|---|
| Academic Rating | 69 |
| Calendar | semester |
| Student/faculty ratio | 17:1 |
| Profs interesting rating | 77 |
| Profs accessible rating | 71 |
| Avg reg class size | 10-19 students |

## STUDENTS SPEAK OUT

### Academics
Washington State University is a large state school that offers a wide range of majors and many research opportunities. Professors at the vaunted Edward R. Murrow School of Communication are "very good" and "in touch with their students." A senior communication major writes, "WSU's professors are highly accessible and have a desire to help the students live up to their potential." A psychology major adds, "Overall, my experience has been amazing." Students "leave Washington State prepared for the real world." A "second-to-none" Honors Program also receives rave reviews. "Seriously," counsels a first-year student, "take honors courses over general education if and whenever possible." The school of veterinary medicine also earns high praise. While students adore many of their professors, teaching assistants don't fare so well, as many "do not speak English very well." One senior accounting major muses, "Part of being a teacher is being able to communicate effectively." Advisors are not held in high regard either at WSU. A junior says, "Advisors need to know what they're telling students to take." Relations between students and administrators responsible for student affairs have gone under a complete rehabilitation; the initial reports are very good. In addition, the computer labs, library, and new bookstore receive kudos.

### Life
Pullman is a "small town," approximately 300 miles from Seattle. For students who expect urban entertainment, the location "means there is not a whole lot to do." But for those who enjoy the outdoors, there are "more opportunities than time," including "excellent intramurals and club sports" (such as snowboarding and lacrosse) and "great" athletic facilities. The plush new Student Recreation Center boasts state-of-the-art equipment and the nation's largest free weight and cardio fitness training area. As a Pac-10 school, sports have a major presence on campus. In 2002–2003, the Cougars played a spectacular 10-2 season in football, catapulting the team to the Rose Bowl. When it comes to recreation, one student explains, "The bars or sporting events are good options. A good day is when you can combine both." While some students pout that "there is nothing [to do] but school because of [WSU's] location," an upbeat junior advertising major points out "fun is all around you. Just open your eyes and you'll find something exciting to do." Greek life is a popular diversion, and "after you turn 21, going to the bars is a big part of social life."

### Student Body
WSU students are extremely friendly. A senior writes that "her favorite thing about Pullman is the people. If you are walking down the street and you go past a total stranger, they always say hello." An advertising major adds, "I love the students here. It's a lovely place to hang your hat." Students celebrate the campus' diversity, and add with a smirk that Washington State has a "great group of people to spend four, five, or six years with." A senior advertising major complains that "the Greek system is emphasized too much," while a journalism major adds that there is "a little tension between the Greek and individual, non-Greek houses." As for the Greeks themselves, "the fraternity members at WSU are half real good guys and the other half are the worst people" one will meet. Still, most students get along and "are great, down to earth, blossoming adults."

708 ■ THE BEST 351 COLLEGES

# WASHINGTON STATE UNIVERSITY

FINANCIAL AID: 509-335-9711 • E-MAIL: ADMISS2@WSU.EDU • WEBSITE: WWW.WSU.EDU

## ADMISSIONS
*Very important factors considered include:* secondary school record, standardized test scores. *Other factors considered include:* essays, extracurricular activities, recommendations, talent/ability. SAT I or ACT required. TOEFL required of all international applicants. High school diploma or GED is required. *High school units required/recommended:* 15 total required; 4 English required, 3 math required, 2 science required (1 science lab), 2 foreign language required, 2 social studies required, 1 history required, 1 elective required.

## The Inside Word
It's a large public-U, formula-driven admission at Washington State. Admission is based on the Admissions Index Number (AIN), a weighted combination of high school GPA (75 percent) and standardized test scores (25 percent). The average AIN for admitted students is 57. Check out the AIN calculator on the University website to estimate your admissibility. An appropriate college-prep high school course selection is required ("core requirements" for students in the state of Washington).

## FINANCIAL AID
*Students should submit:* FAFSA. No deadline for regular filing. The Princeton Review suggests that all financial aid forms be submitted as soon as possible after January 1. *Need-based scholarships/grants offered:* Pell, SEOG, state scholarships/grants, private scholarships, the school's own gift aid. *Loan aid offered:* FFEL Subsidized Stafford, FFEL Unsubsidized Stafford, FFEL PLUS, Federal Perkins, Federal Nursing, alternative loans. Federal Work-Study Program available. Institutional employment available. Applicants will be notified of awards on a rolling basis beginning on or about April 15. Off-campus job opportunities are good.

## FROM THE ADMISSIONS OFFICE
"At Washington State University, you can work side by side with nationally renowned faculty who will help you succeed. Many of the University's academic programs are ranked among the best in the nation. Programs are designed to give you real-world experience through internships, fieldwork, community service, and in-depth labs. You can take part in faculty research, or even conduct your own. Washington State University graduates are considered the best prepared in the state in many fields and are actively recruited by Fortune 500 employers.

"The campus forms the heart of a warm, supportive college town—a community of faculty and friends who can help you achieve your greatest potential. You'll have opportunities to build your leadership skills by getting involved in any of a wide selection of campus organizations. If you have top grades and a passion for learning, apply to the highly acclaimed Honors College. It will challenge you with interdisciplinary studies, rich discussions, and opportunities to study abroad. The priority deadline to apply for admission to Washington State University is March 1.

"In addition to the Pullman campus, WSU has three urban campuses in Spokane, the TriCities (Richland), and Vancouver, plus award-winning Distance Degree Programs."

---

### SELECTIVITY

| | |
|---|---|
| Admissions Rating | 75 |
| # of applicants | 8,986 |
| % of applicants accepted | 77 |
| % of acceptees attending | 41 |

### FRESHMAN PROFILE
| | |
|---|---|
| Range SAT Verbal | 470-580 |
| Average SAT Verbal | 522 |
| Range SAT Math | 480-590 |
| Average SAT Math | 533 |
| Minimum TOEFL | 520 |
| Average HS GPA | 3.4 |

### DEADLINES
| | |
|---|---|
| Priority admission | 3/1 |
| Nonfall registration? | yes |

### FINANCIAL FACTS

| | |
|---|---|
| Financial Aid Rating | 81 |
| In-state tuition | $4,926 |
| Out-of-state tuition | $12,760 |
| Room and board | $6,196 |
| % frosh receiving aid | 42 |
| % undergrads receiving aid | 45 |
| Avg frosh grant | $5,306 |
| Avg frosh loan | $8,533 |

# WASHINGTON UNIVERSITY IN ST. LOUIS

CAMPUS BOX 1089, ONE BROOKINGS DRIVE, ST. LOUIS, MO 63130-4899 • ADMISSIONS: 800-638-0700 • FAX: 314-935-4290

## CAMPUS LIFE

| | |
|---|---|
| Quality of Life Rating | 82 |
| Type of school | private |
| Environment | suburban |

### STUDENTS

| | |
|---|---|
| Total undergrad enrollment | 7,219 |
| % male/female | 47/53 |
| % from out of state | 89 |
| % from public high school | 62 |
| % live on campus | 80 |
| % in (# of) fraternities | 27 (11) |
| % in (# of) sororities | 21 (5) |
| % African American | 8 |
| % Asian | 10 |
| % Caucasian | 66 |
| % Hispanic | 3 |
| % international | 4 |
| # of countries represented | 104 |

### SURVEY SAYS . . .
Students love St. Louis, MO
Registration is a breeze
School is well run
Great on-campus food
Lab facilities need improving
Intercollegiate sports unpopular or nonexistent
Large classes
Ethnic diversity on campus
Students get along with local community

## ACADEMICS

| | |
|---|---|
| Academic Rating | 92 |
| Calendar | semester |
| Student/faculty ratio | 7:1 |
| Profs interesting rating | 91 |
| Profs accessible rating | 92 |
| % profs teaching UG courses | 90 |
| Avg lab size | 10-19 students |
| Avg reg class size | 10-19 students |

### MOST POPULAR MAJORS
Psychology
Biology/biological sciences
Finance

## STUDENTS SPEAK OUT
### Academics
Washington University is widely recognized as one of the top institutions in the country. Most students believe that this reputation is apt. One feature of Wash U is the amount of money that it has available for research and other ventures: "The resources here are endless and the university offers the support to back them." But there's also a downfall to studying at such a "large research institution," a number of professors "are preoccupied with becoming stars in their fields" and consequently devote minimal time to students. But this isn't the norm. Of professors, students write, "They will come in on a Sunday evening before an exam to hold a help session, stay up all night correcting tests, and regularly invite students over to their houses for dinner." The chancellor even "has a bowling alley in his basement, and invites students there sometimes." Because many of the professors are leaders in their fields, they hold high expectations for their students. "The school is really really really tough," reports an undergraduate. "You must work very hard and put a lot of time into what you are doing," writes another. While departments in the pre-medical sciences are particularly popular (more than 1 in every 10 Wash U grads goes directly to medical school), students tell us that every department has its notable strengths.

### Life
There's a motto religiously intoned at Wash U: "Study hard first, then play hard." "I definitely study my butt off during the week," one typical student tells us. But when weekends come around—or free time in general—students at Wash U roll up their sleeves and roll out the party carpet. This work hard/party hard mentality has given rise to the common perception that Wash U undergrads are "the dorkiest students in the world getting [expletive] all the time. Amen. Responsibly of course, Mom." Because the university lies on the skirts of St. Louis, it's not quite urban and not quite suburban—a sort of "in-the-middle" location that makes the school feel like "a self-sufficient bubble." Wash U undergrads get particularly excited "every semester" for the "big party called WILD." WILD "starts at noon on Friday [in the Quad] . . . and they have inflatable games, free food, and music until about 5 P.M. Then bands start playing on stage and at 8 some fairly well-known band will come on. Any student group can register a keg . . . so EVERYONE has a keg (or two or three) . . . and the whole campus is plastered by 6 P.M." Drinking isn't the only activity on campus, though. You'll also find "cafés, sports, religious/political group activities, community service, school-sponsored raves, formal dances, costume parties," and access to about 200 student organizations. When students break out of the Wash U bubble, they often head to "The Loop, which is basically a multi-block collection of restaurants, theatres, etc." Because of the campus' location, students advise that "having a car will increase your quality of life immeasurably."

### Student Body
Washington University students consider themselves Ivy League students without the Ivy League tags. Accordingly, students tell us that their classmates are "all very smart." One student amends this description slightly, writing that they're all "really smart people who like to party." Because of the university's gleaming reputation, it attracts students from "all over." In fact, only about 10 percent come from Missouri, and 55 percent hail from at least 500 miles away. "You have people from all views and walks of life," summarizes one student, "NRA members from the Midwest and rich Jewish girls from Long Island and gay male activists." Most of the causes touted at Wash U are liberal ones, leading a freshman to comment that "conservatives are a distinct minority on this campus." And living in St. Louis is no matter to be taken lightly. One East Coast student declares, "I have to admit that living in the Midwest has almost made me a nicer person."

# WASHINGTON UNIVERSITY IN ST. LOUIS

FINANCIAL AID: 314-935-5900 • E-MAIL: ADMISSIONS@WUSTL.EDU • WEBSITE: ADMISSIONS.WUSTL.EDU

## ADMISSIONS

*Very important factors considered include:* character/personal qualities, class rank, essays, extracurricular activities, recommendations, religious affiliation/commitment, secondary school record, standardized test scores, talent/ability, volunteer work, work experience. *Other factors considered include:* alumni/ae relation, interview, minority status. SAT I or ACT required. TOEFL required of all international applicants. *High school units required/recommended:* 18 total recommended; 4 English recommended, 4 math recommended, 4 science recommended, 4 science lab recommended, 2 foreign language recommended, 4 social studies recommended, 4 history recommended.

### The Inside Word

The fact that Washington U. doesn't have much play as a nationally respected car-window decal is about all that prevents it from being among the most selective universities. In every other respect—that is, in any way which really matters—this place is hard to beat and easily ranks as one of the best. No other university with as impressive a record of excellence across the board has a more accommodating admissions process. Not that it's easy to get in here, but lack of instant name recognition does affect Washington's admission rate. Students with above-average academic records who are not quite Ivy material are the big winners. Marginal candidates with high financial need may find difficulty; the admissions process at Washington U. is not need-blind and may take into account candidates' ability to pay if they are not strong applicants.

## FINANCIAL AID

*Students should submit:* FAFSA, CSS/Financial Aid PROFILE, noncustodial (divorced/separated) parent's statement, student's and parent's 1040 tax returns or signed waiver if there are no tax returns. Regular filing deadline is February 15. The Princeton Review suggests that all financial aid forms be submitted as soon as possible after January 1. *Need-based scholarships/grants offered:* Pell, SEOG, state scholarships/grants, private scholarships, the school's own gift aid, United Negro College Fund. *Loan aid offered:* FFEL Subsidized Stafford, FFEL Unsubsidized Stafford, FFEL PLUS, Federal Perkins, state loans, college/university loans from institutional funds. Federal Work-Study Program available. Institutional employment available. Applicants will be notified of awards on or about April 1. Off-campus job opportunities are excellent.

## FROM THE ADMISSIONS OFFICE

"Washington University students learn in a flexible academic atmosphere that encourages them to cross disciplines, taking courses in any of our five undergraduate divisions: arts & sciences, architecture, art, business, and engineering. We also offer graduate programs in these divisions as well as law; medicine, including occupational therapy and physical therapy; and social work. This interdisciplinary environment allows students to study alongside other academically talented students from across the country and around the world in any subject that interests them. Through research projects that start as early as the freshman year, students can participate with our world-class faculty in the creation of knowledge. This academic exploration takes place in a supportive, friendly community that provides the resources to ensure success. Outside the classroom, students participate in nearly 200 activities, including community service and multicultural groups; musical, dance, and theater groups; fraternities and sororities; intramural sports; student government; and literary groups. We invite you to visit Washington University any time to experience these outstanding opportunities firsthand."

---

### SELECTIVITY

| | |
|---|---|
| Admissions Rating | 97 |
| # of applicants | 19,514 |
| % of applicants accepted | 24 |
| % of acceptees attending | 29 |

#### FRESHMAN PROFILE

| | |
|---|---|
| Range SAT Verbal | 640-730 |
| Range SAT Math | 670-750 |
| Range ACT Composite | 28-32 |
| Minimum TOEFL | 550 |

#### DEADLINES

| | |
|---|---|
| Early decision | 11/15 |
| Early decision notification | 12/15 |
| Regular admission | 1/15 |
| Regular notification | 4/1 |

#### APPLICANTS ALSO LOOK AT AND OFTEN PREFER
Princeton University
Yale University
Stanford University
Harvard College
U Penn

#### AND SOMETIMES PREFER
Cornell University
Duke University
University of Chicago
Northwestern University

#### AND RARELY PREFER
University of Michigan
Emory University
Tulane University
Boston U

### FINANCIAL FACTS

| | |
|---|---|
| Financial Aid Rating | 79 |
| Tuition | $28,300 |
| Room and board | $9,240 |
| Books and supplies | $960 |
| Required fees | $753 |
| % frosh receiving aid | 41 |
| % undergrads receiving aid | 45 |

# WEBB INSTITUTE

298 CRESCENT BEACH ROAD, OCEAN COVE, NY 11542 • ADMISSIONS: 516-674-9838

## CAMPUS LIFE

| | |
|---|---|
| **Quality of Life Rating** | **91** |
| Type of school | private |
| Environment | suburban |

### STUDENTS
| | |
|---|---|
| Total undergrad enrollment | 67 |
| % from out of state | 78 |
| % from public high school | 88 |
| % live on campus | 100 |
| % African American | 1 |
| % Asian | 3 |
| % Caucasian | 96 |

### SURVEY SAYS . . .
Great computer facilities
Great on-campus food
Lab facilities are great
Lots of conservatives on campus
Campus feels safe
Diversity lacking on campus

## ACADEMICS

| | |
|---|---|
| **Academic Rating** | **98** |
| Calendar | semester |
| Student/faculty ratio | 6:1 |
| Profs interesting rating | 92 |
| Profs accessible rating | 94 |
| % profs teaching UG courses | 100 |
| Avg reg class size | 10-19 students |

## STUDENTS SPEAK OUT

### Academics

One thing Webb students needn't worry about is a tuition bill. That's right—the Webb Institute costs "nothing except room and board." While there are only 11 full-time professors at Webb, this number is sufficient to guarantee the 73 students "a great deal of personal attention." And because Webb is such a small school, much of the red tape that crisscrosses most campuses can be avoided. "Since Webb's only major is naval architecture and marine engineering, there is no registration for courses. Everyone takes the same courses, save a few electives each year." With such a specialized educational lens, "Webb is definitely the place to get a degree . . . if you're interested in ship design." One of the unique features of the Webb curriculum is the network of "worldwide internships" that students are required to serve in during the winter, "for two months every year of the four." Students unanimously agree that these hands-on opportunities are at the core of their academic experiences. "We are taught the theory behind the engineering, but it doesn't end there," explains an undergrad. "We are also taught how to apply the theory to real-world problems." An "Honor Code" that is "adhered to by every student" does a good job at structuring the education, and an emphasis on teamwork and interaction ensures that "there is a spirit of cooperation rather than competition."

### Life

All students here have a similar schedule that includes "class from 9 A.M. to 3 P.M. and dinner at 5:30 P.M." And then there are the stacks of homework assignments. To a large extent, the massive amount of "work almost destroys any social life outside of school." When students do find some spare time, they'll go to the campus pub to grab a beer. They'll do some exercising, as well. "Over half the school plays sports, no one is cut from the teams, and everyone gets playing time." For the less competitive athletes, Webb offers "intramural sports almost year round, from basketball to floor hockey, from folf (Frisbee golf) to ultimate Frisbee, and everything in between." The institute provides rent-free boats and a private beach for its students. It also provides tuition-wavers for every student who gets accepted to the school, which allows students to spend late nights talking about things other than how they're planning to pay back college loans. "Speaking for the male population," comments a student, "we spend hours scheming as to how to lure more girls to our school." Some students, however, say to hell with trying to find mates and parties on campus. Day trips to places like nearby New York City provide outlets. "Cutting loose in the city is fantastic after having worked like a dog for five whole days."

### Student Body

"Since Webb is a very small school, it is imperative that the students get along with each other and are able to work well together." And by and large they do. Many of the students at the Webb Institute will agree that they seem "more like an extended family than a student body." Because they "all live in the same damned building" ("a mansion!") during their four years at Webb, the students "become very close," whether or not they want to be. And there's a common interest that binds these students: naval engineering. Typical "Webbies," as they're known, are "Caucasian guys from middle- to upper-class families" and self-declared "nerds." In other words, "there is no—repeat NO—diversity at this school. No gays. No minorities." And as one male student pleads, "Girls . . . we need more girls." But the females who do come are able to fit in well, and they often form tight friendships with each other. A first-year female reports that "all six of the freshman girls bonded within 15 minutes after our parents left orientation." Men and women alike have thick skin and appetites for hard work.

# WEBB INSTITUTE

FINANCIAL AID: 516-671-2213 • E-MAIL: ADMISSIONS@WEBB-INSTITUTE.EDU • WEBSITE: WWW.WEBB-INSTITUTE.EDU

## ADMISSIONS

*Very important factors considered include:* class rank, interview, secondary school record, standardized test scores. *Important factors considered include:* character/personal qualities, recommendations, talent/ability. *Other factors considered include:* extracurricular activities, minority status, volunteer work, work experience. SAT I or ACT required; SAT I preferred; SAT II also required. High school diploma is required and GED is not accepted. *High school units required/recommended:* 16 total required; 4 English required, 4 math required, 2 science required, 2 science lab required, 2 social studies required, 4 elective required.

### The Inside Word

Let's not mince words; admission to Webb is mega-tough. Webb's admissions counselors are out to find the right kid for their curriculum—one that can survive the school's rigorous academics. The applicant pool is highly self-selected because of the focused program of study: Naval Architecture and Marine Engineering.

## FINANCIAL AID

*Students should submit:* FAFSA. Regular filing deadline is July 1. The Princeton Review suggests that all financial aid forms be submitted as soon as possible after January 1. *Need-based scholarships/grants offered:* Pell, state scholarships/grants, private scholarships. *Loan aid offered:* FFEL Subsidized Stafford, FFEL Unsubsidized Stafford, FFEL PLUS. Applicants will be notified of awards on or about August 1. Off-campus job opportunities are good.

## FROM THE ADMISSIONS OFFICE

"Webb, the only college in the country that specializes in the engineering field of Naval Architecture and Marine Engineering, seeks young men and women of all races from all over the country who are interested in receiving an excellent engineering education with a full-tuition scholarship. Students don't have to know anything about ships, they just have to be motivated to study how mechanical, civil, structural, and electrical engineering come together with the design elements that make up a ship and all its systems. Being small and private has its major advantages. Every applicant is special and the President will interview all entering students personally. The student/faculty ratio is 6:1, and since there are no teaching assistants, interaction with the faculty occurs daily in class and labs at a level not found at most other colleges. The college provides each student with a high-end laptop computer they get to keep. The entire campus operates under the Student Organization's Honor System that allows unsupervised exams and 24-hour access to the library, every classroom and laboratory, and the shop and gymnasium. Despite a total enrollment of between 70 and 80 students and a demanding workload, Webb manages to field six intercollegiate teams. Currently more than 60 percent of the members of the student body play on one or more intercollegiate teams. Work hard, play hard and the payoff is a job for every student upon graduation. The placement record of the college is 100 percent every year."

## ADMISSIONS

| | |
|---|---|
| Admissions Rating | 96 |
| # of applicants | 85 |
| % of applicants accepted | 41 |
| % of acceptees attending | 50 |
| # of early decision applicants | 10 |
| % accepted early decision | 70 |

### FRESHMAN PROFILE

| | |
|---|---|
| Range SAT Verbal | 620-710 |
| Average SAT Verbal | 670 |
| Range SAT Math | 700-740 |
| Average SAT Math | 720 |
| Average HS GPA | 3.9 |
| % graduated top 10% of class | 83 |
| % graduated top 25% of class | 100 |

### DEADLINES

| | |
|---|---|
| Early decision | 10/15 |
| Early decision notification | 12/15 |
| Priority admission | 10/15 |
| Regular admission | 2/15 |

### APPLICANTS ALSO LOOK AT AND OFTEN PREFER
Naval Academy
Coast Guard Academy
### AND SOMETIMES PREFER
Virginia Tech
Cooper Union
### AND RARELY PREFER
SUNY Maritime
U of Michigan

## FINANCIAL FACTS

| | |
|---|---|
| Financial Aid Rating | 99 |
| Room and board | $6,950 |
| Books and supplies | $600 |
| % frosh receiving aid | 53 |
| % undergrads receiving aid | 28 |
| Avg frosh grant | $2,750 |
| Avg frosh loan | $2,625 |

# WELLESLEY COLLEGE

BOARD OF ADMISSION, 106 CENTRAL STREET, WELLESLEY, MA 02481-8203 • ADMISSIONS: 781-283-2270 • FAX: 781-283-3678

## CAMPUS LIFE

| | |
|---|---|
| Quality of Life Rating | 85 |
| Type of school | private |
| Environment | suburban |

### STUDENTS

| | |
|---|---|
| Total undergrad enrollment | 2,300 |
| % from out of state | 84 |
| % from public high school | 65 |
| % live on campus | 94 |
| % African American | 6 |
| % Asian | 26 |
| % Caucasian | 48 |
| % Hispanic | 5 |
| % international | 7 |

### SURVEY SAYS . . .
No one cheats
Beautiful campus
Dorms are like palaces
Student government is popular
Political activism is hot
Very little beer drinking
Very little hard liquor
(Almost) no one smokes
No one plays intramural sports

## ACADEMICS

| | |
|---|---|
| Academic Rating | 98 |
| Calendar | semester |
| Student/faculty ratio | 9:1 |
| Profs interesting rating | 96 |
| Profs accessible rating | 99 |
| % profs teaching UG courses | 100 |
| Avg lab size | 10-19 students |
| Avg reg class size | 10-19 students |

### MOST POPULAR MAJORS
English language and literature
Psychology
Economics

## STUDENTS SPEAK OUT

### Academics

Wellesley, an all-women's undergraduate institution near Boston, is not just a college; it is also, according to one typical enthusiast, "a community dedicated to developing women of superior intellect, life skills, and savvy. It's simply the best. Wellesley has shown me that it is okay to be a fabulous woman with so much to offer." Most students here simply can't decide what they like most about the school. It could be that classes "are small and well taught. There's good atmosphere for discussion in and out of the classroom." Or, it might be that students have "access to some of the best lecturers and facilities in the world. World-renowned experts give presentations here." Most likely, though, it's the professors. They "are Wellesley's gold. They give individual attention and that's why I'm here," writes one student. Another explains, "The professors are very knowledgeable but also very approachable. It's obvious they love teaching." Faculty and students "are very fond of each other—but not in a way that could get anyone fired." Students probably are less enthusiastic about the brutal workload the school demands, although most accept it as an essential part of the Wellesley experience. "It'll be the hardest four years of your life, but also the most rewarding," sums up one student.

### Life

Despite the rigorous academic requirements of a Wellesley education, most students try to build an active extracurricular life around their studies, a situation that helps to explain the "popular bumper sticker: 'Wellesley—We'll Sleep When We're Dead.' " Writes one student, "Everyone is always busy. Over-programming for activities can be a problem." Many students become involved in some of the "many student organizations, such as Pre-Law Society and Russian Club. There are also many opportunities to volunteer in this area and the greater Boston region." While there are "student groups doing things, as far [as] parties on campus, sporting events, heavy drinking, etc., it's not here. There is no 'college life' per se. If you want fun, you have to go off campus." Explains one student, "People work hard during the week. On weekends, about one-third of the students get dressed up in tube tops and black pants, hop on the Senate Bus, and go to frat parties; one-third watch movies and do laundry or other on-campus events; and the other one-third study all weekend." Hometown Wellesley, Massachusetts, "is a little too upscale—lots of art dealers and people pushing baby strollers past Ann Taylor. But very safe." Writes one student, "Wellesley is not the best town to go out and have a good time. For fun we usually go to Boston," only 30 minutes away by car or bus. For those who simply choose to stay home, "the campus is beautiful and the dorms are fabulous."

### Student Body

Wellesley's "extremely motivated, dedicated, and ambitious" students are "very intelligent. I have great conversations with everyone. I feel so privileged to be around people who have done fantastic things and will have a major impact on the future." Undergrads enjoy a "very strong sense of community" and the fact that there is "no competition here. Eveyone is competing with themselves." Students "are extremely politically conscious. There is a strong tradition of activism and social efficacy," but they are "sometimes too dogmatic. I get tired of the sidewalk telling me what to do and think." Writes one student, "They don't smile enough. People are so stressed that they (myself included) forget to relax and have fun." As for the "typical" Wellesley woman, "everyone jokes about 'Wendy Wellesley,' but in truth there are a dozen different kinds of typical Wellesley students." Concludes one student, "At an all-women's college, people learn to be themselves, whoever that might be. From Wendy Wellesley, Frat Ho, to Wendy Wellesley, Raging Dyke, we're defining who we are daily, and that is awesome!"

# WELLESLEY COLLEGE

FINANCIAL AID: 781-283-2360 • E-MAIL: ADMISSION@WELLESLEY.EDU • WEBSITE: WWW.WELLESLEY.EDU

## ADMISSIONS

*Very important factors considered include:* essays, recommendations, secondary school record, standardized test scores. *Important factors considered include:* character/personal qualities, class rank, extracurricular activities. *Other factors considered include:* alumni/ae relation, geographical residence, interview, minority status, state residency, talent/ability, volunteer work, work experience. TOEFL required of all international applicants. *High school units required/recommended:* 4 English recommended, 4 math recommended, 3 science recommended, 2 science lab recommended, 4 foreign language recommended, 4 social studies recommended, 4 history recommended.

### The Inside Word

While the majority of women's colleges have gone coed or even closed over the past two decades, Wellesley has continued with vigor. As a surviving member of the Seven Sisters, the nation's most prestigious women's colleges, Wellesley enjoys even more popularity with students who choose the single-sex option. Admissions standards are rigorous, but among institutions of such high reputation Wellesley's admissions staff is friendlier and more open than the majority. Their willingness to conduct preliminary evaluations for candidates is especially commendable and in some form or another should be the rule rather than an exception at highly selective colleges.

## FINANCIAL AID

*Students should submit:* FAFSA, institution's own financial aid form, CSS/Financial Aid PROFILE, noncustodial (divorced/separated) parent's statement, business/farm supplement, parent's and student's tax returns and W-2s. The Princeton Review suggests that all financial aid forms be submitted as soon as possible after January 1. *Need-based scholarships/grants offered:* Pell, SEOG, state scholarships/grants, private scholarships, the school's own gift aid. *Loan aid offered:* FFEL Subsidized Stafford, FFEL Unsubsidized Stafford, FFEL PLUS, Federal Perkins, state loans, college/university loans from institutional funds. Federal Work-Study Program available. Institutional employment available. Applicants will be notified of awards on or about April 1. Off-campus job opportunities are excellent.

## FROM THE ADMISSIONS OFFICE

"A student's years at Wellesley are the beginning—not the end—of an education. A Wellesley College degree signifies not that the graduate has memorized certain blocks of material, but that she has acquired the curiosity, the desire, and the ability to seek and assimilate new information. Four years at Wellesley can provide the foundation for the widest possible range of ambitions and the necessary self-confidence to fulfill them. At Wellesley, a student has every educational opportunity. Above all, it is Wellesley's purpose to teach students to apply knowledge wisely and to use the advantages of talent and education to seek new ways to serve the wider community."

## SELECTIVITY

| | |
|---|---|
| Admissions Rating | 98 |
| # of applicants | 2,877 |
| % of applicants accepted | 47 |
| % of acceptees attending | 44 |
| # accepting a place on wait list | 287 |
| % admitted from wait list | 18 |
| # of early decision applicants | 154 |
| % accepted early decision | 62 |

### FRESHMAN PROFILE

| | |
|---|---|
| Range SAT Verbal | 620-720 |
| Average SAT Verbal | 671 |
| Range SAT Math | 630-720 |
| Average SAT Math | 671 |
| Range ACT Composite | 27-31 |
| Average ACT Composite | 29 |
| Minimum TOEFL | 600 |
| % graduated top 10% of class | 59 |
| % graduated top 25% of class | 92 |
| % graduated top 50% of class | 100 |

### DEADLINES

| | |
|---|---|
| Early decision | 11/1 |
| Early decision notification | 12/15 |
| Regular admission | 1/15 |
| Regular notification | 4/1 |

### APPLICANTS ALSO LOOK AT
**AND OFTEN PREFER**
Brown
Stanford
**AND SOMETIMES PREFER**
Georgetown
UC Berkeley
Dartmouth
Cornell
**AND RARELY PREFER**
U of Chicago
Mount Holyoke

## FINANCIAL FACTS

| | |
|---|---|
| Financial Aid Rating | 80 |
| Tuition | $26,138 |
| Room and board | $8,242 |
| Books and supplies | $800 |
| Required fees | $564 |
| % frosh receiving aid | 56 |
| % undergrads receiving aid | 56 |
| Avg frosh grant | $21,701 |
| Avg frosh loan | $2,360 |

# WELLS COLLEGE

ROUTE 90, AURORA, NY 13026 • ADMISSIONS: 315-364-3264 • FAX: 315-364-3327

## CAMPUS LIFE

| Quality of Life Rating | 85 |
|---|---|
| Type of school | private |
| Environment | rural |

### STUDENTS
| | |
|---|---|
| Total undergrad enrollment | 437 |
| % from out of state | 27 |
| % from public high school | 90 |
| % live on campus | 75 |
| % African American | 5 |
| % Asian | 4 |
| % Caucasian | 76 |
| % Hispanic | 5 |
| % international | 2 |
| # of countries represented | 8 |

### SURVEY SAYS . . .
No one cheats
Musical organizations are hot
Students get along with local community
Very little beer drinking
Student government is popular
Dorms are like palaces
Class discussions encouraged
Theater is hot
Very small frat/sorority scene
Student publications are ignored
Lousy food on campus

## ACADEMICS

| Academic Rating | 86 |
|---|---|
| Calendar | semester |
| Student/faculty ratio | 7:1 |
| Profs interesting rating | 80 |
| Profs accessible rating | 84 |
| % profs teaching UG courses | 100 |
| Avg lab size | 10-19 students |
| Avg reg class size | 10-19 students |

### MOST POPULAR MAJORS
Psychology
English language and literature
Biology/biological sciences

## STUDENTS SPEAK OUT

### Academics
One effusive sophomore calls Wells College "an Ivy League education in disguise as the best time of our lives," and most students on this all-women campus agree. Not only is "advising a very personal encounter at Wells," but the professors also make students "want to sing and dance" with their engaging lectures and personal involvement. "The greatest strength here at Wells is the time that the professors dedicate to tutoring students outside class time," notes a junior. Apparently, a rash of "bad puns" among faculty doesn't impede the "constant exchange of ideas." The cutthroat competition of many top schools is swapped for a spirit of cooperation at Wells. "Everyone wants to help each other," in the experience of one sophomore. The administration is said to have "a well-rounded view of people's abilities" and to be "very in tune with the students." A few complaints are logged regarding the library, which needs "more books from 1970–present." The issue of "low variety of classes and few teachers" is solved by an arrangement that allows Wells students to take courses at nearby Cornell. Some students also suggest putting more money into "educational funding than [campus] aesthetics." But the mentoring students receive plus the influential network of alumnae awaiting them after graduation makes Wells, overall, a "rewarding" place to hit the books.

### Life
Travel for 25 miles in any direction from Wells, and you won't find a whole lot. Thus, students pride themselves on being "self-sufficient" and "making our own fun." On-campus life is described as "one big sleepover" or like "living at home with 400 sisters." Inevitably, this results in an "intimate" community, with more than one student commenting, "Everyone knows you, for better or worse." A senior tells us, "We always find amusement in each other doing something seemingly boring to anyone outside of the 'bubble.' " Some of these activities include, "just being silly, cooking, and playing games" as well as hitting the lone bar in the quiet "village" of Aurora. For a more extensive social life, students utilize the school-sponsored "van runs" to Ithaca and nearby college campuses. Cornell, Ithaca, Syracuse, and Hobart and William Smith are all within striking distance and ready to host the Wells women. "I haven't had any problems meeting guys," comments a junior. To round life out, students take advantage of their picturesque location on Cayuga Lake, especially during the warmer months.

### Student Body
A senior woman characterizes her fellow students thusly: "Wells women tend to be independent thinkers, kind and generous, and mostly very outgoing. They tend to be unusual people, somehow slightly out of the box." These unique individuals are nonetheless still somewhat prone to "gossip" and "way too much drama." Some students observe a "lack of respect for different social classes" and describe their classmates as "prissy." But the consensus is that there is a strong sense of community, where students often "get along more like sisters"; the "very accepting" student body is diverse in nature. A freshman summarizes the warm, fuzzy, estrogen feeling in concluding, "As a community, our ability to communicate is only surpassed by our friendship."

716 ■ THE BEST 351 COLLEGES

# WELLS COLLEGE

FINANCIAL AID: 315-364-3289 • E-MAIL: ADMISSIONS@WELLS.EDU • WEBSITE: WWW.WELLS.EDU

## ADMISSIONS

*Very important factors considered include:* extracurricular activities, recommendations, secondary school record, standardized test scores. *Important factors considered include:* essays, interview. *Other factors considered include:* alumni/ae relation, character/personal qualities, class rank, talent/ability, volunteer work, work experience. SAT I or ACT required. TOEFL required of all international applicants. High school diploma or GED is required. *High school units required/recommended:* 16 total required; 23 total recommended; 4 English required, 3 math required, 4 math recommended, 2 science required, 3 science recommended, 2 science lab required, 3 science lab recommended, 3 foreign language required, 4 foreign language recommended, 2 history required, 3 history recommended, 2 elective required, 3 elective recommended.

### The Inside Word

Wells is engaged in that age-old admissions game called matchmaking. There are no minimums or cutoffs in the admissions process here. But don't be fooled by the high admit rate. The admissions committee will look closely at your academic accomplishments, but also gives attention to your essay, recommendations, and extracurricular pursuits. The committee also recommends an interview; we suggest taking them up on it.

## FINANCIAL AID

*Students should submit:* FAFSA, CSS/Financial Aid PROFILE for early decision Applicants only. No deadline for regular filing. The Princeton Review suggests that all financial aid forms be submitted as soon as possible after January 1. *Need-based scholarships/grants offered:* Pell, SEOG, state scholarships/grants, private scholarships, the school's own gift aid. *Loan aid offered:* FFEL Subsidized Stafford, FFEL Unsubsidized Stafford, FFEL PLUS, Federal Perkins. Federal Work-Study Program available. Institutional employment available. Applicants will be notified of awards on a rolling basis beginning on or about March 1. Off-campus job opportunities are fair.

## FROM THE ADMISSIONS OFFICE

"Sixty percent of Wells women pursue advanced degrees at some point in their careers. Our recent graduates have gained admission to programs at Cornell University, Harvard University, Georgetown University, Duke University, University of California at Berkeley, Yale University, and many others."

## SELECTIVITY

| | |
|---|---|
| Admissions Rating | 80 |
| # of applicants | 404 |
| % of applicants accepted | 86 |
| % of acceptees attending | 31 |
| # of early decision applicants | 23 |
| % accepted early decision | 96 |

### FRESHMAN PROFILE

| | |
|---|---|
| Range SAT Verbal | 530-650 |
| Average SAT Verbal | 580 |
| Range SAT Math | 500-590 |
| Average SAT Math | 550 |
| Range ACT Composite | 22-26 |
| Average ACT Composite | 25 |
| Minimum TOEFL | 550 |
| Average HS GPA | 3.5 |
| % graduated top 10% of class | 30 |
| % graduated top 25% of class | 67 |
| % graduated top 50% of class | 94 |

### DEADLINES

| | |
|---|---|
| Early decision | 12/15 |
| Early decision notification | 1/15 |
| Priority admission | 12/15 |
| Regular admission | 3/1 |
| Regular notification | 4/1 |

### APPLICANTS ALSO LOOK AT
**AND OFTEN PREFER**
Smith College
Mount Holyoke College
Cornell University
**AND SOMETIMES PREFER**
St. Lawrence University
State University of New York at Binghamton
State University of New York College at Geneseo
Syracuse University
**AND RARELY PREFER**
Elmira College, Le Moyne College
Rochester Polytechnic

## FINANCIAL FACTS

| | |
|---|---|
| Financial Aid Rating | 80 |
| Tuition | $13,070 |
| Room and board | $6,450 |
| Books and supplies | $600 |
| Required fees | $680 |
| % frosh receiving aid | 80 |
| % undergrads receiving aid | 78 |
| Avg frosh grant | $9,978 |
| Avg frosh loan | $3,066 |

# WESLEYAN COLLEGE

4760 FORSYTH ROAD, MACON, GA 31210-4462 • ADMISSIONS: 912-757-5206 • FAX: 912-757-4030

## CAMPUS LIFE

| | |
|---|---|
| Quality of Life Rating | 83 |
| Type of school | private |
| Affiliation | Methodist |
| Environment | suburban |

### STUDENTS

| | |
|---|---|
| Total undergrad enrollment | 679 |
| % from out of state | 19 |
| % from public high school | 90 |
| % live on campus | 63 |
| % African American | 35 |
| % Asian | 2 |
| % Caucasian | 58 |
| % Hispanic | 3 |
| % international | 16 |

### SURVEY SAYS . . .
Campus easy to get around
Campus is beautiful
Campus feels safe
Student government is popular
Ethnic diversity on campus
Dorms are like palaces
Students are happy
No one cheats

## ACADEMICS

| | |
|---|---|
| Academic Rating | 91 |
| Calendar | semester |
| Student/faculty ratio | 11:1 |
| % profs teaching UG courses | 100 |
| Avg lab size | 10-19 students |
| Avg reg class size | 100+ students |

## STUDENTS SPEAK OUT

### Academics

"Tradition, community, sisterhood, and southern charm are the heart of Wesleyan College," a small, all-women's liberal arts school in the heart of the Cotton Belt. Students are attracted to Wesleyan by its mission to "teach women of all ages, races, creeds, and colors to think analytically, be independent, and go out into the workplace prepared and with a lot of self-esteem." Once they arrive, however, it is "the experience in the class—the discussions and passion of each of the professors—that has kept me enthralled with the Wesleyan experience." Students agree that profs here "are all extremely well educated, very interested in passing on knowledge to current students, and very available for meetings, study sessions, etc." and that "the curriculum is challenging but satisfying: You sure get your money's worth." Undergrads also love the new president, Ruth Knox, describing her as "an absolute gem to the school" who is "quite easy to carry on a conversation with. . . . You always see her about the school taking care of everyday matters." Student complaints center on budget concerns ("The school could stand to have more money to spend on technology and renovations around campus. I think a lack of available funds is our weakest area," writes a typical undergrad) and the constraints of life in Macon.

### Life

Wesleyan operates on a unique class system in which "each entering class is assigned a color and a mascot." Students love it, telling us it "helps to encourage sisterhood. Without the typical sororities, this provides a way for students to bond with each other." Sisterhood—the spirit that bonds classes as well as the entire student body here—is reinforced by "tons of traditions," including STUNT ("a musical that five members from each class write and direct"); Bandfest ("where local bands come onto campus for an entire day of fun"); Funday ("We basically bring a mini-carnival of blow-up rides and stuff onto campus"); and Sister Sports ("The most popular is class soccer"). A large minority of this tiny student body is "actively involved in student government," under whose auspices the "Student Recreation Council and Campus Activities Board bring new things to campus, and they do an awesome job." All this helps make up for the fact that "there isn't much to do in the town of Macon." Male visitors are kept at bay by "very strict rules," which is why "the majority of social interactions take place off campus." Sometimes way off campus: students tell us that road trips to Atlanta (about 90 minutes away by car) are fairly common. "We often go there and shop, go to the clubs [and] restaurants or just hang out," explains one student.

### Student Body

Students at Wesleyan College strongly believe that "there is no 'typical' Wesleyan student. There are feminists and those who aren't, there are lesbians and those who aren't, there are churchgoers and those who aren't." Students do tend to share a few common traits, however; they are all "incredibly involved, love to have a good time, and we all know how to get serious when it is time to get serious. Everybody here has her own niche, and we all fit very well together." They also share a sense of "sisterhood" that they describe as "unbelievable—it is something that, until you experience it for yourself, you can never know exactly what it is . . . ." The "large international community" and "great ethnic diversity" leave students wondering "if there is any other place in the world where so many different women can come to one place and fit so well together." Although Wesleyan is a Methodist school, the student body includes "numerous Catholics, Baptists, Muslims, and probably any other religion you could possibly think of. People of [different] races or religions or people of different sexual orientations are accepted with open arms."

# WESLEYAN COLLEGE

FINANCIAL AID: 800-447-6610 • E-MAIL: ADMISSIONS@WESLEYANCOLLEGE.EDU • WEBSITE: WWW.WESLEYANCOLLEGE.EDU

## ADMISSIONS
*Very important factors considered include:* secondary school record. *Important factors considered include:* character/personal qualities, class rank, extracurricular activities, recommendations, standardized test scores, talent/ability, volunteer work. *Other factors considered include:* alumni/ae relation, essays, geographical residence, interview, minority status, religious affiliation/commitment, state residency, work experience. SAT I or ACT required. TOEFL required of all international applicants. High school diploma or GED is required. *High school units required/recommended:* 15 total required; 20 total recommended; 4 English required, 3 math required, 4 math recommended, 3 science required, 4 science recommended, 2 science lab required, 3 science lab recommended, 2 foreign language required, 3 foreign language recommended, 3 social studies required, 1 elective recommended.

### The Inside Word
The college has gotten lots of national publicity of late, but its applicant pool is still primarily southeastern in origin. Candidates from outside the usual sphere of influence of any college draw the attention of admissions officers, and it's no exception here. Recommendations are important at Wesleyan; we'd advise that such letters make at least some reference to your interest in and suitability for a women's college; your own essay won't carry nearly as much weight.

## FINANCIAL AID
*Students should submit:* FAFSA, institution's own financial aid form, state aid form, noncustodial (divorced/separated) parent's statement. No deadline for regular filing. The Princeton Review suggests that all financial aid forms be submitted as soon as possible after January 1. *Need-based scholarships/grants offered:* Pell, SEOG, state scholarships/grants, private scholarships, the school's own gift aid. *Loan aid offered:* Direct Subsidized Stafford, Direct Unsubsidized Stafford, Direct PLUS, Federal Perkins, college/university loans from institutional funds, CitiAssist, Wells FARGO, Collegiate Loans, Key alternative loans. Federal Work-Study Program available. Institutional employment available. Applicants will be notified of awards on a rolling basis beginning on or about February 1. Off-campus job opportunities are good.

## FROM THE ADMISSIONS OFFICE
"Mention the term 'women's college' and most people envision ivy-covered towers in the U.S. northeast. However, Wesleyan College in Macon, Georgia, a four-year liberal arts college founded in 1836, has the distinction of having been the world's first degree-granting college for women. Today it is recognized as one of the nation's most diverse and affordable selective colleges. Students value the College's tradition of service, small classes, beautiful residence halls, and a picturesque campus. Wesleyan is committed to the goals of training women to understand and appreciate the liberal and fine arts and preparing them for careers through high-quality professional programs."

### SELECTIVITY

| | |
|---|---|
| Admissions Rating | 69 |
| # of applicants | 449 |
| % of applicants accepted | 72 |
| % of acceptees attending | 47 |
| # of early decision applicants | 39 |
| % accepted early decision | 79 |

### FRESHMAN PROFILE
| | |
|---|---|
| Range SAT Verbal | 500-610 |
| Average SAT Verbal | 574 |
| Range SAT Math | 480-610 |
| Average SAT Math | 562 |
| Range ACT Composite | 19-25 |
| Average ACT Composite | 25 |
| Minimum TOEFL | 550 |
| Average HS GPA | 3.5 |
| % graduated top 10% of class | 36 |
| % graduated top 25% of class | 60 |
| % graduated top 50% of class | 93 |

### DEADLINES
| | |
|---|---|
| Early decision | 11/15 |
| Early decision notification | 12/15 |
| Priority admission | 3/1 |
| Regular admission | 6/1 |
| Regular notification | 12/15 |
| Nonfall registration? | yes |

### APPLICANTS ALSO LOOK AT AND SOMETIMES PREFER
U. Georgia
Emory
Agnes Scott
Mercer

### AND RARELY PREFER
Berry
Rhodes
U. Florida
Florida State

### FINANCIAL FACTS

| | |
|---|---|
| Financial Aid Rating | 91 |
| Tuition | $9,570 |
| Room and board | $7,450 |
| Books and supplies | $600 |
| Required fees | $850 |
| % frosh receiving aid | 58 |
| % undergrads receiving aid | 58 |
| Avg frosh grant | $11,943 |
| Avg frosh loan | $4,094 |

# WESLEYAN UNIVERSITY

THE STEWART M. REID HOUSE, 70 WYLLYS AVENUE, MIDDLETOWN, CT 06459-0265 • ADMISSIONS: 860-685-3000 • FAX: 860-685-3001

## CAMPUS LIFE

| Quality of Life Rating | 78 |
|---|---|
| Type of school | private |
| Environment | suburban |

### STUDENTS

| Total undergrad enrollment | 2,733 |
|---|---|
| % male/female | 48/52 |
| % from out of state | 90 |
| % from public high school | 56 |
| % live on campus | 94 |
| % in (# of) fraternities | 5 (9) |
| % in (# of) sororities | 1 (4) |
| % African American | 9 |
| % Asian | 8 |
| % Caucasian | 67 |
| % Hispanic | 7 |
| % international | 6 |

### SURVEY SAYS . . .
Political activism is hot
Great library
No one cheats
Students aren't religious
Athletic facilities are great
Students don't like Middletown, CT
(Almost) no one listens to college radio
Very small frat/sorority scene

## ACADEMICS

| Academic Rating | 94 |
|---|---|
| Calendar | semester |
| Student/faculty ratio | 9:1 |
| Profs interesting rating | 95 |
| Profs accessible rating | 96 |
| % profs teaching UG courses | 100 |
| % classes taught by TAs | 1 |
| Avg lab size | 10-19 students |
| Avg reg class size | 10-19 students |

## STUDENTS SPEAK OUT

### Academics

"You live with the coolest people in the world, which is interrupted periodically by instruction from the smartest people on campus," says a sophomore about a Wesleyan education. "There is a serious but noncompetitive academic environment," reports a senior art history major. A junior government major says, "When your government professor is on a first-name basis with the White House and is an excellent teacher [to boot], you can't ask for better academics." A senior chemistry major proclaims, "Our hippie, flower-child reputation overshadows the fact that we have a great science department with opportunities you can't get anywhere else." A sophomore writes, "Professors really care about your opinions, and you're treated as an intellectual equal." Still, one junior dance major laments that "diversity university does not have a diverse faculty." Students enjoy their academic freedom. "Wesleyan's academic requirements give you tremendous freedom to design your own curriculum and to take classes you really want to be in." Learning takes place both in and out of class. Writes a sophomore, "I feel like much of my academic experience occurs outside of class because there is so much political activity and passionate discussion about campus and global issues." While the professors are universally admired, the registrar's office is the focus of displeasure. The online registration system might be revolutionary, but "online registration is hell; you're basically racing with all the people on the computers next to you," one junior writes.

### Life

A senior East Asian studies major describes life at Wesleyan thusly: "What do people do for fun? Stage a rally during the president's office hours and simultaneously have a knitting bee and discussion about pro-feminist activism." Though some complain that the party policy is getting too strict, a junior English major says, "If you want frat parties, we've got them. If you want naked parties, we've got those too." Others note that while "the beer flows like water if you know where to look, there's not a lot of pressure to drink." Explains one, "Campus life doesn't revolve around drinking because there are always so many other things going on." Students call Middletown "boring" and "like a sketchy ghost town" but love the university's central New England location and its "great sledding hill." Students don't seem too happy that they are required to remain on the meal plan for four years.

### Student Body

Wesleyan "is a school full of very idealistic people who really want to make a significant impact on the world before they even graduate." Though sometimes described as "self-righteous," Wesleyan is home to a "passionate, involved student body. At best, they change the world. At worst, they're entertaining." While the student body is racially mixed, a senior chemistry major notes that "we are diverse and very accepting as long as you've never worn a white hat or had any Republican sympathies." Still, most students overlook the lack of political heterogeneity because they appreciate that "there is no such thing as a typical Wesleyan student. You can meet a lacrosse jock at a fraternity party and then run into him the next day at an Amnesty International meeting or see him later in a theater performance." Another student adds, "My friends are a motley crew of musicians, artists, intellectuals . . . united by good herb." Even the senior art history major who believes that "the school is populated by a lot of whiny left-wing rich kids who have no concept of reality and how an administration must sometimes make unpopular choices," admits that she "like[s] that students are politically active."

# WESLEYAN UNIVERSITY

FINANCIAL AID: 860-685-2800 • E-MAIL: ADMISSIONS@WESLEYAN.EDU • WEBSITE: WWW.WESLEYAN.EDU

## ADMISSIONS

*Very important factors considered include:* secondary school record. *Important factors considered include:* class rank, character/personal qualities, recommendations, essays, talent/ability, standardized test scores, minority/alumni status, volunteer work. *Other factors considered include:* geographical residence, interview, work experience. TOEFL required of all international applicants. *High school units required/recommended:* 20 total recommended; 4 English recommended, 4 math recommended, 4 science recommended, 3 science lab recommended, 4 foreign language recommended, 4 social studies recommended.

## The Inside Word

Wesleyan stacks up well against its very formidable competitors academically, yet due to these same competitors the university admits at a fairly high rate for an institution of its high caliber. Candidate evaluation is nonetheless rigorous. If you aren't one of the best students in your graduating class, it isn't likely that you will be very competitive in Wesleyan's applicant pool. Strong communicators can help open the doors by submitting persuasive essays and interviews that clearly demonstrate an effective match with the university.

## FINANCIAL AID

*Students should submit:* FAFSA, CSS/Financial Aid PROFILE, noncustodial (divorced/separated) parent's statement, business/farm supplement. Regular filing deadline is February 1. The Princeton Review suggests that all financial aid forms be submitted as soon as possible after January 1. *Need-based scholarships/grants offered:* Pell, SEOG, state scholarships/grants, private scholarships, the school's own gift aid. *Loan aid offered:* FFEL Subsidized Stafford, FFEL Unsubsidized Stafford, FFEL PLUS, Federal Perkins. Federal Work-Study Program available. Institutional employment available. Applicants will be notified of awards on or about April 1. Off-campus job opportunities are good.

## FROM THE ADMISSIONS OFFICE

"Wesleyan faculty believe in an education that is flexible and affords individual freedom, and that a strong liberal arts education is the best foundation for success in any endeavor. The broad curriculum focuses on essential skills and abilities through course content and teaching methodology, allowing students to pursue their intellectual interests with passion while honing those skills and abilities. As a result, Wesleyan students achieve a very personalized but coherent education. Wesleyan's dean of admission and financial aid, Nancy Hargrave-Meislahn, describes the qualities Wesleyan seeks in its students: 'Our very holistic process seeks to identify academically accomplished and intellectually curious students who can thrive in Wesleyan's rigorous and vibrant academic environment, and to also see in a candidate the personal strengths, accomplishments, and potential for real contribution to our diverse community.'"

## SELECTIVITY

| | |
|---|---|
| Admissions Rating | 98 |
| # of applicants | 6,474 |
| % of applicants accepted | 28 |
| % of acceptees attending | 40 |
| # of early decision applicants | 676 |
| % accepted early decision | 46 |

### FRESHMAN PROFILE

| | |
|---|---|
| Range SAT Verbal | 640-740 |
| Average SAT Verbal | 700 |
| Range SAT Math | 650-730 |
| Average SAT Math | 690 |
| Average ACT Composite | 29 |
| Minimum TOEFL | 250 (CBT) |
| % graduated top 10% of class | 73 |
| % graduated top 25% of class | 94 |
| % graduated top 50% of class | 99 |

### DEADLINES

| | |
|---|---|
| Early decision | 11/15 |
| Early decision notification | 12/15 |
| Regular admission | 1/1 |
| Regular notification | 4/1 |

### APPLICANTS ALSO LOOK AT AND OFTEN PREFER
Harvard
Columbia
Brown
Stanford
Yale

### AND SOMETIMES PREFER
Amherst
Princeton
Williams
Bowdoin
Swarthmore

### AND RARELY PREFER
Oberlin
Brandeis
Vassar
Middlebury
Tufts

## FINANCIAL FACTS

| | |
|---|---|
| Financial Aid Rating | 81 |
| Tuition | $29,784 |
| Room and board | $8,226 |
| % frosh receiving aid | 47 |
| % undergrads receiving aid | 47 |
| Avg frosh grant | $23,992 |
| Avg frosh loan | $2,770 |

# WEST VIRGINIA UNIVERSITY

ADMISSIONS OFFICE, PO BOX 6009, MORGANTOWN, WV 26506-6009 • ADMISSIONS: 800-344-9881 • FAX: 304-293-3080

## CAMPUS LIFE

| | |
|---|---|
| Quality of Life Rating | 73 |
| Type of school | public |
| Environment | suburban |

### STUDENTS

| | |
|---|---|
| Total undergrad enrollment | 16,692 |
| % male/female | 54/46 |
| % from out of state | 38 |
| % live on campus | 21 |
| % in (# of) fraternities | 9 (17) |
| % in (# of) sororities | 9 (14) |
| % African American | 4 |
| % Asian | 2 |
| % Caucasian | 92 |
| % Hispanic | 1 |
| % international | 2 |
| # of countries represented | 90 |

### SURVEY SAYS . . .
Everyone loves the Mountaineers
Frats and sororities dominate social scene
Class discussions are rare
(Almost) everyone smokes
High cost of living
Campus difficult to get around
Large classes
Theater is unpopular
Student publications are popular
Ethnic diversity on campus

## ACADEMICS

| | |
|---|---|
| Academic Rating | 64 |
| Calendar | semester |
| Student/faculty ratio | 19:1 |
| Profs interesting rating | 91 |
| Profs accessible rating | 94 |
| Avg lab size | 20-29 students |
| Avg reg class size | 20-29 students |

### MOST POPULAR MAJORS
Engineering
Psychology
Business administration/management

## STUDENTS SPEAK OUT

### Academics

Spread out across three campuses in Morgantown (and several smaller regional campuses), West Virginia University works hard to overcome the usual shortcomings of mammoth undergraduate programs. Operation Jump-Start typifies WVU's efforts to personalize the university. The program groups freshmen in nine residential houses according to academic interest. Faculty couples live close by and serve as mentors for the incoming students, helping them acclimate to the university and quickly achieve a sense of community. Some Jump-Start groups have taken on community service projects, and others have taken trips together. Similarly, "the university Honors Program allows students to have a fulfilling and challenging undergraduate experience" that includes smaller classes and more seminar-style teaching. Professors at WVU run the gamut from wonderful to awful, depending on the department and the individual. Several students in the biological sciences voice such complaints as "I find myself teaching myself through learning centers and excessive studying." Professors in the popular Division of Agriculture and Forestry, however, "run in the good-to-excellent range." The College of Engineering and the College of Human Resources and Education are among the popular and well-regarded options here. According to one dissatisfied student, "Because of problems with the PRT [personnel rapid transit], it usually takes me half an hour to get to class! My advisor has also continually told me wrong information on the classes I need to take."

### Life

Many students love the Morgantown area for its quiet vibe. Explains one, "The town moves at a slow pace when you compare it to some of the larger cities in proximity to Morgantown (i.e., D.C., Pittsburgh, Baltimore, etc.), but that's not a problem. There is always something to do, everything from hiking up to Coopers Rock and taking in the magnificent view from the top, or taking a walk/run along the Monongahela River." They also like its proximity to Pittsburgh, only an hour-and-a-half away by car. Students warn, however, that town-gown relations are extremely strained, except during football games. "WVU students are avid sports fans. Thousands of us go to cheer on our team at each sporting event, be [it] football or basketball." While "WVU was formerly ranked #1 party school in the nation back in 1998 or so . . . now we are nowhere near that ranking. Unfortunately, our president has seen to it that we will never achieve that ranking ever again through [stringent] policies and such." In the place of bleary-eyed beer bashes, "WVU has implemented an alcohol-free program called WVU Up All Night which takes place on Thursday, Friday, and Saturday nights. A lot of free activities and free food are provided during Up All Night. And the turn out is tremendous."

### Student Body

WVU draws students largely from within the state. Maryland, New Jersey, and Pennsylvania also contribute heavily to the student population. Writes one student, "There is a 'country boy meets city boy' situation that occurs for every freshman here at WVU. By this I mean you have a solid in-state population of good ol' West Virginia boys meeting up with the Long Islanders and Jersey boys. . . . I don't want to say there is hostility between these two groups but getting along takes a little effort." Minority populations are tiny, with about 600 African American undergraduates constituting the largest nonwhite group. Complains one black student, "I just wish there were more minorities on campus."

# WEST VIRGINIA UNIVERSITY

FINANCIAL AID: 304-293-5242 • E-MAIL: WVUADMISSIONS@ARC.WVU.EDU • WEBSITE: WWW.WVU.EDU

## ADMISSIONS
*Very important factors considered include:* secondary school record, standardized test scores. *Other factors considered include:* alumni/ae relation. SAT I or ACT required. TOEFL required of all international applicants. High school diploma or GED is required. *High school units required/recommended:* 13 total required; 4 English required, 3 math required, 3 science required, 2 science lab required, 2 foreign language recommended, 3 social studies required.

## The Inside Word
West Virginia's admissions office made an excellent point about rolling admission in their response to us, which applies to candidates for admission at any university that uses such an approach. As the admissions committee gets closer to its enrollment targets, the admissions process becomes progressively more selective. At West Virginia the early bird usually gets a worm, and there is often another one for a late bird. Still, don't hold off on rolling admission applications just because others have more pressing deadlines. Forget that there's a rolling plan, and complete your application as if it has to be in at the same time as all the rest.

## FINANCIAL AID
*Students should submit:* FAFSA. Regular filing deadline is March 1. The Princeton Review suggests that all financial aid forms be submitted as soon as possible after January 1. *Need-based scholarships/grants offered:* Pell, SEOG, state scholarships/grants, private scholarships, the school's own gift aid. *Loan aid offered:* Direct Subsidized Stafford, Direct Unsubsidized Stafford, Direct PLUS, Federal Perkins, Federal Nursing, state loans, college/university loans from institutional funds. Federal Work-Study Program available. Institutional employment available. Applicants will be notified of awards on a rolling basis. Off-campus job opportunities are good.

## FROM THE ADMISSIONS OFFICE
"From quality academic programs and outstanding, caring faculty to incredible new facilities and a campus environment that focuses on students' needs, WVU is a place where dreams can come true. The University's tradition of academic excellence attracts some of the region's best high school seniors. WVU has produced 25 Rhodes Scholars, 24 Goldwater Scholars, 14 Truman Scholars, 5 members of USA Today's All-USA College Academic First Team, and 2 Udall Scholarship winners. Whether your goal is to be an aerospace engineer, reporter, physicist, athletic trainer, opera singer, forensic investigator, pharmacist, or CEO, WVU's 170 degree choices can make it happen. Unique student-centered initiatives include Operation Jump Start, which helps students experience true education extending beyond the classroom. Resident Faculty Leaders live next to the residence halls to mentor students, and WVU All Night provides a way to relax and have fun with free food and activities nearly every weekend. The Mountaineer Parents' Club connects more than 11,000 WVU families, and a parents' helpline (800-WVU-0096) leads to a full-time parent advocate. A new Student Recreation Center includes athletic courts, pools, weight/fitness equipment, and a 50-foot indoor climbing wall. Also, a brand-new life sciences building and completely renovated library complex just opened. With programs for studying abroad, a Center for Black Culture and Research, an Office of Disability Services, and a student body that comes from every WV county, 49 states, and 90 different countries, WVU encourages and nurtures diversity. More than $133 million in annual grant funding makes WVU a major research institution where undergraduates can participate. The main campus is one of the safest in the nation, and the area's natural beauty provides chances to ski, bike, hike, and go whitewater rafting."

## SELECTIVITY

★ ★ ☆ ☆

| | |
|---|---|
| Admissions Rating | 75 |
| # of applicants | 9,147 |
| % of applicants accepted | 94 |
| % of acceptees attending | 46 |

### FRESHMAN PROFILE
| | |
|---|---|
| Range SAT Verbal | 460-560 |
| Average SAT Verbal | 514 |
| Range SAT Math | 470-580 |
| Average SAT Math | 528 |
| Range ACT Composite | 20-25 |
| Average ACT Composite | 23 |
| Minimum TOEFL | 550 |
| Average HS GPA | 3.2 |
| % graduated top 10% of class | 19 |
| % graduated top 25% of class | 43 |
| % graduated top 50% of class | 74 |

### DEADLINES
| | |
|---|---|
| Priority admission | 3/1 |
| Regular admission | 8/1 |
| Nonfall registration? | yes |

### APPLICANTS ALSO LOOK AT
**AND OFTEN PREFER**
Penn State at Univversity Park
Virginia Tech
U of Pittsburgh
**AND SOMETIMES PREFER**
Ohio State U at Columbus
U of Virginia
U of Maryland at College Park
**AND RARELY PREFER**
James Madison
Indiana U of Pennsylvania
U of Delaware

## FINANCIAL FACTS

| | |
|---|---|
| Financial Aid Rating | 82 |
| In-state tuition | $3,240 |
| Out-of-state tuition | $9,710 |
| Room and board | $5,572 |
| Books and supplies | $727 |
| % frosh receiving aid | 38 |
| % undergrads receiving aid | 46 |

# WESTMINSTER COLLEGE

319 SOUTH MARKET STREET, NEW WILMINGTON, PA 16172 • ADMISSIONS: 800-942-8033 • FAX: 724-946-7171

## CAMPUS LIFE

| Quality of Life Rating | 79 |
|---|---|
| Type of school | private |
| Affiliation | Presbyterian |
| Environment | suburban |

### STUDENTS

| Total undergrad enrollment | 1,340 |
|---|---|
| % male/female | 34/66 |
| % from out of state | 21 |
| % from public high school | 90 |
| % live on campus | 78 |
| % in (# of) fraternities | 50 (5) |
| % in (# of) sororities | 50 (5) |
| % African American | 1 |
| % Caucasian | 83 |
| % Hispanic | 1 |

### SURVEY SAYS . . .

Frats and sororities dominate social scene
Diversity lacking on campus
Classes are small
Very little drug use
Lousy food on campus
Political activism is (almost) nonexistent
Lousy off-campus food
Students don't like New Wilmington, PA
Theater is unpopular

## ACADEMICS

| Academic Rating | 77 |
|---|---|
| Calendar | semester |
| Student/faculty ratio | 13:1 |
| Profs interesting rating | 93 |
| Profs accessible rating | 90 |
| % profs teaching UG courses | 100 |
| Avg lab size | 10-19 students |
| Avg reg class size | 10-19 students |

## STUDENTS SPEAK OUT

### Academics

Westminster College, a small Presbyterian school in Western Pennsylvania where "professors have a genuine passion to teach," enjoys an excellent reputation for combining "tough academics" with "real-world preparation." The largely professional-minded student body here is inundated with the essentials of a solid liberal arts education through "the Westminster Plan," a thorough core curriculum in the sciences, humanities, mathematics, computer science, and religion. As a result of the program, every student graduates with at least two majors: a "common" major in the western liberal arts tradition and a specialized major of the student's choosing. While some students complain that these "introductory courses could use some help" and feel that the school "is a slave to tradition" and so refuses to change the program, others feel that the Westminster Plan forms the bedrock of their educational experience. Students happily report that "professors make you welcome to talk with them outside of class, visit their homes, and even eat meals with them." More than a few undergrads bemoan the fact that "the professors teach the classes like you've already had it and fly through the material . . . . They also act like a C is a good grade." Students appreciate the school's president, who "leaves his door open and encourages the students to stop in and say hello."

### Life

According to many Westminster students we heard from, students' social life follows a predictable arc during their four-year tenure here. Explains one, "As a freshman you love the fraternity houses! They're . . . a great way to meet new people. Then things tend to get old as you make it to being a senior. It's a dry town so there aren't any bars; it actually kinda sucks!" Indeed, by senior year, most students find themselves either going home on weekends or heading to nearby Sharon, Youngstown, or Pittsburgh (a little further down the road but with much more to offer) for fun. Until then, most students enjoy a Greek-centered scene. Reports one underclassman, "Greek life is a great way to spend your college experience at school. You get to meet a lot of different people and for the most part they all have your back." Adds another, "Life at Westminster is double-sided. During the day, students are involved in campus organizations, get good grades, go to church. . . . If we are involved, do well in classes, and have faith in God, why not party a little?" Hometown New Wilmington "has one traffic light, so as you can imagine, there's not much to [it], except a significant Amish population." The town does boast "$3 movie theatres that are 10 minutes away, as well as Perkins and Wal-Mart. We couldn't live without 2 A.M. Wal-Mart runs!" While many feel that "besides frat parties, there is nothing to do," they have faith that "the new campus center being built should help things."

### Student Body

Westminster's "very conservative" students, "the majority of whom come from upper-middle-class, white suburban homes," are the type of people who open doors for each other, smile and say 'hi' even to those they don't know, and immerse themselves in extracurriculars and community service. According to many, however, their friendliness "doesn't go beyond the superficial level. Most students form their groups early on in freshman and sophomore year and don't seem to expand those groups much throughout the rest of their college career." Greeks in particular "have some serious rivalries" with each other and also "cause some of the independents to feel like outsiders." Several students reported campus unrest over the issue of sexual preference. Explains one undergrad, "Westminster is a very small school, and as such there isn't a whole lot of diversity held within. Most of the students have never been outside of the area, and all typically share the same dreams and goals . . . . Only a few students break away . . . and some find it too hard to remain on campus because of it."

# WESTMINSTER COLLEGE

FINANCIAL AID: 724-946-7102 • E-MAIL: ADMIS@WESTMINSTER.EDU • WEBSITE: WWW.WESTMINSTER.EDU

## ADMISSIONS

*Very important factors considered include:* interview, secondary school record, standardized test scores. *Important factors considered include:* character/personal qualities, class rank, essays, recommendations. *Other factors considered include:* alumni/ae relation, extracurricular activities, minority status, talent/ability, volunteer work, work experience. SAT I or ACT required. TOEFL required of all international applicants. High school diploma or GED is required. *High school units required/recommended:* 16 total required; 4 English required, 3 math required, 2 science required, 2 science lab required, 2 foreign language required, 2 social studies required, 1 history required, 3 elective required.

### The Inside Word

The vast majority of those who apply to Westminster gain admission, but the applicant pool is strong enough to enable the college to weed out those who don't measure up to the solid entering class academic profile. Candidates who are shooting for academic scholarships should play the admissions game all the way and put a solid effort into the completion of their applications.

## FINANCIAL AID

*Students should submit:* FAFSA, institution's own financial aid form. The Princeton Review suggests that all financial aid forms be submitted as soon as possible after January 1. *Need-based scholarships/grants offered:* Pell, SEOG, state scholarships/grants, private scholarships, the school's own gift aid. *Loan aid offered:* FFEL Subsidized Stafford, FFEL Unsubsidized Stafford, FFEL PLUS, Federal Perkins. Federal Work-Study Program available. Applicants will be notified of awards on a rolling basis. Off-campus job opportunities are good.

## FROM THE ADMISSIONS OFFICE

"Since its founding, Westminster has been dedicated to a solid foundation in today's most crucial social, cultural, and ethical issues. Related to the Presbyterian Church (U.S.A.), Westminster is home to people of many faiths. Our students and faculty, tradition of campus, and small-town setting all contribute to an enlightening educational experience."

---

### SELECTIVITY

| | |
|---|---|
| Admissions Rating | 75 |
| # of applicants | 1,191 |
| % of applicants accepted | 78 |
| % of acceptees attending | 38 |

#### FRESHMAN PROFILE

| | |
|---|---|
| Range SAT Verbal | 480-580 |
| Average SAT Verbal | 544 |
| Range SAT Math | 480-590 |
| Average SAT Math | 543 |
| Range ACT Composite | 19-26 |
| Average ACT Composite | 24 |
| Minimum TOEFL | 500 |
| Average HS GPA | 3.3 |
| % graduated top 10% of class | 20 |
| % graduated top 25% of class | 55 |
| % graduated top 50% of class | 87 |

#### DEADLINES

| | |
|---|---|
| Regular admission | 4/15 |

#### APPLICANTS ALSO LOOK AT AND OFTEN PREFER
College of Wooster
Baldwin-Wallace
**AND SOMETIMES PREFER**
Duquesne U
U of Pittsburg
Grove City College
**AND RARELY PREFER**
Allegheny College
Washington & Jefferson
Thiel College
Slippery Rock U

### FINANCIAL FACTS

| | |
|---|---|
| Financial Aid Rating | 88 |
| Tuition | $18,100 |
| Room and board | $5,590 |
| Books and supplies | $1,700 |
| Required fees | $860 |
| % frosh receiving aid | 82 |
| % undergrads receiving aid | 78 |
| Avg frosh grant | $7,500 |
| Avg frosh loan | $3,100 |

# WHEATON COLLEGE (IL)

501 COLLEGE AVENUE, WHEATON, IL 60187 • ADMISSIONS: 630-752-5005 • FAX: 630-752-5285

## CAMPUS LIFE

| | |
|---|---|
| Quality of Life Rating | 78 |
| Type of school | private |
| Affiliation | other |
| Environment | suburban |

### STUDENTS

| | |
|---|---|
| Total undergrad enrollment | 2,395 |
| % male/female | 49/51 |
| % from out of state | 77 |
| % from public high school | 64 |
| % live on campus | 86 |
| % African American | 2 |
| % Asian | 6 |
| % Caucasian | 88 |
| % Hispanic | 3 |
| % international | 1 |
| # of countries represented | 44 |

### SURVEY SAYS . . .

Lots of conservatives on campus
Diversity lacking on campus
Very little drug use
Campus feels safe
Students are very religious
Very little hard liquor
Beautiful campus
Very little beer drinking
Very small frat/sorority scene
(Almost) no one smokes

## ACADEMICS

| | |
|---|---|
| Academic Rating | 89 |
| Calendar | semester |
| Student/faculty ratio | 11:1 |
| Profs interesting rating | 71 |
| Profs accessible rating | 71 |
| % profs teaching UG courses | 90 |
| Avg lab size | 10-19 students |
| Avg reg class size | 10-19 students |

### MOST POPULAR MAJORS
English language and literature
Business/managerial economics
Music

## STUDENTS SPEAK OUT

### Academics

Book learning means nothing at Wheaton without a Christian basis, and many students comment favorably on the "integration of academic challenges and moral principles" at their school. "It's not that I'm simply studying and earning grades. I am able to grow as a person and a student," writes a first-year undergraduate. Though some professors are accused of being "wrapped up in appearing scholarly," most are described as "personally interested in students. There are always people willing to talk, counsel, or pray with you." The faculty "firmly yet compassionately pushes students," writes a biology student, and lectures are deemed by many as "engaging and challenging." Getting into classes can be tougher than the classes themselves, however. "The registration bureaucracy is a nightmare at worst and an annoying hassle at best," comments a senior in the philosophy department, and reportedly, underclassmen don't stand a chance of landing a spot in certain popular courses.

### Life

The majority of students at Wheaton seem to support the strict rules that govern campus life, concurring that they eliminate "negative peer pressure." A junior tells us, "Although you sign something saying you won't drink, smoke, take drugs, or have sex, it is still on campus. It is just very underground, which is nice. It's there if you want it, but if you don't, it's easy to think it doesn't exist." Others complain that the tight regulations demonstrate that "This school trusts neither its students nor its faculty." With the typical party options abolished, Wheaton students are forced to be "innovative in finding ways to have fun." For example, one sophomore enjoys "dressing up in all polyester and going to Krispy Kreme." Others "sit around thinking about what we could do for fun before resigning to the fact that we will once again either study or do nothing." More commonly, students "go on road trips, see shows in Chicago, play music and sports, and attend museums." Though the dating scene is D.O.A., the school organizes "talent shows, movie nights, and concerts, and dorm life is upbeat and interesting." The Christian environment encourages "open dialogue about campus and personal issues" and builds such an environment of trust that "many of us don't even lock the doors to our rooms."

### Student Body

A transfer student expresses a common view: "The majority of kids on this campus are the smart ones from high school that tended not to drink or party—we're not prudes, though." A senior communications major disagrees, writing, "Students are too worried about academics to have a healthy social life. In our attempt to pursue Godly male-female relationships, we have become sexually and socially repressed." Though some Wheaton kids are undeniably "squares" and "nerds," a freshman generally finds her classmates to be "welcoming, friendly, and inspiring. They challenge me in several aspects of life in the daily examples they set." A junior notes his classmates' personal growth process, telling us, "Many come in rich, protected, and naïve, but they expand their views as they go through." In the diversity department, a black student writes, "As a minority student on campus, I have found this to be an open-minded place."

# WHEATON COLLEGE (IL)

FINANCIAL AID: 630-752-5021 • E-MAIL: ADMISSIONS@WHEATON.EDU • WEBSITE: WWW.WHEATON.EDU

## ADMISSIONS

*Very important factors considered include:* character/personal qualities, essays, recommendations, Christian commitment, secondary school record, standardized test scores, talent/ability. *Important factors considered include:* alumni/ae relation, extracurricular activities, interview, minority status. *Other factors considered include:* class rank, volunteer work. SAT I or ACT required. TOEFL required of all international applicants. High school diploma or GED is required. *High school units required/recommended:* 15 total required; 4 English recommended, 3 math recommended, 3 science recommended, 2 foreign language recommended, 3 social studies recommended.

### The Inside Word

The admissions process at Wheaton is quite rigorous. As at most small colleges, the review of candidates focuses on far more than courses, grades, and test scores. The admissions committee will also carefully consider your essays, recommendations, and other indicators of your character as they assess how well suited you are to the campus community. Wheaton limits acceptance to students who profess Christian faith.

## FINANCIAL AID

*Students should submit:* FAFSA, institution's own financial aid form. The Princeton Review suggests that all financial aid forms be submitted as soon as possible after January 1. *Need-based scholarships/grants offered:* Pell, SEOG, state scholarships/grants, the school's own gift aid. *Loan aid offered:* FFEL Subsidized Stafford, FFEL Unsubsidized Stafford, FFEL PLUS, Federal Perkins, state loans, college/university loans from institutional funds. Federal Work-Study Program available. Institutional employment available. Applicants will be notified of awards on a rolling basis beginning on or about March 1. Off-campus job opportunities are excellent.

## FROM THE ADMISSIONS OFFICE

"At Wheaton, we're commited to being a community that fearlessly pursues truth, upholds an academically rigorous curriculum, and promotes virtue. The college takes seriously its impact on society. The influence of Wheaton is seen in fields ranging from government (the speaker of the house) to sports (two NBA coaches) to business (the CEO of Wal-Mart) to music (Metropolitan Opera National Competition winners) to education (over 40 college presidents) to global ministry (Billy Graham). Wheaton seeks students who want to make a difference and are passionate about their Christian faith and rigorous academic pursuit."

## SELECTIVITY

| | |
|---|---|
| Admissions Rating | 92 |
| # of applicants | 1,968 |
| % of applicants accepted | 54 |
| % of acceptees attending | 53 |
| # accepting a place on wait list | 229 |
| % admitted from wait list | 10 |

### FRESHMAN PROFILE

| | |
|---|---|
| Range SAT Verbal | 620-710 |
| Average SAT Verbal | 661 |
| Range SAT Math | 610-700 |
| Average SAT Math | 658 |
| Range ACT Composite | 26-31 |
| Average ACT Composite | 28 |
| Minimum TOEFL | 550 |
| Average HS GPA | 3.7 |
| % graduated top 10% of class | 54 |
| % graduated top 25% of class | 84 |
| % graduated top 50% of class | 97 |

### DEADLINES

| | |
|---|---|
| Priority admission | 1/15 |
| Regular admission | 1/15 |
| Regular notification | 4/10 |

### APPLICANTS ALSO LOOK AT AND SOMETIMES PREFER
Northwestern U
Taylor U
Calvin College

### AND RARELY PREFER
U of Illinois
Grove City College

## FINANCIAL FACTS

| | |
|---|---|
| Financial Aid Rating | 86 |
| Tuition | $18,500 |
| Room and board | $6,100 |
| Books and supplies | $660 |
| % frosh receiving aid | 47 |
| % undergrads receiving aid | 46 |
| Avg frosh grant | $7,051 |
| Avg frosh loan | $3,754 |

# WHEATON COLLEGE (MA)
OFFICE OF ADMISSION, NORTON, MA 02766 • ADMISSIONS: 508-286-8251 • FAX: 508-286-8271

## CAMPUS LIFE

| Quality of Life Rating | 79 |
|---|---|
| Type of school | private |
| Environment | suburban |

### STUDENTS
| | |
|---|---|
| Total undergrad enrollment | 1,521 |
| % male/female | 36/64 |
| % from out of state | 67 |
| % from public high school | 65 |
| % live on campus | 97 |
| % African American | 3 |
| % Asian | 3 |
| % Caucasian | 83 |
| % Hispanic | 4 |
| % international | 6 |
| # of countries represented | 29 |

### SURVEY SAYS . . .
Lots of conservatives
Registration is a breeze
Students are happy
Students are cliquish
Very little drug use

## ACADEMICS

| Academic Rating | 85 |
|---|---|
| Calendar | semester |
| Student/faculty ratio | 11:1 |
| Profs interesting rating | 96 |
| Profs accessible rating | 97 |
| % profs teaching UG courses | 100 |
| Avg lab size | 10-19 students |
| Avg reg class size | 10-19 students |

### MOST POPULAR MAJORS
Psychology
English language and literature
Fine/studio arts

## STUDENTS SPEAK OUT

### Academics
A comfortable, nurturing environment, Wheaton College offers students a faculty and staff that, as one typical respondant says, feels like "an extension of my family." Even underclassmen enjoy close relationships with professors: "They take special care of freshmen so we don't get forgotten. They spread the love." One senior writes that her professors are "very dedicated to their students and love what they teach," while another characterizes them as "extremely accessible and accommodating." Thanks to the small class sizes, students receive individual attention and perks like "senior seminars conducted in professors' living rooms over tea and cookies." In terms of administration, a senior comments that the Student Life Office is "run poorly and fails to help students." But others note that rather than ride a reputation, the Wheaton administration is "always looking for ways to improve." Internship opportunities and career planning services at the Filene Center are universally lauded by students. One freshman comments, "Our greatest strength is our second transcript—our resume. The school helps you build that while studying."

### Life
Life in the "ghost town" of Norton, Massachusetts, could get boring if it weren't for the "beautiful campus" and "activities that keep students busy and connected" within the "Wheaton bubble." Luckily, both Boston and Providence are within striking distance so students can escape for "nightlife, shopping, and museums." On campus, people hang out at the Lyon's Den café or attend the concerts that frequently come through campus. Most students like the fact that there is no Greek system at Wheaton, but they grumble about school-sponsored social events, including dances that bolster one student's portrayal of Wheaton as "a big high school." A freshman comments, "I think that those who are creative and adventurous find things to do on the weekend." Athletics are popular at this Division III school, with one student stating, "Everyone plays a sport or works out." Synchronized swimming, soccer, and basketball get a lot of attention, but a high percentage of students are also involved in Wheaton's radio station, WCCS. There are complaints of dorm overcrowding, which recently led to some "forced triples," but the opening of a new 100-bed dorm in February alleviated the problem. All in all, students agree that it's "easy to make Wheaton home."

### Student Body
Formerly an all-women school, Wheaton's admissions department is still trying to even out the high female-to-male ratio. "Thank God more men are being admitted!" a female sophomore writes. Generally, the student body is alternately described as "wealthy, snobby, and cliquish" or "rich, white, and preppy." Some students wonder if they've stumbled into an Abercrombie and Fitch advertisement and note a "lack of diversity in interests, ethnicity, and mentality." Though there is "some of that high school grouping" to contend with, others call the student body a "highly interactive community" with a "high level of acceptance." Apparently, "it's almost disturbing how friendly people are." "Everybody says hello," even to people they don't know. Detractors claim that Wheaton-ites are "apathetic" and "should be more political," but others say "people are very concerned with what's going on in the world." Either way, it's maintained that "you won't find a friendlier group."

# WHEATON COLLEGE (MA)

FINANCIAL AID: 508-286-8232 • E-MAIL: ADMISSION@WHEATONCOLLEGE.EDU • WEBSITE: WWW.WHEATONCOLLEGE.EDU

## ADMISSIONS

*Very important factors considered include:* character/personal qualities, essays, extracurricular activities, secondary school record, talent/ability. *Important factors considered include:* alumni/ae relation, class rank, interview, recommendations, volunteer work, work experience. *Other factors considered include:* geographical residence, minority status, standardized test scores, state residency. TOEFL required of all international applicants. High school diploma or GED is required. *High school units required/recommended:* 16 total recommended; 4 English recommended, 3 math recommended, 3 science recommended, 2 science lab recommended, 4 foreign language recommended, 2 social studies recommended.

### The Inside Word

Wheaton is to be applauded for periodically re-examining its admissions process; some colleges use virtually the same application process eternally, never acknowledging the fluid nature of societal attitudes and institutional circumstances. Approaches that emphasize individuals, or even their accomplishments, over their numbers are unfortunately rare in the world of college admission, where GPA and SAT I reign supreme. Wheaton has an easier time than some colleges in taking this step because it isn't prohibitively selective.

## FINANCIAL AID

*Students should submit:* FAFSA, CSS/Financial Aid PROFILE, noncustodial (divorced/separated) parent's statement, business/farm supplement, parent's and student's federal tax returns and W-2s. Regular filing deadline is February 1. The Princeton Review suggests that all financial aid forms be submitted as soon as possible after January 1. *Need-based scholarships/grants offered:* Pell, SEOG, state scholarships/grants, private scholarships, the school's own gift aid. *Loan aid offered:* FFEL Subsidized Stafford, FFEL Unsubsidized Stafford, FFEL PLUS, Federal Perkins, state loans, college/university loans from institutional funds, MEFA, TERI, CitiAssist, other private educational loans. Federal Work-Study Program available. Institutional employment available. Applicants will be notified of awards on or about April 1. Off-campus job opportunities are good.

## FROM THE ADMISSIONS OFFICE

"What makes for a 'best college'? Is it merely the hard-to-define notions of prestige or image? We don't think so. We think what makes college 'best' and best for you is a school that will make you a first-rate thinker and writer, a pragmatic professional in your work, and an ethical practitioner in your life. To get you to all these places, Wheaton takes advantage of its great combinations: a beautiful, secluded New England campus combined with access to Boston and Providence; a high quality, classic liberal arts and sciences curriculum combined with award-winning internship, job, and community service programs; and a campus that respects your individuality in the context of the larger community. What's the 'best' outcome of a Wheaton education? A start on life that combines meaningful work, significant relationships, and a commitment to your local and global community. Far more than for what they've studied or for what they've gone on to do for a living, we're most proud of Wheaton graduates for who they become."

---

### SELECTIVITY

| | |
|---|---|
| Admissions Rating | 82 |
| # of applicants | 3,534 |
| % of applicants accepted | 44 |
| % of acceptees attending | 27 |
| # accepting a place on wait list | 248 |
| % admitted from wait list | 6 |
| # of early decision applicants | 243 |
| % accepted early decision | 66 |

### FRESHMAN PROFILE

| | |
|---|---|
| Range SAT Verbal | 590-670 |
| Average SAT Verbal | 630 |
| Range SAT Math | 550-650 |
| Average SAT Math | 610 |
| Range ACT Composite | 26-29 |
| Average ACT Composite | 27 |
| Minimum TOEFL | 550 |
| Average HS GPA | 3.4 |
| % graduated top 10% of class | 43 |
| % graduated top 25% of class | 76 |
| % graduated top 50% of class | 93 |

### DEADLINES

| | |
|---|---|
| Early decision | 11/15 |
| Early decision notification | 12/15 |
| Regular admission | 1/15 |
| Regular notification | 4/1 |
| Nonfall registration? | yes |

### APPLICANTS ALSO LOOK AT
**AND OFTEN PREFER**
Bates College
Connecticut College
**AND SOMETIMES PREFER**
Skidmore College
University of Vermont
**AND RARELY PREFER**
Boston University
Clark University
Brandeis University

### FINANCIAL FACTS

| | |
|---|---|
| Financial Aid Rating | 85 |
| Tuition | $27,105 |
| Room and board | $7,260 |
| Books and supplies | $1,060 |
| Required fees | $225 |
| % frosh receiving aid | 51 |
| % undergrads receiving aid | 58 |
| Avg frosh grant | $14,416 |
| Avg frosh loan | $3,602 |

THE BEST 351 COLLEGES ■ 729

# WHITMAN COLLEGE

345 BOYER AVENUE, WALLA WALLA, WA 99362-2083 • ADMISSIONS: 509-527-5176 • FAX: 509-527-4967

## CAMPUS LIFE

★ ★ ★ ☆

| | |
|---|---|
| Quality of Life Rating | 89 |
| Type of school | private |
| Environment | rural |

### STUDENTS

| | |
|---|---|
| Total undergrad enrollment | 1,454 |
| % male/female | 43/57 |
| % from out of state | 55 |
| % from public high school | 70 |
| % live on campus | 74 |
| % in (# of) fraternities | 30 (4) |
| % in (# of) sororities | 30 (4) |
| % African American | 1 |
| % Asian | 7 |
| % Caucasian | 80 |
| % Hispanic | 3 |
| % international | 2 |
| # of countries represented | 23 |

### SURVEY SAYS . . .
Great computer facilities
Great library
Hard liquor is popular
No one cheats
Everyone plays intramural sports

## ACADEMICS

| | |
|---|---|
| Academic Rating | 96 |
| Calendar | semester |
| Student/faculty ratio | 10:1 |
| Profs interesting rating | 96 |
| Profs accessible rating | 99 |
| % profs teaching UG courses | 100 |
| Avg lab size | 20-29 students |
| Avg reg class size | 10-19 students |

### MOST POPULAR MAJORS
Biology/biological sciences
Psychology
Political science and government

## STUDENTS SPEAK OUT

### Academics

Students at Whitman College say the caring attention they receive from their professors and administrators is what makes their educational experiences exceptional. Explains one typical undergrad, "The professors are there for you. They know who you are [and] encourage discussion and attendance at office hours. They tell me I can call them at home. I've played with their kids and their dogs and gone to barbeques in their back yards. The admissions officer I interviewed with stops to talk to me, asks what I've been up to, my opinion about whatever. She remembers the essays I wrote." The personal touch reaches all the way to the top here; "[President] Tom Cronin's a really friendly guy. He passes cookies out at the library on Sunday night. He knows almost all of the students on a first-name basis." Faculty members "demonstrate a passion for teaching, learning, and inspiring greatness in their students, and make this evident through their commitment (in the classroom and out) to their field and in discourse with others." These assets help soften the blow dealt by Whitman's extremely rigorous academic program. Writes one undergrad, "Whitman is a very challenging school. The common trend I have noticed is that a student has to do decent work to get a B, but must work their you-know-what off to get an A." Sums up one student, "Everyone is concerned about you here—they don't want you to fail. It is a very challenging school academically, yet it is not undoable. You are never done with your work."

### Life

Because Whitties "are stuck in a really small town, we have to create our own fun on campus." And so they do: reports one undergrad, "On Thursday, Friday, and Saturday night there is always a party somewhere, either at one of the four fraternity houses or at another off-campus house. There's a ton to do. There are always guest lectures or visiting performers. And what with the three choirs, orchestra, wind ensemble, two jazz bands, and flute choir, a musical performance is not hard to come by. The theatre puts up a season of nine shows, but there are usually at least five other off-season shows. Every Friday night is coffee house, where a student group or individual performs. If you're not into performances, there's writer's colony, where you can go and explore the writer in you. The list goes on and on." While students may not love hometown Walla Walla, they do love some of the amenities their surroundings offer. Explains one student, "For someone who likes the outdoors, Walla Walla is a great place. The mountains are close, the rivers of eastern Oregon are only a few hours away, and there are some awesome bike rides. If you don't like the outdoors, you are pretty much out of luck." The campus itself "is absolutely beautiful and on sunny days, the whole school is generally hanging out on Ankeny, the main field, reading, playing games, socializing, and generally just having a good time." The nearest large city, Spokane, is more than two hours away by car; trips to Portland and Seattle each require a four-hour drive.

### Student Body

Students readily admit that "it's a very homogenous student population [at Whitman]. Almost everyone is white, middle class or upper-middle class, and liberal. It would be hard to be a conservative Republican here." Agrees one conservative student, "They are hard on those who do not think like they do—meaning, conservative students are a minority on this campus and are not given their fair opportunity to express their points of view." Students are passionate about their politics, too, leading one student to note that "except for the political debates over the campus listserv, everyone here is really friendly." Students are typically "very bright and highly motivated. As 'Whitties' collectively, we all get along well. Relations, however, between Greeks and non-Greeks are shaky."

# WHITMAN COLLEGE

FINANCIAL AID: 509-527-5178 • E-MAIL: ADMISSION@WHITMAN.EDU • WEBSITE: WWW.WHITMAN.EDU

## ADMISSIONS

*Very important factors considered include:* course selection and grades, character/personal qualities, essays. *Important factors considered include:* extracurricular activities, recommendations, standardized test scores, talent/ability. *Other factors considered include:* alumni/ae relation, class rank, geographical residence, interview, minority status, state residency, volunteer work, work experience. SAT I or ACT required. TOEFL required of all international applicants. High school diploma or GED is required. *High school units required/recommended:* 18 total recommended; 4 English recommended, 4 math recommended, 3 science recommended, 3 science lab recommended, 2 foreign language recommended, 2 social studies recommended, 2 history recommended.

### The Inside Word

Whitman's admissions committee is to be applauded; any admissions process that emphasizes essays and extracurriculars over the SAT I has truly gotten it right. The college cares much more about who you are and what you have to offer if you enroll than it does about what your numbers will do for the freshman academic profile. Whitman is a mega-sleeper. Educators all over the country know it as an excellent institution, and the college's alums support it at one of the highest rates of giving at any college in the nation. Student seeking a top-quality liberal arts college owe it to themselves to take a look.

## FINANCIAL AID

*Students should submit:* FAFSA, CSS/Financial Aid PROFILE, parent's tax return. Regular filing deadline is February 1. The Princeton Review suggests that all financial aid forms be submitted as soon as possible after January 1. *Need-based scholarships/grants offered:* Pell, SEOG, state scholarships/grants, private scholarships, the school's own gift aid. *Loan aid offered:* FFEL Subsidized Stafford, FFEL Unsubsidized Stafford, FFEL PLUS, Federal Perkins, alternative student loans. Federal Work-Study Program available. Institutional employment available. Applicants will be notified of awards on a rolling basis beginning on or about December 20. Off-campus job opportunities are fair.

## FROM THE ADMISSIONS OFFICE

"Whitman is a place that encourages you to explore past the boundaries of disciplines because learning and living don't always fall neatly into tidy little compartments. Many students choose Whitman specifically because they're interested in a particular career such as business or engineering but want the well-rounded preparation that only a liberal arts education provides."

---

### SELECTIVITY

| | |
|---|---|
| Admissions Rating | 95 |
| # of applicants | 2,411 |
| % of applicants accepted | 50 |
| % of acceptees attending | 31 |
| # accepting a place on wait list | 94 |
| % admitted from wait list | 18 |
| # of early decision applicants | 131 |
| % accepted early decision | 82 |

### FRESHMAN PROFILE

| | |
|---|---|
| Range SAT Verbal | 610-710 |
| Average SAT Verbal | 659 |
| Range SAT Math | 610-700 |
| Average SAT Math | 655 |
| Range ACT Composite | 26-31 |
| Average ACT Composite | 28 |
| Minimum TOEFL | 560 |
| Average HS GPA | 3.8 |
| % graduated top 10% of class | 64 |
| % graduated top 25% of class | 90 |
| % graduated top 50% of class | 100 |

### DEADLINES

| | |
|---|---|
| Early decision | 11/15 |
| Early decision notification | 12/15 |
| Regular admission | 1/15 |
| Regular notification | 4/1 |
| Nonfall registration? | yes |

### APPLICANTS ALSO LOOK AT AND OFTEN PREFER
Pomona
Claremont McKenna
Carleton

**AND SOMETIMES PREFER**
Colorado College
Occidental
U of Puget Sound

**AND RARELY PREFER**
U of Washington
Lewis & Clark, Willamette

### FINANCIAL FACTS

| | |
|---|---|
| Financial Aid Rating | 87 |
| Tuition | $25,400 |
| Room and board | $6,900 |
| Books and supplies | $1,000 |
| Required fees | $226 |
| % frosh receiving aid | 43 |
| % undergrads receiving aid | 43 |
| Avg frosh grant | $16,850 |
| Avg frosh loan | $2,650 |

# WHITTIER COLLEGE

13406 East Philadelphia Street, PO Box 634, Whittier, CA 90608 • Admissions: 562-907-4238 • Fax: 562-907-4870

## CAMPUS LIFE

| Quality of Life Rating | 83 |
| --- | --- |
| Type of school | private |
| Environment | suburban |

### STUDENTS

| Total undergrad enrollment | 1,121 |
| --- | --- |
| % male/female | 40/60 |
| % from out of state | 33 |
| % live on campus | 62 |
| % in (# of) fraternities | 12 (4) |
| % in (# of) sororities | 17 (5) |
| % African American | 4 |
| % Asian | 8 |
| % Caucasian | 48 |
| % Hispanic | 25 |
| % international | 5 |
| # of countries represented | 17 |

### SURVEY SAYS . . .
Dorms are like palaces
Campus feels safe
Classes are small
Theater is unpopular

## ACADEMICS

| Academic Rating | 84 |
| --- | --- |
| Calendar | 4-1-4 |
| Student/faculty ratio | 11:1 |
| Profs interesting rating | 95 |
| Profs accessible rating | 98 |
| % profs teaching UG courses | 100 |
| Avg lab size | 10-19 students |
| Avg reg class size | 10-19 students |

### MOST POPULAR MAJORS
Business administration/management
Child development
Biology/biological sciences

## STUDENTS SPEAK OUT

### Academics

The great strengths of Whittier College, a small liberal arts school outside of Los Angeles, include "an interesting and interested faculty, a great student/faculty ratio—during my last term, I was the only student in a class taught by two professors!—and curricular flexibility that allows students to design their own course of study." Students here may choose between two curricular approaches. There is the more conventional Liberal Education track, which requires completion of both an integrated core curriculum and a major course of study. Or, they may select the more adventurous Whittier Scholars Program, in which undergraduates design their own curricula and even their own majors. Students appreciate "the chance for self-motivated growth. It's up to you to be involved, but if you are you will be met with a great college experience." Professors here "are wonderful, very accessible and understanding, and they know what they are doing. They call each student by name and are excited to get to know the students in their classes. The professors ask around to find out why you weren't in class and often invite students into their homes or take them on extra excursions to further the learning process." Student complaints center on the administration and its "lack of communication between offices" (some students concede that "the administration isn't perfect but is getting better") and the need to upgrade facilities. Complains one typical student, "We are behind when it comes to technology on campus."

### Life

Students report a subdued social atmosphere on the Whittier campus, explaining that "The campus is a community without being in your face. There is opportunity for involvement everywhere. If a student is not looking for 24-hour partying and is interested in a calm but valuable social life, this is the place to be." With "80 percent of the students involved in intercollegiate sports," the campus "is pretty busy with sports" at all times. Clubs, lectures, movies, restaurants, study groups, and just hanging out in the student center also contribute to the "many activities during the week," but "on weekends the campus is dead. Most people leave." Although, on-campus parties are deemed nonexistent, as one student cites, "there are societies, which often have parties, especially the ones that have houses off campus. So don't be fooled, the parties are there if you can find them. Other than that, people party in the rooms a lot." Fortunately, "If you are looking for parties, hey, L.A. is only a half-hour away. You just need a car to get there." Students like to head to the beach or "commute to UCSB, USC, or UCLA for a party."

### Student Body

Whittier undergrads brag that "statistics say we're the most diverse, and it's true: you can't turn around without running into someone who defies the 'white, rich, upper-class' stereotype. Asians, blacks, Jews, gays, foreign students . . . we got 'em all." Students "interact without fear of judgment based on race, gender, or sexual orientation" as "a small community where everyone knows everyone else and gets along pretty well together." Interestingly enough, students "tend to be more conservative than the faculty. They seem to be mostly apolitical but a good controversy (like the 2000 presidential elections) seems to bring out their activist tendencies." More than a few undergrads wish their classmates were a bit more academic. "If it could only recruit better students," wrote one undergraduate. "They're very Californian: nice, but slightly vapid," observed another with disgruntlement.

# WHITTIER COLLEGE

FINANCIAL AID: 562-907-4285 • E-MAIL: ADMISSION@WHITTIER.EDU • WEBSITE: WWW.WHITTIER.EDU

## ADMISSIONS

*Very important factors considered include:* essays, secondary school record. *Important factors considered include:* class rank, interview. *Other factors considered include:* alumni/ae relation, character/personal qualities, extracurricular activities, minority status, recommendations, standardized test scores, state residency, talent/ability, volunteer work, work experience. SAT I or ACT required. TOEFL required of all international applicants. High school diploma is required and GED is not accepted. *High school units required/recommended:* 11 total required; 16 total recommended; 4 English required, 3 math required, 1 science required, 3 science recommended, 2 science lab recommended, 2 foreign language required, 3 foreign language recommended, 1 social studies required, 2 social studies recommended, 3 history recommended.

### The Inside Word

The admissions committee at Whittier subjects each candidate to very close scrutiny. Their academic expectations aren't too high, but their interest in making good solid matches between candidates and the college is paramount. If Whittier is high on your list, make sure you put forth a serious effort to demonstrate what you want out of the college and what you'll bring to the table in return.

## FINANCIAL AID

*Students should submit:* FAFSA, CSS/Financial Aid PROFILE. No deadline for regular filing. The Princeton Review suggests that all financial aid forms be submitted as soon as possible after January 1. *Need-based scholarships/grants offered:* Pell, SEOG, state scholarships/grants, private scholarships, the school's own gift aid. *Loan aid offered:* FFEL Subsidized Stafford, FFEL Unsubsidized Stafford, FFEL PLUS, Federal Perkins, college/university loans from institutional funds. Federal Work-Study Program available. Institutional employment available. Applicants will be notified of awards on a rolling basis beginning on or about April 1. Off-campus job opportunities are good.

## FROM THE ADMISSIONS OFFICE

"Faculty and students at Whittier share a love of learning and delight in the life of the mind. They join in understanding the value of the intellectual quest, the use of reason, and a respect for values. They seek knowledge of their own culture and the informed appreciation of other traditions, and they explore the interrelatedness of knowledge and the connections among disciplines. An extraordinary community emerges from teachers and students representing a variety of academic pursuits, individuals who have come together at Whittier in the belief that study within the liberal arts forms the best foundation for rewarding endeavor throughout a lifetime."

### SELECTIVITY

| | |
|---|---|
| Admissions Rating | 76 |
| # of applicants | 1,485 |
| % of applicants accepted | 76 |
| % of acceptees attending | 27 |
| # accepting a place on wait list | 30 |
| % admitted from wait list | 27 |

### FRESHMAN PROFILE

| | |
|---|---|
| Range SAT Verbal | 490-590 |
| Average SAT Verbal | 547 |
| Range SAT Math | 490-600 |
| Average SAT Math | 542 |
| Range ACT Composite | 20-26 |
| Average ACT Composite | 23 |
| Minimum TOEFL | 550 |
| Average HS GPA | 3.1 |
| % graduated top 10% of class | 14 |
| % graduated top 25% of class | 30 |
| % graduated top 50% of class | 52 |

### DEADLINES

| | |
|---|---|
| Priority admission | 2/1 |

### APPLICANTS ALSO LOOK AT AND OFTEN PREFER
Occidental
Redlands

### AND SOMETIMES PREFER
Loyola Marymount
Pitzer

### AND RARELY PREFER
Champman
CMC

### FINANCIAL FACTS

| | |
|---|---|
| Financial Aid Rating | 93 |
| Tuition | $23,192 |
| Room and board | $7,474 |
| Books and supplies | $656 |
| Required fees | $960 |
| % frosh receiving aid | 71 |
| % undergrads receiving aid | 73 |
| Avg frosh grant | $16,531 |
| Avg frosh loan | $7,497 |

# WILLAMETTE UNIVERSITY

900 STATE STREET, SALEM, OR 97301 • ADMISSIONS: 877-LIB-ARTS • FAX: 503-375-5363

## CAMPUS LIFE

| Quality of Life Rating | 82 |
|---|---|
| Type of school | private |
| Affiliation | Methodist |
| Environment | urban |

### STUDENTS

| Total undergrad enrollment | 1,750 |
|---|---|
| % male/female | 46/54 |
| % from out of state | 54 |
| % from public high school | 79 |
| % live on campus | 71 |
| % in (# of) fraternities | 32 (5) |
| % in (# of) sororities | 32 (3) |
| % African American | 2 |
| % Asian | 7 |
| % Caucasian | 62 |
| % Hispanic | 5 |
| % international | 1 |

### SURVEY SAYS . . .
Classes are small
Great food on campus
Low cost of living
Profs teach upper-levels
Dorms are like palaces
Student publications are ignored
(Almost) no one listens to college radio
Students don't like Salem, OR
Very little drug use

## ACADEMICS

| Academic Rating | 87 |
|---|---|
| Calendar | semester |
| Student/faculty ratio | 10:1 |
| Profs interesting rating | 94 |
| Profs accessible rating | 96 |
| % profs teaching UG courses | 100 |
| Avg lab size | 10-19 students |
| Avg reg class size | 10-19 students |

### MOST POPULAR MAJORS
English language and literature
Biology
Political science and government

## STUDENTS SPEAK OUT

### Academics
It's the personal touches that students at Willamette University appreciate most about their school. "One of the best things about Willamette is that the professors are real people," explains one student. "They eat in the cafeteria with us. We call a lot of them by their first names. Sometimes I forget that Bob, my rhetoric professor, is also a leading rhetorical argumentation theorist." Everyone, from faculty to administration officials, "is very friendly. Even our president has student office hours." Professors here are "highly qualified, intelligent, interesting, hard working, and available outside of class." Writes one student approvingly, "They don't point everything out to us. Instead, they allow us to figure some things out for ourselves through class discussion." Students give WU's distribution requirements, designed to expose all undergraduates to math, literature, social sciences, natural sciences, and fine arts, mixed reviews. Most feel that "the intro classes suck, but most upper-level classes are a kick. They make you work, but it's worth it." All students must also complete a senior project, which can be a major scientific research project, a senior thesis, or a professional internship. Students interested in political science benefit from the school's location, right across the street from the state capitol, as well as an internship program in Washington, D.C. Students also speak highly of the "great study abroad programs" offered here.

### Life
Willamette students describe a peaceful, pleasant atmosphere pervading the gorgeous campus. "Willamette spends a lot on campus beauty," notes one student. It's the kind of place where, one student writes, "if I paid tuition and lived here but didn't have to go to classes, I would [remain] here for the rest of my young adult life." It's "very easy to balance your social and academic life here. There's always something happening on campus," whether its "intramural activities (fun and easy to get involved in)," clubs, or just a free movie. Says one undergrad, "I don't come back to my room from 9 A.M. to 9 P.M. Life is busy, fast-paced, and intense. Everyone here is active in rigorous academics, sports, and clubs." Students appreciate the fact that the area is conducive to "good recreation: skiing, beach, kayaking, and hiking in the mountains are nearby." They also point out that "the rain isn't that bad. Goretex is good." Hometown Salem, unfortunately, "isn't tempting. In fact, I rarely leave campus because there isn't much reason to." But "although Salem sucks, Portland is only 45 minutes away." The weekend party scene revolves around the Greek houses and suffers because "the administration wants an alcohol-free campus. In an attempt to get out the beer, they killed the fun. Saturday nights are very quiet at WU because all the parties are off campus, unless the Greeks are partying." And, warns one GDI, "The Greeks never mix with the rest of the university population." Adds another, "If I could change one thing about WU, I would lessen the focus on drinking and the Greek system."

### Student Body
According to the boosters among their ranks, the undergraduates of WU each have "something special to offer: artistic ability, leadership, athletics. Everyone has been successful and is interesting! The nicest people I've ever met." At the other end of the spectrum are those who report that many of their fellow students are "very concerned with how they look and what brand names they are wearing. Abercrombie and Fitch is most popular here." Students would like to see more diversity. However, they temper these complaints as well: "Not enough diversity, but we have the highest in the state," or "there is diversity in thought."

734 ■ THE BEST 351 COLLEGES

# WILLAMETTE UNIVERSITY

FINANCIAL AID: 503-370-6273 • E-MAIL: UNDERGRAD-ADMISSION@WILLAMETTE.EDU • WEBSITE: WWW.WILLAMETTE.EDU

## ADMISSIONS
*Very important factors considered include:* class rank, recommendations, secondary school record, standardized test scores. *Important factors considered include:* character/personal qualities, essays, extracurricular activities, interview, talent/ability. *Other factors considered include:* alumni/ae relation, geographical residence, minority status, volunteer work, work experience. SAT I or ACT required. TOEFL required of all international applicants. High school diploma or GED is required. *High school units required/recommended:* 4 English recommended, 4 math recommended, 3 science recommended, 3 foreign language recommended, 3 social studies recommended.

## The Inside Word
Willamette's admissions process is relatively standard for small liberal arts colleges. Extracurriculars, recommendations, and essays help the admissions committee do some matchmaking, but ultimately it's a candidate's grades that determine admissibility.

## FINANCIAL AID
*Students should submit:* FAFSA, CSS/Financial Aid PROFILE. The Princeton Review suggests that all financial aid forms be submitted as soon as possible after January 1. *Need-based scholarships/grants offered:* Pell, SEOG, state scholarships/grants, private scholarships, the school's own gift aid, United Negro College Fund. *Loan aid offered:* FFEL Subsidized Stafford, FFEL Unsubsidized Stafford, FFEL PLUS, Federal Perkins, state loans, private loans. Federal Work-Study Program available. Institutional employment available. Applicants will be notified of awards on or about April 1. Off-campus job opportunities are good.

## FROM THE ADMISSIONS OFFICE
"And here are what other students have to say about the Willamette experience: 'Willamette students are achievers,' says Tasha Shapiro, a junior politics major from Los Altos, California. 'They're really bright and very eclectic in the activities they do and the interests they have. They're doing great things, they're getting great grades—I always feel surrounded by success.' 'At Willamette, you're accepted for who you are and what you want to do,' says Ben Kessler, a 2002 graduate from Bayside, California. 'You don't have to put on airs—you don't have to act a certain way to be "cool." I don't see any "in" crowd. You just have to be who you are, and you're cool because of that.' And finally, Sharon Long from Gresham, Oregon, sums up her impressions of Willamette by saying, 'I think Willamette creates amazing people. We're determined and ambitions and creative, but we're well-rounded at the same time.'"

## SELECTIVITY

| | |
|---|---|
| Admissions Rating | 85 |
| # of applicants | 1,640 |
| % of applicants accepted | 83 |
| % of acceptees attending | 26 |
| # accepting a place on wait list | 103 |
| % admitted from wait list | 27 |

### FRESHMAN PROFILE
| | |
|---|---|
| Range SAT Verbal | 560-680 |
| Average SAT Verbal | 620 |
| Range SAT Math | 560-660 |
| Average SAT Math | 610 |
| Range ACT Composite | 25-30 |
| Average ACT Composite | 27 |
| Minimum TOEFL | 550 |
| Average HS GPA | 3.6 |
| % graduated top 10% of class | 43 |
| % graduated top 25% of class | 73 |
| % graduated top 50% of class | 94 |

### DEADLINES
| | |
|---|---|
| Priority admission | 2/1 |
| Regular admission | 2/1 |
| Regular notification | 4/1 |
| Nonfall registration? | yes |

### APPLICANTS ALSO LOOK AT
**AND OFTEN PREFER**
Whitman College
**AND SOMETIMES PREFER**
U of Puget Sound
University of Oregon
Lewis & Clark College
**AND RARELY PREFER**
Linfield College
Gonzaga University
Occidental College
U of Portland

## FINANCIAL FACTS

| | |
|---|---|
| Financial Aid Rating | 90 |
| Tuition | $25,300 |
| Room and board | $6,600 |
| Books and supplies | $800 |
| Required fees | $132 |
| % frosh receiving aid | 64 |
| % undergrads receiving aid | 65 |
| Avg frosh grant | $12,000 |
| Avg frosh loan | $4,414 |

# WILLIAM JEWELL COLLEGE

500 COLLEGE HILL, LIBERTY, MO 64068 • ADMISSIONS: 800-753-7009 • FAX: 806-415-5027

## CAMPUS LIFE

| Quality of Life Rating | 82 |
|---|---|
| Type of school | private |
| Affiliation | Baptist |
| Environment | suburban |

### STUDENTS

| Total undergrad enrollment | 1,168 |
|---|---|
| % male/female | 42/58 |
| % from out of state | 20 |
| % from public high school | 95 |
| % live on campus | 71 |
| % in (# of) fraternities | 39 (3) |
| % in (# of) sororities | 37 (4) |
| % African American | 2 |
| % Asian | 1 |
| % Caucasian | 90 |
| % Hispanic | 2 |
| % international | 2 |
| # of countries represented | 12 |

### SURVEY SAYS . . .
Lots of classroom discussion
Great computer facilities
Very little drug use
Student publications are popular
Students are very religious
Registration is a pain

## ACADEMICS

| Academic Rating | 76 |
|---|---|
| Calendar | semester |
| Student/faculty ratio | 13:1 |
| Profs interesting rating | 85 |
| Profs accessible rating | 86 |
| % profs teaching UG courses | 100 |
| Avg lab size | under 10 students |
| Avg reg class size | under 10 students |

## STUDENTS SPEAK OUT

### Academics

One William Jewell student tells a personal story that goes like this: "I was conditionally accepted to William Jewell with a 2.7 GPA. I had to take a study skills class and could only carry 14 hours. I am a real success story for Jewell. In my first semester, I ended with a 3.8 GPA. I was in Emerging Leaders, Alpha Lambda Delta," a national freshman honor society, "and am a student supervisor in the admissions office." The close-knit, nurturing atmosphere at Jewell is what allows students to live up to their potential. Students tell us that the administration cares "not only about the school and admissions and PR, but about the students." And the personal attention that professors lavish on students means that professors are more than teachers; they "become friends, role models, and even 'parents away from home.' " "They are always willing to bend over backward to help their students," adds an undergrad. And they're great teachers, too, "brilliant leaders of their disciplines," according to one student. "Perhaps the most important part of the academic program," writes a student, "is the emphasis put on . . . improving your writing skills." One of the most popular academic tracks at William Jewell is the Oxbridge Honors Program, a four-year program based on one-on-one tutorials, comprehensive exams, and a year of study in England.

### Life

"Jewell is only 20 minutes from downtown Kansas City and only 5 minutes from a field full of cows," explains one undergraduate. The college's proximity to lively Kansas City is a relief to students, since "Liberty is so small that there isn't much to do." When students head to KC, they're usually in search of "eating, drinking, dancing, shopping," and the various other draws of urban life. On campus, a "solid Greek system serves as almost a social backbone for the college." And the "Campus Union Activities," a student-events group, "usually has something planned for most nights." Religious activities are particularly abundant. Writes one freshman, "Thursdays we have chapel in the morning and Worship Jam at night." Dorm life is vibrant, too: "In the residence halls you have a Resident Director, Resident Assistant," and someone called a "Shepherd." These people often join in the late-night conversations or movie-and-popcorn sessions. The party scene picks up on Wednesdays and weekends. Although Jewell's campus is considered "dry," the beer flows plentifully at off-campus frat parties and private parties alike. The restrictive nature of the rules here—from no drinking on campus to limited visitation hours in the dorms—causes some division between students and administration.

### Student Body

William Jewell students are "for the most part very religious and very religiously active." A senior explains that the easiest way to describe the students is to divide them into their preferences for "Christian life" and "Party life." "The Party life . . . is very involved in drinking, dancing, and occasionally drugs. Westport in Kansas City is a favorite site for this group, along with the Corner Bar, Legends, and Lucky's Pizza—all bars that have been known as college hangouts. Now on the other side, there are very large groups of students who are very involved religiously and live a totally different lifestyle. They enjoy just hanging out at Waffle House [or] Steak and Shake late at night, or just playing board games with the Campus Minister and going on mission trips." Despite these distinctions, "the student body is for the most part very friendly and accepting of all people." The fact that most of the students are "white Christians" who "tend to come from Missouri" leads quite a few undergrads to long for "more diversity." Whatever the demographic numbers, however, friendliness is paramount here. But "we are more than just friends," writes a happy student. "We are a family."

# WILLIAM JEWELL COLLEGE

FINANCIAL AID: 800-753-7009 • E-MAIL: ADMISSION@WILLIAM.JEWELL.EDU • WEBSITE: WWW.JEWELL.EDU

## ADMISSIONS

*Very important factors considered include:* class rank, secondary school record, standardized test scores. *Important factors considered include:* essays, recommendations. *Other factors considered include:* alumni/ae relation, character/personal qualities, extracurricular activities, interview, talent/ability, volunteer work, work experience. SAT I or ACT required. TOEFL required of all international applicants. High school diploma or GED is required. *High school units required/recommended:* 20 total recommended; 4 English recommended, 3 math recommended, 3 science recommended, 1 science lab recommended, 2 foreign language recommended, 3 social studies recommended, 2 history recommended, 4 elective recommended.

### The Inside Word

Admission to William Jewell requires the usual suspects: solid grades and test scores. The college is competitive, but admission is not out of reach for the average student. Once admitted, undergrads benefit from William Jewell's leading efforts in experiential learning.

## FINANCIAL AID

*Students should submit:* FAFSA, William Jewell Scholarship application. The Princeton Review suggests that all financial aid forms be submitted as soon as possible after January 1. *Need-based scholarships/grants offered:* Pell, SEOG, state scholarships/grants, private scholarships, the school's own gift aid. *Loan aid offered:* FFEL Subsidized Stafford, FFEL Unsubsidized Stafford, FFEL PLUS, Federal Perkins, Federal Nursing, alternative loans (nonfederal). Federal Work-Study Program available. Institutional employment available. Applicants will be notified of awards on a rolling basis beginning on or about March 1. Off-campus job opportunities are good.

## FROM THE ADMISSIONS OFFICE

"William Jewell College was recently selected by *Time* magazine as the College of the Year in the liberal arts category. *Time* magazine writes, 'In selecting our 2001 Colleges of the Year among candidates recommended by our advisory board, the editors sought institutions with comprehensive freshman programs that have improved retention rates and created a sense of community for students.'

"William Jewell has developed an outstanding reputation for providing students with access to study abroad opportunities. Although students do not have to be in the Oxbridge Honors Program to participate in a year of overseas study, this unique honors program requires a year abroad at either Oxford or Cambridge Universities, England. The **Oxbridge Honors Program** has garnered much national and international attention. Placement rates into graduate school are 100 percent. Oxbridge students will study in the tutorial style of learning traditional in England's finest universities.

"William Jewell College is the ideal place for students who are searching for an integrated leadership development program within the liberal arts curriculum. The College offers a minor in 'not for profit' leadership in addition to a leadership certificate program. In January of 1998, the Pryor Foundation endowed one of the most unique leadership development programs in the country. The leadership certificate curriculum in the Pryor Leadership Studies Program includes a variety of internships; a 15-day Outward Bound excursion in the Florida Everglades, and training on the Tucker Leadership Lab, one of the largest experiential learning courses (ropes course) on any campus in the world."

## ADMISSIONS

| | |
|---|---|
| Admissions Rating | 75 |
| # of applicants | 1,102 |
| % of applicants accepted | 76 |
| % of acceptees attending | 45 |

### FRESHMAN PROFILE
| | |
|---|---|
| Range SAT Verbal | 530-650 |
| Average SAT Verbal | 580 |
| Range SAT Math | 500-640 |
| Average SAT Math | 560 |
| Range ACT Composite | 21-27 |
| Average ACT Composite | 24 |
| Minimum TOEFL | 550 |
| Average HS GPA | 3.6 |
| % graduated top 10% of class | 31 |
| % graduated top 25% of class | 64 |
| % graduated top 50% of class | 93 |

### DEADLINES
| | |
|---|---|
| Nonfall registration? | yes |

### APPLICANTS ALSO LOOK AT AND SOMETIMES PREFER
St. Olaf
Washington U
Hendrix College
**AND RARELY PREFER**
Truman State
Kansas U
Westminster College

## FINANCIAL FACTS

| | |
|---|---|
| Financial Aid Rating | 88 |
| Tuition | $16,500 |
| Room and board | $4,820 |
| Books and supplies | $650 |
| % frosh receiving aid | 69 |
| % undergrads receiving aid | 64 |
| Avg frosh grant | $9,500 |
| Avg frosh loan | $6,629 |

# WILLIAMS COLLEGE

33 STETSON COURT, WILLIAMSTOWN, MA 01267 • ADMISSIONS: 413-597-2211 • FAX: 413-597-4052

## CAMPUS LIFE

| | |
|---|---|
| Quality of Life Rating | 94 |
| Type of school | private |
| Environment | rural |

### STUDENTS

| | |
|---|---|
| Total undergrad enrollment | 1,983 |
| % male/female | 51/49 |
| % from out of state | 80 |
| % from public high school | 54 |
| % live on campus | 93 |
| % African American | 8 |
| % Asian | 9 |
| % Caucasian | 74 |
| % Hispanic | 8 |
| % international | 6 |
| # of countries represented | 52 |

### SURVEY SAYS . . .
Everyone loves the Ephs
(Almost) everyone plays intramural sports
Dorms are like palaces
Registration is a breeze
Campus feels safe
(Almost) no one smokes
Musical organizations are hot

## ACADEMICS

| | |
|---|---|
| Academic Rating | 98 |
| Calendar | 4-1-4 |
| Student/faculty ratio | 8:1 |
| Profs interesting rating | 96 |
| Profs accessible rating | 98 |
| % profs teaching UG courses | 100 |
| Avg lab size | 10-19 students |
| Avg reg class size | 10-19 students |

## STUDENTS SPEAK OUT

### Academics

With only 2,000 undergraduates and no core curriculum, Williams College offers a supportive and idyllic "boot camp for your brain." Professors reportedly "love meeting with us individually" and are personable enough to "let you dog-sit and drive their cars." Many students agree that the Romance language departments fall short, and some note that class sizes are sometimes not as miniscule as advertised. The popular new president, Morty Shapiro, however, who also makes time to teach Economics 101, has "initiated a massive overhaul of the curriculum" to make it "a little less Anglo-Saxon." Distinctive academic programs include rigorous tutorials—"two students, one professor, and a fascinating topic"—and Winter Study, a January term where students study anything from book publishing to the stock market to auto mechanics. Study abroad is widely encouraged at Williams: "They provide lots of grants and fellowships for summer and winter research or travels." The generally "hands-off" administration, one student explains, "knows that I'm a real person, not a number or some drain on their time or energy." After it's all over, loyal alumni serve as "a great family for the rest of your life."

### Life

Reputedly a school for smart jocks, Williams life indeed "revolves around sports," with 40 percent of students participating in varsity athletics. "At Williams people are very proud of our athletes, so we go to support them often." Many undergraduates report meeting their closest friends in their "entry," a residential group of 20 diverse freshmen and two upperclassmen JAs, whose role is to "wipe our noses and take us shopping and buy us alcohol and generally make sure that everyone is surviving and getting along." The dictum "drinking is a way of life" is backed by the administration's attitude of being "concerned with students' health and safety rather than busting people for alcohol." Williamstown shows up as a very small dot on any map; some say it "doesn't even exist." Though the not one, not two, but three local art museums draw high praise, "nothing is open past five," and a new Thai restaurant on Spring Street receives disproportionate buzz. Considering the school's small size and remote Berkshires location, students stay occupied with their "strange devotion to a cappella groups" or the "slightly dorky, albeit well-attended, on-campus events such as movies or lectures." Also, a "ridiculous percentage of the campus knows how to swing dance (well)." When the weather is survivable, the popular Outing Club sponsors excursions through the "amazing fall foliage" and "winter skiing."

### Student Body

The typical Williams student is described as "preppy and athletic," as well as "incredibly driven, even when they pretend to be slackers." One student comments, "Everyone is friendly and down-to-earth, not to mention enormously talented at something." Though they may not be too "interested in the outside world," the inward focus makes for "a cozy atmosphere." In terms of diversity, some note "a polarization of the campus—at one end the minorities and at the other the mainly white jock population." Yet others report, "My group of friends is like a United Colors of Benetton ad." Concurring, another student writes that amid "such diversity of backgrounds and interests, the spirit and unity remains amazingly strong." All in all, "Everyone sees each other all the time, and so there's a real sense of community and caring for each other."

# WILLIAMS COLLEGE

FINANCIAL AID: 413-597-4181 • E-MAIL: ADMISSIONS@WILLIAMS.EDU • WEBSITE: WWW.WILLIAMS.EDU

## ADMISSIONS

*Very important factors considered include:* essays, recommendations, secondary school record, standardized test scores. *Important factors considered include:* class rank, extracurricular activities, talent/ability. *Other factors considered include:* alumni/ae relation, character/personal qualities, geographical residence, minority status, volunteer work, work experience. SAT I or ACT required; SAT II also required. *High school units required/recommended:* 4 English recommended, 4 math recommended, 3 science recommended, 3 science lab recommended, 4 foreign language recommended, 3 social studies recommended.

### The Inside Word

As is typical of highly selective colleges, at Williams high grades and test scores work more as qualifiers than to determine admissibility. Beyond a strong record of achievement, evidence of intellectual curiosity, noteworthy nonacademic talents, and a noncollege family background are some aspects of a candidate's application that might make for an offer of admission. But there are no guarantees—the evaluation process here is rigorous. The admissions committee (the entire admissions staff) discusses each candidate in comparison to the entire applicant pool. The pool is divided alphabetically for individual reading; after weak candidates are eliminated, those who remain undergo additional evaluations by different members of the staff. Admission decisions must be confirmed by the agreement of a plurality of the committee. Such close scrutiny demands a well-prepared candidate and application.

## FINANCIAL AID

*Students should submit:* FAFSA, CSS/Financial Aid PROFILE. Regular filing deadline is February 1. The Princeton Review suggests that all financial aid forms be submitted as soon as possible after January 1. *Need-based scholarships/grants offered:* Pell, SEOG, state scholarships/grants, private scholarships, the school's own gift aid. *Loan aid offered:* Direct Subsidized Stafford, Direct Unsubsidized Stafford, Direct PLUS, Federal Perkins, college/university loans from institutional funds. Federal Work-Study Program available. Institutional employment available. Applicants will be notified of awards on or about April 1. Off-campus job opportunities are fair.

## FROM THE ADMISSIONS OFFICE

"Special course offerings at Williams include Oxford-style tutorials, where students research and defend ideas, engaging in weekly debate with a peer and a faculty tutor. Annually 30 Williams students devote a full year to the tutorial method of study at Oxford; half of Williams students pursue their education overseas. Four weeks of Winter Study each January provide time for individualized projects, research, and novel fields of study. Students compete in 28 Division III athletic teams, perform in 25 musical groups, stage 10 theatrical productions, and volunteer in 30 service organizations. The college receives several million dollars annually for undergraduate science research and equipment. The town offers two distinguished art museums, and 2,200 forest acres—complete with a treetop canopy walkway—for environmental research and recreation."

## SELECTIVITY

| | |
|---|---|
| Admissions Rating | 99 |
| # of applicants | 4,931 |
| % of applicants accepted | 23 |
| # of early decision applicants | 496 |
| % accepted early decision | 39 |

### FRESHMAN PROFILE

| | |
|---|---|
| Range SAT Verbal | 660-760 |
| Average SAT Verbal | 701 |
| Range SAT Math | 660-750 |
| Average SAT Math | 694 |
| Average ACT Composite | 30 |

### DEADLINES

| | |
|---|---|
| Early decision | 11/15 |
| Early decision notification | 12/15 |
| Regular admission | 1/1 |
| Regular notification | 4/8 |

### APPLICANTS ALSO LOOK AT
**AND OFTEN PREFER**
Harvard
Princeton
Yale
MIT
Stanford

**AND SOMETIMES PREFER**
Brown
Dartmouth
Amherst

**AND RARELY PREFER**
Hamilton
Middlebury
Colgate
Haverford

## FINANCIAL FACTS

| | |
|---|---|
| Financial Aid Rating | 83 |
| Tuition | $26,326 |
| Room and board | $7,230 |
| Books and supplies | $800 |
| Required fees | $194 |
| % frosh receiving aid | 45 |
| % undergrads receiving aid | 41 |
| Avg frosh grant | $18,187 |
| Avg frosh loan | $2,533 |

THE BEST 351 COLLEGES ■ 739

# WITTENBERG UNIVERSITY

PO Box 720, Springfield, OH 45501 • Admissions: 800-677-7558 • Fax: 937-327-6379

## CAMPUS LIFE

| | |
|---|---|
| Quality of Life Rating | 83 |
| Type of school | private |
| Affiliation | Lutheran |
| Environment | suburban |

### STUDENTS

| | |
|---|---|
| Total undergrad enrollment | 2,320 |
| % male/female | 43/57 |
| % from out of state | 46 |
| % from public high school | 78 |
| % live on campus | 90 |
| % in (# of) fraternities | 22 (6) |
| % in (# of) sororities | 35 (7) |
| % African American | 8 |
| % Asian | 1 |
| % Caucasian | 84 |
| % Hispanic | 1 |
| % international | 2 |

### SURVEY SAYS . . .
Frats and sororities dominate social scene
Classes are small
Everyone loves the Tigers
Athletic facilities are great
Students don't get along with local community
Students don't like Springfield, OH
Theater is unpopular
(Almost) no one listens to college radio
Lousy off-campus food

## ACADEMICS

| | |
|---|---|
| Academic Rating | 88 |
| Calendar | semester |
| Student/faculty ratio | 14:1 |
| Profs interesting rating | 94 |
| Profs accessible rating | 95 |
| % profs teaching UG courses | 100 |
| Avg reg class size | 20-29 students |

### MOST POPULAR MAJORS
Business/commerce
Biological and physical sciences
Teacher education, multiple levels

## STUDENTS SPEAK OUT

### Academics
Undergrads at Wittenberg University, a small liberal arts and sciences school in Springfield, Ohio, report that their professors "are always there to count on for help with academics, recommendation letters, or just to talk." Students praise the fact that "classes are taught by professors (no TAs) and that they are all generally small, so that each student is given a good amount of attention." One recounts, "I am in a Chinese language class with two other students. That's a total of three students and a professor. It doesn't get any more personal than that." Most Witt faculty members are reputed to be friendly and laid back. A student muses, "It's nice when you can go to the bar with a professor after class on a nice day." One student notes that "the greatest strength of Witt is the academic standards which are set high to inspire achivement." However, students feel that "the administrative offices are not run very effectively and produce more problems than solutions for students."

### Life
Students claim "there is never a dull moment" in "Witt World." This active campus boasts endless "clubs, awareness groups, religious groups for all kinds of religions, and never-ending opportunities for growth amongst the student body." When kicking back, Witt students can be seen at the grassy campus hollow, "a great place to study, sunbathe, nap, play Frisbee golf (on our awesome Frisbee golf course), and of course . . . streak!" Come the weekend, "Union Board usually brings in some cool events, like bands or comedians" and "parties are widespread." In addition, "Greek life is really popular." Nonetheless, students report that "there is very little pressure from others," when it comes to having fun or feeling accepted. One student attests, "Greek life is big here but you can be happy without it . . . . I am living proof!" According to another, "Alcohol is not a must here. I don't drink and have fun with lots of different people."

### Student Body
"Its always easy to strike up an intellectual conversation or dance party," at Wittenberg, where "people make education fun and have fun outside the classroom." Amidst praises, many note with ambivalent disapproval that, "the students at Wittenberg are very friendly but also homogenous." One confides, "We all get along, probably because we come from such similar backgrounds." For the diversity it does have, Wittenberg students are "slightly segregated in terms of race." The lack of diversity does not necessarily translate into a lack of awareness or solidarity at Wittenberg. One student tells this story: "There was a club my freshman year that everyone went to, but the owner of the club made a racist comment to the DJ, who was a Witt student. Once everyone heard about it, the club had to close down due to lack of business."

# WITTENBERG UNIVERSITY

FINANCIAL AID: 800-677-7558 • E-MAIL: ADMISSION@WITTENBERG.EDU • WEBSITE: WWW.WITTENBERG.EDU

## ADMISSIONS
*Very important factors considered include:* secondary school record. *Important factors considered include:* alumni/ae relation, character/personal qualities, class rank, essays, extracurricular activities, interview, recommendations, standardized test scores, talent/ability, volunteer work, work experience. *Other factors considered include:* geographical residence, religious affiliation/commitment, state residency, minority status. SAT I or ACT required. TOEFL required of all international applicants. High school diploma is required and GED is not accepted. *High school units required/recommended:* 16 total required; 4 English required, 3 math required, 3 science required, 3 foreign language required, 3 social studies required.

### The Inside Word
Wittenberg's applicant pool is small but quite solid coming off of a couple of strong years. Students who haven't successfully reached an above-average academic level in high school will meet with little success in the admissions process. Candidate evaluation is thorough and personal; applicants should devote serious attention to all aspects of their candidacy.

## FINANCIAL AID
*Students should submit:* FAFSA. Regular filing deadline is March 15. The Princeton Review suggests that all financial aid forms be submitted as soon as possible after January 1. *Need-based scholarships/grants offered:* Pell, SEOG, state scholarships/grants, private scholarships, the school's own gift aid. *Loan aid offered:* FFEL Subsidized Stafford, FFEL Unsubsidized Stafford, FFEL PLUS, Federal Perkins, state loans, college/university loans from institutional funds. Federal Work-Study Program available. Institutional employment available. Applicants will be notified of awards on a rolling basis beginning on or about February 15. Off-campus job opportunities are good.

## FROM THE ADMISSIONS OFFICE
"At Wittenberg, we believe that helping you to achieve symmetry demands a special environment, a setting where you can refine your definition of self yet gain exposure to the varied kinds of knowledge, people, views, activities, options, and ideas that add richness to our lives. Wittenberg is neither a huge university where students are usually mass produced, nor a very small college with few options, which can provide for the intellectual and personal growth required to achieve balance. Campus life is as diverse as the interests of our students. Wittenberg attracts students from all over the United States and from many other countries. Historically, the university has been committed to geographical, educational, cultural, and religious diversity. With their diverse backgrounds and interests, Wittenberg students have helped initiate many of the more than 100 student organizations that are active on campus. The students will be the first to tell you there's never a lack of things to do on or near the campus any day of the week, if you're willing to get involved."

## SELECTIVITY

| | |
|---|---|
| Admissions Rating | 80 |
| # of applicants | 3,200 |
| % of applicants accepted | 73 |
| % of acceptees attending | 30 |
| # of early decision applicants | 40 |
| % accepted early decision | 83 |

### FRESHMAN PROFILE
| | |
|---|---|
| Range SAT Verbal | 490-680 |
| Average SAT Verbal | 576 |
| Range SAT Math | 484-684 |
| Average SAT Math | 582 |
| Range ACT Composite | 24-29 |
| Average ACT Composite | 26 |
| Minimum TOEFL | 550 |
| Average HS GPA | 3.6 |
| % graduated top 10% of class | 34 |
| % graduated top 25% of class | 65 |
| % graduated top 50% of class | 90 |

### DEADLINES
| | |
|---|---|
| Early decision | 12/1 |
| Early decision notification | 1/1 |
| Priority admission | 12/1 |
| Regular admission | 3/15 |
| Regular notification | rolling |
| Nonfall registration? | yes |

### APPLICANTS ALSO LOOK AT
**AND OFTEN PREFER**
Ohio Wesleyan University
Miami of Ohio
**AND SOMETIMES PREFER**
Allegheny College
Capital University
Denison University
Depauw University, College of Wooster
Ohio State University—Columbus
**AND RARELY PREFER**
Gettysburg College
Ohio Northern

## FINANCIAL FACTS

| | |
|---|---|
| Financial Aid Rating | 91 |
| Tuition | $24,948 |
| Room and board | $6,363 |
| Books and supplies | $800 |
| Required fees | $150 |
| % frosh receiving aid | 74 |
| % undergrads receiving aid | 75 |
| Avg frosh grant | $16,000 |
| Avg frosh loan | $4,400 |

# WOFFORD COLLEGE

429 NORTH CHURCH STREET, SPARTANBURG, SC 29303-3663 • ADMISSIONS: 864-597-4130 • FAX: 864-597-4149

## CAMPUS LIFE

| | |
|---|---|
| Quality of Life Rating | 86 |
| Type of school | private |
| Affiliation | Methodist |
| Environment | urban |

### STUDENTS

| | |
|---|---|
| Total undergrad enrollment | 1,085 |
| % male/female | 49/51 |
| % from out of state | 34 |
| % from public high school | 73 |
| % live on campus | 88 |
| % in (# of) fraternities | 54 (8) |
| % in (# of) sororities | 61 (4) |
| % African American | 8 |
| % Asian | 2 |
| % Caucasian | 89 |
| % Hispanic | 1 |
| # of countries represented | 2 |

### SURVEY SAYS . . .
Frats and sororities dominate social scene
Lots of beer drinking
Hard liquor is popular
Campus is beautiful
(Almost) everyone smokes
Athletic facilities are great
Lab facilities are great
Great computer facilities
Ethnic diversity lacking on campus

## ACADEMICS

| | |
|---|---|
| Academic Rating | 87 |
| Calendar | 4-1-4 |
| Student/faculty ratio | 12:1 |
| % profs teaching UG courses | 100 |
| Avg reg class size | 10-19 students |

### MOST POPULAR MAJORS
Business/managerial economics
Biology/biological sciences
English language and literature

## STUDENTS SPEAK OUT

### Academics

Wofford College, which has a strong history of preparing students for careers in law, the ministry, medicine, and other health sciences, continues to enjoy "a very good regional reputation" as it approaches its 150th anniversary. While this Old South school is also well known for its aristocratic student body, Wofford is by no means a country club. On the contrary, "The school is known as rigorous, and it lives up to its reputation. There's one thing for sure: When you finish a class after a final, you never think to yourself, 'Hey, that wasn't that bad.'" Students warn that "the workload is huge and most classes involve a lot of time outside class" and that "the conflicts with tests and papers are sometimes bad when they all come due at once." Most, however, approve of the "Wofford way," explaining that "tough studies and hard teachers make the student better prepared for life." Students here know that whatever support they need to make it through will be provided them. "Wofford is a place where you are encouraged to do your best because you know that the administration and faculty care about you and expect your best," explains one student. "I'm challenged here every day, but I know that if I ever have trouble I can call my professor or go by his/her office and they're more than willing to help." Also, "tutors are easily accessible." "Great opportunity to travel abroad" further helps to take the sting off the demands of Wofford academics. Sums up one undergrad, "Wofford has been the most difficult challenge that I have faced in my life. I have had to fight for every grade that I've gotten, but it's taught me a lot about myself and life."

### Life

"Not many people go out during the week because there is so much studying that has to be done," students at Wofford agree. Weekends, however, are a different story. "From Thursday night to Saturday night everyone drinks well into the night and sleeps during the day to go back out and drink that night." And where does all this partying occur? At the Greek houses, mostly; students tell us that "social life revolves around the fraternity row on the weekends." Those with less bibulous inclinations appreciate the fact that "it's not like you are totally out of it here if you don't drink. There are plenty of students who don't drink and still have a good time." Some here skip the Greek houses entirely and "simply unwind at the end of the week by going to a movie or to the mall or just out to eat with friends." Others "are very active in the community-service projects, Habitat for Humanity, lots of stuff." Still others "may go mountain climbing or kayaking for the day on the weekend. On weekdays, we'll head to the movies, out to eat, possibly a pick-up game of soccer, or even just grab some friends and head to the gym to socialize while pretending to work out." Students tout the "top-notch athletic facilities," and list the "athletic programs and reputations," especially varsity football and basketball, among the school's strengths. Hometown Spartanburg, unfortunately, doesn't offer much in the way of diversion. "People also sometimes go to Greenville for a little bigger city. Sometimes they go to Asheville or Charlotte." And sometimes those places come to them: "Students from surrounding larger universities come to Wofford a lot for various parties/special weekends," reports one student.

### Student Body

"Most of the students here are alike," Wofford undergrads readily concede. "The atypical student really stands out." Nearly all the "well-dressed and well-put-together," "preppy" students here are "rich, Republican, and very southern. They generally come from good, well-established families." The men are "shaggy-haired, preppy-as-it-gets, frat-tastic guys: pink golf shirts, oxford shirts with their initials on the pocket, and boat shoes required! They study hard but live to drink and party." The women are "Baptist, blond-haired, 'Father, I love you, I need more money,' dot-the-i's-with-hearts girls." Wofford is home to lots of "second- or third-generation Wofford students."

# WOFFORD COLLEGE

FINANCIAL AID: 864-597-4160 • E-MAIL: ADMISSIONS@WOFFORD.EDU • WEBSITE: WWW.WOFFORD.EDU

## ADMISSIONS

*Very important factors considered include:* secondary school record. *Important factors considered include:* character/personal qualities, class rank, essays, extracurricular activities, standardized test scores, talent/ability, volunteer work. *Other factors considered include:* alumni/ae relation, geographical residence, interview, minority status, recommendations, state residency, work experience. SAT I or ACT required. TOEFL required of all international applicants. High school diploma or GED is required. *High school units required/recommended:* 17 total recommended; 4 English recommended, 4 math recommended, 3 science lab recommended, 3 foreign language recommended, 2 social studies recommended, 1 elective recommended.

### *The Inside Word*

Wofford is under-recognized among excellent college options in the South. Matchmaking plays a large part in the decisions of the admissions committee, which means that it takes much more than just above-average grades and solid test scores to get admitted. The admissions staff is friendly and eager to help students put their best foot forward in the process. Wofford is a particularly good choice for those who, while strong academically, are not likely candidates for admission to Duke and other top southern schools.

## FINANCIAL AID

*Students should submit:* FAFSA. The Princeton Review suggests that all financial aid forms be submitted as soon as possible after January 1. *Need-based scholarships/grants offered:* Pell, SEOG, state scholarships/grants, private scholarships, the school's own gift aid. *Loan aid offered:* FFEL Subsidized Stafford, FFEL Unsubsidized Stafford, FFEL PLUS, Federal Perkins, state loans. Federal Work-Study Program available. Institutional employment available. Applicants will be notified of awards on a rolling basis beginning on or about March 25. Off-campus job opportunities are excellent.

## FROM THE ADMISSIONS OFFICE

"Approaching the end of his first year in office in the spring of 2001, Wofford President Benjamin Dunlap (a Rhodes Scholar and Harvard Ph.D.) asked the faculty, "If you had the assurance of sufficient time and institutional support to teach the sort of course you've always dreamed of, what would you do?" In response, using grants from the Andrew Mellon and National Science Foundations, Wofford faculty launched more than 30 new courses and interdisciplinary course sequences during 2001–2002. Some of the new courses are "learning communities," the prototype for which was fashioned by a biologist and an English professor on "the nature and culture of water." A Spanish language course is taught in conjunction with a Latin American and Caribbean history course and a sociology course featuring fieldwork in the local Hispanic community. Handsomely appointed rooms suitable for meetings, meals, and seminars have been included in an ongoing series of major building projects and renovations to forge even closer relationships between faculty and students. Blessed with a Phi Beta Kappa academic tradition, a nationally ranked program of studies abroad, and an economy of scale that encourages innovation and collaboration among faculty and students, Wofford is positioning itself among the national leaders in redefining the liberal arts. More importantly, however, the college community is vigorously pursuing a goal of educating young leaders who can make connections, cross boundaries, and negotiate a world no longer neatly divided into categories of endeavor."

## SELECTIVITY

| | |
|---|---|
| Admissions Rating | 81 |
| # of applicants | 1,349 |
| % of applicants accepted | 78 |
| % of acceptees attending | 28 |

### FRESHMAN PROFILE

| | |
|---|---|
| Range SAT Verbal | 560-660 |
| Average SAT Verbal | 612 |
| Range SAT Math | 580-670 |
| Average SAT Math | 624 |
| Range ACT Composite | 22-27 |
| Average ACT Composite | 25 |
| Minimum TOEFL | 550 |
| Average HS GPA | 3.9 |
| % graduated top 10% of class | 53 |
| % graduated top 25% of class | 79 |
| % graduated top 50% of class | 97 |

### DEADLINES

| | |
|---|---|
| Early decision | 11/15 |
| Early decision notification | 12/1 |
| Regular admission | 2/1 |
| Regular notification | 3/15 |
| Nonfall registration? | yes |

### APPLICANTS ALSO LOOK AT
**AND OFTEN PREFER**
Wake Forest
**AND SOMETIMES PREFER**
U. South Carolina—Columbia
Furman
**AND RARELY PREFER**
Clemson

## FINANCIAL FACTS

| | |
|---|---|
| Financial Aid Rating | 92 |
| Tuition | $19,815 |
| Room and board | $6,100 |
| Books and supplies | $851 |
| Required fees | $795 |
| % frosh receiving aid | 55 |
| % undergrads receiving aid | 54 |

# WORCESTER POLYTECHNIC INSTITUTE

100 INSTITUTE ROAD, WORCESTER, MA 01609 • ADMISSIONS: 508-831-5286 • FAX: 508-831-5875

## CAMPUS LIFE

| | |
|---|---|
| Quality of Life Rating | 74 |
| Type of school | private |
| Environment | suburban |

### STUDENTS
| | |
|---|---|
| Total undergrad enrollment | 2,767 |
| % male/female | 77/23 |
| % from out of state | 48 |
| % from public high school | 79 |
| % live on campus | 83 |
| % in (# of) fraternities | 35 (12) |
| % in (# of) sororities | 25 (2) |
| % African American | 1 |
| % Asian | 7 |
| % Caucasian | 85 |
| % Hispanic | 3 |
| % international | 5 |
| # of countries represented | 68 |

### SURVEY SAYS . . .
Frats and sororities dominate social scene
Class discussions are rare
Student publications are ignored
Students aren't religious
Great computer facilities
Students don't like Worcester, MA
Political activism is (almost) nonexistent
Athletic facilities need improving

## ACADEMICS

| | |
|---|---|
| Academic Rating | 83 |
| Calendar | quarter |
| Student/faculty ratio | 12:1 |
| Profs interesting rating | 91 |
| Profs accessible rating | 96 |
| % profs teaching UG courses | 100 |
| Avg lab size | 20-29 students |
| Avg reg class size | under 10 students |

### MOST POPULAR MAJORS
Mechanical engineering
Electrical, electronics, and communications engineering
Computer science

## STUDENTS SPEAK OUT

### Academics
The WPI undergraduate experience centers around the "WPI Plan," a series of required independent projects designed to build research ability and teamwork skills. Components of the plan include the "Sufficiency," a five-course sequence outside the student's major that culminates in an independent project; the "Interactive Project," which studies the interrelationship of science with social and ethical issues; and the "Major Project," a senior research/design project that allows undergraduates to work closely with graduate students, professors, and occasionally, business leaders. Students approve of WPI's unique approach. Writes one, "The projects force one to apply knowledge in real life, and they are awesome." Another agrees, "The WPI plan forces real-world experience on college students." Adds a third, "If you put the effort in, there are unparalleled opportunities for innovation in the academic experience." The workload is tough at this science, engineering, and computer science heavyweight, made even tougher by a quarterly academic calendar. Warns one engineering major, "You have to work hard here. The classes seem very fast, but it is better because you don't get bored." WPI professors "are different from class to class and really make the difference in your grade. They're like a Clint Eastwood movie: The Good, The Bad, and the Ugly." While many are "always willing to help if you have any questions," others "do not speak much English, making it hard to understand what they are trying to get across." Administrators "are very friendly. It is not uncommon to find the president or vice president walking around campus or eating in the cafeteria."

### Life
A heavy workload and a lopsided male-female ratio leave little time or opportunity for a social life at WPI. Explains one student, "Life is pretty fast. Classes in the morning and afternoon, and games in the evening along with homework." Weekends offer "not much besides fraternities. If you don't belong to a fraternity or a sports team, I don't know what else people would do except visit friends at liberal arts colleges. There are no girls here!" Parties in student apartments are also popular, if not to everyone's taste. Reports one naysayer, "Fun for most is going to one of the party houses off campus. I, however, personally don't like being crammed into a small room with 50 other people huddled around a keg." Under the circumstances, it is not surprising that "school spirit is low," and students feel that they "need more support for athletics and other campus events. A lot of people get involved, but we need a lot more!" Hometown Worcester offers little help; it's a "small, homogeneous city. There are not many opportunities for fun." On the upside, "rooms are spacious and the food is not bad" on campus.

### Student Body
The "international and diverse" students of WPI include "a lot of dorks and weirdoes, but there are also a lot of cool kids." Writes one, "It's a broad range of people from total dorks to total potheads. Frat parties are big with about half the campus. The other half has probably never seen a beer." Students enjoy a spirit of community fostered by a sense that they "have more in common with the students here than I could have at any other school" and because "most people are easygoing and work hard. There is a real sense of helping each other to succeed." On the downside, WPI's "terrible" male-female ratio "causes a strange social scene that most are not used to."

# WORCESTER POLYTECHNIC INSTITUTE

FINANCIAL AID: 508-831-5469 • E-MAIL: ADMISSIONS@WPI.EDU • WEBSITE: WWW.WPI.EDU

## ADMISSIONS

*Very important factors considered include:* class rank, secondary school record, standardized test scores. *Important factors considered include:* essays, extracurricular activities, minority status, recommendations. *Other factors considered include:* alumni/ae relation, character/personal qualities, geographical residence, interview, state residency, talent/ability, volunteer work, work experience. TOEFL required of all international applicants. High school diploma is required and GED is not accepted. *High school units required/recommended:* 10 total required; 4 English recommended, 4 math required, 2 science required, 2 science lab required.

### The Inside Word

Worcester's applicant pool is small but very well qualified. Its high acceptance rate makes it a good safety choice for those aiming at more difficult tech schools and for those who are solid but aren't MIT material. As is the case at most technical institutes, women will meet with a very receptive admissions committee.

## FINANCIAL AID

*Students should submit:* FAFSA, CSS/Financial Aid PROFILE, noncustodial (divorced/separated) parent's statement, parent's and student's prior year's federal tax return and W-2s. Regular filing deadline is March 1. The Princeton Review suggests that all financial aid forms be submitted as soon as possible after January 1. *Need-based scholarships/grants offered:* Pell, SEOG, state scholarships/grants, the school's own gift aid. *Loan aid offered:* FFEL Subsidized Stafford, FFEL Unsubsidized Stafford, FFEL PLUS, Federal Perkins, state loans, college/university loans from institutional funds. Federal Work-Study Program available. Institutional employment available. Applicants will be notified of awards on or about April 1. Off-campus job opportunities are good.

## FROM THE ADMISSIONS OFFICE

"Projects and research are a distinctive element of the WPI plan. WPI believes that in these times simply passing courses and accumulating theoretical knowledge is not enough to truly educate tomorrow's leaders. Tomorrow's professionals ought to be involved in project work that prepares them today for future challenges. Projects at WPI come as close to professional experience as a college program can possibly achieve. In fact, WPI works with more than 200 companies, government agencies, and private organizations each year. These groups provide project opportunities where students get a chance to work in real, professional settings. Students gain experience in planning, coordinating team efforts, meeting deadlines, writing proposals and reports, making oral presentations, doing cost analyses, and making decisions."

## SELECTIVITY

| | |
|---|---|
| Admissions Rating | 87 |
| # of applicants | 3,560 |
| % of applicants accepted | 70 |
| % of acceptees attending | 29 |
| # of early decision applicants | 200 |
| % accepted early decision | 77 |

### FRESHMAN PROFILE

| | |
|---|---|
| Range SAT Verbal | 540-660 |
| Average SAT Verbal | 620 |
| Range SAT Math | 630-730 |
| Average SAT Math | 680 |
| Average ACT Composite | 29 |
| Minimum TOEFL | 550 |
| Average HS GPA | 3.7 |
| % graduated top 10% of class | 47 |
| % graduated top 25% of class | 82 |
| % graduated top 50% of class | 98 |

### DEADLINES

| | |
|---|---|
| Early decision | 11/15 |
| Early decision notification | 12/15 |
| Early action | 11/15 |
| Early action notification | 12/15 |
| Regular admission | 2/1 |
| Regular notification | 4/1 |
| Nonfall registration? | yes |

### APPLICANTS ALSO LOOK AT AND OFTEN PREFER
MIT
Cornell U., Caltech

### AND SOMETIMES PREFER
Rose-Hulman
U. Mass—Amherst
RPI, Case Western Reserve
Carnegie-Mellon

### AND RARELY PREFER
U. Rhode Island
U. New Hampshire, U. Conn
Clarkson U., Drexel

## FINANCIAL FACTS

| | |
|---|---|
| Financial Aid Rating | 86 |
| Tuition | $28,420 |
| Room and board | $8,984 |
| Books and supplies | $692 |
| Required fees | $170 |
| % frosh receiving aid | 77 |
| % undergrads receiving aid | 51 |
| Avg frosh grant | $12,121 |
| Avg frosh loan | $4,620 |

# YALE UNIVERSITY

PO BOX 208234, NEW HAVEN, CT 06520-8234 • ADMISSIONS: 203-432-9316 • FAX: 203-432-9392

## CAMPUS LIFE

| | |
|---|---|
| Quality of Life Rating | 81 |
| Type of school | private |
| Environment | urban |

### STUDENTS

| | |
|---|---|
| Total undergrad enrollment | 5,339 |
| % male/female | 50/50 |
| % from out of state | 92 |
| % from public high school | 53 |
| % live on campus | 87 |
| % African American | 9 |
| % Asian | 17 |
| % Caucasian | 55 |
| % Hispanic | 9 |
| % international | 10 |

### SURVEY SAYS . . .
Registration is a breeze
Ethnic diversity on campus
Students are happy
Lots of classroom discussion
No one cheats
Very little hard liquor
Very little drug use
(Almost) no one listens to college radio
Very small frat/sorority scene

## ACADEMICS

| | |
|---|---|
| Academic Rating | 99 |
| Calendar | semester |
| Student/faculty ratio | 7:1 |
| Profs interesting rating | 92 |
| Profs accessible rating | 90 |
| Avg reg class size | 10-19 students |

## STUDENTS SPEAK OUT

### Academics

Neither professors nor students at Yale rest on their laurels, though there are certainly many laurels to rest upon if they wanted to. Yale's professors, "in addition to being top scholars, actually seem to enjoy teaching undergrads." That's no mean feat at one of the preeminent research institutions in the country. Professors are "incredibly knowledgeable" but also "fascinated with their students, consummately available, and friendly and helpful to an awesome degree." Some, however, "are less talented [than others] in the department of effectively conveying the vast stores of knowledge they possess." Still, students admit that it's sort of thrilling when professors "use their own textbooks in class." Yale can afford to be extremely selective with a huge surplus of applicants beating down the doors, but "once you're in, they will pamper you and support your ambitions." And the university can afford it, too. As one student put it, "Our reputation, and thus our resources, are impressive." Another says, "Yale is so well equipped for students to explore their academic interests that being at a well-known institution almost seems to be only an added bonus." Some students do think, however, that the administration could improve a bit: "The school's administration likes to maintain an official distance from the general student population, but frequently publishes newsletters and responds to articles in the newspaper to keep us informed of its thoughts and plans." Students love the shopping system of registration, which allows them to visit classes for up to two weeks before registering, enabling them to avoid poor instructors and uninteresting classes. Lest you forget, it's worth repeating that "the schoolwork itself is hard, very hard, but rewarding, very rewarding."

### Life

"Yalies take advantage of every free moment," and they have to, balancing rigorous academic requirements with exciting social lives and extracurricular activities. Something has to give, so for some students "sleep becomes a friend you only really get to hang out with on weekends." Yalies applaud the residential college system, where students live together all four years, as "awesome because you really get to know a group of people and get to live with a large portion of them for four years." Residential life also provides access to "key administrators because each college has a master and a dean." Students can depend on help from their college deans when wrangling with university bureaucracy. On campus, Yale provides all kinds of activities, from a cappella performances to parties. Hometown New Haven gets decent marks by students: "The city has its good points (the best pizza in the world among them), and they're doing a good job revitalizing it." New Haven is starkly separate from the university, though students note with pleasure that "the crime rate is down more than 60 percent since 1990." Mostly, Yale students like doing "Lacanian readings of Friends" or just "talking about anything and everything until 4 A.M." And sometimes, Yalies get excited about simply being at Yale, where, "heck, the showers in my building are all solid marble." Still, Yalies are kids like the rest of us, too: "What do we think about? Finishing our work and trying to get laid."

### Student Body

"Yale does a wonderful job selecting students from a broad base," describes one student. "I now have friends in every corner of the globe." With its resources and reputation, Yale manages to bring together students from every racial, ethnic, and socioeconomic background. "The incredible student body provides an education by itself." Over and over, students repeat that what they love best about Yale are their peers. Mind you, Yalies are "intense" ("No one here is lukewarm about anything"), but "no one is trying to fit into a mold." Students are "the smartest people I've ever met." One student glows with pride, "It is easy to believe that we will be the future leaders of tomorrow."

# YALE UNIVERSITY

FINANCIAL AID: 203-432-2700 • E-MAIL: STUDENT.QUESTIONS@YALE.EDU • WEBSITE: WWW.YALE.EDU/ADMIT

## ADMISSIONS

*Very important factors considered include:* character/personal qualities, class rank, essays, extracurricular activities, recommendations, secondary school record, standardized test scores, talent/ability. *Other factors considered include:* alumni/ae relation, geographical residence, interview, minority status, state residency, volunteer work, work experience. SAT I or ACT required; SAT II also required. TOEFL required of all international applicants.

### The Inside Word

There is no grey area here; Yale is ultra-selective with growing applicant pools each year. And there's nothing to be gained by appealing a denial here—the admissions committee considers all of its decisions final. Yale uses a regional review process that serves as a preliminary screening for all candidates, and only the best-qualified, well-matched candidates actually come before the admissions committee.

## FINANCIAL AID

*Students should submit:* FAFSA, CSS/Financial Aid PROFILE, state aid form, noncustodial (divorced/separated) parent's statement, business/farm supplement, tax returns. Regular filing deadline is February 1. The Princeton Review suggests that all financial aid forms be submitted as soon as possible after January 1. *Need-based scholarships/grants offered:* Pell, SEOG, state scholarships/grants, private scholarships, the school's own gift aid, United Negro College Fund. *Loan aid offered:* FFEL Subsidized Stafford, FFEL Unsubsidized Stafford, FFEL PLUS, Federal Perkins, state loans, college/university loans from institutional funds. Federal Work-Study Program available. Institutional employment available. Applicants will be notified of awards on or about April 1. Off-campus job opportunities are good.

## FROM THE ADMISSIONS OFFICE

"The most important questions the admissions committee must resolve are 'Who is likely to make the most of Yale's resources?' and 'Who will contribute significantly to the Yale community?' These questions suggest an approach to evaluating applicants that is more complex than whether Yale would rather admit well-rounded people or those with specialized talents. In selecting a class of 1,300 from approximately 17,700 applicants, the admissions committee looks for academic ability and achievement combined with such personal characteristics as motivation, curiosity, energy, and leadership ability. The nature of these qualities is such that there is no simple profile of grades, scores, interests, and activities that will assure admission. Diversity within the student population is important, and the admissions committee selects a class of able and contributing individuals from a variety of backgrounds and with a broad range of interests and skills."

## SELECTIVITY

| | |
|---|---:|
| Admissions Rating | 99 |
| # of applicants | 15,466 |
| % of applicants accepted | 13 |
| % of acceptees attending | 67 |
| # accepting a place on wait list | 633 |
| % admitted from wait list | 0 |
| # of early action applicants | 1,795 |
| % accepted early action | 29 |

### FRESHMAN PROFILE

| | |
|---|---:|
| Range SAT Verbal | 680-770 |
| Range SAT Math | 680-770 |
| Range ACT Composite | 28-33 |
| Minimum TOEFL | 600 |
| % graduated top 10% of class | 95 |
| % graduated top 25% of class | 99 |
| % graduated top 50% of class | 100 |

### DEADLINES

| | |
|---|---:|
| Early action | 11/1 |
| Early action notification | 12/15 |
| Regular admission | 12/31 |
| Regular notification | 4/1 |

### APPLICANTS ALSO LOOK AT AND SOMETIMES PREFER
Harvard
Stanford
MIT

### AND RARELY PREFER
Brown
Amherst
Williams
Wesleyan U
U of Pennsylvania

## FINANCIAL FACTS

| | |
|---|---:|
| Financial Aid Rating | 80 |
| Tuition | $28,400 |
| Room and board | $8,600 |
| Books and supplies | $2,520 |
| % frosh receiving aid | 42 |
| % undergrads receiving aid | 39 |

# PART 4

## "MY ROOMMATE'S FEET REALLY STINK."

Our survey has seven questions that allow students to answer in narrative form. We tell students that we don't care *what* they write: if it is "witty, informative, or accurate," we try to get it into this book. We use all the informative and accurate essays to write the "Students Speak Out" sections; below are excerpts from the wittiest, pithiest, and most outrageous narrative responses to our open-ended questions.

## LITERARY ALLUSIONS...

"To study at this school is to have infinite control over your destiny: you can crouch in your room like Gregor Samsa transformed into a dung beetle, or you can plunge into the infinite sea of faces that each year flood OSU like a tidal wave."

— A.W., Ohio State University

"Two jokes about St. John's College students:
1. Q: How many Johnnies does it take to change a light bulb?
   A: Let's define 'change' before we go any further.
2. Q: What did the Chorus say to Creon after Oedipus poked out his eyes?
   A: Now that's a face only a mother could love."

— April W., St. John's College

"'Prosperity unbruised cannot endure a single blow, but a man who has been at constant feud with misfortunes develops a skin calloused by time...and even if he falls he can carry the fight upon one knee.' —Seneca on Providence."

— Matthew D., U. of Connecticut

"Very definitely a love/hate relationship here. This is the level of hell that Dante missed."

—Amy P., Caltech

"The Deep Springs Experience is like working in an atrophy factory. Much of what you do in labor and government is fixing, improving, or replacing what came before you. No matter what frame of reference you use—daily, monthly, or yearly—you still feel like Sisyphus. The joy and value comes in building your muscles on so many different rocks."

—Whet M., Deep Springs College

"Lewd quotes on the bathroom walls at least come from great authors."

—Matt J., Simon's Rock College of Bard

# FOOD...

"The food here is really bad; it's either bland or sickening. You're lucky if they don't screw up the bread."

— Scott P., Bentley College

"If you're looking for gray skies, a gray campus, and gray food, then Albany is the place to be!"

— Michele G., SUNY Albany

"When students first arrive, they call the Observatory Hill Dining Facility 'O-Hill.' They soon learn to call it 'O-Hell,' because the food here is beyond revolting."

— Greg F., U. of Virginia

"The food isn't that bad, if you don't mind varying shades of brown. On a good day the food on your tray will remind you of the brown paint sampler at your local Sherwin-Williams dealer."

— Rob P., College of the Holy Cross

"If I had known that I'd be rooming with roaches and poisoned by the cafeteria staff I would have gone to Wayne State. I really can't complain, though, because I have met my husband here, like my mom did twenty years before."

— M.L.P., Fisk University

"You should mention Lil', the lady who has worked in the dining hall for fifty years and who everyone loves. She plays the spoons all the time and runs around."

— Aaron R., Tufts University

"The food here has particularly fancy names, and it seems as though they spend more time thinking of these names than they spend on making decent food."

— Andrew Z., Wheaton College

"We spend more time at the lunch table than George, Jerry, Elaine, and Kramer, except that our cafeteria workers aren't as good looking."

—Chris D., Wake Forest University

## HOMETOWN...

"People ask me, 'Mike Z., why did you come to NYU?' I tell them, 'I didn't come to NYU, I came to New York City.'"

— Mike Z., NYU

"Change the name of UC—Irvine to UC—Newport Beach and we would have more girls."

— Pat M., UC–Irvine

"As this school is located in a tiny Texas town, a favorite activity is called 'rolling.' Rolling entails piling into a car with many drinks and driving the back country roads. Very slowly."

— Anonymous, Southwestern University

"Connecticut is a cute state. It's a great place to go to school, but I wouldn't want to live here."

— Claire S., NJ native, Fairfield University

"Binghamton is always gray. The two days a week we have sun, it's beautiful, but otherwise, sunglasses are not a must unless you're an artsy-fartsy pseudo-chic literature and rhetoric/philosophy major."

— Deborah C., SUNY–Binghamton

"Socially, the surrounding area is so dead that the Denny's closes at night."

— Thomas R., UC–Riverside

"The local liquor stores and towing companies make a lot of money."

— Katherine R., U. of Rhode Island

"Davis is boring; you need a lot of drugs."

— Anonymous, UC–Davis

"It is definitely important to have a car, as the population of Canton frequently matches our winter temperature. 'Canton gray,' our perennial sky color, is one Crayola missed."

— Daniel R., St. Lawrence University

"Contrary to popular belief, cow tipping is definitely passé here."

— Anonymous, U. of Connecticut, Storrs

"Life in New Orleans—'And the people sat down to eat and to drink, and rose up to play.'—Exodus 32:6."

— Theresa W., Tulane University

"Fredericksburg is boring if one is not amused by the simple pleasures of existence such as breathing, sleep, and other things."

— Rich W., Mary Washington College

"I love escaping from Claremont. I wish I had a car! Claremont seems to be stuck in a white, bureaucratic, conservative nightmare. I feel cut off from the rest of the world, like I've fallen into Wonderland—the rules of the outside world don't apply here. However, I do feel like I've gotten and am getting a good education."

— Anonymous, Scripps College

"What do we do for fun? Danville is small, so we go on raids to Wal-Mart. It never fails, no matter what time of day or night that you go to Wal-Mart, you will always run into at least two separate groups of people you know. Plus, Wal-Mart is just a cool place to play around in. Where else can you find [everything from] toy footballs and bikes to goofy hats, clothes, shoes? And let me tell you, those aisles make for a good game of hide and seek."

—Anonymous, Centre College

## SECURITY...

"Campus security is made up of a bunch of midget high school dropouts with Napoleonic complexes who can spot a beer can from a mile away."

— Anonymous, UC–San Diego

"For fun we try to ski around campus on the snow, but campus safety must feel that we should be smoking weed because they allow that more than outdoor activities."

—Male Junior, Clarkson University

"Public safety here is a joke. The public safety officers are like the Keystone Kops on Thorazine."

— Anonymous, Bryn Mawr College

"No doors are locked here—<u>none</u>—but you have to notice the doorknob."

—Female Senior, Simon's Rock College of Bard

## CLASSMATES...

"Sure, our campus is diverse if you call diverse a campus full of white kids looking to make thirty to fifty grand after graduation."

— Joseph M. C., Davidson College

"If you're thinking of applying to MIT, go ahead. Because, believe it or not, most people here are at least as stupid as you are."

— Patrick L., MIT

"My 'life' at school revolves around devising new methods in which to escape and to get away from the nagging, 'supportive' women's environment."

—Caitlin B., Mount Holyoke College

"Students here mostly get along and since it is a business school we all have a common goal of being rich."

—Female Sophomore, Babson College

"People who go to school here are all pretty good-looking, especially the women. It should be renamed UKB, the University of Ken and Barbie."

— Tony H., Arizona State University

"Wesleyan is not only the 'diversity university' but also the 'controversy university,' the 'fight adversity university,' and the 'if we keep trying we might have some unity' university. We satisfy all types."

— John P., Wesleyan University

"Mt. Holyoke students are friendly and respectful with the exception of the occasions when the entire campus gets PMS."

—Abigail K., Mount Holyoke College

"Everyone walks too fast around here. You try to say 'hi' to someone, you've got to time it just right 'cause they aren't going to stop to talk to you. Plus, everyone wears the same clothes!"

— Terry B., Wittenberg University

"Girls over 5'8", watch out—for some reason, guys here have munchkin blood in them or something."

— Robyn A., Tufts University

"A school can be defined by its graffiti and its level of cleverness. Three quarters of our school graffiti is pro- or anti- a specific fraternity, with the other one quarter devoted to homophobic or misogynist theories."

— Matthew E., College of William and Mary

"This is a great university if you're not studying sciences involving animal research, politics, teacher education (certification), or anything that offends any long-haired leftist who's a vegetarian."

— Brock M., U. of Oregon

"This school is filled with wealthy, well-dressed egomaniacs who are about as socially conscious as Marie Antoinette."

— Anonymous, Hofstra University

"For self-absorbed artists my peers are all surprisingly good dancers."

—Jackie G., Bennington College

"When you first come here, you think everybody's really strange. Over time, though, you realize everybody is, and so are you. No big deal."

— Josh B., St. John's College

"University of Chicago's reputation is not entirely deserved. It's not true the place is completely full of nerds. It's only partially completely full of nerds."

— David G., U. of Chicago

"I have this really big booger in my nose that I can't quite handle. What do I do? Pick it in public and look like a typical Brown freak, or just deal with it?"

—"Optional," Brown University

"Don't let anyone try to tell you that this is a diverse but close-knit atmosphere. The people here are about as diverse as a box of nails."

— Cari L., College of the Holy Cross

"UNH is about as diverse as the NHL."

— Curtis E., U. of New Hampshire

"We are cheeseballs, but rather enlightened; thus we condescendingly tolerate almost everyone."

—Cache M., Lawrence U.

"Denison has attempted to lose the 'rich kid party school' image and expand the diversity of the student body, but now it is becoming the 'I wish this were still a rich kid party school.' There is an awful lot available here, but students seem unmotivated and lazy."

— Anonymous, Denison University

"Most of my peers are narrow-minded morons who seem to live in the fifties. Because of this constant annoyance, the rest of us have a camaraderie that allows us to see how the other half lives."

—Gary A., LSU

"Everyone here is too smart for their [sic] own good. As one upper-level executive in the Houston area put it, 'The students at Rice know how to make it rain, but they don't know to come in out of it.'"

— John B., Rice U.

"My roommate's feet really stink."

— Anonymous, Claremont McKenna

"Kids at Bard are like fish in a fish bowl, no blinking but always hitting the glass."

—Zak V., Bard College

"Sometimes people complain about the lack of student involvement. I think someone should really do something about the apathy at St. Lawrence."

— Bill P., St. Lawrence University

"Bates is so diverse! Yesterday I met somebody from Connecticut!"

— Ellen H., Bates College

"Most are either Bible-thumping, goodie-goodie, white, stuck-up, right-wing, straight-A losers or work hard, play harder and party hardy, willing-to-try-anything cool people."

—Male Sophomore, Colorado School of Mines

"Rose-Hulman is one of the few places where it's safer to leave a $20 bill on your desk than it is to forget to log out of the computer network."

— Zac C., Rose-Hulman Institute of Technology

"Wabash College is an all-male institution, so all of my classmates are men."

—Anonymous, Wabash College

"People at F&M are about as original and colorful as the pages of the Encyclopedia Britannica, with different numbers so you can tell them apart, but otherwise arranged much around the same old dull principles."

—Anonymous, Franklin and Marshall College

"I am constantly impressed with the creativity of hell-raisers on campus. One day I walked past the Manor House to find a dozen plastic babies climbing all over the roof! Right before Parents' Weekend, some people hung up signs saying 'Princeton Review reports: "LC students ignore herpes on a regular basis." Please visit the health clinic!'"

—Anonymous, Lewis and Clark College

"I have not met anyone who was horrible."

—Anonymous, UMBC

"When I first visited this campus, I thought, 'Wow, people here are mean. They walk around like they're cold and empty and can't see anyone.' And then I came here and I realized that I was mostly right; people will run right into you and not even turn around."

—Anonymous, University of California–Irvine

## ADMINISTRATION...

"The only thing the administration does well is tasks involving what Kenneth Boulding would call 'suboptimization.' Give them something that really doesn't need doing and it will be accomplished efficiently."

— Dana T., U. of Minnesota–Twin Cities

"Our business office may be the smoothest running machine since the Pinto!"

— Robert C., University of Dallas

"Despite the best efforts of the administration to provide TCNJ students with an inefficient, cold-hearted, red-tape infested, snafu-riddled Soviet-style administrative bureaucracy, The College of New Jersey is a pretty decent place to go for a fairly reasonable amount of money."

— Anonymous, The College of New Jersey

"The admissions office tries to make you apply based on, 'Well, we're very old and . . . and . . . well, we look nice. We'll do whatever it takes to make you happy! Really! I mean it. See my honest smile?' If you visit the school, ditch the tour and the gimmicks and talk to the professors."

— Anonymous, Southwestern University

"Going to a school as small as Emerson means that instead of saying 'screw you, Mr. 90803,' the administration will say, 'screw you, Joe.'"

— "Joe Bloggs," Emerson College

"The administration runs a wonderful school, and the students and teachers have a wonderful school. Fortunately, these are not the same school."

—Male Freshman/Sophomore, Bard College

"Administration is like the stock market, you invest time and money, sometimes you get a return, other times you don't."

—J.W.R., Albertson College of Idaho

"The bursar's office and financial aid are slightly retarded when it comes to communication. The daily walk between the two offices might have contributed to my not gaining 'The Freshman Fifteen.'"

—Brittany R., Wesleyan College

"Columbia is like a fruit truck. It picks up varied and exotic fruits and deposits them rotten at their destination."

— Paul L., Columbia University

"The U. of Minnesota is a huge black hole of knowledge. It sucks things into it from far and wide, compressing to the essence. Unfortunately, it is very hard to get anything out of a black hole. What I have managed to eke out has been both rewarding and depressing."

— James McDonald, U. of Minnesota

"The strangest incident I've ever had in class was when one of my journalism profs burnt our tests in the microwave. But, he decided to give everyone in the class an A, instead of retesting."

—Ashlea K., Ohio University

"Boulder is the world in a nutshell, served with alfalfa sprouts."

— Glenn H., U. of Colorado, Boulder

"Going to Northwestern is like having a beautiful girlfriend who treats you like crap."

— Jonathan J. G., Northwestern University

"Unless you are totally committed to science, do not come. Caltech has as much breadth as a Russian grocery store."

— Daniel S., Caltech

"Being at Marlboro is like having a recurring bizarre dream. You're not quite sure what it all means, but it happens a lot. If it stopped you'd probably wonder why, but then you'd just eat breakfast."

— Mark L., Marlboro College

"Life at school is an oxymoron."

—Dave G., UC–Davis

"One other thing I LOVE about NYU: online registration! God bless the NYU registrar!"

—Timothy A., New York University

"Vassar is like a sexual disease: once you've accepted it, it's great, but when you realize you've got another three years to put up with it, you go see a medical adviser immediately."

— Henry R., Vassar College

"Vassar is like a big walrus butt: lots of hair but also very moist."

— Calder M., Vassar College

"I feel that this school is a maze with snakes and bulls. If you live with a raised fist or a raised phallus, it is easy. If you are earthly, bound to do nothing, come."

— Anonymous, U. of Oregon

"Getting an education from MIT is like getting a drink from a firehose."

— Juan G., MIT

"Financial Aid office needs a complete overhaul. An atom bomb would suffice."

—Male Senior, Duquesne University

"My life here is as the torrential rains of Dhamer upon the Yaktong Valley. I bleat like a llama shedding out of season."

— Ronald M., James Madison University

"This school is like a tight anus: there's tremendous pressure to come out straight and conformed."

— Stephen J., Washington and Lee University

"Intro classes have the consistency of Cheez Whiz: they go down easy, they taste horrible, and they are not good for you."

— Pat T., U. of Vermont

"This school was founded by Jesuits.... However, I believe that it has been hijacked by yuppie prisses."

—Anonymous, Loyola Marymount University

## SEX, DRUGS, ROCK & ROLL...

"This school is no good for people who like art, music, and Sonic Youth. 'Society is a hole.' There's a quote by Sonic Youth."

— Meghan S., Lake Forest College

"Montreal is the city of festivals. It is the party-central of Canada. McGill is located right in the middle of it all."

—Female, McGill University

"The university tries to offer activities as an alternative to alcohol on the weekends. Those are not heavily attended. The weekends are for drinking."

—Maura G., Ohio University

"Beam, Bud, beer, babes—the four essential B's."

— "Jim Beam," Wittenberg University

"William and Mary: where you can drink beer and have sex in the same place your forefathers did."

— Adam L., College of William and Mary

"Yeah, there aren't any guys, but who doesn't like doing homework on a Saturday night?"

— Nicole C., Wellesley College

"UCSB is the only place where U Can Study Buzzed and still ace an exam the next day."

— Tracy B., UC–Santa Barbara

"The dances here are a riot because I love watching nerds and intellectuals dance."

—Male Senior, Columbia University

"When I visited schools, I went to Brown and Northwestern on the same trip. I went to NU on a Wednesday and Thursday night. I partied like a champ. At Brown on Friday I was invited to two parties (I should be psyched) but they were both for NUDE people. AUGH YUCK!"

— Silvy N., Northwestern University

"A Denison student might be quoted as saying, 'Life is a waste of time, and time is a waste of life; so get wasted all the time, and have the time of your life.'"

— Katherine H., Denison University

"This campus is an extremely great place to spend four college years, but it is still plagued, as all other campuses are, including Christian colleges, with sin. Therefore, this campus needs to come under submission to Jesus Christ."

— Laura D., James Madison University

"I have been around the block, you know, sex, drugs, and rock and roll. . . . I was in a sorority . . . . I tend to sleep around, too, but I basically think like a guy, so guys don't disrespect me. I am very picky in who I sleep with, only the best-bodied, best-looking dudes. They feel privileged, and I give them a hell of a time. I am quite the hottie, and I know it, so anyone who has a problem can just stay away."

—Anonymous, University of South Dakota

"St. Mary's College of Maryland Poem:

We are located on the H2O
We get blazed up where ever we go.
You throw your shoes around the tree
When you lose your virginity.
Parties here are just like heaven,
'Cause were all boozed up 24-7.
The girls are cute; the guys are hot,
If you open your window you are bound to smell pot.
If you visit my school I can promise you this,
You'll get so finagled you'll wake up in piss."

—Anonymous, St. Mary's College of Maryland

## NEANDERTHALS

"If U R looking to settle down with an unattractive big woman, Hofstra is the place."

— Anonymous, Hofstra University

"There are lots of complaints about the attractiveness of the female students, but we females have our own saying about the guys at CMU—'The odds are good, but the goods are odd.'"

—Beth M., Carnegie Mellon University

"Girls at BYU are like parking spaces: the good ones are taken, the close ones are handicapped or reserved, and the rest are too far out!"

— Todd P., Brigham Young University

"In Rolla, we have tons of women, but not many of them!"

— Todd O., U. of Missouri–Rolla

"The faculty is great, academics are challenging, but the women are liberated and become difficult to live with. To sum it all up, Hendrix is so cool."

— Mike S., Hendrix College

"The students seem to have serious problems in general, perhaps they all need a little Viagra to perk things up a bit."

—Female Freshman, Albertson College

"UCSD rages—NOT! If you like the ocean and the library and have a fear of parties and girls without facial hair, you've hit the jackpot!!!"

— Spencer M., UC–San Diego

"There's a saying I've heard around: nine out of ten girls in California look good, the tenth goes to UCSD."

— Michael K., UC–San Diego

"U of C is OK if all you want to do is work, but if you are looking for a good social scene or a hot stinkin' babe, go to California, young man!"

—Benjamin D., University of Chicago

"Doesn't matter that we got no women. I'm never in bed anyway."

—Male Sophomore, California Institute of Technology

"Beer, football, and boobies are what Clemson is all about!"

— Paul S., Clemson University

"The men here often complain that there are too few women here; if they took a look in the mirror, maybe they'd realize why girls don't come here!"

— Tara L., Stevens Institute of Technology

"I would have sex more often but the girls are nasty!"

—Anonymous, St. Bonaventure University

"We need some more hot girls. Tell hot girls to come here."

—Anonymous, Macalester College

## SCHOOL VS. THE "REAL WORLD"...

"College is the best time of your life. Never again will you be surrounded by people the same age as you, free from grown-ups and the threat of working in the real world. Your parents give you money when you ask for it, and all you have to do is learn!"

— Jennifer F., Syracuse University

"Real life experience in such concepts—alienation, depression, suppression, isolationism, edge of racial tension, apathy, etc.—before the 'Real World.'"

— Anonymous, NYU

"When we lose a football game to a college with lower academic standards, we console ourselves by saying that one day they will work for us and then we'll get even!"

— Michael J., University of the South, Sewanee

"Going to Chem. review is like masturbating with sandpaper: it's just a bad idea."

—Robby M., California Institute of Technology

## SCHOOLS THAT ARE ALL THAT & A BAG OF CHIPS

"I like Duquesne because it has a mission beyond just educating students—it tries also to educate the heart and soul—and that makes for better students, a better university and a better world."

—Female Senior, Duquesne University

"For the first time in my life I am allowed to think for myself. . . . This is an environment where one can proclaim in class that Socrates is a bastard and, if able to support the statement, be respected for it."

—Female Freshman, Simon's Rock College of Bard

"Best ever dude! Nobody complains if I leave the toilet seat up."

—Derek L., Deep Springs College

"We're small enough that you'll probably hug a significant portion of the population by the time you graduate."

—Male Junior, Bard College

"We play dodgeball at recess and think what it would be like if we could fly."

—Joseph W., Beloit College

"The students here are as diverse as their views and backgrounds. My friends are mostly thespians and lesbians, and they rock!"

—Female Junior, Bennington College

## IN CASE YOU WERE WONDERING...

"You forgot to ask the most pertinent question, which is: 'Have you ever seen Elvis teach your 100 level courses?'"

— Adam L., Alfred University

"I was smart once. I used to sleep. Then I majored in chemical engineering."

— C. C. Smith, Clemson University

"There's about 15 too many classes along the lines of 'Talking Heads: The Politics of Cabbage in 19th Century Guam.'"

—Sarah G., Bennington College

"Classes are hard to get. Usually you have to cheat and just add the class, telling them you are a graduating senior. I've done that for the last three years and it works!"

—Anonymous, UC–Davis

"I am a hermit who enjoys Ramen noodles and skin flicks. In the winter, I sit in a yoga position by a patch of ice on the sidewalk and mock people as they fall. I often bend spoons with my mind."

—Junior, Indiana University of Pennsylvania

"When I'm not trying to free Mumia, experience non-gender orgasm/transgender interpretive dance, contracting any number of venereal diseases, or trying to be hopelessly unique, I obsess to no end in trying to reconcile my existentialist beliefs with paying $30,000 a year to attend this socially legitimizing institution."

—Katherine S., Bard College

"Those who oppose the Dark Lord will be crushed, but those who are its friend will receive rewards beyond the dreams of avarice."

— Anonymous, Sarah Lawrence College

"There is a real problem with moles on this campus; no one is willing to talk about them."

— Alexander D., Bates College

"Bates College is a phallocentric, logocentric, Greco-Roman, linear-rational, ethnocentric, homophobic, patriarchal institution. How's that for a list of catchwords?"

— Stephen H., Bates College

"I think if our generation's parents knew how consumptive, ill-informed, and drug-addicted their children were, they'd suffer a collective nervous breakdown."

— Anonymous, U. of Denver

"Our school is the school of the future and always will be."

— Chuck C., Rhodes College

"To begin, there's an apartment complex on a main road in my college city, and one of the apartments has put up a sign a few times this year that reads 'Honk for a drink.' So anytime someone drives by and honks his/her horn, the guys on the balcony take a swig of beer. I have also heard a story of a guy who turned 21 here and his buddies had a beer tube made that went from the third floor apartments down to the ground filled with beer for the guy to drink . . . . Someone like me would never survive an ordeal like that given my stature. Also, because Interstate 81 cuts through our campus, many drunk girls, especially on homecoming, enjoy giving the truck drivers a little peep show either day or night . . . . One of the great things about our school, though, is that we have a bus service called 'Ride with Len.' This man had a relative die from a drunk driver, and so on the weekends he takes to driving a huge bus around our town to take college kids to their prospective places safely. He has gotten so popular, that more buses and drivers have been added. So I'd say that **although many people drink here, they drink responsibly.**"

—Anonymous, James Madison University

## CONFUSED PEOPLE...

"A crust of bread is better than nothing. Nothing is better than true love. Therefore, by the transitive property, a crust of bread is better than true love."

—Jason G., Gettysburg College

"Bentley College has fulfilled all and more of my expectations than I ever imagined."

— Dawn T., Bentley College

"Everyone seems to be really into political correctness, but in the wake of the recent Supreme Court decision, I don't see that lasting very long."

—John R., Birmingham Southern College

"Sarah Lawrence is a haven of unity and acceptance. Every morning at sunrise the entire campus gathers around the flagpole, holds hands, and sings 'We Are The World.' If you're really lucky, you get to be Dionne Warwick or Willie Nelson. If you show up late you have to be Bob Dylan. But everyone gets free doughnuts, and it's the happiest time of the day for most students. One morning I went hung over and threw up in the middle of the circle. I was so ashamed, but then I looked around at the diverse group of smiling faces from all over the country and the world and suddenly I felt better. I went home and threw up some more, thankful to live in the world of love that is Sarah Lawrence."

— Matt F., Sarah Lawrence College

(On the Academics/Administration) "They think they know a lot but they actually don't know anything, but some of them know that, so they know everything."

—Male Junior, College of the Atlantic

# PART 5

## INDEXES

# INDEX OF SCHOOLS

## A

| | |
|---|---|
| Agnes Scott College | 46 |
| Albertson College | 48 |
| Albion College | 50 |
| Alfred University | 52 |
| Allegheny College | 54 |
| American University | 56 |
| Amherst College | 58 |
| Arizona State University | 60 |
| Auburn University | 62 |
| Austin College | 64 |

## B

| | |
|---|---|
| Babson College | 66 |
| Bard College | 68 |
| Barnard College | 70 |
| Bates College | 72 |
| Baylor University | 74 |
| Bellarmine University | 76 |
| Beloit College | 78 |
| Bennington College | 80 |
| Bentley College | 82 |
| Birmingham-Southern College | 84 |
| Boston College | 86 |
| Boston University | 88 |
| Bowdoin College | 90 |
| Bradley University | 92 |
| Brandeis University | 94 |
| Brigham Young University | 96 |
| Brown University | 98 |
| Bryant College | 100 |
| Bryn Mawr College | 102 |
| Bucknell University | 104 |

## C

| | |
|---|---|
| Cal Poly | 106 |
| California Institute of Technology | 108 |
| Calvin College | 110 |
| Carleton College | 112 |
| Carnegie Mellon University | 114 |
| Case Western Reserve University | 116 |
| Catawba College | 118 |
| Catholic University of America | 120 |
| Centenary College of Louisiana | 122 |
| Centre College | 124 |
| City University of New York—Brooklyn College | 126 |
| City University of New York—Hunter College | 128 |
| City University of New York—Queens College | 130 |
| Claremont McKenna College | 132 |
| Clark University | 134 |
| Clarkson University | 136 |
| Clemson University | 138 |
| Coe College | 140 |
| Colby College | 142 |
| Colgate University | 144 |
| College of Charleston | 146 |
| The College of New Jersey | 148 |
| College of Saint Benedict/Saint John's University | 150 |
| College of the Atlantic | 152 |
| College of the Holy Cross | 154 |
| College of the Ozarks | 156 |
| College of William and Mary | 158 |
| College of Wooster | 160 |
| Colorado College | 162 |
| Colorado School of Mines | 164 |
| Columbia University | 166 |
| Connecticut College | 168 |
| Cooper Union | 170 |
| Cornell College | 172 |
| Cornell University | 174 |
| Creighton University | 176 |

## D

| | |
|---|---|
| Dartmouth College | 178 |
| Davidson College | 180 |
| Deep Springs College | 182 |
| Denison University | 184 |
| DePaul University | 186 |
| DePauw University | 188 |
| Dickinson College | 190 |
| Drew University | 192 |
| Drexel University | 194 |
| Duke University | 196 |
| Duquesne University | 198 |

## E

| | |
|---|---|
| Earlham College | 200 |
| Eckerd College | 202 |
| Elon University | 204 |
| Emerson College | 206 |
| Emory University | 208 |
| Eugene Lang College | 210 |
| The Evergreen State College | 212 |

## F

| | |
|---|---|
| Fairfield University | 214 |
| Fisk University | 216 |
| Flagler College | 218 |
| Florida A&M University | 220 |
| Florida State University | 222 |
| Fordham University | 224 |
| Franklin & Marshall College | 226 |
| Furman University | 228 |

## G

| | |
|---|---|
| George Mason University | 230 |
| George Washington University | 232 |
| Georgetown University | 234 |
| Georgia Institute of Technology | 236 |
| Gettysburg College | 238 |
| Goddard College | 240 |
| Golden Gate University | 242 |
| Gonzaga University | 244 |
| Goucher College | 246 |
| Grinnell College | 248 |
| Grove City College | 250 |
| Guilford College | 252 |
| Gustavus Adolphus College | 254 |

## H

| | |
|---|---|
| Hamilton College | 256 |
| Hampden-Sydney College | 258 |
| Hampshire College | 260 |
| Hampton University | 262 |
| Hanover College | 264 |
| Harvard College | 266 |
| Harvey Mudd College | 268 |

| | |
|---|---|
| Haverford College | 270 |
| Hendrix College | 272 |
| Hiram College | 274 |
| Hobart and William Smith Colleges | 276 |
| Hofstra University | 278 |
| Hollins University | 280 |
| Howard University | 282 |

## I

| | |
|---|---|
| Illinois Institute of Technology | 284 |
| Illinois Wesleyan University | 286 |
| Indiana University—Bloomington | 288 |
| Indiana University of Pennsylvania | 290 |
| Iowa State University | 292 |
| Ithaca College | 294 |

## J

| | |
|---|---|
| James Madison University | 296 |
| Johns Hopkins University | 298 |
| Juniata College | 300 |

## K

| | |
|---|---|
| Kalamazoo College | 302 |
| Kansas State University | 304 |
| Kenyon College | 306 |
| Knox College | 308 |

## L

| | |
|---|---|
| Lafayette College | 310 |
| Lake Forest College | 312 |
| Lawrence University | 314 |
| Lehigh University | 316 |
| Lewis & Clark College | 318 |
| Louisiana State University—Baton Rouge | 320 |
| Loyola College in Maryland | 322 |
| Loyola Marymount University | 324 |
| Loyola University Chicago | 326 |
| Loyola University New Orleans | 328 |

## M

| | |
|---|---|
| Macalester College | 330 |
| Manhattanville College | 332 |
| Marist College | 334 |
| Marlboro College | 336 |
| Marquette University | 338 |
| Mary Washington College | 340 |
| Massachusetts Institute of Technology | 342 |
| McGill University | 344 |
| Mercer University | 346 |
| Miami University | 348 |
| Michigan State University | 350 |
| Michigan Technological University | 352 |
| Middlebury College | 354 |
| Millsaps College | 356 |
| Montana Tech of the University of Montana | 358 |
| Moravian College | 360 |
| Morehouse College | 362 |
| Mount Holyoke College | 364 |
| Muhlenberg College | 366 |

## N

| | |
|---|---|
| New College of Florida | 368 |
| New Jersey Institute of Technology | 370 |
| New Mexico Institute of Mining & Technology | 372 |
| New York University | 374 |
| North Carolina State University | 376 |
| Northeastern University | 378 |
| Northwestern University | 380 |

## O

| | |
|---|---|
| Oberlin College | 382 |
| Occidental College | 384 |
| Oglethorpe University | 386 |
| Ohio Northern University | 388 |
| Ohio State University—Columbus | 390 |
| Ohio University—Athens | 392 |
| Ohio Wesleyan University | 394 |

## P

| | |
|---|---|
| Pennsylvania State University—University Park | 396 |
| Pepperdine University | 398 |
| Pitzer College | 400 |
| Pomona College | 402 |
| Princeton University | 404 |
| Providence College | 406 |
| Purdue University—West Lafayette | 408 |

## R

| | |
|---|---|
| Randolph-Macon College | 410 |
| Randolph-Macon Woman's College | 412 |
| Reed College | 414 |
| Rensselaer Polytechnic Institute | 416 |
| Rhodes College | 418 |
| Rice University | 420 |
| Rider University | 422 |
| Ripon College | 424 |
| Rochester Institute of Technology | 426 |
| Rollins College | 428 |
| Rose-Hulman Institute of Technology | 430 |
| Rutgers University—Rutgers College | 432 |

## S

| | |
|---|---|
| St. Anselm College | 434 |
| Saint Bonaventure University | 436 |
| St. John's College (MD) | 438 |
| St. John's College (NM) | 440 |
| St. Lawrence University | 442 |
| Saint Louis University | 444 |
| Saint Mary's College of California | 446 |
| St. Mary's College of Maryland | 448 |
| St. Olaf College | 450 |
| Salisbury University | 452 |
| Samford University | 454 |
| Santa Clara University | 456 |
| Sarah Lawrence College | 458 |
| Scripps College | 460 |
| Seattle University | 462 |
| Seton Hall University | 464 |
| Siena College | 466 |
| Simmons College | 468 |
| Simon's Rock College of Bard | 470 |
| Skidmore College | 472 |
| Smith College | 474 |
| Sonoma State University | 476 |
| Southern Methodist University | 478 |
| Southwestern University | 480 |
| Spelman College | 482 |
| Stanford University | 484 |
| State University of New York at Albany | 486 |
| State University of New York at Binghamton | 488 |
| State University of New York at Buffalo | 490 |
| State University of New York College at Geneseo | 492 |
| Stephens College | 494 |
| Stetson University | 496 |
| Stevens Institute of Technology | 498 |
| Stony Brook University (SUNY) | 500 |

| | |
|---|---|
| Susquehanna University | 502 |
| Swarthmore College | 504 |
| Sweet Briar College | 506 |
| Syracuse University | 508 |

## T

| | |
|---|---|
| TCU | 510 |
| Temple University | 512 |
| Texas A&M University—College Station | 514 |
| Trinity College | 516 |
| Trinity University | 518 |
| Truman State University | 520 |
| Tufts University | 522 |
| Tulane University | 524 |
| Tuskegee University | 526 |

## U

| | |
|---|---|
| Union College | 528 |
| United States Air Force Academy | 530 |
| United States Coast Guard Academy | 532 |
| United States Merchant Marine Academy | 534 |
| United States Military Academy | 536 |
| United States Naval Academy | 538 |
| University of Alabama—Tuscaloosa | 540 |
| University of Arizona | 542 |
| University of Arkansas—Fayetteville | 544 |
| University of California—Berkeley | 546 |
| University of California—Davis | 548 |
| University of California—Irvine | 550 |
| University of California—Los Angeles | 552 |
| University of California—Riverside | 554 |
| University of California—San Diego | 556 |
| University of California—Santa Barbara | 558 |
| University of California—Santa Cruz | 560 |
| University of Chicago | 562 |
| University of Colorado—Boulder | 564 |
| University of Connecticut | 566 |
| University of Dallas | 568 |
| University of Dayton | 570 |
| University of Delaware | 572 |
| University of Denver | 574 |
| University of Florida | 576 |
| University of Georgia | 578 |
| University of Hawaii—Manoa | 580 |
| University of Idaho | 582 |
| University of Illinois—Urbana-Champaign | 584 |
| University of Iowa | 586 |
| University of Kansas | 588 |
| University of Kentucky | 590 |
| The University of Maine | 592 |
| University of Maryland, Baltimore County | 594 |
| University of Maryland, College Park | 596 |
| University of Massachusetts—Amherst | 598 |
| University of Miami | 600 |
| University of Michigan—Ann Arbor | 602 |
| University of Minnesota—Twin Cities | 604 |
| University of Mississippi | 606 |
| University of Missouri—Rolla | 608 |
| University of Montana—Missoula | 610 |
| University of Nebraska—Lincoln | 612 |
| University of Nevada—Las Vegas | 614 |
| University of New Hampshire | 616 |
| University of New Mexico | 618 |
| University of New Orleans | 620 |
| University of North Carolina—Asheville | 622 |
| University of North Carolina—Chapel Hill | 624 |
| University of North Carolina—Greensboro | 626 |
| University of North Dakota | 628 |
| University of Notre Dame | 630 |
| University of Oklahoma | 632 |
| University of Oregon | 634 |
| University of Pennsylvania | 636 |
| University of Pittsburgh—Pittsburgh | 638 |
| University of Puget Sound | 640 |
| University of Redlands | 642 |
| University of Rhode Island | 644 |
| University of Richmond | 646 |
| University of Rochester | 648 |
| University of San Diego | 650 |
| University of San Francisco | 652 |
| University of Scranton | 654 |
| University of South Carolina—Columbia | 656 |
| University of South Dakota | 658 |
| University of Southern California | 660 |
| University of Tennessee—Knoxville | 662 |
| University of Texas—Austin | 664 |
| University of the Pacific | 666 |
| University of the South | 668 |
| University of Toronto | 670 |
| University of Tulsa | 672 |
| University of Utah | 674 |
| University of Vermont | 676 |
| University of Virginia | 678 |
| University of Washington | 680 |
| University of Wisconsin—Madison | 682 |
| University of Wyoming | 684 |
| Ursinus College | 686 |

## V

| | |
|---|---|
| Valparaiso University | 688 |
| Vanderbilt University | 690 |
| Vassar College | 692 |
| Villanova University | 694 |
| Virginia Tech | 696 |

## W

| | |
|---|---|
| Wabash College | 698 |
| Wagner College | 700 |
| Wake Forest University | 702 |
| Warren Wilson College | 704 |
| Washington and Lee University | 706 |
| Washington State University | 708 |
| Washington University in St. Louis | 710 |
| Webb Institute | 712 |
| Wellesley College | 714 |
| Wells College | 716 |
| Wesleyan College | 718 |
| Wesleyan University | 720 |
| West Virginia University | 722 |
| Westminster College | 724 |
| Wheaton College (IL) | 726 |
| Wheaton College (MA) | 728 |
| Whitman College | 730 |
| Whittier College | 732 |
| Willamette University | 734 |
| William Jewell College | 736 |
| Williams College | 738 |
| Wittenburg University | 740 |
| Wofford College | 742 |
| Worcester Polytechnic Institute | 744 |

## Y

| | |
|---|---|
| Yale University | 746 |

# INDEX OF SCHOOLS BY LOCATION

## ALABAMA
| | |
|---|---|
| Auburn University | 62 |
| Birmingham-Southern College | 84 |
| Samford University | 454 |
| Tuskegee University | 526 |
| University of Alabama—Tuscaloosa | 540 |

## ARIZONA
| | |
|---|---|
| Arizona State University | 60 |
| University of Arizona | 542 |

## ARKANSAS
| | |
|---|---|
| Hendrix College | 272 |
| University of Arkansas—Fayetteville | 544 |

## CALIFORNIA
| | |
|---|---|
| Cal Poly | 106 |
| California Institute of Technology | 108 |
| Claremont McKenna College | 132 |
| Golden Gate University | 242 |
| Harvey Mudd College | 268 |
| Loyola Marymount University | 324 |
| Occidental College | 384 |
| Pepperdine University | 398 |
| Pitzer College | 400 |
| Pomona College | 402 |
| Saint Mary's College of California | 446 |
| Santa Clara University | 456 |
| Scripps College | 460 |
| Sonoma State University | 476 |
| Stanford University | 484 |
| University of California—Berkeley | 546 |
| University of California—Davis | 548 |
| University of California—Irvine | 550 |
| University of California—Los Angeles | 552 |
| University of California—Riverside | 554 |
| University of California—San Diego | 556 |
| University of California—Santa Barbara | 558 |
| University of California—Santa Cruz | 560 |
| University of Redlands | 642 |
| University of San Diego | 650 |
| University of San Francisco | 652 |
| University of Southern California | 660 |
| University of the Pacific | 666 |
| Whittier College | 732 |

## COLORADO
| | |
|---|---|
| Colorado College | 162 |
| Colorado School of Mines | 164 |
| United States Air Force Academy | 530 |
| University of Colorado—Boulder | 564 |
| University of Denver | 574 |

## CONNECTICUT
| | |
|---|---|
| Connecticut College | 168 |
| Fairfield University | 214 |
| Trinity College | 516 |
| United States Coast Guard Academy | 532 |
| University of Connecticut | 566 |
| Wesleyan University | 720 |
| Yale University | 746 |

## DELAWARE
| | |
|---|---|
| University of Delaware | 572 |

## DISTRICT OF COLUMBIA
| | |
|---|---|
| American University | 56 |
| Catholic University of America | 120 |
| George Washington University | 232 |
| Georgetown University | 234 |
| Howard University | 282 |

## FLORIDA
| | |
|---|---|
| Eckerd College | 202 |
| Flagler College | 218 |
| Florida A&M University | 220 |
| Florida State University | 222 |
| New College of Florida | 368 |
| Rollins College | 428 |
| Stetson University | 496 |
| University of Florida | 576 |
| University of Miami | 600 |

## GEORGIA
| | |
|---|---|
| Agnes Scott College | 46 |
| Emory University | 208 |
| Georgia Institute of Technology | 236 |
| Mercer University | 346 |
| Morehouse College | 362 |
| Oglethorpe University | 386 |
| Spelman College | 482 |
| University of Georgia | 578 |
| Wesleyan College | 718 |

## HAWAII
| | |
|---|---|
| University of Hawaii—Manoa | 580 |

## IDAHO
| | |
|---|---|
| Albertson College | 48 |
| University of Idaho | 582 |

## ILLINOIS
| | |
|---|---|
| Bradley University | 92 |
| DePaul University | 186 |
| Illinois Institute of Technology | 284 |
| Illinois Wesleyan University | 286 |
| Knox College | 308 |
| Lake Forest College | 312 |
| Loyola University Chicago | 326 |
| Northwestern University | 380 |
| University of Chicago | 562 |
| University of Illinois—Urbana-Champaign | 584 |
| Wheaton College (IL) | 726 |

## INDIANA
| | |
|---|---|
| DePauw University | 188 |
| Earlham College | 200 |
| Hanover College | 264 |
| Indiana University—Bloomington | 288 |
| Purdue University—West Lafayette | 408 |
| Rose-Hulman Institute of Technology | 430 |
| University of Notre Dame | 630 |
| Valparaiso University | 688 |
| Wabash College | 698 |

## IOWA
| | |
|---|---|
| Coe College | 140 |
| Cornell College | 172 |
| Grinnell College | 248 |
| Iowa State University | 292 |
| University of Iowa | 586 |

## KANSAS
| | |
|---|---|
| Kansas State University | 304 |
| University of Kansas | 588 |

## KENTUCKY
| | |
|---|---|
| Bellarmine University | 76 |
| Centre College | 124 |
| University of Kentucky | 590 |

## LOUISIANA
| | |
|---|---|
| Centenary College of Louisiana | 122 |
| Louisiana State University—Baton Rouge | 320 |
| Loyola University New Orleans | 328 |
| Tulane University | 524 |
| University of New Orleans | 620 |

## MAINE
| | |
|---|---|
| Bates College | 72 |
| Bowdoin College | 90 |
| Colby College | 142 |
| College of the Atlantic | 152 |
| The University of Maine | 592 |

## MARYLAND
| | |
|---|---|
| Goucher College | 246 |
| Johns Hopkins University | 298 |
| Loyola College in Maryland | 322 |
| St. John's College (MD) | 438 |
| St. Mary's College of Maryland | 448 |
| Salisbury University | 452 |
| United States Naval Academy | 538 |
| University of Maryland, Baltimore County | 594 |
| University of Maryland, College Park | 596 |

## MASSACHUSETTS
| | |
|---|---|
| Amherst College | 58 |
| Babson College | 66 |
| Bentley College | 82 |
| Boston College | 86 |
| Boston University | 88 |
| Brandeis University | 94 |
| Clark University | 134 |
| College of the Holy Cross | 154 |
| Emerson College | 206 |
| Hampshire College | 260 |
| Harvard College | 266 |
| Massachusetts Institute of Technology | 342 |
| Mount Holyoke College | 364 |
| Northeastern University | 378 |
| Simmons College | 468 |
| Smith College | 474 |
| Tufts University | 522 |
| University of Massachusetts—Amherst | 598 |
| Wellesley College | 714 |
| Wheaton College (MA) | 728 |
| Williams College | 738 |
| Worcester Polytechnic Institute | 744 |

## MICHIGAN
| | |
|---|---|
| Albion College | 50 |
| Calvin College | 110 |
| Kalamazoo College | 302 |
| Michigan State University | 350 |
| Michigan Technological University | 352 |
| University of Michigan—Ann Arbor | 602 |

## MINNESOTA
| | |
|---|---|
| Carleton College | 112 |
| College of Saint Benedict/Saint John's University | 150 |
| Gustavus Adolphus College | 254 |
| Macalester College | 330 |
| St. Olaf College | 450 |
| University of Minnesota—Twin Cities | 604 |

## MISSISSIPPI
| | |
|---|---|
| Millsaps College | 356 |
| University of Mississippi | 606 |

## MISSOURI
| | |
|---|---|
| College of the Ozarks | 156 |
| Saint Louis University | 444 |
| Stephens College | 494 |
| Truman State University | 520 |
| University of Missouri—Rolla | 608 |
| Washington University in St. Louis | 710 |
| William Jewell College | 736 |

## MONTANA
| | |
|---|---|
| Montana Tech of the University of Montana | 358 |
| University of Montana—Missoula | 610 |

## NEBRASKA
| | |
|---|---|
| Creighton University | 176 |
| University of Nebraska—Lincoln | 612 |

## NEVADA
| | |
|---|---|
| Deep Springs College | 182 |
| University of Nevada—Las Vegas | 614 |

## NEW HAMPSHIRE
| | |
|---|---|
| Dartmouth College | 178 |
| St. Anselm College | 434 |
| University of New Hampshire | 616 |

## NEW JERSEY
| | |
|---|---|
| The College of New Jersey | 148 |
| Drew University | 192 |
| New Jersey Institute of Technology | 370 |
| Princeton University | 404 |
| Rider University | 422 |
| Rutgers University—Rutgers College | 432 |
| Seton Hall University | 464 |
| Stevens Institute of Technology | 498 |

## NEW MEXICO
| | |
|---|---|
| New Mexico Institute of Mining & Technology | 372 |
| St. John's College (NM) | 440 |
| University of New Mexico | 618 |

## NEW YORK
| | |
|---|---|
| Alfred University | 52 |
| Bard College | 68 |
| Barnard College | 70 |
| City University of New York—Brooklyn College | 126 |
| City University of New York—Hunter College | 128 |

| | |
|---|---|
| City University of New York—Queens College | 130 |
| Clarkson University | 136 |
| Colgate University | 144 |
| Columbia University | 166 |
| Cooper Union | 170 |
| Cornell University | 174 |
| Eugene Lang College | 210 |
| Fordham University | 224 |
| Hamilton College | 256 |
| Hobart and William Smith Colleges | 276 |
| Hofstra University | 278 |
| Ithaca College | 294 |
| Manhattanville College | 332 |
| Marist College | 334 |
| New York University | 374 |
| Rensselaer Polytechnic Institute | 416 |
| Rochester Institute of Technology | 426 |
| Saint Bonaventure University | 436 |
| St. Lawrence University | 442 |
| Sarah Lawrence College | 458 |
| Siena College | 466 |
| Simon's Rock College of Bard | 470 |
| Skidmore College | 472 |
| State University of New York at Albany | 486 |
| State University of New York at Binghamton | 488 |
| State University of New York at Buffalo | 490 |
| State University of New York College at Geneseo | 492 |
| Stony Brook University (SUNY) | 500 |
| Syracuse University | 508 |
| Union College | 528 |
| United States Merchant Marine Academy | 534 |
| United States Military Academy | 536 |
| University of Rochester | 648 |
| Vassar College | 692 |
| Wagner College | 700 |
| Webb Institute | 712 |
| Wells College | 716 |

## NORTH CAROLINA

| | |
|---|---|
| Catawba College | 118 |
| Davidson College | 180 |
| Duke University | 196 |
| Elon University | 204 |
| Guilford College | 252 |
| North Carolina State University | 376 |
| University of North Carolina—Asheville | 622 |
| University of North Carolina—Chapel Hill | 624 |
| University of North Carolina—Greensboro | 626 |
| Wake Forest University | 702 |
| Warren Wilson College | 704 |

## NORTH DAKOTA

| | |
|---|---|
| University of North Dakota | 628 |

## OHIO

| | |
|---|---|
| Case Western Reserve University | 116 |
| College of Wooster | 160 |
| Denison University | 184 |
| Hiram College | 274 |
| Kenyon College | 306 |
| Miami University | 348 |
| Oberlin College | 382 |
| Ohio Northern University | 388 |
| Ohio State University—Columbus | 390 |
| Ohio University—Athens | 392 |
| Ohio Wesleyan University | 394 |
| University of Dayton | 570 |
| Wittenburg University | 740 |

## OKLAHOMA

| | |
|---|---|
| University of Oklahoma | 632 |
| University of Tulsa | 672 |

## OREGON

| | |
|---|---|
| Lewis & Clark College | 318 |
| Reed College | 414 |
| University of Oregon | 634 |
| Willamette University | 734 |

## PENNSYLVANIA

| | |
|---|---|
| Allegheny College | 54 |
| Bryn Mawr College | 102 |
| Bucknell University | 104 |
| Carnegie Mellon University | 114 |
| Dickinson College | 190 |
| Drexel University | 194 |
| Duquesne University | 198 |
| Franklin & Marshall College | 226 |
| Gettysburg College | 238 |
| Grove City College | 250 |
| Haverford College | 270 |
| Indiana University of Pennsylvania | 290 |
| Juniata College | 300 |
| Lafayette College | 310 |
| Lehigh University | 316 |
| Moravian College | 360 |
| Muhlenberg College | 366 |
| Pennsylvania State University—University Park | 396 |
| Susquehanna University | 502 |
| Swarthmore College | 504 |
| Temple University | 512 |
| University of Pennsylvania | 636 |
| University of Pittsburgh—Pittsburgh | 638 |
| University of Scranton | 654 |
| Ursinus College | 686 |
| Villanova University | 694 |
| Westminster College | 724 |

## RHODE ISLAND

| | |
|---|---|
| Brown University | 98 |
| Bryant College | 100 |
| Providence College | 406 |
| University of Rhode Island | 644 |

## SOUTH CAROLINA

| | |
|---|---|
| Clemson University | 138 |
| College of Charleston | 146 |
| Furman University | 228 |
| University of South Carolina—Columbia | 656 |
| Wofford College | 742 |

## SOUTH DAKOTA

| | |
|---|---|
| University of South Dakota | 658 |

## TENNESSEE

| | |
|---|---|
| Fisk University | 216 |
| Rhodes College | 418 |
| University of Tennessee—Knoxville | 662 |
| University of the South | 668 |
| Vanderbilt University | 690 |

INDEX OF SCHOOLS BY LOCATION ■ 771

## TEXAS
| | |
|---|---|
| Austin College | 64 |
| Baylor University | 74 |
| Rice University | 420 |
| Southern Methodist University | 478 |
| Southwestern University | 480 |
| TCU | 510 |
| Texas A&M University—College Station | 514 |
| Trinity University | 518 |
| University of Dallas | 568 |
| University of Texas—Austin | 664 |

## UTAH
| | |
|---|---|
| Brigham Young University | 96 |
| University of Utah | 674 |

## VERMONT
| | |
|---|---|
| Bennington College | 80 |
| Goddard College | 240 |
| Marlboro College | 336 |
| Middlebury College | 354 |
| University of Vermont | 676 |

## VIRGINIA
| | |
|---|---|
| College of William and Mary | 158 |
| George Mason University | 230 |
| Hampden-Sydney College | 258 |
| Hampton University | 262 |
| Hollins University | 280 |
| James Madison University | 296 |
| Mary Washington College | 340 |
| Randolph-Macon College | 410 |
| Randolph-Macon Woman's College | 412 |
| Sweet Briar College | 506 |
| University of Richmond | 646 |
| University of Virginia | 678 |
| Virginia Tech | 696 |
| Washington and Lee University | 706 |

## WASHINGTON
| | |
|---|---|
| The Evergreen State College | 212 |
| Gonzaga University | 244 |
| Seattle University | 462 |
| University of Puget Sound | 640 |
| University of Washington | 680 |
| Washington State University | 708 |
| Whitman College | 730 |

## WEST VIRGINIA
| | |
|---|---|
| West Virginia University | 722 |

## WISCONSIN
| | |
|---|---|
| Beloit College | 78 |
| Lawrence University | 314 |
| Marquette University | 338 |
| Ripon College | 424 |
| University of Wisconsin—Madison | 682 |

## WYOMING
| | |
|---|---|
| University of Wyoming | 684 |

## CANADA
### ONTARIO
| | |
|---|---|
| University of Toronto | 670 |

### QUEBEC
| | |
|---|---|
| McGill University | 344 |

## ABOUT THE AUTHORS

**Robert Franek** is a graduate of Drew University and has been a member of The Princeton Review Staff for four years. Robert comes to The Princeton Review with an extensive admissions background, most recently at Wagner College in Staten Island, New York. In addition, he owns a walking tour business and leads historically driven, yet not boring, tours of his home town!

**Tom Meltzer** is a graduate of Columbia University. He has taught for The Princeton Review since 1986 and is the author or co-author of seven TPR titles, the most recent of which is *Illustrated Word Smart*, which Tom co-wrote with his wife, Lisa. He is also a professional musician and songwriter. A native of Baltimore, Tom now lives in Hillsborough, North Carolina.

**Roy Opochinski** is a graduate of Drew University and has been a member of The Princeton Review staff since 1990. He has taught courses for TPR for 11 years and has edited several other books for TPR, including *Word Smart II* and *Math Smart*. In addition, Roy is the executive editor at Groovevolt.com, a music website. He now lives in Toms River, New Jersey.

**Tara Bray** is a resident of New York City by way of Hawaii, New Hampshire, Oregon, and Chicago, and is a graduate of Dartmouth College as well as Columbia University's School of the Arts. When she's not writing, Tara likes to spend her time figuring out how to pay the rent. She is also the author of The Princeton Review's guide to life after college, *Why Won't the Landlord Take Visa?*

**Christopher Maier** is a graduate of Dickinson College. During the past five years, he's lived variously in New York City, coastal Maine, western Oregon, central Pennsylvania, and eastern England. Now he's at an oasis somewhere in the midwestern cornfields—the University of Illinois—where he's earning his MFA in fiction. Aside from writing for magazines, newspapers, and The Princeton Review, he's worked as a radio disc jockey, a helping hand in a bakery, and a laborer on a highway construction crew. He's trying to avoid highway construction these days.

**Carson Brown** graduated from Stanford University in 1998, and after getting paid too much for working for various Internet companies for several years, sold her BMW and moved to Mexico. She has now overstayed her welcome south of the border and is returning to San Francisco to be responsible and further her career working as a writer and editor.

**Julie Doherty** is a freelance writer, Web designer, and preschool teacher. She lives in Mexico City.

**K. Nadine Kavanaugh** is pursuing her Master of Fine Arts at Columbia University. Her fiction has appeared on NYCBigCityLit.com and SlackFaith.com.

**Catherine Monaco**—ACADEMICS: Graduated from Dickinson College and earned a master's degree from Fordham University. STUDENT BODY: Bigger hair, bushier eyebrows (but learned to pluck after junior year). LIFE: Works as NYC public school teacher, lives in Tribeca, and "always has fun quoting other people for The Princeton Review."

**Dinaw Mengestu** is a graduate of Georgetown University and is currently completing his MFA in fiction at Columbia University. He lives in Brooklyn, New York.

# Classroom Courses from The Princeton Review

## The Classic Way to Prep

Classrooms may remind you of school, but in Princeton Review classes the feeling is different. You're in a friendly, supportive place where everyone has the same goal: to beat the test.

**Teachers who really know their stuff.**
Not only do Princeton Review teachers score in the top percentiles on the tests, they complete an intensive training program and must prove themselves again and again by earning outstanding evaluations from their students. Your teacher will keep you interested and involved while helping you master our methods.

**Small, focused classes.**
We never put more than 12 students in any class, so you'll get the personal attention you need, and work at a pace that's right for you. Your time will be spent effectively and efficiently to raise your score.

**Extra help when you need it.**
Most students occasionally need a little bit of extra help. Your Princeton Review teacher is available to meet with you outside of class at no extra charge to help you do your very best.

**Practice Online at Your Convenience.**
Our powerful Online Student Center—included free with your course—gives you as much extra practice as you need, whenever you need it. At any time of the day or night, you can use your own computer to tap into hundreds of supplemental practice questions and drills to help you master the skills and question types you're struggling with. You can even preview upcoming lessons or make up a missed class.

**Materials that work for you.**
Ask anyone who's taken one of our courses: our course manuals are the best. We update them at least once a year to stay current with changes to the test. Plus, you'll take a series of full-length practice tests, so you can monitor your progress and get comfortable with the exam.

**Guaranteed results.**
We know our courses work. In fact, we guarantee it: your SAT score will improve by at least 100 points, or we'll work with you again for up to a year, free.*

*To be eligible for the guarantee, you must complete all assigned homework, attend all your classes, and take the test immediately following your course.

### Classroom Courses Available

- SAT
- ACT
- SAT II – Writing, Math IC, Math IIC, Biology
- Word Smart, Math Smart

Availability of specific courses varies by month and location.

# 1-2-1 Private Tutoring from The Princeton Review

**Tutoring Programs Available**

- SAT
- ACT
- SAT II (all subjects)
- PSAT
- AP tests
- Academic subjects
- ISEE
- SSAT
- SHSAT

Availability varies by location.

## The Ultimate in Personalized Attention

With *1-2-1* Private Tutoring, you'll learn the same effective methods and strategies that we teach in our classroom and online courses, but you'll also get these exclusive benefits:

**Your tutor is your personal coach.**
*1-2-1* tutors are some of our best, most experienced teachers. Your tutor will work side-by-side with you, doing whatever it takes to help you get your best score.

**Prepare at your convenience.**
Whether you want to be taught in your own home or someplace else, your tutor will come to you, and only on the days and times that are most convenient for you.

**Get started when it's right for you.**
You can begin your tutoring sessions as early as freshman or sophomore year to prepare for multiple tests and academic subjects. Or you can choose to focus on a single test one month or more before you take it.

**Benefit from the best materials and tools.**
In addition to all the course manuals and online resources our classroom students get, your tutor may use supplementary materials to focus on the areas where you need more attention.

**Convenient SAT and ACT packages.**
We offer a comprehensive SAT and ACT tutoring package of 18 hours, covering all areas of the test, as well as 9-hour SAT packages of either Math or Verbal tutoring. Additional hours can be purchased if needed, and other tutoring subjects and packages are available depending on your location.

# Online Courses from The Princeton Review

## The Best of Both Worlds

Take the newest and best in software design, combine it with our time-tested strategies, and voilà: dynamic test prep where, when, and how you want it!

**Lively, engaging lessons.**
You'll never passively scroll through pages of text or watch boring, choppy video clips. Our courses feature animation, audio, interactive lessons, and self-directed navigation.

**Customized, focused practice.**
The course software will discover your strengths and weaknesses and will help you to prioritize. Of course, you'll have access to dozens of hours' worth of lessons and drills.

**Real-time interaction.**
Our LiveOnline course includes eight additional classroom sessions that take place in a virtual classroom over the Internet. You'll interact with your specially-certified teacher and up to seven other students in real time using live audio, a virtual whiteboard, and a chat interface.

**Help at your fingertips.**
Any time of the day or night, help is available: you can chat online with a live Coach or check our Frequently Asked Questions database.

**Guaranteed results.**
We stand behind our Online and LiveOnline courses with complete confidence. Your SAT score will improve by at least 100 points—guaranteed.

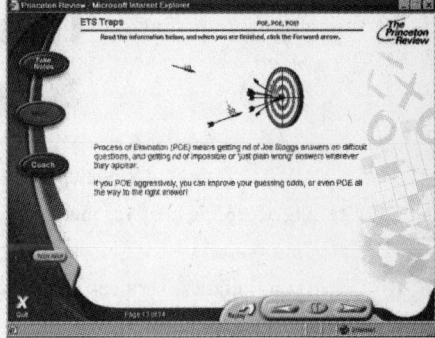
Online Test Prep

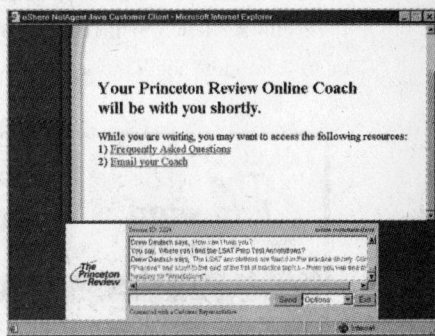
Live chat with an Online Coach

| SAT/ACT Online Course Features and Benefits | LiveOnline | Online | ExpressOnline |
|---|---|---|---|
| Interactive, multimedia lessons | 20–30 hours | 20–30 hours | 3 hours |
| Full-length practice tests | 4 | 4 | 2 |
| Live, online class sessions in real time | 5 sessions | | |
| LiveOnline extra-help sessions | 3 sessions | | |
| Set of printed study materials | ✓ | ✓ | |
| Online Coach to answer your questions 24/7 | ✓ | ✓ | |
| Additional support via email from instructors | ✓ | ✓ | |
| Customized homework assignments | ✓ | ✓ | |
| Estimated time to complete course | 50–70 hours | 40–60 hours | 8 hours |
| Access to course and practice materials | 120 days | 120 days | 30 days |
| Recommended time to complete | 4–8 weeks | 3–7 weeks | Up to 3 weeks |
| Access to online student discussion groups | ✓ | ✓ | ✓ |
| Access to FAQ database | ✓ | ✓ | |
| Score Improvement Guarantee | ✓ | ✓ | |

**ExpressOnline: The Best in Quick Prep**
If your test is less than a month away, or if you just want an introduction to our legendary strategies, this mini-course may be the right choice for you. Our multimedia lessons will walk you through basic test-taking strategies to give you the edge you need on test day. For more details, call us at 888-500-PREP or visit us online at PrincetonReview.com.

**System requirements for online resources:** Netscape Navigator version 4.7 or Internet Explorer version 4.0 or higher; JavaScript-enabled browser; Java-enabled browser; Flash-enabled browser; RealPlayer version 5.0 or higher (for LiveOnline only); sound card; minimum 56K connection.
**Princeton Review online resources are Mac compatible.**

www.PrincetonReview.com

# The Princeton Review Admissions Services

At The Princeton Review, we care about your ability to get accepted to the best school for you. But, we all know getting accepting involves much more than just doing well on standardized tests. That's why, in addition to our test preparation services, we also offer free admissions services to students looking to enter college or graduate school. You can find these services on our website, *www.PrincetonReview.com*, the best online resource for researching, applying to, and learning how to pay for the right school for you.

No matter what type of program you're applying to—undergraduate, graduate, law, business, or medical—**PrincetonReview.com has the free tools, services, and advice you need to navigate the admissions process.** Read on to learn more about the services we offer.

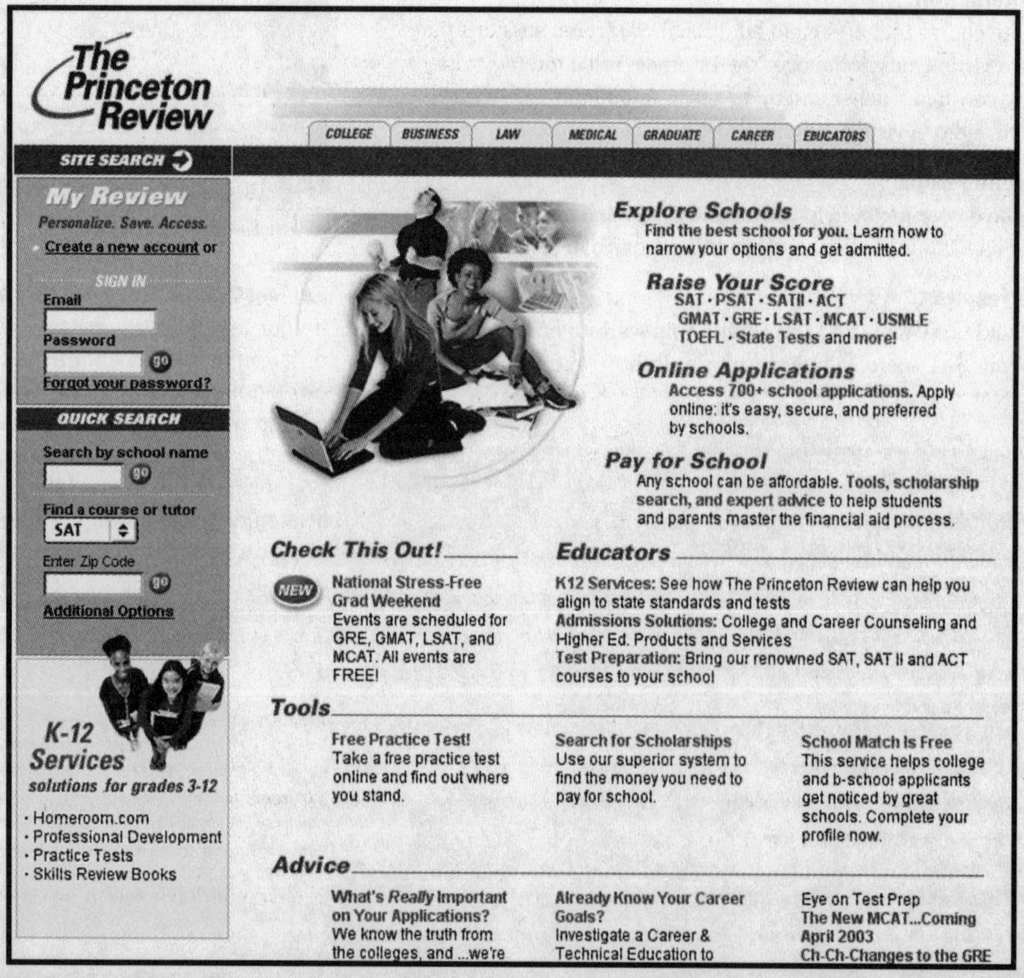

# Research Schools
## www.PrincetonReview.com/Research

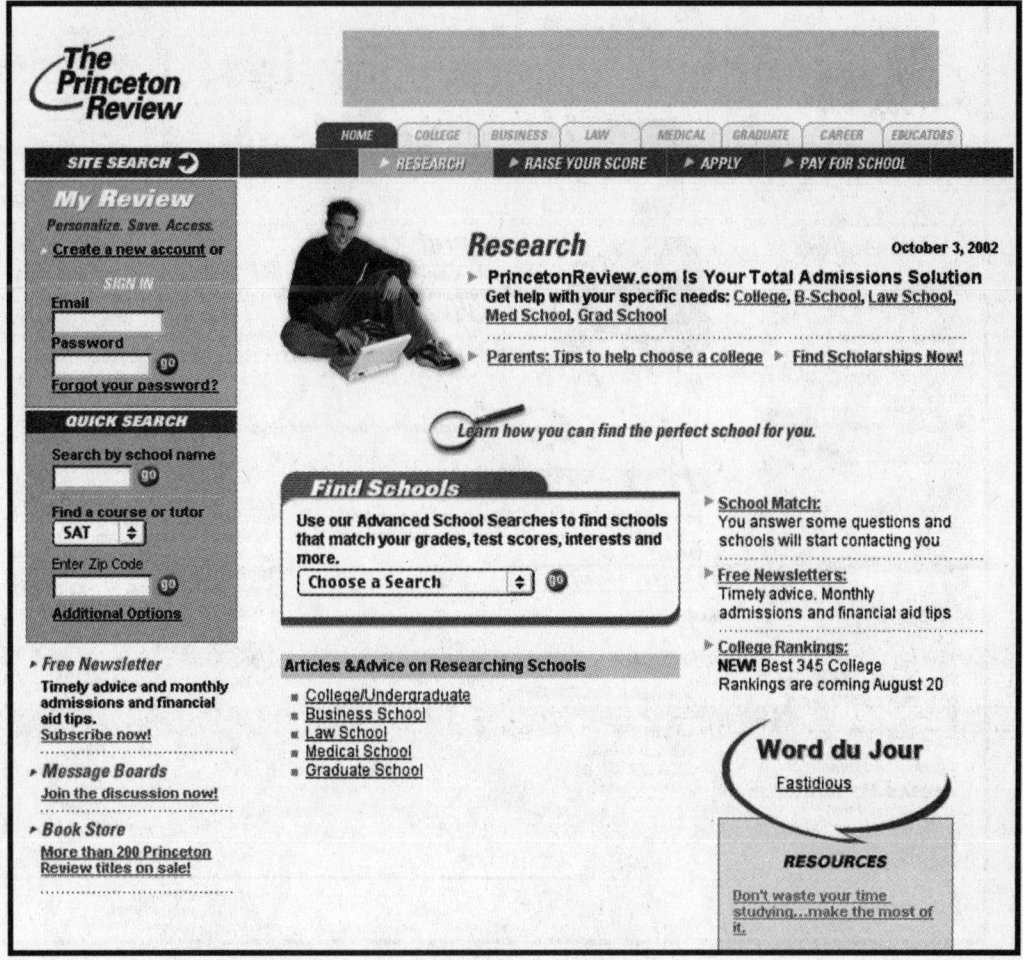

PrincetonReview.com features an interactive tool called **Counselor-O-Matic.** When you use this tool, you enter stats and information about yourself to find a list of your best match schools, reach schools, and safety schools. From there you can read statistical and editorial information about thousands of colleges and universities. In addition, you can find out what currently enrolled college students say about their schools. Once you complete Counselor-O-Matic make sure you opt in to School Match so that colleges can come to you.

Our **College Majors Search** is one of the most popular features we offer. Here you can read profiles on hundreds of majors to find information on curriculum, salaries, careers, and the appropriate high school preparation, as well as colleges that offer it. From the Majors Search, you can investigate corresponding Careers, read **Career Profiles**, and learn what career is the best match for you by taking our **Career Quiz**.

No matter what type of school or specialized program you are considering, **PrincetonReview.com has free articles and advice, in addition to our tools, to help you make the right choice.**

# Apply to School
## www.PrincetonReview.com/Apply

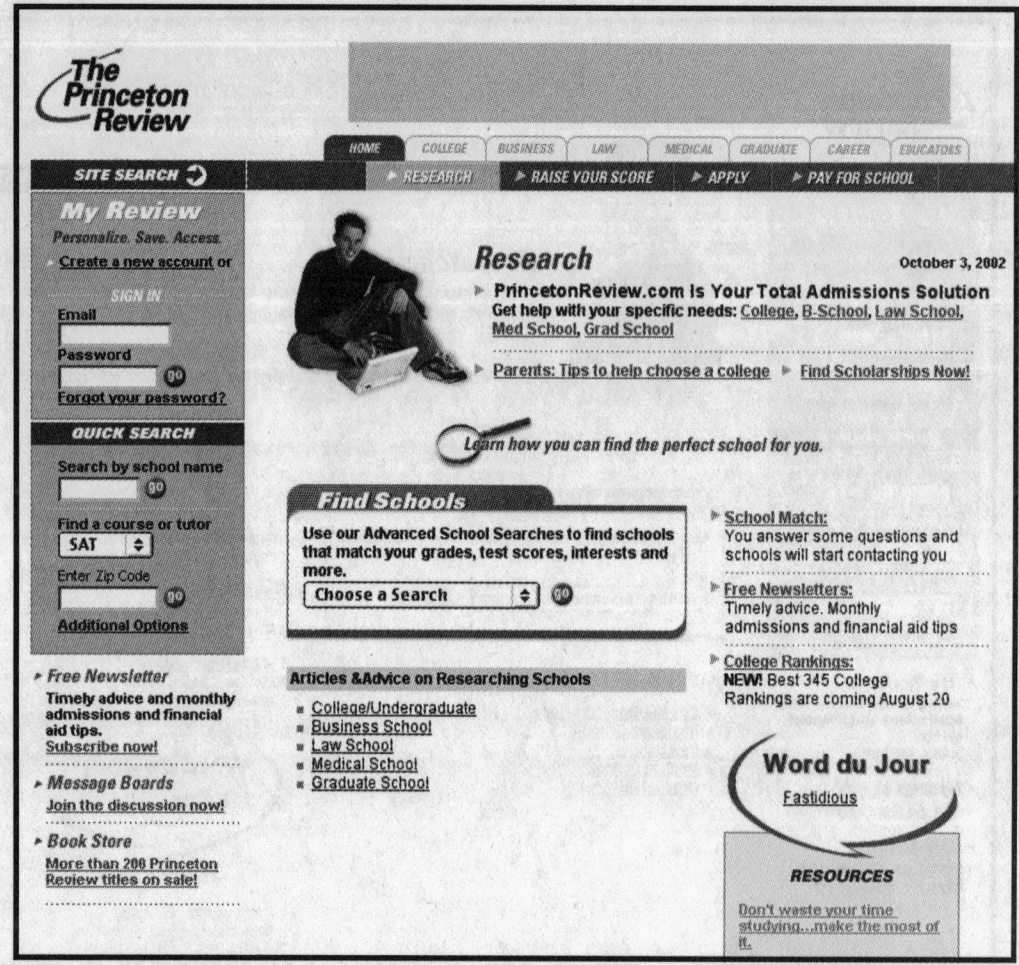

For most students, completing the school application is the most stressful part of the admissions process. PrincetonReview.com's powerful **Online School Application Engine** makes it easy to apply.

Paper applications are mostly a thing of the past. And, our hundreds of partner schools tell us they prefer to receive your applications online.

Using our online application service is simple:

- Enter information once and the common data automatically transfers onto each application.
- Save your applications and access them at any time to edit and perfect.
- Submit electronically or print and mail in.
- Pay your application fee online, using an e-check, or mail the school a check.

**Our powerful application engine is built to accommodate all your needs.**

# Pay for School
## www.PrincetonReview.com/Finance

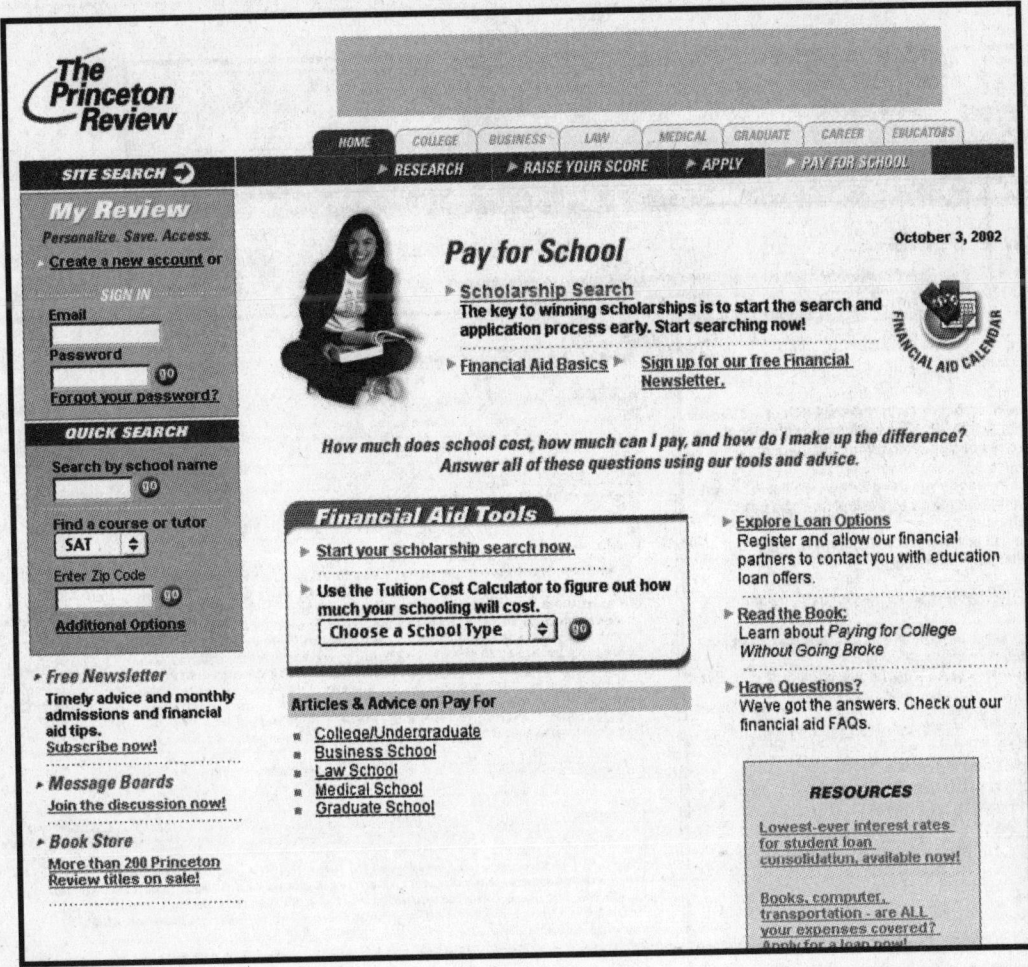

The financial aid process is confusing for everyone. But don't worry. Our free online tools, services, and advice can help you plan for the future and get the money you need to pay for school.

Our **Scholarship Search** engine will help you find free money, although often scholarships alone won't cover the cost of high tuitions. So, we offer other tools and resources to help you navigate the entire process.

Filling out the FAFSA and CSS PROFILE can be a daunting process, use our **Strategies for both forms** to make sure you answer the questions correctly the first time.

If scholarships and government aid aren't enough to swing the cost of tuition, we'll help you secure student loans. The Princeton Review has partnered with a select group of reputable financial institutions who will help **explore all your loans options**.

If you know how to work the financial aid process, you'll learn you don't have to **eliminate a school based on tuition.**

# Be a Part of the PrincetonReview.com Community

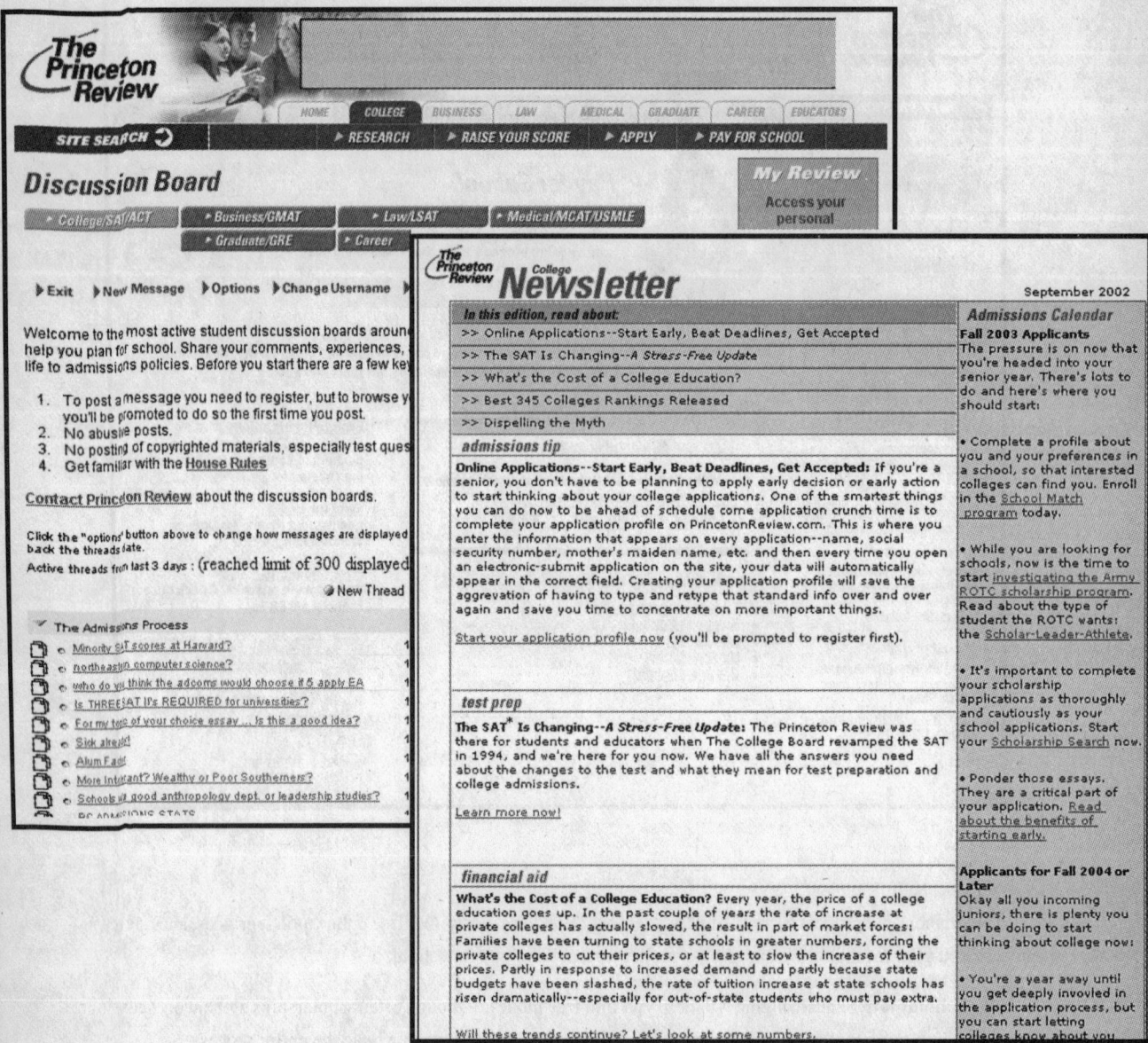

PrincetonReview.com's **Discussion Boards** and **Free Newsletters** are additional services to help you to get information about the admissions process from your peers and from The Princeton Review experts.

# Book Store
## www.PrincetonReview.com/college/Bookstore.asp

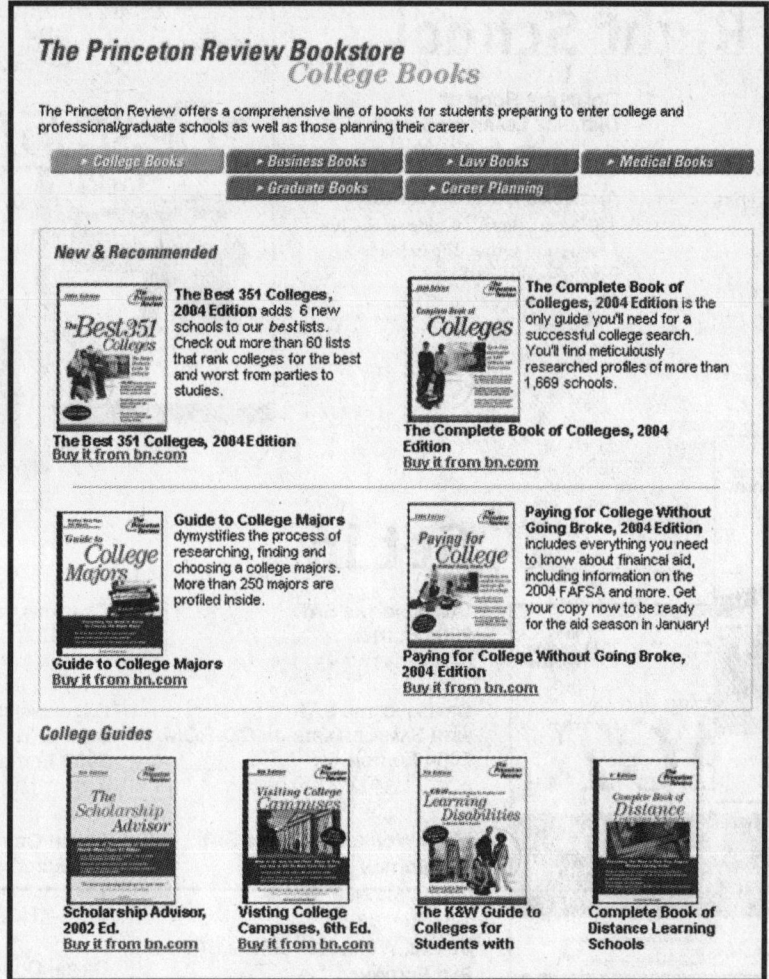

In addition to this book, we publish hundreds of other titles, including guidebooks that highlight life on campus, student opinion, and all the statistical data that you need to know about any school you are considering. Just a few of the titles that we offer are:

- Complete Book of Business Schools
- Complete Book of Law Schools
- Complete Book of Medical Schools
- The Best 351 Colleges
- The K&W Guide to Colleges for Students with Learning Disabilities or Attention Deficit Disorder
- Guide to College Majors
- Paying for College Without Going Broke

For a complete listing of all of our titles, visit our **online book store**:
www.princetonreview.com/college/bookstore.asp

## Find the Right School

**BEST 351 COLLEGES
2004 EDITION**
0-375-76337-6 • $21.95

**COMPLETE BOOK OF COLLEGES
2004 EDITION**
0-375-76330-9 • $24.95

**COMPLETE BOOK OF
DISTANCE LEARNING SCHOOLS**
0-375-76204-3 • $21.00

**AMERICA'S ELITE COLLEGES**
The Smart Buyer's Guide to the Ivy League and Other Top Schools
0-375-76206-X • $15.95

## Get in

**CRACKING THE SAT
2004 EDITION**
0-375-76331-7 • $19.00

**CRACKING THE SAT
WITH SAMPLE TESTS ON CD-ROM
2004 EDITION**
0-375-76330-9 • $30.95

**MATH WORKOUT FOR THE SAT
2ND EDITION**
0-375-76177-2 • $14.95

**VERBAL WORKOUT FOR THE SAT
2ND EDITION**
0-375-76176-4 • $14.95

**CRACKING THE ACT
2003 EDITION**
0-375-76317-1 • $19.00

**CRACKING THE ACT WITH
SAMPLE TESTS ON CD-ROM
2003 EDITION**
0-375-76318-X • $29.95

**CRASH COURSE FOR THE ACT
2ND EDITION**
The Last-Minute Guide to Scoring High
0-375-75364-3 • $9.95

**CRASH COURSE FOR THE SAT
2ND EDITION**
The Last-Minute Guide to Scoring High
0-375-75361-9 • $9.95

## Get Help Paying for it

**DOLLARS & SENSE FOR COLLEGE STUDENTS**
How Not to Run Out of Money by Midterms
0-375-75206-4 • $10.95

**PAYING FOR COLLEGE WITHOUT GOING BROKE
2004 EDITION**
0-375-76350-3 • $20.00

**THE SCHOLARSHIP ADVISOR
5TH EDITION**
0-375-76210-8 • $26.00

# Make the Grade with Study Guides for the AP and SAT II Exams

## AP Exams

**CRACKING THE AP BIOLOGY
2002-2003 EDITION**
0-375-76221-3 • $18.00

**CRACKING THE AP CALCULUS
AB & BC
2002-2003 EDITION**
0-375-76222-1 • $19.00

**CRACKING THE AP CHEMISTRY
2002-2003 EDITION**
0-375-76223-X • $18.00

**CRACKING THE AP ECONOMICS
(MACRO & MICRO)
2002-2003 EDITION**
0-375-76224-8 • $18.00

**CRACKING THE AP ENGLISH
LITERATURE
2002-2003 EDITION**
0-375-76225-6 • $18.00

**CRACKING THE AP
EUROPEAN HISTORY
2002-2003 EDITION**
0-375-76226-4 • $18.00

**CRACKING THE AP PHYSICS
2002-2003 EDITION**
0-375-76227-2 • $19.00

**CRACKING THE AP PSYCHOLOGY
2002-2003 EDITION**
0-375-76228-0 • $18.00

**CRACKING THE AP SPANISH
2002-2003 EDITION**
0-375-76229-9 • $18.00

**CRACKING THE AP STATISTICS
2002-2003 EDITION**
0-375-76232-9 • $18.00

**CRACKING THE AP U.S.
GOVERNMENT AND POLITICS
2002-2003 EDITION**
0-375-76230-2 • $18.00

**CRACKING THE AP U.S. HISTORY
2002-2003 EDITION**
0-375-76231-0 • $18.00

## SAT II Exams

**CRACKING THE SAT II: BIOLOGY
2003-2004 EDITION**
0-375-76294-9 • $18.00

**CRACKING THE SAT II: CHEMISTRY
2003-2004 EDITION**
0-375-76296-5 • $17.00

**CRACKING THE SAT II: FRENCH
2003-2004 EDITION**
0-375-76295-7 • $17.00

**CRACKING THE SAT II:
WRITING & LITERATURE
2003-2004 EDITION**
0-375-76301-5 • $17.00

**CRACKING THE SAT II: MATH
2003-2004 EDITION**
0-375-76298-1 • $18.00

**CRACKING THE SAT II: PHYSICS
2003-2004 EDITION**
0-375-76299-X • $18.00

**CRACKING THE SAT II: SPANISH
2003-2004 EDITION**
0-375-76300-7 • $17.00

**CRACKING THE SAT II:
U.S. & WORLD HISTORY
2003-2004 EDITION**
0-375-76297-3 • $18.00

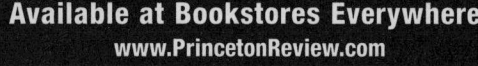

Available at Bookstores Everywhere.
www.PrincetonReview.com

## WE KNOW APPLYING TO COLLEGES IS STRESSFUL.

## Why Not Win $500 for It?

Yeesh. Everyone around you may be weary of your obsessing over every detail of your (or your child's) college search. You know the angst. Location? Academic reputation? Tuition? Majors? Dream school? Safety school? But we're into this stuff even more than you are. So much so that we've created our College Hopes Survey, an opportunity for you to tell us how your search and application experience is going. Our survey's a heck of a lot shorter than any college app you'll face (it's just 10 questions). And it'll only take about five minutes to complete.

But wait, there's more. We're giving a $500 scholarship to one lucky participant (at random). Ten questions. Five minutes. Chance for $500 bucks. You do the math.

Complete this form and mail or fax it back to us. Or visit us at *www.PrincetonReview.com/go/survey* and submit your survey to us online.

In March 2004, we'll post our survey findings on our website, www.PrincetonReview.com and give one participant the happy news that they've won the $500 scholarship. Right about the time you'll be receiving those fat (or not-so-fat) letters from colleges. Hope springs eternal.

## Official Rules:

We will conduct a random drawing in February 2004 to select a winner. The winner of the drawing will receive a $500 scholarship. Your odds of winning depend upon the number of entries received. If you win, you must redeem the scholarship within twelve months of notification. This promotion is not open to employees of The Princeton Review or Random House and is, of course, void where prohibited by law. All taxes are the sole responsibility of the winners. No purchase necessary: if you choose not to buy this book (big mistake!) or fill out the survey (bad decision!), you may enter this drawing by going to our website at: *www.PrincetonReview.com/go/survey* or by sending a postcard with your name, address, and phone number to The Princeton Review, c/o Robert Franek - College Hopes Survey, 2315 Broadway, New York, New York, 10024-4332. You may also write us to get a listing of the prize winner. By the way, we are not responsible for failures in electronic transmission or lost, misdirected, illegible, or mutilated entries.

# College Hopes Survey

Fill out online at *www.PrincetonReview.com/go/survey*

or tear out and snail mail to Robert Franek at The Princeton Review, 2315 Broadway, New York, NY 10024

or fax to Robert Franek at 212-874-0775.

Name _____

Address (optional) _____

City / State / Zip _____

Daytime phone _____

I am ____ a parent of a student   ____ a student applying to attend college beginning in

____ Fall or Spring 2004   ____ Fall or Spring 2005   ____ Later (indicate year: _____ ).

1. What would be your "dream college?" What college would you most like to attend (or see your child attend) if prospects of getting accepted or cost were not an issue?

_____

2. Which of the following would describe your "safety" school? What type of college are you (or your child) applying to that you think you (or your child) will be most likely to get into, and afford? (Choose one.)

____ Private College in my state

____ State or Public College in my state

____ Private College in another state

____ State or Public College in another state

3. When it comes to choosing the actual college you (or your child) will attend, which of the following do you think it is most likely to be? (Chose one.)

____ College with the best academic reputation

____ College that will be the most affordable (with either lowest costs and/or best financial aid package)?

____ College that will be the best overall fit (academically, socially, etc.)

4. How would you gauge your stress level about the college application process? (Choose one.)

____ Very High

____ High

____ Average

____ Low

____ Very Low

5. What's your biggest concern about applying to or attending college? (Choose one.)

　　____ Won't get into first-choice college

　　____ Will get in, but won't be able to afford it

　　____ Will attend a college I (or my child) may later regret

　　____ Taking out loans and graduating with debt

6. What do you estimate your (or your child's) college degree will cost, including four years of tuition, room & board, fees, books and other miscellaneous costs? (Choose one.)

　　____ Up to $25,000

　　____ $25,000 to $50,000

　　____ $50,000 to $75,000

　　____ More than $75,000

# Managing Student Loans and Budgets

**Sponsored by:**

**WHEN IT COMES TO HIGHER EDUCATION, STUDENT LOANS ARE SIMPLY A FACT OF LIFE.**

Most of us will need a student loan at some point on the road to our degree. Chela Financial offers students useful tips for simplifying the loan process.

The goal of a student loan is to help get you through school, not to overload you with debt. Before you take out a student loan, it's a good idea to make sure you understand exactly what your loan entails and what it will take to repay it.

## Loan Repayment and You

Signing your promissory note is the beginning of your process of managing your education financing. Understanding the costs and subtle intricacies of borrowing will help you to manage your debt.

The following are some important lending terms, and understanding them can help you along in your journey:

**Principal:** The amount of money the lender loans to you.

**Interest:** The additional amount that you pay to the lender for the privilege of using the money they are lending you.

**Accrue:** The accumulation of interest.

**Capitalization:** The process of adding accrued interest to the principal amount owed.

When you borrow money from a lender, the total amount you owe is higher than the amount you received because of the interest. For example, if you borrow $10,000 at an interest rate of 8.25 percent, your payback may look something like this:

| | |
|---|---|
| Loan amount: | $10,000 |
| Interest rate: | 8.25% |
| Repayment period: | 10 years |
| Number of payments: | 120 |
| Each payment: | $122.65 |
| Total amount repaid: | $14,718 |

## Making Payments

Remember that loans are structured so that most of your initial payments go toward the interest you owe, rather than toward repaying the principal.

For example, let's say that you have a $5,000 balance at a 17 percent interest rate. If you paid the lender $100 a month for 36 months, your new balance should be approximately $1,400. Right? Wrong. Due to the structure of most credit-based loans, your monthly payment is applied toward the interest first. That means that out of the $3,600 you have paid, only $1,346 went toward the principal. In reality, you still owe $3,654. And if you continue paying $100 each month, it would take 7 1/2 years to pay off the $5,000, and you would have paid a total of $8,819.

To avoid late fees and collection costs, be sure to make loan payments as scheduled.

*Note: The above section does not apply to Federal Stafford Loans.*

## Student Loan Obligations

A student loan is a long-term commitment. Students should explore all of their options before taking out a student loan. Graduates who have loans to repay must include those costs in their monthly budgets.

Repaying your student loans is an opportunity to establish a solid credit record. However, the opposite is also true. Failing to pay your student loans back in a timely fashion, otherwise known as *defaulting*, will cause you to have a bad credit rating and will limit your ability to qualify for other types of credit, including a credit card, a car loan, or a home mortgage.

Keep the following in mind:

- Borrow only what you need
- Keep track of what you owe
- Manage your money wisely

## Plan Ahead

Before you borrow money for school, consider what your anticipated starting salary and living expenses will be when you graduate. Then estimate what you'll be able to afford in monthly loan payments—generally not more than 8% to 10% of your gross monthly salary.

## Establishing a Spending Plan

"Budget" doesn't need to be a nasty word. Having a budget simply means understanding how much you're spending each month and how much you have available. Managing a budget is a key step toward good money management.

**Steps to establishing a budget:**

1. Start by listing all of your available funds—for example, savings, parents' contributions, take-home pay, and any other financial assistance.

2. Itemize all of your expenses, from tuition and fees to meals and entertainment.

3. For a few months track every dollar you spend so you know where your money is going.

4. Add up everything you spend and put that amount in one column on a piece of paper.

5. Compare that amount to how much money you have available.

6. If you find that what you spend exceeds your available funds, it's time to re-evaluate. You either need to increase your income or decrease your spending, or maybe a little bit of both.

7. Always know where you stand.

## Make a Smart Investment

In the end, your education is worth the investment. As long as you spend responsibly, work hard, and remember that financing your education is a commitment that will eventually pay off, you'll be a millionaire before you know it—loan debt or not!

For more information on Chela Financial please visit us at our website www.loans4students.org/tpr where you will find tools and resources to help you make informed decisions about paying for college.